Lecture Notes in Computer Science 12932

More information about this subseries at http://www.springer.com/series/7409

Carmelo Ardito · Rosa Lanzilotti ·
Alessio Malizia · Helen Petrie ·
Antonio Piccinno · Giuseppe Desolda ·
Kori Inkpen (Eds.)

Human-Computer Interaction – INTERACT 2021

18th IFIP TC 13 International Conference
Bari, Italy, August 30 – September 3, 2021
Proceedings, Part I

Springer

Editors
Carmelo Ardito (iD)
Department of Electrical and Information
Engineering
Polytechnic University of Bari
Bari, Italy

Alessio Malizia (iD)
Computer Science Department
University of Pisa
Pisa, Italy

University of Hertfordshire
Hatfield, United Kingdom

Antonio Piccinno (iD)
Computer Science Department
University of Bari Aldo Moro
Bari, Italy

Kori Inkpen (iD)
Microsoft Research
Redmond, WA, USA

Rosa Lanzilotti (iD)
Computer Science Department
University of Bari Aldo Moro
Bari, Italy

Helen Petrie (iD)
Department of Computer Science
University of York
York, UK

Giuseppe Desolda (iD)
Computer Science Department
University of Bari Aldo Moro
Bari, Italy

ISSN 0302-9743   ISSN 1611-3349   (electronic)
Lecture Notes in Computer Science
ISBN 978-3-030-85622-9   ISBN 978-3-030-85623-6   (eBook)
https://doi.org/10.1007/978-3-030-85623-6

LNCS Sublibrary: SL3 – Information Systems and Applications, incl. Internet/Web, and HCI

This Springer imprint is published by the registered company Springer Nature Switzerland AG
The registered company address is: Gewerbestrasse 11, 6330 Cham, Switzerland

Welcome

It is our great pleasure to welcome you to the 18th IFIP TC13 International Conference on Human-Computer Interaction, INTERACT 2021, one of the most important conferences in the area of Human-Computer Interaction at a world-wide level. INTERACT 2021 was held in Bari (Italy) from August 30 – September 3, 2021, in cooperation with ACM and under the patronage of the University of Bari Aldo Moro. This is the second time that INTERACT was held in Italy, after the edition in Rome in September 2005. The Villa Romanazzi Carducci Hotel, which hosted INTERACT 2021, provided the right context for welcoming the participants, thanks to its liberty-period villa immersed in a beautiful park. Due to the COVID-19 pandemic, INTERACT 2021 was held in hybrid mode to allow attendees who could not travel to participate in the conference.

INTERACT is held every two years and is well appreciated by the international community, attracting experts with a broad range of backgrounds, coming from all over the world and sharing a common interest in HCI, to make technology effective and useful for all people in their daily life. The theme of INTERACT 2021, "Sense, Feel, Design," highlighted the new interaction design challenges. Technology is today more and more widespread, pervasive and blended in the world we live in. On one side, devices that sense humans' activities have the potential to provide an enriched interaction. On the other side, the user experience can be further enhanced by exploiting multisensorial technologies. The traditional human senses of vision and hearing and senses of touch, smell, taste, and emotions can be taken into account when designing for future interactions. The hot topic of this edition was Human-Centered Artificial Intelligence, which implies considering who AI systems are built for and evaluating how well these systems support people's goals and activities. There was also considerable attention paid to the usable security theme. Not surprisingly, the COVID-19 pandemic and social distancing have also turned the attention of HCI researchers towards the difficulties in performing user-centered design activities and the modified social aspects of interaction.

With this, we welcome you all to INTERACT 2021. Several people worked hard to make this conference as pleasurable as possible, and we hope you will truly enjoy it.

Paolo Buono
Catherine Plaisant

Preface

The 18th IFIP TC13 International Conference on Human-Computer Interaction, INTERACT 2021 (Bari, August 30 – September 3, 2021) attracted a relevant collection of submissions on different topics.

Excellent research is the heart of a good conference. Like its predecessors, INTERACT 2021 aimed to foster high-quality research. As a multidisciplinary field, HCI requires interaction and discussion among diverse people with different interests and backgrounds. The beginners and the experienced theoreticians and practitioners, and people from various disciplines and different countries gathered, both in-person and virtually, to learn from each other and contribute to each other's growth.

We were especially honoured to welcome our invited speakers: Marianna Obrist (University College London), Ben Shneiderman (University of Maryland), Luca Viganò (King's College London), Geraldine Fitzpatrick (TU Wien) and Philippe Palanque (University Toulouse 3 "Paul Sabatier").

Marianna Obrist's talk focused on the multisensory world people live in and discussed the role touch, taste and smell can play in the future of computing. Ben Shneiderman envisioned a new synthesis of emerging disciplines in which AI-based intelligent algorithms are combined with human-centered design thinking. Luca Viganò used a cybersecurity show and tell approach to illustrate how to use films and other artworks to explain cybersecurity notions. Geraldine Fitzpatrick focused on skills required to use technologies as enablers for good technical design work. Philippe Palanque discussed the cases of system faults due to human errors and presented multiple examples of faults affecting socio-technical systems.

A total of 680 submissions, distributed in 2 peer-reviewed tracks, 4 curated tracks, and 3 juried tracks, were received. Of these, the following contributions were accepted:

- 105 Full Papers (peer-reviewed)
- 72 Short Papers (peer-reviewed)
- 36 Posters (juried)
- 5 Interactive Demos (curated)
- 9 Industrial Experiences (curated)
- 3 Panels (curated)
- 1 Course (curated)
- 11 Workshops (juried)
- 13 Doctoral Consortium (juried)

The acceptance rate for contributions received in the peer-reviewed tracks was 29% for full papers and 30% for short papers. In the spirit of inclusiveness of INTERACT, and IFIP in general, a substantial number of promising but borderline full papers, which had not received a direct acceptance decision, were screened for shepherding.

Interestingly, many of these papers eventually turned out to be excellent quality papers and were included in the final set of full papers. In addition to full papers and short papers, the present proceedings feature's contributions accepted in the shape of posters, interactive demonstrations, industrial experiences, panels, courses, and descriptions of accepted workshops.

Subcommittees managed the reviewing process of the full papers. Each subcommittee had a chair and a set of associated chairs who were in charge of coordinating the reviewing process with the help of expert reviewers. Two new sub-committees were introduced in this edition: "Human-AI Interaction" and "HCI in the Pandemic". Hereafter we list the sub-committees of INTERACT 2021:

- Accessibility and assistive technologies
- Design for business and safety-critical interactive systems
- Design of interactive entertainment systems
- HCI education and curriculum
- HCI in the pandemic
- Human-AI interaction
- Information visualization
- Interactive systems technologies and engineering
- Methodologies for HCI
- Social and ubiquitous interaction
- Understanding users and human behaviour

The final decision on acceptance or rejection of full papers was taken in a Programme Committee meeting held virtually, due to the COVID-19 pandemic, in March 2021. The technical program chairs, the full papers chairs, the subcommittee chairs, and the associate chairs participated in this meeting. The meeting discussed a consistent set of criteria to deal with inevitable differences among many reviewers. The corresponding track chairs and reviewers made the final decisions on other tracks, often after electronic meetings and discussions.

We would like to express our strong gratitude to all the people whose passionate and strenuous work ensured the quality of the INTERACT 2021 program: the 12 sub-committees chairs, 88 associated chairs, 34 track chairs, and 543 reviewers; the Keynote & Invited Talks Chair Maria Francesca Costabile; the Posters Chairs Maristella Matera, Kent Norman, Anna Spagnolli; the Interactive Demos Chairs Barbara Rita Barricelli and Nuno Jardim Nunes; the Workshops Chairs Marta Kristín Larusdottir and Davide Spano; the Courses Chairs Nikolaos Avouris and Carmen Santoro; the Panels Chairs Effie Lai-Chong Law and Massimo Zancanaro; the Doctoral Consortium Chairs Daniela Fogli, David Lamas and John Stasko; the Industrial Experiences Chair Danilo Caivano; the Online Experience Chairs Fabrizio Balducci and Miguel Ceriani; the Advisors Fernando Loizides and Marco Winckler; the Student Volunteers Chairs Vita Santa Barletta and Grazia Ragone; the Publicity Chairs Ganesh D. Bhutkar and Veronica Rossano; the Local Organisation Chair Simona Sarti.

We would like to thank all the authors, who chose INTERACT 2021 as the venue to publish their research and enthusiastically shared their results with the INTERACT community. Last, but not least, we are also grateful to the sponsors for their financial support.

Carmelo Ardito
Rosa Lanzilotti
Alessio Malizia
Helen Petrie
Antonio Piccinno
Giuseppe Desolda
Kori Inkpen

IFIP TC13 – http://ifip-tc13.org/

Established in 1989, the Technical Committee on Human–Computer Interaction (IFIP TC 13) of the International Federation for Information Processing (IFIP) is an international committee of 34 member national societies and 10 Working Groups, representing specialists of the various disciplines contributing to the field of human–computer interaction. This includes (among others) human factors, ergonomics, cognitive science, and multiple areas of computer science and design.

IFIP TC 13 aims to develop the science, technology and societal aspects of human–computer interaction (HCI) by

- encouraging empirical, applied and theoretical research
- promoting the use of knowledge and methods from both human sciences and computer sciences in design, development, evaluation and exploitation of computing systems
- promoting the production of new knowledge in the area of interactive computing systems engineering
- promoting better understanding of the relation between formal design methods and system usability, user experience, accessibility and acceptability
- developing guidelines, models and methods by which designers may provide better human-oriented computing systems
- and, cooperating with other groups, inside and outside IFIP, to promote user-orientation and humanization in system design.

Thus, TC 13 seeks to improve interactions between people and computing systems, to encourage the growth of HCI research and its practice in industry and to disseminate these benefits worldwide.

The main orientation is to place the users at the center of the development process. Areas of study include:

- the problems people face when interacting with computing devices;
- the impact of technology deployment on people in individual and organizational contexts;
- the determinants of utility, usability, acceptability, accessibility, privacy, and user experience ...;
- the appropriate allocation of tasks between computing systems and users especially in the case of automation;
- engineering user interfaces, interactions and interactive computing systems;
- modelling the user, their tasks and the interactive system to aid better system design; and harmonizing the computing system to user characteristics and needs.

While the scope is thus set wide, with a tendency toward general principles rather than particular systems, it is recognized that progress will only be achieved through both general studies to advance theoretical understandings and specific studies on practical issues (e.g., interface design standards, software system resilience, documentation, training material, appropriateness of alternative interaction technologies, guidelines, integrating computing systems to match user needs and organizational practices, etc.).

In 2015, TC13 approved the creation of a Steering Committee (SC) for the INTERACT conference series. The SC is now in place, chaired by Anirudha Joshi and is responsible for:

- promoting and maintaining the INTERACT conference as the premiere venue for researchers and practitioners interested in the topics of the conference (this requires a refinement of the topics above);
- ensuring the highest quality for the contents of the event;
- setting up the bidding process to handle the future INTERACT conferences (decision is made at TC 13 level);
- providing advice to the current and future chairs and organizers of the INTERACT conference;
- providing data, tools, and documents about previous conferences to the future conference organizers;
- selecting the reviewing system to be used throughout the conference (as this affects the entire set of reviewers, authors and committee members);
- resolving general issues involved with the INTERACT conference;
- capitalizing on history (good and bad practices).

In 1999, TC 13 initiated a special IFIP Award, the Brian Shackel Award, for the most outstanding contribution in the form of a refereed paper submitted to and delivered at each INTERACT. The award draws attention to the need for a comprehensive human-centered approach in the design and use of information technology in which the human and social implications have been taken into account. In 2007, IFIP TC 13 launched an Accessibility Award to recognize an outstanding contribution in HCI with international impact dedicated to the field of accessibility for disabled users. In 2013, IFIP TC 13 launched the Interaction Design for International Development (IDID) Award that recognizes the most outstanding contribution to the application of interactive systems for social and economic development of people in developing countries. Since the process to decide the award takes place after papers are sent to the publisher for publication, the awards are not identified in the proceedings. Since 2019 a special agreement has been made with the *International Journal of Behaviour & Information Technology* (published by Taylor & Francis) with Panos Markopoulos as editor in chief. In this agreement, authors of BIT whose papers are within the field of HCI are offered the opportunity to present their work at the INTERACT conference. Reciprocally, a selection of papers submitted and accepted for presentation at INTERACT are offered the opportunity to extend their contribution to be published in BIT.

IFIP TC 13 also recognizes pioneers in the area of HCI. An IFIP TC 13 pioneer is one who, through active participation in IFIP Technical Committees or related IFIP groups, has made outstanding contributions to the educational, theoretical, technical, commercial, or professional aspects of analysis, design, construction, evaluation, and use of interactive systems. IFIP TC 13 pioneers are appointed annually and awards are handed over at the INTERACT conference.

IFIP TC 13 stimulates working events and activities through its Working Groups (WGs). Working Groups consist of HCI experts from multiple countries, who seek to expand knowledge and find solutions to HCI issues and concerns within a specific domain. The list of Working Groups and their domains is given below.

WG13.1 (Education in HCI and HCI Curricula) aims to improve HCI education at all levels of higher education, coordinate and unite efforts to develop HCI curricula and promote HCI teaching.

WG13.2 (Methodology for User-Centred System Design) aims to foster research, dissemination of information and good practice in the methodical application of HCI to software engineering.

WG13.3 (HCI, Disability and Aging) aims to make HCI designers aware of the needs of people with disabilities and encourage development of information systems and tools permitting adaptation of interfaces to specific users.

WG13.4 (also WG2.7) (User Interface Engineering) investigates the nature, concepts and construction of user interfaces for software systems, using a framework for reasoning about interactive systems and an engineering model for developing UIs.

WG 13.5 (Resilience, Reliability, Safety and Human Error in System Development) seeks a framework for studying human factors relating to systems failure, develops leading edge techniques in hazard analysis and safety engineering of computer-based systems, and guides international accreditation activities for safety-critical systems.

WG13.6 (Human-Work Interaction Design) aims at establishing relationships between extensive empirical work-domain studies and HCI design. It will promote the use of knowledge, concepts, methods and techniques that enable user studies to procure a better apprehension of the complex interplay between individual, social and organizational contexts and thereby a better understanding of how and why people work in the ways that they do.

WG13.7 (Human–Computer Interaction and Visualization) aims to establish a study and research program that will combine both scientific work and practical applications in the fields of human–computer interaction and visualization. It will integrate several additional aspects of further research areas, such as scientific visualization, data mining, information design, computer graphics, cognition sciences, perception theory, or psychology, into this approach.

WG13.8 (Interaction Design and International Development) is currently working to reformulate their aims and scope.

WG13.9 (Interaction Design and Children) aims to support practitioners, regulators and researchers to develop the study of interaction design and children across international contexts.

WG13.10 (Human-Centred Technology for Sustainability) aims to promote research, design, development, evaluation, and deployment of human-centered technology to encourage sustainable use of resources in various domains.

New Working Groups are formed as areas of significance in HCI arise. Further information is available at the IFIP TC13 website: http://ifip-tc13.org/.

IFIP TC13 Members

Officers

Chairperson

Philippe Palanque, France

Vice-chair for Awards

Paula Kotze, South Africa

Vice-chair for Communications

Helen Petrie, UK

Vice-chair for Growth and Reach out INTERACT Steering Committee Chair

Jan Gulliksen, Sweden

Vice-chair for Working Groups

Simone D. J. Barbosa, Brazil

Vice-chair for Development and Equity

Julio Abascal, Spain

Treasurer

Virpi Roto, Finland

Secretary

Marco Winckler, France

INTERACT Steering Committee Chair

Anirudha Joshi, India

Country Representatives

Australia
Henry B. L. Duh
Australian Computer Society

Austria
Geraldine Fitzpatrick
Austrian Computer Society

Belgium
Bruno Dumas
IMEC – Interuniversity
Micro-Electronics Center

Brazil
Lara S. G. Piccolo
Brazilian Computer Society (SBC)

Bulgaria
Stoyan Georgiev Dentchev
Bulgarian Academy of Sciences

Croatia
Andrina Granic
Croatian Information Technology
Association (CITA)

Cyprus
Panayiotis Zaphiris
Cyprus Computer Society

Czech Republic
Zdeněk Míkovec
Czech Society for Cybernetics
and Informatics

Finland
Virpi Roto
Finnish Information Processing
Association

France
Philippe Palanque and Marco Winckler
Société informatique de France (SIF)

Germany
Tom Gross
Gesellschaft fur Informatik e.V.

Ireland
Liam J. Bannon
Irish Computer Society

Italy
Fabio Paternò
Italian Computer Society

Japan
Yoshifumi Kitamura
Information Processing Society of Japan

Netherlands
Regina Bernhaupt
Nederlands Genootschap
voor Informatica

New Zealand
Mark Apperley
New Zealand Computer Society

Norway
Frode Eika Sandnes
Norwegian Computer Society

Poland
Marcin Sikorski
Poland Academy of Sciences

Portugal
Pedro Campos
Associacão Portuguesa para o
Desenvolvimento da Sociedade da
Informação (APDSI)

Serbia
Aleksandar Jevremovic
Informatics Association of Serbia

Singapore
Shengdong Zhao
Singapore Computer Society

Slovakia
Wanda Benešová
The Slovak Society for Computer
Science

Slovenia
Matjaž Debevc
The Slovenian Computer Society
INFORMATIKA

Sri Lanka
Thilina Halloluwa
The Computer Society of Sri Lanka

South Africa
Janet L. Wesson & Paula Kotze
The Computer Society of South Africa

Sweden
Jan Gulliksen
Swedish Interdisciplinary Society for
Human-Computer Interaction
Swedish Computer Society

Switzerland
Denis Lalanne
Swiss Federation for Information
Processing

Tunisia
Mona Laroussi
Ecole Supérieure des Communications de
Tunis (SUP'COM)

United Kingdom
José Abdelnour Nocera
British Computer Society (BCS)

United Arab Emirates
Ahmed Seffah
UAE Computer Society

ACM

Gerrit van der Veer
Association for Computing
Machinery

CLEI

Jaime Sánchez
Centro Latinoamericano de Estudios en
Informatica

Expert Members

Julio Abascal, Spain
Carmelo Ardito, Italy
Nikolaos Avouris, Greece
Kaveh Bazargan, Iran
Ivan Burmistrov, Russia
Torkil Torkil Clemmensen, Denmark
Peter Forbrig, Germany
Dorian Gorgan, Romania

Anirudha Joshi, India
David Lamas, Estonia
Marta Kristin Larusdottir, Iceland
Zhengjie Liu, China
Fernando Loizides, UK/Cyprus
Ochieng Daniel "Dan" Orwa, Kenya
Eunice Sari, Australia/Indonesia

Working Group Chairpersons

**WG 13.1 (Education in HCI
and HCI Curricula)**

Konrad Baumann, Austria

**WG 13.2 (Methodologies
for User-Centered System Design)**

Regina Bernhaupt, Netherlands

WG 13.3 (HCI, Disability and Aging)

Helen Petrie, UK

**WG 13.4/2.7 (User Interface
Engineering)**

José Creissac Campos, Portugal

**WG 13.5 (Human Error, Resilience,
Reliability, Safety and System
Development)**

Chris Johnson, UK

**WG13.6 (Human-Work
Interaction Design)**

Barbara Rita Barricelli, Italy

WG13.7 (HCI and Visualization)

Peter Dannenmann, Germany

**WG 13.8 (Interaction Design
and International Development)**

José Adbelnour Nocera, UK

**WG 13.9 (Interaction Design
and Children)**

Janet Read, UK

**WG 13.10 (Human-Centred
Technology for Sustainability)**

Masood Masoodian, Finland

Conference Organizing Committee

General Conference Co-chairs

Paolo Buono, Italy
Catherine Plaisant, USA and France

Advisors

Fernando Loizides, UK
Marco Winckler, France

Technical Program Co-chairs

Carmelo Ardito, Italy
Rosa Lanzilotti, Italy
Alessio Malizia, UK and Italy

Keynote and Invited Talks Chair

Maria Francesca Costabile, Italy

Full Papers Co-chairs

Helen Petrie, UK
Antonio Piccinno, Italy

Short Papers Co-chairs

Giuseppe Desolda, Italy
Kori Inkpen, USA

Posters Co-chairs

Maristella Matera, Italy
Kent Norman, USA
Anna Spagnolli, Italy

Interactive Demos Co-chairs

Barbara Rita Barricelli, Italy
Nuno Jardim Nunes, Portugal

Panels Co-chairs

Effie Lai-Chong Law, UK
Massimo Zancanaro, Italy

Courses Co-chairs

Carmen Santoro, Italy
Nikolaos Avouris, Greece

Industrial Experiences Chair

Danilo Caivano, Italy

Workshops Co-chairs

Marta Kristín Larusdottir, Iceland
Davide Spano, Italy

Doctoral Consortium Co-chairs

Daniela Fogli, Italy
David Lamas, Estonia
John Stasko, USA

Online Experience Co-chairs

Fabrizio Balducci, Italy
Miguel Ceriani, Italy

Student Volunteers Co-chairs

Vita Santa Barletta, Italy
Grazia Ragone, UK

Publicity Co-chairs

Ganesh D. Bhutkar, India
Veronica Rossano, Italy

Local Organisation Chair

Simona Sarti, Consulta Umbria, Italy

Programme Committee

Sub-committee Chairs

Nikolaos Avouris, Greece
Regina Bernhaupt, Netherlands
Carla Dal Sasso Freitas, Brazil
Jan Gulliksen, Sweden
Paula Kotzé, South Africa
Effie Lai-Chong Law, UK

Philippe Palanque, France
Fabio Paternò, Italy
Thomas Pederson, Sweden
Albrecht Schmidt, Germany
Frank Steinicke, Germany
Gerhard Weber, Germany

Associated Chairs

José Abdelnour Nocera, UK
Raian Ali, Qatar
Florian Alt, Germany
Katrina Attwood, UK
Simone Barbosa, Brazil
Cristian Bogdan, Sweden
Paolo Bottoni, Italy
Judy Bowen, New Zealand
Daniel Buschek, Germany
Pedro Campos, Portugal
José Creissac Campos, Portugal
Luca Chittaro, Italy
Sandy Claes, Belgium
Christopher Clarke, UK
Torkil Clemmensen, Denmark
Vanessa Cobus, Germany
Ashley Colley, Finland
Aurora Constantin, UK
Lynne Coventry, UK
Yngve Dahl, Norway
Maria De Marsico, Italy
Luigi De Russis, Italy
Paloma Diaz, Spain
Monica Divitini, Norway
Mateusz Dolata, Switzerland
Bruno Dumas, Belgium
Sophie Dupuy-Chessa, France
Dan Fitton, UK
Peter Forbrig, Germany
Sandnes Frode Eika, Norway
Vivian Genaro Motti, USA
Rosella Gennari, Italy

Jens Gerken, Germany
Mareike Glöss, Sweden
Dorian Gorgan, Romania
Tom Gross, Germany
Uwe Gruenefeld, Germany
Julie Haney, USA
Ebba Þóra Hvannberg, Iceland
Netta Iivari, Finland
Nanna Inie, Denmark
Anna Sigríður Islind, Iceland
Anirudha Joshi, India
Bridget Kane, Sweden
Anne Marie Kanstrup, Denmark
Mohamed Khamis, UK
Kibum Kim, Korea
Marion Koelle, Germany
Kati Kuusinen, Denmark
Matthias Laschke, Germany
Fernando Loizides, UK
Andrés Lucero, Finland
Jo Lumsden, UK
Charlotte Magnusson, Sweden
Andrea Marrella, Italy
Célia Martinie, France
Timothy Merritt, Denmark
Zdeněk Míkovec, Czech Republic
Luciana Nedel, Brazil
Laurence Nigay, France
Valentina Nisi, Portugal
Raquel O. Prates, Brazil
Rakesh Patibanda, Australia
Simon Perrault, Singapore

Lara Piccolo, UK
Aparecido Fabiano Pinatti de Carvalho,
  Germany
Janet Read, UK
Karen Renaud, UK
Antonio Rizzo, Italy
Sayan Sarcar, Japan
Valentin Schwind, Germany
Gavin Sim, UK
Fotios Spyridonis, UK
Jan Stage, Denmark
Simone Stumpf, UK
Luis Teixeira, Portugal

Jakob Tholander, Sweden
Daniela Trevisan, Brazil
Stefano Valtolina, Italy
Jan Van den Bergh, Belgium
Nervo Verdezoto, UK
Chi Vi, UK
Giuliana Vitiello, Italy
Sarah Völkel, Germany
Marco Winckler, France
Dhaval Vyas, Australia
Janet Wesson, South Africa
Paweł W. Woźniak, Netherlands

Reviewers

Bruno A. Chagas, Brazil
Yasmeen Abdrabou, Germany
Maher Abujelala, USA
Jiban Adhikary, USA
Kashif Ahmad, Qatar
Muneeb Ahmad, UK
Naveed Ahmed, United Arab Emirates
Aino Ahtinen, Finland
Wolfgang Aigner, Austria
Deepak Akkil, Finland
Aftab Alam, Republic of Korea
Soraia Meneses Alarcão, Portugal
Pedro Albuquerque Santos, Portugal
Günter Alce, Sweden
Iñigo Aldalur, Spain
Alaa Alkhafaji, Iraq
Aishat Aloba, USA
Yosuef Alotaibi, UK
Taghreed Alshehri, UK
Ragaad Al-Tarawneh, USA
Alejandro Alvarez-Marin, Chile
Lucas Anastasiou, UK
Ulf Andersson, Sweden
Joseph Aneke, Italy
Mark Apperley, New Zealand
Renan Aranha, Brazil
Pierre-Emmanuel Arduin, France
Stephanie Arevalo Arboleda, Germany
Jan Argasiński, Poland

Patricia Arias-Cabarcos, Germany
Alexander Arntz, Germany
Jonas Auda, Germany
Andreas Auinger, Austria
Iuliia Avgustis, Finland
Cédric Bach, France
Miroslav Bachinski, Germany
Victor Bacu, Romania
Jan Balata, Czech Republic
Teresa Baldassarre, Italy
Fabrizio Balducci, Italy
Vijayanand Banahatti, India
Karolina Baras, Portugal
Simone Barbosa, Brazil
Vita Santa Barletta, Italy
Silvio Barra, Italy
Barbara Rita Barricelli, Italy
Ralph Barthel, UK
Thomas Baudel, France
Christine Bauer, Netherlands
Fatma Ben Mesmia, Canada
Marit Bentvelzen, Netherlands
François Bérard, France
Melanie Berger, Netherlands
Gerd Berget, Norway
Sergi Bermúdez i Badia, Portugal
Dario Bertero, UK
Guilherme Bertolaccini, Brazil
Lonni Besançon, Australia

Laura-Bianca Bilius, Romania
Kerstin Blumenstein, Austria
Andreas Bollin, Austria
Judith Borghouts, UK
Nis Bornoe, Denmark
Gabriela Bosetti, UK
Hollie Bostock, Portugal
Paolo Bottoni, Italy
Magdalena Boucher, Austria
Amina Bouraoui, Tunisia
Elodie Bouzekri, France
Judy Bowen, New Zealand
Efe Bozkir, Germany
Danielle Bragg, USA
Diogo Branco, Portugal
Dawn Branley-Bell, UK
Stephen Brewster, UK
Giada Brianza, UK
Barry Brown, Sweden
Nick Bryan-Kinns, UK
Andreas Bucher, Switzerland
Elizabeth Buie, UK
Alexandru Bundea, Germany
Paolo Buono, Italy
Michael Burch, Switzerland
Matthew Butler, Australia
Fabio Buttussi, Italy
Andreas Butz, Germany
Maria Claudia Buzzi, Italy
Marina Buzzi, Italy
Zoya Bylinskii, USA
Diogo Cabral, Portugal
Åsa Cajander, Sweden
Francisco Maria Calisto, Portugal
Hector Caltenco, Sweden
José Creissac Campos, Portugal
Heloisa Candello, Brazil
Alberto Cannavò, Italy
Bruno Cardoso, Belgium
Jorge Cardoso, Portugal
Géry Casiez, France
Fabio Cassano, Italy
Brendan Cassidy, UK
Alejandro Catala, Spain

Miguel Ceriani, UK
Daniel Cermak-Sassenrath, Denmark
Vanessa Cesário, Portugal
Fred Charles, UK
Debaleena Chattopadhyay, USA
Alex Chen, Singapore
Thomas Chen, USA
Yuan Chen, Canada
Chola Chhetri, USA
Katherine Chiluiza, Ecuador
Nick Chozos, UK
Michael Chromik, Germany
Christopher Clarke, UK
Bárbara Cleto, Portugal
Antonio Coelho, Portugal
Ashley Colley, Finland
Nelly Condori-Fernandez, Spain
Marios Constantinides, UK
Cléber Corrêa, Brazil
Vinicius Costa de Souza, Brazil
Joëlle Coutaz, France
Céline Coutrix, France
Chris Creed, UK
Carlos Cunha, Portugal
Kamila Rios da Hora Rodrigues, Brazil
Damon Daylamani-Zad, UK
Sergio de Cesare, UK
Marco de Gemmis, Italy
Teis De Greve, Belgium
Victor Adriel de Jesus Oliveira, Austria
Helmut Degen, USA
Donald Degraen, Germany
William Delamare, France
Giuseppe Desolda, Italy
Henrik Detjen, Germany
Marianna Di Gregorio, Italy
Ines Di Loreto, France
Daniel Diethei, Germany
Tilman Dingler, Australia
Anke Dittmar, Germany
Monica Divitini, Norway
Janki Dodiya, Germany
Julia Dominiak, Poland
Ralf Dörner, Germany

Julie Doyle, Ireland
Philip Doyle, Ireland
Fiona Draxler, Germany
Emanuel Felipe Duarte, Brazil
Rui Duarte, Portugal
Bruno Dumas, Belgium
Mark Dunlop, UK
Sophie Dupuy-Chessa, France
Jason Dykes, UK
Chloe Eghtebas, Germany
Kevin El Haddad, Belgium
Don Samitha Elvitigala, New Zealand
Augusto Esteves, Portugal
Siri Fagernes, Norway
Katherine Fennedy, Singapore
Marta Ferreira, Portugal
Francesco Ferrise, Italy
Lauren Stacey Ferro, Italy
Christos Fidas, Greece
Daniel Finnegan, UK
Daniela Fogli, Italy
Manuel J. Fonseca, Portugal
Peter Forbrig, Germany
Rita Francese, Italy
André Freire, Brazil
Karin Fröhlich, Finland
Susanne Furman, USA
Henrique Galvan Debarba, Denmark
Sandra Gama, Portugal
Dilrukshi Gamage, Japan
Jérémie Garcia, France
Jose Garcia Estrada, Norway
David Geerts, Belgium
Denise Y. Geiskkovitch, Canada
Stefan Geisler, Germany
Mirko Gelsomini, Italy
Çağlar Genç, Finland
Rosella Gennari, Italy
Nina Gerber, Germany
Moojan Ghafurian, Canada
Maliheh Ghajargar, Sweden
Sabiha Ghellal, Germany
Debjyoti Ghosh, Germany
Michail Giannakos, Norway

Terje Gjøsæter, Norway
Marc Gonzalez Capdevila, Brazil
Julien Gori, Finland
Laurent Grisoni, France
Tor-Morten Gronli, Norway
Sebastian Günther, Germany
Li Guo, UK
Srishti Gupta, USA
Francisco Gutiérrez, Belgium
José Eder Guzman Mendoza, Mexico
Jonna Häkkilä, Finland
Lilit Hakobyan, UK
Thilina Halloluwa, Sri Lanka
Perttu Hämäläinen, Finland
Lane Harrison, USA
Michael Harrison, UK
Hanna Hasselqvist, Sweden
Tomi Heimonen, USA
Florian Heinrich, Germany
Florian Heller, Belgium
Karey Helms, Sweden
Nathalie Henry Riche, USA
Diana Hernandez-Bocanegra, Germany
Danula Hettiachchi, Australia
Wilko Heuten, Germany
Annika Hinze, New Zealand
Linda Hirsch, Germany
Sarah Hodge, UK
Sven Hoffmann, Germany
Catherine Holloway, UK
Leona Holloway, Australia
Lars Erik Holmquist, UK
Anca-Simona Horvath, Denmark
Simo Hosio, Finland
Sebastian Hubenschmid, Germany
Helena Vallo Hult, Sweden
Shah Rukh Humayoun, USA
Ebba Þóra Hvannberg, Iceland
Alon Ilsar, Australia
Md Athar Imtiaz, New Zealand
Oana Inel, Netherlands
Francisco Iniesto, UK
Andri Ioannou, Cyprus
Chyng-Yang Jang, USA

Radiah Rivu, Germany
Mehdi Rizvi, Italy
Judy Robertson, UK
Michael Rohs, Germany
Marco Romano, Italy
Anton Rosén, Sweden
Veronica Rossano, Italy
Virpi Roto, Finland
Debjani Roy, India
Matthew Rueben, USA
Vit Rusnak, Czech Republic
Philippa Ryan, UK
Thomas Ryberg, Denmark
Rufat Rzayev, Germany
Parisa Saadati, UK
Adrian Sabou, Romania
Ofir Sadka, Israel
Juan Pablo Saenz, Italy
Marco Saltarella, Italy
Sanjit Samaddar, UK
Ivan Sanchez Milara, Finland
Frode Eika Sandnes, Norway
Leonardo Sandoval, UK
Carmen Santoro, Italy
Pratiti Sarkar, India
Guilherme Schardong, Brazil
Christina Schmidbauer, Austria
Eike Schneiders, Denmark
Maximilian Schrapel, Germany
Sabrina Scuri, Portugal
Korok Sengupta, Germany
Marta Serafini, Italy
Marcos Serrano, France
Kshitij Sharma, Norway
Sumita Sharma, Finland
Akihisa Shitara, Japan
Mark Shovman, Israel
Ludwig Sidenmark, UK
Carlos Silva, Portugal
Tiago Silva da Silva, Brazil
Milene Silveira, Brazil
James Simpson, Australia
Ashwin Singh, India
Laurianne Sitbon, Australia

Mikael B. Skov, Denmark
Pavel Slavik, Czech Republic
Aidan Slingsby, UK
K. Tara Smith, UK
Ellis Solaiman, UK
Andreas Sonderegger, Switzerland
Erik Sonnleitner, Austria
Keyur Sorathia, India
Emanuel Sousa, Portugal
Sonia Sousa, Estonia
Anna Spagnolli, Italy
Davide Spallazzo, Italy
Lucio Davide Spano, Italy
Katta Spiel, Austria
Priyanka Srivastava, India
Katarzyna Stawarz, UK
Teodor Stefanut, Romania
Mari-Klara Stein, Denmark
Jonathan Strahl, Finland
Tim Stratmann, Germany
Christian Sturm, Germany
Michael Svangren, Denmark
Aurélien Tabard, France
Benjamin Tag, Australia
Federico Tajariol, France
Aishwari Talhan, Republic of Korea
Maurizio Teli, Denmark
Subrata Tikadar, India
Helena Tobiasson, Sweden
Guy Toko, South Africa
Brianna Tomlinson, USA
Olof Torgersson, Sweden
Genoveffa Tortora, Italy
Zachary O. Toups, USA
Scott Trent, Japan
Philippe Truillet, France
Tommaso Turchi, UK
Fanny Vainionpää, Finland
Stefano Valtolina, Italy
Niels van Berkel, Denmark
Jan Van den Bergh, Belgium
Joey van der Bie, Netherlands
Bram van Deurzen, Belgium
Domenique van Gennip, Australia

Paul van Schauk, UK
Koen van Turnhout, Netherlands
Jean Vanderdonckt, Belgium
Eduardo Veas, Austria
Katia Vega, USA
Kellie Vella, Australia
Leena Ventä-Olkkonen, Finland
Nadine Vigouroux, France
Gabriela Villalobos-Zúñiga, Switzerland
Aku Visuri, Finland
Giuliana Vitiello, Italy
Pierpaolo Vittorini, Italy
Julius von Willich, Germany
Steven Vos, Netherlands
Nadine Wagener, Germany
Lun Wang, Italy
Ruijie Wang, Italy
Gerhard Weber, Germany
Thomas Weber, Germany
Rina Wehbe, Canada
Florian Weidner, Germany
Alexandra Weilenmann, Sweden
Sebastian Weiß, Germany

Yannick Weiss, Germany
Robin Welsch, Germany
Janet Wesson, South Africa
Benjamin Weyers, Germany
Stephanie Wilson, UK
Marco Winckler, France
Philipp Wintersberger, Austria
Katrin Wolf, Germany
Kim Wölfel, Germany
Julia Woodward, USA
Matthias Wunsch, Austria
Haijun Xia, USA
Asim Evren Yantac, Turkey
Enes Yigitbas, Germany
Yongjae Yoo, Canada
Johannes Zagermann, Germany
Massimo Zancanaro, Italy
André Zenner, Germany
Jingjie Zheng, Canada
Suwen Zhu, USA
Ying Zhu, USA
Jürgen Ziegler, Germany

Partners and Sponsors

Partners

International Federation for Information Processing

In-cooperation with ACM

In-cooperation with SIGCHI

Sponsors

EULOGIC

eusoft

more than a LIMS

Experis™

ManpowerGroup

exprivia

openwork

Just solutions

ORA ZERO

GROUP

sincon

ICT SOLUTIONS

Contents – Part I

Assistive Technology for Cognition and Neurodevelopmental Disorders

Assistive Technology for Mobility and Rehabilitation

Assistive Technology for Visually Impaired

Augmented Reality

Slash Mobiles: A Wearable Light for Online Collaborative Learning
in Video Meetings   112
    Kimihiro Li, Bill Rowden, Jenny Pan, Xinguo Wehr,
    and Michael Shimamura

Supporting Interaction in a Virtual Chorists: Results from a Focus Group . . .   122
    Rita Vincent, Patrizia Marti, and Graziella Tonra

Author Index   131

Keynote Speeches

Human-Centered AI: A New Synthesis

Ben Shneiderman[(⊠)] [iD]

University of Maryland, College Park, MD 20742, USA
ben@cs.umd.edu

Abstract. Researchers, developers, business leaders, policy makers and others are expanding the technology-centered scope of Artificial Intelligence (AI) to include Human-Centered AI (HCAI) ways of thinking. This expansion from an algorithm-focused view to embrace a human-centered perspective, can shape the future of technology so as to better serve human needs. Educators, designers, software engineers, product managers, evaluators, and government agency staffers can build on AI-driven technologies to design products and services that make life better for the users. These human-centered products and services will enable people to better care for each other, build sustainable communities, and restore the environment.

Keywords: Human-computer interaction · Artificial Intelligence · Design · Visualization · Control panels · User interfaces

1 Introduction: A New Synthesis

A new synthesis of disciplines is emerging, in which AI-based intelligent algorithms are combined with human-centered design thinking to make Human-Centered AI (HCAI). This synthesis of disciplines increases the chance that technology will empower rather than replace people. In the past, researchers and developers focused on building AI algorithms and systems, stressing machine autonomy and measuring algorithm performance. The new synthesis values AI and gives equal attention to human users and other stakeholders by raising the prominence of user experience design and by measuring human performance. Researchers and developers for HCAI systems value meaningful human control, putting people first by serving human values such as rights, justice, and dignity, thus supporting goals such as self-efficacy, creativity, responsibility, and social connections.

The higher level goal is to support the 17 United Nations Sustainable Development Goals (https://sdgs.un.org/goals), which were established in 2015 to set aspirations for 2030 (Fig. 1). These goals include elimination of poverty, zero hunger, quality education, and reduced inequalities. Other ambitions address environmental issues such as climate action, life on land, life below water, and sustainable cities and communities. Linking these ambitions to user interface design leads to potent technologies that help people in their relationships, healthcare, education, community efforts and more.

Published by Springer Nature Switzerland AG 2021
C. Ardito et al. (Eds.): INTERACT 2021, LNCS 12932, pp. 3–8, 2021.
https://doi.org/10.1007/978-3-030-85623-6_1

Fig. 1. The 17 United Nations' Sustainable Development Goals (SDGs) (https://sdgs.un.org/goals)

This new synthesis developed in [1–4], is presented in depth in [5] (https://hcil.umd.edu/human-centered-ai/). The supporting concepts come from three fresh ideas for changing technology design so as to bring about a human-centered orientation. These ideas are the:

1) **HCAI framework** that guides creative designers to ensure human centric thinking about highly automated systems [3]. The examples include familiar devices, such as thermostats, elevators, self-cleaning ovens, and cellphone cameras, as well as life critical applications, such as highly automated cars and patient controlled pain relief devices. The dated 1-dimensional model with ten levels of autonomy/automation assumes a zero-sum approach which means that more automation means less human control. However, thoughtful designers can deliver *high levels of human control and high levels of automation*, as we all do with digital cameras and many other devices. In short, the new way of thinking is based on a 2-dimensional model with human control and computer automation as separate axes (Fig. 2). Digital cameras show how high levels of human control (framing, zooming, decisive moment to click, etc.) can be integrated with high levels of automation (aperture, focus, jitter reduction, etc.).

2) **Design Metaphors** suggest how the two central goals of AI research, science and innovation are both valuable, but researchers, developers, business leaders, and policy makers will need to be creative in finding effective ways to combine them to benefit the users [4]. There are four design metaphors that can be used to combine the two goals of AI research:

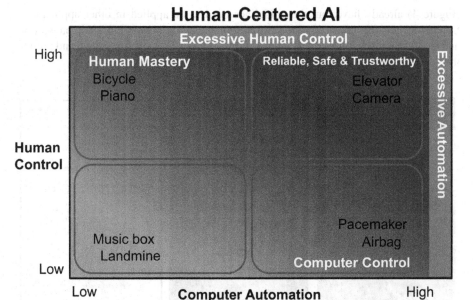

Fig. 2. The HCAI Framework shows a 2-dimensional model with low and high human control and low and high computer automation. It makes clear that it is possible to have high human control and high computer automation. There are also situations in which human mastery or computer control are desired and situations in which excessive human control and excessive automation need to be prevented.

(1) intelligent agents and supertools
(2) teammates and tele-operated devices
(3) assured autonomy and supervised autonomy
(4) social robots and active appliances

Journalists, headline writers, graphic designers, and Hollywood producers are entranced by the possibilities of robots and AI, so it will take a generation to change attitudes and expectations towards a human-centered view. With fresh thinking, researchers, developers, business leaders, and policy makers can find combined designs that will accelerate HCAI thinking. A greater emphasis on HCAI will reduce unfounded fears of AI's existential threats and raise people's belief that they will be able to use technology for their daily needs and creative explorations. It will increase benefits for users and society in business, education, healthcare, environmental preservation, and community safety.

A key change in thinking is to design user interfaces and control panels to give users of supertools and active appliances greater understanding of the state of the machine and what it will do in the next 10, 60, or 600 seconds. Users are in control when they have visual previews (or alternate interfaces for uses with visual impairments) of what their computer could do, so they can select from alternatives and initiate actions, then follow it through during execution. This what users of digital cameras and navigations systems

(Figure 4) already have, but the guidelines need to be applied in other applications. Similar designs for industrial robots, drones, financial trading systems, ship navigation, and medical devices follow the *Human-Control Mantra*: Preview first, select and initiate, then view execution (Fig. 3).

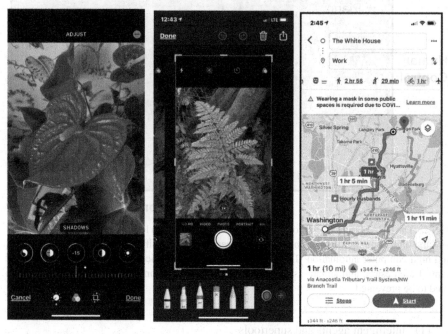

Fig. 3. Digital cameras show users previews of the image they would get and let users control features before, during and after taking photos. Navigation systems show users several possible routes, which they choose from and then they start the system when they are ready.

3) **Governance Structures** bridge the gap between widely discussed ethical principles and the practical steps needed to realize them [3]. Software team leaders, business managers, organization leaders, and government policy makers (Fig. 4) will have to adapt proven technical practices, management strategies, and independent oversight methods [1], so they can achieve the desired goals of:

(1) **Reliable systems** based on proven software engineering practices,
(2) **Safety culture** through business management strategies, and
(3) **Trustworthy certification** by independent oversight and government regulation

These ideas will need to be refined in practice, tuned to the needs of each industry, and adjusted as innovations emerge. They are gaining acceptance, but there is still resistance from those who believe in established ways of working.

Governance Structures for Human-Centered AI

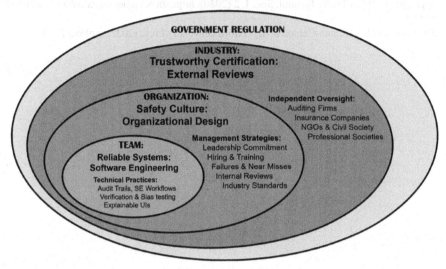

Fig. 4. Governance structures for Human-Centered AI with four levels: reliable systems based on software engineering (SE) practices, a well-developed safety culture based on sound management strategies, trustworthy certification by external review, and government regulation.

I am well aware that my vision for the future is still a minority position, so there is much work to be done to steer researchers, developers, managers, and policy makers to this new synthesis. Other challenges come from the numerous threats such as misinformation, cyber-crime, political oppression, and online bias, hatred and bullying.

However, I feel confident that the future is human-centered -- filled with supertools and active appliances that amplify, augment, and enhance human abilities, empowering people in remarkable ways while ensuring human control. This compelling HCAI prospect enables people to see, think, create, and act in extraordinary ways, by combining engaging user experiences with embedded AI algorithms to support services that users want. The HCAI prospect contributes to hope-filled agendas for healthcare, community safety, economic development, racial justice, and environmental sustainability.

References

1. Shneiderman, B.: Opinion: the dangers of faulty, biased, or malicious algorithms requires independent oversight. Proc. Nat. Acad. Sci. **113**(48), 13538–13540 (2016). http://www.pnas.org/content/113/48/13538.full
2. Shneiderman, B.: Bridging the gap between ethics and practice: guidelines for reliable, safe, and trustworthy human-centered AI systems. ACM Trans. Interact. Intell. Syst. **10**(4), 31 (2020). https://doi.org/10.1145/3419764. Article 26
3. Shneiderman, B.: Human-centered artificial intelligence: reliable, safe, & trustworthy. Int. J. Hum.-Comput. Interact. **36**(6), 495–504 (2020). https://doi.org/10.1080/10447318.2020.1741118

4. Shneiderman, B.: Design lessons from AI's two grand goals: human emulation and useful applications. IEEE Trans. Technol. Soc. **1**, 2 (2020). https://ieeexplore.ieee.org/document/9088114

5. Shneiderman, B.: Human-Centered AI. Oxford University Press (2022, forthcoming)

Multisensory Experiences: Where the Senses Meet Technology

Marianna Obrist[(⊠)] [iD]

Department of Computer Science, University College London,
Gower Street, London WC1E 6BT, UK
m.obrist@ucl.ac.uk

Abstract. Multisensory experiences, that is, experiences that involve more than one of our senses, are part of our everyday life. We often tend to take them for granted, at least when our different senses function normally (normal sight functioning) or are corrected-to-normal (using glasses). However, closer inspection to any, even the most mundane experiences, reveals the remarkable sensory world in which we live in. While we have built tools, experiences and computing systems that have played to the human advantages of hearing and sight (e.g., signage, modes of communication, visual and musical arts, theatre, cinema and media), we have long neglected the opportunities around touch, taste, or smell as interface/interaction modalities. Within this keynote I will share my vision for the future of computing/HCI and what role touch, taste, and smell can play in it.

Keywords: Multisensory experiences · Human-computer interaction · Novel interaction modalities · Multisensory technology · Senses · Touch · Taste · Smell

1 Introduction

"The most profound technologies are those that disappear. They weave themselves into the fabric of everyday life until they are indistinguishable from it" (Weiser 1991). Extending this vision of Mark Weiser, I believe that the most profound future digital technologies are those that unite all the main senses (sight, hearing, touch, taste, smell) into compelling experiences. Here below I outline some relevant developments we can observe today that make this vision for multisensory technologies more feasible than ever, but also leave us still with many challenges and responsibilities to consider.

First, it is key to remind ourselves that our life experiences are multisensory in nature. Think about this moment. You may be reading this article while immersed in a sound atmosphere. There may be a smell in the environment, even if you are not aware of it, and you may be drinking a cup of coffee or eating something, while touching the means through which you read the article. All these different sensory inputs, but perhaps more, influence the experience that you have about reading the article. But what if we could design such multisensory arrangement to create a given, intended, experience? (Velasco and Obrist 2021).

© IFIP International Federation for Information Processing 2021
Published by Springer Nature Switzerland AG 2021
C. Ardito et al. (Eds.): INTERACT 2021, LNCS 12932, pp. 9–13, 2021.
https://doi.org/10.1007/978-3-030-85623-6_2

2 Defining Multisensory Experiences

Multisensory experiences are increasingly changed and enabled through technology (e.g. Lin et al. 2020), and particularly through advances in the field of HCI (e.g. Cornelio et al. 2021; Maggioni et al. 2019; 2020, Vi et al. 2020). Beyond HCI, there are many other disciplines that are contributing to the continuous growth of our understanding of the senses, multisensory experiences, and the relationship between the senses and technology (see Velasco and Obrist 2020).

To account for this growing interdisciplinary interest in multisensory research and practice and enable a dialogue across stakeholders we defined multisensory experiences as *"...impressions formed by specific events, whose sensory elements have been carefully crafted by someone. For example, to create the impression of a sunflower, colours, shapes, textures, and smells are considered. The senses are placed at the centre of the formation of the impression of the sunflower, even in the absence of a real flower."* (Velasco and Obrist 2020, p. 15).

Imagine the experience of a sunflower. Technologies such as virtual and augmented reality (VR, AR) enable the creation of an impression of a sunflower, even in the absence of a real flower. This is enabled through advances in sensory devices and interface that allow us to carefully select and combine sensory stimuli in a virtual or mixed reality environment. The sunflower example is only one of many experiences we can design for and to illustrate a multisensory experience. You can think of any other experiences you have in your everyday life such as eating an apple, watching a movie, or reading this article.

It is worth noting that whilst most of people's experiences are multisensory per se, multisensory experiences are different in that there is intentionality in them. In other words, while, say, walking in a forest or jungle (event) involves a number of sensory elements, a multisensory experience, as we put forward, is carefully designed by someone. Take, as an example, a walk in the jungle that has been designed by a landscape architect in order to evoke specific impressions in a given receiver. Hence, when one refers to multisensory experiences, the "design" part is implied. For this same reason, multisensory experiences and multisensory experience design are often used interchangeably (see further details in Velasco and Obrist 2020, and a primer in Velasco and Obrist 2021).

3 Designing Multisensory Experiences

Technology has revolutionised how we communicate, work, relax, and share experiences. In effect, technology has not only changed the way in which we experience the world around us but has become an experience in itself. Do you remember the one time you forgot your smartphone at home, the Internet connection did not work, or your computer just did not turn on and you stared at a black screen? Experiencing those moments of being "online" and "offline" can be frustrating. It can disconnect us from others and at the same time remind us about what it means to be human, without extensions or augmented capabilities, in an increasingly digital world. Even events that were only partially influenced by technology until recently such as eating, have become increasingly a playground for introducing technology to provide us with completely new dining experiences.

How would it feel to eat your dinner wearing special glasses that make your vegetables look more appealing? How would it feel like to eat in zero gravity without the use of any plateware? Food just floats in front of you and the only thing you need is your mouth to catch the food. It may sound like science fiction, but advances in levitation technology make it possible. You could, for example, levitate a piece of pear to impress your dinner date, as Anakin Skywalker did to impress Princess Amidala in Star Wars: Attack of the Clones. Unexpected and novel experiences can become a reality through technological advances, and thus not only change the experience, but become the experience itself (see TastyFloats by Vi et al. 2017, LeviSense by Vi et al. 2020).

Now, consider how to design a multisensory experience that has no real-world sensory representation. For example, dark matter is often discussed in the general media but difficult to grasp for non-experts. How can we use sensory elements to design an experience that makes the invisible visible, feelable, and much more? Together with astrophysicists from Imperial College, we carefully crafted a multisensory experience of Dark Matter. This experience is facilitated through the integration of multiple technologies, including an ultrasonic mid-air haptic device to create tactile sensations on people's hands (Obrist et al. 2013; Carter et al. 2013), a scent-delivery device to release the smell at specific moments (Maggioni et al. 2019), a projector to create the visual effect of the universe inside the dome, and noise-cancelling headphones to follow the audio narrative (see details in Trotta et al. 2020). Within the field of science communication, there are increased efforts to make those scientific concepts more accessible through the use of technology, sensory experiences, and new ways of storytelling (Hajas et al. 2020).

We only start to understand the design space for multisensory experiences and enabling technologies. With the continuous design and development of multisensory technologies, questions arise such as to what extent are those technologies going to change humans and our everyday lives and become an extension and augmentation of our human capabilities (physical, perceptual, and cognitive) and consequently of ourselves. The growing degree of integration between humans and technology, starting from today's mixed reality spaces, makes us wonder how technology will keep changing us humans (Mueller et al. 2020).

4 Responsible Innovation Around the Senses and Technology

The excitement about multisensory experiences in academia and industry, opens a plethora of opportunities but also needs to be met with responsibility. However, there is, to date, little discussion on the implications of multisensory experiences (e.g. on our body see Brianza et al. 2019, creating illusions Pittera et al. 2019).

Considering the above introduced definition of multisensory experiences, we postulated the three laws of multisensory experiences. These laws focus on acknowledging and debating publicly different questions that are at the heart of the definition of multisensory experiences, namely, the why (the rationale/reason), what (the impression), when (the event), how (the sensory elements), who (the someone), and whom (the receiver), associated with a given multisensory experience.

The three laws indicate (Velasco and Obrist 2020, p. 79):

I. Multisensory experiences should be used for good and must not harm others.
II. Receivers of a multisensory experience must be treated fairly.
III. The someone and the sensory elements must be known.

The first law aims to guide the thinking process related to the question: Why and what impressions and events we want to design for? The answer to this question, should always be: Reasons, events, and impressions must not cause any harm to the receiver, nor anyone else. Multisensory experiences should be used for good. The second law aims to make people reflect about the questions: Who are we designing for? Should we design differently for different receivers? The first question helps to identify the receiver and its characteristics. The final law seeks to address two questions. First, who is crafting the multisensory experience? Second, what sensory elements we select and why? With this law we call for transparency in terms of who designs, what knowledge guides the design, and what sensory elements are chosen to craft an impression. Although it is possible that not all information may be provided upfront to the receiver, they must have easy access to such information if they want.

In summary, today is one of the best moments to design multisensory experiences in that both science and technology are evolving faster than ever and providing us with a deeper understanding of our senses as well as multisensory technologies to stimulate and extend them. Nevertheless, there are still many questions and unknown answers when looking from the present into the future. For example, the growing degree of integration between humans and technology, makes us wonder how technology will keep changing us humans and consequently also inform the design of humanoid robots and future artificial intelligent (artificial intelligence, AI) systems. While humanoid robots still have a long way to go before becoming part of everyday lives, they are surely increasingly becoming ready for it, especially with AI making progress. With it, humanoid robots will be equipped with all the main human senses: sight, hearing, touch, smell, and even taste when it will, if at all, become necessary for them to fully function. Advances in sensor technology facilitate those development.

Only time will tell how the future relationship between humans and technology will look like, although we can be assured that it will be both promising and challenging in the context of multisensory experiences.

Acknowledgements. This work was mainly funded by the European Research Council (ERC) under the European Unions Horizon 2020 Research and Innovation Program under Grant No: 638605. I would like to thank all members of the SCHI Lab for their fantastic contributions to multisensory HCI. Special thanks go to Dr Carlos Velasco, co-author of our book on Multisensory Experiences, that provides the foundation for this keynote.

References

1. Brianza, G., Tajadura-Jiménez, A., Maggioni, E., Pittera, D., Bianchi-Berthouze, N., Obrist, M.: As light as your scent: effects of smell and sound on body image perception. In: Lamas, D., Loizides, F., Nacke, L., Petrie, H., Winckler, M., Zaphiris, P. (eds.) Human-Computer Interaction – INTERACT 2019. INTERACT 2019. Lecture Notes in Computer Science, vol. 11749. Springer, Cham (2019). https://doi.org/10.1007/978-3-030-29384-0

2. Carter, T., Seah, S.A., Long, B., Drinkwater, B., Subramanian, S.: UltraHaptics: multi-point mid-air haptic feedback for touch surfaces. In: Proceedings of UIST 2013, pp. 505–514. ACM (2013)
3. Cornelio, P., Velasco, C., Obrist, M.: Multisensory integration as per technological advances: a review. Front. Neurosci. (2021). DOI: https://doi.org/10.3389/fnins.2021.652611
4. Hajas, D., Ablart, D., Schneider, O., Obrist, M.: I can feel it moving: science communicators talking about the potential of mid-air haptics. In: Frontiers in Computer Science (2020). https://doi.org/10.3389/fcomp.2020.534974
5. Lin, Y.-J., et al.: FoodFab: creating food perception tricks using food 3D printing. In: Proceedings of the 2020 CHI Conference on Human Factors in Computing Systems (CHI 2020), pp. 1–13. ACM, New York (2020). https://doi.org/10.1145/3313831.3376421
6. Maggioni, E., Cobden, R., Obrist, M.: OWidgets: a toolkit to enable smell-based experience design. Int. J. Hum. Comput. Stud. **130**, 248–260 (2019)
7. Maggioni, E., Cobden, R., Dmitrenko, D., Hornbæk, K., Obrist, M.: SMELL SPACE: mapping out the olfactory design space for novel interactions. ACM Trans. Comput. Hum. Interact. **27**(5), 26 (2020). DOI: https://doi.org/10.1145/3402449. Article 36
8. Mueller, F., et al.: Next steps in human-computer integration. In: Proceedings of the 2020 CHI Conference on Human Factors in Computing Systems (CHI 2020), pp. 1–15. ACM, New York (2020). DOI: https://doi.org/10.1145/3313831.3376242
9. Obrist, M., Seah, S.A., Subramanian, S.: Talking about Tactile Experiences. In: Proceedings of the SIGCHI Conference on Human Factors in Computing Systems, pp. 1659–1668. ACM, New York (2013). https://doi.org/10.1145/2470654.2466220
10. Pittera, D., Gatti, E., Obrist, M.: I'm sensing in the rain: illusion of raindrops through multiple incongruent mid-air tactile stimulation. In: Proceedings of the 2019 CHI Conference on Human Factors in Computing Systems (CHI 2019), Paper 132, 15 p. ACM, New York (2019)
11. Trotta, R., Hajas, D., Camargo-Molina, J.E., Cobden, R., Maggioni, E., Obrist, M.: Communicating cosmology with multisensory metaphorical experiences. In: JCOM 2019, p. 2 (2020). https://doi.org/10.22323/2.19020801. N01
12. Velasco, C., Obrist, M.: Multisensory Experiences: Where the Senses Meet Technology. Oxford University Press (2020)
13. Velasco, C., Obrist, M.: Multisensory experiences: a primer. Front. Comput. Sci. (2021). DOI: https://doi.org/10.3389/fcomp.2021.614524
14. Vi, T.C., Ablart, D., Gatti, E., Velasco, C., Obrist, M.: Not just seeing, but also feeling art: mid-air haptic experiences integrated in a multisensory art exhibition. Int. J. Hum. Comput Stud. **108**, 1–14 (2017). https://doi.org/10.1016/j.ijhcs.2017.06.004
15. Vi, C.T., et al.: LeviSense: a platform for the multisensory integration in levitating food and insights into its effect on flavour perception. Int. J. Hum. Comput. Stud. (2020). https://doi.org/10.1016/j.ijhcs.2020.102428
16. Weiser, M.: The Computer for the 21st Century. Scientific American (1991)

Nicolas Cage is the Center
of the Cybersecurity Universe

Luca Viganò[(✉)] [iD]

Department of Informatics, King's College London, London, UK
luca.vigano@kcl.ac.uk

Abstract. Nicolas Cage, prolific actor, Oscar winner but also master of ham acting, star of many excellent films and of at least as many really bad ones. A conspicuous number of these films directly revolve around cybersecurity or can be used to explain cybersecurity notions in such a way that they can be understood by non-experts. This paper is part of a research program that I have been carrying out on how to use films and other artworks to explain cybersecurity notions, and thus provide a form of "cybersecurity show and tell" (in which telling, i.e., explaining notions in a formal, technical way, can be paired with showing through visual storytelling or other forms of storytelling). Here, I focus on 15 of Cage's films in which he has played a wide variety of roles: a stunt motorcyclist, a paroled ex-con and former U.S. Ranger, a U.S. Marine in World War II, an agent of an authoritarian agency, a retired master car thief, a criminal mastermind, an illegal arms dealer, a master sorcerer, a treasure hunter historian, a Batman-like superhero, Spider-Man Noir, Superman, an NSA employee, and a hacker star-nosed mole.

1 Introduction

1.1 "Kevin Bacon Is the Center of the Entertainment Universe"

In 1994, Craig Fass, Mike Ginelli and Brian Turtle, three students of Albright College in Reading, Pennsylvania, invented a game they called "Six Degrees of Kevin Bacon" [21]. The game quickly became very popular on the Usenet newsgroup rec.arts.movies, the forerunner of the Internet Movie Database IMDB, and the three authors were invited to "The John Stewart Show", a late night talk show on MTV, where they proposed the game as a proof of concept for their theory that "Kevin Bacon is the center of the entertainment universe".

As explained by the authors in 1994, the basic idea of the game was that every single Hollywood actor of the previous 15 years or so could be connected to the actor Kevin Bacon (b. 1958) through six or fewer "hops", where a hop is defined as having worked in the same film. The game has since been expanded to include actors and other cast members (in particular, directors and producers) of any movie and any year, although it is quite obvious that more than six hops might be required to connect Kevin Bacon to, say, an international actor of a

C. Ardito et al. (Eds.): INTERACT 2021, LNCS 12932, pp. 14–33, 2021.
https://doi.org/10.1007/978-3-030-85623-6_3

non-Hollywood movie of the beginning of the 20th century. The game can be played online at "The Oracle of Bacon" (https://oracleofbacon.org) or one can simply use Google's search engine to compute an actor's "Bacon number":

- Kevin Bacon himself has a Bacon number of 0;
- those actors who have worked directly with Kevin Bacon have a Bacon number of 1;
- if the lowest Bacon number of any actor with whom actor A has appeared in any movie is n, then A's Bacon number is $n + 1$.

The Six Degrees of Kevin Bacon game is centered around the *six degrees of separation* theory, which postulates that all people are, on average, six, or fewer, social connections away from each other: any two people can be connected in a maximum of six steps by a chain of acquaintances, i.e., a chain of "friend of a friend" statements, which is sometimes also referred to as a chain of "handshakes". As described in detail at [83], the concept was originally set out in the 1929 short story "Chains" (a.k.a. "Chain-Links") by Frigyes Karinthy, where a group of people play a game trying to connect any person in the world to themselves by a chain of five others, and it was popularized in John Guare's 1990 play "Six Degrees of Separation" [27] and the subsequent film adaptation [59].

The six degrees of separation theory is connected to results in *network theory* [80], including the *small-world experiments* lead by Stanley Milgram in the 1960s [45]. Milgram and colleagues carried out a number of studies to examine the average path length for social networks of people in the United States. The studies suggest that human society is a small-world-type network characterized by short path-lengths.[1]

Computer scientists and mathematicians working in cybersecurity might not be familiar with the Six Degrees of Kevin Bacon game and the Bacon number[2], but many of them will likely have heard of the "Erdös number", which measures the collaboration distance with the great and very prolific mathematician Paul Erdös (1913–1996), where two persons are linked if they are coauthors of an article. A small number of people are connected to both Erdös and Bacon and thus have an "Erdös–Bacon number", which combines the two numbers by taking their sum, and an even smaller number of people have an "Erdös–Bacon–Sabbath

---

[1] Interestingly, Kevin Bacon was initially horrified by the Six Degrees of Kevin Bacon game because he believed it was ridiculing him, but he then quickly embraced it, so much so that he wrote the introduction of the book [21] and then, inspired by the game and in the spirit of the "small-world" idea, he created a nonprofit charity called sixdegrees.org "aimed at using everyday activities to connect people and causes" since "at the end of the day, we're all just six degrees from someone who really needs our help, and when we work together, we really can do a great deal of good".

[2] Similarly, younger readers might not be familiar with the Usenet and its newsgroups, and MTV is likely not so popular anymore, but I am confident that they do know who Kevin Bacon is given that he is still very active as a film and TV actor, and as a musician in the "The Bacon Brothers" together with his brother Michael.

number", which is the sum of the Erdös–Bacon number and the collaboration distance to the band Black Sabbath in terms of singing in public [23].[3]

If you have an Erdös–Bacon–Sabbath number, you probably indeed are one of the centers of our universe, embodying the spirit of a true "Renaissance man" as advocated by Leon Battista Alberti, who in the 15th century coined the ideal of a "Universal Man" ("Uomo Universale", in Italian) as "a man who can do all things if he will'. However, it actually turns out that Kevin Bacon is not really the center of the entertainment universe: every few weeks, the Oracle of Bacon algorithm recomputes the list of the "1,000 centers of the Hollywood Universe" that includes the actors that can be linked in the smallest number of hops to all other actors, and at the time of writing (June 2001) Kevin Bacon was number 543 in that list, with Christopher Lee, Harvey Keitel and Christopher Plummer in the top three places. Still, for us movie geeks nothing, not even reality, can dethrone Kevin Bacon from the center of the entertainment universe.

1.2   Is Nicolas Cage the Center of the Cybersecurity Universe?

Nicolas Cage, born Nicolas Kim Coppola in 1964, is one of the most prolific actors of his generation (at the time of writing, he had 106 acting credits on IMDB) and, although he never shared the screen with Kevin Bacon, he has a Bacon number of 2. He is an Oscar winner but also a master of ham acting, and has starred in many excellent films and in at least as many really bad ones, ranging from comedy to drama, from action to animation. A conspicuous number of these films directly revolve around cybersecurity or can be used to explain cybersecurity notions in such a way that they can be understood by non-experts, so, in my view, he is definitely a contender for the title of the center of cybersecurity universe. Let me clarify what I mean.

In my papers "Explaining Cybersecurity with Films and the Arts" [76] and "Don't Tell me the Cybersecurity Moon is Shining... (Cybersecurity Show and Tell)" [77], I discussed how, in the context of research in *Explainable Security (XSec)* [79], popular film and other artworks can be used to explain a number of basic and advanced cybersecurity notions, ranging from security properties (such as anonymity, authentication, confidentiality, integrity and availability) to the algorithms, protocols and systems that have been developed to achieve such properties, and to the vulnerabilities and attacks that they suffer from.

In [76,77], I provided a number of concrete examples of cybersecurity notions and films and other artworks, including a handful of films with Nicolas Cage. In this paper, I will provide even more examples by considering 15 of Cage's films that are related to cybersecurity. I will do so following the structure identified in [77], namely that when using existing films to explain cybersecurity notions there are essentially four sub-categories, from films about hackers, codebreakers

---

[3] There are also a few other similar numbers, such as the "Morphy number", which measures how closely a chess player is connected to the great Paul Morphy (1837–1884) by way of playing chess games, or the "Shusaku number", which similarly measures the distance of Go players to the invincible Honinbo Shusaku (1829–1862).

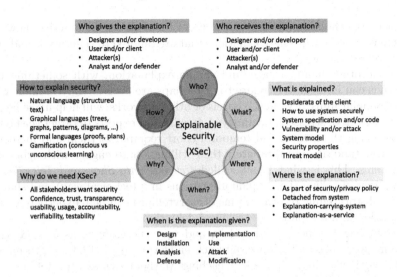

Fig. 1. The Six Ws of explainable security (from [79])

and cybersecurity experts, to films about detectives or spies, to films about ordinary people confronted with cybersecurity, to films that are not explicitly about cybersecurity but can be used to explain cybersecurity notions. Before I give examples of all four sub-categories taken from Nicolas Cage's filmography, let me provide a more detailed summary of the main points of [76,77] as this paper is their natural continuation.

2   Cybersecurity Show and Tell

In [79], Daniele Magazzeni and I introduced XSec and discussed its "Six Ws": Who? What? Where? When? Why? and How?, which are summarized in Fig. 1. We argued that XSec has unique and complex characteristics: XSec involves several different stakeholders (i.e., system's developers, analysts, users and attackers) and is multi-faceted by nature, as it requires reasoning about system model, threat model and properties of security, privacy and trust as well as concrete attacks, vulnerabilities and countermeasures.

The recipients of the explanations might be so varied, ranging from experts to laypersons, that they require quite radically different explanations, formulated using different languages. Experts typically only accept detailed technical explanations, whereas laypersons are often scared off by explanations of cybersecurity (say, how to interact with a system or an app) that are detailed but too technical. Such an explanation might even repulse the laypersons and make them lose all trust in the explanation and, ultimately, in the cybersecurity of the system that is being explained. This repulsion and lack of trust might lead to users interacting with systems in ways that, unbeknownst to the users and possibly even to the developers and administrators of the systems, are vulnerable to attacks (to the systems and to the users themselves). In practice, however, laypersons are rarely given explanations that are tailored to their needs and their ability to understand.

On the other hand, a clear and simple explanation, with something that laypersons can immediately relate to or perhaps are even already familiar with, such as popular films, TV shows, novels or other artworks, will help make laypersons less irritated, stressed and annoyed. It will allow experts to target the laypersons, reducing the mental and temporal effort required of them and increasing their understanding, and ultimately their willingness to engage with cybersecurity systems. This is what I have called *Cybersecurity Show and Tell* [77]: the added power of telling (i.e., explaining notions in a technical way) *and* showing (via visual storytelling or other forms of storytelling) can help experts to convey the intuition in addition to the technical definition.

Storytelling has been used widely, and very successfully, as a pedagogical device in textbooks and science outreach endeavors, e.g., [12,18,89] to name a few. In particular, in their book "Teaching Mathematics as Storytelling" [89], Rina Zazkis and Peter Liljedahl distinguish a number of categories of stories for the teaching of mathematics, ranging from stories that introduce to stories that accompany and intertwine with a mathematical activity.

For what concerns cybersecurity, without limiting the discussion to teaching, but considering all kinds of learning experiences, including scientific communications and public engagement or outreach activities, in [77] I divided the use of artworks to explain cybersecurity into two broad categories:

– *Using existing artworks.*
– *Using new artworks that have been created on purpose.*

My work so far has focused on the first category, but together with a multidisciplinary team we have begun tackling also the second category. I will return to this in the conclusions, but for now let me focus on the first category, which can be further divided into the following 4 sub-categories:

1. *Artworks about hackers, codebreakers and cybersecurity experts*, who make for very interesting hero(in)es or anti-hero(in)es. Notable examples include [1–3,5,10,11,14,19,24,30,37,41,49,54,55,63,65–68,73,84]. Some of these artworks are quite realistic in their depiction of cybersecurity, few are real, most are inventive, giving black/white-hat hackers and codebreakers almost superhero-like abilities, but all of them make for a good "show" companion of the technical telling, as a speaker can discuss how faithfully or not cybersecurity has been portrayed. In fact, bad portrayals can be particularly useful to discuss misconceptions and correct possible prejudices.
2. *Artworks about detectives or spies who use or are confronted with cybersecurity problems and solutions.* This category is closely connected to the previous one and in many cases there are some overlaps, e.g., [20,22,81]. Other notable examples include [8,9,15,16,31–33,40,52,53,58,70,71]. Also these professional and dilettante detectives are typically given abilities that

border on the fantastic as they "see" the solutions of the cryptographic riddles in a matter of minutes, if not seconds. They picture them in their head before anyone can and often when nobody else does. This is "showing" in a way that is exclusive rather than inclusive. Similar to the characters of the first category, this facility for cryptography and cybersecurity creates a clear distinction from ordinary people and turns them into true hero(in)es and anti-hero(in)es. This is, however, quite understandable, as the story would then otherwise risk being quite dull. Still, using such characters and their stories for *showing* can be very effective also thanks to their worldwide popularity.

3. *Artworks about ordinary people confronted with cybersecurity or artworks with references to cybersecurity.* There are in general less examples in this category than the previous two, but still several interesting ones, such as [4,6,25,28, 38,39,64,69,85,86]. This category requires substantial work of the presenter to make the connections between *show* and *tell* but, trust me, it can be lots of fun, especially if one shows excerpts of the animated films.

4. *Artworks that are not explicitly about cybersecurity but can be used to explain cybersecurity notions.* This is, in my view, the most interesting category, but also the most difficult one to populate, as the artworks in this case are symbols or rather allegories of the cybersecurity notions. As an example, consider the famous "I'm Spartacus" scene in the film "Spartacus" [36], which I already discussed in [76]. When the captured rebels all stand up and claim to be Spartacus, so that the Roman soldiers cannot identify (and execute and make an example of) the real Spartacus, they are not only showing friendship and respect to their leader Spartacus, but they are actually also creating what in the context of cybersecurity is called an *anonymity set*. One can of course give a formal definition of *anonymity* [51]—and this is what one would do in front of an expert audience, say in a talk at a conference or in a university lecture on cybersecurity – but the point here is that even non-specialists immediately understand what the rebels are doing and why: they are protecting Spartacus so that he cannot be identified, they are making him anonymous in a crowd. Did Howard Fast, the author of the original novel, or Dalton Trumbo, the author of the screenplay, write the scene in order to explain what an anonymity set is? No, of course not. They probably didn't even have the slightest clue about anonymity sets, but they intuitively knew that anonymity cannot exist in a vacuum (one cannot be anonymous by oneself) but rather requires a large enough set of similar "things", a large enough set of similar people, actions, messages, etc. so that one's identity, actions or messages are not distinguishable from those of the others and thus not identifiable. In fact, I dare say that we all share this intuitive knowledge, which is why that scene is a powerful allegory.

I have been able to identify a number of other examples, such as [17,26,43,44, 87] as well as the stories of authentication and identity that occur extensively in the mythology and fairy-tale literature of most cultures, from Greece to Norway to India to China to Africa (e.g., the "Iliad", the "Odyssey", Ovid's "Metamorphoses", the "Epic of Gilgamesh", "The Arthurian cycle", "The Wolf and the Seven Young Goats", "Ali Baba and the Forty Thieves").

In [77], I give more examples for each category and describe the specific artworks and their relevance and use in detail. Now, it is time to focus on Cage.

3   Nicolas Cage and Cybersecurity

In Fig. 2, I have singled out 15 of Cage's films that are related to cybersecurity notions; there are more, of course, but these 15 provide a good start and cover a wide spectrum. The cells of the table contain keywords that highlight the notions that the films exemplify and the sub-category they belong to. As expected, the number of entries decreases as we move from hackers to allegories. In the following, I discuss each of these films in detail, providing brief plot summaries (mostly taken from IMDB) and discussing the scenes in which cybersecurity plays a role.

Con Air [81]: newly paroled ex-con and former U.S. Ranger Cameron Poe (Nicolas Cage) finds himself trapped in a convict transport plane when the convicts seize control.

- *Steganography*: U.S. Marshal Vince Larkin searches the prison cell of criminal mastermind Cyrus "The Virus" Grissom. He finds a letter from a Colombian law firm, written in Spanish, and a picture of Leonardo Da Vinci's painting "Last Supper" in which the eyes of Jesus Christ and the 12 Apostles have been cut out. Larkin discovers that the letter contains a message in English that can be retrieved by laying the picture over the letter and reading the characters that appear in the holes.
- *Authentication/Deception*: The convicts know that the plane that they have hijacked is tracked by means of a transponder. Hence, they remove it and hide it on another plane so that the FBI and police chase that other plane.

Face/Off [85]: The FBI agent Sean Archer undergoes facial transplant surgery to swap his face (and voice, by means of an implanted microchip) with that of a criminal mastermind Castor Troy (Cage) in order to go "undercover" by assuming Troy's identity and thus find out where Troy has planted a bomb that will destroy the city of Los Angeles. Troy was supposed to be kept sedated in the hospital in the meantime, but he wakes up prematurely and can now pretend to be Archer (as he has Archer's face and voice, after all).

- *Multi-factor authentication* and *Biometrics*: Archer wants to prove to his wife that it is indeed him even though he has Troy's face and voice, but of course she does not believe him. So, what does he do to prove his real identity? He authenticates himself using another biometrics factor, namely his blood type. Moreover, his wife and daughter also recognize him by a specific gesture that he always used to do.

G-Force [88]: A team of very special secret agents, comprising of guinea pigs, flies and the star-nosed mole Speckles (voiced by Cage) is dispatched to stop an evil billionaire from taking over the world by means of the household appliances that he has been selling worldwide and that are all connected with each other over the Internet.

Film title	Keywords	Category
G-Force	Hacking; Password cracking; Worm; Virus; IoT attack	Hackers and cryptologists
Kick-Ass	Anonymity; Tracing	
National Treasure	Steganography; Multiple-stage attack; Masquerading attack; Forging; Pseudonym; Social engineering; Invisible ink; Hacking; Sensor attack; Biometrics; Integrity; Password guessing; Background knowledge; Indistinguishability; Swapping; Tracing; Ottendorf cipher	
National Treasure: Book of Secrets	Playfair cipher; Password guessing; Device cloning; Hacking; Denial of service; Social engineering; Surveillance system; Codes	
Snowden	Cipher machines; Algorithms; Attacks; Malware; Surveillance; Trojan horse; Password protection	
Windtalkers	Codes	
Con Air	Steganography; Authentication/Deception	Detectives and spies
Face/Off	Multi-factor authentication; Biometrics	
Gone in 60 Seconds	Steganography; Codes; Insider attack	
Teen Titans GO! To the Movies	Pseudonyms; Multi-factor authentication; Biometrics; Masquerading attack; Social engineering	
Lord of War	Identity/Authentication; Confidentiality; Integrity; Social Engineering	Ordinary people
Spider-Man: Into the Spider-Verse	Pseudonyms; Identity; Accountability	
The Humanity Bureau	Stolen identity	
Ghost Rider	Biometrics	
	Anonymous	Allegory
The Sorcerer's Apprentice	Authentication	

Fig. 2. Films with Nicolas Cage in the four categories

- *Hacking, Password cracking, Worm, Virus, IoT attack*: Speckles the Mole is a true hacker: he hacks into the evil billionaire's house, cracks the password of his laptop, deploys a worm to decrypt an encrypted file, and deploys a virus to attempt to thwart the Internet of Things (IoT) attack that is taking place via the Internet-connected devices in households worldwide.

Ghost Rider [34]: When motorcycle rider Johnny Blaze (Cage) sells his soul to the Devil to save his father's life, he is transformed into the Ghost Rider, the Devil's own bounty hunter, and is sent to hunt down sinners.

- *Biometrics*: The contract with the Devil is signed with blood rather than with a proper signature.
- *Anonymous*: The demon Blackheart says: "My name is Legion. For we are many.", which is a quote from both the "Gospel according to Mark" and the "Gospel according to Luke" (and there is a similar sentence in the "Gospel according to Matthew"). On January 23, 2008, the international hacktivist collective "Anonymous" outlined what they called a "War on Scientology" by releasing a video on YouTube in which they stated "If you want another name for your opponent, then call us Legion, for we are many."

Gone in 60 Seconds [62]: Reformed master car thief Memphis Raines (Cage) must steal fifty cars with his crew in one night to save his brother's life.

- *Steganography*: The thieves write the list of cars to be stolen on a wall of their warehouse using an ultraviolet-sensitive paint that only becomes visible when a blacklight lamp is shone on it. When the police raid the warehouse, the thieves escape and break the lamp, but a detective finds the shards and has them analyzed by the forensics team. The team tell him that the shards are part of a blacklight lamp, so he deduces that lamp must have been used to read something written somewhere in the warehouse. He gets another blacklight lamp and shines it on the walls of the warehouse until he can finally read the hidden message.
- *Codes*: Memphis Raines and his crew of car thieves, instead, use female code-names to refer to the cars to be stolen: "Why do you call them girls' names?" asks one of the thieves and Raines answers: "It's code. You say Jane, you say Shirley, Lucy, Edna, and nobody listening in on the waves is the wiser."
- *Insider attack*: Two detectives talk about one of the cars that was stolen:
    Detective 1: This is one of three brand-new Mercedes, a car they say is unstealable.
    Detective 2: Yeah, unless you get the laser-cut transponder key sent directly to the US dealer from Hamburg.
    Detective 1: They got somebody working on the inside.

Kick-Ass [75]: Ordinary teenager and comic-book fan Dave Lizewski sets out to become a real-life superhero, calling himself "Kick-Ass", even though he has no powers, training or meaningful reason to do so. Dave gets caught up in a bigger fight when he meets Big Daddy (Cage), a former cop who, in his quest to bring down a crime boss, has trained his eleven-year-old daughter to be the ruthless vigilante Hit-Girl.

- *Anonymity* and *Tracing*: Big Daddy and Hit-Girl pay Dave/Kick-Ass a visit at his home. Dave is surprised that they have been able to find out where he lives, so Big Daddy tells him that if you are a wannabe superhero, it is not a great idea to set up a webpage: "I rerouted your IP address. Finding you was way too easy."

Lord of War [48]: Illegal arms dealer Yuri Orlov (Cage) confronts the morality of his work as he is being chased by an Interpol Agent.

- *Identity/Authentication*: Orlov's container ship is being chased by the Interpol and before they are boarded, they quickly swap their ensign with that of another country and change the ship's name by repainting it.
- *Confidentiality*: One of the containers on the ship contains boxes of guns, but they are covered (encrypted) with potatoes, so that when the Interpol open the container's door, the potatoes fall out and they don't spot the boxes.
- *Integrity*: Orlov convinces his uncle, a former Soviet general overseeing a newly independent Ukrainian Army arsenal, to alter the official documents to state that the warehouse contains only 10,000 guns instead of the 40,000 guns it really contains.
- *Social engineering*: Orlov's wife suspects that he is an illegal arms dealer and tries to open one of his containers to find proof. She successfully guesses that the pin that opens the lock is their son's birthday.

National Treasure [70]: Historian and treasure hunter Benjamin Franklin Gates (Cage) races to find the legendary Templar Treasure before a team of mercenaries.

- *Steganography*: The premise of the film is that on the back of the Declaration of Independence, signed on July 4, 1776, by 55 Founding Fathers (at least nine of whom were Freemasons), hides a coded, unseen map that points to the secret location of the fabled and massive Templar Treasure that was discovered by the Knights Templar and later protected by the Freemasons. This film is a real cybersecurity goldmine, covering a large number of cybersecurity notions in addition to steganography, so let me provide a detailed description. Please, try to stay with me as the plot thickens.
- *Multiple-stage attack, Masquerading attack, Forging, Pseudonym, Social engineering, Invisible ink, Hacking, Sensor attack, Biometrics, Integrity, Password guessing* and *Background knowledge*: In order to protect the Declaration of Independence from the mercenaries and read the hidden message, Gates decides to steal the Declaration himself. To that end, he carries out a multiple-stage attack with the help of his sidekick Riley Poole. First, Gates, pretending to be a tourist shooting some photos while visiting the National Archives, takes a picture of an ID badge of one of the Archive's custodians and then creates a fake ID with his own face. He then smears a rare George Washington's campaign button with invisible ink and sends it to Abigail Chase, an archivist at the National Archives whom he had tried to warn about the impending threat. When he visited Chase in her office, introducing

himself with the pseudonym Paul Brown, Gates noticed that she was missing this button from her collection, so he knows that she will open the gift box he sent her and touch the button to put it in her display case. Poole, in the meantime, has hacked into the network of the Archives and uses a laser hidden in a camera to attack the sensor of the cage that protects the Declaration to raise the temperature over the threshold. The archivists therefore remove the Declaration from display and take it to the Preservation Room for tests. Chase goes to the Room too for a check and types the password on a keyboard, thus unknowingly smearing the keys with the invisible ink that was on the button that Gates sent her. Later that evening, there is a gala at the Archives. Gates masquerades as a custodian using the fake ID badge and, once inside, changes clothes into a Black Tie, the semi-formal Western dress code for evening events, so as to mingle with the other guests. He briefly meets Chase and, with an excuse, takes a glass that she has been drinking from, from which, using a chemical reagent, he reconstructs her fingerprints and puts them on a glove, which he uses to open a door controlled by the fingerprint reader (while the mercenaries, who are also trying to get to the Preservation Room, knock a security guard out and drag him to another reader to open the door with the guard's actual finger). Gates needs now to walk through a corridor, so Poole turns off the surveillance cameras and replaces the feed with an earlier one, so that the security guards watching the monitors see only an empty corridor. There is one final biometric access control device left for Gates: the keyboard that Chase used earlier that day. He shines a blacklight lamp on the keys to see that the ones smeared with the invisible ink are: A E F G L O R V Y. Poole uses an automatic anagram generator to create a list of possible anagrams, but Gates uses background knowledge about Chase, an historian herself, to correctly guess that Chase pressed E and L twice and the password is "Valley forge", the location where the American Continental Army made camp during the winter of 1777–1778 and which is nowadays often called the birthplace of the American Army. Gates can now enter the Preservation Room and take the Declaration.

- *Indistinguishability, Swapping* and *Tracing*: With the Declaration of Independence folded and tucked under his arm, Gates has to go through the shop, which sells actual-size reproductions of the Declaration. A cashier, seeing the real Declaration tucked under Gates' arm, thinks that he is trying to steal one of the reproductions, so he is forced to pay for it. What we the viewers don't know yet, but will soon find out, is that he actually pays both for the real Declaration and for a reproduction, so that when the bad guys catch up with him, he swaps the two declarations and gives them the replica without them noticing at first, and he can get away. "I thought it would be a good idea to have a duplicate. It turned out I was right." Unfortunately, in the shop he did not have enough cash, so he paid with his credit card, which means that the FBI can trace the payment and find out that he is not Paul Brown but discover his real identity and where he lives.
- *Ottendorf cipher*: As a consequence, Gates and Poole cannot use the clean-room environment that they had set up, so, together with Gates' father and

with Chase, who in the meantime has semi-willingly joined them, they use more artisanal methods to reveal the message hidden on the back of the Declaration. Using lemon juice and their own breaths as heat sources, Gates and Chase expose the message, which is constituted by a series of triples of numbers. It is an Ottendorf cipher and the following dialogue takes place to provide a useful explanation for the non-expert viewers:

> **Poole:** Will somebody please explain to me what these magic numbers are?
> **Chase:** It's an Ottendorf cipher.
> **Gates' father:** That's right.
> **Poole:** Oh, OK. What's an Ottendorf cipher?
> **Gates' father:** They're just codes.
> **Gates:** Each of these three numbers corresponds to a word in a key.
> **Chase:** Usually a random book or a newspaper article.
> **Gates:** In this case, the Silence Dogood letters. So it's like *[Pointing to the numbers in a triple, ed]* the page number of the key text, the line on the page, and the letter in that line.

As mentioned earlier in the film, Silence Dogood was the pseudonym that 16 year old Benjamin Franklin used to get his letters published in the "New-England Courant", a newspaper founded and published by his brother James Franklin. Gates and his allies use the cipher (and some additional knowledge they have on the history of the Liberty Bell and on the design of the $100 banknote) to find the hidden message in the letters. This proves to be another clue that allows them to find a special pair of spectacles invented by Benjamin Franklin, which in turn allows them to read another invisible message on the back of the Declaration of Independence, which eventually, after some additional hunting, allows them to find the location of the treasure.

Interestingly, the film also contains a reference to the famous *Monty Hall problem* that originates from the game show "Let's Make a Deal" [61].

National Treasure: Book of Secrets [71]: Benjamin Franklin Gates (Cage) must follow a clue left in John Wilkes Booth's diary to prove his ancestor's innocence in the assassination of Abraham Lincoln.

Like the first National Treasure, this film contains a profusion of cybersecurity references, ranging from hacking, to device cloning and to translating a dead language that thus acts as a code (cf. Fig. 2). Let me discuss three of them.

– *Playfair cipher*: The cipher occurs twice. First, in 1865, Gates' ancestor is asked to decipher a message written with a Playfair cipher and he clarifies that "Cipher's impossible to decode without the key". Then, later in the film, it's the turn of Gates, his father and Poole. They have a fragment of the ciphertext and, after solving a riddle, Gates successfully guesses the cipher's keyword, so that they are able to recover the plaintext with the help of an online "Playfair decoder". In doing so, they quickly explain how the cipher works, although it is imprecisely referred to as a code and they wrongly state that the keyword must be a five-letter word, which is in general not the case as the keyword can actually be of any length.

- *Hacking*, *Denial of Service attack* and *Social Engineering*: In a deleted scene, we get to know how Poole has actually been able to get access to the Buckingham Palace computers, which will be crucial later on. Poole is in the waiting room of the Palace's Curator's Office, while Gates is talking to the curator. Poole uses a device to jam the desktop of the curator's secretary. When she, after having learned in casual conversation that he is a computer expert, asks for his help, Poole ducks under the desk pretending to fix the problem but instead plugs in a small connection device that will later allow him to connect to the network and then simply stops jamming with his other device so that the secretary thinks that he has indeed solved the problem.

- *Hacking* and *Surveillance*: Gates, Chase and Poole have retrieved a wooden plank that contains a clue and a car chase ensues: the bad guys want the plank and the only way out is to give it to them. But first Gates ingeniously creates a copy of the plank: he runs a red right holding the plank in front of his face so that the speed camera on the traffic light takes his and the plank's picture, which Poole is then able to retrieve by hacking into the London Police database to get a copy of the picture. Interestingly, we are not shown, not even in a deleted scene, how Poole does this, but there is a brief dialogue that makes up for this from a dramatic point of view, ensuring that the viewers don't feel the absence of an explanation:

> **Gates:** Hack into the London Police database and get a copy of the picture from that traffic cam.
> **Poole:** Okey-dokey.
> **Gates:** You can't do it?
> **Poole:** No, I can do it. I just don't like that you assume that I can do it.

Snowden [68]: The NSA's illegal surveillance techniques are leaked to the public by one of the agency's employees, Edward Snowden, in the form of thousands of classified documents distributed to the press.

- *Cipher machines*, *Algorithms*, *Attacks*, *Malware*, *Surveillance*, *Trojan horse* and *Password protection*: Given the subject of the film, this is a must-see for everyone interested in cybersecurity and one could easily write a whole paper about it. However, this also makes it perhaps one of the less interesting films for cybersecurity show and tell, so let me only focus here on Hank Forrester, the character played by Nicolas Cage. Inspired by real-life NSA whistleblower William Binney, who appears briefly in news footage in the film, Forrester is a disillusioned NSA employee who acts as an instructor and mentor to Snowden, showing to him, and us viewers, an Enigma machine, its sequel SIGABA, the first hot line between Washington and Moscow, and a Cray 1, the world's first supercomputer. Forrester warns Snowden about the unpleasant realities of intelligence work, which Snowden will then experience throughout the years until he finally decides to reach out to the press.

Spider-Man: Into the Spider-Verse [50]: Teenager Miles Morales becomes the Spider-Man of his universe and must join with five spider-powered individuals from other dimensions to stop a threat for all realities.

- *Pseudonyms* and *Identity*: Thanks to the multiverse, there are actually seven different beings that use the Spidey pseudonym in this Oscar-winner animated film: Peter Parker, Peter B. Parker, Miles Morales, Peni Parker, Peter Porker (Spider-Ham), Gwen Stacy (Spider-Gwen) and Spider-Man Noir (voiced by Cage). Please, see the discussion about superheroes and pseudonyms under "Teen Titans GO! To the Movies" below and in [76].
- *Accountability*: According to NIST, accountability can be defined as "a property that ensures that the actions of an entity may be traced uniquely to that entity. This supports non-repudiation, deterrence, fault isolation, intrusion detection and prevention, and after-action recovery and legal action." In my own experience of teaching cybersecurity, students often struggle to understand what accountability and the other properties it entails really mean. It helps to show them the scene at the beginning of the film that contains the following dialogue between the teenager (and future Spider-Man) Miles Morales and his father Jefferson Davies, a cop who does not like that Spider-Man wears a mask and is thus not accountable for his actions:

  > **Jefferson:** Spider-Man. I mean, this guy swings in once a day, zip-zap-zop in his little mask and answers to no one. Right?
  > **Miles:** Yeah, Dad. Yeah.
  > **Jefferson:** Meanwhile, my guys are out there, lives on the line, no masks.
  > **Miles:** Uh-huh.
  > **Jefferson:** We show our faces. ... With great ability comes great accountability.
  > **Miles:** That's not even how the saying goes, dad.

Teen Titans GO! To the Movies [29]: The maniacal plan for world domination of the villain Slade sidetracks five teenage superheroes who dream of Hollywood stardom like for the adult superheroes.

- *Pseudonyms*: In this animated film, Cage voices Superman, which must have felt for him like a dream finally come true as he had been slated to portray Superman in Tim Burton's canceled Superman film in the 1990s. He even named one of his sons Kal-El, after Superman's birth name. A lifelong comic-book fan, to avoid the appearance of nepotism as Francis Ford Coppola's nephew, Nicolas Coppola changed his name early in his career to Nicolas Cage, inspired by the Marvel Comics superhero Luke Cage. See [76] for more details on pseudonyms and pseudonym resolution in the superhero universes.
- *Multifactor authentication*, *Biometrics*, *Masquerading attack* and *Social engineering*: Slade aims to steal a crystal that would give him the power to control the superheroes, but the Teen Titans initially foil Slade's evil plan by seizing the crystal and safely storing it in the Titan Tower's vault, where access is

controlled by a facial scan and a pin. Then, later in the movie, Slade masquerades as the director Jade Wilson, who is responsible for all the Superhero films being made, and tricks the teen titan Robin into opening the vault for him: Jade is finally shooting his own movie and as he is acting in the final scene and interacts with a prop version of the Titan Tower vault panel, a light falls and knocks him out. He awakens and finishes the scene by opening the vault, but Jade reveals that they are now in the tower for real and that she is actually Slade himself in disguise.[4] Slade steals the crystal but at the end the Teen Titans of course save the day.

The Humanity Bureau [35]: In the future, war, climate and political agendas have robbed the United States of America of their resources. Noah Kross (Cage) is an agent of the authoritarian agency called "The Humanity Bureau", which ensures citizens are productive and deports unproductive citizens to a city called New Eden, which is in reality an extermination camp.

– *Stolen Identity*: Kross learns the truth about New Eden and helps an unproductive single mother, Rachel Weller, and her son, Lucas, escape. During their escape. Kross reveals that he knows the real Rachel Weller, and this woman is not her. Years ago on a Bureau investigation, Kross and the real Rachel conceived a child, who is Lucas. When the famine struck, Rachel tried to sell Lucas. Amanda, her neighbor, got into an argument over this and the resulting fight ended in Rachel's death. Amanda then assumed Rachel's identity and raised Lucas as her own.

The Sorcerer's Apprentice [72]: Balthazar Blake (Cage), an apprentice of the legendary Merlin, must train his old teacher's successor (an introverted but resourceful physics prodigy) in the art of sorcery to defeat Morgana le Fay.

– *Authentication*: In 740 AD, the evil sorceress Morgana le Fay mortally wounds the mighty magician Merlin, but before dying, Merlin gives Balthazar a dragon figurine that will identify the Prime Merlinean, Merlin's descendant and the only one who will be able to defeat Morgana. Balthazar searches for the descendant for centuries, until, at the beginning of the 21st century, he encounters Dave Stutler. When Balthazar gives Dave Merlin's dragon figurine, the statue comes to life and wraps itself around the boy's finger to form a ring, thereby authenticating him as the Prime Merlinean. The authentication process that started 14 centuries earlier, in a pre-technology world, is finally completed when Dave, the film's hero, is able to bring the dragon figurine to life (in fact, it is the figurine that authenticates him). This authentication mode is not surprising if one considers the presence of Merlin in this film as well as in the Arthurian cycle, where Arthur is the only one able to pull out the sword Excalibur from a stone, thereby proving to be the rightful king of Britain. As I already briefly mentioned above, mythologies and fairy tales worldwide have similar allegories of authentication and identity, and I point to [77] for a more detailed discussion.

---

[4] A similar "fake room" attack takes place against phobic con artist Roy Waller (Cage) in "Matchstick Men" [60], which I did not add to the table only for the sake of space.

Windtalkers [86]: Two U.S. Marines in World War II are assigned to protect Navajo Marines, who use their native language as an unbreakable radio code.

– *Codes*: During the Pacific War, the U.S. Marine Corps recruited approximately 500 bilingual Navajo speakers to transmit secret tactical messages over military telephone or radio communications nets using formally or informally developed codes built upon their native language. Code talking was actually pioneered by the Cherokee and Choctaw peoples during World War I, and other Native American codetalkers were deployed by the U.S.A. during World War II in the Pacific, North Africa, and Europe, including Lakota, Meskwaki, Mohawk, Comanche, Tlingit, Hopi, Cree, and Crow soldiers [82]. There are a few scenes in the film that show how the Navajo code worked and why it was crucial to protect it. In particular, we are told that the Japanese were unable to decode the messages when a Japanese radio operator listening to one of the communications says "It sounds like they are under water. Is it English at all?". What do you need to do when your enemy has a code that is virtually unbreakable? You need to get hold of the codebook (that maps Navajo expressions to English), in this case you need to capture one of the codetalkers and torture him until he revels the codebook that he has memorized! Corporal Joe Enders (Cage) is tasked with protecting a codetalker. As Ender's commanding officer tells him "Under no circumstances can you allow your codetalker to fall into enemy hands. Your mission is to protect the code... at all costs." The film's epilogue states that the Navajo code was crucial to the U.S.A.'s success against Japan and that, during the war, like all other Native American codes, the Navajo code was never broken.

4   Conclusions

So, is Nicolas Cage the center of the cybersecurity universe? To provide a definitive answer to this question, one would need to go beyond hop zero (the cybersecurity-related films in which Cage starred) and consider the full "Six Cybersecurity-Degrees of Nicolas Cage"—the database of artworks that I have been collecting for showing and telling cybersecurity will be helpful to that extent. But Cage's 15 films considered here (plus the one in Footnote 4 and other entries in his filmography that could be considered as well) already make a good case for his central position.

This paper completes my personal trilogy on how to use films and other artworks to carry out a cybersecurity show and tell. Such "popular" explanations, which have been explored also for other disciplines (see, e.g., [13,42,47,56,57,74] as well as [7]), are not meant to replace but rather complement the technical definitions and explanations. The synergy of telling and showing via these examples can help go beyond the mere facts and skills by making them more intuitive for the laypersons, more accessible, more interesting, more rewarding.

There is one important stream of research that I have not considered in this paper, namely how to extend and generalize cybersecurity show and tell by means of user studies that will help to support the claims I have made and, possibly, to identify novel research questions. I have been carrying out two such studies together with Diego Sempreboni (a cybersecurity researcher), Sally Marlow (a broadcaster and a researcher in the relationships between mental health and the arts), Hannah Redler Hawes (a contemporary art curator specialized in the intersection between art, data, science and technology) and Alistair Gentry (a writer and artist who makes live art, performance lectures, interventions and live role-playing games). We are currently writing up the results of our two studies, a first one with existing artworks and a second one with an artwork created on purpose, and I can anticipate here that they certify the very positive impact that artworks can have to explain cybersecurity to different kinds of people.

References

1. Alfredson, D. (directed by): The Girl Who Kicked the Hornet's Nest (2009). Screenplay by Jonas Frykberg based on the novel by Stieg Larsson. https://www.imdb.com/title/tt1343097/
2. Alfredson, D. (directed by): The girl who played with fire (2009). Screenplay by Jonas Frykberg based on the novel by Stieg Larsson. https://www.imdb.com/title/tt1216487/
3. Apted, M. (directed by): Enigma (2001). Screenplay by Tom Stoppard based on the novel by Robert Harris. https://www.imdb.com/title/tt0157583/
4. Astley, N., Baker, M. (created by): Peppa Pig, Series 3, Episode 38, "The Secret Club", 2010. 7 seasons, 302 episodes. https://www.imdb.com/title/tt0426769/
5. Badham, J. (directed by): Wargames (1983). Screenplay by Lawrence Lasker and Walter F. Parkes. https://www.imdb.com/title/tt0086567/
6. Bird, B. (directed by): Incredibles 2 (2018). Screenplay by Brad Bird. https://www.imdb.com/title/tt3606756/
7. Blasco, J., Quaglia, E.A.: InfoSec cinema: using films for information security teaching. In: 2018 USENIX Workshop on Advances in Security Education, ASE 2018. USENIX Association (2018)
8. Bond, R.T. (ed.): Famous Stories of Code and Cipher. Rinehart, Providence (1947)
9. Bradbeer, H. (directed by): Enola Holmes (2020). Screenplay by Jack Thorne based on the novel "The Case of the Missing Marquess: An Enola Holmes Mystery" by Nancy Springer. https://www.imdb.com/title/tt7846844/
10. Brown, D.: Digital Fortress. St. Martin's Press, New York (1998)
11. Burt, G. (created by): The Bletchley Circle, 2012–2014. 2 seasons, 7 episodes. https://www.imdb.com/title/tt2275990/
12. Capozucca, A.: Comunicare la matematica. Egea (2018)
13. Champoux, J.E.: Management: Using Film to Visualize Principles and Practice. South-Western, Cincinnati (2000)
14. Donahue, A., Mendelsohn, C., Zuiker, A.E. (created by): CSI: Cyber, 2015–2016. 2 seasons, 31 episodes. https://www.imdb.com/title/tt3560060/
15. Dooley, J.F.: Codes and villains and mystery: the best stories with codes and ciphers 1843–1920. CreateSpace Independent Publishing Platform (2016). See also the "Cryptology in Fiction" document at https://www.johnfdooley.com
16. Doyle, A.C.: The Adventure of the Dancing Men. The Strand Magazine, London (1903)
17. Dumas, A.: Père (avec la collaboration d'Auguste Maquet). Les Trois Mousquetaires. Le Siècle (1844)

18. Erwig, M.: Once Upon an Algorithm: How Stories Explain Computing. MIT Press, Cambridge (2011)
19. Esmail, S. (created by): Mr. Robot, 2015–2019. 4 seasons, 45 episodes. https://www.imdb.com/title/tt4158110/
20. Falacci, N., Heuton, C. (created by): NUMB3RS, 2005–2010. 6 seasons, 119 episodes. https://www.imdb.com/title/tt0433309/
21. Fass, C., Turtle, B., Ginelli, M.: Six Degrees of Kevin Bacon. Plume, New York (1996)
22. Fincher, D. (directed by): Zodiac (2007). Screenplay by James Vanderbilt based on the book by Robert Graysmith. https://www.imdb.com/title/tt0443706/
23. Fisher, L.: What's your Erdös-Bacon-Sabbath number? (2016). https://www.timeshighereducation.com/blog/whats-your-erdos-bacon-sabbath-number. Accessed Jun 2021
24. Gibson, W.: Sprawl Trilogy: Neuromancer, Count Zero, Mona Lisa Overdrive. Victor Gollancz Ltd., London (1984–1988)
25. Gordon, S. (directed by): Identity Thief (2013). Screenplay by Craig Mazin. https://www.imdb.com/title/tt2024432/
26. Grimm, J., Grimm, W.: Kinder-und Hausmärchen (1812–1858)
27. Guare, J.: Six Degrees of Separation: A Play. Random House, New York (1990)
28. Hartman, D. (directed by): Tigger & Pooh and a Musical Too (2009). Screenplay by Nicole Dubuc, Brian Hohlfeld and Dean Stefan, "Password Song" written by Andy Sturmer and Brian Hohlfeld. https://www.imdb.com/title/tt1415904/
29. Horvath, A., Michail, P.R. (directed by): Teen Titans GO! To the Movies (2018). Screenplay by Michael Jelenic and Aaron Horvath. https://www.imdb.com/title/tt7424200/
30. Howard, R. (directed by): A Beautiful Mind (2001). Screenplay by Akiva Goldsman based on the book by Sylvia Nasar. https://www.imdb.com/title/tt0268978/
31. Howard, R. (directed by): The Da Vinci Code (2006). Screenplay by Akiva Goldsman based on the novel by Dan Brown. https://www.imdb.com/title/tt0382625/
32. Howard, R. (directed by): Angels & Demons (2009). Screenplay by David Koepp and Akiva Goldsman based on the novel by Dan Brown. https://www.imdb.com/title/tt0808151/
33. Howard, R. (directed by): Inferno (2016). Screenplay by David Koepp based on the novel by Dan Brown. https://www.imdb.com/title/tt3062096/
34. Johnson, M.S. (directed by): Ghost Rider (2007). Screenplay by Mark Steven Johnson. https://www.imdb.com/title/tt0259324/
35. King, R.W. (directed by): The Humanity Bureau (2017). Screenplay by Dave Schultz. https://www.imdb.com/title/tt6143568/
36. Kubrick, S. (directed by): Spartacus (1960). Screenplay by Dalton Trumbo based on the novel by Howard Fast. https://www.imdb.com/title/tt0054331/
37. Larsson, S.: Millennium Trilogy: The Girl with the Dragon Tattoo, The Girl Who Played with Fire. Knopf, The Girl Who Kicked the Hornet's Nest (2008)
38. Letterman, R., Vernon, C. (directed by): Monsters vs. Aliens (2009). Screenplay by Maya Forbes, Wallace Wolodarsky, Rob Letterman, Jonathan Aibel and Glenn Berger. https://www.imdb.com/title/tt0892782/
39. Loncraine, R. (directed by): Firewall (2006). Screenplay by Joe Forte. https://www.imdb.com/title/tt0408345/
40. Ludlum, R.: Bourne series: The Bourne Identity, The Bourne Supremacy, The Bourne Ultimatum. Richard Marek, Random House (1980, 1986, 1990)
41. Mann, M. (directed by): Blackhat (2015). Screenplay by Morgan Davis Foehl. https://www.imdb.com/title/tt2717822/

42. Marcus, A.S., Metzger, S.A., Paxton, R.J., Stoddard, J.D. (eds.): Teaching History With Film: Strategies for Secondary Social Studies, 2 edn. Routledge (2018)

43. McTeigue, J. (directed by): V for Vendetta (2005). Screenplay by Lilly Wachowski and Lana Wachowski based on [46]. https://www.imdb.com/title/tt0434409/

44. McTiernan, J. (directed by): The Thomas Crown Affair (1999). Screenplay by Leslie Dixon and Kurt Wimmer, story by Alan R. Trustman. https://www.imdb.com/title/tt0155267/

45. Milgram, S.: The Small World Problem. Psychology Today (1967)

46. Moore, A., Lloyd, D.: V for Vendetta. Vertigo (DC Comics) (1982–1989)

47. Mordacci, R. (eds.): Come fare filosofia con i film. Carocci editore (2017)

48. Niccol, A. (directed by): Lord of War (2005). Screenplay by Andrew Niccol. https://www.imdb.com/title/tt0399295/

49. Oplev, N.A. (directed by): The Girl with the Dragon Tattoo (2009). Screenplay by Nikolaj Arcel and Rasmus Heisterberg based on the novel by Stieg Larsson. https://www.imdb.com/title/tt1132620/

50. Persichetti, B., Ramsey, P., Rothman, R. (directed by): Spider-Man: Into the Spider-Verse (2018). Screenplay by Phil Lord and Rodney Rothman. https://www.imdb.com/title/tt4633694/

51. Pfitzmann, A., Hansen, M.: A terminology for talking about privacy by data minimization: Anonymity, Unlinkability, Undetectability, Unobservability, Pseudonymity, and Identity Management (Version v0.34), 10 August 2010. https://dud.inf.tu-dresden.de/literatur/Anon_Terminology_v0.34.pdf

52. Poe, E.A.: A Few Words on Secret Writing (1841)

53. Poe, E.A.: The Gold Bug. The Dollar (1843)

54. Price, T.: Teh Internet Is Serious Business. Bloomsbury Methuen Drama (2014)

55. Robinson, P.A. (directed by): Sneakers (1992). Screenplay by Phil Alden Robinson, Lawrence Lasker and Walter F. Parkes. https://www.imdb.com/title/tt0105435/

56. Rubin, L.C. (ed.): Mental Illness in Popular Media: Essays on the Representation of Disorders. McFarland & Co. (2012)

57. William, B., Russell, III.: The art of teaching social studies with film. Clearing House J. Educ. Strat. Issues Ideas 85(4), 157–164 (2012)

58. Sayers, D.L.: Have His Carcase, Victor Gollancz (1932)

59. Schepisi, F. (directed by): Six Degrees of Separation (1993). Screenplay by John Guare. https://www.imdb.com/title/tt0122241/

60. Scott, R. (directed by): Matchstick Men (2003). Screenplay by Nicholas Griffin based on the book by Eric Garcia. https://www.imdb.com/title/tt0325805/

61. Selvin, S.: On the Monty Hall problem (letter to the editor). Am. Stat. 29(3) (1975)

62. Sena, D. (directed by): Gone in 60 s (2000). Screenplay by H.B. Halicki and Scott Rosenberg. https://www.imdb.com/title/tt0187078/

63. Sena, D. (directed by): Swordfish (2001). Screenplay by Skip Woods. https://www.imdb.com/title/tt0244244/

64. Singh, S.: The Simpsons and Their Mathematical Secrets. Bloomsbury (2013)

65. Softley, I. (directed by): Hackers (1995). Screenplay by Rafael Moreu. https://www.imdb.com/title/tt0113243/

66. Stephenson, N.: Snow Crash. Bantam Books (1992)

67. Stephenson, N.: Cryptonomicon. Avon (1999)

68. Stone, O. (directed by): Snowden (2016). Screenplay by Kieran Fitzgerald and Oliver Stone based on the book by Luke Harding and Anatoly Kucherena. https://www.imdb.com/title/tt3774114/

69. The Pierces. Secret (2007). First track of the album Thirteen Tales of Love and Revenge
70. Turteltaub, J. (directed by): National Treasure (2004). Screenplay by Jim Kouf, Cormac Wibberley and Marianne Wibberley. https://www.imdb.com/title/tt0368891/
71. Turteltaub, J. (directed by): National Treasure: Book of Secrets (2007). Screenplay by Marianne Wibberley and Cormac Wibberley. https://www.imdb.com/title/tt0465234/
72. Turteltaub, J. (directed by): The Sorcerer's Apprentice, 2010. Screenplay by Matt Lopez, Doug Miro and Carlo Bernard based on a screen story by Lawrence Konner, Mark Rosenthal and Matt Lopez. https://www.imdb.com/title/tt0963966/
73. Tyldum, M. (directed by): The Imitation Game, 2014. Screenplay by Graham Moore based on the book by Andrew Hodges. https://www.imdb.com/title/tt2084970/
74. Valeriano, B.: Teaching introduction to international politics with film. J. Polit. Sci. Educ. **9**, 52–72 (2013)
75. Vaughn, M. (directed by): Kick-Ass (2010). Screenplay by Jane Goldman and Matthew Vaughn based on the comic book by Mark Millar and John Romita Jr. https://www.imdb.com/title/tt1250777/
76. Viganò, L.: Explaining cybersecurity with films and the arts. In: Imagine Math 7, pp. 297–309. Springer, Cham (2020). https://doi.org/10.1007/978-3-030-42653-8_18
77. Viganò, L.: Don't tell me the cybersecurity moon is shining... (cybersecurity show and tell). In: Emmer, M. (ed.) Imagine Math 8. Springer, Cham (to appear)
78. Viganò, L., Magazzeni, D.: Explainable Security. CoRR (2018). http://arxiv.org/abs/1807.04178
79. Viganò, L., Magazzeni, D.: Explainable security. In: IEEE European Symposium on Security and Privacy Workshops, EuroS&P Workshops 2020, pp. 293–300. IEEE (2020). A preliminary version appeared as [78]
80. Watts, D.J.: Six Degrees: The Science of a Connected Age. William Heinemann (2003)
81. West, S. (directed by): Con Air (1997). Screenplay by Scott Rosenberg. https://www.imdb.com/title/tt0118880/
82. Wikipedia: Code Talker. https://en.wikipedia.org/wiki/Code_talker. Accessed Jun 2021
83. Wikipedia: Six degrees of separation. https://en.wikipedia.org/wiki/Six_degrees_of_separation. Accessed Jun 2021
84. Wiseman, L. (directed by): Live Free or Die Hard, 2007. Screenplay by Mark Bomback based on a story by Mark Bomback and David Marconi, on an article by John Carlin and on characters by Roderick Thorp. https://www.imdb.com/title/tt0337978/
85. Woo, J. (directed by): Face/Off (1997). Screenplay by Joe Forte. https://www.imdb.com/title/tt0119094/
86. Woo, J. (directed by): Windtalkers (2002). Screenplay by John Rice and Joe Batteer. https://www.imdb.com/title/tt0245562/
87. Wright, E. (directed by): Baby Driver (2017). Screenplay by Edgar Wright. https://www.imdb.com/title/tt3890160/
88. Yeatman, H. (directed by): G-Force (2009). Screenplay by The Wibberleys (Cormac Wibberley and Marianne Wibberley) based on a story by Hoyt Yeatman and David P.I. James. https://www.imdb.com/title/tt0436339/
89. Zazkis, R., Liljedahl, P.: Teaching Mathematics As Storytelling. Sense Publishers (2009)

Future Digital Challenges: Social-Emotional Skills as Critical Enablers for Good Technical Design Work

Geraldine Fitzpatrick[✉]

TU Wien, 1040 Vienna, Austria
geraldine.fitzpatrick@tuwien.ac.at

Abstract. Technology is becoming increasingly entangled in all aspects of our lives often with unintended negative consequences. While there is increasing recognition of the ethical and value-based aspects in our technology design work, and while there is increasing support for the multidisciplinary collaborations needed to address current and future challenges, little focus has been put on the skills needed by people practically engaging in this work. Good technical and design skills are necessary but not sufficient. We also need good social-emotional-ethical skills, with implications for education, collaborations, and leadership development.

Keywords: Digital futures · Social-emotional skills · Soft skills

1 Introduction

The INTERACT2021 theme concepts of 'sense, feel, design' can well be interpreted from the perspectives of how devices can sense human activity or how new multi-sensorial experiences can be enabled for people through technologies; indeed both perspectives raise interesting possibilities for next generation technology design. There can however also be another interpretation that turns these concepts back on to us as the researchers, designers, engineers, etc., who are involved in producing these technologies and the increasing importance of the social and emotional (SE) intelligence skills [4, 13, 14] needed to engage in this work. In particular 'sense and feel' can suggest core SE skills of self and other awareness, related to emotions, empathy and perspective taking. 'Design' can suggest how we actively regulate our own emotions and reactions, how we respond to setbacks and difficulties, and how we manage effective empathic interpersonal inter-actions to communicate effectively, collaborate, negotiate conflict and so on. It is also about values and how we critically engage with complex ethical challenges, and how we creatively approach the hard problems we are needed to solve – this latter is also often referred to as ethical or spiritual intelligence and is included in SE skills learning.

© IFIP International Federation for Information Processing 2021
Published by Springer Nature Switzerland AG 2021
C. Ardito et al. (Eds.): INTERACT 2021, LNCS 12932, pp. 34–38, 2021.
https://doi.org/10.1007/978-3-030-85623-6_4

1.1 Motivating the Importance of Social-Emotional-Ethical Skills for Design

Why are these skills so important to the design of technology? Because computer science and Human Computer Interaction (HCI) have well moved on from a simple focus of what goes on 'inside the box' or how a screen interaction takes place (if it were ever this simple). Now technology is implicated in every aspect of our daily lives and of society, bringing with it complex socio-technical-ethical challenges. A 2008 report from a 2007 Microsoft workshop with leading Human Computer Interaction (HCI) scholars [10] presciently points to these changes and the challenges for HCI. The report asks the question, "what will our world be like in 2020 [recognizing that] digital technologies will continue to proliferate, enabling ever more ways of changing how we live" (p. 10) and argues that we are not just designing technologies but designing "being human" and so needing to put "human values centre stage". In the intervening years we have seen these changes advance, and indeed as HCI researchers and practitioners we have been instrumental in these changes, beyond what we could have even imagined and often with unexpected and undesirable consequences. We're not just building technology, we're fundamentally impacting what it means to be human, whose faces and voices matter, what is society, and, as we have recently seen across world politics, what is democracy.

These complex socio-technical-ethical challenges truly fit the definition of 'wicked problem' [18], with no right or wrong answer, shaping the problem as we explore solutions, negotiating among multiple stakeholder concerns and so on.

I applaud the response to these challenges from the broader computing community to date. There is an increasing turn to taking seriously issues of ethics and values around computing, as seen in the updated ACM Code of Ethics and Professional Conduct [1], the IEEE standard for addressing ethical concerns in system design [11], and various work on values in software engineering, e.g., [22]. HCI also has a long tradition around these concerns, as reflected in the 2008 report previously discussed, and in approaches such as value-sensitive design in HCI [9] and values in computing workshops [6]. And there is a growing number of initiatives and funding schemes that recognize the complexity of these challenges and the need to bring together multiple disciplines to address them, e.g., as exemplified in the Vienna Digital Humanism initiative [20] and the Swedish Digital Futures centre [5].

Frauenberger [7] further encapsulates these concerns in arguing for a new paradigm of 'Entanglement HCI' that moves beyond user centredness and situatedness to recognising the fundamental entanglement of technologies and people and society in ways that are mutually constitutive. In taking this relational view, he argues we are not designing things or interactions but designing the relationships with the things we create.

But there is an elephant in the room – us. The rhetoric often focusses on the aspirations and issues, or on the 'whats' of what we are producing, with values and ethics somehow treated as external properties to be handled. But what is the practical human interactional work of achieving these aspirations? Who are the 'we' that is doing this work? And this is where there is a real skills gap.

How can we effectively work together in teams with people from diverse disciplines? Who do we negotiate the interpersonal and inter-disciplinary conflicts and challenges of multidisciplinary work, or understand the perspectives of diverse potential stakeholders, and negotiate among these perspectives? How will we deal with complex ethical trade-offs? How do we operationalise values, and whose values, in technology? How do we practically engage at multiple levels of scale, and across diverse domains? How do we still make 'good enough' decisions when we don't know what we don't know? How do we identify and weigh the trade-offs of every decision or understand consequences and for whom? How will we deal with uncertainty and failure? And so on.

These are fundamentally human and relational challenges. If we are to properly engage in this work, we need to recognize that core disciplinary skills, core technical and design skills, are necessary but not sufficient for addressing these challenges. The really critical skills will be the so-called soft skills, the social and emotional skills, for example, of being self-aware, being able to manage emotions, being a good communicator and collaborator, being able to see the perspectives of others, being critical thinkers and reflective practitioners. The sensing, feeling and designing skills.

2   Taking Social-Emotional-Ethical Skills Seriously – Challenges

If we take this perspective seriously, it raises a number of challenges[1] for us going forward.

The *first challenge* is nomenclature, and naming these as the essential skills for the 'we' – computer scientists, designers, researchers etc., – engaging in this work. This shift can help put the focus on their core importance rather than as an optional 'nice to have' [21].

The *second challenge* is around education. We are educating the future 'we' who will be solving the complex digital-societal challenges and we need to adequately equip them with future work skills. Reinforcing the importance of SE skills for the future of work, the World Economic Forum has identified top work skills needed in 2025, with eight out of ten top skills, and the top six, related to problem solving, self-management, and working with people, all social-emotional skills [23]. Social-emotional skills are also critical for their learning experiences, as noted by Luca and Tarricone who show "a compelling relationship between students' emotional intelligence and their ability to work effectively within a team" [15].

How can we better embed the development of these skills across all courses? Examples of such initiatives include: the 'Ways of Thinking' course for first year computer science students, developed to replace an introductory HCI course [8] to be able to engage more critically with the implications of their software/design choices; teaching students self-regulation skills to improve programming outcomes [12]; practicing mindfulness with software engineering students to create better conceptual models and improve productivity [3]; and better scaffolding students in support of collaborative group work with structured team-building activities – in our own recent course facilitation we have developed a teamwork module building on Team Playbook tools offered by software company Atlassian [2], complemented with exercises for students to better understand their own values and strengths, and how they could best contribute to teamwork.

---

[1] Many of these are also reflected in Paula Kotze's keynote address at INTERACT2019, 'Is HCI/UX Ready for the Fourth Industrial Revolution?'.

The *third challenge* is around our multidisciplinary collaborations and projects to address these new societal technology challenges. Working with people who are different, whether it is by discipline or culture or life experience or personality and so on, is inherently difficult [19]. It requires strong interpersonal and communication skills to deal with conflicts and differences of opinions and perspectives that will necessarily arise. But research suggests that benefits of doing this are manifold, from more creative solutions to improved performance [ibid].

The *fourth challenge* is leadership development, recognizing the importance of academic leaders at all levels in role-modelling good social-emotional-ethical skills and bringing out the best in their diverse teams [16]. In the top ten skills identified by Google research [17] about what makes a great manager of the best teams at Google, good technical skills only came in at number 8 and almost all of the other skills were around self-regulation, communication, and working with people.

For those of us in any leadership role, the real challenge then is how do we develop our own social-emotional-ethical intelligence skills if we are to address the other three challenges and contribute to creating digital futures that fit with human values.

3 The Call

Good social-emotional-ethical skills will increasingly become the enabler, the fuel, for doing good technical and design work.

It is time we took these essential human skills more seriously for ourselves, for our students and collaborators, and for the sake of our technology-enabled futures.

References

1. ACM Code of Ethics: https://www.acm.org/code-of-ethics. Accessed 25 May 2021
2. Atlassian Team Playbook: https://www.atlassian.com/team-playbook. Accessed 25 May 2021
3. Bernardez, B., Duran Toro, A., Parejo Maestre, J.A., Juristo, N., Ruiz-Cortes, A.: Effects of mindfulness on conceptual modeling performance: a series of experiments. IIEEE Trans. Softw. Eng. 1 (2020). https://doi.org/10.1109/TSE.2020.2991699
4. Brackett, M.A., Rivers, S.E., Salovey, P.: Emotional intelligence: implications for personal, social, academic, and workplace success: emotional intelligence. Soc. Pers. Psychol. Compass **5**, 88–103 (2011). https://doi.org/10.1111/j.1751-9004.2010.00334.x
5. Digital Futures: https://www.digitalfutures.kth.se. Accessed 25 May 2021
6. Ferrario, M.A., Simm, W., Whittle, J., Frauenberger, F., Fitzpatrick, G., Purgathofer, P.: Values in computing. In: Proceedings of the 2017 CHI Conference Extended Abstracts on Human Factors in Computing Systems (CHI EA 2017), pp. 660–667. ACM, New York (2017). https://doi.org/10.1145/3027063.3027067
7. Frauenberger, C.: Entanglement HCI the next wave? ACM Trans. Comput. Hum. Interact. **27**(1), 27 (2020). DOI: https://doi.org/10.1145/3364998. Article 2
8. Frauenberger, C., Purgathofer, P.: Ways of thinking in informatics. Commun. ACM **62**(7), 58–64 (2019). https://doi.org/10.1145/3329674
9. Friedman, B., Kahn, P.H., Borning, A., Huldtgren, A.: Value sensitive design and information systems. In: Doorn, N., Schuurbiers, D., van de Poel, I., Gorman, M.E. (eds.) Early Engagement and New Technologies: Opening Up the Laboratory. PET, vol. 16, pp. 55–95. Springer, Dordrecht (2013). https://doi.org/10.1007/978-94-007-7844-3_4

10. Harper, R. (ed.): Being Human: Human-Computer Interaction in the Year 2020. Microsoft Research, Cambridge, England (2008)
11. IEEE Standard P7000: https://standards.ieee.org/project/7000.html. Accessed 25 May 2021
12. Loksa, D., Xie, B., Kwik, H., Ko, A.J.: Investigating novices' in situ reflections on their programming process. In: Proceedings of the 51st ACM Technical Symposium on Computer Science Education, pp. 149–155. ACM, Portland (2020). https://doi.org/10.1145/3328778.3366846
13. Lopes, P.N.: Emotional intelligence in organizations: bridging research and practice. Emot. Rev. **8**, 316–321 (2016)
14. Lopes, P.N., Brackett, M.A., Nezlek, J.B., Schütz, A., Sellin, I., Salovey, P.: Emotional intelligence and social interaction. Pers. Soc. Psychol. Bull. **30**, 1018–1034 (2004). https://doi.org/10.1177/0146167204264762
15. Luca, J., Tarricone, P.: Does emotional intelligence affect successful teamwork? Meeting at the Crossroads. In: Proceedings of the 18th Annual Conference of the Australasian Society for Computers in Learning in Tertiary Education, Melbourne, Australia (2001). https://ro.ecu.edu.au/ecuworks/4834
16. Parrish, D.R.: The relevance of emotional intelligence for leadership in a higher education context. Stud. High. Educ. **40**, 821–837 (2015). https://doi.org/10.1080/03075079.2013.842225
17. re:Work Learn about Google's manager research. https://rework.withgoogle.com/guides/managers-identify-what-makes-a-great-manager/steps/learn-about-googles-manager-research/. Accessed 25 May 2021
18. Rittel, H.W.J., Webber, M.M.: Dilemmas in a general theory of planning. Policy Sci. **4**(2), 155–169 (1973)
19. Rock, D., Grant, H., Grey, J.: Diverse Teams Feel Less Comfortable—and That's Why They Perform Better, Harvard Business Review (2016)
20. The Digital Humanism Initiative: https://dighum.ec.tuwien.ac.at. Accessed 25 May 2021
21. Warren, C.: "Soft Skills" are the essential skills (2019). https://www.ihhp.com/blog/2019/08/29/soft-skills-are-the-essential-skills/. Accessed 25 May 2021
22. Whittle, J., Ferrario, M.A., Simm, W., Hussain, W.: A case for human values in software engineering. IEEE Softw. **38**(1), 106–113 (2021). https://doi.org/10.1109/MS.2019.2956701
23. World Economic Forum, The Future of Jobs Report 2020: https://www.weforum.org/reports/the-future-of-jobs-report-2020 (2020). Accessed 25 May 2021

POISE: A Framework for Designing Perfect Interactive Systems with and for Imperfect People

Philippe Palanque[✉] ![ORCID]

ICS-IRIT, Université Toulouse III-Paul Sabatier, Toulouse, France
`palanque@irit.fr`

Abstract. The operator is frequently considered as the main sources of vulnerability in command and control systems; for example, in a 2006 survey 79% of fatal accidents in aviation were attributed to "human error." Beyond the case of command and control systems, users' faults occur not only at use time but also during the design and development of systems. Following Avizienis et al.'s taxonomy for faults, human-made error can be characterized as the operator's failure to deliver services while interacting with the interactive system. Non human-made errors are called natural faults and may occur during development or set the interactive system as well as its users into an error-state during its use. Focusing on interactive systems specificities, this paper presents a comprehensive description of faults covering both development and operation phases. In correspondence with this taxonomy, we present mechanisms to avoid, remove, tolerate and mitigate faults in order to design and develop what we call "perfect" interactive systems taking into account the organization, the interactive system, the environment and the people operating them. We define an interactive system as perfect when it blends multiple and diverse properties such as usability, security, user experience, dependability, learnability, resilience … We present multiple concrete examples, from aviation and other domains, of faults affecting socio-technical systems and associated fault-tolerant mechanisms.

Keywords: Faults · Interactive systems · Dependability · Usability · Security · User experience

1 Introduction

Over the last decades, the research work in the field of HCI has been focussing on supporting user-related properties such as **usability** [85], **privacy** [72], **accessibility** [9] or **user experience** [50]. Contributions have been ranging from increased understanding of human behaviour (e.g. motor side [1], perceptive side [58] or cognition [4]) to the design of interaction techniques and innovative input and output devices. Unfortunately, as pointed out in [8] these contributions are rarely incorporated into products that are designed using early understanding of human behaviour (e.g. [22]) and standardized

© IFIP International Federation for Information Processing 2021
Published by Springer Nature Switzerland AG 2021
C. Ardito et al. (Eds.): INTERACT 2021, LNCS 12932, pp. 39–59, 2021.
https://doi.org/10.1007/978-3-030-85623-6_5

interaction (e.g. IBM CUA [13]) incorporated in Operating Systems manufacturers (e.g. touch interactions for Android [3]). While [8] argues that this can be solved by changing the focus of HCI research from user interfaces to interaction, this paper argues that these research contributions should take more into account (an in an integrated way):

- the People (performing the tasks and the work),
- the Interactive System (that is used to perform the work),
- the Organization (providing the work context for the People and being the project owner of the Interactive System)
- the environment (where the People work and where the Interactive System is deployed.

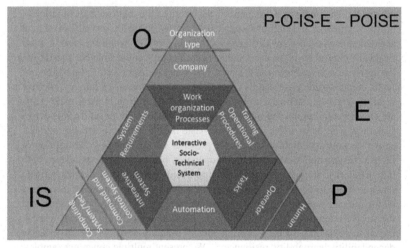

Fig. 1. The POISE framework blending People, Organization, Interactive system and the Environment.

The three vertexes of the triangle represent the three main components POISE framework. These elements are connected to the other ones by dedicated trapeziums (Automation, System Requirements and Training and Operational Procedures). These trapeziums represent explicitly how the element influences the other ones. At the basis of the vertexes of the triangles, the blue trapeziums refine the description of the content of the vertexes. This way, Work organization and Processes are refinement of the organization, Tasks are refinement of the People and Interactive Systems are the relevant part of the Technology component. This is a refinement of the early work from Meshkati [59], claiming that the resilience of socio-technical systems require addressing in the same single framework Human Organization and Technology. Outside of the triangle the grey part corresponds to the Environment where the interactive system is deployed and where the people are working. The environment may be highly dynamic like weather condition for an aircraft or very static and controlled like a dark room of an enroute air traffic control centre.

While the four aspects of POISE have to be taken into account holistically, this paper leaves out aspects related to the organization including standards, training and requirements. Indeed, the focus is here about interaction technologies and their users but taken explicitly into real life concerns imposed by the operational environment. In this context, other properties are relevant (and sometimes of higher importance) that the user-related ones mentioned above. Properties such as **reliability** [54], **dependability** [7], **resilience** [83], **fault-tolerance** [36] or **security** [52] are "usually" related to the interactive system element of POISE while they can also apply to the entire socio-technical systems (including the organization) as argued in [45].

We believe the approaches proposed in this paper would benefit any deployable interactive system (including desktop application or entertainment interactive software) but the benefits are more tangible in the context of safety critical ones.

A safety-critical system is a system in which failures or errors potentially leads to loss of life or injuries of human beings [18] while a system is considered as critical when the cost of a potential failure is much higher than the development cost. Whether or not they are classified as safety-critical or "only" critical, interactive systems have made their way into most of the command and control workstations including satellite ground segments, military and civil cockpits, air traffic control... Furthermore, the complexity and quantity of data manipulated, the amount of systems to be controlled and the high number of commands to be triggered in a short period of time have required the design, development and deployment of sophisticated interaction techniques.

Building reliable and dependable interactive systems is a cumbersome task due to their very specific nature. The behaviour of these reactive systems is event-driven. As these events are triggered by human operators manipulating hardware input devices, these systems have to react to unexpected events. On the output side, information (such as the current state of the system) has to be presented to the operator in such a way that it can be perceived and interpreted correctly. Lastly, interactive systems require addressing together hardware and software aspects (e.g., input and output devices together with their device drivers).

In the domain of fault-tolerant systems, empirical studies have demonstrated (e.g., [62]) that software crashes may occur even though the development of the system has been extremely rigorous. One of the many sources of such crashes is called natural faults [7] triggered by alpha-particles from radioactive contaminants in the chips or neutron from cosmic radiation. A higher probability of occurrence of faults [77] concerns systems deployed in the high atmosphere (e.g., aircrafts) or in space (e.g., manned spacecraft [44]). Such natural faults demonstrate the need to go beyond classical fault avoidance at development time (usually brought by formal description techniques and properties verification) and to identify all the threats that can impair interactive systems.

The paper is structured as follows. The next section focuses on the identification of the specificities of interactive systems. It presents the H-MIODMIT architecture which extends MIODMIT [28] architecture by incorporating the operator. The third section focuses introduces two classifications of faults one dedicated to faults altering the functioning of the interactive system and the other one dedicated to faults altering the behaviour of the operator. The fourth section identifies processes and tools that, when combined, can contribute to the quest for perfect interactive systems by providing means of incorporating and evaluating the presence (or absence) of the properties mentioned above. The fifth section illustrates contributions from the HCI, dependable computing and software engineering domains that support some of the properties and how, by integrating them, they improve the overall quality of interactive systems. Last section concludes the paper and identifies possible paths towards perfect interactive systems.

2   Specificities of Interactive Systems and Their Users

2.1   The H-MIODMIT Generic Architecture

Figure 2 presents an architectural view (from left to right) of the operator, the interactive command and control system, and the underlying system (e.g., an aircraft engine). This architecture is a simplified version of MIODMIT (Multiple Input and Output Devices and Multiple Interaction Techniques), a generic architecture for multimodal interactive systems [28] described in AADL [38]. Following the attribute dimensions of [7] we highlight (top right of Fig. 2) the hardware and software components, and show how the human operator interacts with them (thick dotted lines).

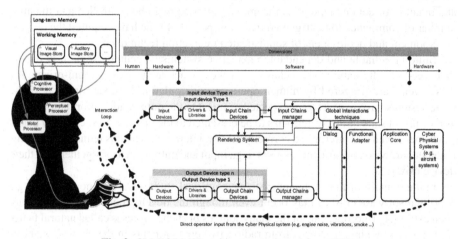

Fig. 2. H-MIODMIT architecture (adapted from [28])

As shown in the figure, interaction mainly takes place though the manipulation of input devices (e.g., keyboard or mouse) and the perception of information from the output devices (e.g., a computer screen or speaker). Another channel usually overlooked is the direct perception by the operator of information produced (usually as a side effect) of the underlying cyber-physical systems (e.g., noise or vibrations from an aircraft engine (represented by the lower dotted line in the figure)).

The Specificities of the Interaction. The top left of the Software section of the diagram corresponds to the interaction technique that uses information from the input devices. Interaction techniques have a tremendous impact on operator performance. Standard interaction techniques encompass complex mechanisms (e.g. modification of the cursor's movement on the screen according to the acceleration of the physical mouse on the desk). This design space is of prime importance and HCI research has explored multiple

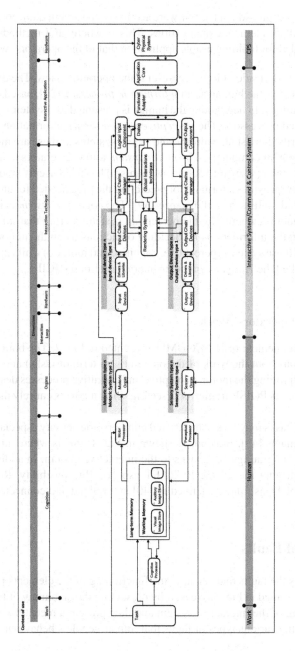

Fig. 3. H-MIODMIT detailed with the explicit representation of motor, perceptive and cognitive capability of operators and their tasks

possibilities for improving performance, such as enlarging the target area for selection on touch screens [64] and providing on-screen widgets to facilitate selection [2].

The System Side. The right side of the Software section of the architecture corresponds to what is usually called interactive applications. This is where HCI methods such as task analysis are needed for building usable application that fit the operators' work [30].

The Human Side. The left side of Fig. 2 represents the operator's view. The drawing is based on work that models the human as an *information processor* [23], based on previous research in psychology. In that model, the human is presented as a system composed of three interconnected processors. The *perceptive system* senses information from the environment – primarily the visual, auditory, and tactile systems as these are more common when interacting with computers. The *motor system* allows operators to act on the real world. Target selection (a key interaction mechanism) has been deeply studied [80]; for example, Fitts' Law provides a formula for predicting the time needed for an operator to select a target, based on its size and distance [39]. The *cognitive system* is in charge of processing information gathered by the perceptual system, storing that information in memory, analyzing the information and deciding on actions using the motor system. The sequential use of these systems (perceptive, cognitive and motoric) while interacting with computers is called the Human-Computer Interaction Loop (HCIL).

2.2 Incorporating Operators' Work

Figure 3 proposes a refinement of H-MIODMIT presented in Fig. 2. The bottom of the figure adds description about the work of the operators (in term of tasks) and how this work is performed exploiting the motor, perceptive and cognitive processes described in [23]. This architecture fits POISE framework (see Fig. 1) as it covers entirely the bottom part of the triangle.

Describing users' tasks may be a complex and cumbersome activity especially when dealing with real domains [48]. Beyond, as shown in Fig. 1, this is where automation design takes place by migrating user's tasks to the interactive system. In addition, this design requires identifying the all the RCRAFT aspects: Responsibility, Resources, Authority and Control Transitions as defined in [40] and refined and connected to task models in [17].

3 Taxonomies of Faults

This section identifies the faults that can alter the functioning of the elements presented in the architecture presented in Fig. 3. We start by presenting the taxonomy of faults that impair the functioning of the interactive system and then present a recent taxonomy of faults that organizes the various types of faults that impair people's behaviour.

3.1 Faults Altering the System

To be able to ensure that the system will behave properly whatever happens, a system designer has to consider all the issues that can impair the functioning of that system. To this end the domain of dependable computing e.g. Avizienis et al. [7] have defined a taxonomy of faults. This taxonomy leads to the identification of 31 elementary classes of faults. Figure 4 presents a simplified view of this taxonomy and makes explicit the two main categories of faults (top level of the figure): i) the ones made at development time (see left-hand side of the figure) including bad designs, programming errors, ... and ii) the one made at operation times (see right-hand side of the figure) including operator errors such as slips, lapses and mistakes as defined in [75].

The leaves of the taxonomy are grouped into five different categories as each of them bring a special problem (issue) to be addressed:

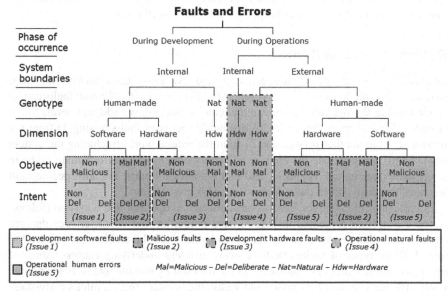

Fig. 4. Taxonomy of faults in computing systems (adapted from [7]) and associated issues for the dependability of these systems

- *Development software faults (issue 1):* software faults introduced by a human during system development. They can be, for instance, bad design errors, bugs due to faulty coding, development mistakes ...
- *Malicious faults (issue 2):* faults introduced by human with the deliberate objective of damaging the system. They can be, for instance, an external hack causing service denial or crash of the system.
- *Development hardware faults (issue 3):* natural (e.g. caused by a natural phenomenon without human involvement) as well as human-made faults affecting the hardware during its development. They can be, for instance, a short circuit within a processor (due to bad construction).

- *Operational natural faults (issue 4):* faults caused by a natural phenomenon without human participation, affecting hardware as well as information stored on hardware and occurring during the service of the system. As they affect hardware faults are likely to propagate to software as well. They can be, for instance, a memory alteration due to a cosmic radiation.
- *Operational human-errors (issue 5):* faults resulting from human action during the use of the system. They include faults affecting the hardware and the software, being deliberate or non-deliberate but don't encompass malicious ones. Connection between this taxonomy and classical human error classification as the one defined in [75] can be easily made with deliberate faults corresponding to mistakes or violations [71] and non-deliberate ones being either slips or lapses. [35] describes precisely how these errors can be connected to the description of operators' work in task models. Even though these sections highlight the negative impact of human error, it is important to note that keeping the human in the loop also adds to the overall system safety as demonstrated in [74] via the concept called human contribution

3.2 Faults Altering the Human

The classification presented in this section expands Avizienis' taxonomy in four ways. First, we extend the *System boundary* dimension to recognize that human faults can be **induced inside the operator** from external causes. Second, we add new levels to the *Phenomenological cause* dimension to distinguish between faults arising 1) from the operator, 2) from another person, and 3) from the natural world (including the system itself). Third, we introduce the *Human capability* dimension to differentiate faults in the operator's perceptual, cognitive, and motor abilities. Fourth, we add specific fault categories that derive from these dimensions. This presentation.

In particular, the complex interactions between an operator and a system (following the architecture presented in Fig. 3) have properties and characteristics that are separate from the operator alone or the system alone, and the architecture can lead to many different types of faults that have many different underlying causes – some of which involve the fault being "induced" in the operator by outside forces. For example, an aircraft's hard landing may arise from within the operator (e.g., a pilot's early-stage Parkinson's disease that reduces their muscular coordination), from another person (e.g., someone shining a laser pointer into the pilot's eyes from the end of the runway), or from effects of the natural world (e.g., air turbulence that shakes a pilot's arm as they try to press a button on the instrument panel). Although these three faults are very different in terms of implications for design, they would all be placed in the same category in the Avizienis framework (i.e., "Operational/External/Human-made/Non-malicious/Non-deliberate/Accidental" operator faults). To address this gap, we need to broaden the dimensions that characterize faults. The classification presented in [66] focusses only on operational faults (leaving aside the development faults and their causes but their types are similar [78]).

The classification expands the *System boundary* dimension to add the architecture of Fig. 3 as a conceptual location for faults that should be considered separately from Avizienis et al.'s categories of "internal to the system" and "external to the system." The idea of internal/external faults separation applied to the architecture of Fig. 3 separates faults that arise from inside the operator (see Fig. 5 bottom) and those that arise external to the operator (see Fig. 5 top).

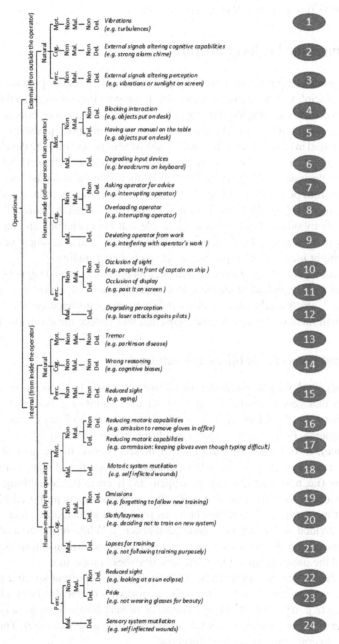

Fig. 5. The taxonomy on Internal and External faults altering the capability of the operator as a service provider (with concrete examples – right-hand side in italics)

This classification covers various types of influential factors for people behaviors such as seven deadly sins [29] (e.g. items 20 and 23 in Fig. 5), cognitive biases [84] (e.g. item 14), aging [87] (e.g. items 13 and 15) as well as more standard human error classification [75] (e.g. items 19 and 21).

4   The Quest for Perfect Software

As other types of computing systems [15], interactive system development follows the three basic principles of incentives in economy: Economic Incentives, Social incentives and Moral incentives (as highlighted in [54]). Economic incentives concern the real development costs and, for instance, detailed information about usability evaluation costs can be found in [14]. Beyond, low quality software exposes software developers and distributors to legal risks [92] that contribute as an economic incentive. Moral incentive will motivate designers and developer to follow their "moral compass" which could prevent them from performing low quality work due, for instance, to laziness [6]. Last, social incentives [34], could be used to develop people's natural desire to be looked upon favorably by others. On the flip side, people fear being shamed and looked upon disfavorably by their peers. This means that control quality and assessment of quality of production might incent them to produce artefacts of better quality.

These three incentives have a strong influence on developers and designers' behavior and might, if well exploited, contribute to the development of interactive systems of better quality. Unfortunately, they are also conflicting as, for instance, increase in quality assessment will increase the development cost and thus reduce the economic incentive.

4.1   Expected Properties of Interactive Software

With the early work on understanding interactive systems [31] came the identification of properties that "good" interactive systems should exhibit (e.g. honesty) and "bad" properties that they should avoid (e.g. deadlocks). Later, guidelines for the design of interactive systems [90] were provided, identifying in a similar way "good" properties (e.g. guidance), in order to favor usability of these systems. In the area of software engineering, early work [51] identified two main good properties of computing systems namely safety (i.e. nothing bad will ever happen) and liveness (i.e. something good will eventually happen). In [55] a hierarchy of software properties is proposed identifying for the first time explicit relationships between properties gathered in a hierarchy (e.g. "reactivity" divided in "recurrence" and "persistence"). While in the area of Human-Computer Interaction the properties were initially expressed in an informal way, [69, 70] proposed the use of temporal logics to describe these properties.

Beyond these "generic" properties, it is of interest to represent specific properties related to the very nature of each system. These properties might also be of a high level of abstraction (e.g. trust for a banking system) or of very low level (e.g. only possible to enter a personal identification number three times on a cash machine). The detailed property would contribute to the high-level one.

Usability and User Experience. These Two Major Properties in Human-Computer Interaction Do not Have Currently the Same Level of Maturity. Usability Has Been

Studied Since the Early 80's and Has Been Standardized by ISO in the ISO 9241 Part 11 Since 1996 [46]. Its Structure is Presented on the a) Section of Fig. 6. The Standard Specializes Usability into Three Sub-properties (Efficiency, Effectiveness and Satisfaction) While Some Researchers Would also Add at Least Learnability and Accessibility [43] as Important Aspects of Usability.

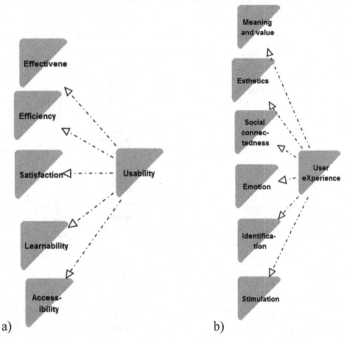

Fig. 6. Representation of the hierarchical relationships between properties and their contributing factors for a) Usability [46, 63] and b) User Experience [68]

User Experience is a more recent concept that is under standardization but still not mature. Sub-properties of User Experience (usually called dimensions) are diverse in terms of level of abstraction and vary widely amongst authors (see [43] for a description of user experience in terms of hedonic and ergonomic qualities – another word for properties). [68] proposes the only set of dimensions that has been carefully check for orthogonality and proposes six dimensions at the same level of abstraction (see right-hand side b) section of Fig. 6).

Dependable and Secure Computing and Concurrent Programs Properties. The first issue of the IEEE transactions on Dependable and secure computing included a paper [7] dedicated to a taxonomy of properties of those systems. The taxonomy is presented in Part a) of Fig. 7. Beyond a very clear definition of each property this classification shows that some sub-properties such as availability are related to higher-level properties namely safety and security. Indeed, a loss of availability might impact dependability of the systems (if the service not available is requested) while security attacks might target at a reduction of availability of service (as in the classical DDoS – Distributed Denial of Service).

The right-hand side of Fig. 7 presents a very old and classical decomposition of properties of concurrent systems: safety and liveness that have been introduced in the introduction. Beyond this separation, Sistla proposed in [79] a refinement of these properties in more precise ones contributing to the presence or the absence of the more high-level ones.

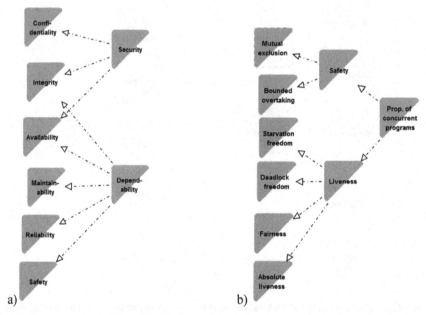

Fig. 7. Representation of hierarchical relationships between properties and contributing factors for Security and Dependability [7] (a) and for concurrent programs [69, 70]

A more comprehensive description of hierarchies of properties for interactive systems and a dedicated notation to represent them and their possible conflicts can be found in [37].

4.2 Processes Supporting the Presence of Expected Properties

User Centered Design Processes. These processes as defined in [47] promotes taking into account usability (especially satisfaction and efficiency) and user experience by iterative processes involving explicitly real users in the design and evaluation phases [41]. Effectiveness is addressed by processes promoting explicit description of user work and tasks as in Cognitive Work Analysis [91] or task-centered processes [57]. while focusing on these "user-centered" properties, these approaches tend to lower the importance of the "system-centered" other properties as this is the case for agile processes focusing of early delivery of low quality systems [88]. According to the classification of faults in Fig. 4 by supporting usability, these processes would support addressing human-made development faults (by having usable integrated development environments) as well as human-made operational faults (by designing usable interactive applications).

Dependability Centered Design Processes. In the field of critical systems, safety standards such as do-178C or IEC 61508 define Development Assurance Levels for software systems (or for functions of software systems). These levels are based on the analysis of consequences or effect of a Malfunction. For instance, if a function failure has high consequences such as multiple fatalities, it is called catastrophic and certification authorities will require that the system manufacturer will provide a development assurance level a (DO-178C standard for aeronautics [32]). If consequences are lower, the required level will decrease. Developing a system of a DAL A is extremely resource consuming and expensive and, as far as software is concerned, the use of formal description techniques is required [33]. In lower DALs, such expensive approaches are not required and for reaching levels such as DAL D rigorous software engineering approaches are sufficient.

According to the classification of faults in Fig. 4 by supporting reliability, these processes would support addressing human-made development faults (by using formal methods to detect defects in the code).

Processes Integrating Dependability, Usability and User Experience. Some processes (such as [11]) which focusses on the use of formal models of the interactive system to assess usability (mainly efficiency and satisfaction) and [56] which focusses on the effectiveness dimension of usability (see decomposition of usability in Fig. 6). merging these two approaches is very difficult and few contributions address it [12]. indeed, this brings specific issues such as the expertise of developers and designers but also the economic benefits in the case of non-critical interactive applications.

5 Techniques and Approaches for Addressing Faults

This section presents several fault-tolerant mechanisms designed in several research domains such as dependable computing, formal methods and human-computer interaction providing means to avoid, detect, remove, tolerate or mitigate the faults presented in Fig. 4 and Fig. 5.

5.1 Techniques for Addressing Human Faults

Heuristic Evaluations. The ten heuristics from [63] aims at support experts in detecting defects in an interactive application and avoiding the operational human-made faults from Fig. 4. In can also support detecting some of the faults affecting the operator in Fig. 5 but more the human-made ones (bottom of the figure) rather than the other ones.

UCD Processes. As explained above, techniques deployed in UCD processes aim at detecting development faults (at design level) by involving users through user testing. Beyond detection, processes focusing on creativity as [20] aim at identifying solutions that would remove the fault by proposing better designs in terms of usability and user experience. However, recent work (e.g. [16] has proposed processes for combining UCD and dependability approaches thus addressing in a unique framework two types of faults.

Debiasing Cognitive Biases. Several hundred of cognitive biases have been identified in the literature. The cognitive biases codex [84] breaks down cognitive errors into four quadrants: memory, meaning, information overload, and need for speed. Others [10] have proposed different grouping according to the general mental problem they attempt to address: too much information, not enough meaning, need to act fast, what should be remembered. In the field of HCI some specific biases have been studied (e.g. peak-end effect [26]) and their use for design (e.g. organizing work over multiple pages taking into account peak-end effect) has been proposed. Similarly, work from Saint-Lot et al. [76] proposes a graphical countermeasure to cognitive tunneling bias (an orange-red flash of 300 ms with a 15% opacity) to improve reaction time of air traffic controller and mitigate attention tunneling bias. However, such research contributions are not connected with each other and propose local solution to selected cognitive biases (on a one by one basis).

Environment Disturbance Tolerance. The environment in which the system is deployed can deeply degrade operators' performance. This is because the environment triggers faults on the operator without possibly affecting the interactive system. This type of fault is represented, for instance, in item 1 of Fig. 5. The turbulences trigger a natural fault that sets the operator in an error mode [65]. If the operator needs to provide input to the interactive system (in that case an aircraft cockpit) the likelihood of error is very high. To prevent such error a new interaction technique called "brace touch" has been proposed that nearly remove all the operators' errors in case of light and severe turbulences [25]. Another approach exploiting stencils overlays on the touch screen is presented in [24].

User Interface Services. Specific function such as copy-paste or undo are added to user interfaces in order to prevent operational faults such as triggering a command inadvertently or making mistake or slips (as defined in [75]) when type the same text in another place. These faults may occur at development and operational times demonstrating the need to encompass these services both in IDEs and in interactive applications.

5.2 Techniques for Addressing Interactive System Faults

Self-checking Software Components (Redundancy, Diversity and Segregation). As introduced in [7] and [53], many dependability strategies rely on replicated self-checking components as they provide error-confinement and can thus be considered as fail-stop components. The COM/MON approach [86] is the basis for various N-Self-checking Programming (NSCP)-based architectures [53]. A self-checking software component can be roughly described as composed of two pieces of software, the first one (functional component) being the classical component and the second one (monitoring component) being in charge of checking its execution and outputs and being able to send error notifications in case of inconsistency. As both pieces receive the same input, fault (e.g. natural faults in Fig. 4) will be detected if both pieces produce inconsistent output. In order to correct the natural faults, more dissimilar (but functionally equivalent) pieces have to be executed in parallel. Having a voting mechanism checking the output of the pieces will allow detecting a fault (if they don't provide the same output) but also remove the fault (by following the majority of outputs that are the same). Self-cheking approach (embedding redundancy, diversity and segregation) have been applied to interactive systems in the area of aircraft cockpits [81]. [82] extends this type of work by providing formal models of the self-checking widgets thus addressing development faults.

Formal Verification. Formal verification aims at exploiting mathematical reasoning over a model (or directly the code) of the system to detect defects (corresponding usually to properties not being true). It thus aims at detecting development faults and usually also provide means or support to remove them. For instance, model checking tools will verify is a property is true on a specification and if not will provide a counter example (a sequence of actions that lead to a state where the property does not hold) [49]. These approaches have been applied for many years to interactive systems, starting from WIMP interaction technique [61] to more sophisticated ones such as multitouch [42] or even brace touch introduced in the previous section [65]. In order to ensure that the verification is performed correctly, tools and tool suites are developed. [27] proposes a systematic comparison of formal tools for interactive systems highlighting both the benefits of these approaches and their limitations. User-related properties can also be checked, at least partly, using formal verification techniques as demonstrated in [67] which demonstrate how to verify ergonomic rules over a formal model of an interactive, post-WIMP, application.

Interactive Software Testing. Software testing is another type of technique for detecting development faults. The basic idea is to run a large number of test cases in order to detect behaviors that are incompatible with the requirements. Software testing has been developed for many years and, in order to deal with the complexity of the cases, model-based testing is nowadays the most prominent approach [89]. As for model-checking, software testing support also the identification of defects and debugging [60]. In the area of interactive systems, testing is a complex tasks as user actions are unpredictable and the number of cases is infinite [19]. Formal model-based approaches offering formal verification have recently been combined [21], to detect and correct defects in interactive systems encompassing both hardware and software aspects of the architecture in Fig. 3.

6 Conclusion and Perspectives

This paper has presented a generic framework called POISE (People, Organizations, Interactive Systems and Environment) that presents in an integrated way four different aspects affecting deeply interactive systems development and exploitation. Based on two complementary on faults taxonomy we have presented a comprehensive coverage of faults altering the functioning of interactive systems (i.e. human-made and natural faults) and the behavior of people (i.e. internal and external to the operator) including cognitive biases, deadly sins and standards operators.

Beyond, the paper has offered an overview of processes, methods and techniques offering various means to address all these faults. These contributions come from different research domains such as Formal Methods, Dependable Computing and Software Engineering and Human-Computer Interaction. While they usually try to tackle a single type of faults, some (which incorporate techniques stemming from multiple domains) have been trying to provide more complex solutions dedicated to the design, development, evaluation and the operation of interactive system embedding multiple (sometimes conflicting) properties such as usability, user experience, reliability, dependability, security, safety … among many other ones [5].

Due to space constraints and for keeping the message simple, the issues related to organizational aspects are not presented. It is however at least as important as the other three aspects as the organization structure the work of operators, define the requirements, select the development processes and techniques to be used by designers and developer and above all plan training and organize operators in teams. Incidents and accidents stemming from the organizations are numerous as demonstrated in [73] as they might jeopardize all the efforts on the other aspects. As stated in the introduction, even though the people are identified as sources of faults, we would advocate that designs should not aim at removing them even though this is the path promoted by Artificial Intelligence (targeting at unmanned systems as drones or so-called autonomous vehicles produced with as limited as possible human intervention. On the opposite, design and development should rely on trained and qualified operators, supported by usable and efficient tools in order to ensure that the human contribution will be fully present in future interactive systems. Knowledge, tools and empowerment of designers and developers is the only path to deploying perfect interactive systems.

Acknowledgements. The author would like to acknowledge support from the ICS team in Toulouse (E. Barboni, D. Navarre and C. Martinie) for working on most of the contributions presented. Special also goes to Yannick Deleris and Christine Gris from Airbus who contributed and funded part of this work.

References

1. Accot, J., Zhai, S.: Refining Fitts' law models for bivariate pointing. In: Proceedings of the SIGCHI Conference on Human Factors in Computing Systems (CHI 2003), pp. 193–200. Association for Computing Machinery, New York (2003). https://doi.org/10.1145/642611.642646
2. Albinsson, P.A., Zhai, S.: High precision touch screen interaction. In: Proceedings of ACM CHI Conference, pp. 105–112 (2003)
3. Android Material Design guidelines: https://material.io/design/guidelines-overview. Accessed 6 Jul 2021
4. Kangasrääsiö, A., Athukorala, K., Howes, A., Corander, J., Kaski, S., Oulasvirta, A.: Inferring cognitive models from data using approximate Bayesian computation. In: Proceedings of the 2017 CHI Conference on Human Factors in Computing Systems, pp. 1295–1306. Association for Computing Machinery, New York (2017).https://doi.org/10.1145/3025453.3025576
5. Ardito, C., Bernhaupt, R., Palanque, P., Sauer, S.: Handling security, usability, user experience and reliability in user-centered development processes. In: Lamas, D., Loizides, F., Nacke, L., Petrie, H., Winckler, M., Zaphiris, P. (eds.) INTERACT 2019. LNCS, vol. 11749, pp. 759–762. Springer, Cham (2019). https://doi.org/10.1007/978-3-030-29390-1_76
6. Armour, P.G.: The business of software estimation is not evil. Commun. ACM **57**(1), 42–43 (2014)

7. Avizienis, A., Laprie, J.-C., Randell, B., Landwehr, C.: Basic concepts and taxonomy of dependable and secure computing. IEEE Trans. Dependable Secure Comput. **1**(1), 11–33 (2004)
8. Beaudouin-Lafon, M.: Designing interaction, not interfaces. In: Proceedings of the Working Conference on Advanced Visual Interfaces (AVI 2004), pp. 15–22. Association for Computing Machinery, New York (2004). https://doi.org/10.1145/989863.989865
9. Beirekdar, A., Keita, M., Noirhomme, M., Randolet, F., Vanderdonckt, J., Mariage, C.: Flexible reporting for automated usability and accessibility evaluation of web sites. In: Costabile, M.F., Paternò, F. (eds.) INTERACT 2005. LNCS, vol. 3585, pp. 281–294. Springer, Heidelberg (2005). https://doi.org/10.1007/11555261_25
10. Benson, B.: Cognitive biases cheat sheet (2016). https://medium.com/better-humans/cognit ive-bias-cheat-sheet-55a472476b18. Accessed July 2021
11. Bernhaupt, R., Navarre, D., Palanque, P., Winckler, M.: Model-based evaluation: a new way to support usability evaluation of multimodal interactive applications. In: Law, E.-C., Hvannberg, E.T., Cockton, G. (eds.) Maturing Usability. HIS, pp. 96–119. Springer, London (2008). https://doi.org/10.1007/978-1-84628-941-5_5
12. Bernhaupt, R., Palanque, P., Manciet, F., Martinie, C.: User-test results injection into task-based design process for the assessment and improvement of both usability and user experience. In: Bogdan, C., et al. (eds.) HCSE/HESSD -2016. LNCS, vol. 9856, pp. 56–72. Springer, Cham (2016). https://doi.org/10.1007/978-3-319-44902-9_5
13. Berry, R.: Common user access – a consistent and usable human-computer interface for the SAA environments. IBM Syst. J. **27**(3) (1988)
14. Bias, R.G., Mayhew, D.: Cost-Justifying Usability: An Update for the Internet Age. Morgan Kaufmann Publishers Inc., San Francisco (2005)
15. Boehm, B., Sullivan, K.: Software economics: a roadmap. In: Proceedings of the Conference on The Future of Software Engineering (ICSE 2000), pp. 319–343 (2000). Association for Computing Machinery, New York. https://doi.org/10.1145/336512.336584
16. Bouzekri, E., Canny, A., Martinie, C., Palanque, P., Gris, C.: Deep system knowledge required: revisiting UCD contribution in the design of complex command and control systems. In: Lamas, D., Loizides, F., Nacke, L., Petrie, H., Winckler, M., Zaphiris, P. (eds.) INTERACT 2019. LNCS, vol. 11746, pp. 699–720. Springer, Cham (2019). https://doi.org/10.1007/978-3-030-29381-9_42
17. Bouzekri, E., Martinie, C., Palanque, P., Atwood, K., Gris, C.: Should I add recommendations to my warning system? The RCRAFT framework can answer this and other questions about supporting the assessment of automation designs. In: IFIP TC 13 INTERACT,Conference, LNCS. Springer (2021)
18. Bowen, J., Stavridou, V.: Formal methods, safety-critical systems and standards. Softw. Eng. J. **8**(4), 189–209 (1993)
19. Bowen, J., Reeves, S.: Generating obligations, assertions and tests from UI models. Proc. ACM Hum. Comput. Interact. **1**, 18 (2017). https://doi.org/10.1145/3095807. EICS, Article 5
20. Buxton, B.: Sketching User Experiences: Getting the Design Right and the Right Design. Morgan Kaufmann Publishers Inc., San Francisco (2007)
21. Canny, A., Martinie, C., Navarre, D., Palanque, P., Barboni, E., Gris, C.: Engineering model-based software testing of WIMP interactive applications: a process based on formal models and the SQUAMATA tool. Proc. ACM Hum.-Comput. Interact. **5**, 30 (2021). https://doi.org/10.1145/3461729. EICS, Article 207
22. Card, S., Moran, T., Newell, A.: The Psychology of Human-Computer Interaction, pp. I–XIII, 1–469. Erlbaum (1983). ISBN: 0898598591

23. Card, S.K, Moran, T.P, Newell, A.: The model human processor: an engineering model of human performance. In: Handbook of Perception and Human Performance, Cognitive Processes and Performance, vol. 2, pp. 1–35 (1986)

24. Cockburn, A., et al.: Turbulent touch: touchscreen input for cockpit flight displays. In: Proceedings of the 2017 CHI Conference on Human Factors in Computing Systems, pp. 6742–6753. Association for Computing Machinery, New York (2017). https://doi.org/10.1145/302 5453.3025584

25. Cockburn, A., et al.: Design and evaluation of braced touch for touchscreen input stabilization. Int. J. Hum.-Comput. Stud. **122**, 21–37 (2019). https://doi.org/10.1016/j.ijhcs.2018.08.005. ISSN 1071-5819

26. Cockburn, A., Quinn, P., Gutwin, C.: Examining the peak-end effects of subjective experience. In: Proceedings of the 33rd Annual ACM Conference on Human Factors in Computing Systems (CHI 2015), pp. 357–366. Association for Computing Machinery, New York (2015). https://doi.org/10.1145/2702123.2702139

27. Creissac Campos, J., Fayollas, C., Harrison, M.D., Martinie, C., Masci, P., Palanque, P.: Supporting the analysis of safety critical user interfaces: an exploration of three formal tools. ACM Trans. Comput.-Hum. Interact. **27**(5), 48 (2020). https://doi.org/10.1145/3404199. Article 35

28. Cronel, M., Dumas, B., Palanque, P., Canny, A.: MIODMIT: a generic architecture for dynamic multimodal interactive systems. In: Bogdan, C., Kuusinen, K., Lárusdóttir, M., Palanque, P., Winckler, M. (eds.) Human-Centered Software Engineering. HCSE 2018. Lecture Notes in Computer Science, vol. 11262. Springer, Cham (2019).https://doi.org/10.1007/978-3-030-05909-5

29. Diamantaris, M., Marcantoni, F., Ioannidis, S., Polakis, J.: The seven deadly sins of the HTML5 WebAPI: a large-scale study on the risks of mobile sensor-based attacks. ACM Trans. Priv. Secur. **23**(4), 31 (2020). https://doi.org/10.1145/3403947. Article 19

30. Diaper, D., Stanton, N.: The Handbook of Task Analysis for Human-Computer Interaction. Lawrence Erlbaum Associates (2003). ISBN 0-8058-4432-5

31. Dix, A.: Abstract, generic models of interactive systems. In: BCS HCI Conference, pp. 63–77 (1988)

32. DO-178C/ED-12C: Software Considerations in Airborne Systems and Equipment Certification, published by RTCA and EUROCAE (2012)

33. DO-333 Formal Methods Supplement to DO-178C and DO-278A, published by RTCA and EUROCAE, 13 Dec 2011 (2011)

34. Eisenberg, N., Miller, P.A.: The relation of empathy to prosocial and related behaviors. Psychol. Bull. **101**(1), 91 (1987)

35. Fahssi, R., Martinie, C., Palanque, P.: Enhanced task modelling for systematic identification and explicit representation of human errors. In: Abascal, J., Barbosa, S., Fetter, M., Gross, T., Palanque, P., Winckler, M. (eds.) INTERACT 2015. LNCS, vol. 9299, pp. 192–212. Springer, Cham (2015). https://doi.org/10.1007/978-3-319-22723-8_16

36. Fayollas, C., Fabre, J.C., Palanque, P., Cronel, M., Navarre, D., Deleris, Y.: A software-implemented fault-tolerance approach for control and display systems in avionics. In: 2014 IEEE 20th Pacific Rim International Symposium on Dependable Computing, pp. 21–30 (2014). https://doi.org/10.1109/PRDC.2014.11

37. Fayollas, C., Martinie, C., Palanque, P., Ait-Ameur, Y.: QBP notation for explicit representation of properties, their refinement and their potential conflicts: application to interactive systems. In: Clemmensen, T., Rajamanickam, V., Dannenmann, P., Petrie, H., Winckler, M. (eds.) INTERACT 2017. LNCS, vol. 10774, pp. 91–105. Springer, Cham (2018). https://doi.org/10.1007/978-3-319-92081-8_9

38. Feiler, P.H., Gluch, D.P., Hudak, J.J.: The Architecture Analysis & Design Language (AADL): An Introduction (No. CMU/SEI-2006-TN-011). CMU Software Engineering Inst (2006)

39. Fitt, P.M.: The information capacity of the human motor system in controlling the amplitude of movement. J. Exp. Psychol. **47**, 381–391 (1954)
40. Flemisch, F., et al.: Towards a dynamic balance between humans and automation: authority, ability, responsibility and control in shared and cooperative control situations. Cogn. Tech. Work **14**, 3–18 (2012). https://doi.org/10.1007/s10111-011-0191-6
41. Gould, I.D., Lewis, C.: Designing for usability: key principles and what designers think. Commun. ACM **28**(3), 300–311 (1985)
42. Hamon, A., Palanque, P., Silva, J.-L., Deleris, Y., Barboni, E.: Formal description of multi-touch interactions. In: Proceedings of the 5th ACM SIGCHI Symposium on Engineering Interactive Computing Systems (EICS 2013), pp. 207–216. Association for Computing Machinery, New York (2013). https://doi.org/10.1145/2494603.2480311
43. Hassenzahl, M., Platz, A., Burmester, M., Lehner, K.: Hedonic and ergonomic quality aspects determine a software's appeal. In: ACM CHI Conference 2000, pp. 201–208. ACM DL (2000)
44. Hecht, H., Fiorentino, E.: Reliability assessment of spacecraft electronics. In: Annual Reliability and Maintainability Symposium, pp. 341–346. IEEE (1987)
45. Hollnagel, E.: How resilient is your organisation? An introduction to the resilience analysis grid (RAG). In: Sustainable Transformation: Building a Resilient Organization, Toronto, Canada (2010)
46. International Standard Organization: "ISO 9241–11." Ergonomic requirements for office work with visual display terminals (VDT) – Part 11 Guidance on Usability (1996)
47. ISO 9241-210: Ergonomics of human-system interaction – Part 210: Human-centred design for interactive systems, Geneva
48. Johnson, P.: Human-computer Interaction: psychology, task analysis and software engineering. McGraw Hill, Maidenhead (1992)
49. Kupferman, O., Vardi, M.Y.: Model checking of safety properties. Formal Methods Syst. Des. **19**, 291–314 (2001). https://doi.org/10.1023/A:1011254632723
50. Lai-Chong, E., Roto, V., Hassenzahl, M., Vermeeren, A., Kort. J.: Understanding, scoping and defining user experience: a survey approach. In: Proceedings of the 27th International Conference on Human Factors in Computing Systems, pp. 719–728. ACM, New York (2009)
51. Lamport, L.: Proving the correctness of multiprocess programs. IEEE Trans. Softw. Eng. **2**, 125–143 (1977)
52. Landwehr, C., Bull, A., McDermott, J., Choi, W.: A taxonomy of computer program security flaws. *ACM Comput. Surv.* 26(3). Sept. **1994**, 211–254 (1994). https://doi.org/10.1145/185403.185412
53. Laprie, J.-C. et al.: Definition and analysis of hardware and software fault-tolerant architectures. IEEE Comput. **23**(7), 39–51 (1990)
54. Levitt, S.D., Dubner, S.J.: Freakonomics: A Rogue Economist Explores the Hidden Side of Everything. William Morrow, New York (2005)
55. Manna, Z., Pnueli, A.: A hierarchy of temporal properties. ACM Symp. Principles Distrib. Comput. **1990**, 377–410 (1990)
56. Martinie, C., Navarre, D., Palanque, P., Fayollas, C.: A generic tool-supported framework for coupling task models and interactive applications. In: Proceedings of the 7th ACM SIGCHI Symposium on Engineering Interactive Computing Systems (EICS 2015), pp. 244–253. ACM (2015). https://doi.org/10.1145/2774225.2774845
57. Martinie, C., Palanque, P., Navarre, D., Barboni, E.: A development process for usable large scale interactive critical systems: application to satellite ground segments. In: Winckler, M., Forbrig, P., Bernhaupt, R. (eds.) HCSE 2012. LNCS, vol. 7623, pp. 72–93. Springer, Heidelberg (2012). https://doi.org/10.1007/978-3-642-34347-6_5
58. Mustafa, M., Lindemann, L., Magnor, M.: EEG analysis of implicit human visual perception. In: Proceedings of the SIGCHI Conference on Human Factors in Computing Systems,

pp. 513–516. Association for Computing Machinery, New York (2012). https://doi.org/10. 1145/2207676.2207746

59. Meshkati, N.: Technology transfer to developing countries: a tripartite micro- and macro ergonomic analysis of human-organization-technology interfaces. Int. J. Ind. Ergon. **4**, 101– 115 (1989)

60. Navabpour, S., Bonakdarpour, B., Fischmeister, S.: Software debugging and testing using the abstract diagnosis theory. In: Proceedings of the 2011 SIGPLAN/SIGBED conference on Languages, compilers and tools for embedded systems (LCTES 2011), pp. 111–120. Association for Computing Machinery, New York (2011). https://doi.org/10.1145/1967677. 1967693

61. Navarre, D., Palanque, P., Bastide, R., Sy, O.: Structuring interactive systems specifications for executability and prototypability. In: Palanque, P., Paternò, F. (eds.) DSV-IS 2000. LNCS, vol. 1946, pp. 97–119. Springer, Heidelberg (2001). https://doi.org/10.1007/3-540-44675-3_7

62. Nicolescu, B., Peronnard, P., Velazco, R., Savaria, Y.: Efficiency of transient bit-flips detection by software means: a complete study. In: Proceedings of the 18th IEEE International Symposium on Defect and Fault Tolerance in VLSI Systems (DFT 2003), pp. 377–384. IEEE Computer Society (2003)

63. Nielsen, J.: Usability Engineering. Morgan Kaufmann Publishers Inc., San Francisco (1994)

64. Olwal, A., Feiner, S.: Rubbing the fisheye: precise touch-screen interaction with gestures and fisheye views. In: Conference Supplement of UIST 2003, pp. 83–84 (2003)

65. Palanque, P., Cockburn, A., Désert-Legendre, L., Gutwin, C., Deleris, Y.: Brace touch: a dependable, turbulence-tolerant, multi-touch interaction technique for interactive cockpits. In: Romanovsky, A., Troubitsyna, E., Bitsch, F. (eds.) SAFECOMP 2019. LNCS, vol. 11698, pp. 53–68. Springer, Cham (2019). https://doi.org/10.1007/978-3-030-26601-1_4

66. Palanque, P., Cockburn, A., Gutwin, C.: A classification of faults covering the human-computer interaction loop. In: Casimiro, A., Ortmeier, F., Bitsch, F., Ferreira, P. (eds.) SAFE-COMP 2020. LNCS, vol. 12234, pp. 434–448. Springer, Cham (2020). https://doi.org/10. 1007/978-3-030-54549-9_29

67. Palanque, P., Farenc, C., Bastide, R.: Embedding ergonomic rules as generic requirements in a formal development process of interactive software. In: Proceedings of IFIP TC 13 Conference on Human-Computer Interaction INTERACT 1999, Edinburg, Scotland, 1–4 Sept 1999 (1999)

68. Pirker, M., Bernhaupt, R.: Measuring user experience in the living room: results from an ethnographically oriented field study indicating major evaluation factors. EuroITV **2011**, 79–82 (2011)

69. Pnueli, A.: Applications of temporal logic to the specification and verification of reactive systems: a survey of current trends. In: de Bakker, J.W., de Roever, W.P., Rozenberg, G. (eds.) Current Trends in Concurrency. Lecture Notes in Computer Science, vol. 224. Springer, Heidelberg (1986). https://doi.org/10.1007/BFb0027047

70. Pnueli, A.: The temporal logic of programs. In: 18th IEEE Symposium on the Foundations of Computer Science, pp. 46–57 (1977)

71. Polet, P., Vanderhaegen, F., Wieringa, P.: Theory of safety related violation of system barriers. Cogn. Technol. Work **4**(3), 171–179 (2002)

72. Raber, F., Kosmalla, F., Krueger, A.: Fine-grained privacy setting prediction using a privacy attitude questionnaire and machine learning. In: Bernhaupt, R., Dalvi, G., Joshi, A., K. Balkrishan, D., O'Neill, J., Winckler, M. (eds.) INTERACT 2017. LNCS, vol. 10516, pp. 445–449. Springer, Cham (2017). https://doi.org/10.1007/978-3-319-68059-0_48

73. Reason, J.: Managing the Risks of Organizational Accidents. Ashgate Publishing limited. (1997)

74. Reason, J.: The Human Contribution: Unsafe Acts, Accidents and Heroic Recoveries. Taylor and Francis, Routeledge (2008)

75. Reason, J.: Human Error. Cambridge University Press, Cambridge (1990)
76. Saint-Lot, J., Imbert, J.-P., Dehais, F.: Red alert: a cognitive countermeasure to mitigate attentional tunneling. In: Proceedings of CHI 2020: CHI Conference on Human Factors in Computing Systems (CHI 2020), 25–30 Apr 2020, Honolulu, HI, USA. ACM, New York (2020). https://doi.org/10.1145/3313831.3376709
77. Schroeder, B., Pinheiro, E., Weber, W.-D.: DRAM errors in the wild: a large-scale field study. In: ACM SIGMETRICS, Seattle, WA, pp. 193–204 (2009)
78. Shah, P., Berges, M., Hubwieser, P.: Qualitative content analysis of programming errors. In: Proceedings of the 5th International Conference on Information and Education Technology (ICIET 2017), pp. 161–166. ACM (2017). https://doi.org/10.1145/3029387.3029399
79. Sistla, A.P.: On characterization of safety and liveness properties in temporal logic. In: Proceedings of the Fourth Annual ACM Symposium on Principles of Distributed Computing, pp. 39–48, ACM (1985)
80. Soukoreff, W., MacKenzie, S.: Towards a standard for pointing device evaluation, perspectives on 27 years of Fitts' law research in HCI. IJHCS **61**(6), 751–789 (2004)
81. Tankeu Choitat, A, Fabre, J.-C., Palanque, P., Navarre, D., Deleris, Y.: Self-checking widgets for interactive cockpits. In: Proceedings of the 13th European Workshop on Dependable Computing (EWDC 2011), pp. 43–48. Association for Computing Machinery, New York (2011). https://doi.org/10.1145/1978582.1978592
82. Tankeu-Choitat, A., Navarre, D., Palanque, P., Deleris, Y., Fabre, J.-C., Fayollas, C.: Self-checking components for dependable interactive cockpits using formal description techniques. In: 2011 IEEE 17th Pacific Rim International Symposium on Dependable Computing, pp. 164–173 (2011). https://doi.org/10.1109/PRDC.2011.28
83. ter Beek, M.H., Faconti, G.P., Massink, M., Palanque, P.A., Winckler, M.: Resilience of interaction techniques to interrupts: a formal model-based approach . In: Gross, T., et al. (eds.) INTERACT 2009. LNCS, vol. 5726, pp. 494–509. Springer, Heidelberg (2009). https://doi.org/10.1007/978-3-642-03655-2_56
84. The cognitive biases codex: 175 cognitive biases: https://medium.com/better-humans/cognitive-bias-cheat-sheet-55a472476b18. Accessed 8 Jul 2021
85. Thoma, V., White, E.P.: In two minds about usability? Rationality and intuition in usability evaluations. In: Campos, P., Graham, N., Jorge, J., Nunes, N., Palanque, P., Winckler, M. (eds.) INTERACT 2011. LNCS, vol. 6949, pp. 544–547. Springer, Heidelberg (2011). https://doi.org/10.1007/978-3-642-23768-3_78
86. Traverse, P., Lacaze, I., Souyris, J.: Airbus fly-by-wire: a total approach to dependability. In: Proceedings of WCC, pp. 191–212 (2004)
87. Trewin, S., et al.: Age-specific predictive models of human performance. In: CHI '12 Extended Abstracts on Human Factors in Computing Systems, pp. 2267–2272. ACM (2012). https://doi.org/10.1145/2212776.2223787
88. Turk, D., France, R., Rumpe, B. Limitations of agile software processes. In: Proceedings of International Conference on eXtreme Programming and Agile Processes in Software Engineering Italy (2002)
89. Utting, M., Pretschner, A., Legeard, B.: A taxonomy of model-based testing approaches. Softw. Test. Verif. Reliab. **22**(5), 297–312 (2012). https://doi.org/10.1002/stvr.456
90. Vanderdonckt, J.: Development milestones towards a tool for working with guidelines. Interact. Comput. **12**(2), 81–118 (1999)
91. Vicente, K.: Cognitive Work Analysis: Toward Safe, Productive, and Healthy Computer-Based Work.Lawrence Erlbaum Associates (1999)
92. Wahl, N.J.: Responsibility for unreliable software. In: Proceedings of the Conference on Ethics in the Computer Age (ECA 1994), pp. 175–177. Association for Computing Machinery, New York (1994). https://doi.org/10.1145/199544.199611

Affective Computing

A Field Dependence-Independence Perspective on Eye Gaze Behavior within Affective Activities

Christos Fidas[1], Marios Belk[2,4(✉)], Christodoulos Constantinides[4],
Argyris Constantinides[3,4], and Andreas Pitsillides[4]

[1] Department of Electrical and Computer Engineering, University of Patras, Patras, Greece
fidas@upatras.gr
[2] Cognitive UX GmbH, Heidelberg, Germany
belk@cognitiveux.de
[3] Cognitive UX LTD, Nicosia, Cyprus
argyris@cognitiveux.com
[4] Department of Computer Science, University of Cyprus, Nicosia, Cyprus
{cconst04,andreas.pitsillides}@cs.ucy.ac.cy

Abstract. Evidence suggests that human cognitive differences affect users' visual behavior within various tasks and activities. However, a human cognitive processing perspective on the interplay between visual and affective aspects remains up-to-date understudied. In this paper, we aim to investigate this relationship by adopting an accredited cognitive style framework (Field Dependence-Independence – FD-I) and provide empirical evidence on main interaction effects between human cognition and emotional processing towards eye gaze behavior. For doing so, we designed and implemented an eye tracking study ($n = 22$) in which participants were initially classified according to their FD-I cognitive processing characteristics, and were further exposed to a series of images, which triggered specific emotional valence. Analysis of results yield that affective images had a different effect on FD and FI users in terms of visual information exploration time and comprehension, which was reflected on eye gaze metrics. Findings highlight a hidden and rather unexplored effect between human cognition and emotions towards eye gaze behavior, which could lead to a more holistic and comprehensive approach in affective computing.

Keywords: Individual differences · Cognitive processing styles · Global and local processing · Human emotions · Eye tracking · User study

1 Introduction

Human emotions are essential in human experience, influencing perception, as well as logical and rational thinking in cognitive processing [1, 2]. Researchers and practitioners in the area of Affective Computing have studied the importance of human emotions in human-computer interaction [2], interactive systems' design [3], and adaptive user

© IFIP International Federation for Information Processing 2021
Published by Springer Nature Switzerland AG 2021
C. Ardito et al. (Eds.): INTERACT 2021, LNCS 12932, pp. 63–72, 2021.
https://doi.org/10.1007/978-3-030-85623-6_6

interfaces [4] that personalize their behavior and responses according to the users' current emotional states.

An important challenge in such research endeavors relates to the non-intrusive and implicit elicitation of users' emotional states. For this purpose, several research works have investigated whether users' visual behavior can be a predictor of their emotional states during memory- and decision-making tasks [5–11]. Lemos et al. [5] introduced an automated method for measuring (un)pleasant emotions and the level of excitement to a stimulus before they are cognitively perceived and interpreted by the human mind by analyzing the gaze properties of a person (eye gaze, blinks, pupil change). Schmid et al. [6] studied how mood states affect information processing during facial emotion recognition by analyzing the users' global and local visual information processing styles. Sears et al. [7] analyzed and investigated visual attention to emotional images in previously depressed individuals. Stanley et al. [8] studied the interplay among cultural differences, visual behavior and emotions utilizing emotional images. Charoenpit and Ohkura [9] explored emotions within eye gaze-driven e-learning systems aiming to detect curiosity, interest and boredom based on low-level eye gaze metrics such as fixations, fixations' duration and pupil diameter. Zheng et al. [10] and Zhen-Fen et al. [11] proposed novel emotion recognition methods by combining electroencephalography (EEG) signals with users' pupillary responses and scan-paths, respectively.

Research Motivation. Visual processing is performed through two distinct information streams of the human brain; the *global* and the *local information streams* [12, 13]. *Global processing* enables individuals to process the visual field holistically to give meaning to an object or a scene [12], while *local processing* enables individuals to process the details out of a whole [13]. Humans process information cognitively through both the global and local information streams by filtering relevant information within a visual scene [14]. Although individuals integrate both streams during cognitive processing, research indicates that *individual differences in cognitive processing styles* exist, which highlight the individuals' preferred mode of visually processing information either *globally (holistically)* or *locally (analytically)* [15]. In addition, prior research suggests that when individuals recognize emotions, they process stimuli globally rather than locally [6, 19, 20], *i.e.*, the stimulus is primarily processed as a whole and not in a fragmented fashion.

Unlike existing works [6, 20], which investigated how mood states affect global and local information processing, in this work, we go a step further by investigating whether there is a systematic effect of human cognitive differences towards eye gaze behavior within affective activities, framed by an accredited human cognition theory (*i.e.*, Witkin's Field Dependence-Independence [15]). Considering such an interplay could lead to a more comprehensive approach in affective computing. To the best of our knowledge, such an interplay has not been investigated so far.

The remainder of the paper is structured as follows. First, we present the underlying theory on human cognitive differences and human emotions. We further present the method of study, analysis of results, discussion on the main findings, limitations, and future steps.

2 Background Theory

Among several cognitive processing style theories, this work focuses on the *Field Dependence-Independence cognitive style theory* [15], which is an accredited and widely applied theory [16–18, 38] that holistically represents how individuals perceive their context and surrounding field in which a task needs to be accomplished. It highlights human cognitive differences into *Field Dependent (FD) (or Wholists)* and *Field Independent (FI) (or Analysts)*. Evidence has shown that FD and FI individuals have differences in visual perceptiveness [15], visual working memory capacity [16], visual search abilities [17], in the way they organize and process information of their surrounding visual field [18]. In particular, FD individuals view the perceptual field as a whole and they are not attentive to detail, while FI individuals view discrete information presented by their visual field as a collection of parts.

Furthermore, affective experiences such as feelings and mood can be defined as combinations of two basic dimensions: *valence* and *arousal* [21, 22]. *Valence* describes the attractiveness or aversiveness of stimuli along a continuum (negative-neutral-positive), while *arousal* relates to the perceived intensity of an event ranging from very calming to highly exciting or agitating [22, 23]. Research has shown that cognitive processing characteristics of individuals affect the way individuals control their emotions, *e.g.*, individuals with enhanced cognitive processing abilities, control their emotions more naturally than those with more limited cognitive abilities [28]. Several works also indicate that emotional arousal affects cognition such as the long-term memory [23, 24].

3 Method of Study

3.1 Research Questions

RQ_1. Are there significant differences in users' visual exploration time between FD *vs.* FI users for images that trigger different emotional valence?

RQ_2. Are there significant differences in users' eye gaze transition entropy between FD *vs.* FI users for images that trigger different emotional valence?

3.2 Apparatus

The research instruments utilized in the study include: *i)* the Group Embedded Figures Test (GEFT) paper-and-pencil test for classifying the participants into FD and FI groups; *ii)* a wearable eye tracking device; *iii)* a wearable electroencephalography (EEG) device for emotion recognition; and *iv)* a conventional desktop computer.

Human Cognitive Style Elicitation. Users' field dependence-independence was measured through the GEFT [29], which is a widely applied and validated paper-and-pencil test [16–18]. The test measures the user's ability to find common geometric shapes in a larger design. The GEFT consists of 25 items. In each item, a simple geometric figure is hidden within a complex pattern, and participants are required to identify the simple figure by drawing it with a pencil over the complex figure. Based on a widely applied cut-off score [16, 32], participants that solve less than 12 items are FD, while participants that solve 12 items and above are FI.

Equipment. An All-in-One HP computer with a 24″ monitor was used (1920 × 1080 pixels). To capture eye movements, we used Pupil Labs Core eye tracker [30], which captures data at 200 Hz. The eye tracker was calibrated individually using a 5-point calibration procedure, and was positioned at an upwards angle roughly 30 cm below eye level and 65 cm away. To capture human emotions, we used Emotiv Epoc+ [31], a 14-channel electroencephalography, which detects emotional states, such as excitement, engagement, relaxation, interest, stress, focus.

3.3 Sampling and Procedure

A total of 22 individuals (9 females) participated, aged between 20–32 years old ($m = 24$, $std = 3.1$). Participants were split into two groups based on the GEFT classification (12 FD, 10 FI).

Aiming to control the effect of image content on creating emotions (positive/negative/neutral), we used an open-source data set of emotionally annotated images (*i.e.*, Open Affective Standardized Image Set (OASIS) [33]). Furthermore, we asked users to think aloud by describing: *i)* the image (to trigger visual exploration and search); *ii)* the feelings the image triggers; and *iii)* the reason the particular feeling was triggered. Throughout the session, participants wore the eye tacking and EEG device for measuring the eye gaze behavior and emotional states respectively (both devices were calibrated at the beginning of each user session). Such a procedure allowed us to triangulate results from subjective feedback (users' expressing their feelings on emotional valence – positive/neutral/negative), and objective measures derived from Emotiv in which the detected emotional states were post-processed and assigned to an emotional valence group (valence – positive/neutral/negative).

Considering that users' cognitive styles and image complexity affect users' visual behavior [32, 34], we chose images of similar complexity between and within images belonging to the three groups. For doing so, we assessed the equivalence of the two image sets by calculating the image complexity using entropy estimators [35, 36]. Following a within-subjects study design, all participants were presented with a series of the same images that were randomly assigned to the participants.

We adopted the University's human research protocol that takes into consideration users' privacy, confidentiality and anonymity. All participants performed the task in a quiet lab room with only the researchers present.

3.4 Image Set

To investigate the research questions, we intentionally chose three image sets: *i) Positive Images:* images that trigger positive valence; *ii) Negative Images:* images that trigger negative valence; and *iii) Neutral Images:* images that trigger neutral valence. For this purpose, we have used the Open Affective Standardized Image Set (OASIS) [33], an open-access online stimulus set containing 900 colored images depicting a broad spectrum of themes, including humans, animals, objects, and scenes along with normative ratings on emotional valence and arousal. Figure 1 illustrates the study images, and Table 1 summarizes the emotional valence and arousal triggered for each image according to OASIS, and the estimated image complexity.

Fig. 1. The set of images used in the study and the corresponding emotions that are triggered.

Table 1. Emotional valence/arousal according to OASIS, and image complexity for each image used in the study.

Image	Emotional valence	Emotional arousal	Complexity in bits
Dog	6.49 (positive)	5.02	7.45
Lake	6.41 (positive)	4.10	7.87
Sidewalk	4.29 (neutral)	2.23	7.34
Yarn	4.20 (neutral)	1.98	7.65
Fire	1.75 (negative)	5.31	7.54
Garbage	1.63 (negative)	4.78	7.23

3.5 Data Metrics

For measuring *visual exploration time*, we measured the time that started as soon as the image was illustrated to the users, until the users expressed loudly their feelings. For capturing the users' *eye gaze behavior*, we used raw fixation metrics (count and duration) using Pupil Labs' built-in methods. We have further extended the software to analyze Areas of Interests (AOI), and gaze transition entropy (based on [37]) to assess whether a user is performing a careful view of AOIs *vs.* more randomness and more frequent switching between AOIs.

4 Analysis of Main Effects

There were no significant outliers in the data based on boxplot inspection, and residuals were normally distributed. Data are mean ± standard deviation.

4.1 Visual Exploration Time Differences Between FD *vs.* FI Users for Images that Trigger Different Emotional Valence (RQ_1)

A two-way mixed analysis of variance was conducted to examine interaction effects among cognitive style (FD/FI) and image type (positive/neutral/negative) on the time to explore the image (Fig. 2). There was no statistically significant interaction between cognitive style and image type on the time to explore the image, $F(2, 60) = .955, p = .391, partial\ \eta^2 = .031$, while there was an effect of image type on the time to explore the image, $F(2, 60) = 7.572, p = .001, partial\ \eta^2 = .202$. Furthermore, there was a significant difference between the time to explore images between FD and FI users, $F(1, 30) = 5.551\ p = .025, partial\ \eta^2 = .156$. Descriptive statistics reveal that affective images (positive and negative) triggered higher exploration times compared to neutral images across cognitive style groups. FD users explored for a longer time all three image types compared to FI users.

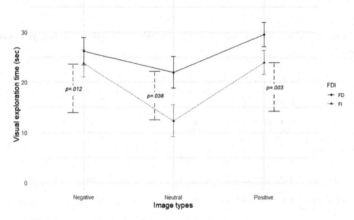

Fig. 2. Mean visual exploration times (sec) among user groups.

Main Finding Related to RQ_1. FD users spent more time viewing affective (positive and negative valence) images than FI users (Fig. 2). Such an observation can be explained by the fact that FD users have a more trained global information processing stream compared to FI users [15–18, 25, 38], and consequently interpreted semantically faster the provided image, which is reflected on their visual behavior. In addition, FD users inherently follow a more holistic and exploratory approach as opposed to FI users that primarily focus their attention on areas of interests, hence, FD users spent more time exploring the image compared to FI users.

4.2 Eye Gaze Behavior Differences Between FD *vs.* FI Users for Images that Trigger Different Emotional Valence (RQ_2)

A two-way mixed analysis of variance was conducted to examine interaction effects among cognitive style (FD/FI) and image type (positive/neutral/negative) on fixation count and fixation duration to assess visual behavior (Table 2). There was no statistically significant interaction between cognitive style and image type on fixation count, $F(2, 60) = 1.397, p = .255, partial\ \eta^2 = .044$, nor on fixation duration, $F(2, 60) = .626, p = .538, partial\ \eta^2 = .02$. Nevertheless, descriptive statistics indicate that for FIs, fixation count and fixation duration was amplified in affective images (positive and negative) compared to neutral images, whereas for FDs, fixation count and duration was similar across image types with a tendency of higher scores in affective images.

Table 2. Mean fixation count and duration among user groups.

Image	Fixation count		Fixation duration (sec)	
	FD (std.)	FI (std.)	FD (std.)	FI (std.)
Positive	24.18 (3.27)	20.68 (2.67)	2.91 (1.50)	2.09 (1.96)
Negative	22.75 (3.99)	23.62 (1.70)	2.59 (1.40)	2.25 (1.55)
Neutral	20.37 (4.31)	12.25 (4.49)	2.71 (2.10)	1.34 (1.67)

To further assess visual search behavior, we compared transition entropy among user groups (Fig. 3). Based on Krejtz et al. [37], lower values of transition entropy H_t indicate more careful/focused viewing of Areas of Interests (AOI), while greater H_t values indicate more randomness and more frequent switching between AOIs. There was a statistically significant interaction between cognitive style and image type on transition entropy, $F(2, 60) = 3.417, p = .039, partial\ \eta^2 = .102$. An analysis of simple main effects shows a statistically significant difference in mean transition entropy among FD and FI users in the positive images, $F(1, 30) = 5.023, p = .033$, as well as for the negative images, $F(1, 30) = 4.522, p = .042$, but not for the neutral images ($p > .05$).

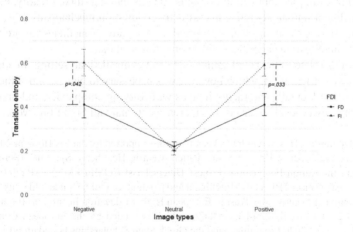

Fig. 3. Mean transition entropy among user groups.

Main Finding Related to RQ_2. FI users switched on a more global visual information processing approach in affective images (positive and negative) compared to neutral images in which they followed their inherent local stream of visual information processing (Table 2) in which they inherited a more analytic approach. While FI users inherently follow an analytic visual exploration approach by using the local information processing stream, in affective images they tend to use their global processing stream as revealed through the analysis of eye gaze metrics. In addition, FD and FI users' visual strategies were amplified significantly on affective images as reflected on eye gaze behavior in terms of eye gaze transition entropy (Fig. 3), which paves the way for considering cognitive style as an important factor in affective computing.

5   Conclusion

In this paper we investigated whether users' inherent and preferred ways of information processing are affected during affective activities, triggered by visual information. For doing so, we conducted an in-lab eye tracking study in which we classified users into Field Dependent (FD) and Field Independent (FI) based on an accredited human cognition theory and cognitive elicitation test, and further exposed them to a series of images, which are known to trigger specific emotional valence.

Beyond our expectations analysis of results point towards a swapping effect in the case of affective images between FD and FI users. In particular, FI users followed a rather holistic approach as opposed to the typical analytical approach, while FD users where not significantly affected. Such an endeavor could pave the path for a new research paradigm for taking into consideration a more holistic and comprehensive approach in interactive system design. Specifically, our work contributes on considering human cognitive differences as an important prediction factor in order to estimate through real-time eye gaze analysis techniques the emotional valence of end-users during affective activities. For example, application domains such as gaming, mixed reality, etc. could deploy intelligent human cognitive and affective elicitation mechanisms (*e.g.*, [26, 27, 39]) by considering the main effects reported in this study. Nonetheless, more research is needed to manifest this approach with more empirical data.

Limitations relate to the small sample size and controlled lab setting. In addition, a specific image set was used, which however was necessary to better control the experiment. Future work entails embracing images with varying complexity, and images that trigger higher/lower levels of arousal to increase external validity of this work.

Acknowledgements. This research has been partially supported by the EU Horizon 2020 Grant 826278 "Securing Medical Data in Smart Patient-Centric Healthcare Systems" (Serums), the Research and Innovation Foundation (Project DiversePass: COMPLEMENTARY/0916/0182), and the European project TRUSTID - Intelligent and Continuous Online Student Identity Management for Improving Security and Trust in European Higher Education Institutions (Grant Agreement No: 2020–1-EL01-KA226-HE-094869), which is funded by the European Commission within the Erasmus+ 2020 Programme and the Greek State Scholarships Foundation I.K.Y.

References

1. Picard, R.: Affective Computing. MIT Press, , Cambridge (1997)
2. Picard, R.: Affective Computing for HCI. Conference on Human-Computer Interaction: Ergonomics and User Interfaces-Volume I. Lawrence Erlbaum Associates (1999)
3. Norman, D.: Emotional Design: Why we Love (or Hate) Everyday Things. Basic Books, New York (2003)
4. Natasha, J., Conati, C., Harley, J., Azevedo, R.: Predicting affect from gaze data during interaction with an intelligent tutoring system. intelligent tutoring systems (2014)
5. Lemos, J., Sadeghnia, G., Ólafsdóttir, Í., Jensen, O.: Measuring emotions using eye tracking (2008)
6. Schmid, P., Mast, M., Mast, F., Lobmaier, J.: How mood states affect information processing during facial emotion recognition: an eye tracking study. Swiss J. Psychol. **70**, 223–231 (2011)
7. Sears, C., Kristin, N., Ference, J., Thomas, C.: Attention to emotional images in previously depressed individuals: an eye-tracking study. Cogn. Therapy Res. **35**, 517–528 (2011)
8. Stanley, J., Zhang, X., Fung, H., Isaacowitz, D.: Cultural differences in gaze and emotion recognition: Americans contrast more than Chinese. Emotion **13**(1), 36–46 (2013)
9. Charoenpit, S., Ohkura, M.: Exploring emotion in an e-learning system using eye tracking. In: Symposium on Computational Intelligence in Healthcare and E-Health, pp. 141–147 (2014)
10. Zheng, W., Dong, B., Lu, B.: Multimodal emotion recognition using EEG and eye tracking data. In: Conference on Engineering in Medicine and Biology Society, pp. 5040–5043 (2014)
11. Zhen-Fen, S., Chang, Z., Wei-Long, Z., Bao-Liang, L.: Attention evaluation with eye tracking glasses for EEG-based emotion recognition. Neural Eng. 86–89 (2017)
12. Hübner, R., Volberg, G.: The integration of object levels and their content: a theory of global/local processing and related hemispheric differences. J. Exp. Psychol. Hum. Percept. Perform. **31**(3), 520–541 (2005)
13. Oliva, A.: Coarse blobs or fine edges? Evidence that information diagnosticity changes the perception of complex visual stimuli. Cogn. Psychol. **34**(1), 72–107 (1997)
14. Davidoff, J., Fonteneau, E., Fagot, J.: Local and global processing: observations from a remote culture. Cognition **108**(3), 702–709 (2008)
15. Witkin, H., Moore, C., Goodenough, D., Cox, P.: Field-dependent and field-independent cognitive styles and their educational implications. Res. Bull. 1–64 (1975)
16. Hong, J., Hwang, M., Tam, K., Lai, Y., Liu, L.: Effects of cognitive style on digital jigsaw puzzle performance: a gridware analysis. Comput. Hum. Behav. **28**(3), 920–928 (2012)
17. Rittschof, K.: Field dependence-independence as visuospatial and executive functioning in working nemory: implications for instructional systems design and research. Educ. Tech. Res. Dev. **58**(1), 99–114 (2010)
18. Belk, M., Fidas, C., Germanakos, P., Samaras, G. : The interplay between humans, technology and user authentication: a cognitive processing perspective. Comput. Hum. Behav. **76**, 184–200 (2017). Elsevier
19. Calder, A., Young, A., Keane, J., Dean, M.: Configural information in facial expression perception. Exp. Psych.: Hum. Percept. Perform. **26**, 527–551 (2000)
20. Prkachin, G.: the effect of orientation on detection and identification of facial expressions of emotion. Br. J. Psychol. **94**, 45–62 (2003)
21. Watson, D., Wiese, D., Vaidya, J., Tellegen, A.: The two general activation systems of affect: structural findings, evolutionary considerations, and psychobiological evidence. J. Pers. Soc. Psychol. **76**(5), 820 (1999)
22. Kensinger, E., Schacter, D.: Processing emotional pictures and words: effect of valence and arousal. Cogn. Affect. Behav. Neurosci. **6**, 110–126 (2006)

23. Costanzi, M., et al.: The effect of emotional valence and arousal on visuo-spatial working memory: incidental emotional learning and memory for object-location. Frontiers Psychol. (2019)

24. Cahill, L., McGaugh, J.: A novel demonstration of enhanced memory associated with emotional arousal. Conscious. Cogn. **4**(4), 410–421 (1995)

25. Belk, M., Fidas, C., Germanakos, P., Samaras, G.: Do human cognitive differences in information processing affect preference and performance of CAPTCHA?. Int. J. Hum. Comput. Stud. **84**, 1–18 (2015). Elsevier

26. Constantinides, A., Belk, M., Fidas, C., Pitsillides, A.: An eye gaze-driven metric for estimating the strength of graphical passwords based on image hotspots. In: ACM IUI 2020, ACM Press, pp. 33–37 (2020)

27. Constantinides, A., Belk, M., Fidas, C., Pitsillides, A.: On the accuracy of eye gaze-driven classifiers for predicting image content familiarity in graphical passwords. In: ACM UMAP 2019, ACM Press, pp. 201–205 (2019)

28. Schmeichel, B., Demaree, H.: Working memory capacity and spontaneous emotion regulation: high capacity predicts self-enhancement in response to negative feedback. Emotion **10**, 739–744 (2010)

29. Oltman, P., Raskin, E., Witkin, H.: A Manual for the Embedded Figures Test. Consulting Psychologists Press, Palo Alto (1971)

30. Kassner, M., Patera, W., Bulling, A.: Pupil: an open source platform for pervasive eye tracking and mobile gaze-based interaction. In: ACM UbiComp 2014 Adjunct, ACM Press, pp. 1151–1160 (2014)

31. Emotiv Epoc+ (2021). https://www.emotiv.com/epoc

32. Katsini, C., Fidas, C., Raptis, G., Belk, M., Samaras, G., Avouris, N.: Influences of human cognition and visual behavior on password security during picture password composition. In: ACM Human Factors in Computing Systems (CHI 2018), ACM Press, p. 87 (2018)

33. Kurdi, B., Lozano, S., Banaji, M.R.: Introducing the Open Affective Standardized Image Set (OASIS). Behav. Res. Methods **49**(2), 457–470 (2016). https://doi.org/10.3758/s13428-016-0715-3

34. Raptis, G., Katsini, C., Belk, M., Fidas, C., Samaras, G., Avouris, N.: Using eye gaze data and visual activities to infer human cognitive styles: method and feasibility studies. In: Conference on User Modeling, Adaptation and Personalization, pp. 164–173 (2017)

35. Cardaci, M., Di Gesù, V., Petrou, M., Tabacchi, M.: A fuzzy approach to the evaluation of image complexity. Fuzzy Sets Syst. **160**(10), 1474–1484 (2009)

36. SciKit Image (2021). https://scikit-image.org/docs/dev/api/skimage.measure.html#skimage.measure.shannon_entropy

37. Krejtz, K., et al.: Gaze Transition Entropy. ACM Trans. Appl. Percept. **13**, 1, article 4 (2015)

38. Fidas, C., Belk, M., Hadjidemetriou, G., Pitsillides, A.: Influences of mixed reality and human cognition on picture passwords: an eye tracking study. In: Lamas, D., Loizides, F., Nacke, L., Petrie, H., Winckler, M., Zaphiris, P. (eds.) INTERACT 2019. LNCS, vol. 11747, pp. 304–313. Springer, Cham (2019). https://doi.org/10.1007/978-3-030-29384-0_19

39. Costi, A., Belk, M., Fidas, C., Constantinides, A., Pitsillides, A. : CogniKit: an extensible tool for human cognitive modeling based on eye gaze analysis. ACM Intelligent User Interfaces (IUI Companion 2020), ACM Press, pp. 130–131 (2020)

A Systematic Review of Thermal and Cognitive Stress Indicators: Implications for Use Scenarios on Sensor-Based Stress Detection

Susana Carrizosa-Botero[✉] ⓘ, Elizabeth Rendón-Vélez ⓘ, and Tatiana A. Roldán-Rojo ⓘ

Universidad EAFIT, Cra 49, #7 sur 50, Medellín, Colombia

Abstract. A systematic literature review aiming to identify the characteristics of physiological signals on two types of stress states - single moderate thermal stress state and moderate thermal stress combined with cognitive stress state – was conducted. Results of the review serve as a backdrop to envision different scenarios on the detection of these stress states in everyday situations, such as in schools, workplaces and residential settings, where the use of interactive technologies is commonplace. Stress detection is one of the most studied areas of affective computing. However, current models developed for stress detection only focus on recognizing whether a person is stressed, but not on identifying stress states. It is essential to differentiate them in order to implement strategies to minimize the source of stress by designing different interactive technologies. Wearables are commonly used to acquire physiological signals, such as heart rate and respiratory rate. Analysis results of these signals can support a user to make a decision for taking actions or to make an automatic system undertake certain strategies to counteract the sources of stress. These technologies can be designed for educational, work or medical environments. Our future work is to validate these use scenarios systematically to enhance the design of the technologies.

Keywords: Physiological signal · Stress states · Thermal environment · Stress · Affective computing · Cognitive load · Use scenario

1 Introduction

Affective computing relates to, arises from, or deliberately influences emotion [1]. Its objective is to allow computers to understand the emotional states expressed by human subjects so that personalized responses can be given accordingly and thus provide an effective and natural interaction between humans and computers [2]. Affective computing systems use physiological features as inputs for emotion detection models [3]. By analyzing, for example, the heart rate variability, respiratory rate, or blood oxygenation, a computer can recognize different emotional states [4]. One of the most studied emotional states is stress. There are several studies on how to perform stress detection by using physiological features [5].

© IFIP International Federation for Information Processing 2021
Published by Springer Nature Switzerland AG 2021
C. Ardito et al. (Eds.): INTERACT 2021, LNCS 12932, pp. 73–92, 2021.
https://doi.org/10.1007/978-3-030-85623-6_7

Stress is defined as the application of a certain stimulus ("stressor") that disrupts an individual's normal function [6]. There are different types of stressors (physical, social, psychological, among others) that generate different states of stress. Current stress detection systems focus on either the detection of an overall stress state induced in a laboratory setting by combining multiple stressors to create acute stress [7] or the acute state of stress generated by a high cognitive demand in mild environmental conditions [8]. However, on a day-to-day basis, people are not only subjected to high cognitive demands but also to exposure to moderate high or low thermal environments. These environments contribute to a stress state called thermal stress that occurs when the body perceives high or low temperatures [9]. People spend 90% of their time indoors [10] and, although many of the enclosed spaces have air conditioning or heating systems that aim to improve people's thermal sensation, these are kept at the same temperature, which is often not considered neutral or satisfactory. For example, 43% of workers are not satisfied with the thermal environment of their workplace according to a report conducted by Karmman et al. (2018) [11]. Even more, an individual can be performing a cognitive task at the same time that the thermal environment has an effect on him. Several researchers have studied the relationship between cognitive loads and the thermal environment in schools [12] or workplaces [13] due to the amount of time people spend in these environments. For example, it has been proven that indoor thermal discomfort has an effect on productivity loss [14].

Although we speak of moderate temperatures, they represent a demand for the body and it must use mechanisms to bring itself into balance [15]. According to the literature, the combination of two demands or two single stressors simultaneously has different effects on human responses than when one stressor acts alone [16, 17]. This suggests that in order to create a detection system that can detect different states of stress, you need to know the specific responses of these different states; that is, you need to characterize the states produced by each single stressor and the state produced by the combination of two or more of these single stressors. Otherwise, it would be impossible to respond accordingly to the stressor in order to counteract the level of stress produced by the specific source.

Given the fact that the state of stress produced by the combination of thermal and cognitive strains is very common (i.e., in school, university or work environments) and that it would be very important for a detection system to be able to detect this state, this paper aims to review the physiological responses that occur when subjected to single thermal stressors or when subjected to the combination of thermal stressors with cognitive stressors. We will not address physiological responses when subjected to a single cognitive stressor because these responses can be easily found in the literature [8, 18]. The features found can be used to design different interactive technologies that work through the acquisition of signals using wearables to identify the state of stress and then perform or implement strategies to minimize the source of stress.

The paper is structured as follows: first, the methodology used to find the physiological indicators in response to the stressors mentioned above is described. Then the results of this review are reported and discussed. From the results, three different use scenarios are presented where physiological indicators could be used to design interactive technologies. Finally, future work and a brief conclusion are presented.

2 Methodology

The search strategy used for this article is derived from the Preferred Reporting Items for Systematic Reviews and Meta-Analyses (PRISMA) [19]. Six research databases were consulted in June 2020: IEEE, Google Scholar, PubMed, APA Psycnet, Science Direct, and Web of Science. The search was performed based on titles, abstracts and keywords of English-written publications to exclude duplicated and nonrelevant studies. The complete text of the remaining publications was reviewed based on the following main topics: physiological response, thermal stress, and temperature (T) of enclosed areas. The search terms were then the combination of the following sets of words:

- "thermal stress", "heat stress", "cold stress".
- "environmental temperature", "indoor temperature" and "moderate temperature".
- "physiological signal", "physiological response", "biosignal".

The first set of words aim to find all papers regarding these types of stressor. The second set of words were used to exclude papers that would address excessive thermal stress and would be outside the scope of this review. Finally, the last terms were added to include these stress measurement methods (alone or in combination with others) and to exclude papers that only relied on other forms of stress measurement. For greater accuracy and to find with more certainty studies that included mental processes, this search was made again adding the keywords "cognition" or "cognitive". These terms encompass any paper that measures cognition or performs some cognitive tasks. Texts published from 2000 onwards were included. The titles submitted were reviewed for relevance and non-repeatability.

The complete selection process can be seen in the following flowchart (Fig. 1). 716 publications were identified and 33 were reviewed. Papers referring to environments other than enclosed ones, as well as those in which some type of physical activity was required (e.g. exercising or driving), were excluded from the review. We did not consider research results where the T analyzed was higher than 40 °C or lower than 10 °C, nor did we include studies where T varied by steps for acclimatization purposes. Only studies with results related to physiological signals were included and no other method to determine the body's physiological responses (e.g. cortisol in saliva) was considered.

Signals were categorized into four different systems: cardiovascular, respiratory, nervous, and integumentary systems. For each one of them the increase, decrease, or significant difference of the indicators of each signal was sought. On each reviewed paper different indicators (also their abbreviations, e.g., for heart rate, "HR") were tracked for each physiological signal of the body systems that changed due to T. Results were divided into "Results of thermal stressors effects on physiological responses" and "Results of combined thermal and cognitive stressors effects on physiological responses". The subcategories included are the body systems mentioned above.

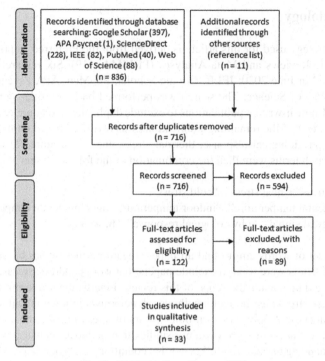

Fig. 1. PRISMA flow diagram [19]

3 Results

To enhance the readability of the following text, Table 1 shows the acronyms of some of the most used physiological indicators, which are grouped according to the human body system to which they belong.

3.1 Results of Thermal Stressors Effects on Physiological Responses

Specific categories of information extracted from the papers reviewed (participants, applied Ts, duration, physiological signals used, and their results) are listed in Table 2.

Cardiovascular System
Some authors agree that heart rate (HR) is higher when T is higher. [21] established that HR increased linearly with T. In [22], the maximum mean HR was seen at 36 °C. [23] found HR statistically significantly higher at 30 °C than at 20 °C. [24] observed that HR increases when thermal conditions depart from the neutral zone (26 °C), i.e. when T drops HR rises. On the other hand, in [25], when T dropped from 26 °C to 16 °C, no significant changes were shown. [26] noticed only a slight difference between cool and warm conditions, a difference that is not significant.

The most studied variable of heart rate variability (HRV) by thermal stress is LF/HF ratio (LF/HF). [27] observed a functional quadratic relationship between LF/HF and

Table 1. Physiological features' acronyms

Cardiovascular system	
HR	Heart rate
RR interval	The interval between two successive heart beats
LF/HF/VLF	High/Low/Very Low frequency activity
BP	Blood pressure
Nervous system	
δ, θ, α, β, γ relative power	Power in δ, θ, α, β, γ frequency bands
Integumentary system	
T	Temperature
Respiratory system	
BR	Breathing rate
SpO2	Oxygen Saturation
ETCO2	End-tidal CO2

room T. Subjects had higher mean LF/HF when exposed both to higher and lower air Ts (from 22 °C to 30 °C). [28, 29] established that ambient T impacts LF and HF. They also found that the minimum value of LF and LF/HF occurred under neutral T (26 °C). [30] performed three experiments setting different Ts in a different order to see if the relationship between T and LF/HF variables was affected by the order in which Ts were presented. In two experiments, LF/HF was higher at a T of 21 °C and 29 °C than at 24 °C and 26 °C. [31] observed significant differences for each T condition in every frequency variable except for LF. Ambient T has little effect on VLF power according to [28, 29]. [31] also performed a temporal analysis of HRV. They found that most of the temporal domain indices values were not significantly different for each T condition. However, the standard deviation of RR intervals (SDNN) commonly showed a significant difference in every T condition.

[25] observed that when T dropped from 26 °C to 16 °C, average skin blood flow decreased. [32] also found that it increased with T. This was also proved by [24]. [33] found that there are statistically significant decreases in mean BP with a T decrease from 28.8 °C to 25.3 °C and with a T increase from 18.7 °C to 25 °C. In another range of Ts, [23] observed that BP was significantly lower at 30 °C than at 20 °C. [34] performed different experiments with T and found that the condition in which there was the greatest increase in systolic BP was 15 °C. At a constant T of 25 °C, BP decreased significantly through time in the experiment [35]. Finally, [22] noticed a fluctuating decrease in systolic BP when T rises from 28 °C to 38 °C.

Nervous System
In two research papers, [28, 29] showed significant differences of α, θ, β δ -band among the temperatures studied. They also identified dominant bands in every T. β-band is dominant under ambient T of 21 °C and 29 °C. α-band under 26 °C. At 24 °C α-band

Table 2. Results of thermal stressors effects on physiological responses

Ref.	Participants	Temperature	Duration	Physiological signal	Physiological response
[34]	2 groups of 8 Subjects All male G1: 20-24 y/o G2: 65-74 y/o	A: AirCon 25°C F: Floor 29°C, air 21°C C: No heating (15°C)	30-min adaptation (25°C) + 90 min on each condition	sT, body T, msT, BP	SBP↑ in C, SBP~ in A and F sT significant change in A and F body T~, msT~ in A and F
[30]	33 Subjects 21 male, 12 female, 23-24 y/o	21, 24, 26,28, 29, 30°C	40 min for each condition	LF, HF	LF/HF↑ 24→21°C LF/HF↑ 28→30°C
[29]	20 Subjects 10 male, 10 female, 21-26 y/o	21, 24, 26, 29°C	Approx. 1 hour per condition	LF, HF, VLF, sT, msT, α, β, θ, δ-band	α, β, θ, δ band significant change LF/HF↑ when T departs from neutral T VLF~, msT, sT significant change
[28]	20 Subjects 10 male, 10 female, 21-26 y/o	21, 24, 26, 29°C	1 hour per condition	LF, HF, VLFn, α, β, θ, δ -Band	21→26°C LF↓ HF↑ LF/HF↓, 26→29°C LF↑ HF~ LF/HF↑ 29→21°C β-band dominant 26°C α-band dominant 24°C α and β-band dominant
[26]	14 Subjects 7 male, 7 female, 19-34 y/o	19, 23, 26°C	30min (23°C) +60min(26°C) +30min (23°C) +60 min (19°C)	HR	HR↑ when T↑
[36]	48 Subjects 24 males, 24 female, 23-27 y/o	26↔38°C G1: Stable G2: 2°C/5 min G3: 2°C/10 min	Depends on the group	sT	when T↓, sT↓ At the same T, sT was higher when T was decreasing compared when it was increasing
[23]	26 Subjects All women >70 y/o	20, 30°C	60 min on each condition	HR, sT, sT, BP	BP↓ HR↑ cT↑ sT↑ at 30°C
[31]	28 Subjects 17 male, 11 female, 19-22 y/o	Approx. 17, 25, 38°C	10 min on each condition	HRV characteristics	LF, HF, VLF significant change at every T, SDNN, RMSSD significant change at 38°C
[35]	200 Subjects 100 male,100 female, 18-29 y/o	25°C	60 min	sT, BP	After 60 min at 25°C BP↓, and sT↓
[25]	30 Subjects All male 18-22 y/o	16, 18, 21, 24°C	30 min (26°C) and 60 min on condition	HR, SkBF, msT	msT↓, SkBF↓, HR~ when T↓
[24]	30 Subjects All male 18-22 y/o	16, 18, 21, 24, 26, 28, 31°C	30 min (26°C) and 60 min on condition	HR, SkBF, msT	sT↑ and SSBF↑ in warm, sT↓ and SSBF↓ in cold, HR↑ when T moves from neutral (26°C) to cold or warm
[37]	50 Subjects All male 20-30 y/o	25, 32°C	30 min (25°C) +35min (32°C) +60min (25°C)	β, θ band	θ-power↑ and β-power↓ when T changes from 32 to 25°C
[27]	6 Subjects All male 18-21 y/o	22, 24, 26, 28, 30°C	20 min on each condition	LF, HF	LF/HF↑ at 22°C and 30°C
[38]	7 Subjects All male 22-28 y/o	15, 18, 21, 24, 28, 31, 34°C	15 min at 24°C + 65 min on each condition	Attention Level (AL)	First 30 min: AL strongest at 21° C Last 30 min: AL strongest at 24,4°C
[20]	30 Subjects 15 male, 15 female, 19-35y/o	20, 23, 26, 29, 32°C	30 min at 26°C and 60 min on condition	HR, msT, sH	msT↑, sH↑, and HR↑ when T↑
[22]	10 Subjects undergraduate students	28, 32, 36, 38°C	24 h on each condition	HR, body T, sT, BP	max mHR↑ at 16°C SBP↓, body T↑, cT~ from 28 to 38°C
[32] *	16 Subjects 8 male, 8 female, 16-24 y/o	18, 22, 26°C	145 min on each condition	msT, SkBF	msT↑, SkBF↑ when T↑
[33] **	22 Subjects 16 male, 6 female, 20-30 y/o	G1:18.7→25°C G2:28.8→25.3°C	60 min on each condition	BP	mean BP↓ in both conditions
[39]	30 Subjects, 15 male, 15 female, 23-28 y/o	G1:20↔26°C G2:22↔26°C G3:26↔30°C G4:26↔32°C	30 min on the first T + 30-40 min condition	msT	msT↑ when T↑

↔: T changes in both ways, →: T changes in one way, ↑: Increase, ~: No significant difference, ↓: Decrease
sT: skin T; msT: mean skin T; sH: skin humidity; SkBF: blood flow rate
*On this experiment, acoustic environment was also a variable, however it was concluded that PRs were not affected by sound pressure level.
**The CO2 concentration was different on conditions A and B, therefore these results are also influenced by this factor.

and β-band were equally regnant. In the experiment of [37], θ-power increased, and β-power decreased when T changed from 32 °C to 25 °C. [38] found that the power of EEG analyzing attention is stronger at 21 °C during the first 30 min and at 24 °C during the last 30. At the end of the experiment, the highest power was observed at 27.6 °C. T of 14.6 °C was the worst condition for attention during the whole experiment.

Integumentary System

[22] showed an increase in skin T when ambient T rises. [23] found that calf T was higher at 30 °C than at 20 °C. [36] drew other conclusions: local skin T changed less as T decreased than as it increased. Local skin T linearly changed with ambient T in a stable thermal environment but nonlinearly in the unstable thermal environment. [29] analyzed local Ts on different body parts. When environmental T varies from 21 °C to 29 °C, local Ts that changed in the following descending order: foot, anterior calf, hand, forearm, and anterior thigh T. The body parts with the lowest changes were the forehead, chest, abdomen, and scapula. [34] experimented with three conditions (C: no heating 15 °C, F: floor heating at 29 °C, air at 21 °C and A: Air conditioning at 25 °C) to monitor each local body location skin T, except abdomen and ilium, finding that these were significantly affected by the conditions proposed by the authors. Significantly higher Ts were found in the forearm, hands back, palms and thigh front for condition A than for condition F, but the opposite occurred in T of the instep and sole. Most local skin T resulting from condition C were significantly lower than those for conditions A and F. [35] maintained a constant T of 25 °C for 60 min; in this time, oral T and skin T decreased.

[34] did not find significant differences in rectal T between conditions A and F. [23] observed that body T was higher at 30 °C than at 20 °C. Furthermore, in the experiment of [22], rectal T fluctuated from 36.6 °C to 37.46 °C among different conditions. [21, 24, 32] stated in their experiments that mean skin T was positively related to T. More specifically, [25] explained that in general when T dropped from 26 °C to 16 °C, mean skin T dropped from 33.8 °C to 30.9 °C. [29] established that when ambient T rises, mean skin T will markedly increase while the maximum difference of skin T all over the body will markedly decrease. [39] observed the same pattern: the lower room T, the lower the mean skin T. [32] observed that at high ambient Ts, skin humidity increased rapidly with an increase of T.

3.2 Results of Combined Thermal and Cognitive Stressors Effects on Physiological Responses

The papers mentioned in this section conducted experiments where participants had to perform cognitive activities while exposed to a thermal stressor. Specific categories of information extracted from the papers reviewed (participants, applied Ts, duration, physiological signals used, and their results) are listed in Table 3. In this table, the name of the applied cognitive activity and a brief description of it can be found.

Cardiovascular System

In the experiments of [12] and [40], subjects had to perform a neurobehavioral test at different Ts. During both experiments, an increase in HR was found at the condition

Table 3. Results of combined thermal and cognitive stressors effects on physiological responses

Ref.	Participants	Temperature	Duration	Physiological signal	Cognitive assessment tool (CT)	Physiological response
[45]	10 Subjects, all men, 20-26 y/o	10, 25°C	90 min (25°C) and 120 min (10°C)	sT, HR, body T, msT, Oxygen consumption, BP	ANAM-ICE: code substitution, logical reasoning, matching to sample, continuous performance, simple reaction time, Stenberg memory search.	$T↓$, HR ↓, Oxygen consumption ↑, BP↑, cT↓, msT↓ at 10°C
[50]	96 Subjects, 48 males, 48 female, 20-23 y/o	20, 23, 26°C	Approx. 250 min on each condition	sT, msT	Measures of mental performance of the subjects were obtained from various tests, i.e. arousal/alertness, concentration, creativity, and reasoning.	sT↓ when T↓, msT decreases with time
[48]*	21 Subjects, 15 male, 6 female, 18-20 y/o	17, 21, 28°C	120 min on each condition	LF, HF, α, β, δ band	Office work: typing and addition tasks. Neurobehavioral: Mental reorientation, Grammatical Reasoning, Digit span memory, Number calculation, Stroop test.	LF/HF ↑ at 28°C, δ band↓, α and β band~ at 17 and 28°C
[42]	12 Subjects, 6 female, 6 male, 21-25 y/o	22, 30°C	The whole exposure lasted 4.5h	HR, respiratory ventilation rate (RVR), SpO2, ETCO2	Office work: typing and addition tasks. Neurobehavioral: Mental reorientation, Grammatical Reasoning, Digit span memory, Number calculation, Stroop test.	HR↑ RVR↑ ETCO2↑ SPO2↓ at 30°C
[40]	12 Subjects, 6 male, 6 female, 21-28 y/o	27, 35°C	3 hours on each condition	HR, pNN50, BR, RVR, msT, ETCO2, SpO2	Neurobehavioral: Mental redirection, grammatical reasoning, digit span memory, visual learning memory, number calculation, one-digit multiplication, Stroop test, visual reaction time.	msT↑, HR↑, pNN50↓, SpO2↓, ETCO2↑, BR~ at 35°C, RVR significant different at sometimes of CT.
[44]	28 Subjects, 23 male, 5 female, 17-30 y/o	Approx. 22, 23, 28°C	Not specified	HR, BP	Reasoning test Battery 5 (BPR-5) (abstract, verbal, numerical, spatial, and mechanical reasoning)	HR↑, BP~ at 28°C
[43]	32 Subjects, 16 male, 16 female, College students	26, 30, 33, 37°C	175 min on each condition	HR, BR, BP, sH, SPO2, ETCO2, sT, body T, msT,	Visual reaction time, Stroop test, redirection, overlapping, addition, multiplication, visual learning	sT↑, HR↑, ETCO2↑, SPO2~, SBP~, BR~, pNN50↓, body T↑, msT↑, sH↑ at 37°C
[49]	22 Subjects, 16 male, 6 females, 26-28 y/o	G1:20→25°C G2: 28→25°C	90 min on each condition	BP	Office work: Visual reaction time, subitizing, Stroop test, backward corsi block-tapping, N-back test, typing	BP↓ in both conditions
[46]	35 Subjects, all male, 20-30 y/o	18, 22, 26, 30°C	50 min on each condition	α, β, θ, δ band, BR	N-back test (3 levels of different complexity)	HR, BR, RMSSD, LF/HF, SDNN significant changes
[47]	20 Subjects, 14 male, 6 female, 18-24 y/o	22.4, 26.2°C	140 min	HR, LF, HF, BR	2-hour university lecture and the Cambridge Brain Science Cognitive Evaluation Tool	HR↓, LF/HF↑, HF↓, BR~ at 26.2°C
[15]	360 Subjects, 252 male, 108 female, 18-30 y/o	20, 24, 30°C	Approx. 1 hour on each condition	HR, BP	Reasoning test Battery 5 (BPR-5) (abstract, verbal, numerical, spatial, and mechanical reasoning)	max HR and BP significant changes
[51]	15 Subjects, 22-33 y/o	21.7, 25.2, 28.6°C	Approx. 1 hour on each condition	Mental workload (MWI)	Computer-based cognitive task: Number addition, Forward digit span, choice reaction, and visual search.	↑MWI at 28.6°C
[41]	12 Subjects, 6 male, 6 females,18-30 y/o	23, 27°C	Approx. 2 hours on each condition	HR, pNN50, BR, SPO2, sT, sH	Office work: typing and addition tasks. Neurobehavioral: Mental reorientation, Grammatical Reasoning, Digit span memory, Number calculation, Stroop test.	sT ↑, sH↑, HR↑, pNN50↓, BR↑, SPO2↓ at 27°C
[12]**	12 Subjects, 6 male, 6 female, 12-14 y/o	26, 29°C	Approx. 80 min on each condition	HR, BP, body T	Neurobehavioral: letter search, Stroop test, graph overlapping, stereoscopic vision, Schulte grid, tow-digit search, visual pattern, visual retention, memory scanning, symbol digit, event sequence, serial addition, serial subtraction.	HR↑, BP~, body T↑ at 29°C, after CT, variation of BP before and after CT was greater at 29°C

←: T changes in both ways, →: T changes in one way, ↑: Increase, ↓: Decrease; sT: skin T; msT: mean skin T; sH: skin humidity; SkBF: blood flow rate; CT: Cognitive Task
* Only 3 subjects had their physiological signs measured.
** In this paper the effect of air velocity was also measured, the conditions of the experiment included not only different temperatures, but also different air velocities (0.1, 0.6, and 1.0 m/s).

with higher T. [41] obtained a similar result where HR was higher at 27 °C than at 23 °C while subjects performed both office and neurobehavioral tests. In a previous study, [42] observed that HR was lower at 22 °C compared to 30 °C; it also decreased during each exposure independently of the condition. [43] established that HR increased with increasing T; they used attentional tasks at different Ts. [44] measured HR before and after the cognitive task; they observed that students HR at the end of cognitive activity was the only value with a significant difference between exposures. According to their study, both the final and mean HR of individuals increased throughout exposure to high Ts. On the other hand, [45] conducted a study with a T condition lower than neutral (10 °C) while performing a cognitive task and found a slight decrease in HR. [46] used the a continuous performance task test and evidenced a significant difference between HR at air Ts. [15] found a significant relationship between maximum HR and Ts while doing a reasoning test battery. Contrary to that, [47] found that HR values were higher at 22 °C compared to 26 °C, but in this study, subjects were students exposed to a 2-h lecture.

[40, 41, 43] agree that pNN50 (proportion of successive heartbeat intervals that differed by more than 50 ms) decreased significantly with increasing T while doing the respective cognitive tasks of each experiment. [46] did not find significant differences in HRV temporal-domain parameters in baseline and exposure conditions with different air Ts, but there was a significant difference in mean values of LF/HF. Moreover, a significant difference was found between mean values of RMSSD (Root mean square of successive heartbeat interval differences), LF/HF, and SDNN in task conditions with low workload, medium workload and high workload in comparison to the baseline considering the Ts of the experiment. The physiological signals in the experiment of [48] were measured while the participants were reading a book or playing games. They found that LF/HF increased with air T, but there was no significant effect. In the experiment of [47], LF/HF was higher at 26 °C compared to 22 °C while indices of HF were lower at 26 °C compared to 22 °C.

[12] measured physiological signals before and after the neurobehavioral test, finding that amplitude variations in diastolic BP before and after the test were small at 26 °C but large at 29 °C. [44] also measured BP before and after the reasoning test and determined that BP levels' distribution was similar between the three experimental conditions. In cold (10 °C), BP was significantly higher compared to control (25 °C) [45]. [49] made different analyses with T changes and cognitive load concerning BP. It increased with work stress regardless of operating T. On the other hand, if operating T was increased from 18.7 °C to 25 °C, BP was reduced only when in seated state (not while neurobehavioral tests were being performed). Furthermore, by lowering operating T from 28.8 °C to 25.3 °C, BP was lowered only in a seated state. In [43], no significant differences were found in BP between Ts.

Nervous System

[51] measured mental workload from the frequency bands. In general, the mental workload was the highest at 28.6 °C among the thermal conditions. Another conclusion of this study was that with a similar mental load, a lower performance was achieved at 28 °C, which means that subjects must make a greater effort to maintain their task performance in a warm environment. On the other hand, they also observed that changes in ambient T causes the mental workload of some subjects to increase but for some others to decrease.

More specifically, [48] analyzed power frequencies of ECG while the participants were reading or playing games. They found that the power of δ-band EEG was significantly affected by air T; it decreased at 17 °C or 28 °C compared with neutral condition (21 °C). Also, α-band and β-band EEG increased at 17 °C and 28 °C, but the change was not significant.

Integumentary System

[41] found that T at temple and hand were systematically higher at 27 °C than at 23 °C while doing office tasks and neurobehavioral tests. Temple T increased significantly when increasing air T in the experiment of [43]. [50] noticed that changes in skin T depended on where it was measured. Forehead T experienced the least fluctuation under all conditions and was the warmest of all measured locations. Something similar happened with T measured on the back and torso. However, T of extremities was different. T of hands and feet at 26.0 °C was maintained, while at 20.0 °C and 23.0 °C it decreased with time of exposure. With a lower T (10 °C), [45] found that T of fingers decreased by 15.3 °C–16.1 °C compared with control conditions (25 °C).

In cold condition (10 °C), rectal T decreased by 0.3 °C–0.4 °C in the experiment of [45]. Similarly, [43] observed an increase in eardrum T as air T increased. [12] also found that body T was higher at 29 °C than at 26 °C. Moreover, at 29 °C, the difference between body Ts before and after the test was larger than that at 26 °C. The behavior of mean skin T was consistent with the results mentioned above. It was significantly higher as air T increased in the experiment of [43]. Similarly, in [40] experiment, mean skin T was higher at 35 °C than at 26 °C. In cold T (10 °C) in [45], mean skin T dropped by 6 °C–6.4 °C compared to control (25 °C). [50] noticed that mean skin T decreased with time in all conditions. [43] reported a significant increase in temple moisture at a T of 33 °C compared to 26 °C and 30 °C. Besides, [41] observed that absolute humidity of skin in the temple was the same in the conditions at the beginning of exposure, and then gradually increased, more at 27 °C than at 23 °C.

Respiratory System

In the experiment of [41] BR was measured at the end of a cognitive task; it was higher at 27 °C than 23 °C. [46] found that independently of the cognitive task, air T influenced BR, but they also reported a significant difference between mean BR changes in task conditions with the low workload, medium workload and high workload and different air Ts. On the other hand, [47] observed no differences in BR between both T conditions. This was also the case of [43]. [40] found BR to be higher at 35 °C compared with 26 °C but not significantly. [42] found that respiratory ventilation rate was lower at 22 °C than at 30 °C. At 22 °C, it decreased during exposure, and at 30 °C, it decreased at first and then increased.

ETCO2 increased significantly with increasing T except between Ts of 30 °C and 33 °C in the experiment of [43]. A similar result was observed by [42]. Although they measured the variable at the end of the cognitive task, they found that ETCO2 was significantly higher at 30 °C than at 22 °C. On the other hand, [40] observed the opposite, although not a significant difference was found, they noted that ETCO2 was lower at 35 °C than at 26 °C, and it tended to decrease throughout each exposure under each condition. In [43], SpO2 did not decrease with increased T nor increased. [40] and [42] found at the end of their experiments a significantly lower SpO2 among the higher Ts. [41] observed an increase in SpO2 overtime at 23 °C, and it was lower at 27 °C. [42] also found that with 22 °C air T, SpO2 did not change significantly between the two periods in which measurements were taken; however, it increased significantly after 15 min of resting at 30 °C. Finally, [45] measured oxygen consumption and found that this increased from 17% to 26% in the cold condition (10 °C) compared to the control (25 °C).

4 Discussion

4.1 Thermal Stressors Effects on Physiological Responses

HR has been used as a proxy of thermal stress [42, 43]. There is a consensus that when T rises, HR also increases [20, 22, 23]. These experiments have a T range of at least 10 °C; therefore it is more likely to see changes in this variable. At low Ts, there is no clear pattern in the behavior of HR, in some experiments, it increases as T drops [24], whereas in others there is no significant noted difference [25, 26]. LF is related to sympathetic and parasympathetic activity, HF infers vagal activity [52]. LF/HF value indicates which type of activity is dominant. Theoretically, if LF/HF is greater than 1, sympathetic and parasympathetic activity is stronger than vagal, placing people in a state of arousal and stress; if it is less than 1, people are in a state of rest or sleepiness, and if LF/HF equals 1, people are in a state of arousal and comfort [28, 53]. Authors agree that LF/HF follows a quadratic function [27–30]. The lowest value of the function is close to 26 °C, a neutral T, and differences between the closer Ts (±2 °C) are not as noticeable. However, those differences become more significant as T increases or decreases, moving further away from neutral T (approx. from 2 °C to 8 °C further away).

The three studies that evaluated skin blood flow rate agree that it is positively related to ambient T regardless of the direction in which it changes [24, 25, 32]. Under high-T environments, the body's sympathetic nervous activity slows, as a consequence, skin vasodilates to increase blood flow and skin T, thus heat dissipation is strengthened [22]. However, skin blood flow was not evaluated with warmer Ts, so it would be interesting to investigate the behavior of this variable at Ts higher than neutral. There is not much consistency in BP's behavior, because of different T ranges and variations between experiments. Several authors showed that BP is lower at high Ts and higher at low Ts [22–24], but further analysis is required in order to draw concrete conclusions.

According to the results, four bands α, θ, δ, and β could be indicators of T changes because they show significant changes with only a 3°C difference. Especially β-band shows dominance in some specific T ranges when they move away from the neutral T [28, 29]. β power widely represents human cognitive function and can also be narrowly correlated to attention and perception [54]. Only one paper was reviewed that analyzed attention [38], and its results show that more experiments should be done with different exposure times and at different Ts because attention level changes according to these variables.

Skin is essential for T regulation, it provides a sensory interface between the body and the external environment [55]. There is a wide agreement between authors regarding body T. There is a directly proportional relationship between T of the environment, mean skin T, and local body Ts [22, 23]. The T of the extremities has a greater variation than that of other parts of the body when changes in ambient T occur [29, 34]. Only one study evaluated skin humidity [20], therefore more studies are needed to draw accurate conclusions, especially in colder environments where this variable was not evaluated.

4.2 Combined Thermal and Cognitive Stressors Effects on Physiological Responses

HR behaves similarly when cognitive tasks are developed in warmer Ts to when they are not, it tends to increase when T rises [12, 40, 41, 42, 43]. This could be since, to ensure oxygen supply to the brain, it is necessary to increase HR [12]. It would be interesting to investigate further the effect of the combination of both stressors, and, in the case of [46] and [15], to review if these significant changes are due to T, cognitive load, or both combined. Some temporal HRV parameters require further study in moderate thermal environments with cognitive loads since no significant difference is found when evaluating different Ts. However, when adding cognitive tasks, a difference between them is found [46], indicating a relationship between both stressors in the body. LF/HF continues to be a promising indicator since, in addition to differentiating Ts, it also presents significant changes between levels of difficulty in cognitive tasks. More information is needed on behavior of LF/HF at different Ts, with different cognitive tasks, and at different levels of these cognitive tasks.

The combination of stressors (cognitive and thermal) have different effects on BP depending on the experiment. [49] observed that BP is changed by the cognitive task regardless of T condition, one hypothesis for this could be that one of the two stressors acts on the other and overrides it, but more research is needed to prove this. On the other hand, [12] found that variation of BP between before and after the cognitive task is different for each T, so there may be an effect of both stressors. On the contrary, [44] found no significant differences in this variable. Because of the previous inconsistency, more research is needed to draw stronger conclusions about BP response to changes in T with or without cognitive load.

Regarding the nervous system, only two studies were found that used measurements from an electroencephalogram, but they are not comparable because one used power bands separately [48] and the other measured mental workload [51]. However, the increase of the task demand results in a significant increase in θ-band activity of the frontal lobe and a decrease in the α-band activity of the parietal lobe [56, 57]. According to this, it would be worth studying the behavior of these bands exposed to different mental loads with different Ts.

Local Ts have a similar effect when doing cognitive tasks or without them. There is a positive relationship between T of the environment, local Ts [41, 43, 45], mean skin T [40, 43, 45, 50] and body T [43, 45]. There is evidence that a slight increase in body T could reduce lapses in attention, improve self-perceived alertness, and elevate neurobehavioral function [58]. It was also found that there is less change of sT in the central parts of the body than in the extremities [50]. It would be useful to investigate the effects of both stressors separately to see if completion of a task increases or decreases its effect on body T. For skin humidity, only two papers were found that measured its change [41, 43], and they found that the higher the T, the higher the skin humidity.

There is agreement among authors that BR rises due to increased T [40, 41]. [46] found that BR changes because of T, regardless of the cognitive task, but it also changes because of task difficulty at different Ts. This suggests that BR is a good indicator for identifying the combination of stressors. For ETCO2, there is an agreement among authors that it increases with increasing T while performing some cognitive activity [42, 43]. This indicates insufficient alveolar ventilation [43]. To better understand this variable, one should compare studies that evaluate it at the same moments of the cognitive task (during or at the end of it). Also, the effect of T alone should be evaluated to see if cognition has a significant effect on these changes. Results of SpO2 are diverse. Some authors do not find significant changes in it [43], while others find that the higher the T, the lower the SpO2 [40–42]. It is reiterated that changes in these indicators must be studied independently to see how much of each stressor contributes to the changes in the variable.

4.3 Limitations

One of the limitations of this review is that PR caused by only cognitive stressors was not evaluated, only thermal stressors independently were reviewed, and the combination of them with cognitive activities. On the other hand, T ranges, samples, and physiological sensors in each study differ, causing variations in the results of the experiments. Finally, cognitive tasks in each experiment evaluate different cognitive functions of the brain and generate a varied strain depending on the difficulty of the task.

5   Implications of the Review Results: Three Use Scenarios

Based on the above result analyses, in this section we present three use scenarios in three contexts' work, education and health. Subsequently, we explore the feasibility of their realization as future work.

5.1   Work Context

Some studies state that one way to improve productivity at work and reduce absenteeism is through a satisfactory thermal environment [13]. There is evidence that a slight increase in body T could reduce lapses in attention [58], affecting worker productivity. According to the review, physiology changes at higher or lower temperatures than a satisfactory thermal environment (approx. temperature 26 °C [26]). With this information, it is possible to design different interactive technology that can detect and act upon stress. According to the results, the physiological features that can identify the state of thermal stress are HR, LF/HF and Body T. Accordingly, different sensors acquire the electrical signals of the heart and the temperature, for example, a smartwatch or any wristband that measures the heart rate and infrared thermometers. These sensors can be implemented in offices, i.e., small infrared thermometers can be placed on computer screens and measure the temperature of workers from time to time. Also, these sensors can be interconnected, and data can be sent to a cloud-based server serving as an IoT platform to provide group or personal reports and respond to thermal changes within the office. The features can be processed to identify the states and levels of stress using machine learning algorithms such as neural networks and support vector machine, which are widely used in the literature to detect stress and other emotional states [59].

Thus, it is possible to design an air conditioning or heating system that lowers or raises the temperature of the offices according to the physiological signals of the workers and that makes temperature adjustments until a balance is achieved. Moreover, according to the results of this review we know that there is an interaction effect reflected in some physiological features when people are in the combined state of stress with thermal stress and cognitive stress. The same features can be used for the detection of this state with the addition of the BR. This specific feature can be obtained from a breathing band or if one wishes to be less invasive it can be taken from any wearable that measures cardiac output [60], such as many wristbands. According to the personalized classification, apps can be designed to block all kinds of pop ups and notifications that can distract the worker when he is concentrating on a task. Or in case of a very high stress level, an app can be created that sends alerts to the worker and recommends him to stop the task and propose activities that minimize his stress, according to whether he is more stressed by a mental activity or by the thermal environment. These interactive technologies would be designed not only to increase the productivity of companies but also to ensure the well-being of workers within them.

5.2 Education Context

In school environments, there is a relationship between the quality of the classroom environment and the mental and physical health of students and their academic performance [12]. Although school settings may be similar to those of an office job, interactive technologies may vary due to different requirements for working with children. Starting with the acquisition methods, children are more active than adults; they are not in an office sitting all the time, they have spaces such as recess, sports classes and didactic games where they are in constant movement. Hence, the sensors have to be as less invasive as possible and appropriate to their daily activity. Body temperature sensors could be integrated into the same wristband that measures heart rate. On the other hand, the physiological indicators evaluated in this review were taken from adult populations, so it would be necessary to study their behavior in children before taking them to a machine learning classifier. Interactive technologies should also be designed according to these young end-users. If children are going to receive personalized feedback of their stress state on tablets or computers, the applications should be intuitive and unobtrusive. For example, if a child's stress level is very high when performing an activity, the child can be shown a slow breathing sequence to regulate the stress without generating a significant stimulus that distracts from the task. But if the technologies are going to be applied by teachers, they can collect information in the cloud and have a wide variety of applications because they have information on the children's stress state and know what times of the day are most stressful for them. In a school day, children are exposed to different subjects that can generate different levels of cognitive demands and consequently different levels of stress states. From there, technologies can be developed in schools to raise comfortable environments that fit the cognitive demands presented to children.

5.3 Health Context

In the context of health, these indicators could have a variety of uses. Heat stress can result in heat stroke, heat cramps, among others [61], but it is not given the importance it deserves because people get used to the environments in which they work or live. One of the applications that could impact the health sector is an interconnected system that contributes to telemedicine. By performing, for example, ambulatory tests such as a holter-exam (portable electrocardiogram), doctors could have access not only to the raw electrocardiographic signal at the end of the exam but also to the data being updated continuously in the cell phones and in the databases where the medical records are stored. In case of diagnosis of a person who works in a hot or cold place, the information sent by this device can be analyzed in the cloud, and the device can send notifications to the doctor showing that this may be a reason for the stress causes. One of the significant advantages, why these technologies should be designed for is that they can improve diagnosis from physiological signals [62]. The processing of machine learning algorithms on physiological signals can detect states of people that doctors cannot see by just analyzing the visible changes in the signals.

5.4 Future Work: Realization of the Use Scenarios

The temperature control systems proposed to be developed could work in countries with changing seasons and climates as well as in tropical countries since the system is not based on the ambient temperature of the places but on the comfort of the users based on their physiology. Even so, before designing any interactive technology based on physiological signals, it should be taken into account that this may lead to some ethical, political and economic dilemmas.

All systems that require sensors, internet connection, interactive platforms require an economical expense [63] that can be considered high depending on the context. For example, public schools may not have the extra resources to invest in such customized temperature regulation technologies. However, the opposite may be the case in large corporate office contexts if it is demonstrated that productivity gains are considerably high with the use of the technology. On the other hand, at the same time that these technologies are advancing, legislation must advance in different countries to regulate the use of data. The acquisition of physiological signals carries a risk of loss of privacy [64] since physiological data are constantly being stored, and companies and governments can access them. The analysis of these data and identifying states in people can lead to the manipulation of situations and people as their day-to-day changes are known. Therefore, parallel to developing these technologies, applications should be studied and designed, taking into account the threats to privacy, security and ethics that they may bring with them [65].

Finally, the technologies to be designed require much more work because the scenarios within the contexts may vary. Some jobs are considered office jobs where workers sit all day in front of a computer, and there, systems installed with sensors on the computer screens can work. But other people work in factories for example, where the sensors must be designed to work in these environments and appropriate to the activities of people. Also, in these places, people can be exposed to other types of stress such as physical stress, and this should be characterized separately to be able to detect it, as well as other office jobs require public speaking, working in teams, which can produce psychological stress, and this should be characterized as well.

To summarize, we identified which characteristics of the physiological signals could be potential indicators for the differentiation of moderate thermal stress states and the combined stress state (cognitive and thermal), which could not, and which need more research to make reliable conclusions. One of the main challenges of affective computing is enabling computers to interact with users in ways relevant to their affective states [3]. The indicators reviewed are part of the affect recognition, in this case of the stress state. This part of the system's design is based on the physiological features found that serve as inputs for machine learning algorithms, such as Bayesian classifiers, neural networks, and fuzzy systems that can classify stress states and, after processed, give an opportune response, indication, or instruction. To the extent that a machine can detect a person's state, it can adapt its behavior to reduce that person's stress levels. This review opens up opportunities to:

- Investigate the effect on physiological signals caused by the other stress states, i.e., combination of different Ts and different types and levels of cognitive loads.
- Research the multidirectional relationship between different temperatures and their effect on cognitive performance and physiological responses, contributing to identifying inputs for a stress state recognition system.
- Initiate the development of models and systems for classifying stress states.
- Design interactive technologies based on these features for different scenarios in different contexts (education, work, health).

6   Conclusion

According to the papers reviewed and analyzed, it can be concluded that the states of stress when a person is subjected to different moderate thermal and cognitive stressors can be reflected in the physiological response of the body. The most promising physiological indicators for identifying a moderate thermal state of stress are body T, LF/HF, and HR. For the identification of the combined stress state, BR can be added to the indicators mentioned above. To enhance human-computer interaction, the machine must have a similar affective recognition as the person to generate a better interaction between the two. The features found in this research can contribute to this interaction, as there is now more information through which machines can identify some human stress states. However, further analysis must be done on physiological indicators caused by different stressors independently and their combination to adjust the physiological features particular to each stress state. Furthermore, challenges for realizing the sensor-based automatic stress detection need to be investigated systematically, thereby identifying cost-effective approaches to overcome them.

References

1. Picard, R.W.: Affective Computing. MIT Media Lab., Cambridge (1997)

2. Cen, L., Wu, F., Yu, Z.L., Hu, F.: A real-time speech emotion recognition system and its application in online learning. In: Emotions, Technology, Design, and Learning, Elsevier Inc., pp. 27–46 (2016)
3. Jerritta, S., Murugappan, M., Nagarajan, R., Wan, K.: Physiological signals based human emotion recognition: a review. In: Proceedings - 2011 IEEE 7th International Colloquium on Signal Processing and Its Applications, CSPA 2011, pp. 410–415 (2011). https://doi.org/10.1109/CSPA.2011.5759912.
4. Plass, J.L., Kaplan, U.: Emotional design in digital media for learning. In: Emotions, Technology, Design, and Learning, Elsevier, pp. 131–161 (2016)
5. Shanmugasundaram, G., Yazhini, S., Hemapratha, E., Nithya, S.: A comprehensive review on stress detection techniques. In: 2019 IEEE International Conference on System, Computation, Automation and Networking, ICSCAN 2019 (2019). https://doi.org/10.1109/ICSCAN.2019.8878795
6. Blanco, J.A., Vanleer, A.C., Calibo, T.K., Firebaugh, S.L.: Single-trial cognitive stress classification using portable wireless electroencephalography. Sensors 19(3), 1–16 (2019). https://doi.org/10.3390/s19030499
7. Karthikeyan, P., Murugappan, M., Yaacob, S.: A review on stress inducement stimuli for assessing human stress using physiological signals. In: 2011 IEEE 7th International Colloquium on Signal Processing and its Applications, CSPA, pp. 420–425 (2011). https://doi.org/10.1109/CSPA.2011.5759914
8. Bong, S.Z., Murugappan, M., Yaacob, S.: Methods and approaches on inferring human emotional stress changes through physiological signals: a review. Int. J. Med. Eng. Inform. 5(2), 152 (2013). https://doi.org/10.1504/IJMEI.2013.053332
9. Keim, S.M., Guisto, J.A., Sullivan, J.B.: Environmental thermal stress. Ann. Agric. Environ. Med. 9(1), 1–15 (2002)
10. Klepeis, N.E., et al.: The national human activity pattern survey (NHAPS): a resource for assessing exposure to environmental pollutants. J. Expo. Anal. Environ. Epidemiol. 11(3), 231–252 (2001). https://doi.org/10.1038/sj.jea.7500165
11. Karmann, C., Schiavon, S., Arens, E.: Percentage of commercial buildings showing at least 80% occupant satisfied with their thermal comfort, April 2018
12. Wang, D., Song, C., Wang, Y., Xu, Y., Liu, Y., Liu, J.: Experimental investigation of the potential influence of indoor air velocity on students' learning performance in summer conditions. Energy Build. 219, 110015 (2020). https://doi.org/10.1016/j.enbuild.2020.110015
13. Li, D., Wang, X., Menassa, C.C., Kamat, V.R.: Understanding the impact of building thermal environments on occupants' comfort and mental workload demand through human physiological sensing. In: Start-Up Creation, pp. 291–341 (2020)
14. Lan, L., Wargocki, P., Lian, Z.: Quantitative measurement of productivity loss due to thermal discomfort. Energy Build. 43(5), 1057–1062 (2011). https://doi.org/10.1016/j.enbuild.2010.09.001
15. Silva, L.B.D., de Souza, E.L., de Oliveira, P.A.A., Andrade, B.J.M.: Implications of indoor air temperature variation on the health and performance of Brazilian students. Indoor Built Environ., pp. 1–12 (2019). https://doi.org/10.1177/1420326X19878228
16. Rousselle, J.G., Blascovich, J., Kelsey, R.M.: Cardiorespiratory response under combined psychological and exercise stress. Int. J. Psychophysiol. 20(1), 49–58 (1995). https://doi.org/10.1016/0167-8760(95)00026-O
17. Myrtek, M., Spital, S.: Psychophysiological response patterns to single, double and triple stressors. Soc. Psychophysiol. Res. 23, 663–671 (1986)
18. Giannakakis, G., Grigoriadis, D., Giannakaki, K., Simantiraki, O., Roniotis, A., Tsiknakis, M.: Review on psychological stress detection using biosignals. IEEE Trans. Affect. Comput. 1–22 (2019) https://doi.org/10.1109/TAFFC.2019.2927337

19. Moher, D., Liberati, A., Tetzlaff, J., Altman, D.G.: Preferred reporting items for systematic reviews and meta-analyses: the PRISMA statement. PLoS Med. **6**(7), e1000097 (2009). https://doi.org/10.1371/journal.pmed.1000097

20. Zhang, Z., Zhang, Y., Khan, A.: Thermal comfort of people from two types of air-conditioned buildings - evidences from chamber experiments. Build. Environ. **162**, 106287 (2019). https://doi.org/10.1016/j.buildenv.2019.106287

21. Zhang, F., de Dear, R., Hancock, P.: Effects of moderate thermal environments on cognitive performance: a multidisciplinary review. Appl. Energy **236**, 760–777 (2019). https://doi.org/10.1016/j.apenergy.2018.12.005

22. Zheng, G., Li, K., Bu, W., Wang, Y.: Fuzzy comprehensive evaluation of human physiological state in indoor high temperature environments. Build. Environ. **150**, 108–118 (2019). https://doi.org/10.1016/j.buildenv.2018.12.063

23. Stotz, A., et al.: Effect of a brief heat exposure on blood pressure and physical performance of older women living in the community—a pilot-study. Int. J. Environ. Res. Public Health **11**(12), 12623–12631 (2014). https://doi.org/10.3390/ijerph111212623

24. Luo, M., Zhou, X., Zhu, Y., Sundell, J.: Revisiting an overlooked parameter in thermal comfort studies, the metabolic rate. Energy Build. **118**, 152–159 (2016). https://doi.org/10.1016/j.enbuild.2016.02.041

25. Luo, M., Ji, W., Cao, B., Ouyang, Q., Zhu, Y.: Indoor climate and thermal physiological adaptation: evidences from migrants with different cold indoor exposures. Build. Environ. **98**, 30–38 (2016). https://doi.org/10.1016/j.buildenv.2015.12.015

26. Choi, J.H., Loftness, V., Lee, D.W.: Investigation of the possibility of the use of heart rate as a human factor for thermal sensation models. Build. Environ. **50**, 165–175 (2012). https://doi.org/10.1016/j.buildenv.2011.10.009

27. Zhu, H., Wang, H., Liu, Z., Li, D., Kou, G., Li, C.: Experimental study on the human thermal comfort based on the heart rate variability (HRV) analysis under different environments. Sci. Total Environ. **616–617**, 1124–1133 (2018). https://doi.org/10.1016/j.scitotenv.2017.10.208

28. Yao, Y., Lian, Z., Liu, W., Jiang, C., Liu, Y., Lu, H.: Heart rate variation and electroencephalograph - the potential physiological factors for thermal comfort study. Indoor Air **19**(2), 93–101 (2009). https://doi.org/10.1111/j.1600-0668.2008.00565.x

29. Yao, Y., Lian, Z., Liu, W., Shen, Q.: Experimental study on physiological responses and thermal comfort under various ambient temperatures. Physiol. Behav. **93**(1–2), 310–321 (2008). https://doi.org/10.1016/j.physbeh.2007.09.012

30. Liu, W., Lian, Z., Liu, Y.: Heart rate variability at different thermal comfort levels. Eur. J. Appl. Physiol. **103**(3), 361–366 (2008). https://doi.org/10.1007/s00421-008-0718-6

31. Shin, H.: Ambient temperature effect on pulse rate variability as an alternative to heart rate variability in young adult. J. Clin. Monit. Comput. **30**(6), 939–948 (2015). https://doi.org/10.1007/s10877-015-9798-0

32. Guan, H., Hu, S., Lu, M., He, M., Mao, Z., Liu, G.: People's subjective and physiological responses to the combined thermal-acoustic environments. Build. Environ. **172**, 106709 (2020). https://doi.org/10.1016/j.buildenv.2020.106709

33. Kim, J., Hong, T., Kong, M., Jeong, K.: Building occupants' psycho-physiological response to indoor climate and CO_2 concentration changes in office buildings. Build. Environ. **169**, 106596 (2020). https://doi.org/10.1016/j.buildenv.2019.106596

34. Hashiguchi, N., Tochihara, Y., Ohnaka, T., Tsuchida, C., Otsuki, T.: Physiological and subjective responses in the elderly when using floor heating and air conditioning systems. J. Physiol. Anthropol. Appl. Human Sci. **23**(6), 205–213 (2004). https://doi.org/10.2114/jpa.23.205

35. Yasuoka, A., Kubo, H., Tsuzuki, K., Isoda, N.: Gender differences in thermal comfort and responses to skin cooling by air conditioners in the Japanese summer. J. Human-Environment Syst. **18**(1), 011–020 (2015). https://doi.org/10.1618/jhes.18.011

36. Liu, Y., Wang, L., Liu, J., Di, Y.: A study of human skin and surface temperatures in stable and unstable thermal environments. J. Therm. Biol. **38**(7), 440–448 (2013). https://doi.org/10.1016/j.jtherbio.2013.06.006
37. Son, Y.J., Chun, C.: Research on electroencephalogram to measure thermal pleasure in thermal alliesthesia in temperature step-change environment. Indoor Air **28**(6), 916–923 (2018). https://doi.org/10.1111/ina.12491
38. Choi, Y., Kim, M., Chun, C.: Effect of temperature on attention ability based on electroencephalogram measurements. Build. Environ. **147**, 299–304 (2019). https://doi.org/10.1016/j.buildenv.2018.10.020
39. Wu, Q., Liu, J., Zhang, L., Zhang, J., Jiang, L.: Study on thermal sensation and thermal comfort in environment with moderate temperature ramps. Build. Environ. **171**, 106640(2020). https://doi.org/10.1016/j.buildenv.2019.106640
40. Liu, W., Zhong, W., Wargocki, P.: Performance, acute health symptoms and physiological responses during exposure to high air temperature and carbon dioxide concentration. Build. Environ. **114**, 96–105 (2017). https://doi.org/10.1016/j.buildenv.2016.12.020
41. Lan, L., Xia, L., Hejjo, R., Wyon, D.P., Wargocki, P.: Perceived air quality and cognitive performance decrease at moderately raised indoor temperatures even when clothed for comfort. Indoor Air, 1–19(2020). https://doi.org/10.1111/ina.12685
42. Lan, L., Wargocki, P., Wyon, D.P., Lian, Z.: Effects of thermal discomfort in an office on perceived air quality, SBS symptoms, physiological responses, and human performance. Indoor Air **21**(5), 376–390 (2011). https://doi.org/10.1111/j.1600-0668.2011.00714.x
43. Fan, X., Liu, W., Wargocki, P.: Physiological and psychological reactions of sub-tropically acclimatized subjects exposed to different indoor temperatures at a relative humidity of 70%. Indoor Air **29**(2), 215–230 (2019). https://doi.org/10.1111/ina.12523
44. Siqueira, J.C.F., Da Silva, L.B., Coutinho, A.S., Rodrigues, R.M.: Analysis of air temperature changes on blood pressure and heart rate and performance of undergraduate students. Work **57**(1), 43–54 (2017). https://doi.org/10.3233/WOR-172533
45. Mäkinen, T.M., et al.: Effect of repeated exposures to cold on cognitive performance in humans. Physiol. Behav. **87**(1), 166–176 (2006). https://doi.org/10.1016/j.physbeh.2005.09.015
46. Abbasi, A.M., Motamedzade, M., Aliabadi, M., Golmohammadi, R., Tapak, L.: The impact of indoor air temperature on the executive functions of human brain and the physiological responses of body. Heal. Promot. Perspect. **9**(1), 55–64 (2019). https://doi.org/10.15171/hpp.2019.07
47. Barbic, F., et al.: Effects of different classroom temperatures on cardiac autonomic control and cognitive performances in undergraduate students. IPEM (2019). https://doi.org/10.1088/1361-6579/ab1816
48. Lan, L., Lian, Z., Pan, L.: The effects of air temperature on office workers' well-being, workload and productivity-evaluated with subjective ratings. Appl. Ergon. **42**(1), 29–36 (2010). https://doi.org/10.1016/j.apergo.2010.04.003
49. Kim, J., Kong, M., Hong, T., Jeong, K., Lee, M.: Physiological response of building occupants based on their activity and the indoor environmental quality condition changes. Build. Environ. **145**(September), 96–103 (2018). https://doi.org/10.1016/j.buildenv.2018.09.018
50. Tham, K.W., Willem, H.C.: Room air temperature affects occupants' physiology, perceptions and mental alertness. Build. Environ. **45**(1), 40–44 (2010). https://doi.org/10.1016/j.buildenv.2009.04.002
51. Wang, X., Li, D., Menassa, C.C., Kamat, V.R.: Investigating the effect of indoor thermal environment on occupants' mental workload and task performance using electroencephalogram. Build. Environ. **158**(March), 120–132 (2019). https://doi.org/10.1016/j.buildenv.2019.05.012

52. Akselrod, S., Gordon, D., Ubel, F.A., Shannon, D.C., Berger, A.C., Cohen, R.J.: Power spectrum analysis of heart rate fluctuation: a quantitative probe of beat-to-beat cardiovascular control. Science, 80 (1981). https://doi.org/10.1126/science.6166045

53. Jaffe, R.S., Fung, D.L., Behrman, K.H.: Optimal frequency ranges for extracting information on autonomic activity from the heart rate spectrogram. J. Auton. Nerv. Syst. **46**(1–2), 37–46 (1993). https://doi.org/10.1016/0165-1838(94)90142-2

54. Perlis, M.L., Merica, H., Smith, M.T., Giles, D.E.: Beta EEG activity and insomnia. Sleep Med. Rev. **5**(5), 365–376 (2001). https://doi.org/10.1053/smrv.2001.0151

55. Hall, J.E., Hall, M.E.: Guyton and Hall Textbook of Medical Physiology, 14th ed. (2020)

56. Lean, Y., Shan, F.: Brief review on physiological and biochemical evaluations of human mental workload. Hum. Factors Ergon. Manuf. Serv. Ind. **22**(3), 177–187 (2012). https://doi.org/10.1002/hfm.20269

57. Klimesch, W.: EEG alpha and theta oscillations reflect cognitive and memory performance: a review and analysis. Brain Res. Rev. **29**(2–3), 169–195 (1999). https://doi.org/10.1016/S0165-0173(98)00056-3

58. Wright Jr, K.P., Hull, C.A., Czeisler, C.A., Kenneth, P., Hull, J.T.: Relationship between alertness, performance, and body temperature in humans. vol. 0354, pp. 1370–1377(2002). https://doi.org/10.1152/ajpregu.00205.2002.

59. Elzeiny, S., Qaraqe, M.: Machine learning approaches to automatic stress detection: a review. In: Proceedings IEEE/ACS International Conference on Computer Systems and Applications, AICCSA, vol. 2018 pp. 1–6 (2019). https://doi.org/10.1109/AICCSA.2018.8612825

60. Dubey, H., Constant, N., Mankodiya, K.: RESPIRE: a spectral kurtosis-based method to extract respiration rate from wearable PPG signals. In: Proceedings - 2017 IEEE 2nd International Conference on Connected Health: Applications, Systems and Engineering Technologies, CHASE 2017, 2017, pp. 84–89 (2017). https://doi.org/10.1109/CHASE.2017.64

61. Sanjog, J., Patel, T., Karmakar, S.: Indoor physical work environment: an ergonomics perspective. Int. J. Sci. Eng. Technol. Res. **2**(3), 2278–7798 (2013)

62. Faust, O., Hagiwara, Y., Hong, T.J., Lih, O.S., Acharya, U.R.: Deep learning for healthcare applications based on physiological signals: a review. Comput. Methods Programs Biomed. **161**, 1–13 (Jul. 2018). https://doi.org/10.1016/j.cmpb.2018.04.005

63. Vannieuwenborg, F., Verbrugge, S., Colle, D.: Choosing IoT-connectivity' A guiding methodology based on functional characteristics and economic considerations. Trans. Emerg. Telecommun. Technol. (2018). https://doi.org/10.1002/ett.3308

64. Stahl, B.C., Wright, D.: Ethics and privacy in AI and big data: implementing responsible research and innovation. IEEE Secur. Priv. **16**(3), 26–33 (May 2018). https://doi.org/10.1109/MSP.2018.2701164

65. Li, X., Zhang, T.: An exploration on artificial intelligence application: From security, privacy and ethic perspective. In: 2017 2nd IEEE International Conference on Cloud Computing and Big Data Analysis, ICCCBDA 2017, pp. 416–420 (2017). https://doi.org/10.1109/ICCCBDA.2017.7951949

Emotion Elicitation Techniques in Virtual Reality

Radiah Rivu[1(✉)], Ruoyu Jiang[2], Ville Mäkelä[1,2,3], Mariam Hassib[1], and Florian Alt[1]

[1] Universität der Bundeswehr München, Neubiberg, Germany
{sheikh.rivu,mariam.hassib,florian.alt}@unibw.de
[2] LMU Munich, Munich, Germany
ville.maekelae@ifi.lmu.de
[3] University of Waterloo, Waterloo, Canada

Abstract. In this paper, we explore how state-of-the-art methods of emotion elicitation can be adapted in virtual reality (VR). We envision that emotion research could be conducted in VR for various benefits, such as switching study conditions and settings on the fly, and conducting studies using stimuli that are not easily accessible in the real world such as to induce fear. To this end, we conducted a user study (N = 39) where we measured how different emotion elicitation methods (audio, video, image, autobiographical memory recall) perform in VR compared to the real world. We found that elicitation methods produce largely comparable results between the virtual and real world, but overall participants experience slightly stronger valence and arousal in VR. Emotions faded over time following the same pattern in both worlds. Our findings are beneficial to researchers and practitioners studying or using emotional user interfaces in VR.

Keywords: Emotions · Elicitation methods · Virtual reality · User studies

1 Introduction

Emotion is a fundamental characteristic of human behavior [24] and crucial for communication. Hence, emotion is subject to extensive research not only in psychology but also in human-computer interaction (HCI) [7]. Researchers have explored various methods to elicit, measure, and quantify emotion, ranging from anger and sadness to excitement and happiness [26,27,33,51]. The methods used to invoke specific emotions on humans are called *emotion elicitation methods* (or *techniques*). These methods include using external stimuli such as video, images, and sound, as well as recalling past events [9,26,35].

In this paper, we explore how various emotion elicitation methods function in virtual reality (VR), and how they compare to real-world use. We see several benefits from this work. First, we envision that VR could be used as a substitute for

© IFIP International Federation for Information Processing 2021
Published by Springer Nature Switzerland AG 2021
C. Ardito et al. (Eds.): INTERACT 2021, LNCS 12932, pp. 93–114, 2021.
https://doi.org/10.1007/978-3-030-85623-6_8

some real-world studies on emotion. VR can provide researchers with opportunities that they would not have in the real world, for example, by being able to manipulate the virtual environment on the fly [32], and researching scenarios that would be difficult or even dangerous in the real world and may put participants at risk (e.g., certain automotive scenarios [14]). Running studies in VR may also be a more cost-effective solution for complex studies. Second, understanding emotions in VR is beneficial to many VR experiences and games as emotions play a key part in the user experience. In particular, designers and practitioners can use this knowledge to effectively invoke the desired emotions in VR users, while also understanding the lasting effects from these emotions. Third, understanding emotions in VR would also be beneficial in medical treatments as VR can aid patients with treatment and therapy, for example treating anxiety in VR [2,4,43].

Existing research has gained only limited understanding on emotion elicitation in VR. In particular, we do not have substantial understanding on whether the different emotion elicitation methods in VR invoke emotions comparable to the real world. Emotion elicitation methods in VR is an under-research area in HCI. Therefore, in this paper, we provide the first exploratory assessment of emotion elicitation methods in VR. Our goal is to understand how different elicitation methods [9,26,35] affect a range of emotions in VR. We also investigate how emotion intensity changes over time and how these results compare to the results from an identical real-world study. To this end, we conducted a mixed-design user study (N = 39), where participants experienced four emotion elicitation methods (audio, video, image, autobiographical recall) and four basic emotions (happy, sad, excited, angry) in a virtual lab setting and an identical real-world setting. Our main research questions were:

- **RQ1:** Can established elicitation methods used in the real world elicit similar emotions in VR?
- **RQ2:** How do the elicited emotions wear off over time?
- **RQ3:** What are the unique characteristics of different elicitation techniques?

Our main results are: (1) Emotion elicitation methods work in a similar manner in both VR and the real world, producing largely comparable results, (2) All elicited emotions take time to fade out, thus there exists a minimum waiting period, and (3) All four elicitation techniques had very small differences between the real-world and virtual conditions. The experienced emotions were generally very slightly stronger in VR. Autobiographical memory recall had a unique challenge, as participants found it difficult to stop recalling their memories further.

We believe this understanding is valuable to researchers, as our work provides evidence that emotions can be researched in VR through emotion elicitation techniques. Our results are also useful for designers and practitioners, as they can inform how certain emotions can best be invoked in VR.

2 Background

Our work draws from previous work on 1) emotion elicitation methods, 2) understanding emotions in VR, and 3) the use of VR for research purposes.

2.1   Emotions and Emotion Elicitation Methods

Emotions have received considerable attention from psychology researchers for more than a century. Researchers have identified various basic emotions [21,31, 42], the most common ones being happiness/joy, sadness, fear, and anger.

Psychologists have also proposed models that use continuous axes to model emotions. Two common axes are *arousal* and *valence*. Arousal refers to the amount of activation in an emotion, in other words, how much calmness or excitement is in the emotion. Valence refers to how positive or negative the emotion is. A third axis often shared by these theories is the *dominance* or control axis. This refers to how much control one has of the emotion, and if it is caused by an internal or external source [41]. Russell presented his Circumplex Model of affect with emotions scattered along both the arousal and valence axis [48]. This model is now commonly used in Affective Computing and HCI research.

To conduct emotion experiments, a broad spectrum of emotions need to be elicited through external stimuli. Exploring emotion elicitation methods is a crucial aspect towards understanding human behaviour and consists of a large research body [47]. Not only do researchers investigate the established approaches towards inducing emotion, but also the opportunity to explore new emotion induction methods such as music [56]. Researchers have also discussed the challenges and concerns of emotion elicitation [54].

Common elicitation methods include showing users various resources such as audio [55], videos [26], and pictures [54], and invoking emotions through past memories through autobiographical recall [28]. Autobiographical recall encourages participants to recall a specific event or memory that can evoke a certain emotion [5,10,20]. Recalling past events can be done via writing, talking aloud or simply remembering. Autobiographical recall has been found to be the preferred method for emotional elicitation in many scenarios, such as automotive research [9], where using videos or pictures is not possible. Researchers have long compared each traditional method of elicitation to understand it's effectiveness and specific application [17,27].

2.2   Utilizing VR as a Research Platform

Recently, advances in VR technologies have brought forth the question of whether studies involving human subjects could be conducted in virtual reality [32]. This approach aims, for example, to produce results that apply in similar real-world conditions [1,18,32], to generate real-world skills through virtual training [15,36,52], or to support real-world behavior change through VR [44].

Conducting studies in VR brings many potential benefits. Researchers have full control of the virtual world and may modify the environment, conditions and variables at will [32]. VR also gives a higher degree of freedom to researchers as it might enable user studies to be conducted remotely [46]. As VR headsets become more ubiquitous, consumers could participate in user studies remotely from the comfort of the users' own homes. In addition, VR has potential to be used for studies that would be difficult or unethical to conduct in the real world, such as certain scenarios in automotive research [14]. We take inspiration from these contexts and explore if VR can further enhance emotion research.

Some studies have briefly touched on emotions in VR. Dickinson et al. [19] investigated the feasibility of using VR to study gambling behaviour. Their findings suggest that participants experience higher levels of arousal and immersion in VR compared to the real world. Guidelines for research in human social interaction using VR is discussed by Pan et al. [37]. The authors compared arousal, immersion, task workload between the real and the virtual world; proposing VR simulations to be beneficial for the study of behaviour. This motivates our research as we comprehend how different emotions are affected in VR in terms of valence, arousal and dominance.

2.3 Emotion Elicitation in VR

Using VR to manipulate and induce emotions is explored by Estupinan et al. [22]. The authors investigated in a pilot study how valence and arousal in VR correlate with the real world. Their findings show that arousal is higher in virtual reality when using images to elicit emotions. Banos et al. [6] explored inducing mood through VR. They created a VR park scene which can adapt based on how the authors wanted to control an emotion after the elicitation phase. The strengths of VR as a platform for investigating emotion are identified by Chirico et al. [12], where they explored how an intense emotion such as *awe* can be elicited in VR. The authors argue in favor of VR allowing experimenters to generate a vast range of complex stimuli to elicit emotions, which are otherwise difficult in the real world. While the authors in this work looked into whether emotions could be elicited in VR, we apply and compare different emotion elicitation methods commonly used in the real word in VR to holistically understand their suitability for VR research and beyond. Riva et al. [45] explored the use of VR to evoke *anxiety* and *relaxation* and analysed the relationship between emotions and presence. Felnhofer et al. [23] covered a range of affective states (joy, sadness, boredom, anger, and anxiety) and found that emotional VR scenarios evoke a higher degree of presence, which in turn affects the intensity of the evoked emotion.

2.4 Summary and Research Approach

The previous sections demonstrate the importance of research on emotion and the need to understand emotion elicitation methods. With VR being an emerging technology which is rapidly becoming more ubiquitous, it is timely to explore how well emotion elicitation methods function in VR. To the best of our knowledge, this is the first work to explore and compare different elicitation methods in VR and the real world in parallel.

3   User Study

We designed a user study to understand the capabilities of different emotion elicitation methods in the virtual world (VW) and how they compare to their real-world counterparts. The participants experienced four different emotions through four different elicitation methods in the real world as well as in a virtual replica of the real-world space.

3.1 Participants

We recruited 39 participants (24 males) with an average age of 28.1 ($SD = 6.9$). We advertised the study via university mailing lists, social media platforms and company notice boards. 25 participants reported to have prior experience with VR. The participants experienced two different environments (real and virtual) on two separate sessions with each session lasting around 40 min. Participants were compensated with 20 EUR in cash for their time.

3.2 Study Design

We conducted a mixed-design experiment with the following three independent variables:

- **Setting (2 levels):** real world (RW) and virtual world (VW).
- **Elicitation Method (4 levels):** audio, video, image, autobiographical recall (ABR)
- **Emotion (4 levels):** happiness, sadness, anger, excitement

Because of the large number of possible combinations (32), we opted for a Graeco-Latin Square to cover the majority of the combinations. Thus, our study was a mixed design, where participants experienced all elicitation methods and all emotions once in both settings, but they did not experience all combinations. Each participant experienced the same combination of emotion and emotion elicitation methods between the real and virtual world in order to compare the results. This resulted in four combinations in both settings per participant, for a total of eight combinations.

We selected four emotions based on Russell's Circumplex model of affect with arousal and valence dimensions as an appropriate model for our investigation, which has been demonstrated to work well in a variety of different studies [48]. The model has two dimensions: *Valence* indicates the positiveness or negativeness of the feeling; *Arousal* indicates how strong the feeling is [8]. We chose to investigate four emotions, one from each quartile of the model of affect [49]: Happiness (low arousal, positive valence), Sadness (low arousal, negative valence), Excitement (high arousal, positive valence), and Anger (high arousal, negative valence).

We selected the elicitation methods based on literature reviews which report these as commonly used approaches [13,47]. For three of the four chosen elicitation methods (video, audio, picture), we needed material that were validated to elicit the desired emotions. These materials were chosen from validated datasets based on literature which shows prolific usage of the datasets in various research directions [3,29,39,40,50,53]. The materials were selected based on the emotion label (we only chose materials that evoke our desired emotions) and the highest valence and arousal values. For autobiographical recall we did not need external materials. Instead, we asked participants to recall past events that had invoked certain emotions in them and it lasted on average two minutes. We showed video and images for 60 s and the audio clips lasted approximately 40–60 s. For audio, video and image we used the following databases:

- **Video:** DEAP: A Database for Emotion Analysis Using Physiological Signals [30]
- **Audio:** The Musical Emotional Bursts (MEB) [38]
- **Picture:** The Geneva affective picture database (GAPED) [16]

For collecting subjective measurements as ground truth for the emotion being elicited we used the 9-point Self-Assessment Manikin scale (SAM) [8] which constitutes our *emotion intensity* dependent variable. The SAM scale uses a visual representation as an indicator of the current emotion while separating the abstract mood into three dimensions: valence, arousal, as described above, and dominance, which indicates how much control the person has over the current feeling. We selected this pictorial representation as this may encourage participants to make reliable assessment of perceived emotion. The databases selected use the same scale (9 point SAM) to visualize Russell's model. We also measured whether emotion induction is dependent on *personality* using the Ten Item Personality Measure (TIPI) [25]. TIPI is a ten-item questionnaire where participants rate statements on a 7-Point Likert scale (1 = strongly disagree; 7 = strongly agree). The ten questions reflect the Big Five dimensions (Extroversion, Agreeableness, Conscientiousness, Emotional Stability, and Openness) using two questions per dimension.

3.3 Apparatus

For the real-world condition, we chose an office space including two tables, chairs, one cabinet, and windows on one side (Fig. 1a). For the VR condition, we built a virtual replica of the same office (Fig. 1b). In the real world, the participants were seated on a chair and the elicitation stimuli were shown through the computer screen placed on the table in front of them (Fig. 1c). In the virtual replica, the exact same procedure was followed. The VR environment was programmed using Unity, running on HTC Vive via SteamVR.

3.4 Study Procedure

The participants experienced each setting (RW and VW) on separate days to eliminate any lasting effects from the first session. We counterbalanced the setting order. In both settings, each participant experienced all four emotion elicitation methods and all four emotions. The combinations of emotions and elicitation methods were kept the same between the settings, but the order of combination was counterbalanced. This was done to ensure that the data remain comparable

Fig. 1. The office environment setups used in the study: a) Real-world study setup, b) Virtual world study setup where we designed the VR environment to closely resemble its real-world counterpart, Participant's sitting position in c) Real world, d) Virtual world.

between RW and VW. For counterbalancing, we used Graeco-Latin Square to cover the majority of the combinations (Table 1); each participant was exposed to four unique combinations of emotions and elicitation methods.

Table 1. The orders for each combination of emotions and methods based on Graeco-Latin Square (AbR = Autobiographical Recall).

Sad - Video	Angry - Audio	Happy - Image	Exciting - AbR
Angry - AbR	Happy - Video	Exciting - Audio	Sad - Image
Happy - Audio	Exciting - Image	Sad - AbR	Angry - Video
Exciting - Image	Sad - AbR	Angry - Video	Happy - Audio

At the beginning of the first session, we explained the purpose of our study to the participants and they signed a consent form. They then filled out their demographic information (age, gender, background, experience with VR), personality questionnaire (TIPI). Before the study, participants were briefed about the elicitation materials and the SAM scale. Participants were then shown how to use the VR equipment and how fill in the SAM scale in VR using controllers.

In each session, participants experienced the elicitation material one at a time, after which they filled in the SAM scale five times with breaks of 30 s in between. We collected five SAM readings to analyze how emotion changes over time and at the same time maintain a reasonable study duration. To the best of our knowledge, no best practices exist regarding the optimal number of readings to study this. After the initial briefing, the participants completed the elicitation without the experimenter in the room. This was done to ensure that the life events narrated by the participants for the autobiographical recall method remained confidential. After finishing both sessions, they filled in the final questionnaire and were interviewed briefly. Each session lasted approximately 40 min. The entire study procedure is visualized in Fig. 2.

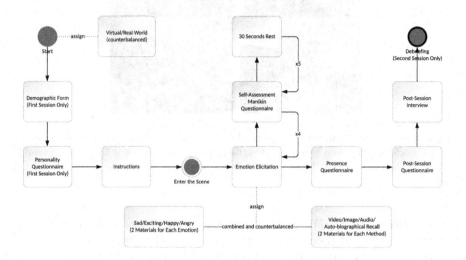

Fig. 2. An overview of the study procedure.

4   Results

In this section, we present the results from our comparative study. We have considered all five SAM readings only for analysing how emotion intensity drops over time. For all the other analyses we only use the first SAM reading after each elicitation.

4.1   Correlations Between Emotions and Personality, Age, Gender, and VR Experience

Using Kruskal-Wallis H Test, we compared the SAM results with the participants' VR experience, their age, gender and TIPI results in each combination of elicitation method, elicited emotion and environment. There was no statistically significant differences between the SAM results and any of the factors ($p > .05$). However, this result may differ if investigated with a larger sample.

4.2   Emotions Between the Real World and the Virtual World

We used non-parametric test as the Shapiro-Wilk Test indicated the SAM values to deviate significantly from normal distribution. Table 2 shows the median values of valence, arousal and dominance from the SAM scale. The median analysis

Table 2. Median and p-values of SAM scores for each elicited emotion between virtual and real world.

Valence scale

	Sadness (n = 39)	Anger (n = 39)	Happiness (n = 39)	Excitement (n = 39)
Virtual	4 ± 2.01	5 ± 1.90	7 ± 1.44	7 ± 1.66
Real	4 ± 1.79	5 ± 1.86	6 ± 1.02	6 ± 1.52
p-value	0.631	0.346	0.24	0.492

Arousal scale

	Sadness (n = 39)	Anger (n = 39)	Happiness (n = 39)	Excitement (n = 39)
Virtual	6 ± 2.05	5 ± 2.05	5 ± 1.97	6 ± 2.31
Real	5 ± 1.93	6 ± 1.80	4 ± 1.88	5 ± 1.81
p-value	0.375	0.766	0.058	0.267

Dominance scale

	Sadness (n = 39)	Anger (n = 39)	Happiness (n = 39)	Excitement (n = 39)
Virtual	6 ± 1.90	6 ± 2.38	7 ± 1.64	8 ± 1.53
Real	7 ± 2.16	7 ± 1.98	7 ± 1.4	7 ± 1.63
p-value	0.693	0.324	0.852	0.421

of each scale indicates that the elicitation methods are capable of eliciting emotions in VR similar to the real world. Friedman test did not show any significant differences between VR and RW with any of the dimensions. The only near-significant difference was observed in *arousal* regarding *Happiness* (p = .058). Therefore, the overall results regarding emotional states are the same between the real world and VR.

Figure 3 shows box plots for each SAM dimension, environment, and elicited emotion. In addition, a Wilcoxon Signed-Rank Test was conducted between virtual and real world regarding the valence, arousal and dominance value for each elicited emotion.

For *Anger*, Wilcoxon Signed-Rank Test did not show any significant difference in valence ($Z = -.943$, p = .346), arousal ($Z = -.297$, p = .766) and dominance ($Z = -.987$, p = .324) values between both worlds. Both environments elicited same median value for valence scale (median = 5). The median values of arousal and dominance dimensions are lower in VR (median of Arousal = 5, median of Dominance = 6) compared to real world (median of Arousal = 6, median of Dominance = 7).

For *Sadness*, no significant difference exists with valence ($Z = -.481$, p = .631), arousal ($Z = -.886$, p = .375) and dominance ($Z = -.395$, p = .693). Though the median values of valence are the same (median = 4), the median arousal value in VR (median = 6) is higher than that in the real world (median = 5). The median dominance in VR (median = 6) is lower than that in the real world (median = 7).

For *Excitement*, no significant difference exists with valence ($Z = -.687$, p = .492), arousal ($Z = -1.109$, p = .267) and dominance ($Z = -.804$, p = .421). The median values for all three SAM dimensions are higher in virtual world (median of Valence = 7, median of Arousal = 6, median of Dominance = 8) compared to

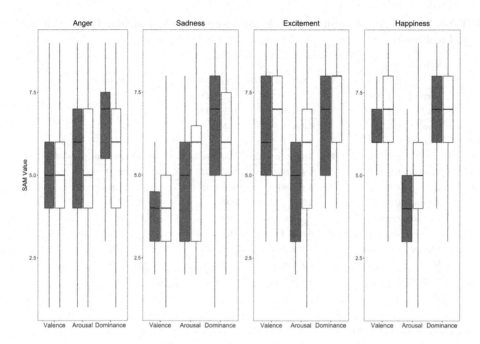

Fig. 3. SAM scores for each elicited emotion in the virtual world and the real world.

real world (median of Valence = 6, median of Arousal = 5, median of Dominance = 7).

For *Happiness*, valence (Z = −1.176, p = .240) and dominance (Z = −.186, p = .852) show no significant differences. Valence in VR (median = 7) has higher median value than the real world (median = 6). While arousal (Z = −1.898, p = .058) scale after emotion Happiness elicitation indicates the two environments being marginally significant. The median value for arousal in VR (median = 5) is higher (median = 4). The median values for dominance are the same for both environments (median = 7).

4.3   Emotion Elicitation Methods

In the next four tables (Tables 3, 4, 5, 6), we present the comparisons of the elicitation methods for *Sadness*, *Anger*, *Happiness*, and *Excitement* respectively.

Video. The results from eliciting *Sadness* through videos show that there was no significant difference between valence and arousal scores between the settings. The median values for arousal were the same across both worlds, though valence was slightly lower in the virtual world. However, dominance was significantly lower in VR than in the real world (p = 0.044). Eliciting *Anger* showed no significant differences among the valence, arousal and dominance scales. The median values for valence and arousal were the same, but dominance was slightly higher

Table 3. Median and p-value of SAM ratings for Video elicitation method between virtual and real world.

Valence scale

	Sadness	Anger	Happiness	Excitement
Virtual world	6.00	6.00	7.50	–
Real world	6.50	6.00	6.00	–
p-value	0.572	0.293	0.251	–

Arousal scale

	Sadness	Anger	Happiness	Excitement
Virtual world	6.00	5.00	4.50	–
Real world	6.00	5.00	3.00	–
p-value	0.666	0.572	0.404	–

Dominance scale

	Sadness	Anger	Happiness	Excitement
Virtual world	6.50	7.00	6.00	–
Real world	8.50	6.00	6.00	–
p-value	0.044	0.206	0.832	–

Table 4. Median and p-value of SAM ratings for Image elicitation method between virtual and real world.

Valence scale

	Sadness	Excitement	Happiness	Anger
Virtual world	4.00	7.00	7.00	–
Real world	4.00	6.00	7.00	–
p-value	0.172	0.374	0.388	–

Arousal scale

	Sadness	Excitement	Happiness	Anger
Virtual world	5.00	6.00	4.00	–
Real world	4.00	5.00	4.00	–
p-value	0.397	0.024	0.407	–

Dominance scale

	Sadness	Excitement	Happiness	Anger
Virtual world	5.5	7.00	8.00	–
Real world	5.5	7.00	8.00	–
p-value	0.886	0.390	0.389	–

Table 5. Median and p-value of SAM ratings for Autobiographical Recall elicitation method between virtual and real world.

Valence scale

	Sadness	Anger	Excitement	Happiness
Virtual world	4.00	3.00	7.50	–
Real world	4.00	3.00	8.00	–
p-value	0.273	0.121	0.465	–

Arousal scale

	Sadness	Anger	Excitement	Happiness
Virtual world	6.00	5.50	4.50	–
Real world	5.00	7.00	6.00	–
p-value	0.433	0.380	0.634	–

Dominance scale

	Sadness	Anger	Excitement	Happiness
Virtual world	5.00	6.50	8.00	–
Real world	6.00	6.00	7.00	–
p-value	0.407	0.546	0.722	–

Table 6. Median and p-value of SAM ratings for Audio elicitation method between virtual and real world.

Valence scale

	Anger	Happiness	Excitement	Sadness
Virtual world	5.00	7.00	5.00	–
Real world	5.00	7.00	5.50	–
p-value	0.391	0.552	0.192	–

Arousal scale

	Anger	Happiness	Excitement	Sadness
Virtual world	5.00	6.00	5.00	–
Real world	4.00	5.00	4.00	–
p-value	0.666	0.110	0.192	–

Dominance scale

	Anger	Happiness	Excitement	Sadness
Virtual world	6.00	6.00	8.00	–
Real world	7.00	7.00	7.00	–
p-value	0.180	0.626	0.917	–

in VR. Eliciting *Happiness* also showed no significant differences in valence, arousal or dominance, although the median values for valence and arousal were slightly higher in the virtual world.

Image. Using image to elicit *Sadness* did not show any significant differences in any dimension between the settings. The medians for both valence and dominance were the same between the real world and the virtual world, but arousal was slightly higher in the virtual world. Eliciting *Happiness* showed no significant differences in any dimension between the settings. Eliciting *Excitement* showed a significant difference in arousal (p = 0.024), but no significant differences in dominance or valence, although valence was slightly higher without significance in the virtual world.

Autobiographical Recall. Eliciting *Sadness* using Autobiographical Recall showed no significant difference between the real and virtual world for valence, arousal or dominance. Median arousal value in the virtual world is higher and the median dominance is lower. Eliciting *Anger* again showed no difference across the dimensions. Median arousal is lower in the virtual world and the median dominance is higher. Eliciting *Excitement* showed no significant difference though the median valence and arousal values are lower in virtual world and dominance is higher.

Audio. Eliciting *Anger* showed no significant difference across the dimensions with the median arousal value being slightly higher and dominance value being slightly lower in the virtual world. For *Happiness* we saw no statistical significance between the worlds for the SAM dimensions. Similar to *Anger*, the median arousal value is higher and the dominance value is lower. For *Excitement*, there was no statistical significance though valence is slightly lower in virtual world and dominance, arousal slightly higher in virtual world.

4.4   Lasting Effects of Emotions

We analyzed how the SAM values for valence, arousal and dominance change over time with each emotion (Fig. 4). SAM readings were taken five times at 30-s intervals. While only the median valence values after emotion *Sadness* in the real world showed an ascending trend; median valence values for the other three emotions remained still over time. For all four emotions across both dimensions, the median arousal values were weaker over time. The median dominance values for *Anger* and *Excitement* in both the environments showed slight increase over time. For *Sadness* and *Happiness* dominance in virtual world showed an increasing trend while it remained at a constant value in the real world.

We also compared how the emotions vary over time with each elicitation method in RW and VR (Fig. 5). Each elicitation method followed a similar pattern except *Audio*, which showed a greater deviation between VR and the real world for all dimensions when compared to other methods.

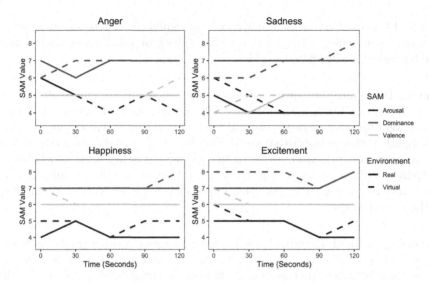

Fig. 4. The lasting effect of arousal, dominance and valence for each emotion in the real world and the virtual world.

4.5   Participants' Perspective

At the end of the study, we interviewed participants about their experiences in the RW and VR settings, particularly about whether or not they found these two experiences similar. Most participants stated that they did indeed perceive the experience between the settings very similar. However, some participants mentioned that the real world had more objects, like noticing extra cables on the table in the real world which was absent in the virtual world, in the room which the virtual world was missing. Nonetheless, this did not seem to be a major factor in the experience, as the layout and most critical objects were the same.

We gained interesting insights from participants regarding autobiographical memory recall. 16 participants mentioned that for emotion elicitation using memory recall, they preferred the real world since VR was perceived more as a game experience. However, 17 participants felt that the virtual world had fewer distractions (such as absence of environmental noise) and helped them concentrate better to recall past events. A few participants also felt that the time given (two minutes) to recall an event was short and they were worried they might not be finished, which may have distracted them.

Several participants mentioned that once they recalled a memory using ABR, continuous memories kept coming back to them even after the emotion elicitation task was over. This might indicate that emotion elicitation through autobiographical memory recall might affect the person for longer periods than other methods, because it is more difficult to fully stop the elicitation when prompted. One participant also mentioned that positive memory recall led to thinking

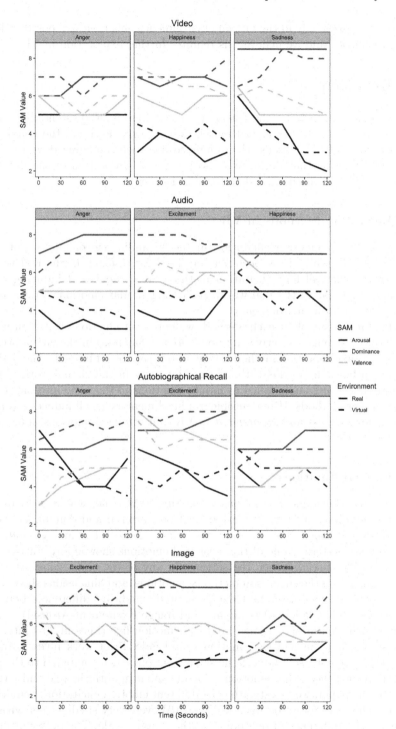

Fig. 5. The lasting effect of arousal, dominance and valence for each emotion with each elicitation method in the real world and the virtual world.

negative memories only in the virtual environment. This indicates possible deviation in behavior and we believe this requires further exploration in VR.

5   Discussion

In this section, we discuss the feasibility of conducting studies entailing emotions and emotion elicitation methods in VR by drawing upon the conducted comparative study. We discuss the differences between the induced emotions in the real and the virtual world. We also present a comparison of the different emotion elicitation methods and the lessons learned.

5.1   Elicitation Methods in VR

We explored four emotion elicitation methods (audio, video, image, autobiographical recall) which have been actively used for research in the real world. We observed that all four elicitation methods were capable of inducing emotions in VR similar to the real world, indicating similar emotional states from participants in both environments.

Taking a closer look at each method, we note that emotion elicitation using video induced stronger negative emotions (*Anger*, *Sadness*) in the virtual world. Similar to video elicitation method, image also is capable of inducing the desired emotions in both the worlds with stronger intensity in the virtual world. Elicitation method using audio failed to induce emotions of the same intensity compared to other methods. Using autobiographical memory recall induces stronger emotions for *Sadness* and *Excitement* in VR, but stronger emotions in the real world for *Anger*.

5.2   Elicited Emotions

We measured the induced emotions using the SAM scale, where participants rated the emotions in three dimensions: valence, arousal and dominance. Generally, our results show that the emotions induced in both RW and VR followed a very similar pattern. None of the measured emotions showed any statistically significant differences between the settings in any of the dimensions. At more detailed analysis of the elicitation methods, emotions, and dimensions shows that only 2 combinations out of the total 36 showed significant differences between the settings (Video-Sadness-Dominance and Image-Excitement-Arousal).

After each elicitation, we measured the emotion five times in 30-s intervals to investigate how quickly the emotion would fade. Prior work investigated if virtual environment itself induces the same emotions when compared to the real world [11] which shows that emotions remain similar in both the real and virtual world. In our paper, we investigated the different emotion elicitation techniques and the differences found between VW and RW were very small, either with no difference or a difference of one point on the 9-point scale. The only exception was the first SAM measure for *Sadness*, where there was a difference of two points between VW and RW. Therefore, the way the emotions developed over time after elicitation was also very similar between the real world and the virtual world.

5.3 The Lasting Effects of the Elicited Emotions

By taking the SAM scale measures five times with 30-s intervals, we measured how each elicited emotion developed during the two minutes that followed the elicitation. In many cases, the emotions still existed after this period, indicating that two minutes may not be enough to diminish the elicited emotion. This is both an opportunity and a challenge. For research purposes, researchers might want to consider a longer waiting period between the elicited emotions, or look for ways to diminish the emotions more quickly. For designers of VR experiences, this could be useful information when designing the experience and the specific scenes within, knowing that elicited emotions can last for some time.

5.4 Lessons Learned

Our results suggest that virtual reality could be used to research emotions and emotion elicitation techniques, and acquire results that translate into the real world. We note that the discrepancies between the RW and VW itself might influence the experienced emotion and that this could be explored in-depth in future work.

Through this study, we gained insight into the differences between emotion elicitation methods. One highlight is the availability of resources for each method. For example, using autobiographical method does not require any additional resources as this is dependent on the participants only. But using other methods would require researchers to have access to verified and established resources to elicit the desired emotion. Obtaining the dataset is also a time consuming process. The other prime difference is the implementation of methods in VR. For example, writing in VR is harder to implement for autobiographical recall compared to "think-aloud" method.

Autobiographical recall has great potential in specific applications where using materials to elicit emotions is challenging (for example, automotive research). However, we observed that many participants found it difficult to stop recalling their life events once they initiated the process. This may affect further actions from the user, thus care must be taken to ensure that users reach a neutral emotional state when needed.

Our results can be translated to clear actionables, allowing researchers to choose the most fitting method of emotion elicitation based on the task at hand and the resulting preoccupation. For example, where visual senses are occupied such as automotive studies, autobiographical recall or audio method is a fitting approach. Where auditory senses are occupied, such as in a speech interface study autobiographical recall (without think-aloud), image or video (without sound) is a fitting approach. It can also help us to know which methods to eliminate from a set of available options. For example, in a task where cognition is occupied, one should avoid autobiographical recall.

Designers can use the results to inform the design of various VR experiences such as Cinematic Virtual Reality (CVR) as well as VR games, where designers want their experience to elicit specific emotions. For example, in a segment where VR players admire a view and designers want to elicit happiness, auditory cues could be used that do not interfere with the visual experience.

5.5   Limitations and Future Work

To measure the elicited emotions, we used a subjective assessment (SAM scale). Emotions could be more thoroughly measured with additional physiological measures such as heart rate and blood pressure [34].

Through our work, we identified three areas that could be addressed in the future:

1) Diminishing elicited emotions in VR. In our work we observed how the elicited emotions fluctuate over a brief period of time. In the future, it would be valuable to investigate how long emotions truly last in VR, and which methods could be reasonably used to accelerate this process (for example, making participants fill in a non-relevant questionnaire). Also, we could investigate how exposure time to emotion-inducing material affects the emotions' duration.

2) Exploring different implementations for autobiographical memory recall. In our study, participants recalled life events without anyone else present in the room. In the real world, this method is often conducted by asking participants to write about their life events or talk about them to another person. Therefore, in the future, it might be valuable to investigate different implementations of autobiographical recall in VR (e.g., writing in VR, reporting the experience to a virtual avatar).

3) Emotion elicitation during tasks. In our work, we focused on studying emotion and emotion elicitation techniques at large. Because most VR experiences and studies conducted in VR involve users being active and engaging in various interactive tasks, it could be valuable to investigate further how tasks of various nature might affect the performance of elicitation methods and the strength of the invoked emotions.

6   Conclusion

In this paper, we explored how established emotion elicitation methods work in virtual reality. In particular, we used four emotion elicitation techniques (audio, video, image, and autobiographical recall) to elicit four different emotions (anger, excitement, happiness, and sadness).

We conducted a user study, where participants experienced the elicitation methods in a real-world study and in an identical virtual study. In particular, we then compared the results between the real world and the virtual world. We learned that: **(1)** Emotion elicitation methods work in a similar manner in both VR and the real world, producing largely comparable results, **(2)** All of the elicited emotions have a lingering effect and it takes time for the emotion to diminish, and **(3)** All four elicitation techniques had very small differences between the real-world and the virtual world. The experienced emotions were in some cases slightly stronger in VR. Autobiographical memory recall had a unique challenge, as participants found it difficult to stop recalling their memories further.

Through our work, we have gained an understanding of the potential, strengths, and weaknesses of emotion elicitation methods in VR. Our work can inform how elicitation methods can be utilized in VR, and in particular, whether or not results from virtual emotion studies can translate into the real world.

Acknowledgements. The presented work was funded by the German Research Foundation (DFG) under project no. 316457582 and 425869382 and by dtec.bw – Digitalization and Technology Research Center of the Bundeswehr [Voice of Wisdom].

References

1. Agethen, P., Sekar, V.S., Gaisbauer, F., Pfeiffer, T., Otto, M., Rukzio, E.: Behavior analysis of human locomotion in the real world and virtual reality for the manufacturing industry. ACM Trans. Appl. Percept. **15**(3), Article 20, July 2018, 19 pages. https://doi.org/10.1145/3230648
2. Anderson, P., Rothbaum, B.O., Hodges, L.F.: Virtual reality exposure in the treatment of social anxiety. Cognitive Behav. Practice **10**(3), 240–247 (2003)
3. Atkinson, J., Campos, D.: Improving BCI-based emotion recognition by combining EEG feature selection and kernel classifiers. Expert Syst. Appl. **47**(2016), 35–41 (2016)
4. Aymerich-Franch, L., Bailenson, J.: The use of doppelgangers in virtual reality to treat public speaking anxiety: a gender comparison. Presented at the (2014)
5. Baker, R.C., Guttfreund, D.O.: The effects of written autobiographical recollection induction procedures on mood. J. Clin. Psychol. **49**(4), 563–568 (1993). https://doi.org/10.1002/1097-4679(199307)49:4⟨563::AID-JCLP2270490414⟩3.0.CO;2-W
6. Baños, R.M., Liaño, V., Botella, C., Alcañiz, M., Guerrero, B., Rey, B.(eds.) Changing induced moods via virtual reality. Presented at the (2006)
7. Beale, R., Peter, C.: The role of affect and emotion in HCI. In: Peter, C., Beale, R. (eds.) Affect and Emotion in Human-Computer Interaction. LNCS, vol. 4868, pp. 1–11. Springer, Heidelberg (2008). https://doi.org/10.1007/978-3-540-85099-1_1
8. Bradley, M.M., Lang, P.J.: Measuring emotion: the self-assessment manikin and the semantic differential. J. Behav. Therapy Exp. Psychiatry **25**(1), 49–59 (1994)
9. Braun, M., Weiser, S., Pfleging, B., Alt, F.: A Comparison of Emotion Elicitation Methods for Affective Driving Studies, pp. 77–81. Association for Computing Machinery, New York (2018). https://doi.org/10.1145/3239092.3265945
10. Chirico, A., Cipresso, P., Gaggioli, A.: Psychophysiological specificity of four basic emotions through autobiographical recall and videos. Presented at the (2018)
11. Chirico, A., Gaggioli, A.: When virtual feels real: comparing emotional responses and presence in virtual and natural environments. Cyberpsychol. Behav. Soc. Networking **22**(3), 220–226 (2019)

12. Chirico, A., Yaden, D.B., Riva, G., Gaggioli, A.: The potential of virtual reality for the investigation of awe. Front. Psychol. **7**(2016), 1766 (2016)
13. Coan, J.A., Allen, J.J.B.: Handbook of Emotion Elicitation and Assessment. Oxford University Press, USA (2007)
14. Colley, M., Walch, M., Rukzio, E.: For a better (simulated) world: considerations for VR in external communication research. In: Proceedings of the 11th International Conference on Automotive User Interfaces and Interactive Vehicular Applications: Adjunct Proceedings (AutomotiveUI 2019), pp. 442–449. Association for Computing Machinery, New York (2019). https://doi.org/10.1145/3349263. 3351523
15. Coyne, L., Takemoto, J.K., Parmentier, B.L., Merritt, T., Sharpton, R.A.: Exploring virtual reality as a platform for distance team-based learning. Currents Pharmacy Teach. Learn. **10**(10), 1384–1390 (2018)
16. Dan-Glauser, E.S., Scherer, K.R.: The Geneva affective picture database (GAPED): a new 730-picture database focusing on valence and normative significance. Behav. Res. Methods **43**(2), 468 (2011)
17. Dean, M., et al.: Comparison of elicitation methods for moral and affective beliefs in the theory of planned behaviour. Appetite **47**(2), 244–252 (2006)
18. Deb, S., Carruth, D.W., Sween, R., Strawderman, L., Garrison, T.M.: Efficacy of virtual reality in pedestrian safety research. Appl. Ergon. **65**(2017), 449–460 (2017). https://doi.org/10.1016/j.apergo.2017.03.007
19. Dickinson, P., Gerling, K., Wilson, L., Parke, A.: Virtual reality as a platform for research in gambling behaviour. Comput. Hum. Behav. **107**(2020), 106293 (2020)
20. Drace, S.: Evidence for the role of affect in mood congruent recall of autobiographic memories. Motivat. Emotion 37(3), 623–628 (2013)
21. Ekman, P.: An argument for basic emotions. Cogn. Emotion **6**(3–4), 169–200 (1992)
22. Estupiñán, S., Rebelo, F., Noriega, P., Ferreira, C., Duarte, E.: Can virtual reality increase emotional responses (Arousal and Valence)? A pilot study. Presented at the (2014)
23. Felnhofer, A., et al.: Is virtual reality emotionally arousing? investigating five emotion inducing virtual park scenarios. Int. J. Hum Comput Stud. **82**(2015), 48–56 (2015)
24. Gendron, M.: Defining emotion: a brief history. Emotion Rev **2**(4), 371–372 (2010)
25. Gosling, S.D., Rentfrow, P.J., Swann Jr., W.B.: A very brief measure of the Big-Five personality domains. J. Res. Personality **37**(6), 504–528 (2003)
26. Gross, J.J., Levenson, R.W.: Emotion elicitation using films. Cognition Emotion **9**(1), 87–108 (1995)
27. Jallais, C., Gilet, A.-L.: Inducing changes in arousal and valence: comparison of two mood induction procedures. Behav. Res. Methods **42**(1), 318–325 (2010)
28. Janssen, J.H., et al.: Machines outperform laypersons in recognizing emotions elicited by autobiographical recollection. Human-Comput. Interaction **28**(6), 479–517 (2013)
29. Jatupaiboon, N., Pan-ngum, S., Israsena, P.: Real-time EEG-based happiness detection system. Sci. World J. 2013 (2013)
30. Koelstra, S.: Deap: a database for emotion analysis; using physiological signals. IEEE Trans. Affective Comput. **3**(1), 18–31 (2011)
31. Leidelmeijer, K.: Emotions: An Experimental Approach. Tilburg University Press (1991)

32. Mäkelä, V., et al.: Virtual field studies: conducting studies on public displays in virtual reality. In: Proceedings of the 2020 CHI Conference on Human Factors in Computing Systems (CHI 2020). ACM, New York. https://doi.org/10.1145/3313831.3376796

33. Mardini, W., Ali, G.A., Magdady, E., Al-momani, S.: Detecting human emotions using electroencephalography (EEG) using dynamic programming approach. Presented at the (2018). https://doi.org/10.1109/ISDFS.2018.8355324

34. Mauss, I.B., Robinson, M.D.: Measures of emotion: a review. Cognition Emotion **23**(2), 209–237 (2009)

35. Mills, C., D'Mello, S.: On the validity of the autobiographical emotional memory task for emotion induction. PloS One **9**(4), e95837 (2014)

36. Moussaïd, M., et al.: Crowd behaviour during high-stress evacuations in an immersive virtual environment. J. Roy. Soc. Interface **13**(122), 20160414 (2016)

37. Pan, X., de C Hamilton, A.F.: Why and how to use virtual reality to study human social interaction: the challenges of exploring a new research landscape. British J. Psychol. **109**(3), 395–417 (2018)

38. Paquette, S., Peretz, I., Belin, P.: The "Musical Emotional Bursts": a validated set of musical affect bursts to investigate auditory affective processing. Frontiers Psychol. **4**(2013), 509 (2013)

39. Paquette, S., Takerkart, S., Saget, S., Peretz, I., Belin, P.: Cross-classification of musical and vocal emotions in the auditory cortex. Ann. NY Acad. Sci. **1423**(2018), 329–337 (2018)

40. Peng, K.-C., Chen, T., Sadovnik, A., Gallagher, A.C.: A mixed bag of emotions: Model, predict, and transfer emotion distributions. Presented at the (2015)

41. Picard, R.W., Vyzas, E., Healey, J.: Toward machine emotional intelligence: Analysis of affective physiological state. IEEE Trans. Pattern Anal. Mach. Intell. **23**(10), 1175–1191 (2001)

42. Plutchik, R.: A general psychoevolutionary theory of emotion. Theories of emotion. Elsevier, pp. 3–33 (1980)

43. Repetto, C., et al.: Virtual reality and mobile phones in the treatment of generalized anxiety disorders: a phase-2 clinical trial. Personal Ubiquitous Comput. **17**(2), 253–260 (2013)

44. Riva, G., Baños, R.M., Botella, C., Mantovani, F., Gaggioli, A.: Transforming experience: the potential of augmented reality and virtual reality for enhancing personal and clinical change. Front. Psych. **7**(2016), 164 (2016)

45. Riva, G., et al.: Affective interactions using virtual reality: the link between presence and emotions. CyberPsychol. Behav. **10**(1), 45–56 (2007)

46. Rivu, R., et al.: Remote VR studies - a framework for running virtual reality studies Remotely Via Participant-Owned HMDs. CoRR abs/2102.11207 (2021). https://arxiv.org/abs/2102.11207

47. Rosenberg, E.L., Ekman, P.: Emotion: Methods of study (2000)

48. Russell, J.A.:1980. A circumplex model of affect. J. Personality Soc. Psychol. **39**(6), 1161 (1980)

49. Russell, J.A., Barrett, L.F.: Core affect, prototypical emotional episodes, and other things called emotion: dissecting the elephant. J. Personality Soc. Psychol. **76**(5), 805 (1999)

50. Sachs, M.E., Habibi, A., Damasio, A., Kaplan, J.T.: Decoding the neural signatures of emotions expressed through sound. Neuroimage **174**(2018), 1–10 (2018)

51. Searles, K., Mattes, K.: It's a mad, mad world: using emotion inductions in a survey. J. Exp. Pol. Sci. **2**(2), 172–182 (2015). https://doi.org/10.1017/XPS.2015.5

52. Shariati, A., et al.: Virtual reality social robot platform: a case study on arash social robot. Presented at the (2018)
53. Soleymani, M., Lichtenauer, J., Pun, T., Pantic, M.: A multimodal database for affect recognition and implicit tagging. IEEE Trans. Affective Comput. **3**(1), 42–55 (2012)
54. Uhrig, M.K., Trautmann, N., Baumgärtner, U., Treede, R.-D., Henrich, F., Hiller, W., Marschall, S.: Emotion elicitation: a comparison of pictures and films. Front. Psychol. **7**(2016), 180 (2016)
55. Västfjäll, D.: Emotion induction through music: a review of the musical mood induction procedure. Musicae Scientiae 5(1_suppl), 173–211 (2001)
56. Woo, S., Chang, D.-S., An, D., Hyun, D., Wallraven, C., Dangelmaier, M.: Emotion induction in virtual environments: a novel paradigm using immersive scenarios in driving simulators. In: SIGGRAPH Asia 2017 Posters (SA '17). Association for Computing Machinery, New York, NY, USA, Article Article 49, 2 pages. https://doi.org/10.1145/3145690.3145693

Expanding Affective Computing Paradigms Through Animistic Design Principles

Arjun Rajendran Menon(✉)🔟, Björn Hedin🔟, and Elina Eriksson🔟

KTH Royal Institute of Technology, Stockholm, Sweden
{armenon,bjornh,elina}@kth.se

Abstract. Animistic and anthropomorphic principles have long been investigated along with affective computing in both HCI and HRI research, to reduce user frustration and create more emotive yet relatable devices, robots, products and artefacts. Yet such artefacts and research have mainly been from user-centric perspectives and the animistic characteristics localised to single objects. In this exploratory paper, we take these principles in a new direction by attempting to invoke animistic characteristics of a room or a space itself. Designing primarily for space itself rather than the user or a single product, allows us to create new interactions and narratives that can induce animism and empathy for the space, in users. This leads to the creation of a prototype space, which we use to investigate how users approach, interact and behave in such a space, yielding several insights and user behaviour, all of which can be used for further studies, capable of generating new interaction perspectives and providing insights into user behaviour. We conclude by discussing the potentiality of such spaces in developing new strategies for behaviour change and HCI.

Keywords: Animism · Spatial interaction · Empathy · HRI

1 Introduction

Affective computing has resulted in computers and devices being sensitive to the emotions and moods of the user. Driven by the initial need to reduce user frustration, research into the field has resulted in several bodies of work that have enabled new, natural and intuitive interactions and experiences in both Human Computer Interaction (HCI) and Human Robot Interaction (HRI) [4].

Emotional design has explored how emotional experiences can be stimulated in users through careful product design [5]. Research has long sought after creating products that elicit positive emotional experiences in users. Going a step further, the fields of HRI and Ubiquitous Computing (Ubicomp) [43] have long utilised and investigated the principles of anthropomorphism (the attribution of human-like characteristics to non-human entities) and animism (the attribution of life-like characteristics to non living entities) to create robots and artefacts

© IFIP International Federation for Information Processing 2021
Published by Springer Nature Switzerland AG 2021
C. Ardito et al. (Eds.): INTERACT 2021, LNCS 12932, pp. 115–135, 2021.
https://doi.org/10.1007/978-3-030-85623-6_9

that are more relatable to users and to try to achieve user empathy and bonding with the artefacts and robots [25]. Entities such as voice assistants are becoming more human-like, for users to relate to them better and be able to use them easier. Norman's Three Levels of Emotional Design have been used for creating a variety of products that we have in our homes today [5] and with the advent of the Internet of Things, these products now have additional functionalities and capabilities that offer new paradigms of interactions with them. Our homes and environments are becoming increasingly filled with such inter-connected and internet-connected devices that seek to become more 'human' to better relate to the user [26].

However, all these products and research focus on the creation of entities that try to achieve user needs and goals. This potentially limits the interactions and possibilities that can be explored. What if the status quo was flipped and the products themselves had needs, moods and requirements that the users must be sensitive to? Could we draw out new experiences, interactions and paradigms from such products/entities? Could users empathise or even form emotional bonds with such products/entities? Research supports the notion of a user forming intimate bonds with technological artefacts and products [27] and new research directions such as Thing-centered Design (TCD) investigates the potentiality of designing from the perspective of the artefact/product being designed, as opposed to the user; i.e. a 'thing-centric' over a 'user-centric' approach [18].

Expanding this perspective, what if instead of creating stand-alone products, designers utilised many such artefacts, that in unison, provide a larger entity such as a room, a park, or any space, with animistic and experiential characteristics? How would users of such spaces behave with them and within them? How differently would they interact with them, if they began to feel that the spaces were 'alive'? Would they be able to empathise or form bonds with the spaces themselves? Could such bonds/interactions be used to achieve secondary goals?

That is what we attempt to investigate with this line of research,exploring further the paradigm of affective systems by creating systems and devices that evoke and stimulate empathy in users for the system itself, rather than systems that simulate empathy. This exploratory study and corresponding paper are part of an ongoing investigation into whether empathy can be stimulated in users for an entity such as a space and how users will behave towards, and in, such spaces. In this first part of the study, we ask how such a space can be created and what are the main takeaways and observations from users interacting with the space? To do so, we first interviewed potential users from various backgrounds to probe them for impressions about the idea of such a space. This allowed us to uncover limits, boundaries and principles with which to create a prototype space, using various connected sensor and actuator artefacts. These interconnected artefacts, in unison, along with the animistic narrative that they were the 'sense organs' of the space, allow the space to be 'alive'. Additionally, we also designed interactions for the spaces that gave it a certain level of autonomy and playfulness; all contributing to the above narrative. This prototype space enabled us to monitor and probe user behaviour and interactions in and with it, which brought out interesting insights that can be used to develop the space further and to design new interactions. The intention is to use such spaces for future studies regarding behaviour change and interaction design.

2   Related Work

There are several areas and domains that this paper touches upon, ranging from affective computing, enhancing emotional user experiences, anthropomorphic and animistic design, to the intermingling of physical and digital spaces in the form of blended spaces.

The idea of merging emotions with computing devices comes from Rosalind Picard's original concept of affective computing, which arose as a means to both reduce user frustration and improve user experiences through the communication and processing of user emotions [4]. Bickmore and Picard state that when a product sympathises with users, it increases the users' appreciation of the product and the product's lifespan [28]. This has led to the development of technological systems that can react to user emotions by detecting emotional cues such as voice tone, facial expressions, etc. [29]. Corresponding research in HRI the communication of emotions has led to the development of robots that are capable of mimicking facial expressions [30]. In the field of product design, Norman's emotional design attempts to elicit positive emotions in users through careful choices about how a product looks, feels and functions. However, this line of research does not explore the opposite, a perspective that attempts to make computing devices or products more likeable, endearing and intimate, to enhance emotional user experiences and also open up new design spaces, although there are other studies that support the concept that users can form intimate bonds with technological products [27].

Animism, the attribution of life-like characteristics to non living entities, and anthropomorphism, the attribution of human-like characteristics to non-human entities, have long been investigated in both anthropology and psychology. Understanding that humans tend to ascribe life-like or human-like characteristics to non-living and non-human entities to make sense of the world, indicates that this is almost primal and basic [3], as opposed to abnormal behaviour. Airenti postulates that anthropomorphism and animism are grounded in interaction rather than any specific belief system [1]. This makes it of particular interest to interaction designers. Animistic and anthropomorphic entities are more relatable to users and therefore, easier to form bonds with. Early design research explored the metaphor of living things to enact intimate intelligent design, as exemplified by the Clippy and other assistants created by Microsoft [40].

Various research has been conducted on using animistic and anthropomorphic principles to make artefacts that are endearing and intimate with users. Work done by van Allen, et al. explores animism as a methodological framework in interaction design through multiple design artefacts (AniThings) [17]. CAMY is a ubicomp product, designed using animistic and zoomorphic (attributing animal characteristics to non-animal entities) principles to investigate the effect of pet-like characteristics on users emotional experiences, specifically intimacy and sympathy [25]. CAMY is a specific example of how animism can be used to improve and enhance the user experience. The work presented in this paper is in line with, and inspired by, these works. However, they are focused on the creation of localised products that exhibit animistic characteristics. This study attempts to expand and extend these characteristics to the environment or space within which such artefacts or products are placed.

In the era of ubiquitous computing, our environments and living spaces are increasingly being imbued with various sensing and computing devices, granting them new capabilities [35,37], particularly with the advent of the Internet of Things. This provides a new design space, rife with opportunities to explore. The notion of extending physical spaces into the digital world can be seen in Blended Spaces, which seeks to merge physical and virtual worlds, in a kind of symbiosis [13,14].

Borgmann defines objects and entities in two categories - Commodities, which are objects having no significant value apart from their principal function and Things, which are objects that have emotional values and meaning associated with it, in addition to their functionality [6]. From this perspective, all previous research relating to emotional design and animism have been centred around turning products from commodities to things. This paper explores how the emotional value and meaning of any space, public or private, can be enhanced through the animism provided by artefacts that exist within them, such that more people will consider them as Things.

Nam et al. in their Design by Tangible Stories method present that having a compelling narrative and adding experiential values to an entity, greatly enhances its propensity to be given animistic characteristics by users [7]. They also state that new design opportunities are found by focusing on 'ludic' or playful values while applying new technologies to everyday products of home environments. This paper expands on this concept by treating the home environment or space itself as the entity to be given a compelling narrative and experiential value. Huizinga [8] explains that people are characterised by play as much as they are by thought or tool use, making playfulness an animistic quality. Thus applying such an animistic quality on a space would both enhance its experiential value, in addition to potentially revealing new forms of interaction between users and the space. Our environments and spaces provide us with both a location and the mechanisms to indulge in ludic activities, yet we do not engage with a space itself as we do with other living beings. If a space were to interact with us in more playful ways, it could potentially change users' relationships with them and bring out new interactions and behaviour. This forms the basis for some of the interaction choices made in this study.

However, animistic and anthropomorphic artefacts are particularly susceptible to the 'uncanny valley' effect [12], wherein a non-human entity behaving akin to a human triggers discomfort and sometimes even fear in users, due to cognitive dissonance. Thus, as designers we must embrace a fine line between what triggers empathy and what triggers fear. Pursuing the drawbacks of animism and anthropomorphism, lead us to the contrasting views regarding the role of anthropomorphism in HCI. Shneiderman [33] embraces an extreme view of this by asserting that employing anthropomorphism in HCI compromises the design, leading to vagueness and unpredictability. He advocates for predictable and comprehensible interfaces that support direct manipulation instead. However, Duffy [16] presents a counter-argument to this by asserting that Shneiderman's comments are not problems relating fundamentally to anthropomorphism, but rather correlating to HCI designers indiscriminately applying certain anthropomorphic qualities to their designs without understanding users' tendencies to anthropomorphize. He also states that Shneiderman's arguments are valid when the system to be designed, is intended as a tool. Since this study intentionally aims to mean the system as something more than a tool, this study is in line with Duffy's counter-argument.

Nass and Moon [29] present experiments through which they show that individuals "mindlessly apply social rules and expectations to computers" but are contradictorily against anthropomorphism as they believe that computers are not people and therefore do not warrant human treatment. Duffy [16] states that the problem here is with portraying lifeless machines and computers as having human-like qualities. The broader psychological perspective of anthropomorphism, which includes metaphorically ascribing human-like characteristics to a system based on the user's interpretation of its actions, is different. While this study does indeed try to portray an inanimate entity with anthropomorphic qualities, it does so by basing this in users' tendencies to anthropomorphize. By including users in the design process, through the initial interviews, the circumstances under which users tend to anthropomorphize are brought out.

3   Method

Since the notion of self-aware computing devices has a lot of prejudices and triggers fear in users, we sought to include the users in as many stages of the study as possible. We conducted the study in three stages, starting with interviews with participants to understand how they relate to their environment and possessions, as well as their impressions on the idea of a 'living space'. These formed a foundation for the prototyping stage that followed, in which various artefacts were built and installed into the chosen space, which was given a narrative of being alive. Finally, we evaluated the prototype space so created, with a focus group of participants who had a discussion within the space, while it interacted with and reacted to them.

3.1   Participants

10 participants (3 female, 7 male) participated in the initial interviews. The initial participants were acquaintances of the first author who referred subsequent participants for the interview. Participants ranged in age from 23 to 63 (M =

38.0, SD = 14.38). This selection of users is, by no means, an 'indicative' group of potential users but rather a snowball sample to identify trends and patterns.

For the focus group, 6 participants (2 female, 4 male) were recruited by the first author from their acquaintances. Participants ranged in age from 24 to 29 (M = 27.5, SD = 1.87). These participants were not included in the initial interviews.

3.2 Procedure

The interview study used a variety of communication tools such as Zoom, Face-Time, and WhatsApp to remotely conduct the interviews. Each interview lasted approximately 45–50 min and was recorded, after asking the participant for consent. Most interviews were conducted in English and relevant quotes were otherwise translated to English. Otter.ai[1], an automatic transcription service, was used to help with the transcription of recorded interviews. The interviewer created and followed an interview guide while conducting the interviews. The interview questions were grouped into various sections and were aimed at probing how the participant related to various entities in their lives, from plants and pets to technology, heirlooms, houses and homes. They also probed the participants reactions to the idea of a animistic space or entity, by posing it as a series of hypothetical questions. Participant comments were coded using initial coding [42] by a single coder. Statements were assigned emergent codes over repeated cycles. A thematic analysis [39] of the codes were then done, identify patterns and trends of note.

After the interviews, prototyping followed, where the Design by Tangible Stories method [7] was used to create narratives for the artefacts created in the prototyping phase. In this context, we define an artefact as a prototype object designed and created by the designers. Technical design and prototyping were done by the first author, in line with agile principles with the goal being to have working, proof-of-concept prototypes at the end of each sprint, followed by testing these artefacts through roleplay. Various interactions were created using the artefacts.

The artefacts were then given the narrative that they were the instruments through which the space experienced events that occurred within it. These were then deployed in a lab space, thereby resulting in the creation of the prototype space, which was then evaluated through the focus group of six users.

The participants of the focus group were not told about the nature and topic of the focus group beforehand, so as to avoid any sort of bias. At the venue, they were told that they were presented with the following narrative:-The participants would be engaging in a focus group discussion in a space that was imbued with technologies that enabled it to be 'alive' in a sense. They were told that the space would also be participating in the discussion as the final member of the group. The creators of the space had created it in such a way that they themselves had no idea or answers as to why the space would choose

---

[1] https://otter.ai.

to behave in certain ways. The space was given certain experiential qualities and a 'personality' and would react to the events that occurred within it and in accordance with its 'personality'. Whenever the space reacted or behaved in accordance to a stimulus or a random event, participants were encouraged to come up with their own theories as to why the space chose to do so. The participants were not told about what interactions the space could or would do but were encouraged to discover them serendipitously. They were also allowed and encouraged to freely move about the space and interact with anything that they found interesting. The interviewer followed a guide for the discussion but broke away from the script, if they deemed anything interesting was transpiring between the space and the users.

4 Results

4.1 Interview Results

The initial interviews with participants generated after thematic analysis, a set of design recommendations. These recommendations are given below in **bold**. *Citations* of the participants are presented together with an identifier Pn, where n is a number that represents each participant.

Anthropomorphic agents should be non-threatening
Presenting hypothetical scenarios where a robot/computer agent was considered as intelligent as a human, triggered discomfort and even fear in most participants, who were wary of having such entities in their homes as exemplified by the following quote -

"I would be frightened if I was in a position where I assigned the same alive-ness to a robot or an Alexa that I assigned to you and even more uncomfortable having it in my house." - P3

Mainstream media portrayal of Artificial Intelligence as the "end of the human race" tends to bias users towards the idea of intelligent robots and AI [2]. However, when presented with a video of Cozmo [41], participants were far more receptive and open towards interacting with it and having it around their homes. They did not consider the robot as intelligent as a human and regarded it as a toy, reflecting its ludic nature and perceived level of intelligence. These indicate that having ludic values and interactions helps soften human prejudice towards anthropomorphic agents.

Occasional randomness and out of the ordinary behaviour instigates curiosity and animistic tendencies in users.
Participants with pets mentioned that they felt curious or concerned when their pets behaved differently. They were able to learn more and understand their pets better when they were able to trace the behaviour to an event or situation. They felt such behaviour and communication made their pets feel more human. Drawing upon this parallel to human-pet interactions, designers designing for anthropomorphism can strive to add occasional randomness and ambiguity in agent behaviour to induce curiosity in users [25]. Enabling users to link the cause

for the 'out of the ordinary behavior' to associated events, additionally serves as a channel for the agent to obliquely interact with users.

Reward for positive interactions and conversely punishment for adverse interactions with the agent induces animism in users.
Inquiries drawing upon human-plant and human-pet interactions revealed that users felt rewarded and joyful when their pets or plants responded positively to their care. Conversely, users also felt guilty when the plants and pets reacted negatively to neglect or adverse interactions. For example, users felt joyful when plants bloomed under their care and guilty when plants withered due to inattention. Participants considered this to be an essential trait of living beings.

"I would hate to have a dying plant in my house. Somehow, I would try to revive it because I feel responsible for it. I would try all sorts of things, before discarding the plant, to see one tiny new leaf coming out. It gives such happiness." - P4

Positive and negative interactions from users should elicit appropriate responses from the agent; taking care of, or interacting with the agent ought to make the user feel rewarded while neglecting it ought to make them guilty.

"It could be silly, but there is a wooden swing in my apartment that I am somewhat attached to, and I feel that it misses me when I'm not there. When I think of home when I'm traveling, along with my family, possibly more than my family, I start thinking of this swing whenever I feel nostalgic." - P4

The above statement, in particular, is an example of an opportunity interaction designers can utilize for inducing animism. For example, designing feedback that manifests the swing's joy upon interaction and its sorrow upon being neglected for prolonged periods, can considerably increase the animistic quality of the swing.

Anthropomorphic agents must indicate privacy palpably and must consistently uphold user trust concerning privacy-related matters.
While technically not in the same domain as anthropomorphism, privacy is of significant concern to users. A majority of the users indicated that they were worried whether an anthropomorphic agent would monitor their behaviour and share private data without their consent or that somebody else would be able to control or manipulate the agent and cause them harm. Such fears are justified as there have been numerous cases where services and products obtained and shared private data without user consent.

"I would be more comfortable with interacting more with Alexa/Siri and the idea of a more intelligent Alexa/Siri if it was just between me and Alexa/Siri. If I know for sure that there is no way anybody else can manipulate the software or the artificial intelligence or the controls of the artificial intelligence, except me." - P3

Privacy concerns influence user trust in agents and therefore are significantly important when designing those agents and interactions. Drawing upon parallels with human-pet and human-plant interactions again, users felt comfortable sharing secrets with plants and pets because they knew that those plants and pets were physically incapable of revealing those secrets. Similarly, in human-human interactions, users would only reveal secrets to people who earned their trust. Thus, user trust is a quality that interaction designers need to assume as unearned.

Since no amount of assurance can ever fully allay user suspicion and fears, palpably indicating that agents either are incapable of sharing private data or cannot share it without user permission, is a means to start earning user trust. Agents must then strive to gradually gain user trust by consistently assuring and proving to their users that private data was not shared (at least not without permission). In cases of breached trust, the agent must strive to be contrite, to regain user trust.

Agents should invoke familiarity and security in users.
When questioned explicitly about objects that they tended to anthropomorphize, several users mentioned various things in their homes that they felt connected to and had a 'personality' of its own. These things varied (ranging from bicycles and cars to swings and guitars) and were given different levels of anthropomorphic qualities (names and quirks to moods and entire personalities). However, they all shared commonalities: they were all objects that users interacted with regularly and had shared experiences with, which is why the users felt attached to the object. They invoked a sense of comfort and familiarity among users.

Therefore, when designing anthropomorphic interactions and characteristics for agents, familiarity and affordances must be maintained. While this is true for interaction design and user experience in general, it is of particular importance to anthropomorphism and animism.

Use the functional and practical values of animistic and anthropomorphic agents to induce users to try them.
In the interviews, hypothetical scenarios relating to autonomous, animistic, and anthropomorphic environments were presented to participants to probe their receptivity to the concept. Most participants were enthusiastic or at least cautiously optimistic and open to the idea of a living house that can take care of itself and interact with them on a more personal level as evidenced by the following quotes -

"I would totally be open to the idea of a house that was capable of taking care of itself. That's where it is going anyways." - P3

"From the utilitarian perspective like it's definitely useful, like a smart house basically. I mean, we've already got a couple of those things in our home. So long as these things like security are tightly regulated." - P6

"I think if the house was entirely automated, I do not think I would feel very involved in it. If the house still required me to be involved in it, I think I would definitely be inclined to do so." - P7

In some cases, the participants were not optimistic about the idea, as seen in the following quote -

"I don't think such a house would make me feel good, because what I make about my room is what I do to it or, like what I inflict in it. I like to clean or take care of it." - P4

Some participants were even able to see new potential uses for such an entity, such as taking care of their pets when they are not at home. From such data, we can deduce that the functional and practical value of a living home appeals to users the most. Pragmatic features are necessary for the initial investment of time and attention from users in animistic or anthropomorphic agents, while subsequent investments require ludic qualities. Thus, applying a blend of anthropocentric and thing-centric design methodologies is essential to the design of animistic and anthropomorphic entities. Designing interactions and features from both perspectives can result in the creation of truly memorable experiences.

4.2   Prototyping Results

The prototyping phase resulted in the creation of several sensors and actuator artefacts which were deployed in a public lab space at a Swedish university. A narrative envisioning the space as an entity limited in its intelligence and capabilities, but still having experiential qualities, was chosen. The above created sensors were embedded into the space, to form the 'senses' and actuators the interactive 'appendages' of the space, similar to their organic counterparts in living beings. These sensor artefacts granted experiential qualities to the space, by functioning as the instruments through which the space experienced events occurring within in it and the actuator artefacts served as instruments and ways for the space to express itself and communicate with users.

The sensor and actuator artefacts developed during prototyping were both inspired by and drew parallels to many organic systems, such as eyes, skin, mouths, etc. etera, leading to an expansion of the narrative for development. Taking cues from Biomimetics, i.e. the imitation of the models, systems, and elements of nature to solve complex human problems [21, 22], it was possible to view the whole system as a metaphorical 'homunculus', with each artefact or subsystem communicating and co-operating, akin to how various organ systems in the human body communicate and co-operate. This anthropomorphic perspective in the design process itself can aid designers and developers in visualizing an abstract entity such as an anthropomorphic space and its subsystems. It also serves as a source of inspiration, making it easier to develop more artefacts and subsystems. However, the homunculus narrative is not presented to users and inhabitants of the space to avoid triggering fear and prejudice.

The narrative for inhabitants instead encourages them to view and treat the space akin to a young pet or being that is just learning to understand the world, in its way. A simplistic way to describe the system is - *"What if your room was a Tamagotchi (the digital pet)?"*.

The space utilizes multiple modalities of interaction to communicate with its inhabitants. Familiarity, inconspicuousness, serendipity, naturalness formed the cornerstones for designing the interfaces and their interactions. Objects and artefacts that are likely to be found in the space served as the basis for the interfaces. The technological aspects of these interfaces were kept as hidden as possible, to avoid prejudicing the inhabitants towards treating the object as a commodity. The emphasis is upon natural physical interaction with natural materials. This was deliberately done to invoke a sense of familiarity with the objects and the space itself, a principle taken from the interview recommendations (Figs. 1 and 2).

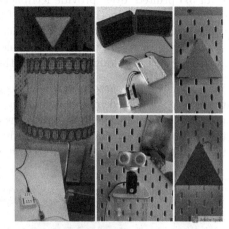

Fig. 1. Sensor artefacts   **Fig. 2.** Actuator artefacts

The following interfaces serve as a starting point -

- Surreptitiously placed mini speakers allowed the space to communicate through sounds. Cartoonish sounds reminiscent of small creatures, were purposely used to both lower fear and prime the inhabitants towards thinking that the space needs care. The modality of speech, offered by interfaces such as smart voice assistants, was purposely avoided to avoid triggering the fear and discomfort in inhabitants, as evidenced by the interviews. Sounds are triggered randomly, in response to events occurring in the space, the space's moods, and interactions with space's other interfaces.
- Haptic feedback, in the form of vibrations and embedded into soft surfaces such as carpets and knitted material, served to both emphasize the audio interface and act as a more persistent channel for communication. Triggered in response to actions such as stroking and pressing the surface, the intensity and frequency of vibrations vary as the strength of the 'emotions' felt by the room and feedback given.
- Visual feedback using LED lights that changed color and intensity depending on the space's mood and as feedback to interactions. Additionally, a lamp already installed in the area also serves as a channel for communication, to mitigate the inhabitants' tendency to localize the anthropomorphic entity to just the interfaces. Similar to the audio and haptic feedback, visual feedback also triggered in response to events and interactions occurring in the space and the space's moods.

- Motion and ultrasonic sensors allowed the use of physical presence as an interaction modality. They allowed for the response to and awareness of inhabitants in the space's vicinity. Additionally, a servo motor actuator with a set of 3D printed 'eyes' provide feedback through rotational movement.
- Electrically conductive threads and fabrics (along with polymers such as Velostat) when sewn or knitted into other fabrics allowed for the creation of pressure and touch sensors. These enabled interactivity to physical actions such as touching, stroking and pressing these soft surfaces.

Sensors were created using Arduino programming kits and the different systems were connected to each other via a local area network using the MQTT protocol [32], with an MQTT broker running on a Raspberry Pi. This allowed the sensors to relay information to other devices by publishing to the relevant topic, to which other devices were subscribed to (Fig. 3).

Fig. 3. Deployment of various artefacts in the studio space. Yellow indicates actuators while Blue indicates sensors (Color figure online)

From the early outset of this study, the idea of individuality was an essential trait in animistic and anthropomorphic agents. To this effect, how an animistic space would utilize the interactions mentioned above to react to various events, was to differ amongst one another. No two spaces would ever react in the same way to the same stimuli. As a result of the analysis of the interviews and related research [31], an element of randomness was introduced into these interactions. User interactions would generally trigger feedback, but not all the time. This was complemented with the narrative that the space better liked users to which it gave feedback.

A few interactions created for the space were as follows -

- Changing and saying the colour of the light actuators depending on the 'mood' of the space.
- Occasional deep breathing and sighing through sounds and fading lights.

– Rotating the 'eyes' to look at the area where motion was detected.
– Turning on the reading lamp when users sat on the sofa where the ultrasonic sensor was placed.
– Random giggling and laughter sounds
– A practical joke intended to reflect a playful and immature personality, wherein the space would randomly make rude farting noise when a user sat on the red chair and start to laugh.
– Gentle sighing when users stroked the soft surfaces such as the carpet or knitted fabric sensor.

Some of the interactions such as turning on the reading lamp also had practical uses as well (in line with interview results), since users generally sat down at that particular place to read. Due to the way they were installed, all the sensors and actuators could be also utilised in a manner similar to how they are normally used in a 'smart space' context as well, such as being used to detect presence or absence, to turn on/off lights, etc. Such interactions, as well as future artefacts would be introduced to the space with the narrative that the space has 'learnt' new skills, greatly increasing the scalability and functionality of the system.

4.3   Focus Group Results

The focus group results are presented as a chronological record of events which generate several observations and insights about how users behave in and feel about the space. These observations yielded several pointers on how to progress the study and corroborated the insights and theories used to develop the prototype space. The observations are presented in **bold**, followed by *quotes* from participants to support them. Citations of the participants are shown together with an identifier FGPn, where n is a number that represents each participant.

The discussion started with general questions similar to the initial interviews, that explored whether the participants could ever consider an entity such as a space or room to be alive. The participants initially chose to remain seated but they were quick to notice the random interactions that space made, such as the lights changing colour, random laughing, giggling and breathing sounds. After a few such events, the participants began asking why the space was behaving in such a fashion. The interviewer repeated the rhetoric that they did not know and encouraged the participants themselves to explore and figure out the reason for the space's behaviour. After this, the participants became more curious about investigating and understanding the room, which brings us to the first observation -

The prototype space instigates curiosity amongst the inhabitants to investigate and explore the space further.
This was an observation that all participants agreed upon. The interactions and feedback of the space greatly stimulated their curiosity to explore the prototype space, which is something they say they would not have done otherwise as evidenced by the following quote -

"I think we have been kind of like... touching different things, just to sort of see if it might cause the room to react." - FGP 6

As participants began to explore the room, they began to uncover some of the interactions with feedback, such as the 'head' rotating to look at the entrance due to a motion sensor detected event and some random events such as sighing or deep breathing sounds and the lights dimming in response. Whenever such events occurred and occupied the participants' attention, the interviewer would ask the participants why they thought the space was behaving in such a fashion. This leads to the second observation -

Participants create their interpretations of the space based on how they perceive the interaction.
Participants sometimes created their own stories and assumptions about the room, even though they were not told anything about the space, as seen in the following quote -

"Even now, for quite some time you've been pretty quiet. And now he just sighed massively and the lights went off. That was sort of interacting to us having a more or no serious conversation. I feel like because we were talking about how we don't want it to interrupt it kind of did that." - FGP 6

Continuing with the discussion, the participants were asked how they felt about such an interactive space and how they would feel if the space could talk or if they were able to talk to the space through voice assistants such as Alexa or Siri or if the space had entities that were moving autonomously in it, such as Roomba vacuum cleaners. This brings us to the next observation -

The prototype space feels like a novel form of interaction.
Participants reported that the space felt like a novel form of interaction different from other types of ambient computing or voice assistants. When asked about introducing moving artefacts and voice assistants such as Alexa or Siri into the space, participants felt that it would detract from the experience currently provided. They felt that such interactions were separate from the level of interactivity offered by the space, as heard from the following quote -

"This has a different kind of feel to it... It feels more subtle and in the background that gives a cozy feel... Moving objects would take away from that." - FGP 6

While the discussion was ongoing, the space would continue to perform random activities and interactions such as making noises and changing light colours. Over time, this began to have effects on the participants as seen in the following observation -

Randomness needs to be balanced.
Participants felt that the randomness of the interactions instigated their curiosity to investigate why the space did a particular action. However, at the same time, participants said that they lost interest if they could not discover a reason for feedback, or if they began to feel that the interaction was too random, as mentioned in the following quote -

"It's like a fine line. If it's super responsive like when you move there, it turns blue or you do something like that, orange. But then if it feels a bit too random, then you'll begin to be like, oh it's just random and that makes it boring." - FGP 2

This also brought the discussion to the topic of annoyances and frustrations, where the participants had some insights

Adaptability was required to prevent interactions from being annoying.
Participants felt that it was important that the space understands their current moods and feelings and adapt its feedback accordingly, to prevent them from getting frustrated with it, as exemplified in the following quote

"...it has to be reactionary. So if you're not in a good mood, then maybe it does cause quiet. It doesn't interact with you too much. Whereas when you're in a good mood or you're waking up for breakfast and you want good music and things like that." - FGP 3

A public or multi-user space has different people who engage with it, each having their own likes and dislikes. So, what is fun and interesting to one person need not be so to another and the space could perhaps behave differently to different users, allowing for different interactions for the same stimulus but different users. A similar parallel can be drawn in the pet analogy, wherein pets such as cats or dogs engage differently with different people depending how they perceive that person.

Exploring the topic of annoyances concerning the space, also brought the discussion to fears and discomfort. The following observation was noted -

Participants felt uncomfortable when an interaction was too human-like.
Interactions that were considered too human-like by the participants, such as the sighing and colour change sounds, made them feel uncomfortable as they did not expect an entity such as a space to behave like a human.

"I don't know, it's too much trying to imitate a human. And, like, at the same time, obviously not a human. Well, I would relate more to it if it was more non-human?" - FGP 1

Making something life-like also runs the risk of making it more human-like as well. This can trigger discomfort in users due to cognitive dissonance. The discomfort so triggered, can even become fear, depending on the user's prior prejudices and perspectives.

In addition to such fears, fears relating to privacy were also brought up in the discussion and yielded the following observation -

Privacy concerns were not considered of significant importance as long as the data remained localised.
Participants did not immediately bring up any privacy concerns with such an environment, but mentioned that they would prefer data collected to be localised.

"I would say like, I need my data to be localised; the data that you collected should not go beyond the house." - FGP 4

Towards the end of the discussion, the participants were asked about how they felt about having the different interfaces (sensor and actuator artefacts), they discovered, spread out in the room. This received the following feedback -

Spreading out and blending of artefacts adds character to the room. Participants felt that the artefacts blended well with the environment, which added to the space's immersive experience. The spacing and placement of the artefacts led to the participants attributing the reactions as a quality of the space itself and not localised to a particular object.

"I think what brings out that this room has this personality is maybe that these elements are placed in different places of the room... so it's not like in one spot. But here you have something to see and it looks like eyes, but there you have a voice." - FGP 5

At the end of the scripted discussion, the participants were debriefed about the purpose of the focus group. They also felt more comfortable wandering about and interacting with the space afterwards, mentioning that they thought it might be impolite to do so, during the discussion. It is also worth mentioning that the participants did not discover all possible interactions with the room. The haptic cloth interface and its vibrations were not discovered. This may have been because the created artefact was too small and inconspicuous to show its affordance. The cushion and associated laughter sound was also not discovered by the participants and was demonstrated at the end by the interviewer.

5   Discussion

By involving users in as many stages of the design process as possible, and by creating a prototype space, we gained insights on how to utilise animistic design principles in spatial interaction design. We also address the issues and criticisms levied on animism and anthropomorphism in design and discuss on how to utilise this in more broader contexts of behaviour studies, behaviour change, affective computing and so on.

What are the main takeaways from the study?
As an exploratory study, our results provide an indication of how users would tend to react to a space that is self aware and the idea of a self-aware space intrigues users as much as it frightens them. The creation of the prototype space and the observation we obtained from observing users in it, provide both a foundation and areas of interest for future studies. The positive aspects identified by users can turn out to become principles that guide the creation of future spaces while the issues pointed out or criticisms that users levied upon the space, provide critical points to ponder on. Could issues such as annoyances from certain interactions or being adaptable to different users provide critical spaces for both the user and space to learn from each other? It also points the

direction for future development of the space, such as both the space and users requiring new interactions to be able to both communicate their frustrations with each other. Coupling randomness with animistic narratives can lead to users behaving differently to interactions that did not occur when stimuli was provided to the space by the user, such as sitting on the chair and not having the space play the prank. Instead of perceiving such an interaction as a failure on the part of the space, users were curious as to why the space did not react to them. These add additional dimensions to interactions in physical systems, outside of the traditional stimulus and response cycle.

Expanding the paradigm of Affective and ubiquitous computing?
Affective computing is often pursued from anthropocentric perspectives, i.e. what can the computer or entity do, if it understands the user's emotions? In this study, we chose to design from the opposite perspective, a thing-centred perspective, i.e. what can the user(s) do if they understand the entity (in this case, the space's) needs? Motivating users to pursue such a line of thought requires additional layers to be added in the design. Animism and anthropomorphism are compelling concepts that can help in achieving this. If users begin to consider the entity as alive, they could interact differently with it and be compelled to take care of it.

Expanding and extending the paradigm of animism to a larger entity such as a space, instead of localising it to single artefacts, opens up the design space and allows for the study of user behaviour which could result in new interactions and design strategies. In addition to using these observations for the creation of animistic spaces, these insights can also be taken as broader recommendations for designers aiming to stimulate empathy and emotion for various designed artefacts.

We argue that animistic characteristics and narratives open new design opportunities. It allows for products and entities to express themselves in new ways that do not need to be explicitly clear to users. Randomness and using environmental data to create new ways of expression could entice curiosity in users to understand the cause of the new behaviour/expression. By spending time with the space, users could slowly understand the cause for said new expression and react accordingly. This also has the side effect of organically prolonging novelty effects that encourage users to try new things [34]. Using strangeness to challenge usual thinking opens a critical space for users to interpret situations for themselves.

If users are able to engage more intimately with spaces and form bonds with them, they can also be a means to gain and increase user trust. A private space such as a room or home, is a very intimate environment. Although smart home technologies are becoming more commonplace, users are still hesitant to include or try them. Animistic and anthropomorphic narratives and features for homes, could provide more compelling reasons for users to try such products, especially if they were obtained with the view of 'helping the home become better' rather than from novelty or functional perspectives, in addition to potentially improving user confidence and trust in such systems, as shown by the study that showed increased levels of user confidence in cars with anthropomorphic characteristics [9].

Future Work and expanding into broader contexts
The aim with this line of research is to investigate through more longitudinal studies in the future on whether emotional and intimate bonds can be formed with animistic spaces and subsequently whether those bonds can be used in creating design strategies for various other domains such as behaviour change, mental health and sustainability. By reframing goals as requirements necessary to the well-being of the space, an entity which its user cares for and takes care of, users could be better motivated to achieve them. Since, home spaces are already being endowed with a great deal of sensing technologies, such as in the smart grid [38], adding a layer of animism and reframing electricity consumption as not a user goal but a requirement for the well-being of the house can potentially help users engage more with such systems, in addition to overcoming their fear and biases towards such sensing technologies. In extension to this, allowing for collaboration and competition between different spaces, and observing how users behave in such scenarios is also a line of research worth pursuing. From a well-being perspective, the Covid-19 pandemic has put the focus on staying at home for a prolonged period of time, and the health issues that might follow from this. Spending time in a room that is 'alive' and that engages you in activities that benefits your health could be explored as future work.

6   Conclusion

This two-part study investigates the application of animism and anthropomorphism in interaction design and HCI, with particular emphasis on spatial interaction. Qualitative research uncovered various insights that designers can use when applying animism and anthropomorphism to their creations, to increase their functionality and emotional value. It also yielded a new perspective that bears merit for further investigation and research. One that designers can employ for inspiration and visualization when designing for complex interconnected systems. Finally, a prototype space with animistic and anthropomorphic qualities was created and evaluated with inhabitants. By opening up the design space, the prototype serves as a foundation and sandbox for future research not just into spatial interaction design, animism and anthropomorphism but also into other domains and concepts to which it can be linked, behavior change and mental health.

Acknowledgments. The authors would like to thank all the participants of the study, especially masters students at the university, where this study was undertaken as the master thesis of the first author. Their valuable contributions through participation, reviews and feedback were much appreciated. The authors would also like to thank all their fellow researchers who gave their feedback on the paper.

References

1. Airenti, G.: The development of anthropomorphism in interaction: intersubjectivity, imagination, and theory of mind. Front. Psychol. **9**, 2136 (2018). https://doi.org/10.3389/fpsyg.2018.02136
2. Złotowski, J., et al.: Anthropomorphism: opportunities and challenges in human-robot interaction. Int. J. Soc. Robot. **7**(3), 347–360 (2015)
3. Guthrie, S.E., Guthrie, S.: Faces in the Clouds: A New Theory of Religion. Oxford University Press on Demand (1995)
4. Picard, R.W.: Affective Computing. MIT Press, Cambridge (2000)
5. Norman, D.: The design of everyday things: Revised and, expanded Basic books (2013)
6. Borgmann, A.: Technology and the Character of Contemporary Life: A Philosophical Inquiry. University of Chicago Press, Chicago (1987)
7. Nam, T.-J., Kim, C.: Design by tangible stories: enriching interactive everyday products with ludic value. Int. J. Des. **5**(1), 85–98 (2011)
8. Huizinga, J.: Nature and significance of play as a cultural phenomenon (1955)
9. Waytz, A., Heafner, J., Epley, N.: The mind in the machine: anthropomorphism increases trust in an autonomous vehicle. J. Exp. Soc. Psychol. **52**, 113–117 (2014)
10. Bell, G., Blythe, M., Sengers, P.: Making by making strange: defamiliarization and the design of domestic technologies. ACM Trans. Comput.-Hum. Interaction (TOCHI) **12**(2), 149–173 (2005)
11. Gaver, W.W., Beaver, F., Benford, S.: Ambiguity as a resource for design. Presented at the (2003)
12. Mori, M., MacDorman, K.F., Kageki, N.: The uncanny valley [from the field]. IEEE Robot. Autom. Mag. **19**(2), 98–100 (2012)
13. O'Keefe, B., et al.: A blended space for heritage storytelling. In: Proceedings of the 28th International BCS Human Computer Interaction Conference (HCI 2014) 28 (2014)
14. Benyon, D., Mival, O., Ayan, S.: Designing blended spaces. Presented at the (2012)
15. Egan, C., O'Dowd, A., Fyffe, N.: Hasten slowly: developing an interactive sustainability storytelling chair. Presented at the (2020)
16. Duffy, B.R.: Anthropomorphism and the social robot. Robot. Auton. Syst. **42**(3–4), 177–190 (2003)
17. Van Allen, P., et al.: AniThings: animism and heterogeneous multiplicity. In: CHI 2013 Extended Abstracts on Human Factors in Computing Systems, pp. 2247–2256 (2013)
18. Cila, N., et al.: Thing-centered narratives: a study of object personas. Presented at the (2015)
19. Seeger, A.-M., Pfeiffer, J., Heinzl, A.: When do we need a human? anthropomorphic design and trustworthiness of conversational agents. In: Proceedings of the Sixteenth Annual Pre-ICIS Workshop on HCI Research in MIS, AISeL, Seoul, Korea. vol. 10 (2017)
20. Pfeuffer, N., et al.: Anthropomorphic information systems. Bus. Inf. Syst. Eng. **61**(4), 523–533 (2019)
21. Bar-Cohen, Y.: Biomimetics: Biologically Inspired Technologies. CRC Press, Boca Raton (2005)

22. Kaufmann, M., Portmann, E.: Biomimetics in design-oriented information systems research. In: At the Vanguard of Design Science: First Impressions and Early Findings from Ongoing Research Research-in-Progress Papers and Poster Presentations from the 10th International Conference, DESRIST: Dublin, Ireland, 20–22 May. DESRIST 2015, 2015 (2015)

23. Al Moubayed, S., Beskow, J., Skantze, G., Granström, B.: Furhat: a back-projected human-like robot head for multiparty human-machine interaction. In: Esposito, A., Esposito, A.M., Vinciarelli, A., Hoffmann, R., Müller, V.C. (eds.) Cognitive Behavioural Systems. LNCS, vol. 7403, pp. 114–130. Springer, Heidelberg (2012). https://doi.org/10.1007/978-3-642-34584-5_9

24. Salles, A., Evers, K., Farisco, M.: Anthropomorphism in AI. AJOB Neurosci. 11(2), 88–95 (2020)

25. Row, Y.-K., Nam, T.-J.: CAMY: applying a pet dog analogy to everyday ubicomp products. Presented at the (2014)

26. Moussawi, S., Koufaris, M., Benbunan-Fich, R.: How perceptions of intelligence and anthropomorphism affect adoption of personal intelligent agents. Electronic Markets, 1–22 (2020)

27. Axelrod, L., Hone, K.: E-motional advantage: performance and satisfaction gains with affective computing. In: CHI 2005 Extended Abstracts on Human Factors. Computing Systems (2005)

28. Bickmore, T.W., Picard, R.W.: Towards caring machines. In: CHI 2004 Extended Abstracts on Human Factors in Computing Systems (2004)

29. Nass, C., Moon, Y.: Machines and mindlessness: social responses to computers. J. Soc. Issues 56(1), 81–103 (2000)

30. Chen, C., et al.: Reverse engineering psychologically valid facial expressions of emotion into social robots. In: 2018 13th IEEE International Conference on Automatic Face and Gesture Recognition (FG 2018). IEEE (2018)

31. Leong, T.W., Vetere, F., Howard, S.: Randomness as a resource for design. Presented at the (2006)

32. Hunkeler, U., Truong, H.L., Stanford-Clark, A.: MQTT-S—A publish/subscribe protocol for Wireless Sensor Networks. Presented at the (2008)

33. Shneiderman, B.: 7, 1 A nonanthropomorphic style guide: overcoming the Humpty Dumpty syndrome. Sparks of innovation in human-computer interaction (1993) 331 (1993)

34. Koch, M., et al.: The novelty effect in large display deployments-Experiences and lessons-learned for evaluating prototypes. Presented at the (2018)

35. Crabtree, A., et al.: Finding a Place for UbiComp in the Home. Springer, Heidelberg (2003)

36. Sundar, S.S., Dou, X., Lee, S.: Communicating in a ubicomp world: interaction rules for guiding design of mobile interfaces. In: Kotzé, P., Marsden, G., Lindgaard, G., Wesson, J., Winckler, M. (eds.) INTERACT 2013. LNCS, vol. 8118, pp. 730–747. Springer, Heidelberg (2013). https://doi.org/10.1007/978-3-642-40480-1_51

37. Greenberg, S.: Opportunities for proxemic interactions in ubicomp (keynote). In: Campos, P., Graham, N., Jorge, J., Nunes, N., Palanque, P., Winckler, M. (eds.) INTERACT 2011. LNCS, vol. 6946, pp. 3–10. Springer, Heidelberg (2011). https://doi.org/10.1007/978-3-642-23774-4_3

38. Siano, P.: Demand response and smart grids-a survey. Renew. Sustain. Energy Rev. 30, 461–478 (2014)

39. Gavin, H.: Thematic analysis. Understanding research methods and statistics in psychology, 273–282 (2008)

40. Maedche, A., et al.: Advanced user assistance systems. Bus. Inf. Syst. Eng. **58**(5), 367–370 (2016)
41. Pelikan, H.R.M., Broth, M., Keevallik, L.: "Are you sad, Cozmo?" How humans make sense of a home robot's emotion displays. Presented at the (2020)
42. Corbin, J., Strauss, A.: Techniques and procedures for developing grounded theory. Sage publications, Basics of qualitative research (2014)
43. Weiser, M.: The computer for the 21st century. Sci. Am. **265**(3), 94–105 (1991)

Assistive Technology for Cognition and Neurodevelopmental Disorders

AI-Based Clinical Decision Support Tool on Mobile Devices for Neurodegenerative Diseases

Annamaria Demarinis Loiotile[1] , Vincenzo Dentamaro[2] , Paolo Giglio[2] ,
and Donato Impedovo[3]([⊠])

[1] Dipartimento di Ingegneria Elettrica e dell'informazione, Politecnico di Bari, Via Orabona 4,
70126 Bari, Italy
[2] Department of Computer Science, Università degli Studi di Bari "Aldo Moro", Via Orabona 4,
70126 Bari, Italy
[3] Digital Innovation S.R.L, Via Orabona 4, 70126 Bari, Italy
donato.impedovo@uniba.it

Abstract. Recently, the role of AI in the development of eHealth is becoming increasingly ambitious since AI is allowing the development of whole new healthcare areas. In many cases, AI offers the possibility to support patient screening and monitoring through low-cost, non-invasive tests. One of the most relevant sectors in which a great contribution from AI is expected is that of neurodegenerative diseases, which represent one of the most important pathologies in Western countries with very serious follow up not only clinical, but also social and economic.

In this context, AI certainly represents an indispensable tool for effectively addressing aspects related to early diagnosis but also to monitoring patients suffering from various neurodegenerative diseases. To achieve these results, AI tools must be made available in test applications on mobile devices that are also easy to use by a large part of the population. In this sense, the aspects related to human-machine interaction are of paramount relevance for the diffusion of these solutions.

This article presents a mobile device application based on artificial intelligence tools for the early diagnosis and monitoring of patients suffering from neurodegenerative diseases and illustrates the results of specific usability tests that highlight the strengths but also the limitations in the iteration with application users. Some concluding remarks are highlighted to face the actual limitations of the proposed solution.

Keywords: Human-computer interaction · Artificial intelligence · Neurodegenerative disease · Mobile applications

1 Introduction

AI is assuming an even more relevant role for the Digital Transitions for a wide range of application area, such as cybersecurity [1], urban safety [2], sustainable mobility [3] and higher education [4].

© IFIP International Federation for Information Processing 2021
Published by Springer Nature Switzerland AG 2021
C. Ardito et al. (Eds.): INTERACT 2021, LNCS 12932, pp. 139–148, 2021.
https://doi.org/10.1007/978-3-030-85623-6_10

In Healthcare 4.0 domain, the increasing frequency with which both patients and health professionals can access and use connected devices for clinical care and for monitoring patients has created abundant opportunities to deliver health and wellness services [5]. Recently, the role of AI in the development of eHealth is becoming more and more ambitious since AI is allowing the development of whole new healthcare areas. In many cases, AI offers the possibility to support patient screening and monitoring through low-cost, non-invasive tests [6]. One of the most relevant sectors in which a great contribution from AI is expected is that of neurodegenerative diseases, which represent one of the most important pathologies in Western countries with very serious follow up not only clinical, but also social and economic.

In this context, AI certainly represents an indispensable tool for effectively addressing aspects related to early diagnosis but also to monitoring patients suffering from various neurodegenerative diseases. To achieve these results, AI tools must be made available in test applications on mobile devices that are also easy to use by a large part of the population. In this sense, the aspects related to human-machine interaction are of paramount relevance for the diffusion of these solutions.

Preemptively diagnosing a form of neurodegeneration is critical to improving the patient's quality of life [7, 8].

This article presents a mobile device application based on artificial intelligence tools for the early diagnosis and monitoring of patients suffering from neurodegenerative diseases. In particular, the article illustrates the smartphone version of some of the pen and paper tasks used by neurologists, psychologists and so on, for monitoring and diagnosis of neuro-muscular degenerative diseases.

The tests considered refer to different cognitive areas and are based on the patient's abilities in constructive praxis, concentration and language. They aim to facilitate and reduce the time of diagnosis, for patients, their relatives and caregivers.

2   Related Work

2.1   Dementia

Dementia is defined as a syndrome of acquired and persistent impairment in cognition and intellectual functioning. The most common cause of dementia is Alzheimer's disease (AD) and the most common dementia syndrome is Alzheimer dementia (AD) [9], which is characterized by a major impairment of episodic memory, while in other types of dementia, other domains are more primarily affected, such as executive functioning in vascular dementia (VaD). Dementia can also develop in people with Parkinson's disease, differing in the relationship between motor and cognitive impairment [10].

Dementia affects memory, thinking, orientation, comprehension, calculation, learning ability, language, and judgment. Consciousness is not impaired. Disorders of cognitive function are commonly accompanied, sometimes preceded, by impairment of emotional control, social behavior, or motivation, which interfere with a person's normal relational and work life.

Doctors diagnose dementia when one or more cognitive functions have been impaired at a significant level. The specific symptoms experienced by a person with dementia depend on the area of the brain that is damaged.

It is increasingly recognized that mixed cases of dementia are commonly encountered, especially in elderly. It is less common for people under age 65 to develop dementia, and in this case, it is referred to as "early-onset dementia." More challenging, however, is distinguishing dementia from more subtle patterns of cognitive impairment that do not fit into standard definitions of dementia but may represent a "pre-clinical" state of dementia, called "mild cognitive impairment" syndrome [11].

Early detection of symptoms is important, as some causes can be treated. In many cases, a person's specific type of dementia may not be confirmed until the person is dead, and the brain is examined [12].

A medical evaluation for dementia generally includes:

- **Medical history**: typical questions generally include taking medications that could cause or worsen a symptom, how and when symptoms occurred, and whether or not there is dementia in the family.
- **Physical exam**: measuring blood pressure and other vital signs can help detect conditions that could cause a dementia state.
- **Neurological testing**: assessing reflexes, cognitive function, balance and sensory response helps identify symptoms early for a more accurate diagnosis.

2.2 Assessment of Cognitive Functioning

Within the neurological testing, there are cognitive tests which are used to assess memory, problem solving, language skills, math skills, and other abilities related to mental functioning. The Mini-Mental State Examination (MMSE) is one of the most frequently used and widely studied with regard to precision and accuracy. A score below 23 has generally been associated with the presence of cognitive impairment [13]. The best screening exam for memory is a short-term memory test: patients with dementia are unable to perform this exam. Neuropsychological testing should be performed when the history and mental status tests performed by the patient are inconclusive. In addition, recent studies point out that the sensitivity of the MMSE is lower when a patient in the early stages of dementia is tested [13].

Another pen and pencil set of tests used by neurologists is the Milan Overall Dementia Assessment (MODA). It is composed by three sections: behavioral and two section of pen and paper testing [14].

This work is organized as follows: Sect. 2 shows the protocol developed, Sect. 3 describes the tasks selected to be implemented as mobile version of the pen and paper. Section 4 shows the SUS usability test results while Sect. 5 sketches conclusions and future remarks.

3 Acquisition Protocol

This protocol can be divided mainly into three phases: an initial screening, a battery of standard cognitive and functional tests and some more relevant graphic and vocal tasks extracted from the medical literature [15].

Initial screening allows the examiner to collect all personal information about the patient, including patient data, caregiver interview, and preliminary testing.

The details of the patient whose cognitive impairment is to be assessed are collected, such as: first name, last name, place of birth, date of birth, social security number, sex, schooling, medications taken and type of dementia. These are sensitive personal data that must be kept confidential; moreover, their treatment, according to the law in force, must be authorized by the user of the test. For this reason, this new mobile version saves the multimedia files (voice and screenshots of tasks) of the patient's exam in a folder with a unique name, to distinguish it from other exams and different from the patient's generalities, to guarantee confidentiality.

Health care providers (caregivers) are involved in gathering information about the patient. Their role is critical to the accuracy of the test outcome. The questions they are asked are regarding the most common symptoms of dementia such as: difficulty in remembering recent conversations; inability to respond to trivial problems; lack of respect for social behavioral rules; tendency to get lost in familiar places, etc.

If the patient, according to the caregiver, would result negative to all the questions indicated, the test would have no reason to continue, because it results a healthy person. If there would be a positive response to at least one question, the test should continue.

4 Implemented Tasks

In this section the tasks that are possible to implement as a smartphone app are discussed. The selection of these tasks is performed, on one hand, keeping in mind the constraints of the device, a smartphone with Android operating system and a touch screen support, and the difficulty of elderly people in approaching the mobile technology. On the other hand, the fact that an app is easily accessible by the majority of people and no special device (Wacom tablet with pen and software) is necessary, would increase the number of people using it and decrease the entry barriers.

Particular attention is dedicated on the design of positive experiences when products and services with AI are developed, using a human-centered design approach [5].

An EC Expert Group defined the potential as well as the need for designing AI systems human-centered, including the ethically and trustworthy development of AI. The Group stated that "AI is not an end in itself, but rather a promising means of enhancing individual and societal well-being and bringing progress and innovation" [16]. This commitment indicates that human-centered approaches have a pivotal role in the development and use of AI technology for the well-being of people [17].

From a Human Computer Interaction perspective, it has been decided to analyze people (mostly elderly) using a smartphone. It has been noticed that elderly tend to bring the device closer to their eyes, they tend to touch the screen several times waiting for feedback, too complex interfaces increase the abandonment of using the app so also interfaces that are too colorful or with low contraction contribute to the abandonment.

Thus, it has been decided to focus on tasks that are feasible given the small screen space of a smartphone.

4.1 Preliminary Tests

Prior to testing, the patient undergoes a series of preliminary tests to ensure that the examinee becomes familiar with the device and application.

They are asked to perform some preliminary tests such as:

- repeating the word "HELLO" aloud;
- connecting two horizontal dots with a straight line;
- connecting two vertical dots with a straight line.

4.2 Attention Matrix

Attention matrix test is a very important test based on an attention task. The patient is shown two matrices and asked to cross out, as quickly as possible, the target numbers. The first two lines, performed by the operator who is reviewing the test, are rehearsal and are used to show the patient how to perform the task.

In Fig. 1, the user is asked to cross all the "6" numbers. A second attention matrix task is to cross 2 numbers at same time: number "2" and "8" at same time.

```
(A) 2 6 5 9 4 5 2
(B) 4 1 2 5 1 3 0
I   0 6 7 6 8 9 8
II  9 0 4 3 0 1 9
III 7 9 5 3 7 2 2
IV  7 3 7 6 2 5 8
```

Fig. 1. Attention Matrix where user is asked to cross one single number, in this case "6"

4.3 Dots Connect

There are several dot linking tasks in the test. They allow the clinician to assess the trait and strategy adopted by the patient. The tasks are listed below:

- Connect 4 points;
- Connect points in numerical order;
- Connect points in alphabetical order.

4.4 Geometrical Figure Copying Task

The patient is asked to copy the figure shown. It is usually asked to copy a square or a rectangular figure given the constraints of the device.

4.5 Copy and Trace of Archimedes' Spiral

The Archimedes spiral is one of the most popular handwriting exercises. In fact, the spiral drawing has frequently been used for motor performance assessment in various movement disorders, particularly Parkinsonians. In these tests, patients are asked to copy an Archimedes spiral and in a second moment to trace it. The chosen Archimede' spiral is the simpler one with only 3 convolving curves, as shown in Fig. 2.

Fig. 2. Archimede' spiral copying (left) and tracing (right)

4.6 "l" and "e" Sequence

The patterns of the cursive letters "l" and "e" are another common exercise in handwriting assessment, this is because such letters are easy to write recurrently and continuously; moreover, their use minimizes the processes of linguistic comprehension. User is asked to draw with one finger three times "le", as shown in Fig. 3:

Fig. 3. "le le" drawing task

4.7 Repeat the Indicated Word Aloud

Speech impairment is a disorder that prevents patients from expressing and/or understanding words. It can result from neuro-muscular alterations. Thus, gradual loss of language is a symptom indicative of Alzheimer's and Parkinson's disease.

Nuances in tone of voice, as well as hand gestures or facial expressions, can be critical in helping to determine the meaning behind the words spoken. In Parkinson's disease, the voice is monotone, raspy, and characterized by low volume; in addition, reduced facial expressions also contribute to greater difficulty in managing the vocal tract. In specific terms, there is a 40% reduction in loudness (sound perception).

For this reason, it has been decided to allow the patient to repeat some very simple words and record the voice, to allow more experienced people to analyze it. The words are administered by visual feedback or by listening to audio.

4.8 Description of the Content of an Image

This task is very similar to the previous one, but the patient is asked to look carefully at a picture and repeat the content orally aloud. The user interface (UI) developed is presented in Fig. 4.

Fig. 4. The UI developed for capturing the aloud description of the image.

5 Usability Tests

Prior to beginning actual data acquisition, a usability assessment was performed, adopting two methodologies:

- SUS (System usability Scale) questionnaire conducted on five young adults;
- Thinking aloud protocol conducted on five healthy older people.

More experiments are of course in progress and data acquisition is still ongoing. In addition, it is important to mention that for both evaluation criteria, users were required to perform the tasks (speech and drawing) without any prior knowledge of the application, the only way to become familiar with the system being the preliminary trials.

The SUS questionnaire is structured by the ten following items:

1. I think I would like to use this [tool] frequently.
2. I find the [tool] unnecessarily complex.
3. The [tool] is easy to use.
4. I think I would need support from a technical person to use this [tool].
5. I find that the various functions of this [tool] were well integrated.
6. I think there is too much inconsistency in this [tool].
7. I imagine that most people would learn to use this [tool] very quickly.
8. I find the [tool] very cumbersome to use.
9. I feel very confident using the [tool].
10. I need to learn a lot of things before I could start this [tool].

The SUS results are presented in Table 1. The overall score is 97 out of 100, which is very high but, because of limited number of people and reflecting only a young population, it is not representative.

Table 1. SUS test results

Subject	Age	Job	Data test	Informatic skill	Score
1	24	Unemployed	30/03/2021	very Good	97,5
2	23	Policeman	02/04/2021	Good	95
3	21	Student	01/01/2021	Good	95
4	25	Student	27/03/2021	Very Good	100
5	24	Healthcare professional	26/03/2021	Very Good	100

The SUS test is less suitable for elderly people, as they are less familiar with technological equipment. For this reason, an assessment based on thinking aloud was adopted only for the sample of elderly people.

The user is encouraged to act and verbalize any thoughts that come to mind while performing the assigned tasks.

The results in Table 2 showed that the users have a good familiarity with the system. The main problem encountered relates to the small screen size. Again, given the low amount of people, reasoning about usability is limited.

Table 2. Think aloud tests results

Subject	Age	Job	Data test	Informatic skill
1	78	Retiree (former public employee)	30/03/2021	Low
2	69	Housewife	02/04/2021	Low
3	73	Retiree (former engineer)	01/04/2021	Sufficient
4	68	Retiree (former teacher)	28/03/2021	Good
5	72	Retiree (former teacher)	01/04/2021	Very low

The aforementioned application is the ground basis for data acquisition, which in turn is represented by the results of the tests previously described. The tests outcomes represent the input to AI algorithms, specifically Convolutional Neural Networks, in order to provide an additional score in terms of probability and confidence of the plausible presence of neurodegenerative pathology [7]. This outcome shall not substitute the physician diagnosis, instead it shall be an additional and objective outcome that the physician could consider during a patient examination.

6   Conclusion and Future Remarks

In this work a mobile app has been developed with the aim to implement some of the most famous pen and pencil tests present in MMSE, IADL and other clinically vali-dated battery tests for assessment of neurodegenerative disease. Taking into account the human centered design approach, it has been decided which tasks to integrate with respect to the constraints of the device and the user. The choice allowed to develop a protocol that, given the widespread availability of smartphones, will be easier to access, at low cost and able to store a great amount of data to be clinically vali-dated in a second stage by merging all information collected. Extended data acquisition and preprocessing session are in progress.

In future, pattern recognition techniques could be applied to the patient data in order to verify that, even though the use of mobile devices, it will be possible to perform early diagnosis of neurodegenerative diseases.

References

1. Dentamaro V., Convertini N., Galantucci S., Giglio P., Impedovo D., Pirlo G.: Ensemble consensus: an unsupervised algorithm for anomaly detection in network security data. Itasec 2021 (2021)
2. Convertini, N., Dentamaro, V., Impedovo, D., Pirlo, G., Sarcinella, L.: A controlled benchmark of video violence detection techniques. Information 11(6), 321 (2020)
3. Nikitas, A., Michalakopoulou, K., Njoya, E.T., Karampatzakis, D.: Artificial intelligence, transport and the smart city: definitions and dimensions of a new mobility era. Sustainability 12, 2789 (2020). https://doi.org/10.3390/su12072789
4. Popenici, S.A.D., Kerr, S.: Exploring the impact of artificial intelligence on teaching and learning in higher education. Res. Pract. Technol. Enhanc. Learn. 12(1), 1–13 (2017). https://doi.org/10.1186/s41039-017-0062-8
5. Adarsha A.S.; Reader K.; Erban S.: AIS transactions on human-computer interaction, vol. 11, no. 4 special Issue on User Experience-driven Innovation User Experience, IoMT, and Healthcare, Article 6 (2019)
6. Dentamaro, V., Impedovo, D., Pirlo, G.: Sit-to-stand test for neurodegenerative diseases video classification. In: International Conference on Pattern Recognition and Artificial Intelligence, pp. 596–609. Springer, Cham, October 2020. https://doi.org/10.1007/978-3-030-59830-3_52
7. Impedovo, D., Pirlo, G.: Dynamic handwriting analysis for the assessment of neurodegenerative diseases: a pattern recognition perspective. IEEE Rev. Biomed. Eng. 12, 209–220 (2018)
8. De Stefano, C., Fontanella, F., Impedovo, D., Pirlo, G., di Freca, A.S.: Handwriting analysis to support neurodegenerative diseases diagnosis: a review. Pattern Recogn. Lett. 121, 37–45 (2019)
9. Olson, E.: Dementia and neurodegenerative diseases - Geriatric palliative care (2003)
10. Rosenblum, S., Samuel, M., Zlotnik, S., Erikh, I., Schlesinger, I.: Handwriting as an objective tool for Parkinson's disease diagnosis. J. Neurol. 260(9), 2357–2361 (2013)
11. Cummings, J.L., Benson, D.F.: Dementia: a clinical approach. Butterworth-Heinemann Medical (1992)
12. «What Is Dementia? Symptoms, Types, and Diagnosis». https://www.nia.nih.gov/health/what-dementia-symptoms-types-and-diagnosis
13. Cockrell, J.R., Folstein, M.F.: Mini-mental state examination. principles and practice of geriatric psychiatry, pp. 140–141 (2002)
14. Brazzelli, M., et al.: A neuropsychological instrument adding to the description of patients with suspected cortical dementia: the Milan overall dementia assessment. J. Neurol. Neurosurg. Psychiatry 57(12), 1510–1517 (1994)
15. Impedovo, D., Pirlo, G., Vessio, G., Angelillo, M.T.: A handwriting-based protocol for assessing neurodegenerative dementia. Cogn. Comput. 11(4), 576–586 (2019)

16. EC: Ethics guidelines for trustworthy AI (2019). Accessed from https://ec.europa.eu/digita lsingle-market/en/news/ethics-guidelines-trustworthy-ai
17. Auernhammer, J.: Human-centered AI: the role of human-centered design research in the development of AI. In: Boess, S., Cheung, M., Cain, R. (eds.) Synergy - DRS International Conference 2020, pp. 11–14. August, Held online (2020). https://doi.org/10.21606/drs.202 0.282

COBO: A Card-Based Toolkit for Co-Designing Smart Outdoor Experiences with People with Intellectual Disability

Giulia Cosentino[1]([✉]) [ID], Diego Morra[2] [ID], Mirko Gelsomini[2] [ID],
Maristella Matera[2] [ID], and Marco Mores[3]

[1] Norwegian University of Science and Technology, Trondheim, Norway
giulia.cosentino@ntnu.no
[2] Politecnico di Milano, Milano, Italy
{diego.morra,mirko.gelsomini,maristella.matera}@polimi.it
[3] Fraternità e Amicizia, Milano, Italy
marco.mores@fraternitaeamicizia.it

Abstract. This paper presents a co-design toolkit that aims to involve people with Intellectual Disability (ID) in the ideation of smart outdoor experiences. We conducted a series of workshops with young adults with ID and special-education professionals of a social-care center, to identify the physical and digital experience that could favour reflection and engagement of the addressed users, and empower them in solving daily-life challenges. Multiple refinements of iterative prototypes led to the design of an interactive toolkit, COBO, that integrates inspirational cards, interactive smart objects and multimedia contents to guide users during the conception of novel ideas. This paper illustrates the main insights of the conducted workshops and the design of COBO. It also reports on a preliminary evaluation we conducted to validate some design choices for the integration of physical and digital components within COBO.

Keywords: Co-design methods · Intellectual Disability · Inspirational cards · Tangible User Interfaces · Smart object design

1 Introduction

Intellectual Disability (ID), also defined as Disorder of Intellectual Development by the International Classification of Diseases (ICD-11 [1], code: 6A00), is a condition arising during the developmental period characterized by often co-occurring challenges in the cognitive, social, communicative, motor, behavioral and emotional spheres [8]. The disorder includes deficits in intellectual functioning (e.g., reasoning, problem solving, planning, abstract thinking, judgment, academic learning) and adaptive behavior (communication, social participation), affecting autonomy in everyday life [31].

© IFIP International Federation for Information Processing 2021
Published by Springer Nature Switzerland AG 2021
C. Ardito et al. (Eds.): INTERACT 2021, LNCS 12932, pp. 149–169, 2021.
https://doi.org/10.1007/978-3-030-85623-6_11

Several studies investigated the use of technology [27] to support people with ID in enhancing their cognitive, behavioral, social, and sensorimotor capabilities. Some works specifically focused on the development of "phygital" interfaces [6,13,36], a specific class of Tangible User Interfaces (TUIs) characterized by the combination of physical and digital contents. The use of such integrated paradigm for people with ID is regarded as a promising approach that is not meant to replace current treatments making use of manipulative interactions, but rather to enhance them with new meanings provided by virtual scenarios. Its potential is driven by theoretical approaches that posit learning as both an intellectual and a physical process. This implies performing tasks through the use of physical materials and emphasizes the formative role of embodiment - i.e., the way sensorimotor capacities enable interacting with the physical environment successfully - in the development of cognitive skills, such as mental imagery, memory, reasoning and problem solving [15,41]. The work presented in this paper explores the potential for young adults with ID of phygital interfaces, and in particular addresses the following research question: *Can a structured co-design method, based on the adoption of phygital material, empower individuals with ID to reflect on and ideate smart outdoor experiences?*

To our knowledge, these aspects have scarcely been addressed in previous studies. The literature mainly reports on the adoption of phygital interfaces as a means to support learning experiences. Our work focuses instead on using this technology to make people with ID protagonists in the ideation of smart outdoor experiences for themselves. These consist in orchestrations of smart devices and behaviors situated outdoors, which can occur in situations users might encounter in their everyday life [7].

For this purpose, our research proposes COBO (COllaborative BOard), a phygital toolkit that we designed by involving a group of young adults with ID and special-education professionals of a social-care center. Based on SNaP [22], a collaborative card-based board game addressing the co-design of smart objects by children, COBO introduces a paradigm that combines multimedia elements (images, animations, sounds) shown on a tablet device, and physical items (deck of cards, an interactive board, some smart objects) that are manipulated by the users. This material is used within a flow of structured activities that favours not only users' reflection, but also group discussion and collaboration. Overall, the users are guided in the ideation of smart interactive artefacts.

This paper illustrates the user-centered design of COBO. It also tries to outline insights related to the adoption of phygital interfaces for engaging people living with ID in the design of interactive technologies, and the potential of these technologies for empowering these users in the design of new interactive solutions. The results of the conducted studies are promising and let us think that, although further experimentation is needed, our work could pave the ground for the definition of methods for the co-design of interactive technologies with people with ID. The paper is organized as follows. After describing our research context in social-care centers and the rationale behind our work, Sect. 2 discusses relevant studies on tangible and phygital interfaces for people with ID. Section 3 describes the user-centered process that led to the design of the COBO toolkit; the main features of COBO are then illustrated in Sect. 4. Section 5 reports on a preliminary evaluation that allowed us to validate some design choices and Sect. 6 discusses the main insights gained throuhg the whole process of design and evaluation. Sections 7 finally draws our conclusions and future directions.

2   Rationale and Background

The research discussed in this paper was conducted in collaboration with young adults living with ID attending a social-care center, and their special-education professionals. Social-care centers, as the one our work is linked with, offer services that reinforce the development of skills such as the physical, cognitive, behavioral and social abilities needed to engage in daily life activities. They provide support for employment skills, self-care (e.g., grooming, dressing, feeding, bathing), leisure (e.g., knitting, playing games), cognitive stimulation.

We worked in close cooperation with Fraternità & Amicizia (F&A), an accredited private non-profit organization that manages social day-care centers in Milan (Italy), offering numerous services to people with ID. In F&A, as well as in most public and private social care institutions in Italy, guests usually work in groups with the intent to promote integration and well-being. Although these services are very valid, the needs of users with ID are often remarkably different and would require customized tools. Therefore, special-education professionals are always looking for innovative and accessible solutions whose use is transverse for different people with ID. Traditionally, most of the materials used are paper-based, yet, in the last decade, digital solutions such as smartphones, tablets and notebooks have been used to provide higher engagement and motivation [40].

In our activities conducted at F&A we wanted to adopt a *Participatory Design* (PD) approach to understand to which extent the use of co-design toolkits could empower users with ID to become protagonists in the design of technology. PD enables the design of products and applications directly with the final users and, more recently, even with users with ID [17] in order to truly develop accessible products. If planned properly, PD can lead to the development of a sense of empowerment and a feeling of competence, which bring beneficial effects on the individuals: they derive satisfaction and fun while feeling useful through their participation [16,29]. We therefore involved young adults with ID throughout the entire process of our toolkit design, with the assumption that their inclusion could have an impact not only on the quality of the final product but also on their experience. We decided to focus on physical interactive materials with the aim to increase their interest and offer, by means of a tangible indicator of progression, a sense of achievement and confidence. The choice of such material also derived from previous research experiences [18,21], which led us to focus our attention on phygital toolkits as a viable solution to involve those users in the ideation of technologies for themselves.

A dimension that characterizes our research is thus the interaction with *smart physical materials*, in the form of *Tangible User Interfaces* (TUIs). TUIs are claimed to be more natural and familiar than other types of interfaces [30], lowering the threshold of participation, enhancing e-accessibility and inclusion, and fostering independent exploratory, assistive and collaborative learning

[33,42]. Research on TUIs, and in particular on their applications for users with ID, is still at a preliminary stage, but initial studies with this population indicate positive effects on engagement, collaboration and initiative [4,5,42] when this technology is meant as a support to professionals in their education activities [11,13,20].

Within the context outlined above, our research aims to define a co-design method, supported by an interactive toolkit, acting on two different levels. At the level of *reflection*, it aims to identify how to lead users with ID to acquire the awareness on their everyday-life challenges, and to reflect on how technology can enhance the situations in which these challenges occur. Also, the mechanisms for smart-object ideation the users are exposed with can help them understand how the surrounding environments they live in, which very often are dense of smart technologies, work. At the level of *empowerment*, we also aim to identify methods that can make people with ID protagonists in the design of smart experiences that are inclusive and adapted to their needs.

2.1 Tangible User Interfaces for People with ID

Tangible User Interfaces (TUIs) enhance physical manipulation, physical-digital mappings, and multisensory exploration, providing richer sensory and learning experiences through the interweaving of computation and physical materials [5,6,13]. They extend the intellectual and emotional potential of interactive artifacts and integrate compelling and expressive aspects of traditional technologies with creative and valuable properties of physical objects [11]. Few empirical studies highlighted the benefits of TUIs for people with ID. Gelsomini et al. explored the use of a system called Reflex [18,21,35]. Inspired by a commercial system named Osmo [39], Reflex provided a number of game-based educational activities, involving the users' manipulation of multimedia contents and physical items. The study unveiled some benefits in the use of TUI-based methods for the development of cognitive and social skills.

Some other studies have shown promising effects of the use of TUIs with children with ID. Falcao [14] studied children with ID playing with different tangible artifacts (Augmented Objects, LightTable, Drum Machine, Sifteo cubes). The author points out the effectiveness of tangible interaction for exploratory learning and suggests that the most efficient gaming paradigm is the one with a clear mapping between specific physical objects and their meanings. A similar mapping characterizes the design of other prominent TUIs. Polipo is a 3D printed smart toy co-designed with special-education professionals, which provides various manipulatory affordances and offers feedbacks and rewards by means of lights, sounds, and music integrated in its body [37]. An exploratory study highlighted its benefits for children with ID in improving fine motor skills and encouraging children's communication with their educators. Similar benefits were also observed with Poma [3], a tangible user interface to improve social and cognitive skills of Sri-Lankan children with autism spectrum disorder (ASD); the authors also identified guidelines to design TUIs for children with ID. The Magic Room is then a more extensive example of physical/digital interaction in a smart space designed specifically for children with special needs, and installed at social-care centers and inclusive schools [2,9,19]. In the Magic Room, multiple connected physical objects and digitally-enhanced soft toys are used as interaction devices and are mapped to digital representations in wall or floor projections.

Recently, some works have proposed TUIs for introducing users with ID to coding. The Magic Cube [28] is an interactive physical toolkit for learning the basics of computer concepts, that allows children with ID to discover, through the interaction with a smart cube, the effects of available input and output. TapeBlocks [12] is then a toolkit for building circuits that aims to be a first point of contact with making for young adults with ID.

In summary, current research mainly highlights the benefits of TUIs for children [43]. With the exception of very few works (e.g., [12]), there is instead a lack of studies on the effects in adolescents and adults with ID. Our work advocates for a better understanding of the advantages and drawbacks of using TUIs with these users, and in particular aims to understand whether the use of TUIs can increase their engagement in co-design processes for technology ideation.

2.2 Co-design Toolkits

Card toolkits are often used in the generative phase of co-design methods to collaboratively build prototype artefacts [34]. They favour the engagement of non-experts in the design process and make it tangible and in some cases playful. In recent years, a number of toolkits have been proposed to help people ideating interactive applications. Tiles Inventor is a general-purpose card toolkit for engaging anybody in the ideation of IoT devices. Khandu [26] is then a card game that aims to bring design thinking to children. It is designed to help children in problem solving and ideation for different contexts. Khandu's approach, however, is non-technology oriented; children are guided to design and prototype ideas without technology. LocaLudo, instead, is a card-based game to design interactive architectures [24] where the outcome are ideas for local-communities. Güldenpfennig [23] created a co-design toolkit to provide senior users with early tangible experiences of their future systems and to iteratively convert them into the final implementations. Tango cards [10] then supports the design of tangible learning games. Overall, to our knowledge, there is a lack of work focusing on people with ID.

2.3 SNaP

Our work takes inspiration from SNaP (Smart Nature Protagonists), a collaborative board game for children aged between 10 and 14 years, designed for 2 to 4 players. As reported in Fig. 1, the main elements of the toolkit are three decks of cards and a game board that aim to inspire the design of augmented environment objects [22].

During the game-play, participants have the role of *Designers* while the game is facilitated by a moderator playing the role of a *City Mayor*. Each player has a mission to accomplish in order to make the elements of the outdoor environment interactive. The game structure recalls the most classic board games and consists of a game board with pawns, dice, coins. There are two types of cards: the

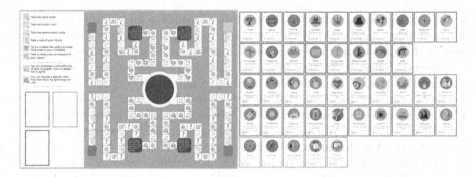

Fig. 1. SNaP toolkit: the game board (left) and the environment, input and output cards (right) [22].

mission cards and the *nature cards*. While the mission cards provide specific objectives that guide the design during the game (e.g., "make the park enjoyable for the visitors"), the nature cards are the central element of the game since they inspire the ideation of interactive artefacts. They consists of 18 *environment cards*, representing objects that can be found in parks or outdoor environments; 20 *input cards*, representing sensors and buttons that trigger an interaction; 5 *output Cards*, representing actuators that react to interactions through sensors and buttons.

In SNaP each player places a token in one corner of the board and tries to reach the central circle by throwing the dice and moving the token. Depending on the space the token reaches on the board, players may be entitled to get one or more cards from the Mayor's deck of cards, get coins to be used to buy further cards, try to combine the cards and take notes, exchange or buy cards. In particular, when *discussion boxes* are reached, the players have rounds of discussion: they have to present their ideas to the rest of the team and to the Mayor. Overall, the goal of the game is to collect and combine different nature cards. At the end, all players "win" the game collaboratively, by presenting to the team their idea inspired by the cards gained during the game-play. The game ends when each player has designed at least an interactive object fulfilling his/her mission.

Given the SNaP capability of facilitating reflection through common discussion, its focus on physical material (i.e., cards, board), and its regular scheme guiding the design activities, we wanted to investigate its potential with people with ID. Trying the SNaP game with the young adults of F&A was the first step that led us to identify the feasibility of adopting such a method, although some adaptations were needed. The following section will describe the process that we followed to frame the opportunities and the limits of SNaP and identify possible benefits deriving from the introduction of TUIs.

3   Design Process

We conducted two workshops involving four users with ID attending the F&A social-care services, supported by two special-education professionals. Through an online survey, we then involved 27 professionals working at F&A. The two professionals attending the workshops were also interviewed to discuss in more details some themes emerged during the workshops and through the survey.

Table 1. Users with ID participating to the Workshops (P1 to P4).

Code	Gender	Age	Diagnosis
P1	M	25	Mild Intellectual Disability, Autism, Chromosomic Disorder
P2	F	29	Mild Intellectual Disability, Learning Disability
P3	M	29	Mild Intellectual Disability, Genetic Syndrome
P4	M	30	Mild Intellectual Disability, Psychotic obsessive-compulsive Disorder

The inclusion criteria for the participants with ID were: mild intellectual disability, no communication disorders, previous experience with experimental technological tools and in working together at F&A (with a consequence of having a strong and efficient relationship)[1]. We thus involved four young adults living with a mild to moderate ID (see Table 1), who are used to working together at F&A, and had participated in other workshops with the use of technological devices. In relation to their level of intellectual functioning, each of them uses public transportation to get to the day-care center; they spend time with friends on the weekends, and they were, or are, all doing internships with the aim of a job placement in protected categories, according to Italian Law 68/99.

The four participants were asked whether they wanted to be involved in the study; after they agreed, we collected informed consents from their legal tutor reporting information about the study goal, the procedure, the planned data treatment and the option to withdraw at any point of the study.

The workshops were held in the day-care center the users with ID generally attend, so to offer a familiar environment and make them feel comfortable. The workshops were moderated by one senior researcher; the two special-education professionals attending the workshops were the ones supervising the activities of the participants at F&A. The two workshops and the interview with the two professionals were audio-video recorded to facilitate the analysis of data.

3.1   Workshop 1: Familiarization with the Game

The first workshop was conducted to favour the familiarization of the participants with the original SNaP board game (see Sect. 2.3); the literature indeed considers familiarization an important element to improve participants' contributions to the final design [30]. The entire session lasted 1 h. The participants (P1–P4) played SNaP following its standard rules (Fig. 2). The two professionals attended the workshop with the aim of assisting the four players in case of need.

---

[1] The study was approved by the Ethical Committee of Politecnico di Milano (n.12/2019).

Fig. 2. Participants familiarizing with the SNaP game in Workshop 1.

An expert researcher played the role of the city Mayor inviting the participants to act as Designers with the mission of making the city park more engaging for the visitors and for themselves. During the game-play, all the players were able to come out with some ideas on which they had discussion rounds. In turn, each one presented his/her ideas to the rest of the team and to the Mayor; the discussion helped refine the initial ideas, for example bringing participants to understand how to combine cards they initially discarded, or how to exchange useless cards with the other participants. The two special-education professionals observed the game, but there were no need for them to support the participants. They encouraged participants' exploration when they encountered a new feature or function that stimulated their interest. They rewarded the participants to increase their confidence in their abilities in ideation.

At the end of the game, the four players in turn presented to the Mayor their final ideas of smart objects supporting playful activities in outdoor environments, as inspired by the cards gained during the game-play. P1 thought of *"street signs that rotate every time someone passes by, to give directions to reach interesting, hidden spots of the park"*. P2 ideated *"a street sign that lights up to indicate the right direction to those who cannot see very well"*. P3 thought of *"a bridge that detects the distance of a person and lights up before s/he passes, to help identify the slope"*. P4 ideated an interactive experience for deaf-blind visitors: *"flowers must be able to sense the proximity of a person and emit scents to offer an olfactory experience"*.

3.2 Online Survey with Special-Education Professionals

After Workshop 1, we invited special-education professionals working at F&A to participate to an online survey. 27 professionals (20 female, with an average age of 40) filled in a questionnaire that was organized in three different parts[2]. The

---

[2] See https://tinyurl.com/COBO-SurveyProfessionals.

first part shortly explained the SNaP game. The second asked for demographic data and experience with technology-based materials. The third one focused on gathering opinions about the adoption of SNaP within the activities held at the day-care center, and how to make it easy to learn, engaging and effective for participants with ID. To give them an idea of possible TUIs, this part also included links to videos of other interactive toolkits proposed in the literature (for example Magic Cube [28]).

The results highlighted that the strongest point of SNaP was the common goal to be achieved collaboratively by the users, which was positively evaluated also due to the participation and fun it can generate. The educators did not report on weaknesses for the game elements, but some of them observed that four players could be too many given the constant and active support that an educator has to devote to assist some users with ID. In this respect, they suggested that the integration of a digital support guiding the game could be useful (also for themselves) to explain the game rules and guide the players step by step.

In their answers to the final open questions, the professionals remarked that the physicality of cards was a strength, because users with ID need to see and touch physical material to improve their understanding of the context they have to focus on. They suggested introducing interactive, physical-digital elements to further help players understand how to combine cards and what the concrete effect of using the depicted sensors and actuators could be. Finally they discouraged the introduction of apps running on the participants' smartphones, as this would distract them from the game and especially from the reflection process.

3.3   Interview with Special-Education Professionals

To deepen the themes emerged with the survey, we conducted an interview with the two professionals participating to Workshop 1[3]. They confirmed what resulting from the survey. In addition, they emphasized the opportunity for the participants to reflect on their needs and possible solutions. Very often, education activities focus on getting people with ID become independent in everyday tasks, especially those to be accomplished outdoor. Experiences at the park can favour the well-being of individual with ID, and can encourage them to go outside; the professionals were therefore in favour of adopting the game for their education activities. They also suggested extensions (e.g., new cards) focusing on further domains: the grocery store, the pharmacy, the best friend's house.

3.4   Workshop 2: Gaining Feedback on the Extensions

The professionals' comments informed the conception of some physical-digital extensions with two main functions: i) showing concretely the effect of card combinations, i.e., how sensors and actuators work; ii) guiding the different steps of the game and recommending how to combine cards. As a result, we started designing an interactive game board, complementing the original paper board,

---

[3] Questions are available here: https://tinyurl.com/COBO-InterviewProfessionals.

Fig. 3. Paper prototype of the interactive board used during Workshop 2.

that could integrate both these functions, with different sensors and actuators to be plugged in to see the effect of card combinations, and a single visual display, also equipped with a conversational UI, offering recommendations to guide the game-play. We therefore wanted to conduct a new workshop to gather the opinions of the users with ID on the introduction of these new elements.

To let the participants understand our idea of tangible interactive board, we created a smart object prototype that, thanks to embedded electronics, could demonstrate the interactive behaviours of the objects depicted on the environment cards, thus giving a concrete feedback on what the game participants would have defined through card combinations. As illustrated in Fig. 3, this new object had an external cardboard case covered by soft plastic grass. Environment elements (e.g., trees, benches and ponds) were positioned on top of the board. Two connectors allowed the participants to plug in one sensor and one actuator at a time to see them work in combination. An Arduino board controlled the behaviour of the plugged digital components.

Workshop 2 lasted one hour and a half and started by asking players to collect cards in the same way they did with the card-only toolkit in Workshop 1. Once the players reached the phase where they had to generate ideas, we proposed them to have a try with the board prototype to see the effect of their choices on card combinations. Each of them orchestrated different inputs and outputs. At the end of the game, we showed participants a prototype of a tablet app aimed to give recommendations on alternative combinations, additional cards to buy, and how to progressively plug corresponding elements into the board.

3.5   Outcomes

We gathered qualitative data from the transcripts of the workshop, from the interview recordings and from the survey answers. We then conducted a thematic analysis to identify opportunities and challenges of adopting SNaP and its phygital extensions. We report below some emerging themes.

Theme 1: Challenges in learning the game. The participants with ID liked a lot manipulating the cards. Even if with different levels of complexity, they were able to come out with meaningful ideas. The involved professionals observed that the game would fit the abilities of users with a moderate ID: in Workshop 1 *"P2 had an initial hesitation in finding card combinations, but she appeared more confident as the game progressed"*. Also, they observed that all the participants were able to understand the dynamics and to make reasonable combinations. Therefore, they did not ask for any simplification of the method, rather they suggested extensions that could lower the entry barriers, for example to demonstrate concretely how electronic components work.

In Workshop 2, the comments of the participants with ID on the new materials highlighted that the meaning of card combinations was clearer than in Workshop 1. P1 for example thought of combining a button as an input, a fountain as an environment object and a light as an output. When trying the combination with the interactive board, P1 said *"So, if I press the button the water lights up in red. It's incredible! Can I decide to make the fountain blue too?"*. Especially the final question let us think that the interactive board stimulated the participants' curiosity on the way things worked, and this can trigger discussions that can facilitate a deeper comprehension of the game and of the designed smart interactive experiences.

Theme 2: Playfulness for engagement. All participants appeared very engaged and enthusiastic of "playing" with SNaP in both the two workshops. The game-play encouraged them all to try ideating interactive objects to enhance their experience at the park, for themselves and also for other visitors. Each one wanted to be protagonist and presented his/her own idea. We did not observe any hesitation, both with thinking about possible combinations of cards, and with sharing their ideas with the others. The meaningfulness of the resulting ideas can be interpreted first of all as an indication of the participants' understanding of the design context, but also as an expression of their engagement in the game-play that motivated them to fulfill the game objective. Indeed, the workshop participants also suggested to *"include tricks during the game to further engage the players (for example, traps or going back a number of positions)."*

Theme 3: Structured game-play and collaboration. The professionals appreciated the regular scheme that the participants must follow to complete the game and the balanced alternation of discussions supporting divergent exploration of possible solutions and convergent refinement of selected ideas. In Workshop 1, the collaboration promoted by these discussion phases guided the participants to identify their ideas and refine them also with the help of their peers. They offered help to each other, and enriched the ideas of the other participants if they were encountering difficulties in combining the cards gained during the game-play. Thanks to this spirit, very few cards remained unused, i.e., outside a combination: every participant tried hard to define combinations also for the others. Participants also liked having missions, because they provide guidance through the game and set a goal. P2 suggested: *"Why don't you add a new (super-)mission for helping the other participants to conceive their new ideas?"*.

Fig. 4. The interactive board prototype.

This is also an indication that they grasped the collaborative spirit of the game, till the point to think of a specific role to encourage ideation by every participant.

Theme 4: Reflection for education. Given the capability of the game to motivate participants to show and discuss their ideas, we identified some evidence for meaningful ideation and social connections. In addition to the benefits that can be achieved from the discussion with the others during the game-play, the two professionals participating to the workshops stressed the mentoring role that the mediator can play. The professionals also highlighted that even if the discussion and the deriving reflections focus on technology and on the role of digital devices in enhancing different activities, *"indirectly this argumentation becomes a means to reflect on the related adversities; the autonomy as a goal would positively influence the user experience of the game"*.

Theme 5: Phygital as a plus. Phygital material facilitated the ability for participants to discover by doing. In Workshop 2, the participants were positive to the introduction of tangible objects representing the park elements as they liked the idea of positioning the objects on the table to mimic the interactive situations they wanted to design. They enjoyed the concrete, immediate feedback provided by the digital devices about the interactive behaviours they were designing (e.g., playing sounds, turning on lights); and expressed their preference to soft sounds. Moreover, manipulating digital components helped them understand better what they were made of and how they worked. They also appreciated having a visual touch point, i.e., the app running on the tablet, to represent in an ordered way the card combinations and to receive guidance on the use of digital devices. They did not dislike having two boards (the paper one, originally devised for the SNaP game, and the new physical-digital one) and they understood very well the aim of having these two elements. This can be considered an indication of the benefit that the proposed paradigm can have on the users'confidence with the game.

4 COBO

Based on the collected information, we expanded the previous design of the toolkit and developed a working prototype: COBO (*COllaborative BOard*). COBO proposes the same game dynamics as SNaP, but introduces new elements in the toolkit: an *interactive board*, showing the effect of card combinations, a *Web application*, running on a tablet integrated into the interactive board and guiding the players in the different steps of the game, and *augmented cards*, equipped with a 2D code that can be read by visual recognition software embedded in the Web application.

Figure 4 illustrates the components of the interactive board:

1. **Actuator bases:** These are the components enabling the multisensory feedback representing the effect of card combinations. They are positioned in the upper side of the board (Fig. 4.1). Their role is to detect up to 8 different plugged-in objects (elements of a park environment) that can be inserted on the top through a 3.5 mm 3 pole male/female stereo audio jack connection. For each object, the bases can generate sound, light and vibration output.
2. **Sensors:** On the front side (Fig. 4.2), the interactive board integrates physical input devices and sensors: a button, a switch, a rotary potentiometer, a distance sensor, a brightness and a motion sensor.
3. **Tablet slot:** The interactive board also includes a housing slot for a 10-inches tablet (Fig. 4.3) for the execution of the Web application.

These components are controlled by an Arduino Mega 2560 board, which is connected to the tablet through an ESP8266 WiFi Module. The external input and output components are instead directly connected to the board.

The cards and the paper board have been re-designed to give a new visual identity to the game (Fig. 5). In addition, on the back, each card has now an AZTEC code that can be recognized by the Web application.

The Web application then includes functionality for:

1. **Visual card recognition:** Through the tablet front camera, it recognizes the card AZTEC code.
2. **Voice-based UI:** A controller allows participants to interact by voice with the app.
3. **Speech recording:** The users can also record and store voice comments.

Given these components and functions, the users interacts with COBO through the following steps:

1. **On-boarding and continuous assistance:** The moderator prepares the playground and positions the deck of cards (Fig. 6A). The role of the moderator (Major) is complemented by Virginia, an avatar/conversational agent provided by the Web application, which supports players both in learning the game rules and in the crucial phases of ideation through card combination (Fig. 6B). Virginia is depicted as a woman university researcher acting as a reference point for interactions. She can assist the players through visual and auditory channels, activated by pressing an always-active help button.

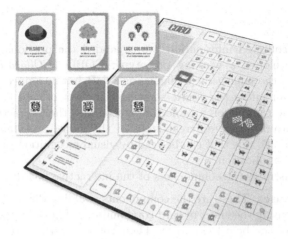

Fig. 5. COBO restyled cards and game board.

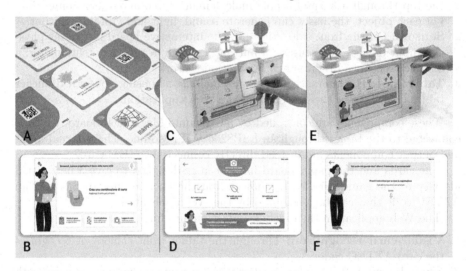

Fig. 6. COBO user experience flow.

2. **Card recognition**: When the player collects enough cards, she can have COBO recognizing them by simply placing their AZTEC code in front of the tablet camera (Fig. 6C). When the card code is recognized, the card name is told and its virtual representation is shown on the screen (Fig. 6D).

3. **Combination feedback**: Once a combination of 3 cards is added (input, environment and output), the user can plug the environment physical objects into the actuator bases (Fig. 6E); while interacting with buttons and sensors, the user sees in real-time a "live" version of the card combination, which is conveyed through the multisensory functions of the board.

4. **Idea recording**: Players can finally voice-record the idea they had in mind. Once the registration is completed, it can be re-played and saved for future listenings (Fig. 6F). In case of any failure (e.g., wrong mounting of the objects on the interactive bases) the application is able to guide the players to undertake the right actions through spoken and written recommendations.

5 Remote Exploratory Study

We run an exploratory study to gather participants feedback on the latest COBO extensions and evaluate their level of engagement and likability of the interactive prototype. In order to get feedback consistent with the previous evaluation sessions, we involved the same four participants with ID. Due to COVID-19 restrictions we could not access the social-care center, thus we organized a Web call on the Google Meet platform. The participants were located at F&A, and were coordinated by one of the two special-education professionals who assisted them in the first two workshops. Two researchers, remotely connected from their offices, guided the whole experience: one acted as moderator, the other provided technical support to ensure the high quality of the streaming. In addition, two other researchers silently attended the call and took notes.

Setting and Materials. A reflex camera was used to frame the moderator, the interactive board prototype, and the cards. A second computer was used by the second researcher to run and share the Web application. The session was audio-video recorded.

During the session, the two researchers guiding the activities used the final prototype of the interactive board, the paper board and the augmented cards. The participants with ID were provided with the cards only.

Procedure. Once all the participants connected to the online room, the moderators briefly recalled the board game rules and illustrated the new features of the augmented cards. The moderator then proceeded by explaining the main functions of the interactive board and the Web application. Since the session was held online, the game was not replicated entirely, while the focus was kept on the phases that most required the use of the new interactive elements (Fig. 7):

1. First of all we showed how the board could recognize the cards. We started from a card combination consisting of an input card (button), an object card (sign) and an output card (color light). While the main moderator with the interactive board were showing to the users how to make the app recognize a card, the second moderator were sharing her screen where the Web app was running. The same procedure was followed for reading other cards and for showing the participants the effect on the Web app.
2. We then proceeded by showing two other card combinations, and how they could be read and managed in the application. Users were asked to interpret the cards, before activating them within the app, and to think of an idea that could refer to the combination they were going to activate.

Fig. 7. A) Users become familiar with the available cards; B) One of the users shows the chosen card; C) Users observe the moderator interacting with the interactive board by showing the effect of the chosen card combination.

3. We then illustrated how the conversational assistant, Virginia, was able to recognize questions such as: "Is there a correct order to add the cards?" or "How do I cancel a card?". For the demonstration, participants were asked if they had any questions on how to proceed; their questions were vocally asked to the conversational agent by the moderator.
4. We showed the procedure to vocally record their ideas, and to save and replay the audio.
5. At the end of the session users were asked whether they had any further questions or concerns about the game and whether they found the game interesting and easy to use.

Final Questionnaire. After the study, participants were asked to fill out a questionnaire to evaluate how much they liked the game and appreciated the various components of the new toolkit[4]. The questionnaire was composed of seven questions to be answered through an iconic Likert scale inspired to the smiley-o-meter representation [32]. One question asked the users to express how much they liked the game in general. Then six questions asked how much they appreciated the different elements of the toolkit: the interactive board, its knobs and sensors, the multisensory effects, the Web application, the card reading mechanisms, the conversational agent. The three last questions, to be answered with "yes" or "no", asked if they perceived the game as easy to use, if it stimulated collaboration among them, and if they wanted to play it again.

Results. The results of the questionnaire, the video-recordings and the taken notes were then analyzed to collect insights. The four participants gave positive feedback about the material, especially the interactive board. As illustrated in Fig. 8, in a scale from 1 to 5, participants, evaluated all the toolkit components with scores equal to 4 and 5 ("satisfying" and "very satisfying"). Only one participant evaluated with 3 the way of reading the cards. Two participants then

---

[4] See https://tinyurl.com/COBO-FinalQuestionnaire.

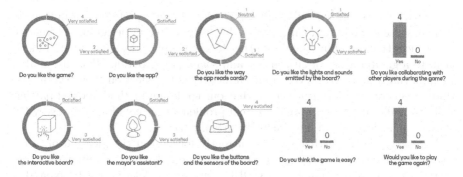

Fig. 8. Answers of the questionnaire submitted to the participants after Workshop 2.

gave the maximum score to all the questions concerning each specific element of the game. The maximum rating given to the question *"Do you like the buttons and sensors of the board"* lets us think that the interaction with tangibles was appealing for the users, and this is in line with the results of others studies [14]. Participants also gave the maximum rate for the question *"Do you like the game?"*, as an expression of their interest in the phygital extension of the game.

In relation to usability, the positive responses received for the question on the *"ease of use"* confirm that the interactive game, grounded on the accessibility guidelines [38], allowed the users to understand how to use the new features. While observing them it emerged that, by exploring card combinations and getting direct feedback, participants were able to build their understanding of how the game works, and this also made interaction easier.

The interactive mechanisms in general were considered easy to use. After illustrating how the application recognizes cards, one of the users said: *"This game is very easy, I like it!"*. All the participants also said they would love to play again with COBO in the future.

6   Discussion

From an educational perspective, we gathered positive feedback during the whole process of design and evaluation. The four participants with ID showed us to feel involved in the design of new interactive artefacts, and at each workshop they asked us to organize further sessions. They also asked if the smart experiences designed in the different sessions had been implemented by some expert developers. We interpret this request as their engagement with the design process.

Considering individual characteristics, we did not observe specific hesitations of the participants to start playing during our workshops. It seemed they did not feel evaluated: they were always willing to express and share their ideas with the other palyers, the researchers and the educators.

The ideas that emerged during the whole process (see Sect. 3.1) also confirmed the willingness of users to think about solutions related to the accessibility of the park for people with disabilities. This can be interpreted as an indication of their sense of empowerment, as they felt responsible in designing interactive experiences that could be useful for other fragile people, a feeling that could lead them to a greater sense of citizenship and social participation. This also makes us think that the use of COBO could induce users to reflect on their own needs. More in general, a relevant aspect is that our co-design method allowed participants to make concrete proposals to real problems that could arise in everyday situations, as designing a new inclusive urban park.

It is worth noticing that COBO currently focuses on the ideation of interactive ideas for the city-park environment and provides participants with cards related to this context. However, COBO was designed to be easily expanded to new environments by simply adding new sets of cards and plug-in objects. The flexibility in expanding the domain of the game is coherent with both the requests of the users participating to the study, who asked to be involved in ideation sessions for other situations, and with the suggestions provided by the professionals in the online survey carried out after the first workshop. Varying the addressed domain would expand the potential of the design process for smart activities, providing people with ID with the opportunity to focus on other environments where they generally act in their everyday life, and where they might potentially encounter situations that can be digitally enhanced.

6.1 Limitations

Although the research had positive findings, there were some unavoidable limitations. First of all, the self-reported data could have introduced biases, such as telescoping, attribution, exaggeration. The difficulty in observing the participants during the remote study might have also induced professionals and researchers to hypothesize some facts [25] leading to further biases. To generalize the results, the study should be replicated with a larger group of participants and for a longer period to observe post-novelty and generalization of effects.

The participants involved had already experienced working together both at the day-care center and with technological devices; furthermore, their communication skills are preserved, both in terms of ideation and phonoarticulatory apparatus, and that made playing with COBO quite easy for them. As a consequence, although we feel·COBO played an important role as a social mediator, we are not able to ascribe whether the method was the principal factor enabling collaboration between them, as the group dynamics were already established.

Finally, to preserve participants' safety during the COVID-19 pandemic, we opted not to enter the center. Giving participants the possibility to share the playground with us would have potentially enhanced the collaboration.

7 Conclusions and Future Work

Our design approach allowed us to collect several insights from the involved young adults with ID, but it also gave them the chance to feel empowered in solving a concrete problem, i.e., the design of smart outdoor experiences. Participants played a crucial role during the process for revising the SNaP method and introducing the phygital elements; they contributed with very important feedback about the game dynamics and the interactive board prototype. Educators' suggestions were valuable as well: they helped us identify tangible and digital interactive material as a viable solution to enhance participants' ability to understand the method and ideate. The final version of the interactive board seemed to allow the participants to enhance their self-accomplishment. Their response during the workshops suggests that it could be helpful for enhancing both the learning and the creativity process.

Our future work will focus on systematically assessing the observed benefits through user studies involving a larger sample of users and in a longer period, also expanding the number of city-related environments available in the game. We plan to involve users who have never worked together in order to verify and evaluate how group dynamics and communication skills evolve during the game. Moreover, it would be interesting to involve people with lower IQ levels and/or with communication disorders, to see whether COBO, together with group dynamics, could promote communication between them.

A long-term goal could be to investigate the use of COBO to help people with ID to improve their communication and logic skills, and to enhance their creative process, which is usually lacking. This would be in line with the results of some recent works (e.g., [12]) that promote tangible toolkits for the playful discovery of electronics, a further form of empowerment that could introduce young adults with ID to making and thinkering practices.

Acknowledgment. This work is partially supported by the Italian Ministry of University and Research (MIUR) under grant PRIN 2017 "EMPATHY: EMpowering People in deAling with internet of THings ecosYstems".

References

1. ICD-11. https://icd.who.int/browse11/
2. Agosta, G., et al.: In: Playful supervised smart spaces (p3s)-a framework for designing, implementing and deploying multisensory play experiences for children with special needs, pp. 158–164. IEEE (2015)
3. Al Mahmud, A., Soysa, A.I.: Poma: a tangible user interface to improve social and cognitive skills of Sri lankan children with asd. Int. J. Human-Comput. Stud. **144**, 102486 (2020)
4. Anderson, R.E.: Social impacts of computing: codes of professional ethics. Social Sci. Comput. Rev. **10**(4), 453–469 (1992)
5. Antle, A.N.: The cti framework: informing the design of tangible systems for children. ACM (2007)
6. Antle, A.N., Wise, A.F.: Getting down to details: using theories of cognition and learning to inform tangible user interface design. Interact. Comput. **25**(1), 1–20 (2013)
7. Ardito, C., Buono, P., Desolda, G., Matera, M.: From smart objects to smart experiences: an end-user development approach. Int. J. Hum. Comput. Stud. **114**, 51–68 (2018). https://doi.org/10.1016/j.ijhcs.2017.12.002

8. Association, A.P., et al.: Diagnostic and statistical manual of mental disorders (DSM-5®). American Psychiatric Pub (2013)
9. Colombo, S., Garzotto, F., Gelsomini, M., Melli, M., Clasadonte, F.: Dolphin sam: a smart pet for children with intellectual disability (2016)
10. Deng, Y., Antle, A.N., Neustaedter, C.: Tango cards: a card-based design tool for informing the design of tangible learning games (2014)
11. Eisenberg, M., et al.: As we may print: new directions in output devices and computational crafts for children. ACM (2003)
12. Ellis, K., Dao, E., Smith, O., Lindsay, S., Olivier, P.: Tapeblocks: a making toolkit for people living with intellectual disabilities. Association for Computing Machinery, New York (2021). https://doi.org/10.1145/3411764.3445647
13. Falcão, T.P.: Action-effect mappings in tangible interaction for children with intellectual disabilities. Int. J. Learn. Technol. **12**(4), 294–314 (2017)
14. Falcão, T.P., Price, S.: Tangibles for students with intellectual disabilities. ACM (2012)
15. Foglia, L., Wilson, R.A.: Embodied cognition. Wiley Interdisc. Rev. Cogn. Sci. **4**(3), 319–325 (2013)
16. Frauenberger, C., Good, J., Alcorn, A., Pain, H.: Supporting the design contributions of children with autism spectrum conditions. In: Schelhowe, H. (ed.) The 11th International Conference on Interaction Design and Children, IDC '12, Bremen, UNK, Germany, 12–15 June 2012, pp. 134–143. ACM (2012). https://doi.org/10.1145/2307096.2307112
17. Frauenberger, C., Good, J., Keay-Bright, W.: Designing technology for children with special needs: bridging perspectives through participatory design. CoDesign **7**(1), 1–28 (2011)
18. Gelsomini, M.: Reflex: learning beyond the screen in a simple, fun, and affordable way (2018)
19. Gelsomini, M., et al.: Magika: a multisensory environment for play, education and inclusion (2019)
20. Gelsomini, M., Garzotto, F., Matarazzo, V., Messina, N., Occhiuto, D.: Creating social stories as wearable hyper-immersive virtual reality experiences for children with neurodevelopmental disorders. ACM (2017)
21. Gelsomini, M., Spitale, M., Beccaluva, E., Viola, L., Garzotto, F.: Reflex: adaptive learning beyond the screen (2019)
22. Gennari, R., Matera, M., Melonio, A., Roumelioti, E.: A board-game for co-designing smart nature environments in workshops with children. In: Malizia, A., Valtolina, S., Morch, A., Serrano, A., Stratton, A. (eds.) IS-EUD 2019. LNCS, vol. 11553, pp. 132–148. Springer, Cham (2019). https://doi.org/10.1007/978-3-030-24781-2_9
23. Güldenpfennig, F.: Tailor-made accessible computers: an interactive toolkit for iterative co-design and embodied interaction, pp. 231–236 (2018)
24. Huyghe, J., Wouters, N., Geerts, D., Vande Moere, A.: Localudo: card-based workshop for interactive architecture. In: CHI'14 Extended Abstracts on Human Factors in Computing Systems, pp. 1975–1980 (2014)
25. Kerr, N.L.: Harking: hypothesizing after the results are known. Pers. Social Psychol. Rev. **2**(3), 196–217 (1998)
26. Khandu: Khandu. https://www.kickstarter.com/projects/1251477973/khandu-building-little-thinkers
27. Kientz, J.A., Hayes, G.R., Goodwin, M.S., Gelsomini, M., Abowd, G.D.: Interactive technologies and autism. Synth. Lect. Assist. Rehabil. Health-Pres. Technol.d **9**(1), 1–229 (2019)

28. Lechelt, Z., Rogers, Y., Yuill, N., Nagl, L., Ragone, G., Marquardt, N.: Inclusive computing in special needs classrooms: designing for all. In: Mandryk, R.L., Hancock, M., Perry, M., Cox, A.L. (eds.) Proceedings of the 2018 CHI Conference on Human Factors in Computing Systems, CHI 2018, Montreal, QC, Canada, 21–26 April 2018, p. 517. ACM (2018). https://doi.org/10.1145/3173574.3174091

29. Malinverni, L., Guiard, J.M., Padillo, V., Mairena, M., Hervás, A., Parés, N.: Participatory design strategies to enhance the creative contribution of children with special needs. In: Iversen, O.S., Markopoulos, P., Garzotto, F., Dindler, C. (eds.) IDC '14, Proceedings of the 2014 Conference on Interaction Design and Children, Aarhus, Denmark, 17–20 June 2014, pp. 85–94. ACM (2014). https://doi.org/10.1145/2593968.2593981

30. Marshall, P.: Do tangible interfaces enhance learning? ACM (2007)

31. Olesen, J., et al.: The economic cost of brain disorders in Europe. Eur. J. Neurol. 19(1), 155–162 (2012)

32. Read, J., MacFarlane, S., Casey, C.: Endurability, engagement and expectations: Measuring children's fun (2002)

33. Sánchez-Morales, A., Durand-Rivera, J., Martínez-González, C.: Usability evaluation of a tangible user interface and serious game for identification of cognitive deficiencies in preschool children. Int. J. Adv. Comput. Sci. Appl. 11, 486–493 (2020)

34. Sanders, E.B.N., Stappers, P.J.: Probes, toolkits and prototypes: three approaches to making in codesigning. CoDesign 10(1), 5–14 (2014). https://doi.org/10.1080/15710882.2014.888183

35. Spitale, M., Gelsomini, M., Beccaluva, E., Viola, L., Garzotto, F.: Meeting the needs of people with neuro-developmental disorder through a phygital approach (2019)

36. Starcic, A.I., Cotic, M., Zajc, M.: Design-based research on the use of a tangible user interface for geometry teaching in an inclusive classroom. Brit. J. Educ. Technol. 44(5), 729–744 (2013)

37. Tam, V., Gelsomini, M., Garzotto, F.: Polipo: a tangible toy for children with neurodevelopmental disorders. ACM (2017)

38. Department of Health: Basic Guidelines for people who commission easy read information. (2009)

39. Tangible Play: Osmo, award-winning educational games system for ipad (2016). https://www.playosmo.com/en

40. Tsatsou, P.: Digital inclusion of people with disabilities: a qualitative study of intra-disability diversity in the digital realm. Behav. Inf. Technol. 39(9), 995–1010 (2020)

41. Wilson, M.: Six views of embodied cognition. Psychon. Bull. Rev. 9(4), 625–636 (2002)

42. Zajc, M., Istenic Starcic, A.: Potentials of the tangible user interface (TUI) in enhancing inclusion of people with special needs in the ICT-assisted learning and e-accessibility. In: Jezic, G., Kusek, M., Nguyen, N.-T., Howlett, R.J., Jain, L.C. (eds.) KES-AMSTA 2012. LNCS (LNAI), vol. 7327, pp. 261–270. Springer, Heidelberg (2012). https://doi.org/10.1007/978-3-642-30947-2_30

43. Zaman, B., Vanden Abeele, V., Markopoulos, P., Marshall, P.: The evolving field of tangible interaction for children: the challenge of empirical validation. Pers. Ubiq. Comput. 16(4), 367–378 (2012)

Digital Producers with Cognitive Disabilities
Participatory Video Tutorials as a Strategy for Supporting Digital Abilities and Aspirations

Petko Atanasov Karadechev[1]([email]) [ID], Anne Marie Kanstrup[1]([email]) [ID],
and Jacob Gorm Davidsen[2]([email]) [ID]

[1] Department of Planning, Aalborg University, A. C. Meyers Vænge 15,
2450 Copenhagen, Denmark
{petko,kanstrup}@plan.aau.dk
[2] Department of Communication and Technology, Aalborg University,
Rendsburggade 14, 9000 Aalborg, Denmark
jdavidsen@hum.aau.dk

Abstract. This paper presents 'participatory video tutorials'—a strategy developed to support the digital empowerment of young people living with cognitive disabilities. The support strategy complements and expands dominant perspectives on the target group, which is often seen as disabled and in need of assistive technology, by foregrounding the young participants' digital abilities and facilitating them as active producers of digital content, which already plays a major role in their everyday social interactions. We present the background and framework for participatory video tutorials and the results from staging digital production with sixteen young participants. Empirically, the results contribute perspectives on this target group as producers (vs. users) with abilities (vs. disabilities). Methodologically, the results outline four principles (socio-technical belonging, technical accessibility, elasticity, and material reusability) that can assist HCI researchers, professionals, and caretakers in their efforts to support the target group in digital production. These principles are guidelines for a participatory staging, driven by the young people's motivation for self-expression. The study and the results contribute an example and a strategy for how to work toward digital inclusion by engaging a marginalized target group in digital production.

Keywords: Cognitive disability · Youth · Content production · Video tutorials · Participatory design

1 Introduction

Video tutorials are commonly used and produced by lay people to share knowledge and skills related to various interests. There are no limits on the uniqueness of topics and interests covered in online video tutorials, and that is perhaps one

© IFIP International Federation for Information Processing 2021
Published by Springer Nature Switzerland AG 2021
C. Ardito et al. (Eds.): INTERACT 2021, LNCS 12932, pp. 170–191, 2021.
https://doi.org/10.1007/978-3-030-85623-6_12

of the reasons tutorials have become a popular format for informal learning. In this paper, we report on research that uses a video tutorial format to engage and support young people living with cognitive disabilities in sharing and advancing their digital abilities. The motivation for this research is grounded in empirical studies identifying an increasing use of digital technology in the everyday life of people living with cognitive disabilities and a subsequent call for strategies to support this target group in their digital abilities and aspirations [3,28]. We present how we have developed and explored video tutorials as a format for supporting digital production with 16 young people (age fourteen through twenty-eight) living with one or more cognitive disabilities. We have named this strategy—'participatory video tutorials'—a strategy that supports the young people as active producers of their own digital content. The producer role comes with responsibilities, skill development, and social relations, and we argue that this support strategy can contribute to the empowerment of our target group.

Both this role and the presented method are enacted in sheltered environments (e.g., participating institutions) due to this study being a part of a pre-approved project. Therefore, the participatory video tutorial incorporates these environments by design, which means that there are inherent choices to be made about the structure of this approach regarding what to engage our participants with and how to keep them involved in the process. We go over this in Sect. 3. The presented research arrangement can answer certain questions (about the specific method it presents) and only give rise to other questions, such as what the results would look like if the participants and researchers had different relationships, and if the presented method were carried out at their homes instead of their schools, if their parents were involved instead of their teachers. As important and valuable as these questions are, they are outside the scope of this study due to the established agreements between the participating institutions. It is, however, important to note that as researchers, we come with a specific focus on our participants' digital interests. This focus is meant to act as a methodological connective tissue between other researchers with interest in this field (e.g., Brereton, Frauenberger, Seale) as well as pedagogues and teachers from institutions that work with youth living with cognitive disabilities.

As discussed by Seale, supportive strategies for digital technology as a tool for empowerment of this target group are challenging [28]. Conflict of interest can easily occur when support of independence clashes with the role of professional or caretaker (family and friends). For example, in situations where those aiming to support people with cognitive disabilities fear backlash from the digital production activities, intentions of support can suppress the young people's ability to speak up. Support of digital production is a difficult balance, with risks of being counterproductive to ambitions of empowerment, which is defined as the power to act with others and by this develop knowledge and abilities to influence personal and social spheres [15]. The developed strategy works with challenges of empowerment by suggesting structure and a process for cooperation with goals that support not only the young people's personal development but also their competence in contributing to collective development (ibid.). The study complements dominant perspectives on this target group as disabled with a need of assistive technology by bringing a conceptual perspective on digital technology as a production tool, as well as by seeing the young participants as active producers of the digital content that plays a major role in their everyday social interactions [7,12,13,26]. Methodologically, this paper contributes guidance to a participatory staging driven by the young people's motivation to self-expression. In the following chapter, we first present background information on cognitive disabilities, related work on this target group's uses of digital technology, and participation in digital production. Secondly, we present the participatory video tutorial format and the principles of the developed participatory video tutorials, and how we staged this approach in four settings with sixteen participants. Thirdly, we present the results, including an analysis of the participants' ways of engaging in the digital production and the developed tutorial format. We discuss these results in relation to the concepts of empowerment and digital technology use for people with cognitive disabilities and conclude with guidelines for using participatory tutorials as support strategies for care workers. Additionally, we make suggestions for future research on approaches to engaging people with cognitive disabilities in research on the design and use of digital technology. The study contributes insights to human-computer interaction (HCI) research on how to engage a marginalized target group in design and use of interactive technologies and bring reflections on strategies for digital inclusion.

2   Background

2.1   Cognitive Disabilities

Cognitive disabilities can be presented through a broad variety of clinical diagnoses that affect cognitive abilities. In the study presented in this paper, all participants live with a neurodevelopmental disorder and have one or more diagnoses including autism, a learning disorder, Down's syndrome, and ADHD. Additionally, some of the participants are diagnosed with anxiety, and sensory impairment is common [20]. Thus, it is difficult to assign the participants specific diagnostic labels since most are challenged by comorbidity and because of diagnostic differences and consequently different individual competencies and potentials even for participants sharing the same diagnosis. Additionally, as for all human beings, possibilities for development for people living with cognitive disabilities are influenced by the dynamics of the individuals and social groups that they interact with [24]. The ecological focus of the World Health Organization [36] is often presented as an important theoretical model for understanding this target group, emphasizing a broad variety of factors influencing individual functioning, including health, context, participation, adaptive behavior, support, and intellectual abilities [20]. On this background, we join HCI researchers arguing for a broad perspective when aiming to understand and engage this target group in HCI research [32].

2.2   Cognitive Disability and Digital Technology—A Call for Participatory Support Strategies

Research on the use of digital technology among young people living with cognitive disability is limited, but some studies show how internet technologies offer opportunities for this target group to develop and maintain social relations [1,9,25,27,30,33,34], such as by participating in social activities mediated by online multiplayer games [27], online dating platforms [21], and by mobile applications more generally [33,34] and a broad variety of consumer applications [3] that support reaching out and sharing experiences through digital technology. However, research has also shown that digital participation is complex and requires support for a target group living with one or several cognitive diagnoses. The target group often benefits from visual communication, known structure and repetition, and social interaction with a limited number of participants. Digital technology can support some of these needs [4,10,16], but challenges related to understanding social codes [9], like challenges related to inclusion in social groups also exist online [21,28]. Research has identified a motivation among the target group to create and share online content to develop friendship [19,29] but also a need to empower the participants to take responsibility and manage online interaction.

Professionals and carers often act as mediators when people with cognitive disabilities engage in digital production [29] and the limited research on empowering this target group in online activities has emphasized the complexity related to this type of support. An empirical study from 2007 of how adults with learning disabilities were supported in online publishing activities concluded that support strategies often have the potential to place this group "in a passive role where they are recipients of technological expertise and protective guardianship" [28]. Hence, there is a call for solutions that encourage carers of people with cognitive disabilities "not to underestimate their ability to cope with the risks of Internet use and to recognize the 'resilience' that might be created through interdependent collaboration with support workers" (ibid.).

We build on the above related research in our development of support strategies for digital production, specifically by anchoring our research in Vygotsky's theory on "defectology" and his concept of Zone of Proximal Development [35]. According to Vygotsky, a child with a disability is no less developed than a child without a disability but develops in different ways than most children ("the norm"). With this perspective, it does not make sense to focus on the disability ("the defect"). What is important is the child's uniqueness since the disabled child represents a qualitatively different development. Further, as captured in the concept of the Zone of Proximal Development, the child is able to perform other activities when guided by a more capable peer. An important aspect of Vygotsky's theorizing is thus to focus on the environment in which the child is learning and support from more capable peers. This perspective has formed the theoretical background for developing participatory video tutorials and grounded our attention on the participants' abilities and aspirations. We term this a *participatory approach*, as it is related to HCI research calling for development of approaches that can support opportunities for people with cognitive disabilities to participate and express experiences and desires digital technology [5]. People with cognitive disabilities tend to participate in design and research by proxy [6]. However, the limited related HCI research shows that this group is able to participate in design and research activities but requires flexible staging [22], careful interpretation [14], and respectful interaction emphasizing attention to mutual learning, self-expression, and self-determination for the participants [26]. In general, this research follows core principles from Participatory Design, treating people as competent practitioners and experts in their own experiences and practices [17] and contributes insights into how to stage participatory settings for marginalized users. In the following, we present how we have used this background in the development of participatory video tutorials.

3   Participatory Video Tutorials

This research was carried out in cooperation with four institutions for young people living with cognitive disabilities. All participants (sixteen in total, aged fourteen through twenty-eight years old) study at or live in the institutions, located in a city in Northern Denmark: (1) a school for children with cognitive disabilities (ages six through seventeen), (2) a high school for young adults with cognitive disabilities (ages eighteen through twenty-two), (3) a sheltered residence for young adults with cognitive disabilities (aged eighteen through twenty-eight), and (4) a sheltered residence for adults with cognitive disabilities (from age 28 - three of the participants in our study moved during this research from the sheltered youth residence, as they turned twenty eight). The research is carried out in close cooperation with these institutions, where staff are confronted with the young people's increasing and extensive use of digital technology and searching support strategies for these activities. The two schools have set up computer areas and dedicated time for a staff member to stage activities such as to support the young participants in online gaming and production of specific content. The residences have tried to initiate conversations with their young residents about digital behavior. All four institutions are interested in exploring ways to engage the young people and develop support strategies that can facilitate their digital abilities and aspirations. The decision to explore opportunities for this through the tutorial format was taken in cooperation with the institutions, where a project team of management, teachers, and pedagogues have participated in ongoing research and development of digital activities.

All participants are Danish and, excluding one minimally verbal person, fifteen can communicate in Danish, eight out of the fifteen can communicate in English, while a further six can partially understand English. English language skills make it easier to engage with the interface of some of the programs used for digital creation (this is especially helpful for participants who watch English-language tutorials on platforms such as YouTube). All participants live with Down's syndrome, ADHD, autism, and/or intellectual disabilities, and several struggle with anxiety and other mental conditions. It is important to note that there is no such thing as a "pure" case of autism or any other neurological condition in this target group. Each individual constitutes a unique experiential case of a person who continuously learns how to live with their conditions in a world that changes its understanding of said conditions constantly [11]. What this means for the present study is that similar diagnoses are translated into a spectrum of experiences (ibid.). Inspired by [35] and participatory design research [31], the point of departure for developing the participatory video tutorial format as a support strategy has been to acknowledge the diversity of the young participants and to enter their world (vs. developing a fixed format). Consequently, it has also been important to openly ask the participants what they feel skilled in doing via digital tools, and how and why they want to present their abilities to friends and fellow peers. Using Vygotsky's concept of the Zone of Proximal Development, we engaged with each participant on their specific terms and needs, acknowledging that the needs and requirements can change during the production process. The participatory video tutorials format allowed us to work on developing a unique tutorial structure, grounded in each participant's specific digital abilities and aspirations. Overall, we adhere to principles of reciprocity and commensurability, where both participants and researchers have shared responsibilities in the common goal to co-create a video tutorial together.

Tutorials as an audio-visual format are well known to the participants, and the participating schools often them to relate to the young people's specific topics of interests. The sheltered residences have had positive experiences producing their own short tutorials about everyday tasks (how to use the dishwasher, etc.), which the residents can access via QR codes, meaning all participants have also had positive experiences with the tutorial format. To facilitate a process that is not only a personal but a collective development [15], we created an unlisted YouTube channel where all participants can upload their own material. Importantly, they can also see material co-produced by friends in their own or other institutions. Producing for a YouTube channel comes with specific commitment to making the process focused, professional, and engaging in a recognizable way. To stage a professional atmosphere around the production, we created a logo and printed it on a large poster, which was set up in rooms at the institutions dedicated to production. The ambition was to underscore the action-oriented approach of the tutorial production and to support the participants in tapping into a co-producer mode.

3.1   Ethical and Methodological Study Design

From an ethical perspective, we can confirm that the research project has received ethical approval in accordance with national rules and the European GDPR legislation. It has been approved by the National Data Protection Agency, and rigorous ethical procedures are followed with support and administration by the office for Grants and Contracts at Aalborg University (registration number: 2018-899/10-0192). All ethical requirements are handled according to national rules and regulations for ethical conduct, GDPR, and anonymity. Due to participants' disabilities, this is extremely important and has high priority—we ensure that all measures and precautions have been taken. Methodologically, we have followed strict ethical codes while obtaining informed consent from our participants, the support staff that works with them, as well as their parents by: (1) taking time to explain to our participants the nature of the project, (2) continuously reminding them that they have to actively agree to be a part of the study and their identities will be kept anonymous, (3) reminding them that they can choose to leave at any time, (4) explaining that data gathered for the project will not be used for any other purposes and is subject to strict GDPR regulations, including deletion after a certain period. These key points were repeated throughout the project, in accordance with the findings from Cameron and Murphy [8].

3.2 Participatory Video Tutorial Production Sessions

To engage the participants with the tutorial format, a production process was developed with three sessions: pre-production, production, and review, elaborated in the following. The process requires coordination with the institutions that prepare the participants for the activity, which is especially important for this target group.

Pre-production: At a one-hour meeting, volunteering participants from all institutions were presented with the video tutorial idea and structure, which includes production a three-to-five-minute video, consisting of three steps: (1) area of interest, in which the young people present an overview of their digital interests, (2) a demonstration of digital skills, in which they show how they pursue their interests, and (3) tips and tricks for solving issues that viewers should consider. The participants were asked about their digital interests and what they would like to make a video about. To help structure their responses, they were given a "tutorial script", using which they could reflect on prompts like "I would like to make a video tutorial about..." and "Who would you like to watch your video tutorial?". The researchers and participants discussed these questions, but answers were not required immediately. After this meeting, the young participants shared their thoughts about the production of tutorials with support staff at the institutions. This worked as preparation for both the young producers but also for the researchers, as an aid to better understand what types of digital skills the participants were interested in sharing and developing (Question 1.) and the social groups or audiences they saw as important (Question 2.). An important part of the preparation was preparing the participants for their role as producers. Hence, the upcoming production sessions were predicated on the idea that the participants are digital producers who have volunteered to demonstrate digital ideas and abilities and share their interests using their digital skills with friends at their school and similar institutions in their city via the YouTube channel. It was clearly communicated that the researchers played a secondary role as co-producers, who supported the participants in their production with recording equipment and with editing the material.

Production of the Tutorials: This part of the study was carried out in two-hour sessions with each participant. The production rooms set up at the institutions were equipped with video cameras (one stationary, one mobile, one 360-degree) and audio recording devices (dictaphone and wired microphones for the participants). Screen capture software was crucial for the sessions, as it allowed the recorded footage of the participants activities to be edited later. For desktops and laptops, we used Open Broadcaster Software (OBS), and for recordings on mobile phones and tablets, we used the integrated screen recording functions of iOS and Android. Once the recordings began, one of the researchers engaged in a semi-structured dialog based on the tutorial script that the participants had prepared before the session. During the recording, the interviewer detailed the script via conversations with the participants as they explained what they were doing and why this was important for the tutorial they were producing. This script used the three-step structure of the tutorial—(1) area of interest, (2) demonstration, (3) tips and tricks—and added notions of visual style (e.g., background music, text, fonts, colors), ensuring that the participants' ideas of content and style are represented as faithfully as possible. Every participant was informed that the screen recorded content and that an impromptu script would be used for draft videos, which they should review in follow up sessions. Immediately after filming, we initiated short and rough video editing sessions, in which we imported footage of the recording session in DaVinci Resolve, a video editing program, and quickly visualized the script into a video timeline. Participants were invited to make corrections on the timeline to clearly reflect the structure they had in mind for their video. Aside from these in-person sessions, video editing took place after the production sessions ended. Researchers edited the original video files outside the institutions and created draft tutorial versions with the explicit intent that they should be reviewed by each participant before finalization.

Review: After the production session, a researcher created draft versions of the tutorials based on the materials and conversations from the production sessions. In a one-hour follow-up session, the researchers played this draft video to each participant individually and asked them for feedback. Participants were encouraged to say what they liked and disliked and point to it on the screen. They were also invited to individually engage with the video editing process by taking control of the editing software and making changes on their own. For some, this involved changing font colors, while others would engage in a narrative exercise, moving video sections around on the timeline and changing the structure and meaning of the video. The review process consisted of one to three iterations, and it ended when participants deemed the tutorial ready for publishing on the YouTube channel. **Sharing the Tutorials:** All tutorials were published on an unlisted YouTube channel (meaning only people with a specific link could access it) and shared with support staff from all institutions. A premiere was set up at two schools and one sheltered residence. Two videos were made at the second sheltered residence, but the participants there did not express a desire for a public premiere, instead opting to have their video tutorials shown at the first institution, where they had lived previously and knew most of the current residents. During the video premieres, fellow students and residents were invited to see the tutorials. At this session, each producer was presented, we watched the tutorial, and in some cases, the audience asked questions. The premieres were staged as a festive activity with a red carpet laid out for the participants, applause, and popcorn. The physical and digital acts of sharing the finished videos were meant to support the social relations the participants have among themselves, as well as those with other students or residents in the participating institutions.

4 Results

The production sessions totaled 143 h and fifty-two minutes of video footage, recorded by the researchers using three cameras and one smartphone. Researchers and participants co-edited the footage into thirteen video tutorials, totaling fifty-two minutes and five seconds and averaging four minutes per tutorial. There were three videos produced by a two-person group, and ten produced by one person. The agreed-upon structure of the tutorials (three to five minutes per video, three sections) was followed and carried out. As stated by staff members at one of the institutions, a main result of our strategy was that the process succeeded in engaging the participants to follow all the production steps and to produce a video. This is especially important, as several of the participants had a history of withdrawing from activities or not finalizing them due to diagnoses (e.g., struggling with symptoms of their diagnosed conditions) and difficulties with coping with demands for focus, conversation and delivering, all of which were a requirement in our format. By supporting their engagement with video production, we established a space where our participants transition from consumers to producers of digital content. To position ourselves in a way that allowed us to analyze this transition, we employed a participatory design approach, in which key aspects of the strategy (story line, video material, directing, co-editing) were delegated solely to the participants. What this means is that by design, our approach would not work without active engagement, and when such engagement occurred, we were in a co-directorial, co-editorial position to see exactly what made it work or not work and offer perspectives on why that might be the case.

In this section, we outline three key insights from our participatory video tutorial strategy, involving: (1) staging a professional setting, (2) embracing multiple production strategies, and (3) sharing digital production. These three insights are based on analysis of video recordings from the production, which have been coded into themes identified as related to the young participants' engagement with the tutorial format. All participant names are anonymized following informed consent with a support person present. The identified three insights come together to offer a framework which is rigid in its constitutive parts (what the video tutorials are made of, and how they are carried out) as well as its output (the videos themselves). The framework nevertheless proved sufficiently flexible, in that it was easy to adapt to each individual participant, either with props during filming or with video style during editing.

4.1   Setting the Stage for Professional Production

An important lesson learned from the production of the thirteen tutorials is that it is vital to set a stage for professional production. The participants all came to the filming sessions with expectations. An example is Malte (all participant names are pseudonyms), who had studied production techniques before we met and came in with the idea to do something with "a green screen" and "video". When he entered the production room for the first time, Malte expressed reservations towards the two 4K cameras we brought to the production room, dismissively asking, "Are they only 4K? Where are the 16K cameras?" and then asked, "What about the green screen?". Malte wanted to make a tutorial that presents techniques for creating a drawbridge in Minecraft. He requested an overlaying image of himself on top of the Minecraft footage, which could be added by manipulating video with the help of the previously requested green screen. School staff provided a green sheet, which was set up on a whiteboard and that seemed to satisfy Malte's needs regarding the production room (cf. Fig. 1). Starting the production, it turned out that Malte did not want his own face to be part of the video. Consequently, the green screen was not a production need but important for staging a professional setting. Malte decided that he wanted to create a digital avatar to be shown instead of himself inside the video tutorial. This start of the production demonstrates two things: first, Malte's individual knowledge of video production, and second—most importantly—the expectations and aspirations of our participants. Creating a tutorial may not technically require 16K or 4K cameras, but it does require staging that feels professional to the participants, as well as a specific goal, a clear framework, a well-suited stage with dedicated time, a quiet room, as well as participants who know their roles, are dedicated to the cause, and can adapt to the demands of the moment. The entire activity seemed to diminish in value if the production setting did not reflect a serious commitment to respectfully and adequately representing the interests of the participants.

The two 4K cameras, 360-degree camera, dedicated software, two microphones and two artificial light sources filmed our participant physically and his Minecraft skills digitally. We figuratively and quite literally put him in the spotlight to physically underscore the video production mode we were engaged in. As we work within a participatory design framework, where the research is not directed at our participants but conducted with them, we highlight the role of the equipment as something that solidifies a fundamental methodological point: Malte is the expert of his activities, who decides what information is important and what needs to be shared. He is a co-producer of a participatory video tutorial format, and we find out what the tutorial will be about together, while we film and edit next to the green sheet and cameras, and in front of the video editing software. The professional setting transforms our efforts from ideas into a specific tutorial script and video.

Fig. 1. A video tutorial recording session with cameras, light, green screen, microphones and computers.

4.2   Embracing Multiple Production Strategies

The role of a digital producer comes with making choices about form and function and requires the participants to pay a different kind of attention to the task at hand. When they engage with the format and present something they care about, they are prompted to pay attention to what is important about their area of interest. This task is inextricably linked with the practical issue of figuring out how to visualize their area of interest for others and for themselves. Both questions require levels of reflexivity and decision-making that turn this video tutorial format into a viable tool for support staff and researchers to better understand what kind of digital production support is needed by youth living with cognitive disabilities and why. The choices our participants make are inherent to the role of a producer of any content. What makes them important for the purposes of this paper is the analytical potential they carry for researchers and support staff, who strive to better understand different digital production strategies developed by the target group. We have identified four approaches that describe how our participants engage with the participatory video tutorial format.

4.2.1   Coping with Ambitions

The first approach deals with ambitions that exceed the participants' current technical abilities. For example, Malte created a digital environment and an avatar in Minecraft. His ambitions for the visual look of the avatar in the tutorial required transparency in the image, which the researchers could not support to a satisfying degree for Malte (the result can be seen in Fig. 2). Frustration was visible when Malte tried to but could not accomplish the task and would not give up on the idea, later returning for a third session with an avatar he had made and was satisfied with. Another participant, Carl, found himself in a similar situation when he saw the draft version of his video tutorial. In a video about setting up and playing a 3D game set in space, Carl felt displeased with the draft narrative we presented him with—the message he felt as most important was not clearly presented, according to him. Carl decided that he should re-record the audio voice-over for the tips and tricks part of the video and fix the issue.

Fig. 2. Digital avatar and environment prepared by a participant. Removing the unequal shading around the avatar was a big technical issue.

These examples serve to highlight how young people with cognitive disabilities struggle to re-formulate their ideas and make sure they are faithfully represented in the final video version. There is a clear desire for digital production, but an unclear way of realizing that desire. The participatory video tutorial format elicited a hands-on approach from some of our participants, in which they attempted to fix what was perceived as a sub-standard technical performance, as well as forcefully alter the agreed-upon script and use their own voice to reformulate specific tips and tricks. These participants show how they take ownership of the video and how they express the strong opinions they have about visuals and narrative. Ambitions that may not be easy to accomplish right away have seemingly not deterred Malte and Carl, but rather inspired them to improve their skills as digital producers. All participants put a great deal of thought into the content and style of the video they produced. This is also important, as staff and family can tend to think that the young people are simply relaxing or playing with digital content, when in fact they are very serious about (in these cases) producing Minecraft environments, 3D games, etc.

4.2.2   Show and Tell

In contrast with the previous production strategy, several participants exerted almost no production control over the form and content of their video tutorials. They would share how they execute certain tasks—e.g., Josephine's communication via iMessage (Fig. 3), and leave the production session relatively earlier than others.

These participants seemed disinterested in the production process but interested in sharing their digital insights and seeing their content in a finished video form. Their relation to the participatory video tutorial format is much more direct, in the sense that they acted only on the explicitly verbalized tasks (e.g., sharing a digital skill, choosing fonts, etc.), rendering their video less truly a product of their own. This type of reaction to the format is important, as it highlights the limits and outlines where it might break down if not adjusted even more to fit each individual's needs. Researchers and support staff should use this type of reaction to also incorporate the format's limitations in their planned activities.

Fig. 3. Participant demonstrating how they attach a video file to an iMessage conversation.

4.2.3   Connecting Physical and Digital Experiences

The third type of reaction to the participatory video tutorial format were two independently requested LAN (Local Area Network) parties at a school and a sheltered center. Participants interpreted the opportunity to create a video as a chance to record a live activity. They expressed a great desire to set up and film a physical activity and shared aspirations to participate in LAN parties. Researchers and support staff facilitated a LAN party, and a producer documented the entire event. The producer recorded the activity with a GoPro camera strapped to their body, as well as a second GoPro camera mounted on a wall, filming a time-lapse (thus condensing around five to six hours of video footage into five to six seconds). At both institutions, participants were either helping with or taking the lead in setting up cables, laptops, desktop computers, physical areas for virtual reality games, and other equipment. Thus, the video was very much a documentary showing how to set-up a LAN party, the joy of gaming with others, and cleaning up.

Fig. 4. Initiator of a LAN Party (red hat) plays a game with friends (Color figure online).

At both institutions, the LAN parties had powerful effects, combining physical, festive events with digital activities to support digital production among the target group. This was largely achieved through a merger of technical aspects (the GoPro cameras strapped to one participant and mounted on walls to capture the entire event) and social conventions (gathering to watch others play in Fig. 4). Both events ultimately featured long gaming sessions (anywhere between 6 and 8 h), and the video tutorials focused on identifying the important building blocks for such coveted activities (e.g., equipment, games, and friends). An interesting observation was that at one LAN party, the participants purposefully invited as many of their friends as possible, whereas the participants at the second LAN party were largely comprised of an already existing group of friends; they did send out an open invitation, but far fewer of their peers joined.

4.2.4 Performative Role

The final reaction to the tutorial format is visible in four examples, where the young people displayed an almost effortless control over their preferred medium of work: the process of preparing for, shooting, editing, and publishing a video on TikTok video import, editing and exporting in the open source ShotCut video editing software, creating landscapes in Roblox Studio; and full recreating of the intro to the Netflix show *Stranger Things* in the 3D modeling program Blender (see Fig. 5).

Fig. 5. Participant demonstrating how he transforms letters in Blender.

The video tutorial format was applicable to the interests of these participants, as they are all visual, with a narrative and somewhat clear structure and goals. The main task these participants focused on as digital producers was to perform what they know well and make clarifying corrections at the review sessions when the researchers, draft videos were not clear enough in visualizing their ideas. As digital producers, the participants' roles were characterized by the need for a good setup—both physical (room, adequate equipment) and digital (video editing software to edit their presentations),—and the time and space to present what they have made. This engagement with the tutorial format is somewhat similar to the first type ("Coping with ambitions") in that this group of participants had a clear idea of what they want to create, and they execute on it. The main difference is that this group is generally pleased with their result and found ways to overcome any issues that arose during filming and editing, in contrast with the first group, whose ambitions always seemed to outgrow their technical skills. The performative role thus requires less technical support (they had already mastered their tools) and more socio-technical presence, where a care-taker or support staffer would learn with this group how their tools (Blender, TikTok, Roblox Studio, etc.) can be used in new and exciting ways (e.g., to gain more followers on TikTok or to create new worlds in Roblox that can be used for game design). Additionally, the performativity extends beyond the production sessions, with one participant somewhat mentoring another in using a specific software (Roblox Studio), which was later used to attract the attention of the researchers.

4.3   Sharing Digital Production

In Sect. 3.1 we described sharing the tutorials as a key part of the participatory video tutorial structure. As emphasized in our theoretical framework, empower-ment is not only about personal development but also about collective develop-ment. The participatory tutorials were developed as a strategy to support this by not only focusing on the individual's digital skills and aspirations but also sharing these and connecting to others via the YouTube platform. The inherent purpose of the tutorial format is sharing with and use by others. This concept is simple, and the format was already familiar to and embraced by our participants. Our experience in this part of the strategy was positive but basic, as we merely created a private YouTube channel and did not research practices of engagement with it. We have not yet conducted research on methods of supporting the shar-ing and viewing of self-produced materials. We have facilitated three premieres, presenting the produced tutorials to an invited audience. While this might seem simple, it was a step that was highlighted by the staff as a success. Several of the participants were generally not keen on sharing with others. Watching the participants present their tutorial as proud producers was a positive conclusion to the process. A teacher at one of the institutions argued that having a result to show and share is important in most activities and this activity resulted in products they were proud of.

Several of the participants appreciated the production process so much that they reached out to the researchers after the premieres to be able to continue their activities as digital producers. Two emailed the researchers a few months after the premieres to request access to the channel so they could view and share their videos with others. Two other participants, Andreas and Thomas specifically requested an altered version of their video tutorials with no mention of their affiliation to the research project. They wanted to republish the videos as their own on their personal social media channels. Emilie, another participant, shared the TikTok video we co-produced on the social platform immediately after the filming session and we monitored engagement with the post for a few weeks (it post did not dramatically alter the participant's follower count). Another participant, Jens, produced a tutorial about German foot soldiers and reached out to the researchers during the draft video editing phase with a coat-of-arms he had made for his personal YouTube channel. Jens wanted the coat-of-arms to be in the video so he could also use it on his personal social media accounts. These are some of the main examples of participants, unprovoked in any direct way, requesting specific actions that would make it easier for them to share their video tutorials with others and continue their activities as digital producers. The participatory video tutorial format was engaging enough to support and stimulate the participants need for sharing self-produced materials with others.

5   Discussion

The participatory video tutorial strategy presented in this paper was developed in cooperation with the young participants and the staff at four institutions in North Denmark [2,18,23]. The processes succeeded in engaging all participants in the process and production of a tutorial, which was identified as a success by the participating institutions, since several of the participants had a history of withdrawing from activities or not finalizing them due to symptoms related to their diagnoses and difficulties with coping with demands for focus, conversation, and delivering. Though the participatory video tutorial format is demanding, as the producer role comes with responsibilities, skill development, and demands for social cooperation, a key finding from this study is that the format has an elasticity that made it possible to meet the needs of the target group, with all its diversity. Surprisingly, the digital arrangement proved to be more fluid and easier to manipulate than the physical arrangement, which required much more thought and care to set up. The tutorial format proved to be able to support the participants not only in producing and developing their own digital materials and skills, but also as a format for sharing their activities and interests and thus supporting their ability to reach out to peers in their own ways. This is an important point, which we want to highlight by referring back to the different approaches to a LAN party (Sect. 4.2.3), which can be described as purposefully open versus somewhat exclusionary access to the events. Additionally, we see that while some participants interacted as little as possible (Sect. 4.2.2), others made a point of supporting each other (Sect. 4.2.4). All this constitutes a rich diversity of reactions to the format. The analysis also showed that the four-step process of engaging young people with cognitive disabilities as producers of digital content relies on their familiarity with the software applications and digital platforms, as well as their desire to create something and make it available for others to watch. A synthesis of these results identified four important principles for supporting this target group in digital production, elaborated in the following section.

5.1   Principles for Participatory Video Tutorials

We have shown how our strategy allowed the sixteen participants to become active co-producers of digital content they enjoy. We found that being a co-producer comes with a set of characteristics: (1) responsibility (to play their role as co-producers in a professional environment), (2) skill development (to have the reflexivity to share existing abilities and developing their abilities through a tutorial process of sharing) and (3) social interactions (establishing a working relationship regarding digital production with the researchers and support staff and sharing the finished material). On this basis, we argue that participatory video tutorials can be used as a support strategy for the digital production needs and ambitions of young people living with cognitive disabilities and thus contribute to digital empowerment and inclusion of this marginalized target group. We have summarized four takeaways from the research process, and we claim that the participatory video tutorials act as a support strategy when they address the principles of:

1. **Socio-technical Belonging.** The tutorials should belong in the socio-technical environment where they are being deployed. Most of our participants were already familiar with the idea of the format, having watched tutorials or made tutorials themselves. The format already had a place in their everyday lives.
2. **Technical Accessibility.** The tutorials should be technologically accessible. It is not necessary to have the same equipment as our research team (with three cameras, lights, microphones, etc.). A similar, if not the same, effect can be reproduced with more common or accessible technologies, such as a smartphone and free video editing software.
3. **Elasticity.** To faithfully represent and clearly visualize unique self-expression by different individuals, the format must be methodologically elastic. This means that its structure (e.g., the three-step tutorial framework) should be equally understandable to participants who act only when they are explicitly asked to as well as to more outgoing participants who want to pursue very specific ideas and outcomes.
4. **Material Reusability.** To ensure that the positive change brought about by the format is permanent, its constitutive parts—the video files, the filming environment—must be easily reusable in different contexts. For example, our co-produced videos were collected in a private YouTube channel that can be used for creative and educational purposes by the participating institutions.

The core contribution of these takeaways is that they refocus the participants as people with abilities (vs. disabilities) and producers (vs. users) of digital content through the production responsibilities of the format. Another important finding is that participatory video tutorials are not just a product of this study, but a process, and sharing activities have an important place in this process. The strategy's ability to support the participants in producing digital content and use it to reach out via digital platforms is an important finding that calls for future research in sharing practices among youth living with cognitive disabilities and how they perceive their own work when it is available on the open internet. The analysis of the production process revealed that each participant displayed different ways of sharing their video tutorials—some wanted to share them on their public YouTube channels, other on their private TikTok accounts, still others more privately. This diversity in the outcome of every tutorial session showed that this kind of production entails different ways of producing and sharing content and highlighted the elasticity of the strategy.

5.2 Challenges for Participatory Video Tutorials as Support Strategies

As presented initially and in related work, developing support strategies for people living with cognitive disabilities is complex. At the end of this process, a key question remains about the future effect of the developed and proposed support strategy. While this study showed positive results with the participatory tutorial format, Seale [28] remind us in her research on the production of digital content for websites, that support strategies are not necessarily empowering if they are only temporary. Seale writes that "there appears to be little point in parents, carers and support workers adopting strategies that help adults with learning difficulties to use home pages as tools to advocate for permanent change if those strategies in themselves are only temporary." ([28], p. 184). In this case, the four types of engagement and the unprovoked requests for materials, which the participants wanted to share and work on after the production process, indicate that our participants have long-term interests in digital production. However, these interests must be addressed seriously, pursued in cooperation with the staff at the institutions, and developed into permanent practices if benefits from the processes of digital production are to be sustained and developed further. As the presented format is focused on engagement and uses participatory design, it inherently comes with a limitation of theoretical and methodological positioning. This positioning prevents us from providing stable definitions for the presented practices that could be used by support staff and other relevant stakeholders, for example. This limitation exists because in a participatory environment, said stakeholders must be directly engaged in all stages of the process, and our method was not set up to incorporate perspectives from staff and institutions, as we exclusively focused on the young people living with cognitive disabilities.

The support staff, however, has professional and personal proximity to our participants that is simultaneously a benefit and a potential challenge. On the one hand, caretakers have a good idea about what engages the young people and what calms them. On the other hand, support staff do not possess the socio-technical skills of gaining proficiency in video production and video management. It is important to stress that our focus on digital interests, and thus on specific video-related skills, narrows both our perspective and potential generalizability of our results. We recognize the danger of reporting on research that is too narrow and thus have strived to make it as useful as possible to all stakeholders. Additionally, we have plans for future research that would build on this foundation and offer insights to a broader audience of researchers, support practitioners, and administrative staff.

Section 4.2 presents us with a complex set of reactions towards the tutorial sessions and reveals four styles of engagement from the target group. To support digital creation and sharing practices, support staff should first recognize the nuanced effects they have on the young people. One way to do this can be to use the produced video tutorials as learning material in their scheduled sessions and learn from them. Second, support staff should dedicate time to exploring digital skill development and digital skill sharing alongside the young people living with cognitive disabilities—not teaching them to do something but learning *with* them. This can be done by refocusing existing pedagogical approaches that require computer time for content creation sessions, applicable to levels the young people are comfortable with. Finally, the caretakers can also support the young people by continuously integrating parts of the video tutorials into the daily lives of the participants, thus ensuring a sort of permanent commitment to digital skill support. Further development of the participatory video tutorial format as a support strategy requires research on how best to integrate this format into the practice of the institutions.

6   Conclusions

The participatory video tutorials presented in this paper proved to be able to engage our participants as digital producers studying at or living in their respective institutions. All participants engaged actively in the four steps of the production process: pre-production, production, review, and sharing. The analysis of this process showed that there are multiple ways of engaging with this format and that the elasticity inherent in it is an important principle for the support strategy. The strategy developed and explored participatory principles grounded in the socio-technical environment of the participants, their ability to access and work with the technology, a methodological elasticity that allowed for structural rigidity (when outlining video structure) and processual adaptability (when customizing the format for each individual participant), and, finally, a product that can be shared and re-purposed by participants and their support staff. As such, the study has contributed new perspectives and empirical examples on a target group that is often regarded as disabled and in need of assistive technology by bringing attention to these young people as producers (vs. users) with abilities (vs. disabilities) and by this contributing insight to HCI research on how to engage a marginalized target group in design and use of interactive technologies. A point for future research, identified during this project, concerns the online sharing practices of young people living with cognitive disabilities, as well as their attitudes towards ownership, reuse, and repurposing of digital content. Finally, this paper highlights the issue of retention and use of existing materials—if the young people's digital productions are not inscribed in the daily practices of the participating institutions in any recognizable way, there is a high risk of losing all the benefits brought about by the production process; benefits that are equally acknowledged by researchers, support staff, and the young co-producers of digital content.

References

1. Alcorn, A., et al.: Social communication between virtual characters and children with autism. In: Biswas, G., Bull, S., Kay, J., Mitrovic, A. (eds.) AIED 2011. LNCS (LNAI), vol. 6738, pp. 7–14. Springer, Heidelberg (2011). https://doi.org/10.1007/978-3-642-21869-9_4

2. Ågren, K.A.: Internet use and digital participation in everyday life: adolescents and young adults with intellectual disabilities, Linköping University Medical Dissertations, vol. 1734. Linköping University Electronic Press, Linköping, September 2020. https://doi.org/10.3384/diss.diva-168070, http://urn.kb.se/resolve?urn=urn:nbn:se:liu:diva-168070

3. Andreasen, D.L., Kanstrup, A.M.: Digital relations among youth with cognitive disabilities: a field study of technology use for developing and maintaining social relations. In: Proceedings of the 9th International Conference on Communities & Technologies - Transforming Communities, pp. 250–254. ACM, Vienna, June 2019. https://doi.org/10.1145/3328320.3328394, https://dl.acm.org/doi/10.1145/3328320.3328394

4. Balasuriya, S.S., Sitbon, L., Bayor, A.A., Hoogstrate, M., Brereton, M.: Use of voice activated interfaces by people with intellectual disability. In: Proceedings of the 30th Australian Conference on Computer-Human Interaction - OzCHI 2018, pp. 102–112. ACM Press, Melbourne (2018). https://doi.org/10.1145/3292147.3292161, http://dl.acm.org/citation.cfm?doid=3292147.3292161

5. Bircanin, F., et al.: The TalkingBox.: revealing strengths of adults with severe cognitive disabilities. In: The 22nd International ACM SIGACCESS Conference on Computers and Accessibility, pp. 1–8. ACM, Virtual Event Greece, October 2020. https://doi.org/10.1145/3373625.3417025, https://dl.acm.org/doi/10.1145/3373625.3417025

6. Brereton, M., Sitbon, L., Abdullah, M.H.L., Vanderberg, M., Koplick, S.: Design after design to bridge between people living with cognitive or sensory impairments, their friends and proxies. CoDesign 11(1), 4–20 (2015). https://doi.org/10.1080/15710882.2015.1009471, http://www.tandfonline.com/doi/abs/10.1080/15710882.2015.1009471

7. Cambridge, P., Forrester-Jones, R.: Using individualised communication for interviewing people with intellectual disability: a case study of user-centred research. J IntelL. Dev. Disabil. 28(1), 5–23 (2003). https://doi.org/10.1080/136682503100008687, https://www.tandfonline.com/doi/full/10.1080/136682503100008687

8. Cameron, L., Murphy, J.: Obtaining consent to participate in research: the issues involved in including people with a range of learning and communication disabilities. Br. J. Learn. Disabil. 35(2), 113–120 (2007). https://doi.org/10.1111/j.1468-3156.2006.00404.x, http://doi.wiley.com/10.1111/j.1468-3156.2006.00404.x

9. Caton, S., Chapman, M.: The use of social media and people with intellectual disability: A systematic review and thematic analysis. J. Intell. Dev. Disabil. 41(2), 125–139 (2016). https://doi.org/10.3109/13668250.2016.1153052, http://www.tandfonline.com/doi/full/10.3109/13668250.2016.1153052

10. Collins, J.C., Collet-Klingenberg, L.: Portable electronic assistive technology to improve vocational task completion in young adults with an intellectual disability: a review of the literature. J. Intellect. Disabil. 22(3), 213–232 (2018). https://doi.org/10.1177/1744629516689336, http://journals.sagepub.com/doi/10.1177/1744629516689336

11. Davidson, J., Orsini, M. (eds.): Worlds of Autism: Across the Spectrum of Neurological Difference. University of Minnesota Press, Minneapolis (2013)

12. Frauenberger, C., Good, J., Keay-Bright, W.: Designing technology for children with special needs: bridging perspectives through participatory design. CoDesign 7(1), 1–28 (2011). https://doi.org/10.1080/15710882.2011.587013, http://www.tandfonline.com/doi/abs/10.1080/15710882.2011.587013

13. Frauenberger, C., Good, J., Pares, N.: Autism and Technology: beyond Assistance & intervention. In: Proceedings of the 2016 CHI Conference Extended Abstracts on Human Factors in Computing Systems, pp. 3373–3378. ACM, San Jose (2016). https://doi.org/10.1145/2851581.2856494, https://dl.acm.org/doi/10.1145/2851581.2856494

14. Frauenberger, C., Spiel, K., Makhaeva, J.: Thinking OutsideTheBox designing smart things with autistic children. Int. J. Hum. Comput. Interact. 35(8), 666–678 (2019). https://doi.org/10.1080/10447318.2018.1550177, https://www.tandfonline.com/doi/full/10.1080/10447318.2018.1550177

15. Freire, P.: Pedagogy of the Oppressed, 30th Anniversary edn. Continuum, New York (2000)

16. Garzotto, F., Gelsomini, M., Gianotti, M., Riccardi, F.: Engaging children with neurodevelopmental disorder through multisensory interactive experiences in a smart space. In: Soro, A., Brereton, M., Roe, P. (eds.) Social Internet of Things. IT, pp. 167–184. Springer, Cham (2019). https://doi.org/10.1007/978-3-319-94659-7_9

17. Greenbaum, J.M., Kyng, M. (eds.): Design at Work: Cooperative Design of Computer Systems. L. Erlbaum Associates, Hillsdale (1991)

18. Gómez-Puerta, M., Chiner, E.: Internet use and online behaviour of adults with intellectual disability: support workers' perceptions, training and online risk mediation. Disabil. Soc. 1–22 (2021). _eprint https://doi.org/10.1080/09687599.2021.1874300. Routledge

19. Hegarty, S.: International perspectives on special education reform. Eur. J. Special Needs Educ. 13(1), 112–115 (1998). https://doi.org/10.1080/0885625980130110, http://www.tandfonline.com/doi/abs/10.1080/0885625980130110

20. Schalock, R.L., et al. (eds.) Intellectual Disability: Definition, Classification, and Systems of Supports. American Association on Intellectual and Developmental Disabilities, Washington, DC, 11th edn. (2010). oCLC: ocn435422270

21. Löfgren-Mårtenson, L.: Love in cyberspace: Swedish young people with intellectual disabilities and the internet1. Scand. J. Disabil. Res. 10(2), 125–138 (2008)

22. Makhaeva, J., Frauenberger, C., Spiel, K.: Creating creative spaces for co-designing with autistic children: the concept of a "Handlungsspielraum". In: Proceedings of the 14th Participatory Design Conference: Full papers, vol. 1, pp. 51–60. ACM, Aarhus, August 2016. https://doi.org/10.1145/2940299.2940306, https://dl.acm.org/doi/10.1145/2940299.2940306

23. Martin, A.J., Strnadová, I., Loblinzk, J., Danker, J.C., Cumming, T.M.: The role of mobile technology in promoting social inclusion among adults with intellectual disabilities. J. Appl. Res. Intellect Disabil. 34(3), 840–851 (2021). https://doi.org/10.1111/jar.12869, https://onlinelibrary.wiley.com/doi/10.1111/jar.12869

24. Ochs, E., Solomon, O.: Autistic sociality. Ethos 38(1), 69–92 (2010). https://doi.org/10.1111/j.1548-1352.2009.01082.x, http://doi.wiley.com/10.1111/j.1548-1352.2009.01082.x

25. Pinchevski, A., Peters, J.D.: Autism and new media: disability between technology and society. New Media Soc. 18(11), 2507–2523 (2016). https://doi.org/10.1177/1461444815594441, http://journals.sagepub.com/doi/10.1177/1461444815594441

26. Rajapakse, R., Brereton, M., Sitbon, L.: A respectful design approach to facilitate codesign with people with cognitive or sensory impairments and makers. CoDesign 17, 159–187 (2019). https://doi.org/10.1080/15710882.2019.1612442, https://www.tandfonline.com/doi/full/10.1080/15710882.2019.1612442

27. Ringland, K.E., Boyd, L., Faucett, H., Cullen, A.L., Hayes, G.R.: Making in minecraft: a means of self-expression for youth with autism. In: Proceedings of the 2017 Conference on Interaction Design and Children, pp. 340–345. ACM, Stanford, June 2017. https://doi.org/10.1145/3078072.3079749, https://dl.acm.org/doi/10.1145/3078072.3079749

28. Seale, J.K.: Strategies for supporting the online publishing activities of adults with learning difficulties. Disabil. Soc. **22**(2), 173–186 (2007). https://doi.org/10.1080/09687590601141626, http://www.tandfonline.com/doi/abs/10.1080/09687590601141626

29. Seale, J.K., Pockney, R.: The use of the Personal Home Page by adults with Down's syndrome as a tool for managing identity and friendship. Br. J. Learning Disab. **30**(4), 142–148 (2002). https://doi.org/10.1046/j.1468-3156.2002.00195.x, http://doi.wiley.com/10.1046/j.1468-3156.2002.00195.x

30. Seymour, W., Lupton, D.: Holding the line online: exploring wired relationships for people with disabilities. Disabil. Soc. **19**(4), 291–305 (2004). https://doi.org/10.1080/09687590410001689421, http://www.tandfonline.com/doi/bs/10.1080/09687590410001689421

31. Simonsen, J., Robertson, T. (eds.): Routledge International Handbook of Participatory Design. Routledge, New York (2013)

32. Sitbon, L., Hoogstrate, M., Yule, J., Koplick, S., Bircanin, F., Brereton, M.: A non-clinical approach to describing participants with intellectual disability. In: Proceedings of the 30th Australian Conference on Computer-Human Interaction, pp. 128–132. ACM, Melbourne, December 2018. https://doi.org/10.1145/3292147.3292206, https://dl.acm.org/doi/10.1145/3292147.3292206

33. Söderström, S.: Offline social ties and online use of computers: a study of disabled youth and their use of ICT advances. New Media Soc. **11**(5), 709–727 (2009)

34. Söderström, S.: Staying safe while on the move. YOUNG **19**(1), 91–109 (2011)

35. Vygotskij, L.S., Cole, M.: Mind in society: the development of higher psychological processes. Harvard University Press, Cambridge (1981). oCLC: 255468763

36. WHO: World Health Organization Homepage (2001). https://www.who.int/standards/classifications/international-classification-of-functioning-disability-and-health. Accessed 5 June 2021

Dot-to-Dot: Pre-reading Assessment of Literacy Risk via a Visual-Motor Mechanism on Touchscreen Devices

Wonjeong Park[1], Paulo Revés[2], Augusto Esteves[2,3(✉)],
Jon M. Kerridge[4], Dongsun Yim[1], and Uran Oh[1]

[1] Ewha Womans University, Seoul, Republic of Korea
{iamwj,sunyim,uran.oh}@ewha.ac.kr
[2] Instituto Superior Técnico, University of Lisbon, Lisbon, Portugal
{paulo.reves,augusto.esteves}@tecnico.ulisboa.pt
[3] ITI/LARSyS, Lisbon, Portugal
[4] Edinburgh Napier University, Edinburgh, UK
j.kerridge@napier.ac.uk

Abstract. While early identification of children with dyslexia is crucial, it is difficult to assess literacy risks of these children early on before they learn to read. In this study, we expand early work on Dot-to-Dot (DtD), a non-linguistic visual-motor mechanism aimed at facilitating the detection of the potential reading difficulties of children at pre-reading age. To investigate the effectiveness of this approach on touchscreen devices, we conducted a user study with 33 children and examined their task performance logs as well as language test results. Our findings suggest that there is a significant correlation among DtD task and series of language tests. We conclude the work by suggesting different ways in which DtD could be seamlessly embedded into everyday mobile use cases.

Keywords: Developmental dyslexia · Pre-reading assessment · Literacy risk · Visual-motor tracing

1 Introduction

The ability to read fluently is considered as a prerequisite for children to be successful in academic settings [59]. Thus, children with reading difficulties have challenging times following class materials at school. It is also reported that children who have trouble reading are more likely to have emotional and behavioral problems compared to the children who do not have reading disorders, and these problems may continue after adolescence [11]. Fortunately, previous studies on children with reading difficulties report that early screening and intervention can prevent from resulting in significant problems in school-age learning [12,14,33,52]. Therefore, it is especially important to screen the children with reading difficulties and to conduct appropriate interventions in educational setting as early as possible.

© IFIP International Federation for Information Processing 2021
Published by Springer Nature Switzerland AG 2021
C. Ardito et al. (Eds.): INTERACT 2021, LNCS 12932, pp. 192–212, 2021.
https://doi.org/10.1007/978-3-030-85623-6_13

To identify children who have trouble reading, language-based tests such as TOWL (Test of Written Language) [19], DIBELS (Dynamic Indicators of Basic Literacy Skills) [51], and CTOPP (Comprehensive Test of Phonological Processing) [57] have been used by professionals. In these tests, children's reading abilities such as phonological awareness, decoding skills, reading fluency, and rapid naming are evaluated through certain methods. However, since most children with reading difficulties are screened during periods after the school year, following the implementation of literacy education, it is a major issue to carry out accurate screening for children at an earlier age before they learn to read for effective interventions.

For this reason, numerous previous studies have been conducted to designing tasks for efficient screening of the children with reading difficulties in their early childhood [7,15,26]. Recently, Phonological Awareness (PA) test and Rapid Automatized Naming (RAN) have been used as representative tasks to identify children with reading difficulties before they learn to read. PA test measures an individual's meta-linguistic abilities to phonetic structures of oral sound to estimate the child's reading development [28]. RAN, on the other hand, is a task consisted with the series of stimuli such as colors, numbers or familiar objects where a participant is required to speak the stimuli as quickly as possible to predicting reading fluency [36]. These two tests have been reported to be strongly linked to current literacy skills of children in early literacy stage, as well as to future reading and academic achievements, and thus commonly used in clinical settings [24]. Yet, these methods are time-consuming and expensive as these require language specialists. Also, it is difficult to get tested unless referred to a clinic by a parent or a teacher.

Meanwhile, there are screening tools which can save time and costs for requiring specialists. For instance, most of these attempted to identify children with reading difficulties by assessing their game performances on smart devices [3,29,44]. However, as language-dependent tools, they cannot be used for children who speak different languages other than the supported ones. Even if the tool supports the very language that the child speaks, a proper evaluation of the child's underlying abilities is not possible if she/he has not learned to read yet.

Inspired by studies on literacy and dyslexia suggesting that reading difficulty is not only a language surface problem but also related to visual, sensory and motor skills [9,41,54,58], we further investigated a non-linguistic approach described as "Dot-to-Dot (DtD)" [4,37] which originally is a desktop application designed to help identifying at-risk behaviors related to reading difficulties for pre-schoolers. This utilizes a simple tracing mechanism, connecting a series of dots, that can potentially facilitate the passive and implicit screening of children at pre-reading age. Our contributions are threefold:

- We expand on the original DtD task which supported indirect, stylus-based input to a separate display with the goal of significantly reducing the manual scoring time and potential bias of experts via an automated screening process (see Fig. 1). We explore instead direct, touch-based input using a single mobile device (see Fig. 3). Our motivation in the context of human-computer interaction (HCI) is the possibility of embedding DtD into everyday touch-screen applications such as games or UI manipulations (*e.g.*, dragging) to enable not only automated but also implicit screening.

– We explore our approach via a user study with 33 pre-school and school-aged Korean-speaking children, widening the participant pool of the original work which reported on the performance of English-speaking children. The empirical data collected from the study revealed that the completion time for DtD task can be used to assess the potential risk of having reading difficulties given the children's age regardless of the input conditions. Direct input condition, in particular, can be used to distinguish between children with low and high literacy group.

– We analyze participant tracing performance using a wider but systematic set of trace characteristics including amplitude, angle, or direction. Our goal is to enable HCI designers and developers to embed DtD into their own applications and systems, e.g., the pervasive SwiftKey keyboard. This with the goal of enabling the implicit assessment of not only children of pre-reading age, but teenagers and adults during they everyday interactions with touchscreen devices.

2   Related Work

Our work was inspired by prior work on dyslexia particularly for children and digital assessment tools for cognitive abilities.

2.1   Possible Causes for Reading Difficulties

The Diagnostic and Statistical Manual of Mental Disorders (DSM-5) defines reading difficulties such as developmental dyslexia within the category of learning difficulties. According to this criteria, reading difficulties refer to children who have deficits in decoding and reading comprehension compared to their peers. These children show significant difficulties in learning academic skills related to reading accuracy, fluency, and recognition [2]; as is the definition we use in our work when talking about developmental dyslexia. Previous studies have shown that children with reading difficulties have lower phonological processing abilities than peers without reading difficulties [6,8,10]. However, it is argued that the reading difficulties cannot be explained only by phonological processing skills. Previous studies have revealed that children with reading difficulties also show a broader range of deficits such as sensory, cognitive, and visual-spatial problems. In particular, many studies have linked the poor visual processing skills of children with reading difficulties to their literacy problems [13,16,53]. These problems of visual processing in reading difficulties also affect the sequential processing of specific stimuli. In addition, children with reading difficulties showed lower performance in tasks using motor skills such as motor coordination [60] and motor sequential learning [56] due to their visual processing deficits. We investigated DtD for assessing literacy of children which involves hand-and-eye coordination on a touchscreen motivated by these prior findings that poor visual-motor skills are closely related to the reading problem.

2.2 Early Identification of Dyslexia

Although the cause of dyslexia is still under debate, there is a widespread consensus that early identification and intervention is crucial in both language remediation and in limiting the low self-esteem and behavioral difficulties often reported in unrecognized dyslexia [48,52]. However, identifying dyslexia is often difficult, time consuming, and expensive as it requires assessments by clinical professionals. As such, its formal identification in many schools typically occurs long after children have failed to learn to read, and interventions are provided only after [49]. Identifications of dyslexia may be further delayed when children do not use their native language at school. Several screening tools have been developed in recent years to estimate the risk of reading difficulties at an early stage in primary-aged children (*e.g.*, [34,50]) for offering early intervention. While effective, drawbacks exists since these often require specialists to administer the procedure and interpret results. Also, these tools lack engagements. While a number of game-based tools have developed both in academia [3,17,18,29,42–44] as well as commercial markets (*e.g.*, *Lexercise Screener*[1], *Nessy*[2]), children who have not acquired reading and writing skills (or who speak different languages) cannot use these tools as they are language-dependent.

2.3 Dyslexia Screening Tools for Pre-schoolers

Others have proposed various approaches on early identification of dyslexia for pre-school-aged children who have not learned to read yet. For example, *DIESEL-X* [18] is a tablet game designed to predict the likelihood of having dyslexia for pre-schoolers by measuring dyslexia-related indicators such as letter knowledge and end-phoneme recognition while a child is playing the game although the effectiveness of their prediction model is unknown. *MusVis* [43] and *DGames* [42] utilize musical-visual cues instead of relying on existing knowledge of literacy or phonological awareness, which pre-school children may not have. While promising, limitations still exist because they can only be applied to children who use specific languages, and they are difficult to use for young children as these approaches screen reading difficulties in a way that assesses children's phonological knowledge involving letters. On the other hand, Bannach-Brown proposed Dot-to-Dot (DtD) [4], a stylus-based dot-connecting task on a computer as a screening tool for young children with potential reading difficulties once they learn to read. Her approach is different from *DIESEL-X* or *DGames* as it is entirely non-linguistic; no prior phonological knowledge is required and thus language-independent. In addition, she showed that DtD could successfully differentiate between children at 'low' and 'high' risks of developing dyslexia

---

[1] https://www.nessy.com/uk/product/dyslexia-screening.
[2] https://www.lexercise.com/tests/dyslexia-test.

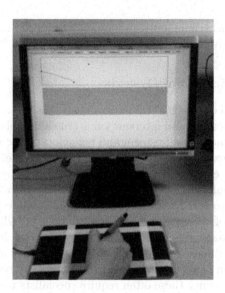

Fig. 1. Photo from the original DtD experiment where participants interacted indirectly with an external display via a stylus [37].

(classified using LUCID Rapid [49]) based on an empirical evidence collected from a user study with 68 English-speaking participants (4 to 8 years old).

We expand this work by exploring the effectiveness of DtD for assessing the potential literacy risks of pre-schoolers via a user study with Korean-speaking children. Moreover, we implemented the task for touchscreen devices to investigate the effects of input modes (direct *vs.* indirect) on detecting potential reading difficulties since direct hand-eye coordination involving one's visual-motor skills of standard touchscreen input is known to outperform indirect input performance [21,45] – as employed in the original DtD work [4,37].

2.4 Digital Tools for Cognitive Assessments

A number of digital tools for assessing one's cognitive abilities have been proposed [5,25,38–40] as an alternative to traditional pen and paper based approach where a trained expert (clinician) is required to examine the test results manually. For instance, Prange *et al.* [39] proposed a multimodal speech-based dialogue system for a questionnaire-based cognitive test called the Mini-Mental State Examination (MMSE). The system could automatically run and evaluate the test with high usability. On the other hand, drawing-based assessments were investigated. Prange *et al.* also implemented a system for detecting signs of dementia or monitoring the stroke recovery progress using the clock drawing test [40]. They showed that their system can reduce the scoring time automating the process and that the its results are clinically reliable. Similarly, Kuosmanen *et al.* [25] developed a smartphone-based clinical tool to detect symptoms of Parkinson's disease with the spiral drawing test. Researchers also focused on Trail

Making Test (TMT) for assessing one's cognitive performance. Barz *et al.* [5], for instance, used TMT performance to predicted the task difficulties in terms of cognitive load. They collected TMT data with six drawing patterns from the Snijders-Oomen Non-verbal intelligence test (SON) with children from elementary school and showed high prediction accuracy. Moreover, a recent study on TMT [38] proposed an automated system that monitors various pen features on a tablet and provides a structured analysis report of the test with explanations for clinicians.

Inspired by the approach for digitizing the assessment process of cognitive performance, we designed an application that utilizes DtD test, which is similar to TMT test but simpler for children, to assess the likelihood of having a dyslexia using off-the-shelf device (*e.g.*, a tablet, a smartphone) so that any sign of reading difficulties can be detected without having to visit a trained expert.

3   The Design of Dot-to-Dot Task

Motivated by prior works on designing digital tools for assessing one's cognitive performance from pen-based tests such as spiral drawings [25] or trail making tests [5,38], our work expands on "Dot-to-Dot" (DtD), a simple dot-connecting task that involves visual-spatial, attentional, and motor mechanisms that often occur in dyslexia [20,22,35]. DtD was initially developed following a series of observations on children tracing their names that highlighted potential visual and motor problems [37]. It was argued by the authors that the difficulty to fixate one's eyes on the screen while moving the stylus on an adjacent trackpad distinguished this task from standard drawing where the eyes gaze just ahead of the hand holding the pen. This ability to dissociate the gaze and the hand may be related to divided attention, and was argued to be likely to reveal developmental delay in control of sensorimotor processing (which may be compromised in individuals with dyslexia).

While the original work by Bannach-Brown [4] and Piotrowska [37] focused on DtD as proof-of-concept for an automated screening process using indirect, pen-based input; we focus instead on the use of the index finger of the dominant hand – a more prevalent form of input with modern touchscreen devices. By exploring how different touch-based strokes relate to at-risk behaviors, we aim to provide interaction designers working on mobile platforms with the knowledge required to pick-up on such at-risk behaviors via already enabled user actions in their mobile apps (or re-think new interaction techniques altogether around these strokes). Regardless of how successful the original DtD task is, a single-purpose application (i.e., a DtD app) will always have a limited reach. Our goal instead is to facilitate the embedding of an implicit DtD screening process into everyday apps and games, which would greatly expand the reach and impact of this approach.

With this in mind, the DtD task we designed for our study requires the user to connect a series of targets (dots) that consecutively appear on a tablet screen as quickly and accurately as possible (without lifting their fingers from the display). At the start of a new task two targets are displayed: the first target in the sequence in red, and the next target in green. Once the user successfully drags his/her finger from the red to the green targets, the next target in the sequence is displayed in green and the previous targets disappear. The user continues to drag its finger towards the latest green target until the sequence is complete. If, for whatever reason, the user lifts the finger from the display during the task, a red target is displayed at the location where this took place. Users can resume the task by moving their fingers from this red target to the green target they were previously pursuing. Five sequences (or patterns) of growing difficulty were designed using eight sequential targets, or seven unique traces, varying index of difficulty and angle to the next target with fixed target width of 0.6 cm:

- **Index of difficulty (approx. amplitude):** 1.5 (1.10 cm), 2 (1.80 cm), 2.5 (2.79 cm), 3 (4.20 cm), 3.5 (6.19 cm)
- **Angle to the next target:** 0, 30, 60, 90, 270, 300, 330 degrees

Index of difficulty (ID) was calculated using Shannon's formulation [30,47]): $ID = \log_2(\frac{A}{W} + 1)$, where A is the amplitude of movement, and W the target width. The five patterns designed can be seen in Fig. 2, accounting for 35 unique traces.

4   User Study

To evaluate the effectiveness of the DtD task in touchscreens, we conducted a user study with 33 children where they were asked to perform a series of dot-connecting tasks. The study was approved by the institutional review board (IRB) of the university where the researchers are affiliated with.

4.1   Participants

Thirty-eight preschool and school-aged children (18 males, 20 females) living in South Korea were initially recruited for this study. We excluded five children from the analysis because two scored less than 85 standard scores on the non-verbal intelligence test, and three had difficulty in handling the tablet PC and thus were severe outliers in the data. As a result, we report on the data from 33 participants in analysis below (13 males, 20 females, mean age of 89.33 months, $SD = 24.29$). Participants were recruited through online and offline advertising on bulletin boards at a private child development center and daycare center; and all children met the following criteria: (1) chronological age was between 5 to 12; (2) the standard score of non-verbal IQ test [31] was higher than 85 ($-1SD$); (3) they speak only Korean; and (4) did not show sensory impairments or psychological problems, as reported by parent and the nursery teacher. Note that we recruited both pre-school (aged 5) and school-aged children (aged 6 to 12) to capture a wide set of data on children with different reading skills and at different points of their development.

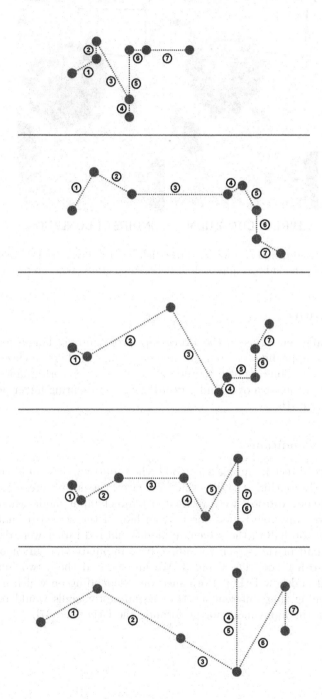

Fig. 2. Patterns 1 to 5 from top to bottom, representing 35 unique traces (5 IDs × 7 angles). These are incrementally harder, represented by traces with average amplitudes of: 2.33 cm, 2.61 cm, 2.85 cm, 3.15 cm, and 5.14 cm. Numbers indicate the tracing order.

DIRECT CONDITION   INDIRECT CONDITION

Fig. 3. Our experimental setting for direct (left) and indirect (right) conditions; the latter emulating the indirect approach of the original study, now via touch input.

4.2 Apparatus

DtD was implemented using the Processing programming language. To make the task more appealing, one out of three recordings of children cheering (<1 s) would play every time a green target was reached. User performance was captured locally in the form of x- and y-coordinates representing finger positions at approximately 60 Hz.

4.3 Input Conditions

In addition to direct manipulation mode where participants could connect the dots by directly touching the dots that appear on the entire screen as described in Sect. 3 (**direct mode**), we investigated indirect input mode where the participants were only able to use the bottom half of the screen to manipulate a cursor on the top half of the screen; an additional red target were displayed at the bottom half of the screen to indirectly manipulate the cursor on the top (**indirect mode**); see Figs. 4 and 3. We investigated these two input modes to examine if and how DtD performance vary depending on which input mode is used assuming that different levels of visual-motor skills would be required depending on the input mode for performing the DtD task [37].

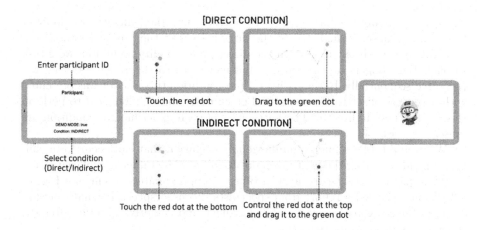

Fig. 4. Procedures of direct (top) and indirect (bottom) conditions. Starting dot was colored as red and the target dot was colored green. (Color figure online)

4.4 Procedure

In accord with IRB regulations, researchers explained the procedure and benefits of the study and received consent from the children and their guardians. All children participated in a language development test, literacy-related tasks, and DtD test. Additionally, we conducted the Korean Receptive and Expressive Vocabulary Test [23] to assess children's language development through evaluation of vocabulary skills. REVT is divided into two tests: the receptive vocabulary test (REVT-R) and the expressive vocabulary test (REVT-E); in which we presented a series of pictures corresponding to different vocabulary (ranked by difficulty level), and evaluated whether the child could vocalize and understand each picture. The total raw scores were kept for further statistical analysis.

The literacy-related tasks included the Rapid Automated Naming (RAN) and Phonological Awareness (PA) test. The RAN test [46] presents a 6×6 matrix on a computer monitor and randomly placed red, yellow, blue, and green colors inside each cell. Children were asked to speak the colors in the cells as quickly as possible, and the time required for the children to speak all the name of colors was measured and used for analysis. The PA is a test that evaluates children's abilities to recognize and modify sound during speech, and consists of two subtests: phonological segmenting and phonological blending. These subtests were conducted at phonemic and syllabic levels, and the total score obtained from this process was recorded. Both RAN and PA have been shown to be strong predictors of a child's literacy skills [15,55].

In our DtD task, participants were asked to trace various sequence of dots on a tablet PC (LG-X760, 10.1") as accurately as possible with their index fingers (without lifting their fingers from the display). The dots in each pattern and condition were presented from left to right as shown in Fig. 2. Motivated by our goal of embedding DtD into everyday mobile devices and by the findings in [3], where children were reported to prefer direct touch (i.e., finger) over indirect touch (i.e., mouse, stylus) due to the intuitiveness of the physical interaction, we examined two input modes. In the direct input condition children were task to place their fingers on the red dot and move this to the green dots that are presented sequentially. In the indirect input condition this red dot was presented with a vertical offset to the sequential green dots, and children had to perform this tracing task indirectly. The particulars of each experimental condition are presented in Fig. 4.

We used a tablet stand to minimize any occlusion that can occur from children's hands covering the next green dot to follow. The tablet was placed at the height of participants heads, at a distance of approximately 30 cm (see Fig. 3). All parents received a report from specialists (licensed speech-language pathologists in South Korea) on the child's language and cognitive abilities after the study as a benefit to participation.

4.5   Data and Analysis

The DtD task performance of all children was analyzed using task completion time and the frequencies of finger lifts per condition and pattern. Each participant's finger lift pattern and trace was represented using x-, y-coordinates. Based on this data, we conducted a series of statistical tests to: (1) examine whether the children's DtD performance correlated with the language development level literacy-related skills; (2) identify whether there is a significant correlation between specific DtD patterns with language and literacy task results; and (3) determine whether there is a significant group difference on DtD performance between high and low literacy groups. For the study purpose, Pearson's correlation and Mann-Whitney U test were conducted using SPSS (v. 26.0).

4.6   Findings

In our study, we found that DtD performance was highly associated with children's reading related variables where the degrees of association between children's age, literacy skills, and the input condition and patterns of the task varied.

Overall Performance in DtD and Literacy-Related Tasks. Prior to the correlation analysis, we examined descriptive statistics of children's literacy-related tasks and DtD performance (see Table 1). Overall, language ability and literacy-related variables, as well as the performance of DtD tend to improve with age. Paired t-tests showed that the time required for performing the direct condition was significantly shorter ($t = -5.481$, $p < .001$), and that the number of finger lifts was less frequent in the direct condition than in the indirect condition ($t = -3.099$, $p = .004$). These indicate that the overall difficulty of DtD was lower in the direct condition as expected [21,45].

Correlation Analysis Across Age Groups. To identify correlations between DtD performance and children's language development and literacy skills, we computed Pearson's correlation coefficients between these. The results

Table 1. Descriptive statistics in age subgroups where DtD-D and DtD-I refer to direct and indirect conditions respectively. Overall, participants who have relatively higher literacy skills took a shorter time to perform the DtD task with fewer finger lifts for both direct and indirect conditions.

	Preschool-age (n=16)	Lower grade (n=10)	Upper grade (n=7)
Age	71.06	90.90	128.86
(month)	(5.99)	(10.94)	(12.66)
REVT-R	64.13	84.50	136.00
	(10.65)	(20.00)	(23.97)
REVT-E	68.19	90.10	144.43
	(15.33)	(19.50)	(23.49)
RAN	42.31	39.80	23.43
(sec)	(8.87)	(25.29)	(3.64)
PA	35.00	73.00	94.29
	(17.81)	(26.83)	(6.86)
DtD-D Time	60151.31	51084.60	35072.57
(ms)	(19902.08)	(12911.64)	(9866.21)
DtD-I Time	91266.56	78160.20	45597.43
(ms)	(25610.86)	(35102.15)	(5967.74)
DtD-D Finger Lift	9.50	4.80	0.14
	(6.70)	(5.92)	(0.38)
DtD-I Finger Lift	16.69	11.40	1.14
	(11.74)	(10.08)	(2.27)

Values are presented as mean(SD)

showed that receptive vocabulary scores (REVT-R), expressive vocabulary scores (REVT-E), and PA showed significant negative correlation with the task duration and the number of finger lifts both in direct and indirect conditions ($p < .050$). The only exception was the correlation between RAN and the number of finger lifts in both conditions ($p > .050$). Additionally, these results also show that children's age has a significant effect on overall performance on DtD task as in the literacy-related tests. This suggests DtD has the potential for estimating one's literacy risk when compared to his/her peers in the same age group.

High Literacy *vs.* Low Literacy Group. We further examined the performance in terms of the literacy skills of participants to explore the potential for our DtD mechanism in detecting children with reading difficulties. For this analysis we rely on the RAN and PA subtests for evaluating children's literacy skills, and to group them based on this performance. Thus, the children who performed below 0.5 standard deviations (*SDs*) from the mean in both RAN and PA tests we considered part of the low literacy group, while children performing above 0.5 *SDs* where considered part of the high literacy group.

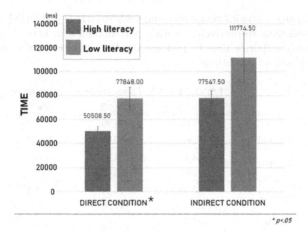

Fig. 5. The average time for both direct and indirect conditions between high literacy group and low literacy group with Mann-Whitney U test results.

Following this criteria, eight similarly aged children were selected: four from each literacy group. As shown in Fig. 5, Mann-Whitney U tests showed that there was a significant difference between the two groups in terms of time only for the direct condition ($U = .000$, $p = .021$); while the number of finger lifts was not found to be significant for either of the two conditions. Still, the number of finger lifts during direct input could also potentially be used to distinguish the two groups with a larger sample size ($U = 1.500$, $p = .056$). This result implies that DtD performance during direct input has potential to identify children with low literacy skills (see Fig. 6 for trace examples produced by children in high and low literacy groups).

Correlation Analysis by Patterns. To examine if the index of difficulty (ID) of each pattern (i.e., trace amplitude) can be a relevant predictor of literacy risk, we conducted a secondary analysis focusing on the direct condition results which were significantly correlated with RAN – one of the representative literacy tests we used for the main analysis above (age-controlled). The results of the correlation analysis suggest *Pattern 5*, with the highest ID, was positively correlated with RAN results ($r = .381$, $p = .031$). Children's pattern-specific performance in the direct input condition and the results of correlation analysis between patterns and RAN performance are presented in Fig. 7.

Analysis by Trace. Continuing our top-down approach, our last analysis focuses on developing a deeper understanding of which individual trace properties can be helpful in predicting literary risk. In order to achieve this, we consider four performance metrics (see Fig. 8): (1) the time to complete a trace in *ms* (*TT*), (2) the distance between the farthest point of a trace to the best fit in *px* (*MD*; the shortest path between two successive points in a pattern), (3) the average distance between each point in the trace to the best fit in *px* (*AD*),

Fig. 6. Example traces from two children during *Pattern 5* (P5): high literacy group on the left and low literacy on the right. Noticeable differences include direction corrections at almost every target for the child with low literacy skills. Further, the pattern on the left was completed in a little over 7 *s* with no finger lifts; while the pattern on the right was completed in over 25 *s* and included 6 finger lifts. The input direction is encoded as a blue gradient towards a lighter shade of blue from left to right. (Color figure online)

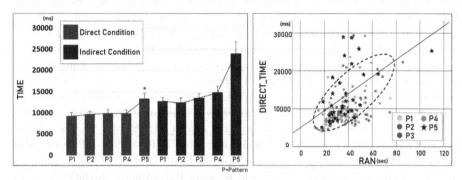

Fig. 7. Left: pattern-specific average time performance per pattern and per input condition. Right: the correlation between time performance and RAN for each of the five patterns. The order of the presentation was the same starting with the first pattern (P1) to the last (P5), whose index of difficulty (ID) is the highest.

and (4) the time to correct the tracing direction at the start of a new trace in *ms* (*TD*). While MD can be used to detect mistakes such as overshooting or sudden changes in direction, AD reflects how well a participant were able to stay close to the shortest path when connecting two dots during the task. TD is the time it takes a participant to start a new trace in the direction of the latest point; this is measured from the time a new point is displayed until the direction of the participant's trace is within 30° s of the target point to quantify visual-motor challenges associated with each new trace if any.

As such, our analysis focused on 48 items: 4 performance metrics × (5 IDs + 7 angles). Following the earlier analysis, we examined solely at the direct condition and RAN performances. We began by filtering these features via a Pearson's correlation matrix between the 48 items and the RAN results, ignoring all items with a correlation coefficient below 0.50. This resulted in six features: 30°-MD (0.50), 90°-TT (0.59), 1.5-TT (0.61), 3.5-TT (0.51), 3.5-MD (0.55), and 3.5-TD (0.58) – the latter three features were not surprising as they played a prominent

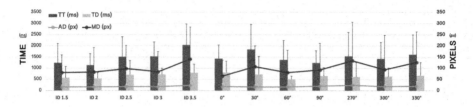

Fig. 8. Participant performance by trace (IDs and angles), measured as: time to complete a trace in ms (TT); maximum distance to best fit in px (MD); average distance to best fit in px (AD); and time to correct the tracing direction at the start of a new trace in ms (TD).

role in *Pattern 5*. We then computed another correlation matrix between these. When two features were correlated (>0.50), the one highest correlated with RAN was selected. This resulted in three final features: 30°-MD, 90°-TT, and 1.5-TT (see Fig. 9). That is, the farthest distance to the best fit between two points at 30° s; the time it takes to drawn an upwards trace (90°); and the time it takes to draw a trace with ID 1.5 (approx. 1.10 cm).

Finally, we computed a Decision Tree Regression using NumPy and Scikit-learn (CART algorithm, default parameters). This reported a mean absolute error (MAE) of 5.71 and root mean squared error ($RMSE$) of 8.50. The importance of each feature was reported as follows: 1.5-TT (0.84), 90°-TT (0.12), and 30°-MD (0.04). With mean RAN results of 37.55 ms ($SD = 16.61$), a MAE of 5.71 ms represents an error 15.21% and is below 0.5 standard deviations representing the RAN results of our low literacy group (i.e., 8.31 ms). In sum, these results start to illustrate the potential of DtD as an implicit tracing mechanism that can assess low literacy risk factors by simply measuring characteristic slow and short traces, particularly if these are performed upwards.

5   Discussion

The purpose of this work was to determine whether DtD on touchscreen devices is a suitable mechanism to assess literary-related factors.

5.1   Relevance to Literacy-Related Factors

Overall, children's performance during the direct condition of DtD was highly correlated with literacy-related variables. These results showed a consistent tendency regardless of age effect, especially with rapid automatized naming (RAN) performance. In other words, children who performed RAN quicker were also were quicker at connecting the dots in the direct condition of the DtD task. As such, it is expected that the properties represented by RAN – children's vocabulary development level, rapid naming, and phonological awareness skills – can also be represented via the DtD task. Unlike vocabulary development tests that recall and produce the lexical knowledge stored in long-term memory, and phonological recognition tasks that manipulate speech sounds

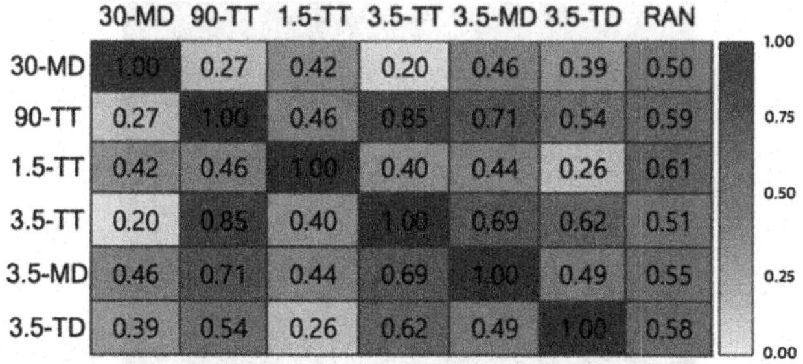

Fig. 9. The Pearson's correlation matrix between the most relevant features. When two features are correlated (> 0.50), the one highest correlated with RAN was selected for analysis.

based on phonemic knowledge and representation, the RAN task requires effective processing skills of visual information. Similarly, in the DtD task users need to be constantly paying attention to moving target points and processing visual information. Common features in performing these tasks can explain this correlation between RAN and DtD performance.

While we found a significant correlation between DtD and RAN, the same cannot be said of phonological awareness (PA) performance. This result is supported by previous work that demonstrates the literacy predictability of PA decreases from the early states of reading education (while the predictability of RAN gradually increases [27,61]). Most of the participants in this study had indeed started to learn how to read, which further explains these observations on RAN and PA performance. In sum, the performance in the direct input condition of the DtD task can be considered as an assessment tool that reflects children's literacy ability; including visual information processing, linguistic features, and the developmental characteristics necessary for reading.

5.2 Feasibility as a Pre-reading Assessment Mechanism

In this paper we have used RAN and PA performances to categorize children's literacy skills as either high or low (above or below 30% from the average performance of their peers). A comparative analysis of the two subgroups showed that children with low literacy had low performance in the direct input condition of the DtD task. Thus, this can be seen as a result of predicting a high probability of diagnosis for children with literacy-related issues such as reading difficulties and dyslexia. Our findings build on the preliminary DtD work showing similar results with British children using indirect input (i.e., stylus pen) [37]. Taken together, this highlights the language-independent features of the DtD task as a potential literacy screening tool.

However, what further sets this work apart from the state-of-the-art is the analysis that shows the potential for the DtD mechanism to work as an abstract layer that can be embedded into every day touch-screen applications. This would ultimately lead to continuous and unsupervised monitoring of literacy problems

Fig. 10. Input via the popular keyboard SwiftKey could be interpreted as a DtD pattern. Future work should investigate if such everyday actions on mobile devices could be used as a quick and seamlessly way to flag for signs of dyslexia in teenagers and adults.

in preschool-age children – shown to interact with tablets as early as 2.5 years old [32]. To do so, applications simply need to measure user performance matching the three features identified in our study. These are highly viable in touch-screen applications as they require short traces of approx. 1.10 cm, combined with upward traces.

5.3   Limitations and Future Work

Although our data showed the potential of using the DtD task as a screening tool for detecting reading difficulties in children, a long-term investigation is needed to confirm if DtD is indeed an accurate predictor. This will be done by following up with children with low DtD performance and assess if they are diagnosed with reading difficulties or dyslexia later on. Additionally, a future study on reliability and feasibility tests for larger clinical groups will also be needed to find out whether the patterns and methods used in DtD itself can be used as a tool to screen children with reading difficulties. For example, a larger clinical group would allow us to do a trace analysis by preschool-age, or by lower and higher grades; allowing us to further validate and fine-tune our findings.

Finally, an exciting future direction for this work is to look at the validity of the DtD task while embedded into various touch-screen applications. This can be explored in children's applications, but could also be used to flag for signs of dyslexia in teenagers and adults. One such way would be to identify applications that already require users to provide direct input in manner resembling a DtD pattern, i.e., applications that require users to sequentially swipe between interface targets without lifting their fingers. One pervasive example would be SwiftKey[3], a popular software keyboard for Android where users write text not by typing, but by swiping between characters. Figure 10 illustrates how writing *Malaysia* with SwiftKey would produce an input with a similar ID to Pattern 5

---

[3] https://www.microsoft.com/en-us/swiftkey.

(depending on screen size and resolution). A machine learning model could also be trained to identify the trace features described earlier (e.g., 1.5-TT, 90°-TT, 30°-MD), potentially allowing the assessment of low literacy factors when users perform slow and short upward traces. These are used often, not only between characters in SwiftKey (e.g., between 'x' and 'e'), but unlocking an iPhone, dragging App icons on them main screen of most touchscreen devices, or various videogames. Further studies would require us to test IDs that vary not only length but target size, backwards traces, and traces that might engage muscle memory in addition to visual-motor coordination (such as the ones performed in SwiftKey). If successful, such approaches could quickly and seamlessly support millions of undiagnosed adults [1] that go through life dealing with academic failure, low self-esteem, and behavioral and motivational difficulties.

6   Conclusion

We have proposed a simple, non-linguistic touchscreen-based task with the goal of predicting a child's likelihood for experiencing reading difficulties based on their visual-motor skills. The effectiveness of this approach was verified through an empirical study conducted with children aged from preschool to elementary school. Results show that children's literacy-related variables have strongly correlated to DtD performance. These results were significant not only in the correlation analysis but also in the comparison analysis between low and high literacy groups. Moreover, we identified specific DtD pattern and trace characteristics that could be effective in screening future learning difficulties. Thus, DtD can contribute to not only an early identification and intervention of children's literacy problems but can also be embedded into any frequently used touchscreen-based applications for implicit detection.

Acknowledgements. We thank all the children and educators who have made this research possible. This was supported by LARSyS (Projeto – UIDB/50009/2020).

References

1. Alexander-Passe, N.: The Successful Dyslexic: Identify the Keys to Unlock Your Potential. Springer, Rotterdam (2017)
2. American Psychiatric Association: Diagnostic and Statistical Manual Of Mental Disorders (DSM-5®). American Psychiatric Pub, Arlington (2013)
3. Van den Audenaeren, L., et al.: DYSL-X: design of a tablet game for early risk detection of dyslexia in preschoolers. In: Games for health, pp. 257–266. Springer, Wiesbaden (2013)
4. Bannach-Brown, A.: Visual-motor integration in developmental dyslexia (2014)
5. Barz, M., Altmeyer, K., Malone, S., Lauer, L., Sonntag, D.: Digital pen features predict task difficulty and user performance of cognitive tests. In: Proceedings of the 28th ACM Conference on User Modeling, Adaptation and Personalization, pp. 23–32, UMAP 2020. ACM, New York (2020). https://doi.org/10.1145/3340631.3394839

6. Boets, B., De Smedt, B., Cleuren, L., Vandewalle, E., Wouters, J., Ghesquiere, P.: Towards a further characterization of phonological and literacy problems in Dutch-speaking children with dyslexia. Br. J. Dev. Psychol. **28**(1), 5–31 (2010)
7. Catts, H.W.: The relationship between speech-language impairments and reading disabilities. J. Speech Lang. Hear. Res. **36**(5), 948–958 (1993)
8. Dandache, S., Wouters, J., Ghesquière, P.: Development of reading and phonological skills of children at family risk for dyslexia: a longitudinal analysis from kindergarten to sixth grade. Dyslexia **20**(4), 305–329 (2014)
9. Eden, G.F., VanMeter, J.W., Rumsey, J.M., Maisog, J.M., Woods, R.P., Zeffiro, T.A.: Abnormal processing of visual motion in dyslexia revealed by functional brain imaging. Nature **382**(6586), 66 (1996)
10. Ehri, L.C., Nunes, S.R., Willows, D.M., Schuster, B.V., Yaghoub-Zadeh, Z., Shanahan, T.: Phonemic awareness instruction helps children learn to read: evidence from the national reading panel's meta-analysis. Read. Res. Q. **36**(3), 250–287 (2001)
11. Eissa, M.: Behavioral and emotional problems associated with Dyslexia in adolescence. Curr. Psych. **17**(1), 39–47 (2010)
12. Elbro, C., Petersen, D.K.: Long-term effects of phoneme awareness and letter sound training: an intervention study with children at risk for dyslexia. J. Educ. Psychol. **96**(4), 660 (2004)
13. Facoetti, A., Paganoni, P., Turatto, M., Marzola, V., Mascetti, G.G.: Visual-spatial attention in developmental dyslexia. Cortex **36**(1), 109–123 (2000)
14. Felton, R.H., Pepper, P.P.: Early identification and intervention of phonological deficits in kindergarten and early elementary children at risk for reading disability. School Psychol. Rev. **24**(3), 405–414 (1995)
15. Furnes, B., Samuelsson, S.: Phonological awareness and rapid automatized naming predicting early development in reading and spelling: results from a cross-linguistic longitudinal study. Learn. Individ. Differ. **21**(1), 85–95 (2011)
16. Gabrieli, J.D., Norton, E.S.: Reading abilities: importance of visual-spatial attention. Curr. Biol. **22**(9), R298–R299 (2012)
17. Gaggi, O., Galiazzo, G., Palazzi, C., Facoetti, A., Franceschini, S.: A serious game for predicting the risk of developmental dyslexia in pre-readers children. In: 2012 21st International Conference on Computer Communications and Networks (IC-CCN), pp. 1–5. IEEE (2012)
18. Geurts, L., et al.: DIESEL-X: a game-based tool for early risk detection of dyslexia in preschoolers. In: Torbeyns, J., Lehtinen, E., Elen, J. (eds.) Describing and Studying Domain-Specific Serious Games. AGL, pp. 93–114. Springer, Cham (2015). https://doi.org/10.1007/978-3-319-20276-1_7
19. Hammill, D.D., Larsen, S.C.: Test of Written Language: TOWL4. PRO-ED, Austin (2009)
20. Hansen, P.C., Stein, J.F., Orde, S.R., Winter, J.L., Talcott, J.B.: Are dyslexics' visual deficits limited to measures of dorsal stream function? NeuroReport **12**(7), 1527 (2001)
21. Hutchins, E.L., Hollan, J.D., Norman, D.A.: Direct manipulation interfaces. Hum. Comput. Interact. **1**(4), 311–338 (1985)
22. Kevan, A., Pammer, K.: Predicting early reading skills from pre-reading measures of dorsal stream functioning. Neuropsychologia **47**(14), 3174–3181 (2009)
23. Kim, Y., Hong, G., Kim, K., Jang, H., Lee, J.: Receptive & Expressive Vocabulary Test (REVT). Seoul Community Rehabilitation Center, Seoul (2009)
24. Kirby, J.R., Parrila, R.K., Pfeiffer, S.L.: Naming speed and phonological awareness as predictors of reading development. J. Educ. Psychol. **95**(3), 453 (2003)

25. Kuosmanen, E., Kan, V., Visuri, A., Hosio, S., Ferreira, D.: Let's draw: detecting and measuring Parkinson's disease on smartphones. In: Proceedings of the 2020 CHI Conference on Human Factors in Computing Systems, pp. 1–9, CHI 2020. ACM, New York (2020). https://doi.org/10.1145/3313831.3376864

26. Landerl, K., et al.: Phonological awareness and rapid automatized naming as longitudinal predictors of reading in five alphabetic orthographies with varying degrees of consistency. Sci. Stud. Read. **23**(3), 220–234 (2019)

27. Landerl, K., Wimmer, H.: Development of word reading fluency and spelling in a consistent orthography: an 8-year follow-up. J. Educ. Psychol. **100**(1), 150 (2008)

28. Lombardino, L.J., Morris, D., Mercado, L., DeFillipo, F., Sarisky, C., Montgomery, A.: The early reading screening instrument: a method for identifying kindergarteners at risk for learning to read. Int. J. Lang. Commun. Disord. **34**(2), 135–150 (1999)

29. Lyytinen, H., Ronimus, M., Alanko, A., Poikkeus, A.M., Taanila, M.: Early identification of dyslexia and the use of computer game-based practice to support reading acquisition. Nordic Psychol. **59**(2), 109–126 (2007)

30. MacKenzie, I.S.: A note on the information-theoretic basis for Fitts' law. J. Motor Behav. **21**(3), 323–330 (1989)

31. Moon, S., Byun, C.: Korean Kaufman assessment battery for children (K-ABC) (2003)

32. Moser, A., Zimmermann, L., Dickerson, K., Grenell, A., Barr, R., Gerhardstein, P.: They can interact, but can they learn? Toddlers' transfer learning from touchscreens and television. J. Exper. Child Psychol. **137**, 137–155 (2015)

33. Nation, K., Cocksey, J., Taylor, J.S., Bishop, D.V.: A longitudinal investigation of early reading and language skills in children with poor reading comprehension. J. Child Psychol. Psych. **51**(9), 1031–1039 (2010)

34. Nicolson, R., Fawcett, A.: The Dyslexia Early Screening Test: DEST-2. Psychological Corporation (2004)

35. Nicolson, R.I., Fawcett, A.J.: Dyslexia, dysgraphia, procedural learning and the cerebellum. Cortex J. Devoted Study Nervous Syst. Behav. **47**, 117–127. (2011). https://doi.org/10.1016/j.cortex.2009.08.016

36. Norton, E.S., Wolf, M.: Rapid automatized naming (ran) and reading fluency: Implications for understanding and treatment of reading disabilities. Ann. Rev. Psychol. **63**, 427–452 (2012)

37. Piotrowska, B.: Investigating the performance and underlying mechanisms of a novel screening measure for developmental dyslexia: implications for early identification. Edinburgh Napier University, Ph.D. thesis, June 2018

38. Prange, A., Barz, M., Heimann-Steinert, A., Sonntag, D.: Explainable automatic evaluation of the trail making test for dementia screening. In: Proceedings of the 2021 CHI Conference on Human Factors in Computing Systems, pp. 1–9 (2021)

39. Prange, A., Niemann, M., Latendorf, A., Steinert, A., Sonntag, D.: Multimodal speech-based dialogue for the mini-mental state examination. In: Extended Abstracts of the 2019 CHI Conference on Human Factors in Computing Systems, CHI EA 2019, pp. 1–8. ACM, New York (2019). https://doi.org/10.1145/3290607.3299040

40. Prange, A., Sonntag, D.: Modeling cognitive status through automatic scoring of a digital version of the clock drawing test. In: Proceedings of the 27th ACM Conference on User Modeling, Adaptation and Personalization, UMAP 2019, pp. 70–77. ACM, New York (2019). https://doi.org/10.1145/3320435.3320452

41. Ramus, F., Pidgeon, E., Frith, U.: The relationship between motor control and phonology in dyslexic children. J. Child Psychol. Psych. **44**(5), 712–722 (2003)

42. Rauschenberger, M., Rello, L., Baeza-Yates, R.: A tablet game to target dyslexia screening in pre-readers. In: Proceedings of the 20th International Conference on Human-Computer Interaction with Mobile Devices and Services Adjunct, pp. 306–312 (2018)

43. Rauschenberger, M., Rello, L., Baeza-Yates, R., Bigham, J.P.: Towards language independent detection of dyslexia with a web-based game. In: Proceedings of the Internet of Accessible Things, pp. 1–10 (2018)

44. Rello, L., Ali, A., Bigham, J.P.: Dytective: toward a game to detect dyslexia. In: Proceedings of the 17th International ACM SIGACCESS Conference on Computers and Accessibility, pp. 307–308. ACM (2015)

45. Saffer, D.: Designing Gestural Interfaces: Touchscreens and Interactive Devices. O'Reilly Media, Inc., Reading (2008)

46. Semel, E., Wiig, E., Secord, W.: Clinical Evaluation of Language Fundamentals, (CELF-4). The Psychological Corporation. San Antonio (2003)

47. Shannon, C.E.: A mathematical theory of communication. Bell Syst. Techn. J. **27**(3), 379–423 (1948)

48. Shaywitz, B.A., et al.: Development of left occipitotemporal systems for skilled reading in children after a phonologically- based intervention. Biol. Psychiatry **55**(9), 926–933 (2004)

49. Singleton, C.: Intervention for dyslexia: a review of published evidence on the impact of specialist teaching. University of Hull (2009)

50. Singleton, C., Horne, J., Simmons, F.: Computerised screening for dyslexia in adults. J. Res. Reading **32**(1), 137–152 (2009)

51. Smith, K., Wallin, J.: Dibels Next Assessment Manual. Dynamic Measurement Group, Eugene (2011)

52. Snowling, M.J.: Early identification and interventions for dyslexia: a contemporary view. J. Res. Spec. Educ. Needs **13**(1), 7–14 (2013)

53. Stein, J.: Dyslexia: the role of vision and visual attention. Current Dev. Disorders Rep. **1**(4), 267–280 (2014)

54. Stein, J., Walsh, V.: To see but not to read; the magnocellular theory of dyslexia. Trends Neurosci. **20**(4), 147–152 (1997)

55. Swanson, H.L., Trainin, G., Necoechea, D.M., Hammill, D.D.: Rapid naming, phonological awareness, and reading: a meta-analysis of the correlation evidence. Rev. Educ. Res. **73**(4), 407–440 (2003)

56. Waber, D,P., et al.: Motor sequence learning and reading ability: is poor reading associated with sequencing deficits? J. Exper. Child Psychol. **84**(4), 338–354 (2003)

57. Wagner, R., Torgesen, J., Rashotte, C., Pearson, N.: Comprehensive Test of Phonological Processing-Second Edition (2013)

58. White, S., et al.: The role of sensorimotor impairments in dyslexia: a multiple case study of dyslexic children. Dev. Sci. **9**(3), 237–255 (2006)

59. Whitehurst, G., Lonigan, C.: Child development and emergent literacy. Child Dev. **69**, 848–872 (1998). Focus on Exceptional Children 44(3) (2011)

60. Wolff, P.H., Michel, G.F., Ovrut, M., Drake, C.: Rate and timing precision of motor coordination in developmental Dyslexia. Dev. Psychol. **26**(3), 349 (1990)

61. Ziegler, J.C., et al.: Orthographic depth and its impact on universal predictors of reading: a cross-language investigation. Psychol. Sci. **21**(4), 551–559 (2010)

Exploring the Acceptability of Graphical Passwords for People with Dyslexia

Polina Evtimova and James Nicholson[✉]

Northumbria University, Newcastle, UK
james.nicholson@northumbria.ac.uk

Abstract. Alphanumeric passwords are still the most common form of user authentication despite well-known usability issues. These issues, including weak composition and poor memorability, have been well-established across different user groups, yet users with dyslexia have not been studied despite making up approximately 10% of the population. In this paper, we focus on understanding the user authentication experiences of people with dyslexia (PwD) in order to better understanding their attitudes towards a graphical password system that may provide a more inclusive experience. Through interactive interviews, participants were encouraged to try three different knowledge-based authentication systems (PIN, password, and graphical password) and then discuss their strategies behind code composition. We found that PwD employed potentially dangerous workarounds when composing passwords, in particular an over-reliance on pattern-based composition. We report on how PwD do not immediately see the benefits of graphical passwords, but upon experiencing the mechanism we see opportunities for more inclusive authentication.

Keywords: Dyslexia · Authentication · Passwords · Graphical passwords · HCI

1 Introduction

Alphanumeric passwords are the most common form of digital authentication and best practice dictates that these should not be reused in order to prevent opportunistic attacks (e.g., credential stuffing). The danger of reusing passwords has become more salient to everyday users recently due to sustained data breaches and the regular publication of large breach compilation on popular hacking forums. In particular, the publication of 3.2 billion individual records, including cleartext passwords, on February 2021 [1] serves as a clear example of the suboptimal nature of user passwords.

However, there are well-known cognitive and social factors [2] that act as disincentives for users to conform to gold standard password advice. Despite recent government

---

Electronic supplementary material The online version of this chapter (https://doi.org/10.1007/978-3-030-85623-6_14) contains supplementary material, which is available to authorized users.

C. Ardito et al. (Eds.): INTERACT 2021, LNCS 12932, pp. 213–222, 2021.
https://doi.org/10.1007/978-3-030-85623-6_14

advice shifting towards usable recommendations, e.g. the National Cyber Security Centre in the UK advocating for length over complexity [3], password management continues to be problematic for many users [4].

People with dyslexia (PwD) account for at least 10% of any given population [5] and exhibit traits that may negatively impact on their password management practices [6]. We know that individuals with dyslexia face concrete problems navigating the online world [7] with many online communications relying on text-based interactions. While audio-visual content continues to proliferate in online platforms, we continue to see a reliance on text-based authentication despite more usable methods such as pattern unlock and biometric recognition being pushed on mobile devices.

In this paper, we focus on understanding the user authentication experiences of PwD and explore the acceptability of graphical passwords – alternatives to alphanumeric solutions that rely on image recognition or pattern generation [8] rather than on textual recall or spelling. We do this through interactive interviews where participants were encouraged to try three different authentication systems and then discuss their strategies behind code composition. This paper makes two distinct contributions: (i) To the best of our knowledge, this is the first paper to explore PwD's experiences of graphical versus alphanumeric authentication schemes in everyday life, and (ii) this work is the first to explore the acceptability of graphical passwords amongst the PwD population.

2 Background

2.1 Computer Users with Dyslexia

Dyslexia is a common neurological and often hereditary learning disability [9]. The prevalence of dyslexia in any given population is not insignificant, with estimates suggesting at least 10% of individuals show symptoms associated with the disability [5]. In the UK, it is estimated that 4% of the population exhibit severe symptoms [10].

Individuals with dyslexia exhibit trouble recognising phonemes and connecting the sounds with the symbols denoting the letters. As such, a word can be misspelled in various different ways by the same user, for example "dalb" and "pald" as variations to "bald". Further, blending sounds into words may be a pronounced difficulty, for example reading and understanding a word correctly, but being unable to read it aloud as it does not compute correctly, resulting in a pronunciation latency. Some people with dyslexia may also exhibit errors regarding semantically-related words: "parrot" for "canary", for example [11]. As a result, people with dyslexia have noticeable trouble reading and spelling, which has been shown to affect day to day online communication [7]. In particular, they have been known to avoid using services that require precise spelling despite being regarded as more trustworthy [12] and avoid combining sources due to working memory limitations [13], which indicates that workarounds are employed by this population in order to overcome systems that rely on textual interactions.

2.2 User Authentication and Graphical Passwords

Passwords, the most common form of user authentication for digital accounts, have also been reported to be problematic for PwD, in particular requiring users to spend longer entering passwords when logging in and the resulting passwords being easier to guess [14]. However, issues with password management are not exclusive to PwD: Users notably engage in insecure practices due to optimistic cognitive biases, or by overlooking immediate consequences, or simply because the trade-off between security and convenience is better in the short term [15, 16]. Often the case is that the users are experiencing a so-called security fatigue [17], which results in a lack of security conscious in daily dealings in the online world, particularly when relating to passwords. Some of the most common issues are creating overly simple and personalised – hence guessable – codes [18], using the same code for more than one account [19], and sharing the codes with friends and family [15].

With these limitations in mind, researchers have looked at other forms of knowledge-based authentication such as challenge questions [20] and graphical authentication systems [8, 21, 22]. Graphical passwords are of particular interest, as we have seen that user groups who typically struggle with either declining cognitive function or with the usability aspects of technology can find this type of authentication suitable: for example, previous work has demonstrated how older users [22] and users with learning difficulties [23] can benefit from the affordances of graphical passwords. This improved performance is in part due to the graphical mechanism bypassing reading and spelling issues, as well as supporting the memorability (e.g. through cued-recall or recognition) of the codes [8]. While issues with scalability have resulted in alphanumeric passwords remaining as the de-facto authentication method for most services, graphical passwords may become a more realistic prospect for both service providers and end users with the proliferation of devices with higher resolution, touch screens, and faster data access.

2.3 Design

The study consisted of semi-structured interactive interviews with internet users with dyslexia (see Fig. 1). Participants were asked to create authentication codes using a bespoke prototype to enable an informed and immersed interview, but the key findings reported here focus on the thematic analysis [24] of the qualitative data (see Sect. 2.6 for details). We recruited 6 participants who reported being diagnosed with dyslexia aged between 18 and 25 years with a 1:1 male-female ratio. Due to ethics procedures, the severity of dyslexia symptoms was not recorded. Participants were recruited through email calls circulated within our institution and through snowball sampling, resulting in all participants being either undergraduate or postgraduate students.

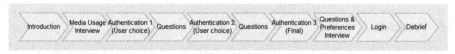

Fig. 1. The interactive interviews consisted of several activities and open-ended questions.

2.4 Materials

In order to understand the user authentication experiences of PwD, we developed a bespoke local website that incorporated three different authentication schemes: an alphanumeric password, a PIN, and a graphical password. The alphanumeric password and PIN implementation consisted of the standard text fields for input. Most apps and websites support the alphanumeric password as the default, if not the only, option for authentication, thus a real-time observation of the user experience with it was the prudent first step in the study. This furthermore served as a 'baseline' of comparison in terms of participant reaction. The PIN was chosen in consideration of the fact that it is a key part of several daily life activities such as banking, physical access devices, and notably even some websites. The graphical password was a simple image pattern cued-recall password similar to Cued Click Points [21] consisting of an image with an overlay of selectable squares that divide the image into sections, any number of which could be selected to create a unique code (see Fig. 2 below). Given the exploratory nature of this work, the interview structure was designed to elicit the mental models of participants with regards to authentication mechanisms as well as to encourage discussion around habits for code creation (see Sect. 2.5 below).

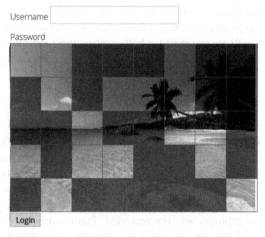

Fig. 2. An example of a code created on the prototype graphical password.

2.5 Procedure

The interview was designed around the task of creating the various types of passwords following a basic structure of create-distract-authenticate (see Fig. 1). First, the participants were asked about their general habits of creating accounts on social media to collect initial behavioural insights. Then, they were tasked with creating an account on the website tool using one mechanism of their choice and their steps and choices were observed while being encouraged to narrate their steps [25]. Participants were asked to follow the steps taken to create a code for a social media website. Following the account creation, participants were asked to reflect on their pick of mechanism and code with some follow-up questions, with a general question about their security consciousness at the end to serve as a distractor task. Participants then followed the same procedure for the other two authentication mechanisms. Once all accounts had been created, they were asked about their experience with dyslexia and online authentication. Finally, participants were asked to authenticate on the website using the same code they devised previously in order to ascertain whether the credentials were memorable (i.e., realistic) within a short time period. In total, the average time taken to complete the interactive interviews, which consisted of 8 open-ended questions, was 30 min. This study was approved by our institution's Ethics Committee.

2.6 Data Analysis

All interviews were audio recorded and transcribed. Then, all transcribed data was analysed using thematic analysis, (e.g. [24]) following the five stages of familiarization, the identification of a thematic framework, indexing, charting, and interpretation. The two members of the research team worked on the data and ensured agreement on the framework and subthemes before they were finalised. We note that the analysis was carried out on all qualitative data collected throughout the interactive interview (including the talk aloud) and not just the pre-defined questions.

3 Results

Here we report on the themes we identified related to user experiences of authentication and dyslexia. Below, we describe in more detail the themes of Familiarity, Effort, and Patterns. First, however, we discuss some similarities that our participants shared with well-known password management behaviours reported in the literature.

3.1 Poor Password Management Behaviours

Supporting vast amounts of previous work reporting on the poor password management behaviours of the general population [15, 16, 18, 19], our participants reported a number of concerning security behaviours and mental models. In particular, the majority of our participants reported reusing their passwords across many platforms, created short passwords, and/or used personal information (e.g., birthdays and names) in their passwords. This is a significant risk for password security as passwords constructed using these characteristics can be very vulnerable to probabilistic context-free grammars (PCFGs) password cracking methods [26].

When analysing the alphanumeric passwords that were created for the password condition in our study, we see that passwords were between 8 and 15 characters. None of the created passwords included special characters, and 5/6 of the passwords included one or more simple dictionary words that would be picked up with a basic dictionary attack. Despite these clear issues, the absence of any historical consequences demotivated participants from changing these behaviours:

"Not really when creating them apart from the fact that the ones I'm making probably aren't that secure. But I've gotten away with having short probably not that secure ones." – Participant 3.

Participants all reasoned that they had not been attacked so far, or that they do not hold any information they deem significant enough to be worried about in their online accounts. This self-fulfilling prophecy is not uncommon with security behaviours and is in line with the studies demonstrating how users generally know and understand good security practices but do not employ them due to a cognitive bias imposed by the lack of immediate negative consequences [16].

3.2 System Familiarity

It was clear from our observations of participants using the three authentication mechanisms that they gravitated towards familiar systems (passwords and PINs) and avoided the unknown system (graphical password).

While our participants were not put off by the graphical password specifically, they preferred erring on the side of the known when they were given an option of mechanism. This behaviour indicates that implementing alternative, more secure and potentially dyslexia-friendly technologies for authentication may be difficult as users would default to the current standard if given a choice. The Technology Acceptance Model (TAM) [27] describes how the perceived usefulness of a system has a significant positive correlation to the actual system use over the perceived ease of use. For an authentication system, this means that its usability and security need to be perceived as being a significant upgrade over traditional alphanumeric passwords to bypass existing defaults, something which is not immediately apparent with graphical passwords.

"That's just a waste of time. I'd rather just type something in because I type faster than I fiddle around. And most of the time when you're doing it, you're going to have a problem where it's going to miss where you dragged, or link somewhere else, or click somewhere else. (…) It's just long." – Participant 5.

As the participant above explains, without much context a graphical password seems like a suboptimal choice for users who are used to authenticating using alphanumeric passwords. However, as discussed in the following subsection, we can begin to see how graphical password may actually be of benefit for PwD and their opinions towards these mechanisms began to improve after use.

3.3 Patterns

A common theme across strategies employed by participants when creating text-based authentication codes was the use of patterns. Our participants reported relying on patterns generated using the keyboard or other input device rather than relying on the actual content of the code.

"If you asked me to tell it to you, I wouldn't be able to. It's a pattern on my keyboard, the same with my work password that I use at work. I don't know the number; I just know where I put my fingers on the keyboard." -Participant 3.

Users employing patterns in passwords is not a new finding [28], but the sheer over-reliance in patterns reported (and observed) by our sample suggests that young PwD may utilise this as a primary technique for key accounts. This is not necessarily surprising, as the disregard of a heavy memory task in favour of the reportedly easier visuospatial pattern [29] seems to make sense.

"I'm trying to make one [password] based on my visual again, rather than making one up that... If I just pick some numbers, I'll forget them." – Participant 3.

The participant above touches on a particular problem that users face when relying on patterns when creating passwords: visual patterns on keyboards are limited, and well-known to cyber criminals. For example, we know that many users rely on simple patterns such as qwerty, qazxsw, and the most popular password 123456 [30], while criminals seek out these patterns when configuring mangling rules for password cracking. As such, PwD who may have an over-reliance on patterns for password creation could be at a higher risk of having them revealed in cyber-incidents.

On the other hand, once participants had an opportunity to create a code using the graphical password, they begun to see the benefits of this scheme. In particular, the fact that the scheme we chose encouraged pattern recognition.

"I think it would be easier just to remember a pattern over specific parts of an image. It was quite basic for me to remember where the squares were on the image." -Participant 5.

While this realisation can be positive for system adoption, an over reliance on basic patterns could also be problematic for graphical passwords. When our participants were given the option to create a code using the graphical password, they mostly picked simple, easy to remember and recreate patterns: a smiley face, a checkerboard pattern, or salient points on the given image such as the shore or the trees. These patterns are not only easily reproducible for the user, but also for any potential attacker [31], which is an undesirable outcome. However, we must note that our participants were not given any prior information about graphical passwords and they were not creating these passwords for valuable personal accounts, so there is scope for future work to understand the types of patterns that are used in high-stakes situations.

3.4 Effort

Participants commonly reported taking extra steps to minimise the effects of dyslexia on their authentication experiences. In particular, participants reported taking extra time to authenticate in order to avoid errors.

"I cannot say, but I do take pauses just to make sure I'm typing the correct numbers and it makes sense to me." -Participant 6.

The participant above further elaborated that sometimes it takes them extra tries because they mistook a 1 for an "l", or they mistyped a number and it would take them a while to find it. This is in line with previous work reporting on the delay in authentication attempts when using alphanumeric passwords [14]. Another participant displaying the typical confusion with "b" and "d," "p" and "q" when reading, reported that such issues typically resulted in slower logins rather than more logins.

The observation that individuals with dyslexia expect to take longer to authenticate can be beneficial for graphical password schemes. The longer login times are often cited as being one of the key issues around adoption [8], yet user groups like PwD and older adults, who usually take longer to authenticate anyway, may not see this as a problem and in fact actual differences in time may not be as pronounced.

4 Discussion

In this study we explored how individuals with dyslexia engaged with authentication mechanisms including alphanumeric and graphical passwords, and reported on how graphical passwords have the potential to serve as inclusive authentication mechanisms for PwD. In particular, we note how PwD take longer to authenticate using passwords and rely on patterns for their codes. This extra login time has traditionally been seen as an obstacle for adoption for graphical passwords [8], yet previous work [14] and our own findings highlight how users with dyslexia take extra time when entering passwords in order to avoid mistakes: this means that in practice the time taken to enter a *strong* password and the time taken to select a pattern on a graphical password may not be as pronounced for this user group.

4.1 Pattern-Based Code Composition

While our participants appreciated the mechanics of the graphical password we tested, which facilitated the use of patterns [21] in the composition of the code, it remains to be seen how PwD may approach other types of graphical passwords – most notably recognition-based systems that do not feature pattern recognition at all. Further investigation into the types of patterns that are generated by users with dyslexia when using graphical passwords is also warranted to ensure that these are not prone to hotspot attacks [31].

However, it is important to also take into consideration how we might approach this population's over-reliance on patterns in the composition of knowledge-based codes. While this insight originates from only six participants – all of which were university students – we know from research into the general population that patterns are a method for creating weaker passwords [28]. Additionally, the insights obtained from our individual participants appear to suggest that the use of patterns as a composition strategy across many accounts serves as a workaround for their well-documented issues with spelling [11] which deserves further inquiry.

4.2 Conclusion

This paper has presented some initial insights on the approaches that users with dyslexia employ when evaluating authentication systems and the potential acceptability of graphical passwords for PwD. Building on other work demonstrating how this type of authentication can benefit marginalised user groups (e.g. older adults [22]), we begin to explore whether graphical passwords could be used as an additional choice to alphanumeric passwords to benefit specific users groups by improving memorability [8] while removing some of the problematic text-based issues that this population faces [11]. We posit that this line of enquiry could be promising but more work is needed to understand how to communicate the benefits to these users in a clear but inclusive way.

References

1. Meyer, B.: COMB: over 3.2 Billion Email/Password Combinations Leaked. https://cybern ews.com/news/largest-compilation-of-emails-and-passwords-leaked-free/
2. Stobert, E., Biddle, R.: The password life cycle. ACM Trans. Priv. Secur. **21**, 13:1–13:32 (2018). https://doi.org/10.1145/3183341
3. National Cyber Security Centre: Password Guidance: Simplifying Your Approach. National Cyber Security Centre (2015)
4. Das, A., Bonneau, J., Caesar, M., Borisov, N., Wang, X.: The Tangled Web of Password Reuse. Presented at the NDSS (2014)
5. Sprenger-Charolles, L., Siegel, L.S., Jiménez, J.E., Ziegler, J.C.: Prevalence and reliability of phonological, surface, and mixed profiles in dyslexia: a review of studies conducted in languages varying in orthographic depth. Sci. Stud. Read. **15**, 498–521 (2011). https://doi.org/10.1080/10888438.2010.524463
6. Renaud, K., Johnson, G., Ophoff, J.: Dyslexia and password usage: accessibility in authentication design. In: Clarke, N., Furnell, S. (eds.) HAISA 2021. IAICT, vol. 593, pp. 259–268. Springer, Cham (2020). https://doi.org/10.1007/978-3-030-57404-8_20
7. Kanniainen, L., Kiili, C., Tolvanen, A., Aro, M., Leppänen, P.H.T.: Literacy skills and online research and comprehension: struggling readers face difficulties online. Read. Writ. **32**(9), 2201–2222 (2019). https://doi.org/10.1007/s11145-019-09944-9
8. Biddle, R., Chiasson, S., Van Oorschot, P.C.: Graphical passwords: learning from the first twelve years. ACM Comput. Surv. **44**, 19:1–19:41 (2012). https://doi.org/10.1145/2333112.2333114
9. Snowling, M.J., Gallagher, A., Frith, U.: Family risk of dyslexia is continuous: individual differences in the precursors of reading skill. Child Dev. **74**, 358–373 (2003). https://doi.org/10.1111/1467-8624.7402003
10. British Dyslexia Association: Dyslexia (2021). https://www.bdadyslexia.org.uk/dyslexia
11. Baddeley, A.D., Logie, R.H., Ellis, N.C.: Characteristics of developmental dyslexia. Cognition **29**, 197–228 (1988). https://doi.org/10.1016/0010-0277(88)90024-8
12. Kvikne, B., Berget, G.: When Trustworthy Information Becomes Inaccessible: The Search Behaviour of Users with Dyslexia in an Online Encyclopedia. IOS Press (2018)
13. Andresen, A., Anmarkrud, Ø., Bråten, I.: Investigating multiple source use among students with and without dyslexia. Read. Writ. **32**(5), 1149–1174 (2018). https://doi.org/10.1007/s11145-018-9904-z
14. Helkala, K.: Disabilities and authentication methods: usability and security. In: 2012 Seventh International Conference on Availability, Reliability and Security. pp. 327–334 (2012)
15. Whitty, M., Doodson, J., Creese, S., Hodges, D.: Individual differences in cyber security behaviors: an examination of who is sharing passwords. Cyberpsychol. Behav. Soc. Netw. **18**, 3–7 (2014). https://doi.org/10.1089/cyber.2014.0179
16. Tam, L., Glassman, M., Vandenwauver, M.: The psychology of password management: a tradeoff between security and convenience. Behav. Inf. Technol. **29**, 233–244 (2010). https://doi.org/10.1080/01449290903121386
17. Stanton, B., Theofanos, M., Spickard Prettyman, S., Furman, S.: Security fatigue. IT Prof. **18**, 26–32 (2016). https://doi.org/10.1109/MITP.2016.84
18. Ur, B., et al.: 'I Added "!" at the End to Make It Secure': Observing Password Creation in the Lab. Presented at the Eleventh Symposium on Usable Privacy and Security ({SOUPS} 2015) (2015)
19. Wash, R., Rader, E., Berman, R., Wellmer, Z.: Understanding Password Choices: How Frequently Entered Passwords Are Re-used across Websites. Presented at the Twelfth Symposium on Usable Privacy and Security ({SOUPS} 2016) (2016)

20. Just, M., Aspinall, D.: Personal choice and challenge questions: a security and usability assessment. In: Proceedings of the 5th Symposium on Usable Privacy and Security, pp. 1–11. Association for Computing Machinery, New York, NY, USA (2009)

21. Chiasson, S., van Oorschot, P.C., Biddle, R.: Graphical password authentication using cued click points. In: Biskup, J., López, J. (eds.) ESORICS 2007. LNCS, vol. 4734, pp. 359–374. Springer, Heidelberg (2007). https://doi.org/10.1007/978-3-540-74835-9_24

22. Nicholson, J., Coventry, L., Briggs, P.: Age-related performance issues for PIN and face-based authentication systems. In: Proceedings of the SIGCHI Conference on Human Factors in Computing Systems, pp. 323–332. Association for Computing Machinery, New York, NY, USA (2013). https://doi.org/10.1145/2470654.2470701

23. Marne, S.T., Al-Ameen, M.N., Wright, M.: Learning System-assigned Passwords: A Preliminary Study on the People with Learning Disabilities. Presented at the Thirteenth Symposium on Usable Privacy and Security ({SOUPS} 2017) (2017)

24. Braun, V., Clarke, V.: Using thematic analysis in psychology. Qual. Res. Psychol. 3, 77–101 (2006). https://doi.org/10.1191/1478088706qp063oa

25. Ericsson, K.A., Simon, H.A.: Verbal reports as data. Psychol. Rev. 87, 215–251 (1980). https://doi.org/10.1037/0033-295X.87.3.215

26. Li, Y., Wang, H., Sun, K.: Personal information in passwords and its security implications. IEEE Trans. Inf. Forensics Secur. 12, 2320–2333 (2017). https://doi.org/10.1109/TIFS.2017.2705627

27. Davis, F.D.: User acceptance of information technology: system characteristics, user perceptions and behavioral impacts. Int. J. Man Mach. Stud. 38, 475–487 (1993). https://doi.org/10.1006/imms.1993.1022

28. Shay, R., et al.: Can long passwords be secure and usable? In: Proceedings of the SIGCHI Conference on Human Factors in Computing Systems, pp. 2927–2936. Association for Computing Machinery, New York, NY, USA (2014)

29. Schnotz, W.: An integrated model of text and picture comprehension. In: Mayer, R. (ed.) The Cambridge Handbook of Multimedia Learning. Cambridge University Press (2005)

30. NordPass: Top 200 Most Common Passwords of 2020. https://nordpass.com/most-common-passwords-list/

31. Thorpe, J., van Oorschot, P.C.: Human-Seeded Attacks and Exploiting Hot-Spots in Graphical Passwords. Presented at the 16th USENIX Security Symposium (2007)

IntraVox: A Personalized Human Voice to Support Users with Complex Needs in Smart Homes

Ana-Maria Salai[1(✉)], Glenda Cook[2], and Lars Erik Holmquist[1]

[1] School of Design, Northumbria University, Newcastle upon Tyne, UK
{ana-maria.salai,lars.holmquist}@northumbria.ac.uk
[2] Nursing, Midwifery and Health, Northumbria University, Newcastle upon Tyne, UK
glenda.cook@northumbria.ac.uk

Abstract. We present IntraVox, a novel voice-based interaction system that supports users with complex needs by introducing a highly personalized, human voice command between smart home devices and sensors. Voice-enabled personal assistants (e.g., Amazon Alexa, Google Home) can be used to control smart home devices and increase the quality of life. However, people suffering from conditions such as dementia or learning disabilities and autism (LDA) can encounter verbal and memory problems in communicating with the assistants. IntraVox supports these users by verbally sending smart home control commands, based on the sensor data collected, to a voice-enabled personal assistant using a human voice. Over 12 months, we conducted 7 workshops and 9 interviews with 79 participants from multiple stakeholder categories - people with LDA, older and frail people, social and health care organisations. Results show that our solution has the potential to support people with complex needs and increase independence. Moreover, IntraVox could have the added value of reinforcing the learning of specific commands and making visible the inner workings of a home automation system, by giving users a clear cause-and-effect explanation of why certain events occur.

Keywords: Home automation · Smart homes · Virtual assistants

1 Introduction

Smart home technologies can increase the quality of life of many user groups. For instance, voice-enabled personal assistants (e.g., Amazon Alexa, Google Home) are becoming increasingly popular [22]. These devices have great potential to support people of all abilities and across the life course to live independently at home and optimize their quality of life [42]. In addition to setting reminders, playing music, and providing information, voice-enabled personal assistants can control various technologies in a home such as light, temperature, and blinds.

© IFIP International Federation for Information Processing 2021
Published by Springer Nature Switzerland AG 2021
C. Ardito et al. (Eds.): INTERACT 2021, LNCS 12932, pp. 223–244, 2021.
https://doi.org/10.1007/978-3-030-85623-6_15

Despite being popular and affordable, certain sectors of the population can encounter issues in interacting with such devices [42]. One issue, particularly relevant for people with speech impairments, memory problems, and cognitive issues, is the verbal requirement to articulate or recall keywords and syntax, such as *"Alexa/Hey Google, turn on the living room lights"* .

In collaboration with a housing association, we undertook a research project to understand how to overcome these issues and support the organisation's customers. Over 12 months, we conducted workshops and interviews with various stakeholder categories - end-users, social and healthcare professionals. Based on their feedback, we developed IntraVox. IntraVox *verbally* sends smart home control commands to a voice-enabled personal assistant (e.g., Amazon Alexa and Google Home, but it could easily be generalized to other platforms) using a *human voice* based on a contextual situation. For instance, when light sensors detect a decrease in the light intensity, IntraVox can enable Alexa to turn on the lights and close the curtains by playing the recording of a human voice (Fig. 1). Our system thus has the potential to reveal the inner workings of home automation, giving users a clear cause-and-effect explanation of why certain events occur. This approach also has the potential of improving the usability of voice-enabled personal assistants by removing the necessity for the user to remember and pronounce specific commands whilst also reinforcing the syntax and usefulness of those commands for future situations (e.g., for when the user wants to turn on the lights themselves). The current implementation of the system is composed of a dedicated computer (Raspberry Pi 4B) to which we attached environmental, touch, proximity, and motion sensors. Using a speaker, the system sends prompts and reminders to householders and commands to a voice-enabled personal assistant which in return controls smart home devices.

Fig. 1. IntraVox is composed of a Raspberry Pi 4B, sensors, speaker, Amazon Alexa and/or Google Home controlling smart home appliances.

This paper is structured as follows. We start by providing an overview of smart homes and voice-enabled personal assistants, followed by the user sessions conducted to develop and evaluate IntraVox. We then discuss the contributions we bring to the design of Human-Computer Interfaces for smart homes and Ubiquitous Computing.

2   Background

In this section, we outline the current research in the area of smart homes and voice-enabled personal assistants. We present how voice-enabled personal assistants can support independent living and the issues some users suffering from various disabilities encounter when interacting with such devices.

Smart home technologies are designed to support people in living comfortably and independently and have caught the attention of researchers working in the field of Human-Computer Interaction and Ubiquitous Computing [1,50]. For example, Dahmen et al. [17] developed a digital memory notebook application for a smart home to help older adults keep track of their daily to-do lists. The application, linked with motion and door sensors, keeps track of the activities performed, and provides prompts when remaining activities need to be completed. By using distortions in the wireless signal, Adib et al. [1] created a system that monitors vital signs such as breathing and heart rate. Rafferty et al. [44] retrofitted an assisted living smart home for older people with activity and environmental sensors to create an intention recognition mechanism based on activity data. Daher et al. [16] used in-depth images extracted from a Microsoft Kinect and accelerometer data to determine falls and to localize and track the daily activities of older people. Suitable for studying the behavior of older and disabled people, Li et al. [29] used a less invasive method and developed an indoor human tracking system based on Wi-Fi signal strength. Vines et al. [54] investigated how home technologies can improve the quality of life of older people by developing a non-invasive monitor system composed of sensors connected to a central hub.

Voice-enabled personal assistants have been introduced in the home to facilitate access to information and control smart home instruments. These devices can also support independent living and improve the quality of life of people suffering from various conditions [42]. Pradhan et al. [42] investigated Alexa's accessibility and how it can improve the quality of life of people with motor, sensory, and cognitive impairments. Alexa was predominantly used for listening to music and playing audiobooks, searching for information (e.g., weather forecast), and home automation (e.g., lights, thermostats). Most users with visual impairments and/or motor disabilities mentioned an increase in independence and quality of life because it saved effort and allowed them to communicate with other family members. Alexa also proved useful in helping people with speech impairments to talk slowly, clearly, and loudly. Setting reminders, medication management, managing calendars, and to-do lists was perceived as useful for people with memory difficulties. Finally, the increase in independence also reduced caregivers' responsibilities. Kowalski et al. [26] conducted workshops with older adults to determine the potential of Google Home in the context of smart homes. Results show that older users face barriers (fear of malfunction) but also benefits (intuitive interaction, friendly manner, no handling of devices) when interacting with the assistant. Simpson et al. [48] designed a conversational agent embodied as a household potted flower to provide companionship to older adults living alone. Using an open source framework for the conversational interface, the device engages in a casual conversation with the user regarding a past memory in their life or by suggesting activities that might be of interest to them.

Despite the above mentioned benefits, some user categories encounter challenges in interacting with voice-enabled personal assistants. For example, Atefi et al. [4] discovered that the length of most Alexa Skill commands is greater than 4 words, with some even requesting 8 words. This has led to a complaint by users who tend to find the commands long and difficult. Vacher et al. [53] evaluated a context-aware voice interface system with seniors and people with visual impairments in an Ambient Assisted Living laboratory. The results show that participants disliked the strict grammar rules for the commands and would have preferred a more natural approach to the interaction. Similarly, Sayago et al. [46] argue that the need of knowing the commands and the *one-size-fits-all* approach adapted has an impact on the user experience. Luger and Sellen [31] investigated users' views on Conversational Agents (e.g., Siri, Cortana) and how this affects everyday use. Results show there is a gap between people's expectations and the agent's capabilities. Users started by interacting with the agent in a natural language but were later forced to limit themselves to just keywords and specific terms to obtain the desired output. Moreover, they had to learn how to speak to the agent to be able to successfully interact with it. Similar to previous findings [18], some users were willing to research in advance the agent's capabilities to maximize the interaction and increase trust. Intuitively, investing time in understanding a system's capabilities and learning how to interact with it becomes bothersome, especially for a person with limited cognitive abilities. Porcheron et al. [41] investigated how families engage with Alexa in their homes. The authors developed a voice recorder composed of a Raspberry Pi and a microphone that would record what happened before and during the conversation with the device. Based on the data from a month-long deployment, the authors argue that voice user interface devices should not be viewed as conversational agents since they are not able to properly understand the meaning of a conversation. The authors suggested that voice-enabled personal assistants should be designed based on a request-response rather than a conversation interaction.

The need to speak clearly and loudly with voice-enabled personal assistants is challenging for people with speech impairments [42]. Moreover, the short amount of time in which the commands need to be spoken and the difficulty in remembering these commands constitutes a problem for people with cognitive impairments [31,42]. Carroll et al. [11] designed and developed an assistive mobile and web platform to support the daily living of people with dementia, by providing voice prompts and task guidance to the users. Being developed as a Skill (a built-in Alexa capability), the system was designed only for people suffering from early stages of dementia as it requires the users to recall specific keywords and phrases. Corbett and Weber [13] developed a mobile voice user interface for people with motor impairments. Regarding speech recognition error rates, the authors highlight that a limited command vocabulary is more effective and accurate than a conversational style interaction. However, from a user experience point of view, the conversational style is the desired and preferred one.

3   Development Process

To address the limitations some users with complex needs face when using voice-enabled personal assistants, we developed a system to support them when using such devices. We developed the system through a process of requirements gathering, system development, feedback interviews, and workshops with social and healthcare organizations and potential end-users. To the best of our knowledge, the resulting *IntraVox* system is unique in that it uses a human voice for Computer-Computer Interaction that aims in increasing the quality of life and independence of people suffering from complex needs (e.g. people with LDA, frail and older people) in the context of a smart home. This interaction focuses on removing the necessity for users to remember specific syntaxes required to enable and control a voice-enabled personal assistant.

3.1   Requirements Gatherings

We started by conducting 2 workshops with 19 Community of Practice (CoP) members from various end-user representation groups such as social care and health organizations, working with and supporting people with LDA. Similar to [30], the workshops aimed to understand how technology can support people with LDA to live independently in their homes. To drive design decisions, we introduced 2 Personas as this User-Centered Design tool proved successful in facilitating design discussions and encouraging participants to engage in a study [10]. The Personas, designed in collaboration with an occupational therapist, represented characters suffering from LDA and behaviours of concern, with reduced independence and significant sensory needs.

During the first workshop (with 11 CoP members), members engaged in timeline analysis to explore the requirements the Personas would have during the day, and how these could be fulfilled through sensing, processing, and actuation. During the second workshop, members engaged in the exploration of challenges and behaviours in relation to daily activities in different locations of a home. The data collected were analysed using elements of thematic analysis [20].

Findings. The outcome of these workshops led to 4 concepts where technology could promote users' independence and increase quality of life: (1) **Concept 1: Smart Home** – the concept of automating the house based on sensors (e.g., sound, light, humidity, temperature, and motion) and use of appliances data (e.g., fridge, kettle, microwave, and toothbrush), (2) **Concept 2: Skills Development and Maintenance** – supporting people to develop personal skills (personal care, interests, and activities), (3) **Concept 3: Prompts and Reminders** – provide people with emotional, nutritional (e.g., cook a meal), daily management support (e.g., appointments and daily activities), and (4) **Concept 4: Behaviour and Environment Monitoring** – allow health professionals access to users' activity data. We used these concepts to drive the cycles of development of the IntraVox system.

3.2   System Explorations

The technologies we used as a starting point (e.g., Alexa as a voice-enabled personal assistant, sensors, smart devices) were shaped by the feedback received during the workshops. The challenge was to integrate the different concepts in a system that was easy to use for our potential user groups. To address Concept 1 and 4, we started by designing a system composed of motion, temperature, sound, and light sensors connected to a Raspberry Pi computer, widely used for home automation. Based on the sensor data collected, the Raspberry Pi would send prompts and reminders (Concept 2 and 3) and activate different smart home commands (Concept 1) such as turn on the lights, close the curtains, play music. A voice-enabled personal assistant was selected to carry out the commands as this is a readily available technology and is compatible with a variety of smart home appliances. Similar to [26,54], it can act as a hub that enables connectivity from different resources and devices. We initially developed 2 ways of sending the instructions in a testing house provided by the housing company partner:

System 1 - *Silent System*: We wanted to have an option where the sensors would control the voice-enabled personal assistant directly without any audible commands. However, Amazon Alexa is fundamentally a voice-enabled personal and home assistant that only accepts verbal commands in its syntax to control devices. This is seen as a shortcoming by some developers, who have created various workarounds. One common way of making it a silent process would require putting a set of headphones on the Amazon Alexa [2]. This is a rather inelegant solution which we did not pursue. Additionally, it can be achieved by using Home Assistant [19], a Python program that can track, control, and automate various smart home devices, and Bespoken [8], a third-party website that creates a virtual/silent Amazon Echo device.

System 2 – *Synthesized Voice System*: Messages verbalized by the Raspberry Pi using voice synthesis created by text-to-speech libraries [45] is another method of enabling Alexa. In our demonstrations, we used an English female voice with emphasis on capitals and speaking slowly. As an example, based on the light sensor data collected, the Raspberry Pi can verbalize a prompt to Alexa to trigger certain processes. Whilst we tried at the beginning to use complex sentences such as *"It is getting dark outside. Alexa, turn on the lights."* or double commands *"Alexa, turn on the lights and close the curtains.",* we soon realized it is hard for Alexa to understand these commands, regardless of accent and delivery pace of the command. Therefore, we limited the instructions to basic keywords and phrases such as *"Alexa, turn on the lights.".*

3.3 Prototype Interviews

Throughout the development phase, we also held 2 interviews with 3 CoP members who could not attend the workshops (one member being a person with a learning disability). The interviews took place in the same house provided by the housing company to ensure that participants can perceive how the systems would fit in a real home. The aim was to confirm the technology decisions taken based on the feedback collected from the 2 workshops. Participants provided positive feedback with respect to the 2 systems and provided suggestions on how they can be improved. Our CoP member suffering from a learning disability noted that the silent system might not be appropriate for a person with LDA as they could find it *"scary"* and the synthesized voice can be perceived as unpleasant and frustrating. Based on their suggestions we developed IntraVox, a human voice-based interaction system.

4 IntraVox

4.1 Proof-of-Concept

As previously described, the synthesized voice used in System 2 for vocalizing the pre-configured messages can be perceived as unpleasant and difficult for the voice-enabled personal assistant to process. The development process took place in the same house provided by the company. We started by creating audio files with a human voice verbalizing the pre-configured messages and used these to send the prompts, reminders, or instructions to Alexa. The audio files were recorded directly on the Raspberry Pi using a microphone and the Audacity software [5]. The voice could be a voice recording of a relative, a carer, or any other familiar person. The intention was to create a sense of security and comfort, as if the person was there to help, rather than commands being carried out automatically by an anonymous computer.

Python software was written to access each sensor's library, read the sensor values and trigger events accordingly based on the user's preferences. As an example, the user, carer or family member can specify an ideal room temperature (e.g., 22°). Based on *if* statements, the Python software would detect whether the temperature sensor values went above or below the ideal value, and would trigger an event, e.g. play an audio file already saved on its internal memory, using Python libraries for playing audio files. IntraVox is agile and these values can easily be changed by simply modifying the lux (for light), decibel (for sound), degrees (for temperature), etc. values in the Python code. Since we were using a human voice and we were not facing any memory or time length constraints, we decided to expand the messages and adapt them to address different scenarios, as follows:

Home Automation: Mennicken et al. [33] highlight that householders do not like smart homes to make decisions for them. The authors suggest that homes should propose rather than impose certain house processes. To address Concept 1 and to promote independence and empower people to make their own decisions, we adapted the messages to the following syntax (based on light sensor data collected): *"It is getting dark outside. Maybe you should turn on the lights and close the curtains."*. However, this type of message would not be appropriate for people lacking the ability to process this information. We, therefore, designed additional messages such as *"It is getting dark outside. Alexa, turn on the lights and close the curtains"* (Fig. 2).

Based on temperature sensor data, the system also alerts users whether it's getting too warm or too cold in a room and to subsequently, turn on or off the heating or open and close a window. This type of message provides a clear justification for why certain types of home automation processes occur.

Fig. 2. IntraVox sends instructions to Alexa to close the bedroom curtains.

Activity: Brewer et al. [9] discuss how voice-enabled personal assistants can support the process of remembering by reminding users about activities that need to be performed in the future and by recalling past information. To address Concept 2–4, if no motion has been detected for a certain amount of time, we designed IntraVox to verbalize a reminder such as: *"You should be a bit more active, it's good for you. How about going for a walk?"*. On the other hand, if the motion sensors detected increased movement which could be a proxy indicator that the user is agitated, IntraVox would verbalize instructions to Alexa to alleviate the situation (based on the user's preferences): *"You seem agitated. Alexa, turn living room lights purple and play calming music"*.

As identified by Kiseleva et al. [25], successful task completion and low level of effort in seeking information are key factors that contribute to users' overall satisfaction when interacting with a voice-enabled personal assistant. Cho et al. [11] also show that interacting with Alexa requires a pre-decision process and a certain level of energy that users view as a burden especially after a tiring day at work. Therefore, since a user (with or without an impediment) is not required to put effort into remembering and vocalizing a command, our solution could contribute to an enhanced user experience.

4.2 First Validation Workshop

We arranged 2 workshops with 2 stakeholder categories - CoP members and potential end-users - to validate IntraVox and evaluate whether our choice of technologies suits end-users. The workshops took place in the same house provided by the company to ensure that participants can perceive how the systems would fit in a real home.

We first conducted a workshop with 9 CoP members from various councils, social care, and health organizations that work with and support people with LDA, to evaluate the technologies deployed. CoP members took part in interactive in-situ demonstrations of the Silent, Synthesized Voice, and IntraVox systems (Table 1 illustrates the IntraVox concepts both stakeholder categories interacted with during the workshop). They also engaged in technical discussions about sensing and actuation, and provided informed feedback about the systems developed based on open-ended questions.

Table 1. IntraVox concepts both stakeholder categories interacted with during the workshop.

Scenario	Activity
Home automation	Using light sensors, IntraVox enables Amazon Alexa to turn on/off lights and blinds
Home automation	Using temperature sensors, IntraVox prompts users to turn on/off the heating and close/open the window
Activity	Using motion sensors, IntraVox prompts users to be more active or provides alternatives if they are agitated

We also organized a workshop with 4 end-users with mild LDA (3 males and 1 female), customers of the housing association that owned the house. The aim was to understand whether the systems developed would be suitable for people with LDA. During the workshop, 4 support workers, employees of the housing association, were also present to offer end-user support. Meetings were held prior to the workshop with one of the support workers to (1) ensure that our workshop structure is appropriate and does not cause any emotional distress in the end-users, and (2) design an easy read version of the information sheet and consent form handed in prior to the workshop.

The workshop lasted for 2 h and was divided into 2 phase: *(1) Phase 1 -* Since no end-user interacted with an Alexa device before, the workshop started by allowing them to familiarize themselves with the device. Similar to [24], end-users were asked to engage with Alexa by conducting short tasks. The tasks varied from asking for cooking recipes, e.g., *"Ask Alexa how to make a sandwich by saying 'Alexa, I want to make a cheese sandwich'"*, to asking Alexa to play funny sounds or booking appointments, *(2) **Phase 2** -* End-users were presented with interactive in-situ demonstrations of the systems (as CoP members) and were asked to provide feedback based on open-ended questions. Notes were taken down and data collected were analysed using elements of thematic analysis [20].

Findings. Our preliminary results show that sensors, IntraVox and Alexa are desired by both stakeholder categories (CoP members and end-users and their support workers). Several themes emerged from the discussions held, as follows:

Interaction. Since a voice-enabled personal assistant such as Alexa is part of the IntraVox system, it was important to understand end-users' views on the device and how they interact with it. Confirming previous findings [42], although people suffering from various disabilities can benefit from using an Alexa, their support workers were not aware of the device's capabilities: *"I have Alexa, but I have no idea how to use it, I only play music."*.

Ease of Use: Despite not being familiar with the device, the end-users were able to interact with it and understand its responses when undertaking basic tasks such as booking an appointment. More complex interactions (e.g. asking for cooking recipes) were perceived as overwhelming and hard to follow: *"She talks too much."*. Confirming previous research findings [42], processing the command of a person with a voice impairment proved problematic for Alexa. For example, one end-user was addressing the device with *"lexa"* in a quick way and found it frustrating when the system did not respond.

Satisfaction: Purington et al. [43] show that personification is associated with an increased level of satisfaction. People who refer to the device using personal pronouns such as *her* and *Alexa*, rather than *Echo* or *it*, tend to have a more friendly interaction with the virtual personal assistant. Our end-users were using personal pronouns such as *she* to describe their interaction with the device and *Alexa* to enable it. Whilst interacting with the device caused frustration in some end-users due to speech recognition errors, all end-users were satisfied with Alexa. Moreover, our end-users tended to have a polite interaction with Alexa using phrases such as *"Alexa, could you please [..]?"* and *"Thank you."* once the command was executed. This is similar to the findings by Nass and Brave [35] who show that voice within technology can encourage social interaction and that people respond to a voice socially even if the voice is synthetic.

Voice. The concept of a voice enabling Alexa received positive feedback from both stakeholder categories. For example, end-users appreciated the Activity Scenario and found it to be *"canny"* (nice). CoP members also expressed interest in such technology in the health system: *"We certainly see a place for products like this within social care."* City council members taking part in the workshop, already trialing the use of Alexa with their customers, also emphasized the system's novelty: *"Interesting to see technology interacting with one another, had* *initially thought these would have stand-alone operations. Importance of personalising where possible the voice used for the instruction.".*

Silent Communication: Previous Human-Robot Interaction research indicates that humans would like to understand what the robots are communicating with each other using voice and gestures [23]. This in return shows humans that robots can communicate with them, making the interaction feel *"natural and smooth"* as during Human-Human Communication. Williams et al. [55] also show that silent communication between robots is perceived as *"creepy"* by humans and highlight that human-robot settings should be sensitive to human expectations. Similarly, with regards to System 1 – Silent System, end-users' feedback varied from *"I wouldn't be bothered"* to *"I'd get frightened as if it was haunted. What's going on? Like a horror movie.".* Additionally, end-users mentioned they would prefer knowing why certain home automation processes occur: *"Good idea to hear what will happen, to warn me.".*

Personification: All end-users preferred IntraVox to the Synthesized Voice System: *"I want a voice that I recognize.",* highlighting the benefits of having such a system: *"A voice that is familiar calms me down.".* This corresponds to the design paradigm that *"Computers are Social Actors"* and that human-computer relationships are in essence social [37]. Indeed, *"Computers that talk"* aim to create *"natural"* and *"real"* experiences, and the use of a human voice can contribute to an enhanced user experience [30] and increased usability [10]. Previous research also indicates that social robots talking in a human voice is preferred to a synthesized voice and a robotic, monotonous voice might not be suitable for emotional interactions [7].

Trust: The results of the workshop also show that designers might also wish to consider the aspect of trust [18] and that importance should be given to the person the familiar voice belongs to and their relationship with the end-users. Large and Burnett [27] investigated how drivers' attitudes towards GPS (automated driver support system) voices and the impact the voices have on trust and attention. Results show that driver's attitudes are influenced by the *"personality"* of the navigation system. For example, drivers may be less likely to follow the instructions provided by an annoying voice but might follow the ones provided by an entertaining voice. Indeed, our end-users provided mixed feedback regarding what type of voice they would prefer: *"I would like Vicky's* [caregiver] *voice."* or *"My voice also."* but *"Not me mam's* [my mother's] *voice!".* It is worth mentioning we used a female voice for the recordings, belonging to one of the workshop's facilitators. Participants also had time to familiarize themselves with the voice before the demonstrations.

4.3   Second Validation Workshop

The findings from the workshops indicated that IntraVox has great potential in supporting people with complex needs. However, the results also show that Alexa might not be suitable for some user categories, as it does not always understand commands, leading to frustration and irritation. This allowed improving the system in cases where users find it challenging to use.

We conducted an additional workshop with 10 CoP members in the same house to understand how IntraVox's functionalities can be expanded and whether it can also improve the quality of life of older adults. As in previous workshops, participants were presented with 2 Personas that were carefully designed by a collaborator in this work, expert in the needs of older people, and an occupational therapist. The Personas represented characters living with long-term health problems (e.g., frailty, dementia, incontinence). CoP members were asked how IntraVox can support the Personas in the context of a smart home, by reflecting also on the 4 Concepts previously discovered.

Findings. CoP participants emphasized the importance of personalization and developing solutions based on the user's needs and preferences. They stressed that the needs of older people should be considered alongside the needs of support workers. At all stages of later life, the needs and preferences of older people change and therefore, it is important for the technology to adapt and respond to different requirements. Following their feedback and in collaboration with the expert in older people's needs, various test scenarios were developed to address common challenges encountered by older people - insufficient hydration and urinary incontinence, prompting and maintaining personal hygiene, etc.

4.4 Integrated System

Given the feedback received, we expanded IntraVox by including additional functionalities and sensors (touch and proximity). We also tested IntraVox on a Google Home device to demonstrate the system's compatibility with other voice-enabled personal assistants available on the market. We, therefore, redesigned the messages to include the specific syntaxes and keywords required to interact with the device, e.g. *"Hey Google, close the curtains."*. To address the test scenarios arising from the workshop findings, the following additional IntraVox prototypes have been implemented (in the same test house):

Activity: Socially assistive robots can support people with dementia by prompting interventions when a behaviour change is detected [14] and motivate them in exercising using personalized messages [15]. We, therefore, expanded the previous Activity Scenario to engage users with home-based exercises. Based on the user's daily routine and necessities, whenever inactivity is being detected, the Raspberry Pi would send an instruction to Alexa to start a workout routine: *"You haven't been active in a while. You should work out, it's good for you. Alexa, start 7min workout [Alexa Skill]"* (Concept 3 and 4).

Hygiene and Dehydration: Using audio and picture prompting proved successful in enhancing the independence of adults with Autism Spectrum Conditions by improving their daily living skills such as washing dishes and doing laundry [49]. To addresses Concept 2 and 3, using a touch sensor attached to

Fig. 3. IntraVox prompts users to wash their hands after using the toilet.

a toilet (Fig. 3), IntraVox can send a verbal notification to the users to wash their hands after using the toilet: *"Remember to wash your hands after going to the toilet."*. Dehydration is a common problem in later life, and it can lead to serious health consequences. Since users must drink sufficient fluid, sensors were deployed to determine the amount of water a person is drinking in a day. If the fluid intake is less than 1.5 l per day [12], a verbal reminder was sent to users to drink the recommended daily intake of fluids. We attached a touch sensor to a glass and an additional temperature sensor at the bottom of a mug that indicates a drink/hot drink is being consumed. In addition, IntraVox can send a message in the morning, afternoon, and evening as a reminder to drink sufficient fluid throughout the day.

Reminder: Using a proximity sensor attached to a front door, users can receive a verbal reminder to take their keys before leaving the house (Concept 2 and 3). Using cloud communications platforms such as Twilio [52] and Plivo [40], IntraVox was programmed to also send an SMS alert to a carer or family member whenever an unexpected or relevant event would occur (e.g., front door opened).

4.5   Online Evaluation Workshops

Following the worldwide lockdown due to the COVID-19 pandemic, evaluating the new IntraVox functionalities during face-to-face workshops was no longer possible. Similar to other research [6], we continued to engage with the same stakeholder categories (potential end-users and CoP members) through internet multimedia platforms and conducted online workshops and interviews.

We organized two online workshops with 15 CoP members and 5 small group interviews involving 14 individuals supporting older and frail people and people with mental health issues. We presented participants with videos of the systems developed (filmed in the same test house) and asked for feedback using open-ended questions. Notes were taken down and data were analyzed using elements of thematic analysis [20]. The workshop focused on understanding how IntraVox can help increase the quality of life of these user categories. In order to validate previous findings, participants were also presented with videos of the Silent and Synthesized Voice Systems.

We also interviewed a frail older man together with his live-in daughter and son-in-law acting as carers, and an older woman together with her daughter who also acted as a carer. Similar to the end-users with LDA workshop, the interviews lasted for one hour were divided into 2 phases: *(1) Phase 1 -* End-users visualized videos that compared the interaction between Alexa and Google Home, e.g., asking both devices for cooking recipes. Previous studies evaluated customer satisfaction of Alexa and Google Home [8, 12]. However, to the best of our knowledge, studies have not been conducted to determine which device is received as better by older people, and *(2) Phase 2 -* End-users were presented with videos of the concepts developed (as CoP members) and were asked to provide feedback based on open-ended questions. Notes were taken down and data collected were analysed using elements of thematic analysis [20].

Findings. Interest was shown by individuals who had not previously considered voice-enabled personal assistants or who have used the assistants in a limited way. There was a consensus among CoP members that products such as sensors and voice-enabled personal assistants have great potential to augment care and support individuals with complex needs to live independently: *"Lots of applications for the technology to support how people may live, manage a long term illness or recover from a health episode.".* Several themes emerged from the discussions held, as follows:

Interaction. Similar to the end-users with LDA workshop, it was important to understand end-users' views on both voice-enabled personal assistants since they are part of the IntraVox system.

Ease of Use: Similar to the end-users with LDA workshop findings, the frail older man and his family members recommended slower, repeated, and short sentences for both voice-enabled personal assistants. They felt that Alexa can be difficult to hear and complicated and that Google Home was *"a very fast talker and needed to slow down".* With regards to asking Google Home or Alexa for cooking instructions, both end-users found Google Home to be better as Alexa offers too much information that is *"difficult to retain in one go".* They also found the instructions given by Alexa to be a bit more complicated than the Google Home ones and found it hard to remember the number of meal choices offered by Alexa. Similar to [32], both end-users thought that Google Home *"sounds good"* with the older woman preferring the female voice to the male one. Although they did not find the instructions to be quick, her daughter mentioned that it might be *"a bit fast whilst doing it but the pace is ok whilst listening".* Similar to the support workers taking part in the previous workshop, the older woman and her daughter were already using Alexa for medication reminders and were not aware of any additional functionalities the device offered such as asking for cooking recipes, playing music, turning off the lights in the entire house.

Certainty: The frail older man and his family members felt that IntraVox could provide independence, security and enhance all of their quality of life. Although they live together, he indicated that being able to alert his daughter when she was away could enhance his sense of security. She and her husband also suggested that this would provide *"peace of mind"* to them and would help enable them to do activities that they enjoyed.

Voice. The high level of personalization offered by IntraVox, in particular, received positive feedback from both stakeholder categories, with CoP members declaring:*"It is helpful to program systems to sound like a family member. This helps in personalising the support provided to the customer.".*

Silent Communication: Confirming previous end-users with LDA workshop and research findings [23,55], the older woman stated that she would prefer voice instructions (regardless of voice) to silent ones (System 1 – Silent System).

Personification: Similar to the end-users with LDA, the frail older man and his family members provided positive feedback regarding the familiar voice that IntraVox provides and stated that the message delivered was at a good pace. They felt that *"IntraVox was the best technology from all the technologies* [systems] *presented"* but they also commented it might be suitable only for mild and moderate dementia (e.g., the familiar voice might confuse the user that the person is physically present in the room). The older woman also found the concept of a human voice enabling Alexa or Google Home to be interesting. She mentioned the computer voice (System 2 – Synthesized System) *"was alright"* but would prefer a human voice. She also found the verbal prompts (Hygiene and Dehydration Scenario) to be useful and would like a reminder to drink more liquids during the day. Her daughter also mentioned that it would be very useful from a carer's point of view to receive a text alert when certain events occur, such as setting up an alert when the door opens in the middle of the night (Reminder Scenario). The older woman did not have a problem sharing this data with her daughter mentioning that: *"I want you* (her daughter) *to know everything.".*

Adherence: CoP members stated that IntraVox *"could be phenomenal"* in helping people adhere to a routine, especially when they are encouraged to conduct tasks related to everyday life. The Activity Scenario received positive feedback and could be useful for people with low motivation.

Personalisation. CoP members highlighted that end-users can encounter difficulties in using technologies as a consequence of mood, lack of confidence, sensory and memory problems. Similar to [39] and as mentioned during previous workshops, CoP members explained that personalisation is a key priority and mentioned that IntraVox can ensure that end-users support would be individualized. End-users have very different requirements: *"Some are visual learners whereas others learn best through listening.".* Therefore, the technology offer should be grounded in a detailed assessment of the end-user's needs and aspirations. CoP members were also keen to stress that further development of IntraVox would be needed to ensure that keywords are easy to understand, and the content motivates end-users. Personalisation is a key aspect of assistive technologies, especially in situations where a person's cognitive abilities are constantly changing [32]. Therefore, CoP members argued that technology should be empowering as well as enabling the end-user. It is important that the end-user could override the automated processes (e.g., switching lighting on/off) or that the system could be altered when the end-users needs change.

5   Discussion

Our studies show how voice-enabled personal assistants can help improve the quality of life of people with complex needs. Similar to previous findings [38], we also encountered issues when engaging with such devices. Here, we discuss some opportunities to improve interaction and user experience.

IntraVox. People suffering from cognitive and speech impairments can encounter major problems in communicating with voice-enabled personal assistants. The need to vocalize the instruction can require a lot of effort for these user categories and can lead to frustration and irritation when the device does not comprehend the command or does not reply accordingly. In our studies, we deliberately used a recording of a human voice (this could be of a relative, a caregiver, a friend) to enable the voice-enabled personal assistant. For some users, this can create a sense of security and comfort, as if the person was there to help, rather than commands being carried out automatically by an anonymous computer or by using a synthetic voice. In our demonstrations, this use of a familiar, recognizable voice for Computer-Computer interaction has received positive feedback from end-users and social and healthcare organizations. IntraVox is also agile; as the purpose evolves, it can be changed over time in response to reflection and assessment of the end-users needs. This change in use could easily be implemented by simply changing the position of sensors and re-programming the message provided by IntraVox. This agile feature can be embedded in an individual's habitual practices and ensures responsiveness to ever-changing needs and health conditions.

We believe that the human voice used in our demonstrations can have an impact on the user experience [46,49] and can play an important role in providing personalisation. Synthetic voices can affect people's social presence feeling of a device and customizing a computer voice according to the user's personality can rise the feeling of social presence [28]. Voice can also have a significant impact on trust and credibility [18,27], with previous studies [36] showing that the emotion in the voice can influence an individual's perception of the content (more than a synthesized speech does). Our findings show that the person the voice belongs to and their relationship with the end-user is also important, as one end-user with LDA stated they would prefer the carer's voice and not the voice of a relative. The familiar, recognizable voice can also be beneficial in learning interventions [9,34] and can help users who have difficulties verbalizing or remembering commands. Previous research [56] shows that older adults can benefit from listening to familiar voices as it can help them identify words in sentences. We believe that IntraVox could have the added benefit of reinforcing the learning of complicated verbal commands. This would allow users to take control of the situation as they learn the commands and take appropriate actions themselves instead of letting the system do it.

Things That Talk. *"Things That Talk"* has been used as a way of describing the Internet of Things (IoT), i.e. the notion that sensors and actuators in the physical world may communicate wirelessly and send data to each other [21]. The paradigm is related to the well-established concepts of Ubiquitous and Pervasive Computing. In our case, we are interested in the use of IoT in the home environment to control smart appliances. However, the way that IoT and home automation are implemented at present is in most cases hidden from human understanding – the things do talk to each other, but we cannot hear them! With IntraVox, by using an audible voice rather than *"silent"* communication between devices, we are purposefully aiming to reveal the inner workings of an IoT system. Rather than things happening without explanation when a sensor is triggered (similar to [55], one end-user described as the house being *"haunted"*), the system explicitly expresses its intentions by speaking out loud.

It is important to stress that this is not a way to increase efficiency – from a purely technical point of view, it makes more sense to send commands directly between systems using a silent communication protocol rather than using voice. Without considering any marketing perspectives [38], we believe that the human element that IntraVox introduces to home automation has a value in itself, something which was also confirmed in our evaluation workshops. In the field of Human-Robot Interaction, Tan et al. [51] show that people perceive robots as more likable if they see them humanly treating each other. Therefore, the use of a personalized human voice within the IntraVox system (rather than anonymous speech synthesis) could create a sense of security and comfort, rather than commands being carried out automatically by an unseen agent. Similar to previous Robot-to-Robot Communication studies in the presence of humans [23,55], our participants appreciated being able to *"hear what will happen"* and know why a certain action would occur.

We think that some principles arising out of this can be applied in other situations, going beyond the users that IntraVox was originally developed for. One way to situate this is to relate to the debate on interface agents versus direct manipulation in HCI [47]. Agents act autonomously, often without the user's conscious input; direct manipulation, on the other hand, puts the control explicitly in the user's hands. In our experiments, the silent control system is akin to an agent, whereas giving commands directly to a voice assistant corresponds to direct manipulation. IntraVox, however, falls in between these 2 interface approaches, as on one hand, it relies on sensors to initiate events, but on the other, it allows the user to be aware of these actions and if needed insert themselves in the process (for instance by counter-acting a command that was issued). We believe IntraVox can suggest an interface principle that we call *Things That*

Talk (Among Themselves) - IoT devices and other context-aware systems that make an event explicit and visible (or audible) to the user, rather than hidden.

6 Limitations and Future Work

IntraVox uses a pre-recorded human voice as the text-to-speech voice generated by the Raspberry Pi was abrasive and often misinterpreted. We started by using free text-to-speech Python libraries as this was the easiest way to produce audio files in terms of time and resources. Using more advanced voice synthesis, e.g. Deep Voice [3] it will be possible to generate not just a more pleasing voice, but also one that is reminiscent of a known and trustworthy person.

There is a need to widen our CoP members to include speech and language therapists to create IntraVox messages that are easy to understand and follow. Instructing the user about what words to say to trigger an action (e.g. *"To close the curtains, say, 'Alexa, close the curtains.'"*) can empower them to make their own decisions. In the current implementation, users cannot reject and stop the command, unless they are able to reverse the command once it is being carried out. One way to overcome this is by using speech recognition and provide users with options: *"Do you want me to ask Alexa to close the curtains? Say yes or no."*. Taking the user's physical presence in the room should also be considered to avoid instances when the system announces its action while the user is out of the room. The resulting user experience of returning to a room to find the blinds closed could be perceived as *"haunted"* as the Silent system.

We also aim to implement a platform to ease the setup process, e.g. select the person the voice recording should belong to and record the audio files, select the desired commands and sensor values. It might also be that the system can learn to change the commands based on the user's behaviour. For example, the system could detect whether the users followed the suggestion of turning on the lights when it's getting dark outside and if not, the system can do it for them.

Alexa uses a built-in technology that is constantly listening for the wake word - the user has little knowledge of when Alexa might be actively listening to them and their environment. We do acknowledge that the microphone must always be enabled to carry out the commands. One way to overcome this aspect would be by controlling Alexa using third-party websites that do not require its microphone to be constantly enabled.

7 Conclusion

In this paper, we introduced IntraVox, a novel voice-based interaction system that allows a Computer-Computer Interaction using a highly personalized, audible human voice. The system was developed and evaluated with multiple stakeholder categories including older and frail people and people with LDA. The system introduces the concept of home automation by allowing sensors, actuators, and IoT devices to verbally communicate with each other using a highly personalized, human voice. This solution has the potential to reinforce the learning of specific commands and make visible the inner workings of a home automation system, removing anxiety and creating a sense of comfort. Situated in between agents and direct manipulation, this approach makes visible the often-hidden workings of a ubiquitous computing system. Our current example uses audible voice commands, but other modalities could also be explored, creating more user-friendly and understandable home automation and IoT environments. We believe that although the initial intended user groups are those with complex needs, many of the lessons learned can be generalize to the general population, making ubicomp systems more understandable, comforting, and easy to use.

References

1. Adib, F., Mao, H., Kabelac, Z., Katabi, D., Miller, R.: Smart homes that monitor breathing and heart rate. In: Proceedings of the 33rd Annual ACM Conference on Human Factors in Computing Systems (2015)
2. Amazon Skills Kit. https://amzn.to/363uZUU, Accessed 23 Jan 2021
3. Arik, S.- Ö., et al.: Deep voice: real-time neural text-to-speech. In: Proceedings of the 34th International Conference on Machine Learning, (ICML'17), vol. 70, pp. 195–204. JMLR.org (2017)
4. Atefi, S., Truelove, A., Rheinschmitt, M., Almeida, E., Ahmed, I., Alipour, A.: Examining user reviews of conversational systems: a case study of Alexa skills. arXiv preprint arXiv:2003.00919 (2020)
5. Audacity. https://www.audacityteam.org/
6. Bakhai, A., Constantin, A., Alexandru, C.A.: Motivate me! an alexa skill to support higher education students with autism. In: International Conferences Interfaces and Human Computer Interaction and Game and Entertainment Technologies (2020)
7. Barnes, J., Richie, E., Lin, Q., Jeon, M., Park, C.-H.: Emotive voice acceptance in human-robot interaction. In: Proceedings of the 24th International Conference on Auditory Display (2018)
8. Bespoken. https://bit.ly/2LO9rVp, Accessed 23 Jan 2021
9. Brewer, R.-N., Morris, M.-R., Lindley, S.-E.: How to remember what to remember: exploring possibilities for digital reminder systems. In: Proceedings of the ACM on interactive, mobile, wearable and ubiquitous technologies, vol. 1, no. 3, pp. 1–20 (2017)
10. Burgoon, J.-K., Bonito, J.-A., Bengtsson, B., Cederberg, C., Lundeberg, M., Allspach, L.: Interactivity in human-computer interaction: a study of credibility, under-standing, and influence. Comput. Human Behav. **16**(6), 553–574 (2000)
11. Cho, M., Lee, S.-S., Lee, K.-P.: Once a kind friend is now a thing: understanding how conversational agents at home are forgotten. In: Proceedings of the 2019 on Designing Interactive Systems Conference (2019)
12. Colley, M.: Use of frequency volume charts and voiding diaries. Nurs. Times **111**(5)(2015)
13. Corbett, E., Weber, A.: What can I say? addressing user experience challenges of a mobile voice user interface for accessibility. In: Proceedings of the 18th International Conference on Human-Computer Interaction with Mobile Devices and Services, pp. 72–82 (2016)

14. Cruz-Sandoval, D., Favela, J.: Co-designing ambient-assisted interventions using digital interlocutors for people with dementia. In: Proceedings of the 2017 ACM International Joint Conference on Pervasive and Ubiquitous Computing and Proceedings of the 2017 ACM International Symposium on Wearable Computers, pp. 813–821 (2017)

15. Cruz-Sandoval, D., Penaloza, C.-I., Favela, J., Castro-Coronel, A.-P.: Towards social robots that support exercise therapies for persons with dementia. In: Proceedings of the 2018 ACM International Joint Conference and 2018 International Symposium on Pervasive and Ubiquitous Computing and Wearable Computers, pp. 1729–1734 (2018)

16. Daher, M., El Najjar, M., Diab, A., Khalil, M., Charpillet, F.: Multi-sensory assistive living system for elderly in-home staying, pp. 168–171. IEEE (2018)

17. Dahmen, D., Minor, B., Cook, D., Vo, T., Schmitter-Edgecombe, M.: Smart home-driven digital memory notebook support of activity self-management for older adults. Gerontechnology **17**, 113–125 (2018)

18. Geeng, C., Franziska Roesner, F.: Who's in control? interactions in multi-user smart homes. In: Proceedings of the 2019 CHI Conference on Human Factors in Computing Systems, pp. 1–13 (2019)

19. Home Assistant. https://www.home-assistant.io/, Accessed 23 Jan 2021

20. Hsieh, H.-F., Shannon, S.: Three approaches to qualitative content analysis. Qual. Health Res. **15**(9), 1277–1288 (2005)

21. Igoe, T.: Making Things Talk: Practical Methods for Connecting Physical Objects, 3rd edn. O Reilly, Sebastopol (2017)

22. Juniper Research. https://bit.ly/3iGO8Ri, Accessed 23 Jan 2021

23. Kanda, T., Ishiguro, H., Ono, T., Imai, M., Mase, K.: Multi-robot cooperation for human-robot communication. In: Proceedings 11th IEEE International Workshop on Robot and Human Interactive Communication, pp. 271–276. IEEE (2002)

24. Kim, D., Park, K., Park, Y., Ju, J., Ahn, J.-H.: Alexa: tell me more: the effect of advertisements on memory accuracy from smart speakers. In: PACIS (2018)

25. Kiseleva, J., et al.: Understanding user satisfaction with intelligent assistants. In: Proceedings of the 2016 ACM on Conference on Human Information Interaction and Retrieval, pp. 121–130 (2016)

26. Kowalski, J., et al.: Older adults and voice interaction: a pilot study with google home. In: Extended Abstracts of the 2019 CHI Conference on Human Factors in Computing Systems (2019)

27. Large, D.R., Burnett, G.E.: The effect of different navigation voices on trust and attention while using in-vehicle navigation systems. J. Saf. Res. **49**, 69-e1 (2014)

28. Lee, K.-M., Nass, C.: Social-psychological origins of feelings of presence: creating social presence with machine-generated voices. Media Psychol. 7(1) (2005)

29. Li, X., et al.: IndoTrack: device-free indoor human tracking with commodity Wi-Fi. In: Proceedings of the ACM on Interactive, Mobile, Wearable and Ubiquitous Technologies, vol. 1, no. 3, pp. 1–22 (2017)

30. Lombard, M., Ditton, T.: At the heart of it all: the concept of presence. J. Comput.-Mediated Commun. **3**(2), JCMC321 (1997)

31. Luger, E., Sellen, A.: "Like Having a Really Bad PA" The Gulf between User Expectation and Experience of Conversational Agents. In: Proceedings of the 2016 CHI Conference on Human Factors in Computing Systems. (2016)

32. McGee-Lennon, M.R., Gray, P.D.: including stakeholders in the design of home care systems: identification and categorisation of complex user requirements. In: INCLUDE Conference (2007)

33. Mennicken, S., Zihler, O., Juldaschewa, F., Molnar, V., Aggeler, D., Huang, E.M.:" It's like living with a friendly stranger" perceptions of personality traits in a smart home. In: Proceedings of the 2016 ACM International Joint Conference on Pervasive and Ubiquitous Computing, pp. 120–131 (2016)

34. Milani, A., Lorusso, M.L., Molteni, M.: The effects of audiobooks on the psychosocial adjustment of pre-adolescents and adolescents with dyslexia. Dyslexia **16**(1), 87–97 (2010)

35. Nass, C.I., Brave, S.: Wired for Speech: How Voice Activates and Advances the Human-Computer Relationship. MIT press, Cambridge (2005)

36. Nass, C.I., Foehr, U., Brave, S., Somoza, M.: The effects of emotion of voice in synthesized and recorded speech. In: Proceedings of the AAAI Symposium Emotional and Intelligent II: The Tangled Knot of Social Cognition. North Falmouth (2001)

37. Nass, C.I., Steuer, J., Tauber, E.R.: Computers are social actors. In: Proceedings of the SIGCHI Conference on Human Factors in Computing Systems, pp. 72–78 (1994)

38. Oppenheimer, A.: From experience: products talking to people-conversation closes the gap between products and consumers. J. Prod. Innov. Manag. **22**(1), 82–91 (2005)

39. Perelmutter, B., McGregor, K.K., Gordon, K.R.: Assistive technology interventions for adolescents and adults with learning disabilities: an evidence-based systematic review and meta-analysis. Comput. Educ. **114**, 139–163 (2017)

40. Plivo. https://www.plivo.com/, Accessed 23 Jan 2021

41. Porcheron, M., Fischer, J.E., Reeves, S., Sharples, S.: Voice interfaces in everyday life. In: Proceedings of the 2018 CHI Conference on Human Factors in Computing Systems, pp. 1–12 (2018)

42. Pradhan, A., Mehta, K., Findlater, L.: "Accessibility Came by Accident" use of voice-controlled intelligent personal assistants by people with disabilities. In: Proceedings of the 2018 CHI Conference on Human Factors in Computing Systems, pp. 1–13 (2018)

43. Purington, A., Taft, J.G., Sannon, S., Bazarova, N.N., Taylor, S.H.: "Alexa is my new BFF" social roles, user satisfaction, and personification of the amazon echo. In: Proceedings of the 2017 CHI Conference Extended Abstracts on Human Factors in Computing Systems, pp. 2853–2859 (2017)

44. Rafferty, J., Nugent, C.-D., Liu, J., Chen, L.: From activity recognition to intention recognition for assisted living within smart homes. IEEE Trans. Human-Mach. Syst. 47(3) (2017)

45. RPi Text to Speech. https://bit.ly/3poEAxf, Accessed 23 Jan 2021

46. Sayago, S., Neves, B.B., Cowan, B.R.: Voice assistants and older people: some open issues. In: Proceedings of the 1st International Conference on Conversational User Interfaces, pp. 1–3 (2019)

47. Shneiderman, B., Maes, P.: Direct manipulation vs. interface agents. Interactions **4**(6), 42–61 (1997)

48. Simpson, J., Gaiser, F., Macík, M., Breßgott, T.: Daisy: a friendly conversational agent for older adults. In: Proceedings of the 2nd Conference on Conversational User Interfaces, pp. 1–3 (2020)

49. Søndergaard, M.L.K., Hansen, L.K. : Intimate futures: staying with the trouble of digital personal assistants through design fiction (2018)

50. Suzuki, Y., Kato, K., Naomi Furui, N., Sakamoto, D., Sugiura, Y.: Cushion interface for smart home control (2020)

51. Tan, X.Z., Reig, S., Carter, E.J., Steinfeld, A.: From one to another: how robot-robot interaction affects users' perceptions following a transition between robots, pp. 114–122. IEEE (2019)
52. Twilio. https://www.twilio.com/, Accessed 23 Jan 2021
53. Vacher, M., et al.: Evaluation of a context-aware voice interface for ambient assisted living: qualitative user study vs. quantitative system evaluation. ACM Trans. Accessible Comput. (TACCESS) 7(2), 1–36 (2015)
54. Vines, J., et al.: Making family care work: dependence, privacy and remote home monitoring telecare systems. In: Proceedings of the 2013 ACM International Joint Conference on Pervasive and Ubiquitous Computing (2013)
55. Williams, T., Briggs, P., Scheutz, M.: Covert robot-robot communication: human perceptions and implications for human-robot interaction. J. Human-Rob. Interact. 4(2), 24–49 (2015)
56. Yonan, C.A., Sommers, M.S.: The effects of talker familiarity on spoken word identification in younger and older listeners. Psychol. Aging 15(1), 88 (2000)

LIFT: An eLearning Introduction to Web Search for Young Adults with Intellectual Disability in Sri Lanka

Theja Kuruppu Arachchi[1,2,4(✉)], Laurianne Sitbon[1], Jinglan Zhang[1],
Ruwan Gamage[2], and Priyantha Hewagamage[3]

[1] Faculty of Science, Queensland University of Technology, Brisbane, QLD, Australia
theja.kuruppuarachchi@hdr.qut.edu.au, {laurianne.sitbon,
jinglan.zhang}@qut.edu.au
[2] National Institute of Library and Information Sciences (NILIS),
University of Colombo, Colombo 3, Sri Lanka
ruwan@nilis.cmb.ac.lk
[3] University of Colombo School of Computing, University of Colombo, Colombo 7, Sri Lanka
kph@ucsc.cmb.ac.lk
[4] Main Library, University of Ruhuna, Matara, Sri Lanka
tka@lib.ruh.ac.lk

Abstract. For users with intellectual disability new to the Internet, mastering web search requires both conceptual understanding and supported practice. eLearning offers an appropriate environment for both self-paced learning and authentic practice since it can simulate the types of interactions encountered during web searching. Yet eLearning approaches have not been explored towards supporting young adults with intellectual disability (YAWID) to search the web or supporting them to learn web search. This paper presents a study that examines the experiences of 6 YAWID learning to search the web with LIFT, an eLearning tool designed with a specific focus on supporting memory through mental models and practice exercises. The content and approach of LIFT are tailored to the Sri Lankan context, incorporating the use of the Sinhala virtual keyboard for Google search and culturally relevant metaphors. We collected a range of observations as the participants used the eLearning tool, subsequently independently searched for information online, and finally described the Google search process to a teacher. We surveyed their understanding through drawings they created about the Internet and Web search. The findings establish the significant potential for eLearning to engage and support YAWID learn web search, with a realistic environment for safely practicing web search and navigation. This study contributes to human-computer interaction by integrating three aspects of eLearning: accessible interface, content, and interactive practice, also accommodating web search in the Sinhala language. It acknowledges that understanding specific users is critical if interaction designs are to be accepted by their users.

Keywords: Interaction design · eLearning · Web search · People with intellectual disability · Sri Lanka · User experience

© IFIP International Federation for Information Processing 2021
Published by Springer Nature Switzerland AG 2021
C. Ardito et al. (Eds.): INTERACT 2021, LNCS 12932, pp. 245–265, 2021.
https://doi.org/10.1007/978-3-030-85623-6_16

1   Introduction

While the rapid development of mobile devices has helped the Internet extend its reach to developing countries. The lack of appropriate training opportunities on the web search for young adults with intellectual disability (YAWID) means that they do not use the web to access information. YAWID are able, with specific computer skills training programs [1] and regular training [2, 3], to learn digital skills, including those to interact with web search interfaces [4]. Information and Communication Technology (ICT) applications that match with learner needs, such as the use of multimedia in instruction for YAWID, support better engagement in learning [5]. In addition to the benefit of learning independently of the skills and pace of an educator, learning web-search in an eLearning environment offers opportunities for practical experience that can be easily transferred to real use [6]. Further research is needed to establish how YAWID in developing countries would engage with and respond to these eLearning experiences if they were made accessible and culturally relevant. We, therefore, designed an eLearning tool called LIFT (Learn Internet skills Facilitated with Technology), introducing Google.lk to search the web in the Sinhala language [7]: Sinhala is used by most people with ID in Sri Lanka as their primary language. LIFT, which was designed for YAWID to develop and apply web search skills, includes both instructions for conceptual understanding and activities to practice, all self-contained in the learning structure. It introduces Google to search the web, since people with intellectual disability (ID) have been previously found to favor Google's simple interface [8].

This study investigated the effectiveness, engagement, and satisfaction aspects of the LIFT through observations, as well as collecting participants' and their teachers' views and expressions during a three-day session. The study sought to answer the following research questions:

RQ1 (Effectiveness): How can the LIFT tool contribute to the learning of web search skills for YAWID?

- How do mental models support understanding and memory about the elements and their functions in Google search by YAWID?
- How do YAWID perform with increased web search abilities during the last two days of the web search workshops?

RQ2 (Engagement): What LIFT features engaged the YAWID?

- What brought enjoyment and self-actualization, in learning for YAWID?

RQ3 (Satisfaction): How satisfied are the YAWID and their teachers about the LIFT tool?

- What are the views of special education teachers about LIFT introducing Google search in a technological environment?

While we report on short-term evidence of learning as an indicator, our focus is on the interaction, effective engagement, and satisfaction, concerning user experience. We observed how participants use LIFT, practice, and explain Google search. Instead of assessment, we asked participants to draw their learning experience about the Internet and web search process, and then to demonstrate the search process to a teacher. Because of teachers' critical role in continuing to support the development of ICT skills at school, we collected the opinions of participants' teachers about the LIFT.

"Human-computer interactions are always situated within someone's life, values, and needs" [9]. This study fills a significant gap in current research targeted at supporting YAWID to search the web. It contributes to the field of human-computer interaction by investigating the user experience of a support approach that pays attention to three aspects of eLearning: accessible interface, content, and interactive practice, also accommodating web search in the Sinhala language. It highlights that observing participant's behavior when applying freshly learned skills and collecting their drawings about their ideas and expression [10] is more appropriate than inquiring whether they can perform different functions through the search process or assigning a search task to complete, at least in this context.

2 Background and Related Work

2.1 Intellectual Disability Definition and the Context of Sri Lanka

The American Association on Intellectual and Developmental Disabilities (AAIDD) [11] defines intellectual disability (ID) as "a disability characterized by significant limitations in both intellectual functioning and in adaptive behavior, which covers many everyday social and practical skills. This disability originates before the age of 18". Focusing on capacities and interests along with the level of support required, Sitbon et al. [12] present the executive function perspective to understanding intellectual disability. The executive function standpoint would be suitable for gaining an understanding, with an ability-based as well as a traditional design point of view. This approach could guide designers to understand users with ID, relative to their level of achievability, and define their potentials and experiences for leveraging them in new technology designs. Participants are therefore introduced in Sect. 3.2, in terms of their existing abilities with MS Word, Paint and Language learning digital tools, rather than through their ID diagnosis.

People with ID and how they are supported in Sri Lanka is a new area of national significance in the educational sector advancements, integrating technology to promote active learning. Sri Lanka, for example, is at the beginning of undertaking fundamental changes in its education sector, integrating technology with teaching; learning facilities available in schools in Sri Lanka vary greatly, with very few facilities in village schools. Students with "special learning needs" (including mild to severe ID) are mostly attending special units in formal or special schools. The language of instruction in special education is Sinhala or Tamil. Most special schools have specially trained teachers, computer labs for ICT training (MS Word & Paint), and language learning programs on computers. There is, however, no support for online learning. Participants in the research presented here were from special schools with these facilities; they had not used the Internet before and neither had their teachers and parents were reported to be familiar with web searching for their information needs.

2.2 ELearning for People with Intellectual Disability

eLearning can be used to enable people with diverse abilities to learn at their own pace and from a convenient place, access learning materials whenever they need, both online and offline [13], with a supporter or independently. Such educational approaches need a "match between designer and learner models" to engage the learner by addressing their needs, both in terms of interface and contents [14]. Interactive content and interface for example can be developed using technologies such as PowerPoint slides and multimedia to present learning content in a visual and auditory form [15].

Interaction Design of eLearning Content. Cognitive theories emphasize the learner's process of knowledge construction through interactions between existing understandings and the new learning experience [16, 17]; the use of metaphors in instruction support learners to process new knowledge using working memory.

Constructivism maintains that people gain new knowledge based on their prior experiences [16]. That means learners create mental models related to their real-world experience and integrate that experience in constructing new knowledge. The introduction of mental models in training can therefore provide opportunities for conceptual understanding where learners can draw links between those representations (designer mental models) and their pre-existing mental models (user mental models). Mental models introduced by the designers, when matched with those user mental models, support interactions with the user interface, and can also improve learning effectiveness. For example, people with previous experience with a typewriter may gain a conceptual understanding of the computer by aligning the functions of the typewriter and computer. Effective mental models can also support the interactions between humans and computers. Uther and Haley [18] found mental models to be helpful to neurotypical learners in a training program on how to use the back button in web navigation. Attention to the user's mental models, through close observations, can be helpful for designers to identify any misconceptions in new designs.

Presenting eLearning content using metaphors, icons, and visual cues, with consistently arranged interface elements, may support a learner's memory [19]. Visual metaphors help to describe or learn new things by comparing them to a well-known thing and developing new mental models [20]. Multimedia images can also act as rewards for learners, offering aspects of persuasive design to support engagement in learning activities and so achieve learning objectives [21, 22]. In LIFT, we describe functions and the elements in Google search using images along with animations to support users' creation of mental models about the Google search process. Drawings can be powerful to elicit user mental models [23, 24]. From drawings about the Internet, Zhang [23] identified mental models with a technical view, functional view, process view, and connection view. LIFT leverages all these four views to introduce the Internet and describe web search. For example, the LIFT tool introduces the functional view of the Internet, providing needed information, by introducing web search for health information. It describes web search advancing the process view or search engine centered view; it presents the search engine as the center of the web to reach the needed information.

Accessible content accompanied by interactive practice exercises draws learners to practice, cementing what they have learned to help memorization. Marshall and Wilson [25] presented their eLearning tool with interactive practice queries for neurotypical users: sequencing questions, visual identification questions, visual multiple-choice questions, and fill-in-the-blank questions that involve what is described in the content. They aimed to support the learners' confidence and satisfaction by providing these questions related to the learned content. In contrast, the approach developed here is different/new in that young adults with ID are guided in their learning using two sets of practice exercises, with and without guidance to repeatedly do and practice the Google search process until they can automatically complete the web search process [26], and effortlessly apply new knowledge.

Interaction Design of eLearning Interface. The interface element of a system determines 'to what extent the system is easy to use'. Sung and Mayer [27] report that navigational aids and signaling aids in an eLearning design for neurotypical people contributed to improving their learning outcomes. Navigational aids such as site maps, concept maps, and outlines support how learners navigate through the eLearning tool and know where they are in a lesson. Signaling aids to direct the learner to the points on the learning content include: highlighting the important text and use of animating objects.

Seo and Woo [28] found that the eLearning design guidelines should acknowledge the capacity of the short-term memory of students with special needs when designing computer-assisted teaching programs. The application of new technology together with such specific design guidelines [29] in the iterative development process of LIFT [7] aimed to increase the accessibility of the design to learners with ID.

It is the blended approach in the eLearning environment that encourages interactions between the eLearning tool, teacher, and learner [30]; provision of on-site support would be supportive for young adults with ID in eLearning, at least until the learners become familiar with the learning interface and content. eLearning tools can be significant, in a blended learning environment, for both the supporters (teachers, family members, or carers) and the learners. Supporters can be relevant for the learners' needs as well as the subject content the learners can learn at a pace that suits them, updating with continued practice with a low trainer-trainee ratio [31]. In developing countries, access to eLearning would be applicable, in general when YAWID practicing web search, and as they need support from their cares and others who are also new to Internet and web search. An initial approach introducing an eLearning tool for practicing Google search would benefit both YAWID and their special education teachers, towards lifting digital inclusion.

3   Methodology

This study investigated the user experience of LIFT along with its interface, content, and interactive practice activities, to further scrutinize the effectiveness, engagement, and satisfaction of its iteratively developed interactions for young adults with ID (YAWID) [7].

3.1 The eLearning Tool - LIFT

The design of the LIFT tool in PPT (Microsoft PowerPoint) format for its target users: new Internet users with ID, who want to learn web search in the Sinhala language using Google search, resulted from iterative participatory design research with YAWID in Sri Lanka [7] and draws on the research team's expertise and field experience in supporting people with ID using online technologies. Arachchi et al. [7] present the full iterative design process that highlighted the applicability of mental models, animations and images, for supporting conceptual understanding and visual memory by YAWID. PowerPoint was selected as a widely used presentation software to create attractive designs, which supports digital story-telling, and can be converted to LMS-supported versions. PowerPoint is also widely accessible, quick, and easy to use, making the LIFT approach easily replicable in other languages, and transferred to new topics of interest.

The LIFT tool covers interface elements and functions in Google search through to selecting a link from the search result list and visiting the corresponding web page. The tool includes an introduction to the Internet and two modules: Module 1 describes the Google search process, and includes a series of activities to practice the web search process; Module 2 presents search strategies to find a web page with a phone number of a health center.

Figure 1 shows the knowledge graph for the concepts introduced in the LIFT, with the relationships between the concepts illustrated using three types of arrows: a) has (e.g. a web page has a web address), b) leads to (e.g. web address leads to a web page), and c) correlation (e.g. between browser and address bar, the address bar and search box).

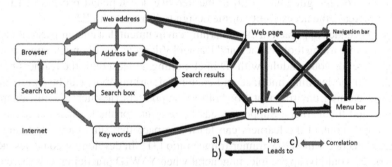

Fig. 1. Knowledge Graph for learning web search and navigation

These concepts have explicit and implicit relationships. Implicit relationships include relationships due to co-location and interaction (Table 1). This study observed partic-ipants' performance in web search focusing on these relationships (listed in Table 3), which are covered in the LIFT, as they were not all possible to study. One such example is the relationship between the address bar and the search box that is converting the address bar to a search box, in the Google Chrome home page, which did not function in Google.lk.

The LIFT used interactive buttons, sound (audio descriptions), and animated images developed in Microsoft PowerPoint. LIFT was designed using guidelines [29] which

Table 1. Relationships between the concepts presented in the Knowledge Graph

		Concepts	Abilities of the learner
Explicit relationships		Browser and address bar	−Finds address bar in the browser
		Browser and search tool	−Finds browser to start a search
		Web address and address bar	−Types web address in the address bar
		Web address and web page	−Knows web address of web page
		Search box and address bar	−Types keyword in the address bar
		Search results and web page	−Identifies listed search results
		Web page and hyperlink	−Uses links to go to web page
Implicit relationships	Due to Co-location	Search tool and search box	−Finds search box in the search window
		Search results and hyperlink	−Finds hyperlinks among search results
		Keyword and hyperlink	−Finds suggested keywords with links
		Web page and menu bar	−Locates menu bar in web pages
		Web page and navigation bar	−Locates navigation bar in web pages
		Hyperlink and navigation bar	−Finds navigation bar links to web pages
		Hyperlink and menu bar	−Finds menu bar links to web pages
	Due to interaction	Search tool and keywords	−Knows search tool needs keywords
		Keyword and search box	−Types keywords in search box
		Browser and web address	−Knows browser needs a web address
		Address bar and search results	−Knows Address bar brings search results
		Search box and search results	−Knows search box brings search results
		Menu bar and navigation bar	−Knows both direct to web pages

enabled us to align the content and interface of our design with both learning theories and usability guidelines.

Clark and Mayer [32] identified that eLearning courses, designed in the form of "multimedia presentations" comprising both words and pictures, can provide a clear meaning for learners. The images and short videos included in LIFT, therefore, aim to support YAWID in creating mental models and to memorize the concepts and Google search functions new to them (Fig. 2). Clark and Mayer [32] highlighted six types of graphics relative to their functions: decorative, representational, organizational, relational, transformational, and interpretive. Motivational graphics were included in the design of LIFT to keep learners engaged. Those graphics are the animating images displayed as an award for the correct performance, further to the feedback with right or wrong marks at the web search practice pages (Fig. 3).

Learners' navigational requirements were addressed by including a navigation bar at the top of each page; the navigation bar directs the learners to the introduction and the first page of each module and the exercises. To avoid accidental multiple clicks, the forward navigation button was set on each page to be displayed and blink at the end of the audio description, signaling the user to click on it [7]. Similarly, the audio button was set to display at the end of the audio track (Fig. 2).

We designed two sets of Google search practice exercises in the LIFT tool for the participants to practice the search process. One set includes instructions about what to do on each page; the other presents the same interface without instructions. Both practice exercises aim to help learners memorize the web-search process (Fig. 3).

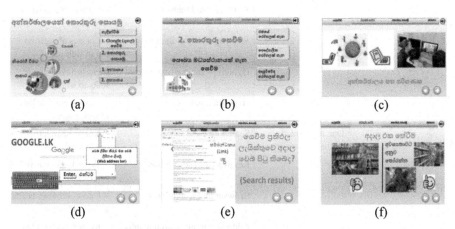

Fig. 2. a–b) Home page and the first page of module two, c) The page introducing the Internet, d–f) Selected pages from module one, describing search process

We also integrated the teachers' advice to use red color in the animating arrows and circles, to attract and engage the learners on the important concepts. The teachers also advised the addition of simple English terms into the text, having read the transcripts of the audio descriptions.

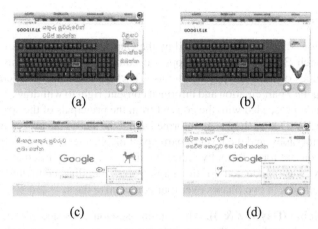

(a)   (b)

(c)   (d)

Fig. 3. Selected practice exercise pages in the LIFT: a) Exercise page with instructions to type the web address, b) Exercise page without instructions to type the web address, c–d) exercise pages with instructions.

3.2 Participants and Their Context

Participants (P) were 6 young adults with ID, 2 female and 4 male recruited from two special schools in Sri Lanka, and from the group of people who contributed 6 months earlier to iterations of LIFT. Selection criteria included: aged 18–30 years, able to read and spell to some extent in their mother tongue 'Sinhala', verbally communicate, and use a computer. Given the qualitative approach of this study, 6 participants is a sufficient number and align with previous studies such as Nielsen's [33].

Before the study commenced, participants demonstrated their current level of abilities developed by working with MS Word, Paint, language learning tools, and web search. Participants were able to use the power button and start the computer; independently use the keyboard and mouse; type their name and other words on the computer; independently navigate through multimedia language learning programs using menus, and forward and backward buttons; locate and click on the close button and close the window after working and shut down the computer by clicking on the power button on the screen. As observed in other studies [31, 34], people with ID did have weak retention of the learned ICT skills over months; we identified our participants had not retained those skills from the iterative design sessions, having not accessed the Internet after that. Their parents, although not included in the study, were not reported to have previous experiences with searching the web for information.

Teachers from the two special schools were specially trained and familiar with the ID levels. They are involved in teaching ICT skills to the YAWID who participated in this study. They helped with participant selection. The teachers had not previously used the Internet for finding information. They were present during all the learning sessions, advising on the specific requirements of YAWID. They reflected and provided ideas about the design/use of LIFT and its applicability and significance in the context of supporting YAWID. They were not involved in data collection.

3.3 Procedure

The study followed procedures approved by the Queensland University of Technology Human Research Ethics Committee (approval number- 1400000673), as well as the ethical guidelines of the two special schools. This research considered ethical issues, including voluntary participation and informed consent, right to withdraw, and confidentiality. The study proceeded with the consent from the principals of the special schools, parents, and YAWID after they were informed about the study; the procedures of taking notes and photographs, and the level of participant involvement. Six YAWID signed the easy-to-read consent form, formally indicating their consent to participate.

The study was conducted in the participants' familiar computer labs in the participants' schools in two phases over four consecutive days.

Phase 1- Training (Day 1, 2 & 3). The training session consisted of three hours per day for the first three days of the study. Health topics were introduced for practicing Google search based on the importance of those topics for life, their interest as stated in the literature, and its relevance for introducing the web to find information.

Day 1. Participants were trained to use the LIFT tool, using the menus, forward and backward buttons, and replaying the recording.

Day 2. Participants used the LIFT tool, the content and practice exercises that incorporate metaphors, animations, and audio recordings, to learn and practice the Google search process (Fig. 4a). They used the LIFT tool and learned the web-search process up to locating a website from the search results list and visiting it, and then performed the practice exercises. They learned that the rewards, in the form of checkmarks or animated images, meant they were correct. They repeated the practice exercises until successfully performing the task.

Day 3: Participants using Google.lk to search for health information were observed. They were asked to select one of the provided health topics in the Sinhala language such as a specific disease or medical problem, diet, nutrition, healthy foods, exercise, a particular doctor or hospital, dental health information [35] in Sinhala terms), and use it for a web search using Google.lk. They also searched for the topics that interest them (e.g. teeth, healthy foods, food pyramid, sleep and rest, exercise, and diseases - in Sinhala terms). Participants proceeded independently unless they requested support, or were not attempting anything for more than 4 min. In these cases, they were advised to use the LIFT tool as a guide.

Phase 2- Demonstrating Knowledge (Day 4). Participants were assigned two tasks: draw what they learned from the LIFT [10], by saying "now you are going to draw what you learned. You can draw anything you learned from LIFT", and describe the web search process to another person, using Google.lk (Fig. 4b and c).

3.4 Data Collection

We collected the data mainly through observations during the four-day session. While participants were being trained to use the eLearning tool and to do a Google search (Day 1 & 2), observations aimed to explore how they interacted with the LIFT tool content and practice activities. Participants' Google search performance on Day 3 and 4 were recorded as an indication of the effectiveness of the LIFT tool. Observations focused on the knowledge graph relationships (Fig. 1) of learning web search and navigation, and whether they were performed independently or with guidance.

During the sessions, we noted a range of behaviors and attitudes, presented in Table 2, as suggested indicators of usability and engagement by existing literature [21, 36]. The non-textual strategy of collecting participants' drawings [10], empowered participants to actively voice their inner senses, in terms of establishing what they had learned about Google search and their mental models.

The views of the two special education teachers were collected to determine their satisfaction with the LIFT tool, as they are involved in teaching ICT skills to the participants. Teachers gave their views about satisfaction, from their perspective as teachers, from that of their participating students in the classroom, and from that of the future of their participating students in the digital society.

Data were coded and grouped into categories, for which different themes were assigned [37, 38]. Interpretations were made with the participation of all coauthors to identify participant needs so that future research involved in educating and designing for young adults with ID with the same level of abilities can be attended to.

Table 2. Participants' facial expressions and body language, to identify attitudes during the sessions

Design elements	Observations	Implications
Courseware screen	Being encouraged to try again, focus their attention for a long time	Great interest [21]
Colorful images and clear sounds	Stares and looks attracted	Draw the attention [21]
	Comments, smiles, laughter, or positive body language	Enjoyment and engagement [36]
	Sighs, and looking around the room	Lack of enjoyment and frustration [36]

4 Findings

Overall, our observations suggested that the LIFT tool did indeed support learning, in terms of user engagement and satisfaction.

(a)   (b)   (c)

Fig. 4. a) Participant practicing web search using the eLearning tool (Day 1, 2 & 3) b) Participants drawing about the Internet and web search process (Day 4) c) Participant describing Google search process (Day 4)

4.1 Effectiveness

Participant drawings (without looking at the eLearning tool) were used to explore what they had learned from the eLearning tool. Participant 2 (P2) drew the picture about the Internet (Fig. 5a) and described in Sinhala that the drawing shows "the Internet connects computers located in different countries", and also mentioned in Sinhala in the title of the drawing ("අන්තර්ජාල සම්බන්ධවීම රටවල් අතර"). While the drawing has similarities with the picture presented in LIFT (Fig. 2c), P2's drawing demonstrates a new mental model integration, with the creativity of adding his country and two persons interacting with computers located in two different countries. P2 included the Wi-Fi icon in the drawing, demonstrating an understanding that Wi-Fi connects computers. P1's drawing (Fig. 5b) demonstrates how he learned to enter a web address in LIFT illustrating his mental models of the relationship between a web address and the address bar, and the use of the "Enter" key to execute the search.

(a)   (b)

Fig. 5. a) Drawing about the Internet (P2), b) Drawing about address bar, web address, and pressing on the "Enter" key (P1)

The eLearning tool introduced how to use keywords related to the information that they needed to search from the web. Participants were interested in searching the web to know more about health topics they had studied at school. They also suggested their own topics and keywords, in line with their interests and daily living information needs;

P2 for example, wanted to search for "Thala", a film currently on theatre. He wanted to find and show it to his friends. P3 had learned the keywords introduced to search for telephone numbers of hospitals in a nearby town (Fig. 6). These are written correctly, however, this participant is still learning to use spaces in between the keywords.

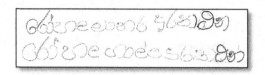

Fig. 6. P3's presentation of keywords to search a phone number of a hospital

Table 3 shows the specific functions where participants demonstrated ability and/or independence in the last two days of the web search sessions. All participants had developed abilities by day 3, and continued to develop their autonomy by day 4.

4.2 Engagement

Participants engaged in learning the search process, following the eLearning content and interactive practice activities. The application of persuasive design principles [21] in the eLearning tool made the learning environment fun. The interactive practice exercises on the web-search process attracted the learner because they rewarded completed actions, as in a game. Participant's smiles and continuing engagement in the activity showed they enjoyed the rewards and praises in multimedia form. They continued showing one another the rewards they were receiving, thus motivating one another to continue and repeat the exercises.

Another indication of their high level of engagement is they spontaneously repeated many of the practice exercises, such as selecting the correct image of the browser icon for starting a web search, and, finding correct letters from the keyboard to type the URL Google.lk. The latter was the page where they stayed for the longest and the most repeated practice activity. Participants liked being supported to find the next letter to type, as animations in letters in the capital form (GOOGLE.LK close to the address bar) had been time set to blink the next letter, parallel to their typing (Fig. 3a and b). On this page, participants enjoyed receiving the reward of 'a flying butterfly' for correctly typing the URL and then performing the click on the Enter key, smiling and showing one another, and engaging others.

Participants showed interest in the activity by extending the activities and suggesting searches using their keywords. P2 was fascinated by the eLearning tool itself and wanted to learn how to create such a PPT document and asked to save the LIFT tool in PPT format to his documents folder in File Explorer, used in the school ICT activities.

The teachers' positive feelings confirmed the value of learning support in an accessible form that incorporates multimedia. Visuals with animations and audio descriptions drew teachers' attention identifying those features with the easy-to-navigate interface to be effective in learning applications for YAWID. The relationship between the link and

Table 3. Participants' abilities to perform web search functions after learning web search with the eLearning tool

Relationship between concepts (functions)	P1		P2		P3		P4		P5		P6	
	D3	D4	D3	D4	D3	D4	D3	D4	D3	D4	D3	D4
Browser and search tool (Finds browser to start search)	X	X	X	X	X	X	O	X	X	X	X	X
Browser and address bar (Finds address bar in the browser)	X	X	X	X	X	X	X	X	X	X	O	X
Web address and web page (Knows web address of web page)	X	X	O	X	X	X	O	X	O	X	O	X
Browser and web address (Knows browser needs web address)	X	X	X	X	X	X	X	X	X	X	X	X
Web address and address bar (Types web address in address bar)	X	X	O	X	X	X	O	O	O	X	X	X
Search tool and search box (Finds search box in search window)	X	X	X	X	X	X	X	X	X	X	X	X
Search tool and keywords (Knows search tool needs keywords)	X	X	X	X	X	X	X	X	O	X	X	X
Search results and web page (Identifies listed search results)	O	X	O	O	X	X	X	X	O	O	O	X
Search results and hyperlink (Finds hyperlinks among search results)	O	X	O	O	O	X	O	O	O	O	O	X
Web page and hyperlink (Uses links to go to web page)	O	X	X	X	X	X	O	O	O	X	X	X
Web page and menu bar (Locates menu bar in web pages)	X	O	O	X	X	X	O	X	O	X	X	X
Keyword and search box (Types keywords in search box)	X	X	X	X	X	X	X	X	O	X	X	X
Browser and web address (Knows browser needs web address)	X	X	X	X	X	X	X	X	X	X	X	X

P- participant, D3- Day 3,   Abilities to perform: X-Independently, O-with guidance

the resultant web page was described using a prompting arrow from a link to an image of a new web page displayed once clicked on the link (Fig. 7a).

Participants responded to the moving red color arrow pointed to a link (Fig. 2e) by investigating the search result list to find a more appropriate link. They learned that the pointer changes its shape to a hand symbol at the link and recognized it during the practice exercises. With an animated red color circle around the back arrow (Fig. 7b), participants rapidly practiced clicking on the browser back button to move back from the resultant web page to the search results page.

Teachers also praised the content arrangement and interface design that supported enjoyment while learning. Teacher (T1) highlighted: "It is very simple. Clear and pleasant, practice exercises are interactive and motivating".

(a)   (b)

Fig. 7. LIFT Interface elements to engage the learner a) Support to identify the functions of the search results list, b) Exercise to click on browser's back button. (Color figure online)

4.3 Satisfaction

Participants expressed their satisfaction with LIFT informally with happy facial expressions. They extended on what they had learned, by sharing their learning experiences with one another. Special education teachers were impressed by LIFT as a guide for them to support young adults with ID in terms of learning the Google search process and finding information from the web. As one teacher said (T1): "I also really like to know about web search in Sinhala. It is a good topic, searching for health information."

Teachers identified that practicing the web search process, particularly in a technological environment with a real interface without needing Internet access, was helpful for participants. A teacher voiced (T2): "They can practice without internet access also. It is good to learn with technology. Rather than written on a book or described on a blackboard. Learning to navigate is also supported while content presents web search process".

LIFT was conceived to be a driver for reinforcing cognitive abilities linked with idea production, visual memory, self-confidence, independent learning, and gaining knowledge on new topics. As it introduces web search for information, teachers highlighted that it will influence the life of YAWID in many ways. "It is good to see their effort describing the search steps. Now they are suggesting new topics to search for. They are very happy and this has motivated them to read. They have learned that they can find some information from the Internet. If they have access to the Internet at home also, it will be helpful".

The interactive practice exercises were identified as enjoyable and engaging for the YAWID to practice the Google search functions and familiarize themselves with the Google search interface. T2 added "Practice exercise for typing Google.lk in the address bar was designed very well, matching with their needs and in an appropriate level. I liked it very much. Its technology strengthened their hand and eye coordination in using the keyboard".

5 Discussion

We designed LIFT to provide an accurate, accessible, and engaging environment for YAWID in Sri Lanka to learn how to search the Web in their native language, Sinhala. The cultural implications of the LIFT program and related support approaches are discussed here.

5.1 ICT for Learning ICT

The LIFT practice exercises help learners visualize and memorize each page and element in a Google search sequence even without internet access. Keskinova and Ajdinski [39] report that people with ID are best at integrative abilities, which would be very important for them to transfer what they learn offline to online web searching. The importance of this type of flexibility in implementing eLearning tools has been emphasized by Lim et al. [40].

This investigation shows that the eLearning tool with the facility to learn and repeatedly practice the Google search process in an ICT environment has helped the participants. Those participants with increased skills were able to show their new abilities by describing the search process and the related concepts to another person, and by demonstrating the Google search for health information (Table 3). This finding strengthens the idea that YAWID's visual memory is better than auditory memory, as Keskinova and Ajdinski [39] previously highlighted, having observed "very good ability for visual memory, and a lot of problems with the ability of auditory memory", in their study that engaged participants with mild ID in special elementary schools and a control group with typical development, from a mainstream elementary school.

Hence, this suggests that the guidelines presented by Arachchi et al. [29] should incorporate these new findings by introducing new guidelines with specifications to multimedia designs; this would increase the comprehensibility of the learning content designs, to keep the learners' attention.

5.2 Training Supporters

Learning online processes in an eLearning environment would be important in the Sri Lankan context, as it can support educators with an offline practice option. It was previously highlighted that the availability of on-site support would increase learner engagement with real-time feedback, which would only be possible with proper training opportunities for supporters: their teachers, parents, and/or caregivers [41]. The eLearning tool we designed would be helpful for supporters to become familiar with Google search in Sinhala and how to search for health information in the Sinhala language, without constant Internet access. LIFT would provide a structure to teach these concepts, and, would address the issues related to different learners obtaining support from different supporters [40]. Internet use especially for finding health information is not a familiar activity for most people living in Sri Lankan villages. The teachers, as well as parents /carers of YAWID from such contexts, would be supported in helping them to learn how to conduct web searches, and especially will become aware of the Internet's usefulness for finding information on topics related to their health.

5.3 The Benefit of the Accessible eLearning Tool Integrating Mental Models

Accessible interface/content would support enjoyment, self-actualization, and therefore engagement in learning. This eLearning tool not only tells and shows the web-search process but also, the learner can experience each step in web-search offline, with the interactive practice exercises. This LIFT design complies with the philosophy of the learning object design strategy introduced by Lao Tze in the 6th century: "If you tell me, I will listen. If you show me, I will see it. If you let me experience, I will learn" [40]. As noted by Lim et al. [40], like learning mathematics, learning web search is comparable to the flow of a stream; YAWID need scaffolding, such as what we have designed in LIFT that serves for participants to learn and practice different steps in the Google search process.

In this four-day study, participants could familiarize themselves with the interface, integrating their previous experiences with navigational and signaling aids in eLearning tools installed on computers. Participants could follow the navigational arrows while few needed support due to continuously clicking on the forward button. Therefore, it is important to design the eLearning tool with a signaling aid that reminds the learner when to click on the forward button. We designed the forward button to blink after the audio recording, played parallel to the animations. Participants were advised to click once on the forward button when it blinks. This could be added as an interface design guideline to the eLearning design guidelines for people with ID presented in [29].

Participants have increased their abilities on web search, especially demonstrating their skills to work with the search results page. They will likely need to continue to seek opportunities to continuously practice and/or to review the eLearning materials [3, 26].

We used mental models in describing the Google search elements and functions in the learning modules; we applied the same mental models in the practice exercises. Participant drawings showed they had created mental models integrating what we presented in the instruction and practice exercises. For example, the presentation of the connection view and the functional view [23] helped to create the mental model that the Internet connects computers, phones, tablets, and those who use them from anywhere in the world, and that the Internet can be used to find information. This shows that mental models are helpful for conceptual understanding and creating memory.

The inclusion of both mental models and practice in LIFT is indeed a good strategy; in that, both are essential for practicing and memorizing each step, and for getting automated in the Google search process [26]. This strategy is already well known and applied for example when a student looks at a teacher describing how to solve a math problem (e.g. $23 + 18 =$) then does the same addition independently.

The LIFT design differs from the eLearning designs focusing on more sophisticated learners [42], as it attends to the needs of learners with diverse cognitive abilities. YAWID would not learn from a video that displays a person describing the web search process, accompanied with PPT slides with static notes [7]. However, some aspects of the theory presented by Zhang et al. [42], such as illustrative video "allow students to view actual objects and realistic scenes, to see sequences in motion, and to listen to narration" are directly applicable to this study and we offered them in the form of mental models, animations and audio recordings.

6 Limitations and Implications for Future Research

Participants for this study were young adults with intellectual disabilities (YAWID) who can use a computer, read their native language, and communicate. Some participants who satisfied the selection criteria for this study, and were interested in this research, left school to join vocational training programs. Most YAWID in Sri Lanka experience limited language ability [43] because they stop applying it after leaving school. These limitations made it difficult to find participants who met all selection criteria, limiting the number of participants for this study to six, which means the quantitative results [44] are purely indicative.

A limited reading ability means disseminating health information in video format would be supportive for people with intellectual disabilities to be informed of health topics. However, early research suggests that interacting verbally with web search engines is attractive for people with ID, but can in some cases cause difficulties and frustrations [45]. Further research that involves a longer duration with more participants with a greater diversity of support needs and communication abilities may be helpful to improve the generalizability of the results. However, limited access to computers and the perceptions of carers towards working with computers may limit the implementation of the eLearning tool for YAWID to learn how to do a Google search at their home or the centers providing care services.

In Sri Lanka, there are Tamil people. Most of them are attending Tamil language schools. The Tamil virtual keyboard displays English letters and generates corresponding Tamil letters in the search box. People with ID cannot be expected to know these corresponding letters and so limiting the accessibility of the virtual keyboard and as a result the generalizability of our approach. Further research is warranted to establish the applicability of Google virtual keyboards in this and 70 other languages, so as to introduce our approach to do a Google search in local languages on any computer, anywhere in the world.

7 Conclusion and Recommendations

This paper described a multimedia-based eLearning tool, called LIFT, designed for helping YAWID learn the web search process, and explored the experience of participants with ID interacting with its contents, interface, and interactive practice activities to be familiar with web search in the Sinhala language. LIFT includes an accessible interface, content, and interactive practice, which are engaging for the participants. To the best of our knowledge, no previous research employs all three aspects in this domain. Observations indicated that LIFT was meeting its goal of increasing participants' abilities to search the web. Teachers commented that the multimedia approach fits with supporting visual memory.

This study confirms the value of applying the persuasive learning theory that describes the positive impact of using rewards and praising in learning designs. Furthermore, it applies the theory that highlights technology-enhanced, well-designed learning environments can be effective in supporting learners with ID; it helped increase their understanding of new concepts and create mental models related to processes, and especially for engaging them in learning activities [46]. During the learning process, we noted that participants need on-site support until they become familiar with the learning environment. Future research is suggested to explore the long-time effect of the eLearning tool on web-search by people with ID and to identify the onsite support requirements.

Acknowledgments. The authors would like to thank the anonymous reviewers from INTER-ACT2021 for their valuable suggestions and comments. Thanks to two special schools, all our participants with intellectual disabilities, and their teachers. We acknowledge the support for this research study from the University Grant Commission, Sri Lanka (UGC/DRIC/QUT2016/RUH/02), Queensland University of Technology, Australia, and University of Colombo, Sri Lanka. Assoc. Prof. Sitbon is supported by the Australian Research Council (FT190100855).

References

1. Wong, A.W.K., Chan, C.C.H., Li-Tsang, C.W.P., Lam, C.S.: Competence of people with intellectual disabilities on using human–computer interface. Res. Dev. Disabil. **30**(1), 107–123 (2009). https://doi.org/10.1016/j.ridd.2008.01.002
2. Rocha, T., Bessa, M., Magalhães, L., Cabral, L.: Performing universal tasks on the Web: interaction with digital content by people with intellectual disabilities. In: Proceedings of the XVI International Conference on Human Computer Interaction, p. 30. ACM, Vilanova i la Geltrú, Spain (2015). https://doi.org/10.1145/2829875.2829897
3. Li-Tsang, C.W.P., Lee, M.Y.F., Yeung, S.S.S., Siu, A.M.H., Lam, C.S.: A 6-month follow-up of the effects of an information and communication technology (ICT) training programme on people with intellectual disabilities. Res. Dev. Disabil. **28**(6), 559–566 (2007). https://doi.org/10.1016/j.ridd.2006.06.007
4. Harrysson, B., Svensk, A., Johansson, G.I.: How people with developmental disabilities navigate the Internet. Br. J. Spec. Educ. **31**(3), 138–142 (2004). https://doi.org/10.1111/j.0952-3383.2004.00344.x
5. Ortega-Tudela, J., Gómez-Ariza, C.: Computer-assisted teaching and mathematical learning in Down Syndrome children. J. Comput. Assisted Learn. **22**(4), 298–307 (2006)
6. Standen, P.J., Brown, D.J., Cromby, J.J.: The effective use of virtual environments in the education and rehabilitation of students with intellectual disabilities. Br. J. Educat. Tech. **32**(3), 289–299 (2001). https://doi.org/10.1111/1467-8535.00199
7. Arachchi, T.K., Sitbon, L., Zhang, J., Gamage, R., Hewagamage, P.: Enhancing internet search abilities for people with intellectual disabilities in Sri Lanka. ACM Trans. Access Comput. **14**(2) (2021). https://doi.org/10.1145/3460202
8. Rocha, T., Carvalho, D., Bessa, M., Reis, S., Magalhães, L.: Usability evaluation of navigation tasks by people with intellectual disabilities: a Google and SAPO comparative study regarding different interaction modalities. Univ. Access Inf. Soc. **16**(3), 581–592 (2016). https://doi.org/10.1007/s10209-016-0489-5
9. Murer, M., et al.: Contextual interaction design research: enabling HCI. In: Abascal, J., Barbosa, S., Fetter, M., Gross, T., Palanque, P., Winckler, M. (eds.) INTERACT 2015. LNCS, vol. 9299, pp. 621–623. Springer, Cham (2015). https://doi.org/10.1007/978-3-319-22723-8_75
10. Literat, I.: "A pencil for your thoughts": participatory drawing as a visual research method with children and youth. Int. J. Qual. Methods **12**(1), 84–98 (2013). https://doi.org/10.1177/160940691301200143
11. The American Association on Intellectual and Developmental Disabilities (AAIDD): Intellectual Disability: Definition, Diagnosis, Classification, and Systems of Supports (2010)
12. Sitbon, L., Hoogstrate, M., Yule, J., Koplick, S., Bircanin, F., Brereton, M.: A non-clinical approach to describing participants with intellectual disability. In: 30th Australian Conference on Human Computer Interaction (OzCHI 2018). ACM Inc., New York, NY (2018). https://doi.org/10.1145/1234567890

13. Hervatis, V., et al.: Offline and computer-based eLearning interventions for medical students' education. Cochrane Database Syst. Rev. **2018**(10), CD012149 (2018). https://doi.org/10.1002/14651858.CD012149.pub2

14. Squires, D., Preece, J.: Predicting quality in educational software: evaluating for learning, usability and the synergy between them. Interact. Comput. **11**(5), 467–483 (1999). https://doi.org/10.1016/S0953-5438(98)00063-0

15. Shafie, A., Wan Ahmad, W.F., Mohd., N., Barnachea, J.J., Taha, M.F., Yusuff, R.L.: "SynMax": a mathematics application tool for down syndrome children. In: Zaman, H.B., Robinson, P., Olivier, P., Shih, T.K., Velastin, S. (eds.) IVIC 2013. LNCS, vol. 8237, pp. 615–626. Springer, Cham (2013). https://doi.org/10.1007/978-3-319-02958-0_56

16. Brandt, D.S.: Constructivism: teaching for understanding of the Internet. Commun. ACM. **40**(10), 112–117 (1997). https://doi.org/10.1145/262793.262814

17. Snowman, J., Biehler, R.: Psychology Applied to Teaching. Houghton Mifflin Company, Boston (2006)

18. Uther, M., Haley, H.: Back vs. stack: training the correct mental model affects web browsing. Behav. Inf. Technol. **27**(3), 211–218 (2008). https://doi.org/10.1080/01449290600956357

19. Buehler, E., Easley, W., Poole, A., Hurst, A.: Accessibility barriers to online education for young adults with intellectual disabilities. In: Proceedings of the 13th Web for All Conference, pp. 1–10. ACM, Montreal, Canada (2016). https://doi.org/10.1145/2899475.2899481

20. Hsu, Y.-C.: The effects of metaphors on novice and expert learners' performance and mental-model development. Interact. Comput. **18**(4), 770–792 (2006). https://doi.org/10.1016/j.intcom.2005.10.008

21. Ng, K.H., Bakri, A., Rahman, A.A.: Effects of persuasive designed courseware on children with learning difficulties in learning Malay language subject. Educ. Inf. Technol. **21**(5), 1413–1431 (2015). https://doi.org/10.1007/s10639-015-9391-7

22. Fogg, B.J.: A behavior model for persuasive design. In: Proceedings of the 4th international Conference on Persuasive Technology, p. 40. ACM (2009)

23. Zhang, Y.: The influence of mental models on undergraduate students' searching behavior on the Web. Inf. Process. Manag. **44**(3), 1330–1345 (2008). https://doi.org/10.1016/j.ipm.2007.09.002

24. Thatcher, A., Greyling, M.: Mental models of the Internet. Int. J. Ind. Ergon. **22**(4–5), 299–305 (1998)

25. Marshall, J., Wilson, M.: Motivating e-learners: application of the ARCS model to e-learning for San Diego Zoo Global's Animal Care Professionals. J. Appl. Instruct. Des. **21**, 012105 (2013)

26. Alonso, F., López, G., Manrique, D., Viñes, J.M.: An instructional model for web-based e-learning education with a blended learning process approach. Br. J. Educat. Tech. **36**(2), 217–235 (2005)

27. Sung, E., Mayer, R.E.: Affective impact of navigational and signaling aids to e-learning. Comput. Hum. Behav. **28**(2), 473–483 (2012). https://doi.org/10.1016/j.chb.2011.10.019

28. Seo, Y.-J., Woo, H.: The identification, implementation, and evaluation of critical user interface design features of computer-assisted instruction programs in mathematics for students with learning disabilities. Comput. Educ. **55**(1), 363–377 (2010). https://doi.org/10.1016/j.compedu.2010.02.002

29. Arachchi, T.K., Sitbon, L., Zhang, J.: Enhancing access to elearning for people with intellectual disability: integrating usability with learning. In: Bernhaupt, R., Dalvi, G., Joshi, A., Balkrishan, D.K., O'Neill, J., Winckler, M. (eds.) INTERACT 2017. LNCS, vol. 10514, pp. 13–32. Springer, Cham (2017). https://doi.org/10.1007/978-3-319-67684-5_2

30. Seale, J., Cooper, M.: E-learning and accessibility: An exploration of the potential role of generic pedagogical tools. Comput. Educ. **54**(4), 1107–1116 (2010). https://doi.org/10.1016/j.compedu.2009.10.017

31. Li-Tsang, C.W.P., Yeung, S.S.S., Choi, J.C.Y., Chan, C.C.H., Lam, C.S.: The effect of systematic information and communication technology (ICT) training programme for people with intellectual disabilities. Br. J. Dev. Disabil. **52**(102), 3–18 (2006)

32. Clark, R.C., Mayer, R.E.: E-Learning and the Science of Instruction: Proven Guidelines for Consumers and Designers of Multimedia Learning. John Wiley & Son, USA (2016)

33. Nielsen, J.: Estimating the number of subjects needed for a thinking aloud test. Int. J. Hum. Comput. Stud. **41**(3), 385–397 (1994). https://doi.org/10.1006/ijhc.1994.1065

34. Li-Tsang, C.W.P., Chan, C.C.H., Lam, C., Hui-Chan, C., Yeung, S.-S.: Evaluations of an information and communication technology (ICT) training programme for persons with intellectual disabilities. In: Miesenberger, K., Klaus, J., Zagler, W.L., Burger, D. (eds.) ICCHP 2004. LNCS, vol. 3118, pp. 1032–1038. Springer, Heidelberg (2004). https://doi.org/10.1007/978-3-540-27817-7_152

35. Fox, S.: Online Health search 2006. Pew Internet & American Life Project, Washington, DC (2006)

36. Sim, G., MacFarlane, S., Read, J.: All work and no play: Measuring fun, usability, and learning in software for children. Comput. Educ. **46**(3), 235–248 (2006). https://doi.org/10.1016/j.compedu.2005.11.021

37. Braun, V., Clarke, V.: Using thematic analysis in psychology. Qual. Res. Psychol. **3**(2), 77–101 (2006). https://doi.org/10.1191/1478088706qp063oa

38. Vaismoradi, M., Turunen, H., Bondas, T.: Content analysis and thematic analysis: implications for conducting a qualitative descriptive study. Nurs. Health Sci. **15**(3), 398–405 (2013). https://doi.org/10.1111/nhs.12048

39. Keskinova, A., Ajdinski, G.: Learning problems in children with mild intellectual disability. Int. J. Cogn. Res. Sci. Eng. Educ./IJCRSEE. **6**(1), 31–37 (2018). https://doi.org/10.5937/ijcrsee1801031K

40. Lim, C.P., Lee, S.L., Richards, C.: Developing interactive learning objects for a computing mathematics module. Int. J. Elearn. **5**(2), 221 (2006)

41. Alfaraj, A., Kuyini, A.B.: The use of technology to support the learning of children with down syndrome in Saudi Arabia. World J. Educ. **4**(6), 42 (2014). https://doi.org/10.5430/wje.v4n6p42

42. Zhang, D., Zhou, L., Briggs, R.O., Nunamaker, J.F., Jr.: Instructional video in e-learning: assessing the impact of interactive video on learning effectiveness. Inf. Manage. **43**(1), 15–27 (2006). https://doi.org/10.1016/j.im.2005.01.004

43. Feng, J., Lazar, J., Kumin, L., Ozok, A.: Computer usage by children with down syndrome: challenges and future research. ACM Trans. Access. Comput. **2**(3), 13 (2010). https://doi.org/10.1145/1714458.1714460

44. Nielsen, J.: Why You Only Need to Test with 5 Users. 2000 https://www.nngroup.com/articles/whyyou-only-need-to-test-with-5-users/. Accessed on 2019

45. Balasuriya, S.S., Sitbon, L., Bayor, A.A., Hoogstrate, M., Brereton, M.: Use of voice activated interfaces by people with intellectual disability. In: Proceedings of the 30th Australian Conference on Computer-Human Interaction, pp. 102–112. ACM (2018)

46. Buzzi, M.C., Buzzi, M., Perrone, E., Senette, C.: Personalized technology-enhanced training for people with cognitive impairment. Univ. Access Inf. Soc. **18**(4), 891–907 (2018). https://doi.org/10.1007/s10209-018-0619-3

Social Robots in Learning Experiences of Adults with Intellectual Disability: An Exploratory Study

Alicia Mitchell[1]([⊠]), Laurianne Sitbon[1], Saminda Sundeepa Balasuriya[1], Stewart Koplick[2], and Chris Beaumont[2]

[1] Faculty of Science, Queensland University of Technology, Brisbane, Australia
{alicia.mitchell,samindasundeepa.balasuriya}@hdr.qut.edu.au,
l.sitbon@qut.edu.au
[2] Endeavour Foundation, Brisbane, Australia
{s.koplick,c.beaumont}@endeavour.com.au

Abstract. The use of social robots has the potential to improve learning experiences in life skills for adults with intellectual disabilities (ID). Current research in the context of social robots in education has largely focused on how children with Autism Spectrum Disorder (ASD) interact with social robots primarily without a tablet, with almost no research investigating how beneficial social robots can be in supporting learning for adults with IDs. This research explores how interactions with a social humanoid robot can contribute to learning for communities of adults with ID, and how adults with ID want to engage with these robots. This exploratory study involved observation and semi-structured interviews of eleven participants with ID (in three groups, supported by their support workers) receiving information from a semi-humanoid social robot and interacting with the robot via its tablet. Two robot applications were developed to deliver content based on the participating disability support organization's life skills curriculum for healthy lifestyle choices and exercise, considering a variety of modalities (visual, embodied, audio). The study identified four ways in which participants interact, and our findings suggest that both the physical presence of the robot and the support of the tablet play a key role in engaging adults with ID. Observation of participant interactions both with the robot and with each other shows that part of the robot's value in learning was as a facilitator of communication.

Keywords: Intellectual disability · Young adults · Communication · Learning · Social robot · Human robot interaction · Tablet applications · Support workers · Pepper humanoid robot

1 Introduction

Around 70% of the Australian National Disability Insurance Scheme (NDIS) users have an Intellectual Disability (ID) or learning disability, and one in eight will access community services for learning and life skills [1]. People with intellectual disability are keen learners, who learn best when presented with embodied and visual information.

© IFIP International Federation for Information Processing 2021
Published by Springer Nature Switzerland AG 2021
C. Ardito et al. (Eds.): INTERACT 2021, LNCS 12932, pp. 266–285, 2021.
https://doi.org/10.1007/978-3-030-85623-6_17

These people are attracted to technology, and prior research suggested that social robots could spark interest and collaboration [2]. Humanoid social robots, such as Pepper (see Fig. 1), combine embodied communication with movement and visual information via a tablet. They have been designed and used as assistants in nursing [3] and hospitality [4], and utilized in clinical contexts for diagnosis and treatment of Autism Spectrum Disorder (ASD) [5]. The purpose of this research is to evaluate how a social humanoid robot, such as Pepper, can contribute to the learning experiences of communities of adults with ID.

People with ID often seek support in community services, where they can learn and practice life skills while socializing. Community services are typically attended by people with diverse abilities, interests and communication preferences. They offer group learning experiences that respect people's individuality. The disability support organization involved in this study only supports people who identify as people who require support and development of life skills. This approach respects the fact that many people with ID do not present with a specific diagnosis. Some people have co-morbidities, such as physical disability or ASD.

The use of social robots, have the potential to contribute to the learning experiences for adults with varying ID. However, the needs and perceptions of support workers must also be considered for that potential to be realized, as they will play a key role in facilitating access to and use of technologies by people they support.

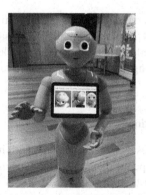

Fig. 1. Pepper robot.

This project explores how adults with intellectual disabilities (IDs) engage with Pepper, a social humanoid robot which can communicate with users through movement, speech, voice and visuals on a tablet (Fig. 1). The project is being undertaken in consultation with an independent, for-purpose organization that provides support to people with intellectual disabilities. This study begins to investigate how and why social robots can improve informational experiences and support communities of people with ID, with the primary purpose to identify how a robot can add value and to raise questions for future research. More specifically, we explore how social robots can use a variety of modalities (visual, embodied, audio) to support communities of people with ID (also including support workers) and improve learning experiences. The research seeks to explore the following questions:

- How do adults with ID want to engage with a social robot?
- How can a social robot contribute to the support network of adults with ID in a learning context?

We approached these questions by porting existing curriculum (both session scripts and visuals), that was about to be introduced in the community centers, in a format that would both be appropriate for and make use of Pepper's abilities. This curriculum forms part of life skills education and focuses on outcomes relating to healthy lifestyle choices (nutrition and exercise). The project included both adult participants with varying IDs, and their support workers. We observed and interviewed them as they took part in, or facilitated, group learning sessions with Pepper.

We first introduce related work which has informed our questions and methodology. We then detail our study methodology and the applications that we created to support our investigation. We present our findings, and finally discuss the implications of this research.

2   Related Work

A literature review was undertaken to investigate existing research involving social robots, education, training and people with intellectual disabilities. Information gathered from this review was used to inform and support the detailed design of this study and the research methodology including identification of the variables, objective and subjective measures.

2.1   Human Robot Interaction

"Social robots are technologies designed to engage with humans on an emotional level through play, sometimes therapeutic play, and perhaps even companionship" [6]. Current publications about social robots in the context of adults with ID and support workers may include studies involving only pictures and concepts of robots, not actual interaction with robots [7, 8]. There has been very little published research involving the Pepper robot, however, an analysis of over approximately 300 studies involving social robots in education, found that around 50% of research involved SoftBank Robotics' small humanoid robot, NAO, which does not have a tablet [9], supporting the perceived research value of humanoid robots. Some papers express concern about artificial interactions and attachment to robots, stating that robots should be designed to assist and support activities, and care should be taken not to try to replace human interaction. Further research investigating actual versus safe imagination is required in relation to how the robot is framed when introduced to users [10]. Currently in many disability support service centers, support workers provide support to groups of 3 to 4 people with ID at a time. Robots to support learning may allow more time for support workers to interact with individuals and could actually increase care and social interactions. As such, it is important to understand the role of support workers and caretakers, and their relationship with the robot.

2.2 Social Robots and Education

Current research in the context of social robots in education has largely focused on social robots primarily without a tablet as platforms for teaching languages [11] and children with ASD [12, 13]. Where a tablet has been connected to a robot, it is often as an additional tool for shared communication.

Social robots have been able to teach children with autism and people with ID to recognize and produce gestures [14]. The children could then generalize what they learned to different scenarios but were unable to reproduce the gestures appropriately when interacting with a human model.

Previous research has observed that people with intellectual disability engage for long periods of learning time when robots were involved in the learning experience [15], however the extent to which delivering information via the robot can improve learning outcomes and knowledge is unknown.

In terms of social skills training, previous studies have shown that robots can be used to improve participation and verbal communication among students with autism or ID [16]. The participants in this study were eager to work with NAO and intrinsic interest in the robot helped them bring about improvements in their communication skills.

A long term study that took place in a public school in South Australia with students with autism or ID showed that the student's eagerness to interact with NAO did not diminish even after 24 months [17]. Skills that they learned from their time with the robot, like turn taking, self-expression, confidence and patience were transferred to general activities.

Parents and teachers of children with ID and autism [17] noticed certain benefits of the children's interactions with NAO and Paro (a furry seal style of robot), stating that the appearance and non-judgmental behavior of the robots were important aspects of their success. The predictability of the robot's behavior and their ability to repeat functions were important to reduce the students' stress and anxiety. A robot can be perceived as an intelligent agent, so it can be used to simulate human behavior [12].

2.3 Social Robots and Intellectual Disability

In a study involving the NAO robot across four activities including guessing and modelling emotions, eliciting behavior such as touch the robot's head, dance choreography and responses to robot characteristics, the researchers observed that participants exhibited a reduced level of disability behavior in comparison to normal situation behaviors, even when the robot was not interacting with them [5]. The findings have supported that of other researchers that attention is comparatively higher during sessions that involve a robot [5, 18]. The six participants aged 33–67, represented conditions ranging from moderate to severe intellectual disability with two also having ASD, two with affective disorder and one with Down Syndrome. The comparative disability behaviors were measured using a questionnaire based on the Gilliam Autism Rating Scale-Second Edition (GARS-2) supplementary screening tool for ASD; the World Health Organization Disability Assessment Schedule 2 (WHODAS 2.0) a tool for assessing functioning and impairment; and the AAMR Adaptive Behaviour Scale (ABS-RC: 2) for assessing adaptive behaviour in mentally handicapped adults.

IDs can cause reduced understanding, challenges in communication, memory recall, focus and attention. Different teaching strategies are required for students with IDs [5]. Disability research often focuses on medical diagnosis narrative however these intellectual disabilities typically occur on a spectrum [5]. Where a robot may be situated in a class with multiple students with varying needs, it is perhaps more appropriate to take a non-clinical approach to describing participants and shift to describing the social narrative in relation to daily living and participation in society [7, 19].

There is limited research for teachers to refer to about using robots to support learning in children with intellectual disabilities, and a preliminary review of existing literature indicates that there has been almost no research investigating how beneficial social robots can be in supporting education for adults with IDs [15]. Despite not being specifically focused on supporting people with IDs, studies of children with ASD also highlighted that the robots offered a number of qualities that also supported suitability for use with children with other IDs, including the predictability, engagement and safety [15]. One user-centered design activity based on the Pepper robot, has reported that people with IDs working in a manufacturing facility felt that robots like Pepper would be useful in demonstrating tasks and explaining activities as the workers rotate through workstation activities [4].

2.4   Social Robots and Support Workers or Caregivers

The social network of people with intellectual disabilities mostly consists of family members and support workers [20]. Support workers that work in disability community activity centers help people with intellectual disabilities exercise control over their daily activities [21]. They are involved in designing and implementing activities that improve the quality of life of people with ID and have many responsibilities including developing skills, conducting leisure activities, daily personal care and monitoring health [22].

A literature review exploring risk and the role of support workers in facilitating technology use by adolescents and adults identified that perceived risk and safety concerns are emerging factors that influence access to technologies [23]. The perceptions of ease of use and safety is linked to uptake of technology [24], and as such, if a support worker is not confident about supervising their clients when using a technology such as Pepper, trial and adoption may be inhibited.

A month-long in-home study involving a social robot with educational content, was situated in a home with young children with ASD revealed that they wanted the robot to stay with them for an extended period of time [25]. Parents of the children stated that they were comfortable leaving their children to interact with the robot independently.

Another study via an online survey, found that whilst support workers saw the potential for robots to perform repetitive tasks, they were concerned about the level of supervision required, and were worried about the robot breaking [8]. They highlighted that robots should not and could not replace human interactions. It is important to note that this survey utilized hypothetical questions and did not show a working model, so the perceptions of participants may change if given an opportunity to experience a live interaction with a physical robot [26].

Support workers watched videos of people with intellectual disability interacting with a small robot named Cozmo and stated that the participants were much more interested in interreacting with Cozmo than they were during the normal workshops [2]. The support workers also commented on behaviors of the participants and mentioned whether they were typical of that person, or a new behavior brought about by Cozmo. For some participants, Cozmo was able to enhance aspects of their personality like competitiveness according to the support workers. But they also noticed moments that they did not expect like some participants who are usually very quiet that engaged in helping their partner out.

2.5   Social Robots – Embodiment and Anthropomorphism

People respond better to robots than computer tablets delivering healthcare instructions, and healthcare apps have been shown to improve patient's adherence to treatment and provide health education information [27].

Comparative studies have found that physically embodied robots show more promise than virtually embodied robots and avatars [28–30], for example one study involving a robot in the form of an exercise coach for the elderly, where the robot acts as a traditional exercise instructor, demonstrates and asks users to imitate, and also involves user activity recognition for the robot to imitate the user [28].

The physical embodiment of the robot makes it more interesting for people to interact with as it allows for tactile exploration and physical movements. The ability to touch is not available in virtual avatars and previous research has shown that children prefer a physical robot over an avatar on a device [31].

Past research with people with ID interacting with Cozmo has shown how they anthropomorphize the robot [2]. They attributed feelings, emotions and a sense of autonomy to Cozmo.

In research incorporating robots with a separate tablet, the tablet appears to be more of a shared communication device, comparable to writing on a board to be observed by the learner, rather than an extension of the robot itself [32, 33]. Pepper's tablet is embedded on the chest, forming a part of the robot rather than a remote device. Users may feel more connected and engaged with the robot when they can touch it [34, 35]. Certainly, the findings by de Wit et al. 2018 [36] and Vogt et al. 2019 [37] support the value of a tablet for user input and display. The use of the tablet not only provides an interactive mechanism for user input, but enhances the multimodal communication capabilities of the robot.

3   Methodology

3.1   Overview

The user study involved running a learning session where participants' interaction with the robot was observed. This exploratory study forms part of a research project which has received ethical clearance by the Queensland University of Technology (1400000673). With consent from all participants and support workers, the sessions were recorded on video to allow further review and analysis by the researchers after the session had been completed. The session was designed in a flexible manner to allow support worker's some autonomy and choice in how to run the session and facilitate use of the robot. Following an introduction about the session approach and objectives, all participants received an interactive induction about how to use Pepper. The user study was then divided into two key activities:

Learning About Healthy Choices. Participants with ID receive the healthy eating life skills education curriculum module via Pepper. This content was developed independently by the disability service organization and adapted for Pepper by the research team. In this session, Pepper delivers some of the content verbally, and some visually (using images on the tablet). Participants can interact with Pepper by touching the screen.

Practicing Healthy Exercise. Participants with ID participate in an exercise class directed by Pepper, mainly based on stretching movements. In this session, Pepper guides participants using speech and displays a video of the full movement on the tablet, and, in one activity, accompanies the video with synchronized arm movements. There is no interaction with Pepper during this session, however participants were encouraged to mimic the movements.

3.2 Apparatus

Robot. The robot used for this study was SoftBank Robotics' Pepper (Model v1.8a). Pepper is a semi-humanoid robot. At 120 cm tall, Pepper is much taller than other robots commonly used in research, but not so tall as to be perceived as threatening. Pepper is sometimes perceived to be equivalent to a 12-year-old child.

Pepper can detect faces and follows people's faces with head movement. The eyes are animated with color change only. A speaker is located with the head, and in this research was programmed with the default female-like voice. There is a microphone to enable speech or sound recognition, however it was not activated during our research. The arms are animated, either with random communication-like movement during speech, or with movement programmed by an application. There are no animated legs, but travel is possible using wheels situated at its base. A 10.1" tactile screen (tablet) is situated on the robot's chest.

Recording Equipment. All sessions were video recorded using three cameras placed in various parts of the room: a Ricoh Theta S 180-degree camera, a Kodak Pixpro SP360 360° camera, and an action camera. An iPhone 8 was used as a backup for recording audio. Having several cameras also ensures that there is always one actively recording. The benefit of having wide angle or 360 cameras for this research is to fully capture all participants reactions and align them with the robot's action naturally. Additionally, these types of cameras are small and unobtrusive, and their quality is sufficient for participant observations.

Furniture. Chairs were available in the room for participants to use if they chose to during the robot interactions, in between interactions and during group discussions.

3.3 Participants

We recruited participants from three of the disability support organization's center locations. They travelled to a University Campus where the sessions were held in order to take part in the research. A total of three trial sessions were run. Each trial had 3–4 participants with IDs and 1–2 support workers. Across the trial there were a total of 11 participants with IDs and 4 support worker participants. Table 1 details the participants and the session which they were involved in.

Table 1. Participants.

Group	Participant ref	Gender	Session
Participants with ID	PA1	F	A
	PA2	M	A
	PA3	M	A
	PA4	M	A
	PB1	M	B
	PB2	F	B
	PB3	M	B
	PC1	M	C
	PC2	F	C
	PC3	M	C
	PC4	F	C
Support worker participants	SWA1	F	C
	SWA2	M	A
	SWB1	F	A
	SWC1	M	B

Participants with Intellectual Disability. Participants were young adults (20–30) with varying abilities and levels of intellectual functioning who attend the support organization's centers/hubs. All participants were physically able to interact with the robot and use the applications via the robot's tablet, despite some displaying limited verbal and reading capabilities. The cohort selected by the support organization were all familiar with and had access to technology such as tablets and computers.

The participants represented conditions ranging from moderate to severe intellectual disability with two also with ASD, and one with Down Syndrome. Whilst it may seem important to provide details about the medical diagnosis and nature of each participant's condition, we argue that this provides a narrow view of the person. The diversity of the participants reflects what is typically observed in disability support centers. As such, we prefer to focus on the evaluation of the robot applications, engagement with the robot and on enhancing informational experiences across a spectrum of individual needs, in the context of group learning.

Support Workers of Adults with Intellectual Disability. An important aspect of this study was to involve the support workers in all aspects of the session. Participants were staff of the support organization, familiar with the people who attended the trials with them. Support workers provide support and supervision through a range of activities and excursions aimed at helping people develop independent life skills, amongst other social and learning skills. It is important to note that support workers typically do not have educational or teaching qualifications or teaching-based backgrounds.

3.4 Applications

The two curriculum applications were developed with varying characteristics and engagement methods to provide insight into the comparative benefits of engagement style. The applications were designed without time limits to complete interactive activities, instead allowing the participant in conjunction with the direction of their support worker to set the pace [38].

Whilst the robot can be programmed to incorporate speech recognition inputs, there are a number of factors that can impact the success of speech interactions, such as background noise, user position in relation to the robot's microphone, timing of speech, choice of words and pronunciation. In this experiment, all programs were run locally on the robot, with no link to external cloud services which may deliver more advanced speech functionality. Without more advanced speech recognition systems and comprehensive user and environmental testing, such technical constraints could result in a high rate of unsuccessful speech interactions. This could, in turn, be discouraging for users and impact their confidence for continuing trying to interact. Thus, a decision was made not to use speech input for this experiment. Instead, we were able to observe where participants maybe were inclined to speak to Pepper, and the language they used, without it impacting the overall success of their interaction and while respecting their varying verbal preferences and abilities. Throughout the applications, an animated speech function was active, where the robot aligns contextual movement and gestures of its body with the content of the speech delivered. When the robot was not speaking, the movement would cease.

Healthy Eating Application. The healthy eating application involved an interactive series of questions which could be answered by an individual user, followed by questions for group discussion with the support worker.

The three interactive questions each gave the user a choice of two pictures for the participants to select the healthy option answer by tapping the screen. For a correct answer, Pepper displayed a green tick on the screen and waved its arms whilst playing a sound of a crowd cheering (see Fig. 2). If the incorrect answer was selected, Pepper displayed a red cross and asked the user to try again. At the end of the three questions, Pepper asked if the user wanted to do the quiz again or move onto the next activity which was the group discussion. eLearning guidelines [39] suggest that frequent learner interaction is necessary to sustain attention. Repeating concepts through discussion can help to facilitate the learning process [38] so the discussion activity was designed with the intent that the support worker would facilitate discussion with the group or with individuals, asking questions about the healthy food pyramid, with the picture displayed on Pepper's tablet (see Fig. 2), and asking participants to identify how many serves of foods were recommended for different genders and ages of people from a table displayed on the tablet. To help reinforce learning through check-point questions [40], the final activity was a facilitator led discussion about what people would like to include in their own food pyramids.

Fig. 2. Pepper robot healthy eating application.

Healthy Exercise Application. This application involved five exercise activities. Each exercise activity was structured in an "I do, We do, You do" format – essentially a basic education strategy for delivery of content. First Pepper showed a video of a person to the participants to demonstrate the exercise, then Pepper asked the participants to try the exercise along with the video, and finally, Pepper asked the participants to try the exercise on their own, whilst displaying a still image of the exercise. The fifth exercise was a repeat of the first exercise, with the addition of a custom animation where Pepper demonstrated the swinging arms movement in time with the video (as shown in Fig. 3).

Fig. 3. Pepper robot exercise application trial.

3.5 Qualitative Data

The sessions involved observation of participant interactions and engagements with the robot, and with other participants in the group. Semi-structured interviews were carried out during the session and at the end of the session to gather information about the participants' previous experience with robots, their thoughts about the robot, if they would like to interact with the robot again, what parts of the robot applications they liked most, and how the robot may be most useful to them. Observations were noted through the session and a thematic analysis [41] was undertaken to look for variances in engagement styles and synthesis across the three study groups. The video and audio recordings were leveraged to look back and verify the observations and gain further insights.

4 Findings

4.1 Overview of Findings

Observing the sessions, we reviewed how participants were engaging with Pepper to look for common themes across the groups. We considered "engagement" to encompass interacting with the robot, displaying interest in the robot, and initiating joint attention such as talking about the robot with others in the group. Engagement was observed both during a participant's turn to interact with Pepper, when other participants were taking their turn, and during group discussion when the application activities had been completed. We identified four commonalities in engagement style:

1. High intensity engagement and emotional attachment
2. Intermittent focus
3. Quiet and obedient
4. Wanting more/distant

Because Pepper is a well-known social robot often appearing in news media, participants may have prior attitudes towards Pepper. None of the participants had interacted with Pepper before.

4.2 Researcher Observations of Participants with Intellectual Disability

High Intensity Engagement and Emotional Attachment. Some participants attempted to engage Pepper in a social interaction when they first saw it. These participants displayed the highest intensity of engagement.

PA1 was clearly drawn to Pepper throughout the session. She went straight up to Pepper at the beginning of the session and stayed close by up until everyone sat down to talk about the healthy eating pyramid. PA1 asked Pepper to shake hands, when no response was received, she threw her hands up a little, then turned away. She then turned to look at Pepper repetitively, often nodding encouragingly, and sometimes speaking, "yes, yes" or "it's ok Pepper" or "that's a good boy, Pepper". During the initial setup, when PA2 had started an application, Pepper gave the instruction to tap its foot. PA1 touched the top of Pepper's bumper, but when nothing happened, she said, "OK, Pepper, please", when nothing happened again, she said, "What are you doing to me Pepper". PA1 seemed fascinated by all parts of Pepper. PA1 answered many of the questions about the healthy eating application correctly, meaning that she paid attention to Pepper's presentation, even when she was not directly involved in the interaction. Even though PA1 had noticed that the robot applications were programmed from the researcher's laptop, she spoke of the robot as an autonomous being, and spoke of "teaching" the robot, rather than programming it, and starting off with simple instructions so that "the robot could get its head around it" to start with. When we asked PA1 what she would like a robot to do for her, she stated that she wanted a robot that could help her around the house, reach high things and push her wheelchair. PA1 also stated that she would trust Pepper more than a doctor to give her medical advice particularly because of her non-threatening face. She also said that she would prefer to talk and give instructions to Pepper verbally than using the tablet.

PC1 was the first in his group to interact with Pepper. He called out "Hello Pepper". In the Healthy Eating quiz, PC1 selected his answers without waiting for the full instruction from Pepper and gave himself a clap. When the robot cheered, he went to touch Pepper's hand. By the third question, where the robot asked "How do you feel? PC1 responded "I feel good" and selected the corresponding picture. At the food pyramid, he verbally answered the questions, then tapped to the next question. At the last question, he knelt down to look closely at the tablet, seemingly not wanting to look away from the robot. Twice during the session, he referred to Pepper as his "best friend" and he thought that robot seemed nice.

PB1 seemed very excited to be meeting a robot for the first time. In the healthy eating application, he seemed to be very concerned with getting the answer correct and seemed surprised when he got the right answer. He loved getting the right answer and seeing Pepper cheer. Unlike PC1 and PA1 who spoke to Pepper more like a friend, PB1 generally referred to Pepper as the "robot" but was amazed when Pepper was "brought back to life".

Intermittent Focus. Some participants switched from highly engaged, and focused on Pepper, to distracted and looking around the room. This may be attributed to a number of factors that have very little to do with the robot, such as the unfamiliar environment, the level of difficulty of the content, and the individual's usual ability to stay on task.

PA4 arrived late at the session and missed out on the earlier play with Pepper. After introducing himself to everyone in the room, he went to look at Pepper and asked, "May I touch it?". PA1 introduced Pepper to him. PA4 was very interested in having a turn to change the application with the support worker. When changing the app, Pepper went into sleep mode. He followed PA1's lead, saying "wakey wakey". When Pepper was awake, he said "Hi Pepper". He found tapping Pepper's screen to be easy. PA4 often sought guidance from SWA2 during his interactions. At the end of each question, PA4 tended to lose focus on the robot. He was less engaged during the exercise class and stated that the exercises were too easy. This could be because of his experience playing basketball.

PB2 celebrated when she got the right answers in the healthy eating application and repeated the activity twice. During the healthy food pyramid section of the application, she walked away from the robot a few times because she thought it was the end of her turn, but it was not.

Quiet and Obedient. Initially PA2 stood back and watched Pepper and PA1, whilst also looking around the room. PA2 pressed icons on Pepper's tablet without being prompted to do so to operate the applications. He seemed very familiar with using tablet functions. He followed along with Pepper's instructions very well, and whilst he seemed quite fascinated by the robot's hands, the majority of his engagement was focused on the tablet.

PB3 did not seem particular interested in Pepper, however SWB1 said that he spoke more to Pepper than in his usual interactions with people.

Wanting More/Distant. Some of the participants did not really engage with Pepper unless asked to. PC2 looked bored and did not seem to be very interested when interacting with Pepper. During the healthy eating pyramid questions, she skipped through to the next question without saying a response. When PC3 got the wrong answers in the healthy eating application, he tried to put Pepper to sleep.

PA3 was the least interested in Pepper. He only engaged in an activity and interacted with Pepper when encouraged by SWB1. He wasn't called over to engage with Pepper until the Healthy Eating pyramid discussion questions. He exhibited a high ability in reading but may have a lower ability to comprehend and contextualize as he said the fruits that he saw, but when asked what the red tick meant, he seemed to have stopped paying attention and for the next two questions he answered incorrectly "fruit" before tapping the next button. He then moved away for PA4 to have their turn and returned to the back of the room. During the Healthy Eating discussion, he answered questions again relating to fruit. When it was time for the exercise class, Pepper asked "Are you ready? And PA3 said yes. We may observe that this participant responded to more active participatory questions rather than quiz questions. He participated in the exercises and was more engaged throughout the exercise application than the healthy eating application. PA3 was quite restless during the session and spent a lot of time walking around the back of the room, which may be due to environmental factors and certain aspects of this participant's disability.

4.3 Support Worker Perspectives

The support workers in each session engaged quite differently. In the first group, SWA2 opted to run the healthy eating application activities as a group, with PA2, PA1 and PA4 each taking a turn to answer a question. He then invited PA3 and PA4 to answer some of the healthy eating pyramid discussion. PA4 asked if he could change the application, and SWA2 then asked him to do it with him.

In the second group, SWB1 was very interactive, discussing the healthy eating topics and encouraging each participant to take their turn and sit down if they liked. SWB1 noted that she was very drawn to Pepper's non-verbal cues, particularly the robot's eyes. SWB1 was active in the exercise application and felt it best for the participants with IDs to be in control of the robot and moving. In the third group, SWC1 allowed the participants to each take a full turn of the whole healthy eating application. SWC1 and SWB1 actively invited the participants to learn to change the application.

The first session involved multiple support workers. SWA1 watched the application, but did not interact with Pepper, encouraging SWA2 to run the session. They agreed that Pepper has a lot of potential to run classes at the support organization's centers while they facilitate. They stated that the robot has the potential to hold the participants attention much better than a human teacher. But they also stated that the lessons will have to be changed up because the novelty factor might wear off after some time. An overall theme was that Pepper would be of benefit to support the consistent delivery of curriculum information. SWA2 stated that a robot with a female voice is better as it is more calming than a male voice.

4.4 Application Structure and Design

Healthy Eating Application. Initially it was thought that each participant would have a turn completing all three questions, however, the first group completed this activity as a group, taking a turn with 1 question each. Some sessions were run with the participants each taking their turn to do all 3 questions of the healthy eating quiz, then they took turns to talk about the healthy eating pyramid. This meant that they had to do the quiz again to get to the discussion questions. In the first session, only three participants had a chance to answer an interactive question.

The image used for the healthy eating pyramid [42] was quite detailed for a small screen. Some participants had difficulty reading the content which may have been in part due to the screen size, but also because the image text and background colors were not web accessibility compliant. Participants were generally able to identify foods, e.g. bananas, but some of the visuals were not as easily identifiable from the images used. When asked to identify a healthy food, PA2 didn't pick an item from the screen, after he hesitated, PA1 asked what he had for lunch, to which he responded "sandwiches". The question, what does the red cross mean, was also challenging for some participants, and SWB1 suggested that a saltshaker may have been more easily identifiable than the imagery used.

This application involved close interaction from the participants to Pepper. Participants in the first group all stood up during this application, but participants in the other group sat in a chair to interact with Pepper. During this time, most participants were looking at the screen, except where Pepper cheered.

Healthy Exercise Application. In all sessions, the participants joined in while the robot was showing the initial demonstration. At the third stage, where participants were supposed to do the exercise by themselves, there was some confusion and participants copied the still image displayed on the tablet. By the fourth exercise, engagement of all participants was starting to wane, however at the fifth exercise, where the robot physically did the exercise as well, all participants reengaged, and except for PC4 and PB1, all participants performed the exercise with more gusto. Most didn't appear to be consciously aware that the robot was doing the activity too. PC4 was so amazed that she didn't do the exercise. PB1 seemed distracted by the fact that the videos showed the researcher doing the exercise.

5 Discussion

We discuss some of the factors that played a role in how participants engaged with Pepper, namely its physical presence and its social features. We also consider the implications of this work in practice, and the limitations of this exploratory study to be considered in future work.

5.1 Social Nature of the Robot and Physical Presence

Participants who wanted to engage with Pepper when they first saw it, may have done so because of its anthropomorphic shape.

Participants were more engaged during the interactive parts of the applications, as interactive activity attracts higher levels of attention [43]. Participants seemed to become less engaged in the exercise application and this may be in part because participants were not required to touch Pepper. This may have a negative effect on participants feelings of social presence and connection to Pepper [34, 44]. As noted by SWB1, the interactive screen is more engaging than playing a video, supporting the findings of other research [5]. In many ways, the tablet is central to this study, and its information delivery and interactions are supplemented by a social robot. Information needs to be visual to appeal to and be easily understood by people with ID. A social robot, offering a personality dimension, can add to user's sense of efficacy and trust in the presented information [45]. While we did not directly measure this in the study, the styles of engagement offer a starting point for future studies examining this aspect more specifically for users responding in a particular way.

The physical presence of the robot performing the arm movements for the final exercise correlated to an improvement in performance and engagement of the participants, even if they did not appear to be consciously following the physical movement of the robot. This supports the finding of other their research which examined the benefits of interactions with physically present robots over video-displayed agents [29].

The most highly engaged participants were also the ones who seemed to be the most emotionally attached, talking both to, and about the robot like a friend. Whilst PA1 and PA2 communicated that they knew that the robot was a machine that could be programmed or rebooted, PA3 did not make such statements. This highlights potential areas of concern about artificial interactions and attachment to the robot [8]. Further research investigating actual versus safe imagination and attachment is required in relation to how the robot is framed when introduced to users.

5.2 Applicability to Support Centers Context

This project started with an opportunity for support workers to be highly engaged and interactive alongside the robot, however, the support workers opted to be less engaged in running the session than was anticipated. The way in which support workers would use the robot, or spend any time and capacity freed up by the robot warrants further exploration, with consideration of factors of perception and acceptance of the robot as a co-facilitator.

The learning material delivered in this study was structured in line with support organization's curriculum requirements, and focus on highly visual and interactive modes of delivery. Pepper's tablet can be used to display video, and this enhances the potential for the robot to be a one stop shop for consistent and repeatable curriculum delivery. Something to consider for future activities is the design and complexity of content displayed on the tablet and the position of users interacting with the robot. Because the tablet is relatively small, it is suggested that content be simple, easy to read, and highly interactive. The participants in the first and second sessions thought that Pepper had potential for supporting sign language education and translation. SWB1 suggested that Pepper may be helpful in guiding meditations and personal hygiene activities. There is an opportunity to explore how robots with tablets may be used to provide information in an unstructured way, including flexible modalities for people to engage with Pepper in the way that best suits them using the tablet, speech or other touch sensor inputs. Beyond traditional curriculum delivery about independent life skills, literacy and numeracy, a social robot like Pepper can foster social relationships and play a role in modeling roles and social stories to support community and social engagement skills development.

As discussed in Lytridis et al.'s 2019 [46] review on measuring engagement, social interactions can be multi-modal and complex. Not all behavioral cues can be detected by equipment, some require trained specialists to detect and assess engagement indicators such as expression, inspection, approach and communications towards the robot. The engagement styles we have identified offer a non-clinical structure for evaluation of robot interactions that follows a social narrative. Observation and thematic analysis to determine styles of engagement enables the nuances of an individual's behavioral cues to be assessed, whilst providing common terms and a way to group participants in a useful way for community-based group learning. This may be useful to determine the kinds of group configurations, types of interaction and curriculum contexts where robot assisted community-based learning may deliver the most benefits, while acknowledging that the robot may not be of interest to everyone.

5.3 Avenues for Future Research

This study involved three separate sessions, with three different groups of participants. Each session was held on the university campus in the morning to align with the participants' morning tea and lunch schedule. Whilst a single interaction session lasting only 5–10 min for each user per activity is of research value [5, 26], as only one session was run with each group, there are limitations on the conclusions that can be drawn. Although the application content was developed from the support organization's standard curriculum, the content may have been of an incompatible complexity for some participants, as such a differentiated model of content warrants further exploration.

The results observed in the experiment may in part be due to the novelty effect of the robot, rather than the interactions with it. In future research, it would be interesting to investigate the long-term effects of the interaction with Pepper. For instance, how well do the participants with ID remember the presented information about the food pyramid? How would their perception of their relationship with the robot change, would they still consider Pepper a friend (PC1) after multiple interactions?

It is also important to note also that the experiments were held at a university, not the participant's regular center environment. As a result of this, further research is needed to determine if there is a difference in interaction and engagement when participants can engage with the robot in familiar surroundings, not just with familiar groups. In the case of participants who appeared to be wanting more/distant, or quiet and obedient, passiveness within the first session may not equate to disinterest over time where participants are given an opportunity to become more familiar and confident in interacting with the robot.

Disability support service organizations are typically for-purpose entities with limited funding. A social robot such as Pepper is currently a significant investment, beyond the initial price of the hardware. At this time there are a very limited range of off the shelf applications available. Longer term studies to observe changes in engagement and use of the robot within a center environment are also required in order to evaluate the novelty effect and intervals at which content should be iterated or changed to maintain results. Once a broader base of participants has had a chance to become familiar with the robot, co-design of applications could be explored.

This research has focused on younger adults and the results may not be generalized across a span of all ages [28]. There is a gap in research about social robots to support older adults (e.g. 45+) with intellectual disability and further research is warranted to examine how social robots can support learning experiences of older people with IDs. The participants invited by the support organization may be more tech savvy than the general population of people and support workers attending the centers, and the applicability of the results to a wider audience should be interpreted with this in mind.

6 Conclusion

This exploratory study provides a new lens on the diversified use of social robots in life skills learning contexts for adults with intellectual disability. We have observed a variety of engagement styles for participants, but also a variety of uses by the learning facilitators. Our study uniquely placed the robot as a co-contributor to the learning experience, rather than as an exclusive learning partner, thus supplementing the social context rather than replacing it. Our findings suggest a way forward for social robots in disability services through engagement, and perhaps co-design with each network of learners and learning facilitators (in this case, support workers), as each group came up with a unique configuration and role for the robot. Many of our participants are eager to further explore the possibilities in the longer term, which we will investigate through a variety of experiences over long periods of time in the future.

Acknowledgements. This research is supported by the Australian Research Council under grant LP160100800, jointly with Endeavour Foundation. We acknowledge the time and dedication of our participants. Gavin Suddrey, Nicole Robinson and Belinda Ward of the ARC Centre of Excellence for Robotic Vision contributed to the development of the robot applications.

References

1. Australian Institute of Health and Welfare: Disability support services: services provided under the National Disability Agreement 2017–18. AIHW, Canberra, Australia (2019)
2. Balasuriya, S.S., Sitbon, L., Brereton, M., Koplick, S.: How can social robots spark collaboration and engagement among people with intellectual disability? In: Proceedings of the 31st Australian Conference on Human-Computer-Interaction, pp. 209–220. ACM, New York (2019)
3. Ahn, H.S., Lee, M.H., MacDonald, B.A.: Healthcare robot systems for a hospital environment: CareBot and ReceptionBot. In: Proceedings of the 24th IEEE International Symposium on Robot and Human Interactive Communication (RO-MAN), pp. 571–576. IEEE, Kobe (2015)
4. Collins, G.R.: Improving human–robot interactions in hospitality settings. Int. Hosp. Rev. **34**(1), 61–79 (2020)
5. Shukla, J., Cristiano, J., Amela, D., Anguera, L., Vergés-Llahí, J., Puig, D.: A case study of robot interaction among individuals with profound and multiple learning disabilities. In: Tapus, A., André, E., Martin, J.-C., Ferland, F., Ammi, M. (eds.) Social Robotics. ICSR 2015. Lecture Notes in Computer Science, vol. 9388. pp. 613–622. Springer, Cham (2015). https://doi-org.ezp01.library.qut.edu.au/10.1007/978-3-319-25554-5_61
6. Shaw-Garlock, G.: Loving machines: theorizing human and sociable-technology interaction. In: Lamers, M.H., Verbeek, F.J. (eds.) HRPR 2010. LNICSSITE, vol. 59, pp. 1–10. Springer, Heidelberg (2011). https://doi.org/10.1007/978-3-642-19385-9_1
7. Williams, A.B., Williams, R.M., Moore, R.E., McFarlane, M.: AIDA: a social co-robot to uplift workers with intellectual and developmental disabilities. In: 14th ACM/IEEE International Conference on Human-Robot Interaction (HRI), pp. 584–585. IEEE, Daegu (2019)
8. Wolbring, G., Yumakulov, S.: Social robots: views of staff of a disability service organization. Int. J. Soc. Robot. **6**(3), 457–468 (2014)
9. Belpaeme, T., Kennedy, J., Ramachandran, A., Scassellati, B., Tanaka, F.: Meta analysis of robots for learning literature. Sci. Robot. **3**(21), eaat5954 (2018)
10. Tanaka, F., Kimura, T.: The use of robots in early education: a scenario based on ethical consideration. In: The 18th IEEE International Symposium on Robot and Human Interactive Communication, pp. 558–560. IEEE, Toyama (2009)
11. Belpaeme, T., et al.: Guidelines for designing social robots as second language tutors. Int. J. Soc. Robot. **10**(3), 325–341 (2018)
12. Pennazio, V.: Social robotics to help children with autism in their interactions through imitation. Res. Educ. Media **9**(1), 10–16 (2017)
13. Pennisi, P., et al.: Autism and social robotics: a systematic review. Autism Res. **9**(2), 165–183 (2016)
14. So, W.-C., et al.: Using a social robot to teach gestural recognition and production in children with autism spectrum disorders. Disabil. Rehabil. Assist. Technol. **13**(6), 527–539 (2018)
15. Hedgecock, J., Standen, P.J., Beer, C., Brown, D., Stewart, D.S.: Evaluating the role of a humanoid robot to support learning in children with profound and multiple disabilities. J. Assist. Technol. **8**(3), 111–123 (2014)
16. Silvera-Tawil, D., Roberts-Yates, C., Bradford, D.: Talk to me: the role of human-robot interaction in improving verbal communication skills in students with autism or intellectual disability. In: Proceedings of the 27th IEEE International Symposium on Robot and Human Interactive Communication (RO-MAN), pp. 1–6. IEEE, Nanjing (2018)
17. Silvera-Tawil, D., Roberts-Yates, C.: Socially-assistive robots to enhance learning for secondary students with intellectual disabilities and autism. In: Proceedings of the 27th IEEE International Symposium on Robot and Human Interactive Communication, pp. 838–843. IEEE, Nanjing (2018)

18. Standen, P., et al.: Engaging students with profound and multiple disabilities using humanoid robots. In: Stephanidis, C., Antona, M. (eds.) UAHCI 2014. LNCS, vol. 8514, pp. 419–430. Springer, Cham (2014). https://doi.org/10.1007/978-3-319-07440-5_39

19. Sitbon, L., Hoogstrate, M., Yule, J., Koplick, S., Bircanin, F., Brereton, M.: A non-clinical approach to describing participants with intellectual disability. In: Proceedings of the 30th Australian Conference on Human Computer Interaction, pp. 128–132. ACM, New York (2018)

20. McVilly, K.R., Stancliffe, R.J., Parmenter, T.R., Burton-Smith, R.M.: "I get by with a little help from my friends": adults with intellectual disability discuss loneliness. J. Appl. Res. Intellect. Disabil. 19(2), 191–203 (2006)

21. Davy, L.: Philosophical inclusive design: intellectual disability and the limits of individual autonomy in moral and political theory. Hypatia 30(1), 132–148 (2015)

22. Iacono, T.: Addressing increasing demands on Australian disability support workers. J. Intellect. Dev. Disabil. 35(4), 290–295 (2010)

23. Seale, J.: The role of supporters in facilitating the use of technologies by adolescents and adults with learning disabilities: a place for positive risk-taking? Eur. J. Spec. Needs Educ. 29(2), 220–236 (2014)

24. Bröhl, C., Nelles, J., Brandl, C., Mertens, A., Schlick, C.M.: TAM reloaded: a technology acceptance model for human-robot cooperation in production systems. In: Stephanidis, C. (ed.) HCI 2016. CCIS, vol. 617, pp. 97–103. Springer, Cham (2016). https://doi.org/10.1007/978-3-319-40548-3_16

25. Clabaugh, C., Becerra, D., Deng, E., Ragusa, G., Matarić, M.: Month-long, in-home case study of a socially assistive robot for children with autism spectrum disorder. In: Companion of the 2018 ACM/IEEE International Conference on Human-Robot Interaction (HRI '18), pp. 87–88. ACM, (2018)

26. Shukla, J., Cristiano, J., Oliver, J., Puig, D.: Robot assisted interventions for individuals with intellectual disabilities: impact on users and caregivers. Int. J. Soc. Robot. 11, 631–249 (2019)

27. Mann, J.A., MacDonald, B.A., Kuo, I.H., Li, X., Broadbent, E.: People respond better to robots than computer tablets delivering healthcare instructions. Comput. Hum. Behav. 43, 112–117 (2015)

28. Fasola, J., Matari, M.J.: A socially assistive robot exercise coach for the elderly. J. Hum.-Robot Interact. 2(2), 3–32 (2013)

29. Bainbridge, W., Hart, J., Kim, E., Scassellati, B.: The benefits of interactions with physically present robots over video-displayed agents. Int. J. Soc. Robot. 3(1), 41–52 (2011)

30. Belpaeme, T., Kennedy, J., Ramachandran, A., Scassellati, B., Tanaka, F.: Social robots for education: a review. Sci. Robot. 3(21) (2018)

31. Sinoo, C., et al.: Friendship with a robot: children's perception of similarity between a robot's physical and virtual embodiment that supports diabetes self-management. Patient Educ. Counsel. 101(7), 1248–1255 (2018)

32. Lemaignan, S., Jacq, A., Hood, D., Garcia, F., Paiva, A., Dillenbourg, P.: Learning by teaching a robot: the case of handwriting. IEEE Robot. Autom. Mag. 23(2), 56–66 (2016)

33. Hood, D., Lemaignan, S., Dillenbourg, P.: When children teach a robot to write: an autonomous teachable humanoid which uses simulated handwriting. Proceedings of the Tenth Annual ACM/IEEE International Conference on Human-Robot Interaction, pp. 83–90. Association for Computing Machinery, Portland, Oregon, USA (2015)

34. Lee, K.M., Jung, Y., Kim, J., Kim, S.R.: Are physically embodied social agents better than disembodied social agents?: The effects of physical embodiment, tactile interaction, and people's loneliness in human–robot interaction. Int. J. Hum Comput Stud. 64(10), 962–973 (2006)

35. Andreasson, R., Alenljung, B., Billing, E., Lowe, R.: Affective touch in human-robot interaction: conveying emotion to the Nao robot. Int. J. Soc. Robot. 10(4), 473–491 (2018)

36. Wit, J.D., et al.: The effect of a robot's gestures and adaptive tutoring on children's acquisition of second language vocabularies. Proceedings of the 2018 ACM/IEEE International Conference on Human-Robot Interaction, pp. 50–58. Association for Computing Machinery, Chicago, IL, USA (2018)

37. Vogt, P., et al.: Second language tutoring using social robots: a large-scale study. In: 2019 14th ACM/IEEE International Conference on Human-Robot Interaction (HRI), pp. 497–505. IEEE, (2019)

38. Lopez-Basterretxea, A., Mendez-Zorrilla, A., Garcia-Zapirain, B., Madariaga-Ortuzar, A., Lazcano-Quintana, I.: Serious games to promote independent living for intellectually disabled people: starting with shopping. In: 2014 Computer Games: AI, Animation, Mobile, Multimedia, Educational and Serious Games (CGAMES), pp. 1–4. IEEE, Louisville (2014)

39. Food and Agriculture Organization of the United Nations: E-learning methodologies: a guide for designing and developing e-learning courses (2011). http://www.fao.org/3/i2516e/i2516e.pdf

40. Australian e-Learning Association: Australian e-learning best practice guidelines: elearning performance criteria – learning methodology and framework (2016). https://www.austra lianelearningassociation.com.au/wp-content/uploads/2016/06/eLearning-Performance-Cri teria-Learning-Methodology-and-Framework.pdf

41. Braun, V., Clarke, V.: Using thematic analysis in psychology. Qual. Res. Psychol. 3(2), 77–101 (2006)

42. Australian Nutrition Foundation Inc.: Healthy eating pyramid (2015)

43. Shukla, J., Cristiano, J., Anguera, L., Vergés-Llahí, J., Puig, D.: A comparison of robot interaction with tactile gaming console stimulation in clinical applications. Proceedings of Robot 2015: Second Iberian Robotics Conference. Advances in Intelligent Systems and Computing, vol. 418. pp. 435–445. Springer, Cham (2015).https://doi.org/10.1007/978-3-319-27149-1_34

44. Lee, K.M.: Presence, explicated. Commun. Theory 14(1), 27–50 (2004)

45. Lopatovska, I., et al.: User perceptions of an intelligent personal assistant's personality: the role of interaction context. Proceedings of the 2021 Conference on Human Information Interaction and Retrieval, pp. 15–25. Association for Computing Machinery, Canberra ACT, Australia (2021)

46. Lytridis, C., Bazinas, C., Papakostas, G.A., Kaburlasos, V.: On measuring engagement level during child-robot interaction in education. In: Merdan, M., Lepuschitz, W., Koppensteiner, G., Balogh, R., Obdržálek, D. (eds.) RiE 2019. AISC, vol. 1023, pp. 3–13. Springer, Cham (2020). https://doi.org/10.1007/978-3-030-26945-6_1

Assistive Technology for Mobility and Rehabilitation

Co-designing Tangible Break Reminders with People with Repetitive Strain Injury

Aditi Singh[1], Sara Nabil[1,2] ⓘ, Anne Roudaut[3], and Audrey Girouard[1(✉)] ⓘ

[1] Carleton University, Ottawa, ON K1S 5B6, Canada
aditisingh3@cmail.carleton.ca, sara.nabil@queensu.ca,
audrey.girouard@carleton.ca
[2] Queen's University, Kingston, ON K7L 3N6, Canada
[3] University of Bristol, Bristol, UK
anne.roudaut@bristol.ac.uk

Abstract. People with Repetitive Strain Injury (RSI) performing computer work for 4+ hours/day should take microbreaks every hour to reduce their symptoms. Unlike apps and notifications, tangible user interfaces offer the opportunity to provide non-focus-demanding and calm break-reminders in users' periphery. This paper explores this design space to identify the design parameters of break-reminders as everyday things. First, we discuss and analyze our initial co-designing study, where 11 participants with RSI created 9 low-fidelity prototypes. Then, we present our results-led high-fidelity prototypes and demonstrate the use of the findings in directing the design decisions of the technical implementation. Finally, we take our designs back to users in a second study to gain deeper insight on their reflection on physical break reminders. Results show how users designed for calmness and ubiquity in their everyday environment, playful user engagement and emotional shape-shifting among other design qualities.

Keywords: Shape-changing interfaces · Workplace · Repetitive strain injury · Well-being · Everyday spaces · Interactive objects

1 Introduction

Computer-dependent lifestyle and work are exacerbating Repetitive Strain Injury (RSI) [1, 2], which has become a prevalent health issue. Lack of attention to ergonomics of various workplace devices [34] combined with psychosocial factors [3–8] are the leading causal factors and aggravators of RSI. Against this, taking microbreaks (30 s to 1 min) is recommended to reduce the load on activated muscles and provide a mental break to increase productivity [9]. But people find it hard to follow a regimented break routine. Notifications (time-based desktop or phone reminders) can help users take breaks, but

Electronic supplementary material The online version of this chapter (https://doi.org/10.1007/978-3-030-85623-6_18) contains supplementary material, which is available to authorized users.

© IFIP International Federation for Information Processing 2021
Published by Springer Nature Switzerland AG 2021
C. Ardito et al. (Eds.): INTERACT 2021, LNCS 12932, pp. 289–311, 2021.
https://doi.org/10.1007/978-3-030-85623-6_18

they are often ill-timed and not aware of the user's natural work pause pattern [10], exacerbating stress and productivity [4]. People with RSI have unique needs regarding notifications, even when a response to promote care and wellbeing would suggest minimizing them. We investigate the need for break reminders that do not disrupt the user's workflow and provide passive awareness while being conducive to productivity. Specifically, we propose actuating everyday objects as a potential solution [11–13] (Fig. 1).

Fig. 1. Interactive everyday objects in the workplace can serve as break-reminders for people with repetitive strain injury. In this illustration, the wilted flower reminds the user to take a break. Once they have, the flower is blooming again.

The study of actuating tangible interfaces as a break reminder so far has only been in preliminary works, which rather focused on the technical implementation with a limited evaluation with end-users (N < 4, without RSI). Our work covers this gap in two rigorous reflective user studies and goes further by engaging people living with RSI symptoms in 4 co-designing activities to ideate and create tangible break reminders for RSI as everyday things that are appropriated for their needs. The first study focused on three research questions: what strategies do people with RSI use to incorporate breaks and other healthy habits? What are user preferences for workplace interactive objects? What do they desire from a tangible object that can support people to take breaks? The second study asked: what impressions, criticisms and reflections did people with RSI have about our implementation of their prototype design?

In doing this research, we further our understanding of the work context in which RSI occurs, contrasting workplace and work-from-home behaviours, the coping strategies, and challenges faced by people with these symptoms. Our goal is not to compare the use of digital or tangible notifiers, but instead to investigate the design space of actuating everyday things as break-reminders by engaging and co-designing with RSI users. We want to inspire designers engaging with actuating physical interfaces and elevate the discussion around tensions between what researchers create as prototypes and what users ideate for themselves. In this sense, our three key contributions are:

- Engaging people living with RSI in discussions by critiquing (2 design probes), ideating (9 low-fidelity prototypes) and reflecting on break-reminding everyday things in a co-design study with 11 participants.

- Proposing 13 findings about break reminders designed by people with RSI in terms of disruption of work, personal preferences, emotional engagement and the social constraints of a workplace versus working from home.
- Designing and implementing 3 high-fidelity actuating prototypes as calm non-focus-demanding break-reminders, using design decisions inferred from the co-designing user study, and gaining user feedback afterwards.

To the best of our knowledge, people with RSI have not been included in user studies related to notifications or break reminders. It is also the first study in investigating tangible devices from a co-designing approach capturing the context and latent needs of the users to formulate a design guideline.

2 Related Work

To explore this design space, we review previous work on RSI, interruptions at work, and actuating everyday things.

2.1 Repetitive Strain Injury

RSI is "pain felt in muscles, nerves and tendons caused by repetitive movement and overuse" [15]. Lack of attention to ergonomics of workplace devices and furniture is a major cause that exacerbates RSI symptoms [1]. While earlier work focused on investigating the impact of repetitive movement, awkward posture, and lack of attention to ergonomics due to prolonged sitting and computer usage [16, 17], recent work demonstrates psychosocial factors like anxiety [3, 4], mental exhaustion [5], social support [6], work organization [7], and time pressure [8] also exacerbate RSI at work. Aside from workplace ergonomics, "healthy behaviour" at work reduces and prevents the symptoms of RSI [18]. These include engaging in regular stretch and rest breaks and incorporating regular physical exercise. The effectiveness of these microbreaks to reduce muscular load is well established [9, 19–21]. Besides releasing muscle strain, microbreaks also reduce the mental strain, which activates the same muscle group as computer usage [5]. This demonstrates the usefulness of incorporating "healthy behaviour" and improving the workplace ergonomics in preventing and reducing RSI.

2.2 Interruptions at Work

Break reminders intervene work to remind the user to move, making it important to understand the cost of interruption on work and well-being. Interruptions in the form of phone and desktop notification do not regard the user's primary tasks, increase task time, and perceived task load [4, 22, 23]. In addition to impacting work and productivity, interruptions in the middle of a user's primary task also increase annoyance by 31% to 106% and double the anxiety [4]. Hence untimely interruptions like generic break reminder software can deter the user's productivity and mental health.

Some HCI research presented non-traditional break reminders to address sedentary behaviour at work [12, 24], using strategies such as interactive breaks [24], non-intrusive reminders [12], or persuasive messages [25]. However, these works do not include the voices of people with RSI who can bring new insights to the study of break reminders. People with RSI may have more experience in trying to incorporate breaks during work as a part of adopting healthy work habits compared to people who do not have RSI. Not much is known about their experience at work and their desires from a device that supports health behaviour such as taking rest and stretch breaks.

2.3 Actuating Everyday Things

Design-led research considerations have shown the value of connecting habitual behaviours in daily lives with acts of checking data through interactive everyday objects [26]. Actuating objects and shape-shifting interfaces are capable of changing their appearance and/or form factors through user interaction or their autonomous behaviour. Several terms have been proposed to encompass this notion such as Shape-changing interfaces [27–29], radical atoms [30] or Organic User Interfaces [31]. Rasmussen et al. [32] and Roudaut et al. [27] have proposed to classify these interfaces depending on their transformations that can include changes in orientation, form, volume, texture, viscosity, or spatiality. Shape-changing interfaces have been used to communicate ambient information through slow movement in the periphery of the user [13, 33]. These changes, when slow and quiet, can exist in the peripheral vision of the user [13]. These functional applications demonstrated in prior work include communicating emotion [34], communicating information [13, 32, 35], dynamic affordances that fit the context [36], and volume change for portability [37].

Further research unfolding the design of everyday computational things [38] suggested experiential qualities that expand the functional purposes of their tangible prototypes. Such examples include furniture [39–43], soft furnishing elements [44–46], decorative objects [26, 47] or fabric [61]. In particular, Shin et al. [43] assessed and proposed to mount a monitor on a robot to slowly correct a desk worker's posture. However, the scope of this research focuses on office desks objects applications and near periphery actuations in the context of break reminding for RSI, not correction.

Limited research has incorporated actuation into everyday objects of the workplace. Seoktae et al. [37] presented an inflatable mouse that facilitates portability through volume change. A few other approaches include: 1) the use of physical and vibrotactile feedback from the chair to facilitate posture change while sitting [48]; 2) shape-change as an ambient notification system during work activities [33, 49]; 3) in-pocket notifications [50]; and 4) deformation for information visualization for diverse datasets (e.g., numeric and textual data, and GIS information) [51]. In BreakAway [12], Jafarniami et al. proposed a shape-changing sculpture resembling a chair placed onto a desktop that suggests breaks through multiple degrees of slouching. They found that the participant appreciated the ability to ignore BreakAway at important moments unlike generic reminders on her calendar. The sculpture succeeded in providing passive awareness as the participant never expected it to completely slouch and took a break as soon as the slouching started. Similarly, Jones et al. [13] and Kobayashi et al. [35] evaluated the effectiveness of shape-changing notifications to provide passive awareness without disrupting the productivity of the user, the first using a self-bending strip, the other propping up a mobile device. They found that the near periphery of the user is ideal for ambient notification to work. Kucharski et al. [14] used a small humanoid robot located on a desk for break reminders, by changing its posture, stomping, and making increasing noise, and participants (4 office workers) indicated potential.

These works demonstrate the potential of interactive everyday objects to provide passive awareness without disrupting the user's primary task. These devices are physical objects that would exist in the environment of the user, the workplace in the case of RSI break reminders. Hence, a co-designing approach that attempts to understand the context, the needs and desires of people with RSI will bring new insights to the existing body of work of interactive break reminders.

3 Study 1: Co-designing Workplace Interactive Objects

In this first study, we conducted 11 individual co-designing sessions to comprehend the potential of interactive everyday objects as break reminders in the workplace for people with RSI. To understand their unique needs, challenges, preferences, and unspoken desires from a break reminder, we divided each session into three activities: 1) User Interview (Q1), 2) Design Critique (Q2), and 3) Co-Design (Q3). Each individual session lasted for an hour, conducted during the winter of 2019. We obtained ethical approval from our institution's research ethics board. Participants received a $30 CAN compensation for their time. The sessions were structured in these three phases to gradually bring participants from a descriptive to a creative state, where each activity was designed to answer a research question:

- Q1 – User Interview: What strategies do people with RSI use to incorporate breaks and other healthy habits?
- Q2 – Design Critique: What are user preferences for workplace interactive objects?
- Q3 – Ideating: What do they desire from a tangible object that can support people to take breaks?

We had 11 participants who had RSI for an average of 7.8 years (21 to 56 years old; mean = 37.6 yo, median = 33 yo; 7 women, 4 men). Their symptoms were in fingers, wrists, back, shoulders, or knees. Nine participants had consulted health experts for their condition and ten of them were actively trying to take breaks. Eight participants were using ergonomic objects or devices including an ergonomic chair, vertical mouse, sit-stand desk, and a document reader. Nine participants had a desk and a cubicle of their own and two participants were moving between different workspaces.

We transcribed 11 h of audio recording from the sessions. For the ideation activity, we supplemented the codes from the audio transcription by interpreting salient design features that were not verbally expressed by the participants and analyzed their sketches and/or low-fidelity designs. The gathered data were all combined and four researchers conducted iterative Thematic Analysis to identify underlying themes, a well-established and rigorous method to analyze qualitative data [52, 53].

We note that to begin this project as well as throughout research process, we talked to experts such as occupational therapists and ergonomists to better understand the requirement from a medical point of view. However, we choose to involve only end-users in this study to fully embrace the benefit of participatory design and better understand how our end-users wanted the intervention to occur within a particular context. Using only end-users within participatory design is a common practice [54].

3.1 Activity 1: User Interviews

We sought to understand the context of working with RSI, challenges faced by our participants and the strategies employed to cope with it. To facilitate the discussion about the participant's work environment, we interviewed six participants in their workplace. The other five participants brought pictures of their office desks.

We supplement the interviews with an observation of the level of privacy, space availability for personal objects, and the presence of personal or decorative objects of preference on or around their desks. We do this to ask specific questions about their personal preferences and feasibility of having a shape-changing device as a break reminder. From the 11 interviews, only one participant was actively using a reminder system. Four talked about having tried notifications and reminders in the past. Another four participants mentioned using their bodies as a reminder to take a break. Rather than following a regular break routine recommended to most of them, they inadvertently waited until the strain in their body triggered them to take breaks.

3.2 Activity 2: Design Critique

To understand the perception of interactive everyday objects as break reminders, we used design probes to encourage participants with RSI to provoke and inspire participants to rethink their environment, and respond in a way that creates a dialogue between the participants and the researcher [55]. Based on the findings of a prior pilot study, we designed two probes to capture users' impressions on introducing interactive objects to their workplace (Fig. 2). The probes gave an actuating form to otherwise static desk objects. We intentionally made the design probes aesthetically crude and in low-fidelity to put less pressure on participants. This will make them more critical, as they do not assume it took a great effort from the researcher to create [56].

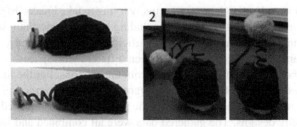

Fig. 2. Design probes: (2.1) springy-mouse (desk object) and (2.2) wilting flower (desk decor).

Probe1. We introduced a mouse probe (Fig. 2.1) with the following fictional story: "The mouse has a small button attached to the spring at the front of the object. The springs extend themselves and the button moves farther away from the mouse indicating a visual cue. You can restore the initial state of the mouse only by taking a break. Tracking the sitting and computer usage happen in the background and the button recoils back to the surface of the mouse once you have taken the break."

Probe2. We introduced a wilting flower (Fig. 2.2) with the following fictional story: "The flower tracks the sitting and computer usage of the user through sensing capabilities that is embedded in the chair and the computer. When it is time for the user to take a break, the flower would wilt, suggesting that users get up and take a break. You can restore the life of the flower by taking a break."

We discussed two versions of each probe: when the flower or mouse was interruptive and whether the wilting and the extension of the spring would affect the user's workflow. When the flower or mouse was disruptive, the withering or spring would decrease the efficiency and potentially prevent the user from continuing work.

3.3 Activity 3: Ideation

While describing their experience and giving their impressions on the design probes, participants often addressed features of the design probes they did not like and made suggestions. We noted these instances to initiate discussion during the design session where we repeated these instances as questions, e.g. *"Earlier you mentioned that you wouldn't relate to a flower, is there an object that you would relate to?"* In answering, participants ideated objects that embodied their preferences and design concepts.

We provided prototyping materials that included a mix of elastic and malleable material to encourage creativity. The elastic materials included elastic bands, foam in the form of sheets, cubes, and rolls. For the malleable materials, we included play dough, pipe cleaners and various types of wires. Additionally, there were small rigid wooden blocks, tape and glue to combine different materials. We also included markers, sticky notes, and drawing sheets to enable sketching during ideation.

Design Concepts. Most participants came up with their own designs of what they personally prefer as a shape-changing object on their desk to remind—and persuade—themselves of their break time. All participants except P1 and P10 used crafting materials to either make a low-fidelity prototype or sketch their design. P1 stated that they were happy with their Outlook reminders and did not find a tangible object desirable due to limited desk space; and P10 preferred *probe2* (the wilting flower) as opposed to another object expressing that the flower would work well for them on their desk. The other design concepts that users developed (Fig. 3) are described below:

- **Snoopy (P2):** A desk toy that stands straight on the desk. When it is time for a break, it collapses and becomes sad. Once the user is back from the break, it stands and greets them with a smile.
- **Blobby (P3):** An animated character pinned on a wall board. It is happy in the default state, but when it is time for a break, it shrinks into a small puddle. Once the user is back from the break, it comes back to life.

- **Sunrise (P4):** A painting that displays a utopian image (sunset) in its default state. As the time to take a break approaches, the painting slowly changes into a dystopian image (sad people, pictured at the bottom). Once a break is taken, the default state is presumed.

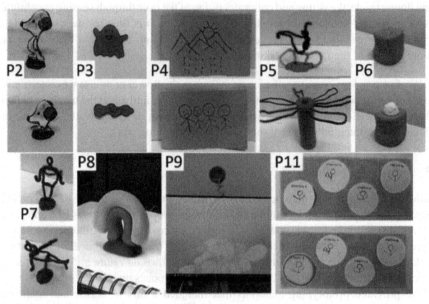

Fig. 3. Low-fidelity prototypes of tangible break reminders that participants with RSI designed for their workplace. Transformations towards the reminding state happen slowly from top to bottom figures in P2-P7, while P8 and P9 rotate, and P11 lights up.

- **Morphy (P5):** A desk toy that changes form from, e.g., a bicycle (top) into a lily (bottom), to give the user a new object to take care of each week. In each case the object has a default behaviour; wheels spinning for the bicycle and the petals blooming for the lily. When it is time to take a break, the wheel stops spinning for the bicycle and petals wither for the lily. When the user is back from the break, the default behaviour is resumed.
- **Luna (P6):** An abstract cyan coloured cylindrical object with a light bulb that emerges out slowly when it is time to take a break and fades in. Once the user is back from the break, it fades out and returns to its default state.
- **Superman (P7):** A desk toy figurine that stands upright in the default mode. When it is time to take a break, it moves to a flying position. When the user is back from the break, it is back to the standing position again.
- **Turbo (P8):** A bright-coloured desk toy designed as an abstract representation of a human. In the default state, it is constantly rotating along a central axis. When it is time to take a break, the rotation slowly stops. Once, the user is back from the break, it starts rotating again.

- **ShyFrame (P9):** A tiny frame with a pleasant scenery (e.g., a picture of the ocean) that hides behind the desk monitor. When it is time to take a break, it slowly moves up to become visible to the user reminding them of positive things. Once the user is back from the break, it goes behind the screen again.
- **Arcade (P11):** A console board with circular buttons representing four stretches. When it is time to take a break, one button lights up, suggesting doing that particular stretch. When the user performs it, they hit the button and the light goes off.

4 Findings

We discuss the results of our thematic analysis drawing on the data from the three activities with 11 participants with RSI. Our choice to use qualitative user interviews, design critiques and ideation as evaluation mechanisms means that the emphasis of our results is less on our "design concepts" and more on a critical reflection of what this user population needs. Accordingly, our themes (i.e. subheadings in this section) unpack the users' own design, preferences and challenges, thereby exploring how they imagine interactive everyday objects can support their well-being while not disrupting their work productivity.

4.1 Ubiquity and Calmness

F1: Disruption and Social Barriers. During the interviews, participants expressed the challenges and barriers to adopt break-reminding digital apps. *Social barriers*, which are issues related to having a group of people working in a social environment, prevented them from setting audible notifications on their mobile phones at the workplace and thus remembering to take frequent breaks. *Workflow barriers*, which are issues relating to their set of tasks to accomplish, were identified as the biggest barrier to taking regular breaks (N = 9) as desktops or mobile apps notifications significantly disrupted their tasks in-hand and negatively affected their work productivity.

While several participants (N = 4) reported using notifications at some point to incorporate more breaks and stretching during their workday, only one was actively using it. They used it for awareness during the day rather than using every reminder to take a break. Others (N = 3) had used it in the past but stopped because it was disruptive to the work and felt too frequent. This aversion to notifications was also due to their existing numerous notifications. P3 said: "*overtime I might get desensitized to it too... I would just ignore it and also be annoyed*", while P8 revealed: "*I already have enough notifications to deal with and I don't want them to interfere with my work but something subtle in the watch maybe, only for that purpose.*"

On this basis, participants preferred *probe2* over *probe1*, critiquing the latter to be disruptive. While participants acknowledged the advantage of good visibility of shape-changing actuation in the mouse, they perceived it intrusive and potentially annoying in the middle of work (N = 9). Moreover, all of their designs were not work-related objects (e.g., mouse/pad, keyboard), but practically decorative desk toys.

F2: Peripheral and Ambient. Participants clearly wanted their break reminders to be in the background of their perceived environment and not demanding much focus. They designed their concept interfaces as part of their workspace i.e., toys, décor or objects on the desk, wall or board. In this sense, interactive objects are in the user's periphery, rather than constantly at the centre of their attention, shifting to their focus only when needed and when appropriate. Such ambient and calm interaction empowers users with selective peripheral focus e.g. "*I want to look at it when I lose my attention*" (P3) and "*it gives something different but without forcing you*" (P11). This aligns with the literature on ambient displays.

F3: Slow Interaction. In addition to preferring an object that is ubiquitously part of the surrounding environment, participants also described their designs as *slow*. This does not only support the previous findings in this theme that interfaces are desired to be calm, ubiquitous and in the user's periphery, but also aligns well with recent research on designing for slowness as an interactive value [35, 36]. For example, P9 designed the *ShyFrame* as hidden from sight, but slowly moves up over time to become completely visible when a break time is due. Even with the spinning *Turbo*, P8 designed it so that the motion is (dis)continued in the periphery and only becomes noticeable as it "*slowly stops*". This notion of (relative) longevity that users desire is contrary to most current technologies that are instant and immediate.

4.2 User Engagement

F4: Playfulness. Most of our participants (N = 8) designed "*desk toys*" as their desired tangible break reminders, for playfulness and multifunctionality (discussed in F10). Playful interaction can be thus employed in designing interactive everyday things as a means of supporting user engagement. What intensifies such engagement is having a delightful design that resonates with personal appeal of toys. For instance, P2 thought their *Snoopy* was "*cute*", P8 made theirs in bright colours to be "*cheerful*". Nevertheless, even abstract designs can have a sense of enjoyment in engaging with them, such as how P11 described the satisfaction of hitting the buttons and how this "*sparks joy*".

F5: Emotional Engagement. Many designed for a relationship between the object and themselves. Several participants (N = 6) mentioned that the need for emotional connection with the object was important to listen to its suggestion without being annoyed. Some also mentioned relatability with the actuation as a determinant factor for emotional engagement with the interface. For example, work-related objects such as *probe1* (i.e., the springy mouse) were harder to relate to, compared to an anthropomorphic object such as *probe2* (i.e., the wilting flower). They described animating objects as feeling happy, sad, in pain or mirroring the user's own RSI state.

F6: Motivation and Care-Giving. Designing something to take care of reoccurred in the data, even with non-animated shape-changing designs. Several participants (N = 7) mentioned the emotional connection and persuasion capability of the object as an important factor to effectively listen to the object when it asks them to take a break. For participants, taking care of something meant taking care of themselves and gave them a motivational objective. This use of caregiving in design is emphasized in anthropomorphic objects such as "*a character or a pet I could take care of, I would care a little bit more*" (P3). However, P5 was worried about *probe2* and the rate of interaction asking "*How often would it die?*". Even, P5 who designed a morphing figure explained that it had a value-based concept of caring for their environment as bikes are eco-friendly: "*gotta keep the bike spinning*".

4.3 Shape-Change and Transformation

F7: Self-awareness. Some users tied up shape-changing interaction with self-reflection. They designed for self-awareness through the shape-shift of their objects. Such transformation included positive feedback as a reinforcement to taking more breaks. These included objects reflecting *self-care* by physicalizing the change, emoting positivity (P5, P6, P7, P9) and enabling the feeling of accomplishment (P11). Participants used both negative and positive scenarios to "making *that connection with taking care of yourself, taking out the time, stretching*" (P8).

F8: Visualizing the Consequences. Negative transformation was used in which the state of the object visualizes and reflects one's state -in proxy- or a representation of the body to remind them of the effects of prolonged sitting. E.g. P2, P3 and P8 made their objects deflate, degrade or break down when their bodies are in need for stretching. P4 depicted a positive imagery that turns into a negative scene explaining this is: "*to see the journey… assuming the longer I work the more I am hurting my back*".

F9: Fading Novelty. Participants pointed out one limitation of actuating break reminders was the wear off of the novelty effect. They expressed concerns around progressive boredom. Some participants suggested designs to overcome this challenge by varying the shape-shifting interaction or changing the object every while as their anti-novelty strategy. Others believed caregiving interaction will turn into a daily healthy routine: "*because once you do it for whatever number of days it becomes a habit*" (P5). Others suggested personalization and customization of their desk objects as their strategy to renew their visceral qualities (P9).

4.4 Design Qualities

F10: Practical Constraints and Multifunctionality. A major constraint was the presence of a plethora of work objects that could obliterate the visibility of the actuating break reminder. Participants frequently expressed aversion to placing more objects on the desks and wanted to utilize their favourite pre-existing objects as multifunctional elements that would do more. The social acceptability of such objects varied per participants: for instance, users in more conservative workspaces were hesitant to have a playful object on the desk. For example, P4 designed an abstract object to avoid attention but still personalized it in their **favourite** colour.

F11: Physical Dimensions. Due to limited desk space, a crucial aspect of shape-changing break reminders in the workplace is the scale of the object. Most participants leaned towards making their break reminders by designing them smaller in size ($N = 8$). Although we introduced our two probes in real-world 1:1 scale, participants suggested they would adopt probe2 if it was in half the size or less. This led to making their object small so that it can sit close to the visual space of the user but is not big enough to be intrusive. Other strategies included pinning the device on the wall or board (P3, P11) or attaching it to the back of the monitor (P9). This included the need for the object to not only require less desk space ($N = 7$), but also to be multifunctional (e.g., a clock that is also a break reminder), and to be in the visual space of the user.

F12: Aesthetic Values. Other physical attributes of the object such as appearance, colour and texture were also discussed by participants. Three participants (P4, P8, P9) discussed the possibility and importance of making the object easy to personalize not just to them but also considering other people's preferences. Participants used both abstraction and anthropomorphism to alter the appearance of their objects. Aesthetic qualities varied from animate characteristics like changing emotions of the object when the user returned from the break (P2, P3, P4), resuming the state of motion of the object (P2, P3, P5, P7, P8) to inanimate characteristics like change in peripheral visibility of the object using light or position of the object (P6, P9, P11).

F13: Personal Preference. We found a correlation between the personal preference of the participant and the design of their break reminding object. For example, P2 chose to have snoopy as the break reminder because it was their favourite character; P3 made an animated object and we observed that they owned a few personal objects depicting similar animated characters; P9 made a small frame with the picture of the ocean because they grew up next to the ocean and it reminded them of home.

5 Prototyping

To enrich the evaluation of our co-designing process, we developed fully-interactive implementations of the design concepts, drawing inspiration from participants' designs and the lessons learnt from our findings (F1–F13). We programmed the prototypes to actuate every 60 min as recommended by healthcare practitioners to reduce RSI symptoms [9]. Our goal is to demonstrate how the experiential expectations and needs of users can be incorporated in the design of things they would want to live with.

We categorized user designs into three categories: 2D planer frames (P4, P9, P11), 3D abstract objects (P5, P6, P8) and animated toys (P2, P3, P7). Then, we developed one from each category (P2, P6, P9) as examples of everyday objects using non-focus demanding, silent, subtle and slow interactive electronics. Emotional engagement is employed through playfulness and caregiving. Their actuation reflects state-change through both positive and negative notions. Finally, the aesthetic qualities consider their practical concerns and reflect their personal and aesthetic preferences. Study 2 will provide an assessment of the prototypes through reflections.

5.1 Snoopy

As an example of the anthropomorphic preference (F4) of users, we prototyped the design of P2, an actuating desk toy as a break reminder (Fig. 4). We stuffed a 10 cm high snoopy plush toy with Shape-Memory Alloy (SMA) springs connected to a MOSFET powered Arduino microcontroller, hidden in the base. Snoopy collapses down when it is time for a break silently and slowly every 60 min.

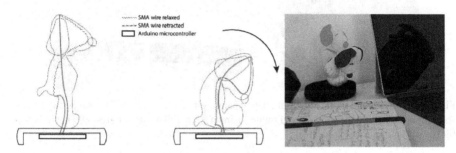

Fig. 4. Snoopy: the interactive desk break-reminder from P2 is a fabric toy that collapses when it is time for a break and deforms its body using sewn SMA wires.

Our goal was to control its shape-change without motors to keep free of audible notifications (F1), due to social barriers in shared workplace. We used SMA wires to deform the body of this object was to make it silent (F1), slow (F3) and subtle, moving in their periphery but not rather distracting (F2). We purposely used a plush snoopy toy rather than a rigid-material model to utilize its softness, furry texture and material affordance in supporting its playfulness (F4), emotional engagement (F5) and caregiving motivation (F6) that would have been somewhat lost or reduced had it been a 2D or rigid figurine. Moreover, the organic twist deformation of the body caused by the fabric stitched with SMA wires accounts to the negative impact of continuous work without breaks and visualizes its entangled consequence (F8).

As much as the creating a shape-changing Snoopy might seem frivolous, more than half of our participants expressed the need for an emotional connection with the object, to strengthen their chances of listening to its suggestion without being annoyed (F5). P2—who already had a Snoopy toy on their desk—wanted to repurpose it to serve as their break-reminder (F10). The incorporation of interactive technology within users' favourite objects reflects and supports their personal preference (F13). We housed the electronics underneath Snoopy—not beside—to save some desk space (F10).

5.2 ShyFrame

As an example of planer desk frames, we prototyped the design of P9, a monitor-mount frame-like break-reminder. To allow the ShyFrame to rotate, appear and hide silently (F1) and slowly (F3) behind the digital display, we used a silent TOKI RC1 motor made of SMA wire. To maintain scale, we used the smallest off-the-shelf Adafruit Trinket 5V mini microcontroller (F11) to control the motor with a USB cable from the user's computer. The challenge of the ShyFrame was to use light-weight materials that can be easily mounted behind the monitor with a magnet and can be moved by the low pull-force of the SMA motor every 60 min (Fig. 5).

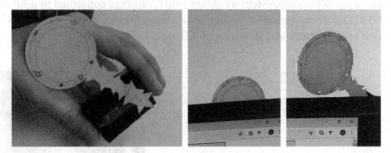

Fig. 5. ShyFrame: the monitor-mount shape-changing break-reminder of P9 saves scarce desk space. It hides behind the monitor and rotates using a silent SMA motor to reveal when it is time for the working user to take a break.

We specifically chose colourful cardboard similar to the user's design (F13) to support aesthetic values (F12) and reflect the *gradual* shape-shifting behaviour (F3), as opposed to a solid colour material. We then laser-cut the material with a design of a star-shaped frame and arm to support delightfulness (F4) and express positivity (F7).

The localized actuation meant that (almost) only the user on this desk could take notice of the slow motion. The choice of the SMA motor meant that the shape-change is not only silent (unlike the sound-producing servo-motors), but is also rotational, moving in a controlled angular path. Although it is using the monitor as its space to consume no desk space (F10), it is not hindering their work productivity (F2) as other desktop break-reminding applications that freeze the monitor for instance.

5.3 Luna

As an example of 3D abstract desk objects, we prototyped the design of P6, a physical artifact that has an emerging light on top. We used a clear flexible resin to 3D print the cylindrical object in dimensions 10×10 cm. We used a servo motor using a gear and a shaft to control the height of the illuminating top section. Inside the body of Luna, an Adafruit Metro Mini microcontroller controls both the motion and an RGB LED for the light. We used a translucent breadboard to avoid obscuring the light and placed all electronic components inside with a connected USB cable to powers the circuit from the user's computer (Fig. 6). The light started from blue and transitioning very subtly to green, yellow, then red (time to take action, i.e., a break) every 60 min.

The light reflection design decisions (using clear acrylic, clear resin, minimal-sized microcontrollers and clear breadboard) to make it calmer (F1), ambient and less distracting (F2). Additionally, the slow (F3) gradual RGB degrade defused the LED light, supporting self-reflection by visualizing the consequences (F8) and physicalizing the state-change (F7). The red light is intentionally not alerting but is still soft, ambient and diffused by the thickness of the 3D design, as interactive break-reminders should not

Fig. 6. Luna: 3D-printed shape-changing desk object as P6's design with an emerging light that moves up slowly and changes its ambient light as break time approaches (Color figure online).

standout (F2), a bright emissive flashing light would have been too focus-demanding. Also, we chose light colours to give the design both emotional associations (F5) and dynamic aesthetics (F12). Moreover, the slow motion (F3) of the "emerging" top part (at a rate of x mm/sec) does not require immediate attention but allows the user to shift their focus only when needed and when appropriate.

We incorporated P6's personal preference (F13) of the abstract cylindrical design with slight curves in the 3D model and the cyan colour using a 1 mm flexible foam sheet lining layer for the aesthetic appearance (F12). However, we note that this is an added object that takes desk space (F10, F11), compared to the other two prototypes.

6 Study 2: User Reflection

Taking our prototypes back to users who designed them, we reinterviewed P2, P6 and P9 to gather their impressions about our implementation of their prototype design, in the form of design crits. We held a 1-h virtual interview with each participant in the summer of 2020. Participants signed consent forms electronically and received $30 CAN eGift Cards as a compensation for their time. Three participants (1F, 2M) are in their 30s, all working around 8 h/day on computer desks (P2 and P9 in administration while P6 in the software industry).

After a brief introduction, we showed the 11 low-fidelity designed concepts and discussed their perceptions. Then, we demonstrated the actuation of the three high-fidelity prototypes built through a video and asked open-ended reflective questions. We audio-recorded the interviews and transcribed them for an iterative process of Thematic Analysis. We report our qualitative analysis by reporting cross-reflections (reflections of participants regarding the prototypes they did not design), and self-reflections (reflections on the implemented prototype designed by them).

6.1 Cross-Reflection

As we showed participants the other low-fidelity designs from Study 1, they reflected individually on other designs ideated by the rest of the participants. The predominance of desk toys in the Study 1 ideas generated particular reflections. They described Actuating desk toys as objects that "*play a role*" (P6), trigger laugh/smile (P9), serves decorative purposes and provides an "*emotional connection*" (P2). For instance, all participants described *Snoopy* as "cute" (F4). P6 explained that *"people need to like what they see on the desks for the object to have the right to remain among the objects that are important for everyday"* (F12). P2 also described this as *"you're keeping something there and you want to keep it happy. That will be helpful to... helping me in that way, I'm taking breaks and happiness, not like 'Oh, I have to break'... [Apps are] dictating to you, but these things are not dictating"* (F5).

Cross-reflection also touched on anthropomorphism—even for abstract objects- and caregiving as a resource for motivation (F6). P6 described Luna as *"a companion"* and P2 described Turbo *"like a virtual pet, you want to keep it alive"* and stated that *"there is kind of a reward... you made him happy or you saved him"* (F7). Alternatively, they also described care-receiving as a value of the ShyFrame *"it feels like it's a person... maybe it's your parent, who's coming out regularly, maybe somebody else that used to have played a role in your life, take care of you, reminding you, and you cannot be impatient to them"* (P6).

Participants also reflected on the variation in designs to meet different preferences (F13) and discussed how the favoured personalization features of such tangible break reminders are different from software customization of apps. For example, P2 said about the Turbo: *"it makes me feel that this thing is, uh, stopped because of me. So I should go away and come back so that it starts spinning again"*. However, some participants refrained from negative transformation (F8) while others noted the potential wear of novelty over time and procrastination (F9) including examples of the alarm clock's snooze button (P2, P6).

Evident in the data is the divergence of personal preference and that there is no one-size-fits-all design (F13). For example, P6 reflected on the *ShyFrame* (designed by P9) saying, *"This shy frame is very interesting. I think it's very cute,"* (F4) while P2 stated, *"Personally, I didn't like that... something rising from my screen... It's more to me, like a distraction came up."* Similarly, P2 reflected on Turbo (designed by P8) *"it will make me notice how it stopped... It's a good emotional connection"* (F5), while P9 said that it's *"so distracting for me... for me, it would be the other way around, like I would like it to be still and then just start to move when I need to take a break"*. Still, all participants expressed their interest in Luna and its design qualities.

6.2 Self-reflection

We asked each participant to reflect on the high-fidelity prototype based on their idea. P2 (who designed *Snoopy*) confirmed its size (F11) and actuation (F7) that in its physicalized form is their *"ideal thing"* and that *"The size's small. So that's really convenient to keep it. It's like a showpiece as well."* He also highlighted the fact that it does not hide or disappear from the periphery (F2) but *"is always there. So it's kind of a constant reminder"*. He also suggested some aesthetic and emotional actuations (F7, F12): *"there's more room to play with the eyes. That feature can be applicable to all these prototypes, which have a character like Snoopy or that toy or others."*

P6 (who designed Luna) praised the prototype saying, *"I still have the same type of excitement when I imagined that object a while ago... I think you guys captured very loyally... with a lot of detail, it's like a very close, super close to my description."* (F5). P6 praised the silent (F1) and slow (F3) movement as an additional user feedback (F7) on top of the light that conveys further information through its colour-change. P6 suggested some design features to be enhanced including thinner material and giving user-control over light brightness to accommodate for ambient conditions.

Finally, P9 (who designed ShyFrame) reflected on the prototype with delight, favouring it over all other designs describing its playfulness as *"something cute, that you could personalize"* (F4, F13) and size (F11). She confirmed the location (F10) and practicality of being monitor-mount to be ideal to grab her attention in her area of periphery (F2). She also elaborated on her positive thoughts of family or adventure photos (F5, F13) to be put in that frame, explaining *"when I see it I need to stop and I need to stretch... the fact that you can put a goal, put something really personal."* P9 recommended that the actuation to be in an exponential motion and start slow (F3) rather than linear with consistent speed. She also suggested some aesthetic changes (F12) including material qualities and polka dots decoration instead of stars.

7   Discussion

Through our 2 user studies with 11 participants who all live with Repetitive Strain Injury (RSI), we learnt about their daily challenges with break reminders. Most people avoid digital alerts and instead use physical objects as reminders to help them adopt a certain behaviour. By engaging them in user-centred design to make tangible break-reminders and analyzing what they created, we were able to draw appropriated design decisions for implementing high-fidelity tangible break-reminders that unfold their needs. Taking these implemented interactive prototypes back to our participants in Study 2 enabled deeper understanding and insight on their design critique reflection. Our hope is that this research would inspire designers engaging with actuating physical interfaces and elevate the discussion around tensions between what we as researchers create as prototypes and what users often ideate for themselves.

To deepen our analysis and discussion our findings, we collated the use of the 13 findings as implemented in the prototypes and correlated them with findings discussed in the second study, through self- and cross-reflections. Table 1 highlights that some findings were implemented and noticed by each participant (e.g., F3), while others were unique to some prototypes. This supports our choices of building three different prototypes. For instance, we find it interesting that while we designed Snoopy and Luna to produce an emotional engagement (F5), the participant who designed the concept of ShyFrame interpreted our prototype as being emotionally engaging. This table also clearly highlights that the finding of fading novelty was not integrated in the designed or discussed in the second study. A long term, in the wild study measuring use and engagement is necessary to address and assess this initial finding.

Our findings can be grouped as challenges (F1, F9, F11), preferences (F2, F3, F12, F13), and unspoken desires (F4, F5, F8) such as self-care (F6, F7). Overall, our participants found desk toys to be interesting as break-reminders (similar to BreakAway [12]) as opposed to computer-related objects (such as keyboard, mouse and pad). Limited desk space, hot-desking and home offices are a current reality that requires relatively small-sized interfaces. Participants also wanted designers to consider wall or monitor mounted devices: while the idea of monitor-mounted artifacts is not new [33], it could be

Table 1. Summary of findings implemented in the 3 prototypes. The circle (●) indicates a finding used in the prototype design (PD), the black square (■) when discussed in the self-reflection (SR), and the white square (□) when discussed in the cross-reflections (CR).

		Snoopy			ShyFrame			Luna		
		PD	SR	CR	PD	SR	CR	PD	SR	CR
F1	Disruption and social barriers	●	■		●	■		●	■	□
F2	Periphery and ambience	●	■	□	●	■	□	●	■	
F3	Slow interaction	●	■		●	■		●	■	
F4	Playfulness	●	■	□	●	■	□			□
F5	Emotional engagement	●	■	□		■		●	■	
F6	Motivation and care-giving	●	■			■	□			□
F7	Self-awareness	●	■		●	■	□	●	■	
F8	Visualizing consequences	●		□				●		
F9	Fading novelty			□	●				■	
F10	Constraints and multifunction	●	■	□	●	■			■	□
F11	Physical dimensions	●	■		●	■			■	
F12	Aesthetic qualities		■		●	■		●	■	□
F13	Personalization	●	■	□	●	■	□	●	■	□

further exploited by the HCI community. We also do note that two participants were not engaged with physical shape change, which strengthens the need for personalized break reminders (F13), whether physical or digital. Other aesthetic and design quality considerations should be considered by workplace designers and researchers to support user adoption of prototypes in situated deployments in shared spaces to avoid possible social barriers, particularly of importance to people who require break reminders because of their RSI. We acknowledge that some findings may feel contradictory: creating a playful desk toy when none exists opposes F4 and F10. However, these tradeoffs are part of designers' reflections when creating new objects or interactions [57].

Our paper presents first-hand lessons learned from people with RSI on how they want to design their break-reminders. The technical implementation of the interaction would not be innovative as there is enough knowledge in the community on how to build it differently if needed. Our focus on the 'design' stems from the research gap found where no prior work has involved people with RSI in designing their own break-reminders, yielding unprecedented insight and deeper knowledge on novel designs that people could benefit from away from mainstream and mass-produced apps and technologies.

Finally, we acknowledge the limitations of interviews in Study 2, both in their reflective nature as well as sample size, and plan for in-situ long-term deployments. As with such study design, our work is limited to the insights of our participants. Perhaps a richer dataset could have emerged from the involvement of RSI experts. However, our goal was not to evaluate between an approach based on the participatory design and another based on the involvement of more expert researchers, which is interesting but is out of scope. Our findings can serve as recommendations that designers may take into account when creating new break reminders for people with disabilities. Although some might perceive these findings as generic to claim relevance to RSI, our approach inherently unfolds a counter-argument. The quality and value of inclusive design lie in putting people with symptoms and their preferences in the centre of the design process and sincerely designing 'with' them. People increasingly do not want to look or feel alienated due to any symptoms they are living with. Therefore, such inclusivity-led research will support designing things they want to live with instead of gadgets, devices and dongles that are often designed 'for' them [58, 59].

8 Conclusion

This paper explores the opportunity of designing tangible everyday objects that can help users mitigate the impact of repetitive strain injury, by reminding them of taking breaks, maintaining good posture and incorporate regular movement during work. Unlike current technology that relies on immediate notifications to achieve this, slow and calm interactive physical objects on their desks can inform users without disrupting their work productivity. We engaged people living with RSI to design their own tangible break-reminders and interviewed each of them to gain deeper knowledge of their challenges and aspirations. We implemented a representative subset of the design concepts, then conducted a second study with the same participants to allow them to reflect on their designs. Through our method of sandwiching the prototyping phase between two rigorous user studies, the design rationale of each prototype we made direct links to the findings of the first study.

Our study findings demonstrated how the interactive everyday objects that users wanted were not focused solely on the state transformation but included notions such as: the emotional engagement of cute and playful objects; the social barriers of owning some designs in a shared environment; visualizing the consequences of negative behaviour; motivating interaction and continuous use through values such as caregiving; and to the value of aesthetic design qualities. Future work will focus on an in-situ deployment of the prototypes to investigate the short term and long term adaption and effects of the tangible objects as reminders for people with RSI. We also look forward to expanding the concept of tangible object, to consider break reminders through the furniture itself, by studying shape-changing desks [39, 43, 60].

Acknowledgements. This work was supported and funded by the National Sciences and Engineering Research Council of Canada (NSERC) through Research and Education in Accessibility, Design, and Innovation (READi) CREATE Training Program (497303-2017), a Discovery Accelerator Supplement (2017-507935). It was also supported by the Royal Society – International Exchanges (ref. IES\R2\170109).

References

1. Mullaly, J., Grigg, L.: RSI: integrating the major theories. Aust. J. Psychol. **40**, 19–33 (1988). https://doi.org/10.1080/00049538808259066
2. Buckle, P.W., Jason Devereux, J.: The nature of work-related neck and upper limb musculoskeletal disorders. Appl. Ergon. **33**(3), 207–271 (2002). https://doi.org/10.1016/S0003-6870(02)00014-5
3. Peper, E., Gibney, K.H., Wilson, V.E.: Group training with healthy computing practices to prevent repetitive strain injury (RSI): a preliminary study. Appl. Psychophysiol. Biofeedback **29**, 279–287 (2004). https://doi.org/10.1007/s10484-004-0388-z
4. Bailey, B.P., Konstan, J.A.: On the need for attention-aware systems: measuring effects of interruption on task performance, error rate, and affective state. Comput. Hum. Behav. **22**, 685–708 (2006). https://doi.org/10.1016/j.chb.2005.12.009
5. Finsen, L., Søgaard, K., Christensen, H.: Influence of memory demand and contra lateral activity on muscle activity. J. Electromyogr. Kinesiol. **11**, 373–380 (2001). https://doi.org/10.1016/S1050-6411(01)00015-3
6. Leclerc, A., Landre, M.F., Chastang, J.F., Niedhammer, I., Roquelaure, Y.: Upper-limb disorders in repetitive work. Scand. J. Work. Environ. Heal. **27**, 268–278 (2001). https://doi.org/10.5271/sjweh.614
7. Christensen, H., Lundberg, U.: Musculoskeletal problems as a result of work organization, work tasks and stress during computer work. Work Stress. **16**, 89–93 (2002). https://doi.org/10.1080/02678370213265
8. Birch, L., Juul-Kristensen, B., Jensen, C., Finsen, L., Christensen, H.: Acute response to precision, time pressure and mental demand during simulated computer work. Scand. J. Work. Environ. Heal. **26**, 299–305 (2000). https://doi.org/10.5271/sjweh.546
9. Henning, R.A., Jacques, P., Kissel, G.V., Sullivan, A.B., Alteras-Webb, S.M.: Frequent short rest breaks from computer work: effects on productivity and well-being at two field sites. Ergonomics **40**, 78–91 (1997). https://doi.org/10.1080/001401397188396
10. Slijper, H.P., Richter, J.M., Smeets, J.B.J., Frens, M.A.: The effects of pause software on the temporal characteristics of computer use. Ergonomics **50**, 178–191 (2007). https://doi.org/10.1080/00140130601049410
11. Gomes, A., Nesbitt, A., Vertegaal, R.: MorePhone: a study of actuated shape deformations for flexible thin-film smartphone notifications. In: Proceedings of the SIGCHI Conference on Human Factors in Computing Systems – CHI 2013,. pp. 583–592. ACM Press, New York, New York, USA (2013). https://doi.org/10.1145/2470654.2470737
12. Jafarinaimi, N., Forlizzi, J., Hurst, A., Zimmerman, J.: Breakaway: an ambient display designed to change human behavior. In: Berlin, L. (ed.) The Man Behind the Microchip, pp. 82–96. Oxford University Press (2007). https://doi.org/10.1093/acprof:oso/9780195163438.003.0005
13. Jones, L., McClelland, J., Thongsouksanoumane, P., Girouard, A.: Ambient notifications with shape changing circuits in peripheral locations. In: Proceedings of the 2017 ACM International Conference on Interactive Surfaces and Spaces, ISS 2017 (2017). https://doi.org/10.1145/3132272.3132291
14. Kucharski, P., et al.: APEOW: a personal persuasive avatar for encouraging breaks in office work. In: 2016 Federated Conference on Computer Science and Information Systems (FedCSIS), pp. 1627–1630 (2016)
15. National Health Services: Repetitive strain injury (RSI). https://www.nhs.uk/conditions/repetitive-strain-injury-rsi/. Accessed 23 Jan 2021
16. Kryger, A.I.: Does computer use pose an occupational hazard for forearm pain; from the NUDATA study. Occup. Environ. Med. **60**, 14e–14 (2003). https://doi.org/10.1136/oem.60.11.e14

17. Fogleman, M., Brogmus, G.: Computer mouse use and cumulative trauma disorders of the upper extremities. Ergonomics **38**, 2465–2475 (1995). https://doi.org/10.1080/001401395089 25280
18. Nieuwenhuijsen, E.R.: Health behavior change among office workers: an exploratory study to prevent repetitive strain injuries. Work **23**, 215–224 (2004)
19. Barredo, R.D.V., Mahon, K.: The effects of exercise and rest breaks on musculoskeletal discomfort during computer tasks: an evidence-based perspective. J. Phys. Ther. Sci. **19**, 151–163 (2007). https://doi.org/10.1589/jpts.19.151
20. Balci, R., Aghazadeh, F.: Effects of exercise breaks on performance, muscular load, and perceived discomfort in data entry and cognitive tasks. Comput. Ind. Eng. **46**, 399–411 (2004). https://doi.org/10.1016/j.cie.2004.01.003
21. McLean, L., Tingley, M., Scott, R.N., Rickards, J.: Computer terminal work and the benefit of microbreaks. Appl. Ergon. **32**, 225–237 (2001). https://doi.org/10.1016/S0003-6870(00)000 71-5
22. Czerwinski, M., Horvitz, E., Wilhite, S.: A diary study of task switching and interruptions. In: Conference on Human Factors in Computing Systems – Proceedings, pp. 175–182 (2004). https://doi.org/10.1145/985692.985715
23. Iqbal, S.T., Horvitz, E.: Disruption and recovery of computing tasks: Field study, analysis, and directions. In: Conference on Human Factors in Computing Systems – Proceedings, pp. 677–686 (2007). https://doi.org/10.1145/1240624.1240730
24. Morris, D., Brush, J.B., Meyers, B.R.: SuperBreak: using interactivity to enhance ergonomic typing breaks. In: Conference on Human Factors in Computing Systems – Proceedings, pp. 1817–1826 (2008). https://doi.org/10.1145/1357054.1357337
25. Van Dantzig, S., Geleijnse, G., Van Halteren, A.T.: Toward a persuasive mobile application to reduce sedentary behavior. Pers. Ubiquitous Comput. **17**, 1237–1246 (2013). https://doi.org/10.1007/s00779-012-0588-0
26. Lee, K., Ju, S., Dzhoroev, T., Goh, G., Lee, M., Park, Y.: DayClo : an everyday table clock providing interaction with personal schedule data for self-reflection. In: Proceedings of DIS 2020, pp. 1793–1806. ACM (2020)
27. Roudaut, A., Karnik, A., Löchtefeld, M., Subramanian, S.: Morphees: toward high "shape resolution" in self-actuated flexible mobile devices. In: Proceedings of the SIGCHI Conference on Human Factors in Computing Systems – CHI 2013, p. 593. ACM Press, New York, USA (2013). https://doi.org/10.1145/2470654.2470738
28. Kim, H., Coutrix, C., Roudaut, A.: Morphees+: studying everyday reconfigurable objects for the design and taxonomy of reconfigurable UIS. In: Conference on Human Factors in Computing Systems — Proceedings (2018). https://doi.org/10.1145/3173574.3174193
29. Alexander, J., et al.: Grand challenges in shape-changing interface research. In: Proceedings of the 2018 CHI Conference on Human Factors in Computing Systems, pp. 1–14. ACM, New York, NY, USA (2018). https://doi.org/10.1145/3173574.3173873
30. Ishii, H., Lakatos, D., Bonanni, L., Labrune, J.-B.: Radical atoms: beyond tangible bits, toward transformable materials. Interactions **19**(1), 38–51 (2012). https://doi.org/10.1145/2065327.2065337
31. Holman, D., Vertegaal, R.: Organic user interfaces: Designing computers in any way, shape, or form. Commun. ACM **51**, 48–55 (2008). https://doi.org/10.1145/1349026.1349037
32. Rasmussen, M.K., Pedersen, E.W., Petersen, M.G., Hornbæk, K.: Shape-changing interfaces: a review of the design space and open research questions. Proceedings of the 2012 ACM Annual Conference on Human Factors in Computing Systems. CHI 2012, pp. 735–744 (2012). https://doi.org/10.1145/2207676.2207781
33. Probst, K., Yasu, K., Seifried, T., Sugimoto, M., Haller, M., Inami, M.: Move-it: interactive sticky notes actuated by shape memory alloys. In: Conference on Human Factors in Computing Systems — Proceedings (2011). https://doi.org/10.1145/1979742.1979780

34. Roy, M., Hemmert, F., Wettach, R.: Living interfaces: the intimate door lock. In: Proceedings of the 3rd International Conference on Tangible and Embedded Interaction, TEI 2009, pp. 45–46 (2009). https://doi.org/10.1145/1517664.1517681

35. Kobayashi, K.: Shape changing device for notification. In: Proceedings of the Adjunct Publication of the 26th Annual ACM Symposium on User Interface Software and Technology, pp. 71–72 (2013)

36. Hemmert, F., Hamann, S., Löwe, M., Zeipelt, J., Joost, G.: Shape-changing mobiles. In: Proceedings of the 28th International Conference on Extended Abstracts on Human factors in computing systems (CHI EA 2010), p. 3075 (2010). https://doi.org/10.1145/1753846.1753920.

37. Kim, S., Kim, H., Lee, B., Nam, T.-J., Lee, W.: Inflatable mouse: volume-adjustable mouse with air-pressure-sensitive input and haptic feedback. In: Proceeding of the Twenty-sixth Annual {SIGCHI} Conference on Human Factors in Computing Systems, pp. 211–224 (2008). https://doi.org/10.1145/1357054.1357090

38. Redström, J.: Designing everyday computational things. PhD Thesis. Gothenbg. Stud. Informatics. 244 (2001)

39. Grønbæk, J.E., Korsgaard, H., Petersen, M.G., Birk, M.H., Krogh, P.G.: Proxemic transitions: designing shape-changing furniture for informal meetings. In: Conference on Human Factors in Computing Systems – Proceedings, pp. 7029–7041., Denver, CO, USA (2017). https://doi.org/10.1145/3025453.3025487

40. Gaver, W., Bowers, J., Boucher, A., Law, A., Pennington, S., Villar, N.: The history tablecloth: illuminating domestic activity. In: Proceedings of the 2017 Conference on Designing Interactive Systems (DIS 2006), pp. 199–208. ACM (2006). https://doi.org/10.1145/1142405.1142437

41. Mennicken, S., Brush, A.J.J.B., Roseway, A., Scott, J.: Finding roles for interactive furniture in homes with EmotoCouch. In: UbiComp 2014 – Adjunct Proceedings of the 2014 ACM International Joint Conference on Pervasive and Ubiquitous Computing, pp. 923–930. Seattle, WA, USA (2014). https://doi.org/10.1145/2638728.2641547

42. Kinch, S., Groenvall, E., Graves Petersen, M., Kirkegaard Rasmussen, M.: Encounters on a shape-changing bench exploring atmospheres and social behaviour in situ. In: Proceedings of the 8th International Conference on Tangible, Embed. Embodied Interact, pp. 233–240 (2014). https://doi.org/10.1145/2540930.2540947

43. Shin, J.G., et al.: Slow robots for unobtrusive posture correction. In: Conference on Human Factors in Computing Systems – Proceedings, pp. 1–10 (2019). https://doi.org/10.1145/3290605.3300843

44. Ueki, A., Kamata, M., Inakage, M.: Tabby: designing of coexisting entertainment content in everyday life by expanding the design of furniture. In: Proceedings of the International Conference on Advances in Computer Entertainment Technology – ACE 2007,. pp. 72–78. ACM Press, Berlin, Germany (2007). https://doi.org/10.1145/1255047.1255062

45. Nabil, S., et al.: ActuEating: designing, studying and exploring actuating decorative artefacts. In: Proceedings of DIS 2018, pp. 327–339. Hong Kong (2018). https://doi.org/10.1145/3196709.3196761

46. Taylor, S., Robertson, S.: Digital Lace: a collision of responsive technologies. In: Proceedings of the 2014 ACM International Symposium on Wearable Computers (ISWC2014 Adjunct), pp. 93–97. ACM, New York (2014). https://doi.org/10.1145/2641248.2641280

47. Zhong, C., Wakkary, R., Zhang, X., Chen, A.Y.S.: TransTexture lamp: understanding lived experiences with deformation through a materiality lens. In: Conference on Human Factors in Computing Systems – Proceedings, pp. 1–13 (2020). https://doi.org/10.1145/3313831.3376721

48. Haller, M., et al.: Finding the right way for interrupting people to posture guidance. In: Proceedings of the 13th IFIP TC 13 International Conference on Human-computer Interaction, pp. 1–18 (2013)
49. QSR International: NVivo 12. https://www.qsrinternational.com/nvivo/nvivo-products/nvivo-12-windows (2019)
50. Dimitriadis, P., Alexander, J.: Evaluating the effectiveness of physical shape-change for in-pocket mobile device notifications. In: Conference on Human Factors in Computing Systems – Proceedings, pp. 2589–2592 (2014). https://doi.org/10.1145/2556288.2557164
51. Everitt, A., Alexander, J.: PolySurface: A design approach for rapid prototyping of shape-changing displays using semi-solid surfaces. In: DIS 2017 – Proceedings of the 2017 ACM Conference on Designing Interactive Systems, pp. 1283–1294 (2017). https://doi.org/10.1145/3064663.3064677
52. Braun, V., Clarke, V.: Thematic analysis. In: Cooper, H., Camic, P.M., Long, D.L., Panter, A.T., Rindskopf, D., Sher, K.J. (eds.) APA Handbook of Research Methods in Psychology, Vol 2: Research Designs: Quantitative, Qualitative, Neuropsychological, and Biological., pp. 57–71. American Psychological Association, Washington (2012). https://doi.org/10.1037/13620-004
53. Braun, V., Clarke, V.: Using thematic analysis in psychology. Qual. Res. Psychol. 3, 77–101 (2006). https://doi.org/10.1191/1478088706qp063oa
54. Preece, J., Sharp, H., Rogers, Y.: Interaction Design: Beyond Human-Computer Interaction, 4th edn. Wiley, USA (2015)
55. Wallace, J., McCarthy, J., Wright, P.C., Olivier, P.: Making design probes work. In: Proceedings of the SIGCHI Conference on Human Factors in Computing Systems, pp. 3441–3450. ACM, New York, NY, USA (2013). https://doi.org/10.1145/2470654.2466473
56. Pernice, K.: UX prototypes: low fidelity vs. high fidelity. https://www.nngroup.com/articles/ux-prototype-hi-lo-fidelity/. Accessed 21 Jan 2021
57. Jacob, R.J.K., et al.: Reality-based interaction: a framework for post-WIMP interfaces. In: Proceeding of the Twenty-Sixth Annual CHI Conference on Human factors in Computing Systems – CHI 2008, p. 201. ACM, New York, NY, USA (2008). https://doi.org/10.1145/1357054.1357089
58. Spiel, K., et al.: Nothing about us without us: Investigating the role of critical disability studies in HCI. In: In: Conference on Human Factors in Computing Systems – Proceedings, pp. 1–8 (2020). https://doi.org/10.1145/3334480.3375150
59. Mankoff, J., Hayes, G.R., Kasnitz, D.: Disability studies as a source of critical inquiry for the field of assistive technology. ASSETS 2010 – Proceedings of the 12th international ACM SIGACCESS conference on Computers and accessibility, pp. 3–10 (2010). https://doi.org/10.1145/1878803.1878807
60. Lee, B., Wu, S., Reyes, M., Saakes, D.: The effects of interruption timings on autonomous height-adjustable desks that respond to task changes. Conference on Human Factors in Computing Systems – Proceedings, pp. 1–10 (2019). https://doi.org/10.1145/3290605.3300558
61. Al Maimani, A., Roudaut, A.: Frozen suit: designing a changeable stiffness suit and its application to haptic games. In: Proceedings of the 2017 CHI Conference on Human Factors in Computing Systems, pp. 2440–2448 (2017)

Exploring User Requirements for an Exoskeleton Arm Insights from a User-Centered Study with People Living with Severe Paralysis

Frederik Victor Kobbelgaard[1]([⊠]) [iD], Anne Marie Kanstrup[1] [iD],
and Lotte N. S. Andreasen Struijk[2] [iD]

[1] Techno-Anthropology and Participation, Department of Planning, Aalborg University,
Aalborg, Denmark
frederik@plan.aau.dk

[2] Neurorehabilitation Robotics and Engineering, Center for Rehabilitation Robotics,
Department of Health Science and Technology, Aalborg University, Aalborg, Denmark

Abstract. It is recognised that assistive technology plays an active role in empowering individuals who live with severe paralysis. Exoskeleton (exo) technology is a promising emerging assistive technology—a wearable robot designed to support the functions of the human body. However, an exoskeleton is a complex technology, and the successful design of exoskeletons depends heavily on the ability to integrate this type of robot in the environments of future users. In this paper, we present insights into user requirements produced through a qualitative study involving adults living with one of the most severe forms of paralysis: tetraplegia, or paralysis from the neck down. The study is based on two iterations of interviews conducted in the homes of future users. The study identifies key user requirements and contextual factors that are important for user acceptance of future exo design. We discuss how to integrate these findings in the design of an exo prototype of an exoskeleton arm targeted at people living with tetraplegia.

Keywords: Exoskeleton · Participatory design · Assistive technologies · User-centered · Tetraplegia · Paralysis

1 Introduction

In this paper, we present the results from a design of human-robot interaction involving an exoskeleton arm targeted at people living with a severe form of paralysis called tetraplegia. An exoskeleton is an assistive technology in the form of a wearable robot designed to support the functions of the human body [13]. Exoskeleton technology has a great potential to rehabilitate and empower individuals who live with some sort of paralysis and therefore depend on caregivers in their daily lives. In the US alone, it was estimated in 2013 that around about 1.7% of Americans live with sort of paralysis

© IFIP International Federation for Information Processing 2021
Published by Springer Nature Switzerland AG 2021
C. Ardito et al. (Eds.): INTERACT 2021, LNCS 12932, pp. 312–320, 2021.
https://doi.org/10.1007/978-3-030-85623-6_19

[1] adding up to around 5.5 million people currently. Tetraplegia is one of the most severe forms of paralysis in all four limbs; however, its victims are usually unaffected cognitively, retaining full potential for education and work if they are only able to, e.g., open doors, control elevators, use computers, eat and drink. A study on selected Activities of Daily Life (ADLs), such as eating and drinking, has shown that the need for assistance could be reduced by up to 41% with the use of an assistive robotic arm [11], and a survey study shows that 86% of disabled participants would consider buying an assistive robotic arm if they could [15]. Further, a study has shown that individuals with complete functional paralysis of the arms and legs are capable of controlling such an assistive robotic arm using the tongue [16].

We present findings on user requirements for assistive robotics. The results are gathered through two iterations of interviews conducted with a total of nine participants, all living with tetraplegia. The ambition is to find an optimal integration between users' visions for robot assistance in their everyday lives and technological opportunities for advancing exo technology. Related research on the design of exoskeletons is primarily technology-driven and based largely on information about future users from Activities of Daily Life. ADLs refer to a clinical list of basic activities of daily living developed based on insights from clinicians and physicians. Hence, future users are primarily included by proxy in the design of exoskeletons [2, 3, 8, 9, 12]. A literature study conducted on the occurrence of user perspectives in exoskeleton technology research in 2017 [6] identified that among 912 articles identified as concerning exoskeleton technologies, only nine papers reported on user perspectives on exoskeleton development—only as far, however, as to state the importance of understanding users. No papers reported on actual user involvement in the design. However, a scoping review found instances of research studies stating that they were either human- or user-centred. Some of these studies involved users by the use of questionnaires, though often without a clear distinction between caregiver and patient [8, 9] and some with a very broad target user group [4]. Additionally, some existing studies report the use of interviews, both with individuals and groups. However, they rarely do so with end users (i.e. people who are paralysed) but with experts (health care professionals) and their perspectives on users' needs [2, 12, 14]. While some papers do focus on the specific context of use and values of the users that are to be designed for [4, 5, 10], the daily lives of the individual end users and the existing technological ecologies employed by the users seem to get lost in previously ascertained notions of building for ADLs.

2 Methods

The recruitment of participants for this study was carried out in collaboration with the Spinal Cord Injury Centre of Western Denmark. The participants recruited for the study were between the ages of 32 and 77. All the participants lived with tetraplegia, albeit with differing degrees of paralysis. Two participants had partial control of their arms, and one was able to stand using a specialised support, though only for brief periods at a time. Because of these abilities, their paralysis is defined as incomplete, although functionally they are still unable to conduct activities requiring even little strength. All but one of the participants interviewed used specialised powered wheelchairs on which several different technologies were mounted. The housing situations for the participants varied. Two of the participants lived in specialised disability housing that was designed for people with physical limitations. One participant lived in a first-floor apartment. The rest of the participants lived in standard housing that had been altered slightly to accommodate their needs. All participants had 24-h personal caregiving, either entirely provided by their municipality or supported by spouses and family. However, all waking hours were covered by professional caregivers. The participants would never be left on their own and always have help available.

2.1 Home Interviews

Two iterations of home interviews were conducted with the participants. The first interviews were based on design games and focused on attaining an understanding of the users' lives, experiences with paralysis, technologies employed and daily activities. The design game that was created for the interviews revolved around a list of activities that each participant would create and prioritise based on activities they carry out during a normal day. Each activity was mapped in relation to assistive technologies and caregivers before being reimagined by the participants to learn about their visions for future scenarios of everyday life with a fully functioning exo arm. The second iteration were based on feedback for a preliminary version of the tongue controlled exoskeleton arm, EXOTIC [17] and zoomed in on the activities prioritised by the participants in the first home interviews. Participants were asked to create timelines for the activities discussed, draw the space in which the activities were currently carried out, and list positive attributes that the arm should possess and negative aspects that should be considered in the design of a future exo arm. For a further explanation of the visual aids and the methodology used, see [7].

3 Results

During the interviews and the design games, a number of different activities (n = 45), artefacts (n = 69), assistants (n = 8) and contextual factors (n = 54) were identified. While the users identified a long list of activities, they agreed on six activities that should be prioritised most highly. These activities were consistently mentioned and prioritised throughout the different interviews. The six activities that the participants prioritised were eating, drinking, itching, reading, brushing teeth and shaving, each of which is described in the following.

Eating was described by the participants as an important activity. However, in contrast to general presentations of eating as an ADL, the participants in this study did not focus on the act of eating a meal as something they would like to have improved. Rather, they focused on the activity of eating as part of a cosy moment defining the activity of eating as being able to eat candy or other snacks over a longer period while, e.g., watching a movie. Independence was not related to being able to have a meal. As explained by one of the participants, "A meal is on the plate as it is and is eaten in a specific tempo, but when you have a bowl of candy, then you will have to keep saying; one more, one more, one more, one more". Another participant explained, "It would be very nice if, at *night, when sitting in front of the television, I could sit and nip at something on my own. That would be a great freedom, to not always have to call and ask for another piece of liquorice".* One participant presented previous experience with an eating robot: *"I think it could be hard. I mean it would be nice to be able to eat on my own, to be able to pick up the pieces, but that machine just grabbed it randomly and then it was cut into pieces like dog food, and that is not fun, that is not a good thing".* Drinking was an equally important activity for the participants. Currently, only a few participants were able to drink by themselves, and they all emphasised that a future use of the exoskeleton arm should be focused on supporting users to be able to drink by themselves. For example, one participant presented the following: *"...and then during the evening with a little glass of red wine so I can sip myself. Especially being with others, drinking, then it is nice to be able to drink on your own."* Another participant described, *"none of us will ever lift anything heavy, it is more to be able to grab a cup of coffee, eat and so on, to me at least, that is important".*

The participants also stated that they were at times annoyed by the lack of ability to scratch themselves when itching. Some participants stated that they believed that they had more itching now than before suffering their paralysis, and that this could be due to medical side effects or imagined itching due to the inability to do anything to mediate it independently. As one participant stated, *"Apparently there are some specific areas on the scalp that are very irritated, I do not know if it is because of medicine or damage to the nerves, but on the scalp it itches so much sometimes".*

Reading was also an important activity that the participants wished could be changed for the better. The participants currently read with the help of their private caregivers, and conversations on possible futures identified a strong wish to not only be able to turn pages themselves, but also that they would be able to fetch some reading materials themselves. As one participant stated, *"...I mean, it would be nice, or an advantage to be able to turn pages in books and newspapers, that is a big wish of mine so I don't have to say all the time: I would like to have the page turned, I would like to have the page turned".* And further, *"...I constantly have to have it fetched, it would be nice to have an arm so one could go over and fetch a magazine and place it".*

An activity that several of the participants also prioritised was the act of grooming, where especially shaving and brushing one's teeth was mentioned. As both of these are activities in which most people have a specific preference as to how it should be done, most participants found it important, or at least desirable, to be able to do these actions by themselves. As one participant stated, *"That with brushing teeth, I can acknowledge that, it is one of the hardest tasks for a caregiver. I have grown a full beard in the process because I realised that it was a challenge to get shaved. I mean I had my own way of shaving, and to have others do it, aaaaaaah, so in the end I gave up and thought that then I was past that problem. Of course, then you have to have it trimmed. But I believe that I have found the best solution for me."* Another participant explains, *"...you could say that those things are very basic things, they occur daily, you brush your teeth twice a day I mean. And it is not good when you have to have another person brushing your teeth and shaving you, because it will never be done the way you want it to be (...) the helpers do their best and it is not on purpose, but it would be nice to be able to do these things yourself".*

In sum, the conversations about present and future activities and artefacts revealed that the participants imagined several activities that an exo arm solution could support them in for future independent living. However, they devoted strong attention to details with, e.g., cosy moments with snacks and wine, grooming, reading and being able to react to itching.

Several activities were discussed during the game but ultimately not deemed important or, at least, less prioritised by the participants as activities to be supported by the future exoskeleton solution. Some of those activities were brewing coffee, using a recreational tabletop bike, printing, opening doors and using a computer. Common to these activities was that most of them were not entirely doable autonomously in the future scenarios. That is, the users could not envision that a future exoskeleton solution would give them independence in completing the activities. Other activities were mentioned that, despite being highly desirable to the participants, could be solved by other existing technologies in a more meaningful or efficient manner, such as doors being opened by electronic door openers. The second round of interviews qualified the findings and gave insights into a deeper contextual understanding of users' design wishes and the use context for an exo arm. The attributes that the future users found important are listed in Table 1. Generally, the attributes that the users found to be important revolve around the look and feel of the future solution. Moreover, most of the mentioned attributes had either been discussed explicitly during the first round of interviews or had, at the very least, been mentioned earlier in the process. Thus, these findings qualified and deepened the results from the first iteration. However, the act of listing them—categorising and visualising the positives and negatives—brought forth some new attributes, such as sharp edges and a wish for the arm to be smaller around the wrist and forearm. In the following sections, the contextual insights and important attributes uncovered throughout the interviews are covered.

Table 1. List of positive and negative attributes that users identified as important to consider in the design of an exo arm

Positive attributes	Negative attributes
Flexibility	Noisy
Small	Robot-like movements
Light	Chunky looking
Smaller at wrist and forearm	Sharp edges
Fast mounting	Requires charge
Must work around the face	Effect on wheelchair battery
Usable in wheelchair	Can be uncomfortable
Can fit clothing underneath	Mounted on wheelchair
Harmonic movements	Should not only have one interfacing option
Can be cleaned	Over-steering
Secure grip	

The home interviews also identified contextual factors. These were especially related to the appearance and functionality of an exoskeleton arm. Regarding statements made by the participants about the design of the exoskeleton arm, most of the participants argued that the most important focus for the development of an exoskeleton arm is functionality. A few of the participants called for close attention to the aesthetics of the exoskeleton design. However, all participants highlighted that the arm should be designed in a manner that makes it as discrete as possible, i.e., none of the participants preferred a "chunky" arm or an arm that makes a lot of noise, as that would draw too much attention in public and make them feel stigmatised. Lastly, the participants stated that the arm should be simple, easily cleaned and require as little time as possible to mount. Due to changing caregivers and the long time spent on getting in and out of bed, this point was emphasised strongly.

Besides appearance and functionality, a lot of information surfaced about the users' lives in general and how they manage a life that is different from that of most people during the home interviews. First and foremost, all the participants that were interviewed identified their own role within their context as that of a manager, employing, scheduling and managing employees in a manner similar to a small company. This was also apparent in the houses in which the users resided, where specific rooms—and in one case, the entire second floor—are dedicated as space for the employees to relax and rest. Secondly, we found that it is not just the wants and needs of the users that decide the success of an assistive technology; it is also a cost-effective assessment made by the municipality in which the users reside as to what technologies can lessen the cost of care. Some participants shared that they had made requests for economic support for electronic door openers that would allow them to move from one room to another on their own. This was denied in all cases, as the participants already had economic support for caregivers who could do this task. Thus, the independence provided by assistive technology like an exo arm will be an important part of the calculation for implementing this future technology in the homes of people living with tetraplegia.

4   Discussion

4.1   Six Key Activities

The analysis has outlined a larger set of activities, among which six activities stand out as user priorities for a future exoskeleton arm. Although activities such as drinking and eating are certainly basic activities of daily life and thereby affirm the choice of using ADLs as a platform upon which to design exoskeleton technologies—as they are sometimes seen in the literature [2, 3, 8, 9, 12]—entirely relying on ADLs would neglect some important insights that we discovered in this paper, such as the different notions and contextual insights into what eating entails. Further, this could mean that the design would not allow for activities such as itching and reading, both of which were highly prioritised by the participants of this study.

In all the prioritised activities, the overall motivation from the users was to attain agency and further their own autonomy and independence. They want to be able to shave in the manner that they prefer. They want to be able to brush their teeth in the manner that they find most comfortable, and perhaps most of all, they want to be able to do repetitive activities without having to ask for help repeatedly, such as eating candy when watching the television at night and reading on their own without having to ask for the pages to be turned. All the activities that were prioritised stood out, as they all entirely replaced the involvement of caregivers with the utility of an exoskeleton arm, indicating that the participants envisioned that the arm should, to the highest degree possible, enable them to independently conduct an activity rather than complement how it is completed today.

The majority of the activities mentioned during the interviews, including the ones that were chosen for further examination, are acted out in a workspace in close proximity to the face of the user. An implication of this is that special attention needs to be paid to the safety of the movements that the arm can make. Furthermore, the participants stated that the mounting of the arm should be both simple and require little time, which is important to the actual use of a future exoskeleton arm—if it is too complicated and time-consuming to mount, there is a strong risk that the arm will not be used, as caregivers will have to prioritise other tasks. Other important findings show that the participants in this study prioritised the functionality of the arm, with a secondary focus on the aesthetics of the final product. The participants want an exoskeleton arm that is as discreet as possible and where functionality and size is balanced towards being able to perform small activities rather than being able to lift heavy loads. Furthermore, emphasis was placed on a wish that the arm is to be as silent as possible and that it should be moving smoothly and as human-like as possible. As an implication of the insights produced, and building upon a users expressions in a previous study [16], it has become evident that careful considerations must be made in regards to meet users' expectations.

Whilst the participants engaged in this study prioritised ADLs, the study expanded the understanding and nuances of the activities. An example is when designing for eating, this should be focused more on snacks that can be picked up independently rather than dinners. The prioritisation of ADLs that the users shared in the study is important, not only in the exo-design itself, but also in the design of clinical tests used for evalutation, in which one of the selected by our research team on the EXOTIC exoskeleton is to grasp plastic strawberries to test the capabilities of the arm.

4.2 Limitations and Future Research

This study was conducted in Denmark, which employs a tax-based and need-based health care and social welfare system. All participants in the study had 24 h of support from this healthcare system, which is likely to have influenced the types of activities that they prioritised. Therefore, it is likely that similar user-centred research in other countries might give differing results. It is also important to note that the insights described in this paper are based on nine interviews, only one of which was with a woman, which might eliminate some gender-based insights that could have been extracted. Why we were unable to attain more female participants can only be speculated. However, as the pool of potential participants that are eligible for the study was extremely limited, the issue has proven very tough to overcome. Additionally, the study did not include caregivers and family members, which we have learned to be instrumental in the participants' lives and the activities they carry out throughout the day. Further, as discussed in the analysis, decision makers in the public care system play a vital role in relation to the participants' technological possibilities. Their opinion is therefore relevant to understanding the larger ecology for an exo arm, i.e., the care systems requirements for an exoskeleton arm.

Lastly, during the interviews, some participants stated that they were anxious about the adoption of the exoskeleton arm, as this might decrease the amount of professional caregiving received by the municipality, which all participants stated that they would not be able to function without. This might have influenced the manner in which the participants thought of and prioritised tasks, which further adds to the notion that decision makers within the municipalities could have been included in the discussions.

5 Conclusion

This paper has presented insights gathered through two iterations of user involvement focused on investigating and integrating users' contextual expertise in the design of future exo technology to support people living with severe paralysis. The results highlight that users identify activities in which they can regain full autonomy and activities that they deemed to be frustrating or invasive. Although this paper does not give a conclusive answer to which activities exoskeleton developers should design for, it identified six situations from the participants' everyday lives that they prioritised as the most important, unfolding the contextual factors related to these activities and how we have worked with integrating these findings in the design of an exo prototype. The findings demonstrate that involving users, in this case individuals living with severe paralysis, and employing their contextual expertise when designing complex technical solutions such as exoskeleton technologies can help to ground the design in the actual context that is being designed for. Further, the paper presented a number of specific design decisions that should be regarded in relation to both the aesthetics and functionality of upper-body exoskeleton solutions. Details of importance are the identification of the facial area as the primary workspace for the interaction and that non-functional requirements, such as the aesthetics, mounting, sound and size of an exoskeleton arm, are key for user acceptance.

Acknowledgements. This work is part of the EXOTIC project at Aalborg. We would like to thank our collaborators on the project: Mikkel Thøgersen, Stefan Bengtson, Mostafa Mohammadi and Muhammad Ahsan Gull. Further, we would like to thank the participants who contributed and collaborated with us in order to create the insights reflected in the article. Finally, we thank the Spinal Cord Injury Centre of Western Denmark for assistance with recruitment and their expertise.

References

1. Armour, B., Courtney-Long, E., Fox, M., Fredine, H., Cahill, A.: Prevalence and causes of paralysis—United States, 2013. Am. J. Public Health **106**(10), 1855–1857 (2016). https://doi.org/10.2105/AJPH.2016.303270
2. Beckerle, P.: Human-Machine-Centered Design and Actuation of Lower Limb Prosthetic Systems (2014)
3. Christ, O., Beckerle, P.: Towards active lower limb prosthetic systems: design issues and solutions. Biomed. Eng. Online **15**(S3), 139 (2016). https://doi.org/10.1186/s12938-016-0283-x

4. Christ, O., et al.: User-centered prosthetic development: comprehension of Amputees' needs. Biomed. Eng./Biomed. Tech. **57**(SI-1 Track-R), 1098–1101 (2012). https://doi.org/10.1515/bmt-2012-4306
5. Ding, D., Cooper, R.A., Pearlman, J.: In: International Conference on Engineering Education – ICEE 2007 Incorporating Participatory Action Design into Research and Education (2007)
6. Hill, D., Holloway, C., Ramirez, D., Smitham, P., Pappas, Y.: What are user perspectives of exoskeleton technology? A literature review. Int. J. Technol. Assess. Health Care **33**(2), 160–167 (2017). https://doi.org/10.1017/S0266462317000460
7. Kobbelgaard, F.V., Kanstrup, A.M., Bødker, S.: Designing a game to explore human artefact ecologies for assistive robotics – basing design games on an activity theoretical framework. In: Proceedings of the 11th Nordic Conference on Human-Computer Interaction—Shaping Experiences, Shaping Society, Tallinn, Estonia (2020)
8. Krishnaswamy, K.: Participatory design: repositioning, transferring, and personal care robots. In: HRI 2017: Proceedings of the Companion of the 2017 ACM/IEEE International Conference on Human–Robot Interaction, pp. 351–352 (2017)
9. Krishnaswamy, K., Moorthy, S., Oates, T.: Preliminary survey analysis in participatory design: repositioning, transferring, and personal care robots. In: HRI 2017: Proceedings of the Companion of the 2017 ACM/IEEE International Conference on Human–Robot Interaction, pp. 171–172 (2017)
10. Lynn, J.D., Armstrong, E., Martin, S.: User Requirements in Multimodal System Design and Robotics. In: Ibáñez, J., González-Vargas, J., Azorín, J.M., Akay, M., Pons, J.L. (eds.) Converging Clinical and Engineering Research on Neurorehabilitation II. BB, vol. 15, pp. 1193–1197. Springer, Cham (2017). https://doi.org/10.1007/978-3-319-46669-9_194
11. Maheu, V., Frappier, J., Archambault, P.S., Routhier, F.: Evaluation of the JACO robotic arm: clinico-economic study for powered wheelchair users with upper-extremity disabilities. In: 2011 IEEE International Conference on Rehabilitation Robotics, Zurich, June 2011, pp. 1–5 (2011)
12. Pedrocchi, A.: MUNDUS project: multimodal neuroprosthesis for daily upper limb support. J. Neuroeng. Rehabil. **10**(1), 66 (2013). https://doi.org/10.1186/1743-0003-10-66
13. Pons, J.L. (ed.): Wearable Robots: Biomechatronic Exoskeletons. Wiley (2008)
14. Power, V., et al.: Exploring User Requirements for a Lower Body Soft Exoskeleton to Assist Mobility (2016)
15. Prior, S.D.: An electric wheelchair mounted robotic arm—a survey of potential users. J. Med. Eng. Technol. **14**(4), 143–154 (1990)
16. Andreasen, L., Struijk, L., Egsgaard, R., Gaihede, M., Bentsen, B.: Wireless intraoral tongue control of an assistive robotic arm for individuals with tetraplegia. J. Neuroeng. Rehabil. **14**, 110 (2017). https://doi.org/10.1186/s12984-017-0330-2
17. Thøgersen, M., Gull, M.A., Kobbelgaard, F.V., Mohammadi, M., Bengston, S.H., Struijk, L.N.S.A.: EXOTIC—a discreet user-based 5 DoF upper-limb exoskeleton for individuals with tetraplegia. In: 2020 3rd International Conference on Mechatronics, Robotics and Automation (ICMRA), pp. 79–83. (2020)

Interactive Modular Tactile Maps of Rooms for Older Adults with Vision Impairments

Miroslav Macik[✉], Tomas Ivanic, and Lukas Treml

Faculty of Electrical Engineering, Czech Technical University in Prague,
Prague, Czech Republic
macikmir@fel.cvut.cz

Abstract. We present an interactive modular tactile map tailored for
older adults with vision impairments, which should help them acquire
spatial knowledge of rooms and their inner equipment. As the outcome of
our iterative design process, we introduced a design concept that employs
skeuomorphic interactive tactile objects that can be placed on a modular
interactive tactile map to resemble real rooms. Qualitative evaluation
(mean age was 81.5 years) indicates our concept's ability to help our
audience build spatial knowledge of rooms and their equipment.

Keywords: Orientation · Tactile maps · Visually impaired · Older
adults

1 Introduction

According to [2] the prevalence of blindness is globally 0.48%, and 2.95% of
the world population deals with moderate to severe vision impairment. The
majority of visually impaired people appear among older adults, as 52.9% of
visually impaired people are older than 70.

Unfortunately, the research attention on older adults with visual impairment
(*VIOA*) is limited. We have analyzed 48 papers focusing on people with VI presented at the last three CHI conferences (2016–2019). When excluding studies
focused mainly on children and young adults, the average age of study participants was 37,3 years (weighted average, sample sizes as weights). Hence, the
current research focus is on VI people is biased in favor of the younger part of
the population.

User research conducted in a specialized residential care facility for *VIOA* [15]
showed that orientation and mobility training is a long and complicated process. This training starts in the client's room, and other locations and routes
are included after the client masters the orientation around his/her room
independently.

© IFIP International Federation for Information Processing 2021
Published by Springer Nature Switzerland AG 2021
C. Ardito et al. (Eds.): INTERACT 2021, LNCS 12932, pp. 321–330, 2021.
https://doi.org/10.1007/978-3-030-85623-6_20

In our previous research, we focused on developing solutions to support orientation in space tailored to the needs and preferences of visually impaired older adults [9,15,19]. It indicated that needs, abilities, and preferences of *VIOA* might differ significantly from the younger and more active part of the community of those challenged with vision impairments, especially when the onset of impairment was recent and at a higher age.

In this paper, we present a method and three generations of related prototypes that primarily aim to help create cognitive map of the environment at the level of detail corresponding to a room. Interactive modular tactile maps of rooms represent room layout and internal equipment like furniture, sinks, toilet, etc. Modular design allows modeling different spatial environments. Multi-modal interaction method involving touch, voice output (audio labels), and visual output allows efficient creation of a cognitive map of the environment for *VIOA*.

2   Related Work

Montello [20] defines spatial cognition as the study of knowledge and beliefs about spatial objects and events worldwide. Term cognitive map refers to internally represented spatial models of the environment [21] which contain knowledge of landmarks, route connections, and distance and direction relations, nonspatial attributes [20]. Fazzi et al. [8] presents methods to teach Orientation and Mobility, including teaching strategies and materials.

According to O'Keefe [17], cognitive maps include at least two types of representations: specific routes to reach some target point in space and more general topographical representation that can be used for inferring shortcuts or alternative pathways. This knowledge can be acquired directly in the environment or by using external representations of the environment like topographic maps.

According to [4,11] maps are two-dimensional, projective, small-scale representations of an environment, presented from an allocentric perspective. People with VI traditionally use tactile maps as a powerful tool for acquiring spatial information [7,22]. Unlike classical maps, tactile maps allow only sequential acquirement of information. As a consequence, they have higher demands on memory.

Jacobson [14] presents a comparative study that showed the efficacy of audio-tactile maps for cognitive map accuracy. Similar results can be found in [7] where tactile maps served as the best means of gaining spatial knowledge. The efficacy of the reading may depend on the chosen scanning strategy. Ungar [22] states that more systematic strategies are better.

Witntjes, in his study [24] identified three strategies used by people with VI for exploration of tactile images: using one hand; using both hands, while a single hand moves and the other hand rests on the image (bimanual strategy); and using both hands simultaneously. Several studies like [12,24] indicate that bimanual strategy is the most effective.

According to [4], using multiple modalities can break down the complexity of communicated information. In [10,13] authors discuss the usage of interactive audio labels, which avoid the necessity to memorize the legend. Various types of gestures can be implemented to activate the labels, e.g., tap, double-tap (examined in [4]), but the sensitivity must be set correctly, not to trigger the audio events too often, and provide clear feedback, as mentioned in [4,10]. Brito in [3] employs conductive filament printed on an image. As the 3D-printed object is touched, the corresponding audio is played to help the user to recognize the object.

Analysis of the related work shows that tactile maps are an effective means to create and improve cognitive maps of environment [7,14], especially when involving multimodal interactivity [3,4,10,13]. However, there is a lack of research focused on suitable methods for *VIOA*.

3   Initial Design - Low-Fidelity Prototype

The design requirements stem from our previous research in a residential care home for *VIOA* [9,19] and from a literature survey. The spatial orientation is essential for the target user audience of *VIOA*. Our previous work focused on creating a cognitive map of the spatial environment on a scale of building floor [19] and support of orientation while traveling indoors [9]. In this paper, we support spatial orientation of *VIOA* by helping the creation of a cognitive map of the indoor environment on a level corresponding to rooms and their equipment.

We set the following design requirements: *1) Modular design:* The artifact enables representing indoor space of different size and layout by means of modules that can be attached to each other. *2) Multi-modal interactivity:* Interactivity by means of touch and audio labels. *2) Skeuomorphism* [6,18]: The interactive objects on the tactile map will resemble their real-world counterparts by shape, texture, or even materials.

Fig. 1. Reference room (left) and Initial design Low-Fidelity prototype (right)

We propose an interactive modular tactile map that represents the indoor environment. It can represent a room (or few rooms when needed) and interior objects, including furniture and equipment like sinks, toilets, or even inner walls. The 3D map elements that represent the objects are easily recognizable by touch as it is a promising direction for VI users [3,23], especially the older adults [9].

As depicted in Fig. 1, the initial design consisted of a board with a matrix of 15 × 15 holes and handcrafted tactile modules. This early prototype was not modular. Its primary purpose was to enable fast evaluation of the concept with representatives of the target user audience. For this prototype, the projection ratio was 20:1.

3.1 Evaluation

The purpose of the evaluation was to get insights into the artifact's efficacy to create a cognitive map of the environment in *VIOA*. Furthermore, we observed the interaction with the interactive tactile room map to evaluate the interaction method and detect the method's potential usability issues. The relatively low number of participants was determined by complicated methods to reach such a specific user group and correspondingly high costs per participant. More information about choosing sample size for a hard-to-reach user audience can be found in [1,5]. The recruitment and execution of all experiments were under the supervision of the special housing authorities.

Table 1. Participants of Low-Fidelity prototype (P1–P5) and High-Fidelity prototype (P6–P12) evaluation.

Participant	Age/Gender	VI category	Impairment onset	In institution
P1	91/F	4	1.5 years	1.5 years
P2	82/F	4	2 years	3 months
P3	83/F	5	60 years	1 month
P4	86/F	4	8 years	6 months
P5	82/F	4	20 years	9 years
P6	52/M	5	27 years	8 years
P7	82/F	4	20 years	9 years
P8	70/M	4	8 years	7 years
P9	89/M	5	6 years	6 years
P10	95/F	3	7 years	6.5 years
P11	75/M	3	9 years	6 months
P12	91/F	4	10 years	4 years

Participants. We recruited five participants (P1–P5, all women, age $MEAN = 84.8$, $SD = 3.83$, $MIN = 82$, $MAX = 90$), representatives of our target user group, they were recruited from residential care institution we cooperate with. Demographic data about the participants are in Table 1.

Procedure. For the experiment, we created all necessary tactile board elements to represent objects in a reference room see Fig. 1. We presented a scenario of a fictive visit to a friend's room to the participant. Before the actual visit, the client will use the tactile board to learn the layout of objects in the room to be visited. The experiment consisted of four phases: *1) Exploration of objects 2) Learning of the room layout. 3) Object finding and distance estimation. 4) Cognitive map – reconstruction from memory.*

Results and Discussion. The physical dimensions of the tactile map enable using booth hands for exploring the represented room. Participants explored the model firstly around the perimeter of the map. They proceeded systematically from the entry door in either direction. Activation of audio labels by pressing the objects was easy to discover and comprehend by all participants. Participants commented in favor of audio labels. However, only P1, P3, P5 activated the audio labels automatically for each discovered object.

The participants recognized most objects. However, the bedside table (recognized by P1, P4), obstacles on high-walls (identified by P1, P2), and the table (none) were hard to recognize. We estimate that the participants did not recognize the table because of confusion caused by its small size compared with a chair. During the exploration, participants described the details of individual objects. A combination of different materials might improve recognizability, i.e., P5 replied, *"Because it has (textile) duvet and pillow."* The evaluation indicates that the tactile map concept represented by the Low-Fidelity prototype is understandable for the target user audience.

4 Basic High-Fidelity Prototype

In comparison to the initial design, this High-Fidelity prototype consisted of modules as depicted in Fig. 2. There were nine modules, each with 16 holes (4×4). A matrix keyboard and micro-controller (ATTiny 48) were embedded into each module. All modules were connected to allow communication with a PC. This technical solution enabled the detection of a press of any contact of any of the nine modules (144 contacts in total). Detected presses trigger audio labels with information about the pressed object. The projection ratio is 80:3, the distance between two holes is 1.5 cm that reflects 40 cm in reality.

4.1 Evaluation

Participants. We recruited seven participants (P6–P12, 4 women, age $MEAN = 77.7$, $SD = 14.0$, $MIN = 52$, $MAX = 95$), representatives of our target user group, they were recruited from residential care institution we cooperate with. Demographic data about the participants are in Table 1.

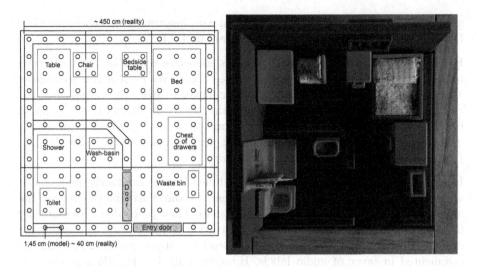

Fig. 2. Basic High-Fidelity prototype – Interactive modular tactile map of rooms

Procedure. The test procedure was similar as for evaluation of initial design, but the first phase (Exploration of objects) was omitted to test whether this phase is necessary. The objects were from the beginning of the experiment placed on the tactile map in the layout of a reference room with inner walls.

Results and Dicussion. There were issues with the recognizability of some objects, mainly those with distinct holes. The water sink was recognized only by P9 and P11. P7 noted, *"Water sink? I could not have guessed"*, P12 noted, *"Isn't that a lamp?"*. Also, objects that have too varying real-world forms were not well recognized. I.e., waste bin. P8 noted, *"I have never seen rectangular waste bin."*

The observation of participants indicated a possible issue with paying attention to long audio labels of objects. The participants did not listen to the full description for some objects and continued by pressing another object. Some participants (P8, P10, P11) also missed the beginning of some audio labels containing information about what kind of object was pressed.

The experiment indicated that modeling more rooms on one tactile map is possible. However, P6, P7 experienced issues with the bedroom's mental projection to the rear left corner of the main room. P8 recognized the inner wall as part of the equipment. After removing the object that represented doors, it was difficult for all the participants to show entrance doors and doors to transit between inner rooms.

Evaluation of the High-Fidelity prototype indicated that the general concept is usable. We showed that the tactile map could create a cognitive map in *VIOA*. Most participants (P6, P7, P8, P10, P11) were after the interactive session able to describe the layout of the represented rooms and inner objects from their cognitive map. However, only P10 and P11 described routes between two objects without any error. We estimate that the primary reason was that the High-Fidelity prototype represented the room with higher layout complexity.

5   Advanced High-Fidelity Prototype

Advanced High-Fidelity Prototype is depicted in Fig. 3. We tried to address issues exposed by evaluation of the previous prototype. New modules have dimensions 75×75 mm. Each module contains 25 holes (5×5) with push buttons on PCB inside the module. Moreover, 25 (grid 5×5) individually addressable

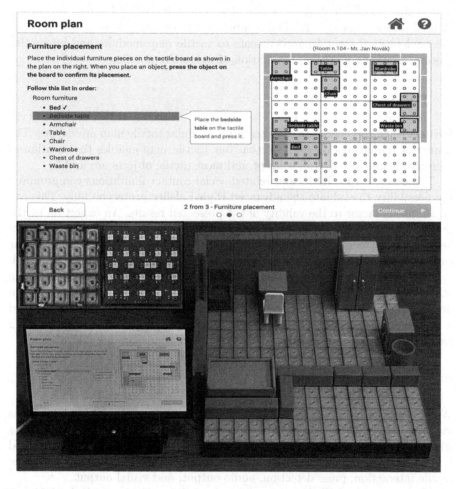

Fig. 3. Advanced High-Fidelity prototype. The user interface of support application for preparation of the tactile map (top). The latest prototype of the modular tactile map (bottom). Module printed combination of translucent and opaque materials and PCB with push buttons and addressable RGB LEDs (left).

RGB LEDs are integrated into each module. The seamless mechanical connection of modules is assured using embedded magnets. Magnets are also used to connect outer walls to the tactile map. The data connection between modules is newly implemented using a chained serial link. This design enables the detection of any push-button press in any hole of any module in the chain.

From the interaction perspective, each module contains negative grooves to help with distance estimation. Outer and inner walls have equidistant pins that correspond to holes in modules. Their purpose is to improve the estimation of distances and make them distinctive from objects objects.

The development of the Advanced High-Fidelity Prototype is currently in progress. The onset of COVID-19 prevented us from contact evaluation with representatives of *VIOA*. A VI expert, that is part of the development team commented and evaluated individual components during the development process. We implemented several improvements to tactile map modules and interactive objects, including a new representation of waste bin or toilet.

6   Discussion

We created three generations of interactive modular tactile map prototypes. The results of the evaluation indicate that our tactile map enables the creation of cognitive maps. The overall concept and most tactile objects are usable.

The onset of COVID-19 and related social-contact limitations compromised the possibility to evaluate the advanced High-Fidelity prototype fully. This can be a limiting factor to the validity of the presented results. An expert on tactile graphics with vision impairment is part of the development team. His comments helped assess the quality of individual prototype components and improve the chance that the prototypes will be usable for the target user audience of *VIOA*.

The community could use tactile exploration with audio-visual feedback in other scenarios related to education and entertainment of those with vision impairments. An example is teaching Braille script where modules connected a row let crating writing exercise book. Also, it is possible to simulate typing using different kinds of Braille typewriters, i.e., Perkins Brailler [16].

7   Conclusion and Future Work

We proposed mapping an indoor environment into a modular interactive tactile map tailored for *VIOA*. We focused on designing interactive objects representing standard equipment of rooms, mainly various kinds of furniture. We introduced a new modular hardware platform to be used in multiple scenarios involving tactile interaction, press detection, audio output, and visual output.

The onset of COVID-19 pandemics limited the evaluation with the *VIOA* as representatives of the target user audience. The health and ethical concerns did not allow in-person evaluation of the advanced High-Fidelity prototype.

It is the subject of future work to evaluate the prototype with the target user audience. We expect the community to use the modular platform in other scenarios to support various tasks related to the education and training of individuals with vision impairments, including those with remaining sight.

Acknowledgments. This research has been supported by the TACR project Proo-Fond (TP01010066) and by research program TE01020415 and the project RCI (reg. no. CZ.02.1.01/0.0/0.0/16_019/0000765) supported by EU.

References

1. Bacchetti, P., Deeks, S.G., McCune, S.G.: Breaking free of sample size dogma to perform innovative translational research. Sci. Transl. Med. **3**(87), 87ps24-87ps24 (2011)
2. Bourne, R.R.A., et al.: Magnitude, temporal trends, and projections of the global prevalence of blindness and distance and near vision impairment: a systematic review and meta-analysis. Lancet Glob. Health **5**(9), e888–e897 (2017)
3. Brito, C., Barros, G., Correia, W., Teichrieb, V., Teixeira, J.M. (eds.): Multimodal augmentation of surfaces using conductive 3D printing. Multimodal augmentation of surfaces using conductive 3D printing. In: ACM SIGGRAPH 2016 Posters, p. 15. ACM (2016)
4. Brock, A.M., Truillet, P., Oriola, B., Picard, D., Jouffrais, C.: Interactivity improves usability of geographic maps for visually impaired people. Hum. Comput. Inter. **30**(2), 156–194 (2015)
5. Caine, K.: Local standards for sample size at CHI. In: Proceedings of the 2016 CHI Conference on Human Factors in Computing Systems, pp. 981–992 (2016)
6. Cho, M., Kwon, S., Na, N., Suk, H.-J., Lee, K.: The elders preference for skeuomorphism as app icon style. In: Proceedings of the 33rd Annual ACM Conference Extended Abstracts on Human Factors in Computing Systems, pp. 899–904 (2015)
7. Espinosa, M.A., Ochaita, E.: Using tactile maps to improve the practical spatial knowledge of adults who are blind. J. Vis. Impair. Blindness **92**(5), 338–345 (1998)
8. Fazzi, D.L., Petersmeyer, B.A.: Imagining the possibilities: Creative approaches to orientation and mobility instruction for persons who are visually impaired. American Foundation for the Blind (2001)
9. Gintner, V., Macik, M., Mikovec, Z.: Perception of tactile symbols by visually impaired older adults. In: Lamas, D., Loizides, F., Nacke, L., Petrie, H., Winckler, M., Zaphiris, P. (eds.) INTERACT 2019, Part I. LNCS, vol. 11746, pp. 325–334. Springer, Cham (2019). https://doi.org/10.1007/978-3-030-29381-9_20
10. Giraud, S., Brock, A.M., Macé, M.J.-M., Jouffrais, C.: Map learning with a 3D printed interactive small-scale model: improvement of space and text memorization in visually impaired students. Front. Psychol. **8**, 930 (2017)
11. Hatwell, Y., Martinez-Sarrochi, F.: The tactile reading of maps and drawings, and the access of blind people to works of art. In: Touching for Knowing: Cognitive Psychology of Haptic Manual Perception, vol. 53, p. 255 (2003)
12. Heller, M.A.: Picture and pattern perception in the sighted and the blind: the advantage of the late blind. Perception **18**(3), 379–389 (1989)
13. Holloway, L., Marriott, K., Butler, M.: Accessible maps for the blind: comparing 3d printed models with tactile graphics. In: Proceedings of the 2018 CHI Conference on Human Factors in Computing Systems, p. 198. ACM (2018)

14. Dan Jacobson, R.: Cognitive mapping without sight: four preliminary studies of spatial learning. J. Environ. Psychol. **18**(3), 289–306 (1998)
15. Macik, M., Maly, I., Balata, J., Mikovec, Z.: How can ICT help the visually impaired older adults in residential care institutions: the everyday needs survey. In: 2017 8th IEEE International Conference on Cognitive Infocommunications (CogInfoCom), pp. 000157–000164. IEEE (2017)
16. Nicolau, H., Guerreiro, J., Guerreiro, T., Carriço, L.: UbiBraille: designing and evaluating a vibrotactile Braille-reading device. In: Proceedings of the 15th International ACM SIGACCESS Conference on Computers and Accessibility, pp. 1–8 (2013)
17. O'keefe, J., Nadel, L.: The Hippocampus as a Cognitive Map. Clarendon Press, Oxford (1978)
18. Page, T.: Skeuomorphism or flat design: future directions in mobile device User Interface (UI) design education. Int. J. Mob. Learn. Organ. **8**(2), 130–142 (2014)
19. Palivcová, D., Macík, M., Míkovec, Z.: Interactive tactile map as a tool for building spatial knowledge of visually impaired older adults. In: Extended Abstracts of the 2020 CHI Conference on Human Factors in Computing Systems, pp. 1–9 (2020)
20. Smelser, N.J., Baltes, P.B.: International Encyclopedia of the Social and Behavioral Sciences, vol. 11. Elsevier, Amsterdam (2001)
21. Tolman, E.C.: Cognitive maps in rats and men. Psychol. Rev. **55**(4), 189 (1948)
22. Ungar, S., Blades, M., Spencer, C.: The role of tactile maps in mobility training. Br. J. Vis. Impair. **11**(2), 59–61 (1993)
23. Voigt, A., Martens, B.: Development of 3D tactile models for the partially sighted to facilitate spatial orientation (2006)
24. Wijntjes, M.W.A., Van Lienen, T., Verstijnen, I.M., Kappers, A.M.L.: The influence of picture size on recognition and exploratory behaviour in raised-line drawings. Perception **37**(4), 602–614 (2008)

Recommendations for the Development of a Robotic Drinking and Eating Aid - An Ethnographic Study

Max Pascher[1,2]([✉]) [iD], Annalies Baumeister[3], Stefan Schneegass[2] [iD],
Barbara Klein[3], and Jens Gerken[1]

[1] Westphalian University of Applied Sciences, Gelsenkirchen, Germany
max.pascher@w-hs.de
[2] University of Duisburg-Essen, Essen, Germany
[3] Frankfurt University of Applied Sciences, Frankfurt am Main, Germany

Abstract. Being able to live independently and self-determined in one's own home is a crucial factor or human dignity and preservation of self-worth. For people with severe physical impairments who cannot use their limbs for every day tasks, living in their own home is only possible with assistance from others. The inability to move arms and hands makes it hard to take care of oneself, e.g. drinking and eating independently. In this paper, we investigate how 15 participants with disabilities consume food and drinks. We report on interviews, participatory observations, and analyzed the aids they currently use. Based on our findings, we derive a set of recommendations that supports researchers and practitioners in designing future robotic drinking and eating aids for people with disabilities.

Keywords: Assisted living technologies · Human-centered computing · Meal assistance · Participation design · People with disabilities · Robot assistive drinking · Robot assistive feeding · User acceptance · User-centered design · User participation

1 Introduction

At the end of 2019, 7.9 million people classed as severely disabled were living in Germany [47]. With over 58% of these cases being attributed to physical disabilities, motor impairments affected an total of 4.6 million people; 11.2% of which are suffering from impaired functionality to a complete loss of motor control of their extremities. Additionally a further 10.4% were also affected by impairments in the spinal and torso region.

© IFIP International Federation for Information Processing 2021
Published by Springer Nature Switzerland AG 2021
C. Ardito et al. (Eds.): INTERACT 2021, LNCS 12932, pp. 331–351, 2021.
https://doi.org/10.1007/978-3-030-85623-6_21

(a) Filling a glass of water   (b) Grasping a glass to drink

Fig. 1. Robotic arms can support users with motor impairments in their everyday drinking and eating task. We explore how such systems should be designed to provide a benefit to the users and support them in living a self-determined life.

Functional loss of the use of extremities can be caused by upper spinal cord trauma and degenerative diseases. Those afflicted are struggling, or are simply unable, to perform every day tasks independently of others. One very prominent area is the one of nutrition. Being self-sufficient in terms of being in control of food and water intake is not only beneficial to ones health but also immensely important for ones self-worth [30].

Assistive technologies are increasingly becoming a vital factor in the field of assisted living; minimising the need for constant care and allowing people with motor impairments to regain some independence [35]. Initial studies by Klein [24] and Merkel and Kurcharski [34] indicated that assistive technology often meets non-acceptance and non-use and propose that devices need to focus more on the needs and preferences of the target group. Using a participatory approach integrating future users in the developing progress is recommended to promote a higher acceptance of the final product [50].

We conducted an ethnographic study in this work to shed light on how users envision future systems supporting them with everyday drinking and eating tasks. We interviewed 15 users with motor impairments, presented a robotic aid as a potential assistive system, and conducted in-situ observations of their drinking and eating behavior and used tools. We gained significant insight into user opinions and derived recommendations regarding structural, social, and collaborative concerns of future assistive systems like a robotic drinking aid (cf., Fig. 1. These recommendations will help designers and engineers in a technology-focused domain to build systems that actually help people.

2   Related Work

Traditionally the focus in the field of developing assistive technologies has been on functionality from an engineering point of view. Recent findings however highlight the need to include future users and their perceived needs in the design process [26]. In this section we first examine previous work done on concepts of user participation and collaborative approaches. In a second step, we present projects that already analysed the use of robotic devices to support people with disabilities and how these aids are valued by their users.

2.1 User Needs

In recent years, there has been growing interest in the concept of user participation in the design of new assistive technologies. Groundwork laid by Thielke et al. [48] and Merkel and Kucharski [34] expressed the need for this collaborated approach to maximize user acceptance. They indicated various methods for integrating the user group as well as family, caregivers and assistants into the innovation process. Focus groups, qualitative interviews, visits of the primary users' homes, and participant observation can provide significant insights into the needs and wants of the user group. The recommendation for this participatory approach that integrates the future users in the developing progress is also noted by Frennert and Östlund [17] and Eftring and Frennert [13], confirming the findings by Klein and Merkel and Kurcharski.

During the development of a robotic therapy support system, Duckworth et al. used three different methods to include the future users preferences into their work [12]. Clinicians and patients were interviewed, given a questionnaire concerning the design of a robotic therapy support system and had the opportunity to use the developed robot during counselling sessions. They came to the conclusion that a participatory design provides essential information for the development of assistive technology and increases the chance of a positive user experience.

Using a similar approach, Mandy et al. conducted a qualitative study with users of the *Neater Eater* to gain an in-depth understanding of their user experience [29]. They report that self-feeding devices increase the life quality of people with disabilities significantly and support a more equal relationship between those who are in need of care and their carers. They stress the need of a positive approach towards assistive technologies for a wide general acceptance.

2.2 Human-Robot Collaboration in the Field of Supporting People with Disabilities

Robotic solutions can make a significant contribution to regaining independence and improving care by supporting and relieving caregivers, thus improving the quality of life of those in need of support [5].

A growing body of literature has examined the impact of assistive robotic systems in supporting people with motor disabilities. Work done by Chen et al. [9] for the *Robots for Humanity* project and Fattal et al. [14] looked into the feasibility and acceptance of robotic systems as assistive technologies. A common finding was that the robotic devices are often designed to assist with several activities of daily living. These devices are usually large; consisting of a robotic arm on a mobile module. They require a barrier-free environment and rooms with sufficient space to fit into and be able to move around safely. In contrast,

Pascher et al. noted the potential of smaller, lightweight solutions designed for individual tasks [36], indicating that a specialized aid would be more accessible in terms of size and portability.

Research by Gallenberger et al. used camera and machine learning for an autonomous robotic feeding system to detect types of food items present and to plan the picking-up and transportation to the mouth of the user [18]. An alternative approach is presented by Canal et al. describing a learning-by-demonstration framework to feed the user [8]. Both projects ensure the ability of the robotic arm to fulfill its autonomous tasks without any fine-control of the user focusing on the technical aspects of the development process of assistive technology.

A 2019 study by Beaudoin et al. focused on the long-term use of the robotic arm JACO [4], a recent advance in assistive technologies. They researched improvements of everyday task capabilities, satisfaction with JACO, psychological impact and the implications for users and their caregivers using a similar quantitative approach as employed in this study. Beaudoin et al. reported that almost all participants gained more autonomy in certain life aspects and experienced a number of positive psycho-social impacts. One such success was the increased capability of participants to drink independently of human support using JACO, thus reducing the amount of care and attention needed and increasing well-being and overall health by having a continuous access to beverages.

Interaction technologies such as gaze-based interaction and head movement have been explored to operate, e.g. a PC [11,38,40] and a robot [22,41,45]. Alternatively, brain-computer interfaces were used to control a robotic arm [1]. However, today's ubiquitous technology interaction scenarios are much more tightly integrated in everyday activities and require different interaction interfaces [28].

3   Study

The goal of this work is to understand users' requirements and demands of assistive technology that supports them with drinking and eating. For this, we conducted an ethnographic study consisting of an interview including a VR presentation of a robotic support system and in-situ participatory observations of their drinking and eating habits, with 15 participants afflicted by a varying degree of motor impairments.

3.1   Participants

In preparation for the main study, we opted to evaluate our methods with a pilot participant allowing us to adapt the study design before approaching the remaining participants. Participants were chosen in collaboration with the *Center for Paraplegic Patients Hamburg*, the *Locked-in-Syndrom e.V. Berlin*, and the *State Association of the German Society for Multiple Sclerosis Hessen e.V.* We recruited 15 participants with a permanent and significant degree of compromised mobility of the extremities and the reliance on support for the consumption of food and drinks. Table 1 presents the participants split by gender, age, and diagnosis. 4 female and 11 male participants took part in the main study; the mean age was 42.07 years (SD = 16.68) and all were categorized as severely disabled.

Table 1. Overview of the pilot and main study participants

ID	Gender	Age	Diagnosis
Pilot	Female	60	Multiple sclerosis
P1	Male	18	Spinal cord injury; incomplete at level C3
P2	Male	46	Spinal cord injury; complete at level C4 & some rudimentary mobility until level C5
P3	Male	41	Spinal cord injury; incomplete at level C3 (right body-side has some mobility until level C5)
P4	Male	30	Spinal cord injury; incomplete at level C3
P5	Female	62	Locked-in syndrom
P6	Male	50	Spinal cord injury; incomplete at level C4
P7	Male	38	Spinal cord injury; incomplete at level C3 & complete at level C5
P8	Male	30	Spinal cord injury; complete at level C3
P9	Male	22	Spinal cord injury; complete from level C3 to C7
P10	Male	48	Spinal cord injury; complete at level C4 & C5
P11	Female	60	Multiple sclerosis
P12	Male	50	Inclusion body myositis
P13	Female	51	Locked-in syndrom
P14	Male	34	Spinal cord injury; complete at level C5 & C6
P15	Female	51	Arthrogryposis

3.2 Procedure

Each session took place in the participants' homes which allowed us to conduct the interview, observation of drinking and eating habits as well as analysis of commonly used aids in a natural setting. In most of the cases a caregiver or assistant was present.

Interview. Due to the nature of the physical impairments faced by the participants, obtaining their consent had to be adapted to their particular capabilities. After reading or listening to a researcher reading the consent form, participants signed the form by themselves or had their spoken agreement recorded. In other cases, an authorized caregiver signed the form on behalf of the participant.

The interview part was structured in four sections; each focusing on a different aspect detailing their living situation, attitudes regarding drinking and eating, level of assistance needed as well as wishes towards an ideal robotic aid. In the first part we aimed to understand their current living situation by establishing how many hours they spend in their wheelchair, where they spend most of the time, and where they eat and drink at home.

Next, we were interested in their value propositions and preferences regarding drinking and eating. The participants were asked to describe a typical mealtime routine, what they generally consume, and which preparations are needed.

Further, we wanted to know if drinking and eating is seen as a necessary task or can also convey enjoyment. Participants were also asked if they consume food and drinks if they are not at home (at work, in a restaurant).

The third step focused on the process of drinking and eating in an assistive setting including the communication with their caregivers/assistants and any improvised aids used.

In the final step of the session, we focused on the use of a proposed robotic arm as a drinking and eating aid. To familiarize participants with the concept they were shown images of different eating support systems and wheelchair-extension-type robotic arms that are already on the market, e.g. iEat [3], Obi [10], JACO [23], and iArm [2]. To simulate the situation of sitting in front of an actual robotic arm performing tasks in a close-contact environment we used Google Cardboard [20] and a stereoscopic video of our in-lab robot setting. Conducting the interviews in the participants' homes made this lightweight solution necessary. Figure 2 shows the robotic arm bringing a glass of water to the user's face (in this case simulated by the camera lens). To further the realism of the situation, participants were able to experience the actual sounds of the robotic aid by simultaneously listening to an audio recording.

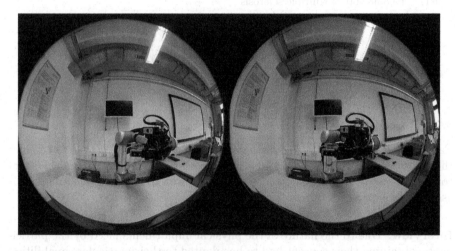

Fig. 2. Stereoscopic video in a first-person perspective of sitting in front of a robotic arm performing tasks in a close-contact environment

Following this experience we inquired about the participants' perception of the robotic aid including their likes and dislikes of the simulation and any changes they would appreciate from an end-user perspective. We encouraged them to express wishful thinking without worrying about current technological capabilities. We were also interested in how the participants would like to interact and collaborate with the robot. Special interest concerned the preferred location of attachment (e.g. table, wheelchair or self-mobile) and which additional functions should ideally be available.

Any additional thoughts, wishes, and suggestions of the participants were recorded for use in future research.

Participatory Observations. This part of the study focused on observing participants consume food and drinks (cf., Fig. 3) with the assistance of their caregiver. Observations of the relative location of the assistant, the methods used, and the communication between both parties were recorded. Depending on the specific type of impairment participants were either laying in their beds or sitting in their wheelchairs. Filming these interactions allowed for easy access during data analysis.

(a) Eating (front view)   (b) Eating (back view)

(c) Drinking with a straw   (d) Drinking with glass contact

Fig. 3. Observation of eating drinking habits together with their caregiver

Analysis of Commonly Used Aids. During the qualitative interviews we found that every study participant uses some kind of aid to facility food and drink consumption (cf., Fig. 4). In order to consume the necessary amount of fluids, tea and water are provided in teapots (cf., Fig. 4b) or in large dispensers (cf., Fig. 4c). Large dispensers contain enough beverages for all day without the need for re-filling by an assistant. We recorded images of these aids to increase our understanding of the help people need and want when confronted with tasks they cannot independently do anymore.

(a) Standard drinking straw for a glass of water

(b) Drinking straw/hose for warm and cold tea

(c) Filling glass with a dispenser

(d) Modification of machines (by adding parts)

(e) Self constructed bottle opener

(f) Portable cutlery set

(g) Hydro flask

(h) Mouth-stick rest

(i) Lifter

Fig. 4. Analyzed aids in the participants' homes which are currently used

3.3   Limitation of Our Study

The main target group of our study were people with quadriplegia caused by spinal cord injury. The noticeable skewed ratio of more male than female participants reflects statistic by the WHO [51] and German Federal Statistical Office (Destatis) [47] of a 2:1 male-to-female ratio for overall recorded spinal cord injuries worldwide [33]. Additionally, a higher number of women refused to take part in our study as they felt uncomfortable with the study design (e.g. getting filmed while eating and drinking).

Use of a Robotic Arm During the Study. One participant (P15) has rudimentary mobility functions in her lower right arm which allows her to use a joystick-controlled robotic arm for nearly every activity of daily living including consuming food and drinks, manipulating objects and basic hygiene. Figure 5 illustrates how she handles the tasks with her robotic arm.

(a) Drinking   (b) Eating

Fig. 5. Observation on the use of a robotic arm (JACO) for the consumption of food and drinks

4   Results and Recommendations

Based on the analysis of interviews, observations, and images we devised a set of user-centered design recommendations for a robotic drinking aid. Recommendations are split into three sections referring to structural, social and collaborative concerns respectively. All materials were transcribed, coded, and categorized independently by two researchers. We focus on processes related to drinking and eating, interactions between participants and caregivers, and additional topics of interest. All participants were interviewed as experts in their own right, as they can accurately describe and explain their situation, their abilities, limitations and needs. Therefore, our analysis method for the interviews and questionnaires followed the qualitative content analysis approach from Mayring [32]. Based on a predetermined interview guide established by the research team, questions belonging into different categories were discussed with study participants. Descriptive and normative statements concerning housing and living situation, individual wishes and needs regarding food and drink intake and attitude towards robotic aids were analysed [7]. The analysis of videos and images was based on the qualitative hermeneutical approach from social sciences by Reichertz and Englert [39] and the photo analysis by Pilarczyk and Mietzner [37]. In a first step, the videos and photos were cataloged according to content (e.g. drinking aid) and subject (e.g. drinking with a straw). Next, the videos were viewed, transcribed and coded. In a last step the photos were viewed again and theme-oriented photo series formed, e.g. photos showing self-made aids. Overall we conclude that photos provide additional information to the videos and interviews or can be used to better describe findings but do not provide much value as standalone objects.

4.1 Structural Concerns

Any design process starts with a structural framework defining size, weight and materials to be used. Whilst the choices might make sense from a purely technical point of view the preferences of the end-user should still be considered. Nobody benefits from the development of an assistive technologies that ends up too big in size to be used in the home of the typical end-user. With the aim being the widespread usage of the new device, taking wishes, where technically possible, regarding size and design into considerations can only be beneficial to future acceptance.

Dimensions of the Robotic Arm. Although all but one of the participants reported living in accessible housing, barriers including narrow hallways remain. During the in-home session we found several of the participants housings to be either too small for current robotic aids or lacking in space due to other large assistive devices present. Care beds and tables, lifters and wheelchairs are essential to support people with disabilities living in their own homes. Adding another large-size device taking up space can be problematic and in some cases impossible.

P10: "There is a second wheelchair somewhere, then maybe there is a bed-side table somewhere, and there is a lifter somewhere and the shower chair somewhere. (...) At some point, many run out of space."

Recommendation 1

A robotic drinking aid should be primarily designed for saving space. The arm has to have the ability to fold itself during waiting/suspended-mode. And include the possibility of space-saving storage when not in use.

Physical Attachment. Types of suitable attachment methods vary depending on individual preferences, type of wheelchair used, and space availability in the participants' homes. Frequent changes between user location (bedroom/living room and bed/wheelchair) is a further factor to consider. Some participants use a chin-controlled electronic wheelchair. This poses an additional challenge for possible attachment methods and hinders both control and movement of the robot during the drinking and eating process because the joystick is in this case directly in front of the mouth.

P13: "It would be great to be able to fix the arm to the table with a small screw clamp. (...) Adding it to the wheelchair might be good too. But in any case it must be easy to dismantle."

Recommendation 2

Different mounting options for the robotic arm have to be available to allow attachment to different surfaces and care devices including mobility aides, resting chairs or overbed/side tables. Special consideration has to be given to the restrictions imposed by types of wheelchairs used.

4.2 Social Concerns

The advantage of an interdisciplinary approach as outlined in this study is the combination between technical necessities and preferences of the end-user. During our analysis we found that the majority of respondents were much more worried about 'social concerns' than technical aspects.

Taking Design Seriously. Stigmatization of people with disabilities is an ongoing problem highlighted in a number of studies and literature e.g. [31]. All participants have reported that they worry about unwanted attention and further stigmatisation by using too-conspicuous aids. Almost all asked for the robotic arm to be unobtrusive and designed with a positive public image in mind.

P14: "I can imagine that design is relatively important, because it is likely the crucial factor whether people accept it and whether they want to integrate it into their environment, right?"

Recommendation 3

The design should range between something plain and unobtrusive to a chic lifestyle product. The arm should be recognizable as a technical tool and not mimic a human arm by using skin-colored coloration or skin-like material.

The Care Situation and Social Aspects. All participants relied on care from in-home relatives for their daily needs. Additionally all but one also employed professional personal care assistants. Due to the limited possibilities of outside interactions the bond with family members and other regular caregivers was observed as particularly strong and important for the mental well-being of the participants.

Interviewer: "Would you describe the exchange between you and your assistant during mealtime as formal or informal?" P4: "Very informal, just about everyday life. Not just about mine. They tell me about themselves. And then you just sit together and talk about everything that is going on. Daily events, personal matters, politics, experiences, about everything really."

Recommendation 4

Disruptions of conversations and social interactions by the drinking aid have to be minimized. The robotic arm should be placed without obstructing the line of sight between user and assistant. Sound and noises have to be kept to an absolute minimum to avoid distractions.

Safety. Safe use must be guaranteed for primary and secondary users from the onset. Teething problems must be avoided at all costs; therefore strict adherence to safety protocols for direct physical proximity is vital. People within the target group are already faced with numerous health concerns [6,46] and many participants expressed worries about additional injury risks posed by the robot. Worries surrounded their inability/decreased ability to move out of the way if the robotic arm does not stop at a certain distance from their face. A frequently suggested solution would be an adjustment to have the robot bringing a cup with a straw close to the mouth - but not directly touching it; thus enabling the user to cover the last few centimeters on their own accord.

Solutions include the aid of a straw to avoid the drinking cup being delivered directly to the mouth. Allowing users the final approach increases their feeling of autonomy, control and safety.

Interviewer: "What could prevent you from using the robotic arm?"
P2: "Teething troubles, something every device has at the beginning. If problems with the programming come up and the whole weight of the robot would fall on me."

Recommendation 5

Apply the principle of *safety first* and design for scenarios of use avoiding body-contact.

Privacy. All participants require 24/7 assistance with results in very limited privacy. They all stated that they have to drink a lot during the day for health reasons. Particularly in the case of paraplegia, it is necessary to consume up to three liters of fluid a day to support digestion and temperature regulation [21]. Being able to regulate fluid intake independently and not having to ask for assistance every time they want to drink would allow users to spend several hours at a time without a caregiver. A frequently recorded hope concerns the increase of time being alone gained by integrating the drinking aid into the users' lives.

P4: "And you really sometimes want to be all alone. And even if I send my assistants to go shopping and have an hour alone here or there, that's not comparable to really being alone."

Recommendation 6

Users have to be able to use the device, once set up, independently or with minimal assistance. Once operational, assistants and caregivers should not need to interact with the device at all. Potential components worn by the user need to fit securely to prevent a constant need of re-adjustments (cf., guidelines for wearability [19]).

Data Privacy and Security. Only a small number of participants were concerned about data protection. Some however expressed concerns about the type of data collected, storage options, as well as access to it.

P6: "If there is a camera then I do not know where these images are going. Especially if the robot is connected to the internet."

Recommendation 7

Transparency about collected and stored data have to be maintained to reduce uncertainty and skepticism about modern technology. Storage of personal data, including camera images, should be avoided and frameworks for voice commands should work offline as much as possible. If data have to be stored, it has to be stored securely.

4.3 Collaborative Concerns

Effective assistive technologies only work if they can be used by the target group without major effort. End-users know best what they are capable of and how they feel most comfortable interacting with the robotic device. Therefore it is important to consider the way they want to collaborate with their robotic aid.

Ease of Use. The aim of using assistive technologies is increased independence of the end-user; something that is only possible if the devices are easy and straight-forward to use. Especially in the case of changing caregivers, it is exhausting for users to repeatedly train others in the use of their robotic aid.

P1: "That means that I might not need a nurse anymore, but a technician. Because I already struggle to instruct the carers; and that is just to trigger three commands on my computer."

> **Recommendation 8**
>
> Ease of use, preferably as *ready-to-use* design, should be the aim of the assistive technology. Given the potential of frequently changing assistants, intuitive design and an obvious command structure are required to ensure a short - if at all necessary - familiarization periods. No prior knowledge or training by secondary users can or should be expected and if anything a short introduction guided by the primary user has to be sufficient. The robotic arm should be - once adjusted to a mounting spot - ready to use and easily used.

Interaction Design and Interaction Technology. Participants in the study indicated various desires regarding the interaction with the robotic aid. Due to the frequent changes in position during the day, it is important that the robotic arm is usable in a lying and in a sitting position either from a bed and from a wheelchair.

The majority of the participants already use voice controlled components in their homes, e.g. telephone, door opener, and lighting fixture. However, these components generally cannot be compared with modern smart devices as they do not connect to the internet. Only one participant used an smart speaker for smart home solutions. Other participants refrained from using devices with internet based voice control due to unreliable internet connections or - more often - out of concerns towards data security.

P14: "So I think it would be great if it was using voice control. (...) I think using a joystick or something similar is also very complex. But if I only have to say: "Give me a glass of water", and that would work, that would be great."

> **Recommendation 9**
>
> Whilst voice control is preferred for control and interaction, speech impairments must be taken into account with the extra requirements they pose. Additionally, data security has been identified as a concern when usage of internet based voice control is suggested. Offline solutions are preferable to address these worries. Alternatively, eye-tracking devices and data glasses can be viable options. Participants preferred the former two options compared to head gestures and headsets. Participants preferred eye-tracking control via gaze-dwelling on either real world components or virtual objects in combination with the data glass's user interface.
>
> For users with residual hand and arm functions, a switch among semi-autonomous mode and manual mode via direct joystick control is interesting as it allows greater flexibility and adaptation to daily needs, due to the fact that in a semi-autonomous mode scenarios have to been learnt by the robot. The current mode has to communicated to the users and

assistants, e.g. by a ring of two-colored LEDs around the robot's flange like a bracelet.

Robotic Arm as Combined Drinking and Eating Aid. All Participants are excited about the prospect of a functional drinking aid, allowing them to independently regulate their fluid intake. In contrast, few participants can imagine regularly using a robotic arm for food consumption. Those who can still eat independently due to residual functionality in their upper extremities would like to use and maintain this ability. A robotic arm as an eating aid is only interesting for this group if food can be cut into small pieces with the help of the arm. A cutting function would further increase their autonomy and enable participation in meal preparation; in their eyes another step towards social integration. Participants who have their food served to them expressed satisfaction with the assistance they receive from other people. They would like to continue in this way because they value this social interaction and note that people can be more flexible and spontaneous in responding to all eventualities. This includes emergency situations such as choking or spillages, a worry of a number of participants from our focus group voiced.

P5: "I would prefer [the aid] of my husband, because we do communicate a little throughout lunch. I think when the robotic arm feeds you, there is just silence."

Recommendation 10

When prioritising the development of robotic assistance the first focus should be on fluid intake. The scenario of eating with a robotic arm is influenced by various complex aspects, such as social interactions, which need further exploration.

Robotic Arm as a General Aid. Participants frequently expressed a desire for a robotic arm with a distinct grasping function beyond a mere drinking aid. Desired functions include manipulating objects, such as picking something up, taking something out of a cabinet, or being able to lift things. Fine motor tasks such as turning the pages of a book or grasping easily breakable items were also desired. In addition, particularly the younger participants would like to be able to operate a game console. Furthermore, some of the participants would also like to use a robotic arm for aspects of basic care, such as combing hair or brushing teeth.

Participants who still eat independently also showed interest in the topic of cooking. A robotic arm that can cut food, handle cooking utensils, and assist with setting the table would increase autonomy and lead to more participation in the entire process of eating. Participants expressed the wish to handle even fragile objects like raw eggs or eat small but delicate snacks like crisps. Although fears of possible stigmatization due to the use of the robotic arm exist, overall the hope that a robotic arm with various functions could promote independent and self-determined living whilst also giving relieve to caregivers was expressed.

P4: "Having such an arm fulfill different functions such as gripping, I think that makes more sense because it would then be more versatile."

Recommendation 11

Apart from functioning as a drinking and eating aid, a robotic arm should be developed to fulfill other everyday tasks. Since participants fear stigmatization over having too many tools, a robotic aid with various functions would meet greater acceptance.

---

5   Discussion

Our ethnographic study provides recommendations for future research and development as well as hypotheses that should be tested for further validation. In the context of our target user group, implementing a solution based on our recommendations will still require adaptation to fit individuals with their specific physical abilities, along with further research to verify that a designed assistive system does indeed support the user. Recommendations regarding "Taking Design Seriously" and "Privacy" concern interaction devices that might lead to further stigmatization by drawing unwanted attention and require asking for assistance for wearing or re-calibration - both aspects the target group wants to avoid.

5.1   End-User Involvement in Assistive Technology

Assistive technologies are on the rise, with a number of different robotic aids already on the market or in various stages of development [15,25]. Studies by Scherer[43] and Verza [49] have shown that these devices, albeit useful in an assistive setting, can have a high rate of non-acceptance and non-usage. There is a growing body of literature indicating that this is due to the exclusion of the end-user from the design process [16]. In recent years the field of collaborative work between developers and end-users (or their advocates) has grown but is still in its infancy as discussed by Lee et al. [27] and Simonsen [44]. Our work represents such a collaborative approach investigating the needs and wants of the end-user in regards to a robotic drinking and eating aid. In fact, participants particularly valued the inclusion in the design process of a device developed specifically for them.

5.2   Potential Autonomy

One important finding is that participants want the possibility of spending time without their assistants. Specifically drinking as continuous hydration throughout the day is vital for people with disabilities which results in a near-constant need of care when drinking independently is not possible [21]. Thus, the most important capability of the robotic system should be to support the users with drinking. On the other hand, however, the participants also noted that the number of assistive systems should be limited and, thus, the system should provide multiple tasks. This trade off will be a core challenge for future developers.

5.3 Importance of Structural Concerns

Our results confirm findings by Fattal et al. [14] and others [34,48] as similar structural concerns are also expressed by our participants. Thus, our results also highlight the need for recommendations related to the physical characteristics of the robotic arm and attachment site.

5.4 In-Home Methodology

In this study we recorded the preferences people with severe motor disabilities have towards a robotic drinking and eating aid in terms of functionality and design. We used in-home sessions to interview our participants and record their everyday behaviours in a familiar setting. We opted for this particular approach to increase authenticity of our observation in accordance with Sakowska [42]. Combining all findings from our conversations and observations allowed us to gain significant insight in the actual living situation and challenges faced by the target group. We believe the in-home methods used in this study to represent a much more accurate picture than studies conducted in artificial laboratory or workshop environments. One downside of this approach, however, is the limitation to a small geographical area, potentially limiting the generalizability.

6 Conclusion

People with motor disabilities face a number of obstacles when confronted with everyday tasks such as drinking and eating. Assistive technologies have the potential to greatly improve the quality of life of the target group; however their user acceptance has been challenged by previous work. In this paper we investigated how drinking and eating aids are perceived by conducting interviews and participatory observations. By analyzing the relationship with food and drink intake as well as analyzing the wishes for future assistive technologies we were able to better understand the needs and wants of the target group.

Our research has highlighted the importance of acknowledging structural, social, and collaborative concerns in respect to the design of a robotic arm, defining a set of recommendations for the designs of robotic drinking aids. These recommendations represent an important step in bridging the gap between technological design and the preferences of the target group, thus increasing the likelihood of acceptance of any further assistive technology.

Acknowledgement. We would like to thank all study participants and their assistants for their valuable opinions and time. The authors are also grateful for the support of the *Center for Paraplegic Patients Hamburg*, the *Locked-in-Syndrom e.V. Berlin*, and the *State Association of the German Society for Multiple Sclerosis Hessen e.V.*. This research is supported by the German Federal Ministry of Education and Research (BMBF, FKZ: 16SV7866K and 16SV7868).

References

1. Achanccaray, D., Chau, J.M., Pirca, J., Sepulveda, F., Hayashibe, M.: Assistive robot arm controlled by a p300-based brain machine interface for daily activities. In: 2019 9th International IEEE/EMBS Conference on Neural Engineering (NER), pp. 1171–1174 (2019). https://doi.org/10.1109/NER.2019.8717042
2. Assistive Innovations B.V.: iARM—Robotic arm for humans, mountable on powered wheelchair. https://www.assistive-innovations.com/robotic-arms/iarm. Accessed 2 May 2021
3. Assistive Innovations B.V.: iEAT Robot—Assistive feeding and eating robot for people. https://www.assistive-innovations.com/eatingdevices/ieat-robot. Accessed 2 May 2021
4. Beaudoin, M., Lettre, J., Routhier, F., Archambault, P.S., Lemay, M., Gélinas, I.: Long-term use of the JACO robotic arm: a case series. Disabil. Rehabil. Assist. Technol. **14**(3), 267–275 (2019). https://doi.org/10.1080/17483107.2018.1428692
5. Bemelmans, R., Gelderblom, G.J., Jonker, P., de Witte, L.: Socially assistive robots in elderly care: a systematic review into effects and effectiveness. J. Am. Med. Dir. Assoc. **13**(2), 114–120 (2012). https://doi.org/10.1016/j.jamda.2010.10.002
6. Bickenbach, J.: International Perspectives on Spinal Cord Injury. World Health Organization, Geneva (2013)
7. Bogner, A., Littig, B., Menz, W.: Interviews mit Experten. QS, Springer, Wiesbaden (2014). https://doi.org/10.1007/978-3-531-19416-5
8. Canal, G., Alenyà, G., Torras, C.: Personalization framework for adaptive robotic feeding assistance. In: Agah, A., Cabibihan, J.-J., Howard, A.M., Salichs, M.A., He, H. (eds.) ICSR 2016. LNCS (LNAI), vol. 9979, pp. 22–31. Springer, Cham (2016). https://doi.org/10.1007/978-3-319-47437-3_3
9. Chen, T.L., et al.: Robots for humanity: using assistive robotics to empower people with disabilities. IEEE Rob. Autom. Mag. **20**(1), 30–39 (2013). https://doi.org/10.1109/MRA.2012.2229950
10. DESiN LLC: Obi—The first dining robot of its kind. https://meetobi.com/. Accessed 2 May 2021
11. Duchowski, A.T.: Gaze-based interaction: a 30 year retrospective. Comput. Graph. **73**, 59–69 (2018). https://doi.org/10.1016/j.cag.2018.04.002
12. Duckworth, D., Henkel, Z., Wuisan, S., Cogley, B., Collins, C., Bethel, C.: Therabot: the initial design of a robotic therapy support system. In: Proceedings of the Tenth Annual ACM/IEEE International Conference on Human-Robot Interaction Extended Abstracts, pp. 13–14 (2015). https://doi.org/10.1145/2701973.2701993
13. Eftring, H., Frennert, S.: Designing a social and assistive robot for seniors. Zeitschrift für Gerontologie und Geriatrie **49**(4), 274–281 (2016). https://doi.org/10.1007/s00391-016-1064-7

14. Fattal, C., Leynaert, V., Laffont, I., Baillet, A., Enjalbert, M., Leroux, C.: SAM, an assistive robotic device dedicated to helping persons with quadriplegia: usability study. Int. J. Soc. Rob. **11**(1), 89–103 (2018). https://doi.org/10.1007/s12369-018-0482-7

15. Federici, S.: Assistive Technology Assessment Handbook. CRC Press, Taylor & Francis Group, Boca Raton (2018)

16. Federici, S., et al.: Successful assistive technology service delivery outcomes from applying a person-centered systematic assessment process: a case study. Life Span Disabil. **18**(1), 41–74 (2015). http://www.lifespanjournal.it/client/abstract/ENG2902.%20Federici.pdf

17. Frennert, S., Östlund, B.: Review: seven matters of concern of social robots and older people. Int. J. Soc. Rob. **6**(2), 299–310 (2014). https://doi.org/10.1007/s12369-013-0225-8

18. Gallenberger, D., Bhattacharjee, T., Kim, Y., Srinivasa, S.S.: Transfer depends on acquisition: analyzing manipulation strategies for robotic feeding. In: 2019 14th ACM/IEEE International Conference on Human-Robot Interaction (HRI), pp. 267–276 (2019). https://doi.org/10.1109/HRI.2019.8673309

19. Gemperle, F., Kasabach, C., Stivoric, J., Bauer, M., Martin, R.: Design for wearability. In: Digest of Papers. Second International Symposium on Wearable Computers (Cat. No. 98EX215), pp. 116–122 (1998). https://doi.org/10.1109/ISWC.1998.729537

20. Google VR: Google Cardboard. https://arvr.google.com/cardboard/. Accessed 2 May 2021

21. Haas, U.: Caring for People with Paraplegia: Problems, Needs, Resources and Interventions (nach "Pflege von Menschen mit Querschnittlähmung Probleme, Bedürfnisse, Ressourcen und Interventionen"). Huber, Bern (2012)

22. Jackowski, A., Gebhard, M., Thietje, R.: Head motion and head gesture-based robot control: a usability study. IEEE Trans. Neural Syst. Rehabil. Eng. **26**(1), 161–170 (2018). https://doi.org/10.1109/TNSRE.2017.2765362

23. Kinova Inc.: Kinova Jaco Assistive Robotic Arm. https://www.kinovarobotics.com/en/assistive-technologies/column-a1/kinovaassistive-robotic-arm. Accessed 2 May 2021

24. Klein, B.: Aides, assistive Technologies, and Robotics: Maintaining Independence and Quality of Life in old age (nach "Hilfsmittel, Assistive Technologien und Robotik: Selbstständigkeit und Lebensqualität im Alter erhalten"). Kohlhammer Verlag (2020)

25. Kyrarini, M., et al.: A survey of robots in healthcare. Technologies **9**(1), 8 (2021). https://doi.org/10.3390/technologies9010008

26. Laitano, M.I.: Developing a participatory approach to accessible design. Int. J. Sociotechnology Knowl. Dev. **9**(4), 1–11 (2017). https://doi.org/10.4018/IJSKD.2017100101

27. Lee, H.R., et al.: Steps toward participatory design of social robots. In: HRI 2017, pp. 244–253. IEEE, Piscataway (2017). https://doi.org/10.1145/2909824.3020237

28. Mahmud, S., Lin, X., Kim, J.: Interface for human machine interaction for assistant devices: a review. In: 2020 10th Annual Computing and Communication Workshop and Conference (CCWC), pp. 768–773 (2020). https://doi.org/10.1109/CCWC47524.2020.9031244

29. Mandy, A., Sims, T., Stew, G., Onions, D.: Manual feeding device experiences of people with a neurodisability. Am. J. Occup. Ther. **72**(3), 7203345010p1–7203345010p5 (2018). https://doi.org/10.5014/ajot.2018.025353

30. Martinsen, B., Harder, I., Biering-Sorensen, F.: The meaning of assisted feeding for people living with spinal cord injury: a phenomenological study. J. Adv. Nurs. **62**(5), 533–540 (2008). https://doi.org/10.1111/j.1365-2648.2008.04637.x
31. Matera, C., et al.: Put yourself in my wheelchair: perspective-taking can reduce prejudice toward people with disabilities and other stigmatized groups. J. Appl. Soc. Psychol. **51**(3), 273–285 (2021). https://doi.org/10.1111/jasp.12734
32. Mayring, P.: Qualitative Content Analysis: Basics and Techniques (nach "Qualitative Inhaltsanalyse: Grundlagen und Techniken"). Beltz, Weinheim (2015)
33. McColl, M.A., Charlifue, S., Glass, C., Lawson, N., Savic, G.: Aging, gender, and spinal cord injury. Arch. Phys. Med. Rehabil. **85**(3), 363–367 (2004). https://doi.org/10.1016/j.apmr.2003.06.022
34. Merkel, S., Kucharski, A.: Participatory design in gerontechnology: a systematic literature review. Gerontologist **59**(1), e16–e25 (2018). https://doi.org/10.1093/geront/gny034
35. Park, D., et al.: Active robot-assisted feeding with a general-purpose mobile manipulator: design, evaluation, and lessons learned. Rob. Auton. Syst. **124**, 103344 (2020). https://doi.org/10.1016/j.robot.2019.103344
36. Pascher, M., Schneegass, S., Gerken, J.: SwipeBuddy. In: Lamas, D., Loizides, F., Nacke, L., Petrie, H., Winckler, M., Zaphiris, P. (eds.) INTERACT 2019, Part IV. LNCS, vol. 11749, pp. 568–571. Springer, Cham (2019). https://doi.org/10.1007/978-3-030-29390-1_39
37. Pilarczyk, U., Mietzner, U.: Picture science methods in research on education and social science (nach "Bildwissenschaftliche Methoden in der erziehungs- und sozialwissenschaftlichen Forschung"). Zeitschrift für qualitative Bildungs-, Beratungs- und Sozialforschung **1**(2), 343–364 (2000). https://www.ssoar.info/ssoar/handle/document/28057
38. Plaumann, K., Ehlers, J., Geiselhart, F., Yuras, G., Huckauf, A., Rukzio, E.: Better than you think: head gestures for mid air input. In: Abascal, J., Barbosa, S., Fetter, M., Gross, T., Palanque, P., Winckler, M. (eds.) INTERACT 2015, Part III. LNCS, vol. 9298, pp. 526–533. Springer, Cham (2015). https://doi.org/10.1007/978-3-319-22698-9_36
39. Reichertz, J.: Introduction to Qualitative Video Analysis – A hermeneutic-sociological Analysis Tool (nach "Einführung in die qualitative Videoanalye – Eine hermeneutisch-wissenssoziologische Fallanalyse"). VS Verlag für Sozialwissenschaften, Wiesbaden (2011)
40. Roig-Maimó, M.F., MacKenzie, I.S., Manresa-Yee, C., Varona, J.: Head-tracking interfaces on mobile devices: evaluation using fitts' law and a new multi-directional corner task for small displays. Int. J. Hum. Comput. Stud. **112**, 1–15 (2018). https://doi.org/10.1016/j.ijhcs.2017.12.003
41. Rudigkeit, N., Gebhard, M.: Amicus—a head motion-based interface for control of an assistive robot. Sensors **19**(12), 2836 (2019). https://doi.org/10.3390/s19122836
42. Sałkowska, M.: Carrying out research among persons with disabilities and their relatives – selected ethical issues. Zoon Politikon **8**, 200–217 (2018). https://doi.org/10.4467/2543408XZOP.18.010.10066
43. Scherer, M.J.: Living in the State of Stuck: How Assistive Technology Impacts the Lives of People with Disabilities. Brookline Books, Brookline (2005)
44. Simonsen, J.: Routledge International Handbook of Participatory Design. Routledge, New York (2013)
45. Stalljann, S., Wöhle, L., Schäfer, J., Gebhard, M.: Performance analysis of a head and eye motion-based control interface for assistive robots. Sensors **20**(24), 7162 (2020). https://doi.org/10.3390/s20247162

46. Statistisches Bundesamt (Destatis): Statistical Yearbook 2019 – Chapter 4 Health (nach "Statistisches Jahrbuch 2019 – Kapitel 4 Gesundheit"). https://www.destatis.de/DE/Themen/Querschnitt/Jahrbuch/jb-gesundheit.pdf (2019)

47. Statistisches Bundesamt (Destatis): Disability Facts and Figures - Brief Report 2019 (nach "Statistik der schwerbehinderten Menschen - Kurzbericht 2019") (2020). https://www.destatis.de/DE/Themen/Gesellschaft-Umwelt/Gesundheit/Behinderte-Menschen/Publikationen/Downloads-Behinderte-Menschen/sozial-schwerbehinderte-kb-5227101199004.html

48. Thielke, S., Harniss, M., Thompson, H., Patel, S., Demiris, G., Johnson, K.: Maslow's hierarchy of human needs and the adoption of health-related technologies for older adults. Ageing Int. **37**(4), 470–488 (2012). https://doi.org/10.1007/s12126-011-9121-4

49. Verza, R., Carvalho, M.L.L., Battaglia, M.A., Uccelli, M.M.: An interdisciplinary approach to evaluating the need for assistive technology reduces equipment abandonment. Multiple Scler. J. **12**(1), 88–93 (2006). https://doi.org/10.1191/1352458506ms1233oa

50. Vines, J., Clarke, R., Wright, P., McCarthy, J., Olivier, P.: Configuring participation: on how we involve people in design. In: Proceedings of the SIGCHI Conference on Human Factors in Computing Systems, pp. 429–438 (2013). https://doi.org/10.1145/2470654.2470716

51. World Health Organization: Spinal cord injury. https://www.who.int/news-room/fact-sheets/detail/spinal-cord-injury. Accessed 2 May 2021

VR Invite: A Project-Independent Smartphone App for VR Observation and Interactivity

Jann Philipp Freiwald$^{(\boxtimes)}$, Sünje Gollek, and Frank Steinicke

Universität Hamburg, Hamburg, Germany
{freiwald,6gollek,steinicke}@informatik.uni-hamburg.de

Abstract. Virtual Reality (VR) is a promising immersive technology, which provides users with place and plausibility illusions in a virtual environment (VE). However, current immersive experiences are often limited to those users wearing a VR head-mounted display (HMD). In this paper we present VR Invite, a project-independent smartphone app, which allows multiple non-immersive bystanders to observe and interact with the VE and the HMD users. Our system renders multiple view ports of the scene on a host computer, and transmits the data via wireless local network to the mobile devices. Furthermore, the position and orientation of the smartphones is tracked to change the viewpoints accordingly.

We conducted a user study with 26 participants in the context of rehabilitation for older adults in retirement homes, with a focus on bystander integration. In the study, a VR user had to play multiple rounds of a memory game, while a bystander provided support. We compared VR Invite with a TV-gamepad-combination as interaction medium for the support role regarding sense of presence, social presence, workload and usability, both with purely verbal and active assistance capabilities. The results indicate that the opportunity for direct interaction positively influences the bystander's sense of presence in the VE and the reported usability of the Smartphone app. However, social presence was rated higher in passive conditions in which the real person was the center of attention, as opposed to the avatar on the screen. Furthermore, users valued the comfort of sitting down over active participation and agency with room-scale movement.

Keywords: Virtual reality · Smartphones · Collaborative Virtual Environments · Multi-user mixed reality interactions · Social VR

1 Introduction

Current virtual reality (VR) setups seldom are a collaborative or social experience for a local group of people. This is due to the requirement of VR being rendered on a single head-mounted display (HMD), with a limited ability to include bystanders. Typically, only passive participation is offered by either mirroring the video feed or rendering the scene from a third person perspective to an external

© IFIP International Federation for Information Processing 2021
Published by Springer Nature Switzerland AG 2021
C. Ardito et al. (Eds.): INTERACT 2021, LNCS 12932, pp. 352–370, 2021.
https://doi.org/10.1007/978-3-030-85623-6_22

stationary monitor. To provide multi-user integration certain applications support the use of a number of HMDs connected via local area network (LAN) or internet. However, those are tailored to a specific use case and require substantial amounts of technical equipment and expertise to use in a local environment.

In single HMD setups exploration of the virtual environment (VE) and social exchange with the HMD user are difficult for bystanders, as there is a need for input devices that are directly connected to the rendering computer, which in turn need to be provided in tandem with the VR setup. Such devices need to be tightly integrated and require an explicit implementation of camera control or other forms of interaction. However, the ubiquitous availability of smartphones allows for integrating bystanders into a social VR experience without the need for proprietary input devices with the "bring your own device" metaphor.

In this paper we introduce a project-independent smartphone app called *VR Invite*, which connects to a self-contained package for the Unity engine on a host computer or standalone VR headset via local wireless network. It allows bystanders hold a view port to the VE and observe the VR from any natural angle or position, as depicted in Fig. 1. The package additionally supports transfer of touch inputs from the smartphone to the host computer. This enables an easy implementation of bystander interactivity for experiences that go beyond passive or verbal participation. Furthermore, we added visualizations of the additional view ports to increase the social presence of the HMD user. These visualizations provide a sense of spatial relation and participation between all users.

VR Invite can be used to extend existing projects with either active or passive participation capabilities, or build applications specifically tailored for an asymmetrical multi-user experience. To test the technical soundness of this library's first prototype, we conducted a user study in the scope of rehabilitation of older adults in a retirement home. Here, we measured the effect of the ability to freely move a handheld VR view port on both an HMD user and a bystander, primarily regarding sense of presence, social presence and usability.

To summarize, the contributions of this paper are:

- Development of VR Invite, a project-independent smartphone VR viewer app &
- a user study to compare bystander integration techniques for the support role in an asymmetrical rehabilitation scenario.

2 Related Work

Our work builds upon three areas of research: Collaborative Virtual Environments (CVEs), asymmetric mixed reality (XR) collaborations, and incorporation of bystanders into XR setups.

2.1 Collaborative Virtual Environments

CVEs enable collaboration and interaction in a shared VE between users who may either use the same physical work space or remotely connect through the

Fig. 1. The VR Invite app allows a bystander to observe and interact with the VE from any perspective.

internet [13]. In 1993 Carlsson et al. published DIVE, one of the first distributed interactive virtual reality systems [11]. They focused on multi-user interaction in VR environments and networking solutions for synchronized databases which reference virtual objects. CVEs now have a widespread use in VR applications, including rehabilitation, education, training, gaming and artistry. For example, Tsoupikova et al. used VR CVEs for rehabilitation in patients that suffered from a stroke [31]. They implemented motoric exercises for up to four patients with a focus on the social component of therapy. Kallioniemi et al. demonstrated how VR CVEs can be used to a help learning a foreign language [24]. In their CityCompass VR application two users move through a virtual city and alternate between the roles of tourist and guide. To reach a common goal, they have to communicate in a foreign language via headset.

Regarding co-located collaboration, Billinghurst et al. [6,7] presented systems that let users perform a variety of interactions and visualizations in augmented reality collaborations. Their goal was to allow communication that is closer to face-to-face dialogue than screen-based interactions. Jones et al. proposed RoomAlive [23], following the concepts of Billinghurst et al. with an implementation of projection-based co-located collaboration. They explored the transformation of a living room into an interactive playing environment for multiple users. The diverse use of CVEs is also evident in areas such as security training [28], medicine [12] or project planning in architecture [22].

2.2 Asymmetric Mixed Reality Collaborations

VR Invite allows a number of bystanders to observe and interact with a virtual environment, using smartphones rather than tracked hand controllers. Hence, their form of interaction is asymmetrical to the HMD wearing user. Several prior works have researched asymmetric interactions in virtual or mixed reality [14–16,21,22,26]. For instance, Oliveira et al. presented a distributed asymmetric CVE for training in industrial scenarios, using screen-based GUIs to guide an HMD wearing user [27]. Their goal was to teach a trainee to operate and repair faulty hardware through remote avatars.

Oda et al. presented an asymmetric case study between a remote user and a local HMD wearing user [26]. They compared the use of traditional 2D interfaces and VR headsets as medium for the remote user regarding their ability to explain a certain task. The results indicate that demonstrating a task with a VR headset was easier to understand than annotations through 2D interfaces.

Lindley et al. compared gamepad-based input to tracked body movements for asymmetric avatar interactions. They found that natural body movements elicited a higher social interaction when compared to predefined animations [25].

2.3   Bystanders in Mixed Reality

Gugenheimer et al. proposed two approaches regarding the incorporation of bystanders in a VR setting. Their FaceDisplay [18] is an extension for conventional HMDs, equipping the headset with three external touch-sensitive displays and a depth camera. This way bystanders can see the VE from the outside and trigger actions by touching the displays on the head. This of course comes with the problem that an active HMD user moves their head frequently, which makes observing the displays and interacting with them difficult. An exploratory user study showed that the FaceDisplay led to a high degree of dominance and responsibility of the bystander over the HMD user.

With ShareVR [17] Gugenheimer et al. investigated an asymmetric gaming scenario, with one HMD user and one bystander. The bystander is equipped with a Vive Wand controller that has a tethered screen attached, acting as a second view port. The scene is rendered from a second point of view on the VR computer and transmitted via standard HDMI cable. Also, a projector shows the VE from a top-down perspective on the floor. The setup showed an improvement in entertainment value, sense of presence and social interaction compared to the common TV-gamepad combination. The Master of Shapes commercial solution used a similar setup, but replaced the Vive Wand with a standalone Vive Tracker for positional tracking of a display [3].

Finally, Owlchemy Labs showed a prototype solution that uses a Smartphone for positional tracking and display of the view port [4]. As long as the front of the headset is in the smartphone's view, their relative position can be calculated. The view port is then rendered on the VR computer and transmitted via wireless LAN.

3   Implementation and Setup

Similar to the approaches of Gugenheimer et al. and Owlchemy Labs we designed a mobile view port solution for desktop and standalone VR experiences. Like Owlchemy Labs we implemented positional tracking on a smartphone and transmit the data to the VR host computer, which then renders the image and streams it back via wireless LAN. Contrary to the aforementioned solutions, we used Google's ARCore library [2] to define a world anchor point, which could be any kind of picture or easily recognized object. For simplicity's sake we used a QR code printed on a piece of paper, detected by ARCore's "Plane Detection", "Augmented Images" and "Anchors" algorithms. The anchor can be placed anywhere in the physical room and is used to calculate the relative pose of a smartphone to the virtual origin point. Once the anchor is established by pointing the smartphone camera at it, ARCore builds and constantly refines a model of the physical room. The world anchor position can be defined in the engine's editor or by using the current position of an arbitrary tracked input device like a Vive Wand at runtime. This approach allows the smartphone user to look in any direction while we retain knowledge about the relative position and orientation to the VR scene's origin point, and transitively the VR player's position.

VR Invite was designed to be self-contained package for the Unity engine. When imported into an existing VR solution, the networking server doesn't need to be configured. At runtime, the server waits for smartphone app clients to connect to it, and then assigns them an in-engine camera object. The camera images are compressed to JPGs, serialized and sent via networking protocol to the client. Our current proof-of-concept prototype uses a simple TCP/IP implementation, which segments the image bytes into several chunks that can easily be reassembled on the client due to TCP/IP's guarantee of package order. Image resolution, compression and frame rate are parameters that can be adjusted depending on the number of clients. Figure 2 illustrates the networking scheme used in the current version of VR Invite.

The client within our smartphone app connects directly to a VR host computer by a given IP address and searches for a predefined anchor image. Upon identification of the world anchor point, the app streams its calculated relative pose to the anchor to the connected server. The camera's pose within the VR scene is now defined as the Vector from origin to world anchor position plus the vector from world anchor position to the smartphone, as determined by the app client.

This approach makes the combination of app and package project-independent, as the client only sends positional tracking data and receives a video stream in return, regardless of the scene's content or interactivity. It also allows a theoretically unlimited number of concurrent smartphone viewers, albeit at the cost of linearly increasing computational requirements for the host computer. The app also transmits touch inputs to the server, allowing optional implementation of project dependent interactivity. For example, touch positions can be interpreted as ray casts from the camera to highlight certain objects or to trigger events tied to virtual buttons or other interactive elements. To increase the VR player's social presence, an avatar should be displayed for each connected client. Obvious approaches are either displaying the image rendered for the view port as floating plane, or using a 3D model positioned where the view port is rendered from. We chose to display a 3D model of a smartphone imitating the pose of the real device to relay a sense of spatial relation.

The source code of both the VR Invite Unity package and smartphone app can be found on GitHub [1].

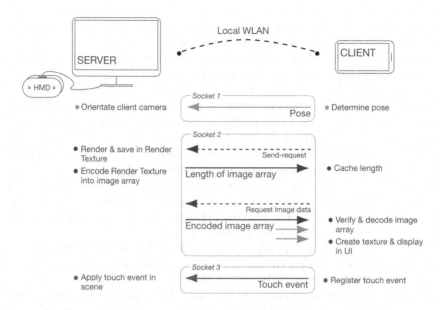

Fig. 2. The networking scheme of VR Invite.

4   User Study

In the context of rehabilitation for older adults in retirement homes, we conducted a user study where a VR player had to play multiple rounds of a memory game, while a bystander supported them. The VR exergame *Memory* of the EXGAVINE project [29] was chosen as a case study. This interdisciplinary project is concerned with the development and evaluation of medically and therapeutically effective VR movement games for the treatment of patients with neurological diseases. While VR Invite can be incorporated into any VR scenario, we focused on use cases which usually have one or multiple bystanders, as opposed to single user or explicit multi user scenarios. The use case of the rehabilitation project is a scenario that not only fulfills this requirement, but could potentially greatly benefit from active bystander integration. Here, bystanders are currently not integrated at all, or only through a passive monitor setup. We expected an increase in sense of co-presence for the older VR users, and thus a positive influence on their enjoyment and engagement with the rehabilitation program. For these reasons, we decided to use this application as a test bed for our case study. Their *Memory* game is meant to be played by older adults with verbal support from family members or nursing staff for training physical and mental capabilities. The term "exergame" is a portmanteau of "exercise" and "gaming" and describes fitness driven game designs. Our goal was to extend the exergame with VR Invite as an uncomplicated and intuitive form of interactivity to increase engagement between players and bystanders. Using the smartphone like a camera view finder was meant to be a concept that is easy to grasp without any knowledge of interactive video games or VR applications.

The focus of the study therefore was to determine if VR Invite is a suitable general purpose tool to observe and interact with a VR scene. To this end we compared VR Invite to a TV-gamepad-combination as input method for the support role regarding sense of presence, social presence, workload and usability, each with purely verbal or active assistance capabilities. In the chosen exergame the player is in a virtual park and has to solve a memory game with eight pairs of tiles (cf. Fig. 3). Selecting a memory tile is done by throwing a virtual ball onto it, which simultaneously trains logical thinking and physical movement. We tested 2×2 combinations of independent variables: *Smartphone* versus *TV*, and *active* versus *passive* interactivity. Thus, each participant had to perform four trials. There was no focus on task performance due to the nature of this exergame's training and gradual self-improvement intent.

Passive TV represents the most common local VR scenario, where one or many bystanders can observe the real HMD user and have a TV screen or monitor showing the viewpoint of the VR user. *Active TV* adds input and a 3rd person perspective to the prior setup. Here, we gave the bystander a gamepad that could control the position and rotation of the TV screens's camera. Pressing any button while a memory tile is under a center crosshair visually highlights the tile in the VE.

The *Passive Smartphone* condition behaves the same as the *Passive TV*. It displays the VE from the HMD user's perspective on the smartphone screen, without the ability to move the camera or interact with the scene. Finally, *Active Smartphone* represents VR Invite. The smartphone can be used as a standalone view port, which can be freely moved. Touching a memory tile on the screen visually highlights it in the VE, as depicted in Fig. 3. The avatar of the HMD user always consisted of a simple head with black HMD and a representation of the controllers. Active view ports were represented with a smartphone 3D model in the VE.

For each condition the workload was measured by the NASA Task Load Index (NASA-TLX) [19], the usability by the System Usability Scale (SUS) [10], the presence by the Slater-Usoh-Steed presence questionnaire (SUSP) [30] and the social presence by the Networked Minds Social Presence Inventory (NMSPI) [8, 9]. The NASA-TLX questionnaire consists of five 7-point Likert scales, and is used to subjectively assess physical and mental workload. The SUS likewise is a ten-item attitude Likert scale, which is used to subjectively assess usability of systems and interfaces. The SUSP again uses Likert scales, with 6 items revolving around the sense of being in a VE and the extent to which the VE becomes the subjective dominant reality. Lastly, the NMSPI is a tool to assess the social and co-presence, as well as psycho-behavioral interactions between multiple study participants. We used the NMSPI version 1.2, consisting of 34 7-point Likert scales. In addition to the questionnaires, we measured the distance covered by the bystander in the VE as well as the duration of visual contact during active conditions as an indication of active participation and social interaction. Here, visual contact was determined by checking if the avatars are within the other participant's camera frustum.

Based on the above described criteria, the experiment was designed as within-subject, and the following hypotheses were formed:

– H_1: Active conditions are rated higher in sense of presence by the bystander.
– H_2: Active conditions are rated higher in social presence by the bystander.
– H_3: Active conditions are rated higher in usability by the bystander.
– H_4: The Smartphone causes a higher workload than the TV for the bystander.
– H_5: There is no difference in sense of presence between all conditions for the HMD user.
– H_6: Active conditions are rated higher in social presence by the HMD user.
– H_7: There is no difference in usability between all conditions for the HMD user.
– H_8: There is no difference in workload between all conditions for the HMD user.
– H_9: The moved distance with active smartphones is greater than with gamepads.
– H_{10}: The visual contact duration with active smartphones is greater than with gamepads.

Fig. 3. The virtual environment of the VR memory game. A bystander with a smartphone highlights a tile.

4.1 Participants and Apparatus

26 participants (9 female, 1 diverse) took part in the experiment in pairs of two. In total, the study lasted about 90 min. Due to current health and hygiene regulations, the study had to be performed predominantly with students rather than

the intended demographic of older adults, their relatives and nursing staff (cf. section 'Limitations'). The age range was between 19–62 years with an average age of 26.81 years ($SD = 10.08, M = 24.5$). All participants had prior experience with stereoscopic displays through VR headsets or 3D cinema, while 57,7% had prior experience with studies in VR. On a scale of 0 to 4, participants reported a mean 3D gaming experience of 2.54 ($SD = 1.10$) and their mean gaming time was 11.17 h ($SD = 15.99$) per week. An HTC Vive Pro with Wand controllers was used for the VR player and depending on the condition a Google Pixel 3XL or XBox One controller for the bystander. A computer equipped with Windows 10, an Intel Core i7-4930K, an NVIDIA GeForce RTX 2080 Ti and 16 GB of RAM was used to render both the VR and the VR Invite view ports.

4.2   Stimuli and Procedure

After giving their informed consent and filling in a demographic questionnaire, participants were introduced to the memory game as well as their assigned device. They were instructed to cooperatively solve the memory challenge. As described above, each trial consisted of a full game of memory, where matching images needed to be turned over consecutively. To select a tile, the VR user had to throw a virtual ball at it. Not hitting two tiles with the same image consecutively resets the last two tiles. The trial ended when all tiles were flipped over. While the VR user selects the tiles, the bystander could assist them purely verbally during passive conditions and additionally by highlighting a single tile during active conditions. The trials were arranged via latin square, each taking circa 5 min. Following each trial, both participants filled out the set of questionnaires. Once all conditions were completed, the pairs switched roles and repeated the experiment.

4.3   Results

In this section the results of the statistical analysis are presented. When the Shapiro-Wilk test showed normal distribution of the samples, a repeated-measure ANOVA and post-hoc paired t tests were used to test for differences between conditions. Otherwise, the Friedman test and Wilcoxon Signed Rank test were used. A 5% significance level was assumed, and only significant results are reported.

Presence. For the sense of presence the SUSP score and the arithmetic mean of the SUSP results were considered. The wilcoxon test shows higher presence values for *Active TV* (score = 1.2) than the passive conditions, *Passive TV* (score = 0.3, p = .005) and *Passive Smartphone* (score = 0.2, p = .007). This is also evident in the arithmetic mean by paired t tests: *Active TV* ($M = 3.6$, $SD = 1.63$) is rated significantly better than *Passive TV* ($M = 2.8$, $SD = 1.33$, p = .003) and *Passive Smartphone* ($M = 2.3$, $SD = 1.04$, p < .0001). *Active Smartphone* ($M = 3.4$, $SD = 1.59$) is also higher than *Passive TV* (p = .007)

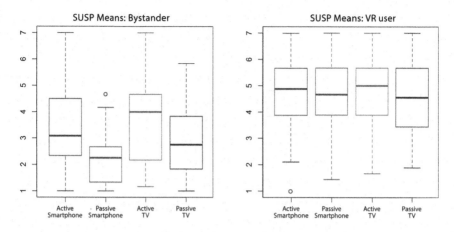

Fig. 4. Mean presence scores for Bystander (left) and VR user (right). Higher is better.

and *Passive Smartphone* (p = 0003). In passive conditions, *Passive TV* performs significantly better than *Passive Smartphone* (p = .019). For the VR user role, no significant differences in sense of presence between the conditions could be observed either in the SUSP score or in the arithmetic mean. Figure 4 depicts the mean SUSP scores for both bystander and VR user.

Social Presence. We found significant differences in the social presence of the bystander. The result of *Passive TV* ($M = 3.2$, $SD = 0.78$) is significantly higher than that of *Active Smartphone* ($M = 2.8$, $SD = 0.82$, p = .0004) and *Active TV* ($M = 2.7$, $SD = 0.87$, p = .0001). *Passive Smartphone* ($M = 3.4$, $SD = 0.89$) shows a significantly higher result than *Active Smartphone* (p = .0002) and *Active TV* (p = .0001). For the VR user role, *Passive TV* ($M = 3.3$, $SD = 0.90$) is higher than *Active TV* ($M = 2.7$, $SD = 1.02$, p = .002) and *Active Smartphone* ($M = 2.9$, $SD = 0.75$, p = .022). *Passive Smartphone* ($M = 3.2$, $SD = 0.79$) was rated significantly higher than *Active TV* (p = .007). Figure 5 depicts the NMSPI scores for both bystander and VR user.

Visual Contact. We observed that some participants deliberately positioned themselves so that they always had the other participant in their view port's frustum, while others focused entirely on the memory tiles. Because of this, the deviations are of considerable size. On average, bystanders looked at the VR users 3.3 times with an *Active Smartphone* ($SD = 3.58$, $min = 0.0$, $max = 14.0$), and 11.3 times ($SD = 7.04$, $min = 1.0$, $max = 28.0$) with an *Active TV*. The average total time looking at the VR user was 11.0 s with an *Active Smartphone* ($SD = 13.34$, median = 7.5, $min = 0.0$, $max = 59.0$) and 82.7 s with the *Active TV* condition ($SD = 77.01$, median = 58.5, $min = 2.0$, $max = 367.0$). Wilcoxon tests showed that both *time* (p < .0001) and *number* of eye contacts (p < .0001) are significantly higher for *TV* overall than for the *Smartphone*. On the other

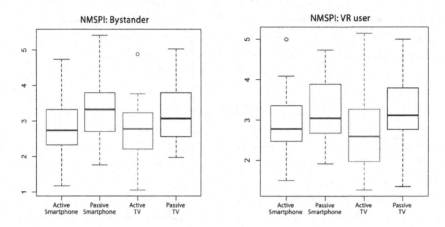

Fig. 5. Social presence scores for Bystander (left) and VR user (right). Higher is better.

hand, the VR user looked at the Bystander an average of 11.5 times in the *Active Smartphone* condition ($SD = 10.09$, $min = 2.0$, $max = 39.0$) and 8.0 times when using the *Active TV* ($SD = 6.12$, $min = 0.0$, $max = 23.0$). The average total time looking at the bystander was 65.1 s during the *Active Smartphone* condition($SD = 63.38$, $min = 7.0$, $max = 309.0$) and 45.6 s when using the *Active TV* ($SD = 64.70$, $min = 0.0$, $max = 320.0$).

Usability. On the SUS, bystanders rated the usability of *Active TV* ($M = 89.5$, $SD = 11.66$) significantly better than all other conditions: *Passive TV* ($M = 81.3$, $SD = 13.75$, p = .009), *Active Smartphone* ($M = 81.0$, $SD = 14.95$, p = .02) and *Passive Smartphone* ($M = 68.9$, $SD = 15.05$, p < .0001). The usability value in the *Active Smartphone* is significantly higher than in the *Passive Smartphone* (p = .0002). The result of *Passive Smartphone* is significantly lower than that of *Passive TV* (p = .003). No significant differences in usability were found for the VR user role. Figure 6 illustrates the SUS score distribution for both bystander and VR user.

Workload. We found a significantly higher workload for the bystander in the condition *Passive Smartphone* ($M = 29.5$, $SD = 14.50$) than in *Active TV* ($M = 19.2$, $SD = 11.56$, p = .0006) and *Passive TV* ($M = 21.4$, $SD = 14.23$, p = .008). *Active Smartphone* ($M = 25.9$, $SD = 16.07$) is significantly higher than *Active TV* (p = .02). There was no significant difference between the workload results for the VR user. Figure 7 show the NASA-TLX scores for both bystander and VR user.

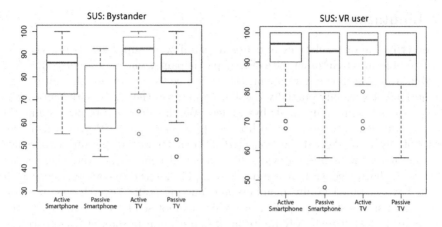

Fig. 6. Usability scores for Bystander (left) and VR user (right). Higher is better.

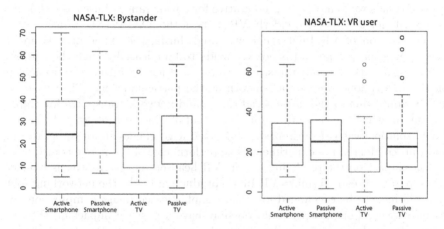

Fig. 7. Workload scores for Bystander (left) and VR user (right). Lower is better.

Bystander Travel. For the calculation of bystander travel two participant pairs had to be removed from the evaluation. Due short losses of ARCore's tracking, the measurements showed huge momentary spikes in covered distance. All other trials showed no tracking data inconsistencies.

A significantly longer distance was covered in the *Active TV* condition than in the *Active Smartphone* condition ($p < .0001$). The average distance in *Active Smartphone* is 15.9 m ($SD = 12.46$, $max = 64.1$) with a minimum value of 6.0 m. In *Active TV* this value is 92.1 m ($SD = 75.43$, $max = 368.0$) with a minimum value of 8.2 m. Only one participant used the provided tools for movement excessively, traveling 64.1 m for *Active Smartphone* and 368.0 m for *Active TV*. When excluding this outlier, the maximum recorded values become 35.5 m for *Active Smartphone* and 177.1 m for *Active TV*. This however has no impact on the significance of the difference between the conditions.

5   Limitations

As described above, relatives and nursing staff were supposed to use the VR Invite mobile app to interact with elderly participants, who are immersed in a VR rehabilitation training environment. However, due to current health and hygiene regulations, it was only partially possible to perform the study with representative participants and only single bystanders. We therefore had to predominantly rely on university students for both roles of bystander and VR user, which will undoubtedly have skewed our collected data in regards to gaming experience and familiarity with input devices like gamepad controllers. Yet, there is an overlap of the tested and targeted demographic for the bystander role, which would have included family members and nursing staff. Nevertheless, the collected data shows strong significances which cannot solely be attributed to the selection of test subjects. VR Invite itself is a general purpose VR cooperation tool, which can be used in a variety of scenarios. Therefore, we believe that the general trends we found are representative for a wide range of use cases, but not necessarily for the intended elderly VR users of the EXGAVINE project.

The version of VR Invite that was used during the experiment is an in-development prototype and is not yet ready to be released. While the tracking was consistent throughout the study, we received feedback that the frame rate on the smartphone was not as smooth as the participants had liked it to be. We attribute this to the naive serialization and network transportation implementation, which we chose to use for our proof of concept prototype. While the tested solution was not optimized, we deemed it good enough for initial testing and thus conducted the experiment. The performance of the image transfer also had no impact on the rendering for the VR headset, as the transfer is handled in a separate thread. To make VR Invite production ready, the networking solution will have to be exchanged for a more sophisticated image compression and transfer stack. This in turn could possibly have a positive impact on the user ratings for usability and possibly sense of presence as well. We don't however expect the reported data to drastically shift with improved frame rates, as the results are quite unambiguous.

6   Discussion

Sense of Presence. The results of the study highlight the connection between active participation in a collaborative experience and an increase in the self-reported sense of presence. When looking at the arithmetic mean, both *Active Smartphone* and *Active TV* received favorable ratings when compared to their passive counterparts. As expected, the ability to independently move and interact with the virtual environment is a major factor in feeling involved in a CVE, confirming hypothesis H_1 (Active conditions are rated higher in sense of presence by the bystander). However, the overall average sense of presence was at a relatively low value of 3.025 out of 7. This can be explained by the fact that the bystanders perceived the CE only via screens and always had the real environment in their field of vision. As mentioned in the limitations section, technical improvements of VR Invite could further shift the bystanders sense of presence in the active conditions favor. We found no significant difference between the conditions for the VR user's sense of presence, which confirms hypothesis H_5 (There is no difference in sense of presence between all conditions for the HMD user). The displayed camera model was perceived equally as present when it was in a fixed location as to it following the bystanders real position. This is most likely due to the fact that bystanders had a tendency to remain standing in the same position for the majority of the trials. They reported an initial wow-effect and tried to move the view port around the tracking space. Once they found a position that was out of the VR user's range from which they could observe the memory tiles, they remained stationary. Because of that, there was no significant difference between the camera model's movement from the VR user's perspective.

Social Presence. Contrary to the hypotheses H_2 (Active conditions are rated higher in social presence by the bystander) and H_6 (Active conditions are rated higher in social presence by the HMD user), the sense of social presence was rated significantly higher by both bystander and VR user in the passive conditions. This might seem counter intuitive at first, but can be explained by two factors. One, the bystander's attention is primarily focused on the VR user in the real world. Instead of looking at a smartphone or TV screen, and thus an avatar, bystanders tended to spend a longer time observing the real human being. Two, when not able to directly interact with the virtual environment, bystanders had to go through the VR user as an intermediary by verbally communicating with them. In the active conditions the pointing interaction was used frequently and reported as joyful. However, the pairs spoke noticeably less with each other. This leads us to believe that verbal communication is a more important factor for sense of social presence than visual communication through cues and individual agency. Thus, autonomy in bystander integration appears to negatively correlate with social presence. Prior studies have found that current VR meetings do not reach the same sense of social presence as a real in-person meeting, which can be applied here as well [20].

Visual Contact. Regarding visual contact, we found that the *Active Smartphone* was used significantly more often to interact with the memory tiles, while the *Active TV* condition showed more visual contacts with the VR user, disconfirming hypothesis H_{10} (The visual contact duration with active smartphones is greater than with gamepads). The *Active Smartphone* incited the bystander to behave autonomous and solve the memory game on their own, and in turn giving more visual cues to the VR user than the *Active TV*. In a sense, *Active Smartphone* users were more engaged with the experience, but less so on a social level. On the other hand, the VR user looked at the Bystander more often and for longer periods of time during the *Active Smartphone* condition, confirming they are not within their reach to accidentally hit them with the Vive Wands (11.5

times versus 8.0 times and 65.1 s versus 45.6 s). Thus, VR users were actively aware of the bystander's location.

We also made the following noteworthy observations regarding visual contact and collected demographic data. Male VR users held visual contact with the *Smartphone* significantly longer than female users. This behaviour was inverted during the *TV* conditions. Overall, while the bystanders used a *Smartphone* as opposed to a controller, they looked at the VR user less often, but the VR user looked at them more often. Vice versa for trials where the bystander used a controller. There was a negative correlation between hours played per week and duration of visual contacts during the *Active Smartphone* condition. A positive correlation was found between age and duration of visual contacts during the *Active Smartphone* condition.

Usability. Bystanders rated the usability higher in the active conditions. *Active TV* achieved the highest rating, followed by *Active Smartphone*. This confirms hypothesis H_3 (Active conditions are rated higher in usability by the bystander). From participant comments we deduced that control over the view port and the interaction made the game easier and more enjoyable, which aligns with the findings of Gugenheimer et al. [17]. The mean values for *Active TV*, *Active Smartphone* and *Passive TV* are above 80 points, a result close to or exceeding the "Excellent" usability category according to the SUS evaluation guidelines of Bangor et al. [5]. *Passive Smartphone* was rated lowest with 68.9 points, which Bangor et al. classify as borderline between "OK" and "Good" usability on the adjective rating scale.

As mentioned above, the technical shortcomings of our implementation could have had an impact on the usability rating. We don't however expect changes to the networking stack to overcome the gap in ratings that presented itself. Not having to actively move within the real space or holding up a smartphone was rated significantly more usable than the opportunity for natural view port manipulation and freedom of movement. The convenience of sitting down outweighed the increase in precision and naturalness of movement.

We found no significant difference for the reported usability of the VR user between the conditions, confirming hypothesis H_7 (There is no difference in usability between all conditions for the HMD user). The visual cues did neither increase or decrease the usability of the entire setup or the memory game as a whole. Looking at the mean values, the active conditions at over 90 points are slightly higher than the passive ones at an average of 88.55 points. All values indicate a satisfactory usability. In the qualitative feedback, especially the visual cues and the avatars were found to be helpful in cooperating with the bystander. Overall this did however not alter the way the VR user interacts with the VE.

Workload. As expected, we also could not find a significant difference for the VR user's workload. While additional visual guidance from the bystanders was perceived as helpful, it also had to be mentally processed and combined with verbal communication and their own memory of the tiles. These two factors effectively canceled each other out, while there was no impact on the physical aspect of the game. This confirms hypothesis H_8 (There is no difference in workload between all conditions for the HMD user). On the Bystanders' side, the workload in the *Smartphone* conditions is reported higher than for the *TV* conditions. This was to be expected; holding up a phone screen is more strenuous than sitting down with a controller. Similarly, actively walking through the real world with a screen in hand less comfortable than sitting down and using the joystick movement. This confirms hypothesis H_4 (The Smartphone causes a higher workload than the TV for the bystander.). Interestingly, bystanders reported a higher workload for holding the *Passive Smartphone* to their face than actively participating with an *Active Smartphone*. It is possible that the smaller screen size compared to the TV resulted in a higher cognitive and physical challenge. However, the average workload values do not exceed 29.5 points in any condition and are thus in a similar range to the values of the VR users.

Travel Distance. A significantly longer distance was covered in the *Active TV* condition than with an *Active Smartphone*, with a factor of 5.8 (92.1 m versus 15.9 m). We expected participants to make use of the freedom of movement, which they did not. This disconfirms hypothesis H_9 (The moved distance with active smartphones is greater than with gamepads). Only one participant used the provided tools for movement excessively, traveling 64.1 m with the *Active Smartphone* and 368.0 m with the *Active TV*. Bystanders tried to avoid the movement radius of the VR user, and were content with a position that let them comfortably see the entire memory board on their screen.

We found several correlations between the traveled distance and demographic data. Participants that were not familiar with gamepad controls generally moved less than those experienced with gamepads, and rated VR Invite more positively overall. There was a negative correlation between *Active TV* and age. Older participants moved significantly less. There was a positive correlation between *Active TV* and hours of playtime per week. More hours of playtime led to a significant increase in travel.

In short, there is an influence of 3D gaming experience on virtual scene exploration. There was no such effect for the *Active Smartphone*. This indicates that VR Invite is an intuitive tool that can be used independently of experience with virtual scenes. The familiarity with smartphones in general and the metaphor of the portable window led to a quick adoption of the technique.

Convenience Over Agency. After the study participants were asked to indicate which input method they preferred overall. Here, *Active TV* was chosen 18 times and *Active Smartphone* 8 times. Participants had an initial "wow-effect" with freedom of motion through VR Invite, but ultimately valued the comfort of sitting down with a controller in hand over room-scale movement and user agency. Screen size and having to hold up the phone over long periods of time were quoted as reasons for preferring the TV condition. It appears that there has to be a balance between convenience and interactivity, where avoidable movement is seen as a cost. The payoff or the incentive for movement seemingly has to be disproportionately big to outweigh the loss of convenience when there is an alternative form of interaction. To summarize, convenience predominates interactivity and agency if the payoff is not disproportionately big.

7   Conclusion and Future Work

We proposed and evaluated a prototype of a project-independent smartphone viewer app, which enables bystanders to explore and interact with PC or standalone VR applications with unexpected and interesting results. In the utilized memory VR exergame, the bystanders in particular reported a higher sense of presence and higher usability of the active conditions compared to the passive ones. However, the self-reported social presence was significantly lower during active than in passive conditions. Bystanders showed a higher independence and agency when using VR Invite, focusing on the task at hand rather than the VR user. However, agency appeared to negatively correlate with social presence in the explored bystander scenario. This indicates that VR Invite is best suited for implementations with active participation rather than pure observation, where a TV screen was preferred thanks to the convenience it provided. Overall, participants preferred the *TV* over VR Invite for single bystander scenarios, quoting convenience as main driving factor. This demonstrates that while user agency and interactivity are welcome and improve the experience over passive participation, convenience cannot be understated as a central factor of interaction paradigms.

VR Invite was rated to have satisfactory usability, and showed promising results that highlight the potential of individual view ports in use cases with multiple bystanders, where a single TV screen is not sufficient for multi user interactivity. The active component of the *TV* condition can also not be applied to multiple users, as the screen has either to be split or only one bystander can have control. Contrary, impromptu social sessions can make use of VR Invite's ability to quickly join an experience, providing multiple viewing angles. TV and VR Invite can of course be combined, with a neutral perspective on the TV and individual view ports for each bystander for personal agency and interactivity. Regarding agency, Gugenheimer et al. reported that mobile systems could significantly increase the enjoyment of a collaborative game [17]. Their findings indicate that VR Invite would be best suited for deliberately designed multi-user applications, making use of the provided touch interactivity.

Our next goal is the optimization of VR Invite with regards to image serialization and networking stack to make it more pleasant and versatile to use. This in turn will enable us to perform further studies with multiple bystanders to investigate social presence in groups of actively supporting users and one or multiple VR users. Furthermore, we plan to extend VR Invite to support augmented and mixed reality. In XR mode, the host computer or standalone XR device should only render the virtual objects of interest on a transparent background instead of the entire VE. The smartphone passes through its built-in camera feed to its display, and layers the video stream received from the rendering host on top. Implementing and testing these capabilities remains as a target for future work.

References

1. Github: VR Invite Source Code (2021). https://github.com/uhhhci/VRInvite. accessed 18 Jan 2021
2. Google: ARCore Overview (2021). https://developers.google.com/ar/discover. Accessed 18 Jan 2021
3. Master of Shapes: Mobile Room Scale (2021). https://masterofshapes.com/work/cover-me/. Accessed 18 Jan 2021
4. Owlchemy Labs: Mobile Spectator (2021). https://owlchemylabs.com/owlchemy-mobile-spectator-ar-spectator-camera/. Accessed 18 Jan 2021
5. Bangor, A., Kortum, P., Miller, J.: Determining what individual SUS scores mean: adding an adjective rating scale. J. Usability Stud. **4**(3), 114–123 (2009)
6. Billinghurst, M., Kato, H.: Collaborative augmented reality. Commun. ACM **45**(7), 64–70 (2002). https://doi.org/10.1145/514236.514265
7. Billinghurst, M., Poupyrev, I., Kato, H., May, R.: Mixing realities in shared space: an augmented reality interface for collaborative computing. In: 2000 IEEE International Conference on Multimedia and expo, ICME 2000, Proceedings. Latest Advances in the Fast Changing World of Multimedia (Cat. No. 00TH8532), vol. 3, pp. 1641–1644. IEEE (2000)
8. Biocca, F., Harms, C.: Networked minds social presence inventory:—(scales only, version 1.2) measures of co-presence, social presence, subjective symmetry, and intersubjective symmetry (2003)
9. Biocca, F., Harms, C., Gregg, J.: The networked minds measure of social presence: pilot test of the factor structure and concurrent validity. In: 4th Annual International Workshop on Presence, Philadelphia, PA, pp. 1–9 (2001)
10. Brooke, J., et al.: SUS-a quick and dirty usability scale. Usability Eval. Ind. **189**(194), 4–7 (1996)
11. Carlsson, C., Hagsand, O.: Dive a multi-user virtual reality system. In: Proceedings of IEEE Virtual Reality Annual International Symposium, pp. 394–400. IEEE (1993)
12. Cecil, J., Ramanathan, P., Rahneshin, V., Prakash, A., Pirela-Cruz, M.: Collaborative virtual environments for orthopedic surgery. In: 2013 IEEE International Conference on Automation Science and Engineering (CASE), pp. 133–137. IEEE (2013)
13. Churchill, E.F., Snowdon, D.: Collaborative virtual environments: an introductory review of issues and systems. Virtual Reality **3**(1), 3–15 (1998)
14. Coninx, K., Van Reeth, F., Flerackers, E.: A hybrid 2D/3D user interface for immersive object modeling. In: Proceedings Computer Graphics International, pp. 47–55. IEEE (1997)
15. Dedual, N.J., Oda, O., Feiner, S.K.: Creating hybrid user interfaces with a 2D multi-touch tabletop and a 3D see-through head-worn display. In: 2011 10th IEEE International Symposium on Mixed and Augmented Reality, pp. 231–232. IEEE (2011)
16. Duval, T., Fleury, C.: An asymmetric 2D pointer/3D ray for 3D interaction within collaborative virtual environments. In: Proceedings of the 14th International Conference on 3D Web Technology, pp. 33–41 (2009)

17. Gugenheimer, J., Stemasov, E., Frommel, J., Rukzio, E.: ShareVR: enabling colocated experiences for virtual reality between HMD and Non-HMD users. In: Proceedings of the 2017 CHI Conference on Human Factors in Computing Systems, pp. 4021–4033 (2017)
18. Gugenheimer, J., Stemasov, E., Sareen, H., Rukzio, E.: FaceDisplay: towards asymmetric multi-user interaction for nomadic virtual reality. In: Proceedings of the 2018 CHI Conference on Human Factors in Computing Systems, pp. 1–13 (2018)
19. Hart, S.G., Staveland, L.E.: Development of NASA-TLX (task load index): results of empirical and theoretical research. Adv. Psychol. **52**, 139–183 (1988)
20. Hodge, E.M., Tabrizi, M., Farwell, M.A., Wuensch, K.L.: Virtual reality classrooms: strategies for creating a social presence. Int. J. Soc. Sci. **2**(2), 105–109 (2008)
21. Holm, R., Stauder, E., Wagner, R., Priglinger, M., Volkert, J.: A combined immersive and desktop authoring tool for virtual environments. In: Proceedings IEEE Virtual Reality 2002, pp. 93–100. IEEE (2002)
22. Ibayashi, H., et al.: Dollhouse VR: a multi-view, multi-user collaborative design workspace with VR technology. In: SIGGRAPH Asia 2015 Emerging Technologies, pp. 1–2 (2015)
23. Jones, B., et al.: RoomAlive: magical experiences enabled by scalable, adaptive projector-camera units. In: Proceedings of the 27th Annual ACM Symposium on User Interface Software and Technology, pp. 637–644 (2014)
24. Kallioniemi, P., Ronkainen, K., Karhu, J., Sharma, S., Hakulinen, J., Turunen, M.: CityCompass VR - a collaborative virtual language learning environment. In: Lamas, D., Loizides, F., Nacke, L., Petrie, H., Winckler, M., Zaphiris, P. (eds.) INTERACT 2019. LNCS, vol. 11749, pp. 540–543. Springer, Cham (2019). https://doi.org/10.1007/978-3-030-29390-1_33
25. Lindley, S.E., Le Couteur, J., Berthouze, N.L.: Stirring up experience through movement in game play: effects on engagement and social behaviour. In: Proceedings of the SIGCHI Conference on Human Factors in Computing Systems, pp. 511–514 (2008)
26. Oda, O., Elvezio, C., Sukan, M., Feiner, S., Tversky, B.: Virtual replicas for remote assistance in virtual and augmented reality. In: Proceedings of the 28th Annual ACM Symposium on User Interface Software & Technology, pp. 405–415 (2015)
27. Oliveira, J.C., Shen, X., Georganas, N.D.: Collaborative virtual environment for industrial training and e-commerce. IEEE VRTS 288 (2000)
28. Passos, C., Da Silva, M.H., Mol, A.C., Carvalho, P.V.: Design of a collaborative virtual environment for training security agents in big events. Cogn. Technol. Work **19**(2–3), 315–328 (2017)
29. Rings, S., Steinicke, F., Dewitz, B., Büntig, F., Geiger, C.: EXGAVINE - exergames as novel form of therapy in virtual reality for the treatment of neurological diseases (2019)
30. Slater, M., Usoh, M., Steed, A.: Depth of presence in virtual environments. Presence Teleoperators Virtual Environ. **3**(2), 130–144 (1994)
31. Tsoupikova, D., Triandafilou, K., Solanki, S., Barry, A., Preuss, F., Kamper, D.: Real-time diagnostic data in multi-user virtual reality post-stroke therapy. In: SIGGRAPH ASIA 2016 VR Showcase, pp. 1–2 (2016)

Assistive Technology for Visually Impaired

"Honestly I Never Really Thought About Adding a Description": Why Highly Engaged Tweets Are Inaccessible

Mallak Alkhathlan$^{(\boxtimes)}$ iD, M. L. Tlachac$^{(\boxtimes)}$ iD, Lane Harrison$^{(\boxtimes)}$ iD, and Elke Rundensteiner$^{(\boxtimes)}$ iD

Worcester Polytechnic Institute, Worcester, MA 01609, USA
{malkhathlan,mltlachac,ltharrison,rundenst}@wpi.edu

Abstract. Alternative (alt) text is vital for visually impaired users to consume digital images with screen readers. When these image descriptions are not incorporated, these users encounter accessibility challenges. In this study, we explore the prevalence and user understanding of alt text in Twitter. First, we assess the availability of alt text by collecting the Twitter Engagement (TWEN) dataset which contains over 1000 high engagement tweets regarding online articles from the most popular Google Keywords. We focused on keywords that create an engagement in Twitter in order to study the possibility of creating priorities of media content that missing alt text then adding descriptions to them by crowdsourcer to help the visually impaired to be equal like others in the social media communities. Our findings reveal approximately 91% of the tweets contained images and videos, less than 1% of the images had alt text. Thus, even highly engaged tweets remain inaccessible to visually impaired individuals. Thus, we designed two guided concepts to raise awareness of high engagement. We then surveyed 100 sighted participants to understand their perception of alt text and evaluate strategies to increase the frequency of alt text for highly engaged content. Our value-based guided concept was well received by the majority of the study participants.

Keywords: Image captions · Image description · Alt text · Accessibility · Visual impairment · Twitter

1 Introduction

Alternative (alt) text, commonly referred to as descriptions, are tags used to describe images, GIFs, diagrams, and illustrations to a non-textual content [50]. Digital images are prevalent, existing on websites, platforms, applications, e-publications, and software. The alt text tag plays a vital role in helping visually impaired users to understand the content. Nowadays assistive technology such as a screen-reader (e.g., Apple Voice-over, Microsoft Narrator, TalkBack) helps

© IFIP International Federation for Information Processing 2021
Published by Springer Nature Switzerland AG 2021
C. Ardito et al. (Eds.): INTERACT 2021, LNCS 12932, pp. 373–395, 2021.
https://doi.org/10.1007/978-3-030-85623-6_23

people who are visually impaired to render screen reader elements into a speech. Recent changes in the world including the ease of use and access to mobile phones with cameras have contributed to the heavy dissemination of images on the internet. In 2014, 1.8 billion digital images were uploaded through social media platforms WhatsApp, Facebook, Instagram, Snapchat, and Flickr [33]. This number is only increasing as social media becomes more popular as evidenced by WhatsApp users alone uploading 4.5 billion digital images in 2017 [38].

In 1999, HTML 4.0 specified standards to meet the needs of visually impaired persons. Now authors need to specify an image description in the "alt" field attribute of the image's HTML tag so screen readers are able to access the image [31,40,47]. Yet, image descriptions are lacking on social media. This results in visually impaired users being unable to access images and GIFs, leading to inequality access among Twitter, Facebook, and Instagram social media platforms [5,16,36,64]. Twitter remains one of the more popular social media platforms. In February 2019, Twitter reported 126 million daily users, an increase of 9% from the prior year [46]. Twitter's simple text-based interface makes it more accessible to screen readers than other more popular social media platforms such as Facebook [8]. As such, Twitter is especially popular with visually impaired users. Specifically, a survey of blind Twitter users revealed 88.4% used Twitter for news and 72% used Twitter for entertainment [36].

Unfortunately, images on Twitter are largely inaccessible to the visually impaired. In 2019 [16], researchers highlighted the barrier of missing descriptions. Findings revealed only 0.1% of tweets with images contained image descriptions [16]. According to the World Health Organization, in 2019, the number of visually impaired in the world was approximately 2.2 billion [65]. Twitter media content (i.e. image, GIF) is one of the most important components of the social network. Users interact on Twitter through liking, retweeting, and/or replying to a tweet. This creates more intellectual communication between members of the Twitter community. Twitter is a way to socialize among the visually impaired, though many studies have shown that the visually impaired face difficult challenges to overcome the amount of media contained in Twitter [32,36,67].

As the visually impaired depend on screen readers to consume tweets, media content is inaccessible if it lacks a description. While there is a feature for adding descriptions, it is optional. Despite the improvements to this feature from 2011 to 2020, many sighted users still neglect to add descriptions to media content. Thus, in our work, we propose using content engagement to measure the priority of adding descriptions to multimedia content. This would make crowdsourcing solutions more effective as descriptions would be added to the content with the highest engagement before content with lower engagement. We designed visual icons to notify users that content has high engagement and needs descriptions.

In this study, we first determine the frequency of descriptions in the media content of tweets about a diverse range of highly engaged topics. Then we survey sighed users to understand how to increase description compliance and the perception of our visual icons on tweets with multimedia content. As far as we know, there is no recent tweet data set available to the public that includes highly engaged keywords that causes missing alt text. Our contributions include:

1. Identifying the type of Twitter content that users engage with the most to build a popular data set,
2. Determining the frequency of media content and descriptions in this set of highly engaged tweets, and
3. Surveying sighted users to understand how to increase the description frequency of highly engaged media content on Twitter through crowd-sourcing.

2   Related Work

Our study urges that the community should share the same social media applications interface with the visually impaired users. We believe that the community is able to increase the percentage of visual content descriptions if the way is paved through the visual notification in the application interface like what propose in our research. Our study builds on previous work by Gleason et al. [16] which focuses on images from the most popular Twitter accounts. Unlike Gleason et al., our research includes other forms of media content such as animated GIFs, videos, and URL previews. Additionally, while Gleason et al. focused on tweets from the most popular twitter accounts, we focus on the tweets containing the most popular keywords. This allows us to capture a tweets about highly engaged topics from a diverse range of Twitter users. In first phase of our study, we hypothesize even highly engaged media content are likely to lack text descriptions on Twitter. Our research is further unique in that it covers the difficulties in finding media content with descriptions on Twitter as well as the important role crowdsourcing could play in providing descriptions for visually impaired users.

2.1   Visually Impaired Users and Twitter

Twitter was founded in 2006 and originally provided a rather simplistic text-based interface thus making it popular for people who are blind [8], but the social media platform started featuring embedded photos in tweets on June 2011 [12]. In 2016 [52] Twitter added a description option on Twitter which needed to be adjusted through the settings. Even users who activated this setting to describe an image did not always provide a description. Furthermore, in May 2020 Twitter modified this feature and users can add the description directly without setting [59]. However, this important feature is not well advertised so many users may be unaware of its existence or the value of including descriptions.

The number of monthly active users on Twitter reached 340 million in 2020 [26]. Tweet engagement is measured through the quantity of likes, retweets, and replies. Engagement and trust are used by influencer marketing to predict the popularity of products [1,61], but many promotions contain visual content without a description [57]. Politics are also frequently discussed on Twitter, in particular during elections [25], and the lack of descriptions impedes the ability of visually impaired users to participate [54]. Regrettably, media content descriptions in tweets are very rare. A study [16] found only 0.1% of 9.22 million tweets with images contained descriptions. Despite the lack of descriptions, Twitter remains popular among visually impaired people who use Twitter to get updates on the latest news, entertainment, and social relations [36]. In addition to images, Twitter also supports videos and GIFs to increase user participation. These media content types allow for expression that static images are unable to capture. However, GIFs are silent animations which make them even more difficult for visually impaired users to consume, creating additional accessibility issues [2]. A survey including 3.7 million accounts found that Tweets with GIFs received 55% greater engagement than those without GIFs [60], demonstrating GIFs are an important tool to increase tweet engagement. Without descriptions, these highly engaged tweets are inaccessible to visually impaired users.

2.2 Methods to Generate Alternative Text

Image-based tweets are highly varied and therefore existing automated image description tools [36,44] are not easily adapted to work on Twitter. In this section we will discuss three strategies for generating content media descriptions.

Human-Powered Approaches. Human-powered approaches specifically refer to human-in-the-loop labeling provided via crowd-powered systems. Researchers [6] have proposed 13 human-powered access technology design principles inspired by both historical and recent technical advances that have potential to make environments more available for people with disabilities. VizWiz [4] is a free iPhone application that allows visually impaired people take pictures, ask questions, and then receive answers from the Amazon Mechanical Turk (mTurk) crowd-sourcing platform in less than 30 s. RegionSpeak [69] is a system that allows blind people to send, receive, and collect more information with crowd-sourcing by providing an easy way to integrate visual details from several images by image stitching which significantly decrease the number of encounters and complete time spent on finding answers. There are also other studies about how to help add image descriptions that rely on human annotators [7,8,42,63].

Automated Approaches. Researchers developed and deployed Automatic Alt-Text (AAT) that applies the computer vision technology to identify images and generates alt text on Facebook [68]. There are other approach to automatically generate image descriptions but these are also not intended for visually impaired individuals [14,30,53,62]. Other research focuses on learning how to recognize objects and relationships. This is generally accomplished with trained computer vision models which input an image to generate a related caption [13,28,41].

Hybrid Approaches. Caption Crawler is a system that proposes a reverse image search to retrieve existing descriptions on the internet for static images [23]. TweetTalk generates human editing descriptions or tags to save time and financial costs for the recruitment of human crowd workers. This is done through the development and assessment of constructed social media image questions that can instruct humans or AI systems to the invention of captions that contain certain types of details most desired by the visually impaired [44]. Research has also leveraged social media posts to explore the value in alternative text formats and how crowdsourcing could answer new questions about popular imagery [45]. Other approaches often consist of combining generated descriptions or tags with human editing [5,43]. Twitter Ally [17] is browser extension to add alt text on to image tweets accessible, however such a system should not be relied upon as an alternative, as it will likely either misidentify objects or not provide an appropriate level of detail in descriptions, especially for scientific purposes [11].

2.3   UI/UX Design Awareness on Social Media

Recently there has been an explosion of data quantity and data sources. For instance, facets of social lives are being increasingly disseminated on social media, essentially allowing for social lives to be transformed into quantifiable information. This increase in data has caused User Interface (UI) and User Experience (UX) design to become increasingly important. In several different contexts, the importance of UX has been studied, especially in the low rate of participatory design awareness. These studies have been used to inform the development of persuasive technologies within the human computer interaction (HCI) community [15,19,20,29,37,66]. The two main ways to portray data is numerically and visually [21,27,39]. Further, research recognizes people historically respond better to evidence when numerical values are involved [39]. Despite enormous research on the accessibility of the Web and on developing standards [22], frameworks and legal standards, awareness of designers [49], and tools to make textbooks accessible [10], access to certain content remains hindered. Unfortunately, creative, dynamic, and adaptable UI/UX design methods that simultaneously benefit both blind users and sighted user have been largely ignored in academic literature. Thus, we explore the use of UX to convey missing alt text using two concepts: (1) numerical guided concept and (2) photo icon guided concept.

3   Twitter Engagement Experiment and Dataset

3.1   Data Collection

In the first phase of our research, we collected the Twitter Engagement (TWEN) data set which consists of data regarding three types of content media on Twitter: image, video, and text. Specifically, this data set is unique as it focuses on Twitter

#	keywords	URL	Total Twitter Engagement (top 3 URL)	Top 3 URL Tweets (15 tweets)														
				1	2	3	4	5	6	7	8	9	10	11	12	13	14	15
1	Weather	5000	26385	I	I	I	I	I	I	V	I	I	I	V	V	V	V	V
2	Maps	5000	25151	I	I	V	I	V	V	I	I	I	I	I	I	I	I	I
3	Translate	5000	6354	I	I	I	I	I	I	I	I	I	I	I	I	I	I	I
4	Calculator	5000	4184	I	I	I	I	I	I	I	I	I	I	I	I	I	I	I
5	Youtube to mp3	116	161	I	I	I	I	I	N	N	N	N	N	I	I	I	I	I
6	speed test	289	1043	N	I	I	I	I	I	I	I	V	V	I	I	B	B	B
7	news	5000	498762	N	V	V	V	V	T	T	T	T	T	I	I	I	I	I
8	thesaurus	375	179	I	T	T	T	I	I	I	B	B	B	I	T	T	T	T
9	poweball	1240	2462	I	T	T	T	B	N	N	N	N	I	I	I	I	I	I
10	donald trump	5000	250554	I	I	I	I	I	I	I	I	I	I	I	I	I	I	I

Fig. 1. Tabular representation of the TWEN data set which indicates the media content of the tweets for the top ten keywords. The tweets are labeled as containing a thumbnail (N), large image (I), video (V), and just text (T). Broken (B) tweets are also noted.

engagement with online articles, thus resulting in a high percent of images and videos. In order to get articles on a variety of popular topics, we choose topics based on the top 100 keywords searched on Google as of June 2018 [48]. We have chosen this list of keywords because they might lead us to find the important tweets that people may interact with often then add description to later, In addition this list is not associated with a brand and has removed porn-related keywords. For each of keyword (such as weather, maps, news, donald trump, game of thrones, etc.), we use Twitter's premium Tweet search API [55,56], to identify the top three articles with the most Twitter engagement by utilizing premium operators to deliver article engagement based on filtering rules where a queries length are the 100 keywords. We defined the article engagement as the number of times tweets mentioning the article were retweeted, replied, and liked. These articles were from June 22, 2019 through April 4, 2020.

For each article, we collect data about the top five tweets with the highest engagement that reference each selected article's URL, resulting in at most 1500 tweets. We removed ten keywords that contains only one letter such as 'g' and 'f' to avoid matches an exact phrase within the body of a Tweet which may return unexpected results (for example 'f' means Facebook). Of the 1350 extracted tweets, 262 were broken due to the tweets being deleted by the user who posted them or blocked on Twitter. Thus, TWEN is comprised of 1088 tweets. While each tweet has a 280 character limit, Twitter Cards allow for the inclusion of images and videos. Our data set consists of four types of cards. First, a Summary Card includes a thumbnail image of the referenced website, description, and text. Second, a Summary Card with Large Image is very similar to a Summary card except the image is larger than a thumbnail. Third, a Player Card allows for the inclusion of audio, videos, and GIFs. Additionally, our data set contains tweets with only text which we refer to as a Text Card. A tabular view TWEN content is displayed in Fig. 1 for the top ten keywords. As seen, there are fifteen tweets, five for each of the articles. We filtered the tweets using operator 'url:' (this refers only to tweets that have URLs that point to media hosted elsewhere). We used 'has:links' and 'has:media' operators to control the API request from the stream. We collect at most 5000 URLs within a tweet for each of the top 100 keywords. Twitter engagement is calculated for the top three article's URLs.

3.2   Findings

Figure 2 contains a summary of TWEN content. Of the 1088 tweets, 902 contain images, 92 contain video, and 94 contain only text. Over 91.4% of the tweets contained content media, demonstrating the prevalence of images and videos in highly engaged tweets about highly engaged articles. In particular, tweets with large images were highly prevalent in TWEN. While videos were less common, Player Cards which support videos were only introduced to Twitter in 2017. None of the videos or thumbnails contained descriptions and only one percent of the 752 large images contained descriptions for visually impaired users. While this alt text can be added to non-textual content on Twitter, it is an optional card property field which is clearly rarely utilized for media content [58].

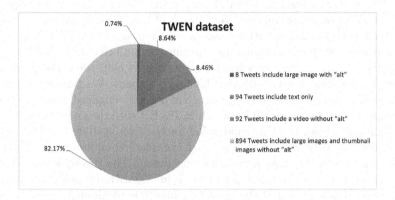

Fig. 2. TWEN shows highly engaged tweets rarely have alt text.

We also compare the content media of the tweets from each of the article URLs, as seen in Table 1. We collected the five most engaged tweets from each of the three most engaged articles for each keyword. Recall, engagement is the summation of the number of likes, retweets, and replays. Tweets referencing the first URL yielded 279 Large Images, which is higher than the second or third URLs. As with the full data set, tweets with Large Images were the most common media content for all URLs. The most engaged (first) URLs have the highest number of tweets with large images and videos. Our threshold of 100,000 engagements serves to prioritize highly-engaged tweets so that they can reach high description compliance. Based on the data, displayed in Fig. 1, we found that the 10 keywords with the highest number of engagements each had more than 100,000 engagements. For example, the keyword 'movies' ranks first with 652,715 engagements. We set our threshold as 100,000 engagements, though this algorithmic threshold could be easily readjusted based on a larger dataset.

Table 1. Distribution of the 1088 TWEN tweets with the article URLs.

Media content	First URL	Second URL	Third URL
Large image	279	239	234
Thumbnail	42	60	48
Video	39	26	27
Text only	32	32	30
Total	392	357	339

TWEN reveals that highly engaged tweets contain plentiful visual content with few descriptions. Large images were the most common type of media content in the tweets. Given the rich visual details in these images, it is most important for them to contain descriptions. Yet, only 8 of the 752 large images contained descriptions. Unfortunately, this poses a major obstacle to Twitter's visually impaired users as they are unable to consume the majority of the most engaged tweets on Twitter. Thus, we consider strategies to help solve the problem of missing descriptions for tweets with high engagement. We propose a publicly visible icon to notify users to the presence of a highly engaged tweet that needs a description. As there were 10 keywords in TWEN with the engagements of over 100 thousand, we set the threshold value for the icon at 100 thousand engagements. We believe if we are unable reach complete compliance, our threshold serves to prioritize the most highly engaged tweets. The threshold can be readjusted as needed. We design a pseudocode in Algorithm 1 which is an informal high-level description of the operating principle to highlight how we add a flag to tweets that have highly engaged media content. We believe this icon will increase description compliance for the most important media content, thus making highly engaged content more accessible for visibly impaired users on Twitter. In the next experiment, we test the effectiveness of this proposed strategy.

3.3   Contributions and Availability

The TWEN dataset contributes information about the variety and types of imagery being shared on Twitter. Upon publication, we will make the entire tabular representation of TWEN, a subset of which is shown in Fig. 1, publicly available at https://osf.io/ksyzx/?view_only=a68dd37bf108424d8006e2d7071e3bdd. Our approach for identifying highly engaged tweets can help inform future research and the design of enhanced automated approaches for captioning.

Algorithm 1. Strategy to identify highly engaged tweets that need a concept flag to encourage descriptions.

```
 1: if the tweet has a media content then
 2:     if media content has a description then
 3:         Don't do anything
 4:     else if the engagement of the tweet ≥ 100,000 then
 5:         Add concept flag to the tweet
 6:     else
 7:         Don't do anything "tweet is not highly engaged"
 8:     end if
 9: else
10:     Don't do anything "tweet has no media content"
11: end if
```

4 UX Accessibility Design Experiment

4.1 Motivation and Research Questions

Building from the results of TWEN, we conducted an experiment to explore themes of encouragement and awareness. The purpose of this experiment is to help understand how extensive the problem is that causes missing alt text in media content. This is done by assisting Twitter users in describing tweets that need more attention, i.e., have very large engagement. We also explored strategies to encourage additions of descriptions to media content. Responses were collected with a survey distributed on Twitter. This experiment was designed to answer three main research questions:

- RQ1: To what extent are our findings from the TWEN data set consistent with surveyed participant experience?
- RQ2: Is there a difference in effectiveness between engagement flags using a numeric value versus a photo icon?
- RQ3: What are guidelines for improving the frequency of media content descriptions on social media?

4.2 Recruitment and Respondents

To ensure applicable results, we purchased an advertisement on Twitter to recruit Twitter users to take our IRB-approved survey. Specifically, we targeted users with location in the United States and English as their language. We sought responses from people of all genders. The recruited participants should be at least 18 years old, have a Twitter account, and participate voluntarily. We used the Qualtrics survey platform and received 101 valid responses. 36.6% identified as female and 63.4% as male. Participants achieved varied highest levels of education: 3% had less than a high school degree, 15.7% had high school diplomas or equivalents, 12.9% had some college but no degree, 13.9% had Associate's degrees, 41.6% had Bachelor's degrees, 8.9% Master's degree,

1% had Doctoral degrees, and 3% had professional degrees. Users identified varied reasons for using Twitter: news and updates (75.5%), following celebrities and brands (32.7%), entertainment (63.4%), social engagement (48.5%), finding a job (1%), and (5.9%) indicated business (note that some respondents select more than one choice in this question). Further self-reported demographics for the 101 participants are in Table 2.

Table 2. Distribution of participant age and frequency/distribution of Twitter use.

Age	%	Frequency of use	%	Duration of use	%
18–24	2%	Multiple times a day	45.5%	<1 year	2%
25–34	39.6%	Once a day	23.8%	1–3 years	18.8%
35–44	35.6%	Multiple times per week	22.7	3–5 years	14.8%
45+	22.8%	Monthly	7.9%	>5 years	64.4%

4.3   Experimental Procedure

There were eight parts to the survey instrument:

1. **Demographic questions:** We presented participants with multiple-choice questions about their Twitter use frequency, age, gender, education, main goals of using Twitter, and length of time they have been using Twitter.
2. **User experience with Twitter:** We first asked respondents to select the type of media they share most on Twitter. Next, we ask them to rank on a Likert scale the frequency they have *written a description when they tweet a media content (i.e. images, GIFs)*. Those who included a description were asked about the source of their descriptions with options including *bot, their own words*, and write-in. Lastly, we presented an screenshot to participants and asked them if *they think image in the bounding box has a description?*
3. **High priority of the engagement:** In the prior experiment, we found only 1% of the highly engaged tweets with media content contained descriptions. As such, this section of questions is to determine if the level of engagement influences users willingness to act as a crowdsourcer by adding a description. We first provide a definition of engagement (like + retweet + replay). We then ask participants to select what media content they would *choose to write a description for* with options varying the level of engagement.
4. **Concept effectiveness:** Respondents were asked to rate on Likert scales the *effectiveness of the numerical value concept* and the *effectiveness the photo guided concept* in comparison to the default concept used by Twitter.
5. **Concept Interest:** Respondents were asked to rate our numerical value and photo guided concepts as well as the Twitter default concept on Likert scales. Options ranged from being *interested* to *disinterested*.

6. **Overall awareness**: We asked respondents to indicate if they are aware of the recent Twitter announcement on May 27, 2020 explaining how descriptions can be added without having enter settings. Participants were also asked to rate on Likert scale their willingness to turn a *screen reader on to see whether or not the image has a description.* We educate the participants on how a screen reader works and why it is used in case they are not aware of this type of technology. As twitter currently hides media descriptions, we also asked participants to rate on Likert scale if they agree with the statement: *Twitter can improve on how it displays invisible descriptions.*

7. **Overall preference**: We asked respondents to select if they preferred the Twitter default, numerical value, or photo guided concept.

8. **Request for further information**: Participants who selected at least *sometimes* regarding their description frequency in part two were automatically prompted to answer the open-ended question: *Why did they add a description to the media content (i.e. images, GIFs)?* Those who selected *Never* were prompted to answer the open-ended question: *Why did they not add a description when they tweeted media content (i.e. images, GIFs)?*

During the survey, participants were asked questions related to our design concepts which we refer to as *guided concepts.* The related questions regarded a news feed on the Twitter interface. Participants compared our numerical value guided concept and photo guided concept with the default concept currently used by Twitter. For this study, we chose a tweet with $likes = 9.9k$, $retweets = 2.7k$ and $replies = 49$. As seen in Figs. 3, 4 and 5, the tweet also contains both text and an image missing a description. Our hypothesis is that many users will fail to distinguish between text at the top of the tweet and the description.

Fig. 3. Numerical value guided concept: the screenshot featuring the numerical value guided concept.

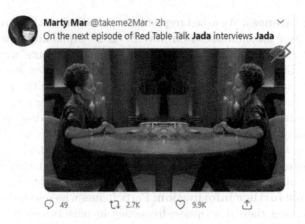

Fig. 4. Photo guided concept: the screenshot featuring the photo guided concept.

Fig. 5. Twitter default concept: displays the screenshot with Twitter's default concept.

For all three concepts, we first asked participants to familiarize themselves with the concept. The screenshot featuring the numerical value guided concept is displayed in Fig. 3. The tweet includes a small icon on the top right-hand side of the image to indicate very high engagement. The screenshot featuring the photo guided concept is displayed in Fig. 4. The tweet includes a depiction of an eye on the top right-hand side of the image to indicate very high engagement. Lastly, Fig. 5 displays the screenshot with Twitter's default concept.

4.4   Analysis

We use qualitative and quantitative analysis in our survey. We focus on three independent variables: 1) *numerical value guided concept*, 2) *photo guided concept*, and 3) *default Twitter concept*. Currently, Twitter hides the descriptions.

Table 3. WN: type of participants responses about why not to add a description.

Category	Description
Time consuming	Statement explaining how adding a description takes time and effort
Type of follower	Statement about personal followers (i.e. friends/family) who are not vision impaired
Misunderstood the necessity of alt text	Statement about how media content can speak for itself without the need to add more explanation
Not expecting blind or low vision (BLV) audience on Twitter	Statement expressing surprise about the existence of users who are blind and might follow them
How to add alt text?	Statement about the location of the option to add description and how it is used

Table 4. WA: the type of participants responses about why to add a description.

Category	Description
Accessible	Statement about how adding descriptions would enable blind users to understand concept of tweets
Post humors	Statement regarding how adding descriptions often makes media content more fun
Easy	Statement about how easy it is to write a description
Deep meaning	Statement about the amount of details when delivering a vague image
More info	statement about how adding descriptions would give clarifications
Out of topic	Statement that is not related to the description

We also focus on a variety of different dependent variables. During the second part of the survey, we collected responses to four questions regarding user experience with Twitter. Participants could respond to *"I often tweet <type of content>* with content types 1 = *text*, 2 = *image*, 3 = *GIF/video*, and 4 = *poll*. A Likert scale ranging from 1 = *always* to 5 = *never* was used to gauge *"if they have ever written a description when they tweet a media content"*. Participants could respond to *"what type of descriptions have been used to write a description"* with 1 = *bot*, 2 = *my own words*, and 3 = *other*. For the question regarding description existence, participants could respond to *"<type of answer> the image has a description"* with answer types 1 = *I think*, 2 = *I don't think*,

$3 = I$ *think there is no way to know if*, or $4 = other$. We will refer to these questions about **user experience with Twitter** as UE1, UE2, UE3, and UE4.

In part three, responses included *very highly engaged, very low engaged, both,* and a write-in option. We will refer to the **high priority of the engagement** as HP1. In part four we collected three Likert scale ratings on the effectiveness of the numerical value, photo guided, and Twitter default concepts. We refer to these five-point scales regarding **concept effectiveness** as EC1, EC2, and EC3. Likewise, in part five, we collect three Likert scale ratings regarding interest in the numerical value, photo guided, and Twitter default concepts. We refer to these five-point scales regarding **concept interest** as ICO1, ICO2, and ICO3.

In part six, we collected one quantitative reply and two Likert scales. Options regarding awareness of Twitter's announcement about descriptions were *aware* and *not aware*. Participants rated their likelihood of screen reader use and the potential Twitter improvement on five-point scales. We refer to these **overall awareness** replies as OA1, OA2, and OA3. In part seven, participants selected whether they preferred the *default Twitter concept, numerical value guided concept,* or *photo guided concept*. We refer to **overall preference** as OP1.

In last part of the survey, we collected open ended answers regarding motivation for adding and not adding descriptions. We performed qualitative analysis by conducting an inductive and deductive reasoning method that performed axial coding [51]. We used inductive logic to identify the reasons for missing image description and deductive reasoning to attribute missing descriptions to a particular concept which allows us to apply it to the theory. We then leverage a semantic analysis technique [18] to identify and code text segments according to the parent codes. According to Braun and Clark [9], when searching for themes one should "not [be] looking for anything beyond what a participant has said or written". Thus, our semantic analysis involves dividing the data into subsets and assigning a unique child code to a parent theme code among all participants' responses. For motivating **description exclusion**, child codes include the statements in Table 3, referred to as WN. For motivating **description inclusion**, child codes include the statements in Table 4, referred to as WA.

4.5   Findings

User Experience with Twitter. *UE1:* 75.2% of participants reported that the majority of their tweets contained only text. 18.8%, 5.0%, and 1.0% reported they most tweeted images, videos, and polls, respectively. *UE2:* 43.6% of participants reported never writing a description while only 1.0% reported always writing descriptions. The remaining participants either wrote descriptions sometimes (31.7%) or half of the time (13.9%). Thus, most participants fail to add a description to most of their media content, even when it is a known option. *UE3:* 98.0% of participants reported using *their own words* when including a description. 2.0% of participants reported using *other* when including a description. None reported using a *bot*. *UE4:* When shown the image, 53.5% of participants reported they thought there was a description while 39.6% of participants reported they thought there was no description. Only 6.9% of participants correctly indicated that there was no way for them to know. This confirms that many people do not know that the description is not visible on the tweet. Currently, the only ways to view descriptions are screen readers or browsers that allow viewing of the HTML source code. We also found a statistically significant relationship between among female and male participants. 71.4% of female participants reported that there was no way to know if there is a description, a view shared by only 28.6% of male participants. To determine the statistical significance, we used Chi-Squared test with p-value = 0.01 and effect size (Cramér's V) = 0.280.

High Priority of the Engagement. *HP1:* About half (53.5%) of participants reported they would add descriptions to the content of highly engaged tweets. A third (32.7%) reported they would want to add descriptions to both tweets with high and low engagement. 1% reported other and the remaining 12.9% would add descriptions to only lowly engaged tweets.

Concept Effectiveness. *EC1-EC3*, respondents rated the perceived effectiveness of the numerical guided *(EC1)*, photo guided *(EC2)*, and Twitter default *(EC3)* concepts. The five-point Likert scale responses were normally distributed. The concept effectiveness for the numerical guided *EC1* (M = 3.25, SD = 1.09) was rated higher than the photo guided *EC2* (M = 2.95, SD = 1.15): t(100) = 2.243, p = 0.027. The effect size using Cohen's d to indicate a standardized difference between two means is 0.264, suggesting a small effect. The concept effectiveness was also rated higher for numerical guided *EC1* (M = 3.25, SD = 1.09) compared to Twitter default *EC3* (M = 2.75, SD = 1.10): t(100) = 2.6, p = 0.026. Cohen's d for this comparison is 0.451, suggesting a medium effect. We do not refer to these differences as statistically significant, however, as a Bonferonni correction for two comparisons would yield an adjusted threshold of p < 0.05/2 or 0.025. We instead refer to these results as weak but inconclusive evidence that the numerical guided concept *(EC1)* is more effective than the photo guided concept *(EC2)* and the default concept *(EC3)*. The results suggest that future experiments in this area may benefit from larger sample sizes or expanded Likert ranges (e.g. a 7- or 9-point scale) to provide more opportunity for participants to relatively order the alternatives.

Concept Interest. *ICO1-ICO3*, respondents rated both the numerical value guided *(ICO1)* than the photo value guided *(ICO2)* and the Twitter default *(ICO3)* concepts. The five-point Likert scale responses were normally distributed. The numerical guided *ICO1* (M = 3.31, SD = 1.18) was rated higher than photo value guided *ICO2* (M = 3.02, SD = 1.11): t(100) = 2.26, p = 0.025. The effect sizes using Cohen's d to indicate a standardized difference between two means is 0.25, suggesting a small effect. The numerical guided *ICO1* (M = 3.31, SD = 1.18) was also rated higher than the Twitter default *ICO3* (M = 2.69,

$SD = 1.18$): $t(100) = 2.61$, $p = 0.01$. The effect sizes using Cohen's d to indicate a standardized difference between two means is 0.52, suggesting a medium effect. Applying the same Bonferroni correction, the latter result favoring numerical guided *ICO1* over the Twitter default *ICO3* would be considered strong statistical evidence. There was little difference in the rated interest between *ICO2* and *ICO3*.

Table 5. WN: category distribution of participants who are not adding descriptions.

Category	%	P	Example quote from participant *P*
Time consuming	9.1%	P99	*"To tweet with the added image description and text takes extra time."*
Type of followers	18.2%	P77	*"None of the people who follow me are visually impaired, so I don't think it's necessary to put in the effort."*
Misunderstood the necessity of alt text	20.5%	P37	*"The ones that i use are specific, they generally speak for themselves when i do tweet media so there is no need to add a description."*
Not expecting BLV audience on Twitter	38.6%	P29	*"Honestly I never really thought about adding a description for those that have vision issues."*
How to add alt text?	13.6%	P33	*"I'd have no idea how to do it. I do not know how to expand on that, sorry. This will have to be enough."*

Table 6. WA: category distribution of participants who are adding descriptions.

Category	%	P	Example quote from participant *P*
Accessible	10.53%	P80	*"I would want them to have the same info I do."*
Post humors	7.0%	P64	*"help to convey the message, usually a parody."*
Easy	1.8%	P12	*"Because its quick to do and easy."*
Deep meaning	19.3%	P73	*"I think that it is necessary in some cases to give some depth or understanding to the image."*
More info	40.4%	P97	*"I think I would do it if people did not understand the context or they can't otherwise read it."*
Out of topic	21.5%	P55	*"I always add GIFS."*

Overall Awareness. *OA1:* Only 16.8% of participants were aware of Twitter's announcement about descriptions. *OA2:* 6.9% of participants reported that they would definitely turn on the screen reader and 20.8% reported that they probably would. 23.8% of participants reported they would definitely not turn on the screen reader and 25.7% reported that they probably would not. The remaining 22.8% were neutral. Almost half of respondents were unwilling to turn on a screen reader while less than a third of participants were willing to turn on a screen reader. As such, We conclude that effective strategies must make descriptions visible to the public. *OA3:* 28.7% and 43.6% of participants strongly and somewhat agreed respectively that Twitter can improve how it displays descriptions. 24.8% were neutral, 3.0% somewhat disagreed, and none strongly disagreed.

Overall Preference. *OP1:* Only 15.8% of participants reported that they preferred Twitter's default concept. 54.5% preferred the numerical value guided concept and 29.7% preferred the photo guided concept. This confirms the participants wanted to know if they can help others by writing a description.

Request for Further Information. *WN:* We found participants who are not adding descriptions can be distributed into five categories, as displayed in Table 5. *WA:* We found participants who are adding descriptions can be distributed into six categories as displayed in Table 6.

5 Discussion

One purpose of this study is to understand how to best integrate the BLV population in social media. Making information accessible to all is an important concept in justice and equality [3]. Currently, fairness [24] and artificial intelligence [34,35] research do not meet the needs of the visually impaired community. Artificial intelligence is not yet capable of accurately describing images. Further, there is a mistrust in image descriptions with prior research [23] indicating visually impaired users desire multiple descriptions to confirm accuracy. Our study reveals new design opportunities for improving UX accessibility technologies by enabling crowdsourcing to involved in adding description. In this study, we found that informing users about the need for descriptions will be useful in urging society to invent multiple ways to adding accurate descriptions to media content on social media. For instance, displaying a guided concept on tweets that have received high engagements and need a description will enable willing members of the community to add descriptions of the image. This could have a significant positive effect to the BLV community by providing multiple descriptions for the most pertinent visual content on social media.

5.1 Implication of TWEN

Through our collection of TWEN, we demonstrate a technique to identify highly engaged tweets across a wide variety of popular topics. This technique could be leveraged in the future and the resulting engagement count inform the threshold for adding a guided concept to highly engaged images missing descriptions. The TWEN data set revealed the need for such a guided concept as less than 1% of the images contained descriptions. The 8 descriptions in TWEN were for the keywords "trump" and "mail". The evidence about keywords corresponding to high engagement is valuable. This knowledge could be used to identify which keywords are correlated with high circulation, thus assisting developers to identify content that may need crowdsourced annotators to provide descriptions. Further, we suggest that Twitter should allow users to add description to the media content when the link's website has Twitter Cards enabled.

5.2   UX Accessibility Design Experiment Research Questions

To answer RQ1, our findings from the second experiment are consistent with our findings from the first experiment. Only 8 of the 902 images in TWEN contained a description. This is not surprising given how many of the surveyed participants did not know what constituted a description. Only 6.9% of participants knew there was no way to know if the image shown to them contained a description (in UE4). Additionally, only 1% of participants always added a description to their posted media content (in UE2). Our participants were mostly avid Twitter users with 45.5% using Twitter more than once a day and 64.6% of them having been a Twitter user for more than 5 years. Yet, only 16.8% knew of the change announced by Twitter regarding the ability to add a description without the need to modify the settings (in OA1).

To answer RQ2, participants preferred engagement flags that used numerical values. 72.3% indicated Twitter's display of descriptions could be improved (in OA3). We presented two alternatives to Twitter's default concept: a numerical value guided concept and a photo guided concept. All three are displayed in Figs. 3, 4 and 5. Participants found the numerical value guided concept more effective (in EC1) and more interesting (in ICO1) than the photo guided (in EC2 and ICO2) and default (in EC3 and ICO3) concepts.

To answer RQ3, we found most participants were amendable to writing descriptions despite only 1% of them always doing so (in UE2). The lack of descriptions seems to stem partially from lack of awareness about descriptions. For instance, only 6.9% of participants knew they could not determine the existence of a description when viewing a tweet containing an image (in UE4). This is confirmed by over a third of participants having replies to why they did not include descriptions (WN) that fell into *misunderstanding* and *How we add alt text?* categories. Another 38.6% of participants were *not expecting BLV to be an audience on Twitter*. Thus it is important to educate social media users on description purpose, how to add descriptions, and the prevalence of visually impaired users. Further, promoting awareness of high engagement may increase willingness to add descriptions. While only a third of participants indicated willingness to always add descriptions, a majority indicated wiliness to add descriptions only to highly engaged media content (in HP1). The 27.3% of open-ended responses (WN) in the *type of followers* and *time consuming* categories also support the need for targeted and effortless solutions. Thus, we must recommend strategies such as our well-received numeric value guided concept for highlighting highly engaged media content without a description.

5.3   Limitations and Future Work

In this study we demonstrated that icons can be used to indicate highly-engaged tweets and encourage users to add descriptions. As there is no international standard icon to indicate BLV in social media platforms, future work involves designing a multicultural icon that could be understood by many people around the world and exploring the pros and cons of different icons. Future icon experiments may include differing formats, shapes, sizes, placements, and colors. However, the icon design is beyond the scope of this paper. Our proposed guided concepts need to be further tested to determine effectiveness, therefore our future work will include more tests to determine effectiveness of guided concepts. As the participants in our study were already are primed to know what the context and meaning of the engagement number, future work involves testing the icons on different populations who have not been asked prior questions about image descriptions and engagement. As it is outside the scope of this research, future research could also involve solutions to the logistical concerns of using crowdsourcing to add descriptions. Notably, there are decorative images that may not require descriptions. Further, some complex images may require domain knowledge to provide a description, so a solution would ideally allow for the people who contribute to writing descriptions specify topics of interest and expertise.

6   Conclusion

In this study we collected the TWEN data set about highly engaged tweets and a surveyed sighted users regarding their experience with descriptions. Over 90% of TWEN included images, suggesting highly engaged tweets frequently have images. However, less than 1% of these images contained descriptions, posing accessibility issues for visually impaired users. The subsequent survey revealed the importance of awareness in increasing description frequency as many participants were unaware of the purpose of descriptions. Despite this, many participants seemed willing to help by providing descriptions for highly engaged content if properly alerted of the need, such as through our well received numerical value guided concept. Thus, if guided concepts are used to draw attention and a method is provided to standardize description writing efforts, adding descriptions to highly engaged content could become more common. Our findings offer a tangible guide regarding what type of media content is available on Twitter and a strategy to increase description frequency.

Acknowledgment. We thank Imam Abdulrahman Bin Faisal University (IAU) and Saudi Arabian Cultural Mission to the USA (SACM) for financially supporting Mallak Alkhathlan. We thank the US Department of Education P200A180088: GAANN grant and the WPI Data Science Department for financially supporting ML Tlachac. We thank Brittany Lewis and the WPI DAISY lab for their advice and support.

References

1. Arora, A., Bansal, S., Kandpal, C., Aswani, R., Dwivedi, Y.: Measuring social media influencer index-insights from Facebook, Twitter and Instagram. J. Retail. Consum. Serv. **49**, 86–101 (2019)
2. Aslam, S.: Twitter by the numbers: Stats, demographics & fun facts (2020). https://www.omnicoreagency.com/twitter-statistics/
3. Bennett, C.L., Keyes, O.: What is the point of fairness? Disability, AI and the complexity of justice. arXiv preprint arXiv:1908.01024 (2019)
4. Bigham, J.P., et al.: VizWiz: nearly real-time answers to visual questions. In: Proceedings of the 23nd Annual ACM Symposium on User Interface Software and Technology, pp. 333–342 (2010)
5. Bigham, J.P., Kaminsky, R.S., Ladner, R.E., Danielsson, O.M., Hempton, G.L.: WebInSight: making web images accessible. In: Proceedings of the 8th International ACM SIGACCESS Conference on Computers and Accessibility, pp. 181–188 (2006)
6. Bigham, J.P., Ladner, R.E., Borodin, Y.: The design of human-powered access technology. In: The Proceedings of the 13th International ACM SIGACCESS Conference on Computers and Accessibility, pp. 3–10 (2011)
7. Brady, E., Morris, M.R., Bigham, J.P.: Gauging receptiveness to social microvolunteering. In: Proceedings of the 33rd Annual ACM Conference on Human Factors in Computing Systems, pp. 1055–1064 (2015)
8. Brady, E.L., Zhong, Y., Morris, M.R., Bigham, J.P.: Investigating the appropriateness of social network question asking as a resource for blind users. In: Proceedings of the 2013 Conference on Computer Supported Cooperative Work, pp. 1225–1236 (2013)
9. Braun, V., Clarke, V.: Using thematic analysis in psychology. Qual. Res. Psychol. **3**(2), 77–101 (2006)
10. Center, D.: Image sorting tool (2014). http://diagramcenter.org/decision-tree.html/
11. Chiarella, D., Yarbrough, J., Jackson, C.A.L.: Using alt text to make science Twitter more accessible for people with visual impairments. Nat. Commun. **11**(1), 1–3 (2020)
12. Dorsey, J.: search+photos (2011). https://blog.twitter.com/en_us/a/2011/searchphotos.html
13. Elzer, S., Schwartz, E., Carberry, S., Chester, D., Demir, S., Wu, P.: A browser extension for providing visually impaired users access to the content of bar charts on the web. In: WEBIST, no. 2, pp. 59–66 (2007)
14. Fang, H., et al.: From captions to visual concepts and back. In: Proceedings of the IEEE Conference on Computer Vision and Pattern Recognition (CVPR), June 2015
15. Georges, V., Courtemanche, F., Senecal, S., Baccino, T., Fredette, M., Leger, P.M.: UX heatmaps: mapping user experience on visual interfaces. In: Proceedings of the 2016 CHI Conference on Human Factors in Computing Systems, pp. 4850–4860 (2016)
16. Gleason, C., Carrington, P., Cassidy, C., Morris, M.R., Kitani, K.M., Bigham, J.P.: "It's almost like they're trying to hide it": how user-provided image descriptions have failed to make Twitter accessible. In: The World Wide Web Conference, pp. 549–559 (2019)
17. Gleason, C., et al.: Twitter A11y: a browser extension to make Twitter images accessible. In: Proceedings of the 2020 CHI Conference on Human Factors in Computing Systems, pp. 1–12 (2020)

18. Goddard, C.: Semantic Analysis: A Practical Introduction. Oxford University Press, Oxford (2011)
19. Gray, C.M., Kou, Y.: UX practitioners' engagement with intermediate-level knowledge. In: Proceedings of the 2017 ACM Conference Companion Publication on Designing Interactive Systems, pp. 13–17 (2017)
20. Gray, C.M., Kou, Y., Battles, B., Hoggatt, J., Toombs, A.L.: The dark (patterns) side of UX design. In: Proceedings of the 2018 CHI Conference on Human Factors in Computing Systems, pp. 1–14 (2018)
21. Grosser, B.: What do metrics want? How quantification prescribes social interaction on Facebook. Comput. Cult. **8**(4), 1–8 (2014)
22. Guidelines, W.C.A.: How to meet WCAG (quick reference) (2019). https://www.w3.org/WAI/WCAG21/quickref/
23. Guinness, D., Cutrell, E., Morris, M.R.: Caption crawler: enabling reusable alternative text descriptions using reverse image search. In: Proceedings of the 2018 CHI Conference on Human Factors in Computing Systems, pp. 1–11 (2018)
24. Guo, A., Kamar, E., Vaughan, J.W., Wallach, H., Morris, M.R.: Toward fairness in AI for people with disabilities SBG@ a research roadmap. ACM SIGACCESS Accessibility Comput. **125**, 1 (2020)
25. Julian Ausserhofer, A.M.: National politics on Twitter: structures and topics of a networked public sphere. Inf. Commun. Soc. **16**(3), 291–314 (2013). https://doi.org/10.1080/1369118X.2012.756050
26. Kemp, S.: Digital 2020: 3.8 billion people use social media (2020). https://wearesocial.com/blog/2020/01/digital-2020-3-8-billion-people-use-social-media
27. Kennedy, H., Hill, R.L.: The feeling of numbers: emotions in everyday engagements with data and their visualisation. Sociology **52**(4), 830–848 (2018)
28. Keysers, D., Renn, M., Breuel, T.M.: Improving accessibility of html documents by generating image-tags in a proxy. In: Proceedings of the 9th International ACM SIGACCESS Conference on Computers and Accessibility, pp. 249–250 (2007)
29. Kitson, A., Buie, E., Stepanova, E.R., Chirico, A., Riecke, B.E., Gaggioli, A.: Transformative experience design: designing with interactive technologies to support transformative experiences. In: Extended Abstracts of the 2019 CHI Conference on Human Factors in Computing Systems, pp. 1–5 (2019)
30. Lin, T.-Y., et al.: Microsoft COCO: common objects in context. In: Fleet, D., Pajdla, T., Schiele, B., Tuytelaars, T. (eds.) ECCV 2014. LNCS, vol. 8693, pp. 740–755. Springer, Cham (2014). https://doi.org/10.1007/978-3-319-10602-1_48
31. Loiacono, E.T., Romano, N.C., Jr., McCoy, S.: The state of corporate website accessibility. Commun. ACM **52**(9), 128–132 (2009)
32. MacLeod, H., Bennett, C.L., Morris, M.R., Cutrell, E.: Understanding blind people's experiences with computer-generated captions of social media images. In: Proceedings of the 2017 CHI Conference on Human Factors in Computing Systems, pp. 5988–5999 (2017)
33. Meeker, M.: Internet trends 2014 (2014). https://cryptome.org/2014/05/internet-trends-2014.pdf
34. Whittaker, M., et al.: Disability, bias, and AI (2019). https://ainowinstitute.org/disabilitybiasai-2019.pdf
35. Morris, M.R.: AI and accessibility: a discussion of ethical considerations. arXiv preprint arXiv:1908.08939 (2019)
36. Morris, M.R., Zolyomi, A., Yao, C., Bahram, S., Bigham, J.P., Kane, S.K.: " With most of it being pictures now, I rarely use it" understanding Twitter's evolving accessibility to blind users. Presented at the (2016)

37. Obrist, M., Wurhofer, D., Beck, E., Karahasanovic, A., Tscheligi, M.: User experience (UX) patterns for audio-visual networked applications: inspirations for design. In: Proceedings of the 6th Nordic Conference on Human-Computer Interaction: Extending Boundaries, pp. 343–352 (2010)

38. Online, B.: Whatsapp users share 55 billion texts, 4.5 billion photos, 1 billion videos daily (2017). https://www.businesstoday.in/technology/news/whatsapp-users-share-texts-photos-videos-daily/story/257230.html

39. Porter, T.M.: Trust in Numbers: The Pursuit of Objectivity in Science and Public Life. Princeton University Press, Princeton (1996)

40. Power, C., Freire, A., Petrie, H., Swallow, D.: Guidelines are only half of the story: accessibility problems encountered by blind users on the web. In: Proceedings of the SIGCHI Conference on Human Factors in Computing Systems, pp. 433–442 (2012)

41. Ramnath, K., et al.: AutoCaption: automatic caption generation for personal photos. In: IEEE Winter Conference on Applications of Computer Vision, pp. 1050–1057. IEEE (2014)

42. Rodríguez Vázquez, S.: Measuring the impact of automated evaluation tools on alternative text quality: a web translation study. In: Proceedings of the 13th Web for All Conference, pp. 1–10 (2016)

43. Rowe, N.C.: Marie-4: a high-recall, self-improving web crawler that finds images using captions. IEEE Intell. Syst. **17**(4), 8–14 (2002)

44. Salisbury, E., Kamar, E., Morris, M.R.: Toward scalable social alt text: conversational crowdsourcing as a tool for refining vision-to-language technology for the blind. In: 5th AAAI Conference on Human Computation and Crowdsourcing (2017)

45. Salisbury, E., Kamar, E., Morris, M.R.: Evaluating and complementing vision-to-language technology for people who are blind with conversational crowdsourcing. In: IJCAI, pp. 5349–5353 (2018)

46. Shaban, H.: Twitter reveals its daily active user numbers for the first time (2019). https://www.washingtonpost.com/technology/2019/02/07/twitter-reveals-its-daily-active-user-numbers-first-time/

47. Shi, Y.: E-government web site accessibility in Australia and China: a longitudinal study. Soc. Sci. Comput. Rev. **24**(3), 378–385 (2006)

48. Siegemedia: The 100 most popular google keywords, March 2020. https://www.siegemedia.com/seo/most-popular-keywords

49. Spyridonis, F., Daylamani-Zad, D.: A serious game to improve engagement with web accessibility guidelines. Behav. Inf. Technol. **39**(4), 1–19 (2020). https://doi.org/10.1080/0144929X.2019.1711453

50. Stangl, A., Morris, M.R., Gurari, D.: " Person, shoes, tree. Is the person naked?" What people with vision impairments want in image descriptions. Presented at the (2020)

51. Strauss, A., Corbin, J.: Basics of Qualitative Research Techniques. Sage Publications, Thousand Oaks (1998)

52. todd: Accessible images for everyone (2016). https://blog.twitter.com/en_us/a/2016/accessible-images-for-everyone.html

53. Tran, K., et al.: Rich image captioning in the wild. In: Proceedings of the IEEE Conference on Computer Vision and Pattern Recognition Workshops (2016)

54. Tumasjan, A., Sprenger, T.O., Sandner, P.G., Welpe, I.M.: Predicting elections with Twitter: what 140 characters reveal about political sentiment. In: Fourth International AAAI Conference on Weblogs and Social Media (2010)

55. Twitter: Rules and ltering: Premium (2020). https://developer.twitter.com/en/docs/twitter-api/premium/rules-and-ltering/operators-by-product

56. Twitter: using-premium-operators (2020). https://developer.twitter.com/en/docs/twitter-api/premium/rules-and-filtering/using-premium-operators
57. Twitter, I.: Promoted tweet (2020). https://business.twitter.com/en/help/campaign-setup/advertiser-card-specifications.html
58. Twitter, I.: The suggested minimum properties for cards (2020). https://developer.twitter.com/en/docs/twitter-for-websites/cards/overview/summary-card-with-large-image
59. @TwitterA11y: Adding descriptions to images (2020). https://twitter.com/TwitterA11y/status/1265689579371323392
60. @TwitterBusiness: Fun fact: A study of twitter accounts (2020). https://twitter.com/TwitterBusiness/status/1070423034467540992?s=20
61. Vilenchik, D.: The million tweets fallacy: activity and feedback are uncorrelated. In: Twelfth International AAAI Conference on Web and Social Media (2018)
62. Vinyals, O., Toshev, A., Bengio, S., Erhan, D.: Show and tell: a neural image caption generator. In: Proceedings of the IEEE Conference on Computer Vision and Pattern Recognition, pp. 3156–3164 (2015)
63. Von Ahn, L., Ginosar, S., Kedia, M., Liu, R., Blum, M.: Improving accessibility of the web with a computer game. In: Proceedings of the SIGCHI Conference on Human Factors in Computing Systems, pp. 79–82 (2006)
64. Voykinska, V., Azenkot, S., Wu, S., Leshed, G.: How blind people interact with visual content on social networking services. In: Proceedings of the 19th ACM Conference on Computer-Supported Cooperative Work & Social Computing, pp. 1584–1595 (2016)
65. WHO: Blindness and vision impairment (2020). https://www.who.int/news-room/fact-sheets/detail/blindness-and-visual-impairment
66. Wood, G., et al.: Rethinking engagement with online news through social and visual co-annotation. In: Proceedings of the 2018 CHI Conference on Human Factors in Computing Systems, pp. 1–12 (2018)
67. Wu, S., Adamic, L.A.: Visually impaired users on an online social network. In: Proceedings of the SIGCHI Conference on Human Factors in Computing Systems, pp. 3133–3142 (2014)
68. Wu, S., Wieland, J., Farivar, O., Schiller, J.: Automatic alt-text: computer- generated image descriptions for blind users on a social network service. In: Proceedings of the 2017 ACM Conference on Computer Supported Cooperative Work and Social Computing, pp. 1180–1192 (2017)
69. Zhong, Y., Lasecki, W.S., Brady, E., Bigham, J.P.: RegionSpeak: quick comprehensive spatial descriptions of complex images for blind users. In: Proceedings of the 33rd Annual ACM Conference on Human Factors in Computing Systems, pp. 2353–2362 (2015)

'Did You See That!?' Enhancing the Experience of Sports Media Broadcast for Blind People

Cagatay Goncu[1,2(✉)] and Daniel J. Finnegan[3]

[1] Monash University, Melbourne, Australia
cagatay.goncu@monash.edu
[2] Tennis Australia, Melbourne, Australia
[3] Cardiff University, Cardiff, UK
finnegand@cardiff.ac.uk

Abstract. Accessibility in sports media broadcast (SMB) remains a problem for blind spectators who wish to socialize and watch sports with friends and family. Although popular, radio's reliance on low bandwidth speech results in an overwhelming experience for blind spectators. In this paper we focused on two core issues: (i) how SMB can be augmented to convey diegetic information more effectively, and (ii) the social context in which SMB are consumed. We chose tennis broadcasts for our investigations. Addressing issue (i), we developed a system design and prototype to enhance the experience of watching tennis matches, focusing on blind spectators using audio descriptions and 3D audio, and evaluated our system with (n = 12) in a controlled user evaluation. Our results indicate how audio descriptions gave clear information for the tennis ball placements, 3D audio provided subtle cues for the ball direction, and radio provided desired human commentary. For issue (ii), we conducted an online questionnaire (n = 15) investigating the social context in which blind spectators consume SMB. Participant feedback indicated there is a demand for more accessible SMB content such that people can consume SMB by themselves and with their friends. Participants were enthusiastic for a revised system design mixing elements from 3D audio and audio description. We discuss our results in the context of social SMB spectatorship, concluding with insights into accessible SMB technologies.

Keywords: Accessibility · Blind and low vision people · Sports broadcasting · Tennis · Spectatorship

1 Introduction

Sports Media Broadcast is a hugely popular pastime enjoyed by millions of people, and for many is a viable alternative to attending events in person. SMB lets viewers experience what attending the event is like by simulating the experience of co-presence: microphones and cameras capture events happening on and around the sports pitch, delivering content regarding actions in the sport

© IFIP International Federation for Information Processing 2021
Published by Springer Nature Switzerland AG 2021
C. Ardito et al. (Eds.): INTERACT 2021, LNCS 12932, pp. 396–417, 2021.
https://doi.org/10.1007/978-3-030-85623-6_24

event and the reactions of fans in the arena. The most dominant form of SMB is on-demand televised (TV) experience, where events are broadcast with audio narration and commentary from professional commentators, celebrities, and journalists who dictate all the action as it happens in the arena. While providing a state of the art experience for sighted spectators, blind spectators must tune in to radio broadcasts to receive information which is normally captured in the video stream, for example team formation provided via info graphics.

Both radio and TV SMB suffer from problems with respect to accessibility: for example blind people may miss out on essential action happening within the SMB if the actions are not described. Broadcast media for blind people typically requires extra information in the audio channel: for example, audio descriptions which provide context and detail around what is happening in the TV broadcast. Television shows typically insert brief snippets of spoken audio in between dialogue to convey information that is captured in the video, for example the emotions of the characters like disgust and fear on their faces [36]. However, this is not systematically described in a fast paced environment like SMB: instead, blind spectators are encouraged to consume a separate channel such as radio, removing them from the shared social experience. In a social setting, blind people may therefore depend on social interventions: friends dictating parts of the action or describing the meta data around a game event, for example, who scored the recent goal which won the soccer game. Interestingly, in the early 1920s, the genesis of sports broadcasting, the British Broadcasting Commission (BBC) radio commentators used an experimental structured commentary technique for soccer[1]. Sports commentators using this system coined the phrase 'back to square one' as the soccer field was divided into 8 cells, and commentators used each cell's associated number to relay the position of the ball and the players. For example, during a match the commentator would provide real time audio commentary while their colleague would declare 'Square 2' ... 'Square 6' as the ball moved around the pitch[2]. Though innovative at the time and providing essential information for spectators, this technique of structured commentary providing clear descriptions of where the football is has been forgotten in time and is no longer used in main stream sports broadcast commentary [18].

Our goal is to innovate and provide a better blind spectatorship experience than de facto radio broadcasting. Potential avenues lie in creating augmented broadcasts which add extra information such as audio descriptions and sonifications to the original SMB: here we focus on augmentations conveyed using 3D audio as it provides spatial information without the need of description or commentary. These augmentations could provide blind spectators with a better experience, with information regarding events and actions that go unreported in the SMB commentary. This will provide a complete picture of what is happening, without impacting the experience of sighted users in social consumption environments, and help the blind spectators form a mental image as similar to graphical information [20].

---

[1] An image of the football pitch showing the demarcation of zones can be found at http://news.bbc.co.uk/sport2/hi/football/1760579.stm.

[2] https://www.theguardian.com/notesandqueries/query/0,5753,-1811,00.html.

Therefore, we seek to address the following research questions:

RQ 1: How do blind spectators consume SMB and what, if any, preferences do they have regarding radio or TV?

RQ 2: Is augmented SMB more effective in conveying SMB information compared to radio?

To facilitate social SMB consumption, we present an iteratively designed prototype system for spatializing tennis SMB events using an augmented audio channel to aid blind spectators interpret the event. The system captures key information during the SMB event and renders it in real time so that blind people can consume broadcasts with their sighted friends and family without negatively affecting one another's overall experience. We also present the results of a questionnaire which investigates the current methods of consuming SMB by blind spectators and their overall experience.

We chose tennis because: (i) it is a very structured game, (ii) during game play it has long quiet time slots which creates opportunities for SMB augmentation, and (iii) we can access detailed match data from Tennis Australia. Our system incorporates elements from different modern day SMB–commentary from radio, multi channel information from TV–, to enhance the experience for blind spectators. Our main contribution is an analysis of the shortcomings in SMB: particularly how it falls short of presenting the full content of a sport event to blind spectators, and a potential prototype system that can remove some of these shortcomings. We conclude that SMB for blind spectators may, and arguably should, raise a new design challenge for the HCI community.

2   Background

The dominant forms of technology mediated broadcast for sports spectatorship are radio and television, with both providing real time commentary describing what is happening throughout the broadcast. For blind spectators, radio remains the most effective mode of consumption as greater emphasis is placed on describing what is happening via commentary due to the lack of a visual broadcast channel. Technology has been applied over the past few decades to enhance the experience of sports spectatorship [37]. Most work around augmenting media broadcast revolves around enhancing the experience through the use of predominantly visual displays [12,34], via augmented reality [48], automated processing of statistical data [2,35], and enabling consumption of ever growing repositories of visual information. Existing methods for making pre-recorded videos accessible to the visually impaired community use audio descriptions (AD)–spoken dialogue detailing what is displayed on the screen. However, ADs may not be suitable for live broadcast: they require identifying appropriate gaps in the video, so that descriptions do not overlap with other spoken dialogue content. In a live broadcast, one does not know when appropriate gaps for inserting ADs may appear. Recent work has investigated automatic generation of ADs applied to live sports, showing subjective improvement in understanding by blind SMB consumers [19,24,43]. However, these systems focus on very simple event based commentary, for example a point was scored, and are limited in their ability to capture more nuanced play which spectators may wish to follow, for example, the trajectory of the ball. Recent work concerning a system designed for general audience to sonify soccer games used computer vision techniques to capture movement of the ball and the players, generating sonifications for key features such as possession, passes, steals, and goals [39]. In this study pitch mapping was used to map the ball's distance to goal to the pitch of the sound, and this was found more enjoyable. It was also reported that key moments sonification which provided events that focused on passes, steals, and goals were found more useful. The study also reported the need for a more deeper investigation in improved spectator experience.

Why Focus on the Spectator Experience? SMB is a popular pastime for blind people [32] with many people spending a significant amount of time spectating sports events on television. Sports are seen as extremely difficult to follow when watching television [32]: factors contributing to this difficulty involved the clarity of dictation, long scenes of quiet exposition where much attention is focused on visual camera panning with little to no audio description, and poor sound quality. While work from the HCI community has sought to develop systems to aid blind participation in sport [10,17,22], it has curiously neglected sports spectatorship and the problem of creating accessible environments for spectating live sports events. We are interested in the role of HCI in sports spectatorship for blind people due to several benefits it may bring, for example, to health and wellbeing [21] and social opportunities [9]. For example, the feeling of catharsis that can come from "vicarious participation in sports" achieved through spectatorship [47], and the sense of recreation accompanying SMB consumption. Other work has developed systems to enable blind participation in sport for exercise and recreation, for example using sonification techniques to render player and ball movement [38], and using spatial audio for locating the ball positions in virtual reality games [42,46].

We begin by observing the motivations: what drives sport spectatorship? Several studies refer to the appeal of vicarious achievement or achievement gained through observing others [33], but also the social factors surrounding sports spectatorship [27,44]. One may infer the motivations driving sports spectatorship for blind people are the same, however research is scarce in this regard. Classic work in HCI has created taxonomies of interaction and how to provide meaningful engagement for the spectator [37], however these taxonomies are not discussed in the context of accessible design, for example being able to observe one perform gestures in public without necessary audio description or tactile information pertaining to the gesture or other event. Designing for and facilitating the spectator experience for blind people is what we focus our attention on in this paper.

Augmenting SMB via Sports Commentary: Modern approaches to augmentation generally operate by broadcasting meta information in another representation, for example audio descriptions, to a client's companion device. One core issue persists with these approaches: they rely on the meta information that is broadcast with the main channel. This meta-information takes the form of a descriptive narrative over what is happening on the screen. Users are required to concentrate on this descriptive content while simultaneously paying attention to the main content of the program e.g. dialogue and action sounds. Thus, content consumers are subjected to divide their attention between diegetic events–events happening within the broadcast content that they can perceive, such as crowds roaring–and non-diegetic descriptive information. In e-sports, researchers have explored how to enhance the spectator experience of live game streams through enhanced communication channels [28], focusing not on what to present but how and when to present it [5]. As e-sports events are inherently digitally mediated, all the relevant information is immediately available and thus the risk of missing any information which the commentator fails to report may be mitigated by displaying the raw information directly to the observer in whatever format they choose. However these options are still limiting for blind consumers, creating barriers and compounding the issue with information overload and confusion by requiring the spectator to attend to even more channels. Attending to multiple sources of information is a difficult task, causing higher cognitive load and even stress on the consumer, and attention is known to be poor unless people are trained in divided attention tasks [41].

Since the early days of radio, sports has been broadcast with a commentator whose role is to provide a real time account of what is happening in the game. Sports commentary itself is typically provided in two concurrent flavors: the first providing descriptive content regarding the event while the other provides more dramatic commentary, known as 'color commentary'. One aspect of SMB color commentary is the added value brought by the commentator who creates a narrative discourse [26]. Their role focuses on conveying the emotional aspect of sports, and their commentary is thus fuelled with passion and exuberance. As they seek to augment the broadcast experience for listeners by storytelling based on similar events in previous games, this value proposition hinges on the listener's capability to map current events in the game to the story being told.

Finally, color commentators provide contextualized information for listeners: for example, if a player wins a point by hitting a between-the-legs shot, the color commentator may explain this as extraordinary as the player is normally right footed. If listeners can't fully comprehend the current game events then this will negatively impact their ability to enjoy the story. Furthermore, they may begin to confound the story with current events and misinterpret historical from current events in the broadcast. With respect to tennis, commentary typically comes between points where color commentators discuss the players themselves and their historical games. Consequences for blind spectators can be severe and can lead to further barriers: for example, missing commentary impacts a blind spectator's ability to engage with particular events happening in the game. As social peers may begin a discussion regarding an event with missing commentary, blind spectators cannot engage fully with the shared social discourse. Although follow up discussions (i.e. post broadcast analyses) provide opportunities for in-depth and discussion which blind spectators may engage in, this would fall short of the same problems in programming/broadcasting where programme directors and media personalities may not share the same events and/or prioritize some events over others.

3 Pilot Studies and Initial Prototype Design

Thus, there are opportunities for the role of technology to enhance SMB and provide a better blind spectatorship experience than de facto radio broadcasting. Before embarking on our system design, we conducted pilot studies with two blind spectators to identify the level of access to tennis SMB. In the pilot studies, we did unstructured interviews with one male and one female participant both of whom follow sports, in particular tennis matches, on both radio and TV. We conducted these interviews iteratively while we were doing improvements in the prototype system. In each iteration (in total 3) we asked the questions to both pilots participants.

The first study involved informal discussions around the context in which they consume SMB. They reported that they use radio to follow tennis matches, while using their mobile phone to browse various applications and web sites. They also commented how they use radio receivers with headphones in public spaces so not to ruin the experience for others. From their comments, it was clear that they could get a general description of the game, but they could not get a lot of information about how the game is actually played, for example where the ball bounced and/or other game specific actions such as whether the players hit the ball hard or with a heavy top spin. For instance, if a player hits a down-the-line forehand after having a long sprint and wins the point, radio commentators have just enough time to describe this action: in this case there is no time to describe the ball's movement and/or the player locations. Our pilots also reported watching the matches on TV is not a good option either, as the commentary does not describe much about the game play.

Based on the first pilot study, we considered augmenting tennis SMB in a way that blind spectators can access game play information. Our system is designed for blind spectators to consume SMB using an augmented broadcast channel delivering audio description and 3D audio content which a) does not overwhelm the spectator and b) does not occlude other elements of the original broadcast. This facilitated the investigation of our **RQ 1**. Our system is designed to be used in a setting similar to watching a live-TV broadcast at home or in a public space, instead of going to a match in a stadium. As the radio broadcasts are already fully occupied, we decided to augment the TV broadcasts. In tennis, crowd noise is kept to a minimum during game play and broadcast commentators also keep quiet during this period. This gives us commentator free time slots that can be used to add additional information about the game play including audio descriptions and 3D audio content covering events and actions that go unreported in the SMB commentary. This facilitated the investigation of our **RQ 2**.

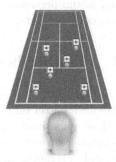

(a) System prototype user interface

(b) Tennis court grid system used for audio descriptions.

(c) Sample 3D audio placements used for 3D audio

Fig. 1. System components

A screenshot of our system prototype's user interface is shown in Fig. 1a. The prototype uses pre-recorded video footage and 3D positional data to create augmented SMB content consumable using off the shelf headphones. The 3D positional data are provided from the ball tracking system, an industry standard system for tracking ball movements in major sporting games. The ball tracking data (JSON files containing timestamped Cartesian coordinate system positional information about the ball) are used to select synthesized audio descriptions, and as input to a 3D audio rendering subsystem. Our prototype takes video recordings of tennis matches and the ball tracking data as its inputs and generates the augmented videos with audio description and 3D audio as its output. Pre-recorded video are used for conducting the user evaluation in an easier fashion, however the prototype is suitable for live consumption as it uses the ball tracking data format that is identical to the real time tracking data which can be received within 100ms. Our prototype also features simple slider bar elements for adjusting the volume of the original broadcast and audio description/3D sounds separately.

In the prototype, left and right of the tennis court are defined from the spectator's perspective sat behind the nearest tennis player as in Fig. 1a. The server is not fixed to a particular side of the screen, so the server can be either the bottom player or the top one. Each side of the court is divided into a 3 by 3 grid providing finer detail as shown in Fig. 1b. The audio descriptions provide information about the bounce location of each ball during the play. These are vocalized using synthesized speech from descriptions provided by an expert tactile graphics transcriber.

We use binaural audio to implement our 3D audio augmentation. Binaural is a form of 3D audio based on how we hear sounds naturally. It requires only stereo channels which are filtered using anthropomorphic models of the human head and pinnae called head related transfer functions (HRTFs). Though it is possible to create bespoke HRTF models for individual listeners, this is logistically challenging and was not feasible for our prototype. Instead we used a generic (HRTF) which is good enough for sound localization when users are given the opportunity to train using them [1,7]. During piloting, the comments from participants regarding their use of headphones to not disturb others in public spaces was the main factor driving our design decisions for spatialized audio. As our system leverages headphones for 3D, the participants will use our system as they do their radios. We decided on using a binaural HRTF design for 3D audio due to it not requiring specialized equipment, for example multi channel headphones.

3.1 Issues with Pilot System Design

The second pilot study involved gathering feedback on the initial prototype design. Discussions with our pilot participants focused on issues around audio descriptions and the augmented SMB channel. For example, we first used 'short' and 'long' to describe the ball bounce location as an indication of its distance to the net. Although these labels were accurate, they caused problems for our pilot participants because of their game specific meanings. In tennis, the term 'long' is used to represent an out-of-bounds hit due to the ball landing beyond the opposing baseline. Similarly the term 'short' is used when the ball bounces near the service line.

For 3D audio, initially we had conceived an egocentric perspective where the listener is placed in the middle of the court. In this setup, sounds are rendered in 3D based on the actual ball bounce location obtained from the ball tracking data. For example, when the ball hits the upper left corner of the tennis court, our 3D sound augmentation would be heard to the front left of the listener while a ball hitting the lower right of the court would be heard from behind and to the right of the listener. This initial design caused two problems: first, the 3D audio was difficult for users to interpret as they found it disconcerting to imagine themselves standing in the center of the court during game play. Secondly, the 3D sounds did not correlate with the typical coordinate system used in tennis commentary. This caused further confusion for the pilot study participants who found it cognitively demanding to interpret. To summarize, the issues identified in our pilot studies are: **I1**) *Terminology used in audio descriptions regarding the location of the ball must consider game specific factors.* and **I2**) *3D audio must consider listener perspective and the coordinate system used in SMB commentary.*

4   Final System Design

To solve **I1**, we changed the terminology for 'short' and 'long' to 'near' and 'far' respectively. Thus, the grid squares are labelled left far (cell 7), centre far (cell 8), right far (cell 9) for the row furthest from the net; left near (cell 1), centre near (cell 2), right near (cell 3) for the row closest to the net; and left middle (cell 4), centre middle (cell 5), right middle (cell 6) for the middle of the court. The labels are converted to synthesised speech recordings by using the

Speech Synthesis manager[3] on macOS. These recordings are then used as audio descriptions which can be reused in every match without any modification.

As an example, consider the following play: (i) the server starts the point with a serve to the centre middle service line, (ii) the receiver returns a short ball to the left side, and (iii) the server hits the ball down-the-line on the right side on the court, but misses the shot. The system gets the exact ball bounce positions from the ball tracking data, and matches it to one of the cells in the grid. Using this match it uses the relevant audio description. Thus, for this particular 3 shot point, the system provides 'centre middle', 'left near', and 'right far' audio descriptions at the time the ball bounces on the court.

The audio descriptions only describe the locations of ball bounces. They will not let you know whether the ball is in or out. This is based on the design consideration for not occluding other elements of the original broadcast. Original TV broadcast still has the line umpire calls in the video, so the out-calls will still be audible. Therefore, for this particular example, the final output starts with the original TV broadcast sounds, i.e. crowd noise, at the beginning. Then, 'centre middle', 'left near', and 'right far' audio descriptions will be heard at the specific times of the ball bounces. As before, the out-call from the umpire that comes from the original TV broadcast will be heard.

To solve I2, we placed the viewer behind the court and rendered 3D audio from the perspective of the video camera capturing the TV footage. This provided a 1:1 mapping between the visual scene and our 3D audio augmentation. This was done to mimic the same conditions of a blind spectator watching a tennis match in front of a TV. Though TV broadcasts use different view angles during a match, for example focusing on individual players in between serves for dramatic effects, they use a fixed view angle when the ball is in play as seen in Fig. 1a. This view does not change based on the server position. As the players change over after every two games, the server will be seen either at the top or the bottom of the view. We use this view for the audio augmentation to avoid any disorientation. A short click sound was used for our 3D audio augmentation. Therefore, for the same example described in Sect. 3, 3D positioned click sounds are rendered in time when the ball bounces off the tennis court. As with audio descriptions, out-calls from the original broadcast umpire are heard.

5   Questionnaire and User Evaluation

We conducted a mixed methods approach involving an online questionnaire and a controlled user evaluation, both with blind participants. The online questionnaire probed participants on their spectating experience. Their comments give insight into how blind spectators consume SMB, and what their preferences and experiences are (**RQ 1**). Their comments give insight into how blind spectators consume SMB. In the controlled user evaluation, we evaluated how our system may enhance the experience for blind spectators using augmented SMB

---

[3] https://developer.apple.com/documentation/applicationservices/speech_synthesis_manager.

delivered through audio descriptions and 3D audio. We tasked participants with answering questions based on what they viewed during the evaluation, and their preferences in three different forms of SMB. Task performance in the evaluation determined the effectiveness of SMB augmentations compared to radio (**RQ 2**).

We recruited 14 blind participants (8 female), all legally blind (i.e., a visual acuity of 20/200 or less). using opportunity sampling advertised using social media channels and email lists. We disseminated the online questionnaire to 14 participants, 12 of which were included in the user evaluations: 2 participants could not do the user evaluations due to poor internet connections. Participants ranged from 26 to 74 years old ($\bar{x} = 49$, sd $= 17$), and granted their consent to take part. A \$30 e-gift card was given to participants for their time.

Online Questionnaire. Participants completed the questionnaire before the user evaluation, so that our system design would not effect their comments. We used an online system (Google Forms) to disseminate the questionnaire. To ensure the questionnaire was accessible for our participants, we used simple radio buttons and text field controls instead of drop down menus and linear scales. The questionnaire contained open ended questions on sports media broadcast consumption, asking participants which sports they follow and/or play, how they follow these sports, what they like/dislike about SMB, what type of SMB they want to have, and the social environment of consumption. Two questions specifically focused on tennis were: (i) "If tennis is one of the sports that you have been following, how do you follow the tournaments and matches?", and (ii) "Do you play tennis? Which other sports do you play or would like to play?".

User Evaluation. COVID-19 forced us to conduct evaluations remotely over video conferencing. Thus we presented our prototype system output as pre-recorded videos on a single platform (Google Forms) that both serves the stimuli and records participants' responses. Doing so minimizes context switching between apps, avoiding additional stress on participants. As we aware of disadvantages and problems around conducting remote evaluations with participants with disabilities [31], we gathered feedback on the online form from a member of the blind community working at Monash University before recruiting our participants. Based on their feedback we updated the form to ensure screen readers can read it without any issues on desktop and mobile platforms, for example partitioning the form into sections so that participants could navigate it easier. We disseminated the controlled user evaluation links to them by email at the beginning of the sessions to mitigate difficulty issues accessing the chat messages on the video conferencing platforms

Our user evaluation consisted of 3 presentation conditions (audio description, 3D audio, and radio). We did not consider the combination of presentation methods to keep the study duration under 90 minutes, avoiding participant fatigue. In creating videos for our user evaluation, we sampled points from three different tennis matches: Osaka vs. Kvitova, 2019; Cilic vs. Federer, 2018; and Djokovic vs. Nadal, 2019. We created 4 MP4 videos (1 for training, and 3 for testing) for each condition, resulting in 12 videos in total for our evaluation. These videos were counterbalanced to avoid learning effects. Each video captures a different point in one of these matches: for example, video 2 in the 3D audio condition was the 3rd point of the 7th game in the 2nd set of the Osaka vs. Kvitova, 2019 match, and video 1 of the radio condition was the 1st point of the 3rd game in the 1st set of the Djokovic vs. Nadal, 2019 match. Using video recordings of our prototype system output enabled us to conduct the user evaluations remotely, as participants would not need to install our software locally. Each of these videos represent a point of a tennis match with increasing complexity having 2, 3 and 5 shots each, including the training material. The videos were then uploaded to a private online repository and embedded into the online form. For each video we gave participants three tasks, designed by an expert tennis player, to represent the game and player's actions: one of the fundamental needs of spectators [14]:

T1: Which player (server or receiver) won the point?
T2: Can you describe the movement of the ball?
T3: How competitive/skilful was the point in a scale of 1 (low skilful) to 5 (high skilful)?

T1 is simply a binary choice between the server or receiver, T2 is a multiple choice question (each choice is a textual description of a point play), and T3 is a numeric value from a 5 point scale, with the correct answer pre-determined by one of the researchers involved in this study who is also an expert reviewer.

Each participant performs the tasks for each of the 3 presentation conditions in a repeated measures design: audio description (AD), 3D audio, and radio (R). The order of the presentation conditions was balanced using a Latin square. Participants were presented the training video first, followed by 3 test videos. They answered T1, T2 and T3 for each of these test videos. After completing all the trials, participants were asked to rank their preferred presentation conditions. We used preference rankings as they are an important factor in evaluating spatial audio reproduction systems [11]. They were then invited to provide comments explaining what they like and dislike for each of the presentation conditions. Additionally, they were asked about the main considerations that affected their preferences. We used video conferencing software to monitor participants during the evaluation. Participants used screen sharing to let us observe their progress. They also shared their computer sound with us, so that we could hear the screen reader prompts. Each evaluation took on the order of 90 min to complete.

6   Results

Online Questionnaire. *What blind people like and dislike about SMB content:* Radio was the preferred medium for following sports due to several distractions from the TV broadcast. Comments from the online questionnaire raised issues with TV advertisements interrupting the game and causing confusion, and TV providing a worse *'picture' (P4)* compared to the one perceived from listening to radio commentary. However some preferred the color commentary from TV commentators as they add a *'sense of humour' (P6)* while others found this to be *'excessive' (P13)*. Though radio was perceived as providing more detail about what is happening compared to TV broadcasting, one participant commented on the declining quality of radio broadcasting. They described how commentators spend more time *'having a chat with one another' (P12)* and growing interest in *'chemistry between broadcaster and expert summariser [sic] rather than a focus on the game itself' (P12)*.

> "I like that radio is designed to not be able to see the picture so they often describe visual aspects of the game as well as commenting eg. weather, crowd numbers and they add a lot more statistics and description to their commentary. It makes it very difficult if radio commentary or TV commentary gets distracted and they go off track and are discussing things that are not relevant to the game. ... the TV tends to do this more often because the assumption is made that you can keep up by watching they [sic] vision while they discuss something else. Also TV commentary often uses less descriptive language, eg. <u>did you see that</u>, have a look at that kick." (P3, emphasis ours)

The Social Context(s) in Which Blind People Consume SMB Content: Several participants noted how they typically watch SMB content with others as a social activity. The context in which social interaction takes place differed across participants: for some, SMB content was enjoyed at home with family and friends while others would go to pubs and bars. Finally, a select few would attend live events and bring with personal radios to listen to live commentary while watching the game. *"I tend to listen on my own via radio, or with family/friends. I sometimes go to the pub to watch football with friends." (P12).* Almost all participants said they would also watch tennis broadcasts by themselves.

Summary: Results from our online questionnaire reveal the diversity in participants' relationship with modern SMB and the issues they face. Most participants declared radio as their first preference, and had strong opinions on the commentary provided in traditional broadcasting and its impact on their consumption experience and ability to comprehend the action in and around the game. They were also concerned about others as they mostly consume SMB in social contexts: key issues revolve around not wanting to negatively impact the experience of others while at the same time relying on friends and family for bespoke descriptions about what is happening.

User Evaluation. To analyse the results from the user evaluation tasks (T1, T2, T3), we conducted a Cochran's Q test, a significance test suitable for repeated measures block designs where the response variable is binary. For determining the victor of the match point (T1), a Cochran's Q test determined that there was no difference in the proportion of participants who were correct over the different presentation conditions, $\chi^2(8) = 10.0, p = .26$. There was also no difference in the proportion of participants who could correctly determine the

408   C. Goncu and D. J. Finnegan

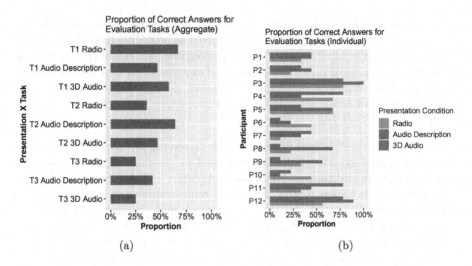

(a)　　　　　　　　　　　　　(b)

Fig. 2. User evaluation results: proportions of correct answers for all participants, and individually.

movement of the ball (T2) (χ^2 (8) $= 12.5, p = .13$) nor who could determine the skillfulness of the players (T3) in the broadcast event (χ^2 (8) $= 7.7, p = .46$). Figure 2a shows the proportion of correct answers for each task in each presentation condition. Figure 2b shows the proportion of correct answers for each participant[4]. Some participants (P3, P12) are 'power users' and score highly in each presentation. Most of the participants performed better with audio description than radio. Half of the participants (P1, P2, P4, P7, P11, P12) did better with 3D audio than radio. With the exceptions of P6 and P10, all participants performance with radio is at best on par with audio descriptions and 3D audio.

To test for a difference in preference rankings between all three presentation conditions, we conducted a Friedman Test on the preference votes. There was no difference between preferences across all participants for Radio, 3D audio, or Audio Description, χ^2 (2) $= 0.5, p = .78$. Figure 3, Panel A shows the preference rankings (1st, 2nd, and 3rd) for each presentation condition, and Panel B shows the proportion of correct answers across all tasks in each presentation condition. Audio description has 51%, 3D audio has 44%, and Radio has 43% correct answer proportion. This is striking: participants can't correctly interpret *more than half of the game play information for radio–the de facto medium–yet it is the most preferred presentation condition.*

We used thematic coding to analyse participant comments, explaining what they like or dislike about the presentation conditions, and the main considerations for their comments. We used two independent coders to look through the comments, and identified keywords and phrases to construct codes. Finally, we then categorized these codes into the following themes: the context where they

---

[4] P3 and P11 indicated that they passionately follow sports.

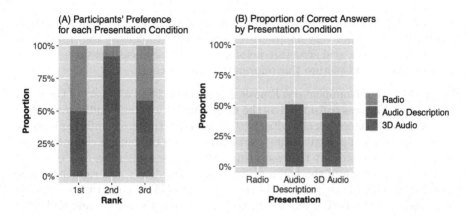

Fig. 3. Participant preference towards each SMB medium used in our user study.

Table 1. The mappings between codes and themes used in the thematic analysis, and the total number of times the codes are mentioned by the participants. The themes that have more relevance to tennis are marked with a star (*).

Themes	Codes	No. of mentions
Tracking the ball (*)	Position of the ball	10
	Precision	5
	Raw play information	10
Pros and cons of commentary	Capturing player emotions	2
	Natural feeling of radio	9
	Dislike of synthetic speech	9
	Randomness of commentary	8
Information load	Overwhelming	7
	High concentration for AD and 3D audio	9
Spectator experience	Radio with headphones	11
	Social desire to follow the action with others	3
	Distractions from others	3
Accuracy and consistency of the augmentation (*)	Density of information	6
	Expanding bandwidth of information	7
Usefulness of the augmentation (*)	3D audio providing subtle feedback	3
	3D audio difficult at first	2

can use each condition, the cognitive load introduced by the augmentations, the ability of tracking the ball location, the amount of information each condition provide, the quality of information they get, the distractions they experience, and the factors effecting their overall experience. For each theme, we report the number of participants in parenthesis. See Table 1 for our map between codes and themes generated.

Tracking the Ball: Participants liked how our system gave consistent and precise ball locations in contrast to radio that depends on the human commentators (10). Many participants stated they want to get raw play information about the status of activity (including ball and player positions) on the field (10):

Some participants liked the clear audio description for the placement of the ball, however they were not very happy with the way they took away the crowd noise (5). They found the grid structure helpful for ball placement locations, and the fact that they could picture this information on the court.

Pros and Cons of Commentary: Emotions were considered as a part of the experience (2). Radio was considered as the most natural way, and audio description was considered a mechanical feedback (9). Radio was the most familiar presentation condition for the participants. Participants liked the human commentators, however they pointed out that sometimes they missed the play, and they had to guess the position of the ball and the players (8). They also said that radio provided the vibe of the game better than the others (5). Another issue regarded the random information given by commentators about the players and their shot selections (3). Some participants found this distracting (5), while others said that this information helped them understand the player strategies (2). Some participants complained about radio's lack of timeliness and consistency, being prone to human commentator error, bias, and irrelevant chat during points (8). Some participants said that they had their own favorite commentators who describe the game better than others (3). So, the style of commentating is a factor for the overall radio experience, and could sometimes give no clue what was happening in the game.

Information Load: Participants commented how the SMB augmentation provided by our prototype did not overwhelm or hinder their enjoyment of the experience (7). However, some participants mentioned high concentration levels for 3D and AD, but described how their cognitive load reduced as points were watched (2). Some also reported that they would use ADs by themselves at home, and 3D at home (3). ADs are preferred to get detailed information and keep up with every shot and its location (4). 3D audio is treated as a presentation condition which can be used when they want to get detailed information as well as not distracting friends (3).

Spectator Experience: Participants were asked about the context in which they want to use each of the presentation conditions. They reported that they would use radio with headphones when at home, at sports venues, outside in public spaces, or with others (11). Regarding the social context, it was surprising to see that participants were worried for other people in the same environment if they use radio and audio descriptions. They commented that these would create noise for their friends, and would ruin their overall experience (3). However, they said that this would not be an issue if they could use 3D audio as this would reduce the need for excessive commentary which participants perceived as the main factor creating noise and distractions for their friends (3).

Accuracy and Consistency of the Augmentation: Participants also commented on the amount of information given by each of the presentation conditions. Some said that radio broadcasts were too busy to include any other information such as the location of the ball and the player (6). ADs helped with the ball position, adding similar information about players, umpire, and the crowd would be distracting (7). 3D audio gave more space for other sounds that can be used for the players, umpire, and the crowd (6).

Usefulness of the Augmentation: 3D audio was found to be a presentation condition that participants had the least positive experience with. They liked the subtle feedback and how it did not remove the experience of the crowd noise and other broadcasting sounds such as calls for balls going out of bounds (3). Some participants commented that it would be useful for people who want to experience a new way of watching tennis matches, pointing out that adjustment of 3D audio could improve the experience (2).

7 Discussion

It's clear there is a need for improving the spectator experience for blind people. Although radio is the traditional way of consuming SMB, it cannot provide the information that blind spectators want to know. Our participants could not fully comprehend what was happening in the games with radio commentary provided. High speed speech is intelligible by blind people [30], and can be improved further with training [45], however the information content of fast speech is typically limited. In SMB the pace is fast and the information is vast, adding an extra barrier to consumption for blind people. Our presentation conditions provide these missing information in an accessible way (**RQ 2**), yet participants still struggle to fully interpret the shots made.

It is surprising that none of our presentation conditions had a higher preference than the others (**RQ 1**). They were equally as poor in conveying the details of what was happening in the SMB. Though our audio descriptions were developed to ensure direct mapping with the tennis court, and were refined through pilot testing, perhaps they remained unclear. Rapid successive shots from players may have led to short time intervals between bounces of the ball, which in turn would reduce the time between descriptions. Another issue may be the synthesized nature of descriptions: although generally considered acceptable, human speech is both preferred and easier to understand for audio descriptions [23]. We used a generic HRTF for rendering 3D audio because it was unfeasible to capture individual HRTFs. Although 'good enough' [1], this approach has its disadvantages as some sounds remain difficult to localize. More advanced techniques exist for synthesizing 3D sounds [6] may alleviate some of these problems and produce better 3D audio SMB augmentation.

Although radio was a popular medium amongst our participants, its information bandwidth is already occupied with dense commentary. This is a common disadvantage for blind people [29]. The commentaries help blind spectators to understand how the game is played on a higher level while omitting details such as the ball placements, player locations, and shot types. Our results demonstrate how radio broadcasting is inadequate in addressing the needs of blind spectators. Although it is very popular and the most relied on medium, it falls short in delivering game play details. In contrast TV broadcasts have more space to augment the experience. Tennis is one of the sports where the crowd and the commentators do not speak during game play, providing opportunities for augmenting the broadcast by adding audio description and/or 3D audio. However limitations for concurrent audio and speech should be considered [4,8,15,16]. Color commentators typically focus on building the buzz and excitement around the event, emphasizing the reaction of the crowd, and therefore their commentary may only capture what the commentators themselves perceive as significant, restricting the listener's experience to only events commentators acknowledge. Thus there are limitations to consider regarding the type of the commentary which can prime listeners, and further inhibits understanding [13]. Also blind spectators may confuse broadcast effect sounds with game events, having detrimental effects on attention and the spectator experience [25].

We note the striking contrast between a qualitative preference towards radio broadcast with inconclusive quantitative results. Results from our user evaluation show no difference in performance (quantitative) when SMB is augmented with things participants say they want (qualitative). Though radio was preferred, it did not improve participants' accuracy in interpreting what is happening in the game (**RQ 2**). Perhaps our participants simply regressed to their comfort zone: radio is familiar and they understand how it operates, where 3D audio is difficult to interpret at first and requires some training to acquire competency in using it (**RQ 1**). Participants found the augmentations difficult to interpret at first, though this may have been due to unfamiliarity with 3D audio and the content of the audio descriptions. Previous work has highlighted how, particularly for information gathering tasks, efficiency with technological use is key for blind people [40]. We can see this insight replicated in our results: participants described how they could see the benefit of an augmented broadcast channel providing discrete spatiotemporal information regarding the ball and player movement, and would likely use an augmented broadcast channel similar to our system if improvements were made to the design (**RQ 2**). Given the limitations of the de facto system (radio), our attempt to improve the quality of life for participants, however small it may seem, was met with much praise from our participants.

Of upmost importance to our participants was the need to be on a level spectating field as their sighted peers. Although participants enjoyed the benefits of a social context with respect to bespoke commentary, at the same time there is a strong desire for independence (**RQ 1**). They want to be able to enjoy the SMB with others: this requires a level of independent consumption so they can feel part of the group and engage in social discussions about the SMB while simultaneously consuming it. Participants said they would follow up post-match statistics to ensure they understood the match outcome correctly, enabling them to engage in social conversation with sighted peers. Delivering real time information to blind spectators in a format they can understand will help elevate them to the same level as their peers, and include them in the discussion so they may enjoy SMB.

The results of our questionnaire and evaluations support this, indicating how blind spectators want to experience what sighted people experience. We would like to finish with the following quote which captures this succinctly:

"I would like to hear the details that sighted people can see." (P1)

8   Limitations

We could only use two blind spectators for the pilot studies. We could not do a comprehensive pilot study due to logistic reasons. Our initial attempts with pilot participants to do a remote study overwhelmed them [3]. We acknowledge that this imposed limitations on the development of the prototype. However, we believe that our iterative development that includes multiple evaluations provided a reasonable final prototype. We also did not investigate sustained consumption of the SMB. We would like to identify the features of the best possible prototype system before further investigations. We believe this type of consumption requires more control over the augmentations added to the original broadcasts by the users. We listed supporting social consumption as one of the main motivations. Though pursuing this motivation in a formal study was out of scope for our work here, our prototype system, which fulfills the requirements of effective conveyance of information, serves as the prerequisite for future social consumption studies. SMB consumption is a complex experience, with many factors driving people towards consuming content. In this early stage we have focused on developing a system that is up to the challenge of delivering accurate information to create a good experience for spectators. We acknowledge that more elaborate studies are needed to investigate factors such as color commentary engagement, social spectating, and why people prefer one presentation condition over another.

9   Conclusion

Our main contribution is providing insights into how radio broadcasting falls short of presenting a sport event to blind spectators. We have presented our work exploring how blind spectators approach sports media broadcast content. We built a prototype system for augmenting SMB content to enhance the spectator experience of blind and low vision people, and evaluated our prototype in a controlled user evaluation. We also conducted an online questionnaire to understand the social and technological context in which blind people consume SMB. Results showed a contrast between qualitative and quantitative responses in peoples' preference regarding augmented broadcast channels and traditional broadcast commentary. Though participants would repeatedly tout the benefit of radio over other ways to present information in the sport, they were no better at answering basic questions regarding the outcome of a game when listening to radio compared to augmented broadcast channels. Care must be taken when designing augmentations so as not to interfere with other aspects of the SMB itself and the external social context in which SMB spectating takes place. We hope our work raises a new design challenge for HCI, and provides principles to designers, engineers, researchers, and broadcasters in the HCI community producing more inclusive broadcast material.

Acknowledgments. Cagatay Goncu is supported by the Australian Research Council (ARC) grant DE180100057, and thanks the Faculty of Information Technology at Monash University for their support. Daniel J. Finnegan thanks the School of Computer Science & Informatics at Cardiff University for their continued support. We also thank Tennis Australia, particularly the Game Insight Group members Machar Reid, Touqeer Ahson and Stephanie Kovalchik for their support, and finally Kate Stephens for providing insightful feedback during development.

References

1. Berger, C.C., Gonzalez-Franco, M., Tajadura-Jimenez, A., Florencio, D., Zhang, Z.: Generic HRTFs may be good enough in virtual reality. Improving source localization through cross-modal plasticity. Front. Neurosci. **12** (2018). https://doi.org/10.3389/fnins.2018.00021

2. Bielli, S., Harris, C.G.: A mobile augmented reality system to enhance live sporting events. In: Proceedings of the 6th Augmented Human International Conference, AH 2015, pp. 141–144. Association for Computing Machinery, New York, March 2015. https://doi.org/10.1145/2735711.2735836

3. Brinkley, J., Huff, E.W., Boateng, K.: Tough but effective: exploring the use of remote participatory design in an inclusive design course through student reflections. In: Proceedings of the 52nd ACM Technical Symposium on Computer Science Education, SIGCSE 2021, pp. 170–176. Association for Computing Machinery, New York, March 2021. https://doi.org/10.1145/3408877.3432527

4. Cherry, E.C.: Some experiments on the recognition of speech, with one and with two ears (1953). https://doi.org/10.1121/1.1907229

5. Cheung, G., Huang, J.: Starcraft from the stands: understanding the game spectator. In: Proceedings of the SIGCHI Conference on Human Factors in Computing Systems, CHI 2011, pp. 763–772. Association for Computing Machinery, New York, May 2011. https://doi.org/10.1145/1978942.1979053

6. Cobos, M., Lopez, J., Spors, S.: A sparsity-based approach to 3D binaural sound synthesis using time-frequency array processing. EURASIP J. Adv. Signal Process. **2010**(1), 415840 (2010). https://doi.org/10.1155/2010/415840

7. Dong, M., Wang, H., Guo, R.: Towards understanding the differences of using 3D auditory feedback in virtual environments between people with and without visual impairments. In: 2017 IEEE 3rd VR Workshop on Sonic Interactions for Virtual Environments (SIVE), pp. 1–5, March 2017. https://doi.org/10.1109/SIVE.2017.7901608

8. Donker, H., Klante, P., Gorny, P.: The design of auditory user interfaces for blind users. In: Proceedings of the Second Nordic Conference on Human-Computer Interaction, pp. 149–156 (2002). https://doi.org/10.1145/572020.572038

9. Eastman, S.T., Land, A.M.: The best of both worlds: sports fans find good seats at the bar. J. Sport Soc. Issues **21**(2), 156–178 (1997). https://doi.org/10.1177/019372397021002004

10. Ferrand, S., Alouges, F., Aussal, M.: An electronic travel aid device to help blind people playing sport. IEEE Instrum. Meas. Mag. **23**(4), 14–21 (2020). https://doi.org/10.1109/MIM.2020.9126047. conference Name: IEEE Instrumentation Measurement Magazine

11. Francombe, J., Brookes, T., Mason, R.: Evaluation of spatial audio reproduction methods (part 1): elicitation of perceptual differences. J. Audio Eng. Soc. **65**(3), 198–211 (2017)

12. Funakoshi, R., Okudera, Y., Koike, H.: Synthesizing pseudo straight view from a spinning camera ball. In: Proceedings of the 7th Augmented Human International Conference 2016, AH 2016, pp. 1–4. Association for Computing Machinery, New York, February 2016. https://doi.org/10.1145/2875194.2875236

13. Goldschmied, N., Sheptock, M., Kim, K., Galily, Y.: Appraising Loftus and Palmer (1974) post-event information versus concurrent commentary in the context of sport. Q. J. Exp. Psychol. **70**(11), 2347–2356 (2017). https://doi.org/10.1080/17470218.2016.1237980

14. Gregory Appelbaum, L., Cain, M.S., Darling, E.F., Stanton, S.J., Nguyen, M.T., Mitroff, S.R.: What is the identity of a sports spectator? Personality Individ. Differ. **52**(3), 422–427 (2012). https://doi.org/10.1016/j.paid.2011.10.048

15. Guerreiro, J.: Towards screen readers with concurrent speech: where to go next? ACM SIGACCESS Accessibility Comput. **115**, 12–19 (2016). https://doi.org/10.1145/2961108.2961110

16. Guerreiro, J., Gonçalves, D.: Scanning for digital content: how blind and sighted people perceive concurrent speech. ACM Trans. Accessible Comput. (TACCESS) **8**(1), 1–28 (2016). https://doi.org/10.1145/2822910

17. Hermann, T., Zehe, S.: Sonified Aerobics - Interactive Sonification of Coordinated Body Movements, June 2011. https://smartech.gatech.edu/handle/1853/51764. Accessed 21 May 2014. T16:35:15Z Publisher: International Community for Auditory Display

18. Huggins, M.: BBC radio and sport 1922–39. Contemp. Br. Hist. **21**(4), 491–515 (2007). https://doi.org/10.1080/13619460601060512

19. Ichiki, M., et al.: Study on automated audio descriptions overlapping live television commentary. In: Miesenberger, K., Kouroupetroglou, G. (eds.) ICCHP 2018. LNCS, vol. 10896, pp. 220–224. Springer, Cham (2018). https://doi.org/10.1007/978-3-319-94277-3_36

20. Kamel, H.M., Landay, J.A.: A study of blind drawing practice: creating graphical information without the visual channel. In: Proceedings of the Fourth International ACM Conference on Assistive Technologies, Assets 2000, pp. 34–41. Association for Computing Machinery, New York, November 2000. https://doi.org/10.1145/354324.354334

21. Kim, J., Kim, Y., Kim, D.: Improving well-being through hedonic, Eudaimonic, and social needs fulfillment in sport media consumption. Sport Manag. Rev. **20**(3), 309–321 (2017). https://doi.org/10.1016/j.smr.2016.10.001

22. Kim, S., Lee, K.p., Nam, T.J.: Sonic-Badminton: audio-augmented badminton game for blind people. In: Proceedings of the 2016 CHI Conference Extended Abstracts on Human Factors in Computing Systems, CHI EA 2016, pp. 1922–1929. Association for Computing Machinery, New York, May 2016. https://doi.org/10.1145/2851581.2892510

23. Kobayashi, M., O'Connell, T., Gould, B., Takagi, H., Asakawa, C.: Are synthesized video descriptions acceptable? In: Proceedings of the 12th International ACM SIGACCESS Conference on Computers and Accessibility, ASSETS 2010, pp. 163–170. Association for Computing Machinery, New York, October 2010. https://doi.org/10.1145/1878803.1878833

24. Kumano, T., et al.: Generation of automated sports commentary from live sports data. In: 2019 IEEE International Symposium on Broadband Multimedia Systems and Broadcasting (BMSB), pp. 1–4, June 2019. https://doi.org/10.1109/BMSB47279.2019.8971879

25. Kwon, Y.S., Lee, S.E.: Cognitive processing of sound effects in television sports broadcasting. J. Radio Audio Media **27**(1), 93–118 (2020). https://doi.org/10.1080/19376529.2018.1541899

26. Lee, G., Bulitko, V., Ludvig, E.A.: Automated story selection for color commentary in sports. IEEE Trans. Comput. Intell. AI Games **6**(2), 144–155 (2014). https://doi.org/10.1109/TCIAIG.2013.2275199. conference Name: IEEE Transactions on Computational Intelligence and AI in Games

27. Lee, M., Kim, D., Williams, A.S., Pedersen, P.M.: Investigating the role of sports commentary: an analysis of media-consumption behavior and programmatic quality and satisfaction. J. Sports Media **11**(1), 145–167 (2016). https://doi.org/10.1353/jsm.2016.0001. https://muse.jhu.edu/article/626349

28. Lessel, P., Vielhauer, A., Krüger, A.: Expanding video game live-streams with enhanced communication channels: a case study. In: Proceedings of the 2017 CHI Conference on Human Factors in Computing Systems, CHI 2017, pp. 1571–1576. Association for Computing Machinery, New York, May 2017. https://doi.org/10.1145/3025453.3025708

29. Lopez, M., Kearney, G., Hofstädter, K.: Audio description in the UK: what works, what doesn't, and understanding the need for personalising access. Br. J. Vis. Impair. **36**(3), 274–291 (2018). https://doi.org/10.1177/0264619618794750

30. Moos, A., Trouvain, J.: Comprehension of ultra-fast speech-blind vs. 'normally hearing' people, p. 4 (2007). http://www.icphs2007.de/conference/Papers/1186/1186.pdf

31. Petrie, H., Hamilton, F., King, N., Pavan, P.: Remote usability evaluations with disabled people. In: Proceedings of the SIGCHI Conference on Human Factors in Computing Systems, CHI 2006, pp. 1133–1141. Association for Computing Machinery, New York, April 2006. https://doi.org/10.1145/1124772.1124942

32. Pettitt, B., Sharpe, K., Cooper, S.: AUDETEL: enhancing television for visually impaired people. Br. J. Vis. Impair. **14**(2), 48–52 (1996). https://doi.org/10.1177/026461969601400202

33. Pizzo, A.D., Na, S., Baker, B.J., Lee, M.A., Kim, D., Funk, D.C.: eSport vs. Sport: a comparison of spectator motives. Sport Market. Q. **27**(2), 108–123 (2018)

34. Popovici, I., Vatavu, R.D.: Towards visual augmentation of the television watching experience: manifesto and agenda. In: Proceedings of the 2019 ACM International Conference on Interactive Experiences for TV and Online Video, TVX 209, pp. 199–204. Association for Computing Machinery, New York, June 2019. https://doi.org/10.1145/3317697.3325121

35. Rafey, R.A., Gibbs, S., Hoch, M., Le Van Gong, H., Wang, S.: Enabling custom enhancements in digital sports broadcasts. In: Proceedings of the Sixth International Conference on 3D Web Technology, Web3D 2001, pp. 101–107. Association for Computing Machinery, New York, February 2001. https://doi.org/10.1145/363361.363384

36. Ramos, M.: The emotional experience of films: does Audio Description make a difference? Translator **21**(1), 68–94 (2015). https://doi.org/10.1080/13556509.2014.994853

37. Reeves, S., Benford, S., O'Malley, C., Fraser, M.: Designing the spectator experience (2005). https://doi.org/10.1145/1054972.1055074

38. Saidi, N.L.: Sound guided football/basketball game for blind people, October 2007. https://patents.google.com/patent/US20070238557A1/en

39. Savery, R., Ayyagari, M., May, K., Walker, B.N.: Soccer sonification: Enhancing viewer experience. Georgia Institute of Technology (2019). http://hdl.handle.net/1853/61512

40. Shinohara, K., Tenenberg, J.: A blind person's interactions with technology. Commun. ACM **52**(8), 58–66 (2009). https://doi.org/10.1145/1536616.1536636

41. Spelke, E., Hirst, W., Neisser, U.: Skills of divided attention. Cognition **4**(3), 215–230 (1976). https://doi.org/10.1016/0010-0277(76)90018-4

42. Swaminathan, M., Pareddy, S., Sawant, T.S., Agarwal, S.: Video gaming for the vision impaired. In: Proceedings of the 20th International ACM SIGACCESS Conference on Computers and Accessibility, ASSETS 2018, pp. 465–467. Association for Computing Machinery, New York, October 2018. https://doi.org/10.1145/3234695.3241025

43. Toupal, R., Schmid, D.: System and method for automatically generating a narrative report of an event, such as a sporting event, December 2005. https://patents.google.com/patent/US6976031B1/en

44. Trail, G.T., Kim, Y.K.: Factors influencing spectator sports consumption: NCAA women's college basketball. Int. J. Sports Market. Sponsorship **13**(1), 55–77 (2011)

45. Walker, B.N., et al.: Spearcons (speech-based earcons) improve navigation performance in advanced auditory menus. Hum. Factors **55**(1), 157–182 (2013). https://doi.org/10.1177/0018720812450587

46. Wedoff, R., Ball, L., Wang, A., Khoo, Y.X., Lieberman, L., Rector, K.: Virtual showdown: an accessible virtual reality game with scaffolds for youth with visual impairments. In: Proceedings of the 2019 CHI Conference on Human Factors in Computing Systems, CHI 2019, pp. 1–15. Association for Computing Machinery, New York, May 2019. https://doi.org/10.1145/3290605.3300371

47. Zillmann, D., Bryant, J., Sapolsky, B.S.: Enjoyment from sports spectatorship. In: Sports, Games, and Play: Social and Psychological Viewpoints, vol. 2, pp. 241–278 (1989). https://www.taylorfrancis.com/books/e/9780203728376/chapters/10.4324/9780203728376-14

48. Zollmann, S., Langlotz, T., Loos, M., Lo, W.H., Baker, L.: ARSpectator: exploring augmented reality for sport events. In: SIGGRAPH Asia 2019 Technical Briefs, SA 2019, pp. 75–78. Association for Computing Machinery, New York, November 2019. https://doi.org/10.1145/3355088.3365162

An Enriched Emoji Picker to Improve Accessibility in Mobile Communications

Maria Teresa Paratore[1] , Maria Claudia Buzzi[2](✉) , Marina Buzzi[2] ,
and Barbara Leporini[1]

[1] ISTI – CNR, via Moruzzi 1, 56124 Pisa, Italy
{mariateresa.paratore,barbara.leporini}@isti.cnr.it
[2] IIT – CNR, via Moruzzi 1, 56124 Pisa, Italy
{claudia.buzzi,marina.buzzi}@iit.cnr.it

Abstract. We present an emoji picker designed to enrich emojis selection on mobile devices using audio cues. The aim is to make emojis selection more intuitive by better identify their meanings. Unlike the typical emoji input components currently in use (known as "pickers"), in our component each emotion-related item is represented by both an emoji and a non-verbal vocal cue, and it is displayed according to a two-dimensional model suggesting the pleasantness and intensity of the emotion itself. The component was embedded in an Android app in order to exploit touchscreen interaction together with audio cues to ease the selection process by using more than one channel (visual and auditory). Since the component adds non-visual information that drives the emoji selection, it may be particularly useful for users with visual impairments. In order to investigate the feasibility of the approach and the acceptability/usability of the emoji picker component, a preliminary remote evaluation test involving both sighted and visually impaired users was performed. Analysis of the data collected through the evaluation test shows that all the participants, whether sighted or visually impaired, rated the usability of our picker as good, and also evaluated positively the model adopted to add semantic value to emojis.

Keywords: Emojis · Accessibility · Inclusive design · Visual impairments ·
Audio affect bursts · Circumplex model of affect · Mobile communication

1 Introduction

Computer-mediated communication, i.e., communication delivered through networks of computers (in short, CMC), is now pervasive and affects our daily social interactions, especially in text-based formats, both synchronous (instant-messaging applications) and asynchronous (email, social media, blogs) [3]. This phenomenon has dramatically grown worldwide during the recent COVID-19 pandemic, when nationally imposed lockdowns and forced self-isolation have led to a massive adoption of social media and messaging applications to replace face-to-face interactions. Not only business meetings and school lessons [29, 30] have been held in virtual mode, but also social relations with friends

C. Ardito et al. (Eds.): INTERACT 2021, LNCS 12932, pp. 418–433, 2021.
https://doi.org/10.1007/978-3-030-85623-6_25

and relatives have been carried out via electronic devices on a regular basis. In these exceptional circumstances, CMC has fully shown its potential, becoming the safest (and sometimes the only possible) communication channel among people located in different places. Thanks to CMC, co-workers have been able to exchange and comment documents from different locations and store copies on their personal devices, while friends could chat through virtual groups via messaging applications such as WhatsApp. Although the term "Mobile Mediated Communication" may be found in the literature to identify interactions that occur via smartphones or tablets, for simplicity's sake we will adopt the term "CMC" in these cases as well.

1.1 Adding Empathy to CMC: Emoticons and Emojis

Despite the aforementioned advantages, text-based CMC presents a major shortcoming compared to face-to-face communication; the lack of non-verbal cues, such as facial expressions or different tones of voice, creates a sort of psychological distance and makes it less "empathic" and more prone to misunderstandings [6, 8].

Since the time when emails became a widely adopted communication medium, users have strived to add socioemotional cues to their messages. Examples of such a behavior are the use of capitalized words to simulate a loud tone of voice, or typing nonverbal interjections such as "ehm", "oh-oh", etc.

The way users manage timing in asynchronous CMC may also convey socioemotional hints to messages; a reply may in fact be perceived differently depending on its promptness, suggesting a different degree of intimacy/liking or dominance/submissiveness with respect to the sender [3, 9]. Emoticons are one of the earliest expedients adopted to enrich text-based communication, ever since the spread of emails and SMS text-messaging, and are still in use nowadays.

An emoticon is formed by a sequence of text characters (typically punctuation and symbols) that represent facial expressions when viewed sideways (e.g. :-) to describe a smiling face). In the literature, many studies confirm the function of emoticons as effective substitutes of non-verbal cues. Derks et al. [6] examined the role of emoticons in synchronous textual CMC (chat sessions) with respect to the social context (socioemotional vs task-oriented). Their findings show that emoticons are mainly used in socioemotional contexts (i.e., with friends), in both positive and negative situations, in accordance with what happens in face-to-face communication. Moreover, Walther and D'Addario [8] found that when communicating via email (i.e., asynchronously), emoticons add a significant bias to the interpretation of messages when associated with a negative emotional valence (e.g. :-("sad face", >:-("angry face").

Emojis are single-character pictographs used to add non-verbal emotional cues, and can be considered an evolution of emoticons [7]. Unlike emoticons, which are not subjected to any standard or supervision, they are standardized according to an encoding maintained by the Unicode Consortium [11].

At the time of writing, the Unicode standard (release 13.1) [12] accounted for 3521 emojis, according to the classification shown in Table 1.

Emojis are more expressive than emoticons, since they provide a graphical rendering. However, their rendering depends on platforms and applications, which may cause misunderstandings. Miller et al. [23] explored whether emoji renderings or differences

Table 1. The number of emojis according to official Unicode classification release 13.1 [12].

Smileys and emotions	People and body	Components	Animals and nature	Food and drink	Travel and places	Activities	Objects	Symbols	Flags	Total
156	2049	9	140	129	215	84	250	220	269	3521

across platforms give rise to diverse interpretations of emojis. To this aim, they distributed an online survey to solicit people's interpretations of a sample of the most popular emojis, each rendered for multiple platforms. The survey was completed by 304 users and the variance in interpretation of the emojis, quantifying which emojis were most (and least) likely to be misinterpreted, which were analyzed both in terms of sentiment and semantics. Results showed that in many cases, when two people consider the same emoji rendering, they may interpret both the sentiment and semantic meaning differently. Disagreement about both sentiment and semantic interpretations across different platforms was also highlighted.

According to Cramer et al. [10], the contextual meaning of a particular emoji or sequence of emojis can be quite difficult to untangle, since the linguistic function for both sender and recipient is flexible and open to interpretation. Emojis can depict facial expressions, but also pictorial representations of objects, symbols and actions, and their intended meanings can go far beyond their definition according to the Unicode standard. They suggest that when interpreting emojis, it is important to detect the sender's intent, before 'translating' [10]. Semantic ambiguities may arise from cultural, interpersonal and social differences between sender and receiver [7, 13, 14]. The variety of emojis usages and interpretations will depend on specific social practices and norms, e.g. a private long-standing group of friends may send messages containing emojis with meanings not interpretable without an intimate knowledge of their shared history. Volkel et al. [7] assert that emojis may be misunderstood since their intended meaning often remains ambiguous. They present the results of an online large survey (N = 646) showing that personality traits influence the choice of emojis, and that an emoji's choice and interpretation varies greatly between users, even if it is presented in a defined message context. They also infer that emojis interpretations differ depending on whether users are in a public (Twitter, blog posts, etc.) or private context (text chat).

Barbieri et al. [13] explore the meaning and usage of emojis across a number of languages and dialects, also comparing the language-specific models of each emoji. Results suggest that although the overall semantics of the most frequent emojis are similar, some emojis are interpreted in a different way from language to language, and this could be related to socio-geographical differences. Lu et al. [14] analyze how smartphone users adopt emojis based on a very large data set collected from a popular emoji keyboard, extracting a complete month of emoji use by 3.88 million active users from 212 countries and regions, in order to compare user behaviors and preferences across countries and cultures. Their findings show that categories and frequencies of the emojis used provide rich signals for the identification and the understanding of cultural differences among smartphone users.

Emojis' ambiguities are also confirmed in more recent works. Alismail and Zhang [24] conducted a study focused on the perception, interpretation, and liking of a facial emoji-based Likert scale as a means of evaluation assessment in online surveys; their research highlights different experiences of usage among participants.

Herring and Dainas [25] performed an online survey to assess how English-speaking social media users interpreted the pragmatic functions of emojis in examples adapted from public Facebook comments. Their findings show that while female and male interpretations of emojis are generally similar, there are differences in the appreciation and understanding of their usage depending on age, older males being the least likely to use and appreciate emojis, the opposite of the younger females.

1.2   Emojis and Accessibility for Users with Visual Impairments

Tigwell et al. [4] conducted a survey to find out the problems faced by people with visual impairments in relation to emojis. Their findings highlight the issue that assistive technologies, instead of facilitating the inclusion of emojis in CMC, may complicate it, thus being an obstacle to social inclusion.

Screen readers translate emojis into textual descriptions. When a screen reader user receives a message, they perceive an emoji as extra text embedded in the current conversation, which may become very annoying, especially if it contains many emojis. Moreover, the text that is read aloud by the screen reader for an emoji may be a source of misinterpretation itself, since the associated description may not correspond to the emotion that the sender meant to convey.

Searching for an emoji to embed into a message as it is composed emerges as one of the most challenging tasks. Figure 1 shows two screenshots of the emoji picker provided by the Twitter client for Android; the picker comprises a panel containing some controls and a grid of selectable items. The left screenshot shows how emojis are presented according to the frequency of use, while the right one shows the grid for the 'smileys and people' category. In both cases, choosing an emoji via an assistive technology may be cumbersome, given the number of items the user has to navigate. Moreover, default descriptions associated with pictographs may be misleading, if not cryptic, and as a

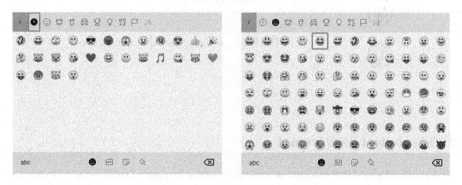

Fig. 1. Two screenshots of the emoji picker from the Twitter client for Android.

result, it may be difficult to understand whether a chosen emoji actually conveys the desired meaning.

A good example of such ambiguity is given by the emoji whose Unicode name is "Face with Look of Triumph", which was originally meant to convey positive emotions associated with pride and personal satisfaction [4]. In spite of its Unicode definition and original meaning, the emoji is currently used on many platforms to suggest negative feelings, such as frustration, anger or contempt. As a result, a recipient might be puzzled on how to interpret this character in a message; should they intend it as a "cool" expression ☻(described as a "smiling face with sunglasses" according to the Unicode specifications), or rather as an "angry" one ☻(described as an "angry face")?

The redundancy of symbols used to express essentially the same feeling is another problem. Table 2 shows a number of emojis currently in use to express happiness. Different graphic representations for the same emotion are meant to convey intensity or qualitative differences, but they are not very simple to differentiate and can be confusing for users with visual impairments.

Table 2. Windows 10 rendering, unicode encoding and unicode standard textual description of "smiley" emojis

Windows 10 rendering	Encoding	Description
☺	U+1F642	Slightly smiling face
☺	U+1F60A	Smiling face with smiling eyes
☺	U+263A	Smiling face
☺	U+1F603	Grinning face with big eyes
☺	U+1F600	Grinning face
☺	U+1F601	Beaming face with smiling eyes

2 Theoretical Background

We have highlighted that emoticons, and later emojis, originated from the need to enrich textual CMC with emotional cues. In this section, we will provide an overview of psychological models related to emotions.

2.1 Basic Emotions Theories and Models

Many different theories exist that identify basic emotions [1]. Plutchick [2] devised eight primary emotions as an evolutionary development of the human being; anger, disgust, fear, sadness, anticipation, joy, surprise, trust. Primary emotions are strictly related to the survival of the human species. Plutchick later developed a circular graphic scheme called the 'wheel of emotions', a two-dimensional model that relates different emotions and attitudes to each other by means of spatial distribution and colors. The model, shown in Fig. 2, highlights how primary emotions are pairwise opposites; joy vs. sadness, anger vs. fear, trust vs. disgust, and surprise vs. anticipation.

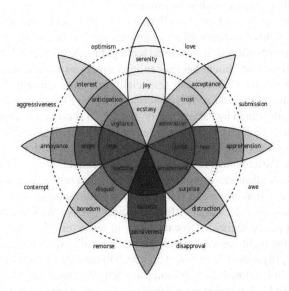

Fig. 2. The Plutchick wheel of emotions.

Ekman and Friesen [28] identified a different set of basic emotions related to non-verbal communication. Their studies on facial expressions led to the definition of six "modal" emotions (anger, disgust, fear, sadness, surprise, happiness), associated with well-defined facial expressions, which constitute the "Ekman faces"; a validated set of grayscale photographs that portrait different actors' faces expressing the modal emotions, plus a neutral expression. The number and quality of Ekman's basic emotions are subject to debate [18], although the Ekman faces are widely adopted in research as a valid tool to assess emotions, primarily due to the fact that Ekman faces refer to cross-cultural non-verbal stimuli.

According to Russell et al. [1, 2, 18], a state of mind can always be described in terms of a linear combination of two neuropsychological states, the valence (the level of pleasure/displeasure) and the arousal, or alertness. This model is well-known as the "Circumplex Model of Affect", and introduces the concept of "core affect" as a consciously recognizable feeling in a certain moment. Based on Russell's theory, core affects are placed in a two-dimensional space, where the X-axis represents the pleasantness and the Y-axis the arousal experienced in a certain state of mind. Yik et al. [2] identify 12 such core emotional components, evenly distributed as 12 sectors on a circular surface. Their model is referred to as the 12-Point Affect Circumplex, and is shown in Fig. 4 (Sect. 3.1).

2.2 Theories of Emotions and Auditory Perception

Ekman and Frieser's theories have mainly been criticized [15, 18] because many emotions are not referable to a characteristic facial expression; moreover the same facial expressions can be related to different emotions (e.g., a smile may be used to convey happiness as well as commiseration or sarcasm).

Alongside the analysis of emotions based on facial expressions, research has been conducted in the field of auditory affective processing, focused on the role of nonverbal interjections in manifestations of emotional feelings [19, 20]. The results of these studies essentially highlight that human beings can infer emotions from nonverbal vocal cues exactly as occurs for the Ekman faces (especially in a cross-cultural way). Belin et al. [15], in particular, propose an auditive alternative to the Ekman faces, in which facial expressions are substituted by "affect bursts" (i.e., eight short non-verbal vocal interjections). According to their study, eight basic emotions (anger, disgust, fear, pain, sadness, surprise, happiness, and sensual pleasure) can be associated with the same number of nonverbal bursts. Participants (15 of them male, 15 female), were asked to evaluate an initial set of 198 vocalizations reproduced by actors, each related to a basic emotion. At the end of the evaluation process, a validated set of audio samples was obtained, which constitutes the so-called Montreal Affective Voices (MAV). MAV is composed of 90 audio samples, i.e., the registered vocalizations of ten actors (5 males and 5 females), each portraying the eight basic emotions, plus a "neutral" expression.

Cowen et al. [16] adopted a different approach to classify emotions in terms of vocal bursts. These authors refined the two-dimensional model based on valence and arousal, and theorized a multi-dimensional semantic space where each emotion is obtained as a combination of emotion categories. Categories do not belong to a discrete set; on the contrary, they blend into each other with smooth gradients that determine a continuous semantic difference. In order to infer the dimensionality of the space, a large-scale, multi-stage experiment was conducted, at the end of which 24 semantic dimensions were identified: adoration, amusement, anger, awe, confusion, contempt, contentment, desire, disappointment, disgust, distress, ecstasy, elation, embarrassment, fear, interest, pain, realization, relief, sadness, surprise (negative), surprise (positive), sympathy, triumph. As in [15], in this study as well a possible limitation may arise from cultural bias. Actually, while vocalizations were gathered from participants from four different countries, only US-English speaking users participated in the task of recognizing emotions. The result of the experiment is available within an online interactive map [17], in which the 2032 vocal bursts analyzed in the study are clustered according to the identified semantic components.

3 Designing a Novel Emoji Picker Based on "Real" Emotions

As we previously highlighted, standardized Unicode emojis bear intrinsic semantic ambiguities and accessibility issues due to their graphical nature, which may hinder the quality of social relationships via CMC. This is even more true if the sender and/or the recipient of a message is a person with visual impairments. Picking one or more emojis from the standard set while typing a message may prove to be an overwhelming task, given the enormous number of items available. In order to address these shortcomings, we designed an emoji picker that guides the user through the choice of an emoji thanks to auditory cues and an arrangement of the pictographs on the screen oriented by their emotional components. In order to test the emoji picker, we integrated it in an Android app; one of the authors, who is totally blind, actively collaborated on the interface design, and on the prototype evaluation throughout all phases of development. Moreover, intermediate versions of the emoji picker were periodically published as beta tests on the Google Play Store, so that other users could give us feedback. Beta testers were recruited through specialized email groups and comprised both sighted users and users with visual impairments who relied on Android's screen reader, namely TalkBack.

3.1 Arranging Emotions on the Screen

In order to make the browsing functionality more intuitive, we associated the action of sliding one's finger across the screen with a coherent change in the emojis' semantic value. This solution was straightforward once we decided to adopt Russell's circumplex model, in a similar way as proposed in [5]. The graphical user interface (GUI) of the emoji picker was modelled upon a circular shape, similar to a wheel divided into sectors, where each sector corresponds to an emotion. Thanks to the underlying semantic structure of Russell's model, users can adjust the characteristics of the emotion they want to convey by sliding the finger on the screen of the mobile device. Figure 3 shows how the movement of the finger on the GUI is related to the emoji that is going to be selected.

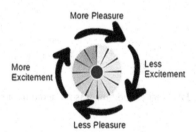

Fig. 3. Sliding the finger across the GUI helps find emojis according to degree of pleasure and excitement.

Our design strategy aimed to create a compromise between a fair range of emotions and a narrow space, since our emoji picker was expected to be mostly used on medium-sized smartphones. Thus, one of our main design requirements was to achieve a good compromise between expressiveness and usability. Prototypes of wheel-shaped GUIs existing in the literature [31, 32] rely on the Plutchick model and the Geneva Emotion Wheel [33], which also account for the intensity of emotions. In our case, due to the small size of the screen, implementing a wheel of reduced size with concentric sectors would result in very poor user interaction, especially when selecting emojis close to the center of the wheel. A very small movement of the finger in that area would in fact result in hearing a confusing rapid succession of different vocal bursts. If the interaction were performed by a person with visual impairment, especially via screen reader, the emoji picker would actually become not usable.

Concerning the number of emotions to be considered, in spite of the many categories existing nowadays, the most frequently used emojis in messaging apps and social media are those related to feelings and emotions, in accordance with the primary function of these special characters [21]. Unicode statistics [34] also show that only a very limited subset of emojis classified as "smileys and emotions" appears within the first ten positions of the most frequently used. This encouraged us to adopt the 12-Point Circumplex Model of Affect (12-PAC) by Yik, Steiger and Russell [12, 22], which presents an adequate granularity of emotions for our purpose.

Figure 4 shows the 12-PAC model and our rendering of it as a wheel with 12 sectors associated to emojis. In order to associate each core emotion with a pictogram, we referred to the aforementioned statistics and our personal experiences with social media, instant messaging apps and emails. While some associations are immediate (e.g., Scared, Disgusted), others may be ambiguous (Excited, Satisfied), but we were confident that audio hints would have conveyed clearer information.

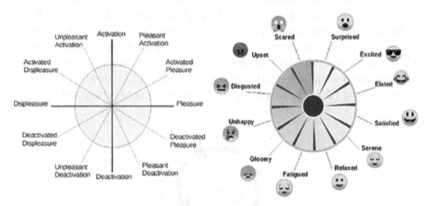

Fig. 4. The 12-PAC model and how it is rendered in our emoji picker.

3.2 Associating Affective Vocal Bursts

We adopted non-verbal emotional hints from the MAV set [15], integrated with vocal bursts provided by [16], in order to reduce semantic ambiguity and further improve accessibility. For each emotion sector in our wheel, a validated auditory, non-verbal counterpart was associated.

Our circumplex-based model maps the following emotional states; surprised, excited, elated, satisfied, serene, relaxed, fatigued, gloomy, unhappy, disgusted, upset, scared.

MAV model [15], on the other hand, only accounts for eight emotions, i.e., anger, disgust, fear, pain, sadness, surprise, happiness, and sensual pleasure. We hence chose two sets of eight MAV audio files, one per gender, and inferred the four missing emotions from [16] using the online interactive map provided [17]. Given the wide range of nuances available, we used the interactive map to identify the missing vocal cues according to the percentage composition of emotional components.

Table 3 shows the four missing emotional bursts (one per gender) chosen from the map (Excited, Elated, Fatigued, Gloomy) and their emotional components.

Table 3. The vocal bursts chosen from the model proposed by Cowen et al. [16, 17]

Gender	Emotional burst	Composition
M	Excited	84% awe, 8% surprise (positive), 8% sympathy
M	Elated	53% elation, 25% triumph, 8% contempt, 8% awe, 8% ecstasy, 8% pride
M	Fatigued	35% pain, 17% distress, 8% confusion, 8% desire, 8% elation, 8% embarrassment, 8% fear, 8% neutral
M	Gloomy	58% sadness, 18% pain, 8% contentment, 8% disappointment, 8% distress
F	Excited	50% elation, 26% triumph, 8% contempt, 8% ecstasy, 8% pride
F	Elated	67% elation, 17% triumph, 8% confusion, 8% contentment
F	Fatigued	34% distress, 17% confusion, 17% embarrassment, 8% contempt, 8% desire, 8% disappointment, 8% sadness
F	Gloomy	29% distress, 21% embarrassment, 8% confusion, 10% disappointment, 8% disgust, 8% fear, 8% pain, 4% contempt, 4% elation

4 Testing the Emoji Picker

As previously mentioned, in order to test the emoji picker, we integrated it in an Android app. The app's distribution was provided worldwide in English and Italian. In order to address aspects related to accessibility and the rendering of audio hints, we actively involved our co-author, who is blind, in the design phase along with two volunteers with visual impairments recruited via a specialized Facebook group. Their suggestions and feedback were important in defining the interactions of our emoji picker with Android's assistive technologies.

After a first phase of internal testing within our research group, the Android app with the emoji picker was released for evaluation as an "open test app" on the Google Play Store. Participants to the evaluation phase were recruited via social media and mailing lists; invitations to participate were posted on Facebook and email groups focused on accessible technologies for users with a visual impairment. Overall, 30 testers were recruited, 12 of whom were visually impaired and regular TalkBack users.

The test was divided into two phases; in the first part, the users were presented with the consent form to participate in the study and then were introduced to the emoji picker with a detailed description of how it works. At the same time, they were asked to customize the emoji picker by choosing a gender for the voice that will utter the affect bursts. Finally, the emoji picker was displayed and users were invited to practice with it (see Fig. 5) in order to become more familiar with the different interaction modalities.

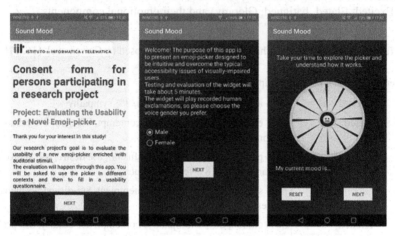

Fig. 5. Screenshots of the app: first part of the evaluation process.

Once users had completed the phase of familiarization with the emoji picker, they were asked to complete three sentences by adding an emoji as if they were using an instant messaging app. Each sentence was conceived to fit with an emoji from a different quadrant as shown in Fig. 6, so that test users were encouraged to explore most of the

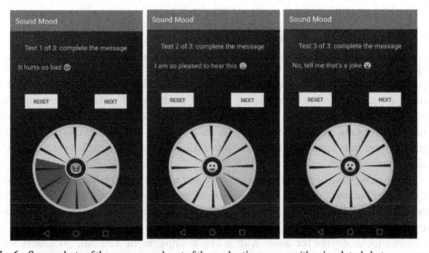

Fig. 6. Screenshots of the app: second part of the evaluation process (the simulated chat messages).

wheel to complete the test. In the case that an assistive technology was in use, each sentence was read aloud by the screen reader as soon as it was presented to the user; while dragging with the finger on the GUI, only emotional audio bursts were heard to announce the underlying emojis. As the user chose an emotion, the focus returned to the sentence and the screen reader read again the whole sentence and reproduced the emoji in terms of its pictogram's description.

After the test, users were invited to fill out an evaluation questionnaire, which was anonymized via a unique identifier. The goal of the questionnaire was to assess the usability of the emoji picker and the validity of our model, hence we adopted the ten-question System Usability Scale (SUS) [23, 24], to which three questions were added, related to the model:

- The position of the emotions on the screen helped me find what I wanted to pick (Q1)
- The audio cues (exclamations) helped me find what I wanted to pick (Q2)
- The audio cues (exclamations) gave a good description of the emotions (Q3)

All the questions used 5-point Likert items, answered in the same way as the SUS, from Strongly Disagree (1) to Strongly Agree (5). To complete the questionnaire, testers were finally asked to provide their gender, age, level of education and if they had visual impairments.

5 Results

Once all the questionnaires were completed, we checked data for inconsistencies and consequently eliminated six questionnaires in which the answers showed obvious inconsistencies. SUS scores [26, 27, 29] were then evaluated for each of the 24 remaining participants (ten of whom with visual impairments).

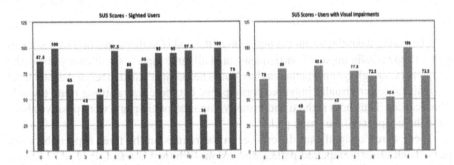

Fig. 7. SUS scores collected for each participant in our study.

SUS values for both evaluation groups are described in Fig. 7. In the sighted group there are some high values (8 higher than 80/100) but also three values below 60/100. In the visually impaired group there are only two values higher than 80/100 and three values below 60/100; anyway, the overall analysis of the results shows a substantial

Table 4. Means and standard deviations for SUS for sighted and visually impaired participants

Evaluation group	M	SD
Sighted (N = 14)	79.46	21.6
Visually impaired (N = 10)	69.25	18.41

equivalence between sighted and visually impaired participants in their SUS scores ($t = -1.21$, $df = 22$, n.s.) (Table 4).

The ratings on the three questions about the model were very skewed towards the "Strongly Agree" end of the scale, so non-parametric statistics, as shown in Table 5, were appropriate.

Table 5. Median and interquartile range (IQR) for ratings on the three questions related to the model for sighted and visually impaired participants, with one sample Wilcoxon Signed Rank test results

Evaluation group	Median	IQR	W	Probability
Sighted (N = 14)				
Q1: position of emotions	4.5	1.0	81.5	0.009
Q2: auditory cues helped	5.0	1.0	99.0	0.002
Q3: auditory cues good description	4.0	1.0	67.0	0.021
Visually impaired (N = 10)				
Q1: position of emotions	4.0	1.0	42.0	0.018
Q2: auditory cues helped	4.0	1.0	37.5	0.068
Q3: auditory cues good description	4.0	2.0	48.0	0.031

Comparing the ratings with the midpoint of the scale (neither agree or disagree) both sighted and visually impaired participants rated all three aspects significantly above the midpoint (although Q2 on whether auditory cues helped just failed to reach the 0.05 level of significance for visually impaired participants, but there was a strong trend towards significance). Thus both sighted and visually impaired participants were positive about these three aspects of the emoji picker.

There were no significant differences in the ratings on the three aspects between sighted and visually impaired participants (Mann-Whitney U test, Q1: $U = 77.5$, n.s.; Q2: $U = 92.0$, n.s.; Q3: $U = 56.0$, n.s.).

In relation to the participants' personal characteristics there was a significant difference between men and women in their ratings of Q1, but not the other two questions (see Table 6). There were no significant differences due to age, but the number of participants in each age group was probably not sufficient for a robust analysis.

Table 6. Median and interquartile range (IQR) for ratings on the three questions related to the model for men and women participants, with Mann–Whitney U test results

	Men (N = 16)		Women (N = 7)		U	Probability
	Median	IQR	Median	IQR		
Q1: position of emotions	4.0	1.0	5.0	0.0	24.0	0.033
Q2: auditory cues helped	4.0	2.0	5.0	1.0	36.5	n.s
Q3: auditory cues good description	4.0	1.0	4.0	1.0	47.5	n.s

6 Discussion and Conclusions

We have presented an emoji picker for mood and emotions based on a model inferred from theories of emotions. The aim of the emoji picker is to provide users with spatial and auditory hints related to the semantics of emotions, in order to overcome the typical problems of ambiguity and misinterpretation posed by the choice of an emoji. At the same time, our picker is aimed at overcoming the accessibility issues met by users with visual impairments when they wish to express feelings through emojis. The emoji picker relies on 12 basic emotions (the 12-PAC emotion model) and on a validated set of emotional vocal hints (the Montreal Affective Voices, plus four audio cues selected from among those identified by Cowen et al.). The 12-PAC model enabled us to arrange the emojis based on a semantic structure, while the purpose of the audio cues was to provide immediate, non-ambiguous descriptions of the emotions, especially helpful when accessing the emoji picker via a screen reader. While exploring the wheel by touch, audio feedback that reproduces a non-verbal description of emotions is triggered and immediately perceived, so that users do not need to listen to a long and possibly ambiguous description spoken by a voice synthesizer.

An evaluation study was conducted via an Android app, which was completed by 24 participants, ten of whom have visual impairments. The app presented the emoji picker, proposed a series of short tests and finally administered a questionnaire to assess the SUS score and an evaluation of the model. Values obtained for the SUS score are encouraging, since the results collected showed that both sighted and visually impaired participants rated the emoji picker's usability as good. The spatial and auditory model's evaluation was also positive for both categories of users, even though the ratings suggest that improvements must be considered, for users with visual impairments, in finding more effective techniques to convey audio hints. Future efforts in the improvement of the emoji picker will be mainly devoted to finding effective solutions to express the emotions' intensity and add more customization options (e.g., personalized associations between emotions and vocal bursts).

In order to gather more test users, we are planning to develop a prototype of our tool for the iOS platform. This will enable us to make a comparison between different assistive technologies (i.e., TalkBack vs VoiceOver).

Finally, we are aware that ambiguities in the interpretation of emojis may persist on the recipient's side, but the design of a software component such as a "recipient's translating layer" was beyond the scope of this study. However, this topic will be a subject of our research in the near future.

Acknowledgments. We wish to thank the following email groups devoted to accessibility and users with visual impairments, who showed particular interest in our study and helped us find participants: tech-vi@groups.io, accessible@googlemail.com. We wish to also thank the Blind & Visually Impaired Android Users on Facebook.

References

1. Russell, J.A.: A circumplex model of affect. J. Pers. Soc. Psychol. **39**, 1161–1178 (1980)
2. Yik, M., Russell, J.A., Steiger, J.H.: A 12-point circumplex structure of core affect. Emotion **11**(4), 705–731 (2011)
3. Walther, J., Tidwell, L.C.: Nonverbal cues in computer-mediated communication, and the effect of chronemics on relational communication. J. Organ. Comput. **5**, 355–378 (1995)
4. Tigwell, G.W., Gorman, B.M., Menzies, R.: Emoji accessibility for visually impaired people. In: Proceedings of the 2020 CHI Conference on Human Factors in Computing Systems (2020)
5. Toet, A., Erp, J.V.: The EmojiGrid as a tool to assess experienced and perceived emotions. Psychology **1**, 469–481 (2019)
6. Derks, D., Bos, A.E., Grumbkow, J.V.: Emoticons in computer-mediated communication: social motives and social context. Cycberpsychol. Behav. **11**(1), 99–101 (2008)
7. Völkel, S.T., Buschek, D., Pranjic, J., Hußmann, H.: Understanding emoji interpretation through user personality and message context. In: Proceedings of the 21st International Conference on Human-Computer Interaction with Mobile Devices and Services (2019)
8. Walther, J., D'Addario, K.P.: The impacts of emoticons on message interpretation in computer-mediated communication. Soc. Sci. Comput. Rev. **19**, 324–347 (2001)
9. Liebman, N., Gergle, D.: It's (not) simply a matter of time: the relationship between cmc cues and interpersonal affinity. In: Proceedings of the 19th ACM Conference on Computer-Supported Cooperative Work and Social Computing (2016)
10. Cramer, H., Juan, P.D., Tetreault, J.: Sender-intended functions of emojis in US messaging. In: Proceedings of the 18th International Conference on Human-Computer Interaction with Mobile Devices and Services (2016)
11. Unicode Inc.: Unicode® Full Emoji List, v13.1. https://www.unicode.org/reports/tr51/ (2020). Accessed: 12 October 2020
12. http://unicode.org/emoji/charts/full-emoji-list.html
13. Barbieri, F., Kruszewski, G., Ronzano, F., Saggion, H.: How cosmopolitan are emojis? Exploring emojis usage and meaning over different languages with distributional semantics. In: Proceedings of the 24th ACM international conference on Multimedia (2016)
14. Lu, X., Ai, W., Liu, X., Li, Q., Wang, N., Huang, G., Mei, Q.: Learning from the ubiquitous language: an empirical analysis of emoji usage of smartphone users. In: Proceedings of the 2016 ACM International Joint Conference on Pervasive and Ubiquitous Computing. (2016)
15. Belin, P., Fillion-Bilodeau, S., Gosselin, F.: The Montreal affective voices: a validated set of nonverbal affect bursts for research on auditory affective processing. Behav. Res. Methods **40**, 531–539 (2008)
16. Cowen, A., Elfenbein, H., Laukka, P., Keltner, D.: Mapping 24 emotions conveyed by brief human vocalization. Am. Psychol. **74**(6), 698–712 (2019). https://doi.org/10.1037/amp000 0399
17. https://s3-us-west-1.amazonaws.com/vocs/map.html

18. Posner, J.D., Russell, J., Peterson, B.: The circumplex model of affect: an integrative approach to affective neuroscience, cognitive development, and psychopathology. Dev. Psychopathol. **17**(3), 715–734 (2005)
19. Banse, R., Scherer, K.: Acoustic profiles in vocal emotion expression. J. Pers. Soc. Psychol. **70**(3), 614–636 (1996)
20. Schröder, M.: Experimental study of affect bursts. Speech Commun. **40**, 99–116 (2003)
21. Updated Emoji Statistics: https://www.emojipedia.org/stats/
22. Zhong, K., Qiao, T., Zhang, L.: A study of emotional communication of emoticon based on Russell's circumplex model of affect. In: HCI (2019)
23. Miller, H., Thebault-Spieker, J., Chang, S., Johnson, I.L., Terveen, L., Hecht, B.J.: "Blissfully happy" or "ready to fight": varying interpretations of emoji. In: ICWSM (2016)
24. Alismail, S., Zhang, H.: Exploring and understanding participants' perceptions of facial emoji Likert scales in online surveys. ACM Trans. Soc. Comput. **3**, 1–12 (2020)
25. Herring, S., Dainas, A.: Gender and age influences on interpretation of emoji functions. ACM Trans. Soc. Comput. **3**, 1–26 (2020)
26. Brooke, J.: SUS: a "quick and dirty" usability scale. In: Jordan, P.W., Thomas, B., Weerdmeester, B.A., McClelland, A.L. (eds.) Usability Evaluation in Industry. Taylor and Francis, London (1986)
27. Brooke, J.B.: SUS—a retrospective. J. Usabil. Stud. **8**(2), 29–40 (2013)
28. Ekman, P., Friesen, W.V.: Constants across cultures in the face and emotion. J. Pers. Soc. Psychol. **17**(2), 124–129 (1971)
29. Bangor, A., Kortum, P.T., Miller, J.T.: Determining what individual SUS scores mean: adding an adjective rating scale. J. Usabil. Stud. Arch. **4**, 114–123 (2009)
30. Sirait, E.R., Zellatifanny, C.M.: An empirical study: computer-mediated communication and collaboration among government employees during flexible working arrangements. In: 2020 International Conference on Information Technology Systems and Innovation (ICITSI), pp. 95–100 (2020)
31. Runge, N., Hellmeier, M., Wenig, D., Malaka, R.: Tag your emotions: a novel mobile user interface for annotating images with emotions. In: Proceedings of the 18th International Conference on Human-Computer Interaction with Mobile Devices and Services Adjunct (2016)
32. Warpechowski, K., Orzeszek, D., Nielek, R.: Tagging emotions using a wheel user interface. In: Proceedings of the 13th Biannual Conference of the Italian SIGCHI Chapter: Designing the Next Interaction (2019)
33. Sacharin, V., Schlegel, K., Scherer, K.: Geneva Emotion Wheel Rating Study. https://archive-ouverte.unige.ch/unige:97849 (2012)
34. Frequency of Emoji Use: https://home.unicode.org/emoji/emoji-frequency/

Analyzing the Design of Tactile Indoor Maps

Christin Engel[✉] and Gerhard Weber[✉]

Institute for Applied Computer Science, Human-Computer-Interaction,
Technische Universität Dresden, Dresden, Germany
{christin.engel,gerhard.weber}@tu-dresden.de

Abstract. Tactile maps are feasible to increase the mobility of people with blindness and to achieve spatial information of unknown environments. Exploring tactile maps could be a hard task. Research on the design of tactile maps, especially the design and meaningfulness of tactile symbols, mostly addresses outdoor environments. The design of tactile indoor maps has been studied less frequently, although they differ significantly from outdoor environments. Therefore, in this paper, 58 tactile indoor maps have been investigated in terms of the design of the headline, additional map information, legend, walls and information presentation types used. In addition, the design of common objects for indoor environments, such as doors, entrances and exits, toilets, stairs and elevators, has been examined in more detail and commonly used symbols have been extracted. These findings form the basis for further user studies to gain insights into the effective design of indoor maps.

Keywords: Tactile indoor map design · Accessible building maps · People with blindness and visual impairments

1 Introduction

The ability to travel is an essential requirement not only for the equal participation of people with impairments in social life, but also in many professional areas. Whether attending workshops, training sessions, networking meetings or conferences - many professions require independent mobility in unfamiliar outdoor and indoor environments. For people with blindness (PB) it is challenging to orient and navigate themselves especially in unknown environments. Tactile mobility and orientation maps are feasible to explore unknown areas and information points as well as to acquire different type of knowledge (landmarks, routes, configurations) [4] and thus support increasing mobility for PB. Tactile maps (TM) consist of raised lines, symbols and textures and can be perceived sequentially by touch. However, reading tactile maps (TM) is a hard task which is why they should be well-designed in regard to the specific requirements of the tactile sense. This requires at least enlargement of symbols and textures as well as the use of Braille letters. Consequently, generalization is an important aspect

© IFIP International Federation for Information Processing 2021
Published by Springer Nature Switzerland AG 2021
C. Ardito et al. (Eds.): INTERACT 2021, LNCS 12932, pp. 434–443, 2021.
https://doi.org/10.1007/978-3-030-85623-6_26

for the design of TM which implies not least a decision about which details are shown at a specific scale [19]. Still, the usefulness of TM has been shown in prior research. Furthermore, several studies investigated the design of TM (e.g. [8,10,16] that highly influences the readability. However, TM for outdoor environments are mostly considered, only a few studies have been conducted on the design of TM for indoor environments (e.g. [17,19]) although indoor and outdoor environments differ significantly. Indoor maps of buildings are more complex than outdoor representations and include multiple levels. They are primarily large-scaled indoor maps, showing more details than outdoor and geographical maps. Well-designed tactile maps are also needed for the development of effective audio-tactile applications.

In conclusion, more detailed research on effective design of tactile indoor maps is needed to increase the mobility of PB, even within unfamiliar buildings. Therefore, as a first step in our development process, we investigated existing tactile indoor maps in terms of the applied design. The goal of the analysis was to identify different design characteristics as well as repeating design elements, thus deriving first insights into the design of tactile indoor maps and generating research questions for upcoming user studies.

2   Research on Tactile Maps

The design of TM is influenced by many factors, e.g. the production method [4], the function of the map, the context of use [9] or the experiences and abilities of the user. In order to be able to decrease the amount of data on maps, in recent years, lots of research have been done developing interactive TM for PB (e.g. [2,3,6]). Effective interactive TM require effective tactile map design. For this reason, a number of studies have examined specific design aspects. First, general guidelines for tactile graphics (e.g. [1,15]) recommending minimal distances and sizes, can be applied. However, these guidelines are not sufficient and do not address specific aspects of indoor maps. Although there is no common standard for the use of symbols [11], much research focused on the distinguishability and design of symbols (e.g. [7,11]). Rowell et al. [16] use interviews to investigate which properties are important when designing symbols. The authors identified texture, spacing, type, shape, size, elevation and standardisation as key factors. Other researchers examine the meaningfulness of symbols in maps (e.g. [9,10]). Lambert et al. [9] found out that meaningful symbols are better remembered. According to the authors, the physical characteristics of symbols should help to understand their meaning. Lee et al. [10] investigated the usefulness of visual symbols, collected from visual maps, for use in TM. There is no discussion of how useful it is to assign further meaning to the symbols, for example, the orientation of the symbols. Only Lobben et al. [11] introduce modifiers paired with symbols to expand their meaning (e.g. a triangle to indicate elevation changes). Additionally, a number of papers dealt with increasing availability of TM by proposing an automated creation process (e.g. [18,20,21]).

However, the majority of previous research focused on spatial maps with streets and buildings [3] so their findings can usually be applied specifically to outdoor environments. The orientation strategies, structure, objects, scale and information needs for indoor and outdoor environments differ greatly, so specific research is needed for indoor environments [12]. Some approaches already exist that address information needs for orientation in buildings as well as orientation strategies. Rowell et al. [17] investigate in interviews with PB to find out preferences of different map features, characteristics and which types of information to include on a mobility map. The authors point out the usefulness of indoor maps and large scale mapping for mobility purposes. In a recent survey with 106 participants with blindness and visual impairments we investigated [5] the information need in indoor environments, applied orientation strategies, important orientation features and as well specific challenges arising in indoor environments. The study shows the lack of availability of tactile indoor maps, which is due in part to the fact that building data is often not freely available [19]. Till now, it is unclear which information should be included in tactile indoor maps and how to represent the information effectively and highly readable for different purposes. Furthermore, existing studies evaluating the effectiveness of maps often used highly simplified maps without much details (e.g. [4]).

In summary, most of the specific research on design of TM is almost limited to outdoor environments and cannot directly be transferred to indoor environments. Effective design implies the use of meaningful design elements, especially symbols, which must be considered for indoor maps to provide effective design. In addition, the context of use is clearly relevant for the design [14] so it is needed to evaluate symbols and other design characteristics in context of the map [9].

3   Analysing the Design of Tactile Indoor Maps

Due to the lack of studies on specific design aspects for indoor maps, we started our research by analyzing existing indoor maps in terms of design. Therefore, only a few examples of tactile indoor maps are available, which is why we analyzed examples from practice, and extracted the symbols and design approaches used for further user studies.

3.1   Methods and Materials

In total, we collected 58 photos of different tactile indoor maps. As mentioned before, only a few research examples (e.g. [13]) of tactile indoor maps could be used as a basis for the design analysis. Nevertheless, a number of companies produce commercially tactile indoor maps as part of building guidance systems [1]. Many of them reference their projects and the maps created on their websites. Some of these maps were used for the analysis, retrieved from the websites of 12 companies. Three maps come from publications and research projects, four maps have been photographed by ourselves directly in a building, six were provided on the website

---

[1] e.g. https://www.schilder-systeme.com, https://www.mdsignworx.at, https://www. meng.de or https://www.ilis-leitsysteme.de (last visited: 09. June 21).

of a library for the blind (DZB)[2] and few maps were provided by building websites (e.g. website of a university). Due to the corona crisis, it was not possible to visit various buildings to search for building maps, so these could only be obtained online. For this reason, we have no further information about most of the maps (e.g. about the expertise of the creators, feedback from users, quality of the maps, exact size, etc.).

The majority of analyzed TM are large UV prints (64%) that have been set up or hung to a fixed position (74%) in a building for visitors. The physical size of the maps can only be estimated, some companies indicated page lengths of at least 60 cm. Besides using UV printing, 10% of the maps were produced with swellpaper and 12% as foil reliefs. A minority consists of metal or a plastic composition. About 22% are suitable for the mobile use (maximum size of A3). Furthermore, almost all maps (except three) support both - visual and tactile objects and letters and are therefore feasible for people with and without sights. One map provides further information by adding QR-codes to points-of-interest that can be scanned by mobile devices. The maps come from 11 different countries, with the majority from Germany (60%) and 17% from Sweden and just few maps from China. Only one example is represented from each of the other countries (e.g. Great Britain, Czech Republic, Switzerland, USA).

First, we analyzed related work and extracted basic building features that are important for orientation and may be relevant for indoor maps. On that basis, we defined categories that are relevant for indoor map design. We then analyzed the retrieved indoor maps manually in regard to the defined attributes. If maps contain relevant properties that were not previously considered, this category was added and all other maps were also examined in this regard. A descriptive analysis has been applied on the results, followed by an extraction of outlying features and symbols.

4   Results of the Design Analysis

We examined the design with regard to design of symbols, textures, lines, legend as well as Braille labels. We paid particular attention to the different design characteristics as well as the common features and differences of the maps. The majority of maps were made for public buildings, with the exception of shopping centers and hotels. Most indoor maps were made for museums or theaters as well as universities (26%). About 10% also represent sports or swimming halls. Building types that are typically frequently visited by people with disabilities, such as health centers or train stations, are less frequently represented. However, it cannot be assumed that the frequency with which building types are represented in the sample reflects the population of available TM. It is also possible that additional indoor maps are not publicly available.

Headline. The headline of a map is very important for orientation and understanding the map's content. Most maps provide a headline, at least representing

---

[2] https://www.dzblesen.de/index.php?site_id=4.2 (last visited: 09. June 21).

Table 1. The first value column shows the percentage of maps containing basic elements like Headline, Legend, Walls, Symbols etc. The second column contains additional characteristics that frequently occur in relation to the first column values (average value calculation without 0).

	Available	Frequent characteristics
Headline	81%	Building name (50%), level number (45%)
Legend	88%	Position above map (31%)
Walls	95%	All walls same width (57%)
Symbols	95%	6 per map in average (SD = 3.3)
Textures	59%	3.1 per map in average (SD = 2.6)
Line styles	98%	1.6 per map in average (SD = 0.6)
Labels	54%	6 per map in average (5.1)
Keys	40%	8.2 per map in average (SD = 6.9)
Doors	86%	Gap in the wall (76%)
Entries/Exits	81%	Shown as symbol (76%)
Elevator	66%	Shown as symbol (62%)
Stairs	83%	Shown as symbol (79%)
Toilets	76%	Shown as symbol (43%), indicators for gender (64%)
Location	65%	Shown as symbol (65%)

the building name or the name or number of the most common level (see Table 1). 25% of the analyzed maps provide the type of the map (e.g. orientation or evacuation plan). A description of the shown area is given for 12% of the TM (e.g. exhibit name, building wing). 25% of the headlines provide multiple information types (e.g. building name and level name).

Further Information. Overall, most maps do not include further information about the map. In particular, no map makes use of a grid for orientation, just five maps provide a visual or labelled marker for scale and four present a marker to indicate north direction. Only two maps support a schematic overview specifying the location of the map shown in the building.

Legend. The majority of maps comes with a legend, that is most often placed directly above the map and quite often on the right side (26%), followed by the left side (21%). Two maps (handheld ones) provide the legend on a separated sheet. The design of the legend is mostly similar, with a reference on the left (e.g. key, texture, symbol used in the map) and an explanation on the right. The legend is essential for the comprehension of almost all maps and mostly describes all elements on the map. Some maps do not reference the stair symbol in the legend.

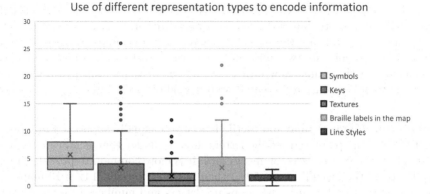

Fig. 1. Box plot that shows how many different symbols, keys, textures, Braille labels and line styles were used on average on one map to provide information (maps without occurrence included as 0 value) .

Walls. The structure of the building is represented by the floor plan and, if necessary, by the labeling of rooms and areas. When exploring TM, lines are followed to identify the dimensions of the building and its layout. Most of all analyzed maps support the representation of inner and outer walls. While most maps present walls with same width, about 30% support line tracing and thus recognition of the outline, by designing outer walls thicker than inner walls. 14% of the TM represent the wall thicknesses in the building very differently, as they correspond to the real thickness of walls. Only 19% reference the line style for walls in the legend.

Encoding of Information. Information on maps can be provided using Braille labels, textures, line styles, and point symbols. It is up to the author's decision which information the map should contain and which of these encoding types are used. The main focus was on analyzing which representations occur in the maps and how many different elements of an object class (e.g. symbols) were represented. Almost all maps make use of different symbols to represent relevant information (see Fig. 1). An amount of 5 to 8 different symbols on the map is very common, where the maximum number of different symbols per map is 15. While some maps provide only a few basic symbols, others use them as the main information carriers. Textures, line styles (at least one to represent walls), and braille labels in the map are used less consistently, but still by the majority of maps (see Table 1). According to this, there is partly a high variance in the number of objects used. For example, while 46% do not provide any braille label in the map for areas and objects, the number of labels used varies greatly for the remaining maps. Most of the maps use less than 10 different keys. Textures and line styles were used relatively rarely to encode information. Textures were often used to determine restricted areas or to indicate functions of areas (e.g. corridors, exhibition areas). Filled areas occurred most frequently. Areas are often visually separated with colors, but not filled with raised textures. A maximum of three different line styles (5%) were used on a map, with solid lines assigned to walls. Most maps present only two different line styles to distinguish walls and routes. About 45% of the maps show either a route (e.g. escape route) or a guidance system, which is mainly represented with dotted or dashed lines.

Labels and Keys. Visual and tactile labels were equally supported in most of all TM. Most maps placed Braille letters directly under the visual counterpart. Visual letters are also raised on most maps. It is more common to provide Braille labels just in the legend (about 50%) than in the map only (14%). 12 maps use numeric indicators for keys, two maps use letters and numbers to separate keys in two categories, and seven maps use abbreviations with single letters.

Doors. Doors are important for orientation for many PB (e.g. by counting the doors). The majority of the maps show at least the positions of doors. The majority represent normal doors with a gap in the wall, the remaining representations use symbols. These indicate not only the position of doors, but also their opening direction. The different symbols appearing in the maps are shown in Fig. 2. The symbols used are very similar to those applied for visual indoor maps. Many maps explicitly identify entrances or exits of the building by special symbols, Braille labels (5%) or both (9%). A total of 38% identify emergency exits separately, although some maps also distinguish between normal exits and emergency exits. Most entries (56%) can be identified by a filled triangle or arrowhead (see Fig. 2 Entrance (a) to (d)), while 22% apply an arrow that points in the direction of the entry. One map indicates a revolving door with an unfilled circle with a gap (Fig. 2 Doors (f)). Exits or emergency exits were often represented with the same symbol (Fig. 2 (Emergency) Exit (a) and (b)). Three times, a combination of an arrow and a further symbol (e.g. wheelchair or iconic person) was given for this purpose.

Stairs and Elevators. Stairs and elevators are an important orientation feature and can be found in almost all buildings. The majority of maps include stairs and elevators and represent it with a symbol. 69% of the stair symbols consist of parallel lines in different variations (e.g. with or without border). About 40% of the represented stairs have indicators for their direction, for example, an open side of a rectangle indicates the bottom (13%), decreasing width of steps from top to bottom (8%), an arrow pointing to the top (6%), applying three elevation levels (8%), or a point on the highest step (6%), as shown in Fig. 2. Symbols for elevators mostly represent variations of a square with (47% of all symbols for elevators) or without an open site indicating the entry, whereby some contain a cross (24%), two arrows (18.4%) or a key/ label (8%). The elevator symbol most often used is a rectangle with one side open and an arrow pointing in (29%, Fig. 2 Elevators (c)).

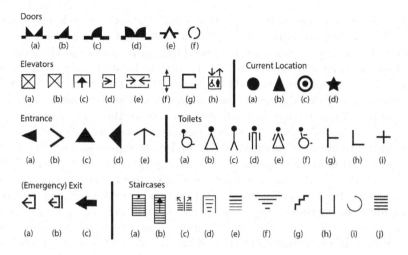

Fig. 2. Different types of symbols extracted from the analyzed maps

Toilets. The location of toilets is a very important feature for many people, especially those with disabilities. Most maps show the location of toilets, represented by a single symbol in more than half of the maps or just by labels (26%). While 21% of the toilets do not distinguish between different types of toilet rooms, 64% use indicators for male, female, and accessible toilets, with more than half illustrating these with iconic stick figures. The label "WC" was commonly used (33%).

Infopoints and Current Location. Especially for mobility maps it is essential to know the current location. However, in the case of static maps, this is only meaningful when maps were permanently installed. More than 50% of the symbols represent a filled circle and 23% a filled triangle, similar to many visual maps. In particular, PB also have great interest in the location of information points or personal contacts in the building. This information is rarely given: just 10% of the maps provide information on receptions or info points, mostly marked with an "I" symbol.

5 Discussion and Outlook

We analyzed a wide range of different indoor maps in regard to the representation of important building information as well as design concepts and spaces for the design of tactile building maps. The results show that although the design of the maps is very heterogeneous and not standardized, some design aspects are very similar. For example, there seems to be a consensus on the design of some symbols as the applied symbols were often similar and meaningful relating to the represented feature, e.g. symbols for stairs, elevators and exits. In contrast, different line styles and textures play a minor role for the analyzed indoor maps. Symbols were more often used than Braille labels to encode information. We could also identify important building objects that were represented with the majority of maps. Consequently, a headline, walls, stairs and elevators, toilets, doors and exits/ entries as well as the current location (in case of fixed or dynamic maps) should be provided by the map. We extracted the different types of symbols for individual objects from the maps, traced them and adapted the size to at least 6 mm per site (according to guidelines). Based on our many years of experience, we will adapt the most common symbols according to guideline requirements to evaluate their readability and meaningfulness with PB in well-designed indoor maps. For example, it would be interesting to find out whether encoding of additional information with symbols, such as the opening direction of elevators or the direction of staircases, can be represented and understood by PB. In addition, the choice of symbols should be made not only in terms of readability but also concerning their meaningfullness and consistency with outdoor map symbols. In particular, the level-of-detail of tactile indoor maps still needs to be investigated.

Acknowledgements. This paper is funded by the Federal Ministry of Labour and Social Affairs (BMAS) under the grant number 01KM151112.

References

1. Braille Authority of North America and Canadian Braille Authority: Guidelines and standards for tactile graphics (2010). http://www.brailleauthority.org/tg
2. Brock, A., Oriola, B., Truillet, P., Jouffrais, C., Picard, D.: Map design for visually impaired people: past, present, and future research. MEI-Médiation et information, pp. 117–129 (2013)
3. Brock, A.M.: Touch the map! designing interactive maps for visually impaired people. SIGACCESS Access. Comput. (105), 9–14 (2013). https://doi.org/10.1145/2444800.2444802
4. Brock, A.M., Truillet, P., Oriola, B., Picard, D., Jouffrais, C.: Interactivity improves usability of geographic maps for visually impaired people. Human-Comput. Interact. **30**(2), 156–194 (2015)
5. Engel, C., Müller, K., Constantinescu, A., Loitsch, C., Petrausch, V., Weber, G., Stiefelhagen, R.: Travelling more independently: a requirements analysis for accessible journeys to unknown buildings for people with visual impairments. In: The 22nd International ACM SIGACCESS Conference on Computers and Accessibility, ASSETS '20. Association for Computing Machinery, New York (2020). https://doi.org/10.1145/3373625.3417022
6. Götzelmann, T.: Lucentmaps: 3d printed audiovisual tactile maps for blind and visually impaired people. In: Proceedings of the 18th International ACM SIGACCESS Conference on Computers and Accessibility, ASSETS '16, pp. 81–90. Association for Computing Machinery, New York (2016). https://doi.org/10.1145/2982142.2982163
7. James, G.: A kit for making raised maps. Cartographic J. **12**(1), 50–52 (1975)
8. Lambert, L., Lederman, S.: An evaluation of the legibility and meaningfulness of potential map symbols. J. Visual Impair. Blindness **83**(8), 397–403 (1989)

9. Lambert, L., Lederman, S.: An evaluation of the legibility and meaningfulness of potential map symbols. J. Visual Impair. Blindness **83**(8), 397–403 (1989). https://doi.org/10.1177/0145482X8908300808

10. Lee, C.L.: An evaluation of tactile symbols in public environment for the visually impaired. Appl. Ergon. **75**, 193–200 (2019)

11. Lobben, A., Lawrence, M.: The use of environmental features on tactile maps by navigators who are blind. Prof. Geographer **64**(1), 95–108 (2012). https://doi.org/10.1080/00330124.2011.595619

12. Loitsch, C., Müller, K., Engel, C., Weber, G., Stiefelhagen, R.: AccessibleMaps: addressing gaps in maps for people with visual and mobility impairments. In: Miesenberger, K., Manduchi, R., Covarrubias Rodriguez, M., Peňáz, P. (eds.) ICCHP 2020. LNCS, vol. 12377, pp. 286–296. Springer, Cham (2020). https://doi.org/10.1007/978-3-030-58805-2_34

13. Papadopoulos, K., Barouti, M., Charitakis, K.: A university indoors audio-tactile mobility aid for individuals with blindness. In: Miesenberger, K., Fels, D., Archambault, D., Peňáz, P., Zagler, W. (eds.) ICCHP 2014. LNCS, vol. 8548, pp. 108–115. Springer, Cham (2014). https://doi.org/10.1007/978-3-319-08599-9_17

14. Perkins, C.: Cartography: progress in tactile mapping. Prog. Human Geography **26**(4), 521–530 (2002)

15. Guidelines on Conveying Visual Information on Information Access for People with Print Disabilities Inc. (2005)

16. Rowell, J., Ongar, S.: The world of touch: an international survey of tactile maps. part 2: design. Brit. J. Visual Impair. **21**(3), 105–110 (2003)

17. Rowell, J., Ungar, S.: Feeling our way: tactile map user requirements-a survey. In: International Cartographic Conference, La Coruna (2005)

18. Štampach, R., Mulíčková, E.: Automated generation of tactile maps. J. Maps **12**(sup1), 532–540 (2016)

19. Trinh, V., Manduchi, R.: A multi-scale embossed map authoring tool for indoor environments. In: Miesenberger, K., Manduchi, R., Covarrubias Rodriguez, M., Peňáz, P. (eds.) ICCHP 2020. LNCS, vol. 12376, pp. 459–466. Springer, Cham (2020). https://doi.org/10.1007/978-3-030-58796-3_53

20. Wabiński, J., Mościcka, A.: Automatic (tactile) map generation–a systematic literature review. ISPRS Int. J. Geo-Inf. **8**(7), 293 (2019)

21. Watanabe, T., Yamaguchi, T., Koda, S., Minatani, K.: Tactile map automated creation system using openstreetmap. In: Miesenberger, K., Fels, D., Archambault, D., Peňáz, P., Zagler, W. (eds.) ICCHP 2014. LNCS, vol. 8548, pp. 42–49. Springer, Cham (2014). https://doi.org/10.1007/978-3-319-08599-9_7

Understanding Motivations and Barriers to Exercise Among People with Blindness in India

Gesu India, Mohit Jain[✉], and Manohar Swaminathan

Microsoft Research, Bangalore, India

Abstract. People with vision impairments (PVIs) have inferior physical fitness compared to sighted individuals. Several studies have been conducted to understand concerns, motivations, barriers, and experiences with exercise in the blind population. However, these studies have been limited to the developed regions. India is home to one-third of the world's blind population and hence it is crucial to understand exercise patterns among PVIs in India. In this work, we interviewed 24 Indian PVIs to uncover novel insights, including minimal use of exercise technology, crucial role of blind schools, and infrastructural and social barriers. We conclude the paper with design recommendations, such as exploiting the design space of restricted walking, emphasizing on schools for the blind, and forming support groups to promote exercises among PVIs.

Keywords: Accessibility · Blind · Visual impairments · PVI · Exercise · Walking · Motivation · Barrier · ICTD · HCI4D · India · Developing region

1 Introduction

People with vision impairments engage in less physical exercises, and therefore have inferior physical fitness compared to sighted adults [6,22]. Weit *et al.* [20] found that the odds of being obese or overweight for PVIs were 1.5 times greater than for sighted individuals. Several studies have been conducted to understand concerns, motivations, barriers, and experiences with exercise in the blind population, and also understand the role of technology in encouraging exercise among them [16,17,22]. They found PVIs face several barriers, including inaccessible fitness infrastructures, discouragement by parents due to safety concerns, limited social opportunities to exercise with a partner, lack of experience and interest, and misperceptions related to the importance of exercise [10,16,17].

This has triggered accessible exercise technologies to be an emerging area of research in the HCI and accessibility community [15,23,24]. To promote physical activities, several sports have been invented and/or made accessible for PVIs, such as goalball [2], beep baseball, and blind cricket. These sports use a combination of audio and vibrotactile-based stimuli to replace the visual stimuli.

© IFIP International Federation for Information Processing 2021
Published by Springer Nature Switzerland AG 2021
C. Ardito et al. (Eds.): INTERACT 2021, LNCS 12932, pp. 444–454, 2021.
https://doi.org/10.1007/978-3-030-85623-6_27

However, participation in these sports is very limited, due to safety concerns, lack of resources, and perceived requirement of athletic abilities and competence [17]. Exergames can mitigate these barriers, as they combine playful video gaming with exercise and can be played indoors, thus motivating PVIs to engage in more exercising. Several accessible exergames have been developed, which are either accessible versions of famous exergames for sighted individuals (*e.g.*., VI-Tennis [11], Blind Hero [23]), or exergames specifically designed for PVIs (*e.g.*, Eyes-Free Yoga [15], Pet-N-Punch [13]). However, these exergames require expensive hardware, thus limiting their global adoption.

Importantly, research around understanding exercise among PVIs and accessible exercise technologies have been limited to the developed world. On the other hand, India is home to one-third of the world's blind population [3]. Due to the social, cultural, economic, and infrastructural differences, results from the developed regions cannot be generalized to the Indian settings. Thus, it is crucial to understand motivations, barriers, and role of technology in exercising among PVIs in the global south, to develop accessible exercise technologies for them.

In this paper, we conducted semi-structured interviews of 24 Indians with vision impairments, to understand their exercise patterns, motivations and barriers in performing exercise, their learning and experiences, and the role of technology in contributing to their exercise habits. We found novel insights, including minimal use and awareness of accessible exercise technologies, the pivotal role of blind schools in teaching accessible sports, and support structure of friends, family and peers to motivate individuals to be physically fit. We conclude with design recommendations to help accessible exercising in developing regions.

2 Study Design

2.1 Participants

Twenty four adults (5 female) with an average age of 25.4 ± 5.6 years, participated in the study. Sixteen of them were blind since birth, and four (P4, P9, P16 and P20) had partial vision impairments. On average, participants had vision impairments for 21 ± 8.9 years. The participants were from across India: 11 participants from Tier-1 cities, 6 from Tier-2 cities, and 7 from Tier-3 cities [21]. Four participants have post-graduate degrees, eleven have graduate, and seven have high school degrees. Participants have been using Android phones with Talk-Back for 6.1± 3.6 years and have access to the Internet; 8 participants owned low-range (below $150) smartphones, 12 mid-range ($150–$300) smartphones, and four high-range (above $300) smartphones. For mobility, all, except one, have been using a white cane for 9.6±7.0 years. A majority of participants (21) reported doing regular exercises (more than thrice a week).

2.2 Methodology and Data Analysis

We conducted IRB-approved semi-structured, in-depth interviews of the 24 participants to learn about their current exercise habits, experiences with physical activities since childhood, associated motivations, barriers and influencing factors, and use of technology in exercising. We also collected demographic information. Two local NGOs helped us in recruitment, by circulating the recruitment email in their respective networks and WhatsApp groups. All interviews were conducted remotely by the first author in English, over Google Meet. They were audio-recorded and later transcribed with the consent of the participants. The interview lasted for 30–75 mins; participants were paid 500 INR.

We analyzed the transcripts using an inductive and iterative approach. Three authors participated in the coding process and iterated upon the codes until consensus was reached. Over the course of the analysis, we (1) discussed coding plans, (2) developed a preliminary codebook, (3) reviewed the codebook and refined/edited codes, and (4) finalized categories and themes (see Table 1).

3 Findings

3.1 Physical and Mental Fitness

Participants acknowledged improving physical fitness as their primary motivation for regularly participating in exercises. They considered exercise to be crucial for a healthy life and strive to integrate fitness activities into their daily routine.

"I have a love-hate relationship with physical activities. People say that it makes them feel very fresh, but I feel very sweaty and sticky. Still, I do it, as it's just something that I know it's healthy for me." - P2.

Most participants (21) performed preliminary physical activities, such as (brisk) walking and stretching, regularly. Only four of them had fitness goals, such as improving body stamina, strengthening arms/legs, *etc..*, and hence were engaged in strenuous activities like martial arts, squat and rope skipping. Apart from fitness reasons, participants varied physical activities to reduce monotony. P18 attended weekly lessons in dance, yoga, martial arts, and aerobics, to minimize boredom. Moreover, growing concerns about their declining health after quitting exercise led participants to re-engage in fitness activities. E.g.:

"I left school at 16, and stopped exercising. I was healthy back then. Later, my health got a little upset, so I started exercising at home." - P1.

Participants mentioned the benefits of exercise on mental health, and the importance of mental health in general, quoting *"a healthy mind in a healthy body"*. Further, they were also engaged in mental health exercises, like meditation.

"Meditation, which I do as part of yoga, makes my mind free." - P1.

Besides physical and mental impact, performing regular exercises has helped in boosting self-defence morale for female participants. Two participants who actively participate in blind sports mentioned social interactions that happened in and out of the playfields, as the key motivator. P20 was proud about finishing a marathon, his newly discovered potential, which boosted his self-confidence.

"It was amazing for me that I won! It changed my life! I thought, if seven days of exercise can be so worthwhile, I should keep doing it." - P20.

3.2   Family, Friends and Peer Support

Participants reported support of family members, friends, and peers to be crucial in sustaining fitness routine, as they taught them the benefits of regular exercising. Their family members helped them by providing verbal encouragement, purchasing fitness equipment (treadmill, weights, *etc.*.), and assisting them in attending fitness classes and sports events. At times, the parents of our participants not only encouraged, but also forced them to exercise.

"I didn't like (doing) any physical activity. I was not interested. But I started doing it because my parents wanted me to. They were concerned about my physical health. They got me a treadmill when I was 12." - P2.

Five participants were accompanied by their friend or a family member for their daily yoga, walking or workout sessions. This also helped in strengthening the relationship between them. Due to the time commitment by their sighted peers, our participants felt more *'accountable'* towards their own health.

"My dad asks me to join him for evening walks. We talk about things that happened that day. I also made him install this step counter app and now we track each other's step count records." - P16.

Although peer and family support helped PVIs, a few participants reported lacking motivation due to the absence of it. A participant mentioned being limited to indoor exercises, due to the lack of *"company for outdoor walks or for playing games"* (similar to [16]). Failure to gain support from family members to continue playing sports after losing eyesight led P16 to stop playing, while P19 continues to play (blind) cricket but with internal conflicts.

"I lost my eye while playing, with a cricket ball. My parents started hating cricket and did not want me to play anymore. That was very difficult for me. They wanted me to play chess, other indoor games. Later, they were convinced that blind sports are helping me mingle with people." - P19.

3.3   Stigmatization by Society

A broad range of social factors influenced the exercising behavior of our participants. Negative perceptions and stereotyping associated with vision impairment [4] was one of the main barriers. For instance, P2 explained her internalized social stigma related to white cane, resulting her not been able to walk independently till adulthood, thus curtailing her exercise options.

"There was a lot of stigma around white cane, a lot of internalized ableism. As a child, my only motivation was to look less blind. Using a cane would make me look more blind. Hence, I never used it." - P2.

Due to similar reasons, P18 stopped her classical dance training, and P16 stopped walking on the streets as he was once mistaken for a beggar.

The perception of sighted people that PVIs are always in need of their assistance, acted as a barrier as well. P2 shared her experience:

"In college, everyone would always be concerned about me walking on my own. I would always get interrupted with them providing help. I have to explain 'I'm only walking, I don't need you to take me anywhere.'" - P2.

To minimize such unwanted help offerings by strangers, P17 mentioned taking phone calls in public places, thinking *"people won't come, or offer help, when they see I am on a phone call."* On the contrary, P4 shared his experience of not receiving help from people on the road, when in need. This resulted in him going out for walks only with his sighted friends, thus curtailing his opportunity for independent outdoor exploration, and limiting it to walking indoors.

3.4 Role of Technology

We use the term *technology* to refer to a variety of support tools, similar to [16], including smartphone apps, fitness bands and treadmills. In spite of the regular exercising behaviour of 21 participants, we found them using technology minimally to support that. Ten participants reported not using any technology to help with their exercises; eight participants reported using an app to track step count, heart rate, calories burned (Google Fit (3), Pedometer (2), Samsung Health (2), etc.); seven used apps to keep them engaged during the (monotonous) exercise routines (YouTube (4), Netflix (2), Spotify (2), Audible (2), *etc.*).

"When I walk on the terrace, I usually call someone on the phone... That walk is not boring anymore." - P2.

Moreover, seven participants wanted to track their walking, but were unaware of self-tracking phone apps which can help them with their physical fitness goals.

Affordability is a key factor in choosing technology by our participants. Only four participants owned phones costing more than US$300 (considered high-range in India), two participants owned health-tracking wearable devices, and two participants mentioned having access to a treadmill. Most of the apps reported by our participants were free apps, except paid video-streaming services and subscription-based audio-book apps used by four participants. Interestingly, most participants reported walking regularly, mainly because it is accessible, and does not require any additional equipment/infrastructure.

Even when the technology was available, participants complained about the missing accessibility component. For instance, three participants tried using Cult.Fit app to access exercise-related video tutorials:

"I tried Cult.Fit but unfortunately, they don't tell me what to do. They just keep on doing the exercises, so for me, it's of no use. I still use their app for meditation since those instructions are accessible, maybe because everyone has to close their eyes during meditation (laugh)". - P10.

3.5 Importance of Educational Institutions

In developed countries, children with vision impairments attend mainstream schools (also known as integrated/inclusive schools) with trained educators [19]. In contrast, in India, 40% of children with vision impairments in the age group of 5–19 years do not attend any school [18], while the rest mainly attend schools for the blind [9,14]. Out of our 24 participants, 18 attended schools for the blind, while 6 (four of them had low vision) attended mainstream schools. In India, most children who attend schools for the blind have to reside in the school hostel, to receive holistic training, including orientation, mobility, personal care, independent living, and physical well-being, in addition to schooling [9].

A key characteristic of schools for the blind, relevant to our study, is the emphasis on physical exercises and outdoor games. Participants who studied in schools for the blind mentioned playing freely in grounds with their school friends. They were introduced/trained in one or more of these activities in school: yoga, blind cricket, blind football, kho-kho, kabaddi, handball, discus throw, basketball, cycling, and running. The positive perception towards physical fitness and enjoyment of playing team sports were seeded during their childhood years.

"I studied in a residential school. We had a compulsory physical education class every day 8:30 to 9. Also, the wardens, the teachers used to encourage us to play more. I played Kabaddi and Hide-and-Seek." - P17.

In contrast, participants who attended integrated school, faced difficulty:

"There was a subject called physical training. I did whatever the teacher told, like stretching my hands and legs. Everyone else after doing these exercises would leave to play... I sat alone in the class." - P20.

This highlights the importance of peer support and trained instructors, which are available by default in schools for the blind.

Moving to adulthood, participants highlighted the importance of being associated with a university or higher-education institution, in order to have infrastructural support for games and exercising, including gyms, pools, and trainers.

"Playing cricket was a happy thing during my graduation. Every evening, we used to play. At times, my sighted friends would cover their eyes and play." - P19. *"My hostel had a gym. I used to do treadmill daily."* - P2.

However, such facilities are available only in elite institutions. Moreover, to access these facilities, individuals need to be either residents or stay in close proximity to be able to travel for utilizing these facilities. For instance, P14 complained that he could not continue sports after school, as his college had minimal infrastructure:

"In my blind school, we used to play cricket daily... also handball. Now I don't play. It stopped when I left school and joined college." - P14.

3.6   Access to City Infrastructure

Though usage of smartphone apps for exercise was minimal, we found participants using navigation apps (like Google Maps) frequently in combination with exploration apps (like Lazarillo, Nearby Explorer) to hear updates on landmarks in their route. Seven participants mentioned walking outside their homes regularly, and six participants shared their eagerness to walk outdoors but were unable to because of *"bad road"* and/or *"unavailability of nearby parks"*. Thirteen participants complained about the poor road infrastructure.

"I don't go out for any leisure walk because unfortunately Bangalore city is not that accessible. The roads, especially the footpaths, are not proper, there are too many pits and drainages." - P10.

Poor road infrastructure hinders walking, the most common exercise among PVIs. Even apps supporting neighbourhood exploration to encourage people to walk on the road, are of limited relevance for PVIs in India. Moreover, participants stated their struggles in finding other city infrastructures to support physical activities, including accessible playgrounds and player communities. *E.g.*,

> *"Even when I have a (tennis) court, it's very difficult to find someone to play with me."* - P19.

The infrastructure needs expressed by our participants are minimal, which are taken for granted in developed countries, such as open public spaces, parks, and accessible roads, to pursue basic physical activities, including walking, jogging and games requiring minimal equipment (blind cricket, blind football). The availability of such spaces may attract other PVIs, thus enabling team sports.

3.7 Impact of COVID-19

The pandemic severely impacted our participants, uncovering barriers in their pursuit to physical fitness. To fight COVID-19, the government of India has been imposing restricted mobility, forcing people to stay at home. This negatively impacted the already fragile outdoor movement of our participants.

> *"I used to go to the football camp, but that stopped due to COVID."*-P6.
> *"I used to go for a walk outside daily morning with my family members, mostly to a park which have some gym equipment. I walked and also used those equipments. But yeah, now we stopped due to COVID."* - P15.

The pandemic triggered participants' concern about their physical health. Eight participants expressed decline in their physical and mental health due to the COVID-forced sedentary lifestyle. To counter this, participants mentioned changing their eating habits to improve health, and walking throughout the day in and around their homes as a form of physical activity.

4 Discussion and Design Implications

In this paper, we studied the exercise patterns of PVIs in India and factors influencing it, by conducting semi-structured interviews of 24 adults with visual impairments. We discovered patterns that were novel and/or in contrast to previous findings [16,17], such as intrinsic motivation, minimal use of technology, infrastructural and societal barriers, role of blind schools, and support of friends, family, and peers. Prior exercise-related work for blind people has been restricted to developed regions, which assumes accessible road infrastructure and prevalence of latest technologies, which are not true for India. Thus, the novel findings of our work have potential to influence the design of accessible physical activities for a majority of the global blind population living in developing regions.

Next, we briefly discuss design implications for accessible exercising.

Minimal Technological Solution: In spite of our participants being well-educated and technology-friendly, we found their investment in exercise-related technology to be minimal. Ten of them did not even use their phones to help with their exercising, and a majority of them were unaware of existence of such apps. Prior work in resource-rich environments has investigated a range of technologies for self-tracking and exergames [11–13,15,16] involving body sensors, depth cameras, and smart exercise equipment. However, such technologies are not affordable for our participants. Enabling accessible exercise technology in the Indian context requires a novel approach, which increases awareness about the influential role of technology in exercises, may be in their educational/workplace settings, and exploits existing technologies (like inbuilt smartphone sensors). For instance, VStroll [7] uses smartphone sensors to promote walking among PVIs, by enabling them to virtually explore real-world locations while walking.

Schools for Blind: A majority of PVIs in India attend schools for the blind, instead of inclusive school. Prior work has reported various shortcomings of such blind schools especially with respect to lack of access to STEM education [8]. However, from the perspective of learning life-skills and physical activities, the role played by such special schools need further research. On the flip side, to make inclusive schools accessible, it should have well-trained instructors to teach accessible sports/exercises, and provide peer support to PVIs [22]. A hybrid approach, wherein blind children attend schools for the blind during their early years of education and transition to an integrated school setting, is worth exploring.

Restricted Walking: Walking was the most common exercise among our participants. Health experts recommend 150 min of brisk walking per week [1]. However, due to poor road infrastructure and safety concerns, walking in restricted spaces – home, terrace, nearby parks – is the only viable option for our participants. There is scope to design future apps that can provide engaging experience to PVIs while they walk in such restricted spaces (similar to [7]).

Family and Peer Support: Prior work in developed regions found that with the increase in vision loss, parents' expectations for their children's ability to be physically active decreased [17]. In contrast, friends and family not only motivated our participants to take part in physical activities, but also enabled it by facilitating their transportation to attend sports events and fitness classes. However, non-availability of such support systems acted as barrier to pursue these activities. Hence, efforts to enhance exercise behavior of PVIs in India should consider creating and optimally utilizing such support groups.

Limitations: This study was conducted during COVID-19 outbreak in India and restricted the recruitment of participants via email/WhatsApp. As a result, we could not recruit PVIs who are illiterate, or do not have phones (for instance, older adults) or Internet connectivity. In addition, participants of our study predominantly represent the middle-income, urban population of India, usually considered as the early adopters of technology. Reduced access to education and technology create barriers to physical fitness for PVIs [5], thus findings from our work cannot be generalised to the entire population of PVIs in India.

5 Conclusion

We emphasize the specificity of our study here as a reminder that this study is at best a first step towards characterizing exercising patterns among PVIs outside of the developed regions context. We found novel insights which are in sharp contrast to prior findings from the developed world. Our participants minimally used exercise technology with no/rare access to fitness bands and exergames, studied in special schools for blind instead of inclusive schools, and faced severe infrastructural and social barriers. An understanding of such differences can help with a global exploration of issues around exercise and accessibility.

A Codebook

Table 1. Codebook from our analysis of interview transcripts. The codebook shows seven themes (bold), 15 codes, prevalence (%) for each theme, and the total count of each theme and code.

Theme/Code	Count	Theme/Code	Count
Access to city infrastructure (24.11%)	**116**	**Family, Friends and Peer support (13.92%)**	**67**
Poor road infrastructure	50	Friends and peer support	25
Public fitness infrastructure	45	Family support	21
Safety concerns on roads	21	Exercise partner	21
Physical and Mental Health (20.58%)	**99**	**Role of Technology (12.26%)**	**59**
Exercise habits	66	Exercise-related apps	46
Improved physical health	17	Accessibility issues	13
Improved mental health	16	**Stigmatization by Society (9.14%)**	**44**
Importance of Educational Institution (15.8%)	**76**	Disability stigma	44
Sports/exercises in school	40	**Impact of COVID (4.15%)**	**20**
Schools for the blind	36	Impact of COVID	20

References

1. CDC: How much physical activity do adults need? (2019). https://www.cdc.gov/physicalactivity/basics/adults/index.htm
2. Çolak, T., Bamaç, B., Aydin, M., Meriç, B., Özbek, A.: Physical fitness levels of blind and visually impaired goalball team players. Isokinetics Exerc. Sci. 12(4), 247–252 (2004)
3. Correspondent, H.: Number of blind to come down by 4m as india set to change blindness definition (2017). https://bit.ly/3aXHKB7
4. Dawn, R.: The portrayal of disability in Indian culture: an attempt at categorization (01 2015)

5. Dwyer, A.: Factors That Increase Physical Activity in Youth Who Are Visually Impiared. Kinesiology, Sport Studies, and Physical Education Synthesis Projects (May 2017). https://digitalcommons.brockport.edu/pes_synthesis/22
6. Hopkins, W.G., Gaeta, H., Thomas, A.C., Hill, P.N.: Physical fitness of blind and sighted children. Eur. J. Appl. Phys. Occup. Phys. **56**(1), 69–73 (1987). https://doi.org/10.1007/BF00696379
7. India, G., Jain, M., Karya, P., Diwakar, N., Swaminathan, M.: VStroll: An audio-based virtual exploration to encourage walking among people with vision impairments. In: ASSETS 2021, ACM (October 2021). https://doi.org/10.1145/3441852.3471206
8. India, G., Ramakrishna, G., Pal, J., Swaminathan, M.: Conceptual learning through accessible play: Project Torino and computational thinking for blind children in India. In: ICTD 2020 (June 2020)
9. Kumar, P.: Evolving role of special schools for children with visual impairment in India (2019). https://ncert.nic.in/pdf/publication/journalsandperiodicals/journalofindianeducation/JIE_May_18.pdf
10. Lieberman, L.J., McHugh, E.: Health-related fitness of children who are visually impaired. J. Vis. Impairment Blindness **95**(5), 272–287 (2001). https://doi.org/10.1177/0145482X0109500503
11. Morelli, T., Foley, J., Columna, L., Lieberman, L., Folmer, E.: Vi-tennis: a vibro-tactile/audio exergame for players who are visually impaired. In: FDG 2010, New York, pp. 147–154. ACM (2010). https://doi.org/10.1145/1822348.1822368
12. Morelli, T., Foley, J., Folmer, E.: Vi-bowling: a tactile spatial exergame for individuals with visual impairments. In: ASSETS 2010, New York, pp. 179–186. ACM (2010). https://doi.org/10.1145/1878803.1878836
13. Morelli, T., Foley, J., Lieberman, L., Folmer, E.: Pet-n-punch: upper body tactile/audio exergame to engage children with visual impairments into physical activity, presented at the. In: Proceedings of Graphics Interface 2011 (2011)
14. NAB: Nan department of education (2019). https://www.nabindia.org/education/
15. Rector, K., Bennett, C.L., Kientz, J.A.: Eyes-free yoga: An exergame using depth cameras for blind amp; low vision exercise. In: ASSETS 2013, New York, ACM (2013). https://doi.org/10.1145/2513383.2513392
16. Rector, K., Milne, L., Ladner, R.E., Friedman, B., Kientz, J.A.: Exploring the opportunities and challenges with exercise technologies for people who are blind or low-vision. In: ASSETS 2015, New York, pp. 203–214. ACM (2015). https://doi.org/10.1145/2700648.2809846
17. Stuart, M.E., Lieberman, L., Hand, K.E.: Beliefs about physical activity among children who are visually impaired and their parents. J. Vis. Impairment Blindness **100**(4), 223–234 (2006). https://doi.org/10.1177/0145482X0610000405
18. UNESCO: N for nose: State of the education report for India 2019: Children with disabilities (2019). https://en.unesco.org/news/n-nose-state-education-report-india-2019-children-disabilities
19. View, S.: Where do children who are blind or visually impaired go to school? (2015). https://sandysview1.wordpress.com/2015/06/04/where-do-children-who-are-blind-or-visually-impaired-go-to-school/
20. Weil, E.: Obesity among adults with disabling conditions. JAMA **288**(10), 1265 (2002). https://doi.org/10.1001/jama.288.10.1265
21. Wikipedia: Classification of Indian cities (2020). https://en.wikipedia.org/wiki/Classification_of_Indian_cities

454 G. India et al.

22. Williams, C., Armstrong, N., Eves, N., Faulkner, A.: Peak aerobic fitness of visually impaired and sighted adolescent girls. J. Vis. Impairment Blindness **90**(6), 495–500 (1996)
23. Yuan, B., Folmer, E.: Blind hero: Enabling guitar hero for the visually impaired. In: ASSETS 2008, New York, pp. 169–176. ACM (2008). https://doi.org/10.1145/1414471.1414503
24. Zhu, Y., Wang, C., Liu, W., Lv, Y.: Running guide: Design of a marathon navigation system for visually impaired people. In: Chinese CHI 2019, New York, pp. 7–15. ACM (2019). https://doi.org/10.1145/3332169.3333579

Augmented Reality

Acceptance of an AR-Based In-Store Shopping Advisor - the Impact of Psychological User Characteristics

Jesús Omar Álvarez Márquez[✉] and Jürgen Ziegler

University of Duisburg -Essen, Forsthausweg 2, 47057 Duisburg, Germany
{jesus.alvarez-marquez,juergen.ziegler}@uni-due.de

Abstract. We present a study on the acceptance of augmented reality-based product comparison and recommending in a physical store context. An online study was performed, in which a working prototype for head-mounted displays, developed in previous research, was used to showcase the concept. The survey included questionnaires to assess shopping behaviour, decision styles and propensity to adopt new technologies of the participants. A cluster analysis of these psychological traits reveals the existence of different types of customers, who also differ on their assessment of the system. While the technology adoption propensity index is the better predictor of the acceptance of an augmented reality shopping advisor, the results suggest that factors such as the user's previous experience, a high experiential chronic shopping orientation, or an intuitive decision style have a significant impact on it as well. Thus, predicting user acceptance solely based on one of the investigated psychological traits may be unreliable, and studying them in conjunction can provide a more accurate estimation.

Keywords: Technology acceptance · Augmented reality · Retailing · Shopping advisors

1 Introduction

AR technology has made considerable advances in recent years [7], making it more readily available in a wider range of domains. Its usage has been successfully implemented in industry, specially concerning areas such as quality control, training and assistance in complex tasks [36]. AR is being well regarded in entertainment and marketing spheres too, due to the possibilities that it offers in terms of consumer engagement [14]. However, the use of AR in retailing is still scarce and most of the time e-commerce is the centre of attention, while physical retailing is left aside [34]. Bringing AR to physical stores requires finding more u-tilitarian uses for it [46], as well as suitable scenarios and proper visualization

Supported by European Regional Development Fund, project "FairWays" [EFRE-0801448].

© IFIP International Federation for Information Processing 2021
Published by Springer Nature Switzerland AG 2021
C. Ardito et al. (Eds.): INTERACT 2021, LNCS 12932, pp. 457–479, 2021.
https://doi.org/10.1007/978-3-030-85623-6_28

and interaction methods. Furthermore, it is essential that an AR-based solution brings clear added value in contrast to more traditional options in order to be acceptable.

With all of this in mind, a promising use of AR is that of supporting in-store product comparison. Physical retailing lacks the ease with which online stores provide their customers with plenty of useful data and shopping tools. AR could be used precisely for closing this gap by letting customers explore product attributes via augmentations, while also allowing their comparison by assisting clients in the process of finding and understanding their differences. A potential benefit of the approach is that users are free to inspect attributes directly on the physical object they belong to, which may be of help for obtaining a better understanding of its qualities and, thus, make a more satisfactory purchase decision. In combination with recommending functions, AR can build a bridge between physical stores and online shopping to create multi-channel options [27,55], more so if the recommendations include products from the vendor's online catalogue. A system like this offers the rarely seen combination of digital and physical items of the same type, where the characteristics of all of them are accessible through a unified medium. This aspect may also have an impact on the decision making process of users by influencing how they explore the digital space and learn about physical and digital items.

However, it is unclear whether the use of AR technology in such context is acceptable to all users and which psychological characteristics may determine acceptance and attractiveness. Different general attitudes towards new technologies and user-specific shopping and decision-making behaviours may influence the acceptance of an AR system in a shop environment. Such factors may be particularly relevant when the system involves wearing an AR headset, which is conspicuous and may attract other customers' attention. Although research on the topic of AR acceptance already exists and even spans through different disciplines [18,37], it approaches the investigation mostly from a technical angle (e.g. users proficiency, availability of learning tools or current reliability of AR) or contextual elements, but overlooks the involvement of other psychological factors and the interactions that may occur between them. Thus, the following research questions are raised:

RQ1 How useful do users consider the possibility to explore and compare products across physical and online spaces?
RQ2 What is the impact of individual and combined personal characteristics on the acceptance of AR-based support functions?

This paper makes a further contribution to existing literature by presenting a exploratory study where, unlike previous research, users are defined by a set of psychological traits. These traits are based on how clients make decisions in a shopping scenario with a heavy technological component; that is, by assessing their technology adoption propensity, decision-making styles and shopping orientation. Participants are then grouped into types of clients to study their acceptance of an AR shopping advisor running on a head mounted display, in an attempt to find out which characteristics are more significant and uncover possible interactions that may exist between them.

2   Related Work

2.1   Use and Value of AR in Retailing

Studies show that AR has a positive impact on the shopping experience, particularly regarding customer satisfaction, consumer engagement and purchase intention [39,43]. Modern retailing can take advantage of AR at various consumer touch points, supported on the exponential growth of mobile technology [28] (e.g. IKEA's popular app [9]). Previous research shows that Mobile AR apps are perceived as valuable in retail contexts and provide benefits beyond the regular shopping experience [17]. Furthermore, due to its ability to merge digital and physical worlds together, AR acts as an enabler of omni-channel experiences by supporting the seamless integration of the different retailing channels [10,17,23]. Thus, it seems important for retailers to, at least, consider the adoption of AR-based experiences. However, the adoption of AR also presents its own challenges, such as taking the risk of its implementation, the initial investment in new technology or the need of training employees [17].

Previous approaches to AR in physical retailing include the PromoPad [59], an early application capable of providing context-aware information; Välkkynen et al. [54] explore the possibility of visualizing the content of a package before opening it; Rashid et al. [44] combined RFID with AR to browse product shelves; Cruz et al. [16] created an AR mobile application for retail stores that detects where the user is located and provides guidance to the item that the user is looking for. As of today and in terms of commercial success, virtual try-on [28] (or "magic-mirrors") are the most widely spread implementation of AR in physical contexts.

2.2   Shopping Advisors

Shopping advisors are very common in online settings, including features such as comparison tools [29,41], customer reviews and ratings [31] and product recommendations [50]. Per contra, it is difficult to find such elements in physical stores. An approach that brings such functionality into physical retailing can be found in Kourouthanassis et al. [30], where the authors present a system able to automatically create and keep track of a shopping list, and offer product information and personalized recommendations of promotions. APriori [47] is another example of a system that provides in-store product data, recommendations and user ratings.

Concerning AR, it has been stated that the technology offers improved search of information at the point of sale [52] and supports clients in making a purchase decision [15], characteristics that are desirable in a shopping advisor. Fully fledged AR shopping advisors are still rare, although some research exists on the topic: Ahn et al. [3] explore the benefits of using AR for product search in retail stores; Acquia Labs [13] developed a demo for a shopping assistant that provides, among other features, product information and in-store navigation support; Gutiérrez et al. [21] present a prototype for an AR shopping assistant that offers health-related information and discus different visualization layouts; Ludwig et al. [35] developed a working prototype to study the benefits of using AR to expose the underlying technical features of physical products. Commercial apps exist too: Aisle411 and Tango partnered to develop an app for Walgreens stores [1] that delivers product information, promotions and in-store navigation; or the Olai Skin Advisor [2], which offers recommendations of products after detecting the consumer's face skin conditions. Nonetheless, despite the existence of previous research on AR-based in-store shopping assistants, the combination of digital and physical products that can be seamlessly compared and recommended remains unexplored.

2.3   Acceptance of Augmented Reality Technology

Technology acceptance is defined by Dillon [19] as *"the demonstrable willingness within a user group to employ IT for the tasks it is designed to support"*. Despite what intuition might tell us based on that definition, the results provided by Roy et al. [49] suggest that technology readiness (i.e. an individual's propensity to embrace and use new technologies) may only influence customer acceptance towards smart retail technologies to some extent, that is, under certain conditions and for certain customers, while other factors such as perceived usefulness (PU), perceived ease of use (PEOU), and perceived adaptiveness play a larger role. Precisely, the review of existing literature [42] shows that one of the most widely used approaches to assess user acceptance of augmented reality in retail is the Technology Acceptance Model (TAM) [33], which considers that PU and PEOU are the main drivers of technology acceptance. The model has undergone several revisions through the years by both original and independent researchers [11], and it is often criticized because of its simplicity, which neglects the differences in decision-making and decision makers across technologies [8]. However, it is still a widely used model and considered valid for AR applications [18]. The extended versions of the TAM often discuss the addition of new factors such as perceived enjoyment (although the findings about its impact on user acceptance are conflicting) and perceived informativeness [24,42]. As a contrasting note, several authors opt for using flow theory instead [57], which focuses on the four dimensions of immersion, curiosity, fun and control.

Security and privacy aspects have been flagged as other relevant factors that influence the acceptance of AR technology, where previous literature [46,56] show that AR systems do not currently offer enough protection in that regard or, at the very least, do not sufficiently transmit the feeling of it.

When exploring the different factors involved in the acceptance of AR, existing studies mostly focus on the impact of aspects such as the characteristics of the technology (real or as perceived by users), psychological factors and environmental influences [18,42]. However, the existence of different types of consumers (defined by the combination of several of these elements), and how they may differ in their perception of AR in retailing settings, are questions that have been generally overlooked.

3   Research Questions

3.1   RQ1: How Useful Do Users Consider the Possibility to Explore and Compare Products Across Physical and Online Spaces?

Supporting the comparison process is a key component of the prototype that is evaluated here. This is justified by the great relevance of comparing in how human beings learn about their environment [20] and, consequently, the significant role that it plays in consumer behaviour, where comparing products is the most natural way to reach a purchase decision [32]. A previous evaluation of the system [6] suggested that combining digital recommendations and physical items may be beneficial for understanding the qualities of the not physically present products, due to the possibility of learning about them through the examination of the real ones. Moreover, it also seems to exist some connection regarding how users navigate the digital space and what products are physically available, in a way that digital items are intuitively filtered out by exploring only the recommendations provided for already suitable, physical products. These points indicate some potential benefits of offering such in-store services, but there is still a need to confirm these results by surveying a larger population sample.

3.2   RQ2: What Is the Impact of Individual and Combined Personal Characteristics on the Acceptance of AR-based Support Functions?

There is a research gap concerning how different decision-making-related psychological traits participate in a user's acceptance of in-store AR applications. To determine what these traits could be, we take the work by Alavi and Joachimsthaler [4] as reference, where the psychological variables involved in the acceptance of a decision support system are examined. *Cognitive style, personality traits, user situational variables* and *demographics* are identified as the most relevant factors. In the following, the measurement of each factor (as defined by Alavi and Joachimsthaler) is discussed.

Cognitive style refers to how information is processed and used. Different scales exist that allow its analysis, such as the Decision Styles Scale [22], which only requires 10 items to provide an outcome on two different scales (*rational* and *intuitive*); or the more complete and commonly used approach by Scott and Bruce [51], which distinguishes between *rational, avoidant, intuitive* and *dependent* decision-making styles, but at the expense of a greater number of items.

Personality traits are such as need for achievement, degree of defensiveness, locus of control or risk-taking propensity. Given that the matter at hand consists in the inclusion of a very intrusive technological component (a head mounted display) in a physical retailing context, we aim at the assessment of those traits involved in both technology adoption and shopping behaviour.

Concerning technology adoption, it has already been stated that the Technology Acceptance Model [33] is the most popular theory. The Technology Readiness

Index [40] is another well-known tool for measuring an individual's propensity to adopt and embrace new technology, and it focuses on four different dimensions that act as motivators (*optimism, innovation*) or inhibitors (*discomfort, insecurity*). Consistent with this idea, the Technology Adoption Propensity index [45] also considers the existence of positive (*optimism, proficiency*) and negative (*dependence, vulnerability*) attitudes in the assessment of technology acceptance, but uses a more contained set of items.

Among the alternatives for measuring consumer-related traits, the most prominently used is the Consumer Styles Inventory [53], which profiles individuals by analysing eight basic characteristics. Westbrook and Black [58] propose another widely used approach based on *hedonic* and *utilitarian* shopping motivations. A more recent study by Büttner et al. [12] discusses the creation of a 7-items long Chronic Shopping Orientation Scale, which aims at the prediction of the consumer's stable shopping disposition (*experiential* or *task-focused*).

Demographic data on gender, age and education can be easily collected. As for user-situational variables, the work by Alavi and Joachimsthaler [4] refers to user training and experience, which in our case could be associated with the user's previous knowledge about augmented reality.

Gathering information on each one of these personal characteristics would allow the investigation of their role in the judgement of a system like the one described in the following section. Furthermore, by uncovering possible relationships between these characteristics, it would be possible to determine the existence of distinguishable customer types and any variations in their acceptance of the system.

4   Description of the Prototype

A prototype for an AR-shopping advisor designed for Microsoft HoloLens was developed [5,6]. As of today, using a smartphone could have been a more practical approach. However, this research chose to use a head mounted display as AR enabler because of its growing relevance and availability, and its facility to provide a more engaging experience (which is specially relevant in shopping contexts) and allow for more interesting interaction possibilities (e.g. hands-free direct inspection of products).

Vacuum cleaners were chosen as the product domain, since they are common, technical commodity products. The approach, however, could have been applied to a wide range of products, so long as they are rich in attributes and their physical qualities are relevant for consumers. It is also necessary to keep in mind that this approach may not be best suited for standard shopping environments, but in stores whose activities include working as show-rooms: spaces where a carefully selected range of products are presented (usually specialized in a specific type of items), and where clients have enough space to wander around and freedom to examine them.

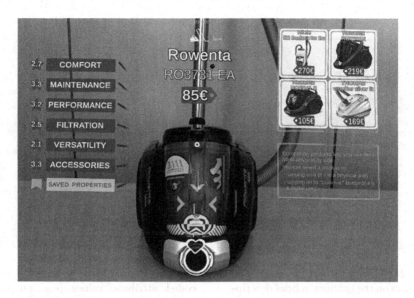

Fig. 1. Main view of the system. Attribute categories and recommendations are placed on the left and right sides of the product.

4.1 Access to Product Information

When a user looks to a product that is physically present in the store, relevant information is displayed surrounding it (Fig. 1). Clients can then move from one product to another to inspect them individually. Product information is organized in categories that group attributes based on their impact over a certain aspect. Within a category, the system shows the values of the attributes that belong to it. They can be selected, which shows extra information (Fig. 2).

Against the argument that similar results could be achieved by more standard means (e.g. a smartphone app with object recognition capabilities), an AR approach enables the inclusion of relevant spatial information for each attribute (i.e. where they are located), bringing into play a new layer of interaction between digital and physical worlds where their connexion is made more apparent. Such union should call for direct exploration and testing of physical items, while improving the understanding of their digitally displayed properties.

4.2 Product Comparison

Taking online comparison tools as a reference, the prototype lets users select up to three different products to be compared. When the user looks to one of the selected items, the attributes of the other one(s) (not directly in the client's line of sight) are shown next to the attributes of the former, in a side-by-side manner (but maintaining the same attribute organization and exploration methods that have been previously explained). Each product is assigned a specific colour that helps to distinguish their properties. The system highlights in green or red the

Fig. 2. Selecting an attribute shows its location on the product, a brief description and critiquing buttons (+/−).

Fig. 3. Comparison view. Colour-coded attribute values (e.g. purple) belong to products not in the client's line of sight. (Color figure online)

attributes of the current product to easily identify in which ones it performs better or worse than the other selected items (Fig. 3).

4.3   Product Recommendation

Product recommendations are obtained likewise attribute information is retrieved: just by looking at a certain product. Items similar to the product directly in the line of sight of the client are shown next to it (Fig. 1). These recommendations can be directly compared without requiring users to find the real objects they represent. This allows the inclusion of recommendation of products that are not physically present at the store, effectively expanding the store's catalogue.

Recommendations can be modified, either by directly removing those that are not wanted (which brings new ones in their place) or by critiquing the attributes of the item for which they have been recommended (users can choose whether they seek for products with higher or lower values in a particular property).

5   Online Study

An online study has been conducted to assess the acceptance of an AR-based in-store shopping advisor designed for head-mounted displays and the specific functions described in the previous section. An online study design was chosen to get a broader feedback following an initial lab study[1] [6]. The goals of the study

---

[1] Conducting another, larger lab experiment was also considered, but that option had to be discarded due to restrictions related to the COVID-19 pandemic.

include defining different consumer profiles based on their propensity to adopt technology, shopping orientation and decision styles, and to analyse whether differences exist in their judgement of the system. Finding possible relationships between the psychological traits that characterize those profiles and their impact on the acceptance of the concept is also within the scope of this investigation.

5.1 Settings of the Study

Participants were asked to complete an online questionnaire with three distinct parts. The first one focused on determining the psychological profile of the participants and included questionnaires to that effect. Then, since participants could not experience the system by themselves, a video was included that had an initial part where the concept was introduced, followed by a thorough description of the prototype's functionality, showcased with real images of the system as seen from the user's point of view. The last part of the survey was comprised by a set of questions in relation to the aforementioned video with the purpose of collecting information about the acceptance of the prototype.

5.2 Method

A total of 63 participants (40 females, average age of 34.1, σ 12.29) took part in the study. They were recruited through the online platform *Prolific*[2] and received a monetary award of £1.50 after successfully completing a survey (as per the site's policy). As it can be seen in Table 1, the majority were residents of the United Kingdom, while most of them had achieved a master's degree level of education and worked either as employees or were self-employed. Furthermore, many of them reported to have limited knowledge about augmented reality and its possible applications (Table 2).

Table 1. Demographic information of the sample

Country	#
United Kingdom	43
United States	8
Ireland	4
Netherlands	2
Canada	2
Other	4

Education level	#
Secondary school	2
High school	9
Apprenticeship	1
Bachelors degree	19
Masters degree	32

Working status	#
Pupil/in school	3
Training/apprenticeship	1
University student	8
Employee	28
Civil servant	4
Self-employed	10
Unemployed	9

---

[2] www.prolific.co.

Table 2. Knowledge about augmented reality technology

I know nothing about it	8
I know the name, but not much more	21
I know a bit about it and its possible applications	30
I have followed its development and know it well	4
I know a lot and could be considered an expert in the field	0

The survey itself was hosted by *SosciSurvey*[3]. The first part of the survey comprised questionnaires that were to be used in the creation of the participant's psychological profile. Since different traits had to be measured, and to prevent response fatigue and collect more truthful answers [38], the length of the questionnaires included in the survey was an important factor when selecting them. Even though the chosen questionnaires might not offer as much information as others available, their combination should suffice to create a reliable user profile:

- *Technology Adoption Propensity* (TAP) index [45], a 14-items-long questionnaire that provides a score that represents how likely a person is to adopt new technology by considering four sub-scales: *optimism, proficiency, dependence* and *vulnerability*. A TAP score is equal to the sum of the average scores on each of the four factors, with inhibiting factors reverse coded. Each individual item is rated using a 5-point Likert scale.
- *Chronic Shopping Orientation* (CSO) scale [12], which assesses whether a person has a stable consumer disposition to shop under an experiential or a task-focused shopping orientation. It uses a 7-points Likert scale, ranging from *task-oriented* (lower values) to *experience-based* (higher values) shopping orientations.
- *Rational and Intuitive Decision Styles* (RDS and IDS) scale [22], which reflects the prevailing manner by which individuals make decisions. Each decision style is measured independently, hence two scores (in a 5-point Likert scale) are provided.

Following these questionnaires, a video that explains the concept and showcases the implemented prototype for Microsoft HoloLens was presented to participants[4]. After watching it, a final set of system-related questions were presented to assess the acceptance of the concept. These questions were designed to measure the constructs *perceived usefulness* and *perceive ease of use* (the two main constructs in TAM), extended with *decision-making support, hedonic motivation* and *intention to use*. Items regarding *social acceptance* and *privacy* were also part of it, which have been highlighted as inhibitors in the adoption of AR headsets [46].

---

[3] www.soscisurvey.de.

[4] The video is available on www.youtube.com/watch?v=k4nyTDQ-n7U.

In the following, to examine the overall acceptance of the concept and the usefulness of the AR functions provided (RQ1), the results obtained for the sample are examined as a whole. Afterwards, psychological data is used to find how different psychological traits influence the adoption of an in-store AR advisor, either individually or combined to define consumer types (RQ2).

5.3   General Results

Table 3 reports descriptive data obtained for each one of the investigated constructs and the items within them, which are relevant for determining the overall acceptance of the system and the usefulness of the combination of digital and physical elements (RQ1). *Perceived usefulness* and *decision support* received the highest scores among all the constructs, while *privacy* and *social acceptance* obtained the lowest ones. However, it has to be noted that all constructs fall into the positive side of the scale (their scores are higher than 3). Furthermore, although the construct *importance of physical items* appears in fourth position, the score for the single item *"Inspecting products will help me to make a more informed buying decision"* is among the most highly rated.

The data in Table 4 shows that providing *comparison support* is perceived as the most important feature of the system. *Product recommendations* and *access to a digital catalogue* are close to each other, while *interaction with physical items* falls a bit behind, in the last position. These results are in line with the scores given to the constructs, where *decision support* (comparing and recommending) obtained higher ratings than *importance of physical products*.

Finally, when having to choose between using the system or being assisted by sales personnel, 21 participants stated that they would use the system only; other 29 said that they would use the system first, and ask for support if required; 10 would first ask for support, and likely use the system afterwards; and the remaining 3 would not use the system at all.

An analysis of the Pearson's product-moment correlation between psychological traits and the questionnaire's constructs was performed to study the impact of individual personal traits on the acceptance of the system (RQ2). After the adjustment of the p-values by using the Benjamini-Hochberg procedure, only a moderately negative correlation between intuitive decision style and *social acceptance* ($r(89) = -.37, p < .05$) was found. Although the results hint at other possible correlations, they are not strong enough to be reported here.

5.4   Cluster Analysis

In order to find combinations of user characteristics that may have an effect on system acceptance (RQ2), it is first necessary to classify users into customer types, which allows the comparative analysis of their responses. In our case, this classification considers the scores that subjects obtained in TAP, CSO, RDS and IDS scales, that is: how likely they are to adopt a new technology, the way they approach shopping and how they make decisions. To this end, a two-step process was performed: first, data was classified through a hierarchical cluster analysis

Table 3. Overall results for the system-related items

Constructs and items from higher to lower mean	Mean	σ	95% CI Lower	Upper
Perceived Usefulness	**4.18**	**0.84**	**3.97**	**4.39**
I find the system will be useful	4.21	0.85	3.99	4.42
I believe that the use of Augmented Reality is beneficial in the given scenario (physical retailing)	4.16	0.90	3.93	4.39
Decision Support	**3.94**	**0.81**	**3.74**	**4.15**
I can have a better view of all the available choices with the help of the system	4.16	0.94	3.92	4.39
The system will help me to discover new products	4.13	0.92	3.89	4.36
By using the system, I think it will be easier to find an item that I like	4.00	0.90	3.77	4.23
This recommender system will increase my confidence in my selection/decision	3.98	1.04	3.72	4.25
By using the system, I think it will be easier to find an item to buy	3.86	1.00	3.61	4.11
Using the system will help me to make a decision more quickly	3.52	1.06	3.26	3.79
Interface Adequacy	**3.94**	**0.95**	**3.70**	**4.18**
The information provided for the recommended items will be sufficient for me to make a purchase decision	3.94	0.95	3.70	4.18
Importance of Physical Products	**3.78**	**0.70**	**3.60**	**3.95**
Inspecting products will help me to make a more informed buying decision	4.11	0.85	3.90	4.32
Interacting with physical products will help me to understand the features of similar, digital ones	3.89	0.81	3.69	4.09
I would use the system even if a digital catalogue were not available (the system would only recommend physically available products)	3.69	1.06	3.42	3.95
If the same catalogue is available at an online store and a physical one, I generally prefer to do the extra effort of travelling to the physical one to inspect the products by myself	3.43	1.10	3.15	3.71
Intention to Use	**3.67**	**0.95**	**3.43**	**3.91**
Assuming I had access to the system, I would likely use it	3.89	0.99	3.64	4.14
Being able to use the system will be a reason for choosing one store over another	3.57	1.20	3.27	3.87
When in a physical store, I would rather use this system than a more traditional web-based recommender	3.54	1.11	3.26	3.82
Perceived Ease of Use	**3.64**	**0.92**	**3.40**	**3.87**
Learning how to use the system will be easy for me	3.94	1.08	3.67	4.21
I think that the interaction with the system will be clear and understandable	3.70	1.01	3.44	3.95
I find the system will be easy to use	3.52	1.03	3.26	3.78
Interacting with the system will be an effortless task	3.38	1.07	3.11	3.65

(continued)

Table 3. *(continued)*

Constructs and items from higher to lower mean	Mean	σ	95% CI Lower	Upper
Hedonic Motivation	**3.61**	**1.16**	**3.32**	**3.90**
Using the system will be fun	3.71	1.18	3.42	4.01
Using the system will be entertaining	3.51	1.19	3.21	3.81
Privacy (reversed)	**3.25**	**1.14**	**2.97**	**3.54**
I would be concerned that my data is stored and used for other purposes	3.05	1.25	2.73	3.36
I would have privacy concerns if someone uses the glasses around me (e.g. when that person looks at me)	2.44	1.20	2.14	2.75
Social Acceptance (reversed)	**3.22**	**0.88**	**3.00**	**3.44**
Being able to share the experience with my shopping partner (e.g., we both see and interact with the same AR elements in real time) is relevant for deciding whether to use the system or not	3.35	1.17	3.06	3.64
I would not feel comfortable using the system while other people are around	2.64	1.24	2.32	2.95
I would find it annoying/irritating when other person uses the system nearby	2.35	1.21	2.05	2.65

based on average linkage between groups, which provided information on outliers and an initial distribution of participants; second, a K-means clustering analysis was conducted to confirm the results obtained in the first step. Since the variables involved have different scales, their z-scores were used for clustering purposes.

The outcome shows that four well-distinguishable groups can be identified, although 9 out of the total of 63 participants are considered as outliers and can thus not be classified. The silhouette scores [48] for each cluster are reported in Fig. 4, and the average results that each group obtained in the psychological tests are shown in Table 5. It is possible to identify what traits characterize each cluster by considering the relation between their means and the average of the sample (in the following, "group" and "cluster" are used interchangeably):

Table 4. Importance assigned by participants to each feature of the system (1–5 scale).

Feature	Mean	σ	95% CI	
			Lower	Upper
Product comparison support	4.60	0.61	4.45	4.76
Access to product recommendations	4.33	0.78	4.14	4.53
Access to a digital catalogue	4.27	0.77	4.08	4.46
Interaction with physical products	3.94	1.03	3.68	4.20

Group 1 is composed of average technology users (relative to this sample). This group is the most experiential one when it comes to shopping and has an over the average intuitive decision-making style. It is also the largest group, gathers the youngest participants and is mostly composed of females.

Group 2 includes people with higher probabilities of adopting new technology, who also see shopping as a task-oriented experience. The group presents a notable polarization between rational and intuitive decision scales: their RDS is the highest among groups, while their IDS shows the lowest value.

Group 3 has the lowest probabilities of adopting new technology: its members do not perceive it as useful, are not proficient at it and believe themselves to be very dependant and vulnerable. Consequently, they know the least about AR. They also show the lowest rational decision style score.

Group 4 has a TAP value similar to that of group 2, but its CSO, RDS and IDS scores are more moderate, and has more knowledge of AR technology than any other cluster. The average age is higher than that of the other groups and it is the only one composed predominantly of male participants.

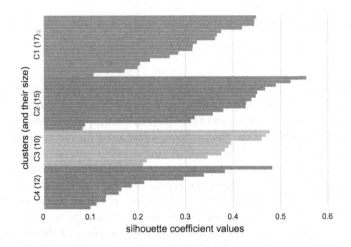

Fig. 4. Silhouette scores by clusters. Average silhouette width = 0.32.

Table 6 shows the scores obtained by cluster in each construct, which already suggests a difference in their assessment of the system. Although the ranking of the constructs is mostly maintained between groups (with perceived usefulness and decision support in the first places and privacy and social acceptance in the last), the range of scores differs: group 2 has the most positive view of the system and group 3 the most negative; group 1, on the other hand, is the most polarized (it provides some of the highest and some of the lowest scores of the sample), while, in contrast, group 4 shows a more uniform and moderate rating distribution.

Table 5. Psychological traits per group. From left to right: group size; percentage of females; average age; AR knowledge (on a 1–5 scale); TAP sub-scales (1–5): Optimism, Proficiency, Dependence, Vulnerability; total TAP score; Chronic Shopping Orientation (1–7); Rational and Intuitive Decision Styles (1–5); and the difference between them. Values of the psychological traits are relative to the average of the sample without outliers (last row of the table). Coloured cells identify those values where a group's mean noticeably differs from the total.

	#	Fem.	Age	AR Kno.	Opt.	Pro.	Dep.	Vul.	TAP Score	CSO Score	RDS Score	IDS Score	RDS - IDS
G1	17	88%	28.53	-0.09	0.10	0.01	0.30	0.20	-0.39	1.23	0.05	0.58	0.72
G2	15	47%	34.53	0.09	0.06	0.35	-0.36	-0.52	1.28	-0.84	0.46	-0.91	2.63
G3	10	70%	33.70	-0.44	-0.30	-0.96	0.78	0.76	-2.80	-0.37	-0.50	0.22	0.54
G4	12	33%	37.75	0.39	0.03	0.36	-0.62	-0.27	1.29	-0.37	-0.24	0.13	0.88
			Avg.	2.44	4.27	3.68	2.95	3.60	13.40	3.58	4.25	3.00	1.25

Table 6. Differences in the assessment of the system among user groups.

	Group 1		Group 2		Group 3		Group 4		Total	
	Mean	σ	Mean	σ	Mean	σ	Mean	σ	Mean	σ
Perceived Usefulness*	4.44	0.58	4.43	0.65	3.75	0.79	3.83	1.03	4.18	0.80
Decision Support	4.20	0.62	4.19	0.47	3.52	0.81	3.89	0.72	4.00	0.68
Interface Adequacy	4.06	0.90	4.27	0.88	3.40	0.84	3.92	0.79	3.96	0.89
Imp. of Physical Products	4.04	0.54	3.93	0.70	3.78	0.77	3.40	0.58	3.82	0.67
Hedonic Motivation*	4.06	1.00	4.00	1.02	3.00	1.00	3.54	0.81	3.73	1.02
Intention to Use*	3.98	0.69	4.11	0.87	3.27	0.94	3.28	0.84	3.73	0.89
Perceived Ease of Use	3.72	0.96	3.88	0.60	3.23	1.10	3.71	0.80	3.67	0.87
Privacy	3.09	1.08	3.77	1.05	2.90	1.02	3.38	0.12	3.31	1.06
Social Acceptance*	2.86	0.53	3.87	0.75	2.93	0.93	3.19	0.93	3.23	0.86

*There is statistically significant difference between groups ($p < .05$)

The analysis of the means by performing a Kruskal-Wallis test revealed statistically significant differences between clusters for *perceived usefulness, hedonic motivation, intention to use* and *social acceptance*. Subsequent Dunn-Bonferroni pairwise comparison tests reported a significant difference between groups 1–3 in terms of *hedonic motivation*, and groups 1–2, and 2–3 regarding *social acceptance* ($p < .05$ in all cases). In that regard, group 1 shows the highest *hedonic motivation* but, at the same time, it seems to be the most worried about *social acceptance*, in contrast to groups 3 (the least attracted by the system) and 2 (the least concerned about *social acceptance*). These results agree with the previously established negative correlation between intuitive decision style and *social acceptance* because, as a matter of fact, group 1 comprises the most intuitive participants. As for the remaining statistically significant constructs, post-hoc tests were not able to specify the groups for which the differences were significant, which suggests the existence of more complex relationships. Further testing of different group combinations showed that there is a statistically significant difference between the union of groups 1 and 2 and the union of groups 3 and 4 for *perceived usefulness* and *intention to use* ($p < .01$ in a Mann-Whitney U test).

Performing the same procedure over individual items of the questionnaire shows more significant differences, but most of them are in line with the test involving constructs and, therefore, are not reported here. However, some new disparities were found in relation to *decision support*, more specifically for *"This RS will increase my confidence in my selection/decision"* (between groups 1–3, $p < .05$) and *"I can have a better view of all the available choices"* (between groups 2–3, and 2–4, both $p < .05$).

Regarding what features are more important (Table 7), groups with higher TAP (2 and 4) seem to prioritize exploration-related functions (comparison and digital catalogue). On the other hand, group 3, the least technologically proficient and rational, finds product recommendations to be the most valuable feature. It also seems that the lower the TAP value is, the more importance is given to physical interaction with products.

Lastly, Table 8 shows the distribution of answers concerning users intention to use the system when sales personnel is also available. The responses are consistent with each group's assessment of the system. Interestingly, it is in group 4 (the one with the highest knowledge about AR) where, given the chance to use the system, one of its members would choose not to do so.

Table 7. Importance assigned by groups to each feature of the system (1–5 scale, 'R' is for rank).

Feature	Group 1			Group 2			Group 3			Group 4		
	m	σ	R	m	σ	R	m	σ	R	m	σ	R
Product comparison	4.59	0.51	1	4.73	0.46	1	4.40	0.70	2	4.67	0.65	1
Product recommendations	4.53	0.51	2	4.07	0.88	3	4.60	0.96	1	4.25	0.75	3
Digital catalogue	4.18	0.64	3	4.20	0.77	2	4.20	0.92	3	4.33	0.78	2
Int. with physical products	4.12	0.86	4	4.00	1.25	4	4.20	0.79	3	3.42	0.90	4

Table 8. Intention to use the system by group.

If i need support and the system is available ...	G1	G2	G3	G4
... I would use it to find what i need	6	7	1	4
... I would use the system and ask for assistance only in case of doubt	9	8	4	5
... I would first ask for assistance and likely use the system afterwards	2	0	5	2
... I would prefer to receive assistance from sales personnel only	0	0	0	1

5.5   Discussion

In relation to the usefulness of the hybrid physical-digital approach (RQ1), the feedback received on the AR-based shopping advisor can generally be considered positive. While it was not possible to assess the prototype against a baseline due to the lack of a system with comparable functionality, the scores received for the different functions and interaction methods are all in the positive range. The constructs *perceived usefulness* (considered one of the main drivers of user acceptance in conjunction with *perceived ease of use*) and *decision support* received particularly high ratings. Although interacting with physical products is overshadowed by the other features, it is still regarded as helpful to make a more informed buying decision.

As for the impact of the traits investigated here (RQ2), none of them appear to fully determine the acceptance of in-store AR-based advisors. In some cases, participants with apparently opposing psychological profiles seem to coincide in their assessment of the system. For instance, both persons with a heavily task-oriented CSO and a rational DS and those with an experiential CSO and an intuitive DS are more likely to perceive the system as useful and to use it. In contrast, those with a low TAP score who also have little knowledge about AR and those with a high TAP score and knowledgeable in AR technology are less inclined to its usage. However, their reasons for accepting or rejecting the system may as well be very different: perhaps they see a practical value in it, or think that it may offer an enjoyable experience; maybe they simply do not like technology in general or, if they do, they have had a higher exposure to AR already, in a way that they are less impressed by its novelty and more aware of its current limitations. In general terms, a lower TAP score appears to be the better predictor of the rejection of the system, but average to high TAP scores seem to be moderated by previous experience with AR technology. This may be a reflection of how quickly the novelty of AR fades away [25] and the difficulty of finding reasons to use it on a regular basis instead of a more traditional method [26]. Finally, a prominent experiential CSO and an intuitive DS seem to lead to a good acceptance of the concept too, although overexposure to AR could have the same moderating effect as with high TAP values.

The outcome of the study also indicates that rejection of the system due to privacy or social acceptance concerns is more likely to happen on subjects with higher intuitive decision styles and lower TAP scores. In spite of that, it must be noted that these worries were present in all groups to a certain degree. This finding agrees with previous research on the topic where privacy and social acceptance are identified as challenges in the adoption of AR [46, 56]. Some participants left comments where they defined the glasses as *"too creepy"* or would express their fear to *"be pick-pocketed or robbed when not on guard"*. These worries are mostly related to 1) the insecurity of not knowing what operations are being performed when other person is wearing the glasses and 2) the vulnerability derived from having a reduced view of the surroundings and few control over the collected data when the client is the one wearing them. It seems that there is a need for finding less obtrusive solutions for AR glasses as well as to make sure that users know and understand their capabilities and how their personal data is going to be treated. Additionally, some time is still required until wearing such devices in public is more socially acceptable, factor that seems to affect to a greater extent to people with an intuitive decision style. In the meantime, other ways for alleviating this issue could be explored, like more natural interaction methods that do not involve unusual gestures (as "air tapping" could be considered) or that help to better discern the wearer's intentions, so that other people around are more aware of them and less worried.

Some participants were also troubled about the trustworthiness of the recommendations and whether they could be biased towards the store's particular interests. Making clear the source of the provided information and its neutrality may be another relevant factor to increase the acceptance of applications like the one presented here.

What do these results mean for physical stores? Current AR technology is still young and well under development. Challenges in terms of social acceptance and privacy concerns can be expected to be overcome the more mature and available the technology becomes. As of today, however, it may be difficult to find a selling point to convince those users preoccupied for such matters, which stresses the importance of increasing customer awareness of privacy regulations and device capabilities. Nonetheless, AR is able already, at its current state, to provide a number of useful in-store functions, and there seems to be a great portion of consumers who are willing to try them. Stores may contribute in developing the potential of AR in physical retailing, while also making profit from it, by focusing on attracting these types of clients: those who enjoy shopping and those who find AR technology to be useful. That means developing applications and designing settings that contribute to an improved shopping experience and offer utilitarian benefits. Precisely this last part, focusing on the practical side of AR, may be a crucial factor in drawing the interest of those who have used AR in the past and no longer feel the so-called "wow" effect. Due to the current limitations of AR, it would be necessary to create specialized areas with different set-ups, more appropriate for experimenting and learning about products. In that regard, systems like the one here described may be more suitable for event-like shopping scenarios (such as trade fairs) where customer experience in a special setting is of the highest importance.

Limitations. Participants only watched a video of the system and were not able to test the prototype by themselves nor had access to the physical products; thus, they were not able to experience the "physical side" of the approach, perhaps the hardest part to imagine in conjunction with the other features of the system. Besides, participants were recruited through an online platform, which increases the probabilities for them to be more proficient in the use of technology and to have more trust on it than the average of the population. These factors may have had an impact on the assessment of the acceptance of the approach. There is also a probability of finding new types of customers if a bigger sample is used. In the same manner, the measurement of different psychological traits than the ones proposed here could uncover other still unknown relationships between them and the acceptance of the concept. Finally, few differences found between groups were actually statistically significant. However, considering the exploratory nature of this study, the observed results strongly suggest that such differences may indeed exist and offer a starting point for further research on the topic.

6 Conclusions

Related work on the topic of in-store AR acceptance has mainly focused on the independent assessment of technological, psychological and environmental factors. However, it is generally overlooked that connections between these aspects may exist that could be used to obtain a better understanding of how different types of clients accept the technology and what the obstacles are. To that end, this paper presents an exploratory study that investigates the interactions between a set of decision-making-related traits and their effects on the acceptance of an in-store AR advisor that runs on a head-mounted display.

Personal characteristics were defined by the Technology Adoption Propensity (TAP) [45], Chronic Shopping Orientation (CSO) [12] and Decision Styles (irrational, IDS, and rational, RDS) [22]. Using them to group participants uncovers the existence of four types of users within the sample, and a further analysis suggest differences between them in the acceptance of the system. There is an indication that technology-related aspects are not entirely responsible for defining AR acceptance, but that other factors are involved as well (and even negate the effects of high TAP scores). Overall results show that the approach is generally well-received, but users with low TAP scores are less convinced about its benefits and, thus, are less likely to make use of it. Both persons who know and trust technology (high TAP) and those who are experiential shoppers (high CSO) seem to be related to higher acceptance values. However, AR knowledge above the average seems to have a moderating effect on high TAP values. The most relevant issues to overcome involve concerns about privacy and social acceptance, opinion that is shared by all groups. Nevertheless, an intuitive decision style seems to be correlated with greater worries about the social acceptance of the approach.

The results indicate the existence of some psychological traits that have an impact on the acceptance of an AR-based in-store advisor and that relationships between them exist. Some of these relationships are revealed here, which may provide a deeper insight into how the concept could be introduced as a new in-store service by focusing on specific types of clients and making sure to cover privacy-related concerns. Nonetheless, further technology-dependant advances are still required in terms of intrusiveness for the approach to be more socially acceptable.

Future research should focus on discovering other underlying factors and on how to use them in both the improvement of the system to adapt to the specific needs of targeted consumer-types, and its successful introduction in real shopping environments.

References

1. Walgreens - aisle 411 and tango. http://aisle411.com/walgreens/ (2014) Accessed 19 May 2020
2. Olay Skin Advisor. https://www.olay.com/en-us/skinadvisor (2020). Accessed 22 May 2020
3. Ahn, J., Williamson, J., Gartrell, M., Han, R., Lv, Q., Mishra, S.: Supporting healthy grocery shopping via mobile augmented reality. ACM Trans. Multimedia Comput. Commun. Appl. **12**(1s), 16:1–16:24 (2015). https://doi.org/10.1145/2808207
4. Alavi, M., Joachimsthaler, E.A.: Revisiting DSS implementation research: a meta-analysis of the literature and suggestions for researchers. MIS Q. **16**(1), 95–116 (1992). https://doi.org/10.2307/249703, publisher: Management Information Systems Research Center, University of Minnesota
5. Álvarez Márquez, J.O., Ziegler, J.: Augmented-Reality-Enhanced Product Comparison in Physical Retailing. In: Proceedings of Mensch und Computer 2019, MuC 2019, Association for Computing Machinery, Hamburg, Germany, pp. 55–65 (September 2019). https://doi.org/10.1145/3340764.3340800
6. Álvarez Márquez, J.O., Ziegler, J.: In-store augmented reality-enabled product comparison and recommendation. In: Fourteenth ACM Conference on Recommender Systems, RecSys 2020, pp. 180–189. Association for Computing Machinery, New York (September 2020). https://doi.org/10.1145/3383313.3412266
7. Arth, C., Grasset, R., Gruber, L., Langlotz, T., Mulloni, A., Wagner, D.: The history of mobile augmented reality (2015)
8. Bagozzi, R.P.: The legacy of the technology acceptance model and a proposal for a paradigm shift. J. Assoc. Inf. Syst. **8**(4), 3 (2007)
9. Baier, D., Rese, A., Schreiber, S.: Analyzing online reviews to measure augmented reality acceptance at the point of sale: the case of Ikea. In: Successful Technological Integration for Competitive Advantage in Retail Settings, pp. 168–189. IGI Global (2015)
10. Beck, N., Rygl, D.: Categorization of multiple channel retailing in multi-, cross-, and omni-channel retailing for retailers and retailing. J. Retail. Consum. Serv. **27**, 170–178 (2015). https://doi.org/10.1016/j.jretconser.2015.08.001
11. Benbasat, I., Barki, H.: Quo vadis tam? J. Assoc. Inf. Syst. **8**(4), 7 (2007)
12. Büttner, O.B., Florack, A., Göritz, A.S.: Shopping orientation as a stable consumer disposition and its influence on consumers' evaluations of retailer communication. Eur. J. Market. (2014)
13. Buytaert, D.: Shopping with augmented reality. https://dri.es/shopping-with-augmented-reality (2018). Accessed 25 Jan 2021
14. Chatzopoulos, D., Bermejo, C., Huang, Z., Hui, P.: Mobile augmented reality survey: from where we are to where we go. IEEE Access **PP(99)**, 1–1 (2017)
15. Chylinski, M., De Ruyter, K., Sinha, A., Northey, G.: Augmented retail reality: Situated cognition for healthy food choices. In: ANZMAC (Australian and New Zealand Marketing Academy) (2014). 2017-09-11T01:54:50Z ISSN: 1447–3275

16. Cruz, E., et al.: An augmented reality application for improving shopping experience in large retail stores. Virtual Reality **23**(3), 281–291 (2019). https://doi.org/10.1007/s10055-018-0338-3
17. Dacko, S.G.: Enabling smart retail settings via mobile augmented reality shopping apps. Technol. Forecast. Soc. Change **124**, 243–256 (2017). https://doi.org/10.1016/j.techfore.2016.09.032
18. Dalim, C.S.C., Kolivand, H., Kadhim, H., Sunar, M.S., Billinghurst, M.: Factors influencing the acceptance of augmented reality in education: a review of the literature. J. Comput. Sci. **13**(11), 581–589 (2017)
19. Dillon, A.: User acceptance of information technology. Taylor and Francis, London (2001). 2006-07-20T00:00:01Z
20. Gentner, D., Medina, J.: Comparison and the development of cognition and language. Cogn. Stud. **4**(1), 1_112–1_149 (1997)
21. Gutiérrez, F., Htun, N.N., Charleer, S., De Croon, R., Verbert, K.: Designing Augmented Reality Applications for Personal Health Decision-Making (January 2019). https://doi.org/10.24251/HICSS.2019.212. 2019-01-02T23:56:24Z
22. Hamilton, K., Shih, S.I., Mohammed, S.: The development and validation of the rational and intuitive decision styles scale. J. Pers. Assess. **98**(5), 523–535 (2016)
23. Hilken, T., Heller, J., Chylinski, M., Keeling, D.I., Mahr, D., de Ruyter, K.: Making omnichannel an augmented reality: the current and future state of the art. J. Res. Interact. Market. **12**(4), 509–523 (2018). https://doi.org/10.1108/JRIM-01-2018-0023, publisher: Emerald Publishing Limited
24. Holdack, E., Lurie-Stoyanov, K., Fromme, H.F.: The role of perceived enjoyment and perceived informativeness in assessing the acceptance of AR wearables. J. Retail. Consum. Serv. 102259 (Septeber 2020). https://doi.org/10.1016/j.jretconser.2020.102259
25. Hopp, T., Gangadharbatla, H.: Novelty effects in augmented reality advertising environments: the influence of exposure time and self-efficacy. J. Curr. Issues Res. Advertising **37**(2), 113–130 (2016)
26. Huang, T.L., Liao, S.: A model of acceptance of augmented-reality interactive technology: the moderating role of cognitive innovativeness. Electron. Commer. Res. **15**(2), 269–295 (2015)
27. Huré, E., Picot-Coupey, K., Ackermann, C.L.: Understanding omni-channel shopping value: a mixed-method study. J. Retail. Consum. Serv. **39**, 314–330 (2017). https://doi.org/10.1016/j.jretconser.2017.08.011
28. Javornik, A.: Augmented reality: Research agenda for studying the impact of its media characteristics on consumer behaviour. J. Retail. Consum. Serv. **30**, 252–261 (2016). https://doi.org/10.1016/j.jretconser.2016.02.004
29. Kocas, C.: Evolution of prices in electronic markets under diffusion of price-comparison shopping. J. Manage. Inf. Syst. **19**(3), 99–119 (2002). https://doi.org/10.1080/07421222.2002.11045740
30. Kourouthanassis, P., Spinellis, D., Roussos, G., Giaglis, G.M.: Intelligent cokes and diapers: mygrocer ubiquitous computing environment. In: First International Mobile Business Conference, pp. 150–172 (2002)
31. Lackermair, G., Kailer, D., Kanmaz, K.: Importance of Online Product Reviews from a Consumer's Perspective (2013). https://doi.org/10.13189/aeb.2013.010101
32. Lancaster, K.J.: A new approach to consumer theory. J. Polit. Econ. **74**(2), 132–157 (1966)
33. Lee, Y., Kozar, K.A., Larsen, K.R.: The technology acceptance model: past, present, and future. Commun. Assoc. Inf. Syst. **12**(1), 50 (2003)

34. Linzbach, P., Inman, J.J., Nikolova, H.: E-commerce in a physical store: which retailing technologies add real value? NIM Market. Intell. Rev. **11**(1), 42–47 (2019). https://doi.org/10.2478/nimmir-2019-0007, publisher: Sciendo Section: NIM Marketing Intelligence Review

35. Ludwig, T., Hoffmann, S., Jasche, F., Ruhrmann, M.: Vacuumcleanar: augmented reality-based self-explanatory physical artifacts. In: Proceedings of the Conference on Mensch und Computer, pp. 291–302 (2020)

36. Masood, T., Egger, J.: Augmented reality in support of industry 4.0–implementation challenges and success factors. Robot. Comput. Integr. Manuf. **58**, 181–195 (2019). https://doi.org/10.1016/j.rcim.2019.02.003

37. McLean, G., Wilson, A.: Shopping in the digital world: Examining customer engagement through augmented reality mobile applications. Comput. Hum. Behav. **101**, 210–224 (2019). https://doi.org/10.1016/j.chb.2019.07.002

38. Narayana, C.L.: Graphic positioning scale: an economical instrument for surveys. J. Market. Res. **14**(1), 118–122 (1977)

39. Pantano, E.: Innovation drivers in retail industry. Int. J. Inf. Manage. **34**(3), 344–350 (2014). https://doi.org/10.1016/j.ijinfomgt.2014.03.002

40. Parasuraman, A.: Technology readiness index (tri) a multiple-item scale to measure readiness to embrace new technologies. J. Serv. Res. **2**(4), 307–320 (2000)

41. Park, Y., Gretzel, U.: Influence of consumers' online decision-making style on comparison shopping proneness and perceived usefulness of comparison shopping tools (2010)

42. Perannagari, K.T., Chakrabarti, S.: Factors influencing acceptance of augmented reality in retail: insights from thematic analysis. Int. J. Retail. Distrib. Manage. **48**(1), 18–34 (2019). https://doi.org/10.1108/IJRDM-02-2019-0063, publisher: Emerald Publishing Limited

43. Poushneh, A., Vasquez-Parraga, A.Z.: Discernible impact of augmented reality on retail customer's experience, satisfaction and willingness to buy. J. Retail. Consum. Serv. **34**, 229–234 (2017). https://doi.org/10.1016/j.jretconser.2016.10.005

44. Rashid, Z., Pous, R., Melià-Seguí, J., Morenza-Cinos, M.: Mobile augmented reality for browsing physical spaces. In: Proceedings of the 2014 ACM International Joint Conference on Pervasive and Ubiquitous Computing: Adjunct Publication, UbiComp 2014 Adjunct, pp. 155–158, New York, ACM (2014). https://doi.org/10.1145/2638728.2638796, event-place: Seattle, Washington

45. Ratchford, M., Barnhart, M.: Development and validation of the technology adoption propensity (tap) index. J. Bus. Res. **65**(8), 1209–1215 (2012)

46. Rauschnabel, P.A., He, J., Ro, Y.K.: Antecedents to the adoption of augmented reality smart glasses: a closer look at privacy risks. J. Bus. Res. **92**, 374–384 (2018)

47. von Reischach, F., Guinard, D., Michahelles, F., Fleisch, E.: A mobile product recommendation system interacting with tagged products. In: 2009 IEEE International Conference on Pervasive Computing and Communications. IEEE (Mar 2009). https://doi.org/10.1109/percom.2009.4912751

48. Rousseeuw, P.J.: Silhouettes: a graphical aid to the interpretation and validation of cluster analysis. J. Comput. Appl. Math. **20**, 53–65 (1987)

49. Roy, S.K., Balaji, M.S., Quazi, A., Quaddus, M.: Predictors of customer acceptance of and resistance to smart technologies in the retail sector. J. Retail. Consum. Serv. **42**, 147–160 (2018). https://doi.org/10.1016/j.jretconser.2018.02.005

50. Schafer, J.B., Konstan, J., Riedi, J.: Recommender systems in e-commerce. In: Proceedings of the 1st ACM conference on Electronic commerce - EC 99. ACM Press (1999). https://doi.org/10.1145/336992.337035

51. Scott, S.G., Bruce, R.A.: Decision-making style: the development and assessment of a new measure. Educ. Psychol. Measur. **55**(5), 818–831 (1995)
52. Spreer, P., Kallweit, K.: Augmented reality in retail: assessing the acceptance and potential for multimedia product presentation at the pos. Trans. Market. Res. **1**(1), 20–35 (2014)
53. Sprotles, G.B., Kendall, E.L.: A methodology for profiling consumers' decision-making styles. J. Consum. Aff. **20**(2), 267–279 (1986)
54. Välkkynen, P., Boyer, A., Urhemaa, T., Nieminen, R.: Mobile augmented reality for retail environments. In: Proceedings of Workshop on Mobile Interaction in Retail Environments in Conjunction with MobileHCI (2011)
55. Verhoef, P.C., Kannan, P., Inman, J.J.: From multi-channel retailing to omni-channel retailing. J. Retail. **91**(2), 174–181 (2015). https://doi.org/10.1016/j.jretai.2015.02.005
56. Wassom, B.: Augmented Reality Law, Privacy, and Ethics: Law, Society, and Emerging AR Technologies. Syngress, Waltham (2014)
57. Webster, J., Trevino, L.K., Ryan, L.: The dimensionality and correlates of flow in human-computer interactions. Comput. Hum. Behav. **9**(4), 411–426 (1993). https://doi.org/10.1016/0747-5632(93)90032-N
58. Westbrook, R.A., Black, W.C.: A motivation-based shopper typology. J. Retail. **61**(1), 78–103 (1985)
59. Zhu, W., Owen, C.B.: Design of the promopad: an automated augmented-reality shopping assistant. JOEUC **20**, 41–56 (2008)

Character Input in Augmented Reality: An Evaluation of Keyboard Position and Interaction Visualisation for Head-Mounted Displays

Maite Frutos-Pascual$^{(\boxtimes)}$ ⓘ, Clara Gale, Jake M. Harrison, Chris Creed, and Ian Williams ⓘ

DMT Lab, School of Computing and Digital Technology,
Birmingham City University, Birmingham, UK
`maite.frutos@bcu.ac.uk`

Abstract. Character input in immersive environments is a non trivial task that has attracted much attention in recent years. This paper presents an evaluation of keyboard position, orientation and interaction together with the influence of visual interaction feedback in a controlled character input task with 27 participants in Augmented Reality (AR). It presents 5 different keyboard locations (3 bounded to the headset and 2 bounded to the non-dominant hand of the user) and 3 visual interaction feedback methods (finger raycast, fingertip glow and both combined). Objective (completion time, accuracy, Key per Minute (KPM)) and subjective (After Scenario Questionnaire (ASQ)) metrics are presented. Results showed that keyboard placement had an effect on accuracy, KPM metrics and subjective preference, with keyboard visualisation parallel and bounded to the headset position and orientation outperforming other keyboard locations.

Keywords: Augmented reality · Text input · Usability · User evaluation · Visualisation

1 Introduction

Text input is a non-trivial [31] and fundamental task [7] which is an integral component of interaction in immersive environments. Subsequently text input has recently received increased attention, notably in Virtual Reality (VR), with authors focusing on interaction visualisation challenges [13,14,21,34], typing performance [7,29] and feedback methods [26,28], among others. Typing in Augmented Reality (AR) has also been explored, with the key focus on the use of mid-air gestures [22], combined input mechanisms [8,40] and keyboard representations [22].

ⓒ IFIP International Federation for Information Processing 2021
Published by Springer Nature Switzerland AG 2021
C. Ardito et al. (Eds.): INTERACT 2021, LNCS 12932, pp. 480–501, 2021.
https://doi.org/10.1007/978-3-030-85623-6_29

Multi-modal approaches have been extensively evaluated, with speech recognition being a major input method for Head-Mounted Displays (HMDs). However, this presents environmental limitations such as noise, social acceptance [22] and privacy concerns for sensitive information (i.e. passwords and personal messages). Alternative approaches suggest the use of head-gaze and eye-tracking interaction combined with dwell time and click interaction [33] or touch gestures [1] for typing. While these offer hands free interaction, they have been deemed to be constrained and present challenges associated to performance, user strain and motion sickness [33].

As an alternative, hand-held controllers are presently one of the most common interaction paradigms in VR [40] with existing consumer-grade HMDs often relying on indirect pointing mechanisms via hand-held controllers or head-gaze direction [26] for interaction and typing. While these offer benefits for locating and selecting targets, they are not suitable for interactions where hand tracking is posed as a valuable input technology [9]. Hand-tracking based studies in AR typing have predominantly focused on interaction, presenting gesture-based [9], pointing and selection mechanisms [40] and novel paradigms based on statistical models for improved typing reliability [8]. While these enable advancements in the field of AR/VR typing, configuration to their ergonomics, and specially the evaluation of position, orientation and location of virtual keyboards have not been previously explored.

Selecting character keys on virtual keyboards is often error-prone and inefficient [17,22], as users may experience difficulties to locate small characters or have problems when performing locomotion tasks. Therefore, understanding the additional feedback methods that may aid users to improve their typing performance is an additional key challenge largely unexplored in the literature. The use of visual feedback such as glow effects have been explored with positive usability and performance results while interacting with virtual objects of different sizes in VR [11], mid-air typing in standard QWERTY layouts have received positive performance outcomes [42] while augmented visual effects have been explored in AR [45] with positive usability outcomes. The use of ray-casting methods have been proven helpful in AR typing while using handheld controllers [40], however to what extent ray-casting is still useful while using hand-tracking based approaches has not been explored.

This paper presents the first study comparing different AR keyboard positions and orientations alongside visual hand based interaction feedback methods in AR character input scenarios. It contributes to the growing body of work in character input in immersive environments, where the delivery of productive and enjoyable input methods remains a challenge [7]. We present the results of a formal user study with 27 participants; evaluating 5 different keyboard locations (3 bound to HMD, and 2 bound to the non-dominant hand of the user) and 3 interaction feedback mechanisms (fingertip raycast, fingertip glow and both combined) as in Fig. 1. This study reports on precision (time to completion, accuracy, Key Per Minute (KPM) and interaction metrics (After-Scenario Questionnaire (ASQ)). The paper is structured as follows; firstly we present a literature review of text input in immersive environments, methodology of the conducted study is then presented, followed by the precision and interaction metrics used. We then present the results analysis and conclusion to the work, detailing key aspects contributing to AR/VR typing.

2 Related Work - Text Input in AR/VR

2.1 Physical Keyboards and External Devices

Physical keyboards have extensively been integrated in virtual environments, as a way of reducing the learning curve of new text input methods while keeping a familiar input mechanism [28]. Logitech released their own Software Developer Kit (SDK) as a consumer-ready solution to use physical keyboards in VR [4]. McGill *et al.* integrated physical keyboards; augmenting the virtuality of typing tasks in VR and suggesting positive outcomes when enabling a partial view of hands and keyboard while interacting [24]; they followed up their study by integrating a realistic and co-located virtual representation of the keyboard in VR [25]. Grubert *et al.* also integrated standard physical keyboards in virtual environments, reporting on the effect of keyboard layouts and hand representations [13] on user performance [14]. Gupta *et al.* integrated physical keyboards while investigating different vibrotactile feedback conditions in typing tasks in

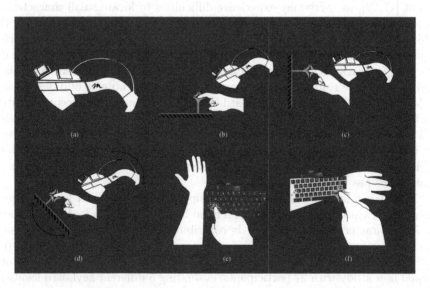

Fig. 1. Representation of the meta 2 HMD with attached leap motion on top of the headset (a) and keyboard positions and visual feedback configurations (b–f). Keyboard positions: horizontal bound view flat (VF) (b), Vertical bound view parallel (VP) (c) and HMD bound view adaptive (VA) (d), Wrist bound wrist side (WS) (e) and Wrist back (WB) (f). Interaction feedback visualisation conditions raycast and glow depicted together in illustrations (b) to (f).

VR [16], while Walker *et al.* investigated virtual assistants to assist in typing VR tasks when integrating physical keyboards [37]. Schneider *et al.* and Otter *et al.* further explored keyboard layouts while using touch-sensitive physical keyboards [29,34]. Pham and Stuerzlinger presented portable keyboard mounted on a hawker's tray for text entry while navigating or moving in VR [30].

Other devices such as haptic gloves [18,39], custom-made wearables [15,20] and hand-held controllers [3,19,44] have been studied for typing in AR/VR.

The majority of approaches involving physical keyboards have been developed for fully virtual environments, where the availability of consumer-ready VR equipment has resulted in in VR applications [6]. While physical keyboards can be connected to current AR HMDs such as the HoloLens, the use of traditional input devices such as mice and keyboard in AR environments are not suitable for outdoors or move-around/locomotion scenarios, as they require a surface to operate on [40] while proposing unique challenges, such as as the need for users to constantly switch from their virtual environment to the spatial layout and their surroundings to locate the physical keyboard [24]. Wearable and external devices have proven to be useful for text entry in virtual environments while providing a haptic feeling. However, they often rely on ad-hoc hardware or keyboard layouts and interaction metaphors, limiting transferability and adoption.

2.2 Virtual Keyboards in Immersive Environments

Grubert *et al.* compared the use of virtual and physical keyboards using a QWERTY layout [14] while Dudley *et al.* proposed a method to improve typing performance in AR environments [8]. Xu *et al.* investigated text entry mechanisms for virtual typing in AR environments. Results suggested that the combination of a controller and raycasting feedback methods outperformed other conditions [40].

Wang *et al.* presented PalmType a solution mapping the standard QWERTY keyboard layout to the palm as a text input method for smart-glasses [38]. This approach offered a novel QWERTY configuration and enabled passive feedback through the use of the body as a surface for binding AR typing interfaces.

Lee *et al.* developed a dynamic virtual keyboard layout for AR where the characters were positioned depending on their probability within the current input. However, they found dynamic layouts led to low accuracy and mediocre text input, so they proposed a 1-line solution keyboard that improved user performance [22].

Yu *et al.*, Grossman *et al.* and Ogitani *et al.* explored different hand gestures and keyboard layouts to overcome spatial interaction limitations in smart-glasses [12,27,43].

Yu *et al.* presented a radial layout for text input using an standard game controller. This alternative presented characters in groups of 4 in alphabetical order, inside a circle partitioned in 7 slices [44]. Jiang and Weng also investigated a radial layout in combination with handheld devices as an alternative text input solution in VR environments [19].

Non-QWERTY alternatives have been explored predominantly to mitigate spatial and input restrictions in immersive environments. However, the main limitation of these approaches is that Users rarely invest time in learning new keyboard layouts [2, 22], and they are often not transferable limiting their wider adoption and suggesting that standard QWERTY layouts may be preferable.

2.3 Multi-modal Approaches

Multi-modal approaches combining speech input, gaze tracking or head gaze rotation on their own or with handheld controllers or hand tracking methods have been explored in the literature. Speech input has been deemed to be the fastest medium for long text entry solutions [13]. Pick *et al.* presented a multi-modal interaction approach for text editing complementing speech input with point-and-click [31]. Other authors have used eye-tracking and head gaze in combination with dwell time, click interaction [33] and touch gestures [1] to reinforce gaze and head-gaze as interaction paradigm.

While these combination approaches have been deemed usable, no consideration have been given to the input of sensitive information or its usage in noisy and/or shared environments [13], while gaze interaction has previously shown to cause strain and motion sickness with prolonged text input tasks [33].

2.4 Visual Feedback in Typing Interaction

Providing Interaction feedback while typing has a crucial impact on users' performance using HMDs [36]. Virtual keyboards in immersive environments are limited in size and FOV of the devices. Therefore, improvement in pointing performance and key aiming accuracy without interference is vital to the design of virtual keyboards [41]. Lee *et al.* used visual feedback as an additional support mechanism for text input in AR, using a colour changing ray-cast to showcase interaction state and width of the area [22].

The effect of hand representations on typing performance, workload and presence in VR was also explored [13, 21], while a minimalist representation of the users' fingertips did also enhance keyboard visibility [13]. Yang *et al.* used visual feedback in the shape of enhanced magnified raised keys to showcase when the fingers or participants were pointing to a particular key on the virtual keyboard in the VR environment [41].

Visual feedback have proven to be efficient in guiding user interaction while typing on immersive environments, supporting the use of novel interaction methods, increasing intuitiveness and influencing the feeling of presence, while reduced feedback could result in higher error rates [36]. Most of the approaches relied on ray-casting and pointing metaphors, and Xu *et al.* suggested the use of ray-casting as the preferred visual interaction feedback method for AR HMDs, linked to reduced motion sickness while using hand-held controllers [40]. However, to what extent this is maintained in freehand interaction have not been explored, while other aspects of visual enhancements, such as colour changes or other types of virtual highlighting, may also influence input performance [41].

3   Study Design

3.1   Apparatus

We built a custom experimental AR typing framework using Unity 2017.4.20f2 LTS, a Leap Motion sensor and the Leap Motion Core 4.4.0 SDK[1] for hand tracking and the Meta2 headset for visualisation purposes as a head mounted display. C# was used as scripting language. The leap Motion sensor was mounted above the visor of the Meta2 headset, using a 3D printed structure tilted downwards following the shape of the device to facilitate hand tracking (Fig. 1a). We used the Meta 2 headset for visualisation due to its wider Field of View (FOV), however, we did not use built-in hand tracking capabilities due to reported limits with its tracking area and reliability [40].

Participants performed the test in a controlled environment under laboratory conditions. An non-cluttered room layout was used for all tests. The interactive space dimensions were 270 cm by 180 cm. The test room was lit by a 2700k (*warm white*) fluorescent with controlled external light source. A regular office chair (50 cm height) was used as participants were seated during the experiment. The chair was placed in the centre of the interaction space.

3.2   Interaction

Previous typing studies have highlighted the difficulty of typing using multiple fingers in immersive environments, while proving that novice participants using a single digit per hand can perform better than users using all digits in multi-target selection tasks [7]. Therefore, we enabled dominant-hand interaction using the index finger, for direct interaction with the keyboard. Interaction was triggered upon collision detection of the fingertips with the keyboard position.

3.3   Conditions

Five different keyboard positions were evaluated in combination with three visual interaction feedback representations *(5 × 3 = 15 unique conditions)*. Keyboard positions were not adjustable by participants.

Keyboard Positions. The keyboard position conditions are categorised into two primary conditions, viewpoint bound conditions (Fig. 1b–d) and non-dominant hand bound conditions (Fig. 1e–f). The virtual keyboard size was 26 cm width by 10 cm height. All keyboard positions were anchored relative to the user position and the position of the headset.

---

[1] https://developer.leapmotion.com/, *(Last accessed 7th November 2020)*.

Viewpoint bound conditions: The conditions showcased below were defined based on the position and orientation of the HMD. The keyboard was placed in a fixed plane 35 cm away in the Z axis and 10 cm below in the vertical plane from the camera (the HMD), changing its orientation as described in the conditions below. These are inspired by the tag-along User Interface (UI) paradigm common in current HMDs[2].

- **View Flat (VF):** In this condition the keyboard was shown always horizontal (flat) in front of the user and anchored to the plane mentioned above. The position and orientation were calculated using the sensor information provided by the HMD. A representation of this condition is shown in Fig. 1(b).
- **View Parallel (VP):** In this condition the keyboard was parallel to the HMD point of view. Thus was anchored parallel to the front facing position of the user, tilting its angle with head-gaze orientation and fixed to the plane mentioned earlier. A representation of this condition is shown in Fig. 1(c).
- **View Adaptive (VA):** In this condition, the keyboard was anchored to the plane above but changed orientation between 2 tilting planes, one horizontal and one vertical, depending on HMD orientation. This transition between planes was performed using a threshold of 20° below the horizon line of the HMD to avoid jittering, therefore removing the noise for involuntary head movements. A representation of this condition is shown in Fig. 1(d).

Non-dominant hand bound conditions: The conditions showcased below were defined based on the position and orientation of the non-dominant hand.

- **Wrist Side (WS)** - In this condition the keyboard was displayed to the side of the users' wrist, floating in mid-air and 3 cm away from the wrist point. This was inspired by the Hand Menu UX pattern proposed by Microsoft in their Hololens 2[3]. The keyboard orientation was bound to the rotation of the wrist. A representation of these keyboard location is showcased in Fig. 1(e).
- **Wrist Back (WB)** - The keyboard was displayed as an overlay between the elbow and wrist. This approach was inspired by previous research showcasing the benefits of passive feedback for interactions in virtual environments [7, 38]. A representation of this keyboard location is shown in Fig. 1(f).

Interaction Feedback. To support the interaction between the user's digit and the key to be pressed we evaluate two forms of visual feedback and guidance notably Raycast and Glow. These visual feedback methods are used for guiding the user and providing feedback about the key they are aiming at with their interaction.

---

[2] https://docs.microsoft.com/en-us/windows/mixed-reality/design/billboarding-and-tag-along, *(Last accessed 14th January 2021).*

[3] https://docs.microsoft.com/en-us/windows/mixed-reality/design/hand-menu, *(Last accessed 14th January 2020).*

(a) Raycast   (b) Glow   (c) Both combined

Fig. 2. Interaction feedback modes. Raycast depicting a continuous guidance ray to the keyboard (a), Glow depicting the tip of the dominant hand index finger (b) and both combined (c). Black hand represents the AR hand segmentation alpha mask for the occlusion handling of the interaction hand, grey region is rendered to the real environment on the AR HMD.

Raycast (R): This feedback method showed a continuous solid pointer connecting the users dominant hand index finger to the closest part of the surface of the keyboard. This feedback method is inspired by virtual pointing, one of the most common approaches used for object selection in immersive environments [32]. The raycast acts as a visual trajectory guidance method in locating the key for direct tap selection. A representation of this feedback condition is shown in Fig. 2(a) and combined with the keyboard modes in Fig. 3(r), 3(n), 3(j), 3(b) and 3(f).

Glow (G): In this condition the index fingertip in participants' dominant hand displayed a glow. Fingertip feedback has proven to enhance keyboard visibility [13] and has recently been adopted by Microsoft UX guidelines for direct object manipulation using their Collidable Fingertip paradigm[4]. This glow represented the contact point that will be used for interaction with the keyboard, changing its size and intensity with proximity to the target. This glow effect is inspired by previous work [11], where authors evaluated glow effects as an interaction trigger in VR. A representation of this feedback conditions is shown in Fig. 2(b) and combined with the keyboard modes in 3(s), 3(o), 3(k), 3(c) and 3(g).

Both combined (B): This condition combined both the raycast and glow feedback to display both concurrently. A representation of this feedback conditions is shown in Fig. 2(c) and combined with the keyboard modes in Fig. 3(t), 3(p), 3(l), 3(d) and 3(h).

---

[4] https://docs.microsoft.com/en-us/windows/mixed-reality/design/direct-manipulationinteraction, *(Last accessed 7th November 2020).*

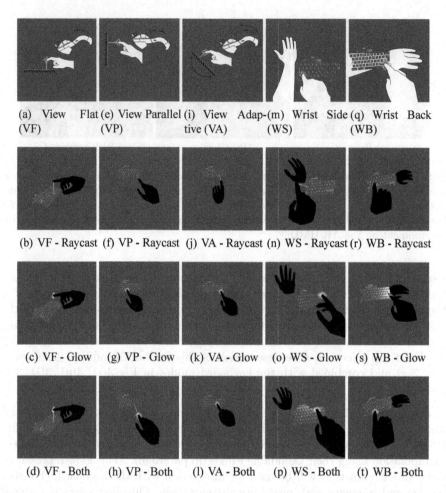

(a) View Flat (VF)   (e) View Parallel (VP)   (i) View Adaptive (VA)   (m) Wrist Side (WS)   (q) Wrist Back (WB)

(b) VF - Raycast   (f) VP - Raycast   (j) VA - Raycast   (n) WS - Raycast   (r) WB - Raycast

(c) VF - Glow   (g) VP - Glow   (k) VA - Glow   (o) WS - Glow   (s) WB - Glow

(d) VF - Both   (h) VP - Both   (l) VA - Both   (p) WS - Both   (t) WB - Both

Fig. 3. Interaction modes for the keyboard and the visual feedback in the test. Representations of the five keyboard positions with the corresponding representations of the feedback modes for each keyboard representation.VF stands for View Flat, VA for View Adaptive, VP for View Parallel, WS for Wrist Side and WB for Wrist Back keyboard placement conditions Black hand represents the AR hand segmentation mask for the occlusion handling of the interaction hand, grey region corresponds to the real environment of the user. The virtual keyboard and feedback mechanisms were the only elements rendered in the device.

3.4   Task

We proposed these tasks under the scenario of security/sensitive character input (as in passwords), where hand interaction will be preferred over speech commands for privacy. The input task was defined to involve the use of special characters, numbers and capital letters in character strings, in compliance with standardise guidelines for secure passwords. Therefore, participants were asked to input a randomised 7-character sequence containing a) 4 letters (2 of them uppercase) b) 2 numbers and c) 1 special character (e.g. G2+hDf8). Sequences were presented above the keyboard in the UI layout and they maintained the same level of complexity for every condition under study, each participant completed a total of 15 unique sequences. Lower case L and upper case I were removed from all sequences for clarity.

3.5 Participants

27 right-handed participants (1 non-binary, 6 female, 20 male) from a population of university students and staff members were recruited to take part in this study. Participants' mean age was 24.3 (SD: 4.78).

All participants performed the task described in Sect. 3.4 under the keyboard placement and feedback conditions explained in Sect. 3.3. Participants completed a standardised consent form and were not compensated. Visual acuity of participants was measured using a Snellen chart, each participant was also required to pass an Ishihara test to exclude for colour blindness. Participants with colour blindness and/or visual acuity of < 0.80 (where 20/20 is 1.0) were not included in this study.

Participants were asked to self-assess their level of experience with AR and VR systems, with 5 participants reporting to have an average level of experience and the remaining 22 reported being novice to immersive technologies. None of the participants had any substantial previous experience using an AR HMD or hand tracking devices.

3.6 Protocol

A within participants test protocol design was used. All participants tested the 5 keyboard positions and 3 interaction methods, inputting a total of 15 string sequences. Participants were only allowed to proceed to the next sequence when the current input was correct. The overall duration of the experiment ranged between 30 and 45 min, including pre-test and post-test questionnaires.

Pre-Test. Prior to the study, participants were given a written consent form, where the test protocol was described. Additionally, participants completed a pre-test questionnaire enquiring about their background level of experience with immersive systems, recognition sensors and the use of HMDs.

Calibration. Before each test, the test coordinator helped participants to fit the HMD in the most suitable and comfortable way to ensure successful hand tracking from the Leap motion. Once the system was calibrated participants were asked to confirm that the characters on display were clearly legible.

Training. Once participants were comfortable with the device and the hand tracking, recognition and interaction system, they were trained with an specific task-related scenario. This consisted of 3 training tasks introducing different levels of typing complexity: 1) participants were asked to input a lowercase 3 character sequence, 2) participants were introduced to the SHIFT key for upper-case and special characters, 3) participants were asked to use the arrow keys and delete button to edit their inputs. Each training sequence was a predefined string with 3 characters. This task training was the same for every participant and they were trained in a representative version of every keyboard position.

Test. Once participants were comfortable with the interaction conditions, we presented the main experimental task. Participants were asked to complete the task as accurately as possible in the shortest amount of time. Tasks reported in Sect. 3.4 for every condition reported in Sect. 3.3 were loaded in counterbalanced random order.

Post-Test. After each of the keyboard-location conditions were completed, participants were asked to fill the After Scenario Questionnaire (ASQ). Once all 5 keyboard location conditions were completed and all the interaction tests were finished, participants were asked to fill a post-test questionnaire asking about their overall experience with the system and keyboard location and visual feedback preferences.

3.7 Metrics

Completion Time. Completion time was defined as the time it took to complete the string input task per condition under study. It was measured as the time in seconds from the start of every condition until the participant successfully input the character string.

Accuracy. Accuracy was calculated as $\frac{correct\ key\ presses}{total\ key\ presses}$ per task (task defined as the combination of keyboard location and interaction feedback).

Each key-press was labelled as correct or incorrect at run-time based on the considerations listed below:

Labelled as correct: a) After a key-press, if the input matches the character sequence up to that point. b) If the key-press is BACKSPACE, if there was a mistake behind the cursor. c) If the key-press is CLEAR, if there was any mistake in the text. d) LEFT if there is an error more than one character to the left of the cursor. e) RIGHT f there is an error to the right of the cursor, or there are no errors and the cursor is in the middle of the input. f) RETURN if the input matches the character sequence.

Labelled as incorrect: a) If the key-press is a letter/special character and the input does not match the character sequence. b) If the key-press is SHIFT and it would result in the next input character not matching the next sequence character.

Key per Minute (KPM). Entry rate was measured in keys per minute (KPM). KPM was calculated as the number of key-press in a minute calculated based on the ratio of input obtained for every task as in $\frac{key\ input\ \times\ 60\ seconds}{time\ in\ seconds}$.

After Scenario Questionnaire (ASQ). This questionnaire was used to assess participants' satisfaction or frustration after the completion of each task per condition. This three-item questionnaire address ease of task completion, time to complete a task, and adequacy of the support information [23]. It gives a value from 1 *strongly agree* to 7 *strongly disagree*; being 1 the ideal.

3.8 Statistical Analysis

The Shapiro-Wilk [35] normality test found the data to be not normally distributed. We tested for significance between the conditions and the metrics described using a non parametric Friedman test [10]. 95% Confidence Intervals (CI) and pair-wise Effect Sizes (ES) are reported.

4 Results

A comprehensive analysis of completion time, accuracy and KPM with Effect Sizes (ES) and 95% Confidence Intervals (CIs) per keyboard position and interaction feedback condition is presented in Tables 2 and 3 respectively. A comprehensive statistical analysis of ASQ responses is presented in Table 1.

4.1 Completion Time

Completion time results by keyboard position condition are shown in Fig. 4(a). Completion times ranged from 62.35 sec (SD = 45.03 sec) for Wrist-Back Glow condition to 25.70 sec (SD = 10.04 sec) for the View-Parallel Glow condition.

By Keyboard Position. Statistically significant differences were found for the different interaction feedback modes for Wrist-Side keyboard position, with medium ES between a) Glow and Both combined b) Raycast and Both combined. No statistically significant differences were found for the remaining keyboard conditions comparing interaction feedback modes for each position (i.e. *raycast* vs. *glow* and *glow* vs. *both* for *View Parallel*). An in-depth analysis of these results is presented in Table 2.

By Feedback Mode

– **Raycast:** Statistically significant differences were found between keyboard locations for the raycast feedback condition with large ES shown between a Wrist-Back and View-Parallel.

- **Glow:** Statistically significant differences were found between keyboard locations for glow feedback mode. Large ES were shown between a) Wrist-Back and View-Parallel, b) Wrist-Back and View-Adaptive c) View-Parallel and View-Flat.
- **Both:** Statistically significant differences were found between keyboard locations for the combined feedback mode. While medium ES where shown as in Table 3 no large ES were found.

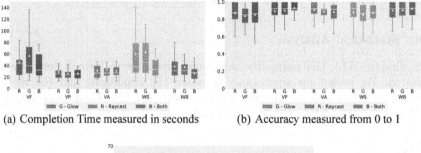

(a) Completion Time measured in seconds   (b) Accuracy measured from 0 to 1

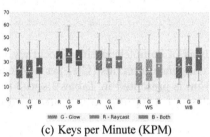

(c) Keys per Minute (KPM)

Fig. 4. Completion time 4(a), accuracy 4(b) and KPM 4(c) per keyboard position and feedback condition displayed in seconds with white triangles showcasing mean value, where VF stands for View Flat, VA for View Adaptive, VP for View Parallel, WS for Wrist Side and WB for Wrist Back keyboard placement conditions, with R standing for Raycast feedback condition, G for Glow and B for both feedback conditions.

4.2 Accuracy

Accuracy results per keyboard location and feedback mode are displayed on Fig. 4(b). Average accuracy levels were high for all conditions, ranging from 0.93 (SD = 0.07) for View-Parallel Both condition to 0.85 (SD = 0.12) for the Wrist Back Glow condition.

No statistically significant differences were found between the visual feedback modes when comparing them for each keyboard placement position. The comparison between different keyboard positions when comparing them by feedback mode did not show statistically significant differences either. This suggested that the interaction feedback modes and keyboard positions under study did not have statistically significant effects on input accuracy.

4.3   Key per Minute (KPM)

Key per Minute (KPM) values are shown on Fig. 4(c). Average values ranged from 36.29 kpm (SD = 9.47 kpm) for the View-Parallel Glow condition to 24.7 kpm (SD = 10.06 kpm) and 24.29 kpm (SD = 9.45 kpm) for the View-Flat Raycast and Glow conditions.

By Keyboard Position. Statistically significant differences were found again for Wrist-Back keyboard condition, with medium ES showing between a) Glow and both feedback combined.. No statistically significant differences were found for the remaining keyboard conditions comparing interaction feedback modes for each position. An in-depth analysis of this is presented in Table 2.

By Feedback Mode

– **Raycast:** Statistically significant differences were found between keyboard locations for raycast feedback. Large ES were shown between a) Wrist-Back and View-Parallel b) Wrist-Back and View-Adaptive c) View-Parallel and View-Flat.
– **Glow:** Statistically significant differences were found between keyboard locations for glow feedback. Large ES were found for a) Wrist-Side and View-Parallel b) Wrist-Back and View-Parallel c) View-Parallel and View-Flat.
– **Both:** Statistically significant differences were found between keyboard locations for combined feedback. While medium ES where shown as in Table 3 no large ES were found.

4.4   After-Scenario Questionnaire (ASQ)

Statistically significant differences were found between keyboard location conditions for ASQ questionnaire, as in Table 1. Overall scores per condition are showcased in Fig. 5. Mean scores ranged from 1.88 (SD = 1.03) for *View Parallel* condition to 3.48 (SD = 1.59) for the *Wrist Back* condition, with Wrist Side scoring 2.41 (SD = 1.16), View Adaptive 2.14 (SD = 1.26) and View Flat 2.96 (SD = 1.27). Large ES were found between a) Wrist-Back and View-Parallel b) Wrist-Back and View-Adaptive.

4.5   Preferences

Participants were asked to rank keyboard locations and interaction feedback modes in preference order (from 1 to 5 for keyboard locations and 1 to 3 for feedback conditions). No tracking issues were reported by participants and results are presented in Figs. 6(a) and 6(b).

– **Keyboard position:** 13 participants chose "View-Parallel" as their preferred keyboard position, while 15 participants declared that "Wrist-Back" was their

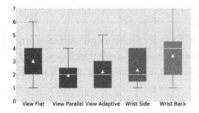

Fig. 5. ASQ Scores by keyboard location with white triangles showcasing mean value, where VF stands for View Flat, VA for View Adaptive, VP for View Parallel, WS for Wrist Side and WB for Wrist Back keyboard placement condition.

Table 1. ASQ questionnaire response statistics, showcasing p, effect sizes ($|ES|$) and 95% confidence intervals where WS stands for Wrist Back, WB for Wrist Back, VP for View Parallel, VA for View Adaptive and VF for View Flat.

ASQ Questionnaire	p	(Stat = 17.08, p = 0.02)*	
	$|ES|$	WS $vs.$ WB= 0.75 WB $vs.$ VA= 0.90	
		WS $vs.$ VP= 0.46 WB $vs.$ VF= 0.32	
		WS $vs.$ VA= 0.21 VP $vs.$ VA= 0.22	
		WS $vs.$ VF= 0.39 VP $vs.$ VF= 0.78	
		WB $vs.$ VP= 0.95 VA $vs.$ VF= 0.55	
	95% CI	WB WS VA VP VF 0 1 2 3 4 5 6 7 Score	

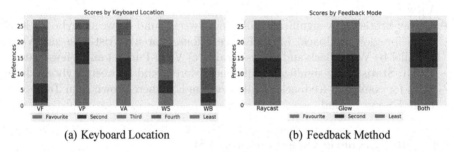

(a) Keyboard Location   (b) Feedback Method

Fig. 6. Participants' reported preferences. With (a) showcasing preferences by keyboard position and (b) showcasing preferences by feedback condition.

least preferred position for text input interaction. This results are in alignment with the performance metrics presented earlier, where View Parallel had one of the shortest completion times and highest KPM and accuracy values. Results for all the location conditions are presented in Fig. 6(a).

5   Discussion

We presented a study to evaluate different keyboard locations and interaction feedback conditions in a controlled environment for text entry in AR. Currently, there are no standard methods for AR/VR text entry, with current commercial systems implementing their own often differing techniques [36]. Our proposed conditions rely on the standard QWERTY keyboard configuration and a free-hand interaction paradigm using a commercially available sensor. We altered

Table 2. Completion time, accuracy and Key per Minute (KPM) statistics, displaying effect sizes (|ES|) and 95% confidence intervals (CI) where G stands for Glow feedback mode, R for Raycast feedback mode and B for Both feedback combined for all keyboard location conditions.

		Wrist Side	Wrist Back	View Adaptive	View Parallel	View Flat
Completion Time	*p*	(**Stat = 8.22,** **p = 0.01)***	(*Stat* = 1.85, *p* = 0.39)	(*Stat* = 1.18, *p* = 0.55)	(*Stat* = 0.29, *p* = 0.86)	(*Stat* = 1.55, *p* = 0.45)
	|ES|	B *vs.* G = 0.51 B *vs.* R = 0.61 R *vs.* G = 0.01	B *vs.* G = 0.25 B *vs.* R = 0.19 R *vs.* G = 0.05	B *vs.* G = 0.19 B *vs.* R = 0.03 R *vs.* G = 0.14	B *vs.* G = 0.04 B *vs.* R = 0.19 R *vs.* G = 0.23	B *vs.* G = 0.09 B *vs.* R = 0.26 R *vs.* G = 0.30
	95% CI					
Accuracy	*p*	(*Stat* = 0.43, *p* = 0.80)	(*Stat* = 0.42, *p* = 0.81)	(*Stat* = 0.64, *p* = 0.73)	(*Stat* = 0.92, *p* = 0.63)	(*Stat* = 2.58, *p* = 0.27)
	|ES|	B *vs.* G = 0.17 B *vs.* R = 0.18 R *vs.* G = 0.03	B *vs.* G = 0.25 B *vs.* R = 0.02 R *vs.* G = 0.23	B *vs.* G = 0.03 B *vs.* R = 0.34 R *vs.* G = 0.31	B *vs.* G = 0.31 B *vs.* R = 0.37 R *vs.* G = 0.07	B *vs.* G = 0.1 B *vs.* R = 0.2 R *vs.* G = 0.32
	95% CI					
Key per Minute (KPM)	*p*	(**Stat = 6.66,** **p = 0.03)***	(*Stat* = 2.28, *p* = 0.32)	(*Stat* = 0.47, *p* = 0.78)	(*Stat* = 1.41, *p* = 0.49)	(*Stat* = 1.27, *p* = 0.52)
	|ES|	B *vs.* G = 0.54 B *vs.* R = 0.48 R *vs.* G = 0.01	B *vs.* G = 0.26 B *vs.* R = 0.45 R *vs.* G = 0.20	B *vs.* G = 0.09 B *vs.* R = 0.03 R *vs.* G = 0.06	B *vs.* G = 0.22 B *vs.* R = 0.06 R *vs.* G = 0.31	B *vs.* G = 0.22 B *vs.* R = 0.17 R *vs.* G = 0.04
	95% CI					

the spatial position of the virtual AR keyboard and the visual feedback method used. This enables an evaluation of performance without changing the user's input habits, which has been successfully evaluated previously in AR/VR environments creating a one-to-one mapping of virtual and real worlds [36,41].

The range of tasks presented were a representative version of what could be expected in a password input scenario, where speech-based interaction will not be suitable due to privacy concerns. These tasks are common in HMD interaction, specially when connecting the device to a WiFi network or inputting account credentials.

Most current text entry solutions present the virtual keyboard location anchored and fixed in 3D space, with current text input methods for immersive

Table 3. Completion time, accuracy and key per minute (KPM) statistics, showcasing effect sizes (|ES|) where WS stands for Wrist Back keyboard placement, WB for Wrist Back keyboard placement, VP for View Parallel keyboard placement, VA for View Adaptive keyboard placement and VF for View Flat keyboard placement for all feedback conditions.

		Raycast	Glow	Both
Completion Time	p	(Stat = 16.50, p = 0.02)*	(Stat = 24.5, p < 0.01)*	(Stat = 9.27, p = 0.05)*
	|ES|	ws vs. wb= 0.55 wb vs. va= 0.77 ws vs. vp= 0.49 wb vs. vf= 0.34 ws vs. va= 0.38 vp vs. va= 0.12 ws vs. vf= 0.26 vp vs. vf= 0.69 wb vs. vp= 0.84 va vs. vf= 0.60	ws vs. wb= 0.63 wb vs. va= 0.80 ws vs. vp= 0.59 wb vs. vf= 0.15 ws vs. va= 0.20 vp vs. va= 0.48 ws vs. vf= 0.52 vp vs. vf= 0.92 wb vs. vp= 0.90 va vs. vf= 0.73	ws vs. wb= 0.70 wb vs. va= 0.61 ws vs. vp= 0.09 wb vs. vf= 0.16 ws vs. va= 0.27 vp vs. va= 0.36 ws vs. vf= 0.60 vp vs. vf= 0.61 wb vs. vp= 0.74 va vs. vf= 0.54
	95% CI	Time [sec]	Time [sec]	Time [sec]
Accuracy	p	($Stat$ = 1.63, p = 0.80)	($Stat$ = 5.82, p = 0.2)	($Stat$ = 5.80, p = 0.21)
	|ES|	ws vs. wb= 0.18 wb vs. va= 0.30 ws vs. vp= 0.08 wb vs. vf= 0.04 ws vs. va= 0.12 vp vs. va= 0.21 ws vs. vf= 0.21 vp vs. vf= 0.13 wb vs. vp= 0.11 va vs. vf= 0.36	ws vs. wb= 0.51 wb vs. va= 0.34 ws vs. vp= 0.05 wb vs. vf= 0.05 ws vs. va= 0.19 vp vs. va= 0.14 ws vs. vf= 0.58 vp vs. vf= 0.53 wb vs. vp= 0.46 va vs. vf= 0.41	ws vs. wb= 0.45 wb vs. va= 0.07 ws vs. vp= 0.08 wb vs. vf= 0.18 ws vs. va= 0.39 vp vs. va= 0.50 ws vs. vf= 0.57 vp vs. vf= 0.66 wb vs. vp= 0.56 va vs. vf= 0.25
	95% CI	Accuracy	Accuracy	Accuracy
Key per Minute (KPM)	p	(Stat = 25.44, p < 0.01)*	(Stat = 35.82, p < 0.01)*	(Stat = 10.31, p = 0.03)*
	|ES|	ws vs. wb= 0.51 wb vs. va= 0.85 ws vs. vp= 0.49 wb vs. vf= 0.27 ws vs. va= 0.26 vp vs. va= 0.26 ws vs. vf= 0.26 vp vs. vf= 0.83 wb vs. vp= 0.93 va vs. vf= 0.58	ws vs. wb= 0.32 wb vs. va= 0.55 ws vs. vp= 0.87 wb vs. vf= 0.02 ws vs. va= 0.25 vp vs. va= 0.65 ws vs. vf= 0.33 vp vs. vf= 0.97 wb vs. vp= 0.95 va vs. vf= 0.57	ws vs. wb= 0.48 wb vs. va= 0.30 ws vs. vp= 0.05 wb vs. vf= 0.06 ws vs. va= 0.24 vp vs. va= 0.30 ws vs. vf= 0.60 vp vs. vf= 0.64 wb vs. vp= 0.52 va vs. vf= 0.41
	95% CI	KPM	KPM	KPM

environments not allowing the user to change the position or size of keyboard representations [36]. This study presented a unique approach to varying the position and orientation of the virtual keyboard based on participants position and orientation.

The results showcased a preference for the *View Parallel* condition for completion time, ASQ scores and KPM metrics. Key input metrics for this condition were in alignment with those reported in the literature and deemed as tolerable [8]. We envisage participants performance will improve with experience and practice. Therefore, we presented these results as an indication of achievability under the circumstances outlined.

While previous studies have shown a preference for tilted keyboards in VR [5,41], they have mostly evaluated keyboard positions anchored to spatial surroundings. We proposed these alternatives to spatially fixed keyboards to support on demand access to typing capabilities, specially for inputting confidential information.

Limitations of current HMD devices and tracking solutions have showcased limits in the use of horizontal keyboards. Primarily due to tracking inaccuracies while maintaining a low head posture which may end in increased neck pressure [41] and discomfort for users. This is in alignment with the results presented, where the *View Flat* condition received poor ASQ scores. Therefore, the use of horizontal keyboards, akin to current interaction with physical keyboards, may require further technical support [41] for them to be adopted. While passive feedback has been successfully explored in immersive environments before [38], we did not find the same results. While no tracking issues were reported during the study, this could be due to current limitation of the display and hand tracking technologies and may need to be further explored with improved tracking capabilities in the future.

We paired keyboard location with the evaluation of visual interaction feedback to further assess visual guidance and its effect on perceived usability and character input performance. While no statistically significant differences were found, ray-cast and fingertip feedback have been used widely in AR/VR environments and our suggestion would be for it to be considered and implemented as a guiding technique. Previous literature suggested that reduced visual feedback could result in decreased performance [36], therefore we suggest supportive visual feedback to be considered when enabling text input.

Overall, the main findings of the study related to short character input, akin to password and confidential information input, in AR environments were as follows:

- Keyboard locations bounded to the user and following the same orientation of the viewpoint of the HMD were preferred for interaction (*i.e. always in front keyboards*).
- While there was no clear preference for a visual feedback mode, our suggestion would be to continue to use ray-cast and fingertip visual feedback for guiding typing tasks in immersive environments.
- Multi-modal interaction (i.e. speech and gaze) and haptic feedback should be considered, specially for longer non-confidential typing tasks.

5.1   Limitations

Freehand input has been deemed as the most realistic text entry method for immersive environments [36]. This technique relies on hand tracking capabilities, therefore we employed the Leap Motion sensor mounted on the front of the AR HMD. While this approach has been previously used for text entry studies [41], it is worth highlighting that the tracking limitations of this device may negatively impact performance and preference results. However, the Leap Motion was chosen as it is the current most affordable and consumer available method for finger input. Future developments in hand tracking technology, specifically related to robustness and accuracy, may influence the results presented here. Furthermore, while external and high-quality motion tracking solutions could be employed to track the user, the current system presents a deployable solution that can easily be adopted and utilised in wider studies with comparable HMD setups, as motion capture solutions are not portable or mobile [21].

5.2   Future Work

Our evaluation was conducted in a laboratory environment, under controlled conditions. This supports repeatability and transferability of the findings, however, future work should consider more realistic locomotion situations and environments i.e. outdoors, on the move, while commuting, etc. This will expand the finding from this work into text input interaction paradigms and keyboard locations that enable the user to fully move and explore the AR environment. These situations may also require keyboards and interactive elements to be bound to the user and not the environment, thus leveraging the learned keyboard interaction behaviour and exploiting the additional dimensions of the space available in AR [8]. This future research can be informed by the results of the current experiment and be extrapolated to wider interaction scenarios such as user interface widgets and buttons.

We solely evaluated visual feedback for typing guidance, future work should consider the role of audio feedback and haptics as further guidance support for typing tasks in AR.

Although the presented solution may be suitable for short character input sequences or sensitive information such as passwords, it may be worth considering combination approaches using speech input for longer text editing or writing tasks. It is worth exploring these to support text entry techniques that are more involved [40].

6   Conclusion

We have conducted a study comparing five different keyboard locations and three visual feedback modes in a controlled AR environment for text input. We followed a within participants study design and we reported on completion time, KPM, accuracy and ASQ questionnaire metrics. Our results suggest that *View*

Parallel condition outperformed all keyboard locations while the visual feedback used did not have a statistically significant effect.

Our findings have some interesting implications for the design and implementation of text input tasks in AR. Overall, the results of this study can guide the design of typing on immersive environments by applying the keyboard location and input feedback considerations presented here, specially for tasks that require the input of sensitive content of login credentials.

References

1. Ahn, S., Lee, G.: Gaze-assisted typing for smart glasses. In: Proceedings of the 32nd Annual ACM Symposium on User Interface Software and Technology, pp. 857–869 (2019)
2. Bi, X., Smith, B.A., Zhai, S.: Quasi-qwerty soft keyboard optimization. In: Proceedings of the SIGCHI Conference on Human Factors in Computing Systems, pp. 283–286 (2010)
3. Boletsis, C., Kongsvik, S.: Text input in virtual reality: a preliminary evaluation of the drum-like vr keyboard. Technologies **7**(2), 31 (2019)
4. Bovet, S., et al.: Using traditional keyboards in vr: steamvr developer kit and pilot game user study. In: 2018 IEEE Games, Entertainment, Media Conference (GEM), pp. 1–9. IEEE (2018)
5. Dang, N.-T., Mestre, D.: Effects of menu orientation on pointing behavior in virtual environments. In: Shumaker, R. (ed.) VMR 2011. LNCS, vol. 6773, pp. 144–153. Springer, Heidelberg (2011). https://doi.org/10.1007/978-3-642-22021-0_17
6. Dube, T.J., Arif, A.S.: Text entry in virtual reality: a comprehensive review of the literature. In: Kurosu, M. (ed.) HCII 2019. LNCS, vol. 11567, pp. 419–437. Springer, Cham (2019). https://doi.org/10.1007/978-3-030-22643-5_33
7. Dudley, J., Benko, H., Wigdor, D., Kristensson, P.O.: Performance envelopes of virtual keyboard text input strategies in virtual reality. In: 2019 IEEE International Symposium on Mixed and Augmented Reality (ISMAR), pp. 289–300. IEEE (2019)
8. Dudley, J.J., Vertanen, K., Kristensson, P.O.: Fast and precise touch-based text entry for head-mounted augmented reality with variable occlusion. ACM Trans. Comput.-Hum. Interact. (TOCHI) **25**(6), 1–40 (2018)
9. Fashimpaur, J., Kin, K., Longest, M.: Pinchtype: text entry for virtual and augmented reality using comfortable thumb to fingertip pinches. In: Extended Abstracts of the 2020 CHI Conference on Human Factors in Computing Systems Extended Abstracts, pp. 1–7 (2020)
10. Friedman, M.: A comparison of alternative tests of significance for the problem of m rankings. Ann. Math. Stat. **11**(1), 86–92 (1940)
11. Frutos-Pascual, M., Harrison, J.M., Creed, C., Williams, I.: Evaluation of ultrasound haptics as a supplementary feedback cue for grasping in virtual environments. In: 2019 International Conference on Multimodal Interaction, pp. 310–318 (2019)
12. Grossman, T., Chen, X.A., Fitzmaurice, G.: Typing on glasses: adapting text entry to smart eyewear. In: Proceedings of the 17th International Conference on Human-Computer Interaction with Mobile Devices and Services, pp. 144–152 (2015)
13. Grubert, J., Witzani, L., Ofek, E., Pahud, M., Kranz, M., Kristensson, P.O.: Effects of hand representations for typing in virtual reality. In: 2018 IEEE Conference on Virtual Reality and 3D User Interfaces (VR), pp. 151–158. IEEE (2018)

14. Grubert, J., Witzani, L., Ofek, E., Pahud, M., Kranz, M., Kristensson, P.O.: Text entry in immersive head-mounted display-based virtual reality using standard keyboards. In: 2018 IEEE Conference on Virtual Reality and 3D User Interfaces (VR), pp. 159–166. IEEE (2018)

15. Gupta, A., Ji, C., Yeo, H.S., Quigley, A., Vogel, D.: Rotoswype: word-gesture typing using a ring. In: Proceedings of the 2019 CHI Conference on Human Factors in Computing Systems, pp. 1–12 (2019)

16. Gupta, A., Samad, M., Kin, K., Kristensson, P.O., Benko, H.: Investigating remote tactile feedback for mid-air text-entry in virtual reality. In: 2020 IEEE International Symposium on Mixed and Augmented Reality (ISMAR), pp. 350–360. IEEE (2020)

17. Hincapié-Ramos, J.D., Guo, X., Irani, P.: The consumed endurance workbench: a tool to assess arm fatigue during mid-air interactions. In: Proceedings of the 2014 Companion Publication on Designing Interactive Systems, pp. 109–112 (2014)

18. Hsieh, Y.T., Jylhä, A., Orso, V., Gamberini, L., Jacucci, G.: Designing a willing-to-use-in-public hand gestural interaction technique for smart glasses. In: Proceedings of the 2016 CHI Conference on Human Factors in Computing Systems, pp. 4203–4215 (2016)

19. Jiang, H., Weng, D.: Hipad: text entry for head-mounted displays using circular touchpad. In: 2020 IEEE Conference on Virtual Reality and 3D User Interfaces (VR), pp. 692–703. IEEE (2020)

20. Kim, J., Delamare, W., Irani, P.: Thumbtext: text entry for wearable devices using a miniature ring. In: Proceedings of Graphics Interface, pp. 18–25 (2018)

21. Knierim, P., Schwind, V., Feit, A.M., Nieuwenhuizen, F., Henze, N.: Physical keyboards in virtual reality: analysis of typing performance and effects of avatar hands. In: Proceedings of the 2018 CHI Conference on Human Factors in Computing Systems, pp. 1–9 (2018)

22. Lee, L.H., Braud, T., Lam, K.Y., Yau, Y.P., Hui, P.: From seen to unseen: designing keyboard-less interfaces for text entry on the constrained screen real estate of augmented reality headsets. Pervasive Mob. Comput. 64, 101148 (2020)

23. Lewis, J.R.: IBM computer usability satisfaction questionnaires: psychometric evaluation and instructions for use. Int. J. Hum.-Comput. Interact. 7(1), 57–78 (1995)

24. McGill, M., Boland, D., Murray-Smith, R., Brewster, S.: A dose of reality: overcoming usability challenges in vr head-mounted displays. In: Proceedings of the 33rd Annual ACM Conference on Human Factors in Computing Systems, pp. 2143–2152 (2015)

25. Mcgill, M., Kehoe, A., Freeman, E., Brewster, S.: Expanding the bounds of seated virtual workspaces. ACM Trans. Comput.-Hum. Interact. (TOCHI) 27(3), 1–40 (2020)

26. Menzner, T., Otte, A., Gesslein, T., Grubert, J., Gagel, P., Schneider, D.: A capacitive-sensing physical keyboard for vr text entry. In: 2019 IEEE Conference on Virtual Reality and 3D User Interfaces (VR), pp. 1080–1081. IEEE (2019)

27. Ogitani, T., Arahori, Y., Shinyama, Y., Gondow, K.: Space saving text input method for head mounted display with virtual 12-key keyboard. In: 2018 IEEE 32nd International Conference on Advanced Information Networking and Applications (AINA), pp. 342–349. IEEE (2018)

28. Otte, A., Menzner, T., Gesslein, T., Gagel, P., Schneider, D., Grubert, J.: Towards utilizing touch-sensitive physical keyboards for text entry in virtual reality. In: 2019 IEEE Conference on Virtual Reality and 3D User Interfaces (VR), pp. 1729–1732. IEEE (2019)

29. Otte, A., Schneider, D., Menzner, T., Gesslein, T., Gagel, P., Grubert, J.: Evaluating text entry in virtual reality using a touch-sensitive physical keyboard. In: 2019 IEEE International Symposium on Mixed and Augmented Reality Adjunct (ISMAR-Adjunct), pp. 387–392. IEEE (2019)

30. Pham, D.M., Stuerzlinger, W.: Hawkey: efficient and versatile text entry for virtual reality. In: 25th ACM Symposium on Virtual Reality Software and Technology, pp. 1–11 (2019)

31. Pick, S., Puika, A.S., Kuhlen, T.W.: Swifter: design and evaluation of a speech-based text input metaphor for immersive virtual environments. In: 2016 IEEE Symposium on 3D User Interfaces (3DUI), pp. 109–112. IEEE (2016)

32. Pietroszek, K.: Raycasting in Virtual Reality, pp. 1–3. Springer, Cham (2018). https://doi.org/10.1007/978-3-319-08234-9_180-1

33. Rajanna, V., Hansen, J.P.: Gaze typing in virtual reality: impact of keyboard design, selection method, and motion. In: Proceedings of the 2018 ACM Symposium on Eye Tracking Research and Applications, pp. 1–10 (2018)

34. Schneider, D., et al.: Reconviguration: reconfiguring physical keyboards in virtual reality. IEEE Trans. Visual. Comput. Graph. **25**(11), 3190–3201 (2019)

35. Shapiro, S.S., Wilk, M.B.: An analysis of variance test for normality (complete samples). Biometrika **52**(3/4), 591–611 (1965)

36. Speicher, M., Feit, A.M., Ziegler, P., Krüger, A.: Selection-based text entry in virtual reality. In: Proceedings of the 2018 CHI Conference on Human Factors in Computing Systems, pp. 1–13 (2018)

37. Walker, J., Li, B., Vertanen, K., Kuhl, S.: Efficient typing on a visually occluded physical keyboard. In: Proceedings of the 2017 CHI Conference on Human Factors in Computing Systems, pp. 5457–5461 (2017)

38. Wang, C.Y., Chu, W.C., Chiu, P.T., Hsiu, M.C., Chiang, Y.H., Chen, M.Y.: Palm-type: using palms as keyboards for smart glasses. In: Proceedings of the 17th International Conference on Human-Computer Interaction with Mobile Devices and Services, pp. 153–160 (2015)

39. Wu, C.M., Hsu, C.W., Lee, T.K., Smith, S.: A virtual reality keyboard with realistic haptic feedback in a fully immersive virtual environment. Virtual Reality **21**(1), 19–29 (2017)

40. Xu, W., Liang, H.N., He, A., Wang, Z.: Pointing and selection methods for text entry in augmented reality head mounted displays. In: 2019 IEEE International Symposium on Mixed and Augmented Reality (ISMAR), pp. 279–288. IEEE (2019)

41. Yang, Z., Chen, C., Lin, Y., Wang, D., Li, H., Xu, W.: Effect of spatial enhancement technology on input through the keyboard in virtual reality environment. Appl. Ergon. **78**, 164–175 (2019)

42. Yi, X., Yu, C., Zhang, M., Gao, S., Sun, K., Shi, Y.: Atk: enabling ten-finger freehand typing in air based on 3D hand tracking data. In: Proceedings of the 28th Annual ACM Symposium on User Interface Software & Technology, pp. 539–548 (2015)

43. Yu, C., Sun, K., Zhong, M., Li, X., Zhao, P., Shi, Y.: One-dimensional handwriting: inputting letters and words on smart glasses. In: Proceedings of the 2016 CHI Conference on Human Factors in Computing Systems, pp. 71–82 (2016)

44. Yu, D., Fan, K., Zhang, H., Monteiro, D., Xu, W., Liang, H.N.: Pizzatext: text entry for virtual reality systems using dual thumbsticks. IEEE Trans. Visual. Comput. Graph. **24**(11), 2927–2935 (2018)

45. Yumura, T., Nakamura, S.: Augmented typing: augmentation of keyboard typing experience by adding visual and sound effects. In: Asian CHI Symposium 2019 (2019)

Co-watching 360-Films in Nursing Homes

Anders Lundström[1,2(✉)], Sharon Ghebremikael[2], and Ylva Fernaeus[2]

[1] Umeå University, Umeå, Sweden
Anders.lundstrom@umu.se
[2] KTH Royal Institute of Technology, Stockholm, Sweden
{andelund,sharong,fernaeus}@kth.se

Abstract. This work investigates experiences and practical aspects of co-located and co-watched 360-videos in head mounted displays by groups of older people at nursing homes. In a study involving 19 residents at two different nursing homes, co-watching screenings were arranged with 360-videos produced in the local area by filmmakers. Data was collected through non-participant observation and semi-structured interviews with the participants. Input from nurses and facilitators were also collected. We found this to be a much appreciated, feasible, and enjoyable immersive experience improving short-term well-being, expressed through (e.g.) new conversations, pride in participation, and spontaneous movements. However, the value of co-watching was mainly captured for residents who already knew each other, and we found limited indications of virtual co-presence. We further recognized the value of the videos themselves and the desire for new 360-video experiences. But also, a need for better headsets suitable for older people and shared use at nursing homes to avoid social isolation due to the introduction of VR technology.

Keywords: 360-films · Virtual reality · Nursing homes · Co-watching

1 Introduction

Social isolation and loneliness are well-recognized health problems among older people [22, 30]. To prevent these issues nursing homes typically arrange social activities. However, limited and restricted mobility still lowers the sense of life quality, simply through the lack of new experiences and limited variety of environments and happenings to experience. Notably, although not our focus, the situation has worsened by the current and ongoing Covid-19 pandemic. Within the era of social distancing as prescribed by the pandemic, older citizens are like never before isolated with limited activities. To counter these issues, a broad range of new technologies are being explored and tested.

This work concerns an intervention conducted by Swedish filmmakers in collaboration with the caregiver Tiohundra in Norrtälje municipality in Sweden. Using short 360-videos recorded in the local area, the aim was to improve the quality of life of the older people living at the nursing homes through new social virtual experiences. Examples of films featured were a boat trip in the archipelago, a canoe ride in a local

© IFIP International Federation for Information Processing 2021
Published by Springer Nature Switzerland AG 2021
C. Ardito et al. (Eds.): INTERACT 2021, LNCS 12932, pp. 502–521, 2021.
https://doi.org/10.1007/978-3-030-85623-6_30

canal, a fortress, an art walk, and the fascinating lemurs at a nearby zoo. This case has conceptual similarities to The Photostroller by Gaver et al. [19], though their design exploration concerned navigation of FIckr images rather than 360-video VR content.

The purpose of this work was to study how co-watched 360-films are experienced among older people living in nursing homes, as well as practical aspects and the feasibility of facilitating 360-video screenings at nursing homes. Co-watching, in this case experiencing short 360-videos in a group setting, presumes that several residents are watching synchronously and co-located in a room. This is novel research as there is generally little research on experiences of 360-videos viewed in HMDs, particularly in contexts such as nursing homes. Although some research has been done on co-watching regular films in VR on a virtual TV [21, 35], none of these studies have looked at 360-videos, which is a very different media covering the whole field of view in all directions. This allows for looking around as if being in a real environment. Furthermore, the medium is different to TV since everyone wears an HMD and is therefore visibly shielded from each other.

Using non-participant observation, we followed five screenings with 19 participants at two different nursing homes. The screenings were facilitated and arranged by the nurses. Without intervention we filmed these screenings and afterwards we interview the participating residents in groups. Post screenings, we also collected input from other stakeholders such as nurses and head of divisions at the nursing homes. Our overall aim was to examine how this technology played out when residents co-watched synchronized 360-videos in head mounted displays (HMDs) as a social group activity. The recorded data was thematically analysed focusing on practical implications and experiences, feasibility, and potential improvements regarding setup and design.

The project has received substantial attention in Sweden, which has caused a widespread interest at other nursing homes. Currently, without our involvement, the approach is spreading to new nursing homes and municipalities in Sweden.

2   Background

Virtual Reality (VR) is a well-established research area in HCI, concerned with methods that let people take part of three-dimensional visual material using different types of stereoscopic displays, a topic that has been explored from an artistic and technical standpoint ever since the 1950s [55].

2.1   VR in Medical and Clinical Settings

In the medical domain, there are several dedicated centres and programs for VR-based treatment methods, such as the VR Medical Center[1] and the VR treatment program at Duke University[2]. Examples of applications include pain management for adults [1, 23, 33, 45] and children [4], post-stroke rehabilitation [31], treatment of stress-related disorders [6], tinnitus [32], balance impairment [43], intellectual disabilities [9],

---

[1] http://www.vrphobia.com/.

[2] http://psychiatry.duke.edu/divisions/general-psychiatry/virtual-reality-therapy-phobias/.

dementia [22], exposure-based cognitive behaviour therapy (CBT) [42] for self-treatment of spider phobia [11, 37], rehabilitation of neck injuries [13], fear of heights [16, 49], social phobia [26], fear of flying [39], and PTSD for war veterans [48]. Studies have shown that VR can save time and lead to more effective exposure therapy [34] in safe and controlled environments [47]. There is also evidence that cognitive behaviour therapy using VR is an attractive entry to real environments [29]. VR has also been used for education in dental [50] and medical [46] school where simulators allows student to practice procedures without human subjects and less supervision.

The above examples are based on systems where 3D graphics have been produced specifically for a clinical case. However, immersive 360° videos are also considered a form of VR [2]. Similar to 3D graphics-based VR, 360-films [30] are experienced via head-mounted displays (HMDs), but are based on real recorded video footage instead of computer-generated graphics. Recently, several research groups have, like us, experimented with this new media format in various applied interactive settings [8, 27, 58]. Examples from the healthcare domain include preparing patients for anaesthesia [53], MRI scanning [3] and exposure therapy [17].

One technical limitation of VR [18] is the limited horizontal view. In newer HMD's, the field-of-view (FOV) is usually limited to around 110° [61]. Another limitation is network delays, such as transmission of data which could cause delays in an experience, especially when users are in different geographical locations [18].

2.2 VR and Related Technology for Older Adults

HCI research in relation to older adults are diverse. For example, there are studies focusing on different methods of digital game design for older adults [24], and studies focusing on using multimodal interfaces to allow users to communicate with their social network [14]. In healthcare, HCI for older adults is used as an intervention for, e.g. cognitive training to slow down deterioration of cognitive function [65] or to encourage physical movement and counteract loneliness through games [10].

Examining the use of VR in a group setting, one study [15] investigated how the use of VR, by older adults in assisted living communities, over a two-week period of time might contribute to the residents social and emotional well-being. The study consisted of two groups, the control group watched the same content on a regular TV, the other group co-watched virtual TV using HMD's. The VR group was reported less socially isolated, being less likely to show signs of depression, experiencing positive effects more frequently, and feeling better about their overall well-being.

A case study [40] showed that the first encounter with VR-glasses elicited positive feedback and an overall positive experiences in long-term care facilities in Austria. Furthermore, the residents reported being interested in the technology and desired to see different types of nature scenes in Austria. Another study [57] examined how the well-being of older adults could be improved with VR and found that the experience stimulated positive emotions, triggered memories, and led to discussions. However, it only partially affected the participants' measured subjective well-being (SWB). The weight of the HMD have also been highlighted as a concern when designing to enhance the virtual reality presence for older people [36].

Wallace, Wright et al. [62] has identified characteristics of anchoring, capturing and supporting sense of self and connecting relationships to work as guides within design for personhood, particularly for people with dementia. Personhood in dementia is distinguished by focusing on the immediate social circle becoming active in maintaining their sense of self. One conclusion was that while reminiscence is seen as a potential value of digital technologies, there is a risk that looking back can be perceived as of loss of self and what has been lost. Hence, they emphasize on the importance to focus on the present and imagined futures as well as remembering the past. In an associated study, Wallace et al. [63] found that in dementia, possessions including places, groups and local culture, are essential in preserving parts of a person's sense of self and this can be supported by the ones in proximity (e.g. staff at nursing home) finding "ways in" to the person with dementia. This means that design needs to encourage conversations in which the people with dementia can share their knowledge and expertise.

Hodge et al. [22] has studied VR-experiences for people with dementia and their caretakers to outline implications for design and use in future experiences. They found that the weight and the fit of the HMD is of concern for the participants and that they wanted to share the experience with their caretakers. The authors suggest that the latter can be helped by having caretakers follow their experience on an additional screen displaying the same view. Another finding was that it is important to personalize the experience to the preferences of the user.

A related non-VR study [19] used a device called the Photostroller, designed for older people at care homes. It showed continuous slideshow of pictures from predefined categories with the aim to support older people's experiences with pleasure, engagement and sociability, while allowing for diversities by designing for flexibility in interpretation. They found that the elderly was happy with drifting along with an ambiguous slideshow that allowed an openness to reminisce and socialize about their own memories rather than prescribed and closed topics.

2.3 Co-watching and Co-location

The act of watching film together, e.g., on TV or YouTube, can be described with different, yet not always synonymous terms. In the present study, the term co-watching will be used to describe the act of a group watching something synchronized. The research done on co-watching has mainly focused on watching TV (long formats) [5, 38] and watching online videos (shorter formats) [59]. In terms of online videos, there are systems with the purpose to enable co-watching, such as Zync [52], by allowing people to watch videos synchronized.

In this study, we focus on co-watching of 360-films in VR in a co-located setting. Co-location, according to according to the Merriam-Webster, means to "be located together", this may both concern physical or virtual co-location. In a virtual environment, it can be described as the subjective "sense of being there" [36] together as if it was reality through "virtually generated streams of sensory information" [51]. Perceiving co-location in virtual environments hence also entails perceiving co-presence with others, to sense others presence. We define a co-watching experience – as different to a watching experience – in VR as the perceived experience of virtually watching a 360-film together, in opposition to experience a film in isolation.

One study explored the co-watching process and suggested that co-watching was a way for people to manage "other's impressions of themselves" [54]. The results also indicated that co-watching could alter the engagement and intentionality depending on, for instance, where the users are located (e.g., public space). Another study [35] showed that co-watching using an HMD at-a-distance was preferred over watching TV at-a-distance. The participants were co-located and could perceive each other through virtual representations. However, note that they watched a virtual "regular" TV set inside the virtual environment and not 360-films – which is the focus of this study. Therefore, they did not test the increased immersion that 360-films offers.

In a related study [21] on watching regular TV inside a virtual environment, the struggle to communicate while wearing a HMD and how it can create a social barrier was recognized. In the study, users could see each other in a 360° virtual space sitting around a table and was represented with 2D video streams in which they all wore HMDs as captured by the camera. The study found that the framework helped provide high immersion and co-presence, but it acknowledged that there is still a great deal left to work on. However, this approach may not be suitable for 360-films as the others representation would occlude the film.

Fig. 1. Example pictures from two screenings in which residents were watching synchronized 360-films.

3   Method

In order to study the experiences, challenges and practicalities around facilitating older people to co-watch 360-films for increased wellbeing, a study at two nursing homes was devised. The study consisted of five screenings (see Table 1 for group and resident coding and Fig. 1 for context) with 19 residents in which they co-watched one to three 360-films using HMDs. Data was collected using non-participant observations [64], video, and semi-structured interviews [20]. This data was then thematically analyzed [7]. We also collected input from six nurses and four head of divisions through surveys and group discussions. Additionally, we interviewed a film consular involved in the screenings and a playmaker who had done 360-films screenings with about 50–70 nursing home residents. Finally, to determine the extent the 360-medium was used we analyzed residents head rotations.

The data was collected during what we refer to as *screenings* and consisted of a preliminary survey, screenings of the films, and interviews. Five screenings were arranged on three separate occasions at two different nursing homes during a one-month period. Different residents and nurses were involved in all screenings. One nursing home was located in the center of the town Norrtälje with a population of 22000. The other nursing home was in the small town Rimbo with a population of 5000. The size of the groups varied across the screenings (2–8 residents/screening). Prior to the VR-screenings, the residents filled out a short preliminary survey with background questions such as age, gender and information about their technological habits.

Fig. 2. The HMD Oculus Go. Multiple devices were used, and they were connected through the Showtime VR application, controlled by nurses using a tablet or smartphone.

Non-participant Observation, Video Recordings and Displayed 360-Films. Non-participant observation [64] is a method where the object is to gather data without the observer participating in the activities being observed. This can be conducted with the observer either being present in the natural setting of the activity or not, in our study a researcher was present. The screenings were facilitated by trained nurses. This included fitting the headset onto the residents, getting the settings right, starting films, supporting, and engaging the residents throughout the screenings. The residents were seated during the screenings. Each screening was video recorded with consent.

The number of screened 360-films varied in the different screenings. The nurses were familiar with the films prior to the screenings. During the screenings the nurses could follow what the residents was seeing on a separate screen. All showed 360-videos were recorded in the local area and were filmed by Film Stockholm. The films used was a boat trip to Norrtälje archipelago (F1), lemurs at Skansen Zoo (F2), a guided tour at Siaröfortet (F3, underground mountain fortress), an art exhibition/walk (F4), and a canoe ride on the Åkersberga canal (F5). Table 1 provide an overview of films screened in each screening along with resident codes and video lengths.

Oculus Go and Viewing Platform. The head mounted device (HMD) that was used in this study was the Oculus Go (see Fig. 2). This HMD's is designed to be worn with glasses [41]. Focus adjustments is limited to moving the HMD itself for the best possible experience. However, it is possible to purchase tailored prescription lenses for Oculus Go, but this was not possible within this study as it requires prior knowledge about resident's visual defects. To be able to watch videos synchronized, the third-party application Showtime VR was used. Showtime VR allows a facilitator to control and start synchronized videos on multiple devices through either a tablet or smartphone.

Table 1. Resident coding (with gender and age), group composition and films watched

Group	Resident code (gender, age)	Films screened
G1	P1 *(M, 84)*, P2 *(F, 77)*, P3 *(M, 88)*	F1, F2
G2	P4 *(M, 93)*, P6 *(F, 85)*, P8 *(F, 90)*	F1, F2
G3	P9 *(F, 64)*, P10 *(F, 82)*, P11 *(F, 75)*, P12 *(F, 87)*, P13 *(F, 89)*, P14 *(F, 89)*, P15 *(F, 78)*, P16 *(F, 84)*	F3, F4, F5
G4	P17 *(F, 55)*, P18 *(F, 79)*, P19 *(M, 81)*	F3, F4, F5
G5	P20 *(M, 78)*, P21 *(M, 78)*	F1, F2

F1 – Boat trip (7:00 min), F2 – Lemurs at zoo (7:30 min), F3 – Guided tour at fortress (5:20 min), F4 – Art exhibition/walk (7:15 min), F5 – canoe ride (7:20 min)

Interviews. After the screening, semi-structured group interviews [20] was held to capture experiences and thoughts around co-watching 360-films. The questions were based on four aspects: feelings, group connection, technology and user experience.

Residents. In total 21 residents (P1-P21) took part in the study over five screenings. However, two residents (P5, P7) dropped out early so only 19 residents were included, 13 women and 6 men. The residents were aged between 55 to 93 years (average 81 years). In this paper we refer to our participants primarily as 'residents' of a nursing home or 'older people'. While these residents are typically aged over 65 and considered 'older adults', some of our residents – and other residents at nursing homes – are, due to medical conditions, aged under 65. Moreover, while our participants are predominantly aged over 65, they may not identify as 'old'. Twelve residents (63,2%) had owned a computer and six had owned a smartphone.

Thematic Analysis. A thematic analysis [60] was used to get a direct understanding [64] of the residents experiences and the screenings in its natural element by identifying and analyzing patterns [7]. The second authors initially conducted a cursory analysis by listening to and transcribing the interviews. This was used to identify more prominent and recurrent themes. With preliminary themes identified, deeper analysis and validation was made independently by the first author. No other coders were involved.

Post-screening Follow-ups with Stakeholders. Several activities were performed to follow-up on the nurses, their head of divisions, one so called playmakers, and one film consular. All involved nurses (N = 6) discussed their experience and thoughts in smaller groups. The heads of division (N = 4) answered a survey, and interviews was conducted with the Playmaker and film consular.

Post-Analysis of HMD Head Rotations. To quantify how much residents looked around in the virtual environment we performed a video analysis of their head movements during the screenings. The purpose was to determine the degree the medium was used. If not actively used the added value of the medium could be questionable. The analysis was done by scrubbing the videos back and forth looking at each resident's HMD rotations. We marked each resident approximate total HMD rotation horizontally in degrees. All residents were classified as active, or passive, based on how much they looked around. Active classification was determined for frequent movements regardless of the magnitude of the rotation, this was obvious when scrubbing the film. Infrequent movements with long duration without movement was classified as passive.

4   Results

Here we summarize the findings from the study around five themes: general experiences and ideas expressed regarding 360-videos as a resource for enriching of everyday life, issues related specifically to the use of HMDs, participants sense of immersion and togetherness while co-watching, and finally, follow-up reflections by nurses, facilitators of the screenings as well as people involved in the technical production.

4.1   General Experiences

Before the experience no residents expressed having any prior expectations. The general interest was to explore something new. After the screenings were finished, many expressed positive experiences such as it being fantastic (P2, P6, P17), wonderful (P15), exciting (P18), happiness (P1). In fact, no one had any adverse comments. Overall, the experience was highlighted as captivating and more intense than simply watching a regular movie on a TV (P10, P15), comparable to IMAX but in a smaller size (P10).

For several residents, the experience prompted old memories that triggered feelings and even bodily sense perceptions. For instance, P17 could strongly recall the smell of a salt mine only by watching the film from the underground fortress (F3):

> *"when she walks into that mine you could actually smell it [...]. I haven't been to that mine, but what I could smell was like a salt mine [...] which I have been in many times. That smell is what I felt"*

Another resident (P4) was familiar with the area in the boat trip film (F1), which led to reminiscing previous boat trips, places visited, and boats previously owned. Notably, the boat trip film was strongly emotional for group G5, so much that P20 cried after taking of the HMD in pure enjoyment over being able to revisit these waters he had visited earlier in his life. Both P20 and P21 was anglers. Post the screening P20 and P21 talked about (e.g.) where the best fishing waters were in the area and what fish species most easily takes the bait, indicating a social value post the screening as it led to deeper conversations not covered but rather triggered by the 360-film.

Several residents expressed a desire for more videos and experiences. Their requests included previously visited areas and places. However, many rather desired to visit places that they never had the chance to see before, to go on new adventures. One example is how P1 wanted to visit particular Swedish mountains as his wife was born there and he had never been there. Another resident (P19) openly said that he really wanted to see things and places that he never had seen before, as if he was urging for new experiences and adventures, connotating possibilities no longer practically possible in real life at the nursing home. Other common suggestions circled around nature, and many residents were quite detailed and vivid in their suggestions, such as birds chirping (P13) and colorful forest sceneries with blueberries and lingonberries (P20).

One positive aspect of the experience was that it provided the opportunity to simply experience new technology. This was mentioned as technology that they have heard about on TV or in newspapers, but never had gotten access to. Residents highlighted that they are used to adopt new technology as they have experienced advances in technology throughout their entire life. However, recent developments had been difficult to catch up with. The value of this experience – in itself – was perhaps best expressed by P8, in which we could sense the excitement and curiosity:

> *"it's that we've been following [technology] during our lifetime and a lot has happened. So, to get to experience something I've only heard about was fun!"*

In our analysis, we also associated P8s statement with a sense of preserved dignity and the sense of staying relevant with present age. P4 was thinking in similar paths and implied that this type of expanding experience should be an everyday element to maintain well-being through smaller and reoccurring portions of new experiences:

> *"You, of course, get happier, that's certain. A little while every morning"*

4.2 Experiences and Issues Specific to the Head-Mounted Displays

Since the HMD was an integral part of the experience, one question asked to the residents after the screening was how it felt to wear it, and if they experienced any difficulties. The majority (14 out of 19) of the residents did not express any issues in comfort or otherwise felt that it affected their experience. However, five experienced some noteworthy problems. First, three residents (P9, P16, P18) expressed that they encountered visual problems during the screening and that the films looked blurry. Notably, all three were wearing glasses. For instance, P18 elaborated:

> *"I got used to it […]. It was blurry, maybe it has something to do with my eyes or my glasses […] but it always had that little tremble"*

It is unclear exactly what P18 experienced and what she meant by "tremble", but 360-vidoes often flickers a bit when moving the head fast or if the video quality is either low, or too high, for the HMD to handle. However, it is important to highlight that most residents wearing glasses did not explicitly state any visual problems or discomfort.

Another concern was for P3 who also expressed having severe problems seeing, saying: *"You could not see anything!"*. However, looking at the recorded video it was evident that the resident had trouble holding his head up, indicating that the HMD was too heavy. The result would be that P3 was looking down on the ground in the videos, where also a black circle was places to mask the camera stand, and hence there was little to see. Despite this, P3 did not report any discomfort using the HMD. Similarly, P10 stated that the HMD was too heavy and P1 was observed to have difficulties with the weight of the HMD.

Another practical problem concerned how P1 found it weird that *"you could not blow your nose"* when being in the virtual environment. In the video material, it is also evident how P1 is trying to blow his nose but not managing to do so because of the HMD covering his nose.

4.3 Immersion and Togetherness While Co-watching

As regards the social aspects of co-watching 360-videos in HMDs, almost all residents expressed paying no attention towards other residents in the room, indicating a low level of perceived virtual co-location and co-presence. Hence, a limited sense of a virtual co-watching experience. As regards to immersion, seven residents explicitly noted that they felt as if they really were in the 360-films being viewed, immersed and present in the virtual environment. The focus was clearly on digesting and experiencing the films as a strong medium which overshadowed the physical presence of others in the room. One illustrative example was expressed by P9:

> *"I was just looking at what was in front of me [in the HMD], not thinking too much about what was happening around me [in the physical room]" (P9)."*

On a group level, in the second group, G2, it could be seen that during that screening there was a lot of sounds and commotion around them, apart from the screening, but we observed no distractions or breaking of immersion. This could also be said for quieter groups, residents were focused during the screening and immersed in the virtual environment. The residents in G3 and G4 spent almost the whole screening being completely quiet, except for initial sporadic comments on how *"cool"* it was. From an observation point they all appeared to be inside their own little bubbles.

As regards being immersed in VR, some weird expressions of feelings were recorded. First, P10 explained how she felt a sudden urge to ask a question to the guide in the film but then *"realized that there was no [real] guide here!"*, indicating a high degree of presence and immersion in the film.

When asked if they thought it was better to watch together in a group or if it made any difference to the overall experience, the consensus during this first experience with VR was that it did not make much difference (all except P20 and P21). Three residents (P4, P17, P18) explicitly stated that they were so absorbed by the environment presented in the film that they forgot about the social surroundings in the physical room. For instance, a sense of being *"in the archipelago"* (P4), being *"in your own little world"* (P18) or being *"just me there"* (P17).

However, in post follow-up, it became apparent that these responses were affected by how well the residents knew each other. In groups where they knew each other (G1 and G5), they commented on the films and socialized more during the screening. This contrasted with the other groups (G2, G3 and G4) composed by people not knowing each other, in which remarkably less communication took place. Group G5, was also the only group that stated that the experience was better and more enjoyable when sitting in a group. These gentlemen new each other well prior to the screening. Here expressed through a dialogue between two residents:

> *"you can actually talk about [what's happening] and that does add something".* *(P20)*
>
> *"Yeah, I think that it's good, it gets better by not sitting by yourself" (P21)*

Not knowing what the other residents were looking at created a case in group G1 where P2 was trying to get P3 to look at a specific thing in the film. Calling out *"look over there"* while pointing. This created some confusion, as P3 had no idea where to look, as no virtual indicators were directing attention towards the object in question. While there was only one explicit instance of this, there were indications observed that this could have been a social hindrance for a common social experience also in other groups. For instance, we recorded several instances were dialogues caused other residents to look around as if searching for the objects or happening in question.

4.4 Video-Analysis of HMD Movements

The Oculus Go have 101° field of view (FOV). So, a resident turning 180° takes advantage of approximately 280° of the 360-film. In the study, 16 residents rotated their HMD 90° or more, thus taking advantage of at least 190° of the 360-film. One rotated the HMD 120° (seeing 220°), two rotated 135° (seeing 235°), five rotated 180° (seeing 280°), and one even 210° (seeing 310°). All these 16 residents were classified as actively looking around. Interestingly, the remaining three residents all rotated less than 90° and were also classified as passive in their head movements, bordering to almost no head movements at all. Two rotated as little as 40° (seeing 140°) and one rotated 65° with very few movements overall. These three (all older males) had severe mobility issues and were the only residents in wheelchairs.

4.5 Follow-Up with Stakeholders

The nurses were positive to the whole intervention and stated that it was a good addition to otherwise more mundane activities. First, they highlighted positive aspects such as spontaneous movements, particularly among otherwise passive residents. Their impression was that the residents was strongly immersed and that the 360-films evoked many memories. Generally, they noticed a sense of pride among the residents having been invited to try VR for the first time. Regarding the films screened they highlighted that films should be short (maximum 5–10 min) and that more films are needed. Suggestions was to add town walking tours, the main square, churches, seasonal happenings such as when cows are let out for summer bait, other specific local places, as well as films of elephants and lions. Furthermore, they noted some practical issue in managing the films on all the headsets, which required manual transfer to each headset. Therefore, they required that the tablet should be able to download new films and synchronize all headsets to reduce workload. Furthermore, they thought it would be good to be able to record their own films. They also reported some issues with the wi-fi connection in their facilities related to problems downloading films. Furthermore, as Showtime VR needed a little onboarding it would be good with a manual since it was not always straightforward to use.

The head of divisions confirmed much of the nurses' positive picture, and similar issues of using 360-films in nursing homes. Overall, either they wanted to borrow equipment again or purchase their own. In fact, three nursing homes had already purchased their own VR equipment and two others was considering purchasing to continue with screenings. Indicating both a perceived value to the care and the feasibility of distributed large scale VR screenings in these settings. Overall, all respondents leaned towards strongly recommending other nursing homes to test 360-films, simply because of the added value to their operations and the residents.

The playmakers' role was to engage residents through activities, his experiences was not concerned with co-watching experiences, rather individual viewings of 360-films. At the time of the interview, he estimated that he had screened 360-films for around 50–70 elderly (not the same as in this study) prior to the Covid-19 outbreak. Generally, he confirmed the strong immersive experience that 360-films provides for the residents compared to TV, as it situates them in a surrounding context. Some ethical considerations that he mentioned was the importance of dedicating time after screenings to discuss the experience, in particular for people with dementia, in order to manage any triggered negative emotions. He also highlighted that sometimes films need to be chosen together with caregivers or family as it sometimes can be difficult to tell what residents want to see, in particular when dementia is prevalent.

5 Discussion

The purpose of this work was to study how co-watching of 360-films can be experienced among elderly people in nursing homes, as well as practical aspects and the feasibility of such screenings. This is novel research as there is generally little research on experiences of 360-films viewed in HMDs, especially at nursing homes. Although some research has been done on co-watching regular films in VR on a virtual TV [21, 35], none of these studies have looked at 360-films, which is a very different media that covers the whole field of view in all directions, as if being in a real environment.

Overall, all 19 participating residents was strongly positive to the whole experience and expressed a wish to watch 360-videos on a regular basis. Thus, the results overall indicate that this was a pleasant and enjoyable experience that they would like to have recurringly. The majority actively used the medium to the fullest and utilized between 190° and 310° of the 360-films. Regarding how the experience enriched their life, they felt that it was an enriching experience that also made them reminisce and think of old memories that made them happy. The viewings spurred lots of discussions and suggestions for new experiences after the screenings, suggesting that the experience extended in a positive way also after the actual screening. Furthermore, nurses and other actors involved confirmed that it enriched their otherwise ordinary everyday life and led to conversations. Furthermore, they noticed a sense of pride about having gotten the opportunity to try new technology. During screenings nurses also noticed positive spontaneous movements and excitement, also among otherwise passive residents.

Who this experience is shared with also seemingly affects social interactions. The results indicate, overall, that in groups where the residents were familiar with one another there was more interaction, both during and after screenings. Being familiar with each other surely makes it easier to engage in conversations. However, it should be noted that this was a single event for the residents, recurring screenings with the same residents may have led to new bonds forming and increased social activity. This may also be the reason why all groups but one stated that they might as well have watched the movies alone, although they did not rule co-watching as negative. Those who knew each other beforehand was positive about co-watching and said it was better than watching alone. This indicates that co-watching may have positive sides not fully captured in this study due to social barriers caused by not knowing the others beforehand.

While high immersion is at the core of VR [35], little virtual co-presence was captured during the screenings. One reason may be that there were no signs of the others in the virtual environment. Although there was only one explicit, and a few more implicit instances of this, when residents were pointing at or talking about particular objects or happenings in the 360-videos, we believe it highlights that there are missing properties for social interactions to take place and let shared experiences unfold.

Looking at ideas [12, 21] that are available to improve co-watching, finding ways to somehow make it known where the others are present, or as with this current situation where they are looking or pointing, might be difficult to achieve while maintaining and an immersive experience. One issue in the present study was that the users were not represented in the virtual environment, and while it could be sorted with a solution such as the one Gunkel et al. [21] have, the occlusion of the 360-video would likely lead to a less immersive experience. As a comparison, to have someone standing in front of the TV would occlude and disturb the watching experience. This is a clear trade-off and tension between immersion and co-presence somewhat unique to 360-films in which the films are visible in all directions leaving no free directions for additional add-ons. The question is how to unobtrusively make users aware of one another, without losing the level of immersion in the films and avoiding occlusion.

Concerning the residents who experienced difficulties with the HMD, some of the problems could be attributed to being unfamiliar with the device. The problems stated was visual blur and heavy HMD. The problem with the weight of the device is highly individual and a potential workaround is to support the device with their hands. However, HMDs for older people should clearly have less weight – or otherwise be more balanced in their weight not forcing the head forward – to be accessible technology. This is also supported by Hodge et al. [22]. As regards eyewear, according to the manufacturer [41], it should be possible to use glasses with this specific HMD and most residents with glasses did not have any problems. It is possible that the blurry experiences recorded might be due to individual differences and eye conditions. The used HMD offers prescription lenses that would likely solve these issues. However, although this would be a good option for personal HMDs that option appears less appropriate within contexts such as nursing homes where HMDs are shared. Repeated use could potentially make using and adjusting the HMD correctly easier for the few who suffered from these problems. Although this was a marginal problem in the study, care should be taken to avoid social isolation for those who HMDs does not work for. The best option would be to design

HMDs for this target group. However, other options may concern prescription lenses or testing other HMDs for specific individuals, and if this does not work, another possibility could be to participate using a tablet similarly to how the nurses followed the screening. Although the latter would take away much of the immersive 360-video experience, it would potentially lead to better social inclusion.

Another alternative to HMDs would be to use a large curved display. Although this could potentially work and also have co-watching benefits over individual HMDs, this option is not feasible in practice. Both because it would require large investments and it needs dedicated spaces for viewings at the nursery home. In our results we could also see that most of the residents with good mobility rotated their HMD to take advantage of between 190° and 310°, which rather suggests a dome than a curved display, something that is even more unfeasible to host at a nursing home. Furthermore, portable solutions are beneficial for nursing homes as this allows for flexibility and sharing of equipment between different facilities and divisions. As we have seen, the nursing home have the economy and sees the added value to purchase HMDs, indicating that HMDs are indeed a good option despite some minor issues.

Regarding the extent the participants took advantage of the 360-films, our post analysis shows that the vast majority actively looked around. However, three residents were classified as passive and also rotated their heads less. Notably, these were the only residents sitting in wheelchairs and having more severe mobility issues. Although they were still positive to the experience and did indeed look around to some degree, this highlights that people with mobility issues may have more challenges in these contexts. On the other hand, albeit speculative, this medium could potentially also be used for training by naturally inviting to explore in the 360-films. There is research looking at how VR can be used for various types of rehabilitation [e.g. 10, 34], and having the technology already integrated at nursing homes may be an untapped opportunity.

The results indicate that watching these films created an immersive enough feeling that succeeded in shielding from outside disturbances. At least our residents explicitly ruled 360-films as more immersive than TV and sometimes the media blurred the boundary between real and virtual. For instance, when residents occasionally tried to ask questions to people in the 360-films.

The enrichment of the everyday life is a measurement that is, in nature, highly subjective. Subjective, in the sense that what one person found would make their everyday more enjoyable, might be something others liked less. All the residents in the present study expressed their experience to be positive, which could be considered to have made their everyday life better, at least for a moment. The scope of the study was not sufficient to conclude if their everyday life became better for long term. However, the involved nurses noted positive effects and that it was a positive addition to the nursing home to activate and stimulate the residents. Moreover, loneliness and isolation are common within the older population [25, 44], e.g. by not being able to do the same things as before. Afterall, there is evidence [15] that VR experiences in groups can combat some of these problems. Although any type of new experience could be enriching, the quality and suitability of the experience should be considered [24].

For many of the residents the value of their first-time experience seemed to be in the actual content of the films, which for some brought back memories. Experiencing VR-technology enables people, who are no longer able to do things they would have been doing previously (e.g., traveling), to still be able to at least simulate experiencing them again, this time in a virtual environment. It is also a way to see places and happenings not seen before. This appears to be a sought-after value proposition for the residents in this study, as 360-vidos may provide the opportunity to virtually experience places and happenings that no longer is practically possible in their life. This potentially offers opportunities to fill gaps and develop as a human in the autumn of their life. It is our impression that the value of this should not be understated. Another potential is to also offer films purposely made to be a catalyst for discussion and activation through intellectual or emotional stimulation.

In this study, the films used were from places in their vicinity that the majority was highly likely to have already seen, but even if not, the films are open enough to prompt memories. This openness was described by Gaver et al. [19] as an important factor in the design of the Photostroller. Overall, from what could be seen in the screenings, this connection to location seemed to have a positive effect, as it made them revisit memories and places they had not been to in a very long time. Therefore, this type of experiences, where the films have a geographical connection, becomes a way to continue to have a connection to another – or past – part of one's life. However, there is a risk that looking back at old memories could be seen as a loss of self or what has been lost, as described by Wallace et al. [62]. Therefore, it probably wise to also focus on the present and potential future. This could be done by having films that show new places and happenings, something that residents also asked for.

Besides this, results also suggests that the value of the experience is not entirely in the viewing itself, but in a bigger context. It is not only about viewing a film that might bring you back to old memories, but also about the discussion that occurs before, during and after watching. In many ways the experience became a "ticket-to-talk". Similar effects have been reported for both television [56] and robots [28]. This supports the notion that VR experiences cannot replace social interaction [22], and should instead be used as a tool to engage the residents and through that enrich their lives. Additionally, in some way, it is also about keeping older people in the loop with technology and letting them experience it. Perhaps the conversations that came forth in the interviews are our best glimpse of how these 360-videos led to increased well-being since their responses and reactions was so overwhelmingly positive and rich in all its simplicity.

5.1 Reflection on Method

In hindsight, the varying groups sizes may have had an impact on the group interviews. In bigger groups it was hard to dig deeper as some residents tended to agree with more vocal residents. Although we wanted similarly sized groups this was not fully in our control as it was arranged by the nursing homes.

Some aspects in the study, perhaps particularly social aspects, may have benefited from several screenings with each group over a longer period to allow more time for social interactions to form. Preferably with the same facilitator and residents every time. Such study setup could potentially also measure long-term effects.

Another aspect was that the screenings did not allow the residents to freely choose films. This could have influenced the outcome since films might have resonated differently for different residents and thereby affect their experiences.

6 Implications for Design

These key design implications should be considered for co-watching 360-films screenings with elderly at nursing homes.

HMDs Designed for Social Inclusion. Not all older people have the strength to use HMDs. In order to make HMDs accessible for this group this calls for efforts on reducing weight – and weight distribution – not to force the head forward. Furthermore, HMD designs for nursing homes should better account for a broader scope of visual problems. This is a matter of social inclusion.

Content is King. It is important to provide a rich and diverse set of films to allow screenings to be tailored to residents' personal interests, background and memories. This is also important to allow for reoccurring 360-video events in nursing homes. Examples of desired videos as expressed by the participants in this study includes known places, nature and new interesting places and experiences.

Increased Virtual Co-Presence. Although functional, co-watching 360-videos in the form we have studied, lacks the co-presence component that makes the users aware of each other and what they are doing. This could potentially be helped with additional tools (e.g., to allow pointing and better virtual co-presence).

7 Future Work

On a general level, we need more research in the areas of 360-films to better understand the benefits of this medium. We also need follow-ups and long-term studies in nursing homes to better determine the long-term effects of using 360-films at nursing homes. Furthermore, since there was low virtual co-presence among our residents, we need more research on how to increase co-presence when co-watching 360-films and new studies on how that influences the perceived value of co-watching. Finding unobtrusive ways to (1) make it possible for users to know where others are, (2) what they are pointing at, and (3) what they are looking at, could be potential paths forward.

8 Conclusions

The aim of this work was to gain insight into how older residents at nursing homes experience co-watching 360-videos in HMD's by having them watch synchronized 360-videos in groups. But also, to investigate practical aspects for this target group, potential improvements and the feasibility of 360-video screenings in this setting. This study found that 360-videos was experienced positively by the residents and that 360-videos may be a good addition to increase – at least – short-term well-being in nursing homes through new experiences leading to new conversations. This general impression was also confirmed by the professionals working with the residents, who noticed excitement, pride to get to try new technology, and spontaneous movements. The feasibility was acknowledged as several nursing homes purchased own equipment and continues on their own. Showing that a self-going practice was established.

During the study we also captured weight and visual problems with the used HMDs that may lead to social isolation for individuals. This calls for designing better HMDs for older people in these settings, it may be particularly important with adjustable and weight balanced HMDs in settings where HMDs are shared among older people with a vast array of visual and mobility issues.

However, the intended social benefits from co-watching were not immediately obvious and the social interactions observed during screenings was limited, except for residents who knew each other beforehand. Overall, this indicates that other social aspects may strongly influence the perceived value of co-watching. But also, that the potential social value of watching together was hampered as there was little virtual co-presence. We believe that this is particularly challenging for 360-videos and suggest more research on pointing and perceiving the presence and gaze of others.

Finally, we conclude that it is largely the media content itself (the 360-videos) that creates valuable and enjoyable experiences. The films prompted different memories and discussions among the residents based on their previous experiences. We also noted a strong desire and opportunity for this user group to experience new places never experienced in their life. Because of their age and health, these may be out of reach in real life during their remaining time, but possible through this medium. Albeit difficult for young and healthy to imagine, it appears that such experiences could fill important gaps for people with more restricted life situations.

References

1. Ahmadpour, N., et al.: Virtual reality interventions for acute and chronic pain management. Int. J. Biochem. Cell Biol. **114**, June, 105568 (2019). https://doi.org/10.1016/j.biocel.2019.105568
2. Argyriou, L., et al.: Engaging immersive video consumers: challenges regarding 360-degree gamified video applications (2016). https://doi.org/10.1109/IUCC-CSS.2016.028
3. Ashmore, J., et al.: A free virtual reality experience to prepare pediatric patients for magnetic resonance imaging: cross-sectional questionnaire study. JMIR Pediatr. Parent. **2**, 1 (2019). https://doi.org/10.2196/11684
4. Atzori, B., Vagnoli, L., Messeri, A., Lauro Grotto, R.: Virtual reality for pain management among children and adolescents: applicability in clinical settings and limitations. In: Antona, M., Stephanidis, C. (eds.) UAHCI 2018. LNCS, vol. 10908, pp. 15–27. Springer, Cham (2018). https://doi.org/10.1007/978-3-319-92052-8_2
5. Banjo, O.O., et al.: Co-viewing effects of ethnic-oriented programming: an examination of in-group bias and racial comedy exposure. J. Mass Commun. Q. **92**(3), 662–680 (2015). https://doi.org/10.1177/1077699015581804
6. Baños, R.M., et al.: A virtual reality system for the treatment of stress-related disorders: a preliminary analysis of efficacy compared to a standard cognitive behavioral program. Int. J. Hum. Comput. Stud. **69**(9), 602–613 (2011). https://doi.org/10.1016/j.ijhcs.2011.06.002

7. Braun, V., Clarke, V.: Using thematic analysis in psychology (2006)
8. Brown, A., et al.: Subtitles in 360-degree Video. In: Adjunct Publication of the 2017 ACM International Conference on Interactive Experiences for TV and Online video - TVX '17 adjunct. pp. 3–8. ACM Press, New York, New York, USA (2017). https://doi.org/10.1145/3084289.3089915
9. Brown, R., et al.: Design insights into embedding virtual reality content into life skills training for people with intellectual disability. In: Proc. 28th Aust. Comput. Interact. Conf. OzCHI, pp. 581–585 (2016). https://doi.org/10.1145/3010915.3010956
10. Brox, E., et al.: Exergames for elderly: social exergames to persuade seniors to increase physical activity (2011). https://doi.org/10.4108/icst.pervasivehealth.2011.246049
11. Carlin, A.S., et al.: Virtual reality and tactile augmentation in the treatment of spider phobia: a case report. Behav. Res. Ther. **35**(2), 153–158 (1997). https://doi.org/10.1016/S0005-7967(96)00085-X
12. Chan, L., Minamizawa, K.: FrontFace: facilitating communication between HMD users and outsiders using front-facing-screen HMDs (2017). https://doi.org/10.1145/3098279.3098548
13. Daniel, N.: StarGazer: a virtual reality exergame for neck pain rehabilitation (2015)
14. Dias, M.S., et al.: Multimodal user interfaces to improve social integration of elderly and mobility impaired. Stud. Health Technol. Inform. **177**, 14–25 (2012)
15. Eichhorn, C., et al.: Human aspects of IT for the aged population. Appl. Health Assist. Entert. **10927**, 526–545 (2018)
16. Emmelkamp, P.M.G., et al.: Virtual reality treatment in acrophobia: a comparison with exposure in vivo. Cyberpsychol. Behav. **4**(3), 335–339 (2001)
17. Flobak, E., et al.: Participatory Design of VR Scenarios for Exposure Therapy. 1–12 (2019)
18. Fraser, M., et al.: Revealing the realities of collaborative virtual reality (2000). https://doi.org/10.1145/351006.351010
19. Gaver, W., et al.: The photostroller: Supporting diverse care home residents in engaging with the world. In: Conf. Hum. Factors Comput. Syst. - Proc., pp. 1757–1766 (2011). https://doi.org/10.1145/1978942.1979198
20. Given, L.M.: The SAGE Encyclopedia of Qualitative Research Methods. United States, California, Thousand Oaks: SAGE Publications, Inc., Thousand Oaks (2008). https://doi.org/10.4135/9781412963909.
21. Gunkel, S.N.B., et al.: Virtual reality conferencing: multi-user immersive VR experiences on the web. In: Proceedings of the 9th ACM Multimedia Systems Conference, pp. 498–501 ACM (2018)
22. Hodge, J., et al.: Exploring the design of tailored virtual reality experiences for people with dementia. In: Conf. Hum. Factors Comput. Syst. - Proc. 2018-April, 1–13 (2018). https://doi.org/10.1145/3173574.3174088
23. Hoffman, H.G., et al.: Effectiveness of virtual reality-based pain control with multiple treatments. Clin. J. Pain. **17**(3), 229–235 (2001). https://doi.org/10.1097/00002508-200109000-00007
24. Ijsselsteijn, W., et al.: Digital game design for elderly users (2007). https://doi.org/10.1145/1328202.1328206
25. Jakobsson, U., Hallberg, I.: Loneliness, fear, and quality of life among elderly in Sweden: a gender perspective. Aging Clin. Exp. Res. **17**(6), 494–501 (2005). https://doi.org/10.1007/BF03327417
26. Kampmann, I.L., et al.: Behaviour research and therapy exposure to virtual social interactions in the treatment of social anxiety disorder: a randomized controlled trial. Behav. Res. Ther. **77**, 147–156 (2016). https://doi.org/10.1016/j.brat.2015.12.016
27. Kavanagh, S., et al.: Creating 360° educational video. In: Proceedings of the 28th Australian Conference on Computer-Human Interaction - OzCHI '16, pp. 34–39 ACM Press, New York, New York, USA (2016). https://doi.org/10.1145/3010915.3011001

28. Lazar, A., et al.: Rethinking the design of robotic pets for older adults. In: DIS 2016 - Proc. 2016 ACM Conf. Des. Interact. Syst. Fuse. Pp. 1034–1046 (2016). https://doi.org/10.1145/2901790.2901811

29. Liebert, M.A., et al.: Redefining therapeutic success with virtual reality exposure therapy. Cyberpsychol. Behav. 4(3), 341–348 (2001)

30. Lin, Y.-C., et al.: Tell me where to look. In: Proceedings of the 2017 CHI Conference on Human Factors in Computing Systems - CHI '17, pp. 2535–2545. ACM Press, New York, New York, USA (2017). https://doi.org/10.1145/3025453.3025757

31. Luque-Moreno, C., et al.: A decade of progress using virtual reality for poststroke lower extremity rehabilitation: systematic review of the intervention methods. Biomed Res. Int. 2015, February (2015). https://doi.org/10.1155/2015/342529

32. Malinvaud, D., et al.: Auditory and visual 3D virtual reality therapy as a new treatment for chronic subjective tinnitus: results of a randomized controlled trial. Hear. Res. 333(January), 127–135 (2016). https://doi.org/10.1016/j.heares.2015.12.023

33. Mallari, B., et al.: Virtual reality as an analgesic for acute and chronic pain in adults: a systematic review and meta-analysis. J. Pain Res. 12, 2053–2085 (2019). https://doi.org/10.2147/jpr.s200498

34. Maples-keller, J.L., et al.: The use of virtual reality technology in the treatment of anxiety and other psychiatric disorders. Harv. Rev. Psychiatry. 25(3), 103–113 (2018). https://doi.org/10.1097/HRP.0000000000000138

35. Mcgill, M., et al.: Examining the role of smart TVs and VR HMDs in synchronous at-a-distance media consumption. ACM Trans. Comput.-Hum. Interact. 23(5), 1–57 (2016)

36. McGlynn, S.A., Rogers, W.A.: Design recommendations to enhance virtual reality presence for older adults. In: Proc. Hum. Factors Ergon. Soc. Annu. Meet. 61(1), 2077–2081 (2017). https://doi.org/10.1177/1541931213602002.

37. Miloff, A., et al.: Single-session gamified virtual reality exposure therapy for spider phobia vs. traditional exposure therapy: Study protocol for a randomized controlled non-inferiority trial. Trials. 17(1), (2016). https://doi.org/10.1186/s13063-016-1171-1

38. Mora, J.-D., et al.: Television co-viewing in Mexico: an assessment on people meter data. J. Broadcast. Electron. Media. 55(4), 448–469 (2011). https://doi.org/10.1080/08838151.2011.620905

39. Mühlberger, A., et al.: One-session virtual reality exposure treatment for fear of flying: 1-Year follow-up and graduation flight accompaniment effects. Psychother. Res. 16(1), 26–40 (2007). https://doi.org/10.1080/10503300500090944

40. Mühlegger, V.: A first encounter of residents of a long-term care facility with virtual reality glasses. September (2018). https://doi.org/10.20944/preprints201809.0410.v1

41. Oculus: Oculus Go

42. Opriş, D., et al.: Virtual reality exposure therapy in anxiety disorders: a quantitative meta-analysis. Depress. Anxiety 29(2), 85–93 (2012). https://doi.org/10.1002/da.20910

43. Öst, L.-G.: Cognitive behavior therapy for anxiety disorders: 40 years of progress. Nord. J. Psychiatry. 62(sup47), 5 (2008). https://doi.org/10.1080/08039480802315590

44. Paul, C., et al.: Psychological distress, loneliness and disability in old age. Psychol. Health Med. 11(2), 221–232 (2006). https://doi.org/10.1080/13548500500262945

45. Pourmand, A., Davis, S., Marchak, A., Whiteside, T., Sikka, N.: Virtual reality as a clinical tool for pain management. Curr. Pain Headache Rep. 22(8), 1–6 (2018). https://doi.org/10.1007/s11916-018-0708-2

46. Rahm, S., et al.: Performance of medical students on a virtual reality simulator for knee arthroscopy: an analysis of learning curves and predictors of performance (Report). BMC Surg. 16(1), (2016). https://doi.org/10.1186/s12893-016-0129-2

47. Rizzo, A.S.: A SWOT analysis of the field of virtual reality rehabilitation. Presence 14(2), 119–146 (2005)

48. Rothbaum, B.O., et al.: A randomized, double-blind evaluation of D-clycoserine or alprazolam combined with virtual reality exposure therapy for posttraumatic stress disorder in Iraq and Afghanistan War Veterans. Am. J. Psychiatry. **171**(June), 1–9 (2014). https://doi.org/10.1176/appi.ajp.2014.13121625

49. Rothbaum, B.O., et al.: Virtual reality graded exposure in the treatment of acrophobia: a case report. Behav. Ther. **26**, 547–554 (1995)

50. Roy, E., et al.: The need for virtual reality simulators in dental education: a review. Saudi Dent. J. **29**(2), 41–47 (2017). https://doi.org/10.1016/j.sdentj.2017.02.001

51. Sanchez-vives, M.V., Slater, M.: From presence to consciousness through virtual reality. Nat. Rev. Neurosci. **6**(4), 332–339 (2005). https://doi.org/10.1038/nrn1651

52. Shamma, D., et al.: Enhancing online personal connections through the synchronized sharing of online video (2008). https://doi.org/10.1145/1358628.1358786

53. Sulliyan, B.O., et al.: Creating Low-Cost 360-Degree Virtual Reality Videos for Hospitals : A Technical Paper on the Dos and Don'ts. 20 (2018). https://doi.org/10.2196/jmir.9596.

54. Sun, E., et al.: Challenges on the Journey to Co-Watching YouTube (2017). https://doi.org/10.1145/2998181.2998228

55. Sutherland, I.E.: A head-mounted three dimensional display *. 5–10

56. Svensson, M.S., Sokoler, T.: Ticket-to-talk-television: designing for the circumstantial nature of everyday social interaction BT - NordiCHI 2008: Building Bridges - 5th Nordic Conference on Human-Computer Interaction, October 20, 2008 - October 22, 2008. 358, 334–343 (2008)

57. Tahar Aissa, S.: Improving well-being with virtual reality for frail elderly people: A mixed method approach letting them into the three-dimensional world. Independent (2018)

58. Tang, A., Fakourfar, O.: Watching 360° videos together. In: Proceedings of the 2017 CHI conference on human factors in computing systems - CHI '17. pp. 4501–4506. ACM Press, New York, New York, USA (2017). https://doi.org/10.1145/3025453.3025519

59. Thorson, E., et al.: Co-viewing, tweeting, and facebooking the 2012 presidential debates. Electron. News. **9**(3), 195–214 (2015). https://doi.org/10.1177/1931243115593320

60. Vaismoradi, M., et al.: Content analysis and thematic analysis: implications for conducting a qualitative descriptive study. Nurs. Health Sci. **15**(3), 398–405 (2013). https://doi.org/10.1111/nhs.12048

61. VR ARVILab: What do we need to know about HMD?

62. Wallace, J., et al.: A design-led inquiry into personhood in dementia. In: Proceedings of the SIGCHI Conference on human factors in computing systems. pp. 2617–2626 (2013). https://doi.org/10.1145/2468356.2479560

63. Wallace, J., et al.: Enabling self, intimacy and a sense of home in dementia: an enquiry into design in a hospital setting. In: Proceedings of the SIGCHI Conference on human factors in computing system, pp. 2629–2638 (2012). https://doi.org/10.1145/2207676.2208654

64. Wiebe, E.: Encyclopedia of case study research. United States, California, Thousand Oaks: SAGE Publications, Inc., Thousand Oaks (2010). https://doi.org/10.4135/9781412957397

65. Zhuang, J.-P., et al.: The impact of human-computer interaction-based comprehensive training on the cognitive functions of cognitive impairment elderly individuals in a nursing home (2013). https://doi.org/10.3233/JAD-130158

Exploring the Visual Space to Improve Depth Perception in Robot Teleoperation Using Augmented Reality: The Role of Distance and Target's Pose in Time, Success, and Certainty

Stephanie Arévalo Arboleda(✉)(iD), Tim Dierks, Franziska Rücker,
and Jens Gerken

Westphalian University of Applied Sciences, Gelsenkirchen, Germany
{stephanie.arevalo,tim.dierks,franziska.ruecker,jens.gerken}@w-hs.de

Abstract. Accurate depth perception in co-located teleoperation has the potential to improve task performance in manipulation and grasping tasks. We thus explore the operator's visual space and design visual cues using augmented reality. Our goal is to facilitate the positioning of the gripper above a target object before attempting to grasp it. The designs we propose include a virtual circle (Circle), virtual extensions (Extensions) from the gripper's fingers, and a color matching design using a real colormap with matching colored virtual circles (Colors). We conducted an experiment to evaluate these designs and the influence of distance from the operator to the workspace and the target object's pose. We report on time, success, and perceived certainty in a grasping task. Our results show that a shorter distance leads to higher success, faster grasping time, and higher certainty. Concerning the target object's pose, a clear pose leads to higher success and certainty but interestingly slower task times. Regarding the design of cues, our results reveal that the simplicity of the Circle cue leads to the highest success and outperforms the most complex cue Colors also for task time, while the level of certainty seems to be depending more on the distance than the type of cue. We consider that our results can serve as an initial analysis to further explore these factors both when designing to improve depth perception and within the context of co-located teleoperation.

Keywords: Human-robot interaction · Depth perception · Augmented reality · Robot teleoperation · Visual cues · Certainty

1 Introduction

One of the most common tasks in Human-Robot Interaction (HRI) is pick-and-place since it presents a basic interaction for teleoperation of robotic arms.

Electronic supplementary material The online version of this chapter (https://doi.org/10.1007/978-3-030-85623-6_31) contains supplementary material, which is available to authorized users.

C. Ardito et al. (Eds.): INTERACT 2021, LNCS 12932, pp. 522–543, 2021.
https://doi.org/10.1007/978-3-030-85623-6_31

These tasks are common in non-standardized assembly workspaces, where target objects often change in shape and position, which may require the human operator to fine-control (semi-autonomous) robotic arms to succeed in the tasks.

Picking an object can be further segmented into **1) (Coarse) Pointing**, which requires the user to identify the location of a target object and consequently move the gripper of the robotic arm roughly to that location; **2) Positioning**, which requires to align the gripper with the target object to successfully grasp it; and **3) Grasping** then requires the user to move the gripper to the point in space where the object can finally be acquired. While this, at first sight, might sound straightforward, it often requires many trial-and-error attempts from the operator due to misjudgments regarding the position in space of either the gripper or the object. This can lead to precarious situations when handling hazardous material.

The crucial point in this process takes place while positioning the gripper. It might not always be possible for the operator to accurately determine the gripper's position relative to the target object due to the visual perception of distance and object's pose, both factors related to depth perception. Even in co-located scenarios (robot and operator located in the same physical space) operators could have a fixed viewpoint due to physical mobility restrictions, e.g., people with disabilities, or due to environmental limitations, e.g., safety measures due to the manipulation of hazardous materials. As a result, spatial abilities are impeded, hindering the operator to correctly identify the shape, pose, and distance of a target object relative to the gripper and other objects within the workspace.

Augmented Reality (AR) creates opportunities to improve depth perception of real-world objects by enhancing the visual space to provide awareness of their position in the workspace. Some studies present evidence that AR counteracts visual feedback limitations in teleoperation [19,39,53]. Some of these limitations are related to the manner in which humans perceive distance and judge depth. Humans perceive visually the environment through different visual cues (monocular, binocular, dynamic) [14]. These cues can be enhanced through AR and thus refine the visual space. Here, it is important that these cues provide a message that can be clearly interpreted by the observer, avoiding unnecessary extra mental processing due to conflicts among cues [29].

In this paper, we contribute to the exploration of the design space to improve depth perception. Therefore, we first propose three designs of visual cues in AR that systematically build on each other. Each one considers different design elements that could foster depth perception in co-located robot teleoperation and provide a foundation for future HRI designs. Second, we present a systematic experiment investigating the relationship between the design of visual cues, the operator's distance, and the target object pose to evaluate the advantages and downsides of each visualization concept. Third, we include the operator's perceived certainty during picking as a novel measure to better understand if and how· objective measures of performance such as success (certainty accuracy or effectiveness) and time (efficiency) correlate with the subjective certainty of the operator.

2   Background

We first review theoretical foundations of visual perception regarding distance and depth, the use of AR to improve depth perception in robot teleoperation, and the role of time, success, and certainty in visual perception.

2.1   Visual Perception of Depth

Visual perception can be defined as a complex representation of the visual world, where features of objects in the environment are collected visually to then be interpreted through computations in multiple areas of the brain [49]. In order to visually determine the depth of objects, factors such as size, shape, and distance are determinants to gain an accurate perception of objects in the environment [24]. Brenner and Smeets [9] present the relation between size and distance as straightforward, e.g., smaller sizes provide hints about how distant an object might be, while shape and distance present a more complex relation. Distance can compromise determining the shape of objects, e.g., problems in accurately determining the shape of far-away objects. Further, perceived objects' shape varies depending on the manner that they are positioned (pose). Here, having different perspectives acquired by motion assists with accurately determining an object's shape.

Within the visual space, it is relevant to explain the perceived location. This is understood as the perception of direction and distance from the observer's viewpoint (egocentric distance) or the distance between two external points (exocentric distance) [34]. Related to perceived location, the space layout of a person is determinant for evaluating distance and depth as farther distances compromise the manner how objects in the surroundings are perceived. Cutting and Vishton [12], divide the layout of space around a person into three: personal space (within 2 m), typically a stationary working space; action space (from 2 m to 30 m), which is the moving and public action space; and vista space (>30 m). Different authors agree that humans underestimate egocentric distances (distance relative to the observer) in the real-world [33,34]. Distance can be evaluated through different measures, e.g., verbal reports, walking around a target, visually matching distances to a familiar one, and blind walking [47]. It can also be estimated through bisection or fractionation, which consists of determining the midpoint of a distance from the observer's perspective to a target, and specify that bisection does not provide absolute measures of egocentric distances [7].

Humans perceive and interpret distance through a set of visual cues: monocular (perceived using one eye), binocular (perceived using both eyes), and dynamic (perceived by movement) [14]. Nonetheless, interpreting all the cues perceived under some environmental conditions is not a straightforward process. Laramee and Ware [31] describe it as an ambiguity solving process, where different cues need to be primed over others to get an accurate picture of the environment (cue dominance). Further, Howards and Rogers [25] highlight that the reliability of cues is determined by cue average, cue dominance, cue specialization, range extension, and probabilistic models.

Rolland et al. [46] already found a relation between object size and distance in virtual objects displayed in ARHMD. In Mixed Reality (MR) environments, this problem can be not only inherited from the real-world but can be exacerbated [26,40]. Further, El Jaimy and Marsh [14] present a survey on depth perception in head-mounted displays (HMDs) and highlight the importance of evaluating not only depth but also distance perception in virtual and augmented reality environments.

2.2 Designing to Improve Depth Perception in AR Environments

We consider the work of Park and Ha [41] as a keystone to improving depth perception in virtual and mixed reality environments. They provide a classification of visual enhancements techniques that offer spatial information as follows: geometric scaling, understood as the variation of size to provide a distance relationship; symbolic enhancements, which are visual representations that allow creating associations, e.g., a grid surface or ground plane to transfer spatial information; visual cues, which are a combination of monocular cues to improve the perception of depth; a frame of reference that provides a mental model of the environment; and visual momentum, referring to providing perceptual landmarks to reduce visual inconsistency among different displays/scenes. Following this line of research, Cipiloglu et al. [11] grouped a series of methods for depth enhancement in 3D scenes focusing on perspectives, focus, shading and shadows, among others.

Heinrich et al. [21] provided a state-of-the-art overview of visualization techniques using AR for depth perception. They presented different visualization concepts that have been applied to improve depth perception with an emphasis on projective AR without using HMDs. Also, Diaz et al. [13] explored different factors that influence depth perception in AR such as aerial perspective, cast shadows, shading, billboarding, dimensionality, texture, and the interaction of cues. They presented two experiments where they evaluated the effect of these factors in participants' perception of virtual objects' depth relative to real targets. Their results showed that among all their designs, the use of cast shadows improved depth estimation the most. This aligns with other studies [56] that used casting shadows through AR as depth cues. They used pictorial cues (color encoded markers) to provide information about egocentric distance together with shadows and aerial perspective, showing similar results in distance perception.

When aiming to enhance the visual space through AR the work of Kruijff et al. [29] is of particular importance. They identified and classified a series of factors that affect the augmentations related to the environment, capturing, augmentations, display devices, and users. These provide a framework to identify the potential factors that influence depth perception.

2.3 AR for Depth Perception in Robot Teleoperation

Previous studies present evidence that AR diminishes visual feedback limitations in teleoperation by providing additional information to the operator [19,39,52].

Presenting cues through AR could enhance the perception of depth and distance in the real world. Choi et al. [10] present reinforcement of the user's cognitive abilities as the purpose of AR. Moreover, the use of AR for robot control has been found to reduce the mental load in robot programmers [48].

Depth perception is still an issue in MR and teleoperation [10] that invites further exploration. Casting shadows using AR has been used in the teleoperation of aerial robots [53,60] since it has proven to support aerial navigation by improving the spatial relationships between the environment and the aerial robot. Zollman et al. [60] used different techniques that aim to maintain or replicate natural depth cues to design visual hints (waypoints and pathlists) that provide flight-relevant information. In pick-and-place tasks, AR has also been used to present a projection-based AR interface that provides task instructions [18]. Here, shadows have been used to highlight intended target positions and thus provide instructions to operators.

2.4   Certainty, Time, and Accuracy in Visual Perception

Certainty can be defined as a sense of conviction and is considered as a foundation of people's beliefs [42]. In order to achieve "good visual certainty", observers need to consider information that goes beyond monocular, binocular, or motion parallax cues and acknowledge sources of uncertainty, being thus able to predict an outcome [35]. In order to measure the degree of certainty, people need information derived from evidence and time, wherein evidence, in turn, contributes to accuracy [27].

Evidence can be acquired from experience, where certainty plays a pre-and-post-decision-confidence role. Pre-decision confidence relates to the current incoming information and post-decision confidence is the information derived from experience [20]. Also, evidence can be acquired through perceptual evaluation, wherein visual perception has a relevant role. Here, findings of [17] show that the amount of evidence has a positive correlation with accuracy.

Time plays a significant role in relation to attitude certainty. This relation has received special attention in neuroscience. Willis and Todorov [55] shown that a longer period of time allows to form greater impressions of certainty, yet it does not necessarily improve the impression of accuracy. In line with this view, Barden and Petty [4] provided evidence that greater thoughtfulness leads to greater certainty. However, there are controversial results about the influence of time on certainty. Some studies [2,3] associate longer times with lower certainty. Further, Kiani et al. [27] showed that time alone cannot explain fluctuations in certainty but time together with difficulty have a critical role in certainty.

In visual perception, accuracy is bound to the ability to make a good judgment of the visual stimulus, while certainty relates to the ability to make a good judgment on the validity of a perceptual decision [35]. Accuracy has been suggested to be connected to the amount of evidence from the environment that can be collected [44]. Perceived visual certainty can be dissociated from accuracy [35], and adding to that, a line of research suggests that time can also be disassociated from accuracy [27]. Visual certainty is a topic with controversial findings that has several factors that influence it. Barthelme and Mamassian [5] found that visual uncertainty predicts objective uncertainty. Interestingly, Gardelle and Mamassian [16] showed that subjective uncertainty is abstract and task-independent. They compared identical and perceptual different task-trials in succession in a visual discrimination task, e.g. the orientation of a bar, and found no difference between conditions.

3   Exploration of Visual Cues for Co-located Teleoperation

Building on the research mentioned in Sects. 2.2 and 2.3, we present three designs of visual cues to help operators to evaluate distance and depth which in turn could allow to better estimate the position of the gripper relative to a target object for successful grasping. In particular, our designs of visual cues capitalize on previous findings of the effectiveness of cast and drop shadows [13], symbolic enhancements [41], and matching physical and virtual landmarks [60] to provide better awareness of the position of the gripper on the workspace. While some related work has focused on improving depth perception of virtual objects and their interaction in the real-world, we focus our designs on using virtual elements to improve the depth perception of real-world objects. Consequently, all our designs augment the environment through AR using the Microsoft HoloLens. As can be depicted in Fig. 1, each of our designs builds upon the previous one. Thereby, the Extensions include the Circle visual cue and the Colors include both, the Extensions and Circle.

3.1   Virtual Circle Using Cast Shadows (Circle)

In this design, we provide a virtual cue derived from the real-world (the gripper) which in turn acts on the physical world (workspace). We cast the real grip region as a virtual representation of it through a virtual circle. This virtual circle's diameter matches the width of the grip region and is shown right under the real gripper on the workspace, see Fig. 1a. We base our design on previous findings of the efficacy of cast shadows to improve depth perception [13]. Cast shadows can be described as the shadow of an object that is reflected on a different surface [59]. This first design of visual cue is minimalistic and intends to provide a simple and comprehensible hint of the location of the gripper on the workspace.

3.2   Virtual Extensions as a Symbolic Enhancement (Extensions)

In this design, in addition to the Circle, we virtually extend an object from the physical world (the gripper). Based on previous work about symbolic enhancements [41] and considering Walker et al.'s framework for AR in HRI [52], we augment the robot's end-effector, through a virtual elongation of the gripper's fingers. We present three virtual elongations, one at the tip of each finger, and

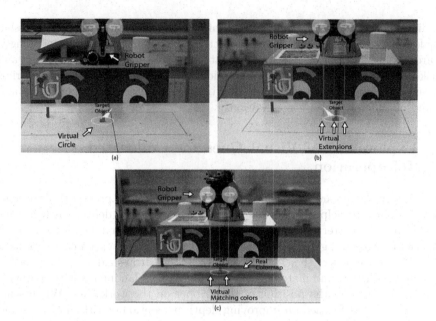

Fig. 1. (a) Circle. (b) Extensions. (c) Colors: Physical color map with matching virtual circles at the end of the Extensions. (Color figure online)

another one rendered at the center of the grip region, see Fig. 1b. These virtual extensions are designed to allow for a better visualization of the exact gripper position on the workspace. Through these visualizations, the operator can determine if the target object is within reach or if there are any potential collisions, e.g., between the fingers and some surface of the target object or other elements in the environment.

3.3 Mixed Reality Color Gradient Using Physical Landmarks (Colors)

Building on the Circle and Extensions, the Colors cues aim to provide a connection to the real-world by matching physical landmarks with virtual ones. This could potentially improve the mapping and alignment between the augmentation and the real-world objects as it provides more information about the spatial arrangement of the environment. Here, we take into account the work of Zollman et al. [60], who explored this connection in flying aerial robots. We considered these findings and applied them to our scenario by providing a real physical landmark that connect the gripper and the workspace.

Our landmark is a physical colormap. It presents 5 different color gradients (6 cm per stripe) that cover the workspace, signaling incremental depth, see Fig. 1c. Our reasoning behind the use of a colormap comes from the problems that have been found of determining with precision a position in monochromatic surfaces, e.g. previous research showed that the human eye loses depth cues on uniform surfaces [29]. Further, the use of colors has proven to be effective to signal depth [56]. Through a colormap, the operator can identify a color in the workspace where a target object is located and then position the gripper with greater precision above it. To facilitate pointing at the target area of the workspace, the cursor also adopts the color of the area that is being pointed at. Additionally, we added small colored circles at the end of the virtual extensions, which adopt the color of the current area.

3.4   Interaction Design for Teleoperation

This research is part of a larger project that takes a closer look at hands-free multimodal interaction. Our interaction design consists of head orientation to point, head yaw for positioning, and voice commands to commit an action. Previous studies have shown that the use of speech and head movements are an intuitive interaction concept for human-robot collaboration in pick-and-place tasks [30]. Further, these modalities are natively supported by the HoloLens, and are common for MR environments. The initial and resting position of the robotic arm can be seen in Fig. 1 and the interaction is explained as follows:

Pointing. The operator sees a white head pointer which moves with the operator's head movements. Once an intended position has been determined, the operator gazes at that position and commits the action with the command "Move". After the command has been recognized, the head pointer turns green in a "pie timer" manner for one second. During this time, the operator can decide to keep (remain still) or modify (change head position) the pointer's position before the gripper starts moving to the selected position on the x,y plane. This helps to counter slight inaccuracies that can result from unintended head movements which can happen while uttering the voice command.

Positioning. Once the gripper is located over the desired position. We placed a set of virtual buttons anchored to the real gripper. These virtual buttons rotate the gripper to the left or right and allow the operator to ensure that the fingers' grasping points match the affordances of the object, see Fig. 1. In addition, the operator can activate a fine control mode through the command "Precision". This fine control is executed through the operator's head yaw, where the gripper moves slowly following the head's yaw. In this mode, we display (on the edges of the circle) an arrow to indicate the direction that the gripper is moving towards.

Grasping. When the operator has determined that the gripper is located at an adequate grasping position, the command "Pick" commits the action of grasping, i.e., the gripper moves with the fingers opened along the z-axis towards the object, stops at 0.5 cm above the tabletop, closes the fingers, and moves back up to the resting position.

4 Study

We present a study with 24 participants that aims at exploring the relationship between the different designs of cues (Circle, Extensions, Colors) and depth-related variables distance (2 m and 3 m) and object pose (clear, ambiguous) when teleoperating a co-located robotic arm. In particular, we looked at measures of effectiveness (success), efficiency (time), and perceived certainty. In the study, participants wore the Microsoft HoloLens to visualize our designs of visual cues while teleoperating a robotic arm.

4.1 Hypotheses

Distance perception of the bare eye has an imminent effect on depth perception. Based on this, we hypothesize that our designs of visual cues will reduce the impact of distance (H1). Similarly, objects' pose can reduce depth perception, we thus hypothesize that our visual cues will reduce the impact of pose (H2). Based on the fact that the individual designs of each visual cue builds systematically on each other, subsequently adding more depth information, we expect a step-wise rise between each of them. This means that the performance with Circle will be exceeded by Extensions and Extensions by Colors for the evaluated metrics (H3). Further, building upon visual perception and certainty, we designed our visual cues provide more information (evidence) about the workspace, which will in turn show a correlation between these two metrics (H4). Specifically, we hypothesize that:

H1. Our designs of visual cues will lead to similar results in grasping time, success, and certainty at 2 m and 3 m.

H2. Our design of visual cues will leading to similar results in success and time but a higher degree of certainty for the clear pose.

H3. Colors will lead to a higher success rate, shorter execution time, and higher perceived certainty compared to Extensions and Circle. Similarly, the Extensions would perform better on those metrics compared to the Circle alone.

H4. Our results will point to a positive correlation between certainty and success rate.

4.2 Participants

We recruited 24 participants among students and university staff with an average age of 28.67 (SD = 7.72). The pre-test questionnaire revealed that 6 participants had previous experience using the Microsoft HoloLens 1 and 11 participants had some experience with robots (not necessarily a robotic arm). One participant reported having red-green colorblindness but did not experience problems in distinguishing the colors used. Participants received 7 euros for their participation.

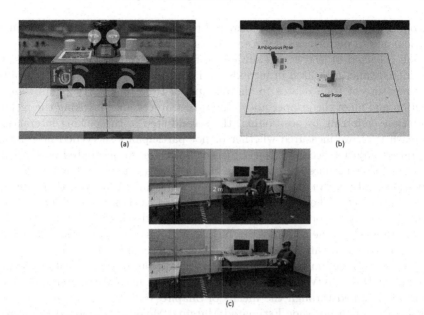

Fig. 2. (a) Experiment set-up for Circle and Extensions. (b) Upper view from the workspace with the target objects. (c) An operator located at different distances from the workspace. (Color figure online)

4.3 Study Design

We designed a full factorial $2 \times 2 \times 3$ within-subject experiment (2 distances $\times$ 2 poses $\times$ 3 designs of visual cues) where participants executed 3 trials per condition, yielding 36 trials per participant and 864 trials in total. The conditions were counter-balanced through a Latin-square design.

Our independent variables were the type of visual cue (Circle, Extensions, Colors), distance (2 m, 3 m), and pose (clear, ambiguous). For distance, we varied the egocentric space between the workspace and the stationary position of the operator (Fig. 2c). We chose 2 m and 3 m as distances to represent realistic co-located scenarios covering the egocentric personal (2 m) and action space (3 m) respectively. We did not vary the size of the object due to kinetic invariance—when an object varies in size it affects how the observer perceives the size and distance of the object [22].

Different poses were achieved by manipulating the position and orientation of an L-shaped target object. To differentiate the poses, we used two objects of the exact same size and shape but with different colors. A green object was deemed as the "clear" pose. It was located roughly in the center of the workspace and oriented in such a way that the shape was fully visible. A red object was deemed as the "ambiguous" pose. It was located in the left corner, almost at the border of the workspace and oriented in such a way that participants could only see one side of the object. We considered this pose ambiguous since it required participants to perform mental rotations (see Fig. 2).

We collected objective and subjective measures. As objective measures, we considered time, measured in seconds, and success, measured as a binary value. Our measure of time relates to the amount of time that participants took to position and align the gripper above the target object until invoking the picking operation—referring to positioning, the second step of the picking interaction. For each trial, we measured whether or not participants succeeded in grasping the target object (success). As a subjective measure, we prompted participants with the following question directly in the HoloLens whenever they invoked the picking operation: "In this position, how certain (in %) are you that you can grasp the object". The percentages were provided as choices on a 7-point scale. Tormala [50] argues for a 7-point scale to measure attitude certainty, as in certain circumstances extreme attitudes can be held with less certainty. Also, qualitative data were collected through a short interview at the end of the study.

We used a mixed-methods approach to evaluate our data. The data were analyzed using RM-ANOVA for time and certainty, as a normal distribution of data could be assumed through the means of Shapiro-Wilk test. For pairwise comparisons (through post-hoc Estimated Marginal Means), we applied Bonferroni corrections to control for Type I errors. For the analysis of the binary variable grasping success, we could not assume a normal distribution and therefore opted for GEE (Generalized Estimating Equations). GEE accounts for correlations within-participants in repeated measures designs and has been commonly used for binary outcome variables [32,57]. To investigate potential associations between our dependent variables (certainty and success/time), we applied Spearman's partial correlation controlling for the effect of our independent variables.

4.4   Task

Our main task simulated a grasping task inspired from manufacturing workspaces. The task comprised of teleoperating the robotic arm to grasp an "L-shaped" object $(4 \times 1 \times 2)$ cm placed at two different positions and with the different poses on the workspace. The operator performed this task at 2 m and 3 m from the workspace, see Fig. 2c. Participants were instructed to remain seated in a comfortable position and avoid movements to the left or right or tilt their heads to change their visual perspective. This instruction helped to evaluate the effects of distance and pose using our designs of visual cues on depth perception.

We performed a pilot test with 3 users to identify potential factors that may affect our experiment. We discovered learning effects due to the position invariance of the target objects during trials. Thus, we moved each object 1 cm apart from the last position for each trial for the experiment, see Fig. 2b.

4.5   Procedure

The experiment took approximately 60 min divided into (1) introduction, (2) calibration, (3) training (4) task, and (5) post-test questionnaires and interview.

(1) During the introduction participants were handed a standardized consent form and pre-test questionnaire. They were briefed about the devices, the objects that they will be interacting with, and the interaction modalities. Also, we showed an explanatory video depicting the interaction techniques, interface, and visual cues. (2) Next, participants calibrated the HoloLens, where the interpupillary distance was recorded for each participant. (3) Then, they proceeded to perform a training task, consisting of teleoperating an industrial robot arm to pick an L-shaped object, similar to the one to be used in the real task but bigger in size, at 1m from the robot. (4) Following, participants executed the experiment. Half of the participants started the task at 2 m and after finishing all designs of cues and pose combinations repeated the same procedure at 3 m. The other half started at 3 m and then at 2 m. For pose and designs of cues, we followed a Latin square distribution. (5) Finally, we carried out a short interview about their experiences.

4.6 Apparatus and Communication

We used a Kuka iiwa 7 R800 lightweight robotic arm with an attached Robotiq adaptive 2-Finger Gripper. Both are controlled via the Kuka iiwa's control unit. For our visual cues and the user interface, we used the Microsoft HoloLens 1, which is equipped with inside-out tracking, an HD video camera, and microphones allowing the use of head movement, speech, and gestures as input options [36]. The HoloLens has a field of view (FOV) of $30° \times 17.5°$ with a resolution of 1268×720 px per eye. The application running on the HoloLens was programmed with Unity 2018.1.2 and the HoloToolkit Plugin [38].

The Kuka iiwa and the HoloLens communicate via the User Datagram Protocol in a local network. The control unit of the Kuka iiwa runs a specially designed back-end program that processes the received messages, moves the robot according to the receiving data, and returns its current status. To communicate position data between devices, we first converted the pose from Unity's left-handed coordinate system to the robot's right-handed one and used common length units (cm). Then, this cartesian position, rotation and velocity is sent to the control unit. This recognizes the command and allows the robot to plan the movement via internal inverse kinematics to then physically move the robotic arm.

A calibration process is important to achieve accuracy when using AR. The HoloLens adjust the hologram display according to the interpupillary distance. When it is not accurate, holograms may appear unstable or at an incorrect distance [37]. Thus, we ran the Microsoft calibration application for each user. Also, in order for the virtual tracking to be transferred to the real world, the position and alignment of the robot must be known in the virtual-world. For this, we use a 2D marker and the camera-based marker detection from Vuforia [45] when starting the application. Since the position of the 2D marker in relation to the robot is known, the position of the robot in the virtual'world can be determined and set as world anchors. The stability of world anchors has been previously evaluated and found a mean displacement error of 5.83 ± 0.51 mm [51]. This is precise enough to handle grasping tasks.

5 Results

5.1 Objective Measures

Time (Efficiency). Analyzing the time spent to perform the tasks, we opted for a RM-ANOVA with the design of cues, distance, and object pose, as independent variables and time as a dependent variable. For time, we used the average across the three trials for each condition. Testing the assumptions with Shapiro-Wilk, the distribution of some residuals showed a slight deviation from the normal distribution. The inspection of QQ-plots as well as skewness and kurtosis analysis, revealed that all residuals in question were skewed in the same positive direction and within an acceptable range [28]. In addition, the literature [6] suggests that a slight deviation from a normal distribution can be handled by ANOVA procedures, which is why we kept this approach. For pairwise comparisons, we refer to the estimated marginal means and report p-values and standard errors.

Results show that there were no significant three-way ($F(2, 46) = 0.225$, $p = .8$) or two-way interaction effects for our independent variables (design of cues per distance $F(2, 46) = 2.31$, $p = .11$; pose per distance $F(1, 23) = 0.979$, $p = .333$; pose per design of cues, Greenhouse-Geiser corrected due to sphericity violation $F(1.562, 35.93) = 2.036$, $p = .154$).

We found a significant main effect for each of our independent variables. For distance ($F(1, 23) = 7.124$, $p = .014$, $\eta p^2 = .236$), grasping objects at 2 m ($M = 26.25$ s, $SE = 1.67$) was significantly faster than at 3 m ($M = 30.95$ s, $SE = 2.12$), Fig. 3b. For pose ($F(1, 23) = 7.145$, $p = .014$, $\eta p^2 = .237$) participants completed the ambiguous pose ($M = 26.46$ s, $SE = 1.94$) significantly faster than the clear pose ($M = 30.74$ s, $SE = 1.79$), Fig. 3d. Finally, we also found significant differences in grasping times for the three design of cues ($F(2, 46) = 13.029$, $p < .001$, $\eta p^2 = .362$). Post-hoc pairwise comparisons (Bonferroni adjusted) showed significant differences for Colors ($M = 33.14$ s, $SE = 1.78$) compared to Circle ($M = 26.12$ s, $SE = 2.04$, $p = .001$) and Extensions ($M = 26.54$ s, $SE = 1.91$, $p = .003$).

Success (Efficacy). For the dichotomous variable success, we applied a GEE model for which we used the GENLIN procedure in SPSS. As the working correlation matrix, we applied an exchangeable structure, and we used a binary logistic response model. For pairwise comparisons, we refer to the estimated marginal means and report p-values and standard errors.

Our results show no significant three-way or two-way interaction effects for our independent variables (design of cues per distance Wald $\chi^2(2, N = 864) = 3.74$, $p = .154$; distance per pose Wald $\chi^2(1, N = 864) = 3.59$, $p = .058$; pose per design of cues Wald $\chi^2(2, N = 864) = 3.59$, $p = .166$).

Again, we found significant main effects for each of our independent variables. For distance (Wald $\chi^2(1, N = 864) = 28.35$ $p < .001$), grasping objects at 2 m ($M = 0.71$, $SD = 0.46$) was significantly more successful compared to 3 m ($M = 0.43$, $SD = 0.495$). For pose (Wald $\chi^2(1, N = 864) = 11.526$, $p = .001$), the clear pose ($M = 0.66$, $SD = 0.475$) shows a significantly higher success compared to the ambiguous pose (M = 0.48, SD = 0.5). Finally, we also see a significant difference between the design of cues (Wald $\chi^2(2, N = 864) = 42.96$, p < .001). Post-hoc pairwise comparisons (Bonferroni adjusted) revealed that Circle (M = 0.72, SE = 0.03) showed a significantly higher success compared to both Extensions (M = 0.58, SE = 0.05, p = .004) and Colors (M = 0.45, SE = 0.04, p < .001). Also, there is a significant difference between Extensions and Colors (p = .02).

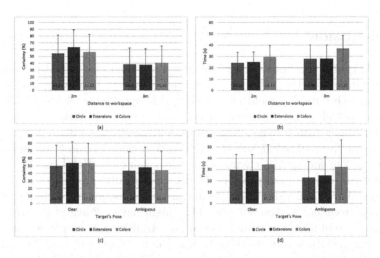

Fig. 3. Summary of M and SD with each design of visual cue (a) Shows certainty vs distance. (b) Shows time in seconds vs distance. (c) Shows certainty vs pose. (d) Shows time vs pose.

5.2   Subjective Measures

Certainty. We calculated the mean certainty rating across the three trials for each participant in each condition. Shapiro-Wilk tests and inspection of QQ plots showed that for the residuals normality could be assumed, we thus applied a RM-ANOVA. We found no significant three-way interaction ($F(2, 46) = 0.65$, p = .94) but a significant two-way interaction for distance per design of cues ($F(2, 46) = 4.01$, p = .025). Looking at the simple main effects for this interaction (post-hoc Estimated Marginal Means, Bonferroni adjusted), we found that for the 2 m distance, the Extensions led to significantly higher certainty (M = 63.30%, SE = 4.27) compared to both Colors (M = 56.53%, SE = 4.11, p = .01) and Circle (M = 54.58%, SE = 4.83, p = .015). However, this is not the case for the 3 m distance, where Extensions reached the lowest perceived certainty (Extensions M = 37.64%, SE = 4.06; Colors M = 40.66%, SE = 4.32; Circle M = 38.40%, SE = 4.01; differences not significant). We found a significant main effect both for pose ($F(1, 23) = 7.41$, p = .012, $\eta p^2 = .24$) and distance ($F(1, 23) = 32.96$, p < .01, $\eta p^2 = .589$). For pose, the clear pose led to a higher certainty (M = 52.13%, SD = 27.42) compared to the ambiguous pose (M = 44.91%, SD = 26.02), Fig. 3c.

For distance, the closer distance of 2 m led to a higher certainty (M = 58.14%, SD = 26.43) compared to 3 m (M = 38.90%, SD = 23.89), Fig. 3a.

To understand the relationship between perceived certainty and measures success and time we calculated a Spearman Partial Correlation, controlling for design of cues, distance, and pose. Results show that there is a significant positive partial correlation between certainty and success (rs(859) = 0.144, p < .001) but not between certainty and time (rs(859) = 0.021, p = .53).

6   Discussion

First (**H1**), we hypothesized that our design of visual cues would perform similarly regardless of the different egocentric distances, improving hence depth perception. Our results could not support this hypothesis. A smaller distance prompted better results in terms of time, certainty, and success compared to 3 m. This aligns with previous findings of depth perception decaying at greater distances in the real-world and in AR [43]. Further, Microsoft recommends a distance of 2 m for an MR environment when using the HoloLens 1 as further distances can induce perceptual problems. Specifically, problems derived from capturing (flares and calibration) that can provoke scene distortion and problems in environment abstraction [29]. This might have influenced the results and the experience of using our visual cues at 3m. Additionally, all participants mentioned that performing the grasping task at 3 m was harder than at 2 m, e.g., P3, "The farther distance was exponentially more difficult." P19, "The farther away, the harder it is to understand depth independently of the virtual supporters." These results lead us to think that teleoperation in co-located spaces should be performed within the personal space (up to 2 m) for better depth perception and thus performance. Despite that, we highlight the importance of further exploring distances beyond 2 m to better understand the dynamics of teleoperation within the operator's action space.

Second (**H2**), we hypothesized that our design of visual cues would reduce the effect of the target's pose, which would be reflected in similar results of success and time. However, we expected a higher degree of certainty for the clear pose compared to the ambiguous pose. Our results partially support this hypothesis. The effect of pose proved to be still present in spite of our designs of visual cues. Our results show that the clear pose prompts indeed higher certainty but also a significantly higher success with a compromise in terms of time (longer time) compared to the ambiguous pose. These results align with the findings of Barden and Petty [4] in terms of a direct relation between certainty and time. During our interview, we asked participants if they deemed one pose harder than the other for grasping, while most of them found the ambiguous pose harder, many also stated that they did not find differences among them, which could possibly be an effect of our visual cues. For instance, P7, "Both objects were equally hard," P9, "There was no difference between the 2 objects," "I did not find any object harder than another." Another factor that might have influenced these results is the type of task. Grasping tasks in a workspace with no other objects in vicinity that partially or completely occlude the target objects, may not highlight the potential benefits of our designs of cues.

Third **(H3)**, we hypothesized about potential differences between our design of cues with respect to time, success, and certainty. We assumed that Colors would perform best, followed by Extensions, and then Circle. Our results indeed showed that our designs of visual cues had different effects on our dependent variables, but the effects were different from what we hypothesized.

Regarding time, we found that our participants were faster using both the Circle and Extensions compared to using Colors. Additionally, no significant differences were found with respect to time between Circle and Extensions. When analyzing success, we found higher success rates when using Circle compared to using Extensions and Colors. Also, using Extensions showed a higher significant success compared to Colors.

Concerning certainty, we found a significant interaction effect for distance per design of cues. These point to differences at 2 m, where Extensions prompted the highest level of certainty, which in turn was significantly higher compared to both Circle and Colors. Since our designs were incremental, Extensions, which included the Circle, seemed to provide the necessary information about depth without the visual complexity of Colors. The absence of this effect at 3 m might be due to the fact that the effect of distance alone overshadowed any potential difference among our designs of cues. While Audley [2] remarked that the amount of information (evidence) that can be collected from the environment influences the amount of perceived certainty, e.g., the more evidence that is collected, the higher certainty that is evoked. Our results show that one must be careful when designing to provide more information about the environment. While the Colors certainly provided the most depth cues, our results point towards the fact that this information was not always usable to our participants. This is also reflected by our participants' comments, who mostly pointed out the simpler cues, Circle and Extensions, and deemed them as helpful: P1, "The visual extensions were good for the further distance." P10, "The most helpful thing was the circle. I used it the most to align the gripper." P11, "The circle was what helped the most." We attribute the preferences towards the Circle, to the fact that it did not fully occlude the real object, and when it did it was an indicator of misalignment of the gripper over the target object. Further, participants' subjective preferences for Extensions and Colors together with higher efficiency and effectiveness lead us to recommend a simpler design of visual cues.

In H3, we did not expect Colors to perform the worst across conditions. In consequence, we further explored the reasons behind the low scores in time and success by analyzing the participants' comments. During our interview, participants expressed confusion when using the Colors due to lack of color opponency. Specifically, they expressed problems with the color gradient on the physical colormap, e.g., P13, "The gradient of the colormap made it a little bit confusing. I could not tell if it was already yellow or still blue?" P15, "I would prefer stripes, not gradient colors, that would have made it easier to distinguish where I was on the tabletop." Added to that, participants expressed difficulties in distinguishing the real and physical colors, which is related to focal rivalry—the human visual system cannot focus on two elements at the same time, e.g., P14, "I had to concentrate to match the colors;" P15, "It was hard to see the real and the virtual colors because they were right above each other." Therefore, we believe that this lack of color opponency added to focal rivalry worsened depth perception. This accords to the observations of Ellis and Menges [15], who determined that physical surfaces influence depth perception misestimation.

Fourth (H4), we hypothesized about finding a correlation between certainty and success as a possible pointer to better depth perception. Our results confirmed the correlation between certainty and success, even when controlling for our independent variables (distance, pose, and design of cues). We still found a positive and significant, albeit rather weak, correlation. This aligns with a line of research suggesting that subjective certainty correlates closely with objective success [8,58]. We consider that all our design cues provided additional evidence about the position of the gripper in the workspace, which in turn influenced certainty. A note of caution is due here since, as mentioned in Sect. 2.4, there have been controversial findings related to the influence of time and success in certainty. We acknowledge that other factors can influence certainty and were not considered in our experiment such as fatigue and changes in attention, and these have proven to influence perceived certainty [20]. Further, when evaluating depth perception in 3D environments, it is necessary to separate "the amount of depth that an object is seen to have (mind independent property) and the realism of the experience (mind dependent property)" [23]. In fact, we consider that this construction can also be applied to AR environments and is related to certainty. This in consequence might have influenced the perceived certainty during our experiment.

7   Limitations

A limitation of our work relates to the multimodal interaction technique used. While a joystick or a control pad are commonly used in robot teleoperation, we aim to explore hands-free multimodal interaction. This type of interaction has raised interest in the research community, especially in HRI. Our previous experiences have shown that using speech and head movements is simpler to learn than using a control pad or even a joystick. Additionally, these modalities are natively supported by the technology used (Microsoft HoloLens 1). We further stress that the modalities were kept stable among conditions to avoid them causing a major influence on the evaluation of the other factors in our experiment.

This work may be also limited to the technology used. For instance, our design of the Colors cue, which combines a real-world colormap with virtual colors displayed over it, could have contributed to focal rivalry problems. However, this problem is present not only in the Microsoft HoloLens 1 but in the current generation of MR headsets [31]. Additionally, current ARHMDs have a limited field of view which do not cover human's peripheral vision. This presents a disadvantage when using AR, as mentioned by Williams et al. [54].

Our experimental design also presents certain limitations. We did not consider a condition without cues since a previous study [1] already evaluated the use of visual cues versus the absence of them, suggesting potential improvements in certainty. This study thus builds upon those findings and further explores the influence of distance and pose. We did not consider grasping accuracy, defined by the distance to an ideal grasping position, since we realized that the effect of the displacement of the virtual visual cues at 3 m influences greatly this measure.

Our main goal is to capture first experiences with certain designs of visual cues that can provide direction for a better design that improves depth perception. Furthermore, people can perceive distance and depth differently due to individual differences in visual acuity, eye dominance, color vision, and spatial abilities [29]. We considered different color visions for the colors used in the colormap but left aside the other factors which might have influenced on how each participant experienced not only the types of cues but depth perception.

8 Conclusions

In this paper, we evaluated how egocentric distances and target objects' pose affect co-located teleoperation when using certain designs of visual cues presented through AR. To this end, we performed an experiment with 24 participants. Our results align with previous studies about depth perception within the observer's personal space. Teleoperating a robot at 2 m with our designs of visual cues leads to a higher success rate, shorter time, and a higher degree of certainty compared to 3 m. A clearer pose leads to higher success and certainty but requires longer time. As time and certainty are closely tied, i.e., greater thoughtfulness is required to achieve higher certainty and success. We also found a positive correlation between success and certainty, but we are careful with these findings since other factors, e.g., attention and fatigue, have an effect on certainty and were not considered in our experiment. Additionally, we found differences of our designs of visual cues. The Circle and Extensions cues prompted shorter times and higher success compared to Colors, wherein Circle showed the highest success. These findings suggest that simplicity of design leads to higher efficiency and effectiveness.

We consider that our findings are thought-provoking and present a detailed analysis of distance and target pose in co-located teleoperation. These, further contemplate the role of certainty as a factor that can shed some light about depth perception. Besides, our designs of visual cues suggest advantages and downsides of using cast shadows, symbolic enhancements, and combining real and virtual landmarks to enhance the visual space when teleoperating a robotic arm in co-located spaces. Although our study focuses on evaluating specific factors related to depth perception, our findings may well have a bearing on designing cues using AR to improve perception of real objects and facilitate teleoperation of robotic arms.

Acknowledgements. This research is supported by the German Federal Ministry of Education and Research (BMBF, FKZ: 13FH011IX6).

References

1. Arévalo Arboleda, S., Dierks, T., Rücker, F., Gerken, J.: There's more than meets the eye. In: Companion of the 2020 ACM/IEEE International Conference on Human-Robot Interaction, pp. 104–106. ACM, [S.l.] (2020). https://doi.org/10.1145/3371382.3378240
2. Audley, R.J.: A stochastic model for individual choice behavior. Psychol. Rev. **67**, 1 (1960). https://doi.org/10.1037/h0046438
3. Baranski, J.V., Petrusic, W.M.: Probing the locus of confidence judgments: experiments on the time to determine confidence. J. Exp. Psychol. Hum. Percept. Perform. **24**(3), 929–945 (1998). https://doi.org/10.1037//0096-1523.24.3.929
4. Barden, J., Petty, R.E.: The mere perception of elaboration creates attitude certainty: exploring the thoughtfulness heuristic. J. Pers. Soc. Psychol. **95**(3), 489–509 (2008). https://doi.org/10.1037/a0012559
5. Barthelmé, S., Mamassian, P.: Evaluation of objective uncertainty in the visual system. PLoS Comput. Biol. **5**(9), e1000504 (2009). https://doi.org/10.1371/journal.pcbi.1000504
6. Blanca, M.J., Alarcón, R., Arnau, J., Bono, R., Bendayan, R.: Non-normal data: is ANOVA still a valid option? Psicothema **29**(4), 552–557 (2017). https://doi.org/10.7334/psicothema2016.383
7. Bodenheimer, B., et al.: Distance estimation in virtual and real environments using bisection. In: Proceedings, APGV 2007, p. 35. ACM (2007). https://doi.org/10.1145/1272582.1272589
8. Boldt, A., Yeung, N.: Shared neural markers of decision confidence and error detection. J. Neurosci. **35**(8), 3478–3484 (2015). https://doi.org/10.1523/JNEUROSCI.0797-14.2015
9. Brenner, E., Smeets, J.B.J.: Depth perception. In: Stevens' Handbook of Experimental Psychology and Cognitive Neuroscience, pp. 1–30. John Wiley & Sons, Inc (2018). https://doi.org/10.1002/9781119170174.epcn209
10. Choi, H., Cho, B., Masamune, K., Hashizume, M., Hong, J.: An effective visualization technique for depth perception in augmented reality-based surgical navigation. Int. J. Med. Robot. Comput. Assist. Surg. **12**(1), 62–72 (2016). https://doi.org/10.1002/rcs.1657
11. Cipiloglu, Z., Bulbul, A., Capin, T.: A framework for enhancing depth perception in computer graphics. In: Proceedings of the 7th Symposium on Applied Perception in Graphics and Visualization, p. 141. ACM (2010). https://doi.org/10.1145/1836248.1836276
12. Cutting, J.E., Vishton, P.M.: Perceiving layout and knowing distances. In: Perception of Space and Motion, pp. 69–117. Elsevier (1995). https://doi.org/10.1016/B978-012240530-3/50005-5
13. Diaz, C., Walker, M., Szafir, D.A., Szafir, D.: Designing for depth perceptions in augmented reality. In: 2017 IEEE International Symposium on Mixed and Augmented Reality, pp. 111–122. IEEE (2017). https://doi.org/10.1109/ISMAR.2017.28
14. El Jamiy, F., Marsh, R.: Survey on depth perception in head mounted displays: distance estimation in virtual reality, augmented reality, and mixed reality. IET Image Process. **13**(5), 707–712 (2019). https://doi.org/10.1049/iet-ipr.2018.5920
15. Ellis, S.R., Menges, B.M.: Localization of virtual objects in the near visual field. Hum. Factors J. Hum. Factors Ergon. Soc. **40**(3), 415–431 (1998). https://doi.org/10.1518/001872098779591278

16. de Gardelle, V., Mamassian, P.: Does confidence use a common currency across two visual tasks? Psychol. Sci. **25**(6), 1286–1288 (2014). https://doi.org/10.1177/0956797614528956
17. Gherman, S., Philiastides, M.G.: Neural representations of confidence emerge from the process of decision formation during perceptual choices. NeuroImage **106**, 134–143 (2015). https://doi.org/10.1016/j.neuroimage.2014.11.036
18. Gong, L.L., Ong, S.K., Nee, A.Y.C.: Projection-based augmented reality interface for robot grasping tasks. In: Proceedings of the 2019 4th International Conference on Robotics, Control and Automation - ICRCA 2019, pp. 100–104. ACM Press (2019). https://doi.org/10.1145/3351180.3351204
19. Hedayati, H., Walker, M., Szafir, D.: Improving collocated robot teleoperation with augmented reality. In: HRI 2018, pp. 78–86. ACM (2018). https://doi.org/10.1145/3171221.3171251
20. Heereman, J., Walter, H., Heekeren, H.R.: A task-independent neural representation of subjective certainty in visual perception. Front. Hum. Neurosci. **9**, 551 (2015). https://doi.org/10.3389/fnhum.2015.00551
21. Heinrich, F., Bornemann, K., Lawonn, K., Hansen, C.: Depth perception in projective augmented reality: an evaluation of advanced visualization techniques. In: 25th ACM Symposium on Virtual Reality Software and Technology, pp. 1–11. ACM (2019). https://doi.org/10.1145/3359996.3364245
22. Hershenson, M.: Size-distance invariance: kinetic invariance is different from static invariance. Percept. Psychophysics **51**(6), 541–548 (1992). https://doi.org/10.3758/BF03211651
23. Hibbard, P.B., Haines, A.E., Hornsey, R.L.: Magnitude, precision, and realism of depth perception in stereoscopic vision. Cogn. Res. Principles Implications **2**(1), 25 (2017). https://doi.org/10.1186/s41235-017-0062-7
24. Howard, I.P.: Depth perception. In: Stevens' Handbook of Experimental Psychology, pp. 77–120 (2002)
25. Howard, I.P., Rogers, B.J.: Perceiving in Depth, vol. 29. Oxford University Press (2012)
26. Jones, A., Swan, J.E., Singh, G., Kolstad, E.: The effects of virtual reality, augmented reality, and motion parallax on egocentric depth perception. In: IEEE Virtual Reality 2008, pp. 267–268. IEEE (2008). https://doi.org/10.1109/VR.2008.4480794
27. Kiani, R., Corthell, L., Shadlen, M.N.: Choice certainty is informed by both evidence and decision time. Neuron **84**(6), 1329–1342 (2014). https://doi.org/10.1016/j.neuron.2014.12.015
28. Kim, H.Y.: Statistical notes for clinical researchers: assessing normal distribution (2) using skewness and kurtosis. Restorative Dent. Endodontics **38**(1), 52–54 (2013). https://doi.org/10.5395/rde.2013.38.1.52
29. Kruijff, E., Swan, J.E., Feiner, S.: Perceptual issues in augmented reality revisited. In: 9th IEEE International Symposium on Mixed and Augmented Reality (ISMAR), 2010, pp. 3–12 (2010). https://doi.org/10.1109/ISMAR.2010.5643530
30. Krupke, D., Steinicke, F., Lubos, P., Jonetzko, Y., Gorner, M., Zhang, J.: Comparison of multimodal heading and pointing gestures for co-located mixed reality human-robot interaction. In: 2018 IEEE/RSJ International Conference on Intelligent Robots and Systems (IROS), pp. 1–9. IEEE (2018). https://doi.org/10.1109/IROS.2018.8594043
31. Laramee, R.: Ware colin: rivalry and interference with a head-mounted display. ACM Trans. Comput.-Hum. Interact. **9**(3), 238–251 (2002). https://doi.org/10.1145/568513.568516

32. Lee, J.H., Herzog, T.A., Meade, C.D., Webb, M.S., Brandon, T.H.: The use of gee for analyzing longitudinal binomial data: a primer using data from a tobacco intervention. Addict. Behav. **32**(1), 187–193 (2007). https://doi.org/10.1016/j.addbeh. 2006.03.030

33. Livingston, M.A., Zanbaka, C., Swan, J.E., Smallman, H.S.: Objective measures for the effectiveness of augmented reality. In: Virtual Reality 2005, pp. 287–288. IEEE (2005). https://doi.org/10.1109/VR.2005.1492798

34. Loomis, J., Knapp, J.: Visual perception of egocentric distance in real and virtual environments. In: Virtual and Adaptive Environments, pp. 21–46. Lawrence Erlbaum (2003). https://doi.org/10.1201/9781410608888.pt1

35. Mamassian, P.: Visual confidence. Annu. Rev. Vis. Sci. **2**, 459–481 (2016). https://doi.org/10.1146/annurev-vision-111815-114630

36. Microsoft: Microsoft hololens. https://www.microsoft.com/en-us/hololens

37. Microsoft: Microsoft hololens calibration. https://docs.microsoft.com/en-us/hololens/hololens-calibration

38. Microsoft: Mixed reality toolkit (2017). https://github.com/microsoft/MixedRealityToolkit-Unity/releases

39. Mosiello, G., Kiselev, A., Loutfi, A.: Using augmented reality to improve usability of the user interface for driving a telepresence robot. Paladyn, J. Behav. Robot. **4**(3), 174–181 (2013). https://doi.org/10.2478/pjbr-2013-0018

40. Paris, R., Joshi, M., He, Q., Narasimham, G., McNamara, T.P., Bodenheimer, B.: Acquisition of survey knowledge using walking in place and resetting methods in immersive virtual environments. In: Proceedings of the ACM Symposium on Applied Perception, pp. 1–8. ACM (2017). https://doi.org/10.1145/3119881. 3119889

41. Park, J., Ha, S.: Visual information presentation in continuous control systems using visual enhancements. In: Contact-free Stress Monitoring for User's Divided Attention. INTECH Open Access Publisher (2008). https://doi.org/10.5772/6307

42. Petrocelli, J.V., Tormala, Z.L., Rucker, D.D.: Unpacking attitude certainty: attitude clarity and attitude correctness. J. Pers. Soc. Psychol. **92**(1), 30–41 (2007). https://doi.org/10.1037/0022-3514.92.1.30

43. Ping, J., Weng, D., Liu, Y., Wang, Y.: Depth perception in shuffleboard: depth cues effect on depth perception in virtual and augmented reality system. J. Soc. Inf. Disp. **28**(2), 164–176 (2020). https://doi.org/10.1002/jsid.840

44. Pleskac, T.J., Busemeyer, J.R.: Two-stage dynamic signal detection: a theory of choice, decision time, and confidence. Psychol. Rev. **117**(3), 864–901 (2010). https://doi.org/10.1037/a0019737

45. PTC: Vuforia engine in unity. https://library.vuforia.com/articles/Training/getting-started-with-vuforia-in-unity.html

46. Rolland, J.P., Meyer, C., Arthur, K., Rinalducci, E.: Method of adjustments versus method of constant stimuli in the quantification of accuracy and precision of rendered depth in head-mounted displays. Presence Teleoperators Virtual Environ. **11**(6), 610–625 (2002). https://doi.org/10.1162/105474602321050730

47. Rosales, C.S., et al.: Distance judgments to on- and off-ground objects in augmented reality. In: Proceedings, 26th IEEE Conference on Virtual Reality and 3D User Interfaces, pp. 237–243. IEEE (2019). https://doi.org/10.1109/VR.2019. 8798095

48. Stadler, S., Kain, K., Giuliani, M., Mirnig, N., Stollnberger, G., Tscheligi, M.: Augmented reality for industrial robot programmers: workload analysis for task-based, augmented reality-supported robot control. In: 2016 25th IEEE International Symposium on Robot and Human Interactive Communication (RO-MAN), pp. 179–184 (2016). https://doi.org/10.1109/ROMAN.2016.7745108
49. Shimojo, S., Paradiso, M., Fujita, I.: What visual perception tells us about mind and brain. Proc. Nat. Acad. Sci. U.S.A. **98**(22), 12340–12341 (2001). https://doi.org/10.1073/pnas.221383698
50. Tormala, Z.L.: The role of certainty (and uncertainty) in attitudes and persuasion. Curr. Opin. Psychol. **10**, 6–11 (2016). https://doi.org/10.1016/j.copsyc.2015.10.017
51. Vassallo, R., Rankin, A., Chen, E.C.S., Peters, T.M.: Hologram stability evaluation for Microsoft hololens. In: Medical Imaging 2017: Image Perception, Observer Performance, and Technology Assessment, p. 1013614. SPIE Proceedings, SPIE (2017). https://doi.org/10.1117/12.2255831
52. Walker, M., Hedayati, H., Lee, J., Szafir, D.: Communicating robot motion intent with augmented reality. In: Kanda, T., Šabanović, S., Hoffman, G., Tapus, A. (eds.) HRI 2018, pp. 316–324. ACM (2018). https://doi.org/10.1145/3171221.3171253
53. Walker, M.E., Hedayati, H., Szafir, D.: Robot teleoperation with augmented reality virtual surrogates. In: HRI 2019, pp. 202–210. IEEE (2019). https://doi.org/10.1109/HRI.2019.8673306
54. Williams, T., Hirshfield, L., Tran, N., Grant, T., Woodward, N.: Using augmented reality to better study human-robot interaction. In: Chen, J.Y.C., Fragomeni, G. (eds.) HCII 2020. LNCS, vol. 12190, pp. 643–654. Springer, Cham (2020). https://doi.org/10.1007/978-3-030-49695-1_43
55. Willis, J., Todorov, A.: First impressions: making up your mind after a 100-ms exposure to a face. Psychol. Sci. **17**(7), 592–598 (2006). https://doi.org/10.1111/j.1467-9280.2006.01750.x
56. Wither, J., Hollerer, T.: Pictorial depth cues for outdoor augmented reality. In: ISWC 2005. IEEE (2005). https://doi.org/10.1109/ISWC.2005.41
57. Xie, F., Paik, M.C.: Generalized estimating equation model for binary outcomes with missing covariates. Biometrics **53**(4), 1458 (1997). https://doi.org/10.2307/2533511
58. Yeung, N., Summerfield, C.: Metacognition in human decision-making: confidence and error monitoring. Philos. Trans. R. Soc. Lond. Ser. B Biol. Sci. **367**(1594), 1310–1321 (2012). https://doi.org/10.1098/rstb.2011.0416
59. Yonas, A., Granrud, C.E.: Infants' perception of depth from cast shadows. Percep. Psychophysics **68**(1), 154–160 (2006). https://doi.org/10.3758/bf03193665
60. Zollmann, S., Hoppe, C., Langlotz, T., Reitmayr, G.: Flyar: augmented reality supported micro aerial vehicle navigation. IEEE Trans. Vis. Comput. Graph. **20**(4), 560–568 (2014). https://doi.org/10.1109/TVCG.2014.24

Looking for Info: Evaluation of Gaze Based Information Retrieval in Augmented Reality

Robin Piening[1,2]([✉]), Ken Pfeuffer[1], Augusto Esteves[3], Tim Mittermeier[1], Sarah Prange[1,2], Philippe Schröder[2], and Florian Alt[1]

[1] Universität der Bundeswehr München, Neubiberg, Germany
{robin.piening,ken.pfeuffer,tim.mittermeier,sarah.prange,
florian.alt}@unibw.de
[2] LMU Munich, Munich, Germany
{robin.piening,sarah.prange,philippe.schroder}@campus.lmu.de
[3] ITI / LARSyS, IST, ULisbon, Portugal
augusto.esteves@tecnico.ulisboa.pt

Abstract. This paper presents the results of an empirical study and a real-world deployment of a gaze-adaptive UI for Augmented Reality (AR). AR introduces an attention dilemma between focusing on the reality vs. on AR content. Past work suggested eye gaze as a technique to open information interfaces, however there is only little empirical work. We present an empirical study comparing gaze-adaptive to an always-on interface in tasks that vary focus between reality and virtual content. Across tasks, we find most participants prefer the gaze-adaptive UI and find it less distracting. When focusing on reality, the gaze UI is faster, perceived as easier and more intuitive. When focusing on virtual content, always-on is faster but user preferences are split. We conclude with the design and deployment of an interactive application in a public museum, demonstrating the promising potential in the real world.

Keywords: Gaze interaction · AR · Eye-tracking · Adaptive UI

1 Introduction

Head-worn AR displays, that superimpose graphics and text over the appropriate objects in the user's view, have the potential to enable a new way of seeing the world [10]. Users can be assisted in a range of activities from everyday scenarios to obtain contextual information of the world (e.g., restaurants, streets, sights) to interactive architecture and museum tours to gain guidance and knowledge about the artifacts. This introduces a key user interface (UI) challenge of user access to contextual information through interfaces in form of panels or windows anchored to real world environments. Virtual content can occlude the visibility and distract users when attending to the real world, and environments cluttered with too many panels can feel overwhelming.

© IFIP International Federation for Information Processing 2021
Published by Springer Nature Switzerland AG 2021
C. Ardito et al. (Eds.): INTERACT 2021, LNCS 12932, pp. 544–565, 2021.
https://doi.org/10.1007/978-3-030-85623-6_32

Fig. 1. Gaze-adaptive UIs in AR enable one of the most effortless and implicit access methods to context information inherent in world objects. For example, interactive objects have subtle visual indicators that, when fixated with the eyes, open information panels (a). When opened, further UI elements utilise the eyes' dwell-time as a technique to browse more pages or activate sound files on-the-fly (b).

As an alternative to always-on interfaces, adaptive context-aware AR pursues the idea to present appropriate information at the right time through analysis of context information [12]. This is particularly useful in scenarios where the hands may not be available or desired to employ for the selection and deselection of casual AR information. A promising method of adaptation is to exploit the user's visual attention as context information, being highly indicative of what we are interested in [33,45]. Eye-tracking modules are increasingly integrated with AR devices such as the Microsoft HoloLens 2 or Magic Leap One. Gaze, as the point where our eyes converge, can be harnessed to adapt information availability and density. Several prototypical gaze-adaptive UIs were proposed in the literature [1,23,33]. However, there is a lack of empirical evidence with regards to user experience and performance, making it difficult to assess the feasibility of the concept in the maturing AR landscape.

Our work aims to fill this gap, by presenting an empirical experiment in the lab, and a field study of the gaze-adaptive UI in a real world scenario. Figure 1 provides an overview of the concept, technical prototypes and the two studies. Users can access additional information of an object by looking at an indicator located nearby. After a time threshold, the UI element is 'activated' and opens a window of appropriate information. For example in a virtual city environment, the user can look around the scene, and fixate objects of interests such has the lamp to quickly open a definition of it (a).

Our first contributions is an empirical comparison of the gaze-adaptive to an always-on UI. the latter is representative of the default way to visualise AR contextual information in the world. This allows us to establish a ground truth for future developments and studies with gaze in AR. The comparison is two-fold, to understand both perspectives of the attention dilemma in AR. First, users focus on the reality, tasked to find "real-world" objects in this environment while AR panels can be in the way. Second, users focus on virtual content, by searching particular information in the AR panels anchored to objects in the vicinity. The results of the study provide insights on the performance, user experience, and occlusion trade-off:

- For the reality focused task, users performed faster with gaze-adaptation, found it easier, more intuitive, and preferred it.
- For the virtual UI task, as expected users were faster when seeing all information, but user preferences were split between the two techniques (11 gaze-adaptive vs. 10 always-on UI).
- Across both tasks, most users prefer using the gaze-adaptive UI, and find it less distracting.

Furthermore, to understand gaze-adaptation in practice, we present a novel gaze-adaptive AR application specifically tailored to a museum scenario. Figure 1b shows the application in action in a real museum where we deployed it. Wearing the AR headset, users view the museum artifacts and can interact with superimposed information. Complementary to physical information on a desk, users can directly read and hear about the artifacts by looking at visual indicators close to each artifact. The opened information interface has further buttons, to browse more information by dwell-time. We conducted a field study where participants report on their experience, overall showing a positive reception of this method and further ideas for improvements.

Together, these findings allow to gain a better understanding of the various trade-offs and the overall viability of gaze-activated AR information, of value for designers and researchers working to bring AR applications beyond the lab toward an efficient and natural way in everyday environments.

2   Background and Related Work

2.1   Gaze Interaction

Eye-tracking has the potential to facilitate our interactions with computers, making them more intuitive and responsive [6]. A major usability challenge with gaze input is the involuntary selection of elements when these are being gazed at by the user ("Midas Touch" problem [17]). Several selection confirmation mechanisms were investigated for objects including mouse press [17], gestures [35], touch input [34,41], controllers [21,42] and menus [36].

A popular approach is dwell time. It gives users a time window to look at an object before the user's gaze is interpreted as a command, e.g., to trigger a selection [4,17,30,40,44]. The limitations of dwell are response time, as the user needs to wait until the timer finishes, and false triggers, if accidentally dwelling on objects for too long. We focus on revealing information based on user interest. This is a more forgiving task, as users can simply avert their gaze if not interested, but requires a different design of timing parameters we introduce later.

Gaze has been explored for head mounted AR devices. Kyto et al. studied different selection techniques in head mounted AR displays, comparing their use of gaze or head ray as primary input with secondary refinement methods like hand gestures or external devices [21]. Ishiguro et al. used gaze as a filtering mechanism to avoid occlusion when visual information is overlaid [16]. They explored annotations at the edges of the display, with symbols that could be recognized peripherally. Upon being gazed at, these annotations would expand with detailed information. Tonnis et al. explored a mechanism, presenting contextual information at an offset from the user's gaze point. This allows the user to freely interact with an interface or the world, and only when attending to the information, it will stay in place [43]. Rivu et al. developed a prototype for a face-to-face AR interface for people, where information is indicated next to the user and gazing at them allows to reveal them [38].

Our work is complementary, focusing on the more general approach of providing information in the vicinity of objects through an implicit gaze activation, and then allow users to explicitly trigger more content. Such an implicit approach is closely related to Vertegaal's Attentive User Interfaces (AUIs) [45], a general concept where displays adapt to the user's attention capacities. We investigate this approach for AR, where it is a more significant problem of attention management between real world and digital augmentation.

2.2 Adaptive AR

AR display technology affords many use cases where virtual content overlays real content in everyday environments [10], and creating such mixed reality content is becoming increasingly possible for a range of users [32]. A major challenge is that the virtual content can be informative, but also obstruct the user's view and important real-world information. This is recognized in AR research as the "label placement problem" [2,39].

Several researchers have thus investigated particular placement parameters for information close to objects [13,24]. Bell et al. introduced view management techniques that used scaling, transparency, and repositioning to avoid occluding places of interest or other annotations, while enabling functional grouping [3]. Julier et al. used different rule-based filtering methods to avoid information overload, employing distance, visibility, object importance, and task relevance [18]. Keil et al. used camera and motion based techniques to minimize information overload [19], while Fender et al. explored automated placement optimization of visualizations based on user behavior and information quality [11].

AR systems can be improved by making them adaptive to context information on user and environment. Ajanki et al. [1] used gaze patterns, implicit speech recognition, the user's task, and physical location, to deliver highly relevant augmented information retrieved from the web. Feiner et al. described a system that took into account user's environment to determine an optimal data density [9]. Lages and Bowman investigate adaptive interfaces during walking, where information is offered through 2D windows that follow the user and adapt to the environment [22]. Lindlbauer et al. developed a context aware system that responded to cognitive load, reducing the augmentation density, positioning, and time accordingly [7]. Further potential of mobile AR has been explored by Höllerer et al. via eye-tracking and location awareness [14]. White et al. explored situated pattern visualization for urban planning and site visits, eliminating the memetic accuracy loss experienced with attention switches between, e.g., a map and the real environment [46].

Little work empirically studied gaze for context-aware AR. Kim et al.'s Shop-i concept demonstrated that users recognized the value of gaze-aware digital labels laid over the real-world in a shopping environment [20]. McNamara et al. demonstrated that having gaze dictate 'where' and 'when' to display such labels improved users' performance when searching for contextual information in VR [26,27]. Their studies compare early prototypes of various methods such as always-on labels, labels using a clamped squared relationship between their anchor and the user's gaze point, labels remaining visible for a short amount of time after being gazed at, and labels with a trigger and exit radius [28,29]. They found a combination of the latter two to be ideal, which we build upon.

Closely related is the research on Glanceable AR [8,15,23]. We share focus on temporary accessible information, and the potential integration of gaze for interaction. Lu et al. focus on a personal UI that allows notifications to be triggered and typical apps as found in a smartphone to be accessed quickly [23]. Inamov et al. studied positioning information relative to the object [15]. We extend their work by focus on 1) world-fixed interfaces which is different to a personal UI [23] (e.g., having a large number of information UIs), 2) eye based input which has been shown to be different to head direction [5] ([8,15] do not use eye gaze), and 3) contributing insights from a controlled lab and a field study.

Lastly, our work is inspired by recent work on the ARtention design space of gaze for AR scenarios proposed in [33]. They formulate three roles for gaze: reveal information, select information, and browse information, demonstrated in three applications. We extend their work by providing 1) an empirical evaluation of using gaze to transition from reality to virtual UI focus, and 2) design a new application that integrates all three roles of the design space.

3 Looking for Info: Gaze Adaptive AR

Building on the prior work, the main idea is to utilise eye gaze input of the user to access information bits in AR. Meaning, users can look at meaningful points of the real environment, and when indicating interest by gazing at a particular point, the system provides the user with additional information. In order to better ground our design and study efforts, we formalize the properties of a gaze adaptive AR system across three dimensions:

Temporal Activation. This is defined as how long a user needs to look at a real-world object to trigger any embedded AR panel. In some tasks (e.g., information retrieval) the user might prefer immediate AR panel activations, while in others a delay can make for a more pleasant and seamless experience.

Spatial Activation. This is defined as the area a user needs to gaze at to trigger an AR panel, and its size can vary in different ways. For simple, self-contained application where the user is not required to move, each activation area can have the same size for UI consistency. For an in-the-wild application these activation areas can match the scale of the objects as they are perceived by the user, facilitating the activation of AR panels in their immediate vicinity.

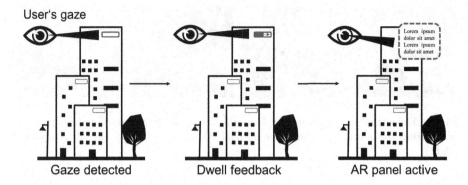

User's gaze

Gaze detected   Dwell feedback   AR panel active

Fig. 2. The concept of gaze-adaptive AR UI from the user's perspective. The user views a city and can gaze at one of the panel's indicators. Then, the feedback indicates progress of the dwell time, which leads to opening the content.

User Feedback. Finally, we need to consider the various states an adaptive AR panel can be in (Fig. 2). Before being gazed at, an object can already display an icon or symbol that highlights it holds a gaze-adaptive panel to explore. During dwell this icon or symbol can be used as progress bar not only so the user receives feedback the system understands its intent, but also to give users a chance to advert their eyes if they do not wish to trigger the AR panel.

4   User Study: AR vs World Focus

Our first study investigates the effect on user performance and experience when using a gaze-adaptive UI compared to a baseline condition. We use two tasks to vary whether the user focuses on interaction with real objects, or on interaction with the virtual content provided by AR. In the task, the user either searches for a specific AR information, or for an object in the environment.

Baseline Rationale. We use a baseline of showing information all the time, as this is a common depiction of AR use in everyday environments such as Feiner's illustration of a AR-mediated city [10]. We considered several baselines. A button-triggered UI baseline is popular, but with our focus on lightweight information access [8,23,33] it may not be ideal. It is possible that the hands may be occupied or otherwise unavailable. It is also overhead for simple information access, e.g., the user would point & click on each information panel in each single trial. Similarly, in peripheral vision approaches [16], the user would have to divert their eyes off to the periphery for each panel. We also considered a context adaptation baseline. But we consider these approaches as different and complementary. It uses knowledge from context data to suggest a potential selection. If context data is insufficient to make a selection, the user can utilise a method where they are in more control by gaze.

Fig. 3. The virtual city environment from the first study from a participant's perspective during the *always on* condition. A trial displaying 20 (left) and 40 AR panels (right).

We chose always-on information as baseline. This is as Feiner's vision [10] is still desirable today, i.e. that the world is augmented with informative context information. But it is an open question how to design access to those, and how adaptive methods such as eye gaze are different to such an always-on method.

Research Questions. The research questions of this study include:

- **User performance**: How is user performance affected in the object search? While the gaze-adaptive UI shows up to one AR panel at a time, they dynamically appear at gaze – it is unclear how this affects the task performance.
- **User experience**: Even if always-on is faster in one task, performance is not necessarily linked to preference. Which method do users prefer for each task, and across both tasks as a generic UI mode?

4.1   Experimental Design

Our study followed a within-subjects design (balanced using a Latin Square) with two independent variables: AR panel behavior (all on, gaze adaptive) and search task (information, object). Participants interacted in a city-like environment that is inspired by Feiner's illustration of a AR-mediated city [10], representative of these types of search tasks while using AR. We implemented this experience using a VR setup for increased fidelity and ecological validity [25].

AR Panel Adaptation Method. As the name implies, in the *all on* condition all AR panels were displayed concurrently. In the *gaze adaptive* condition we employed a triggering mechanism that relied on a *temporal activation* of 300 ms. We chose this as our pilot tests have shown that this provides a good compromise between fast activation and minimal accidental activation. In our pilot, 15 users tested object activation times from .3 s to 3 s in a simplified environment and provided preferences. The *spatial activation* was implemented by a 2×2 m which allowed to easily gaze on objects without interference from the eye-tracker's precision. *User feedback* consisted of a progress bar (see Fig. 4 – top). These parameters are optimised for our study task – and can be adapted when used in other use cases (e.g., as in the following study).

Fig. 4. Elements from the conditions in the first study. Top: three states of our gaze adaptive mechanism: (a) progress bar associated with an AR panel before being gazed at; (b) progress bar during dwell; and (c) the AR panel after being triggered. Bottom: objects a participant had to find in the *object* condition.

Task. In the *information* condition participants were tasked with finding the year in which a building was completed. This information was present in each AR panel associated with the various buildings in the scene – the year in which each building was completed was randomized at the start of each new trial. In the *object* condition participants were tasked with finding a 2D representation of a person, animal or object (see Fig. 4 – bottom) randomly placed in the scene at the start of each trial. An object was "found" when gazed at for 2 s.

Repetitions. Finally, to add variety to our trials in terms of potential occlusion and information overload, we varied the number of AR panels available in the scene between 20 and 40. This was randomized but equally distributed among conditions so that each user experienced each layout once (see Fig. 3). This leads to 2 adaptation methods ×2 tasks ×2 repetitions = 8 trials per user.

4.2   Experimental Setup

The city-like environment was implemented and deployed using the same setup as in the pilot study (Unity, HTC Vive Pro Eye). This included various buildings such as skyscrapers and apartments, a grocery store and a fuel station, and other pedestrians and cars that moved around. The AR panels associated with these elements had similar properties: a headline and a body of 250 characters displayed in white on a semi-transparent black background. These panels displayed appropriate content, such as opening times or the age of the building, and were displayed on average at 16.56 m ($SD = 16.6$) from participants' starting position ($\approx 7.15°$ of visual angle). This made them easy to gaze at with the eye-tracker employed in the study. In case of occasional occlusions, the AR panel closest to the participant was triggered. Finally, participants were free to move in a small area of 3×3 m at the center of the scene – the bird's eye view of this scene, together with all AR panel locations can be seen in Fig. 5.

4.3   Procedure

The study took place in a quiet and empty laboratory. Hygiene measures as required in the institution were ensured for each user as of COVID-19. After providing consent and filling in the demographic questionnaire, participants calibrated the eye-tracker and started the study. Only brief instructions were given as training, as the task was straightforward for all users to perform. At the beginning of each trial, the participant's goal was displayed in VR, either as question (i.e. information search) or as the person, animal or object they had to find in the scene (i.e., object search). This was displayed for five seconds, after which we would start measuring task completion time. We also told participants that during object search trials no hints were hidden in any of the AR panels and that these were of no use to the task. After participants completed both search conditions for each of the AR panel behaviors they filled in a brief usability survey using a 5-point Likert scale.

Survey questions were specifically chosen based on what we aim to find out: how easy and intuitive the task was and how stressed and distracted participants felt. The 4 Likert questions were: *"Performing the task using this adaptation was easy/intuitive/stressful/distracting"*. They were chosen to assess the trade-off between performance and experience. After completing all tasks, participants reported on their favorite conditions and provided a brief rationale.

4.4   Participants

26 people participated in the study (5F) with a mean age of 29.2 years ($SD = 10$). Using a 5-point Likert scale participants reported high affinity with technology ($M = 4.23$, $SD = 0.86$) and moderate VR/AR affinity ($M = 2.88$, $SD = 1.24$).

4.5   Results

Below we report on task completion times, usability and user feedback/preference. As two users were identified as outlier as of large times, we excluded them from the statistical analysis.

Task Completion Times. We conducted a Shapiro-Wilk test using SPSS. It showed that the data of all conditions follow a normal distribution: information task + all on ($p = .11$), information task + gaze ($p = .51$), object task + all on ($p = .39$), object task + gaze ($p = .2$). An ANOVA showed a significant effect of task ($F(1,25)=257.4$, $p < .001$, $r = .88$) and adaptation method ($F(1,25) = 12$, $p = .002$, $r = 1$) on task completion time, as well as a significant interaction effect ($F(1,25) = 12$, $p < .001$, $r = .63$). Post-hoc pairwise comparisons with Bonferroni corrections showed the two techniques had a significant effect on task completion time in the object ($p = .035$) and information search task ($p = .002$). In information search the particular times are *all on* ($M = 21.48$ s, $SD = 12.01$ s), *gaze adaptive* ($M = 37.3$ s, $SD = 17.4$ s); in object search *all on* ($M = 12.4$ s, $SD = 6.5$ s),

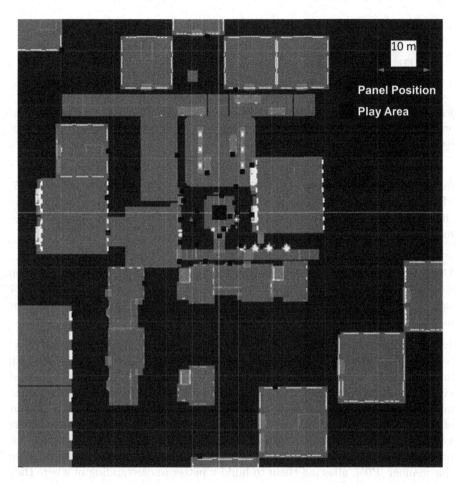

Fig. 5. The city-like environment used in the search study. All the AR panels are displayed in green, and participants' play area is displayed in red (i.e., the area in which participants were free to move in during the study). (Color figure online)

gaze adaptive (M = 9.4 s, SD = 3.7 s). This shows that the *All_on* method was faster in information search, and the *Gaze* $t_a = 0$ method faster in the object search task.

Usability. Usability results are shown in Fig. 6b) and c). We used a Friedman test with post-hoc Wilcoxon signed rank tests with Bonferroni corrections, of which we report the significant results only. For the information search task, the effect of the adaptation method was statistically significant for the category "distracting" (Z = −2.8, p = .006, r = .4). For the object search task, significant effects were revealed in categories "ease" (Z = −2, p = .047, r = .29), "intuitiveness" (Z = −2, p = .042, r = .29), and "distracting" (Z = −3.6, p < .001, r = .52). Users

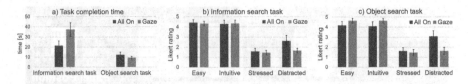

Fig. 6. Results of the search study: a) Average task completion time for the two tasks and conditions. Likert rating for information b) and object search task c). The error bars denote 95% CI.

found *Gaze_adaptive* (M=4.62, SD=.58) easier to use than *All_on* (M=4.17, SD=.96). Users perceived *Gaze_adaptive* (M=4.62, SD=.58) as more intuitive than *All_on* (M=4.1, SD=1.1). Lastly, they found *All_on* (M=3.1, SD=1.35) more distracting than the *Gaze_adaptive* technique (M=1.63, SD=.86).

User Feedback. The general concept of gaze-based AR activation was well received and described as "immersive" [P7, P12] and "practical" [P17]. P17 said: "this could replace looking at your phone while walking (...) to find out information about a shop or something (...)".

Information Search Task. 10 out of 26 participants preferred the *all on* panel behavior setting, with nine participants highlighting the speed and ease at which information could be scanned. Other reasons for this preference were the reduced visual movement necessary [P18] and the reduced likeliness of overlooking some information [P4]. The *gaze adaptive* condition was preferred more often (11 out of 26 participants), with six participants mentioning reduced information overload. Two participants reported that this was a "more pleasant" mechanism for prolonged use, and others reported they could focus better on a single panel in this manner [P05], allowing them to build a better understanding of where they had looked already [P23]. More generally [P6, P14, P22] reported preferring the "feel of it", but [P23] suggested a more explicit gaze behavior to trigger the AR panels (e.g., a "blink or similar"). The remaining five participants did not express any preference.

Object Search Task. 24 out of 26 participants preferred the *gaze adaptive* AR panels, citing being less distracting (14), not getting in the way of the search task (6), and how intuitive it was [P6, P13]. On the other hand, the all on behavior was preferred by one participant who could "easily search around the panels" [P22]. Finally, one participant reported no preference as it felt the progress bars that responded to gaze could be distracting [P25].

Concurrent Search Tasks. Lastly, we asked participants to imagine a more representative scenario where they would often have to alternate between information and object search tasks. In this scenario most participants still preferred the *gaze adaptive* behavior (22 out of 26), with one participant highlighting how AI could play a crucial role in this domain: "maybe the adoption of different

Fig. 7. Various examples of AR panels from our museum AR prototype application: (a) shows a first AR panel after it has been triggered, simply displaying the name of the object it is matched to and a green controller that can trigger further content (b and c). Gazing at content in purple plays back audio (b). Finally, the purple line is purely illustrative of the user's gaze and was not shown in the UI. (Color figure online)

(dwell) times for different objects (...) according to your interests". [P25]. Further, one participant referred that the dwell user feedback was quite effective at promoting exploration. Finally, two participants reported no preference in this scenario, and one reported preferring the *all on* panel behavior.

4.6 Discussion

We studied a gaze-adaptive UI for AR in a virtual city with a plethora of information, firstly quantifying the trade-off between performance, user experience, and occlusion issues. The main insight is that users, after experiencing both tasks, find the gaze-adaptive UI more suitable as a UI mode. Users found the always-on condition, a default AR viewing mode, more distracting in both tasks.

In the task where users focused on the VR environment, we discovered that users are faster with the gaze-adaptive UI and found it easier and more intuitive. Note that it would be misleading to assume that this is an expected result. The gaze-adaptive UI dynamically triggers information on gaze, which could as well be distracting, and affect performance, compared to a static information visualisation. Yet, our study showed that this is not the case in the tested condition.

In the task where users focused on retrieving information from AR panels, interestingly we find that even when users are faster with the *All_on* condition, users preferences were split, and they also found the constant display as more distracting. Thus, in cases when usability is prioritised over performance, as it can be with many open AR environments, the gaze-adaptive UI is a promising alternative UI mode.

Our study has several limitations to consider when interpreting the findings. It was focused on an abstract virtual city task (not real AR), and a basic task of visual search. Such an abstraction allows to gather a more generalisable result, however real world situations can be different and the UI is likely to need adaptations. To better understand the utility in practice, in the following we investigate gaze-adaptation for a real use case.

5   Field Study: Museum Application

Following prior work in which deployments in museum were used as a powerful approach for in-situ studies of novel technologies and concepts and to validate lab findings [37], we implemented a prototype application for use in a museum. The application came and was a classic example of an AR application that can provide relevant information and media-rich content without getting in the way of the user's experience. This was studied during a museum's standard opening hours and lasted for three days. We recruited 50 participants on the spot as they visited one of the museum's exhibitions. We observed a balanced split between young/senior adults, no gender bias, and high diversity in nationality, but did not collect specific demographics to minimize the study duration.

5.1   Experimental Setup

Our prototype was developed for the German Museum in Munich[1], Germany and augments a music studio exhibition spanning approximately 4×2 m and featuring 15 objects. The studio featured historic sound generators/transformers and was chosen as the location due to a favorable, undisturbed position and because the available content suited our setup. Participants' movements were tracked in front of the exhibition in an area of 3.5×3 m using Vive base stations, and static hit boxes were placed over each object. The entire interaction was controlled via gaze, and unlike the previous study, each AR panel had between two to four layers of information that could contain more content and media (triggered after a dwell times of 300 ms, see Fig. 7). Sound in particular was played while participants looked at the appropriate AR panel; these were displayed at 35% opacity so that the exhibition was always perceivable, and always facing the participant for improved readability.

Since the setup was not a controlled study, we used the chance to test new ideas and react to participant feedback on the fly. Adjustments and implementations were done during downtime or before visitors arrived. As such, we completely refrained from markers indicating interactable objects in initial runs, in fear they'd obscure the exhibit too much. However, they proved very necessary according to comments and behaviour of the first < 10 participants (see visual feedback results). Following participant feedback from the previous study, we designed a simpler user feedback mechanism that displays a relevant character over an object when this is not being gazed at, instead of progress bar (see Fig. 8). Additionally, these characters faded out once the corresponding AR panel has been interacted with. These could still be triggered, but now required a dwell time of 600 ms. This way, viewed panels were less prone to accidental activation, as they are now only offering old, possibly boring information. Since users are still likely to scan these objects again in search for new, it seemed logical to raise the respective threshold of confidence for inferred interest, i.e. activation time. Finally, we used the same hardware as before with the addition of a Zed Mini

---

[1] Deutsches Museum: http://www.deutsches-museum.de/.

Fig. 8. The museum scene when none of the AR panels are active. A simple and relevant character is displayed over each object, indicating these can be gazed at for further content. Two of these characters appear faded out to indicate users already interacted with them ("G" and "C").

Mixed-Reality[2] camera for high-resolution video see-through AR (2560×720 p, 60 fps, $110°$ FoV), and thus a more pleasant experience of the exhibition.

5.2   Procedure and Metrics

Participants were acquired by a sign at the exhibition, by evoked interest due to other users testing the setup, or verbal invitation by the experimenter. Instructions included a brief explanation of hardware, the UI, and gaze adaptation, as well as an instruction on how to put on and adjust the headset, which was helped with if asked for. No particular task was given to participants other than casually engaging with the augmented exhibition. This was preceded by the calibration of the eye-tracker and some simple instructions on the functionality of our application. Afterwards, the UI was immediately active and reactive to gaze. Participants interacted with the prototype for approximately seven to 10 min, viewing over 80% of all AR panels developed (including its layers). We took notes of participants verbal comments and actions, and asked for optional feedback on ease of use, speed, and how natural the interaction felt (via a 5-point Likert scale). From mental reconstructions, most verbal comments were positive, with only a few negative ones. Of the 50 users, 22 left written comments not referring to technicalities (e.g. headset fit). 14 gave general positive feedback along the lines of "interesting", "interactive" and "easy to use". Others gave constructive feedback regarding functions and behaviour, e.g. activation time. The other 28 users only left ratings.

5.3   Results

The application was well received, with median scores of 4 for ease of use ($\sigma^2 = 0.33$), 5 for speed of use ($\sigma^2 = 0.45$), and 4 for how natural the experience was (σ^2

---

[2] https://www.stereolabs.com/zed-mini/.

= 0.68). Participants described it as "interesting" [P17, P28, P43], "intuitive" [P28], "effective" [P29, P36, P49], "wonderful" [P37] and "very cool" [P50].

Temporal Activation. As for the previous implementation, participants were positive about the short dwell times (300 ms): "It was so fast it almost felt supernatural at times."/"I especially liked the fast and prompt reaction". Only two users preferred longer dwell times [P50]: "it was like I was being flooded by information"; "some sort of confirmation for the activation (...) as I was having a hard time viewing the objects without AR information" [P49]. In early runs, longer dwell times were tested to allow spectating the exhibit better, but proved impractical, as users didn't gaze long enough to trigger the UI.

Visual Feedback. At the first prototypes without visual indicators, participants reported a feeling of "missing out", i.e., not knowing if there was an AR panel left they had not seen yet. We changed it afterwards and added visual feedback in form of letters, as described in the description of the application – which eliminated this type of question. The experimenter also observed that with this prototype, users were revisiting the same panels in search for new and partly missing out on others. For this reason, we added another feature of whether users have already visited a panel: the corresponding indicator had lower opacity to indicate that it has already been viewed, allowing users to quickly assess their prior interaction. Also, one user suggested enhancing the letters we used. We could use descriptive symbols or short names instead of such characters. Nonetheless the response was quite positive: "it felt a little too technological at first, but turned out to be quite useful to find what you had not seen yet".

Multi-layered AR Panels. One concern was the newly added multi-layered AR panels, which potentially could occlude large portions of participants FoV. This was proven not to be the case: "while you are reading the text, you do not want to view anything else anyway". Also, while participants managed to unfold AR panels up to four times, they reported that more than this could quickly become cumbersome. Finally, the main issue reported was the amount of text in each AR panel and how this demanded more attention than participants might want to provide in a casual exploration.

5.4 Discussion

Through this field study we have validated some of our findings from the prior lab experiment such as the dwell time and the overall use of gaze adaptive AR panels. We have also expanded on this mechanism by allowing participants to not only trigger these panels but navigate between layered content using solely their gaze.

The overall results are very positive, particularly taking into account these were every day museum attendees with no particular training in AR or eye-tracking technologies (and despite any novelty effects). Participants seemed motivated by our user feedback to fully engage with the exhibition, but were not shy of ideas on how to improve the visual elements of our UI. This included animations or more focused textual descriptions.

Notably, this was quite a different task from the ones proposed in the previous study, and future work should consider some of our participant feedback regarding temporal activations (i.e., it could be found to be too fast for casual, leisurely explorations). While it's possible, that results might be affected by the filter, that only people open to technology were willing to try the prototype, it's probably not significant, as most people seemed to be of average technological understanding. The exhibit, while quite technological itself, was situated in a non technological part of the museum featuring music instruments in general.

6 Overall Discussion

We discuss the main trade-offs of gaze adaptive AR interfaces in light of the study findings and our experiences across the two studies.

Search vs. Occlusion Trade-off. One of the main themes investigated in the paper is the contrast between the gaze-based adaptation with a default mode where it is always visible. Our research indicates that it depends on a search versus occlusion trade-off. The default is best for highest performance to find a specific information in one out of many panels in the environment, useful for tasks that prioritise virtual content. The gaze-adaptive UI provides a trade-off where the reality is temporally occluded, making it easier to perceive and search in reality, albeit still able to instantly access context information in the vicinity. Thus, a hybrid technique that prioritizes more real world viewing but also supports virtual content. We believe our implementation showed promising results, as users rated it significantly less distracting in both tasks. Future work could explore different gaze-adaptive UIs to improve search performance, e.g., panels that are always-on, but fade out when the user do not fixate them.

Multi-layer Information. Our museum application demonstrated a qualitative advantage to an always-on condition. If all the information panels of this application would be active, the entire field of view is occluded, whereas the gaze-adaptive UI allowed users to interact with panels on demand. Occlusion is substantially minimised, as the panels only open when fixating a small indicator dot on the object, while the remaining object area is free for viewing. Moreover, by integrating an advanced functionality where users can navigate more pages by gaze selections allowed to substantially increase the amount of information that users can experience. This points to thinking of gaze-adaptive UIs for a different class of use cases, where users often shift their focus between real objects and the information it could encapsulate.

Advanced Gaze Behaviour Adaptation. By deploying the gaze-adaptive application in the museum, we gained insights into the applicability and features of the system. Visitors who experienced the system enjoyed the subtly appearing augmentations around the museum artifacts they are looking at, and saw the potential to enrich the experience of exhibits. In addition, we believe that further mechanisms to adapt to the user's gaze behaviour can be beneficial, such as subtle indicators that communicate where AR panels reside before active, or historic gaze information to mark what has been already viewed. The order of appearance of gaze adaptive panels can be based on what the user has seen before, enabling a story-telling experience that gradually unfolds new information.

Transfer to VR Interaction. As the user study shows, many of our findings regarding gaze adaptive AR interfaces are also applicable in VR. Using gaze as a modality to access context information seems to be independent from the type of mixed reality interface, as long as interactable objects are highlighted in an appropriate way, e.g. by a visual marker.

Effect of 2D Targets. In the object search task of the user study, we chose to use 2D targets, that always face towards the user and stand out from the 3D background. This tends to make the task easier in comparison to 3D objects, that might be occluded or face away from the user. Assuming that the differences in the task completion time are founded on the distraction of the user by the panels, it could be stated that the gaze-adaptive method is faster for object search, even if the task gets more difficult to complete.

7   Design Recommendations

Across the two user studies, we derived the following design recommendations:

- We recommend a fast activation time (0.2–0.5 s), because in our context users tended to miss interactive objects as they did not dwell long enough on them otherwise.
- In the context we studied, occlusion was not a major issue as people seem to want to view the occluding information anyway most of the time.
- Still, a mechanism for returning to no augmentation is necessary, which could be simply the user's action of averting gaze in a less densely augmented area, or other means of input, e.g. a gesture or gaze reactive HUD element.
- A visual marker indicating interactable objects should be employed to ensure a good applications experience where users are aware of the interactions possible. The marker can carry a low level of information, e.g. a letter, symbol or a short name, as long as it is unobstructive. Moderate colors and reduced opacity are recommended.
- To give users even more reference for navigation, markers can react to being activated and change color like a clicked link.

8   Future Work

To assess the effect of the minimal occlusion in the gaze-adaptive UI, it would be interesting to compare gaze-adaptive UIs to not using AR at all. Additionally, comparing against a manual activation of the AR panels is important to understand further trade-offs and identify the limitations of the techniques. In principle we believe manual input is more useful for highly interactive applications like games or messaging, while gaze-adaptive UIs allow light information retrieval in everyday situations. Nonetheless, our study reveals, and contributes a first empirical assessment of the contrasting interaction properties in comparison to a more basic always-on AR experience. Another challenge to consider is handling and mitigating occlusions as well as testing different methods of conveying visual information surpassing text, such as animations, 3d models, or screen space augmentations corresponding to the currently viewed object.

Furthermore, an examination of additional types of content will be necessary to exploit the full potential of gaze adaptive interfaces. While gaze adaptation as technique for activation is principally independent of the content's type, parameters, like dwell or fade out time may be varied.

Our system and subsequent evaluations were based on pass-through AR with a large headset. The field of view, lower resolution (than real world) and weight can have an effect on users. We envision our concept to be applied with lightweight AR devices to fulfill its full potential in everyday settings.

Prior research on interaction in public space shows, people are often in groups and that user interfaces can be designed to account for this [31]. Future work could look into how the concept could be applied to multi-user scenarios. This can point to interesting new ideas, for example, in the museum context, in a group of people it would be easy to observe if other group members are inspecting an exhibit or are reading relevant information. If both are wearing AR glasses, this might be less obvious. Future work could look at mitigating such cases, for example by providing indicators what fellow visitors are currently engaging with, or which parts of an exhibit have received more attention by the people.

9   Conclusion

We explored a gaze adaptive UI that allows users lightweight access of context information about real objects in the environment. Such a method provides a unique trade-off between reality perception and virtual UI access. We firstly present an empirical comparison that reveals how user performance and experience is affected in tasks that focus on either reality or virtual UI. We demonstrate the utility of the method by a museum application of the concept, that allows users to consume multi-level information at a glance, and report on user feedback from its field deployment. Our research offers insights into trade-offs and UI design of gaze in more open AR scenarios, and the positive user reception is a promising result to employ gaze adaptation as an always-on UI mode when AR becomes more lightweight and populated in the consumer market. In future, we aim to extend our investigation to more optical see through AR devices and to broader use cases such as tourism and shopping, as well as effects and preferences of long term use.

Acknowledgments. We thank the German Museum in Munich and in particular Claus Henkensiefken for their collaboration in the context of this project as well as all visitors who participated in our research. The presented work was funded by the German Research Foundation (DFG) under project no. 425869382 and by dtec.bw – Digitalization and Technology Research Center of the Bundeswehr [MuQuaNet].

References

1. Ajanki, A., et al.: An augmented reality interface to contextual information. Virtual Reality **15**(2–3), 161–173 (2011)
2. Azuma, R., Furmanski, C.: Evaluating label placement for augmented reality view management. In: Proceedings of the 2nd IEEE/ACM International Symposium on Mixed and Augmented Reality, p. 66. IEEE Computer Society (2003)
3. Bell, B., Feiner, S., Höllerer, T.: View management for virtual and augmented reality. In: Proceedings of the 14th Annual ACM Symposium on User Interface Software and Technology, UIST 2001, pp. 101–110. ACM, New York (2001). https://doi.org/10.1145/502348.502363
4. Bernardos, A.M., Gómez, D., Casar, J.R.: A comparison of head pose and deictic pointing interaction methods for smart environments. Int. J. Hum.-Comput. Interact. **32**(4), 325–351 (2016)
5. Blattgerste, J., Renner, P., Pfeiffer, T.: Advantages of eye-gaze over head-gaze-based selection in virtual and augmented reality under varying field of views. In: Proceedings of the Workshop on Communication by Gaze Interaction, COGAIN 2018, pp. 1–9. ACM, New York (2018). https://doi.org/10.1145/3206343.3206349
6. Bolt, R.A.: Gaze-orchestrated dynamic windows. In: ACM SIGGRAPH Computer Graphics, vol. 15, pp. 109–119. ACM (1981)
7. Lindlbauer, D., Feit, A., Hilliges, O.: Context-aware online adaptation of mixed reality interfaces. In: Proceedings of the 32th Annual ACM Symposium on User Interface Software and Technology, UIST 2019, pp. 213–222. ACM, New York (2019)
8. Davari, S., Lu, F., Bowman, D.A.: Occlusion management techniques for everyday glanceable AR interfaces. In: 2020 IEEE Conference on Virtual Reality and 3D User Interfaces Abstracts and Workshops (VRW), pp. 324–330. IEEE (2020)
9. Feiner, S., Macintyre, B., Seligmann, D.: Knowledge-based augmented reality. Commun. ACM **36**(7), 53–62 (1993). https://doi.org/10.1145/159544.159587
10. Feiner, S.K.: Augmented reality: a new way of seeing. Sci. Am. **286**(4), 48–55 (2002)
11. Fender, A., Herholz, P., Alexa, M., Müller, J.: Optispace: automated placement of interactive 3D projection mapping content. In: Proceedings of the 2018 CHI Conference on Human Factors in Computing Systems, p. 269. ACM (2018)
12. Grubert, J., Langlotz, T., Zollmann, S., Regenbrecht, H.: Towards pervasive augmented reality: context-awareness in augmented reality. IEEE Trans. Vis. Comput. Graph. **23**(6), 1706–1724 (2017). https://doi.org/10.1109/TVCG.2016.2543720
13. Hartmann, K., Götzelmann, T., Ali, K., Strothotte, T.: Metrics for functional and aesthetic label layouts. In: Butz, A., Fisher, B., Krüger, A., Olivier, P. (eds.) SG 2005. LNCS, vol. 3638, pp. 115–126. Springer, Heidelberg (2005). https://doi.org/10.1007/11536482_10
14. Höllerer, T., Feiner, S.: Mobile Augmented Reality. Telegeoinformatics: Location-Based Computing and Services. Taylor and Francis Books Ltd., London (2004)

15. Imamov, S., Monzel, D., Lages, W.S.: Where to display? How interface position affects comfort and task switching time on glanceable interfaces. In: 2020 IEEE Conference on Virtual Reality and 3D User Interfaces (VR), pp. 851–858 (2020). https://doi.org/10.1109/VR46266.2020.00110

16. Ishiguro, Y., Rekimoto, J.: Peripheral vision annotation: noninterference information presentation method for mobile augmented reality. In: Proceedings of the 2nd Augmented Human International Conference, AH 2011, pp. 8:1–8:5. ACM, New York (2011). https://doi.org/10.1145/1959826.1959834

17. Jacob, R.J.K.: What you look at is what you get: eye movement-based interaction techniques. In: Proceedings of the SIGCHI Conference on Human Factors in Computing Systems, CHI 1990, pp. 11–18. ACM, New York (1990). https://doi.org/10.1145/97243.97246

18. Julier, S., Baillot, Y., Brown, D., Lanzagorta, M.: Information filtering for mobile augmented reality. IEEE Comput. Graph. Appl. 22(5), 12–15 (2002). https://doi.org/10.1109/MCG.2002.1028721

19. Keil, J., Zoellner, M., Engelke, T., Wientapper, F., Schmitt, M.: Controlling and filtering information density with spatial interaction techniques via handheld augmented reality. In: Shumaker, R. (ed.) VAMR 2013. LNCS, vol. 8021, pp. 49–57. Springer, Heidelberg (2013). https://doi.org/10.1007/978-3-642-39405-8_6

20. Kim, M., Lee, M.K., Dabbish, L.: Shop-i: Gaze based Interaction in the physical world for in-store social shopping experience. In: Proceedings of the 33rd Annual ACM Conference Extended Abstracts on Human Factors in Computing Systems, CHI EA 2015, pp. 1253–1258. Association for Computing Machinery, Seoul (2015). https://doi.org/10.1145/2702613.2732797

21. Kytö, M., Ens, B., Piumsomboon, T., Lee, G.A., Billinghurst, M.: Pinpointing: precise head- and eye-based target selection for augmented reality. In: Proceedings of the 2018 CHI Conference on Human Factors in Computing Systems, CHI 2018, pp. 81:1–81:14. ACM, New York (2018). https://doi.org/10.1145/3173574.3173655

22. Lages, W., Bowman, D.: Adjustable adaptation for spatial augmented reality workspaces. In: Symposium on Spatial User Interaction, SUI 2019, Association for Computing Machinery, New York (2019). https://doi.org/10.1145/3357251.3358755

23. Lu, F., Davari, S., Lisle, L., Li, Y., Bowman, D.A.: Glanceable ar: evaluating information access methods for head-worn augmented reality. In: 2020 IEEE Conference on Virtual Reality and 3D User Interfaces (VR), pp. 930–939. IEEE (2020)

24. Madsen, J.B., Tatzqern, M., Madsen, C.B., Schmalstieg, D., Kalkofen, D.: Temporal coherence strategies for augmented reality labeling. IEEE Trans. Vis. Comput. Graph. 22(4), 1415–1423 (2016)

25. Mäkelä, V., et al.: Virtual field studies: conducting studies on public displays in virtual reality. In: Proceedings of the 2020 CHI Conference on Human Factors in Computing Systems, CHI 2020, pp. 1–15. Association for Computing Machinery, New York (2020). https://doi.org/10.1145/3313831.3376796

26. McNamara, A., Boyd, K., George, J., Suther, A., Jones, W., Oh, S.: Information placement in virtual reality. In: 2019 IEEE Conference on Virtual Reality and 3D User Interfaces (VR), pp. 1078–1079 (2019). https://doi.org/10.1109/VR.2019.8797910, iSSN: 2642-5246

27. McNamara, A., Boyd, K., Oh, D., Sharpe, R., Suther, A.: Using eye tracking to improve information retrieval in virtual reality. In: 2018 IEEE International Symposium on Mixed and Augmented Reality Adjunct (ISMAR-Adjunct), pp. 242–243 (2018). https://doi.org/10.1109/ISMAR-Adjunct.2018.00076

28. McNamara, A., Kabeerdoss, C.: Mobile augmented reality: placing labels based on gaze position. In: 2016 IEEE International Symposium on Mixed and Augmented Reality (ISMAR-Adjunct), pp. 36–37 (2016). https://doi.org/10.1109/ISMAR-Adjunct.2016.0033

29. McNamara, A., Kabeerdoss, C., Egan, C.: Mobile user interfaces based on user attention. In: Proceedings of the 2015 Workshop on Future Mobile User Interfaces, FutureMobileUI 2015, pp. 1–3. Association for Computing Machinery, Florence (2015). https://doi.org/10.1145/2754633.2754634

30. Miniotas, D., Spakov, O., Tugoy, I., MacKenzie, I.S.: Speech-augmented eye gaze interaction with small closely spaced targets. In: Proceedings of the 2006 Symposium on Eye Tracking Research & Applications, ETRA 2006, pp. 67–72. ACM, New York (2006). https://doi.org/10.1145/1117309.1117345

31. Müller, J., Walter, R., Bailly, G., Nischt, M., Alt, F.: Looking glass: a field study on noticing interactivity of a shop window. In: Proceedings of the SIGCHI Conference on Human Factors in Computing Systems, CHI 2012, pp. 297–306. Association for Computing Machinery, New York (2012). https://doi.org/10.1145/2207676.2207718

32. Müller, L., Pfeuffer, K., Gugenheimer, J., Pfleging, B., Prange, S., Alt, F.: Spatialproto: exploring real-world motion captures for rapid prototyping of interactive mixed reality. In: Proceedings of the 2021 CHI Conference on Human Factors in Computing Systems, CHI 2021. Association for Computing Machinery, New York(2021). https://doi.org/10.1145/3411764.3445560

33. Pfeuffer, K., et al.: ARtention: a design space for gaze-adaptive user interfaces in augmented reality. Comput. Graph. **95**, 1–12 (2021). https://doi.org/10.1016/j.cag.2021.01.001. http://www.sciencedirect.com/science/article/pii/S0097849321000017

34. Pfeuffer, K., Alexander, J., Chong, M.K., Gellersen, H.: Gaze-touch: combining gaze with multi-touch for interaction on the same surface. In: Proceedings of the 27th Annual ACM Symposium on User Interface Software and Technology, UIST 2014, pp. 509–518. ACM, New York (2014). https://doi.org/10.1145/2642918.2647397

35. Pfeuffer, K., Mayer, B., Mardanbegi, D., Gellersen, H.: Gaze + pinch interaction in virtual reality. In: Proceedings of the 5th Symposium on Spatial User Interaction, pp. 99–108. ACM (2017)

36. Pfeuffer, K., Mecke, L., Delgado Rodriguez, S., Hassib, M., Maier, H., Alt, F.: Empirical evaluation of gaze-enhanced menus in virtual reality. In: 26th ACM Symposium on Virtual Reality Software and Technology, VRST 2020. Association for Computing Machinery, New York (2020). https://doi.org/10.1145/3385956.3418962

37. Prange, S., Müller, V., Buschek, D., Alt, F.: Quakequiz: a case study on deploying a playful display application in a museum context. In: Proceedings of the 16th International Conference on Mobile and Ubiquitous Multimedia, MUM 2017, pp. 49–56. Association for Computing Machinery, New York (2017). https://doi.org/10.1145/3152832.3152841

38. Rivu, R., Abdrabou, Y., Pfeuffer, K., Esteves, A., Meitner, S., Alt, F.: Stare: gaze-assisted face-to-face communication in augmented reality. In: ACM Symposium on Eye Tracking Research and Applications, ETRA 2020 Adjunct. Association for Computing Machinery, New York (2020). https://doi.org/10.1145/3379157.3388930

39. Rosten, E., Reitmayr, G., Drummond, T.: Real-time video annotations for augmented reality. In: Bebis, G., Boyle, R., Koracin, D., Parvin, B. (eds.) ISVC 2005. LNCS, vol. 3804, pp. 294–302. Springer, Heidelberg (2005). https://doi.org/10.1007/11595755_36

40. Sibert, L.E., Jacob, R.J.K.: Evaluation of eye gaze interaction. In: Proceedings of SIGCHI Conference on Human Factors in Computing Systems, CHI 2000, pp. 281–288. ACM, New York (2000). https://doi.org/10.1145/332040.332445

41. Stellmach, S., Dachselt, R.: Look & touch: gaze-supported target acquisition. In: Proceedings of the SIGCHI Conference on Human Factors in Computing Systems, CHI 2012, pp. 2981–2990. ACM, New York (2012). https://doi.org/10.1145/2207676.2208709

42. Tanriverdi, V., Jacob, R.J.K.: Interacting with eye movements in virtual environments. In: Proceedings of the SIGCHI Conference on Human Factors in Computing Systems, CHI 2000, pp. 265–272. ACM, New York (2000). https://doi.org/10.1145/332040.332443

43. Tönnis, M., Klinker, G.: Boundary conditions for information visualization with respect to the user's gaze. In: Proceedings of the 5th Augmented Human International Conference, AH 2014, pp. 44:1–44:8. ACM, New York (2014). https://doi.org/10.1145/2582051.2582095

44. Velichkovsky, B., Sprenger, A., Unema, P.: Towards gaze-mediated interaction: collecting solutions of the Midas touch problem. In: Howard, S., Hammond, J., Lindgaard, G. (eds.) Human-Computer Interaction INTERACT '97. ITIFIP, pp. 509–516. Springer, Boston (1997). https://doi.org/10.1007/978-0-387-35175-9_77

45. Vertegaal, R., et al.: Attentive user interfaces. Commun. ACM **46**(3), 30–33 (2003)

46. White, S., Feiner, S.: Sitelens: situated visualization techniques for urban site visits. In: Proceedings of the SIGCHI Conference on Human Factors in Computing Systems, CHI 2009, pp. 1117–1120. ACM, New York (2009). https://doi.org/10.1145/1518701.1518871

On the Use of Handheld Augmented Reality for Inventory Tasks: A Study with Magazine Retailers

Peter Mitts and Henrique Galvan Debarba[✉]

IT University of Copenhagen, Copenhagen, Denmark
hend@itu.dk

Abstract. In this paper we investigate if handheld augmented reality, in the form of an application running on a mainstream smartphone, can serve as a practical and effective tool for inventory tasks. Taking magazine retail as an example, we have applied a user-centered design process to research, design, implement and evaluate a handheld AR application prototype. We conducted a qualitative user study at magazine retail stores, where staff responsible for magazines were interviewed ($n = 8$) and their primary magazine handling tasks observed. After an analysis of the study findings, we selected a key task as the basis for the design, implementation and test of an AR app prototype. The task consisted of collecting and registering a list of magazines for return to the distributor. We evaluated the AR app prototype in a user study ($n = 22$), where participants used it to perform the selected task. They also performed the task using the paper list currently in use, and a second, simplified app prototype, without AR features. Task performance was measured based on time and error rate. The participant's subjective experience was also captured in the form of a post-task survey and interview. Our findings suggest that handheld AR can prove effective when used for specific, focused tasks, rather than more open-ended ones.

Keywords: Augmented reality · Handheld devices · User-centered design · User studies

1 Introduction

Augmented Reality (AR) has the capability to improve logistics workflows across a number of areas, from warehousing operations [8,17], transportation optimization and last-mile delivery [27], to enhanced value-added services [9,26]. In fact, AR technologies excel in situations where it is required to present information and functionality in a spatial, three-dimensional context, in relationship to physical objects and locations [13]. Notably, mobile augmented reality (MAR) applications are widely available today, on devices ranging from industrial grade headsets to smartphones [7]. Technological advances across the board, from mobile

© IFIP International Federation for Information Processing 2021
Published by Springer Nature Switzerland AG 2021
C. Ardito et al. (Eds.): INTERACT 2021, LNCS 12932, pp. 566–589, 2021.
https://doi.org/10.1007/978-3-030-85623-6_33

displays, cameras and sensors to broad availability of wireless network connectivity, and through it access to cloud computing resources, provide the building blocks to enable widespread implementation of MAR for professionals as well as consumers [2].

Here we explore how MAR can be used in inventory tasks, and in particular, in the management of a magazine inventory. Physically handling a store's magazine inventory can require a significant investment of working hours spent on tasks such as receiving magazines, correctly placing them on stands, and locating outdated magazines to be returned to the distributor. Traditional tools, like paper pick lists and shipping waybills, leave a lot of work for the store staff. For example, the physical magazines still have to be checked against their identifying details from the list (name, volume, etc.), and the correct magazine stands located and eventually memorized.

An AR solution for magazine retail can leverage the built-in computer vision features of the mainstream AR platforms, coupled with magazine cover image databases, to more easily identify magazines without having to check a list or scan a barcode. While distributors can potentially provide supporting resources like these, they do not have the authority to dictate any specialized hardware purchases by the customer stores they serve. Therefore the smartphone is the most realistic hardware candidate, since it is likely to already be available, ready for installation of a new AR application. Being handheld, however, means that the benefits of AR have to be balanced against the drawback of requiring a hand to hold the device.

To better understand the specific challenges of AR for inventory management and analyze potential avenues for AR functionalities, we conducted a qualitative field research with seven magazine retail stores. We interviewed the staff responsible for magazines ($n = 8$), and carried observations as they performed typical inventory management tasks. This research informed the selection of a realistic task to be used as the basis for the design of a smartphone app prototype with AR features. The task consists of collecting and registering a list of magazines that have to be returned to the distributor. A user study was conducted to evaluate the AR app prototype ($n = 22$), compared to the paper list currently in use, and a second, simplified app prototype, without AR features. Our results indicate that different aspects of the task could be improved by adopting a combination of the AR app and the simplified list based app, over the commonly used paper list.

In summary, this study contributes to AR design research by:

- Investigating the potential role of AR in retail stores, with a focus on magazine retail, where current research on AR and logistics may not apply due to differences in scale, tasks and environments.
- Designing and evaluating a mobile AR application prototype developed to address some of the problems uncovered in the qualitative investigation.
- Providing reflections and design guidelines based on the results and observations of the user evaluation.

2   Background

2.1   Augmented Reality in Logistics

In [15], Porter et al. argue that AR can create business value in two broad ways; by becoming part of the product itself, or by improving performance across the whole value chain. This paper is particularly concerned with the latter, where AR can be used to enhance the flow of information from a database to the operator by presenting contextualized information. This can benefit many ordinary tasks in logistics and the industry, such as wayfinding, where AR is used to issues contextualized navigation instructions with the path to a given destination [4,22], object search, where AR emphasizes the object of interest [10,17], assembly instructions, where AR is used to detect the current stage of assembly and present step-by-step 3D information to an operator [24], and remote guidance, where a remote instructor can issue contextualized instructions to an AR supported operator [18,23,25].

Cirulis and Ginters [5] present the basics of logistics processes, and possibilities for improvement, such as reducing workload and easing decision making in routine operations. They claim that solutions built on AR technology can decrease object pickup time and error rates in human-operated warehouses by providing workers with the information they need to make better decisions. This information can be visualized in the worker's physical environment, to further simplify its interpretation. For example, guidance and wayfinding instructions can be displayed as 3D graphics that shows, rather than tells, where to go. Providing a more concrete example, Cirulis and Ginters [5] describe a process for designing an AR solution for order picking, which is a common warehouse task. First, a virtual model of the warehouse is constructed. It can be as simple as a 2D floor plan, or significantly more elaborate with areas, locations and paths represented in 3D space. An optimal pathfinding solution can then be generated for a given set of objects in the order they should be picked up. The worker is typically equipped with a mobile AR device such as head-mounted display (HMD) or a handheld screen device, such as a tablet or smartphone, that will present a sequence of steps to be followed as a visual overlay. In fact, assisted indoor navigation is a recurrent topic in AR research, and while warehouse research normally focus on head-mounted AR, the topic has also been investigated for a range of devices and from different perspectives. For instance, Chung et al. focused on the use of projection based AR [4], while Soulard [22] explored user interfaces for handheld devices.

According to Reif et al. [17,21], the hardware in an AR system consists of three distinct parts; the visualization, interaction, and tracking system. They develop a concrete AR-based solution for warehouse workers, Pick-by-vision, that includes the first two components. A HMD is used for visualization, and the user interacts with the system using an adjusting knob and speech input. Evaluation of the system in a real warehouse environment shows that users are faster and make fewer errors, compared to using a paper list. While the results of the study were very promising, the paper also concludes with recognizing the challenge of porting research systems built on similar hardware into practical industry use.

Moreover, a functional tracking and visualization system can be used for other inventory management tasks, besides wayfinding. Notably, Chen et al. [3] propose using the tracking and processing capabilities of mobile devices for registering the location of inventory items in a library, which can enable a system to effectively be used for both, navigation guidance and maintenance of the stock database.

Here we focus on a related but significantly different problem. The logistical challenges in magazine retail, and retail more generally, are quite different from the ones in warehouses. The distances to cover within the store are shorter, so wayfinding is less complicated. Conversely, a store presents a more dense, "target-rich" environment when it comes to actually spotting the magazine to find on a given stand. The environment is also less controllable and stable than a warehouse. As customers browse magazines, they are put back in different locations than where they initially were.

Moreover, literature that investigates the use of AR in retail settings seems to focus mostly on marketing strategies and consumer engagement, with the objective to enhance the experience of users with a specific product, brand or store. For instance, Bonetti et al. [1] investigate the augmentation of physical stores with a virtual model of the store and product information. Their exploration suggest that augmenting the store with AR can increase consumers' desire to shop at a particular retailer. In contrast to that, here we are concerned with how handheld AR can improve the work of store employees.

2.2   Designing for Handheld Augmented Reality

Augmented reality is a relatively recent technological development, and user interface conventions have not reached the same maturity level as traditional 2D user interfaces. According to de Sá and Churchill [19], challenges when designing for handheld, or any form of mobile, AR include discoverability, interpretability and usability.

AR applications need to remain usable while displaying their augmented world realistically. However, since they tend to present their content in a layered way, this can sometimes result in an inherently messy appearance [2]. To ensure an adequate user experience, Kourouthanassis et al. offer a set of general design principles [12]:

- Use the context (e.g. location) for providing content.
- Deliver relevant-to-the-task content (filter and personalize the AR content).
- Inform the user about content privacy.
- Support different application configurations, to ensure an adequate user experience based on the available processing power, system resources, network connectivity etc.
- Make it easy for the user to learn how to use the application.

Instead of trying to fit 2D User Interface (UI) conventions to a 3D AR UI, or attempting to create a set of new conventions from scratch, we can be inspired by other fields. Video games are such a field, which has already tackled the challenges of viewing and interacting with a 3D world through a 2D display. In [6] Dillman et al. reviewed the cues in a selection of video games, and classified into a framework based on three dimensions; purpose, markedness and trigger, i.e. the goal of the cue, how distinct the interaction cue is from the environment and what makes the cue become visible, respectively.

The three dimensions are mapped to AR, followed by a series of examples describing visual interaction cues from existing AR applications in terms of the framework. The framework is also presented as a tool for generating new interaction cue design ideas.

3 Prototype

3.1 Field Research

This research was developed in collaboration with one of the largest postal companies in Denmark. Their magazine vendor customers are comprised of different types of businesses, from corner shops and grocery stores to specialty magazine stores. For many of them receiving, handling and returning of magazines requires a significant investment of working hours. The purpose of the field research was to achieve a more detailed understanding of current magazine handling and its physical context, and specifically to identify routine, error-prone tasks where AR methods may be a good fit.

The field research was conducted as a series of magazine vendor visits that included the following activities:

- A semi-structured interview, where the participant was asked about their magazine handling routines, and where and how the tasks were performed. They were also asked to freely talk about any specific things they perceived as working well, or less so, in the current system.
- Task observation, where the participant was asked to think aloud while performing their routine magazine handling tasks.
- General inspection of the store layout, focused on the placement of magazine stands in relation to the other areas where magazine tasks were performed.
- Inspection of magazine placement in the stands.

Seven magazine vendors were recruited around the greater Copenhagen, Denmark, area in a collaboration with the distribution company. The smallest store managed 68 different magazine titles whereas the largest store managed 689 different titles. At each vendor one or more employees responsible for magazine handling were interviewed, for a total of 9 staff interviews. However, one vendor later decided against participating in the interview, so the visit was limited to the inspection of store layout and magazine placement. All participants read and agreed to an informed consent form.

During the field observations two primary task candidates for prototyping and test were identified, replacing old magazines with new ones and registering magazines to return. The vendor needs to return the magazines that were replaced by newer issues and only gets billed for the difference between the original delivery and the returned amount. Therefore, it is important for the vendor to carry these tasks without mistakes since they can affect the profitability of the operation.

Replacing Old Magazines with New Ones. When new magazines are received, they are first registered in the store's point of sale system and the price checked. New price labels may be attached if needed. Then the magazines are carried out to the magazine stands. One magazine at a time, the old issue needs to be found and replaced with the new issue. Note that the old magazine may of course be sold out, so the staff member needs to first determine if this is the case, and then decide where the new issue should be placed. Finally, the old magazines are taken out to the back room. When performing this task, the main challenges are determining what stand (and where on that stand) to look for the old magazine issue, and then identifying the physical magazine issue itself. An AR app prototype could help by indicating the expected location and then further positively identifying it (using image recognition) and indicating it more precisely. Also, simply showing the cover image for the old magazine is likely to simplify the search for it, even before the addition of AR. It would also be possible to display additional product information, but that is less likely to be important to complete this particular task.

Registering Magazines to Return. Near the end of each week, the vendor receives a paper recall list, containing all the magazine issues to find, count, register and pack up in bundles for return at the end of that week. This workflow starts by going through the magazines in the back room that have already been taken down during the week (see the first task described above). Each magazine issue in the stack in the back room is checked against the list, and if it's on the list, the number of copies are registered by writing it in a designated field. The ID of the next unused bundle label (from the distributor) is also written in a separate field. Then the magazines are put in a new stack to the side. This is repeated for all the magazines in the stack. Any magazines that are not on the list are put to the side for later. Next, any remaining magazines on the list need to be found out on the magazine stands. Each remaining magazine issue on the list is looked for, and if found counted and registered on the list. Note that, as in the first workflow above, magazine issues may be sold out. Finally, the registered magazines are taken out to the back room.

This task has two distinct phases. During the first phase, the main challenge is matching a physical magazine issue with text on a row on the recall list, especially since the texts may not be identical in either content or format. The field for writing the count is also at the opposite side of the row from the title, so simply writing in the correct field can be an issue as well. An AR app prototype could help by positively identifying the magazine (using image recognition), so that the list lookup would be fully automated, and only entering the magazine count done manually. Also, simply showing the cover image for each magazine on the list is likely to simplify matching physical magazines to list items, even before the addition of AR.

During the second phase, the main challenges are determining what magazine stand (and where on that stand) to look for the magazine issue on the list, and then identifying the physical magazine issue itself. Similar to the first workflow above, an AR app prototype could help by indicating the expected location and then further positively identifying it (using image recognition) and indicating it more precisely. Again, simply showing the cover image for each magazine on the list is likely to simplify the search for it, even before the addition of AR.

Additional Findings. We have also observed other user related aspects that may affect efficiency while carrying out the tasks.

Typically only one staff member was responsible for magazines at each vendor. Other staff members may call them if they are not at work when there is a magazine related issue, like customers asking for a particular magazine. The "magazines responsible" is typically the only one on the staff who is familiar in detail with the placement scheme for the magazine stands. When less experienced staff place magazines on the stands, which can happens somewhat often, they are likely to spend significantly more time on the task, and frequently place magazines incorrectly. We believe that AR features can be particularly helpful to the naive employee that may need to carry these tasks on occasion, and we consider them as potential users later in the development and evaluation of the prototype and during the discussion.

Many of the vendors did not find the current recall list helpful, and did not register their returns on it. This meant that they did not have a record of their returns to check against the invoice later. Therefore, they cannot anticipate the cost of the invoice, having to rely solely on the verification made by the distributor. This could lead to disagreements between the vendor and the distributor as the vendor cannot verify the correctness of the invoice. We believe that the digitalization of the inventory management alone can improve the transparency in the relation between both parts.

Finally, the vendors perceived it as problematic that, for many magazines, the recall week could be weeks after the next issue has been received. This was mainly due to the fact that they did not have any extra storage space for magazines no longer for sale, but it also implies that they have to search the magazines that need to be returned from larger piles, instead of simply registering these magazines for return.

3.2   Design

The task "Registering magazines to return" was selected as a basis for the user test and prototype concept. This was due to the fact that the two distinct phases the task consists of allows for addressing two different types of user challenges; quickly identifying magazines in a stack, and finding a set of magazines on multiple magazine stands. Moreover, there is an opportunity to facilitate how vendors keep a record of the magazines that they return, which is critical to improve the transparency in the relation of the distributor with retailers.

The AR App prototype includes three main features; List, Scan and Find:

List includes a list of magazines to return, the ability to enter the return counts for each magazine and then register the counts on the list. It can also display a large version of each magazine's cover. This feature was included to address the complexity of matching a physical magazine issue with its information as presented in the recall lists, which can be time consuming. It provides users with visual information of the stock item in addition to name and issue number.

Scan allows for automatically selecting a magazine that is in front of the camera by recognition of its cover image. This simplifies the process of mapping physical items in the magazine stack with list entries in the recall list since it can immediately select a recalled magazine based on the cover of a physical copy, or indicate to the user that this magazine does not need to be returned just yet. It is an automated alternative to searching that aims to reduce the workload and number of errors of the operator.

Finally, *Find* indicates the expected locations of all the magazines on the list still without a return count entry. It combines wayfinding and image recognition to facilitate a picking task, similar to what was described earlier, but adapted to smaller and cluttered environments. This functionality should help staff with locating the recall magazines in the stands, even when they are not familiar with the layout of the shop and the different magazine categories. Therefore, we believe that this can be particularly helpful for naive users, who have little or no experience with the task.

The prototype UI includes the screens below:

Magazine List Screen: This screen contains a list of all the magazines to be returned. For each magazine, the cover, title, issue and category are displayed (see Fig. 1a). A magazine in the list can be selected by tapping it. The same scan functionality as described below for the Scan screen is also active here, so a magazine can also be selected by pointing the camera at the physical magazine's cover. When a magazine is selected, entry controls are revealed (see Fig. 1b). Initially there is no value, but tapping the + button increases the count to 0, 1, 2 and so on. The - button decreases the value. Tapping the cover opens the Large magazine cover screen. At the bottom of the list is a registration button that becomes active when all the magazines in the list have their return count entered (see Fig. 1c). Tapping the button submits the list and displays the Confirmation screen.

Large Magazine Cover Screen: This screen contains a large version of the selected magazine's cover as well as the other information displayed for it in the magazine list (see Fig. 1d). The next or previous magazine in the list can be selected by swiping left or right. The same scan functionality as described below for the

Scan screen is also active here, so a magazine can also be selected by pointing the camera at the physical magazine's cover. The return count can be increased and decreased with a pair of + and − buttons, just like on the Magazine list screen.

Scan Screen: This screen includes a large camera view, where any magazine cover recognized by the camera is selected and indicated with an outline frame. Below the camera view, the selected magazine is displayed with entry controls, so the return count can be entered directly (see Fig. 2a).

Find Screen: This screen provides indicators for finding all magazines that remain on the list without an entered return count. If the camera is not pointed towards an area where a magazine should be, the area is instead indicated by an off-screen indicator arrow, showing where to point the camera (see Fig. 2b). Once the area of a magazine stand where a magazine should be is in view, it is indicated by a category area frame around it. This frame is based on the magazine's category, and the location where magazines of that category should be placed (see Fig. 2c). Finally, if the camera comes close enough to the magazine itself to recognize it, the category area frame is replaced with a frame around the magazine (see Fig. 2d).

Confirmation Screen: This screen displays a message confirming that the entered return counts have been registered.

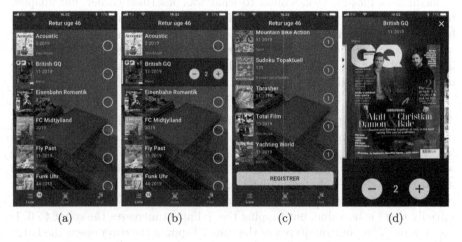

(a)   (b)   (c)   (d)

Fig. 1. Screenshots from the prototype: (a) Magazine list; (b) Item selected and entered value; (c) Active registration button; (d) Large magazine cover.

3.3   AR Scan Feature

The magazine cover Scan feature was intended to allow for selecting a magazine in front of the camera automatically by recognizing its cover image. It was initially implemented only as a separate camera viewport screen, where the

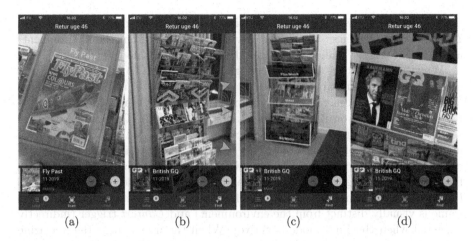

(a)   (b)   (c)   (d)

Fig. 2. Screenshots from the prototype: (a) Scan; (b) Find, displaying off-screen indicator arrows; (c) Find, displaying category area frames; (d) Find, displaying a frame around an identified magazine.

recognized magazine cover was indicated with an AR frame and title around it (see Fig. 2a). New ideas and experimentation during technical design iterations implementation resulted in also enabling the Scan functionality, without the AR graphics, on the List and Large cover screens (see Fig. 1). Our intent was to offer test participants multiple ways of scanning, without necessarily having to have a dedicated camera viewport visible.

In the Dillman et al. [6] framework, the magazine frames map to the *Discover* purpose (inform the user that the magazine can now be acted upon), *Emphasized* markedness (the frame is visually distinct from the environment) and *Player* trigger (directly triggered by the user pointing the camera at a magazine to scan it when the Scan mode is active).

3.4   AR Find Feature

The magazine *Find* feature was intended to provide a form of local wayfinding, indicating the expected locations of the remaining unregistered magazines on the magazine stands. Since a typical store and its few magazine stands represent a concentrated environment, with short distances, and large numbers of potential targets (magazines), it is more critical to be able to indicate a location on the vertical axis than in a warehouse such as the one used by Reiff et al. [16,17]. Thus, the *Find* feature was implemented with three different levels of precision.

At a very short distance, magazine frames are the same AR frame and title (see Fig. 2d) used to indicate an identified magazine as in the *Scan* feature. The difference is that *Find* uses it to indicate magazines still on the magazine stands. It should be noted that while the cropped tracking cover images increased the probability of a positive match, they also appeared to reduce the distance at which they could be identified. In the Dillman et al. [6] framework, the magazine frames map to the *Look* purpose (make the user look at the identified magazine), *Emphasized* markedness (the frame is visually distinct from the environment) and *Context* trigger (indirectly triggered when the Find mode is active).

When magazines are not close enough to the camera to be identified, their approximate locations are indicated with category area frames. The test magazines had been placed realistically by category, so these categories could then be mapped to areas on the magazine stands (see Fig. 2c). Then, the AR representations of the magazine stands were constructed, with a titled frame for each magazine category placed in front of the part of the magazine stand where magazines of that category should be placed (see Fig. 3b). In the Dillman et al. [6] framework, the category area frames map to the *Go* purpose (make the user go towards the magazine stand where the frame is), *Emphasized* markedness (the frame is visually distinct from the environment) and *Context* trigger (indirectly triggered when the Find mode is active). When the user is near the magazine stand, it can be argued that the frame acts as a *Look*, rather than a *Go* purpose cue, since it is now directing the gaze of the user.

When the camera is facing away from the magazine stands, the locations of the relevant category area frames (with remaining unregistered magazines) are indicated by off-screen indicator arrows. These were inspired by a common convention in video games for indicating objects of interest (e.g. enemies) outside the screen area. They are implemented as 2D arrows lying "flat" on the screen, rather than in 3D space (see Fig. 2b). This ensures that they are always equally visible (when shown), regardless of the angle of the smartphone. Each arrow points towards a specific category area frame with unregistered magazines, and once the frame is in view, the arrow is hidden. In the Dillman et al. [6] framework, the off-screen indicator arrows map to the *Look* purpose (make the user look in the direction of the arrow), *Overlaid* markedness (the arrows are placed on top of the viewport, rather than 3D space) and *Context* trigger (indirectly triggered when the Find mode is active).

3.5 Design Variations

The initial idea was to construct the AR-based app prototype, and then test it against the current paper-based method. However, since so many issues with the current paper list were uncovered during the field research, it was considered likely that simply going from a paper list with text to a digital list with more relevant text and magazine cover images, would bring significant improvement, before introducing AR features. Thus, the scope of the test was increased to include testing three different methods to solve the same type of task. Three prototypes were needed for testing.

- AR App - a smartphone app with AR features, in addition to a basic magazine recall list and cover images.
- Paper List - a paper list similar to the current magazine recall list layout.
- List App - a smartphone app with only the magazine recall list and cover images.

The List App prototype was implemented by stripping out all the AR features from the prototype described above, keeping only the list and large cover screens. Identical to Fig. 1, but with the camera disabled and a different color scheme to help distancing the two prototypes.

The Paper List is simply a set of printed mockups of the paper list format currently in use, filled with the actual magazines that are used in the test and a field to write the number of magazines.

3.6 Implementation

The prototype was build on the *Unity*[1] game engine, using the cross-platform AR framework, *AR Foundation*[2], that works as a wrapper around the frameworks offered by Apple's iOS (ARKit[3]) and Google's Android (ARCore[4]). We run all the tests, including the user study, on an iPhone 8, but using AR Foundation meant we also had the option of installing on Android phone, if needed.

Database: the Magazine data needed by the AR App prototype consists of *display cover* images, *tracking cover* images and *magazine attributes*. The *display cover* is used in the magazine list and large cover magazine, as presented in Fig. 1. They were created by taking pictures of the magazines. The *tracking cover* are images used by the *AR Foundation* subsystems to identify each magazine. Magazines are often layered when placed in the stand, and only a small portion of the cover is visible for identification. To increase the relative image area visible to the camera, these *tracking cover* images are cropped versions of the full cover, which only include the top-left corner of the cover. Finally, the *magazine attributes* consits of magazine title, issue and category.

4 User Study

4.1 Task

Participants were asked to perform the same task for each test, with a different prototype and a different set of magazines. The task consisted of two subtasks.

Subtask 1 - Register Magazines from the Stack: They started at the "back room" table, facing away from the "store". For each magazine in the stack on the table they should count the number of copies, register the count on the list, and then put the counted copies in a stack on the right side of the table.

Subtask 2 - Find and Register Magazines from the Stands: Afterwards, for the remaining magazines on the list, they needed to go into the "store". They should find the magazines on the stands, gather them on the table next to the stands, and register them on the list.

---

[1] https://unity3d.com.

[2] https://docs.unity3d.com/Packages/com.unity.xr.arfoundation@3.1/manual.

[3] https://developer.apple.com/augmented-reality/.

[4] https://developers.google.com/ar.

Participants were also told that magazines may be sold out, in fact exactly one title for each test was sold out, so they would not be able to find it, and should just register a count of zero once they had determined which one it was.

Finally, they should take the registered magazines back to the "back room" table and put them on the same stack as the others. The task was complete when all magazines were on the table, and the filled-out list had been submitted.

4.2   Experiment Design

The purpose of the prototype evaluation tests was to acquire and compare objective task performance and subjective experience between three different prototypes, namely: the *AR App*; the *List App*; and the *Paper list*. The experiment followed a within subject design. Thus, participants completed the whole task three times, once with each of the prototypes. The presentation order of the prototypes was counterbalanced to control for learning effect due to task repetition.

4.3   Test Environment

The test environment was set up with two magazine stands in one corner (the "store"), and a small table (the "back room") in a room (Fig. 3a). A large table in the center of the room served as a means to separate the two areas from each other and also recreate the relatively narrow space available in front of the magazine stands in a store.

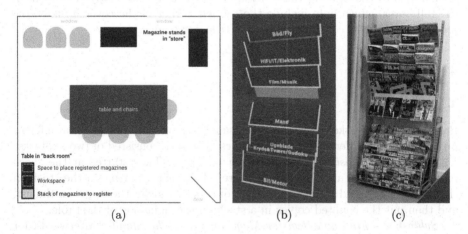

(a)   (b)   (c)

Fig. 3. (a) Test room layout diagram. (b) Magazine category area frames objects, a placeholder plane for the anchor banner can be seen in the center. (c) Magazine stand with anchor banner.

The stands were realistically filled with magazines based on typical magazine categories and placement in stores. Three test magazine sets were prepared, so that participants would not repeat the same set while testing the three different prototypes. Each set consisted of:

- 10 titles, in a stack on the "back room" table;
- 5 titles, in the magazine stands. One of these always had a title that was very similar to two other magazines nearby;
- 1 "sold out" title, that was neither in the stack nor on the stands.

The number of copies of each title varied, from one to four, but all stacks consisted of 20 copies, and the copies to find on the stands were always 15, adding up to 35 copies in each magazine set. The total of "sold out" copies were obviously 0. To control the systematic influence that the magazine visual attributes and placement could have on task performance, the use of the magazine sets was randomized.

A fourth smaller set was prepared for the introductory task training. It consisted of two magazine titles in a stack, and a single title on one of the magazine stands.

4.4 Dependent Variables and Procedure

Objective performance was measured by capturing the time to complete each of the two sub-tasks, total task time and number of errors. These metrics are relevant to the task and application context since shorter completion times could translate into productivity gains, whereas errors when documenting and returning stock can affect reimbursement and profit for store owners. Each participant's subjective experience was captured in a survey, as well as a brief post-test interview. We were particularly interested on perceived workload and ease to use of the prototypes, since a common argument for AR applications is the potential to reduce the mental workload of users, as Cirulis and Ginters discuss in [5].

To be able to test participants that had a basic pre-existing familiarity with the environment, task and tools, participants were given basic training prior to the three tests themselves. After an initial introduction to the agenda for the test session they were given a couple of minutes to get acquainted with the magazine stands and their contents, paying special attention to what categories of magazines they could see.

Before each test the participant was introduced to features of the prototype they would use, and given a small hands-on training task to familiarize themselves with how to perform the real test task. They were informed about technical limitations and known issues of the prototype, and also encouraged to ask questions about anything they were unsure of. It's worth noting that while all the features of the List App prototype are included in the AR App prototype, participants were explicitly instructed to make use of the AR features, and only use other features if they felt necessary to be able to proceed.

After this the participant was to perform the actual test itself. They were encouraged to think aloud during the test, but prioritize performing the task as fast as made sense to them, without feeling rushed. They were also told that they could ask for help if stuck, and that this would also be recorded as part of the result.

After each test, the participant was asked to fill out a short survey, where they assessed their workload level with the NASA Task Load Index[5] [11], adapted to a 7-point Likert scale. They were also asked to answer a Single Easy Question [20] to assess the overall difficulty of the task ("Overall, how difficult was this task?") on a 7-point scale and write down any other free-form comments they had about their experience. This procedure was repeated for each of the three conditions during a testing session.

After completing all of the tests, participants were asked to fill out a survey to capture more general information about them, as well as their smartphone usage and previous experience with AR, VR (virtual reality) and video games. The test session concluded with a brief interview about their experience with the AR features in the AR App prototype. Each test session lasted about 60 min.

5   Results

A total of 22 participants took part in the experiment (age from 22 to 51, median of 28, 15 female), three of which have been removed due to malfunctioning of the prototype during the experiment, leaving a total of 19 participants. Recruitment was carried through the university mailing lists. Originally, we planned to test the AR App prototype with store employees, but this turned out not to be possible. However, our sample is representative of typical temporary employees hired in these stores, since it was composed mostly by students. In fact, one participant had previous experience with managing magazine inventories for a store. Participants did not know the experimenter before and were compensated with a gift card. All participants read and agreed to an informed consent form.

The statistical significance of the differences in task duration between prototypes was verified using the repeated measures ANOVA test, followed by pairwise comparisons with the t-test. The violation of the assumptions of normality of residuals and sphericity were verified using the Shapiro-Wilk test and Mauchly's sphericity test. The statistical significance of the differences in the Single Easy Question and Task Load ratings between prototypes was verified using the Friedman test, followed by pairwise comparisons with the Wilcoxon Signed Rank test. The significance threshold α was set to 0.05 for all tests. The collected data (time and questionnaire responses) and analysis code are available for download at [14].

5.1   Duration

During the first subtask, registering magazines from the stack in the "back room", participants were generally faster using the AR App (mean $\mu = 90.84$, standard deviation $\sigma = 25.45$) than List App ($\mu = 111.05$, $\sigma = 24.17$) and Paper List ($\mu = 107.9$, $\sigma = 29.09$), as shown in Fig. 4a. A statistically significant difference was found ($F_{(2,36)} = 7.24$, $p < .003$), with a decrease in task duration for the AR App compared to both the Paper List ($t_{(18)} = 2.66$, $p < .02$) and

---

[5] https://humansystems.arc.nasa.gov/groups/tlx/downloads/TLXScale.pdf.

List App ($t_{(18)} = 4.22$, $p < .001$). We did not observe a statistically significant difference between the two list methods ($t_{(18)} = .54$, $p = .59$).

During the second subtask, finding and registering magazines from the stands in the "store", the List App ($\mu = 177$, $\sigma = 73.3$) was generally faster than AR App ($\mu = 231.3$, $\sigma = 77.1$) and Paper List ($\mu = 209.7$, $\sigma = 65.1$), as shown in Fig. 4b. However, the difference was not statistically significant ($F_{(2,36)}$, $p = .06$). We note, however, the presence of outliers in both App conditions, which could indicate that the App prototypes were more challenging to some users than others.

Looking at the full task, the App prototypes did not appear to decrease duration (Fig. 4c). The AR App ($\mu = 322.2$, $\sigma = 84.9$), List App ($\mu = 288.1$, $\sigma = 82.5$) and Paper List ($\mu = 317.6$, $\sigma = 81.1$) presented similar total time, with a small advantage for the List App prototype. However, we did not observe a statistically significant difference in duration between the three prototypes ($F_{(2,36)} = 1.15$, $p > .33$).

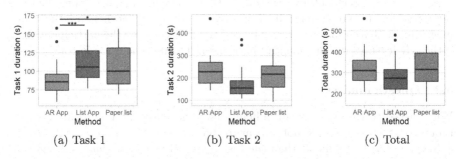

(a) Task 1   (b) Task 2   (c) Total

Fig. 4. Box plots showing the duration of the two subtasks as well as full task duration: (a) registering magazines from the stack; (b) finding and registering magazines from the stands; (c) total time. '*' indicates $p < .05$ and '***' indicates $p < .001$.

5.2   Errors

None of the recorded errors below were noticed by the participants themselves. There was a small number of basic entry errors for the List App and AR App prototypes, where participants appeared to enter a value that was 1 less than the correct value, due to how the return count entry controls work, i.e. the first button press would set the count to zero, in case there were not magazines to return, but users naturally expected that it would set it to one and would not visually inspect the input number. Even after being informed of this behavior prior to the tests, some participants on occasion overlooked the mistake of only counting the number of button taps without checking the value on the screen. These errors (2 for the List App, 7 for the AR App, 9 in total) have been removed from further analysis.

The number of errors for all three prototypes was low, and no conclusions about differences in error rates could be drawn. However, different types of errors occurred for the different prototypes. These error types were split into two major categories; physical magazine picking errors, and list entry errors.

For the Paper List, the picking errors were picking a magazine with a similar title to the correct one (two errors in total). The entry error was writing in the wrong field on the paper list, most likely due to the title being on the left side of each row, and the entry field at the right side (two errors in total). When this occurred, it automatically triggered a second error, when the participant wrote the count for the next title in the remaining field.

For the List App, while there were no errors based on similar magazine titles, there were instead errors based on similar covers (two errors in total). In one case, while registering magazines from the stack, the count was incorrectly entered for a magazine that was on the stands. This in turn triggered another error; that the magazine on the stand was not searched for and picked. In another case, the same error occurred while searching for magazines on the stands (two errors in total).

For the AR App, a single entry error occurred when the camera was briefly turned so that it accidentally scanned another magazine, and the count then was registered for the wrong magazine (one error in total). In another case the wrong magazine, with a similar cover, was picked and registered by the participant, even if the AR features did not identify it as the right one (one error in total).

5.3   Questionnaires

When asked to rate the overall difficulty of performing the test task with each prototype, participants did not appear to consider the AR App ($Q1 = 2$, *Median* $= 3$, $Q3 = 3.5$) less difficult than the List App ($Q1 = 1.5$, *Median* $= 2$, $Q3 = 3$) or Paper List ($Q1 = 2$, *Median* $= 3$, $Q3 = 4.5$). No statistically significant difference was found for this question ($\chi^2_{(2)} = 4.41$, $p = .11$).

Participants were also asked to rate their task load using the NASA Task Load Index questions (Fig. 5). No statistically significant difference was found with regard to Mental ($\chi^2_{(2)} = 4.72$, $p = .094$), Physical ($\chi^2_{(2)} = 4.03$, $p = .133$) or Temporal ($\chi^2_{(2)} = 5.41$, $p = .067$) Demand.

Participants rated their success in performing the task relatively highly, regardless of the prototype used ("Performance" score in Fig. 5), and no statistically significant difference was found for this particular question ($\chi^2_{(2)} = 4.1$, $p = .129$).

A statistically significant difference was found for the "Effort" question ($\chi^2_{(2)} = 10.24$, $p = .006$). The effort required to use the AR App was rated lower than the Paper List, with a significant difference ($p < 0.05$). This was also true for the List App compared to the Paper List ($p < 0.004$). The List App did not appear to require a significantly different level of effort, compared to the AR App ($p = .35$).

A statistically significant difference was also found for the "Frustration" question ($\chi^2_{(2)} = 6.12$, $p = .047$). The List App was less frustrating than the Paper List, with a significant difference ($p < .04$). However, the ratings did not suggest that participants were less frustrated while using the AR App, compared to the Paper List or the List App, there was no significant difference ($p = .53$ and $p = .057$ respectively).

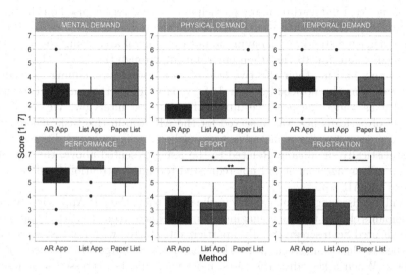

Fig. 5. Box plots showing the ratings for the NASA Task Load Index questions: Mental Demand; Physical Demand; Temporal Demand; Performance; Effort; and Frustration. '*' indicates $p < .05$ and '**' indicates $p < .01$.

5.4   Key Observations

Here we highlight the key observations obtained in the semi-structured interview and through the observation of participants while performing the task using the AR App. Since we believe that the malfunction of the prototype did not affect these aspects of the user study we consider all 22 participants here.

The AR Scan feature was perceived by participants as being very fast and easy to use. In fact, some participants mentioned that it might almost be "too fast", as it immediately selects any magazine that the camera is pointed at. During the tests, we observed situations where the participant, when about to register the return count for one magazine, briefly turned the camera so that it accidentally scanned and selected another magazine instead. This kind of error was observed once, as described above. Several participants stated that they felt like they were on "auto-pilot" while using the AR Scan feature; just trusting the app, without having to think about what they were doing. This was not always perceived as positive, because afterwards they could not know for sure if the task had been completed without errors. Moreover, we recall that we have recorded a significant gain in performance with this feature, where participants were faster at registering magazines to return from a pile by scanning than by searching it on a list.

The AR Find feature's indication of multiple target magazines using arrows and frames was reported as overwhelming by several participants. They cited a feeling of lack of control over the app in this situation, and a preference for instead manually selecting and finding a single magazine at a time. During the test of the AR Find feature, many participants stayed very focused on the smartphone screen. Rather than e.g. trying to find the magazines by looking directly at the magazine stand, after having found the general area using the app, they appeared to continue to view their environment through this "lens". This behavior, severely limiting their effective field of view and still remaining "locked" to the screen, was also noticed by several of the participants themselves. They mentioned it as something negative during the post-test interview. We recall that no gain of performance was observed for the AR App in this task, whereas the List App seem to offer some advantage, although the recorded difference was not statistically significant. Related to the issue presented above, the List App had the advantage that it did not requested too much attention from the user, as with the AR App.

While registering the magazines in the stack using the AR App, slightly more participants elected to scan magazines using the List screen (12 participants) over the dedicated Scan screen (8). Two participants started with the List screen and switched to the Scan screen mid-task. None used the Large cover screen for this subtask. When asked after the tests, most participants expressed a preference for the AR Scan (12) feature over the AR Find (6) feature in the AR App. The most common reasons to prefer the AR Scan feature were its speed and ease of use, and the expectation that in a real work situation, one would learn the physical locations of the magazines categories in the store within a week or so. Only five participants mentioned that having to hold the smartphone could be a challenge while performing the magazine tasks, while several have complained about the ergonomics of handling a paper list during the second sub-task.

6   Discussion

As expected, moving from registering magazines using a paper list, to using a smartphone app resulted in improved performance and, to some extent, user experience. However, the AR App itself did only show a performance improvement for the entire task. For the first subtask, registering magazines from a stack, the AR App performed the best of the prototypes. Test participants were offered a choice of three different screens where they could use the Scan functionality in the AR App. Interestingly, the majority chose the List screen, that used the camera to identify and select magazines, but did not have a dedicated AR camera viewport. This choice appeared to be primarily due to the List offering a better overview of the remaining list of magazines, while the participant scanned them one by one.

For the second subtask, finding and registering magazines from the magazine stands, participants were not given the same freedom. Rather, they were to use the single Find screen, which indicates the approximate location of all the remaining magazines on their list. The intent was to explore if participants would themselves choose a suitable order, as well as opportunistically pick up nearby magazines. However, we found that this higher level of complexity in the AR App did not perform well. Participants were often overwhelmed by the multiple graphic elements on the screen (see the arrows on the right of Fig. 2b for an example), and would have preferred selecting a single magazine at a time to locate. Moreover, the Find functionality can be appealing for new or temporary employees, who are naive about the store layout and location of the magazine categories, and possibly even for consumers, but not for the employees who are used to manage the magazine inventory. They will quickly become familiar with the layout of the store and typical location of the items.

Participants committed very few errors during the tests, and the number of errors were also similar between prototypes. We found it interesting to see a few cases where a magazine with similar cover image was picked instead of the target magazine. This occurred for both the List App as well as the AR App. This type of error appeared similar in nature to when users picked a magazine with similar title, instead of the target magazine, when using the Paper List. Participants were likely doing a quick pattern match (e.g. "Does the cover image contain a row of band member faces?", "Does the title begin with 'Eisenbahn'?"), rather than confirming that it was exactly the correct cover or title.

Overall the AR App performed the best when there was less information to interpret for the participant, and a clear next action, like when registering magazines in a stack. When presented with more complex graphics, and having to make a decision on what to do next, performance decreased significantly, back down to similar levels as the Paper List. Thus there seemed to occur a significant mental mode shift for participants when going from using AR Scan to AR Find. Some participants reported that they worked "on automatic" when using AR Scan. AR Find then felt overwhelming, as the participant now was forced to interpret the graphics and make decisions.

While using the AR App, most participants stayed focused on the smartphone screen, as expected. But this also meant that they viewed their environment through a relatively narrow viewport, instead of directly looking first at the magazines they were scanning the magazine stands where they needed to find more magazines. This behavior did not appear to have any adverse effect on how fast they were able to register the magazines from a stack, but did afterwards seem to impede how quickly they could find the magazines on the stands. There the magazine covers were partially obscured by other magazines, and the distance to the smartphone camera was typically greater, so the app could not help by identifying magazines as fast and consistently as in the stack.

Generally speaking, the value of AR-based order picking appears greater when navigating a larger, complex space, with walls or tall shelves blocking the user's view. For example, a warehouse (as in [5, 16, 17]). Going to the wrong area costs time, both in terms of transport and then searching for the target product. In a magazine store environment, we found that AR is often more valuable as a means of directing the user's gaze towards the part of a magazine stand where the target product is likely to be, rather than providing wayfinding to the magazine stand itself. In the store, distances are short, and the product may already be visible from where the user is standing.

In lieu of having individually named locations for magazines, we used a category-based method to show the approximate location where the target magazine is likely to be. This method should also be applicable in other contexts where object categories map to physical locations. One such context is a library. The off-screen indicators and category area frames could be employed by library visitor to find the shelf where a book is located. While the cover of the book is unlikely to be visible, image recognition or even optical character recognition (OCR) could be used to identify the book by the title on its spine. Both recognition of the book's spine and front cover could be used when registering the books to be borrowed, extending the ideas presented by [3].

A library visitor would be an occasional, relatively inexperienced user of such a handheld AR app. Similarly, the target user group for our magazine handling AR app concept is less experienced, temporary or part-time, store staff. They need a straightforward tool, that does not require lengthy, specialized training. Such an app could reduce the variance in how long it takes to perform inventory tasks between the experienced and less experienced staff. The AR Scan feature could benefit all, while a revised AR Find feature would be most valuable to new staff, who are not yet familiar with the store's magazine stands. As they become familiar over time, the AR Find feature would recede in importance.

6.1   Recommendations

Finally, based on the weaknesses that were identified in our prototype through the user study, we compiled a set of recommendations, that we believe could improve the prototype and may be useful for designers and researchers developing mobile AR applications:

- AR features as a strong supporting cast - The basic list and cover image UI is a solid set of baseline functionality. The AR features should be available and quick to use when needed, but not dominate the user experience.
- Separation of registered magazines in list - As the return count is entered for magazines, move them to the top of the list, so that the remaining magazines are together at the bottom, near the Register button. This will continuously decrease the effective length of the list the user needs to pay attention to.
- List scan with toggle - Being able to scan magazines in the list (without a dedicated Scan screen) is sufficient to use the feature and was preferred by most users. Remove the Scan screen and add the ability to turn the scanning on/off on the List screen. Communicate a successful scan more explicitly to avoid accidental selections, by e.g. flashing the selected item, coupled with an audible beep.
- Numeric keyboard entry - Replace the ± buttons with a numeric keyboard when a magazine is selected for entry. This will increase the physical size of the input buttons, and consistently place them in the same screen location. Also, if

the scan feature is temporarily disabled until the keyboard is dismissed again, it effectively removes the risk of involuntarily scanning another magazine cover.

– Find selected magazine - Make Find accessible from a single selected magazine at a time, to reduce the number of magazines the user has to find at the same time. This addresses the problem that users often felt overwhelmed when information about all missing magazines were presented at the same time.

7   Conclusion

In this paper we addressed the question of whether handheld AR can serve as a practical and effective tool for inventory tasks. To answer the question, we applied a user-centered design process, starting with a round of field research. We interviewed magazine retail staff and observed them performing work tasks. This research informed the selection of a realistic task to be used as the basis for the design of a smartphone app prototype with AR features. This prototype was then evaluated in a user study, where it was also compared to the paper list currently in use, and a second, simplified app prototype, without AR features.

Based on the results of the user study, we conclude that the answer is yes. Handheld AR can indeed serve a practical and effective role in inventory tasks. However, our findings indicate that this role is best played as a supporting actor, rather than a dominant one, since it did not always improve performance and satisfaction of the users in our study. The limited handheld AR viewport afforded by a smartphone was most effective to use when the task itself was also focused, like when registering magazines in a stack.

Acknowledgments. We wish to thank the store staff and prototype evaluation participants for their time, and the anonymous reviewers for their valuable comments. This research was supported by Bladkompagniet, which provided materials and compensation for the studies and participants. Their team participated in initial planning, field research recruitment, prototype evaluation environment construction and provided feedback. This research was also supported by Charlie Tango, which provided the infrastructure for the prototype evaluation. We wish to thank Ulla Tønner, who provided valuable feedback on the design of the prototype evaluation. Peter Mitts also wishes to thank Tessa, for her support during the development of this project.

References

1. Bonetti, F., Pantano, E., Warnaby, G., Quinn, L., Perry, P.: Augmented reality in real stores: empirical evidence from consumers' interaction with AR in a retail format. In: tom Dieck, M.C., Jung, T. (eds.) Augmented Reality and Virtual Reality. PI, pp. 3–16. Springer, Cham (2019). https://doi.org/10.1007/978-3-030-06246-0_1

2. Chatzopoulos, D., Bermejo, C., Huang, Z., Hui, P.: Mobile augmented reality survey: from where we are to where we go. IEEE Access **5**, 6917–6950 (2017). https://doi.org/10.1109/ACCESS.2017.2698164

3. Chen, D.M., Tsai, S.S., Girod, B., Hsu, C.H., Kim, K.H., Singh, J.P.: Building book inventories using smartphones. In: Proceedings of the 18th ACM International Conference on Multimedia, pp. 651–654 (2010)

4. Chung, J., Kim, I.J., Schmandt, C.: Guiding light: Navigation assistance system using projection based augmented reality. In: 2011 IEEE International Conference on Consumer Electronics (ICCE), pp. 881–882. IEEE (2011)

5. Cirulis, A., Ginters, E.: Augmented reality in logistics. Procedia Comput. Sci. **26**, 14 – 20 (2013). https://doi.org/10.1016/j.procs.2013.12.003, iCTE in Regional Development, December 2013, Valmiera, Latvia

6. Dillman, K.R., Mok, T.T.H., Tang, A., Oehlberg, L., Mitchell, A.: A visual interaction cue framework from video game environments for augmented reality. In: Proceedings of the 2018 CHI Conference on Human Factors in Computing Systems, CHI 2018, ACM, New York (2018). https://doi.org/10.1145/3173574.3173714

7. Elia, V., Gnoni, M.G., Lanzilotto, A.: Evaluating the application of augmented reality devices in manufacturing from a process point of view: an ahp based model. Expert Syst. Appl. **63**, 187–197 (2016)

8. Fang, W., Zheng, S., Liu, Z.: A scalable and long-term wearable augmented reality system for order picking. In: 2019 IEEE International Symposium on Mixed and Augmented Reality Adjunct (ISMAR-Adjunct). pp. 4–7. IEEE (2019)

9. Glockner, H., Jannek, K., Mahn, J., Theis, B.: Augmented reality in logistics. changing the way we see logistics–a dhl perspective. DHL Customer Solutions Innov. **28** (2014)

10. Guo, A., et al.: A comparison of order picking assisted by head-up display (hud), cart-mounted display (cmd), light, and paper pick list. In: Proceedings of the 2014 ACM International Symposium on Wearable Computers, ISWC 2014, pp. 71–78. ACM, New York (2014). https://doi.org/10.1145/2634317.2634321

11. Hart, S.G., Staveland, L.E.: Development of nasa-tlx (task load index): results of empirical and theoretical research. In: Hancock, P.A., Meshkati, N. (eds.) Human Mental Workload, Advances in Psychology, vol. 52, pp. 139–183. North-Holland (1988). https://doi.org/10.1016/S0166-4115(08)62386-9

12. Kourouthanassis, P.E., Boletsis, C., Lekakos, G.: Demystifying the design of mobile augmented reality applications. Multimed. Tools Appl. **74**(3), 1045–1066 (2015). https://doi.org/10.1007/s11042-013-1710-7

13. Milgram, P., Takemura, H., Utsumi, A., Kishino, F.: Augmented reality: a class of displays on the reality-virtuality continuum. In: Das, H. (ed.) Telemanipulator and Telepresence Technologies, vol. 2351, pp. 282–292. International Society for Optics and Photonics, SPIE (1995). https://doi.org/10.1117/12.197321

14. Mitts, P., Debarba, H.G.: On the use of handheld augmented reality for inventory tasks: a study with magazine retailers - dataset (2021). https://doi.org/10.5281/zenodo.4926619

15. Porter, M.E., Heppelmann, J.E.: Why every organization needs an augmented reality strategy. HBR'S 10 MUST, p. 85 (2017)

16. Reif, R., Günthner, W.A.: Pick-by-vision: augmented reality supported order picking. Vis. Comput. **25**(5), 461–467 (2009). https://doi.org/10.1007/s00371-009-0348-y

17. Reif, R., Günthner, W.A., Schwerdtfeger, B., Klinker, G.: Evaluation of an augmented reality supported picking system under practical conditions. Computer Graphics Forum **29**(1), 2–12 (2010)

18. Robert, K., Zhu, D., Huang, W., Alem, L., Gedeon, T.: Mobilehelper: remote guiding using smart mobile devices, hand gestures and augmented reality. In: SIGGRAPH Asia 2013 Symposium on Mobile Graphics and Interactive Applications, pp. 1–5 (2013)
19. de Sá, M., Churchill, E.F.: Mobile Augmented Reality: A Design Perspective, pp. 139–164. Springer New York, New York (2013). https://doi.org/10.1007/978-1-4614-4205-9_6
20. Sauro, J., Dumas, J.S.: Comparison of three one-question, post-task usability questionnaires. In: Proceedings of the SIGCHI Conference on Human Factors in Computing Systems, CHI 2009, pp. 1599–1608. ACM, New York (2009). https://doi.org/10.1145/1518701.1518946
21. Schwerdtfeger, B.: Pick-by-vision: Bringing hmd-based augmented reality into the warehouse. Ph.D. thesis, Technische Universität München (2010)
22. Soulard, O.: Development of an adaptive user interface for mobile indoor navigation. Master's thesis, Lehrstuhl für Medientechnik, Fachgebiet Verteilte ... (2012)
23. Teo, T., Lawrence, L., Lee, G.A., Billinghurst, M., Adcock, M.: Mixed reality remote collaboration combining 360 video and 3d reconstruction. In: Proceedings of the 2019 CHI Conference on Human Factors in Computing Systems, pp. 1–14. ACM, New York (2019). https://doi.org/10.1145/3290605.3300431
24. Vidal-Balea, A., Blanco-Novoa, O., Fraga-Lamas, P., Vilar-Montesinos, M., Fernández-Caramés, T.M.: Creating collaborative augmented reality experiences for industry 4.0 training and assistance applications: Performance evaluation in the shipyard of the future. Appl. Sci. 10(24), 9073 (2020)
25. Wang, P., et al.: Ar/mr remote collaboration on physical tasks: a review. Robot. Comput.-Integr. Manuf. 72, 102071 (2021). https://doi.org/10.1016/j.rcim.2020.102071
26. Wang, W., Wang, F., Song, W., Su, S.: Application of augmented reality (ar) technologies in inhouse logistics. In: E3S Web of Conferences, vol. 145, p. 02018. EDP Sciences (2020)
27. Winkel, J.J., Datcu, D.D., Buijs, P.P.: Augmented reality could transform last-mile logistics. In: Symposium on Spatial User Interaction, pp. 1–2 (2020)

Placement of Teleported Co-users in AR

Jens Reinhardt[1], Marco Kurzweg[2(✉)], and Katrin Wolf[2]

[1] University of Applied Science Hamburg, Hamburg, Germany
jens.reinhardt@haw-hamburg.de
[2] University of Applied Science Berlin, Berlin, Germany
{marco.kurzweg,katrin.wolf}@beuth-hochschule.de

Abstract. Teleportation and conversations with virtual representations of remote people have been made possible by recent developments in augmented reality (AR) technology. This paper aims at understanding how such AR telecommunication systems should be implemented by asking where to display 3D scans of potential remote users. As the perfect interaction design solution may be different while walking versus while staying in one place, we conducted a user study comparing both. We also varied the placement of the remote user in the co-user's field of view (FoV) and where the coordinate system in which the 3D scan is visualized has its origin. We found that remote users we talk to should, in general, be visualized in AR in front of us, but in situations in which the physical world requires attention a visualization in the periphery is better. Re-placing the co-user through gestures is not desired, but the ability to look away from them should be supported, which strongly supports placing virtual co-users in AR relatively to the user's body.

Keywords: Augmented reality · Hologram · Teleportation · Co-user · Remote user visualization

1 Introduction

Teleportation using Augmented Reality (AR) can enormously enrich telecommunication and realizes an old humankind's dream of talking to remotely located people and seeing them as if they would be in the same place we are. The affordability of AR glasses and recent technological advantages, e.g., to display remote people in real-time on AR glasses, enable us to talk to remote people more naturally than through traditional telecommunication technology. Besides a potential increase of sensed co-presence [22], seeing the face of a speaking person helps to understand the spoken word [27], and to see the lips of the speaker enables the listener to hear and thus better understand [25]. We believe that such

---

Electronic supplementary material The online version of this chapter (https://doi.org/10.1007/978-3-030-85623-6_34) contains supplementary material, which is available to authorized users.

hologram-like telecommunication will change the way we live and work together. We could better maintain relationships with friends and family when being away, and we would not need as many business travels as today if meetings using a technical solution like Microsoft's *Holoportation* [22] would become ubiquitous.

Holoportation displays a remote user on AR glasses so that they seem to stand beside us. While this seems to be perfectly fine when being at home while communicating with remote users, other (more mobile) solutions may be better suited for telecommunication on the go. Previous research on AR and VR video- or hologram based communication investigated technical solutions for recording, transmitting, and visualizing the remote conversation partners [6,22,32]. It has also been investigated how digital content, like text, has to be arranged and positioned when using smart glasses [8,21,23,29]. Different aspects influence the placement of AR content. While AR content placed in the center may occlude important real-world content, peripheral vision is limited [26]. However, peripheral cues can also grab the user's attention [12] as humans can well perceive motion in their visual periphery [7]. Thus, the question of where to position a remote user's visual representation during AR telecommunication remains unclear and defines the research gap that we target in this paper.

In a user study, we varied the position of remote users' visual representation, placing them in the space beside the user (fixed world position), around the user in a way that the visualization would "follow" the user if they walk, or in the user's field of view (FoV). As peripheral visualizations versus centered visualizations lead to different attention [5] and perception [26], we also vary that attribute. Our results indicate no differences between scenarios, but indicate that placement gestures lack usability while a center placement and attaching the AR co-user to the user's body works best as it allows the user to look away if real-world content requires attention, while otherwise facing the co-user make the conversation most natural.

With this work, we contribute by recommending how we can display remote users we are talking to, which can improve the usability of next-generation telecommunication software for future AR glasses. Furthermore, it will enable us to stay in better contact with distant family and friends and reduce the need to travel, for example, to business meetings.

2   Related Work

This paper aims to improve communication with remote users displayed at AR head-worn optical see-through (OST) devices. Thus, we discuss works that previously explored AR telepresence systems; content presentation, arrangement, and positioning for AR glasses; and techniques to visualize remote co-users in AR.

2.1   AR Telepresence Systems

Billinghurst and Kato introduced an AR conferencing system that uses the superimposition of virtual images with the real world [13]. Remote co-workers are displayed on virtual monitors that can be freely placed in space by a user with the help of tracking markers.

Velamkayala et al. investigated AR collaboration with an interface that allowed the *HoloLens* user to see the face of the remote collaborator [30]. They compared the performance of teams in a navigation task performed while using the *HoloLens* and smartphone when using *Skype*[1]. Their results showed that the task completion time was longer when using the *HoloLens*, but the number of errors was lower when using that device. They concluded that the longer completion time was due to the design and unfamiliarity with the new technology. In contrast to our research focus, neither co-presence, telepresence, and social presence were evaluated, nor alternative placement of the remote user was explored. Lawrence et al. performed a pilot study to investigate the influence of video placement in AR conferencing for an assembly and a negotiation task [16]. They evaluated the different positions of the video window (fixed position in the head-mounted display's (HMD) field of view (FoV), fixed world-position, only audio) of Skype for the *HoloLens* for the different tasks. They evaluated communication, co-presence, and user preference. Their findings show that co-presence was rated significantly higher in the assembly task than in the negotiation task for the fixed world position. Moreover, they found that users preferred the two video conditions and rated the pure audio condition significantly lower. While this work varied placement of AR communication partners in static setups, we also compare the positioning of co-users' visualization depending on the mobility of the user (on the go versus staying in place).

2.2 Presentation and Arrangement of Content in AR Glasses

AR allows superimposing the real environment with additional information [10] that can be perceived while working on a real object and without losing focus on the object being worked on. A large body of research investigated how to present, arrange, and position this additional information.

Tanaka et al. investigated how information must be arranged on AR glasses focusing on viewability [28,29]. Although the HMD can display information without interfering with the user's view, the information displayed may be complicated to see if the view behind the display is too structured, the background is too bright, or the contrast is too low. Their research focuses on the automated alignment of AR content based on the environment. Users' preferences are not taken into consideration. Chua et al. investigated the influence of the physical position of the display of monocular smart glasses on the performance in dual-task scenarios [5]. They compared nine display positions for displaying notifications and found that the notifications at the middle and lower-middle positions were noticed more quickly. Moreover, they found that the upper and peripheral positions were more convenient, less obtrusive, and favored. In particular, the best compromise of performance and usability in a dual-task scenario was obtained by the center-right position. The positioning of content at AR glasses often concerns textual

---

[1] https://news.microsoft.com/de-de/videos/microsoft-hololens-skype/.

information, which is targeted by research discussed in the following paragraphs. Orlosky et al. investigated a text management system for AR headsets in mobile outdoor scenarios that actively manages the movement of text in a user's FoV [21]. Camera tracking is used to identify dark areas in the user's FoV, which are then used to display textual content to maximize readability. Their results indicate that dynamic text placement is preferred over text placement at fixed positions due to better text readability in dark areas. Rzayev et al. investigated text presentation on AR smart glasses and how walking, text position, and presentation type affect comprehension, reading and walking speed, and workload [23]. They found that text displayed in the upper right corner of smart glasses increases the subjective workload and reduces comprehension. Klose et al. investigated how the reading of text on AR glasses and the simultaneous execution of three real-world tasks influence each other [14]. They compared text placed in a head-locked coordinate system, a body-locked coordinate system as well as text placement at the top and bottom during the following tasks: a visual stimulus-response task, a simple walking task, and an obstacle course task. For the head-locked presentation, the text was fixed relative to the AR glasses FoV (top and bottom). For the body-locked presentation, the text was fixed at the height relative to the user (top and bottom). Their findings show that AR reading negatively influenced performance in all three tasks. The statistical analysis of user preferences showed no main effects of task, height, or coordinate system, but an interaction effect of task and coordinate system attachment was found. Participants preferred head-locked positions during the visual stimulus-response task. Simultaneous reading in AR during the obstacle course was significantly more distracting than when merely walking. Furthermore, the body-locked text was significantly more disturbing for the visual stimulus-response task than the head-locked text. At the same time, the anchoring of the coordinate system made no difference for the other two tasks.

While previous research examined the placement of textual and static content for AR in head-worn OST devices, we explored the placement of animated content, which is the co-user's visual representation. It is commonly known that moving objects are well perceivable in the periphery, while static objects are not [2,26]. Hence, it is worth exploring where to best place moving content on AR glasses.

2.3   Co-user Visualization in AR

In the area of AR co-user visualization, research has been conducted on the realistic representation of gaze as well as on the virtual co-user integration in the local user's environment. Furthermore, work on partially obstructed transparent displays is related to this project and will be presented here.

Orts-Escolano et al. introduced *Holoportation*, a technique for augmented reality, which transfers a remote user into the augmented environment [22]. The work focuses on the capturing and 3D reconstruction of the remote user, but not on their placement. An immersive teleconferencing system, which seats participants at a virtual table while allowing each participant to gauge each other's gaze, was proposed by Zhang et al. [31]. Another approach to achieve a realistic meeting experience was introduced through *TELEPORT* by Gibbs et al. [11]. Here, a power wall is used to create a virtual extension of the meeting room wherein the communication partner is placed. *TELEPORT* is designed to give users a realistic physical context, and realistically represent the remote user's gaze. Nassani et al. explored if changes in visual representation, proximity, or a combination thereof, depending on social relations, influence how natural the experience is [19]. They discovered that visual representation is preferred over proximity, and that visual representation and the combination with proximity is preferred over the lack thereof. *Tracs*, introduced by Lindlbauer et al., is an approach on transparent displays, which allows for privacy in parts of the screen while facilitating collaboration by making areas of the screen transparent or shared with the other side [17,18]. Lindlbauer suggests that this might promote collaboration with close spatial co-workers. Angos et al. presented an approach for dynamically manipulating scale, orientation, and the position of miniaturized co-users as holograms, which guarantees eye-contact [1]. In a preliminary study, they found that dynamic scaled remote people help obtain eye contact by considering differences in height, positioning, orientation, and the characteristics of the surrounding space.

Previous research investigated the visual representation, capturing, display, and transmission of the co-user. We are interested in the influence of positioning and spatial referencing of the co-user in different scenarios. Therefore we researched the placement in a static setup as well as when walking around.

2.4   Summary

Previous research has been focused on technical feasibility, capturing, transmission, and presentation of life-like 3D representations of co-users in AR. Moreover, while research on placement of content in AR, particularly on the placement of textual information and video call windows has been done, no previous work looked at the placement of 3D reconstructed remote users in head-worn OST AR devices. Research on the positioning of a life-like 3D representation of the co-user in AR distinguishing mobile and stationary scenarios has not yet been carried out. This research gap is addressed in this paper.

3   Method

To better understand how and where the virtual representation of a co-user has to be positioned in AR, we conducted an experiment. We compared three different positions of a virtual co-user in a controlled experiment with three different reference coordinate systems for a video call task in a walking and stationary situation.

3.1   Design

Our study had a $3 \times 3 \times 2$ within subjects design with the independent variables *point of reference* (head-fixed, body-fixed, world-fixed), *placement* (center, periphery, interactive), and *scenario* (mobile, stationary). As a Latin square would not equally distribute 18 conditions across 18 participants, we had varied our 3×3 conditions in a Latin square order while having the last variable randomized within that order [3]. The dependent variables were *self reported co-presence, perceived others co-presence, social presence, telepresence*, and *usability*.

3.2 Measurements

Self reported co-presence, perceived others co-presence, social presence, and *telepresence* were measured by the Nowak and Biocca questionnaire [20].

Co-presence: is the feeling of belonging between two people [20]. Co-presence was measured on two different scales, one relating to the participants' perception of their partner's contribution to the interaction (*perceived others' co-presence*) and the other relating to the self-report of their contribution to the interaction (*self-reported co-presence*) [20].

Social Presence: is the perceived ability of the medium to connect people [20].

Telepresence: is a measure of the feeling of "being there" to be "within" a virtual environment that a person has [20].

Usability was recorded using the System Usability Scale (SUS) questionnaire [4]. To better understand the quantitative data, we collected additional qualitative feedback in semi-structured interviews. Here, we were asking regarding the interactive *placement* condition:

- If you have the free choice to place the co-user to get the maximal usability, where would you place them?
- Why would you place them there?

Alternatively, we asked for the center, and periphery *placement* condition:

- Regarding the usability, what was beneficial about the co-user's position?
- Regarding the usability, what was obstructive about the co-user's position?

3.3 Participants

The experiment was conducted with 18 participants (6 females, 12 males) aged between 22 and 35 years and an average age of 27.8 years ($SD = 4.0$), recruited at our university campus. 17 (6 female) participants had experience with AR.

3.4 Apparatus

Meta 2 glasses[2] were used as visual AR output device. We used the backpack computer (MSI VR ONE, i7 7820HK/2,9 GHz, 16GB RAM, GTX 1070) to run our prototype software, as the Meta 2 glasses have no data processing unit.

---

[2] https://www.metavision.com.

Fig. 1. Screenshots of our prototype of the female (left) and male (right) representation of the co-user.

The apparatus was implemented in Unity3D[3] presenting the co-user as two randomly selected visualizations of a virtual phone caller (male/female) on the AR glasses. For these two virtual user representations, we recorded separate volumetric videos using Microsoft Kinect.

The user interface for the study participants was kept as simple as possible and solely displayed the virtual co-user (see Fig. 1). For the virtual representation of the co-user (remote teleconferencing caller), we used three different reference points that define where the coordination system (in which the co-user is visualized) is attached to (or fixed to, see Fig. 2). For the co-user's representation, we decided to use pre-recorded videos instead of live recordings and transmissions to keep the system's performance as high as possible. Moreover, this ensured that all participants would see the same performance of the callers' presentation, regardless of any errors in the live generation of the volumetric video or the transmission of it. The volumetric video consisted of a textured point cloud. To display the silhouette and surface of the co-user, the individual points of the point cloud were enlarged until the impression of a flat texture was created. To avoid gender biases, we recorded one female and one male person representing the callers.

---

[3] https://unity.com.

Fig. 2. *Point of Reference*: *head-fixed*, which means that the AR content is fixed to the head position and follows head movements (left), *body-fixed*, which means that the AR content is fixed to the user's feet and follows when the user walks or rotates their body (center), *world-fixed* means that the AR content stay in the real world even if the user looks or moves away (right).

Point of Reference. We compared three different coordinate systems where the co-user's virtual visualization referenced (see Fig. 2.)

Head-Fixed: The *head-fixed* coordinate system had its origin (or reference point) directly at the user's forehead. Therefore, the coordinate system is affected by head movements and the virtual visualization is following head rotations and tilts. Consequently, this coordinate system is representing the FoV (see Fig. 2 (left)). As the origin, we used the origin of the virtual Meta 2 camera in the Unity scene with applied camera rotation to ensure that the virtual visualization follows the FoV.

Body-Fixed: The *body-fixed* coordinate system had its origin (or reference point) at the feet of the user. When moving through space, this coordinate system is carried by the user, but the origin remained unaffected when the user turned its head (see Fig. 2 (center)). As the origin, we used the camera (head) position of the virtual Meta 2 camera in the Unity scene and subtracted the participant's height (which we measured at the beginning of the experiment). The origin was placed at users' feet to ensure the virtual visualization is always located at the ground, which was realized by subtracting the height of a participant from the origin.

World-Fixed The *world-fixed* coordinate system had its origin (or reference point) at the origin of the Unity scene (see Fig. 2 (right)).

Placement. Within the coordinate system that might be *head-*, *body-*, or *world-fixed*, we compare three possibilities where the co-user's virtual visualization is placed (see Fig. 3).

Center: The virtual co-user was positioned centrally (see Fig. 3 (left)). For the *head-fixed point of reference* the co-user was placed 2m in front of the user, while for the *body-fixed* and *world-fixed point of reference* the co-user was placed 3m in front of the user. The vertical alignment was three degrees downwards so

Fig. 3. *Placement* conditions: *center* (left), *periphery* (middle), *interactive* (right).

that the co-user is fully visible and at eye level. The horizontal alignment was 0 degrees, exactly centered. We have chosen a smaller distance for the head-fixed coordinate system due to the walking course's nature. When participants walked and turned their heads in the direction of a wall bordering the course, the possibility of clipping the co-user into the wall possibly occurred. These clippings were greatly reduced by the decreased distance of the co-user's representation.

Periphery: The virtual co-user was positioned in the right periphery (see Fig. 3 (center)). For the *head-fixed point of reference*, the co-user was again placed 2m in front of the user and vertically aligned three degrees downwards. The horizontal alignment was 15° to the right. This angle was chosen because the density of sensory cells on the human eye's retina decreases very strongly from 15° eccentricity [9,24]. For the *body-fixed* and *world-fixed point of reference* the co-user was placed 3 m in front of the user. The vertical alignment was the same as for the *head-fixed point of reference*. The horizontal alignment was 25° to the right.

Interactive: Here, participants had to interactively set the position of the co-user's visual representation through a pinch gesture, whose realization is described below (see Fig. 3 (right)).

Although the Meta 2 has gesture recognition, it was too error-prone for our purposes. Therefore, we implemented a prototypical pinch gesture using Python[4] and OpenCV[5]. We equipped the index finger and the thumb with a red and blue marker and implemented a color tracking algorithm to recognize the fingertips. If both fingertips touched each other, a pinch gesture, similar to the commonly known HoloLens gesture, was recognized. The user "clicked" on a position on the ground, as seen from its perspective, using the pinch gesture. The co-user then was placed on this location on the ground. The Python application ran as a separate application as a separate process. The communication with the Unity application was realized via network sockets.

Scenario. For our experiment, we compared a stationary and a mobile scenario.

Stationary Scenario: In the standing scenario, we placed every participant in the same position and with the same viewing direction into the room that an unobstructed view into the room was ensured. The participant was not allowed

---

[4] https://www.python.org.
[5] https://opencv.org.

to leave the position, but head and body movements were allowed for better observation of the caller.

Mobile Scenario: In the mobile scenario, the participant had to follow a marked rectangular path. All participants were placed on the same starting point. Head and body were allowed to be turned as desired while walking. They were not permitted to leave the path. The path was chosen in a way that there were no obstacles on the track. The side lengths of the chosen rectangle were 6m × 4 m. Thus, a distance of 20 m was completed per lap. The participants were free to choose their running speed. Thus, the walking distance varied from participant to participant.

3.5   Procedure and Task

First participants were welcomed and then asked to complete a consent form and fill in a demographic questionnaire. We also collected information about previous experience with AR. We measured the height of the participants to align the correct position of the ground plane.

At the beginning of the experiment, participants got an introduction to the Meta 2 device and were then shown how to execute the pinch gesture to place the co-user interactively. To avoid sequence effects, the order of conditions in which we varied *point of reference*, *placement* and *scenario*, followed a Latin square design. We equipped the participants with a VR backpack and the Meta 2 glasses. We asked the participants to proceed to the starting point marked on the ground, depending on the scenario.

The participant's task was to observe the caller. The participant should imagine a conversation situation with the remote caller and then evaluate their positioning and referencing. The caller informed the subscriber that a book borrowed from the participant was still in possession, that the book was very enjoyable, and that it would be returned soon. The spoken text of the virtual co-user text was chosen unemotionally to not bias the ratings. We have deliberately chosen not to engage in a real dialogue so as not to distract the participant.

Once the participants were in the right position, we showed them the caller. We used a Wizard of Oz design, so the experimenter actively performed the actions of the pre-recorded caller. The caller's visual appearance was previously communicated to the participants as a visual ringing and symbolized the incoming call. If the placement condition was interactive, the participant first had to place the caller through the interaction gesture. If the participants were ready to answer the call, they should loud and clearly say "Answer". The experiment leader had to start the recorded volumetric video by manually press a button in our prototype software. The volumetric video was placed according to the *placement* and referenced in the 3D space according to the *point of reference* conditions. In each condition, a male and a female co-user were shown simulating a video call. Both the co-user's appearances, the female and the male, were displayed in random order for each condition. Finally, the participants filled in the questionnaires and repeated this procedure for all 18 conditions of our

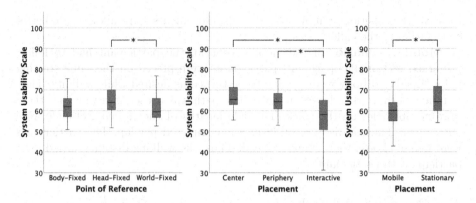

Fig. 4. *System usability scale for point of reference,placement, and scenario*

experiment. The experiment lasted between two and three hours, including the completion of the individual questionnaires, and several breaks.

4   Results

We used independent Friedman tests with *point of reference* (head-fixed, body-fixed, and world-fixed), and *placement* (center, interactive, and periphery) as independent variables to indicate significant effects on the ordinal data *self reported co-presence, perceived others' co-presence, social presence, telepresence,* and *usability.* Post-hoc analysis with Wilcoxon signed rank tests were conducted with a Bonferroni correction applied. Moreover, we used Wilcoxon signed-rank tests with the independent variable *scenario* (mobile, stationary) to indicate significant effects on the ordinal data *self reported co-presence, perceived others' co-presence, social presence, telepresence,* and *usability.*

4.1   Quantitative Results

Usability. Descriptive statistics led to the following median values for the *SUS* scale sorted by *point of reference*: $Mdn_{\text{body-fixed}} = 61.875$, $Mdn_{\text{head-fixed}} = 63.384$, and $Mdn_{\text{world-fixed}} = 59.375$, by *placement*: $Mdn_{\text{center}} = 65.417$, $Mdn_{\text{periphery}} = 64.375$, and $Mdn_{\text{interactive}} = 58.125$, and by *scenario*: $Mdn_{\text{mobile}} = 60.139$, and $Mdn_{\text{stationary}} = 64.306$.

Independently performed Friedman tests indicate significant differences for the *usability* between the different coordinate systems for *point of reference*, $\chi^2(2) = 6.958$, $p = .031$, and for the *placement* conditions, $\chi^2(2) = 16.085$, $p < 0.001$, see Fig. 4.

Post-hoc analyzes performed with a Wilcoxon Signed-Rank test show a significantly higher *usability* for the *head-fixed* compared to the *world-fixed* coordinate system, $Z = -3.291$, $p = 0.001$. However, Wilcoxon Signed-Rank tests did not show significant differences for the *usability* between the differently used coordinate systems, neither for the *body-fixed* compared to the *head-fixed*, $Z = -1.962$, $p = 0.05$, nor for the *body-fixed* compared to the *world-fixed* coordinate system, $Z = -.853$, $p = 0.394$. Moreover, Wilcoxon Signed-Rank tests show a significant higher *usability* when the co-user was placed in the *center*, $Z = -3.378$, $p = 0.001$, and also when the co-user was placed in the *periphery*, $Z = -3.420$, $p = 0.001$ compared to the *interactive placement*, see Fig. 4. A Wilcoxon Signed-Rank test shows a significantly higher *usability* for the *stationary* compared to *mobile scenario*, $Z = -2.962$, $p = 0.003$, see Fig. 4.

Self Reported Co-presence. Descriptive statistics led to following median values for the *self reported co-presence* sorted by *point of reference*: $Mdn_{\text{body-fixed}} = 18.083$, $Mdn_{\text{head-fixed}} = 18.833$, and $Mdn_{\text{world-fixed}} = 18.583$, by *placement*: $Mdn_{\text{center}} = 18.167$, $Mdn_{\text{periphery}} = 17.917$, and $Mdn_{\text{interactive}} = 19.000$, and by *scenario*: $Mdn_{\text{mobile}} = 18.389$, and $Mdn_{\text{stationary}} = 18.444$.

Individual Friedman tests did neither indicate significant differences for the *self reported co-presence* between the differently used coordinate systems for *point of reference*, $\chi^2(2) = 1.701$, $p = .427$, nor significant differences between the different *placement* conditions, $\chi^2(2) = 5.382$, $p = .068$.

A Wilcoxon Signed-Rank test did not show significant difference for the *self reported co-presence* score between the *scenario* conditions *mobile* and *stationary*, $Z = -.047$, $p = .962$.

Perceived Others' Co-presence. Descriptive statistics led to following median values for the *perceived others' co-presence* sorted by *point of reference*: $Mdn_{\text{body-fixed}} = 39.250$, $Mdn_{\text{head-fixed}} = 40.417$, and $Mdn_{\text{world-fixed}} = 39.583$, by *placement*: $Mdn_{\text{center}} = 39.667$, $Mdn_{\text{periphery}} = 38.917$, and $Mdn_{\text{interactive}} = 40.167$, and by *scenario*: $Mdn_{\text{mobile}} = 38.889$, and $Mdn_{\text{stationary}} = 40.000$.

Individual Friedman tests did neither indicate significant differences for the *perceived others' co-presence* between the different coordinate systems for *point of reference*, $\chi^2(2) = 2.257$, $p = .323$, nor significant differences between the different *placement* conditions, $\chi^2(2) = 3.200$, $p = .202$.

A Wilcoxon Signed-Rank test did not show a significant difference for the *perceived others' co-presence* score between the *mobile* and *stationary scenario*, $Z = 1.111$, $p = .267$.

Social Presence. Descriptive statistics led to following median values for the *social presence* sorted by *point of reference*: $Mdn_{\text{body-fixed}} = 9.398$, $Mdn_{\text{head-fixed}} = 9.373$, and $Mdn_{\text{world-fixed}} = 9.469$, by *placement*: $Mdn_{\text{center}} = 9.183$, $Mdn_{\text{periphery}} = 9.660$, and $Mdn_{\text{interactive}} = 9.142$, and by *scenario*: $Mdn_{\text{mobile}} = 9.409$, and $Mdn_{\text{stationary}} = 8.930$.

Individual Friedman tests did neither indicate significant differences for the *social presence* between the different coordinate systems for *point of reference*,

$\chi^2(2) = 0.778$, $p = .678$, nor significant differences between the different *placement* conditions, $\chi^2(2) = 5.944$, $p = .051$.

A Wilcoxon Signed-Rank test did not show a significant difference in the *social presence* score for the *scenario* conditions *mobile* and *stationary*, $Z = -2.069$, $p = .039$.

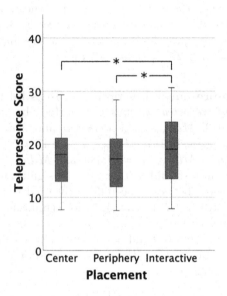

Fig. 5. *Telepresence score for placement condition (center, periphery, interactive)*

Telepresence. Descriptive statistics led to following median values for the *telepresence* sorted by *point of reference*: $Mdn_{\text{body-fixed}} = 16.417$, $Mdn_{\text{head-fixed}} = 17.250$, and $Mdn_{\text{world-fixed}} = 19.000$, by *placement*: $Mdn_{\text{center}} = 18.083$, $Mdn_{\text{periphery}} = 17.250$, and $Mdn_{\text{interactive}} = 19.083$, and by *scenario*: $Mdn_{\text{mobile}} = 17.167$, and $Mdn_{\text{stationary}} = 18.889$.

Whilst a Friedman test did not indicate significant differences for *telepresence* between the different coordinate systems for *point of reference*, $\chi^2(2) = 4.324$, $p = .115$, a Friedman test indicated significant differences between the different *placement* conditions, $\chi^2(2) = 17.333$, $p < .001$, see Fig. 5.

Post-hoc analysis with Wilcoxon Signed-Rank tests showed a significant higher *telepresence* when the co-user was placed *interactively* by the user, compared to the placement in the *center*, $Z = -2.813$, $p = .005$, and also a significant higher *telepresence* when the co-user was placed *interactively* by the user, compared to the placement in the *periphery*, $Z = -3.050$, $p = .002$. No significant difference could be found for placing the co-user in the *center* compared to the *periphery* condition, $Z = -1.767$, $p = .077$, see Fig. 5.

Furthermore, a Mann-Whitney U test did not show significant difference in the *telepresence* score for the *scenario* conditions *mobile* and *stationary*, $Z = 0.523$, $p = .601$.

4.2 Qualitative Results

We analyzed the qualitative data collected during semi-structured interviews through closed coding. The categories were structured according to our independent variables to find explanations for our quantitative analyses' results.

Point of Reference. Our quantitative results did indicate a significant favor for the *head-fixed point of reference* of the coordinate system in which the co-user should be visualized. The qualitative results indicate that a majority of our participants (15) prefer to have the co-user always in view. This is a strong argument for the *head-fixed* coordinate system:

- *"The caller was always in my view and I could focus on the object of the conversation"* (P14, *center, mobile*).

Reasons given for the *head-fixed* favor were:

- *"The conversation felt more direct."* (P8, *center, mobile*),
- *"Position right in front of me, I was able to keep eye contact with the caller"* (P17, *center, mobile*),
- *"I was able to change my head position for comfort without risking loosing eye contact"* (P16, *center, stationary*).

Although the majority of the participants favored the *head-fixed point of reference*, advantages for a *body-fixed* coordinate system were also named. A real advantage of the *body-fixed* referenced coordinate system was that (while having the benefits of the *head-fixed* position, such as eye contact, etc.), one could spontaneously focus on other things in the environment:

- *"Center position but fixed through room tracking is a good way to focus on the caller, but it still feels natural to move the head around."* (P18, *center, stationary*)
- *"The direction of the caller was more or less clear and I could control if I want to look at them or not"* (P13, *center, mobile*).

Placement. Our quantitative results indicate a significantly higher *usability* if the co-user is placed in the *center* and in the *periphery* than if *interactively* placing the co-user.

The majority (12) of the participants commented positively on the *placement* in the *center* of the FoV and stated that the co-user would be easy to focus, for example:

- *"Was always in view and easy to focus on"* (P7, *body-fixed, stationary*),

- *"The caller was always in my view and I could focus on the object of the conversation"* (P14, head-fixed, mobile),
- *"The caller was in the middle of my view.... so I don't have to turn my head or move my eyes"* (P7, head-fixed, stationary).

Moreover, participants indicated when they preferred the *placement* in the *periphery*. There were also comments explaining when the *center placement* lacks usability, and the *periphery placement* works better. The *center placement* can, for example, be obstructive and can cause occlusion, especially during *mobile* scenarios and when the coordinate system was *head-fixed*:

- *"The caller was always in the center of my view, so could not see my surroundings as good as I wanted sometimes"* (P2),
- *"Always in view. Can not look away. Obstructing the middle of the FoV. Due to not being always on eye level felt more like looking at a screen instead of a real person."* (P3),
- *"It would take the focus out of my normal vision. This would be bad in some situations (driving a car, shopping...)"* (P8).

For the *interactive placement*, the responses showed that users tended to place the caller in the center position (11), which confirms the preference for the *placement*:

- *"In the center of my view."* (P18, head-fixed, interactive, mobile),
- *"Directly in front of me or slightly to the side."* (P7, world-fixed, interactive, stationary), or
- *"More or less in front of me but a little bit out of the middle axis."* (P11, head-fixed, interactive, mobile).

Also, the *interactive placement* was often put in the center, which was, e.g., done for the following reason:

- *"So I can see their reactions and gestures"* (P2, head-fixed, stationary).

The alternative and only slightly less favored placement was the *periphery*, which was confirmed by seven positive comments, such as:

- *"On my right-hand side, like a good friend who walks a few steps with me"* (P15, head-fixed, interactive, mobile).

Scenario. Our quantitative results show a significant favor for the *stationary scenario*. Participants (7) stated that if the scenario was *mobile*, it was irritating and felt uncomfortable communicating with a *world-fixed* co-user:

- *"The caller was an obstacle in my route, so i had to pass through him/her. Not really comfortable."* (P2, periphery),
- *"Sometimes you go through the person, weird feeling"* (P5, periphery).
- *"... moving away from the person, while listening to the caller, seemed counter-intuitive"* (P14, center).

5   Discussion

We structured and discussed the obtained quantitative and qualitative results according to our independent variables.

5.1   Point of Reference

From a *usability* point of view, the *head-fixed* condition was rated significantly higher by the users. This is in line with our qualitative results that indicate that the participants preferred head-fixed referencing. Participants preferred such referencing as it supports a sense of the remote user's presence by enabling face-to-face conversation and maintaining eye contact. This can serve as an explanation for the *usability* favor of always seeing the co-user, which is also in line with psychological research on non-verbal communication cues, such as [15] as the understanding of the co-user is increased when the face of the co-user [27] or lips are visible [25]. Moreover, participants perceived the *world-fixed* and *body-fixed* referenced co-user equally. In the *stationary* condition, both references seemed nearly identical. We did not measure differences in any presence score, which could be because the co-user was theoretically always and under each condition visible within the FoV. As our walking circle was relatively small, the *mobile* scenario allowed the user to see the *world-fixed* person still when walking "away". Hence, a mobile scenario in which users walk further away and leave the room could show the lack of *presence* when communicating with a *world-fixed* virtual co-user. The qualitative data shows that participants, in general, like the *body-fixed* reference system as well as the *head-fixed* system, but from time to time, the *head-fixed* system can lead to occlusion of real-world content through the co-user's visualization. Especially if the co-user is placed in the center, the *head-fixed* system does not allow for looking away as even when turning the head, the co-user would always be in the center of the view. The *body-fixed* system allows for looking away and focusing on real-world content, which would be especially crucial in multi-task scenarios or when walking through big cities with traffic.

5.2   Placement

Considering the *usability*, the *center* and the *periphery* conditions were rated significantly higher compared to the *interactive placement*. The answers in the semi-structured interviews provide more information about the intends of our participants. The participants considered whether the user's placement directly in the *center* or in the *periphery* was advantageous, depending on the situation. If the focus is on the conversation, the center placement is preferred. Like mentioned before, the placement in the *center* of the FoV corresponds to everyday face-to-face conversations where the conversation partners face each other, and eye contact can be maintained. If the surroundings must be taken into account, peripheral placement is preferred. Not having the co-user in the center of the FoV means the possibility to see the surroundings better and to be able to spend attention on other activities besides the conversation. With regard to *usability*, the interactive placement seems to have proved to be a greater effort. Users had chosen a placement in the *center* or the *periphery* when they placed the co-user interactively. The qualitative data show this. Thus the same *placement* led to an increased effort, which is reflected in the lower usability. Interestingly, the sense of *telepresence* for the *interactive placement* of the co-user was rated significantly highest. While costing cognitive effort and time, one can interpret the data in a way that the free placement of the co-user increases the feeling of being in the virtual environment, as the co-user is positioned in the position that suits the individual needs of users which leads to an increased sense of *telepresence*. We did not measure differences in the other presence scores except the *telepresence*, which could be because the co-user was theoretically always and under each condition visible within the FoV.

5.3   Scenario

Our results did show significantly higher usability for the *stationary scenario*. When the study participants were standing in one place, the covering of the co-user's view was not perceived as disturbing, which had a positive effect on usability. Users could focus on the caller and the talk. When walking in the mobile condition, each condition of the co-user placement resulted in parts of the view being obscured. Walking and simultaneous focusing on the co-user was perceived as disturbing and obstructive. On the one hand, the path to be walked could not be entirely perceived due to the environment's partial occlusion and led to uncertainties when moving. On the other hand, distractions seem to occur because simultaneous visual focusing on the caller and walking is a cognitive load. If one has to be careful when walking, for example, to pay attention to traffic, a *center placement* might be disturbing. Furthermore, if walking further away from the co-user's visualization, results for the *mobile scenarios* might show that the *world-fixed* condition lacks usability.

5.4   Design Recommendations

Scenario: We do not recommend scenario-dependent placements as we address the scenario dependency shown in our results through the recommendation of a dynamically changeable *reference system*.

Reference System: When focusing on the conversation, we recommend using the *head-fixed* referenced coordinate system. Keeping the co-user in view supports the remote user's presence by enabling face-to-face conversation and maintaining eye contact as an important social signal. From time to time, the *head-fixed* system can lead to occlusion of real-world content through the co-user's visualization. Especially if the co-user is placed in the *center*, the *head-fixed* system does not allow for looking away as even when turning the head, the co-user would always be in the *center* of the view. The *body-fixed* system allows for looking away and focusing on real-world content, which would be especially crucial in multitasking scenarios or when walking through big cities with traffic.

If the conversation is not in focus and other tasks require attention, we recommend using the *body-fixed* referenced coordinate system. This referencing leaves the control of content placement to the user through head-turning, for example during a multitask situation when attention sharing and cognitive load matter.

Placement: Placing the co-user in the *center* is often favored as this positioning represents natural face-to-face communication. Such natural communication is supported when placing the co-user in the *center* of the FoV. For tasks that require little attention and where the co-user has an instructing function, we recommend the placement in the *periphery*. Suppose the task has a high cognitive load and requires much attention. In that case, we recommend the *center* or *periphery* placement with the *body-fixed* referencing of the coordinate system. This allows the user to place the co-user through head rotations, representing a natural visual attention switch.

Future Work. While a face-to-face set up, just like in natural inter-social communication was always given in the head-fixed coordinate system, it was partly missing in the body- and floor-fixed version due to users' movements and rotation. Such difference in communication quality due to partly missing eye contact could be compensated through automatic avatar rotations, especially for the body-fixed coordinate system. If such rotation is desired might be worth investigating in future work.

6   Conclusion

Exploring where visualizations of remote communication partner should be placed in AR, we focused on three research questions:

(1) Where shall we display co-users we talk to in AR relative to us: somewhere in the room, somewhere around us or in our FoV? In other words, where shall the reference of a coordinate system be in which the co-user is visualized: world attached, body attached, or attached to our FoV?
(2) Where within such coordinate system shall the co-user's visualization be placed: in the center, in the periphery, or chosen by the user (through gesture interaction)?
(3) How are placement and coordinate systems favored in different scenarios comparing a mobile and a stationary scenario?

Through a user study, we found that remote users we talk to should be visualized in AR in front of us, but in situations in which the physical world requires attention, visualization in the periphery is better.

In short, for pure communication situations, AR co-users should be placed in the *center* of the FoV using a *head-fixed* referencing. For task situations, AR co-users visualizations should be referenced *body-fixed* to allows the user to place the co-user through head rotations.

Acknowledgements. This work is funded by the German Ministry of Education and Research (BMBF) within the GEVAKUB project (01JKD1701B) and by the Deutsche Forschungsgemeinschaft (DFG, German Research Foundation) – 425869442 and is part of Priority Program SPP2199 Scalable Interaction Paradigms for Pervasive Computing Environments.

References

1. Anjos, R.K.D., et al.: Adventures in hologram space: exploring the design space of eye-to-eye volumetric telepresence. In: 25th ACM Symposium on Virtual Reality Software and Technology. VRST 2019. Association for Computing Machinery, New York, NY, USA (2019). https://doi.org/10.1145/3359996.3364244, https://doi.org/10.1145/3359996.3364244

2. Basler, A.: Über das sehen von bewegungen. Archiv für die gesamte Physiologie des Menschen und der Tiere **115**(11), 582–601 (1906). https://doi.org/10.1007/BF01677292, https://doi.org/10.1007/BF01677292

3. Bradley, J.V.: Complete counterbalancing of immediate sequential effects in a Latin square design. J. Am. Stat. Assoc. **53**(282), 525–528 (1958). https://doi.org/10.1080/01621459.1958.10501456, https://amstat.tandfonline.com/doi/abs/10.1080/01621459.1958.10501456

4. Brooke, J.: SUS: a quick and dirty usability scale (1996)

5. Chua, S.H., Perrault, S.T., Matthies, D.J.C., Zhao, S.: Positioning glass: investigating display positions of monocular optical see-through head-mounted display. In: Proceedings of the Fourth International Symposium on Chinese CHI, pp. 1:1–1:6. ChineseCHI2016, ACM, New York, NY, USA (2016). https://doi.org/10.1145/2948708.2948713, http://doi.acm.org/10.1145/2948708.2948713

6. Du, R., Chuang, M., Chang, W., Hoppe, H., Varshney, A.: Montage4d: interactive seamless fusion of multiview video textures. In: Proceedings of the ACM SIGGRAPH Symposium on Interactive 3D Graphics and Games, pp. 5:1–5:11. I3D 2018. ACM, New York, NY, USA (2018). https://doi.org/10.1145/3190834.3190843, http://doi.acm.org/10.1145/3190834.3190843

7. Finlay, D.: Motion perception in the peripheral visual field. Perception **11**(4), 457–462 (1982)

8. Fiorentino, M., Debernardis, S., Uva, A.E., Monno, G.: Augmented reality text style readability with see-through head-mounted displays in industrial context. Presence: Teleoperators Virtual Environ. **22**(2), 171–190 (2013)

9. Fischer, B.: Blick- Punkte. Neurobiologische Prinzipien des Sehens und der Blicksteuerung. Huber, Bern (1999)

10. Gabbard, J.L., Swan, J.E., Hix, D., Schulman, R.S., Lucas, J., Gupta, D.: An empirical user-based study of text drawing styles and outdoor background textures for augmented reality. In: IEEE Proceedings. VR 2005. Virtual Reality, 2005, pp. 11–18, March 2005. https://doi.org/10.1109/VR.2005.1492748

11. Gibbs, S.J., Arapis, C., Breiteneder, C.J.: Teleport— towards immersive copresence. Multimedia Syst. **7**(3), 214–221, May 1999. https://doi.org/10.1007/s005300050123, http://dx.doi.org/10.1007/s005300050123

12. Gruenefeld, U., Löcken, A., Brueck, Y., Boll, S., Heuten, W.: Where to look: exploring peripheral cues for shifting attention to spatially distributed out-of-view objects. In: Proceedings of the 10th International Conference on Automotive User Interfaces and Interactive Vehicular Applications, pp. 221–228. AutomotiveUI 2018. Association for Computing Machinery, New York, NY, USA (2018). https://doi.org/10.1145/3239060.3239080, https://doi.org/10.1145/3239060.3239080
13. Kato, H., Billinghurst, M.: Marker tracking and HMD calibration for a video-based augmented reality conferencing system. In: Proceedings of the 2nd IEEE and ACM International Workshop on Augmented Reality, p. 85. IWAR 1999, IEEE Computer Society, USA (1999)
14. Klose, E.M., Mack, N.A., Hegenberg, J., Schmidt, L.: Text presentation for augmented reality applications in dual-task situations. In: 2019 IEEE Conference on Virtual Reality and 3D User Interfaces (VR), pp. 636–644, March 2019. https://doi.org/10.1109/VR.2019.8797992
15. Krauss, R.M., Chen, Y., Chawla, P.: Nonverbal behavior and nonverbal communication: what do conversational hand gestures tell us? In: Advances in Experimental Social Psychology, vol. 28, pp. 389–450. Elsevier (1996)
16. Lawrence, L., Dey, A., Billinghurst, M.: The effect of video placement in AR conferencing applications. In: Proceedings of the 30th Australian Conference on Computer-Human Interaction, pp. 453–457. OzCHI 2018. Association for Computing Machinery, New York, NY, USA (2018). https://doi.org/10.1145/3292147.3292203, https://doi.org/10.1145/3292147.3292203
17. Lindlbauer, D., et al.: A collaborative see-through display supporting on-demand privacy. In: ACM SIGGRAPH 2014 Emerging Technologies, pp. 1:1–1:1. SIGGRAPH 2014. ACM, New York, NY, USA (2014). https://doi.org/10.1145/2614066.2614095, http://doi.acm.org/10.1145/2614066.2614095
18. Lindlbauer, D., et al.: Tracs: transparency-control for see-through displays. In: Proceedings of the 27th Annual ACM Symposium on User Interface Software and Technology, pp. 657–661. UIST 2014. ACM, New York, NY, USA (2014). https://doi.org/10.1145/2642918.2647350, http://doi.acm.org/10.1145/2642918.2647350
19. Nassani, A., Lee, G., Billinghurst, M., Langlotz, T., Lindeman, R.W.: Using visual and spatial cues to represent social contacts in ar. In: SIGGRAPH Asia 2017 Mobile Graphics & Interactive Applications, pp. 15:1–15:6. SA 2017. ACM, New York, NY, USA (2017). https://doi.org/10.1145/3132787.3139199, http://doi.acm.org/10.1145/3132787.3139199
20. Nowak, K.L., Biocca, F.: The effect of the agency and anthropomorphism on users' sense of telepresence, copresence, and social presence in virtual environments. Presence 12(5), 481–494 (2003). https://doi.org/10.1162/105474603322761289
21. Orlosky, J., Kiyokawa, K., Takemura, H.: Dynamic text management for see-through wearable and heads-up display systems. In: Proceedings of the 2013 International Conference on Intelligent User Interfaces, pp. 363–370. IUI 2013. ACM, New York, NY, USA (2013). https://doi.org/10.1145/2449396.2449443, http://doi.acm.org/10.1145/2449396.2449443
22. Orts-Escolano, S., et al.: Holoportation: virtual 3d teleportation in real-time. In: Proceedings of the 29th Annual Symposium on User Interface Software and Technology, pp. 741–754. UIST 2016. ACM, New York, NY, USA (2016). https://doi.org/10.1145/2984511.2984517, http://doi.acm.org/10.1145/2984511.2984517

23. Rzayev, R., Woźniak, P.W., Dingler, T., Henze, N.: Reading on smart glasses: the effect of text position, presentation type and walking. In: Proceedings of the 2018 CHI Conference on Human Factors in Computing Systems, pp. 45:1–45:9. CHI 2018. ACM, New York, NY, USA (2018). https://doi.org/10.1145/3173574. 3173619, http://doi.acm.org/10.1145/3173574.3173619

24. Schandry, R.: Biologische Psychologie. Beltz (2011)

25. Schwartz, J.L., Berthommier, F., Savariaux, C.: Seeing to hear better: evidence for early audio-visual interactions in speech identification. Cognition 93(2), B69–B78 (2004). https://doi.org/10.1016/j.cognition.2004.01.006, http://www.sciencedirect.com/science/article/pii/S001002770400054X

26. Strasburger, H., Rentschler, I., Jüttner, M.: Peripheral vision and pattern recognition: a review. J. Vis. 11(5), 13 (2011). https://doi.org/10.1167/11.5.13

27. Sumby, W.H., Pollack, I.: Visual contribution to speech intelligibility in noise. J. Acoust. Soc. Am. 26(2), 212–215 (1954). https://doi.org/10.1121/1.1907309

28. Tanaka, K., Kishino, Y., Miyamae, M., Terada, T., Nishio, S.: An information layout method for an optical see-through HMD considering the background. In: 2007 11th IEEE International Symposium on Wearable Computers, pp. 109–110, October 2007. https://doi.org/10.1109/ISWC.2007.4373791

29. Tanaka, K., Kishino, Y., Miyamae, M., Terada, T., Nishio, S.: An information layout method for an optical see-through head mounted display focusing on the viewability. In: Proceedings of the 7th IEEE/ACM International Symposium on Mixed and Augmented Reality, pp. 139–142. ISMAR 2008, IEEE Computer Society, Washington, DC, USA (2008). https://doi.org/10.1109/ISMAR.2008.4637340, https://doi.org/10.1109/ISMAR.2008.4637340

30. Velamkayala, E.R., Zambrano, M.V., Li, H.: Effects of Hololens in collaboration: a case in navigation tasks. In: Proceedings of the Human Factors and Ergonomics Society Annual Meeting, vol. 61(1), pp. 2110–2114 (2017). https://doi.org/10. 1177/1541931213602009, https://doi.org/10.1177/1541931213602009

31. Zhang, C., Cai, Q., Chou, P., Zhang, Z., Martin-Brualla, R.: Viewport: a distributed, immersive teleconferencing system with infrared dot pattern. IEEE MultiMedia 20(1), 17–27, January 2013. https://doi.org/10.1109/MMUL.2013.12, http://dx.doi.org/10.1109/MMUL.2013.12

32. Zhang, L., Amin, S.O., Westphal, C.: VR video conferencing over named data networks. In: Proceedings of the Workshop on Virtual Reality and Augmented Reality Network, pp. 7–12. VR/AR Network 2017. ACM, New York, NY, USA (2017). https://doi.org/10.1145/3097895.3097897, http://doi.acm.org/ 10.1145/3097895.3097897

Projection Grid Cues: An Efficient Way to Perceive the Depths of Underground Objects in Augmented Reality

Cindy Becher[1,2]([✉]) [ID], Sébastien Bottecchia[1] [ID], and Pascal Desbarats[2] [ID]

[1] Univ. Bordeaux - ESTIA Institute of Technology, 64210 Bidart, France
c.becher@estia.fr
[2] LaBRI, UMR 5800 - Université de Bordeaux, 33405 Talence, France

Abstract. Augmented Reality is increasingly used for visualizing underground networks. However, standard visual cues for depth perception have never been thoroughly evaluated via user experiments in a context involving physical occlusions (e.g., ground) of virtual objects (e.g., elements of a buried network). We therefore evaluate the benefits and drawbacks of two techniques based on combinations of two well-known depth cues: grid and shadow anchors. More specifically, we explore how each combination contributes to positioning and depth perception. We demonstrate that when using shadow anchors alone or shadow anchors combined with a grid, users generate 2.7 times fewer errors and have a 2.5 times lower perceived workload than when only a grid or no visual cues are used. Our investigation shows that these two techniques are effective for visualizing underground objects. We also recommend the use of one technique or another depending on the situation.

Keywords: Projection techniques · Depth cues · Visualization · Underground objects · Augmented reality

1 Introduction

In this article, our goal is to help the understanding of underground objects by visualizing them using an Augmented Reality Head-Mounted Display. According to Milgram *et al.* [21], Augmented Reality (AR) is part of a continuum between real and virtual environments and consists of augmenting reality by superimposing virtual content on it. On the one hand, AR is a promising way of representing many kinds of information, such as 2D data, 3D data, texts, images, or holograms, directly in situ and with better immersion. On the other hand, a bad perception of the distances between or of the positions of the augmentations can considerably alter the experience of AR, especially with direct perception systems like a Head-Mounted Display (HMD).

Several studies [8,19,28] focus on the problems of perception in AR. They show that virtual content cannot be naively added to reality: visual cues are

© IFIP International Federation for Information Processing 2021
Published by Springer Nature Switzerland AG 2021
C. Ardito et al. (Eds.): INTERACT 2021, LNCS 12932, pp. 611–630, 2021.
https://doi.org/10.1007/978-3-030-85623-6_35

necessary. Indeed, human perception is influenced by our experience of our environment, and virtual objects do not follow the same physical rules as real objects. This work focuses on removing the ambiguities of interpreting a complex underground scene in AR. This open issue has been recently highlighted in a course taught by Ventura *et al.* [34].

In this work, we focus on a specific optical see-through HMD: the first generation of the HoloLens. The design of this device allows parallax movement and stereoscopic disparity, both of which are natural features for enhancing perception as mentioned in the work of Cutting [6]. In this paper, we focus on cues for improving the visualization of underground objects. One cue is a synthetic projection on the floor of the virtual object's silhouette, linked to the object by an axis, i.e., Projection Display (PD). We combine this projection with a grid that represents the virtual floor and overlays the real floor, i.e., Projection Grid Display (PGD). We conducted two experiments to determine whether these visualization techniques improved spatial perception. More specifically, we evaluated the benefits and drawbacks of three visualization techniques in comparison to the naive technique used to display buried objects in AR.

The contributions in this paper are the following:

- Two hybridizations of visualization techniques for displaying underground objects in AR.
- A comparison of how four visualization techniques affect the user's perception of the absolute positioning of underground virtual objects in AR.
- A comparison of how four visualization techniques affect the user's perception of the relative positioning and altitude of underground virtual objects in AR.

Fig. 1. Comparison of two classical methods, Naive Display and Grid Display (ND-GD), with hybridized visual cues, Projection Grid Display and Projection Display (PGD-PD), for depth perception methods, including both relative and absolute methods: Projection Display (PD), Projection Grid Display (PGD), Naive Display (ND), and Grid Display (GD).

2   Motivation

In recent years, underground facilities (e.g., for electricity, water, or natural gas networks) have been precisely referenced to prevent accidents during future works. They are typically reported on 2D maps with depth information, but sometimes are reported directly in 3D. Ventura *et al.* [34] observed that these maps can be used for many tasks: information querying, planning, surveying, and construction site monitoring.

We focus on the marking picketing task, which consists of reporting map points of interest directly in situ in the field. While carrying out these tasks, workers have many constraints. We conducted interviews beforehand to collect needs and constraints during these tasks and, more generally, during the use of these 2D/3D maps on 2D displays (paper or screen).

According to workers, these plans are very difficult to interpret in the field. As Wang *et al.* [35] mentioned, reading 3D GIS data from a 2D display affects the user cognition and understanding of 3D information. For example, at a construction site during an excavation, the underground elements are indicated by a color code. They are classified according to what they consist of. Workers are in a dangerous environment (construction site) and want to keep their hands free. In addition, they need to quickly visualize and understand the information being displayed.

We choose AR to facilitate the visualization of 2.5/3D data in the field. In our case, we need to display underground virtual objects. We opted for a non-realistic rendering to allow workers to quickly target important information. Rolim *et al.* [24] classified some perception issues into three main categories: visual attention, visual photometric consistency, and visual geometric consistency. Due to our industrial background, we choose to focus on the last category, visual geometric consistency. This choice is appropriate because our focus is the display of underground pipes using the data from 2D plans. Following the example of Zollmann *et al.*, [43,45] who displayed underground pipes, our major challenges are to maintain the coherence between the real environment and the virtual data (management of occlusions by the ground) and to provide a correct perception of distances and spatial relationships between objects.

3 Related Work

The display of 3D underground virtual objects involves two main problems: occlusion management and depth perception.

3.1 Occlusion Management

The link between real and virtual worlds can be made by managing the occlusion of virtual objects by the ground. According to Zollmann *et al.* [41], if occlusions are not considered, it always leads to poor depth perception. Our goal is to account for occlusions without losing the precision or the resolution of underground object information (as can be the case for solutions that use transparencies or patterns that partially mask underground objects).

There are several methods for managing occlusion. One method consists of revealing the interior of an object by maintaining and/or accentuating its edges [7,17,20]. This type of solution works well for small objects that are included in larger objects (for example, organs in a body). The user can see the whole object and therefore better understand the spatial relationships between the larger object and the smaller, virtual objects inside it. However, such a method must be adapted when the occlusion occurs in a large plane without visible bounds (such as occlusion by the floor or walls).

Another method is to apply occlusion masks as demonstrated in many works [22,23,26,27,37,40]. The different areas of interest are separated layer by layer, and the virtual objects are displayed at the appropriate level of depth in the image by managing their occlusions with other layers. Since our goal is to display underground objects, such a method is not directly possible.

Transparency is a solution that takes advantage of the benefits of the previous two solutions. Ghosting techniques render occluding surfaces onto semitransparent textures to reveal what is behind them. For example, some works [2,4,10,27,42,45] used important image elements for occlusion, sometimes with different levels of transparency, to give a feeling of depth. We do not want to lose any information about underground objects or compromise their accuracy; However, this is likely to occur when using ghosting techniques alone since they add semitransparent layers in front of the hidden objects. These solutions have therefore been discarded. Some transparency methods have been combined with other techniques [15,16]. With the visualization proposed by Kalkofen et al. [16], all nearest edges overlap the information and all objects appear to be on the same plane despite their different depths. In Kalkofen et al.'s other work [15], occluders are displaced to better understand relationships, but perception of their real position is lost. It seems that transparency techniques allow ordering objects but do not quantify the distance between them.

Another very useful technique is the excavation box [9,14,46]. This is a synthetic trench identical to the excavation during construction. Virtual excavation offers valuable visual cues; however, if it is not combined with transparency techniques, the contained objects will only be visible when the user's point of view allows it. Virtual excavation alone does not offer a complete visualization of virtual objects from all points of view.

3.2 Depth Perception

There are some solutions to understand occlusion by a plane, but it is still difficult to perceive virtual objects position and negative altitude. Rosales et al. [25] studied the difference in perception between objects on or above the ground. Their work demonstrates that objects above the ground were seen on it, but further from the observer than their actual distance. Distance and altitude are intrinsically related. We can hypothesize that there would be a similar perception disparity with our underground objects: they would be perceived as being underground and stuck to the ground but they would appear closer to the observer than they actually are.

Many factors influence the perception of an object's position. These factors include the conditions of the experiment: display [1], being indoors or outdoors [18]. Other factors also include the elements of realism [33] in the scene:

the coherence of shadows [5,31] and illuminations [11] improve the user's perception of positions. However, perception can also be influenced by the focal distance, the age of the user (physiological characteristics of the user), or luminosity (characteristics of the scene) [29] as well as interpupillary distance or parallax [39].

The anatomical characteristics of the users are not something that can be changed. In addition, our system must work outdoors on an optical see-through HMD device. Another factor that has a great impact on the perception of an object's position is the visualization technique used [9,13], which can include many factors, such as shadows or realism. Several visualization techniques have been proposed. In our context, some visual cues, such as those described by Luboschik *et al.* [19] would be unusable. Indeed, their use of perspective lines is interesting, but these lines must be adapted to our context, as they could easily be confused with pipes when visualizing many networks. The system must work despite the influence of all the factors incurred by our technical and technological choices.

The visualizations that we compare are inspired by those of Ware *et al.* [36], Skinner *et al.* [30] or even Heinrich *et al.* [13]. Ware *et al.* and Skinner *et al.* worked on virtual object projection on a surface (grid for the first, ground for the second). Heinrich *et al.* worked with a projective AR display and compared many methods for displaying 3D holograms that improve the user's understanding of their position (both vertical position and object distance to the user). They asked their users to sort objects according to these two dimensions and found that their supporting lines approach is the best approach for removing ambiguity from scene perception. The same kinds of projections have been named dropping lines by Ware *et al.* [36] or shadow anchors by Ventura *et al.* [34], but these methods always involve objects that are above the ground.

Our study is closely related to some aspects of the work done by Zollmann *et al.* [44]. However, nothing during their study suggested that their visual cues would provide the same results for underground objects within a small range of distances (up to 1.50 m deep in our case). Additionally, our problem is slightly different: the relative (spatial relationship between objects) and absolute (absolute distance) perception of the positions of underground objects needs to be improved, even for objects which are below the ground and not above, and we want to provide an evaluation of absolute positioning perception.

4   Concepts

We describe the design of two visualizations for underground objects that are based on different visual cues.

- **Projection:** In various works [13,36,38], projection facilitates better estimates of the relative distances between objects. Because underground objects need to be displayed, we choose a hybridization of this approach. The silhouettes of underground objects are projected onto the ground in an unrealistic way. These silhouettes are also connected to the corresponding objects with a vertical axis. All the projections are on the same plane and could be compared side by side. Additionally, the heights of the projection axes could be compared to allow a better perception of the negative altitude.

– **Grid:** Projection alone allows all objects to be referenced on a single plane, however, sometimes it is difficult to discern nearby objects and identify that they are underground. As a result, we choose to add a visual cue to reference the floor. Zollmann *et al.* [45] help to materialize this real surface in the virtual world using a ghosting technique with a semitransparent chessboard. In AR, however, transparent layers cannot be numerous due to the brightness of the screens, which would make it difficult to see all the layers and objects behind them. Therefore, we choose to use a grid. This allows us to implement a visual cue for the ground without obscuring underground objects. The grid is regular and orthogonal, so we hypothesize that it can improve distance perception. In addition, the grid allows users to integrate their perception of their own body into the virtual world. Thus, they can have a better understanding of the spatial relationships between the ground, objects (relative altitude), and themselves.

5   Implementation

We calibrate the position of the ground using an ARToolKit marker[1] (Hiro pattern) that is printed and placed on the real scene. The size of this marker is 8 by 8 cm. The user must look at the marker continuously for 5 consecutive seconds. The system then evaluates the position of the marker using the HoloLens camera. We previously informed the system of the camera's intrinsic parameters. Then, we obtain the ground's height and save it.

We choose this solution instead of the traditional spatial mapping of the HoloLens because we do not find this spatial mapping to be precise enough [4]. Indeed, the ground is estimated at 10 cm above its real position. We implement the two cues as follows:

– **Projection:** We project the silhouettes of underground objects directly onto the ground. We also connect them with a vertical axis. The axis and silhouette are rendered in a semitransparent shader to distinguish the object from visual cues, making it more perceptible.
– **Grid:** The grid is made up of 3D lines. The grid is green because the user needs to distinguish it from other cues such as projections, and additionally, green is a color well perceived by the human eye [12]. The grid is rendered with a semitransparent shader. The grid is displayed at the same height as the ground horizontally, and its rotation is not modified (HoloLens has a stabilization method).

We therefore implement four visualization techniques, one using projection, one using a grid, one using a combination of the two and one without any visual cues.

---

[1] http://www.hitl.washington.edu/artoolkit/.

6   Experiments

The goal of the experiments is to compare the designed visualization techniques in the case of buried networks. We consider only points of interest (specific components of an installation or parts of a pipe that are not straight) on buried network maps. Indeed, the links between these points can provide additional visual cues due to their appearance and their geometry. We choose to display points of interest as cubes. Later, we will expand our exploration of our techniques by considering the entire network topology and test our techniques using more complex scenes.

Rosales *et al.* [25] revealed that there is an ambiguity for cubes of 0.20 m per side that are 0.20 m above the ground. We therefore choose to evaluate the perception at 6 underground depth levels, from 0.20 m to 1.5 m (most of the objects in the industrial context are in this interval).

Rosales *et al.* also carried out a preliminary study to determine the range of distances in which their method worked. They found the HoloLens to be reliable up to an 8 m distance. Additionally, it is difficult to test a higher distance under laboratory conditions. Even for the high range of the average interpupillary spacing interval, the parallax reconstruction is only viable to just under 5 m. We, therefore, choose to evaluate objects from a distance of 5 m (to minimize this natural cue) to 8 m. We define the distances d_A and d_E, visible in Fig. 2 as being the altitude (negative in our case) and the egocentric distance, respectively. For the experiments, we define an orthogonal coordinate system O (X, Y, Z) (see Fig. 2). We conducted two experiments: one to evaluate the absolute spatial position and another to evaluate the relative spatial relationships.

6.1   Procedure, Apparatus, Tasks

Our experiments used Microsoft 1st generation HoloLens. The applications were built using Unity3D 2018.3.f1. The tests took place as follows: one participant entered the empty test room, with no marks or indicators on the ground. Participants had an open space in front of them measuring 5 by 10 m. They calibrated the HoloLens using the native application so that the display was adapted to their vision. Then, they launched the test application (Absolute or Relative), and in both cases, they stared at a Hiro marker to calibrate the height of the ground. After that, the test started, and participants used a large gray cube to their right to switch scenes. Participants stared at the cube for 5 s, and the gray cube then became greener until it disappeared to make way for a new scene. We used the same behavior for both applications.

For the "Absolute" experiment, participants only had one task:

- **Task 1 (T1)**: Participants observed a scene composed of one small gray cube that could be at 6 different distances ([5; 5.6; 6.2; 6.8; 7.4; 8] m, named d_E on Fig. 2) and 6 different depths ([0.20; 0.46; 0.72; 0.98; 1.24; 1.50] m, named d_A on Fig. 2). The cube was randomly rotated and scaled (0.20–0.30 m per side) to avoid a comparison bias with the floor or the previous scenes. The cube

The cube was randomly rotated and scaled (0.20–0.30 m per side) to avoid a comparison bias with the floor or the previous scenes. The cube appeared for 10 s using a random visualization technique and then disappeared. During this phase, participants had to observe the cube and its position. Then, they had to walk to the position they had estimated the cube to be and place a black cross on the ground. If the cube was perceived to be above or below the ground, participants placed the black cross below or above the real position of the cube, respectively, directly on the ground. They mentally projected the cube on the ground. Participants had begun walking to this position by the time the cube disappeared.

For the "Relative" experiment, participants had to complete two tasks in the same scene:

- **Task 2 (T2)**: The scene was composed of six simple gray cubes. All cubes are at 6 different distances (defined in Task 1) and 6 different depths (defined in Task 1). They were randomly rotated and scaled (defined in Task 1) to avoid a comparison bias between the cubes themselves and with the ground. The cubes were separated by 0.5 m along the X-axis (see Fig. 2). During this phase, participants had to classify the cubes by altitude (d_A), from highest to lowest.
- **Task 3 (T3)**: During the same scene, participants had to order the cubes by egocentric distance (d_E), from nearest to farthest.

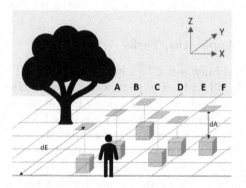

Fig. 2. Apparatus schema

After the practical part of the test, each participant was invited to sit down to answer some questions and to complete some surveys (see Sect. 6.3). First, images rendered using the four visualization techniques were presented, and then, participants were asked to fill out a NASA-TLX survey for each visualization technique.

Then, for each experiment (relative and absolute), we asked the participant to answer a few questions: which visualization technique did you prefer and why? Rank them in order of preference. Do you have any thoughts on which cue helped you more or less? We then conducted a small interview to better understand their choices and feelings. Participants used each visualization technique twice. We randomly chose the visualization methods' order of appearance.

6.2 Participants

We recruited 40 participants, 20 for each experiment. For the "Absolute" experiment, their ages ranged from 21 to 54. Ages ranged from 22 to 53 for the "Relative" experiment (see Table 1 for ages and gender distribution). All participants had perfect color perception, 4 wore glasses for the absolute experiment and 6 wore glasses for the "Relative" experiment. For each experiment, we conducted a preliminary survey of their familiarity with AR, which indicates self-rated familiarity on a scale from one (not familiar—never) to five (familiar—every day). For each experiment, participants were not familiar with AR.

Table 1. Ages and distribution of participants for each experimentation

	Ages						Gender			Familiarity	
	20s	30s	40s	50s	$\bar{x}$	σ	Male	Female	Total	σ	$\bar{x}$
Absolute	9	5	4	2	33	1.52	13	7	20	10.98	1.9
Relative	9	6	3	2	33	1.62	10	10	20	9.35	1.9

6.3 Measures and Surveys

Understanding the effects of the grid, the projection, and the combination of both was important. These methods' comparison to a naive visualization is also important. Therefore, our experiments involved both independent and dependent variables. We also present our hypothesis for this work.

Independent Variables: Our independent variables were the four visualization techniques (visible on Fig. 1). Cues from the Sect. 4 were used to construct them:

- Projection Display (PD) = projection
- Projection Grid Display (PGD) = projection + grid
- Grid Display (GD) = grid
- Naive Display (ND) = no hint

Dependent Variables: For both experiments, we examined the NASA-TLX scores for each visualization technique: Mental Demand (MD), Physical Demand (PD), Temporal Demand (TD), Performance (P), Effort (E), Frustration Level (FL), and Total score (Total). These scores were the main factors we focused on improving.

- "Absolute" Experiment: We evaluated the distance differences (Diff-D) between the perceived distance and the real distance during T1, in meters.
- "Relative" Experiment: For T2, the participant sorted the cubes according to d_A. We computed the inversion score (Error d_A) according to the real positions of the cubes. The sorting error score was calculated using the number of inversions that existed between the combination given by the participant and the perfect combination (the real positions of the cubes). For example, if the perfect combination was A-B-C and the participant chose B-A-C, there was only one inversion (A and B, Error = 1). However, if the participant chose C-A-B, there were two inversions (B and C but also A and C, Error = 2). We also recorded the sorting time (Time d_A), in seconds. Similarly, for T3, we evaluated the sorting error score according to d_E (Error d_E). We also recorded the sorting time (Time d_E), in seconds.

Hypothesis: For the "Absolute" experiment we hypothesize the following:

- The perceived workload is less when using PGD and PD than when using ND and GD – **Total NASA-TLX score (H1)**: PGD-ND (H1a); PGD-GD (H1b); PD-ND (H1c); PD-GD (H1d).
- PGD has a lower perceived workload than PD – **Total NASA-TLX score (H1bis)**.
- PGD and PD are more accurate in terms of egocentric distance estimation when compared to ND and GD – **Diff-D (H2)**: PGD-ND (H2a); PGD-GD (H2b); PD-ND (H2c); PD-GD (H2d).
- PGD is more accurate in terms of egocentric distance estimation when compared to PD – **Diff-D (H2bis)**.

For the "Relative" experiment we hypothesize that:

- PGD and PD reduce the perceived workload for sorting tasks when compared to ND and GD – **Total NASA-TLX score (H3)**: PGD-ND (H3a); PGD-GD (H3b); PD-ND (H3c); PD-GD (H3d).
- PGD reduces the perceived workload for sorting tasks when compared to PD – **Total NASA-TLX score (H3bis)**.
- PGD and PD are more efficient at ordering virtual objects by their altitude than ND and GD over similar periods of time – **Error d_A/Time d_A (H4)**: (PGD-ND (H4a); PGD-GD (H4b); PD-ND (H4c); PD-GD (H4d)).
- PGD is more efficient at ordering the virtual objects by their altitude than PD over similar period of time – **Error d_A/Time d_A (H4bis)**.

- same supposition as in H4 but for egocentric distance rather than altitude –
  Error d_E/Time d_E (H5): PGD-ND (H5a); PGD-GD (H5b); PD-ND (H5c); PD-GD (H5d).
- The same supposition as in H4 is proposed here, but for egocentric distance rather than altitude – **Error d_E/Time d_E (H5bis)**.

7   Results

Table 2. Table of t-values (Conover's results) on the left, mean and standard deviation on the right, each for both experiments (NASA-TLX data rounded to the nearest whole number).

	a	b	c	d	BIS	PGD $\overline{X}$	σ	PD $\overline{X}$	σ	GD $\overline{X}$	σ	ND $\overline{X}$	σ
H1	-4.918	-2.705	-3.689	-1.476	-1.230	20.71	11.017	23.13	10.478	31.67	10.044	39.63	15.305
H2	-3.965	-3.111	-5.185	-4.331	1.220	0.57	0.792	0.38	0.803	1.42	0.916	1.70	1.082
H3	-5.887	-3.618	-3.863	-1.594	-2.023	31.50	13.579	51.75	15.357	54.75	13.049	73.25	18.236
H4	-3.089	-4.521	-2.788	-2.788	-1.733	0.20	0.516	0.55	1.061	1.12	1.682	0.82	1.217
H5	-3.382	-4.651	-2.396	-3.664	-0.986	0.28	0.784	0.55	1.358	2.070	1.35	1.10	1.751
MD (rel)	X	X	X	X	-2.991	31.50	20.203	51.75	21.901	X	X	X	X
P (rel)	X	X	X	X	-1.999	31.00	16.591	43.00	22.266	X	X	X	X

All results were obtained using R [32] scripts and R Studio[2]. We set the risk parameter, α, at 5%. The p-values must therefore be less than 0.05 to make the test meaningful.

We analyzed the results of each experiment separately. Since participants tested the four visualization techniques, experiments were within-subject, so all data were paired. We used a Friedman test with a post-hoc Conover test. The Friedman test is the equivalent of a nonparametric repeated measures ANOVA, which can be applied to ordinal qualitative variables or when the conditions of the ANOVA are not met (normality of the residuals and homogeneity of variances). During the Conover post-hoc, we chose the Bonferroni method to adjust the p-values.

7.1   "Absolute" Experiment

Table 3 shows the p-values, while Table 2 shows the means, standard deviation and Conover's t-values. Figure 3 presents boxplots of the NASA-TLX scores, arranged by theme, as well as total scores for the absolute experiment. Figure 4 shows boxplots of differences in absolute distance estimation.

Based on Table 3, the differences in terms of perceived mental workload between PGD-ND and PD-ND were not due to chance. PGD and PD both appear to lower the perceived mental load in comparison with the baseline ND technique.

---

[2] https://rstudio.com/, Version 1.2.1335 on Windows.

Table 3. P-values of the "Absolute" experiment – White: Conover post-hoc - Grey: Friedman - Bold: significant p-values.

	PGD-ND H*a	PGD-GD H*b	PD-ND H*c	PD-GD H*d	PGD-PD H*bis	ND-GD	P-value (Friedman test)	χ^2 df=3
MD	3.237×10^{-05}	**0.015120**	0.082802	1.0000000	0.096939	0.408922	$\mathbf{8.827\times10^{-06}}$	26.161
PD	0.78331	1.0000000	1.0000000	1.0000000	1.0000000	1.0000000	0.4429	2.6842
TD	0.18389	0.48906	1.0000000	1.0000000	1.0000000	1.0000000	0.1399	5.4783
P	**0.002863**	0.059806	**0.020445**	0.291242	1.0000000	1.0000000	**0.0004363**	18.017
E	$\mathbf{8.1487\times10^{-05}}$	0.22487126	**0.00070701**	0.82905500	1.0000000	0.06549875	$\mathbf{5.24\times10^{-06}}$	27.238
FL	**0.0035119**	**0.0439828**	**0.0065033**	0.0744200	1.0000000	1.0000000	**0.000148**	20.276
Total (H1*)	$\mathbf{4.6635\times10^{-05}}$	0.0539280	**0.0030283**	0.8734384	1.0000000	0.1853742	$\mathbf{5.388\times10^{-06}}$	27.184
Diff-D (H2*)	**0.00082901**	**0.00873809**	$\mathbf{1.7818\times10^{-05}}$	**0.00030423**	0.45502326	0.45502326	$\mathbf{4.382\times10^{-08}}$	37.101

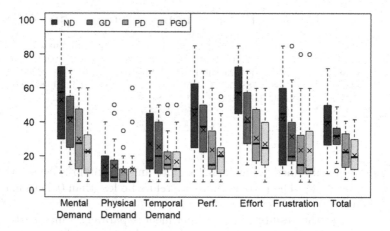

Fig. 3. NASA-TLX scores of the absolute experiment

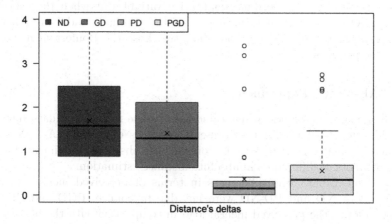

Fig. 4. Boxplots of differences of absolute distances estimation

Concerning the perceived distance, there is a very high probability that the observed differences between PGD and PD and the other two visualization techniques are not due to chance. We can thus say that PGD allows for better precision in the evaluation of these distances than ND and GD. We find the same result when comparing PD to ND and GD.

7.2 "Relative" Experiment

All of the p-value results are displayed in Table 4, and Table 2 displays the means, standard deviation and t-values from Conover's post-hoc test. Additionally, see Fig. 5 for NASA-TLX scores by theme and total NASA-TLX score for the relative experiment. See Fig. 6 for the boxplots of Errors d_E and Error d_A, made during sorting.

Table 4. P-values of the "Relative" experiment – White: Conover post-hoc - Grey: Friedman - Bold: significant p-values.

	PGD-ND H*a	PGD-GD H*b	PD-ND H*c	PD-GD H*d	PGD-PD H*bis	ND-GD	P-value (Friedman test)	χ^2 df=3
MD	3.237×10^{-05}	**0.015120**	0.082802	1.0000000	0.096939	0.408922	**8.827×10⁻⁰⁶**	26.161
PD	0.78331	1.0000000	1.0000000	1.0000000	1.0000000	1.0000000	0.4429	2.6842
TD	0.18389	0.48906	1.0000000	1.0000000	1.0000000	1.0000000	0.1399	5.4783
P	**0.002863**	0.059806	**0.020445**	0.291242	1.0000000	1.0000000	**0.0004363**	18.017
E	**8.1487×10⁻⁰⁵**	0.22487126	**0.00070701**	0.82905500	1.0000000	0.06549875	**5.24×10⁻⁰⁶**	27.238
FL	**0.0035119**	**0.0439828**	**0.0065033**	0.0744200	1.0000000	1.0000000	**0.000148**	20.276
Total (H1*)	**4.6635×10⁻⁰⁵**	0.0539280	**0.0030283**	0.8734384	1.0000000	0.1853742	**5.388×10⁻⁰⁶**	27.184
Diff-D (H2*)	**0.00082901**	**0.00873809**	**1.7818×10⁻⁰⁵**	**0.00030423**	0.45502326	0.45502326	**4.382×10⁻⁰⁸**	37.101

It is very likely that the observed differences between the averages of the total NASA-TLX scores between PGD and ND and between PGD and GD are not due to chance. We deduce that using PGD induces a lower mental load than using GD or ND (H3a and H3b validated). Similarly, PD seems more effective for reducing mental load than ND.

It is likely that PGD is more efficient than ND for sorting objects according to d_A. To compare PGD and GD according to this same factor, it is very likely that PGD is more efficient than GD. When comparing PD and GD on this criterion, PD seems more efficient than GD. Although statistically significant, this comparison would require further testing.

With sorting by d_E, PGD is most likely more efficient than ND and GD. For comparisons between PD and other visualization techniques, we can only say that it is very likely that this visualization technique is more efficient than GD. Regarding hypotheses H1bis, H2bis, H3bis, H4bis and H5bis, none of them can be validated by the experiments carried out in this paper. But some NASA-TLX themes in the "Relative" experiment show significant differences between PD and PGD. In both cases, the statistical tests indicate that there seems to be an advantage when using the PGD visualization technique, which has a lower score on average on these two themes. We conclude that PGD implies a lower mental load than GD or ND.

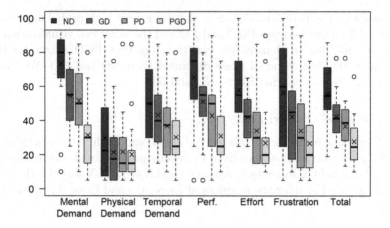

Fig. 5. NASA-TLX scores of relative experiment

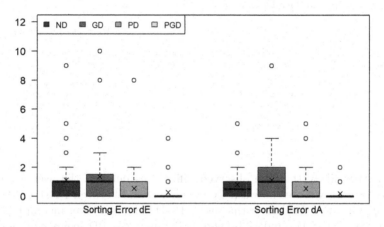

Fig. 6. Boxplot of the number of sorting errors

8   Discussion

The statistical results show that Projection Display (PD) and Projection Grid
Display (PGD) supplant the other two techniques (ND and GD). However, some
of the results can also be better understood through the interviews with participants. Moreover, the results obtained can be moderated due to the conditions
of the experiments and many other factors.

8.1 "Absolute" Experiment

Regarding the projection, some participants were very confident about their performance using ND or GD, more than with PD or PGD. We did not explain to them what the cues looked like or how to use them, so some participants preferred to trust their perception and chose to ignore these visual cues. However, given the overall results, we see that the projection greatly improves performance, whether using PD or PGD. These few users, therefore, were incorrect in their assertion that they could be more efficient without cues.

Four participants said that the grid helped but overloaded the visualization compared to ND or PD. Two participants said the grid might be too thick. We can hypothesize that having the ability to change the visualization mode or change the thickness or transparency of the grid will probably lead to better results. In addition, the position of the grid was determined using the position of the marker. Although the accuracy was higher than that with HoloLens spatial mapping, the grid was still a few centimeters above the ground. The combination of these inaccuracies with an overloaded visualization can induce an incorrect interpretation of the position of the projection, which is supposed to stick to the grid. In addition, H2 and partially H1 have been validated, but H1bis and H2bis have not.

Regarding hypotheses H1bis, H2bis, H3bis, H4bis and H5bis, none of them are validated by the two experiments carried out in this paper. On the other hand, some NASA-TLX themes in the relative experiment show significant differences between PD and PGD (Mental Demand: p-value $= 0.0246120$ t-value $= -2.991$; Performance p-value $= 0.03020057$ t-value $= -1.999$). In both cases, the statistical tests indicate that there seems to be an advantage when using the PGD visualization technique, which has a lower score on average on these two themes. Regarding the perceived workload, the observed difference between PGD and GD was not statistically significant. Nevertheless, it is close to the alpha risk. Further experiments with new samples would need to be carried out to study whether there is a significant difference between PGD and GD. The nonsignificance of the results when comparing PGD and PD can be explained by the appearance chosen for the grid (e.g., thickness or color). Indeed, an evaluation of the influence of these parameters might be helpful. Additionally, consideration should be given to whether the appearance of the grid may cause participants to change their minds about feeling visually overloaded.

8.2 "Relative" Experiment

If we consider the PGD-GD and PGD-ND comparisons, all hypotheses are validated (H3a, H4a, H5a, H3b, H4b, H5b). However, in regard to PD comparisons, the hypotheses are not all verified because of the nonsignificance of some of the p-values (H3c, H4d, H5d validated). This confirms the results of the "Absolute" experiment.

In this experiment, although the tests between PGD and PD are not decisive, PGD outperforms ND and GD for these tasks, while PD does not. We also see that PGD is better than PD in terms of Mental Demand, while it is not in the absolute experiment. This difference can be explained by the nature of the task: it is useful to have a grid while comparing two objects that are far from each other but at similar distances from the user (d_E). Indeed, according to the participants, the grid is useful for comparing distances since it is regular and therefore allows measurement. Participants also added that the grid allowed them to map the room. More experiments must be conducted to further study the differences between PGD and PD, such as evaluating different thicknesses and/or colors of the grid.

9   Conclusion and Perspectives

In this article, we evaluate four visualization techniques in regard to the perception of vertical and horizontal distances in the case of buried objects. Based on the experimental results, the hybridization techniques are promising. However, some users think that the grid overloads the visualization, although it improves the understanding of the scene. We can thus envision implementing several options to let users decide how much information they need as they go. For example, projection is precise enough to visualize the absolute position of virtual objects under the ground. However, in regard to comparing the positions of objects relative to each other, the grid is useful for nearby objects and to better understand that objects are underground.

Additionally, absolute depth perception was evaluated in only one direction, d_E, and not d_A. It would be interesting to find a way to assess this issue to see if the results would be different. Another question to address would be to assess if the same conclusions can be drawn with objects that are above the ground. We plan to test projection alone and its combination with the grid with more objects and assess the impact of the density of displayed objects. We also want to test these methods with a more complex geometry, for example, cubes linked by pipes, and improve visualization by changing the appearance of the data. The final step will be to integrate real data from 3D underground network maps and study how they are perceived by the user.

10   Health Crisis

The tests were carried out outside of a lockdown at a time when national laws and laboratory rules allowed it. We ensured that our protocol was validated by our hierarchy. We, therefore, followed a very strict sanitary protocol, with individual protective equipment (e.g., masks, disposable caps), disinfection of all surfaces, all equipment, and the HMD to perform the tests.

Note

This article is a translation of a French article from the IHM20.21 conference with permission [3].

Acknowledgements. We gratefully acknowledge the support of ANRT (French National Association for Research and Technology). We also warmly thank Professor Laurence Nigay for her help during the shepherding process.

References

1. Ahn, J., Ahn, E., Min, S., Choi, H., Kim, H., Kim, G.J.: Size perception of augmented objects by different AR displays. In: Stephanidis, C. (ed.) HCII 2019. CCIS, vol. 1033, pp. 337–344. Springer, Cham (2019). https://doi.org/10.1007/978-3-030-23528-4_46
2. Avery, B., Sandor, C., Thomas, B.H.: In: Improving spatial perception for augmented reality X-ray vision, pp. 79–82. IEEE (2009). https://doi.org/10.1109/VR.2009.4811002
3. Becher, C., Bottecchia, S., Desbarats, P.: Projection Grid Cues: une manière efficace de percevoir les profondeurs des objets souterrains en Réalité Augmentée. In: IHM 2020–2021 (To appear) (2021). https://doi.org/10.1145/3450522.3451247
4. Chen, J., Granier, X., Lin, N., Peng, Q.: In: On-line visualization of underground structures using context features, pp. 167–170. ACM, New York (2010). https://doi.org/10.1145/1889863.1889898
5. Cöster, J.: The effects of shadows on depth perception in augmented reality on a mobile device. Technical report (2019)
6. Cutting, J.E.: How the eye measures reality and virtual reality. Behav. Res. Methods Instrum. Comput. **29**(1), 27–36 (1997). https://doi.org/10.3758/BF03200563
7. De Paolis, L.T., Luca, V.D.: Augmented visualization with depth perception cues to improve the surgeon's performance in minimally invasive surgery. Med. Biol. Eng. Comput. **57**(5), 995–1013 (2018). https://doi.org/10.1007/s11517-018-1929-6
8. Dey, A., Cunningham, A., Sandor, C.: In: Evaluating depth perception of photorealistic mixed reality visualizations for occluded objects in outdoor environments, vol. VRST 10, p. 211. ACM Press, New York (2010). https://doi.org/10.1145/1889863.1889911
9. Eren, M.T., Balcisoy, S.: Evaluation of X-ray visualization techniques for vertical depth judgments in underground exploration. Vis. Comput. **34**(3), 405–416 (2017). https://doi.org/10.1007/s00371-016-1346-5
10. Fukiage, T., Oishi, T., Ikeuchi, K.: In: Reduction of contradictory partial occlusion in mixed reality by using characteristics of transparency perception, pp. 129–139. IEEE (2012). https://doi.org/10.1109/ISMAR.2012.6402549
11. Gao, Y., Peillard, E., Normand, J.M., Moreau, G., Liu, Y., Wang, Y.: Influence of virtual objects shadows and lighting coherence on distance perception in optical see-through augmented reality. J. Soc. Inf. Disp. **28**(2), 117–135 (2019). https://doi.org/10.1002/jsid.832
12. Gross, H.: Handbook of Optical Systems, vol. 1. Wiley-VCH (September 2005). https://doi.org/10.1002/9783527699223

13. Heinrich, F., Bornemann, K., Lawonn, K., Hansen, C.: In: Depth perception in projective augmented reality: an evaluation of advanced visualization techniques, pp. 1–11. ACM, New York (2019). https://doi.org/10.1145/3359996.3364245

14. Junghanns, S., Schall, G., Schmalstieg, D.: In: VIDENTE-What lies beneath?, A new approach of locating and identifying buried utility assets on site, vol. 08), p. showcase. p. 28, Salzburg, Austria (2008)

15. Kalkofen, D., Tatzgern, M., Schmalstieg, D.: Explosion diagrams in augmented reality. In: 2009 IEEE Virtual Reality Conference, pp. 71–78. IEEE (March 2009). https://doi.org/10.1109/VR.2009.4811001

16. Kalkofen, D., Mendez, E., Schmalstieg, D.: Interactive focus and context visualization for augmented reality. In: 6th IEEE and ACM International Symposium on Mixed and Augmented Reality, pp. 1–10. IEEE (November 2007). https://doi.org/10.1109/ISMAR.2007.4538846

17. Kalkofen, D., Veas, E., Zollmann, S., Steinberger, M., Schmalstieg, D.: In: Adaptive ghosted views for augmented reality, pp. 1–9. IEEE (2013). https://doi.org/10.1109/ISMAR.2013.6671758

18. Livingston, M., Ai, Zhuming, Swan, J., Smallman, H.: In: Indoor vs. Outdoor depth perception for mobile augmented reality, pp. 55–62. IEEE (2009). https://doi.org/10.1109/VR.2009.4810999

19. Luboschik, M., Berger, P., Staadt, O.: In: On spatial perception issues in augmented reality based immersive analytics, vol. 16, pp. 47–53. ACM Press, New York (2016). https://doi.org/10.1145/3009939.3009947

20. Mendez, E., Schmalstieg, D.: In: Importance masks for revealing occluded objects in augmented reality, vol. VRST 2009, p. 247. ACM Press, New York (2009). https://doi.org/10.1145/1643928.1643988

21. Milgram, P., Takemura, H., Utsumi, A., Kishino, F.: Augmented reality: a class of displays on the reality-virtuality continuum. In: Das, H. (ed.) Telemanipulator and Telepresence Technologies. SPIE (1995). https://doi.org/10.1117/12.197321

22. Montero, A., Zarraonandia, T., Diaz, P., Aedo, I.: Designing and implementing interactive and realistic augmented reality experiences. Univ. Access Inf. Soc. **18**(1), 49–61 (2017)

23. Otsuki, M., Kamioka, Y., Kitai, Y., Kanzaki, M., Kuzuoka, H., Uchiyama, H.: Please show me inside. In: SIGGRAPH Asia 2015 Emerging Technologies on - SA 2015, pp. 1–3. ACM Press, New York (2015). https://doi.org/10.1145/2818466.2818469

24. Rolim, C., Schmalstieg, D., Kalkofen, D., Teichrieb, V.: Design guidelines for generating augmented reality instructions. In: IEEE International Symposium on Mixed and Augmented Reality, pp. 120–123. IEEE (September 2015). https://doi.org/10.1109/ISMAR.2015.36

25. Rosales, C.S., et al.: In: Distance judgments to on- and off-ground objects in augmented reality, pp. 237–243. IEEE (2019). https://doi.org/10.1109/VR.2019.8798095

26. Roxas, M., Hori, T., Fukiage, T., Okamoto, Y., Oishi, T.: In: Occlusion handling using semantic segmentation and visibility-based rendering for mixed reality, vol. VRST 2018, pp. 1–8. ACM Press, New York (2018). https://doi.org/10.1145/3281505.3281546

27. Sandor, C., Cunningham, A., Dey, A., Mattila, V.V.: In: An Augmented Reality X-Ray system based on visual saliency, pp. 27–36. IEEE (2010). https://doi.org/10.1109/ISMAR.2010.5643547

28. Schall, G., et al.: Handheld augmented reality for underground infrastructure visualization. Pers. Ubiquit. Comput. **13**(4), 281–291 (2008). https://doi.org/10.1007/s00779-008-0204-5

29. Singh, G., Ellis, S.R., Swan, J.E.: The effect of focal distance, age, and brightness on near-field augmented reality depth matching. IEEE Trans. Vis. Comput. Graph. **26**(2), 1385–1398 (2020). https://doi.org/10.1109/tvcg.2018.2869729

30. Skinner, P., Ventura, J., Zollmann, S.: Indirect augmented reality browser for GIS Data. In: Adjunct Proceedings - 2018 IEEE International Symposium on Mixed and Augmented Reality, ISMAR-Adjunct 2018, pp. 145–150. Institute of Electrical and Electronics Engineers Inc. (July 2018). https://doi.org/10.1109/ISMAR-Adjunct.2018.00054

31. Sugano, N., Kato, H., Tachibana, K.: The effects of shadow representation of virtual objects in augmented reality. Presented at the (2003)

32. Team, R.C.: R Core Team. R: A language and environment for statistical computing. Foundation for Statistical Computing (2013)

33. Vaziri, K., Liu, P., Aseeri, S., Interrante, V.: In: Impact of visual and experiential realism on distance perception in VR using a custom video see-through system, vol. 17, pp. 1–8. ACM Press, New York (2017). https://doi.org/10.1145/3119881.3119892

34. Ventura, J., Zollmann, S., Stannus, S., Billinghurst, M., Driancourt, R.: In: Understanding AR inside and out – Part Two, pp. 1–243. ACM, New York (2020). https://doi.org/10.1145/3388769.3407543

35. Wang, W., et al.: Holo3DGIS: leveraging Microsoft Hololens in 3D geographic information. ISPRS Int. J. Geo-Inf. **7**(2), 60 (2018). https://doi.org/10.3390/ijgi7020060

36. Ware, C.: Information Visualization: Perception for Design: Second Edition. Elsevier (2004). https://doi.org/10.1016/B978-1-55860-819-1.X5000-6

37. Wilson, A., Hua, H.: Design and prototype of an augmented reality display with per-pixel mutual occlusion capability. Opt. Express **25**(24), 30539 (2017). https://doi.org/10.1364/OE.25.030539

38. Wither, J., Hollerer, T.: In: pictorial depth cues for outdoor augmented reality, vol. ISWC 2005, pp. 92–99. IEEE (2005). https://doi.org/10.1109/ISWC.2005.41

39. Woldegiorgis, B.H., Lin, C.J., Liang, W.Z.: Impact of parallax and interpupillary distance on size judgment performances of virtual objects in stereoscopic displays. Ergonomics **62**(1), 76–87 (2018). https://doi.org/10.1080/00140139.2018.1526328

40. Zhu, J., Pan, Z., Sun, C., Chen, W.: Handling occlusions in video-based augmented reality using depth information. Comput. Animation Virtual Worlds **21**(5), 509–521 (2009). https://doi.org/10.1002/cav.326

41. Zollmann, S., Grasset, R., Langlotz, T., Lo, W.H., Mori, S., Regenbrecht, H.: Visualization techniques in augmented reality: a taxonomy, methods and patterns. IEEE Trans. Vis. Comput. Graph. (2020). https://doi.org/10.1109/TVCG.2020.2986247

42. Zollmann, S., Grasset, R., Reitmayr, G., Langlotz, T.: In: Image-based X-ray visualization techniques for spatial understanding in outdoor augmented reality, vol. 14, pp. 194–203. ACM Press, New York (2014). https://doi.org/10.1145/2686612.2686642

43. Zollmann, S., Hoppe, C., Kluckner, S., Poglitsch, C., Bischof, H., Reitmayr, G.: Augmented reality for construction site monitoring and documentation. Proc. IEEE **102**(2), 137–154 (2014). https://doi.org/10.1109/JPROC.2013.2294314

44. Zollmann, S., Hoppe, C., Langlotz, T., Reitmayr, G.: FlyAR: augmented reality supported micro aerial vehicle navigation. IEEE Trans. Vis. Comput. Graph. **20**(4), 560–568 (2014). https://doi.org/10.1109/TVCG.2014.24
45. Zollmann, S., Kalkofen, D., Mendez, E., Reitmayr, G.: In: Image-based ghostings for single layer occlusions in augmented reality, pp. 19–26. IEEE (2010). https://doi.org/10.1109/ISMAR.2010.5643546
46. Zollmann, S., Schall, G., Junghanns, S., Reitmayr, G.: Comprehensible and interactive visualizations of GIS Data in augmented reality. In: Bebis, G., et al. (eds.) ISVC 2012. LNCS, vol. 7431, pp. 675–685. Springer, Heidelberg (2012). https://doi.org/10.1007/978-3-642-33179-4_64

Simplifying Robot Programming Using Augmented Reality and End-User Development

Enes Yigitbas[(✉)], Ivan Jovanovikj, and Gregor Engels

Paderborn University, Zukunftsmeile 2, 33102 Paderborn, Germany
{Enes.Yigitbas,Ivan.Jovanovikj,Gregor.Engels}@upb.de

Abstract. Robots are widespread across diverse application contexts. Teaching robots to perform tasks, in their respective contexts, demands a high domain and programming expertise. However, robot programming faces high entry barriers due to the complexity of robot programming itself. Even for experts robot programming is a cumbersome and error-prone task where faulty robot programs can be created, causing damage when being executed on a real robot. To simplify the process of robot programming, we combine Augmented Reality (AR) with principles of end-user development. By combining them, the real environment is extended with useful virtual artifacts that can enable experts as well as non-professionals to perform complex robot programming tasks. Therefore, Simple Programming Environment in Augmented Reality with Enhanced Debugging (SPEARED) was developed as a prototype for an AR-assisted robot programming environment. SPEARED makes use of AR to project a robot as well as a programming environment onto the target working space. To evaluate our approach, expert interviews with domain experts from the area of industrial automation, robotics, and AR were performed. The experts agreed that SPEARED has the potential to enrich and ease current robot programming processes.

Keywords: Augmented Reality · Robot programming · Usability

1 Introduction

Robots are becoming ubiquitous and they are used nowadays in different settings with typical application domains like education, household, or industry. They come in diverse forms and shapes depending on the task they were designed for. In the manufacturing industry, an increasing number of robots are used for assembly tasks such as screwing, welding, painting or cutting [16].

Tasks are domain-dependent as different contexts of use demand different precision/safety regards (i.e., educational robots in school vs. robots in the manufacturing industry). Describing a task requires process knowledge as well as

© IFIP International Federation for Information Processing 2021
Published by Springer Nature Switzerland AG 2021
C. Ardito et al. (Eds.): INTERACT 2021, LNCS 12932, pp. 631–651, 2021.
https://doi.org/10.1007/978-3-030-85623-6_36

domain knowledge. Transferring this as an executable movement to the robot demands (robot) programming proficiency. However, robot programming is a complex and time-consuming task, where programming errors may occur, e.g., minor offsets in coordinates or differences between the test environment and real environment [20]. On a real robot, these may cause hardware damage up to irrecoverable damage to a person. Thus, the reduction of errors and their prevention is important. Consequently, different challenges exist which cause the high complexity of robot programming. Based on an extensive literature research (see Sect. 2) related to the topics of AR-assisted robot programming and robot programming by demonstration, we have identified the following major challenges:

C1 Program State Visualization: In robot programming, the visualization of the robot and its parameters at a current state can be challenging. For validation purposes and to simplify trajectory programming an intuitive visualization of context information concerning path trajectory, the goal of the next movement, and end-effector status is required [6, 8, 23]. Developers need to be able to validate whether the execution of the current program causes the expected effect. For supporting robot programmers in identifying the current state of the robot and possible configuration errors, feedback about current path trajectories or states of different robot parts is required.

C2 Root Cause Analysis: Enabling a correct root cause analysis of programming errors is important as logic errors may occur when programming [34]. Such errors can lead to unintended actions in the robot behavior. Hence, a common challenge robot programmers need help with, is finding root causes for these failures. Problems in source code can be solved if the robot programmer is able to identify these causes for a specific problem, e.g., imprecise coordinates or wrong end-effector state at a specific code point.

C3 Vendor Robot Programming Language Proficiency: The reduction of needed vendor robot programming language proficiency should also be addressed. Here, the focus lies on approaches using code or code-alike representations of robot programs. Usually, every vendor has its own programming language [19]. Being manufacturer-independent reduces barriers to integration [15]. Furthermore, it removes the need to learn a new programming language for every robot vendor. Thus, it probably reduces the mental-load when programming and also allows vendor-independent, uniform programming.

C4 3-Dimensional Thinking: The correct determination of 3-dimensional data is important as robots operate in their own 3-dimensional space. A correct interpretation of coordinates and their translation from/into source code is necessary to create working programs. The interpretation can be hard because parts of the robot may have different coordinate origins than the real world. Translating and mapping them to each other is not trivial. Especially 3D models represented on 2D Screens cause issues in positioning because of missing depth [23]. Humans intuitively locate things in 3D-space and dynamically adapt their estimations as they get closer. Hence, an intuitive definition of targets or coordinates, as well as an understandable representation of (arbitrary) targets, are required for simplifying robot programming.

C5 Environment-Specific Information: The correct representation of environmental constraints is also very important. For example, when an object the robot might want to grab could be a couple of centimeters off since the last development state. Furthermore, there could be physical obstacles in the working environment of the robot. Therefore, representing this kind of information, as fixtures [1] or cues [2], as well as integrating them at development time, e.g., interacting with a virtual clone of the real object, should be addressed. This is especially important when the recreation of a full simulation for every difference [10] is not possible or a considerable option.

C6 Modification of Existing Code: When working with existing source code bases of robot programs, it has to be ensured that functional modifications are causing the expected change in behavior. For supporting robot programmers in adjusting and adaptation of existing robot code it is important to import existing parts of the code and enable a modification in the same manner as the creation of new programs. This of course means to consider above-mentioned challenges and to reload the modified code to the robot so that the changes in the behavior can be reflected to the robot system.

To tackle the above-mentioned challenges, we have developed a novel AR-assisted robot programming environment called SPEARED. A general overview of the solution idea of SPEARED is depicted in Fig. 1.

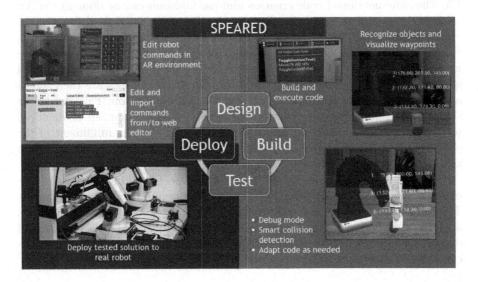

Fig. 1. Overview of the AR-assisted robot programming environment (Color figure online)

SPEARED is an AR-assisted robot programming environment that supports the different phases of the robot programming process, namely *design*, *build*, *test*, and *deploy* while addressing the aforementioned challenges. To address *Challenge C1*, a head-mounted AR device is used which shows the robot model (current working state), detected objects, and goals of the next movement (refer to top-left and top-right screenshots of Fig. 1). Furthermore, the current robot code is shown (refer to the "AR DoBot Code Panel" in the top middle of Fig. 1 or refer to Fig. 6), so the user knows which code is executed and is able to find errors. Thus, tackling *Challenge C2*. To handle the *Challenge C3*, the code in the "AR DoBot Code Panel" is written in a domain-specific language (DSL) that is vendor-independent. New code can be created, existing code adapted and both of them executed. This is done by using building blocks (e.g. move the robot to coordinate A, enable the end-effector of the robot). These building blocks have placeholders (i.e. the point A or whether the end-effector should be enabled or disabled). To tackle *Challenge C4*, these programming building blocks can also be set in the AR environment. The code component is visualized in the top-left image of Fig. 1. The AR environment enables the previously mentioned code interactions as well as some quality of life features e.g. voice commands, transforming the User Interface (UI) (resize, rotate, move) based on gestures, etc. To simplify programming inside the AR environment, the above mentioned simple and lightweight DSL allows the users to abstract from scenario-dependent settings (e.g. speed of movement, movement type). This block-based DSL enables the user to perform movement tasks as well as changing the state of the end-effector. Furthermore, specific interaction objects are emphasized (refer to the detected object/yellow cube in Fig. 1). This enables the handling of *Challenge C5*. The aforementioned code creation and modification can be done in the AR application as well as in a non AR setting (refer to the top-left of Fig. 1). The created artifacts can be synchronized in both directions. Here the translation to the aforementioned block-language enables a consistent programming experience for old and new code. Thus, it tackles *Challenge C6*. The code being executed is sent to a simulator that moves the robot. These movements are then shown and subscribed to the model of the robot in the AR application. This also allows the user to visualize the current working state. The final code can be deployed to the real robot (see bottom left of Fig. 1). To evaluate the fulfillment of the challenges, the AR solution has been evaluated based on expert interviews from the domain of industrial automation, robotics, and AR.

The rest of the paper is structured as follows. Section. 2 introduces and discusses related work in the areas of robot programming and augmented reality. The conceptual solution and the implementation of the SPEARED framework are presented in Sect. 3 and Sect. 4, respectively. In Sect. 5, we present and discuss the main results of the expert interviews. Finally, Sect. 6 presents conclusions and directions for future work.

2   Related Work

Augmented Reality (AR) and Virtual Reality (VR) have been a topic of intense research in the last decades. In the past few years, massive advances in affordable consumer hardware and accessible software frameworks are now bringing AR and VR to the masses. While VR interfaces support the interaction in an immersive computer generated 3D world and have been used in different application domains such as training [30], robotics [31], education [33], or healthcare [28], AR enables the augmentation of real-world physical objects with virtual elements. In previous works, AR has been already applied for different aspects such as product configuration (e.g., [11,12]), prototyping [13], planning and measurements [32] or for realizing smart interfaces (e.g., [14,29]). Besides this broad view of application domains, in recent years, several approaches have addressed the problem of enabling non-programmers to program robots. Apart from classical programming approaches based on end-user development [5], two major fields of related work in this direction are robot programming by demonstration and augmented reality-assisted robot programming approaches.

2.1   Robot Programming by Demonstration

Robot Programming by Demonstration (PbD), also known as imitation learning, is a widespread technique to teach robots how to perform tasks. Hence, PbD is used as an alternative or addition to traditional programming. In PbD, the resulting artifact is not necessarily a program that can be executed. It can be a more generic representation of the task presented, as in Aleotti et al. [3]. Here, a visuo-haptic AR interface was used for robot programming by demonstration. The task *lay the table* was taught to a robot. To be specific, the precedence relations that hold were learned e.g. the dinner plate has to be put on the table first, then the soup plate has to be put on top of it. These relations were learned via multiple demonstrations of the task. The demonstration was done with a haptic input device for performing the interaction and a camera-based AR system for visual feedback. A further PbD based approach is presented by Orendt et al. [18]. In contrast to [3], it enables the execution of the created artifact on the real robot. To be precise, they focused on one-shot learning by kinesthetic teaching. In other words, the task was demonstrated one time (one-shot) by moving the robot arm. Instead of using a real robot, a visual AR environment for PbD was used in Fang et al.[7]. Here, a pick and place task and path following operations were taught by kinesthetic teaching. Therefore, a tracker marked cube was used as a demonstration instrument. The results were saved as sets of points with end-effector orientation. These were visualized after recording the task. Another PbD-based approach is presented in [4], where Alexandrova et al. present a method to generalize from programming by demonstrations. They have developed a Graphical User Interface (GUI) which was able to edit actions after they were demonstrated. In total, as depicted in Fig. 2, we can see that existing PbD approaches do not fully cover the mentioned challenges *C1 - C6*. Still, the presented works offer insight about relevant approaches and their upsides and downsides: One-shot learning offers high intuitiveness, but does often lack the integration of adaptation capabilities. Having these integrated, one-shot learning as well as using multiple demonstrations allows tackling the challenges *C1* and *C2*. Using visual depth information, or force-feedback as in [3], by utilizing AR tackles *Challenge C4* and enables a possible integration of environment-specific information (*Challenge C5*). PbD often relies on environments that defer from using a programming language. Thus, *Challenge C3* is often missing by design because a code-alike representation itself is missing. In conclusion, existing PbD approaches do not tackle all challenges to serve as a solution for this work.

Legend: ● Completely fulfills ◐ Partially fulfills ○ Does not fulfill	C1 Program State Visualization	C2 Root Cause Analysis	C3 Vendor Robot Programming Language Proficiency	C4 3-D Thinking	C5 Environment Specific Information	C6 Modification Of Existing Code
Aleotti et al. [3]	◐	◐	◐	◐	◐	○
Alexandrova et al. [4]	●	◐	◐	◐	◐	◐
Orendt et al. [14]	◐	○	○	◐	◐	○
Fang et al. [7]	●	●	◐	●	◐	●

Fig. 2. Evaluation of PbD approaches

2.2 Augmented Reality-Assisted Robot Programming

In the following, we briefly present and evaluate related approaches that follow the idea of augmented reality-assisted robot programming.

Shepherd et al. [23] used a video-based AR approach for robot programming. A block-based Integrated Development Environment (IDE) was embedded onto the screen. The block-based IDE is a CoBlox derivate. CoBlox is designed for offline robot programming and normally features a robot and environment simulation [22,26,27]. However, in contrast to the simulation, in this paper, a real robot was used. Additionally, waypoints, showing the current planned path, were projected in the AR environment. In [23] it was also noted, that programming with controllers as well as having to move the real robot with hands is cumbersome. Another approach is to use hands for both interactions. This approach was used in Gadre et al. [9] where Mixed Reality (MR) interface was proposed for creating and editing waypoints. The created waypoints could be grouped, the resulting action previewed, and the resulting program executed on the real robot. The solution was tested against a monitor interface in a usability study using Microsoft HoloLens. Ong et al. [25] proposed an AR-assisted robot programming system that allows users to program pick-and-place as well as welding tasks by demonstrating the task/path. These paths can be selected by showing the full path, showing the start and endpoints, or selecting features based on Computer-Aided Design (CAD), e.g., edges. The robot motion was simulated and augmented in AR. Rosen et al. [21] proposed an MR interface for programming robots. Here a manipulation of the movement starting point and goal, as well as end-effector orientation, via hand interaction, is possible. The AR device used is a Microsoft HoloLens. MoveIt is the motion planning tool used to calculate a path between the two aforementioned points (start point and endpoint).

As summarized in Fig. 3, none of the existing AR-based approaches for robot programming fully address the introduced challenges C1 - C6. Most of these approaches represent robot programs with waypoints, code, or occluding robot arm movements. These representations address C1. Hand interaction or pointer interaction, with the User Interface (UI) or with the real robot, as well as a

Head-Mounted AR device ensure depth information and human-like interaction with AR objects, thus tackling *C4*. This reflects the identified benefits of using AR. Furthermore, *C3* is either tackled implicitly, by using a high-level block-based Domain-Specific Language (DSL) or not at all, by using no code as a representation. Still, challenge *C5* is not sufficiently covered as integration of environment-specific information is missing e.g. picking up real objects by making a virtual copy. In summary, while identifying and tackling similar challenges as described in this work, the reviewed approaches for AR-based robot programming do not fully support all of them.

Legend	C1 Program State Visualization	C2 Root Cause Analysis	C3 Vendor Robot Programming Language Proficiency	C4 3-D Thinking	C5 Environment Specific Information	C6 Modification Of Existing Code
● Completely fulfills ◖ Partially fulfills ○ Does not fulfil						
Gadre et al. [9]	●	●	◖	●	◖	●
Ong et al. [21]	●	◖	○	●	◖	○
Rosen et al. [17]	●	◖	○	●	◖	◖
Shepherd et al. [19]	●	●	●	●	◖	◖

Fig. 3. Evaluation of AR-based robot programming approaches

3   Conceptual Solution

In this section, the conceptual solution of the Simple Programming Environment in Augmented Reality with Enhanced Debugging (SPEARED) framework is presented. As depicted in Fig. 4, the SPEARED framework can be divided into three main parts: *Head-mounted AR Device, Robot Simulator*, and *Non-AR Device*. The *Robot Simulator* is responsible for simulating the robot, its movements, and detected objects. As SPEARED supports robot programming on AR Devices (e.g., HoloLens) and Non-AR Devices (e.g., Laptop or Desktop-PC using an editor), we have two separate components for visualization and interaction: *Head-mounted AR Device* and *Non-AR Device*. In the following, each of the three main parts will be described in more detail.

3.1   Robot Simulator

As stated in *Challenge C1*, it is necessary to visualize the current program state. The *Robot Simulator* (see Fig. 4) enables the simulated execution of the current program state. Furthermore, it removes the need of setting up a real robot. Please not that if needed, it is possible to register the coordinate system of the virtual robot and the real one. Using a simulation also supports to address *Challenge C2*. Additionally, the *Robot Simulator* enables the simulation of the effect of environmental constraints, as described in *Challenge C5*. The simulation itself depends on two components: The *Physics Simulation* is responsible for realistic

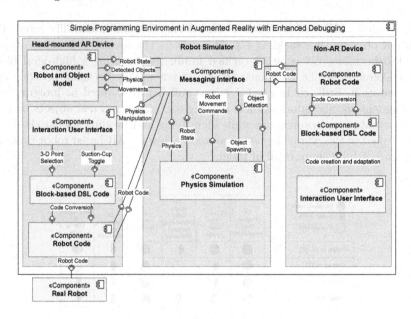

Fig. 4. An architectural overview of the SPEARED framework

robot movements and collisions. The *Messaging Interface* allows communication from and to the simulator. For example, movement commands can be received and executed or the joint states published for other programs. In the following, the *Physics Simulation* and *Messaging Interface* components are described in more detail.

Physics Simulation. The *Physics Simulation* is mimicking real-world physical constraints regarding movements, gravity, etc. It serves as an endpoint for doing robot physics simulation. It enables a simulation of a robot according to pre-defined properties (e.g., joint position, Computer-Aided Design (CAD) model, etc.) and the execution of movement commands in the same manner as the real robot (e.g. by using inverse kinematics). Additionally, reachability constraints are preserved. Thus, the simulation tackles the execution part of *Challenge C1*. Furthermore, the creation of other objects is possible (e.g., import of existing 3D models). Collisions with these objects are represented realistically. The collision detection is necessary for *Challenge C5*. Finally, the possibility to execute code together with collisions tackles *Challenge C2*. Interfaces to simulation information, e.g., state of the robots' joints and path trajectories, are available to be consumed. Finally, physical properties, e.g., speed up execution, slow down execution, or change gravity can be manipulated.

Messaging Interface. The *Messaging Interface* serves as a communication facility for interactions with the *Physics Simulation*. It abstracts from simulation specific endpoints and offers more generic communication methods. Therefore, conversion routines between the requests are necessary. The interface provides endpoints for physics manipulation, robot state, robot movement, and robot code. For physics manipulation, the endpoints speed up, slow down, pause, and resume physics are available to be consumed. For robot state endpoints, the joint states, the robot parts' orientation and position, the end-effector state, and the idle state can be requested. For robot movement endpoints, the movement command to a specific point in the robot or simulation space can be issued. Furthermore, path trajectories for the planned path can be requested. For robot code endpoints, the interface offers the possibility to convert movement commands to actual robot (simulation) movements. Thus, the *Messaging Interface* offers the endpoints to transfer the execution simulation information for challenges *C1*, *C2*, and *C5* to their respective visualizations.

3.2   Head-Mounted AR Device

The AR visualization contains four different components. The *Robot and Object Model*, the *Robot Code*, the *Block-based DSL Code*, and the *Interaction User Interface*. In the following, the components are described and the visualization and interaction possibilities are presented. As described above, SPEARED relies on a robot simulation to visualize and validate created robot programs. To enable users to see these validations in real-time, the simulated robot has to be visualized. The *Robot and Object Model* describes the robot, as well as other detected objects, and its properties e.g. joints, CAD-model, etc. It acts as a representation of the real robot, and detected objects. It is updated based on the movements done in the *Robot Simulator*. Thus, it is necessary for tackling the challenges *C1*, *C2*, and *C5*. The model does not depend on the other components, as it is for visualization purposes only. However, the movement and model information is received from the *Robot Simulator* and not generated inside the AR device itself. The current robot program is displayed in the *Robot Code* component. It allows a vendor-independent representation of e.g. movement and end-effector commands. Thus, it is tackling *Challenge C3*. The programming component of the AR visualization is based on the *Block-based DSL Code* component. It acts as a programming environment. Here, it represents the different movement commands and end-effector commands and enables their adaptation. Thus, it addresses *Challenge C3*. Furthermore, both the *Robot Code* component as well as the *Block-based DSL Code* component help tackling the challenges *C1* and *C2*. The *Interaction User Interface* provides interaction and visualization facilities to the user. It visualizes the current robot movement target and the robot end-effector state. The interface enables the user to perform coding activities. These are: Adding new commands, deleting existing commands, modifying existing commands, changing the order of commands, executing the current program, and synchronizing the current program with the non-AR environment. Furthermore, *User Interface (UI)* manipulation is possible. The robot model as well as other UI elements can be moved, rotated, and resized. These operations are specific to the target platform and are supported based on hand gestures on the *Head-mounted AR device* and respective interactions on the *Non-AR Device*. The interface also provides access to the *Robot Simulator* endpoint e.g. the manipulation of physics. Finally, the interaction methods are either gaze, together with hand gestures, or voice commands. The interface enables the challenges *C4* and *C6*.

3.3 Non-AR Device

The non-AR interface consists of the components *Robot Code*, *Block-based DSL Code*, and the *Interaction User Interface*. Its visualization consists of the coding environment, the movement commands, and the end-effector commands. The interface enables the user to perform coding activities. These consist of: adding new commands, deleting existing commands, modifying existing commands, changing the order of commands, and synchronizing the current robot program with the AR environment. Thus, it tackles the challenges *C3* and *C6*.

3.4 Execution Logic and Interplay Between Components

To describe the execution logic of SPEARED in more detail, in the following the intra-component and inter-component interfacing tasks are explained.

Intra-component Execution Logic. Inside the components *Head-mounted AR Device*, *Robot Simulator*, and *Non-AR Device* the following interfacing tasks exist. In the *Head-Mounted AR Device*, the *Interaction User Interface* allows the parameterization of robot code commands. These parameterizations are shown in Fig. 4 on the left side with the labels "3D-Point Selection" and "Suction-Cup Toggle". Therefore, the target of movement commands can be set and the state of the end-effector toggled. Thus, enabling *Challenge C6*. "3D-Point Selection", as in the *Challenge C4*, is the process of setting a movement target by hand and gaze interaction in the AR environment. "Suction-Cup Toggle" is the process of toggling the state of the end-effector e.g. a suction cup. Furthermore, a code-conversion between the created code (with the aforementioned interactions) and robot code is possible. Therefore, the UI elements have to be converted to robot code and vice-versa. This tackles the *Challenge C3*. Inside the *Robot Simulator*, the *Messaging Interface* provides translation capabilities of robot code to movement commands. Here, the robot code has to be translated to physical movements e.g. by using inverse kinematics. Furthermore, the information regarding detected objects, physics, and the robots' state (e.g. end-effector state) is transferred between the components. This is necessary to allow a realistic simulation and to tackle the challenges *C1*, *C2*, and *C5*. Inside the non-AR device, the Interaction User Interface allows the code creation and adaptation. As a result, the block-based Domain Specific Language (DSL) represents the robot program created. Furthermore, the conversion between the block-based DSL and the robot code is possible. The blocks need to be translated to robot code and vice-versa. This tackles the challenges *C3* and *C6*.

Inter-component Execution Logic. The different devices allow the synchronization of robot code with each other. Therefore, the *Robot Simulator*, or to be specific, the *Messaging Interface*, provides a service to store and load the current robot program. Both devices can upload and download their current code to that place. This also enables *Challenge C6*. Between the *Robot Simulator* and the *Head-mounted AR Device* the robot's movements, the robot's state (e.g. end-effector state or whether the robot currently idle), and physics properties are published. This interaction allows the AR device to present the current state of the robot. Furthermore, the detected objects are forwarded to the AR device. This is necessary for the challenges *C1*, *C2*, and *C5*. The manipulation of physics is forwarded to the *Messaging Interface*. Implicitly, the conversion between coordinate systems of the AR-device and *Robot Simulator* has to be done, when detected objects or movements are transferred. This is required for the *Challenge C4*. Additionally, the code can be executed on the *Real Robot*.

4   Implementation

In this section, we describe implementation-specific details of the SPEARED framework which is publicly available as an open-source software project at GitHub[1]. Figure 5 shows the architecture of the SPEARED framework annotated with the used technologies.

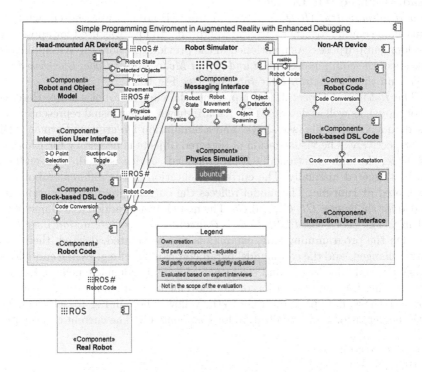

Fig. 5. Used technologies in SPEARED

---

[1] https://github.com/VARobot-PG/application.

Robot Simulator

The *Robot Simulator* is based on *Gazebo*[2] as a *Physics Simulation* and *Robot Operating System (ROS)*[3] as a *Messaging Interface*. It is deployed in a *Docker*[4] container using Ubuntu. To mimic the behavior of the real robot, a *Physics Simulation* is needed. For this purpose, *Gazebo* was chosen which is able to simulate robots and physics as well as offers graphical and programmatic interfaces. To simulate the robot in *Gazebo*, the robot model has to be created. It is based on an XML macro (XACRO) file[5]. It is spawned inside the simulation context. This robot model describes the different properties of the robot. It includes the visuals, the physics e.g. mass, etc., and the collisions for each part of the robot. Additionally, *Gazebo* offers ROS endpoints for physics manipulation. The *Messaging Interface* component is based on ROS, which provides a communication interface based on asynchronous and synchronous communication. ROS offers a parameter server that enables the sharing of relevant information. Here, the server is used for code synchronization. Furthermore, topics are used for publishing the current position of the robot arm or information about whether the robot is idle. The Real Robot is a *DoBot Magician*[6]. It offers the same ROS endpoints as the AR simulation. Hence, on the implementation side, it does not matter whether the code is being sent to the real robot or the simulation.

Head-Mounted AR Device

As a *Head-mounted AR-Device*, the Microsoft HoloLens was chosen, while the Unity game engine together with the Microsoft MRTK[7] was used for application development purposes. As mentioned in the previous section, the AR application consists of the components *Robot and Object Model*, *Robot Code*, *Blockbased DSL Code*, and the *Interaction User Interface* (see Fig. 6).

The *Robot and Object Model* represents the current robot's state. Here, the robot model, as well as detected objects, are shown. Their visual representation is based on a XACRO file (see above) and a Simulation Description Format (SDF) file respectively. The visualization of detected objects is necessary for *Challenge C5*. Here, the aforementioned self-programmed service is used. This endpoint can be triggered manually. The current orientation of the different robot parts is adapted at runtime. The model reflects the current program execution. It is needed for challenges *C1*, *C2*, and *C5*. The model itself is added as a GameObject in Unity. The *Block-based DSL Code* is controlled via the *Interaction User Interface*. On the programming side, commands can be created, deleted, their order can be changed, and the commands' parameter can be set e.g. switch end-effector on, switch end-effector off, and set target coordinate for movement commands. For selecting the target position of the movement command, a target sphere is moved to the wanted position (refer to the yellow sphere in Fig. 6), which enables both the definition and visualization for *Challenge C4*. The current coordinate of

---

[2] http://gazebosim.org.

[3] https://www.ros.org.

[4] https://www.docker.com.

[5] https://ni.www.techfak.uni-bielefeld.de/files/URDF-XACRO.pdf.

[6] https://www.dobot.us/.

[7] https://github.com/microsoft/MixedRealityToolkit-Unity.

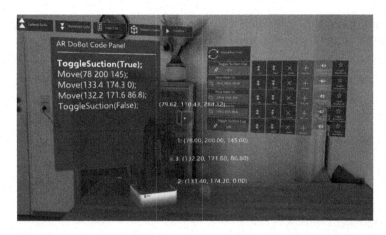

Fig. 6. Robot code, Robot model in an AR application and block-based DSL code (f.l.t.r.) (Color figure online)

the sphere can be selected as a target by pressing the respective move-statement in the *Block-based DSL Code* component (Fig. 7).

The *Block-based DSL Code* component, shown in Fig. 7, together with its interaction capabilities via the *Interaction User Interface* component, is needed for the challenges *C6, C3, C4* for coordinate definition purposes.

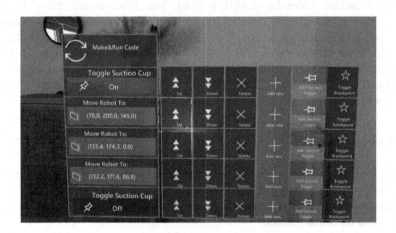

Fig. 7. AR block-based coding environment

Non-AR Device

The *Non-AR device* solution is based on *Google Blockly*[8] and *roslibjs*[9] for interfacing purposes. It consists of the *Interaction User Interface*, the *Block-based*

---

[8] https://developers.google.com/blockly.

[9] https://github.com/RobotWebTools/roslibjs.

DSL, and the *Robot Code* component. It resembles the programming experience of a simple Integrated Development Environment (IDE).

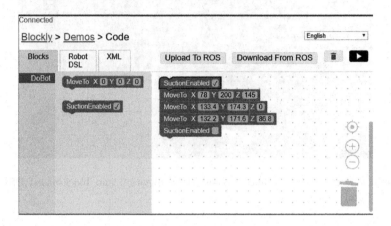

Fig. 8. Adapted blockly environment with custom blocks (above) and for robot code (below)

Additionally, code modifications can be synchronized between the non-AR and the AR environment. To provide a uniform experience across the different devices, a similar *Block-based DSL* is used. The *Block-based DSL* is based on custom blocks. They were defined for movement commands, which consist of three coordinates, and end-effector commands, which enable or disable the suction cup. Here, the name as well as e.g. parameters and their types had to be set. This enables the usage of features independent from the vendor language, thus, tackling *Challenge C3*. The adaptation of values tackles *Challenge C6*. The layout with instances of these definitions can be seen in Fig. 8.

5   Evaluation

For the evaluation of the SPEARED framework concerning the introduced challenges in Sect. 1 we have conducted expert interviews. In the following, we first describe the setup and execution of the expert interviews. After that, we present and discuss its main results.

5.1   Setup and Execution of Expert Interviews

Unfortunately, due to the current situation (COVID-19), we could not conduct usability tests with a larger group of heterogeneous end-users as initially planned. Instead expert interviews were conducted as semi-structured interviews [17]. We conducted expert interviews with 9 experts from the area of robotics, automation, and augmented reality. Inside the interview, a pre-defined question set was asked to every participant. To derive the questions for the expert interviews, a

GQM (Goal Question Metric) model is used [24]. The evaluation consists of six goals. These goals describe whether SPEARED fulfills the respective challenges

Statement ID / Statement	Description
1.1 Defect finding through visualization **C2**	The waypoints drawing, code visualization, and robot simulation have the potential to improve finding software defects. Improved software defect finding implies the ability to find the root causes.
1.2 Coordinate handling target sphere **C4**	The robot target sphere-based coordinate selection has the potential to improve the handling of coordinates for robot programmers. Improved handling of coordinates implies easier handling of coordinates in 3-Dimensional selection processes.
1.3 Environmental constraints through robot projection **C5**	The projection of the robot into the working environment has the potential to reflect environmental constraints. The visualization of environmental constraints implies the handling of environment-specific information.
1.4 Easy adaptation of existing code **C6**	The code adaptation inside SPEARED of existing code (e.g. legacy code) is easy. Easy code adaptation implies SPEARED being able to handle the modification of existing code.
2.1 Validation Through Visualization **C1**	The waypoints drawing, code visualization, robot simulation, suction cup highlighting, and object detection have the potential to improve robot program validation. An improved robot program validation through visualizations implies that the visualizations are helpful and that they were noticed.
2.2 Step-by-step defect finding **C2**	The 'step-by-step' execution has the potential to improve the identification of robot program defects. Improving the identification of robot program defects implies that the root cause analysis of defects is possible.
3.1 Smart collision detection error finding **C2**	Smart collision detection has the potential to improve the finding of errors in robot program code. Finding errors in robot code implies that the root cause analysis is possible.
3.2 Time ghosts object localization **C4**	Time Ghosts facilitate an understanding of where objects e.g. the robot have been before collisions. The understanding of previous locations implies an understanding of 3-Dimensional representations.
3.3 Time ghosts Environmental information **C5**	Time ghosts should show the recent past of all moved objects (real and simulated ones). The integration of environmental information (i.e. real objects) into collisions implies the handling of environment-specific information.
3.4 Environmental information through object detection **C5**	Object detection has the potential to improve the handling of environmental constraints when doing robot programming. The detection and simulation of real object interactions imply not only the visualization but also the integration of environment-specific information into the development process.
4.1 Understandability through uniform representation **C1**	The uniform representation of uploaded/downloaded code has the potential to improve the understanding of existing code. An improved understanding through code representations implies a recognizable program state visualization.
4.2 Defect finding through uniform representation **C2**	The uniform representation and adaptation capabilities have the potential to speed up defect finding. A speedup defect finding also implies the ability to find defects.
4.3 Multi-device code modification **C6**	The code synchronization feature (uploading and downloading of code) has the potential to improve code modification tasks along different end-devices. An improved modification of existing code implies that modification of existing code is possible.
4.4 Learnability through code abstraction **C3**	The abstraction from concrete robot code in the Code Panel and Integrated Development Environment (IDE) has the potential to reduce learning time. The reduced learning time through abstraction implies a vendor-independent programming experience.
4.5 Entry-barrier reduction through uniform code **C3**	The independency of vendor-specific robot code has the potential to reduce robot programming entry barriers Reduced entry barriers imply the successful integration of vendor-independent coding.

Cn   Corresponding Challenge

Fig. 9. Overview of the main statements and their corresponding challenges

motivated in Sect. 1. For each goal, different statements, describing specific components of the respective challenge, were created (see Fig. 9).

5.2 Evaluation Results

In the following, the answers, expressing the expert's degree of agreement to the provided statements are presented. For each statement, the experts' degree of agreement was measured on a 7-point Likert scale. For evaluation purposes, metrics on a per statement and a per challenge basis were used where the median, arithmetic mean, minimum rating, and standard deviation of the aggregated answers were calculated. An overview of the extracted metrics - per statement - is depicted in Fig. 10. As explained before, the statements are mapped to the challenges. To evaluate the challenges, the answers to the respective statements are combined e.g. *Challenge 2* is equal to the combination of the answers to Statement 1.1., 2.2, 3.1, and 4.2 (Fig. 9). Every single feedback of each statement mapped to a challenge is aggregated to calculate the median, average (arithmetic mean), minimum, and standard deviation on a challenge level. The results, showing an overview of the aggregated metrics - per challenge - is shown in Fig. 11.

Statement	Experts Feedback (n=9)				
	Median	Average	Min	Max	Std. Dev.
1.1 Defect finding through visualization	6	5,44	1	7	1,71
1.2 Coordinate handling target sphere	6	5,67	2	7	1,41
1.3 Environmental constraints through robot projection	7	6,44	5	7	0,68
1.4 Easy adaptation of existing code	5	5,22	3	7	1,47
2.1 Validation Through Visualization	7	6,11	2	7	1,52
2.2 Step-by-step defect finding	6	6,22	5	7	0,63
3.1 Smart collision detection error finding	7	6,56	5	7	0,68
3.2 Time ghosts object localization	6	5,89	3	7	1,29
3.3 Time ghosts Environmental information	4	4,00	1	7	1,63
3.4 Environmental information through object detection	7	6,33	5	7	0,82
4.1 Understandability through uniform representation	6	6,33	5	7	0,67
4.2 Defect finding through uniform representation	6	6,22	5	7	0,79
4.3 Multi-device code modification	7	6,67	6	7	0,47
4.4 Learnability through code abstraction	7	6,33	5	7	0,82
4.5 Entry-barrier reduction through uniform code	7	6,78	6	7	0,42

Fig. 10. Feedback to statements overview

Challenge	Experts Feedback (n=9)				
	Median	Average	Min	Max	Std. Dev.
C1 Program state visualization	7	6,22	2	7	1,18
C2 Root cause analysis	5	6,11	1	7	1,12
C3 Vendor robot programming language proficiency	7	6,56	5	7	0,68
C4 3-Dimensional Thinking	6	5,78	2	7	1,36
C5 Environment specific information	6	5,59	1	7	1,59
C6 Modification of existing code	7	5,94	3	7	1,31

Fig. 11. Feedback to challenges overview

Based on the results above and the informal feedback we have received, we will discuss in the following how the experts rated the SPEARED framework in addressing the challenges.

Challenge 1: The majority of the experts agreed that the AR-based visualization and simulation of the robot helps to increase the understandability of the robot code. Especially the visualization of robot part information, e.g., the suction cup status (on/off) was identified as helpful. Here, one expert concluded that this status shows the potential to integrate other helpful information, e.g., current weight load, heat, and motor force. Still, the experts claimed that the current visualization state is not end-user ready and potentially hard to understand without prior introduction. Nevertheless, they see the potential of the approach and believe that further development and better AR hardware will circumvent the current User Interface (UI) problems.

Challenge 2: In general, the experts see SPEARED's potential to aid in root cause analysis processes. Especially the smart collision detection feature using the benefits of AR for object recognition and projection facilities was agreed to have potential to improve defect finding. However, some experts noted the fact that some of the existing solutions already provide sophisticated ways of finding software defects through intelligent debugging mechanisms. With this regard they suggested to enrich those solutions with AR capabilities to combine the strength of both solutions.

Challenge 3: The experts expressed that the abstraction from concrete robot code is especially helpful for lay people as they do not need to learn a new language every time they change the robot. Furthermore, it was stated that the focus on the Block-based Domain Specific Language (DSL) may also reduce the possible mistakes and ensures a smoother programming process for beginners. This goes hand in hand with the feedback to *Statement 4.5* which received two ratings of "6-Agree" and seven ratings of "7-Strongly Agree". However, multiple experts stated that they see the advantages mainly in supporting lay people in the programming process and further more sophisticated or fine grained commands could be provided to also support the experts.

Challenge 4: The received feedback suggests that coordinate handling is challenging and SPEARED does help in tackling these difficulties with the coordinate selection mechanism and the waypoints drawing. One of the experts stated that problems may occur when trying to select coordinates where different axial combinations are possible. This feature was intentionally not implemented in SPEARED due to simplicity reasons. Also, SPEARED is using a sample robot system (Dobot Magician) which does not have different axial combinations to reach a specific coordinate. Nevertheless, the experts agreed that SPEARED supports "3-dimensional thinking" which is enabled through the projection of the simulated robot arm in the real-world setting.

Challenge 5: In general, the experts agreed that SPEARED's object detection has the potential, to improve the handling of environmental constraints when doing robot programming. This feedback also shows that the experts see the representation and integration of environmental constraints into the programming environment as beneficial. However, Statement 3.3 received one rating of "1-Strongly Disagree" and one "2-Disagree" with the others being "4-Neutral" or higher. Here, the feedback of the experts showed that either the meaning of the statement was quite unclear or the experts opinions differed. Nevertheless, the majority of the informal feedback indicates that it is helpful when environmental context information are integrated into the AR programming environment e.g. pick yellow cube. Hence, the realization of integration of environment specific information has been considered as a helpful feature for AR-assisted robot programming.

Challenge 6: Concerning the addressing of this challenge, we received different opinions from the experts. This leads to believe that the experts were not sure about the feature or the meaning of the statement. The ambiguity of the statement is also reflected in one expert asking for explicitly stating the meaning of legacy code and its adaptation capabilities in the context of the statement. However, after explaining the meaning, most experts agreed that SPEARED offers easy code adaptation capabilities. All experts were sure that SPEARED has potential to improve code modification tasks along different end-devices.

The discussion above shows preliminary results regarding the fulfillment of the challenges. However, multiple experts stated that some statements were subjectively unclear for them. Here, the authors tried to explain the respective statement without being too biased. Still, technical difficulties like video stuttering, audio delays, and missing webcams made the process of remote expert interviews more challenging and may lead to additional bias.

6   Conclusion and Outlook

The usage of robots promises support in a plethora of activities in e.g. households, education, care, and businesses. However, robot programming faces high entry barriers due to the complexity of robot programming itself. Even for experts robot programming is a cumbersome and error-prone task. In this paper, an Augmented Reality (AR)-assisted robot programming environment is presented. Usability evaluation results based on expert interviews show that the solution approach has the potential to enrich current robot programming processes and thus could reduce complexity and entry barriers of robot programming.

In future work, we plan to investigate the efficiency, effectiveness, and user satisfaction of the SPEARED framework based on usability tests with end-users from different domains. Furthermore, Programming by Demonstration (PbD) could be used to further simplify the programming complexity of robots. PbD allows users to program robots by demonstrating a task. Using PbD for generating source code in the AR Framework, which can then be adopted, could allow an even more intuitive way of programming.

Acknowledgement. We would like to thank Jonas Eilers and Michael Wieneke for their support during the implementation and evaluation of the presented approach.

References

1. Aleotti, J., Caselli, S., Reggiani, M.: Leveraging on a virtual environment for robot programming by demonstration. Robot. Auton. Syst. **47**(2–3), 153–161 (2004). https://doi.org/10.1016/j.robot.2004.03.009
2. Aleotti, J., Caselli, S., Reggiani, M.: Evaluation of virtual fixtures for a robot programming by demonstration interface. IEEE Trans. Syst. Man Cybern. Part A **35**(4), 536–545 (2005). https://doi.org/10.1109/TSMCA.2005.850604
3. Aleotti, J., Micconi, G., Caselli, S.: Programming manipulation tasks by demonstration in visuo-haptic augmented reality. In: 2014 IEEE International Symposium on Haptic, Audio and Visual Environments and Games, HAVE 2014, Richardson, TX, USA, 10–11 October 2014, pp. 13–18. IEEE (2014). https://doi.org/10.1109/HAVE.2014.6954324
4. Alexandrova, S., Cakmak, M., Hsiao, K., Takayama, L.: Robot programming by demonstration with interactive action visualizations. In: Fox, D., Kavraki, L.E., Kurniawati, H. (eds.) Robotics: Science and Systems X, University of California, Berkeley, USA, 12–16 July 2014 (2014). https://doi.org/10.15607/RSS.2014.X.048
5. Coronado, E., Mastrogiovanni, F., Indurkhya, B., Venture, G.: Visual programming environments for end-user development of intelligent and social robots, a systematic review. J. Comput. Lang. **58**, 100970 (2020). https://doi.org/10.1016/j.cola.2020.100970
6. Fang, H., Ong, S.K., Nee, A.: Orientation planning of robot end-effector using augmented reality. Int. J. Adv. Manuf. Technol. **67**(08) (2012). https://doi.org/10.1007/s00170-012-4629-7
7. Fang, H., Ong, S.K., Nee, A.: Novel ar-based interface for human-robot interaction and visualization. Adv. Manuf. **2**(12) (2014). https://doi.org/10.1007/s40436-014-0087-9
8. Fang, H., Ong, S., Nee, A.Y.C.: Robot programming using augmented reality. In: Ugail, H., Qahwaji, R., Earnshaw, R.A., Willis, P.J. (eds.) 2009 International Conference on CyberWorlds, Bradford, West Yorkshire, UK, 7–11 September 2009, pp. 13–20. IEEE Computer Society (2009). https://doi.org/10.1109/CW.2009.14
9. Gadre, S.Y., Rosen, E., Chien, G., Phillips, E., Tellex, S., Konidaris, G.D.: End-user robot programming using mixed reality. In: International Conference on Robotics and Automation, ICRA 2019, Montreal, QC, Canada, 20–24 May 2019, pp. 2707–2713. IEEE (2019). https://doi.org/10.1109/ICRA.2019.8793988
10. Gianni, M., Ferri, F., Pirri, F.: ARE: augmented reality environment for mobile robots. In: Natraj, A., Cameron, S., Melhuish, C., Witkowski, M. (eds.) TAROS 2013. LNCS (LNAI), vol. 8069, pp. 470–483. Springer, Heidelberg (2014). https://doi.org/10.1007/978-3-662-43645-5_48
11. Gottschalk, S., Yigitbas, E., Schmidt, E., Engels, G.: Model-based product configuration in augmented reality applications. In: Bernhaupt, R., Ardito, C., Sauer, S. (eds.) HCSE 2020. LNCS, vol. 12481, pp. 84–104. Springer, Cham (2020). https://doi.org/10.1007/978-3-030-64266-2_5
12. Gottschalk, S., Yigitbas, E., Schmidt, E., Engels, G.: ProConAR: a tool support for model-based AR product configuration. In: Bernhaupt, R., Ardito, C., Sauer, S. (eds.) HCSE 2020. LNCS, vol. 12481, pp. 207–215. Springer, Cham (2020). https://doi.org/10.1007/978-3-030-64266-2_14

13. Jovanovikj, I., Yigitbas, E., Sauer, S., Engels, G.: Augmented and virtual reality object repository for rapid prototyping. In: Bernhaupt, R., Ardito, C., Sauer, S. (eds.) HCSE 2020. LNCS, vol. 12481, pp. 216–224. Springer, Cham (2020). https://doi.org/10.1007/978-3-030-64266-2_15

14. Krings, S., Yigitbas, E., Jovanovikj, I., Sauer, S., Engels, G.: Development framework for context-aware augmented reality applications. In: Bowen, J., Vanderdonckt, J., Winckler, M. (eds.) EICS 2020: ACM SIGCHI Symposium on Engineering Interactive Computing Systems, Sophia Antipolis, France, 23–26 June 2020, pp. 9:1–9:6. ACM (2020). https://doi.org/10.1145/3393672.3398640

15. Lambrecht, J., Chemnitz, M., Krüger, J.: Control layer for multi-vendor industrial robot interaction providing integration of supervisory process control and multifunctional control units. In: 2011 IEEE Conference on Technologies for Practical Robot Applications, pp. 115–120 (2011). https://doi.org/10.1109/TEPRA.2011.5753492

16. Lasi, H., Fettke, P., Kemper, H., Feld, T., Hoffmann, M.: Industry 4.0. Bus. Inf. Syst. Eng. **6**(4), 239–242 (2014). https://doi.org/10.1007/s12599-014-0334-4

17. Newcomer, K.E., Hatry, H.P., Wholey, J.S.: Conducting semi-structured interviews. In: Handbook of Practical Program Evaluation, pp. 492–505 (2015)

18. Orendt, E.M., Fichtner, M., Henrich, D.: Robot programming by non-experts: Intuitiveness and robustness of one-shot robot programming. In: 2016 25th IEEE International Symposium on Robot and Human Interactive Communication (ROMAN), pp. 192–199 (2016). https://doi.org/10.1109/ROMAN.2016.7745110

19. Pan, Z., Polden, J., Larkin, N., van Duin, S., Norrish, J.: Recent progress on programming methods for industrial robots. In: ISR/ROBOTIK 2010, Proceedings for the joint conference of ISR 2010 (41st Internationel Symposium on Robotics) und ROBOTIK 2010 (6th German Conference on Robotics), Munich, Germany - Parallel to AUTOMATICA, 7–9 June 2010, pp. 1–8. VDE Verlag (2010). http://ieeexplore.ieee.org/document/5756855/

20. Pettersen, T., Pretlove, J., Skourup, C., Engedal, T., Løkstad, T.: Augmented reality for programming industrial robots. In: 2003 IEEE / ACM International Symposium on Mixed and Augmented Reality (ISMAR 2003), Tokyo, Japan, 7–10 October 2003, pp. 319–320. IEEE Computer Society (2003). https://doi.org/10.1109/ISMAR.2003.1240739

21. Rosen, E., Whitney, D., Phillips, E., Chien, G., Tompkin, J., Konidaris, G.D., Tellex, S.: Communicating and controlling robot arm motion intent through mixed-reality head-mounted displays. Int. J. Robot. Res. **38**(12–13) (2019). https://doi.org/10.1177/0278364919842925

22. Shepherd, D.C., Francis, P., Weintrop, D., Franklin, D., Li, B., Afzal, A.: [Engineering paper] an IDE for easy programming of simple robotics tasks. In: 18th IEEE International Working Conference on Source Code Analysis and Manipulation, SCAM 2018, Madrid, Spain, 23–24 September 2018, pp. 209–214. IEEE Computer Society (2018). https://doi.org/10.1109/SCAM.2018.00032

23. Shepherd, D.C., Kraft, N.A., Francis, P.: Visualizing the hidden variables in robot programs. In: Proceedings of the 2nd International Workshop on Robotics Software Engineering, RoSE 2019, Montreal, QC, Canada, May 27, pp. 13–16. IEEE/ACM (2019). https://doi.org/10.1109/RoSE.2019.00007

24. Solingen, R., Basili, V., Caldiera, G., Rombach, D.: Goal Question Metric (GQM) Approach, January (2002). https://doi.org/10.1002/0471028959.sof142

25. Thanigaivel, N.K., Ong, S.K., Nee, A.: Augmented reality-assisted robot programming system for industrial applications. Robot. Comput. Integr. Manuf. **61** (2019). https://doi.org/10.1016/j.rcim.2019.101820

26. Weintrop, D., Shepherd, D.C., Francis, P., Franklin, D.: Blockly goes to work: Block-based programming for industrial robots. In: 2017 IEEE Blocks and Beyond Workshop (B B), pp. 29–36 (2017). https://doi.org/10.1109/BLOCKS. 2017.8120406

27. Weintrop, D., Afzal, A., Salac, J., Francis, P., Li, B., Shepherd, D.C., Franklin, D.: Evaluating coblox: A comparative study of robotics programming environments for adult novices. In: Mandryk, R.L., Hancock, M., Perry, M., Cox, A.L. (eds.) Proceedings of the 2018 CHI Conference on Human Factors in Computing Systems, CHI 2018, Montreal, QC, Canada, 21–26 April 2018, p. 366. ACM (2018). https:// doi.org/10.1145/3173574.3173940

28. Yigitbas, E., Heindörfer, J., Engels, G.: A context-aware virtual reality first aid training application. In: Alt, F., Bulling, A., Döring, T. (eds.) Proceedings of Mensch und Computer 2019, pp. 885–888. GI/ACM (2019)

29. Yigitbas, E., Jovanovikj, I., Sauer, S., Engels, G.: On the development of context-aware augmented reality applications. In: Abdelnour Nocera, J., Parmaxi, A., Winckler, M., Loizides, F., Ardito, C., Bhutkar, G., Dannenmann, P. (eds.) INTER-ACT 2019. LNCS, vol. 11930, pp. 107–120. Springer, Cham (2020). https://doi. org/10.1007/978-3-030-46540-7_11

30. Yigitbas, E., Jovanovikj, I., Scholand, J., Engels, G.: VR training for warehouse management. In: Teather, R.J., Joslin, C., Stuerzlinger, W., Figueroa, P., Hu, Y.,Batmaz, A.U., Lee, W., Ortega, F.R. (eds.) VRST 2020: 26th ACM Symposium on Virtual Reality Software and Technology. pp. 78:1–78:3. ACM (2020)

31. Yigitbas, E., Karakaya, K., Jovanovikj, I., Engels, G.: Enhancing human-in-the-loop adaptive systems through digital twins and VR interfaces (2021). https:// arxiv.org/abs/2103.10804

32. Yigitbas, E., Sauer, S., Engels, G.: Using augmented reality for enhancing planning and measurements in the scaffolding business. In: EICS 2021: ACM SIGCHI Symposium on Engineering Interactive Computing Systems, Virtual, 8–11 June 2021. ACM (2021). https://doi.org/10.1145/3459926.3464747

33. Yigitbas, E., Tejedor, C.B., Engels, G.: Experiencing and programming the ENIAC in VR. In: Alt, F., Schneegass, S., Hornecker, E. (eds.) Mensch und Computer 2020, pp. 505–506. ACM (2020)

34. Yoshizawa, Y., Watanobe, Y.: Logic error detection algorithm for novice programmers based on structure pattern and error degree. In: 9th International Conference on Awareness Science and Technology, iCAST 2018, Fukuoka, Japan, 19–21 September 2018, pp. 297–301. IEEE (2018). https://doi.org/10.1109/ICAwST. 2018.8517171

Computer Supported Cooperative Work

"WhatsApp in Politics?!": Collaborative Tools Shifting Boundaries

Himanshu Verma[1,3], Jakub Mlynář[2], Camille Pellaton[1], Matteo Theler[1], Antoine Widmer[1], and Florian Evéquoz[1(✉)]

[1] University of Applied Sciences of Western Switzerland (HES-SO Valais-Wallis), Sierre, Switzerland
{Himanshu.Verma,Camille.Pellaton,Matteo.Theler,Antoine.Widmer, Florian.Evequoz}@hevs.ch
[2] Charles University, Prague, Czech Republic
jakub.mlynar@ff.cuni.cz
[3] TU Delft, Delft, Netherlands
H.Verma@tudelft.nl

Abstract. We examine the technological aspects of political collaborative practices in one of the first studies of participatory constitution writing in the course of its progression. In particular, we examine how digital collaborative and communicative tools can facilitate (or inhibit) the permeation of boundaries, which manifest through the differences in political ideologies and partisan beliefs. Our study is grounded in interviews with 15 members of the Constituent Assembly in the canton of Valais, Switzerland, and its primary contribution is in constructing a fine-grained contextualized understanding of political collaborations, their evolution, and their relationship with collaborative tools. Our findings demonstrate the centrality of versatile and widely available digital tools (such as WhatsApp and Google Docs) in political work. In addition, elected lawmakers prefer tools that allow them to organize their collaborative and communicative actions based on dynamic social boundaries, and their need for asynchronous work practices. We observed a tendency of simultaneously using multiple digital tools to accomplish specific political objectives, and leveraging them in plenary sessions for strategic advantages. On the one hand, collaborative tools enabled strategic advantages by *selective permeation* of boundaries across political ideologies. On the other hand, lack of awareness about boundaries between 'private' and 'public' on social networks were considered as privacy blind spots. By focusing on boundaries of different kinds, our paper elucidates how the introduction of digital technologies into political process transforms the long-established categories, distinctions and divisions that are often taken for granted.

Keywords: CSCW · Participatory politics · Constitution writing · Collaborative and communicative tools · Political boundaries

© The Author(s) 2021
C. Ardito et al. (Eds.): INTERACT 2021, LNCS 12932, pp. 655–677, 2021.
https://doi.org/10.1007/978-3-030-85623-6_37

1 Introduction

Politics[1] is defined through the boundary between participation and exclusiveness. Even in the most open political systems the responsibility for government and decision making is placed in the hands of a selected group. The boundary between those who are in power, and those who are not, is one of the fundamental structural aspects of modern societies. Nevertheless, boundaries matter to politics in a number of other senses, from ideological delineation between political parties, through barriers in political participation, to borders in a geographical or national sense. In this paper, we use the notion of *boundaries* as a sensitising concept for an empirical exploration of how technologies –particularly, digital collaborative and communicative tools– can assist in making various boundaries more (or less) permeable, and facilitate (or impede) overcoming diverse differences. The boundaries which we examine in this article are particularly the partisan and ideological boundaries which are ubiquitous and inflexible within the domain of political work. Furthermore, we seek to understand the ways in which these boundaries are rendered (more or less) permeable through digital collaborative/communicative tools and assist politicians in overcoming the aforementioned differences. More specifically, our study aims to analyze a particular *constitutional moment* [1] –defined as *"brief periods in which, through the unending contestation over democracy, basic rules of political practice are rewritten, whether explicitly or implicitly, thus fundamentally altering the relations between citizens and the state"* [25]– in the canton (or state) of Valais in Switzerland, where the new constitution is being produced in a bottom-up fashion by several groups of constituents and members of political parties.

Participatory democracy has been linked to digital communication technologies since the inception of the Internet, and recently also to the variety of social media and networks [32]. Digital communication was often seen, in an utopian way, as a transformative tool in the political engagement within the Habermasian "public sphere" [20]. Lately, many scholars focused on ICT "as part of the mundane activities of 'everyday life'" [58], and in the context of politics analyzed their subversive potential (for example, [6,21,30,54]). Our research is based on a qualitative study of a quite different case: ICT is not utilized for politically *disruptive activities* [32] but rather for *constitutive activities*, i.e. mediated interactions of participants who are taking part in the officially approved, mundane, daily work of "doing politics" and "co-writing a constitution". In this regard, our study examines actual uses of ICT in a constituent assembly consisting of elected officials who were mandated by the citizens to write a new constitution.

Our contributions are two-fold. *Firstly,* we document and examine the communicative and collaborative actions in the domain of participatory politics – particularly addressing an electoral mandate aimed at the complete revision and re-writing of the state constitution. *Secondly,* by focusing on boundaries of different kinds, we investigate how the introduction of digital technologies into the

---

[1] https://www.merriam-webster.com/dictionary/politics (Last visited on 23rd January 2021).

political process transforms the established categories, distinctions and divisions that are often taken for granted.

1.1 Background and Context

In the Swiss canton of Valais (or Wallis in German), the new state constitution is being written since 2019, and will replace the old constitution –last written in 1907– in the year 2023. The process of complete revision of the state constitution started in March 2018, when the general populace voted to accept a popular initiative to revise and replace the existing constitution. The initiative also entrusted the work of re-writing the constitution to a *'Constituent Assembly'* (henceforth '**CoA**'), which was elected by the general public on November 25th, 2018 and comprised of 130 members (elected from 13 districts of the canton).

The work presented in this article began shortly after the CoA *1)* adopted the regulations which underpinned the *modus operandi* within the Assembly, and *2)* appointed the members of the different –10 *thematic* and 3 *institutional*– commissions (see Table 1) which formally started the process of collective planning, negotiations, discussions and co-creation of the content (set forth as Articles and Paragraphs) that will manifest as the blueprints of the new constitution. Each thematic commission comprises of 13 members and every member of the CoA is part of exactly one thematic commission. The representation of different political movements within these commissions is proportional to their overall representation in the CoA. Moreover, besides thematic commissions, there are also 3 institutional commissions, the members of which also belong to thematic commissions (i.e., Citizen Participation Commission, Coordination Commission, and Drafting Commission).

It is worth noting that the majority of elected members of the CoA (95 of the 130 members) do not have a prior background in politics and never had an electoral mandate. All members hold ordinary jobs and their work on the new constitution only makes up a small part (approximately 10%) of their monthly work percentage. In addition, most of the elected members, on the one hand, represent the different political parties of the region within the CoA. On the other hand, there are also some elected members (16 out of 130) in the CoA who belong to a non-partisan movement which was conceived especially to allow citizens not affiliated with a political party to participate in the process. Members of this non-partisan movement also contested the election for the CoA, and were elected by the general populace.

Through our research, we examine *a)* the way diverse digital (communicative/collaborative) tools are used by the members of the CoA, *b)* the entailed effort to change one's practices while adopting a certain tool (owing to group pressure, for instance), and *c)* how recent advancements in these tools are profoundly changing the established –*collaborative* and *communicative*– practices, protocols, and experiences of policy makers. Moreover, we contribute to the domains of HCI and CSCW by examining the context of participatory politics, and by establishing the potential routes of designing collaborative tools which are well-suited and integrated into the modern political landscape, and can support participatory political efforts in a seamless and meaningful manner. Still, it is worth noting that these collaborative practices lie within the scope of normal democratic practices (within the CoA), and do not refer to the practices unique to the digital or internet democracy (such as e-voting). Additionally, the co-writing of constitution is just an observational context and not an objective i.e., it is not our goal to evaluate the quality of procedures for effectively co-writing a constitution, but to examine how it was done in our context.

2   Related Work

The presented work is situated at the intersection of participatory policy-making and the tools used in accomplishing the collective political objectives. The latter aspect is extensively and rigorously investigated within the domains of CSCW and HCI, especially in the context of personal and organizational collaborations. Consequently, in this section, we will review the relevant researches which inform and inspire our work.

2.1   Participatory Constitution Writing

Over the past three decades, there have been numerous cases where a participatory approach was adopted in drafting of a constitution. Among the earliest examples, even before the age of digital networking and social media, there is the constitution of Brazil written in 1988, which collected over 70,000 amendments from citizens [4]. Other similar cases include Uganda in 1995, South Africa in 1996, and Kenya in 2001. With the advent of social media platforms such as Facebook and Twitter, citizens' participation in constitutional processes appears to be more frequent, such as in Egypt in 2012, Iceland in 2012 [23,29], Chile in 2016 [18], and Ireland in 2016–2017. For example, several existing studies investigate the use of instant messaging in the context of public involvement in politics [27,46].

Besides these numerous instances of participatory constitution writing, in recent years, we have also seen technological developments which enable such large-scale participative endeavors in policy making. In 2012, the Net Democracy Foundation (a non-profit organization) released an open-source web-based platform called 'DemocracyOS[2]', to facilitate dialogue and deliberation between politicians and general populous on legislative aspects [35]. This platform has since been incorporated by numerous local governments and communities to engage in matters of policy making by enabling communities to vote on legislative motions, and also allowing law makers to gather opinions and concerns from their constituencies. 'Consider.it[3]' is another open-source web-based platform, which affords for *"personal deliberation in the realm of public deliberation* [28,51]"*. Precisely, it allows users to *a)* add opinions/arguments along with

---

[2] DemocracyOS URL: http://democracyos.org/ (Last visited on 20th January 2021).
[3] Consider.it URL: https://consider.it/ (Last visited on 20th January 2021).

reflections regarding their arguments' position being in favor or against a specific motion, *b)* highlight crucial attributes behind their contributions, *c)* consider others' contributions and adopt them in their own arguments, and *d)* emphasize the salient elements of their personal deliberations in relation to the proposed motion.

Therefore, by far, the case of Valais is not the first example of participatory constitution writing. However, it is still specific in a number of aspects, which were discussed in the previous section. Furthermore, our research differs in its focus on the constitution writing as an ongoing social activity, which is currently (at the time of our study and the writing of this article) in progress and engages both the citizens and politicians.

2.2   Communicative Aspects of Technologies

Owing to the nature of communicative practices in the Constituent Assembly, which are asynchronous in time and happen over a distance (Space-Time Taxonomy by [15,17]), here, we will review works which have examined technological aspects of supporting such communicative practices. In particular, we focus on the utilization of technological devices in communicative practices as part of the daily work on the constitution. Previous research shows that users of communication technologies tend to distribute their social relationships across different apps and appropriate the features and technical constraints of these apps (such as the ability to monitor the delivery status of a message [22]), in order to serve specific aims and purposes [40]. Even while engaging in communication through one particular tool such as Facebook, users "maintain independent social spheres", which can lead to perceived tensions and conflicts [3]. Current organization of work involves "media toolboxes" within "communicative ecologies" [53,59], where users might show preference for a certain tool. Such "media toolboxes" provide users with a number of technological tools that they can use and combine in order to achieve a certain task in a given context [59]. In making a selection from the range of available communication tools, users' decisions are influenced by a number of factors, such as material features of the tool, familiarity with it, and the situated local circumstances of a particular communicative process [26]. In particular, WhatsApp is perceived as more intimate [41], utilizable in mediated interaction within small groups, even while in physical co-presence [5]. It is seen as a tool for chatting rather than formal message exchange, which is the case with SMS [10]. At the same time, people use multiple communication tools and devices simultaneously in "temporal and sequential interdependence" [52].

Besides supporting communicative practices in diverse social and public spheres, digital communication tools, in particular Social Media, have been linked to the global protest movements and their disruptive effects on the political landscape (e.g., Arab Spring [60], Hong Kong protests [45], and Black Lives Matter [14]). Shah et al. [49] has referred to this phenomena as "personalized politics" where diverse individuals and communities have rallied behind multiple causes which comprise of public's demand for fair democratic establishments, economic justice, human rights, and environmental protection. Yet another politically relevant aspect of the use of social media is the dissemination of conspiracy theories [11]. Moreover, Semaan et al. [48] have observed the ways in which social media tools support users' interactions with others in the context of political deliberations. Their findings reveal the relationship between affordances of different social media platforms and how they support or inhibit users' engagement and dissemination of political information, and particularly, users' adaption of alternate tools in the face of external impositions that challenge their civic agency [47,48].

2.3 Technological Support for Co-writing Activities

In particular relevance to our study, large-scale distributed and asynchronous collaboration facilitated by technologies has been extensively studied in the context of collaborative writing (on platforms such as Google Docs and GitHub). Ishtaiwa and Aburezeq [24] examined the impact of Google Docs on collaborative learning amongst students and their instructors, and observed an enhanced interactivity with the content. In addition, the authors suggest putting in place a comprehensive set of regulations and task-division to ensure effective moderation of co-created content as well as improved collaboration experience. Olson et al. [42] also studied collaborative writing within student teams at undergraduate levels with Google Docs, and found variability in collaborative writing strategies ranging from synchronous to asynchronous. Moreover, they also observed the inherent dynamism in acquisition and transfer of roles during writing and editing activities, and found that balanced participation and exhibited leadership in student teams resulted in high-quality writing (similar observations in collocated student teams were also reported by [55,56]). Awareness tools that visualize individual contributions, document change history, and overall collaboration synthesis have also been developed and evaluated in the context of collaborative writing with Google Docs [57]. On the other hand, GitHub –a popular online service for software development within large distributed teams– has also been widely studied for collaborative writing of software, owing to its attributes of transparency and versioning [12,16]. GitHub has also been appropriated for other collaborative scenarios which differ from software development, for example, management of archival activities in libraries [13], and open collaboration on textual documents [33]. Furthermore, the use of GitHub in collaborative writing projects aiming to develop non-software digital artifacts has been examined by Pe-Than et al. [43]. The authors reported observing online or face-to-face meetings as the prominent activities in the early stages of the project, while GitHub was found useful especially in the later stages requiring audience participation and project management activities.

3 Research Questions and Methods

In this article, we generally aim to inquire the emerging patterns of usage of digital collaborative tools, and the evolution of these patterns, amongst the members of the Constituent Assembly (CoA) who are co-writing the constitution of Valais.

Particularly, we seek to comprehend the means of organizing and maintaining communication, negotiation, and coordination at different levels of social conformity – amongst closest colleagues, peers from the same commission, colleagues from the same/different political group(s), or with all members of the CoA. In addition, what factors necessitate the formation of these different levels of social conformity, and more importantly, how permeable and temporal are these social boundaries (implying how easily they change and how long do they last)? Moreover, which digital tools assisted or inhibited the seamless achievement of aforementioned intended social objectives? In order to address these inquiries, we conducted an interview study with 15 elected members of the CoA.

3.1 Interview Study

Initially, a formal e-mail of invitation to participate in our study was sent to the President of the Constituent Assembly (CoA), who disseminated our invitation to the elected members. 15 members (7 females and 8 males between 25 and 74 years old), some of them with a previous experience in politics, accepted to participate in our study (see Table 1). Next, we sent an e-mail containing *1)* the general objective of our research without revealing the specifics of the questions we intended on asking, in order to prevent biasing their responses, and *2)* the description of our research approach including the approximate time required on the participants' part. In addition, the participants were also informed that we will properly acknowledge them in our research publications and that there was no financial compensation.

We have opted for interviewing as the primary method for several reasons. First, it was not possible to observe and interview participants *in situ*. Our participants often work asynchronously and over distance, and so there were simply no collocated sessions of collaborative work to be directly observed. Moreover, political work within commissions is not open to the public (based on the regulations of the CoA) and potentially sensitive in nature, hence disqualifying the possibility of observations and contextual inquiry. Although plenary sessions are public, citizens are seated in different areas separated from the politicians. This all hindered the use of observational methods.

The interview study was designed to gather fine-grained insights about participants' –individual and collaborative– work in the CoA, and the nature of its entanglement with diverse digital tools. Starting with specific questions about participants' political work and background, their involvement and role in commissions, and their familiarity with digital tools and modern technologies, the significant part of the interviews focused on specific themes relevant to our study. In particular, we discussed about participants' *1)* experiences with the ongoing policy making practices and protocols in the CoA, *2)* perceptions about how different tools support or impede their attainment of specific political objectives, *3)* reflections about the strategic advantages inspired by the accessibility to an ecosystem of digital tools and how they are profoundly changing policy making, *4)* concerns about security and privacy issues, and *5)* perspectives about the role and position of digital tools and technologies in the future constitution.

Table 1. The table illustrates the participants' involvement in our interview study. In addition, it also describes the participants' memberships to different thematic (T) and institutional (I) commissions. The only thematic commission which is not represented by any of our participants is "10. Municipalities and territorial organization".

Participant	Gender	Commission memberships
P01	MALE	T04: Principles, finance and economic development
P02	FEMALE	T06: Social and other tasks of the State
P03	FEMALE	T02: Fundamental rights, social rights and civil society
P04	MALE	T01: General provisions, social cohesion, preamble and church-state relations, final provisions
P05	MALE	T02: Fundamental rights, social rights and civil society
P06	FEMALE	T03: Political rights IB: Coordination
P07	FEMALE	T01: General provisions, social cohesion, preamble and church-state relations, final provisions
P08	FEMALE	T09: Judicial power IA: Citizen participation IB: Coordination
P09	MALE	T07: Legislative power IA: Citizen participation
P10	MALE	T04: Principles, finance and economic development IA: Citizen participation
P11	MALE	T05: Territorial development and natural resources IB: Coordination
P12	FEMALE	T08: Executive power IA: Citizen participation
P13	MALE	T03: Political rights IA: Citizen participation
P14	FEMALE	T06: Social and other tasks of State
P15	MALE	T03: Political rights

The interviews were conducted in semi-structured manner and lasted for approximately an hour. Interviews were conducted in the participants' preferred venue (cafeteria, home, or office). Three interviews were conducted over Skype, and one over telephone. The interviews were audio recorded and were later transcribed by two researchers, followed by open coding with recurrent topics and themes that emerged from the repeated reading of the interview transcripts by three researchers. After the open coding phase, the co-authors organized two sessions to interpret and consolidate the codes into relevant categories and themes. During this phase, relevant segments of the interviews were aggregated into categories and further compared in order to identify common approaches to discussed topics among the participants [9].

4 Analysis and Results

The interviews aimed at eliciting fine-grained aspects of communicative and collaborative activities within the Constituent Assembly (CoA). Particularly, we sought insights into the participants' use of digital tools and technologies, and how they are appropriated in the interplay between malleable social boundaries and the temporality of collaborative routines and practices. Next, we will describe the emergent themes from the semi-structured interviews. Our findings are organized in the following sections along *five* binary distinctions: *1)* Informal and Formal, *2)* Novice and Expert, *3)* Private and Public, *4)* Advertence and Multiplicity, and *5)* Instruments and Environments. These binary distinctions are guided by the notion of boundaries, which we use as a sensitising concept. However, we need to stress that it is a post-hoc analytical construction, and boundaries (in a general sense) were not explicitly discussed with the interviewees, although the term is nevertheless occasionally mentioned by them.

4.1 Informal and Formal

Reflections about the use of digital collaborative/communicative tools often led to associations whether the tool, or its intended usage, was 'informal' or 'formal'. This boundary, and its perception, can be attributed to the well-established and normative nature of political customs and protocols (in democratic societies), which in turn are the manifestation of the dichotomy between *"what is visible"* and *"what happens backstage"* (cf. [2]).

The members of the CoA work asynchronously, part-time, and remotely, with less possibilities for frequent collocated meetings – *"we are like the 'militia', we live our normal lives and do our normal jobs, but we also contribute to the constitution"* (P09). As a consequence, our participants unanimously affirmed that e-mails are the accepted channel for *formal* and *official* communication. They afford for lengthy and complete information exchange with multiple stakeholders, while allowing for the transfer of documents and links (also observed by [7,26]). However, the use of e-mail does not necessarily guarantee a reply from the recipient (P05, P09, P10). Furthermore, the use of multiple e-mail accounts and the "Reply All" feature often floods the inboxes, and sometimes important e-mails are marked as spam (P12), which in-turn leads to messages getting lost and overwhelming its users (P08, P09, P11). P11 referred to this phenomenon as the *"e-mail ping-pong"* which *"requires a lot of effort to remain up-to-date"*.

On the other hand, WhatsApp was referred to as a *lighter, informal,* and *rapid* alternative to e-mails (as reflected by P03, P05, P08, P09, P11, and P12), which affords for approachability –since it is mostly used on a phone and people generally carry it with them– and the push notifications increase the likelihood that messages are seen. The participants, however, added that WhatsApp is not an ideal channel for deep and meaningful conversations unlike telephone calls or e-mails (P03, P12), and sending short messages might lead to misunderstandings (P09). Also, push notifications were reported as *"intruding in private life, where the boundary between politics and home is blurred"* (P05, P08, P09,

P14; cf. [31]). Moreover, the membership to a high number of WhatsApp groups and the numerous messages received on a daily basis, overwhelmed the participants and caused a *"catching-up"* fatigue (P07, P14). In addition, the lack of a functionality to search old messages/conversations (unlike e-mail) complicates the process of navigating amongst old messages (P03, P05). Finally, Facebook's ownership of WhatsApp was also reported as disadvantageous in terms of privacy concerns. However, a lack of a popular alternative gives WhatsApp a competitive advantage. P09 expressed this by noting that *"It's again the classical freedom versus convenience dilemma"*.

Contrary to the use of WhatsApp, phone calls were reported as another *informal* channel for discussions. Attributed with the qualities of enabling a clear medium and facilitating elaboration of ones' ideas or concerns, which assist in swift attainment of conversational agreement, phone calls were reported as affording *"a large space for discussion in uncertain situations or with people who are not proficient with digital tools"* (P09, P10). However, it requires prior synchronization and planning to set-up the call (which was also referred to as *"messy"* by P09), and at the end of a long call there is no tangible trace of what was discussed (P06, P12).

With regards to collaborative activities, such as the co-creation, modification, and review of documents, participants preemptively and collectively formalized the rules of engagement. Google Docs was reported as the popular choice for co-creation by our participants, especially for the ongoing work within the different commissions. P05 and P09 noted that they collectively organized a workshop for their colleagues to familiarize them with Google Docs, especially the elderly members who had never used Google Docs before (see also Sect. 4.2). Specific rules for fair usage (or best-practices) of these tools were explicitly predefined (*"Please do not delete others' comments or work!"*, *"Be respectful to others and their contributions"*, etc.), and roles were assigned to individuals who were responsible for resolving conflicts and preparing the final version of the documents.

These findings underline a tension between the "formal" and the "exceptional" use of collaborative tools – in particular, how this boundary is intentionally constructed to enable better coordination and fair collaboration practices while creating documents. On the other hand, this boundary is shifted, or even temporarily deconstructed, to resolve immediate urgent concerns over WhatsApp and phone calls.

4.2   Novice and Expert

Before the commencement of work on the constitution, a working procedure for solving routine tasks had been negotiated within the Constituent Assembly (CoA), including an implicit agreement (which was open to future adaptations) on the use of different collaborative and communicative tools. Additionally, such negotiations about the choice of appropriate digital tools happened within different political groups. However, the specific level of knowledge regarding different tools varies for each participant – they belong to different age groups and have varied professional backgrounds. During the interviews, we asked participants to self-assess themselves on a scale from "physical" to "digital" (spontaneously, some of them used a scale from 1 to 10). Cumulative results of responses to this question are displayed in Fig. 1. Still, it should be noted that the distribution of participants is approximate, since their understanding of the scale reflects two concurrent conceptions of being digital or non-digital. On the one hand, it pertains to *knowledge and familiarity* with various collaboration/communication tools, on the other hand, there is the aspect of *usage preferences*, and related attempts to intentionally limit the digitality of their lives (for example, putting their phone into flight mode while at home [P09]).

In organizing collaborative work in the CoA, general preference seems to be given to popular and widespread tools, apps, and devices. The process of selecting a tool for the group takes into account several factors: *"You have to balance the interest between the time it takes to understand a new tool, make people use it, and what it can offer"* (P12). It is also important to note that the decision does not happen only once, but it is often temporary, in the *wait-and-see* fashion. The need for a new tool can emerge in real time while working on specific tasks, as the same participant explains: *"When we were working on the rules of the CoA, we were discussing between several parties on WhatsApp, and shortly after starting, we realized that we had to move to something like a Word document and share it if we wanted to get things done, or pick up the phone and talk to each other."* A possible explanation for the specific role of technology in policy-making in the CoA was provided by P15 – who has a prior political background unlike many of the elected members in the Assembly. Comparing his work at the CoA with his parallel duties at the Legislative Council, he noted that *"there is a bit more technology use in the CoA than in the Legislative Council, because of a different and younger population ... On the contrary, in politics we are not educated about these tools"*.

Thus, in some cases, in order to be able to collaborate with others smoothly within the Assembly, participants had to start using technologies that they did not know before. Several participants stated that their work in commissions heightened their familiarity with Google Drive (P04, P06, P08, and P14). They find it useful overall: *"Being able to collectively interact on the same document at the same time is really time saving for us"* (P08). On the other hand, working in a group of people with uneven knowledge of collaborative tools can also create

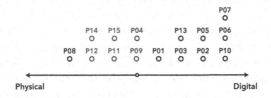

Fig. 1. Distribution of interview participants along the digital-physical scale, according to their self-assessment.

an environment of "peer pressure" for more tech-savvy users, who are required to use means that they might not find very efficient or beneficial. P03 criticized her colleagues' way of using Doodle: *"they do not use the orange checkbox ... they just wait until everyone is there"*. WhatsApp seems so ubiquitous that it almost appears as a necessity: *"WhatsApp is not necessarily a group pressure, but it's simply so well established in society that [communication] can't be done without it"* (P02). However, some participants pointed to certain negative aspects of this tool: *"If the number of groups grows more, then it would lose its efficiency"* (P08). In addition, *"WhatsApp can be annoying when people are sending a lot of things about their holidays ... But you can always shut it down"* (P06).

4.3 Private and Public

Participants reflected about the boundary between private and public in relation to the use of social networks (primarily Facebook). In particular, participants who are new to politics and relatively younger, used the platform in the campaigning phase before their election, which compelled them to add strangers and acquaintances to their network. This phenomenon was reported as causing a major shift in their perceptions and experiences with privacy. P08 reflected that *"with Facebook the boundaries between what is private, and what is public are becoming thin, almost invisible"*. Others (P01, P02, P09, P13, and P14) also reported having similar experiences where their private and public personas were perceived as indistinguishable by the outside world. Moreover, this influenced participants to put in place varied self-identified best practices. For example, P02 created a separate Facebook profile for her political objectives, whereas P08, P09, and P14 subjected their posts to extra scrutiny. P09 recollected an anecdote from his personal experience that *"within the political context, [he] learned quickly that it is not wise to criticize or joke about another party on Facebook"*, as the controversy led him to *"exercise discretion"* and treat every post since this incident *"as a public statement you give to a journalist"*. P08, on the other hand, *"stopped adding [her] opinions along with the posts [she] shared"*. P13 and P14 reported that their posting activity on Facebook has been significantly reduced since their election into the CoA, and they use the platform primarily to *"follow and observe social opinions, concerns, and movements"*.

Between the younger and the elder participants, we observed a disparity in the awareness about privacy aspects, and the means of effectively managing it. Amongst the elderly participants, P04 (who is over 70 years) expressed a feeling of pride that he has over 1500 members in his social network, and he frequently shares his ideas and opinions over Facebook. Furthermore, P05 recalled an incident involving an elderly colleague, whose post on the social network platform was regarded as incongruous with their political ideology. Consequently, other members of the party urgently demanded the responsible person to remove the post, and addressed the gaps in their colleague's awareness about the potential risks with privacy on social networks. P05 further added that *"these permeable boundaries between private and public on social network platforms are awareness blind-spots for people who are not knowledgeable about the risks"*, and expressed a desire to *"make this distinction more salient"* by adopting the principles of 'seamful design' [8] concerning privacy on social networks.

Few participants also expressed their concerns about the risks associated with Facebook's use in light of the recent global scandals surrounding the platform. P01 stated that *"... trust in politics and politicians has suffered as [Facebook] was used to influence elections. Consequently, the entanglement of politics and Facebook is not good as the trust is clearly lacking"*. Furthermore, both P01 and P09 referred to Godwin's Law[4] as a reason to avoid organizing discussions or canvassing opinions on the platform. P02 further noted that *"seeking neutral and honest opinions on Facebook has a certain 'tiredness', and [she] would rather prefer to subscribe to several newspapers to inform [herself] about public concerns"*. Finally, P07 informed us that the CoA has commissioned an ad-hoc and secure participatory tool that will enable the citizens to engage with the commissions and their work in the Assembly.

As discussed in the previous section, participants noted using Google Docs to collectively create, review, and edit documents. In response to a question whether participants perceived risks in using a commercial third-party platform, which can be subjected to malicious activities such as hacking, most replied *"the nature of our work is public, and we have nothing to hide"* since prior measures have been collectively taken to define best practices. Furthermore, P09 elaborated that the preemptive policy of establishing accepted behaviors a priori, and defining regulations mitigate the likelihood that, in the event of a leak, the content and comments cannot be used adversely.

4.4 Advertence and Multiplicity

Participants reported conventionally using multiple digital tools simultaneously in their political work. In addition, the tools themselves have become versatile and support multiple concurrent activities, for example, *"... Google enables searching for articles and laws from other states and countries, translating them, and sharing it with your colleagues in less than a minute"* (P05). Still, the most striking revelation was the appropriated use of WhatsApp during plenary sessions to facilitate *'Silent Lateral Communication'*. P05, P09, and P11 noted this phenomenon in response to the question – Does the accessibility of digital tools make the modern political work different from past efforts in constitution writing?

Plenary sessions of the Constituent Assembly (CoA) are important public events attended by the general public and journalists, and the proceedings are broadcasted live on state television. P05 stated that *"the use of smartphones by the elected members during these sessions are not perceived well by the public, as they might presume that you are inattentive or distracted ... but since WhatsApp is also available on our laptops, we frequently use it to coordinate in real time to strategically present our ideas and prepare our arguments"*. Moreover, similar to parliamentary proceedings, each member is awarded a 5 min time-window

---

[4] https://en.wikipedia.org/wiki/Godwin%27s_law (Last visited on 23rd January 2021).

to speak, which is primarily used to propose a new motion, present arguments in response to existing discussion, and answer questions raised by others. This adherence to protocol, time constrains, and social perceptibility entails microscopic collective planning, negotiation, and organization which are afforded by WhatsApp. Since these recurrent sideways communicative actions co-occur with the proceedings of the Assembly, and are invisible to the eyes of the public and press, we refer to them as 'Silent Lateral Communications'. Both P09 and P11 recollected engaging in such conversations which also involved members from different parties. This finding confirms that chat at work is used when information is *"timely* and *pertinent to ongoing work"* [38].

The multiplicity of tools –different tools supporting different tasks– was observed by a few participants as *"adding to the complexity"* which makes it more likely to *"exclude some people from actual discussions"* (P15). Further illustrating his argument, P15 used an example scenario: *"Before a meeting, discussions happen primarily over e-mail or Google Drive, however, during the meeting people who did not contribute online would be at a disadvantage"*. Moreover, combined influence of aspects related to the partial nature of work in the CoA, and the varying levels of accessibility afforded by different tools, resulted into a *"catching-up fatigue"* (P06, P07). The affordances of WhatsApp (availability on phone and push notifications) render it permanently accessible, and subsequently a source of *"frequent intrusion in private and family time"* (P05, P08). Participants also noted establishing different coping mechanisms to prevent such intrusions resulting from numerous notifications. For instance, P09 stated that *"when at home, [he] puts [his] phone on the flight mode, and turns it back ON again after [his] kids are sleeping"*.

4.5   Instruments and Environments

Finally, we will review the results related to more general questions focusing on the role of technological tools in the daily political work of the participants, in the foreseeable future, and on the overarching role of ICT in contemporary society as a whole.

Nearly all of the participants see technologies primarily as means to an end. What will ultimately count is only the result of their work – that is the final text of the constitution, which is *"the end product"* (P04). P01 noted that *"the technological tools are there to optimize and simplify the writing process ... If the final constitution is there, no one is interested in what the process was like"*. Or even more concisely, as P07 put it: *"The tool is a mean, the constitution is a value"*. Once the goals are reached, the road and the obstacles will be simply forgotten. Grasping the technology as an *instrument* –a pragmatic mean for achieving a definite goal– can be conceived as one pole of a conceptual scale.

The understanding of technology as an instrument is also reflected in response to the question about the imagined position of technology in the future constitution. Most of the constituents do not see a real reason to dedicate any articles of the constitution specifically to digital technologies. Our interviewees often mentioned that a need might emerge for approaching the digitization of society in a generic way in the constitution, but that it is rather a topic which should be regulated at the level of laws (P02, P04, P11, P12, and P13).

In addition to the instrumental conception of technology, on the other end of the scale, we encounter the notion of technology as an *environment*. While reflecting on the difference between their own work on the constitution and the creation of previous constitution in 1907, the role of technologies is seen as central and beneficial: *"Every element that you used to have when you wrote the constitution, 100 years ago, you always had to meet. That's very cumbersome"* (P01). The lower necessity of face-to-face meetings and possibility of distant working is seen as an advantage by some (P12, P01), and many appreciate that the whole process is much faster (P03, P06, P08, P10, P13, P14). Although generally positive, several participants also noted disadvantages of mediated interaction as a basis for political work: *"I believe that the dynamics of face-to-face discussions can have an impact on the outcome, although I am not so sure, just a feeling ... In real meetings, there is a lot in the attitudes ... You know, the non-verbal attitudes, ability to convince or manipulate the opinions, this doesn't happen while editing the documents collaboratively online"* (P09). In addition, the easy and quick availability of information online was also evaluated critically: *"In the past it was about knowledge, which you had to have, today it is more about where you can get knowledge. But there can also be a surplus of information and distractions"* (P11).

Although sometimes reserved about the true value of technologies, participants also reported that the digital communication tools are not used in their full potential: *"In this respect we are at the beginning of a great journey to discover what technology can still do and what possibilities it will still offer"* (P01). Several participants (P02, P03, P12, P15) emphasized the disparity in the rate of changes in digital technologies and the change in human practices: *"Everything is getting faster at the moment, and its overwhelming to keep up to it"* (P02). Indeed, this is only part of the story, as in many cases the inefficient use of technology is not caused by insufficient cognitive capacities, but rather lack of technical skills and sometimes also unwillingness: *"Skills of people are not enough. It would be good to educate people...But a change of culture is also needed. Some people still think that everything should be discussed during face-to-face meetings only. We can do much better, and I have the feeling that culture will change in the future"* (P15).

5   Discussion

In this section, we discuss the presented findings from the interview study, and elaborate the implications for our project context and the overarching role of HCI/CSCW research in the political landscape.

5.1   Adapting Collaborative Tools for Political Practices

Owing to the *a)* peculiarity of the participatory constitution writing process, *b)* amalgamation of elected members with varying political experiences, and *c)* temporal positioning of our qualitative inquiry, our research work has certain uniqueness. In addition, we present one of the first studies which examine the participatory constitution writing process in its progression. In this way, our contributions to the domains of HCI and CSCW are not limited to the extension and reinforcement of existing literature by adding the context of participatory politics, but can also open up avenues for designing tools that can better support the communicative and collaborative activities within politics.

The part-time engagements of politicians in the Constituent Assembly (CoA), and limited opportunities for collocated collective efforts ostensibly favor digital tools which support asynchronous collaboration over a distance. These factors, thus, explain the centrality and affinity to tools like WhatsApp and Google Docs in the CoA. On the other hand, tools that support synchronous communicative actions (such as Skype and phone calls) were discouraged because they require prior planning, which was not in agreement with the varied professional responsibilities of elected members. Furthermore, our study was conducted prior to the onset of the COVID-19 pandemic, and despite the disruptions caused in the ways of working and collaborating, the work in the CoA continued as before. Consequently, the onset of pandemic does not invalidate our findings, but reinforces them as the foundations of our social fabric are being redefined and restructured by the changes brought forth by this situation.

Another interesting finding that seems to underpin the value of these tools in the constitution writing process is related to the phenomenon of *catching-up*. This cultural phenomenon captures the purposeful and systematic set of activities that a person undertakes, in order to minimize an epistemic gap created by the tension between a possible immediate knowledge of happenings and the current point in time. Moreover, this social phenomenon is not limited to the use of digital tools to support collaborative and communicative actions *per se*. It has also been observed in the conduct of 'fly-in-fly-out families' [37], as well as in the context of social media and political protests [44], and immigration [61]. Still, this phenomenon may be the consequence of transformation of social time in the modern era [50], such as the *time-space distanciation* [19]. In our context, both WhatsApp and Google Docs enable the opportunity of checking-in and catching-up at a chosen point of time, thus, affording participants a chance to manage their own time in a very flexible, personalized way. This is important, especially since the elected members have daily jobs beside their involvement in the CoA.

We consider the '*temporal permanence*' of collaborative/communicative tasks, and '*levels of social conformity*' (or the dynamic social boundaries which are opportunistically created to afford strategic political advantage) as the two dimensions to assess the functional quality of varied tools used by the participants. Both WhatsApp and Google Docs occupy a wider spectrum across these dimensions. As noted by the participants, their memberships to numerous groups – including peers from the same party, colleagues from the same commission, as well as friends within and outside the CoA, affirms that the scope of WhatsApp and Google Docs is effortlessly adaptable for collaborations with individuals as well as groups. Furthermore, keeping several, yet distinct, WhatsApp groups and conversations is also an elegant solution to the classical issue of role conflict, especially in conflicting political roles that one individual has in respect to other individuals [39]. In addition, they are well suited to short-term transitory (for example, creating a group for a specific plenary session) as well as long-term (keeping a record of commission work for the whole duration of constitution writing process) collaboration needs. However, e-mails and phone calls present only a narrow spectrum within this two-dimensional space. On the one hand, phone conversations are relatively ephemeral and afford one-to-one communications; on the other hand, e-mails are episodic in terms of temporality but simultaneously adapt to varying levels of social conformity. Also, this two-dimensional space has implications for technology designers to assess the scope and scale of their tools, in order to ascertain their seamless diffusion in contexts such as participatory politics.

Collaborative tools and political practices are related to each other in a reflexive way: the tools and practices mutually influence and establish each other. The tools are designed with practices in mind, but once introduced, they are repurposed by users in ways that were not previously imagined by the designers and engineers. In this sense, the shifting boundaries of political work open new spaces for intervention from the HCI and CSCW communities.

5.2 Shifting Boundaries of Political Landscape: HCI's Space for Intervention

Access to a wide variety of digital tools is fundamentally changing the policy-making practices, enabling politicians to look beyond their region or state, and seek inspiration from global events and movements. As revealed in our studies, participants proactively sought inspiration and ideas from constitutions written in other states and countries. In addition, the ubiquity of social networks and accessibility to public opinions and trends have brought the politicians closer to their constituents, and enabled the realisation of efforts to write a constitution in a participatory manner.

The versatility of instant messaging tools like WhatsApp have also fostered the emergence of new collaborative practices like 'Silent Lateral Communication' (see Sect. 4.4 above), especially in public proceedings during plenary sessions. These practices manifest as opportunistic and improvised cooperative acts between elected members with homogeneous political objectives – often involving members from different political parties. The elected members' need to attain a real-time strategic advantage coupled with the peculiar affordances of WhatsApp and its simultaneous availability on computers, have led to the wider acceptance of this emergent practice in the Constituent Assembly (CoA). Furthermore, the concerns about privacy and third-party ownership of these tools has led the politicians to establish rigorous regulations and best practices as preemptive prevention against malicious activities. Aforementioned findings illustrate the evolving nature of policy-making practices, and present numerous opportunities and implications for the HCI community to intervene and design effective and secure tools which can support and encourage the participatory approaches within the political landscape.

Our article contributes novel insights into the shifting boundaries of evolving political practices in the context of current digital societies. We have shown how collaborative technologies shift boundaries of informal and formal activity, the categories of novice and expert in relation to the use of ICT, the sphere of the public and the private, and facilitate simultaneous communicative actions. In some aspects, these boundaries are rather "*selectively permeated*" to gain strategic political advantages in plenary sessions (for example, Silent Lateral Communication). In other cases, they are "*selectively constructed*" to facilitate better coordination (for example, predefined regulations and best practices), and to mitigate adverse effects of security and privacy breaches. Our use of the term 'selective' underlines the inherently dynamic and opportunistic manner in which social objectives are constantly redefined in such political collaborations, and conformity to specific groups is malleable over time.

Yet another conceptual outcome that emerged from our analysis of empirical materials is the distinction of *technological tools as instruments and environments*. Instruments and environments are two opposite conceptions of technology, exemplified in our data in the tension between "means to an end" on the one hand, and, on the other hand, conditions structuring more fundamentally the social activities that constitute political work. The central difference is that *tools as instruments* are tied to solving clearly outlined *problems* (such as "writing a document together"), while *tools as environments* transform the horizon of *possibilities* in a more essential sense (such as the faster pace of work under digital conditions). In this sense, it is also easier to assess the digital *tools as instruments*, because their utility can be judged by measuring whether, or to what extent, the tool helps us reach the goal. Evaluating digital *tools as environments* seems to be more complex and problematic, because the ontological changes it brings around –for instance the pace of communication– can have both positive (volume of work) and negative (cognitive overload) impacts. While formulated on the grounds of our specific study of collaborative constitution writing, we believe that the conceptual relationship of instruments and environments merits further advancement and verification in other social settings.

In conclusion, our examination of collaborative constitution writing provides valuable insights into an understudied area of politics, particularly focusing on the role of ICT. It is clear that –at least in our context– technologies play an important role in supporting politics and political issues. As demonstrated throughout the paper, the use of digital communication tools is omnipresent and ubiquitous in political work, reflecting and reinforcing the broader social developments in recent decades [34, 36]. Moreover, although the role and impact of communicative/collaborative tools is more pronounced in relation to the varied everyday activities and tasks that constitute political work, their role in the evolution of politics is still nuanced, spontaneous, gradual and hard to assess in the time frame of a study such as ours.

Our research shows that the constitutive boundaries which have been characteristic of politics for centuries (for example, the clear partisan divisions, or citizens' detachment from the actual details of everyday political work) are being profoundly transformed by the use of ICT. Interestingly, many of the ways technologies are currently utilized in our interviewees' political work have been redeployed from other domains of work, such as industry, business and services. It remains an open question how these changes can be effectively evaluated within the specific domain of political work, taking into account its unique disposition.

Although it was not our purpose in this paper to formulate assessments of our participants' work practices, we rest confident that the reported results can serve as grounds for further research in this important direction.

Finally, the design implications of our work seem to be grounded in the existence of two types of boundaries. First, there are *desirable boundaries*, which are necessary or inevitable – for example, the private/public dichotomy. These are not to be overcome or removed but they should be made explicit and transparent. Second, there are *undesirable boundaries*, where the designers/researchers should provide instruments and environments that actively hinder emergence of boundaries – for example, between novice and expert users. In short, spaces are open in political work for HCI and CSCW to *design for* and *design against* the frictions we identified and described in politicians' everyday praxis, oriented to the collaborative constitution writing. Indeed, such design solutions need to be created in close collaboration with the practitioners themselves, serving their variable and multifarious needs and requirements.

6   Concluding Remarks

We present a qualitative examination into an ongoing participatory effort of constitution writing in the Swiss canton of Valais (or Wallis). With an aspiration to comprehend the dynamic and multi-layered collaboration practices within the political landscape, we present an interview study about the ways politicians use ICT to collaborate and acquire a strategic political advantage in public spheres. Our study documents how a relatively rigid and steady domain of social life has undergone substantial transformations in the last decade. Various boundaries which have been built into in the cultural understanding of political activities –such as the line between public and private, or the difference of formal and informal– seem to shift and merge in novel and sometimes surprising ways due to the increasing use of ICT for routine everyday communication. In this paper, while aiming somewhat "impatiently" to analyse an ongoing political process of collaborative constitution writing still in its course, we hope to have also identified and specified some of the more general ongoing societal tendencies.

Acknowledgements. We would like to thank Blaise Crettol, Emilie Praz, Laurence Vuagniaux, and other interviewees who preferred to remain anonymous. We greatly appreciate their participation and engagement in our study.

References

1. Ackerman, B.A.: Reconstructing American Law. Harvard University Press, Cambridge (1983)
2. Alexander, J.C.: Performance and Power. Polity Press, Cambridge/Malden (2011)
3. Binder, J., Howes, A., Sutcliffe, A.: The problem of conflicting social spheres: effects of network structure on experienced tension in social network sites. In: Proceedings of the SIGCHI Conference on Human Factors in Computing Systems, CHI 2009, pp. 965–974. ACM, New York (2009). https://doi.org/10.1145/1518701.1518849

4. Brazil, P.: Brazil's democratic constitution of 1988 was built by society (2018). http://www.brazil.gov.br/about-brazil/news/2018/11/brazils-democratic-constitution-of-1988-was-built-by-society

5. Brown, B., O'hara, K., Mcgregor, M., Mcmillan, D.: Text in talk: lightweight messages in co-present interaction. ACM Trans. Comput. Hum. Interact. **24**(6), 42:1–42:25 (2018). https://doi.org/10.1145/3152419

6. Castells, M.: Communication, power and counter-power in the network society. Int. J. Commun. **1**(1), 238–266 (2007)

7. Cecchinato, M.E., Sellen, A., Shokouhi, M., Smyth, G.: Finding email in a multi-account, multi-device World. In: Proceedings of the 2016 CHI Conference on Human Factors in Computing Systems, CHI 2016, pp. 1200–1210. ACM, New York (2016). https://doi.org/10.1145/2858036.2858473

8. Chalmers, M., Galani, A.: Seamful interweaving: heterogeneity in the theory and design of interactive systems. In: Proceedings of the 5th Conference on Designing Interactive systems: processes, Practices, Methods, and Techniques, pp. 243–252. ACM (2004)

9. Charmaz, K., Liska Belgrave, L.: Qualitative interviewing and grounded theory analysis. In: Gubrium, J.F., Holstein, J.A., Marvasti, A.B., McKinney, K.D. (eds.) The SAGE Handbook of Interview Research: The Complexity of the Craft, pp. 347–365. SAGE, Thousand Oaks (2012)

10. Church, K., de Oliveira, R.: What's up with WhatsApp?: comparing mobile instant messaging behaviors with traditional SMS. In: Proceedings of the 15th International Conference on Human-Computer Interaction with Mobile Devices and Services, MobileHCI 2013, pp. 352–361. ACM, New York (2013). https://doi.org/10.1145/2493190.2493225

11. Cosentino, G.: Social Media and the Post-Truth World Order: The Global Dynamics of Disinformation. Palgrave Pivot, Cham (2020)

12. Dabbish, L., Stuart, C., Tsay, J., Herbsleb, J.: Social coding in GitHub: transparency and collaboration in an open software repository. In: Proceedings of the ACM 2012 Conference on Computer Supported Cooperative Work, pp. 1277–1286. ACM (2012)

13. Davis, R.C.: Git and GitHub for librarians. Behav. Soc. Sci. Libr. **34**(3), 158–164 (2015)

14. De Choudhury, M., Jhaver, S., Sugar, B., Weber, I.: Social media participation in an activist movement for racial equality. In: Tenth International AAAI Conference on Web and Social Media, pp. 92–101 (2016)

15. Desanctis, G., Gallupe, R.B.: A foundation for the study of group decision support systems. Manag. sci. **33**(5), 589–609 (1987)

16. Dias, L.F., Steinmacher, I., Pinto, G., da Costa, D.A., Gerosa, M.: How does the shift to GitHub impact project collaboration? In: 2016 IEEE International Conference on Software Maintenance and Evolution (ICSME), pp. 473–477. IEEE (2016)

17. Ellis, C.A., Gibbs, S.J., Rein, G.: Groupware: some issues and experiences. Commun. ACM **34**(1), 39–58 (1991)

18. Fierro, C., Fuentes, C., Pérez, J., Quezada, M.: 200k+ crowdsourced political arguments for a new chilean constitution. In: Proceedings of the 4th Workshop on Argument Mining, Copenhagen, Denmark, pp. 1–10. Association for Computational Linguistics (2017). https://www.aclweb.org/anthology/W17-5101

19. Giddens, A.: The Consequences of Modernity. Stanford University Press, Stanford (1990)

20. Habermas, J.: The Structural Transformation of the Public Sphere. Polity Press, Cambridge (1962)

21. Hill, K.A., Hughes, J.E. (eds.): Cyperpolitics: Citizen Activism in the Age of the Internet. Rowman and Littlefield, Oxford (1988)
22. Hoyle, R., Das, S., Kapadia, A., Lee, A.J., Vaniea, K.: Was my message read?: privacy and signaling on Facebook messenger. In: Proceedings of the 2017 CHI Conference on Human Factors in Computing Systems, CHI 2017, pp. 3838–3842. ACM, New York (2017). https://doi.org/10.1145/3025453.3025925
23. Hudson, A.: When does public participation make a difference? Evidence from Iceland's crowdsourced constitution. Policy Internet 10(2), 185–217 (2017)
24. Ishtaiwa, F.F., Aburezeq, I.M.: The impact of google docs on student collaboration: a UAE case study. Learning, Learn. Cult. Soc. Interact. 7, 85–96 (2015)
25. Jasanoff, S.: Constitutional moments in governing science and technology. Sci. Eng. Ethics 17(4), 621–638 (2011). https://doi.org/10.1007/s11948-011-9302-2
26. Jung, Y., Lyytinen, K.: Towards an ecological account of media choice: a casestudy on pluralistic reasoning while choosing email. Inf. Syst. J. 24(3), 271–293 (2014). https://doi.org/10.1111/isj.12024
27. Kligler-Vilenchik, N.: Imagine we're all in the living room talking about politics: Israeli WhatsApp groups devoted to informal political talk. In: Paper Presented at AoIR 2016: The 17th Annual Conference of the Association of Internet Researchers, pp. 1–4. Berlin, Germany: AoIR (2016). http://spir.aoir.org
28. Kriplean, T., Morgan, J., Freelon, D., Borning, A., Bennett, L.: Supporting reflective public thought with considerit. In: Proceedings of the ACM 2012 Conference on Computer Supported Cooperative Work, CSCW 2012, pp. 265–274. ACM, New York (2012). https://doi.org/10.1145/2145204.2145249
29. Landemore, H.: Inclusive constitution making and religious rights: lessons from the Icelandic experiment. J. Polit. 79(3), 762–779 (2017). https://doi.org/10.1086/690300
30. Leigh, D., Harding, L. (eds.): Wikileaks: Inside Julian Assange's War on Secrecy. Guardian Books, London (2011)
31. Licoppe, C.: The crisis of the summons: a transformation in the pragmatics of notifications, from phone rings to instant messaging. Inf. Soc. 26(4), 288–302 (2010)
32. Loader, B.D., Mercea, D.: Networking democracy? Inf. Commun. Soc. 14(6), 757–769 (2011). https://doi.org/10.1080/1369118X.2011.592648
33. Longo, J., Kelley, T.M.: Use of GitHub as a platform for open collaboration ontext documents. In: Proceedings of the 11th International Symposium on Open Collaboration, OpenSym 2015. ACM, New York (2015). https://doi.org/10.1145/2788993.2789838
34. Lupton, D.: Digital Sociology. Routledge, Oxon/New York (2014)
35. Mancini, P.: Why it is time to redesign our political system. Eur. View 14(1), 69–75 (2015)
36. Marres, N.: Digital Sociology: The Reinvention of Social Research. Policy Press, Cambridge (2017)
37. Mayes, R.: Mobility, temporality, and social reproduction: everyday rhythms of the 'FIFO family' in the Australian mining sector. Gend. Place Cult. 27(1) 126–142 (2019). https://doi.org/10.1080/0966369X.2018.1554555
38. McGregor, M., Bidwell, N.J., Sarangapani, V., Appavoo, J., O'Neill, J.: Talking about chat at work in the global south: an ethnographic study of chat use in India and Kenya. In: Proceedings of the 2019 CHI Conference on Human Factors in Computing Systems, CHI 2019, pp. 1–14. ACM, New York (2019). https://doi.org/10.1145/3290605.3300463
39. Merton, R.K.: Social Theory and Social Structure. The Free Press, New York, NY (1968)

40. Nouwens, M., Griggio, C.F., Mackay, W.E.: WhatsApp is for family; messenger is for friends: communication Places in app ecosystems. In: Proceedings of the 2017 CHI Conference on Human Factors in Computing Systems, CHI 2017, pp. 727–735. ACM, New York (2017). https://doi.org/10.1145/3025453.3025484

41. O'Hara, K.P., Massimi, M., Harper, R., Rubens, S., Morris, J.: Everyday dwelling with WhatsApp. In: Proceedings of the 17th ACM Conference on Computer Supported Cooperative Work and Social Computing. CSCW 2014, pp. 1131–1143. ACM, New York (2014). https://doi.org/10.1145/2531602.2531679

42. Olson, J.S., Wang, D., Olson, G.M., Zhang, J.: How people write together now: beginning the investigation with advanced undergraduates in a project course. ACM Trans. Comput. Hum. Interact. **24**(1), 1–40 (2017).https://doi.org/10.1145/3038919

43. Pe-Than, E.P.P., Dabbish, L., Herbsleb, J.D.: Collaborative writing on GitHub: a case study of a book project. In: Companion of the 2018 ACM Conference on Computer Supported Cooperative Work and Social Computing, CSCW 2018, pp. 305–308. ACM, New York (2018). https://doi.org/10.1145/3272973.3274083

44. Poell, T.: Social media, temporality and the legitimacy of protest. Soc. Mov. Stud. **19**, 609–624 (2019)

45. Purbrick, M.: A report of the 2019 Hong Kong protests. Asian Aff. **50**(4), 465–487 (2019).https://doi.org/10.1080/03068374.2019.1672397

46. Resende, G., Messias, J., Silva, M., Almeida, J., Vasconcelos, M., Benevenuto, F.: A system for monitoring public political groups in WhatsApp. In: Proceedings of the 24th Brazilian Symposium on Multimedia and the Web, pp. 387–390. ACM (2018)

47. Semaan, B., Faucett, H., Robertson, S.P., Maruyama, M., Douglas, S.: Designing political deliberation environments to support interactions in the public sphere. In: Proceedings of the 33rd Annual ACM Conference on Human Factors in Computing Systems, pp. 3167–3176. ACM (2015)

48. Semaan, B.C., Robertson, S.P., Douglas, S., Maruyama, M.: Social media supporting political deliberation across multiple public spheres: towards depolarization. In: Proceedings of the 17th ACM Conference on Computer Supported Cooperative Work and Social Computing, CSCW 2014, pp. 1409–1421. ACM, New York (2014). https://doi.org/10.1145/2531602.2531605

49. Shah, D.V., Friedland, L.A., Wells, C., Kim, Y.M., Rojas, H., Bennett, L.W.: The personalization of politics: Political identity, social media, and changing patterns of participation. ANN. Am. Acad. Polit. Soc. Sci. **644**(1), 20–39 (2012). https://doi.org/10.1177/0002716212451428

50. Sorokin, P.A., Merton, R.K.: Social time: a methodological and functional analysis. Am. J. Soc. **42**(5), 615–629 (1937). https://doi.org/10.1086/217540

51. Stiegler, H., de Jong, M.D.: Facilitating personal deliberation online: immediate effects of two considerit variations. Comput. Hum. Behav. **51**, 461–469 (2015). http://www.sciencedirect.com/science/article/pii/S0747563215003891

52. Su, N.M.: Temporal patterns of communication: media combos. In: Proceedings of the ACM 2009 International Conference on Supporting Group Work, GROUP 2009, pp. 387–388. ACM, New Yor (2009). https://doi.org/10.1145/1531674.1531737

53. Turner, T., Qvarfordt, P., Biehl, J.T., Golovchinsky, G., Back, M.: Exploring the workplace communication ecology. In: Proceedings of the SIGCHI Conference on Human Factors in Computing Systems, CHI 2010, pp. 841–850. ACM, New York (2010). https://doi.org/10.1145/1753326.1753449

54. Velasquez, A., LaRose, R.: Youth collective activism through social media: the role of collective efficacy. New Media Soc. **17**(6), 899–918 (2015), https://doi.org/10.1007/s11948-011-9302-2

55. Verma, H.: Latent social information in group interactions with a shared workspace. Technical report, EPFL (2015)

56. Verma, H., Roman, F., Magrelli, S., Jermann, P., Dillenbourg, P.: Complementarity of input devices to achieve knowledge sharing in meetings. In: Proceedings of the 2013 Conference on Computer Supported Cooperative Work, pp. 701–714. ACM (2013). https://doi.org/10.1145/2441776.2441855

57. Wang, D., Olson, J.S., Zhang, J., Nguyen, T., Olson, G.M.: DocuViz: visualizing collaborative writing. In: Proceedings of the 33rd Annual ACM Conference on Human Factors in Computing Systems, CHI 2015, pp. 1865–1874. ACM, New York (2015). https://doi.org/10.1145/2702123.2702517

58. Wellman, B., Haythornthwaite, C. (eds.): The Internet in Everyday Life. Blackwell, Oxford (2002)

59. Woerner, S.L., Orlikowski, W.J., Yates, J.: The media toolbox: combining media in organizational communication. In: Proceedings of the Academy of Management, pp. 1–36. Orlando (2004)

60. Wulf, V., Misaki, K., Atam, M., Randall, D., Rohde, M.: On the ground in Sidi Bouzid: investigating social media use during the Tunisian revolution. In: Proceedings of the 2013 Conference on Computer Supported Cooperative Work, CSCW 2013, pp. 1409–1418. ACM, New York (2013). https://doi.org/10.1145/2441776.2441935

61. Zhou, R.: Time-lag and catching up: managing polysemic temporality in the context of immigration. In: Paulin, A.A., Anthopoulos, L.G., Reddick, C.G. (eds.) An Interdisciplinary Forum on Time and Globalization, Globalization Working Papers 12/3, Institute on Globalization and the Human Condition, Hamiltoh, pp. 6–10 (2012)

Designing Cyber-Physical Production Systems for Industrial Set-Up: A Practice-Centred Approach

Aparecido Fabiano Pinatti de Carvalho[1]([envelope]) [iD], Sven Hoffmann[1] [iD], Darwin Abele[2] [iD], Marcus Schweitzer[3] [iD], and Volker Wulf[1] [iD]

[1] Institute of Information Systems and New Media, University of Siegen, Siegen, Germany
fabiano.pinatti@uni-siegen.de
[2] Institute of Production Engineering, Industrial Science and Ergonomics,
University of Siegen, Siegen, Germany
[3] Siegen Institute of Small and Medium-Sized Companies,
University of Siegen, Siegen, Germany

Abstract. Industrial set-up has long been a focus of scientific research, largely because it entails substantial cost overhead for manufacturing companies. Whilst various efforts have been made to optimise this process, mainly in terms of time and other resources needed to accomplish it, to date little can be found in the HCI literature about how digital technologies can support workers who engage in it. This article sets out to addresses this gap in the literature by introducing a design case study carried out for the conception of a CPPS (Cyber-physical Production System) to support machine operators with industrial set-up. Our contribution is therefore threefold: first, we describe and discuss the results of an in-depth ethnographic study, carried out under the premises of the grounded design research paradigm, to uncover practices of machine operators to inform design. Second, we introduce a series of design implications drawn from those results. Finally, we demonstrate how those design implications have informed the participatory design activities pursued for the conception of the CPPS in question. In so doing, we advance the state of the art on the design of digital technologies to support people working with industrial set-up and open new research directions on the subject.

Keywords: Practice-centred design · Design case studies · Industrial contexts · Cyber-physical systems · Augmented-reality · Sensors · Design implications

1 Introduction

Industrial set-up refers to a set of preparatory actions on a machine or a tool prior to the start of a production cycle [1]. This is a core and time-critical operation in manufacture

Electronic supplementary material The online version of this chapter (https://doi.org/10.1007/978-3-030-85623-6_38) contains supplementary material, which is available to authorized users.

and in many cases without set-up there is no production. Therefore, supporting it is key to maximising efficient production and to address the challenges from the trend towards decreasing order/delivery sizes and increasing the range of produced artefacts [2, 3]. Furthermore, the resulting need for flexibility stemming from increasing globalization, customer expectation, intense competition, as well as short innovation and product life cycles faced by either large, small or medium-sized enterprises for many years now [4, 5] has direct implications for industrial set-up. On the one hand, there is a need to reduce resource allocation and, on the other hand, there is a demand for ever more flexible production cycles and ever more varied quality demands [6]. This need for flexibility ramifies at a worker level too, through the demand for flexible competences to handle heterogeneous set-up processes. This may entail being able to handle a large range of different products, use a variety of materials with varying degrees of acceptable tolerance, and all of this on a number of different machines. This leads to a variety of KES (Knowledge and Expertise Sharing) issues [7, 8], which can be potentially addressed by CPPS (Cyber-physical Production Systems) [3].

A review of the HCI literature demonstrate that little is known about how these systems can be designed to effectively support machine operators in industrial set-up [3, 4]. In view of the relevance of human-centred methods for the conception of systems that can effectively support users, this article aims to contribute towards filling or, at least, mitigating this gap. To fulfil our goals, we conducted an ethnographically informed investigation in four SMEs where the goals were to better understand the practices inherent in the set-up of bending machines and how CPPS could potentially support these practices. So, the research questions that this article sets out to answer are:

1. What challenges do machine operators face in practicing industrial set-up?
2. What HCI aspects must be considered in the design of CPPS, so that the resulting solution can successfully support machine operators to overcome the challenges they face in regard to industrial set-up?

Our study is oriented towards the GD (Grounded Design) research paradigm: a praxeological worldview, which highlights the importance of understanding practices for the design of useful and usable digital technologies [9]. This is a well-stablished paradigm for HCI research, increasingly being used by the community, rooted on a pragmatic approach to design research and predicated on clear scientific practices [9–11].

Our research questions are clearly informed by GD and go to the heart of HCI. The first research question focuses on understanding practices: according to GD, clearly understanding practices is key to identify the design space for the conception of new and innovative technologies that can effectively be used and appropriated. Designing useful and useable technologies is a central aspect of HCI since its very beginning [12–14].The second research question focuses specifically on identifying the HCI aspects that would contribute for the design of usable and useful CPPS to support machine operators. With this question we set out to investigate, among other things, aspects of the user interface and the interaction with it, seeking to advance the state of the art of the HCI literature in terms of designing CPPS for similar contexts and processes.

The presented findings are based on rich descriptions of the work processes involved in industrial set-up, shedding light on the practices of machine operators and the difficulties they face with such processes. They allowed us to elaborate a set-up model to unpack possible opportunities for the design of CPPS for industrial set-up. Hence, our contribution is threefold: (1) we present an in-depth user study in manufacturing contexts, which remains visibly under-addressed in HCI and CSCW, exploring the potential of CPPS to support machine operators in industrial set-up (Sect. 4); (2) we introduce a set of design implications, providing useful directions to follow when designing CPPS to support industrial set-up, drawing attention to important interaction challenges (Sect. 5); (3) we illustrate how those design implications can be applied in the design of a CPPS to support industrial set-up (Sect. 5).

2   Related Work

In this section we provide relevant background information regarding the concept of CPPS and reflect on how these systems can potentially support industrial set-up. We also examine current HCI und CSCW literature on KES, which we found to be a central aspect of industrial set-up and the challenges that machine operators face on a daily basis, as discussed in our empirical sections. It is worth noticing that this section is neither meant to cover all research studies on the subjects above, nor to deeply discuss the reviewed studies. Instead, this section is meant to setting the scene for the analytical developments of Sects. 4 and 5, which further elaborate on them.

2.1   Cyber-Physical Production Systems and Their Potential for Supporting Industrial Set-Up

CPPS consist of autonomous and cooperative elements and subsystems, e.g. Smart Machines and Smart Factories, which are connected to one another from the process level to the production level, depending on the situation or context [15]. Their characteristic features include the networking of various production components, such as machines or tools, as well as the data sets characterizing them [15, 16]. Concrete application examples of CPPS exist in both the industrial context and inter alia in aerospace, healthcare, civil infrastructure, logistics, military or defence, automotive, energy network and agriculture [17–19].

Lee et al. [20] introduce a structure and architecture for CPS (Cyber-Physical Systems) – and consequently CPPS, which are nothing else than CPS designed specifically for production contexts – starting with data collection, moving through analysis, up until final value creation. This architecture, according to the authors, should serve as a guideline for the implementation of such systems in the industry. These guidelines are supplemented by practical applications and techniques that underpin the theoretical architecture with practical implementation possibilities. Nevertheless, the design and development of useful and usable CPPS has proven to be challenging, which calls upon further research and development in the area.

Authors such as Lee [21], Monostori [15] and Paelke and Röcker [22] have discussed some of the challenges associated with the design and implementation of CPPS. These are usually described in terms of increased technical complexity, the need for new inter-action concepts that can consider the unpredictability of interaction between physical and the virtual worlds and the lack of prototyping and test tools. All of these challenges are relevant to HCI research and yet underexplored [23]. In particular, qualitative insights that explore contextual variation and the need for better tailoring of solutions are hard to find. In view of its relative novelty, this lack of research regarding CPPS is understand-able. However, this is likely to change within the next 10 to 15 years, as investment in Industry 4.0 from national governments begins to kick in [24]. Together with the poten-tial advantages of CPPS, e.g., enhanced productivity and flexible production systems [15, 22, 25], this trend underscores the timeliness and relevance of our own contribution.

2.2   The Social Nature of Knowledge and Its Relevance in Industrial Contexts

Knowledge is a socially constructed and often distributed asset, whose management is deemed an important strategic resource for companies and a source of competitive advantages in the market [7, 8, 26–30]. In CSCW, the focus on issues of knowledge has been rather more on the sharing than on the management of such an asset. CSCW researchers have long since been investigating those issues under manifold designa-tions, e.g., organisational memory, collective memory, collective intelligence, expertise location, etc. [7, 31] at least since the 1990s. All of these studies examine the role of information in organisational settings, concentrating on the social context and empha-sising communication amongst knowledgeable workers in contexts like safety critical environments and office environments [7].

The HCI literature has also touched upon the matter, particularly with regard to the design of digital visualisation technologies for KES. Burkhard and Meier [32], for instance, address issues of sharing by introducing two theoretical concepts for knowledge visualisation, based on the use of visual metaphors and knowledge maps. The authors discuss how visual metaphors are powerful for KES but yet underused in organisations. Their results demonstrate the usefulness of visual metaphors in motivating people to engage in knowledge exchanges and in supporting learning processes. In particular, the authors found visual metaphors to support the presentation of new perspectives, increase remembering, enhance the focus and concentration of the viewer, and structure and coordinate communication. Many other studies followed Burkhard and Meier's. However, most of them have focused on teaching and learning [e.g., 33, 34] or issues of information overload [see for instance 35], rather than on KES within organisational contexts. In manufacturing contexts, even less material has been produced.

The assumption that the primary issue in relation to KES lies in making the previously tacit somehow more explicit has been challenged within the HCI and CSCW [3, 7, 36]. Research on the field has shifted the emphasis to the social, processual and other contextual factors which may influence KES. This, effectively, can be thought of as a specific element of the 'turn to practice' which characterises much CSCW work. This re-emphasis is particularly important when the potentially transferable skills under examination are 'embodied', relying as it were on a 'feel' for things [3, 37].

3 Methodology

In this section, we provide an overview of our overall methodological approach. We will not delve into details here, as these are given in Sects. 4 and 5 ahead. We will also address the limitations of our methodology in turn, so that the readers can judge its *trustworthiness* and *authenticity*, in assessing the quality of this research [38].

For our own purposes, we have drawn on Wulf et al. [10]'s DCS (Design Case Study) framework for GD [9]. GD is a solid and well-established design research paradigm, which puts focus on practices for the understanding of issues of design and the quality of designed artefacts. DCS, on the other hand, is a research design for this paradigm. Case studies, which have its origins in the social sciences, have been consistently used across different disciplines (e.g., psychology, sociology, HCI, and CSCW) to investigate and shed light on assorted types of phenomena [39]. DSC is built around this socio-scientific tradition and is, therefore, of highly scientific relevance.

The framework is mainly organised in three phases. The first phase sets out to understand user practices that can potentially be supported by technological solutions. The second phase, and actual design of the technology, comprises traditional user-centred and participatory design methods – see e.g., [13, 40] – to build a socio-technical system concept. The final phase encompasses a longitudinal study to investigate and document the deployment and appropriation of designed technological artefacts in the users' social systems. This article's contributions are based on activities of the first two phases of the DCS framework, namely *pre-study* and *design*. In particular, we focus on the results of the shadowing, eye-tracking, in-depth interview, document analysis, scenario-based design, DW (Design Workshop) activities and high fidelity prototyping activities. It is worth pointing out that the design phase was not constrained to scenario-based design, DW and high-fidelity prototyping; medium-fidelity prototyping, heuristic evaluation [41], cooperative evaluation and lab usability test were also involved in this phase, as seen in Fig. 1, although these are not addressed in this article – therefore they are greyed out.

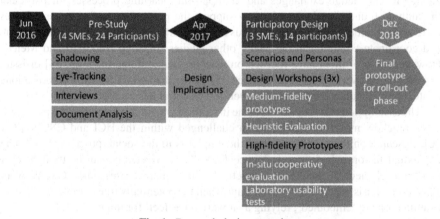

Fig. 1. Research design overview

Our pre-study consisted of an in-depth ethnographic study carried out over a period of 10 months (Jun 2016–April 2017). By the end of this phase, we devised a series of initial design implication for AR-based CPPS to support machine operators with KES concerning context-specific industrial set-up, as seen in Sect. 5. These design implications have been based on the machine operator practices and the challenges stemming from them, as introduced in Sect. 4 below.

The identified design implications informed the design activities of the second phase, which started with a series of DWs, carried out between April and August 2017. These workshops have been carried out with representative users, therefore, observing the premises of PD (Participatory Design) approaches, which entails the involvement of the participants in the design decisions across all the design phase [40]. The results of the workshops fed into the prototyping activities, which resulted in the design concepts presented across Sect. 5, as the design implications are discussed. The design phase activities extended until December 2018, as seen in Fig. 1.

4   Uncovering User Needs Concerning Industrial Set-Up Processes

In this section, we introduce our findings regarding machine operators' practices concerning industrial set-up and associated user needs stemming from it. These findings underpin the elaboration of a practice-centred model for industrial set-up as well as the design implications and envisaged solutions introduced across Sect. 5.

The case we examine involves the set-up of machines used to bend material like metal tubes. In order to produce different products, these machines must be equipped with different tools. Figure 2 shows the rough flow of the process, which is described in more detail across Sect. 4.1. Overall, the process starts with the machine being prepared for the process. This includes, for example, moving machine axes to certain set-up positions, so that parts can be removed and new ones can be installed. Subsequently, the necessary tools for the process must be found in the storage areas and organised in a desktop nearby the machine to be set up, therefore requiring certain logistics. The set-up process includes dismantling tools that were previously in the machine and assembling new ones for the manufacture of the new product. After the (dis)assembly operations, the production starts. As these machines are CNC (Computer Numerically Controlled), they must be configured through a variety of parameters. These parameters influence the efficiency and cost of the production by determining its cycle time and the quality of the product. An inspection establishes the quality and, if necessary, a new iteration cycle happens. For this purpose, the error pattern is viewed and the corresponding parameter is adjusted in the CNC code.

In order to understand the user needs regarding the process, we carried out a 10-month ethnographic study. Our study included investigations in 4 SMEs in 2 European countries. The main data collection instruments were: *shadowing,* for in situ data collection about the participants' work practices and the social system in which they unfold; *eye-tracking,* for detailed information about the steps involved in the process; and *in-depth semi-structured interviews,* to discuss design opportunities for a CPPS support and issues arising from the shadowing and eye-tracking data. Eye-tracking sessions were recorded with both the eye-tracker cameras and a stationary video camera, giving us micro and macro representations for post hoc analysis. The in-depth interviews were audio recorded and later transcribed. We performed a total of 14 shadowing sessions, with each session also featuring at least one eye-tracking session. Interactions observed before, during and after these sessions were documented through fieldnotes. A total of 24 in-depth interviews ranging from 45 to 120 min were performed.

Overall, 24 workers across the 4 SMEs participated in the study. Out of these, 7 were from company A; 13 from company B; 2 from company C; and 2 from company D. All companies are medium-sized and produce components for various customers. The age of the participants varied from 20 to 60. They occupied different roles in the companies, as for example foreman (n = 5), production engineer (n = 3), machine operator (n = 9), process owner, etc. They also had different educational backgrounds, for instance, graduated unspecialised (n = 2), graduated specialised (n = 6), masters specialised (n = 8) and job tenures (varying from 1 to 20 years of experience). This diverse group facilitates a better representation of the different stakeholders of the system [13].

We are aware that this is a relative small sample and that the findings of our study cannot be generalised. This is a widely acknowledged and accepted limitation of qualitative studies [39]. However, we have been careful to address issues of *trustworthiness* and *authenticity* [38] to assure the quality of our research. For that, we have used two strategies. First, we have used different data collection methods to allow for triangulation during the data analysis, i.e. cross-checking the consistency of the findings resulting from the data collected from these different methods [39]. Second, we have drawn on a systematic data analysis technique [42], to support us in the generation of the findings, as made clear below. The triangulation performed demonstrated consistency of the findings across the different data sources, reinforcing the trustworthiness and authenticity of the findings. This becomes visible when the findings coming from the pre-study interview presented in Sect. 4 are corroborated by the ones coming from the DW in Sect. 5.

The interview transcripts, fieldnotes and eye-tracking recordings were subjected to a TA (Thematic Analysis) according to Braun and Clarke approach [42], which entails a set of well-established steps involving open coding of the media excerpts, systematic revision of the coded segments and the identification of code-families and their relationships, to elaborate a deep understanding of the explored contexts and/or phenomenon. In relation to the eye-tracking material, we have gone through the videos recurrently, using the Tobii Pro Lab software and have also coded the relevant video excerpts. Information about the start and end time of the excerpt was recorded in a spreadsheet and assigned a referent code. Memos about the excerpt were also written to support posterior processing of the analysis.

The pre-study data sources were coded thoroughly. More than *70 codes* were identified and developed during this initial phase – e.g., *sequential execution of steps, expertise-based solutions, strategies to find answer to set-up problems*. These codes were further developed into themes, through careful analysis and characterisation of their relationships. *Four main themes* emerged from our analysis: (1) the workflow nature of industrial set-up; (2) the mixed relationship of dynamic and static elements with mechanic and non-mechanic operations; (3) the highly knowledge intensive character of the process; and the (4) potential challenges in interacting with any digital technology while working on it. We address each of these themes in turn in the next sub-sections and illustrate

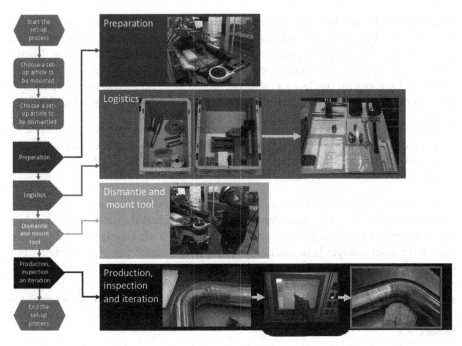

Fig. 2. Presentation of the general steps of a set-up process on a bending machine

them with quotes from our participants. The quotes are associated with the participants who provided them. We refer to the participants through the notation *(participant number, job position, company, data source)*, where data source refers to the data collection instrument that originated the quote – i.e., interview, shadowing, eye-tracking or DW.

4.1 A Workflow-Like Process

Our analysis of machine operators' practices concerning industrial set-up suggested that the process can be clustered in *6 interdependent* phases which resembles in many aspects a workflow. Based on the practices involved, we have named these phases as: *Preparation* (Phase 1), *Logistic* (Phase 2), *Tool and machine set-up* (Phase 3), *Production* (Phase 4), *Inspection* (Phase 5) and *Programme iteration* (Phase 6).

Workflows have been discussed in CSCW research as a sequence of subtasks in work processes that are carried out cooperatively. These subtasks are assigned to different workers, which contribute towards the accomplishment of a common goal. The route of the work is automatically defined as subtasks are completed and directed to the person responsible for the next subtask [43]. Like workflows, the industrial set-up can be split in several subtasks that will route the flow of work to the next subtask(s) upon their completion. Unlike workflows, these tasks are performed by the same worker and can happen in parallel with each other at times. This has important implications for the design of computer-aids to support it, as observable in Sect. 5. In the following, we discuss and illustrate each of the industrial set-up phases that we have identified through the analysis of our empirical data.

Preparation Phase. Our observations show that industrial set-up starts with preparation activities that specify the production process and are based on existing production resources, e.g., semi-finished products and machine and personnel availability. To efficiently carry out a set-up, machine operators need clear planning guidelines regarding the set-up to be carried out *"[...] so that you have a more rational and orderly set-up"* (P7, Operator, Comp. A, Interview). However, this is not always easily achieved:

> On the one hand, the stock must be minimised by making the production variable and carrying out many set-up operations. Conversely, it is important to keep the overall set-up times low by means of a small number of procedures. (P4, Production Engineer, Comp. A, Interview)

Hence, there is constant tension regarding how to respond to divergent production demands, which relates not only to the final product but also to the economics of production. We observed that participants would benefit from a working environment where there were fewer changes in production planning and therefore fewer interruptions. For the participants a lack of continuity is not just a disturbance, but is suboptimal. This results in time lost to both reconfiguring and restarting the process. Thus, the preparation phase includes a planning problem which should somehow be overcome, for example, by providing virtual process data to support planning decisions, as suggested in Sect. 5.2.

Logistic Phase. Parallel to all set-up phases, operators must deal with the logistics of the process, which refers mainly to bringing the tools and materials necessary to the set-up to the place where set-up will happen. Unsurprisingly, this is a critical step, which can potentially impact on the overall set-up time. If parts are not where they are expected to be, set-up time will increase [6, 44]. This is an issue concerning KES, as discussed in the design implication introduced in Sect. 5.4.

Even the most experienced operators have problems with logistics from time to time. Analysis of the eye-tracking records showed that logistic activities can account for up to 21% of the set-up time. In the course of the observations we noted, in particular, that additional paths followed during the set-up contributed to disturbances in an ordered set-up sequence. For instance, the set-up of the same machine, with the same tools, for the same product, by machine operators with comparable experience varied from 63 to 97 min (mean = 79 min). Closer analysis of the eye-tracking data also showed that the routes leading to increased set-up times could have been avoided if a clear assessment of logistic activities had happened at the beginning of the process. These aspects informed the elaboration of the design implication presented in Sect. 5.1.

Tool and Machine Set-Up Phase. In this phase, the necessary tools and machines components from the previous production order must be removed from the machine and the new ones should be assembled. Our observations showed that much of the set-up time was invested in this phase. Uncertainties here had a serious impact on the overall set-up time and it was not uncommon for workers to draw on the knowledge of their colleagues to solve particular problems. P5 (Operator, Comp. A, Interview), for instance says: *"if i cannot solve a problem, i can call at any time or use WhatsApp and then we do that in this way"*. Indeed, the relevance of experience-based knowledge for the tools and set-up phase was a strong feature of our fieldwork data from the outset. Although it has been acknowledged in the literature that set-up procedures are highly dependent on the skills of the workers on the shop floor [6, 45], so far this has not been appropriately explored. Our own data sheds light on this issue, drawing attention to the need for a system that can support seamless KES among workers, in particular those demanding particular know-how: *"Mounting the tools, every beginner with support would be able to do this. changing values and parameters is, in turn, a matter of experience."* (P7, Operator, Comp. A, Interview)

Hence, as the complexity of the mechanical activities increases, the know-how of the machine operators becomes decisive for a successful and efficient set-up. In principle, knowledge of the set-up process qualifies employees to perform these activities without further restrictions. As discussed in the next section, this raises relevant issues of KES, which are addressed in the design implication discussed in Sect. 5.4.

Overall, our findings suggest a need for instructions that generally represent the steps concerning the tool or machine set-up in question. This tool *"should actually have a representation of how the tool should be mounted on the machine"* (P6, Operator, Comp. A, Interview), so as to ensure that the set-up runs smoothly. This also relates to the implications in Sects. 5.2 and 5.3.

Production, Inspection and Programme Iteration Phase. These three remaining phases have been found to be seamlessly interleaved and, therefore, are presented together here. Overall, our analysis suggests that the production phase – when the arte-facts are really manufactured – does not present any special challenges with regard to time or content concerning set-up. The Inspection phase – where optical tests and tactile measurement are carried out in a test run component – did reveal some issues, however. In the course of the actual set-up, the verification of component quality plays a special role because the results of any tests have direct implications for the set-up itself and the subsequent programme iteration phase. *"If the part is not true to gauge, i must intervene in the process and change machine parameters."* (P1, Foreman, Comp. A, Interview).

Bending processes generally provide for a gauge test by the operator. The key thing about gauge tests is that geometrical deviations are directly recognised and converted into changes to the machine programming. This programme iteration phase can be described as success-critical. It is characterised by intensive parameter adjustments on the man–machine interface (MMI) as deviations in the manufactured product are spotted. These aspects connect directly with the design implications presented in Sects. 5.1 and 5.2, as will become observable.

4.2   Static and Yet Dynamic

Another relevant finding from our analysis is that industrial set-up involves both a static and a dynamic dimension, which have certain relationships with mechanical and non-mechanical set-up operations performed during it. Figure 3 introduces a model that we have elaborated out of the practices that we have observed in this regard. This model is organised into four abstracted areas of activity, concerning characteristics relating to the documentability and explicability of the set-up operations we have observed.

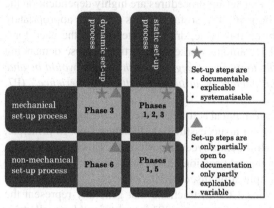

Fig. 3. Practice-based model for industrial set-up.

From our perspective, this model represents a relevant advancement in the understanding of industrial set-up. Existing models, like the SMED model proposed by Shingo [6], depicts a twofold process consisting of external and internal set-up operations, our findings suggest this is a limited way of seeing industrial set-up. Our findings suggest that set-up is far more complex than it has been depicted to date. Our model therefore provides a more nuanced treatment of the practices relating to set-up.

In principle, our findings showed that it is possible to distinguish between relatively constant, or repetitive, set-up operations (static) and highly variable set-up operations (dynamic). For instance, some of the findings previously introduced demonstrate how industrial set-up refers to a rational and orderly process, which can be carefully planned. During our triangulation activities, the eye-tracking and the observation data of the logical activities showed that the *Logistics* phase also displays characteristics of static operations, since tools and other components required for the set-up must be placed at defined locations in order to allow easy access and quick handling. The *Tool and machine set-up* phase also involves some static operations, for example dismantling tool and machine components, although some of the operations from this phase would better fit the dynamic aspect of the process.

With regard to the mechanical and non-mechanical characteristics of the process, our findings suggest that the mechanical part of the set-up includes mounting and disassembly, whereas the non-mechanical part contains interactions with the user interface of the machine – e.g., configuring the CNC code. As a matter of example, the *Preparation, Logistic* and *Tool and machine set-up* phases are characterised by mechanical operations, within which the machine operator has to do physical work to complete the set-up process. The *Preparation* and *Inspection* phases have some operations which do not involve any mechanical interaction.

In terms of the characteristics of the steps involved in industrial set-up, our findings suggest that some of them are documentable. In other words, there are steps within the set-up process that can be easily documented by virtue of their simple and quick explicability. In Nonaka et al.'s [46] words, these steps can be easily made explicit. From our own observations, these steps are also easily 'systematisable', for instance, by the use of checklists, as suggested by the SMED approach [6].

Despite the fact that many set-up steps are explicable, documentable and systematisable, *many of them are not*, either because the machine operators cannot always articulate the reasons for their actions or because the underlying set-up actions display high variability, as illustrated by previous findings. This is particularly the case with non-mechanical operations and mechanical operations related to the dynamic dimension of our model. An example of the former are manual adjustments of the machine programme and, of the latter, adjustment of the position of a tool on the machine axis. These issues have implications, as discussed in the Sect. 5.5.

4.3 Highly Dependent on Knowledge

The findings presented so far suggest that industrial set-up is a knowledge intensive process. The high proportion of knowledge intensive operations gives KES a decisive role here. Our analysis revealed a strong need to initiate KES among colleagues because expert knowledge lies within a very restricted cohort. Moreover, as contingencies arise in this context, the knowledge needed is held by relatively few [31, 47]:

> [...], there is just a lack of documentation so this mainly remains 'in the head' knowledge of the individual employees. If today three employees leave the company and tomorrow three new ones are hired, then a massive problem arises. (P4, Production Engineer, Comp. A , Interview)

This is particularly relevant for new employees, who often lack experience. However, the knowledge in question is both extensive and diverse, so conventional KES [7, 31, 48] is especially challenging:

> Even if everything has been shown [to you], you have to make your own experiences. There are many tricks that you do not immediately master. It is incredibly extensive what can happen there. These are many things that cannot be passed on. You can manage a large amount, but everything will never be passed on. (P5, Operator, Comp. A , Interview)

Furthermore, personal transmission of experience can become burdensome: *"Over time, that is exhausting. I had to explain every step what he should do."* (P14, Operator, Comp. B, Interview). There are two issues that contribute to this. First, as visible before, there is a systematic lack of documentation. Another is that the existing documentation is usually very abstract and often outdated. As a result, the existing documentation generally ends up not being used. Sharing knowledge and expertise emerged as a success-critical basis for allocation of resources – see implication for design in Sect. 5.2. If an effective system for KES were in place, *"I would not sit here and I would be released [to be working on something else]"* (P5, see earlier, Interview).

Nevertheless, such a system is not easy to devise. In general, various information formats are considered helpful: *"Visual and written information and also a video"* (P6, Operator, Comp. A, Interview). The persistence of embodied knowledge emerges as an important requirement for the tool: *"If you get help from the experienced co-workers, they make the changes and explain, but in the end, you look only and then you forget at some point"* (P6, see earlier, Interview). This relates directly to the fact that experience-based knowledge is mostly of the embodied kind [3]. In other words, much of the understanding of how to handle particular parts of the process only becomes visible when it is observed in action. This is difficult to convey [29, 48]. Such difficulties call for innovative ways to record and visualise this type of knowledge. CPPS, it has been claimed, is about to result in a revolution in the way that knowledge and expertise can be shared, by providing ways to conveniently capture and display knowledge embodied in action [3], without the need to translate this knowledge into propositional knowledge, the driving approach in industrial and organisational management [46], as discussed in the design implication introduced in Sect. 5.1.

4.4 Interaction Challenges in Industrial Contexts

Set-up processes take place in real production environment contexts. Requirements for the design and development of a system support to help machine operators, need to take into account the realities of these kinds of physical environments. For instance, both our observations and interviews stressed the fact that operators must have *"both hands"* (P10, Operator, Comp. B, Interview) available to carry out set-up work. Moreover, we have observed that the workspace where industrial set-up unfolds is very limited, *"due to the large number of tools and tools combined with limited storage space, we always have a problem with space"* (P5, Operator, Comp. A, Interview). Last but not least, *"dirt and noise"* (P10, see earlier, Interview) must also be taken into consideration. One the one hand, the system must be sturdy enough to take on eventual accidents without breaking: *"You need to have something you can work with. If it falls off, don't break it"* (P11, Operator, Comp. B, Interview). Conversely, the environmental noise must not interfere on its functioning or in the interaction with it, as observed in our fieldwork, meaning that voice commands, at least in the current stage of the art, would be an unfeasible mechanism to interact with the envisioned technology. These aspects have informed the elaboration of the design implication discussed in Sect. 5.6.

5 Designing CPPS to Support Industrial Set-Up

As previously mentioned, the findings from our pre-study led to the identification of a series of design implications for the design of CPPS to assist machine operators with industrial set-up. These implications had mainly to do with the six identified phases of the set-up process that have been elaborated out of the understanding of the machine operator practices concerning the process. We brought these implications to the attention of our fieldwork participants in a series of DWs, discussing with participants the extent to what the identified implications would correspond to their needs and expectations. In these workshops, potential technologies that could be used to address those requirements have also been discussed. The results from these activities have ultimately led to the design solutions that we introduce and thoroughly discuss in the course of this section.

In total, 3 DWs have been carried out – 1 with participants from Comp. A, 1 with participants from company B and, 1 with participants from Comp. C. Identified requirements have been introduced to participants by means of scenarios and personas, following a scenario-based approach to design [49]. DWs lasted from 4 to 8 h. Around 6 participants were involved in each of them. Most participants in the DWs had also participated in the pre-study, and therefore could confirm or disconfirm our interpretation of the data. DWs have been audio recorded. The audios have been transcribed and also submitted to TA, as the pre-study data, i.e., code categories have been identified and revised and the relationship between those categories have been explored elaborated and formalised in themes [42].

In summary, *6 themes* have been identified in terms of implications for design, namely: (1) use of sensors to collect real data; (2) use of digital simulations in situations there is no real data available; (3) support for aggregation digital data to work practices; (4) support for KES; (5) support for data configuration; (6) provision of feasible inter-action in industrial contexts. These themes are not only based on the data analysis of the DW data, but also on the pre-study data.

Interestingly enough, the identified themes resonated to a large extent to with Lee et al.'s 5-level architecture for the design of CPS, introduced in our related work section [20]. Nevertheless, our findings extend Lee et al.'s architecture, as Lee et al.'s architecture concentrates solely on the technical aspects and does not engage with the socio-technical aspects of the design and the affordance of creating an environment in which KES processes can take place. The following sub-section details how these 6 design implications can extend Lee et al.'s 5-level architecture for the design of CPS and what they meant for our design decisions [20].

5.1   Use Sensors to Collect Real Set-Up Process Data for Subsequent Use

Our findings suggest that contextual information relevant to the process is something that can be captured, combined and prepared using a CPPS that draws on human practices or technical sensor technology. This somehow relates to Lee et al.'s smart connected level of CPPS [20]. Appropriate sensor technology could be implemented through different identification systems, like barcodes or RFID systems [50] and connected to the CPPS. In so doing, the system would be able to support machine operators with operations from phases 1 and 2 introduced before:

> The Holo-Lens would be connected via the W-LAN. That means I can access everything that is available via W-LAN, i.e., if we have such a reader for an RFID chip that we can access via the network. (P23, Comp. B, DW2)

This design implication led to a series of design decisions for the AR-based CPPS elaborated during the participatory activities carried out during the design phase of our DCS. Figure 4 illustrate how this have been implemented in practice.

In summary, for logistic activities, sensor technologies have been employed. Sensor technologies can play an important role in recording paths and providing data for sub-sequent optimisation (see Fig. 4[b]). As evident in the quote below, this sort of tracking would be a relevant aid in optimising the time used for the set-up process:

> From the methodological point of view this is a typical SMED procedure [...] (T)here is a so-called spaghetti diagram where the paths covered by setter during this set-up process are shown. (P25, Comp. B, DW2)

In addition to that, machine operators can be assisted in unambiguously identifying the tools as well as in determining their position on the machine axis by selecting the tools through sensor-based recognition (see Fig. 4[a]). Not only that, by means of sensor technology, local knowledge embodied in action can potentially be recorded in videos and shared (see Fig. 4[c]). In other words, sensor technology has the potential to show product-specific characteristics to workers in real time, enabling context-sensitive dispositions, so to avoid wasting time and other resources in the accomplishment of the set-up process.

Real machine data can also be beneficial if individual values can be assigned to a quality image of the article. This speaks directly to user needs that were captured in phases 5 and 6. Furthermore, there is a need to share knowledge about the machine settings that could be used for different situations, i.e., the knowledge about the different parameters that can be defined for each tool axis, which describe the geometry of the article to be manufactured and the procedural. Capturing and sharing this knowledge in a contextualised way can offer a significant added value for other operators in the course of the dynamic set-up process.

Fig. 4. First level: Sensory check of the size and position of the mounted tools [a], the recording of the set-up paths [b] and the video recording of the set-up interaction [c]

5.2   Provide Virtual Process Data to Support Decisions in Situations Where Real Process Data is not Available

The results we have presented across this article implies that CPPS should not only be consisted of real data, but should also be enriched with virtual data, as for example, by blending 3D holograms with the real machines as demonstrated in Fig. 5[a], or by providing simulation data as seen in Fig. 5[b]. This resonates with Lee et al.'s *Conversion* level of CPPS architecture, which suggests that CPPS should generate smart analytics for machine component health, multidimensional data correlation and degradation and performance prediction. Phase 3 introduces requirements for a virtual confirmation of the assembly process.

In this case, a virtual construction environment can potentially circumscribe this activity [51, 52]. Separately, the assembly process must be free of collisions. This can be ensured through virtual kinematic simulations in the preparation phase and with the help of AR visualisations on the real machine during the set-up process (Fig. 5[a]). In addition to that, phase 6 presents an even more complex requirement for virtual data concerning the configuration of the machine parameters. Hence, virtual production data, which considers the material reactions of the semi-finished products in detail, can offer some added value, because the settings can be derived in advance of the real set-up process. At the same time, the need for specific settings can be clarified by means of material stress parameters (Fig. 5[b]). Here an operator can interpret the colour coding of the places with the highest stress and introducing specific countermeasures, locating the exact position of maximum load and tracing it back to a tool movement with the aid of the diagram.

The virtual generation of process data, then, can allow for the translation of certain aspects of local knowledge into propositional content, to be used during the performance of actual mechanical processes. This virtual data can potentially complement the real data generated by the use of sensors.

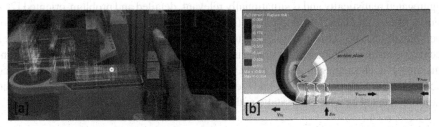

Fig. 5. Second level: The recording of the virtual set-up interaction [a], the generation of virtual process data by means of an FEM simulation [b]

5.3 Supporting Human-Centred Aggregation of Data

From our results, it is relevant to support a human-centred aggregation of data, or in other words the aggregation of experience-based knowledge 'owned' by workers. Put differently, data has to provide an added value for KES:

> If I first use this system to create a kind of story book for the set-up process, to link individual data to a manual and then afterwards have the possibility to move or change this data again in a different order in my office, then from my point of view I have all the possibilities I need to create a knowledge base. (P25, see earlier, DW2)

However, this is limited by the capacity of people to recall all of the specific details [8, 53]. For instance, the demands from phases 1 and 2 represent the need for data aggregation in the form of (primarily) master data about an article and its associated tools. The master data serves as a cornerstone of an article to be produced. Likewise, they form the foundation for their digital representation [54]. This resonates with the third level of Lee et al.'s architecture for CPPS, which has to to do with a *Cyber* level where twin models for components and machines are generated and managed. The twin model is a virtual representation of the real machine and describes the behavior of the machine in the virtual world.

Our results also indicate that a set-up operation can benefit from a digital representation of the haptic aspects of the process (see Fig. 3 'static set-up process') as well as essential data for the machine's adjustment (see Fig. 3 'dynamic set-up process').

> If I have the 6 different positions in front of me [where I can assembly a tool] in the machine, the HoloLens must show me the position with a virtual representation

of the tools. In addition, information about the assembly is stored in a window above the machine. All information must be directly visible when looking at the machine, but must not obscure the assembly location. (P31, Comp. C, DW3)

Figure 6[a] and [b] show the implementation. The data recorded on the lower two levels are assigned to a set-up step and saved afterwards. The virtual data is stored in an AR animation of the set-up interaction and machine data is visualised on a dashboard. However, the data only adds value for a learning-friendly environment if it is aggregated realistically and is situationally relevant, detailed and problem-oriented [20]. Furthermore, the data must come directly from the production process. A reduction of complexity can be achieved: by a) ensuring the provision of the data takes place in a context-sensitive fashion and b) that it is directed to support key elements of decision-making [19]. The aggregation of real and virtual data and their representation in embodied action and through propositional knowledge correlate strongly with the mechanical and non-mechanical as well as the static and dynamic set-up components.

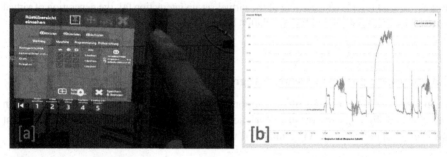

Fig. 6. Third level: The storage of the recorded set-up data in the HoloLens [a], the visualisation of the machine data [b]

5.4   Support Knowledge and Expertise Sharing (KES)

Integrated simulation, connected systems, remote visualisation for human and collaborative diagnostic and decision making are some issues addressed by the fourth level of Lee et al.'s [20] CPS architecture, namely *Cognition* level. Not surprisingly, the long-term storage of knowledge and the individual and independent accessibility of multimedia content is an important advantage in an industrial environment [30, 55–57]. This has been extensively discussed within the CSCW and HCI literature, which has been investigating OM (Organisational Memory) and KES issues since the early 1990s [7].

As discussed across Sect. 4, some critical operations of the set-up process are intensively influenced by experience-based knowledge. Nevertheless, we have observed that written documentation is fragmentary, not up-to-date and does not capture the necessary level of detail:

I think it would be cool if we could manage to get the mediation that you can say, I get for the respective tools that I want to install now, with which torque they theoretically have to be tightened and which screws, for example, or all of which must be used for this tool. That I really only have to grab my belt and I have everything I need. I also know with which pretension. (P23, see earlier, DW2)

Advanced systems have significant potential to support the contextuality information
[22]. De Carvalho et al. [3] introduces a discussion about how CPPS can support KES
by allowing new ways to convey information
embedded in embodied action. We have further
pursued the authors' initial ideas and have made
it concrete in the technological aid that we put
together to support machine operators in carrying out machine set-up. Figure 7 shows the visualisation of the set-up interaction, which was
recorded on the second level of the CPS archi-

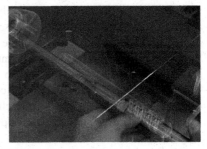

Fig. 7. Fourth level: The replay of the recorded set-up data

tecture and now is aggregated on the fourth level to a complete set-up instruction, using an AR visualisation. On the basis of this interactive instruction, set-up information is available independently of people's availability and a KES can take place on the basis of the recorded and visualised set-up information.

5.5 Support Knowledge and Data Configuration

The findings concerning the phase 1 stress the importance of standardised processes and therefore the need to provide interactive checklists according to well-defined and clear foundations in order to avoid failures. During the DWs, it was made clear that for supporting machine operators with their daily set-up activities, the system has to be able to access databases that contain logistic real-time information with regard to the name, storage location and condition of the respective target object:

So, there are databases for certain things and links for certain things, so I know which tools are necessary for this article [...] it would make sense for our set-up editor to continue thinking in databases, i.e., we create a complex tool database. (P7, Operator, Comp. A, DW1)

In a second step, users can potentially interact with the system by confirming or verifying physical availability as well as the target state of the target object. Moreover, by such means, users can be guided step-by-step through the working task and receive multimedia support in terms of texts, pictures and videos [58]:

If I can see a 3D model, then that is certainly not bad. Additionally, it can be enhanced with pictures and videos. With this data a standard set-up instruction can be created [...] probably not perfect yet [...] Because at the beginning the experience knowledge is not there yet, it is only built up with time. (P33, Comp. C, DW3)

The observations above resonates with the fifth Lee et al.'s [20] architecture for CPPS, namely *Configuration* level. Iterative approaches where machine operators evaluate a best practice, then modify accompanying processes such as logistic tasks, influence the actual set-up tasks. Although, some mechanical set-up operations are static, it is possible that there will be an impact on the handling processes as well. Existing set-up instructions need to offer adaption options for these changes.

This implication resonates with the realisation that frameworks, which actively support learning processes of the worker, must adapt to innovations and changes [5]. Overall, then, any support system will need to meet these requirements. In particular, changes in set-up order need to be developed cooperatively and, if appropriate, through actual interaction. For this purpose, a tablet client, which can adjust the aggregated set-up data by changing the sequence of the set-up steps, was implemented (see Fig. 8).

5.6   Provide Feasible Interaction Mechanisms for the Manufacturing Context

A final implication for design that we have identified concerns a vertical level that permeates all other 5 levels of Lee et al.' [20] architecture: it concerns the interaction challenges faced in the everyday life activities of machine operators. These challenges mainly emerge from the interactions between users and the system in the environment where the system is deployed:

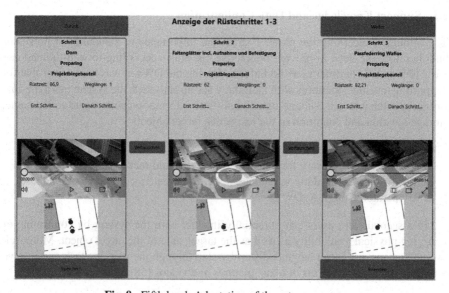

Fig. 8. Fifth level: Adaptation of the set-up process

[…] weight of the glasses, […] the wearing comfort [should be] there. The recording quality of the videos has to be good, that you don't have to focus so exactly on the window, but that you can move freely. The same with the sound quality.

When I record something, I want to make sure that it is of the appropriate quality, that the background noise is not so present and that you can understand what the colleague is saying [...] (P30, Comp. C, DW3)

In more detail, these challenges encompass: 1) allowing the machine operator to operate hands-free; 2) local, mobile and decentralised access to information because of the manual reconfiguration processes which are performed directly at the machine; 3) recognising the limited working space around the machine. Therefore, the central ergonomic design aspects of the CPPS should be oriented to the principle that the interaction of the machine operator will not be affected negatively during the whole process. The aim is not to achieve the simplest possible interaction, but rather to sensitively adapt the complexity to the field of application [59]. Moreover, the support system should support shift work, which is pervasive in industrial settings. Thus, the CPPS needs to facilitate communication regarding KES between the separate steps, firstly, to offset temporal variability, and secondly, to provide teaching and training material. These requirements cannot be limited to specific phases, but they are essential for all phases of the set-up process. For the reasons listed here, we decided to use AR-visualisation with the help of Microsoft HoloLens. The set-up instructions, as described above, are recorded and also played back with the HoloLens. In addition, the HoloLens serves as a sensor for recording the set-up paths. The main advantage of using the HoloLens is the gesture-based interaction and the visibility of the set-up information – independent of the position of the set-up person – spatially adapted to the real machine.

6 Conclusion

This article introduces a series of timely and relevant contributions to the HCI research. Timely because they refer to the design of CPSS, a type of system that has been receiving increasingly attention of the community and the market, but has not yet been fully explored in the HCI literature, especially because only recently it has been proposed as a solid concept to be explored in design [15, 60]; relevant, because they address a context not yet widely explored in HCI (manufacturing contexts) and introduce findings shedding light on how these systems should be designed, in order to be useful and usable and to fit to users practices. These three last aspects are key for system acceptability and appropriation, as discussed extensively in the literature [10].

In answering our first research question, we have demonstrated that industrial set-up is a knowledge intensive process involving an ecology of practices that make it really challenging. Our findings certainly overlap with other CSCW studies on KES, as for instance the case of sharing knowledge about technical questions in organisations [31, 47] or about medical diagnosis and care activities in medical settings [61, 62]. Nevertheless, our findings point towards a case of knowledge concentrated in the hands – or the heads, if one will – of very few actors, where the 'social distribution of expertise' is of a highly concentrated kind. Different from Bardram and Bossen [61], who discuss how medical and care knowledge was distributed across different actors and its implication for mobility work, our case reports on a small number of experienced machine operators that hold important knowledge concerning the set-up of the varied machines.

The manufacturing context explored also has its particularities, as demonstrated by our findings, as has the addressed process, i.e., industrial set-up. All those elements sum to the novelty of our contribution. Furthermore, our implications for CPPS, which have not yet been extensively explored for KES [3], provide us with opportunities to advance the state of the art.

In terms of our second research question, our findings suggest that CPPS should be able to capture and support both the static and dynamic dimensions of set-up, ultimately leading to more effective KES by the machine operators. The use of sensors can potentially support operators in capturing different set-up scenarios that can then be learnt from down the line. Furthermore, the subdivision into processual knowledge which is represented by embodied action, as well as the presence of propositional knowledge can be reflected in the representation. While the static and mechanical set-up process is primarily characterized by embodied action components, the dynamic and non-mechanical set-up process is characterized by propositional knowledge components. Furthermore, as discussed by de Carvalho et al. [3], CPPS can support effective KES by providing new ways to capture, process and visualize relevant knowledge that can potentially trigger improvements in the process.

All in all, the findings regarding manufacturing contexts (e.g., re. noise in the environment) can potentially be transferred to other similar contexts (e.g., construction contexts). The same applies for the findings concerning processes which are workflow like and demand the use of both hands to be accomplished. The observations and the solutions herein presented can, we argue, inspire other design solutions or even sparkle new HCI research.

Acknowledgements. The findings presented in the article have been generated as part of the Cyberrüsten 4.0 project funded by the European Union and EFRE.NRW through the grant EFRE-0800263. We are thankful for the financial support. We are also thankful to Professor M. Diaz Perez for her valuable comments and improvement suggestions on previous versions of this article.

References

1. Palanisamy, S., Siddiqui, S.: Changeover time reduction and productivity improvement by integrating conventional SMED method with implementation of MES for better production planning and control. Int. J. Innov. Res. Sci. Eng. Technol. (An ISO Certif. Organ.) **3297**, 7961–7974 (2007)
2. Van Goubergen, D., Van Landeghem, H.: Rules for integrating fast changeover capabilities into new equipment design. In: Robotics and Computer-Integrated Manufacturing, pp. 205–214 (2002). https://doi.org/10.1016/S0736-5845(02)00011-X
3. de Carvalho, A.F.P., et al.: Of embodied action and sensors: knowledge and expertise sharing in industrial set-up. Comput. Supp. Cooperat. Work (CSCW) **27**(3–6), 875–916 (2018). https://doi.org/10.1007/s10606-018-9320-6
4. Hoffmann, S., de Carvalho, A.F.P., Abele, D., Schweitzer, M., Tolmie, P., Wulf, V.: Cyberphysical systems for knowledge and expertise sharing in manufacturing contexts: towards a model enabling design. Comput. Support. Cooperat. Work (CSCW) **28**(3–4), 469–509 (2019). https://doi.org/10.1007/s10606-019-09355-y

5. Vicente, K.J.: HCI in the global knowledge-based economy: designing to support worker adaptation. ACM Trans. Comput. Interact. **7**, 263–280 (2000). https://doi.org/10.1145/353 485.353489

6. Shingo, S.: A Revolution in Manufacturing: The SMED System. CRC Press (1985)

7. Ackerman, M.S., Dachtera, J., Pipek, V., Wulf, V.: Sharing knowledge and expertise: the CSCW view of knowledge management. Comput. Support. Cooperat. Work (CSCW) **22**(4–6), 531–573 (2013). https://doi.org/10.1007/s10606-013-9192-8

8. Argote, L., Ingram, P., Levine, J.M., Moreland, R.L.: Knowledge transfer in organizations: learning from the experience of others. Organ. Behav. Hum. Decis. Process. **82**, 1–8 (2000). https://doi.org/10.1006/obhd.2000.2883

9. Rohde, M., Brödner, P., Stevens, G., Betz, M., Wulf, V.: Grounded design – a praxeological IS research perspective. J. Inf. Technol. **32**, 163–179 (2017). https://doi.org/10.1057/jit.2016.5

10. Wulf, V., Müller, C., Pipek, V., Randall, D., Rohde, M., Stevens, G.: Practice-Based Computing: Empirically Grounded Conceptualizations Derived from Design Case Studies. In: Wulf, V., Schmidt, K., Randall, D. (eds.) Designing Socially Embedded Technologies in the Real-World. CSCW, pp. 111–150. Springer, London (2015). https://doi.org/10.1007/978-1-4471-6720-4_7

11. Wulf, V., Pipek, V., Randall, D., Rohde, M., Schmidt, K., Stevens, G.: Socio-Informatics: A Practice-based Perspective on the Design and Use of IT Artifacts. Oxford University Press, Oxford (2018)

12. Harper, R., Rodden, T., Rogers, Y., Sellen, A.: Being Human: Human-Computer Interaction in the year 2020. Microsoft Research Ltda, England (2008)

13. Sharp, H., Rogers, Y., Preece, J.: Interaction Design: Beyond Human-Computer Interaction. John Wiley & Sons, West Sussex (2006)

14. Benyon, D.: Designing Interactive Systems: A Comprehensive Guide to HCI and Interaction Design. Addison Wesley (2010)

15. Monostori, L.: Cyber-physical production systems: roots, expectations and R&D challenges. In: Procedia CIRP, pp. 9–13. Elsevier B.V. (2014). https://doi.org/10.1016/j.procir.2014.03.115

16. Marcus, A.: Design, user experience, and usability: design discourse. In: Marcus, A. (ed.) 4th International Conference, Design, user experience, and usability: Design discourse DUXU 2015 Held as Part of HCI International 2015 Los Angeles, CA, USA, August 2-7, 2015 proceedings, Part I. LNCS, pp. 75–85. Springer International Publishing, Cham (2015). https://doi.org/10.1007/978-3-319-20886-2

17. Baheti, R., Gill, H.: Cyber-Physical Systems: From Theory to Practice (2011). https://doi.org/10.1145/1795194.1795205

18. Rajkumar, R.: A Cyber Physical Future. Proc. IEEE. **100**, 1309–1312 (2012). https://doi.org/10.1109/JPROC.2012.2189915

19. Schuh, G., Gartzen, T., Rodenhauser, T., Marks, A.: Promoting work-based learning through industry 4.0. Procedia CIRP. **32**, 82–87 (2015). https://doi.org/10.1016/j.procir.2015.02.213

20. Lee, J., Bagheri, B., Kao, H.-A.: A Cyber-Physical Systems architecture for Industry 4.0-based manufacturing systems. Manuf. Lett. **3**, 18–23 (2015). https://doi.org/10.1016/j.mfglet.2014.12.001

21. Lee, E.A.: Cyber physical systems: design challenges. In: 11th IEEE Int. Symp. Object Oriented Real-Time Distrib. Comput. 10 (2008). https://doi.org/10.1109/ISORC.2008.25

22. Paelke, V., Röcker, C.: User interfaces for cyber-physical systems: challenges and possible approaches. In: Marcus, Aaron (ed.) DUXU 2015. LNCS, vol. 9186, pp. 75–85. Springer, Cham (2015). https://doi.org/10.1007/978-3-319-20886-2_8

23. Schuh, G., Potente, T., Wesch-Potente, C., Weber, A.R., Prote, J.-P.: Collaboration mechanisms to increase productivity in the context of industrie 4.0. Procedia CIRP **19**, 51–56 (2014). https://doi.org/10.1016/j.procir.2014.05.016

24. Kagermann, H., Wahlster, W., Helbig, J.: Recommendations for implementing the strategic initiative INDUSTRIE 4.0. Final Rep. Ind. 4.0 WG. **82** (2013). https://doi.org/10.13140/RG. 2.1.1205.8966
25. Post, T., Ilsen, R., Hamann, B., Hagen, H., Aurich, J.C.: User-guided visual analysis of cyber-physical production systems. J. Comput. Inf. Sci. Eng. **17** (2017). https://doi.org/10.1115/1. 4034872
26. Grant, R.M.: Toward a knowledge-based theory of the firm. Strateg. Manag. J. **17**, 109–122 (1996). https://doi.org/10.1002/smj.4250171110
27. Grant, R.M., Baden-Fuller, C.: A knowledge accessing theory of strategic alliances. J. Manag. Stud. **41**, 61–84 (2004). https://doi.org/10.1111/j.1467-6486.2004.00421.x
28. Levin, D.Z.: Organizational learning and the transfer of knowledge: an investigation of quality improvement. Organ. Sci. **11**, 630–647 (2000). https://doi.org/10.1287/orsc.11.6.630.12535
29. Spender, J.-C.: Making knowledge the basis of a dynamic theory of the firm. Strateg. Manag. J. **17**, 45–62 (1996). https://doi.org/10.1002/smj.4250171106
30. Watson, S., Hewett, K.: A multi-theoretical model of knowledge transfer in organizations: determinants of knowledge contribution and knowledge reuse. J. Manag. Stud. **43**, 141–173 (2006). https://doi.org/10.1111/j.1467-6486.2006.00586.x
31. Randall, D., O'Brien, J., Rouncefield, M., Hughes, J.A.: Organisational memory and CSCW: supporting the "Mavis Phenomenon." In: Proceedings Sixth Australian Conference on Computer-Human Interaction, pp. 26–33. IEEE Computer. Soc. Press (1996). https://doi. org/10.1109/OZCHI.1996.559984
32. Burkhard, R.A., Meier, M.: Tube map visualization: evaluation of a novel knowledge visualization application for the transfer of knowledge in long-term projects. J. Ucs. **11**, 473–494 (2005). citeulike-article-id:4469994
33. Patterson, R.E., et al.: A human cognition framework for information visualization. Comput. Graph. **42**, 42–58 (2014). https://doi.org/10.1016/j.cag.2014.03.002
34. Keller, T., Tergan, S.-O.: Visualizing Knowledge and Information: An Introduction. In: Tergan, S.-O., Keller, T. (eds.) Knowledge and Information Visualization. LNCS, vol. 3426, pp. 1–23. Springer, Heidelberg (2005). https://doi.org/10.1007/11510154_1
35. Mengis, J., Eppler, M.J.: Visualizing instead of overloading: exploring the promise and problems of visual communication to reduce information overload. In: Information Overload, pp. 203–229. John Wiley & Sons, Inc., Hoboken, NJ, USA (2012). https://doi.org/10.1002/ 9781118360491.ch10
36. Schmidt, K.: The trouble with "tacit knowledge." Comput. Support. Coop. Work. **21**, 163–225 (2012). https://doi.org/10.1007/s10606-012-9160-8
37. Clarke, K., et al.: Dependable red hot action. In: Proceedings of the 2003 European CSCW Conference (ECSCW '03). pp. 14–18 (2003)
38. Guba, E.G.: Criteria for assessing the trustworthiness of naturalistic inquiries. ECTJ. **29**, 75–91 (1981)
39. Bryman, A.: Social Research Methods. Oxford University Press, New York (2008)
40. Muller, M.J., Kuhn, S.: Participatory design. Commun. ACM. **36**, 24–28 (1993). https://doi. org/10.1145/153571.255960
41. Nielsen, J., Molich, R.: Heuristic Evaluation of User Interfaces (1990). https://doi.org/10. 1145/97243.97281
42. Braun, V., Clarke, V.: Thematic analysis. APA Handb. Res. methods Psychol. Vol 2 Res. Des. Quant. Qual. Neuropsychol. Biol. **2**, 57–71 (2012). https://doi.org/10.1037/13620-004
43. Poltrock, S., Grudin, J.: CSCW, Groupware and Workflow: Experiences, State of Art, and Future Trends. In: Howard, S., Hammond, J., Lindgaard, G. (eds.) Human-Computer Interaction INTERACT '97. ITIFIP, pp. 661–662. Springer, Boston, MA (1997). https://doi.org/ 10.1007/978-0-387-35175-9_121

44. MacKelprang, A.W., Nair, A.: Relationship between just-in-time manufacturing practices and performance: a meta-analytic investigation. J. Oper. Manag. **28**, 283–302 (2010). https://doi.org/10.1016/j.jom.2009.10.002

45. Van Goubergen, D., Lockhart, T.E.: Human Factors Aspects in Set-Up Time Reduction. In: Zülch, G., Jagdev, H.S., Stock, P. (eds.) Integrating Human Aspects in Production Management. IICIP, vol. 160, pp. 127–135. Springer, Boston, MA (2005). https://doi.org/10.1007/0-387-23078-5_10

46. Nonaka, I., Toyama, R., Konno, N.: SECI, Ba and leadership: a unified model of dynamic knowledge creation. Long Range Plann. **33**, 5–34 (2000). https://doi.org/10.1016/S0024-6301(99)00115-6

47. Ackerman, M.S.: Augmenting organizational memory: a field study of answer garden. ACM Trans. Inf. Syst. **16**, 203–224 (1998). https://doi.org/10.1145/290159.290160

48. Nonaka, I.: The Knowledge-Creating Company. Harvard Business Review Classics, Brighton, MA, USA, MA, USA (1991)

49. Carroll, J.M.: Five reasons for scenario-based design. Interact. Comput. **13**, 43–60 (2000). doi:10.1016/S0953-5438(00)00023-0

50. Finkenzeller, K., Waddington, R.: RFID Handbook: Fundamentals and Applications in Contactless Smart Cards and Identification. Wiley (2003). doi:10.1002/9780470665121

51. Altintas, Y., Brecher, C., Weck, M., Witt, S.: Virtual machine tool. CIRP Ann. **54**, 115–138 (2005). https://doi.org/10.1016/S0007-8506(07)60022-5

52. Jönsson, A., Wall, J., Broman, G.: A virtual machine concept for real-time simulation of machine tool dynamics. Int. J. Mach. Tools Manuf. **45**, 795–801 (2005). https://doi.org/10.1016/J.IJMACHTOOLS.2004.11.012

53. Sweller, J.: Cognitive load theory, learning difficulty, and instructional design. Learn. Instr. **4**, 295–312 (1994). https://doi.org/10.1016/0959-4752(94)90003-5

54. Tantik, E., Anderl, R.: Industrie 4.0: Using cyber-physical systems for value-stream based production evaluation. Procedia CIRP. **57**, 207–212 (2016). https://doi.org/10.1016/j.procir.2016.11.036

55. Caudell, T.P., Mizell, D.W.: Augmented reality: an application of heads-up display technology to manual manufacturing processes. In: Proceedings of the Twenty-Fifth Hawaii International Conference on System Sciences, vol. 2, pp. 659–669. IEEE (1992). https://doi.org/10.1109/HICSS.1992.183317

56. Goh, S.C.: Managing effective knowledge transfer: an integrative framework and some practice implications. J. Knowl. Manag. **6**, 18–35 (2001)

57. Roberts, J.: From know-how to show-how? Questioning the role of information and communication technologies in knowledge transfer. Technol. Anal. Strateg. Manag. **12**, 429–443 (2000). https://doi.org/10.1080/713698499

58. Fillatreau, P., Fourquet, J.Y., Le Bolloc'H, R., Cailhol, S., Datas, A., Puel, B.: Using virtual reality and 3D industrial numerical models for immersive interactive checklists. Comput. Ind. **64**, 1253–1262 (2013). https://doi.org/10.1016/j.compind.2013.03.018

59. Janlert, L.-E., Stolterman, E.: Complex interaction. ACM Trans. Comput. Interact. **17**, 1–32 (2010). https://doi.org/10.1145/1746259.1746262

60. Lee, J., Bagheri, B., Kao, H.: Recent advances and trends of cyber-physical systems and big data analytics in industrial informatics. In: Int. Proceeding Int Conf. Ind. Informatics. (2014). https://doi.org/10.13140/2.1.1464.1920

61. Bardram, J., Bossen, C.: Mobility work: The spatial dimension of collaboration at a hospital. Comput. Support. Coop. Work CSCW An Int. J. **14**, 131–160 (2005). https://doi.org/10.1007/s10606-005-0989-y

62. Strauss, A., Fargerhaugh, S., Suczek, B., Wiener, C.: Social Organisation of Medical Work. University of Chicago Press, Chicago & London (1985)

Me-to-We Design: How Can a Makerspace Nurture the Building of a Collaborative Community?

Árni Már Einarsson(✉) ⓘ and Morten Hertzum ⓘ

University of Copenhagen, Karen Blixens Plads 8, 2300 Copenhagen, Denmark
{arni.mar.einarsson,hertzum}@hum.ku.dk

Abstract. Makerspaces provide communal access to resources such as 3D printers, laser cutters, electronics equipment, and sewing machines. This way, makerspaces aspire to facilitate their users – the so-called makers – in acquiring craft skills, creating products, learning about technology, and meeting other makers. The collaborative qualities of the makerspace community are key to this aspiration. Yet, just like many non-makerspace initiatives, makerspaces often struggle to foster and sustain a collaborative community. In this study, we use the model of me-to-we design to analyze a makerspace that has succeeded in nurturing a collaborative community. We disentangle the makerspace activities into the five stages of the model and, on that basis, arrive at six principles for nurturing collaborative makerspace communities: (1) accept diverse entry and end points, (2) plan for transitions, (3) help makers devise meaningful projects, (4) encourage sharing and lightweight documentation, (5) collaborate toward communal goals, and (6) attend to the social.

Keywords: Makerspace · Making · Co-design · Designing social experiences

1 Introduction

Makerspaces are communal facilities that provide their users with access to resources such as 3D printers, laser cutters, electronics equipment, and sewing machines. The users – known as makers – are a mix of creative people who seek to express themselves with the makerspace tools [9] and skillful technicians who seek to share their interest in technology with others [28]. The collaborative qualities of a makerspace are important in attracting makers. To thrive, a makerspace must provide a sense of community that nurtures information exchange, social encounters, informal collaboration, and other forms of sharing among the makers. Yet, many makerspaces struggle to foster and sustain an inclusive and collaborative community, and it is unclear from the existing research under what circumstances such collaboration succeeds. Similarly, many non-makerspace initiatives struggle to capitalize on the capabilities of social activities (e.g., [18, 19]). Thus, there is a need for models of how to design for collaborative experiences. One such model is me-to-we design [24].

© IFIP International Federation for Information Processing 2021
Published by Springer Nature Switzerland AG 2021
C. Ardito et al. (Eds.): INTERACT 2021, LNCS 12932, pp. 702–711, 2021.
https://doi.org/10.1007/978-3-030-85623-6_39

In this study, we apply the model of me-to-we design to the activities in a makerspace in a rural municipality in Denmark. Importantly, the model does not imply that collaborative activities must replace individual activities. Rather, the makerspace must support activities that span from individual to collaborative. By analyzing the activities in the makerspace, we provide a case-based answer to the research question: *How can a makerspace nurture the building of a collaborative community?* The studied makerspace has managed to build and sustain a collaborative community in which individual projects coexist with social and collaborative activities. We investigate how this is accomplished and arrive at six principles for nurturing collaborative communities.

2 Makerspace Communities

Many studies mention the social and collaborative qualities of makerspaces [6, 8, 12, 26]. Yet, in the existing body of research, these qualities tend to be scaffolded in predefined activities such as courses [27], distributed in wider maker networks [10], directed at actors external to the makerspace [17], or assumed as part of the informal exchanges among individuals [13]. Only few studies have investigated discretionary collaborations among users around a shared objective: Hui and Gerber [12] report of a group of makers who collaboratively make objects for an educational program. Davies [4] discovers collaborative projects where makers contribute with diverse skills and value the interdisciplinarity. Toombs et al. [28] emphasize the collaborative effort that goes into taking care of a makerspace.

Most makerspace research investigates how makerspaces facilitate individual makers in creating products on their own and learning about technology [2, 27, 30]. These studies emphasize the creative, immersive, and practical aspects of making [9, 22]. They also emphasize that makers obtain help and inspiration from peers in the makerspace [13] and from online videos and tutorials [9, 29]. For some makers, the social relations in the makerspace are as important as the possibilities for making tangible products [4, 26]. These makers value that makerspaces provide a place to meet others with similar interests.

In spite of their qualities, makerspace communities also cause problems. For example, some regular users stake claims to machinery, even when they are not currently using it, thereby blocking other makers' access to the machinery [1]. Furthermore, several studies find that the community of regular users can constitute a barrier for newcomers, who experience the community as difficult to enter [5, 7, 25]. To make the communities more inclusive, research has suggested recruitment through structured object-focused activities [6], promotion of arts and crafts practices [15], and reconfiguration of the community [25]. Such changes are not easy to accomplish and may have unintended consequences on the long-term evolution of the community [23]. Sustainable models for balancing the individual (me) and social (we) have yet to be developed.

3 Me-to-We Design

Simon [24] originally devised me-to-we design to reconnect museums with their audiences. The overarching aim was to engage museum visitors through the creation of personally rewarding, social experiences. When people have such experiences, they enjoy themselves and want to revisit the museum in the future. The challenge is to design a context in which people are prepared to collaborate confidently with other museum visitors, that is, with strangers. Me-to-we design posits that this preparedness can be fostered by enabling people to engage through personal, not social, entry points. Thus, the basic principle in me-to-we design is that personal entry points (me) are an effective means of scaffolding social experiences (we).

Me-to-we design provides a five-stage model for moving from individual to social experiences, see Table 1. The stages are progressive in that higher-level stages presuppose the groundwork provided by the lower-level stages. To illustrate the broad applicability of me-to-we design, Simon [24] supplements the museum-related examples with the example of turning the individual, and sometimes loathed, activity of running into a screen-supported social competition. At Stage 1, you listen to music on your phone while running on your own. You can create motivational playlists, but essentially "you consume music as the pavement consumes your shoes" [24]. At Stage 2, your phone tracks your location in real time and provides statistics about your performance. Reviewing your statistics helps you stay disciplined. At Stage 3, you share your statistics online with other runners and use theirs as inspiration. Even without connecting with them directly, you get a sense of community: If they can run that long or fast, maybe you can too. At Stage 4, you form online teams with other runners and take on collective challenges. These challenges make you accountable to your virtual teammates. Running is no longer just about your personal exercise, but also about being part of the team. At Stage 5, you meet with your virtual teammates for real-life running events or for real-time chatting while each of you are running in your own neighborhood. In total, running has been transformed from an exercise that requires personal discipline to an experience that is socially driven – from me to we.

Table 1. The five stages of me-to-we design, based on Simon [24].

	Stage	Definition	Museum example
We	5	Individuals engage with each other socially	Visitors experience the museum as a place full of potentially enriching social encounters
	4	Individual interactions are networked for social use	Visitors connect with particular people – staff and other visitors – who share their interests
	3	Individual interactions are networked in aggregate	Visitors can see where their interests and actions fit in the wider community of visitors
	2	Individual interacts with content	Visitors are provided with an opportunity for inquiry, for taking action, and for asking questions
Me	1	Individual consumes content	Visitors are provided with access to the content that they seek

4   Method

To examine how makerspaces can nurture a collaborative community, we conducted a multimethod case study [14] in a Danish library makerspace. The case, Vordingborg

Makerspace, was selected for its communal qualities as it was open to all citizens in the local municipality, established in a citizen-driven process, and had a community of about thirty regulars, who to a large extent ran the makerspace. Vordingborg Makerspace is situated in a medium-sized city and occupies three rooms in its public library. These rooms have tools and materials for 3D printing, laser cutting, soldering, CNC milling, t-shirt printing, sewing, and tinkering with electronics and robotics.

The data material for this study comprises 25 h of observation and interviews with six users and two staff members. The observations were conducted over seven sessions. Six sessions were in the makerspace when the community met on Tuesday evenings; one was from a makerspace trip to the local dump yard to scout for materials. The observations were documented in field notes describing the place, the users, and their activities – individual as well as social. Furthermore, the makerspace Facebook group was monitored. The interviewed users were mainly regulars. These interviews lasted on average 50 min and concerned the users' motivation, history of becoming makers, affiliation to the makerspace, accounts of projects, and descriptions of how making interacted with their life. The staff interviews included the main makerspace facilitator and the library manager. They were interviewed about the objectives of the makerspace, the activities in it, the barriers they experienced, and the relation between the makerspace and the library. All interviews were recorded and transcribed.

The observations and interviews showed many activities happening in parallel. In analyzing the data, we used the model of me-to-we design [24] to disentangle the activities and structure our analysis. We acknowledge that the model was originally devised to facilitate design, but contend that it can also be used analytically. As an analytic framework, the model served to deconstruct a case in which a mix of individual and collaborative practices already existed. The analysis proceeded by identifying activities at different model stages and accounting for how makers entered and transitioned among the stages. That is, we coded the field notes, interview transcripts, and Facebook posts according to model stages (Table 1), personal entry points, and transitions among stages. In addition, we recorded differences in which stages the makers preferred.

5   Results

The community in Vordingborg Makerspace meets on Tuesday and Thursday evenings. From 6.30 in the afternoon, the regulars gather in the makerspace and engage in multiple activities spread across its three rooms. In the first room (which during regular office hours is the library staff's lunchroom), makers can attend courses. Only separated by a sliding door, the second room is a large open space with tables, 3D printers, and stocks of electronic components. This room also features a coffee cart where makers gather and socialize. The third room is for noisy activities such as laser cutting, CNC milling, and crafting. At times, all participants assemble to receive practical information, see an example, or discuss a project. But most of the time, they are engaged in a multitude of different activities. Because these activities run in parallel, the makers have ample opportunity for seeking assistance, sharing objects, observing what others are doing, and feeling connected to the community. In the following, we disentangle this mix of activities using the five stages of the me-to-we model.

Individuals Consuming Content (Stage 1): The entry point for participating in the makerspace is an interest in technology or a curiosity about the possibilities afforded by the makerspace. The makerspace supports exploration by providing new users a tour of the space and hosting courses about tools and techniques every second week. One week, the course was about 3D modeling. For this course, the participants were handed a computer and instructed to follow along while modeling a nut (i.e., adding the octangular shape, the thread at the center, etc.). One of the participants was a retired engineer and collector of industrial CNC mills. He was already familiar with the makerspace but only visits it to attend courses and discuss technology informally with the other participants. Consuming the course content is suitable for him. Because he does not have a specific project he wishes to complete, he contentedly remains at Stage 1. To transition to the next stage, the makers must have a project idea they wish to pursue.

Individuals Interacting with Content (Stage 2): A project can be a technical exercise proposed by a course instructor, but most projects are defined by the makers themselves. Many makers enter the makerspace with such a project idea as their motivation for arriving. For them, the courses provide the prerequisites for proceeding to work on their projects. Through their projects, they interact with content in ways they experience as pleasurable and rewarding. For example, the interviewed makers enjoyed *"figuring out how things work"* (User 1), *"seeing the final outcome"* (User 1), *"taking on a challenge"* (User 2), *"immersing into a different world"* (User 2), and *"making something where you are not accountable for your time [in opposition to work]"* (User 6). Two of the six interviewed makers avoid the community evenings because they prefer unrestricted tool access and space to immerse themselves. However, the other four make their projects during the community evenings to have easy access to assistance and be able to share their ideas with others. The co-presence during the community evenings also affords makers in transitioning to the next stages.

Individual Interactions are Networked in Aggregate (Stage 3): Both the interviews and observations showed that makers are prepared to share. For example, User 4 stated that *"In the makerspace we exchange information just like you in books pass on knowledge and wisdom. It is a place where you can access knowledge."* Most of the sharing occurs through face-to-face exchanges, but sharing is also made manifest in the Facebook group and curated in the makerspace. The Facebook group counts 390 members. In addition to posts with practical information, the makers share inspirational articles, ask for help, and showcase completed projects. The showcased projects include role-playing objects, engraving in phones, a laser-cut Eiffel tower, and a device to translate Morse code (inputted on an Arduino-based device) to text.

In the makerspace, examples and demonstration projects are kept on display. For instance, example objects are curated near the 3D printers, completed projects are curated in a glass display, and a bulletin board lists the competences of the regular users (Fig. 1). Along with the Facebook group, the examples, projects, and other information curated in the makerspace are aggregates of the makers' activities. These aggregates support additional activity and stage transitions in two ways. First, they help new makers get a sense of the possibilities afforded by the makerspace. Second, they provide inspiration for new projects and higher aspirations: If other makers have been able to complete these projects, then my project idea may be feasible too.

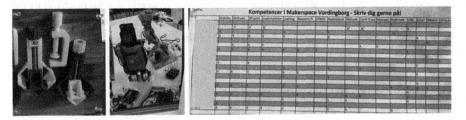

Fig. 1. Aggregates of participation displayed in the makerspace.

Individual Interactions are Networked for Social Use (Stage 4): While the majority of the makers perform their individual projects, our observations also include examples of collaborative projects, such as parents making with their children. One collaborative project was especially large and involved making an unmanned underwater vehicle (UUV). The idea for the UUV project arose from a makerspace field trip to a technical university. After the field trip, the project was announced on the makerspace Facebook page to encourage participation and, then, a private Facebook group was established for the project. The project was undertaken by four of the regulars, who contributed expertise in different areas. For example, one was responsible for the Arduino programming, while another made the 3D drawings and printed propellers. In addition to the delegated technical tasks, the project required a lot of discussion and coordination among the participants. Many of these collective activities took place at a whiteboard in the makerspace and were summarized in Facebook postings. The makerspace welcomes collaborative projects because they create ties among the makers and make grander project ideas feasible. Therefore, the makerspace supports these projects by financing materials. However, the UUV project eventually stalled, maybe because it lacked an external purpose. In an interview, one of the participants explained that the motivation behind the project was to have "*something to fall back on when we are there [i.e., in the makerspace] anyway*" (User 4). Over time, this motivation gave way to other activities in the makerspace and outside of it.

Individuals Engage with Each Other Socially (Stage 5): The social qualities of the makerspace are found at all stages. Specifically, the course participation and UUV project demonstrate that many users value the makerspace as much for the social encounters as for the project outcomes. Stage 5 stands out by having contribution to the community as a distinct element. The contribution may be internal to the makerspace or by promoting it externally. For example, one maker described that his entry point was to bring his individual hobby of electronics tinkering from his home to the makerspace where he could talk with others with similar interests. From that starting point, his participation soon transitioned into helping others and promoting the makerspace with a demonstration project at a local conference. Others are motivated by communal goals such as making youth interested in science, technology, engineering, and mathematics (STEM) disciplines. These makers have transitioned out of the project focus characteristic of Stages 2–4. Instead, they enjoy contributing to the makerspace and the local community by helping others, servicing tools, giving courses, organizing field trips, promoting the makerspace, and the like. Without their contributions, it would not be possible to run courses every second week on the community evenings, thereby limiting Stage 1 and the possibilities for new makers to become part of the community.

6 Concluding Discussion

The studied makerspace succeeds in facilitating activities that span all five stages in the model of me-to-we design [24]. This way, the makerspace nurtures a collaborative community that attracts new makers and remains attractive to the regulars. On the basis of the analysis, we propose six principles for establishing and sustaining a collaborative makerspace community. With these principles, we aim to articulate the practical implications of our analysis. That is, we aim to support me-to-we *design*. We acknowledge that the principles are based on one case. The six proposed principles are:

Accept Diverse Entry and End Points. Consistent with prior research [9, 26], our results show that makers enter the makerspace at different stages and end their cross-stage transitions at different stages. Many of the observed and interviewed users value the community evenings because they provide ready access to help, add social qualities, and allow for contributing to the community. Another group of makers avoids the community evenings. These makers are motivated by immersing themselves in their creative processes, prefer to work alone, or feel underrepresented in the community [7, 25]. They have the opportunity to share their projects or attend the community evenings but prefer not to. In the studied makerspace, both staff and users acknowledge the makers' diverse motivations and accept participation at all stages of the me-to-we model.

Plan for Transitions. The analytic benefit of the me-to-we model [24] is that it calls attention to the transitions among its stages. The co-situated activities on the community evenings afford transitions because the makers are exposed to courses, projects made by peers, and inevitable social encounters all at once. The me-to-we model shows how participation can gradually transition from individual toward communal activities. This appears an intuitive approach to the inclusion of new makers [6]. However, we also find that transitions are multidirectional. For example, some newcomers transition back and forth between courses and projects (Stages 1 and 2). Relatedly, some experienced makers transition back and forth between communal activities (Stage 5) and the early stages of participation (Stages 1 to 3) when they volunteer for teaching, guide new users, and share completed projects. Makerspace staff may enrich makers' participation by reflecting on the qualities of the stages and scaffolding transitions among them.

Help Makers Devise Meaningful Projects. Makers are interested in the technical and expressive possibilities of physical computing and fabrication tools [10]. These tools enable ordinary people to engage in advanced fabrication, and the makerspace assembles the tools in the local community. While insufficient technical skills can be a barrier to makerspace participation [6], newcomers in the studied makerspace can acquire these skills through courses, exercise sheets, and peer assistance. We find less support for the transition from being familiar with tools (Stage 1) to making projects (Stage 2). Prior research has emphasized that meaningful projects are key drivers of learning [2, 20]. However, we (and others [4]) find that makers are presumed to have a meaningful project idea and the self-sufficiency to pursue it. Without support for devising meaningful projects, makers may struggle to identify worthwhile project ideas. Better support for devising projects could include assistance in refining an initial idea, but it could also involve a shared catalogue of projects proposed by other makers or needed by citizens who are not themselves able to undertake the projects.

Encourage Sharing and Lightweight Documentation. Like in other makerspaces [12], our case displays a community with much willingness to share information through file sharing, material exchanges, peer tutoring, course teaching, and the informal flow of advice, news, and creative input. Yet, documentation of completed projects is only shared to a limited extent. Makers may use their documentation of their own projects for reflection and learning about the project process [29]. But documentation may also support others in developing new meanings and mediate contacts among people [11]. By aggregating interactions (Stage 3), shared documentation makes some of the otherwise invisible makerspace activities visible. Thereby, documentation such as a short video may show how key steps in a project were accomplished. Users may however abstain from making or sharing documentation because they feel that their projects do not demonstrate enough skill or because documentation is a time-consuming activity that may require users to repeat parts of their process for the purpose of video-recording them [29]. Makerspaces should encourage the sharing of documentation but should also emphasize lightweight documentation to make it manageable to produce.

Collaborate Toward Communal Goals. Collaboration connects makers around a shared goal [9] and allows for undertaking advanced projects. While valued, projects with interdependence and a shared objective are rare in the studied makerspace. We find two reasons for this. First, collaboration adds complexity [21] because objectives require negotiation, work must be divided, activities must be articulated, and mutual interdependences may stall progress. Because making is a leisure activity centered around a pragmatic identity of 'just doing' [3], the complexity can cause more frustration than joy. Second, the UUV project was not motivated by an actual need; the makers merely wanted to have a project to fall back on. While we acknowledge the difficulty of balancing leisure and obligation, we suggest that makerspaces consider reaching out to the local community outside the makerspace with an invitation to collaborate about projects that matter to the local community. Being anchored in local needs, these projects will likely be meaningful to makers who resonate with the needs. Proposals for such projects could be catalogued and kept on display in the makerspace or they could be presented on a community evening to stir interest and make connections.

Attend to the Social. The social qualities of makerspaces should not be underrated. Studies have found that makerspaces provide conditions conducive of wellbeing for both youth and adults. Makers feel empowered by immersing in productive activity, but they also enjoy meeting others and being part of a community [16, 26]. We observed intense engagement among users with similar interests as well as unexpected encounters among users across age and group boundaries. Sustaining a constructive social atmosphere requires ongoing care [28]. The staff in the studied makerspace cared for the social atmosphere by serving coffee, facilitating meetings among users who could learn from one another, providing opportunities for users to take ownership, organizing social activities that celebrate the community, and so forth.

References

1. Annett, M., Grossmann, T., Widgor, D., Fitzmaurice, G.: Exploring and understanding the role of workshop environments in personal fabrication processes. ACM Trans. Comp. Hum. Interac. **26**(2), 1–43 (2019)
2. Blikstein, P.: Digital Fabrication and 'making' in education: the democratization of invention. In: Walter-Herrmann, J., Büching, C. (eds.) FabLabs: Of Machines, Makers and Inventors, pp. 203–222. Transcript, Bielefeld (2014)
3. Davies, S.R.: Characterizing hacking: Mundane engagement in US hacker and makerspaces. Sci. Technol. Hum. Values **43**(2), 171–197 (2018)
4. Davies, S.R.: Hackerspaces: Making the Maker Movement. Polity Press, Cambridge, UK (2017)
5. Dreessen, K., Schepers, S., Leen, D.: From hacking things to making things. Rethinking making by supporting non-expert users in a FabLab. Interact Des. Arch. J. **30**, 47–64 (2016)
6. Dreessen, K., Schepers, S.: Three strategies for engaging non-experts in a fablab. In: Proceedings of the 10th Nordic Conference on Human-Computer Interaction, pp. 482–493. ACM (2018)
7. Eckhardt, J., Kaletka, C., Pelka, B., Unterfrauner, E., Voigt, C., Zirngiebl, M.: Gender in the making: An empirical approach to understand gender relations in the maker movement. Int. J. Hum. Comp. Stud. **145**, 102548 (2021)
8. Einarsson, Á.M., Hertzum, M.: How is learning scaffolded in library makerspaces? Int. J. Child Comp. Interact. **26**, 100199 (2020)
9. Gauntlett, D.: Making is Connecting: The Social Power of Creativity, from Craft and Knitting to Digital Everything. Polity Press, Newark, UK (2018)
10. Gershenfeld, N.: How to make almost anything: The digital fabrication revolution. Foreign Aff. **91**(6), 43–57 (2012)
11. Hertzum, M.: Six roles of documents in professionals' work. In: Proceedings of the Sixth European Conference on Computer Supported Cooperative Work, pp. 41–60. Copenhagen, Denmark, Springer (1999). https://doi.org/10.1007/978-94-011-4441-4_3
12. Hui, J.S., Gerber, E.M.: Developing makerspaces as sites of entrepreneurship. In: Proceedings of the 2017 ACM Conference on Computer Supported Cooperative Work and Social Computing, pp. 2023–2038. ACM (2017)
13. Koh, K., Abbas, J., Willet, R.: Makerspaces in libraries: Social roles and community engagement. In: Lee, V.R., Phillips, A.L. (eds.) Reconceptualizing libraries: Perspectives from the information and learning sciences, pp. 17–36. Routledge, New York (2019)
14. Lazar, J., Feng, F., Hochheiser, H.: Research Methods in Human-Computer Interaction, 2nd edn. Morgan Kaufmann, Cambridge, Massachusetts (2017)
15. Lewis, J.: Barriers to women's involvement in hackspaces and makerspaces. Access as spaces. https://access-space.org/wp-content/uploads/2017/04/Barriers-to-womens-involvement-in-hackspaces-and-makerspaces.pdf (2015). Accessed 12 April 2021
16. Li, X., Todd, R.J.: Makerspace opportunities and desired outcomes: Voices from young people. Libr. Q. **89**(4), 316–332 (2019)

17. Mikhak, B., Lyon, C., Gorton, T., Gershenfeld, N., McEnnis, C., Taylor, J.: Fab Lab: An alternate model of ICT for development. In: Proceedings of the 2nd International Conference on Open Collaborative Design for Sustainable Innovation (2002)

18. Putnam, R.D.: Bowling alone: America's declining social capital. J. Democr. **6**(1), 68–78 (1995)

19. Rapp, A., Tirassa, M., Tirabeni, L.: Rethinking technologies for behavior change: a view from the inside of human change. ACM Transact. Comp. Hum. Interact. **26**(4), 22:1–22:30 (2019)

20. Resnick, M.: Lifelong Kindergarten: Cultivating Creativity Through Projects, Passion, Peers, and Play. MIT Press, Cambridge, Massachusetts (2017)

21. Schmidt, K., Bannon, L.: Taking CSCW seriously. Comput. Support. Coop. Work **1**(1), 7–40 (1992)

22. Sennett, R.: The Craftsman. Yale University Press, London (2008)

23. Seravalli, A.: Infrastructuring urban commons over time: Learnings from two cases. In: Proceedings of the 15th Participatory Design Conference, pp. 1–11. ACM (2018)

24. Simon, N.: The Participatory Museum. Museum 2.0, Santa Cruz, CA (2010)

25. Smit, D., Fuchsberger, V.: Sprinkling diversity: Hurdles on the way to inclusiveness in makerspaces. In: Proceedings of the 11th Nordic Conference on Human-Computer Interaction, pp. 1–8 (2020)

26. Taylor, N., Hurley, U., Connolly, P.: Making community: The wider role of makerspaces in public life. In: Proceedings of the 2016 CHI Conference on Human Factors in Computing Systems, pp. 1415–1425. ACM (2016)

27. Thanapornsangsuth, S.: Using human-centered design and social inventions to find the purposes in making. In: Proceedings of the 6th Annual Conference on Creativity and Fabrication in Education, pp. 17–25. ACM (2016)

28. Toombs, A.L., Bardzell, S., Bardzell, J.: The proper care and feeding of hackerspaces: Care ethics and cultures of making. In: Proceedings of the 33rd Annual ACM Conference on Human Factors in Computing Systems, pp. 629–638. ACM (2015)

29. Tseng, T., Resnick, M.: Product versus process: representing and appropriating DIY projects online. In: Proceedings of the 2014 Conference on Designing Interactive Systems. pp. 425–428. ACM (2014)

30. Tuhkala, A., Wagner, M., Iversen, O., Kärkkäinen, T.: Technology comprehension — combining computing, design, and societal reflection as a national subject. Int. J. Child Comp. Interact. **20**, 54–63 (2019)

Study Marbles: A Wearable Light for Online Collaborative Learning in Video Meetings

Yanhong Li[(✉)], Bill Bapisch, Jenny Phu, Thomas Weber,
and Heinrich Hußmann

LMU Munich, Frauenlobstr. 7a, 80337 Munich, Germany
{yanhong.li,thomas.weber,hussmann}@ifi.lmu.de,
{bill.bapisch,jenny.phu}@campus.lmu.de
http://www.medien.ifi.lmu.de

Abstract. Video meetings gained popularity for remote communication, both for work and education. As a result, collaborative online learning has become increasingly widespread. However, it is a challenge to make students feel engaged and connected during video meetings. In this study, we addressed this problem with a prototype for a wearable user interface called *Study Marbles*. It aimed to create a more social and active sense of remote, collaborative learning in video conferences. Our device is a tangible necklace with attachable, illuminated marbles that can be worn during video meetings. It could visualize students' learning status, moderate group discussions, and enable voting. The user study showed that participants perceived our prototype as a good way to create a more active and connected environment and to improve the interaction between group members in video conferences.

Keywords: Tangible user interfaces · TUI · Tangible learning · Online learning · Remote tangible interaction · Group learning · Collaboration · Distance learning

1 Introduction

Video meetings have become increasingly common in the past years, especially during the COVID-19 pandemic. Online video conferences have made it feasible for people to communicate and collaborate from distributed locations. This also applies to the learning domain where collaborative online learning with video conferencing (VC) systems, such as Zoom, has become common. However, compared to face-to-face classroom learning, VC was found to be less interactive and less encouraging to discussions [6]. Therefore, there is an issue of how to

---

Y. Li, B. Bapisch, J. Phu–Contributed equally to this study and were parallel first author.

make remote video communication more engaging. Andel et al. [2] argue that it is "more important now than ever [...] to effectively optimize and enhance the online learning experience".

Research has shown that Tangible User Interfaces (TUIs) can be helpful to increase motivation by offering playful interaction with tangible objects [11,13]. TUIs show a good potential for online learning, but currently there are few studies of TUIs for remote collaborative learning, and even fewer for use in video conferences.

In this paper, we present and evaluate a TUI prototype named "Study Marbles", which is a tangible necklace worn by each call member in a video meeting for augmenting communication with tangible, illuminated marbles. The reason why we chose a tangible, light-based interface for communication instead of traditional digital video overlays is to achieve a stronger coupling of bits and atoms [9] and interaction independent from video conferencing software. Study Marbles has three main functions: 1) status visualisation, 2) discussion moderation and 3) multiple choice voting. We aim to design a tangible tool to create a more involving, motivating and social environment for group video meetings.

2   Related Work

Online learning has grown rapidly over the last years. There are many online learning platforms enabling people in different locations to study together, for instance to access learning materials, attend online lectures and communicate in video conferences. However, there is a concern that virtual learning might reduce the learning quality [1]. For example, students in remote learning environments might feel a lack of focus, lower commitment and support [8]. In addition, a study showed that the majority of students thought that the use of Video Conference (VC) technology "discouraged classroom discussions" and was a "barrier to their interaction with the instructor" [6]. Therefore, online education needs engaging and connected learning environments.

One solution to achieve this is social presence. Indicating social presence in video-central online learning environments through features like comments was shown to result in higher motivation to participate and better performance [2]. In addition, there are different approaches to make people feel more connected in remote group settings. One study showed that visualisations help collaboration in remote synchronous group work [3]. Another solution was BuddyWall [14], a tangible ambient wall to visualise "an awareness of group presence". Lastly, wearables in this area were also studied, like a tangible apps bracelet [7] for non-verbal communication and reminders. Successful conversational learning requires more than a communication channel, it takes a mutual understanding and methods to make a conversation successful and efficient. One way to facilitate this is through specialized learning devices [16]. These devices need to be "highly portable", "unobtrusive", "available anywhere", "useful, suited to everyday needs" and "intuitive to use" [15].

Even though it is possible to use digital overlays to visualise different states in video meetings, the goal of specialised tangible learning devices is to counteract

Fig. 1. Illuminated marbles in the video call show the current status of each call member using traffic light color coding. The participant in the lower left corner has not selected a marble and the necklace remains empty as the marbles are detachable.

the strong influence of digital communication in online learning. In the following, we combine wearable devices with the ability of haptic interaction and ambient light in the real world. Thereby we want to use the approach"People, Bits and Atoms" [9] to bridge the gap between the digital and the real world. For this purpose we associate digitally available information with physical objects (marbles), similar to Durrell Bishop's Marble Answering Machine [12]. We extend this idea to represent information using light in the real environment and then send it through the digital channel (VC).

3   Study Marbles

In the following section we share several concept ideas and walk through the design process, which led to our final prototype of a wearable light-based interface to enhance communication in video meetings.

3.1   Concept Ideas

Our process for gathering concept ideas started with the question: "How might we support groups collaborating and learning remotely with a tangible light-based tool?". We considered different aspects of learning, such as learning through acquisition, inquiry, discussion, practice and collaboration [10]. Based on these, we examined the following common use cases in more detail: communicating availability, calling a meeting, leading a discussion, collaborative voting, requesting breaks and asking a teacher for help, with the use of an ambient light on the desk or in the periphery. In parallel, we collected light-based interactions for communication such as turning light on/off, dimming, flashing, changing light temperature, brightness, colors, color gradients, light and shadow or using light stencils or projections.

In the end, we decided on a wearable necklace to enhance collaboration and group communication in video meetings because of its good visibility in the view of the video camera. At the same time, we were inspired by Bishop's Marble Answering Machine [12], which used marbles as physical visualisations of messages. Therefore, we developed the idea of light-emitting marbles attachable to the necklace through tangible interactions (see Fig. 1). More specifically, our prototype has the following functions: (1) providing status information with different colors associated with different meanings; (2) moderating the group discussion with tangible interactions, for example attaching and detaching marbles to the necklace; (3) supporting learning through multiple-choice voting.

One of our aims was to design intuitive tangible interactions with this wearable interface, so we integrated the following actions: touching buttons on sides of the hexagon to change color, shaking/swinging the necklace (detected by accelerometer) and attaching and detaching marbles with magnetic latches. Finally, we planned a central database and a mobile app for further development.

3.2 Design Process

An important aspect of the design process was the overall shape of the wearable object. The size needed to be small in order to be light enough to be worn, however, it should also be large enough to be visible in a video meeting. Because of the relatively small size of the prototype, it was important to select the right components early on. The ESP32 D1 mini was chosen for its compact size and important functionalities for our prototype, such as WiFi. Other components included the MPU-6050 accelerometer and RGB LEDs based on the WS2811.

The hardest challenge was to design and build a detachable marble that contains an LED and provided reliable electronic contacts when inserted and removed. Therefore, we split our design process into two parts: necklace design and marbles design. For designing the marbles, the goal was to create a connection that prevented improper electronic connection and at the same time guaranteed a strong and stable connection. To differentiate between different types of marbles and accordingly control the color of the RGB LED, we used a voltage divider to detect different voltage levels for different marbles, with resistors between the marble and micro-controller. In total, we needed four leads connecting the lamp to the body (ground, 5 volt, LED color control and a lead for the resistors).

The design decision that turned out to be very effective was to use pogo pins as electrical contacts between the marbles and the necklace. These were built into the necklace and the marbles were fitted with matching concave connectors. In order to facilitate effortless and firm attachment of the marbles to the pogo pins, there are two strong magnets in the lid of the necklace and two smaller ones hidden inside each marble.

The hexagonal design was chosen to allow up to six capacitive touch buttons on each side. We decided to only use four in order to have space at the bottom and top to grip the device and also for the micro-USB port to upload new firmware. In order to fabricate a reliable and sturdy prototype, as shown in Fig. 2, the entire assembly was first designed as a 3D model and later 3D printed.

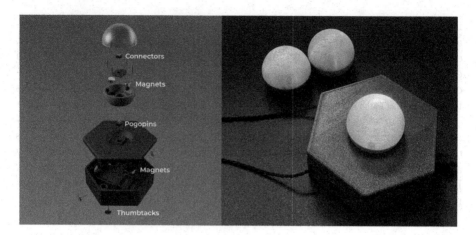

Fig. 2. Left: 3D model render of components; Right: *Study Marbles* prototype with an inserted illuminated color marble. (Color figure online)

3.3   Prototype

The finished model for the hexagonal necklace and marbles can be seen in Fig. 2. Each pin is used to set one of the colors: red, yellow, green and blue. We included two different types of marbles with the same design. However, there was one difference: the *color marble* lights up when it is attached to the necklace; while the *action marble* used for the discussion and vote mode does not, it lights up only when it's your turn or you have voted. We designed three use cases for it:

(1) **Status:** To visualise the users' current status, for example their feeling regarding a task or the status of their progress on a worksheet in a learning context, users can insert the *color marble* into the necklace. The color marble lights up in a color, which can be changed by pressing one of the four touch pins on the sides of the hexagon. Additionally, we implemented light effects: By *shaking* the necklace, a flashing/blinking light can be triggered, for example to signal distress. *Swinging* the hexagon on the necklace string can trigger a breathing/fading light effect to show a relaxed state.

(2) **Discussion:** The *Study Marbles* can moderate group discussion by lighting up the marble of the current speaker. The discussion mode can be started, after everyone inserts the *action marble*. The action marble turns off at first. One person can start the discussion mode in the app. The system then chooses one random person whose marble turns on as a random speaker. After the speaker removes his/her marble or when the Skip button is pressed in the app, the next random speaker is chosen. This ensures that everyone gets a turn to speak.

(3) **Multiple-choice voting:** The vote mode is also started by inserting the *action marble*, which is off in the beginning. One person can start the voting in the app. Subsequently participants can vote by pressing one of the four

sides of the hexagon, which represent a multiple choice answer (a, b, c, d). When someone has voted, their marble lights up in white. After everyone has voted, the votes can be revealed by pressing a button in the app and the colors of all marbles change to the answers chosen by their users.

The discussion and vote mode can be started with a smartphone app, which we built with Thunkable[1], a tool for fast prototyping of cross-platforms apps. The communication between the smartphone app and the ESP32 inside the necklace works by accessing variables in a cloud database and polling it for updates, e.g. to know the start of a new mode or the detachment of a marble.

4   Findings

In order to know users' practical impressions and suggestions for *Study Marbles*, we conducted an online survey. The online format of the survey (due to the pandemic situation) is a limitation of our user study, however, we included detailed videos to show all the functions, together with text descriptions. Finally, we got 41 participants (19 females and 22 males). Eighteen of the 41 participants were 18–24 years old and 10 were 26–34 years old. The rest were 35–74 years old. More than half of them were students. 35 participants had a higher education and 31 used video meetings multiple times a week or more often. The most common reasons for using VC were "attending university lectures, classes and work meetings".

We asked participants to rate *Study Marbles'* usability with the *System Usability Scale* (SUS) [4]. The average of the result SUS scores was 69.15, with a standard deviation of 13.16, which shows a good usability rating [5].

In addition, we have ten items grouped in three areas, to know participants' feeling and opinions of *Study Marbles*, which can be seen in Fig. 3.

Wearable: 63% of participants liked our wearable design and 83% thought that the light of the marbles was a good way to convey information. On the other hand, participants' opinions were more divided when asked if it is desirable to have a wearable tool for online meetings.

Video Meetings: 76% of participants thought they would pay more attention to the video when using *Study Marbles*, however only 39% thought they would feel more comfortable to turn on their video when using *Study Marbles*. The last two questions about video meetings asked if *Study Marbles* could be distracting during video calls. This was approved by almost half of the participants. This raises the question if *Study Marbles* is more likely to distract the users than help. Here, the participants were rather uncertain, as this is still a very new area and they lacked experience with the technology.

---

[1] https://thunkable.com/.

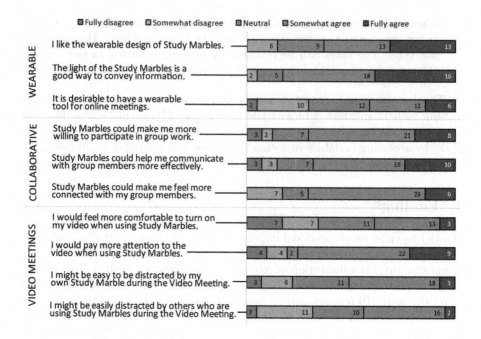

Fig. 3. Users' experience about *Study Marbles*'s wearable, collaborative and video meeting characteristics

Collaborative: Regarding *Study Marbles'* effect on collaboration, the majority of participants thought that it could make them more willing to participate in group work and would help to communicate with group members more effectively. Most agreed that it could make them feel more connected with group members. All in all, *Study Marbles* was rated to have a positive impact on collaboration.

Participants commented: *"I think this is a good way to enforce participation in a lecture setting", "Study Marbles is especially advantageous in video conferences with many people to make the participants feel more included", "Good idea to make everyone more active in the meeting".*

5   Discussion

In this section, we will discuss challenges, possibilities of using *Study Marbles* and limitations of this work. One of the disadvantages of *Study Marbles* is accessibility for (partially) color-blind people, as the color of the light is used for the status and vote mode. The visibility of the light could be another issue, which could be dependent on video quality and the posture of the wearer. Some people commented *Study Marbles* could be distracting from the meeting itself and that it would be more suited for smaller groups. Two people thought that there could be misinterpretations of the light meanings, which have to be clarified before using the system. Some mentioned the concern that the necklace might be too heavy. Since the participants could only watch a video of the *Study Marbles*, this was rather difficult to estimate, but the necklace actually weighs only 70g. The vote mode could also be improved by displaying a chart of the vote results and one person noted they would like to keep votes hidden to not be under pressure while voting. Some participants commented that *Study Marbles* could be integrated into a video conferencing tool to reduce the number of devices, for example combining it with the "hand-raising"- function in Zoom.

Study Marbles can also be extended with different functions, such as a timer or reminder before a meeting, group allocation or used in completely different settings, such as real-life meetings or classrooms. As alternative use cases, participants suggested using it for games, in Agile teams, in combination with task boards or as a timer for Pomodoro learning. Nonverbal light signals can also be useful to ask for help in a classroom or when talking is not possible, for example one participant suggested it could be used in hospitals.

In the survey, we asked the participants what other kinds of wearables they would like to use instead of a necklace. Most people thought that the necklace was the best option. Arguments for a necklace design was portability and visibility during the video meeting. Only one person said that they would never wear a necklace for that. Other ideas for wearables included a bracelet, a wristband or a watch, pin-buttons, a cap, hat or headband. Some unique ideas were lights attached to headphones or a modified pair of glasses.

Limitations of our survey were that it was just an online survey, in which the participants could not try the prototype in real life. Also, we did not test the prototype in a learning or teaching scenario, so this could be investigated more. We did not specifically search for participants with a background of teaching or studying, however most of our participants were students. Future work could recruit teachers to evaluate our prototype and also children and teenagers, since all our participants were older than 18.

6   Conclusion

In this paper we presented *Study Marbles*, a concept idea for a tangible, wearable interface with illuminated marbles to support online, remote collaboration, particularly for online learning. So far, the concept is still in its early stages and there is still a lot of potential for future research. Our review of related work showed that tangible interaction with light-based interfaces is still a new area, which is promising, not only for collaborative remote learning. Main results of our online survey were that the usability of *Study Marbles* was mostly rated positively, and that it could help to make group members feel more included and motivated to participate.

Beyond a field evaluation, future work could explore if users prefer tangible interaction *vs.* software-integrated interaction in common digital devices (PC, tablet, smartphone) to control the marbles and if there are any advantages or performance differences between both. Variations of *Study Marbles* using different wearables or other types of tangible objects and alternative interactions with illuminating marbles could also be studied in the future. Since *Study Marbles* does not have to be limited to virtual online meetings or learning contexts, there are still numerous possible use cases that can be investigated, for example real-life meetings, classrooms, games or work settings.

Acknowledgements. This research is funded by the Elite Network of Bavaria (K-GS-2012-209).

References

1. Amelung, C., Laffey, J., Turner, P.: Supporting collaborative learning in online higher education through activity awareness, pp. 75–77 (2007). https://doi.org/10.3115/1599600.1599611
2. Andel, S., de Vreede, T., Spector, P., Padmanabhan, B., Singh, V., de Vreede, G.J.: Do social features help in video-centric online learning platforms? A presence perspective. Comput. Hum. Behav. **113**, 106505 (07 (2020). https://doi.org/10.1016/j.chb.2020.106505
3. Balakrishnan, A., Fussell, S., Kiesler, S.: Do visualizations improve synchronous remote collaboration? pp. 1227–1236 (2008). https://doi.org/10.1145/1357054.1357246
4. Brooke, J.: SUS: a quick and dirty usability scale. Usability Eval. Ind. **189**, 4–7 (1995)
5. Brooke, J.: SUS: a retrospective. J Usability Stud. **8**, 29–40 (2013)
6. Doggett, M.: The videoconferencing classroom: what do students think? Architectural and Manufacturing Sciences Faculty Publications (2007)
7. Fortmann, J., Root, E., Boll, S., Heuten, W.: Tangible apps bracelet: designing modular wrist-worn digital jewellery for multiple purposes, pp. 841–852 (2016). https://doi.org/10.1145/2901790.2901838
8. Hussein, E., Daoud, S., Alrabaiah, H., Badawi, R.: Exploring undergraduate students' attitudes towards emergency online learning during COVID-19: A case from the UAE. Child Youth Serv. Rev. **119** (2020). https://doi.org/10.1016/j.childyouth.2020.105699
9. Ishii, H., Ullmer, B.: Tangible bits: towards seamless interfaces between people, bits and atoms. In: Conference on Human Factors in Computing Systems - Proceedings (1998). https://doi.org/10.1145/258549.258715
10. Laurillard, D.: Teaching as a design science: building pedagogical patterns for learning and technology. Teaching as a Design Science: Building Pedagogical Patterns for Learning and Technology, pp. 1–258 (2012). https://doi.org/10.4324/9780203125083
11. O'Malley, C., Fraser, D.S.: Literature Review in Learning with Tangible Technologies (2004). https://telearn.archives-ouvertes.fr/hal-00190328, a NESTA Futurelab Research report - report 12
12. Polynor, R.: The hand that rocks the cradle (1995)
13. Price, S., Rogers, Y., Scaife, M., Stanton, D., Neale, H.: Using 'tangibles' to promote novel forms of playful learning. Interact. Comput. **15**, 169–185 (04 (2003). https://doi.org/10.1016/S0953-5438(03)00006-7
14. Quintanilha, M.: BuddyWall: a tangible user interface for wireless remote communication, pp. 3711–3716 (2008). https://doi.org/10.1145/1358628.1358918

15. Sharples, M.: The design of personal mobile technologies for lifelong learning. Comput. Educ. **34**, 177–193 (2000). https://doi.org/10.1016/S0360-1315(99)00044-5
16. Sharples, M.: Disruptive devices: mobile technology for conversational learning. Int. J. Continuing Eng. Educ. Lifelong Learn. **12** (2002). https://doi.org/10.1504/IJCEELL.2002.002148

Supporting Interaction in a Virtual Chorus: Results from a Focus Group

Rita Francese[1]([⊠]), Patrizia Bruno[2], and Genoveffa Tortora[1]

[1] Università degli Studi di Salerno, Fisciano, Italy
{francese,tortora}@unisa.it
[2] Ministero della Pubblica Istruzione, Rome, Italy
patrizia.bruno@ic-carduccitrezza.edu.it

Abstract. To get effective participation in a virtual chorus is particularly difficult because there is the need of artificially creating that common sense of union among all the group members. This paper aims at understanding how technology may enhance virtual chorus members' interaction through a focus group involving three chorus masters with experience in conducting virtual chorus. We used the Thematic Analysis Template (TAT) for planning and analyzing the results. Results revealed that three types of interaction modalities have been employed: asynchronous audio/Video multi tracking recording grouping the participant single tracks, synchronous teleconferencing with one participant speaking, and social gaming. These activities are surrogates of F2F choir rehearsals because present technology is not adequate for real synchronous interaction. While waiting for connection empowerment, participants expressed their needs for enhancing present videoconferencing tools, including simultaneous recording of participants in an individual way and integration of the various environments.

Keywords: Virtual chorus · Multimedia interaction · Focus group · Requirements · Multi-user interaction/cooperation

1 Introduction

Singing together on a chorus has many health benefits [12]. Unfortunately, pandemic restrictions are very heavy for chorus activities. In many countries, as in Italy, singing in groups in presence modality is forbidden. One of the main challenges is to avoid the chorus dispersion, that is avoiding that the group identity is wasted by the perduration of the pandemic situation and the consequent desegregation of the contacts. Many choir masters in all the world decided to adopt distance technology to keep on the singing group. But singing in a chorus is an activity that benefits participants far more than the other "social" activities, by enabling them to perform a shared creation of music through the coordinated physical action of singing together within the same physical space [4]. For this

© IFIP International Federation for Information Processing 2021
Published by Springer Nature Switzerland AG 2021
C. Ardito et al. (Eds.): INTERACT 2021, LNCS 12932, pp. 722–730, 2021.
https://doi.org/10.1007/978-3-030-85623-6_41

reason, to get effective participation in a virtual chorus is particularly difficult, because there is the need to artificially creating that common sense of unity among all the group members.

In this paper we try at answering the following research questions:

- **RQ1:** *Which are the virtual chorus interaction modalities adopted during the pandemic period?*
- **RQ2:** *How technology may improve the interaction experience of the virtual chorus?*

In this study, we aim at understanding the chorus masters' opinions on the support offered by the technology solutions they adopted in the pandemic period for conducting the chorus activities; what features provide an effective value, how and why, and what aspects may be improved. We conducted a focus group with three chorus masters collecting impressions on their virtual chorus experience, on the support offered by technology, and on their needs. We used the Thematic Analysis Template (TAT) for planning and analyzing the recordings of the focus group session.

This paper is structured as follows: Sect. 2 introduces the background concepts, while Sect. 3 details the planning of the focus group. Section 4 discusses our findings. Finally, Sect. 5 concludes the paper.

2   Background

It is widely recognized that to be part of a chorus has many health and social benefits [5,12]. But Face-to-Face chorus interaction has been strongly impacted by the covid-19 pandemic and many chorus masters organized virtual sessions for keeping on their activities. The experiences, activities, and reflections of choir singers during lockdown are reported by Daffern et al. [4] who conducted a user study involving 3948 choristers. Unlike them, we focus our attention on the support offered by the software platforms and on the chorus masters' technological needs.

Many applications require Internet connectivity for communication and data exchange and do not suffer from latency problems. The case of the virtual chorus is different, because an application for multi-user singing synchronously in Real-Time belongs to a specific type of applications, named Networked Music Performance (NMP) systems [9]. One of the major challenges for NMP systems is to maintain the synchronization of the group, due to high latency [7]. A solution may use an audio connection using software such as Soundjack [2], a teleconferencing software for the video, such as Zoom or Skype. Soundjack requires deep technical knowledge of networks and is difficult to use.

There exist some applications supporting virtual chorus activities aiming at simplifying some problems. For example, choristers when recording audio/video have to use the PC to listen to the base and the phone for registering their voice. The Gala application [1] enables choristers to listen to the guide track with their headphones on, and record themselves with their audio/video camera. Gala integrates also video recording and editing features.

3 The Focus Group

In this paper, we follow the guidelines proposed by Kontio *et al.* [8] concerning the planning and execution of the focus group.

3.1 Defining Research Question

A focus group involves a small group of carefully selected participants that are representative of the target population. The goal is to interact with the participants and collect their opinions on a specific subject [10]. Our study aims at understanding how technology has been exploited by virtual choruses for supporting the interaction among the chorus members in the pandemic period and how interaction may be improved. We investigated the following research questions:

- **RQ1:** *Which are the virtual chorus interaction modalities adopted during the pandemic period?*
- **RQ2:** *How technology may improve the interaction experience of the virtual chorus?*

3.2 Selecting Participants

We conducted a focus group involving three chorus masters, namely M1, M2, and M3. M1 and M2 were both masters of a gospel chorus, size 40 and 36 members, respectively. M3 was the master of a pop chorus with 53 members.

All the participants have actively conducted distance sessions for keeping on the chorus activities. During this period they have performed virtual rehearsals and organized various group activities. Participants were volunteers.

3.3 Planning and Conducting the Focus Group Session

The focus group was held in about one-hour session. It was held the on April the 9th 2021 on the platform Microsoft Teams. It started at 10.05 a.m.

The first author explained the aim of the study and the discussion rules. We also assured that the discussion would be anonymous and confidential. The discussion was conducted in Italian and recorded for further analysis. The first author acted as facilitator and checked that all the topics were considered while encouraging the participants to express their ideas. Another author took the discussion notes. We defined the topics of the discussion but did not formulate specific questions. In this way, during the discussion all the relevant arguments were addressed, leaving participants free to dialogue.

We transcribed and anonymized the focus group recordings and notes, on which we conducted our analysis. These data have been analyzed by exploiting the thematic analysis templates (TAT) [3]. It is based on a qualitative method, the thematic analysis, which is adopted to determine patterns, themes, and to understand data [13]. TAT performs thematic analysis by following a template, which provides a set of initial discussion themes that can evolve while the analysis goes ahead. The templates we adopted in this study were designed by considering our previous experience in conducting focus groups for the Software Engineering field [6].

The template was manually filled in by all the researchers, which were all agree to the selected themes. In Table 1, we show the template we created.

4   Results

This section presents the results from the identified themes.

4.1   Virtual Chorus Experience

Positive points. Participants appreciated the distance activity because it allows them to work in a more in-depth way on listening. It is possible to individually work and to have more time to prepare the material. Also, the use of audio/video during the rehearsal was considered a very positive aspect.

There is a new possibility: putting together musicians of any places in the world or inviting special guests. Also to avoid traveling is a good advantage for people living far from the rehearsals meeting point.

Negative Points. All participants agreed that the main drawback is not being able to play/sing in sync with the choristers. Not having the opportunity to leverage the "network" of emotions that the group generates in presence. The repertoire to be proposed is very limited. There is no executive interactivity.

Table 1. Template for TAT analysis.

ID	Theme	Discussion
1.1	Virtual chorus experience	Reveals what were the positive and negative points encountered when managing a chorus at distance
1.2	Participation	How do you describe the participation (also in therms of presence) of your chorus members?
2	The adopted interaction modalities	Reveals appreciations and bias of the adopted interaction modalities
3	The supporting software	a) helps in the interaction between the chorus members b) does not help in the interaction between the chorus members c) which features a supporting tools tools should offer to improve chorus interaction?

Maintaining attention is much more difficult. Having a medium/high quality standard of the test is tiring.

Many choristers had serious problems with the use of technology.

Fig. 1. Asynchronous interaction modality.

4.2   Participation

All the participants lamented a reduction in the choristers' participation. In particular, for M1 more than half of the choristers remained assiduous to the rehearsals, but there is a 25–30% who is less constant, even in the delivery of the assigned parts. 8 singers neither longer log in, nor are active in the choir chat. Also, 40% of M2 participants abandoned the activities, while M3 lost the 45%.

4.3   RQ1: Which Are the Virtual Chorus Interaction Modalities Adopted During the Pandemic Period?

The answers to RQ1 are summarized in Table 2, where we report the results of the discussion on the adopted interaction modalities. They may be grouped in three categories:

- *asynchronous interaction*, where the master collects audio (or separated audio and video) produced singularly by participants. From them, she produces audio (resp. video) performance in which the chorus members seem singing together (see Fig. 1). This requires a great effort of the master and high technological skills.

Table 2. Adopted virtual chorus interaction modalities and their characteristics.

	Asynchronous	Synchronous	Socialization
Output	Audio/Video multitracking recording grouping the participant single tracks	None	None
Master preparatory work	Reparations of the separate parts for voices. Realization of backing tracks	Creating scores and musical pieces	Preparation of the game, collection of sources, photos, images, videos. Creativity and the ability to be ironic
Master work during the session	Edit the video/audio by composing the single participant tracks	Managing the online meeting, playing accompaniment or sharing the base, checking technology working appropriately	None
Software	Teleconferencing (Zoom), audio editing (mix pad) video editing (moravi/video pad editor/wondeshare filmora) musical notation software (finale/ musiscore/sibelius) Google drive	Music notation software (finale/musiscore/ sibelius)	Wardwall, google form, prezi, powerpoint, powtoon
Requirements	Good participants microphone and camera, good master technical skills	Good internet connection, medium master's technical skills	Medium internet connection, medium master's technical skills
Required scheduling	One registration every 15 days	Fixed deadlines, scheduled meetings	None
Participants' preparation work	Audio (or separate audio and video) to prepare and send	None	None
Commitment required of participants during the session	Follow the directions given for each exercise. Commitment of about 20/30 min	Pay attention to reading. Take notes for the execution to be carried out later remotely	A few minutes of attention
Optimal number of participants	20/25	20/25	No limit

- *synchronous interaction*, conducted by using a video-conference tool, such as Zoom (see Fig. 2). When singing, they have the microphone muted and listen to the music base played by the master. It is not possible to sing together because the platform makes one person sing at a time. This produces a sense of frustration but enables the people to have the sense of being together.

- *social interaction*, where the master creates games by using gaming applications, or quizzes, or organize activities on a social network, such as "post the image of a painting that has a particular meaning for you and say the reason".

DRAW ME CLOSE

Draw me close to you
Never let me go
I lay it all down again
To hear you say that I'm your friend
You are my desire
No one else will do
'Cause nothing else can take your place
To feel the warmth of your embrace
Help me find the way
Bring me back to you

You're all I want
You're all I've ever needed
You're all I want
Help me know you are near

Fig. 2. Synchronous interaction modality.

4.4   RQ2: How Technology May Improve the Interaction Experience of the Virtual Chorus?

Help in the Interaction Between Chorus Members. Through audio and video editing chorus members get the impression of singing together. Even if the preparation is singularly performed, the final result is very satisfying. Another positive aspect is the attitude of many choristers to feel more relaxed when they are online. This lets them express themselves more freely than they are in presence.

Does Not Help in the Interaction Between Chorus Members. Some singers have difficulty in using Zoom, the platform adopted by all the three interviewed, because of their low technological skills. Many of them often have difficulty in basic operations such as turning on the microphone, activating the camera, zooming in, etc., and need family support.

Other difficulties occurred when making the audio recording. The audio produced is rarely of good quality: rustling, background noises, electric shocks, etc. are often heard. Of course, no chorister has instruments and/or software that allow high-quality recordings.

New Features. Needs of an integrated environment for non-expert users. Switching between all the various systems is too complicated for them.

In addition to the requirement of reducing latency time, one of the main features may be to have a software platform that lets participants listen to a common base while singing and, at the same time, records the single voices, which are muted for the others. This may be very useful to create an audio track with all the voices.

The chorus activities are full of social aspects: choristers spend time together before, during, and after rehearsals. They meet in many social activities unrelated to the music, often they create personal relationships with some chorus members, and also may generate conflict among them. Thus, social aspects have to be included in the virtual chorus activities. This may be done by integrating the platform with a social environment, which may use also immersive technologies. Creating a virtual music room where, in virtual reality modality, choristers may sing together.

Having at disposal a common archive where all the chorus material (sheet music, video and audio registration, social-cultural contents) are available and easy to search by the chorus members. It would be nice to have a platform with which one does not have to stay rigidly in the squares assigned to each user, but in a way that can visually simulate, as much as possible, the real one of "being together" in an interactive environment, a little as it happens in virtual reality through visors, gloves, and headphones. Also, Loveridge [11] suggests using virtual reality for conducting virtual chorus activity because it enhances the "presence" sensation.

5   Final Remark

In this paper, a focus group study has been conducted with the involvement of three chorus masters performing virtual chorus activities. We used thematic analysis template (TAT) when discussing the adopted interaction modalities, the support offered by the adopted software, and how the interaction may be improved with the technology support.

During the pandemic period, the choral activities have been completely transformed by forcing the groups to hold remote rehearsals. The seal of the group, as well as on the proposed musical activities, is based on the friendships that exist between the participants. The chorus masters have exploited all their creativity and technical skills to let the chorus members keep on social interaction. Virtual chorus masters use different communication modalities that try to offer some aspects of in presence experience and that are accepted because of the persisting needs of socialization and singing. To this aim asynchronous technologies have been adopted, such as multitracking audio/video recording and production, synchronous videoconferencing platforms for singing in the group, and social technologies for maintaining the group identity.

The digital aspect to which the choir was forced to use to perform activities, aroused first resistance in most of the choristers and, only later, week after week, a gradual overcoming of the many difficulties that had arisen.

Our results revealed that the first need is to have a tool for real-time multi-user singing, which is not supported by actual technology. Several further interesting suggestions implementable by using present technology are related to the integration of the various tools for providing a single and easy-to-use interface suitable for not expert users, and tools for singular recording the performance of each participant during videoconferencing. The use of multi-user, immersive reality may also be investigated.

References

1. Gala website. https://galachoruses.org/resource-center/quarantined-choirs/virtual-choir-performances/. Accessed 3 Apr 2021
2. Carôt, A., Werner, C.: Distributed network music workshop with soundjack. In: Proceedings of the 25th Tonmeistertagung, Leipzig, Germany (2008)
3. Cassell, C., Symon, G.: Essential Guide to Qualitative Methods in Organizational Research. Sage, Thousand Oaks (2004)
4. Daffern, H., Balmer, K., Brereton, J.: Singing together, yet apart: the experience of UK choir members and facilitators during the COVID-19 pandemic. Frontiers in Psychology **12**, 303 (2021). https://doi.org/10.3389/fpsyg.2021.624474, https://www.frontiersin.org/article/10.3389/fpsyg.2021.624474
5. Dingle, G.A., Brander, C., Ballantyne, J., Baker, F.A.: 'To be heard': the social and mental health benefits of choir singing for disadvantaged adults. Psychol. Music **41**(4), 405–421 (2013)
6. Francese, R., Risi, M., Scanniello, G., Tortora, G.: Users' perception on the use of metricattitude to perform source code comprehension tasks: a focus group study. In: 2017 21st International Conference Information Visualisation (IV), pp. 8–13. IEEE (2017)
7. Iorwerth, M., Knox, D.: The application of networked music performance technology to access ensemble activity for socially isolated musicians (2019)
8. Kontio, J., Lehtola, L., Bragge, J.: Using the focus group method in software engineering: obtaining practitioner and user experiences. In: Proceedings 2004 International Symposium on Empirical Software Engineering, 2004. ISESE 2004, pp. 271–280. IEEE (2004)
9. Lakiotakis, E., Liaskos, C., Dimitropoulos, X.: Improving networked music performance systems using application-network collaboration. Concurrency Comput. Pract. Experience **31**(24), e4730 (2019)
10. Lehtola, L., Kauppinen, M., Kujala, S.: Requirements prioritization challenges in practice. In: Bomarius, F., Iida, H. (eds.) PROFES 2004. LNCS, vol. 3009, pp. 497–508. Springer, Heidelberg (2004). https://doi.org/10.1007/978-3-540-24659-6_36
11. Loveridge, B.: Networked music performance in virtual reality: current perspectives. J. Netw. Music Arts **2**(1), 2 (2020)
12. Moss, H., Lynch, J., O'Donoghue, J.: Exploring the perceived health benefits of singing in a choir: an international cross-sectional mixed-methods study. Perspect. Public Health **138**(3), 160–168 (2018)
13. Orosz, J.: Qualitative data analysis: an expanded sourcebook. Public Adm. Rev. **57**(6), 543–550 (1997)

Author Index

Printed in the United States
by Baker & Taylor Publisher Services

Printed in the United States
by Baker & Taylor Publisher Services